The Skeptical Environmentalist

The Skeptical Environmentalist challenges widely held beliefs that the environmental situation is getting worse and worse. The author, himself a former member of Greenpeace, is critical of the way in which many environmental organizations make selective and misleading use of the scientific evidence. Using the best available statistical information from internationally recognized research institutes, Bjørn Lomborg systematically examines a range of major environmental problems that feature prominently in headline news across the world. His arguments are presented in non-technical, accessible language and are carefully backed up by over 2,900 notes allowing readers to check sources for themselves. Concluding that there are more reasons for optimism than pessimism, Bjørn Lomborg stresses the need for clear-headed prioritization of resources to tackle real, not imagined problems.

The Skeptical Environmentalist offers readers a non-partisan stocktaking exercise that serves as a useful corrective to the more alarmist accounts favoured by campaign groups and the media. It is essential reading for anybody with a serious interest in current environmental debates.

BJØRN LOMBORG is an Associate Professor of Statistics in the Department of Political Science, University of Aarhus, Denmark. He has published in international journals in the fields of game theory and computer simulations.

Advance praise for *The Skeptical Environmentalist*

"Bjørn Lomborg raises the important question whether the costs of remedying the damage caused by environmental pollution are higher than the costs of the pollution itself. The answer is by no means straightforward. He has written a pioneering book."

Professor Richard Rosecrance, Department of Political Science, University of California, Los Angeles

"The well-publicized, but failed doomsday predictions made by some well-known environmentalist writers have inspired a number of rejoinders. This is the best one, by a wide margin. Its author teaches statistics in the Department of Political Science at Aarhus University in Denmark. He has marshaled an extremely impressive array of data to buttress his optimism about long-term and current trends in environment and development. On the environmental side, the book covers traditional problems like food, energy, water, and pollution, but also future problems like biodiversity and the greenhouse effect. In each of these areas, he argues that environmental problems can be managed (and in many cases have been managed already), and that trying to turn the clock back will be costlier in economic as well as human terms. On the development side, Lomborg points to encouraging trends in life expectancy, welfare, the decline of population growth, and the reduction of hunger. While he may occasionally make things difficult for himself by insisting that the world is making progress in virtually every area, this is also what makes the book such an impressive tour de force. This volume is a revised version of a much-debated Danish book from 1998, but the documentation is truly international – much more so than in the extensive US literature that promotes a similar message. Since theories of environmental conflict are generally predicated on a premise of scarcity, Lomborg's argument is of great potential importance to peace research."

Nils Petter Gleditsch, Editor, *Journal of Peace Research*, Research Professor, International Peace Research Institute, Oslo (PRIO), Professor of International Relations, Norwegian University of Science and Technology (NTNU), Trondheim

"For many scientists working with developing country issues it has long been difficult to reconcile findings from our field studies in Africa, Asia and Latin America with the pronouncements from environmental pressure groups in the industrialized world. With much better access to media and politicians a number of influential institutes and individuals have created images of a rapidly deteriorating world which is not always apparent to a significant section of the world population. What is even more disturbing is that much of the negative statements on environmental issues and on the global food situation seem to stem from relatively short-term time series, with apparent bias in selection of begin-points and end-points to make development look gloomy. There seems a sharp reluctance in some media and political circles to accept that much progress has been made in providing food for a population which is twice the size of what it was when the Club of Rome issued its doomsday scenarios. Indeed there is reluctance in the North to accept that poor people in the South have mostly done it themselves. It seems almost universally accepted in the North that the forests of the South are disappearing, depriving the globe of its green lungs, whilst serious study of forestry data indicate a much more mixed picture, with India arguably having more forests than 50 years ago.

Lomborg's book is a warning to scientists who have abandoned statistical prudence in their work. Anecdotal science can become biassed science or lead to wrong conclusions. The magnifying glass of crisis-focussed media, the scramble for competitive grants funding among scientists, and the need for pressure groups to sustain themselves, obscure less obvious and often less dramatic trends. And in particular they obscure a great deal of good news for the poor.

The concern for the environment and for the global food situation is honourable. We are all *for* a better environment and high biodiversity, and *against* food insecurity. There is a general consensus against pollution of the environment, wasteful food production methods, inequalities in access to food. There is a growing awareness of the dangers of global climate change. Lomborg does not argue against these legitimate concerns. He argues against lax and biassed use of data, particularly of time series. He warns that it is degrading science by allowing bits to be picked out of context. He is afraid that pompous statements based on flimsy evidence that also attract the media and the politicians constitute a threat to the integrity of science itself. If, in the long run, opportunistic behaviour of scientists leads to disregard of some of the basic tools of science – and statistical analysis is certainly one of them – then science itself will ultimately be the loser.

Lomborg's book questions the scientific basis why good news is suppressed and bad news amplified. But given that the environment is under pressure, it also questions whether we apply the correct remedies. In a world where around 1.5 billion people live on less that one US dollar a day and 2.5 probably on less than two dollars a day, we should be seriously concerned about the human dimension of our interactions with the environment. In our efforts to rescue the environment Lomborg suggests that exorbitant sums may be invested in environmental efforts that mean little to the poor, whilst only a handful of countries set aside as much as 0.7% of their GDP for development aid. If we are developing a setting, based on flawed data analysis, where rich people let butterflies count more heavily in their budgets than hungry and sick people, then we are morally on very thin ice. In a long string of examples Lomborg suggests that there is growing evidence that we may not have got our priority setting right, and that poor people may suffer from our careless handling of scarce data sets.

Lomborg questions most of our common views on the environment, the global food situation, and strategies for development assistance to the poor. He may not be right on all issues, but his plea for scientific stringency in analysis, and his exposure of false environmental prophets, are all very credible."

Stein W. Bie. Director General, International Service for National Agricultural Research (ISNAR)

"Those who feel strongly about poverty always emphasize how deep and widespread it is. But they seldom mention the great amount of people who have been lifted out of poverty over the last few hundred years or, especially, over the last few decades. A similar observation applies to those who care deeply about the environment. They tell us about the inroads of degradation and pollution all over the world, but seldom direct our attention to the results achieved in turning this process around, at least in significant parts of the world.

These attitudes have always amazed me. Although it is important to know the depth and width of a problem, it is no less important to know how it is being met and what results are thus being achieved. It is only in light of that knowledge that we can move forward with force and confidence. Such a view from both sides is the essential asset of Bjørn Lomborg's book. It presents the nature and extension of the problems we are faced with, as well as the ways along which they are being challenged and the results that are being obtained. The outcome is a hopeful view which should hearten all those who feel anxious about poverty and environment."

Jonas H. Haralz, Former Executive Director of the World Bank for the Nordic Countries.

"Based on facts and figures that are common ground to all sides of the ecological debate, this book will change forever the way you think about the state of the world. It is a remarkable, no, an extraordinary achievement."

Tøger Seidenfaden, Executive Editor-in-Chief, *Politiken*

The Skeptical Environmentalist

Measuring the Real State of the World

Bjørn Lomborg

PUBLISHED BY THE PRESS SYNDICATE OF THE UNIVERSITY OF CAMBRIDGE
The Pitt Building, Trumpington Street, Cambridge, United Kingdom

CAMBRIDGE UNIVERSITY PRESS
The Edinburgh Building, Cambridge CB2 2RU, UK
40 West 20th Street, New York, NY 10011–4211, USA
477 Williamstown Road, Port Melbourne, VIC 3207, Australia
Ruiz de Alarcón 13, 28014 Madrid, Spain
Dock House, The Waterfront, Cape Town 8001, South Africa

http://www.cambridge.org

Originally published in Danish as *Verdens Sande Tilstand* 1998
and © Bjørn Lomborg 1998

This revised and updated version,
partially translated by Hugh Matthews
first published in English by
Cambridge University Press 2001
as *The Skeptical Environmentalist*

First published 2001
Ninth reprint 2002

Printed in the United Kingdom at the University Press, Cambridge

Typeface Swift 9/12 pt *System* QuarkXPress™ [SE]

A catalogue record for this book is available from the British Library

Library of Congress Cataloguing in Publication data

Lomborg, Bjørn, 1965–
The skeptical environmentalist: measuring the real state of the world / Bjørn Lomborg.
p. cm.
Originally published in Danish as Verdens sande tilstand, 1998.
This revised and updated version first published in English by Cambridge University Press, 2001–T.p. verso.
Includes bibliographical references and index.
ISBN 0 521 80447 7 – ISBN 0 521 01068 3 (pb.)
1. Global environmental change. 2. Pollution. 3. Human ecology. I. Title.
GE149 .L65 2001
363.7–dc21 00-068915

ISBN 0 521 80447 7 hardback
ISBN 0 521 01068 3 paperback

This is my long-run forecast in brief:

The material conditions of life will continue
to get better for most people, in most countries,
most of the time, indefinitely. Within a century or two,
all nations and most of humanity will be at or above
today's Western living standards.

I also speculate, however, that many people will continue
to *think and say* that the conditions of life are getting *worse*.

Julian Simon (1932–98), Professor of Economics,
University of Maryland (Regis 1997:198)

The book is dedicated to my mother, Birgit Lomborg.

Contents

Part III: Can human prosperity continue?

Part IV: Pollution: does it undercut human prosperity?

Part V: Tomorrow's problems

Part VI: The Real State of the World

List of figures

List of tables

Preface

The idea for this book was born in a bookstore in Los Angeles in February 1997. I was standing leafing through *Wired Magazine* and read an interview with the American economist Julian Simon, from the University of Maryland. He maintained that much of our traditional knowledge about the environment is quite simply based on preconceptions and poor statistics. Our doomsday conceptions of the environment are not correct. Simon stressed that he only used official statistics, which everyone has access to and can use to check his claims.

I was provoked. I'm an old left-wing Greenpeace member and had for a long time been concerned about environmental questions. At the same time I teach statistics, and it should therefore be easy for me to check Simon's sources. Moreover, I always tell my students how statistics is one of science's best ways to check whether our venerable social beliefs stand up to scrutiny or turn out to be myths. Yet, I had never really questioned my own belief in an ever deteriorating environment – and here was Simon, telling me to put my beliefs under the statistical microscope.

In the fall of 1997 I held a study group with ten of my sharpest students, where we tried to examine Simon thoroughly. Honestly, we expected to show that most of Simon's talk was simple, American right-wing propaganda. And yes, not everything he said was correct, but – contrary to our expectations – it turned out that a surprisingly large amount of his points stood up to scrutiny and conflicted with what we believed ourselves to know. The air in the developed world is becoming less, not more, polluted; people in the developing countries are not starving more, but less, and so on.

I asked myself why I was so definitely convinced that the environmental situation is bad and ever deteriorating. And if I was wrong in my beliefs about the environment, I was probably not the only one. Thus, I contacted one of the leading Danish newspapers, the centre-left, *Guardian*-like *Politiken*, and suggested to them that I write some articles about our understanding of various environmental problems. The outcome was four articles, that gave rise to one of the biggest Danish debates, spreading to all newspapers, and covering well over 400 articles, commentaries and critiques. Later, I tried to follow up on the debate with a book, covering a much wider area and attempting to address all our main worries.

However, the entire debate seemed peculiarly incomplete. To begin with, I was surprised that the only reaction from many environmental groups was the gut reaction of complete denial. Sure, this had also been my initial response, but I would have thought as the debate progressed that refusal would give place to reflection on the massive amounts of supportive data I had presented, and lead to a genuine reevaluation of our approach to the environment. Surprisingly, I met many, even amongst my close friends, who had only read the critical commentaries and drawn the simple conclusion that I was wrong, and that we could comfortably go on believing in the impending doomsday. This suggested that doomsday-visions are very thoroughly anchored in our thinking.

I teach statistics at the University of Aarhus and basically my skills consist in knowing how to handle international statistics. Normally you associate statistics with a boring run-through of endless rows of numbers – a problem I must every term convince new students is not necessarily true. Actually, statistics can be thoroughly exciting exactly because it confronts our myths with data and allows us to see the world more clearly. This excitement, I hope, is also apparent throughout the book. Though it contains much quantitative information, knowing the state of our world should be stimulating and invigorating, the challenge to our world view healthy and rewarding.

If I mention my profession at a party, it is seldom that I avoid a comment which rightly or wrongly builds on something which the English Prime Minister Benjamin Disraeli (1804–81) is supposed to have said: "There are three kinds of lies: lies, damned lies and statistics."[1] And it's actually true that statistics can be used to manipulate the truth. But used judiciously statistics is the best source of information about our world.

Why? Because the small part of the world that we see amongst our friends and acquaintances and in the media seldom shows a balanced picture of the whole world. For many different reasons our friends and acquaintances are much more similar to ourselves than the average population. Thus, basing our impressions of the world from friends alone will bias our views. Likewise, on TV we often get to hear stories which are twisted and sensationalized in many different and predictable ways (see chapter 2 on the problems of truth and the media).

In this way, statistics offers us a way to see the world more clearly. Indeed, statistics is in many areas the only way we can make a scientifically sound description of the world.

I have let experts review the chapters of this book, but I am not myself an expert as regards environmental problems. My aim has rather been to give a description of the approaches to the problems, as the experts themselves have presented them in relevant books and journals, and to examine the different subject-areas from such a perspective as allows us to evaluate their importance in the overall social prioritization.

The key idea is that we ought not to let the environmental organizations, business lobbyists or the media be alone in presenting truths and priorities. Rather, we should strive for a careful democratic check on the environmental debate, by knowing the real state of the world – having knowledge of the most important facts and connections in the essential areas of our world. It is my hope that this book will contribute to such an understanding.

Language and measures

This book presents a lot of data. In making complete sentences out of specific data, I have often selected fluency over cumbersome accuracy, which nevertheless should be available through the endnotes or the figure captions. When I write 'today' it typically implies the most recently available data, which could be anywhere from 1997 to 2001, depending on the speed of data collection and the time span involved.

Any data book in the English market has to consider the question of measures. This book mainly uses metrics, but whenever 'human-size' data are involved, I try also to indicate the imperial measures.[2] Thus, when discussing the American waste production (Figure 114, p. 207), the national waste is denoted in million metric tons. (I doubt if anyone truly has a feel for the magnitude of 150 million tons of landfill waste, and it would probably not help much to say 330 billion pounds instead.) Here, the important comparison is with the – equally incomprehensible – figures from 1960 or from 2005. However, when talking about the average daily waste per American, a change from 3 pounds in 1985 to 2.5 pounds in 2000 is readily comprehensible.

Timing throughout the book is in Common Era (CE) and Before Common Era (BCE). Energy is denoted by Joule (J) or kilo-watt-hours (kWh). Exponentials are used to denote large numbers, i.e. 5e6 means $5x10^6$, or a five followed by six zeros (5 million). The conventional prefixes are used throughout, with k (kilo, thousand), M (mega, million), G (giga, billion), and for really large numbers E (eta, 1e18) and Z (zeta, 1e21).[3] Celsius is used for temperature, with one degree Celsius being 1.8 degrees Fahrenheit, and 0°C being 32°F.

Acknowledgements

In writing this book, I have been fortunate to have had help and inspiration from a lot of different people. I would like to thank my student helpers, who have always been ready to key in another statistic, touch up a graph, locate an obscure research report, call for a reference, rummage the internet or do the zillion other, less glamorous and (yes, I know!) often quite boring tasks. Thanks to David Nicolas Hopmann for his unflinching commitment to get the data (and for all the extra info on *Star Trek*), thanks to Helle Dam Sørensen for her amazing ability to keep track of all my odd requests (and her seemingly infinite patience with the Xerox machine), and thanks to Jesper Strandsbjerg Pedersen for his persistence in getting data in and good-looking graphs out (and even biking for an hour and a half to get an obscure CD-ROM). I am also grateful for all the skilled help and effort from Ida Pagter Kristensen, Siggi Brandt Kristoffersen, Ulrik Larsen and Kenneth Thue Nielsen.

Acknowledgement also goes to the large number of researchers who have read through different parts of the book. For different reasons, not all have wished to be mentioned, but they have all contributed with constructive suggestions and useful information, although definitely not all agree with my overall conclusions. Naturally, the customary caveat holds – only I am responsible for the contents of this book.

A big thanks to leader of research at the Center for Development Research, Jannik Boesen, administrative consultant Dr. Arne Høst at the University Hospital in Odense, professor of geology Henning Sørensen, Martin Einfeldt and Søren Fodgaard from the Danish Forestry Association, senior consultant Helle Buchardt Boyd from the Danish Center for Toxicology, Stefan Brendstrup from the Center for Social and Environmental Research, physicist Peter Thejll from the Danish Meteorological Institute, and Jes Fenger, National Environmental Research Institute of Denmark, who commented on large parts of the book.

The most gratitude goes to all the scientists in the field, from universities and research institutes, who actually measure the world in so many different ways, and all the statisticians within government agencies and international organizations who painstakingly assemble and publish the bits and pieces of the information that is presented in this book. A special thanks to the many scientists who have helped with some of the more particular requests: Mark Aldrich from the World Conservation Monitoring Centre, Chuck Allen, Michael Grillot and Harriet McLaine from the Energy Information Agency under the US Department of Energy, Ed Dlugokencky and P. Tans from the Climate Monitoring and Diagnostics Laboratory of the US National Oceanic and Atmospheric Administration, John H. Dyck from the US Department of Agriculture, Dr. Johann Goldammer at the Max Planck Chemistry Institute, Dr. Jim Hammitt at the Department of Health Policy and Management, Harvard Center for Risk Analysis, Dr. Annette Pernille Høyer at the Copenhagen Centre for Prospective Population Studies, senior researcher Alan McHughen at the University of Saskatchewan, Kåre Kemp at the National Environmental Research Institute of Denmark, chief librarian Patricia Merrikin at

FAO headquarters in Rome, crop physiologist Shaobing Peng at the International Rice Research Institute, Dr. Niels Skakkebæk of the Danish National Research Hospital, Dr. Henrik Svensmark from the Danish Space Research Institute, and Shanna H. Swan at the California Department of Health Services.

A lot of good friends have spent an inordinate amount of their time reading different chapters and excerpts of the book. Carol Anne Oxborrow has read through heaps of material, and she has given me a better feel for the subtleties of British English while sharpening my expositions in many places. Bill Jeffrey has – despite the recurrent interruptions of his two 3-years olds – managed to get all through the first draft of the book, and his comments have forced me to clarify and strengthen the arguments, while he has also showed me the difficulty of mastering the American side of English. I also want to thank Lars Nørgaard, Martin Ågerup, Simon Henriksen, Henrik Kjærsig, Henrik Kjærgaard, Tom Yoo Kjær Nielsen, Jacob Heide Pedersen and Ulrik Wittendorff. Their good suggestions, constructive criticisms and honest reactions have contributed to making a much better book. In particular, I want to express my gratitude to my long-term friend, colleague and mentor, professor Jørgen Poulsen for his inspiring and always challenging thoughts. Likewise, I want to thank Nikolaj Vibe Michelsen, who has helped shape a lot of the arguments and who willingly let me test out a lot of new (if not always smart) ideas. Finally, I would like to thank my patient students, my good colleagues and here especially professor Søren Risbjerg Thomsen at the Department of Political Science, University of Aarhus. They have supported my research and provided me with an impetus to carry on, while they have also been wonderfully forgiving when sometimes I have turned up late or forgotten a deadline.

I have been fortunate to have a publisher who has supported me all along. My editor, Chris Harrison, has throughout believed in the book and carried it through the many Byzantine quirks of book publishing, while contributing with many good questions and useful advice. Likewise, production controller Caroline Murray, senior design controller Peter Ducker and David Barrett and his colleagues at Servis Filmsetting have all given the book a great layout and handled all the intricacies of getting graphs designed on the screen to look good on paper. Also, marketing director Sloane Lederer and Diane Goddard have worked enthusiastically on promoting the book.

While every effort naturally has been made to ensure that all the information in this book is correct, errors will undoubtedly still have crept in. In the days of old one would have to wait till the book – maybe – was reprinted and the statements could be corrected, but with the internet, this can be done immediately. Thus, I will endeavor to post any mistakes on the book's web-site: www.lomborg.org.

When I first read the interview with Julian Simon in Los Angeles, February 1997, I had no idea that checking up on his statements would end up taking more than four years of my life. But it has been an exhilarating and challenging experience and it has taught me a lot about our world and about my own myths.

The world is not without problems, but on almost all accounts, things are going better and they are likely to continue to do so into the future. The facts and information presented here should give us an opportunity to set free our unproductive worries and allow us to focus on the important issues, so that we may indeed help make an even better world for tomorrow.

Aarhus, 22 May 2001

Permissions

I have tried wherever possible to give full details of sources for all data and am grateful to the following for permission to reproduce copyright material: Figure 44 is reproduced from figure 8 in Jesse H. Ausubel and Arnulf Grübler, "Working less and living longer: long-term trends in working time and time budgets." *Technological Forecasting and Social Change* 50:113–31. Reprinted with permission from Elsevier Science. Figure 59 reproduces the WWF Forests for Life web page (http://www.panda.org/forests4life.htm). Printed by permission of the WWF's Forest for Life Campaign and Tori Lyall. Figures 96, 97, 109, and 113 are reproduced from page 764 of Nemat Shafik, "Economic development and environmental quality: an econometric analysis." *Oxford Economic Papers* 46:757–73. Reprinted with permission from Oxford University Press and Nemat Shafik. Figure 98 is reproduced from page 529 in J. Laurence Kulp, "Acid rain," in Julian Simon, *The State of Humanity*. Oxford: Blackwell. Reprinted with permission from Blackwell Publishers. Figure 101 is reproduced from page 607 in D. Jarvis and P. Burney, "The epidemiology of allergic disease." *British Medical Journal* 318:607–10. Reprinted with permission from BMJ Publishing Group. Figure 151 is reproduced from Figures 2 and 3 in Ujjayant Chakravorty, James Roumasset and Kinping Tse, "Endogenous substitution among energy resources and global warming." *Journal of Political Economy* 105(6):1,201–34. Reprinted by permission from The University of Chicago Press.

While every effort has been made to identify the owners of copyright material, I may have overlooked some cases, and I therefore take this opportunity to offer my apologies to any copyright holders whose rights I have unwittingly infringed.

The Litany

PART I

1 Things are getting better

What kind of state is the world really in?

Optimists proclaim the end of history with the best of all possible worlds at hand, whereas pessimists see a world in decline and find doomsday lurking around the corner. Getting the state of the world right is important because it defines humanity's problems and shows us where our actions are most needed. At the same time, it is also a scorecard for our civilization – have we done well with our abilities, and is this a world we want to leave for our children?

This book is the work of a skeptical environmentalist. Environmentalist, because I – like most others – care for our Earth and care for the future health and wellbeing of its succeeding generations. Skeptical, because I care enough to want us not just to act on the myths of both optimists and pessimists. Instead, we need to use the best available information to join others in the common goal of making a better tomorrow.

Thus, this book attempts to measure the real state of the world. Of course, it is not possible to write a book (or even lots and lots of books for that matter) which measures the entire state of the world. Nor is this my intention. Instead, I wish to gauge the most important characteristics of our state of the world – the *fundamentals*. And these should be assessed not on myths but on the best available facts. Hence, the *real* state of the world.

The Litany

The subtitle of my book is a play on the world's best-known book on the environment, *The State of the World*. This has been published every year since 1984 by the Worldwatch Institute and its leader Lester Brown,[4] and it has sold more than a million copies. The series attempts to identify the world's most significant challenges professionally and veraciously. Unfortunately, as we shall see, it is frequently unable to live up to its objectives. In many ways, though, *The State of the World* is one of the best-researched and academically most ambitious environmental policy publications, and therefore it is also an essential participant in the discussion on the State of the World.[5]

On a higher level this book plays to our general understanding of the environment: the Litany of our ever deteriorating environment. This is the view of the environment that is shaped by the images and messages that confront us each day on television, in the newspapers, in political statements and in conversations at work and at the kitchen table. This is why *Time* magazine can start off an article in 2000, stating as entirely obvious how "everyone knows the planet is in bad shape."[6]

Even children are told the Litany, here from Oxford University Press' *Young Oxford Books*: "The balance of nature is delicate but essential for life. Humans have upset that balance, stripping the land of its green cover, choking the air, and poisoning the seas."[7]

Equally, another *Time* article tells us how "for more than 40 years, earth has been sending out distress signals" but while "we've staged a procession of Earth Days . . . the decline of Earth's ecosystems has continued unabated.[8] The April 2001 Global Environment Supplement from *New Scientist* talks about the impending "catastrophe" and how we risk consigning "humanity to the dustbin of evolutionary history." Our impact is summarized with the headline "Self-destruct":

> We humans are about as subtle as the asteroid that wiped out the dinosaurs . . . The damage we do is increasing. In the next 20 years, the population will increase by 1.5 billion. These people will need food, water and electricity, but already our soils are vanishing, fisheries are being killed off, wells are drying up, and the burning of fossil fuels is endangering the lives of millions. We are heading for cataclysm.[9]

This understanding of the environment is all pervasive. We are all familiar with the Litany:[10] the environment is in poor shape here on Earth.[11] Our resources are running out. The population is ever growing, leaving less and less to eat. The air and the water are becoming ever more polluted. The planet's species are becoming extinct is vast numbers – we kill off more than 40,000 each year. The forests are disappearing, fish stocks are collapsing and the coral reefs are dying.

We are defiling our Earth, the fertile topsoil is disappearing, we are paving over nature, destroying the wilderness, decimating the biosphere, and will end up killing ourselves in the process. The world's ecosystem is breaking down. We are fast approaching the absolute limit of viability, and the limits of growth are becoming apparent.[12]

We know the Litany and have heard it so often that yet another repetition is, well, almost reassuring. There is just one problem: it does not seem to be backed up by the available evidence.

Things are *better* – but not necessarily *good*

I will attempt over the course of this book to describe the principal areas which stake out humankind's potentials, challenges and problems – in the past, the present and the future. These areas are selected either because it is immediately obvious that they are important (e.g. the number of people on earth), because models show they will have a decisive influence on human development (air pollution, global warming) or because they are frequently mentioned in the discussion on the state of the world (chemical fears, e.g. pesticides).[13]

In presenting this description I will need to challenge our usual conception of the collapse of ecosystems, because this conception is simply not in keeping with reality.

We are not running out of energy or natural resources.[14] There will be more and more food per head of the world's population. Fewer and fewer people are starving. In 1900 we lived for an average of 30 years; today we live for 67. According to the UN we have reduced poverty more in the last 50 years than we did in the preceding 500, and it has been reduced in practically every country.

Global warming, though its size and future projections are rather unrealistically pessimistic, is almost certainly taking place, but the typical cure of early and radical fossil fuel cutbacks is way worse than the original affliction, and moreover its total impact will not pose a devastating problem for our future. Nor will we lose 25–50 percent of all species in our lifetime – in fact we are losing probably 0.7 percent. Acid rain does not kill the forests, and the air and water around us are becoming less and less polluted.

Mankind's lot has actually improved in terms of practically every measurable indicator.

But note carefully what I am saying here: that by far the majority of indicators show that mankind's lot has *vastly improved*. This does not, however, mean that everything is *good enough*. The first statement refers to what the world looks like whereas the second refers to what it ought to look like.[15]

While on lecture tours I have discovered how vital it is to emphasize this distinction. Many people believe they can prove me wrong, for example by pointing out that a lot of people are still starving: "How can you say that things are continuing to improve when 18 percent of all people in the developing world are still starving?"

The point is that ever fewer people in the world are starving. In 1970, 35 percent of all people in developing countries were starving. In 1996 the figure was 18 percent and the UN expects that the figure will have fallen to 12 percent by 2010.[16] This is remarkable progress: 237 million fewer people starving. Till today, more than 2000 million more people are getting enough to eat.

The food situation has vastly improved, but in 2010 there will still be 680 million people starving, which is obviously not *good enough*.

The distinction is essential; when things are not going well enough we can sketch out a vision: fewer people must starve. This is our political aim.

But when things are improving we know we are on the right track. Although perhaps not at the right speed. Maybe we can do even more to improve the food situation, but the basic approach is not wrong. We are actually saving lives and can look forward to fewer people starving in future.

Exaggeration and good management

The constant repetition of the Litany and the often heard environmental exaggerations has serious consequences. It makes us scared and it makes us more likely to spend our resources and attention solving phantom problems while ignoring real and pressing (possibly non-environmental) issues. This is why it is important to know the real state of the world. We need to get the facts and the best possible information to make the best possible decisions. As the lead author of the environmental report *Our Common Future*, Gro Harlem Brundtland, put it in the top scientific magazine *Science*: "Politics that disregard science and knowledge will not stand the test of time. Indeed, there is no other basis for sound political decisions than the best available scientific evidence. This is especially true in the fields of resource management and environmental protection."[17]

However, pointing out that our most publicized fears are incorrect does not mean that we should make no effort towards improving the environment. Far from it. It will often make good sense to make some effort towards managing our resources and tackling our problems in areas like forest and water management, air pollution, and global warming. The point here is to give us the best evidence to allow us to make the most informed decision as to where we need to place most of our efforts. What I will show throughout the book is that our problems are often getting *smaller* and not bigger, and that frequently the offered solutions are grossly inefficient. What this information should tell us is not to abandon action entirely, but to focus our attention on the most important problems and only to the extent warranted by the facts.

Fundamentals: trends

If we are to understand the real state of the world, we need to focus on the *fundamentals* and we need to look at *realities*, not myths. Let us take a look at both of these requirements, starting with the fundamentals.

When we are to assess the state of the world, we need to do so through a comparison.[18] Legend has it that when someone remarked to Voltaire, "life is hard," he retorted, "compared to what?"[19] Basically, the choice of comparison is crucial. It is my argument that the comparison should be with *how it was before*. Such comparison shows us the extent of our progress – are we better or worse off now than previously? This means that we should focus on *trends*.

When the water supply and sanitation services were improved in cities throughout the developed world in the nineteenth century, health and life expectancy improved dramatically.[20] Likewise, the broadening of education from the early nineteenth century till today's universal school enrolment has brought literacy and democratic competence to the developed world.[21] These trends have been replicated in the developing world in the twentieth century. Whereas 75 percent of the young people in the developing world born around 1915 were illiterate, this is true for only 16 percent of today's youth (see Figure 41, p. 81). And while only 30 percent of the people in the developing world had access to clean drinking water in 1970, today about 80 percent have (see Figure 5, p. 22). These developments represent great strides forward in human welfare; they are huge improvements in the state of the world – because the trends have been upwards in life expectancy and literacy.

In line with the argument above, it is a *vast improvement* that people both in the developed and in the developing world have dramatically increased their access to clean drinking water. Nevertheless, this does not mean that everything is *good enough*. There are still more than a billion people in the Third World who do not have access to clean drinking water. If we compare the world to this *ideal* situation, it is obvious that there are still improvements to be made. Moreover, such a comparison with an ideal situation sets a constructive, political ambition by showing us that if access has become universal in the developed world, it is also an achievable goal for the developing world.

But it is important to realize that such a comparison constitutes a political judgment. Of course, when asked, we would probably all want the Third World to have better access to clean drinking water, but then again, we probably all want the Third World to have good schooling, better health care, more food security, etc. Likewise, in the developed world we also want better retirement homes for our elders, better kindergartens, higher local environmental investments, better infrastructure, etc. The problem is that it all costs money. If we want to improve one thing, such as Third World access to clean drinking water, we need to take the resources from other areas where we would also like to make things better. Naturally, this is the essence of politics – we have to prioritize resources and choose some projects over many others. But if we make the state of the world to be a comparison with an *ideal* situation we are implicitly making a political judgment as to what projects in the world we should be prioritizing.

Thus, with this assessment of the state of the world I wish to leave to the individual reader the political judgment as to where we should focus our efforts. Instead, it is my intention to provide the best possible information about how things have progressed and are likely to develop in the future, so that the democratic process is assured the soundest basis for decisions.

And this means focusing on trends.

Fundamentals: global trends

The *Global Environmental Outlook Report 2000* tells us much about the plight of Africa.[22] Now, there is no doubt that Africa, and especially Africa below the Sahara, has done less well than other continents, an issue to which we will return (p. 65ff). Sub-Saharan Africa has by far the greatest numbers of starving people – almost 33 percent were starving in 1996, although this was down from 38 percent in 1970 and is expected to fall even further to 30 percent in 2010.[23]

In the most staggering prediction of problems ahead, *Global Environmental Outlook Report 2000* tells us that soil erosion is a pervasive problem, especially in Africa. Indeed, "in a continent where too many people are already malnourished, crop yields could be cut by half within 40 years if the degradation of cultivated lands were to continue at present rates."[24] This, of course, would represent a tragedy of enormous proportions, causing massive starvation on the African continent. However, the background for this stunning prediction stems from a single, unpublished study from 1989, based on agricultural plot studies only in South Africa.[25] And it is in stark opposition to the estimates of the major food production models from the UN (FAO) and IFPRI, expecting an annual 1.7 percent yield increase over the next 20–25 years.[26] Although the growth in yield in the 1990s was small but positive, the absolute grain production increased more than 20 percent.[27]

In many ways this is reminiscent of one of the most cited European soil erosion estimates of 17 tons per hectare.[28] This estimate turned out – through a string of articles, each slightly inaccurately referring to its predecessor – to stem from a single study of a 0.11 hectare sloping plot of Belgian farmland, from which the author himself warns against generalization.[29] In both examples, sweeping statements are made with just a single example. Unfortunately, such problematic argumentation is pervasive, and we will see more examples below. The problem arises because in today's global environment, with massive amounts of information at our fingertips, an infinite number of stories can be told, good ones and bad.

Should you be so inclined, you could easily write a book full of awful examples and conclude that the world is in a terrible state. Or you could write a book full of sunshine stories of how the environment is doing ever so well. Both approaches could be using examples that are absolutely true, and yet both approaches would be expressions of equally useless forms of argumentation. They resemble the classic fallacy that "my granddad smoked cigars all his life and was healthy until he died at the age of 97, so smoking isn't dangerous." Such a fallacy is clearly not rectified by accumulating lots of examples – we could easily find many grandfathers who had smoked heavily and lived into their late nineties, but still this is no argument for smoking not being dangerous. The argument fails because it systematically neglects all the men who smoked and died of lung cancer in their late forties, before they even got to be grandfathers.[30] So if we are to demonstrate the problems of smoking, we need to use comprehensive figures. Do smokers get lung cancer more or less often compared with non-smokers?[31]

In the same way we can only elucidate global problems with global figures. If we hear about Burundi losing 21 percent in its daily per capita caloric intake over the past ten years,[32] this is shocking information and may seem to reaffirm our belief of food troubles in the developing world. But we might equally well hear about Chad gaining 26 percent, perhaps changing our opinion the other way.[33] Of course, the pessimist can then tell us about Iraq loosing 28 percent and Cuba 19 percent, the optimist citing Ghana with an increase of 34 percent and Nigeria of 33 percent. With 120 more countries to go, the battle of intuition will be lost in the information overload.[34] On average, however, the developing countries have increased their food intake from 2,463 to 2,663 calories per person per day over the last ten years, an increase of 8 percent.[35]

The point is that global figures summarize *all* the good stories as well as *all* the ugly ones, allowing us to evaluate how serious the overall situation is. Global figures will register the problems in Burundi but also the gains in Nigeria. Of course, a food bonanza in Nigeria does not alleviate food scarcity in Burundi, so when presenting averages we also have to be careful only to include comparable countries like those in the developing world. However, if Burundi with 6.5 million people eats much worse whereas Nigeria with 108 million eats much better, it really means 17 Nigerians eating better versus 1 Burundi eating worse – that all in all mankind is better fed. The point here is that global figures can answer the question as to whether there have been more good stories to tell and fewer bad ones over the years or vice versa.

This is why in the following chapters I shall always attempt to present the most comprehensive figures in order to describe the development of the entire world or the relevant regions. What we need is global trends.

Fundamentals: long-term trends

In the environmental debate you often hear general discussion based on extremely short-term trends. This is dangerous – a lone swallow does not mean that summer has arrived.

Food prices have fallen dramatically during the last centuries (see Figure 25, p. 62). However, Lester Brown said in early 1998 that he could detect the beginnings of a historic increase in the price of wheat. From 1994 to 1996 wheat got more expensive and now we were headed for the abyss. In Figure 49 (p. 94) you will see that he was wrong. The wheat price in 2000 was lower than ever before.

Unfortunately, looking at short-term counter-trends was already firmly established in the first Worldwatch *State of the World* publication in 1984. Here, they worried about an international trade setback. "Nor is future growth in international trade likely to be rapid. According to the International Monetary Fund, the value of world exports peaked at $1,868 billion in 1980 and fell to roughly $1,650 billion in 1983, a decline of nearly 12 percent."[36] This claim can be evaluated in Figure 1. The 12 percent trade setback occurred mainly because of the second oil crisis, and it hit trade in goods but not services. However, Worldwatch Institute measures only goods and only presents figures that are not corrected for inflation – actually the alleged trade setback for inflation-adjusted trade in both goods and services is almost non-existent. Since 1983, international trade has more than doubled from $3.1 trillion to $7.5 trillion in 1997. And yes, the years 1980–83 show the *only* multi-year setback since data start in 1950.[37]

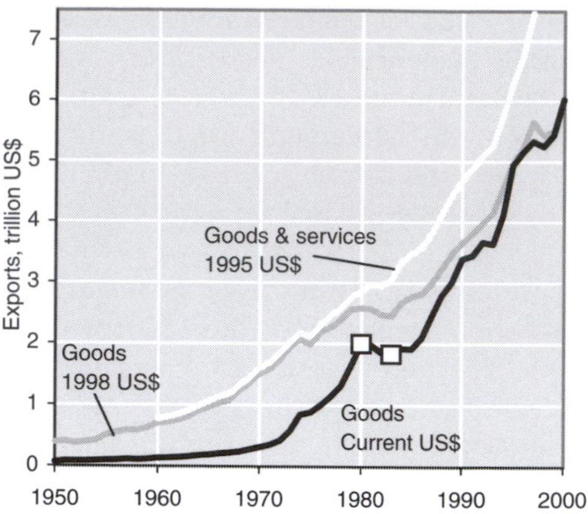

Figure 1 World exports of goods in current US$ 1950–2000, in 1998 US$ 1950–98, and goods and services 1960–97. Worldwatch Institute's worry of declining trade from 1980 to 1983 is marked out. Source: WTO 2000:27, IMF 2000d:226, 2000e, WI 2000b:75, 2000c, World Bank 2000c.[38]

Equally, Lester Brown wants to tell us how grain yields are no longer growing as fast or have perhaps even stopped completely, because increasingly we are reaching the physiological limits of the plants[39] (we will look more at this line of argument in chapter 9). Trying to discredit the World Bank grain predictions, he points out that "from 1990 to 1993, the first three years in the Bank's 20-year projection period, worldwide grain yields per hectare actually declined."[40] This claim is documented in Figure 2. Here it is evident that while Brown's claim is technically true (the grain yield did decline from 2.51 t/ha to 2.49 t/ha), it neglects and misrepresents the long-term growth. Moreover, it ignores the fact that this decline did not take place in the more vulnerable developing countries, where yields have steadily grown. Actually, the reason Brown finds grain yield declines in the early 1990s is primarily due to the breakup of the Soviet Union, causing grain yields there to plummet, but this is hardly an indication of physiological limits of the plants.

Isaac Asimov, worrying about more hurricanes from global warming (something we will look into in Part V), cites some seemingly worrying statistics: "The twenty-three years

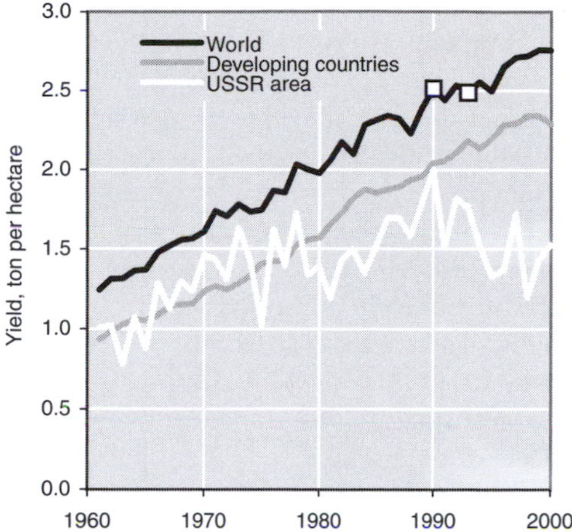

Figure 2 Grain yields for the world, the developing world and the USSR area, 1961–2000. Brown's proof of declining grain yields from 1990 to 1993 is marked out. Source: FAO 2001a.

from 1947 to 1969 averaged about 8.5 days of very violent Atlantic hurricanes, while in the period from 1970 to 1987 that dropped by three-quarters, to only 2.1 days per year . . . and in 1988–1989 rose again to 9.4 days a year."[41] This seems threatening. Now the hurricane rate is higher than ever. But notice the time-spans: 23 years, 17 years and then just two years at the end. Maybe the two years have been singled out just because they can be made spectacular? Well, at least the two years immediately preceding have 0 and 0.6 violent Atlantic hurricane days. And yes, the two years just after had only 1 and 1.2 days.[42] Documenting these trends, the original researcher points out that Atlantic violent hurricane days "show a substantial decrease in activity with time."[43] Since then, only hurricane days have been documented, and they too show a decline of 1.63 days/decade.[44]

In 1996 the World Wide Fund for Nature told us that the rate of forest loss in the Amazon rainforest had increased by 34 percent since 1992 to 1,489,600 hectares a year.[45] What they did not tell us was that the 1994/5 year had been a peak year of deforestation, at an estimated 0.81 percent, higher than any other year since 1977.[46] The year 1998/9 is estimated at 0.47 percent or nearly half of the top rate in 1994/5.

In a highly interconnected world, statistical short-term reversals are bound to occur in long-term trends. If we allow environmental arguments – however well-meaning – to be backed merely by purported trends of two or three carefully selected years, we invariably open the floodgates to any and every argument. Thus, if we are to appraise substantial developments we must investigate long periods of time. Not the two or five years usually used, but as far back as figures exist. Of course, we must be aware that a new tendency may be developing, and we must also be extra careful to include and analyze the latest available figures. But insisting on long-term trends protects us against false arguments from background noise and lone swallows.

In the chapters that follow, I will endeavor always to show the longest and the newest time trends.

Fundamentals: how is it important?

When we are told that something is a problem we need to ask how important it is in relation to other problems. We are forced constantly to prioritize our resources, and there will always be good projects we have to reject. The only scarce good is money with which to solve problems. But when the Litany is recited, it is often sufficient to point out that indeed there *is* a problem. Then you have won.

We all hear about pesticides getting into the groundwater. Since pesticides can cause cancer, we have a problem. Thus, they must be banned. Not many other fields would be able to sustain that sort of argument. "The Department of Defense has uncovered that State X has developed so-called Y6 missiles, which is a problem. We will therefore have to develop and set up a missile defense system." Most of us would probably ask how probable it was that State X would attack, how much damage a Y6 missile could do and how much the necessary defense system would cost. As regards pesticides, we should also ask how much damage they actually do and how much it would cost to avoid their use. Recent research suggests that pesticides cause very little cancer. Moreover, scrapping pesticides would actually result in *more* cases of cancer because fruits and vegetables help to prevent cancer, and without pesticides fruits and vegetables would get more expensive, so that people would eat less of them.

Likewise, when the World Wide Fund for Nature told us about the Amazon rainforest loss increasing to 1,489,600 hectares a year, we also have to ask, how much is that?[47] Is it a lot? One can naturally calculate the classical rate of "football pitches per hour." But have we any idea how many football pitches the Amazon can actually accommodate?[48] And perhaps a more important piece of information is that the total forest loss in the Amazon since the arrival of man has only amounted to 14 percent.[49]

The magazine *Environment* told us in May 2000 how we can buy a recyclable toothbrush to "take a bite out of landfill use."[50] At $17.50 for four toothbrushes, each comes with a postage-paid recycling mailer, such that the entire toothbrush can be recycled into plastic lumber to make outdoor furniture. The president of the company producing the toothbrush tells us how he "simply cannot throw plastic in the garbage. My hand freezes with guilt . . . The image of all that plastic sitting in a landfill giving off toxic gases puts me over the top."[51] Never mind that traditional plastics do not decompose and give off gases.[52] The more important question is: how important will this toothbrush effort be in reducing landfill?

If everyone in the US replaced their toothbrush four times a year as the dentists recommend (they don't – the average is 1.7), *Environment* estimates the total waste reduction at 45,400 tons – what the company thinks would "make a pretty significant impact on landfills."[53] Since the municipal waste generated in the US last year was 220 million tons,[54] the total change (if *everyone* brushed their teeth with new brushes four times a year and *everyone* bought the new recyclable toothbrush) is a reduction of 0.02 percent, at an annual cost of more than $4 billion. Equivalently, of the daily generated 4.44 pounds of waste per person, recycling one's toothbrush would cut 0.001 pound of waste a day (a sixtieth of an ounce), down to 4.439 pounds of daily waste.[55] Not even considering the added environmental effects of the postal system handling another billion packages a year, the cost is huge, while the benefit seems slight at best. Moreover, as we shall see in the section on waste, we are not running out of storage space – the entire waste generated in the US throughout the rest of the twenty-first century will fit within a square landfill less than 18 miles on the side (see Figure 115, p. 208).

In the following example Worldwatch Institute combines the problems of looking at short-term counter-trends and not asking what is important. In 1995 they pointed out how fertilizer use was declining. In their own words: "The era of substituting fertilizer for land came to a halt in 1990. If future food output gains cannot come from using large additional amounts of fertilizer, where will they come from? The graph of fertilizer use and grainland area per person may capture the human dilemma as the twenty-first century approaches more clearly than any other picture could."[56] (We will deal with the question of grainland area below.) The graph they showed us is the world fertilizer consumption (upper line) in Figure 3.

First, if we worry about food production, we should focus not on the *world* average, but on the average of where the potential food problem is – the developing world. And here we see that the fertilizer use per person has been almost continuously increasing, hitting an all-time high at 17.7 kg/person in 1999. When Worldwatch Institute finds a trend to worry about, it is mainly because they neglect to ask

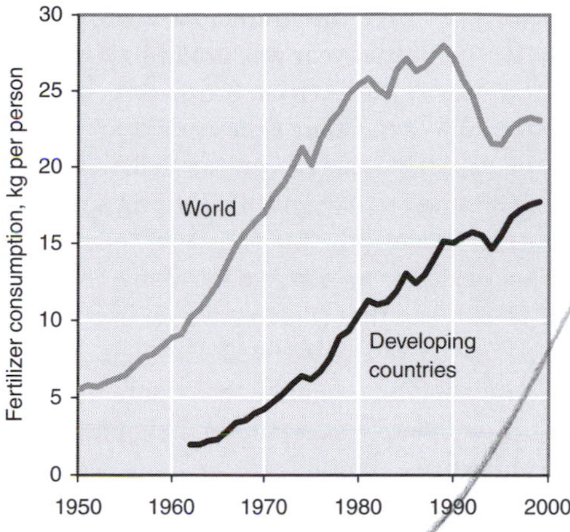

Figure 3 Fertilizer use, kg per person for the world (1950–99) and for the developing world (1962–99). Source: IFA 2000, WI 1999b.

what information is important. Second, this "human dilemma" is also a product of looking at short-term trends. With their data naturally stopping in 1994, Worldwatch Institute finds a clear reversal of trends – but why? Mainly because of the breakdown of the Soviet Union, which the Worldwatch Institute also acknowledges elsewhere.[57]

Another neat example is the way many commentators merely regard one environmental solution as the beginning of another problem.[58] Isaac Asimov informs us that "what has happened to the problem of air pollution is only what happens to most of the world's environmental problems. The problems don't get solved. They simply get pushed aside, because they are swamped with unexpected newer and even worse ones."[59]

Of course, such a sweeping statement should at least have a good foundation in its example. Here, Asimov tells us how the British tried to solve London's air pollution by building "very tall smokestacks so that the particulate pollution rose high into the air and only fell to earth as soot hundreds of miles away. Like most technological fixes, that one didn't really fix the problem, it only removed it to a different place. In the final analysis, all London had done was to export its smog, in the form of acid rain, to the lakes and forests of Scandinavia."[60] Former vice president Al Gore tells us the exact same story: "Some of what Londoners used to curse as smog now burns the leaves of Scandinavian trees."[61] And since Britain and most other developed nations have begun removing the sulfur from the smokestack emissions, environmentalists now point out that depositing the removed sulfur slurry constitutes a major health hazard.[62]

In essence, first we had one problem (bad air in London), then we had another (acid rain in Scandinavia), and then came a third (slurry waste). But we still had a problem. So things are not getting better. Or, in the judgment of Asimov, the problem has apparently become even worse. But such argument entirely avoids asking the question "how important?" Urban air pollution in London has decreased by more than 90 percent since 1930.[63] The former urban air pollution probably killed at least 64,000 extra people each year in the UK.[64] Depositing slurry waste causes far less than one cancer death every fifty years.[65] Thus, to describe the transition from one problem to another as simply exchanging one problem for another is to miss the point entirely: that more than 63,999 people now live longer – every year.

Without asking the essential question of "how important" we cannot prioritize and use our resources where they make the most impact.

Fundamentals: people

Counting lives lost from different problems also emphasizes a central assumption in my argument: that the needs and desires of humankind represent the crux of our assessment of the state of the world. This does not mean that plants and animals do not also have rights but that the focus will always be on the human evaluation.[66]

This describes both my ethical conception of the world – and on that account the reader can naturally disagree with me – but also a realistic conception of the world: people debate and participate in decision-making processes, whereas penguins and pine trees do not.[67] So the extent to which penguins and pine trees are considered depends in the final instance on some (in democracies more than half of all) individuals being prepared to act on their behalf. When we are to evaluate a project, therefore, it depends on the assessment by *people*. And while some of these people will definitely choose to value animals and plants very highly, these plants and animals cannot to any great extent be given particular rights.[68]

This is naturally an approach that is basically selfish on the part of human beings. But in addition to being the most realistic description of the present form of decision-making it seems to me to be the only defensible one. Because what alternative do we have? Should penguins have the right to vote? If not, who should be allowed to speak on their behalf? (And how should these representatives be selected?)

It is also important to point out that this human-centered view does not automatically result in the neglect or elimination of many non-human life forms. Man is in so many and so obvious ways dependent on other life forms, and for this reason alone they will be preserved and their welfare appreciated. In many places man actually shares common interests with animals and plants, for example in their desire for clean air. But it is also obvious that a choice frequently has to be made between what is good for humans and what is good for animals and plants. If we choose to allow a forest to stand untouched this will be a great advantage to many animals but a lost opportunity for man to cultivate timber and grow food.[69] Whether we want an untouched forest or a cultivated field depends on *man*'s preferences with regard to food and undisturbed nature.

The conclusion is that we have no option but to use humans as a point of reference. How can we otherwise avoid an ethical dilemma? When Americans argue for cutting nitrogen emissions to the northern Gulf of Mexico to save the bottom-dwelling animals from asphyxiation, this is a statement of a *human* desire or preference for living sea-floor fauna. It is not that such a cut is in itself mandated to save the sea-bed dwellers – not because they have inalienable rights in some way. If we were to use the inalienable rights argument we could not explain why we choose to save some animals at the bottom of the sea while at the same time we slaughter cattle for beef. Why then should these cattle not have the same right to survive as the fauna at the bottom of the Gulf?

Reality versus myths

It is crucial to the discussion about the state of the world that we consider the fundamentals. This requires us to refer to long-term and global trends, considering their importance especially with regard to human welfare.

But it is also crucial that we cite figures and trends which are true.

This demand may seem glaringly obvious, but the public environment debate has unfortunately been characterized by an unpleasant tendency towards rather rash treatment of the truth. This is an expression of the fact that the Litany has pervaded the debate so deeply and for so long that blatantly false claims can be made again and again, without any references, and yet still be believed.

Take notice, this is *not* due to primary research in the environmental field; this generally appears to be professionally competent and well balanced.[70] It is due, however, to the communication of environmental knowledge, which taps deeply into our doomsday beliefs. Such propaganda is presented by many environmental organizations, such as the Worldwatch Institute, Greenpeace and the

World Wide Fund for Nature, and by many individual commentators, and it is readily picked up by the media.

The number of examples are so overwhelming that they could fill a book of their own. I will consider many of them in the course of this book, and we will look specifically at their connection to the media in the next chapter. However, let us here look at some of the more outstanding examples of environmental mythmaking.

Reality: Worldwatch Institute

Often the expressions of the Litany can be traced – either directly or indirectly – to Lester Brown and his Worldwatch Institute. Its publications are almost overflowing with statements such as: "The key environmental indicators are increasingly negative. Forests are shrinking, water tables are falling, soils are eroding, wetlands are disappearing, fisheries are collapsing, range-lands are deteriorating, rivers are running dry, temperatures are rising, coral reefs are dying, and plant and animal species are disappearing."[71] Powerful reading – stated entirely without references.[72]

Discussing forests, Worldwatch Institute categorically states that "the world's forest estate has declined significantly in both area and quality in recent decades."[73] As we shall see in the section on forests, the longest data series from the UN's FAO show that global forest cover has *increased* from 30.04 percent of the global land area in 1950 to 30.89 percent in 1994, an increase of 0.85 percentage points over the last 44 years (see Figure 60, p. 111).[74] Such global figures are not referred to, however; we are only told that "each year another 16 million hectares of forests disappear"[75] – a figure which is 40 percent higher than the latest UN figure.[76] Nor is reference made to figures regarding the forests' quality – simply because no such global figures exist.

Blatant errors are also made with unfortunate frequency. Worldwatch Institute claims that "the soaring demand for paper is contributing to deforestation, particularly in the northern temperate zone. Canada is losing some 200,000 hectares of forest a year."[77] Reference is made to the FAO's *State of the World's Forests 1997*, but if you refer to the source you will see that in fact Canada grew 174,600 *more* hectares of forest each year.[78]

In their 2000 overview, Worldwatch Institute lists the problems staked out in their very first State of the World publication from 1984. Here is the complete list: "Record rates of population growth, soaring oil prices, debilitating levels of international debt, and extensive damage to forests from the new phenomenon of acid rain."[79] Naturally, assessing this list at the turn of the millennium could be a good place to take stock of the important issues, asking ourselves if we have overcome earlier problems. However, Worldwatch Institute immediately tells us that we have not solved these problems: "Far from it. As we complete this seventeenth *State of the World* report, we are about to enter a new century having solved few of these problems, and facing even more profound challenges to the future of the global economy. The bright promise of a new millennium is now clouded by unprecedented threats to humanity's future."[80]

Worldwatch Institute does not return to look at the list but merely tells us that the problems have not been solved and that we have added even more problems since then. But does the Litany stand up, if we check the data? The level of international debt may be the only place where we have not seen significant improvement: although the level of debt declined steadily throughout the 1990s, it declined only slightly, from 144 percent of exports in 1984 to 137 percent in 1999.[81]

However, and as we shall see, acid rain while harming lakes did very little if any damage to forests. Moreover, the sulfur emissions responsible for acid rain have declined in both Europe and the US – in the EU, emissions have been cut by a full 60 percent since 1984 (as you can also see in Figure 91, p. 172).[82]

The soaring oil prices which cost the world a decade of slow growth from the 1970s into the mid-1980s declined throughout the 1990s to a price comparable to or lower than the one before the oil crisis (as can be seen in Figure 64, p. 123). Even though oil prices have doubled since the all-time low in mid-1998, the price in the first quarter of 2001 is on par with the price in 1990, and the barrel price of $25 in March 2001 is still way below the top price of $60 in the early 1980s.[83] Moreover, most consider this spike is a short-term occurrence, where the US Energy Information Agency expects an almost steady oil price over the next 20 years at about $22 a barrel.[84]

Finally, speaking of record rates of population growth is merely wrong, since the record was set back in 1964 at 2.17 percent per year, as you can see in Figure 13, p. 47.[85] Since that record, the rate has been steadily declining, standing at 1.26 percent in 2000, and expected to drop below 1 percent in 2016. Even the absolute number of people added to the world reached its peak in 1990 with 87 million, dropping to 76 million in 2000 and still decreasing.

Thus, in its shorthand appraisal of the state of the world since 1984, Worldwatch Institute sets out a list of problems, *all* of which have improved since then, and all but one of which have improved immensely, and one of which is just plain wrong. Not a great score for 16 years that have supposedly been meticulously covered by the Worldwatch reports. The problem, of course, is not lack of data – Worldwatch Institute publishes fine data collections, which are also used in this book – but merely a carelessness that comes with the ingrained belief in the Litany.

Such belief is also visible in the future visions of the Worldwatch Institute. After all, in their 2000 quote above, they promise us that we will face "even more profound challenges" and "unprecedented threats," clouding humanity's future.[86] These threats are often summarized in a connection that has almost become a trademark of the Worldwatch Institute, namely that the ever expanding economy will eventually undermine the planet's natural systems. In the 2000 edition it proclaims: "As the global economy expands, local ecosystems are collapsing at an accelerating pace."[87] Of course, we should like to see such an accelerating pace being documented. But Worldwatch Institute immediately continues:

> Even as the Dow Jones climbed to new highs during the 1990s, ecologists were noting that ever growing human demands would eventually lead to local breakdowns, a situation where deterioration would replace progress. No one knew what form this would take, whether it would be water shortages, food shortages, disease, internal ethnic conflict, or external political conflict.[88]

Notice, we are not being offered any documentation as to these breakdowns. Moreover, the (unnamed) ecologists are sure that they will come, but apparently "no one" knows what form this breakdown will take. And finally, creating a list as broad as above, including even internal ethnic conflicts, seems like hedging your bets, while they have an entirely unexplicated and undocumented connection to ecological breakdown.

But right after this, Worldwatch Institute gives us its main example of the breakdown, caused by an ever expanding economy crushing the local ecosystems: "The first region where decline is replacing progress is sub-Saharan Africa. In this region of 800 million people, life expectancy – a sentinel indicator of progress – is falling precipitously as governments overwhelmed by rapid population growth have failed to curb the spread of the virus that leads to AIDS."[89] To make the implication perfectly clear, Worldwatch Institute points out that this AIDS infection "suggests that some countries may already have crossed a deterioration/decline threshold."[90]

This prime example of an ecosystem collapse is surprising, to say the least. It is true that HIV/AIDS has decreased and is decreasing life expectancy in sub-Saharan Africa, and within some states has caused shockingly great declines (this we will look at in Part II). However, is this caused by an ever increasing economy crushing the ecosystem? In one of the newest reviews of AIDS in Africa, the main cause is staked out fairly clearly:

> The high levels of AIDS arise from the failure of African political and religious leaders to recognize social and sexual reality. The means for containing and conquering the epidemic are already known, and could prove effective if the leadership could be induced to adopt them. The lack of individual behavioral change and of the implementation of effective government policy has roots in attitudes to death and a silence about the epidemic arising from beliefs about its nature and the timing of death.[91]

Equally, in a review in *The Lancet*, it is argued that:

> two principal factors are to blame [for the AIDS epidemic in the developing countries]: first, the reluctance of national governments to take responsibility for preventing HIV infection; and second, a failure by both national governments and international agencies to set realistic priorities that can have an effect on the overall epidemic in countries with scarce resources and weak implementation capacity.[92]

To put it differently, the rapid spread of AIDS in Africa is primarily caused by *political* and *social* factors. The tragedy is obvious and demands the attention and efforts of the developed world, but it is *not* an indication of an ecological collapse brought on by an ever expanding economy. Moreover, the Worldwatch Institute's obsession with pointing out how they have finally found an example of concrete decline replacing progress seems ill placed and unfounded.[93]

But Worldwatch Institute also gives us another concrete example of ecological collapse, when pointing out the dangers of complex interactions. Let us quote the entire paragraph to see the extraordinary transition from general claims to concrete examples:

> The risk in a world adding nearly 80 million people annually is that so many sustainable yield thresholds will be crossed in such a short period of time that the consequences will become unmanageable. Historically, when early civilizations lived largely in isolation, the consequences of threshold crossings were strictly local. Today, in the age of global economic integration, a threshold crossing in one major country can put additional pressure on resources in other countries. When Beijing banned logging in the upper reaches of the Yangtze River basin in 1998, for example, the increased demand for forest products from neighboring countries in Southeast Asia intensified the pressure on the region's remaining forests.[94]

Thus, the best example that Worldwatch Institute can give us of the world's unmanageable collapses is a change in timber production of an undocumented size, which by most economists would be described exactly as an efficient production decision: essentially the Chinese government has discovered that producing trees in the upper reaches of the Yangtze is all in all a bad deal, because the trees are better used to moderate flooding. Ironically, Worldwatch Institute actually claims that this logging ban is a proof that "the principles of ecology are replacing basic economics in the management of national forests."[95] The reason is that the Beijing viewpoint "now is that trees standing are worth three times as much as those cut, simply because of the water storage and flood control capacity of forests."[96] Of course, this is just plain and simple (and probably sound) social cost-benefit analysis – good economics, and not ecology.

Thus, the prominent and repeated statements of the Worldwatch Institute analyzed here seem to indicate that the Litany's claims of ecological collapse are founded on very fragile examples or merely offered on faith. (It is also worth pointing out how these quotes underline the danger of arguing from single examples and not global trends, as pointed out above.)

Of course, while these quotes show some of the strongest arguments for the Litany in *State of the World*, Worldwatch Institute offers a long list of other examples and analyses within different areas, and we shall comment on these as we go through the subjects in this book.

Reality: World Wide Fund for Nature

World Wide Fund for Nature (WWF) focused towards the end of 1997 on the Indonesian forest fires which were pouring out thick clouds of smoke over much of Southeast Asia. There is no doubt that these were obnoxious for city dwellers, but WWF stressed how the forest fires were a signal that the world's forests were "out of balance" – tidings which the Worldwatch Institute actually announced as one of the primary signs of ecological breakdown in 1997.[97]

WWF proclaimed 1997 as "the year the world caught fire," because "in 1997, fire burned more forests than at any other time in history."[98] Summing up, the WWF president Claude Martin stated unequivocally that "this is not just an emergency, it is a planetary disaster."[99] But on closer inspection, as can be seen in the forests section later in the book, the figures do not substantiate this claim: 1997 was well below the record, and the only reason that 1997 was the year when Indonesia's forest fires were noticed was that it was the first time they really irritated city dwellers.[100] In all, Indonesia's forest fires affected approximately 1 percent of the nation's forests.

Likewise, WWF in 1997 issued a press release entitled "Two-thirds of the world's forests lost forever."[101] Both here and in their *Global Annual Forest Report 1997*, they explained how "new research by WWF shows that almost two-thirds of the world's original forest cover has been lost."[102] This seemed rather amazing to me, since most sources estimate about 20 to 25 percent.[103] I therefore called WWF in England and spoke to Rachel Thackray and Alison Lucas, who had been responsible for the press release, and asked to see WWF's research report. All they were able to tell me, however, was that actually, *no report had ever existed* and that WWF had been given the figures by Mark Aldrich of the World Conservation Monitoring Centre. Apparently, they had looked at some maximum figures, and because of problems of definition had included the forests of the northern hemisphere in the original overview of forest cover, but not in the current one.[104]

From this non-report, WWF tells us that: "now we have proof of the extent of forest already lost . . . The frightening thing is that the pace of forest destruction has accelerated dramatically over the last 5 years and continues to rise."[105] The UN, however, tells us that the rate of deforestation was 0.346 percent in the 1980s and just 0.32 percent in the period 1990–5 – not a dramatic increase in pace, but a *decrease*.[106]

WWF confides in us that nowhere is deforestation more manifest than in Brazil, which "still has the highest annual rate of forest loss in the world."[107] In actual fact the deforestation rate in Brazil is among the lowest as far as tropical forest goes; according to the UN the deforestation rate in Brazil is at 0.5 percent per year compared to an average of 0.7 percent per year.[108]

In more recent material, WWF has now lowered their estimate of original cover from 8,080 million hectares to 6,793 million hectares (some 16 percent), while they have increased their estimate of the current forest cover from 3,044 million hectares to 3,410 million (some 12 percent), although their current estimate is still some 100 million hectares lower than the UN estimate.[109] This means that WWF has lowered its estimates from 62.3 percent to 49.8 percent of the earth's forest that have been lost.[110]

Still, this is much more than the 20 percent commonly estimated. However, two independent researchers at the University of London and the University of Sussex[111] have tried to assess the sources and data used by WWF, the World Conservation Monitoring Centre and others in making such gloomy estimates of vast forest reductions. Considering the enormous amount of data, they have focused on the assessments of forest loss in West Africa, a place where WWF/WCMC estimates a forest loss of 87 percent or some 48.6 million hectares.[112] However, when looking at the documentation, it turns out to be based mainly on problematic bio-climatic forest zones, essentially comparing today's forests with where there *may* have been forests earlier. In general, the researchers find that "the statistics for forest loss in general circulation today massively exaggerate deforestation during the twentieth century."[113] The result is that for West Africa the actual deforestation is about 9.5–10.5 million hectares, *or about five times less than what is estimated by WWF/WCMC.*[114]

Finally, WWF uses among other measures these forest estimates to make a so-called Living Planet Index, supposedly showing a decline over the past 25 years of 30 percent – "implying that the world has lost 30 per cent of its natural wealth in the space of one generation."[115] This index uses three measures: the extent of natural forests (without plantations), and two indices of changes in populations of selected marine and freshwater vertebrate species. The index is very problematic. First, excluding plantations of course ensures that the forest cover index will fall (since plantations are increasing), but it is unclear whether plantations are bad for nature overall. Plantations produce much of our forest goods, reducing pressure on other forests – in Argentina, 60 percent of all wood is produced in plantations which constitute just 2.2 percent of the total forest area, thus relieving the other 97.8 percent of the forests.[116] While WWF states that plantations "make up large tracts of current forest area,"[117] they in fact constitute only 3 percent of the world's total forest area.[118]

Second, when using 102 selected marine and 70 selected freshwater species there is naturally no way of ensuring that these species are representative of the innumerable other species. Actually, since research is often conducted on species that are known to be in trouble (an issue we will return to in the next chapter, but basically because troubled species are the ones on which we need information in order to act), it is likely that such estimates will be grossly biased towards decline.

Third, in order to assess the state of the world, we need to look at many more and better measures. This is most clear when WWF actually quotes a new study that shows the total worth of the ecosystem to be $33 trillion annually (this problematic study estimating the ecosystem to be worth more than the global production at $31 trillion we will discuss in Part V).[119] According to WWF, it implies that when the Living Planet Index has dropped 30 percent, that means that we now get 30 percent less from the ecosystem each year – that we now lose some $11 trillion each year.[120] Such a claim is almost nonsensical.[121] Forest output has not decreased but actually increased some 40 percent since 1970.[122] And the overwhelming value of the ocean and coastal areas are in nutrient recycling, which the Living Planet Index does not measure *at all*. Also, marine food production has increased almost 60 percent since 1970 (see Figure 57, p. 107). Thus, by their own measures, we have not experienced a fall in ecosystem services but actually an increase.

Reality: Greenpeace

In the Danish press I pointed out that we had long been hearing figures for the extinction of the world's species which were far too high – that we would lose about half of all species within a generation. The correct figure is closer to 0.7 percent in 50 years. This led to the Danish chairman of Greenpeace, Niels Bredsdorff, pointing out that Greenpeace had long accepted the figure of 0.7 percent.[123] However, Greenpeace's official biodiversity report stated that "it is expected that half the Earth's species are likely to disappear within the next seventy-five years."[124] The chairman has never officially commented on this report, but he did manage to persuade Greenpeace International to pull the report off the internet, because it did not contain one single scientific reference.

Norwegian television also confronted Greenpeace in Norway with this report and rather forced them into a corner. Four days later they decided to hold a press conference in which they raised all the general points which I had mentioned and reevaluated their effort. The Norwegian daily *Verdens Gang* reported:

> We have had problems adapting the environment movement to the new reality, says Kalle Hestvedt of Greenpeace. He believes the one-sided pessimism about the situation weakens the environment organizations' credibility. When most people do not feel that the world is about to fall off its hinges at any moment, they have problems taking the environmental organizations seriously, Hestvedt maintains.[125]

By way of summary Greenpeace says in brief: "The truth is that many environmental issues we fought for ten years back are as good as solved. Even so, the strategy continues to focus on the assumption that 'everything is going to hell'."[126]

Reality: wrong bad statistics and economics

There is an amazing amount of incorrect statements in many other sources. Let us just try to summarize a few, and also display the often lax attitude to economic arguments.

One of the new anxieties, about synthetic chemicals mimicking human and animal hormones, has received a great boost with the publication of the popular scientific book *Our Stolen Future*.[127] We will look at the arguments in Part V, but here we can state that the book hinges a large part of its argument on a purported connection between synthetic hormones and breast cancer. It states, that "by far the most alarming health trend for women is the rising rate of breast cancer, the most common female cancer."[128] The link? "Since 1940, when the chemical age was dawning, breast cancer deaths have risen steadily by one percent per year in the United States, and similar increases have been reported in other industrial countries. Such incidence rates are adjusted for age, so they reflect genuine trends rather than demographic changes such as a growing elderly population."[129] A 1 percent increase since 1940 would mean a 75 percent increase in breast cancer deaths by publication in 1996.[130] However, this claim is plain wrong, as you can also see in Figure 119, p. 220. At the time of writing *Our Stolen Future*, the age-adjusted death rate had *dropped* some 9 percent since 1940; the latest figures for 1998 indicate a drop of 18 percent.[131]

The *Global Environmental Outlook Report 2000* also tells us of the Earth's many water problems.[132] These we shall look at in Part IV, but when *GEO 2000* actually mentions numbers, it gets carried away. "Worldwide, polluted water is estimated to affect the health of about 1200 million people and to contribute to the death of about 15 million children under five every year."[133] However, the *total* number of deaths among children under 5 is estimated by WHO to be about 10 million.[134] Equally, the report claims that "the growth of municipal and industrial demands for water has led to conflicts over the distribution of water rights. Water resources are now a major constraint to growth and increased economic activities envisioned by planners, especially in the west and southwestern arid lands of the United States."[135] But its only reference does not even mention water constraints influencing economic growth in the US.[136]

Virtually every year, Worldwatch Institute makes much of the fact that the use of renewable energy sources grows much faster than use of conventional fuels – in the 1990s at 22 percent compared to oil at less than 2 percent.[137] But comparing such growth rates is misleading, because with wind making up just 0.05 percent of all energy, double-digit growth rates are not all that hard to come by. In 1998, the amount of energy in the 2 percent oil increase was still 323 times bigger than the 22 percent increase in wind energy.[138] Even in the unlikely event that the amazing wind power growth rate could continue, it would take 46 consecutive years of 22 percent growth for wind to outgrow oil.[139]

Likewise, the environmental movement would love renewable energy to be cheaper than fossil fuels. But using economic arguments, there often seems to be an astounding lack of rigor. Many argue simply on faith that if the costs on environment and humans from coal pollution and waste products were taken into account, renewable energy would indeed be cheaper.[140] However, three of the largest projects – one European and two American – have attempted to examine *all* costs associated with electricity production, all the way from the mortal risks of mining coal, the traffic hazards of transportation and occupational hazards of production including consequences of acid rain, soot, sulfur dioxide, nitrogen oxides and ozone on lakes, crops, buildings, children and old people and up to the consequences of tax codes and occupation plus a long, long list of similar considerations and costs.[141] And they still find the extra costs to be less than the gap between renewables and fossil fuels (see also the discussion in Part III).[142] However, there is no doubt that renewables will be cheaper in the near-to-medium future, and this will probably be a big part of the reason why we need to worry less about global warming in the long run (see Part V).

An equivalent laxness in economic arguments is obvious when Worldwatch Institute tells us that "wind power is now economically competitive with fossil fuel generated electricity."[143] However, they also tell us that in the future it is necessary that "sufficiency replaces profligacy as the ethic of the next energy paradigm."[144] But according to Worldwatch Institute this will be okay, since it is not a major cut-back: "Modest changes, such as owning smaller cars and homes, or driving less and cycling more, would still leave us with lifestyles that are luxurious by historical standards."[145] Thus, while it may be true that if we merely accept less convenience we will still be better off than by "historical standards," it nevertheless means that we will be *less* well off. Possibly, it will be a more sustainable society with a better environment, but at least the choice should be stated clearly as a trade-off.

Likewise, Worldwatch Institute wants to downplay the costs of avoiding global warming by reducing CO_2 emissions. Quoting Thomas Casten, a CEO from a smaller renewable energy firm, they point out that "the small, extraordinarily efficient power plants his company provides can triple the energy efficiency of some older, less efficient plants. The issue, he says, is not how much it will cost to reduce carbon emissions, but who is going to harvest the enormous profits in doing so."[146] However, Worldwatch Institute also envisions how in the twenty-first century "the climate battle may assume the kind of strategic importance that wars – both hot and cold – have had during" the twentieth Century.[147] Backed up by a number of leading scientists writing in *Nature*, Worldwatch Institute actually asserts that to develop the necessary technologies to combat climate change will require a monumental research effort, conducted with the urgency of the Manhattan Project.[148] It is perhaps as well to note that both the cold war and the Manhattan Project were rather expensive projects.

Reality: water problems

A lot of worries go into the question of water – do we have enough, will scarcity cause water wars, etc. In recent years water scarcity has become one of Worldwatch Institute's favorite

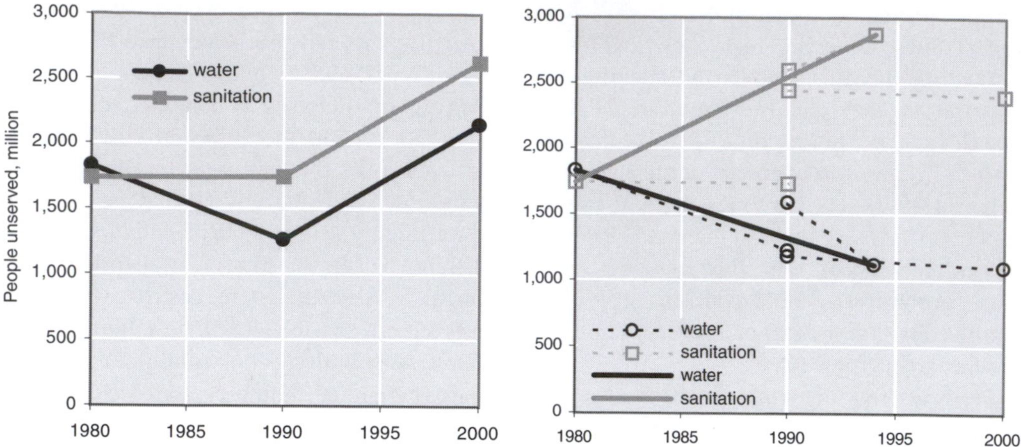

Figure 4 Two attempts at showing the development of access to clean water and sanitation. Left, number of people unserved 1980–2000. OBS: Numbers for 1990–2000 are incorrect. Right, number of people unserved 1980–90, 1990–4, 1990–2000 in broken lines. OBS: Solid lines for 1980–94 are incorrect. Source: Gleick 1993:10, 187–9. 1998:262, 264, 1999, Annan 2000:5.

examples of future problems. While we will discuss these water questions more thoroughly in chapter 13, we will here look at two of the most common claims.

One of the most widely used college books on the environment, *Living in the Environment*, claims that "according to a 1995 World Bank study, 30 countries containing 40 percent of the world's population (2.3 billion people) now experience chronic water shortages that threaten their agriculture and industry and the health of their people."[149] This World Bank study is referred to in many different environment texts with slightly differing figures.[150] Unfortunately, none mentions a source.

With a good deal of help from the World Bank, I succeeded in locating the famous document. It turns out that the myth had its origin in a hastily drawn up press release. The headline on the press release was: "The world is facing a water crisis: 40 percent of the world's population suffers from chronic water shortage."[151] If you read on, however, it suddenly becomes clear that the vast majority of the 40 percent are not people who use too much water but those who have no access to water or sanitation facilities – the exact opposite point. If one also reads the memo to which the press release relates, it shows that the global water crisis which Lester Brown and others are worried about affects not 40 percent but about 4 percent of the world's population.[152] And, yes, it wasn't 30, but 80 countries the World Bank was referring to.

However, it is true that the most important human problem with water today is not that we use too much but that too many have no access. It is estimated that if we could secure clean drinking water and sanitation for everyone, this would avoid several million deaths every year and prevent half a billion people becoming seriously ill each year.[153] The one-off cost would be less than $200 billion or less than four times the annual global development aid.[154]

Thus, the most important water question is whether access to water and sanitation has been improving or declining. Peter Gleick, one of the foremost water experts, has edited a substantial, engaged book about water, *Water in Crisis*, an erudite Oxford publication of almost 500 large pages. However, when estimating water and sanitation access, Gleick seems to stumble on the Litany, as illustrated in Figure 4.

From 1980 to 1990, Gleick makes the same general point as this book, i.e. that things have become better: fewer people in the world are denied access to water, and because 750 million more souls came into the developing countries in the same period, 1.3 billion more people have actually gained access to water. The proportion of people in developing countries with access to water has thus increased from 44 percent to 69 percent, or by more than 25 percentage points. As far as sanitation is concerned, more or less the same number of people are denied access (about 6 million more), but once again, because of the growth in the population, almost three-quarters of a billion more people have access to sanitation – making the proportion increase from 46 percent to 56 percent.[155] However, the period from 1990 to 2000 in the left side of Figure 4 indicates that things will now get worse. Far more people will end up without water or sewage facilities. In fact the proportion will again fall by 10–12 percentage points. But if you check the figures it turns out that all Gleick has done is to expect that 882 million more people will be born in the nineties. Since none of these from the outset will have access to water or sewage facilities their number has simply been added to the total number of unserved.[156]

Of course, this is an entirely unreasonable assumption. In essence, Gleick is saying that in the decade from 1980 to 1990, 1.3 billion people had water supplies installed, so we should assume that for the period 1990 to 2000 the figure will be *zero*? However, the graph has been reproduced in many places, and has for instance been distributed in a seminal article on the shortage of water.[157]

In 1996, the UN published its official estimates for access to water and sanitation in the period 1990 to 1994.[159] What constitutes water and sanitation access is naturally a question of definition. (How close to the dwelling need a water pump be? Is a hole in the ground sanitation?) In 1996, the UN used its most restrictive definition of access on both 1990 and 1994.[160] This caused the UN estimate for the 1990 number of unserved to increase substantially.[161] Thus, in the right-hand side of Figure 4 we can see how the number of people without access to water in 1990 was no longer 1.2 billion but 1.6 billion, now declining to 1.1 billion in 1994. Equally, the number of people without sanitation was not 1.7 billion but 2.6 billion, increasing to 2.9 billion in 1994. Gleick gives us both sets of numbers in his academic book,[162] but when presenting the evidence in a popular magazine only the original 1980 and the revised 1994 figures are presented.[163] This, of course, compares two entirely non-comparable figures. It suggests that the decline in the number of water-unserved has been much smaller than it really is, and suggests that the increase in sanitation-unserved has been much higher than it really is.

In April 2000, the UN's latest estimate for 1990–2000 was published, indicating that unserved of both water and sanitation had indeed declined over the decade.[164] Since the decade added some 750 million people to the developing world, this means that more than three-quarters of a billion more people got access to clean drinking water and sanitation. Thus, the share of people with access increased substantially. In Figure 5 you can see how the share of people in the developing countries with access to drinking water has increased from 30 percent in 1970 to 80 percent in 2000. Equally, the share of people with access to sanitation has increased from 23 percent in 1970 to 53 percent in 2000.

Although there is still much left to do, especially in sanitation, the most important water problem is indeed improving.

Reality: Pimentel and global health I

Most basic environmental research is sound and unbiased, producing numbers and trends as inputs to evaluations such as Worldwatch Institute's *State of the World* or indeed this

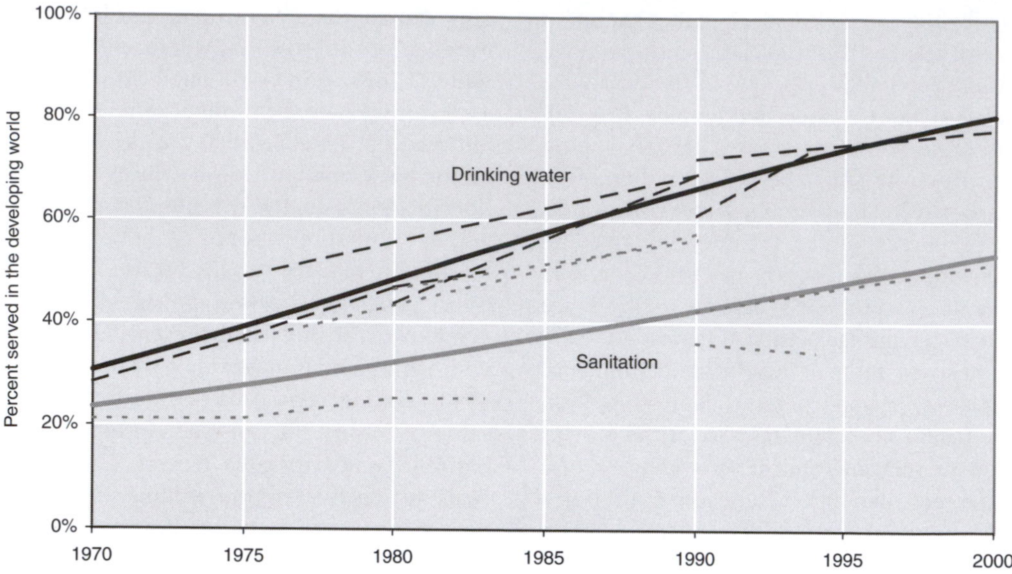

Figure 5 Percentage of people in the Third World with access to drinking water and sanitation, 1970–2000. Light, broken lines indicate individual, comparable estimates, solid lines is a logistic best fit line – a reasonable attempt to map out the best guess of development among very different definitions.[158] Source: World Bank 1994:26 (1975–90), WHO 1986:15–18 (1970–83), Gleick 1998:262, 264 (1980–90, 1990–4), Annan 2000:5 (1990–2000).

book. However, there is a significant segment of papers even in peer-reviewed journals trying to make assessments of broader areas, where the belief in the Litany sometimes takes over and causes alarmist and even amazingly shoddy work. Most of these poor statements are documented throughout this book, but nevertheless it might be instructional to take a look at the anatomy of such arguments. As I do not want just to show you a single example or pick out a lone error, but to show you the breadth and depth of the shoddiness, we will actually have to touch a number of bases that we will return to during the book.

Professor David Pimentel of Cornell University is a frequently cited and well-known environmentalist, responsible – among many other arguments – for a global erosion estimate far larger than any other (we will discuss this in Part III) and for arguing that the ideal population of a sustainable US would be 40–100 million (i.e. a reduction of 63–85 percent of the present population).[165]

In October 1998, Professor Pimentel published as lead author an article on the "Ecology of increasing disease" in the peer-reviewed journal *BioScience*.[166] The basic premise of the paper is that increasing population will lead to increasing environmental degradation, intensified pollution and consequently more human disease. Along the way, many other negative events or tendencies are mentioned, even if many have very little bearing on the subject.

The Pimentel article repeatedly makes the mistakes we have talked about above, but most importantly it is wrong and seriously misleading on all of its central conclusions. However, this has not hindered the article in being cited and frequently used in pointing out the decline of the world.[167]

When looking at trends, Pimentel happily uses very short-term descriptions. He looks at the biggest infectious disease killer, tuberculosis, claiming it has gone from killing 2.5 million in 1990 to 3 million in 1995, and citing an

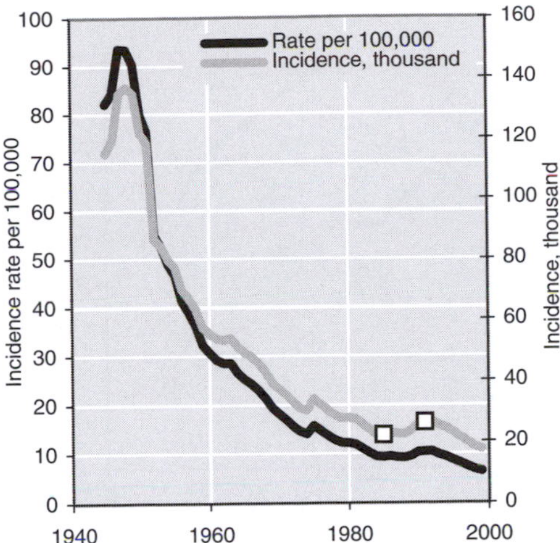

Figure 6 Number and rate of tuberculosis cases in the US, 1945–99. The two years, 1985 and 1991, picked by Pimentel, are indicated. Source: CDC 1995:69–79, CDC 1999g:79, 2000a:858, USBC 2000c.

expected 3.5 million dead in 2000.[168] However, in 1999, the actual death toll from tuberculosis was 1.669 million, and the WHO source that Pimentel most often uses estimates an almost stable 2 million dead over the 1990s.[169]

Although predictions can excusably prove wrong, Pimentel's comparison with tuberculosis in the US is seriously problematic: "Patterns of TB infection in the United States are similar to the world situation, in which TB cases increased by approximately 18 percent from 1985 to 1991."[170] While technically true, it is obvious from Figure 6 that this quote is misleading. Pimentel has taken the lowest number of tuberculosis cases (22,201 cases in 1985) and compared it with the almost top in 1991 (26,283 cases). But using almost any other years would more correctly have indicated a decline. Even in 1996, two years before Pimentel's article, the total number was below 1985. The latest figures from 1999 show 17,531 cases.

Moreover, comparing absolute numbers is problematic; when the population in the US increased 6 percent from 1985 to 1991,[171] we should expect tuberculosis cases to increase equivalently. If we look at the rate per 100,000, the increase from 1985 to 1991 almost disappears (slightly less than 12 percent) and the rate has since dropped some 31 percent since 1985, some 38 percent since 1991. Similarly, the tuberculosis death rate has declined more than 40 percent since 1985.[172] The only reason Pimentel can find an increase in tuberculosis cases is because he picks the exact years to show a counter-trend.

Equally, pointing out the danger of chemicals and pesticides, Pimentel tries to make a connection by pointing out that "in the United States, cancer-related deaths from all causes increased from 331,000 in 1970 to approximately 521,000 in 1992."[173] However, this again ignores an increasing population (24 percent) and an aging population (making cancers more likely). The age-adjusted cancer death rate in the US was actually *lower* in 1996 than in 1970, despite increasing cancer deaths from past smoking, and adjusted for smoking the rate has been declining steadily since 1970 by about 17 percent. You can see the data in Part V (Figure 117, p. 217) where we will discuss such arguments in more detail.

Pimentel picks and chooses a lot of numbers to show that things are getting worse, as when he accepts that malaria incidence outside Africa has declined till 1980 and remained stable since then – and then nevertheless only lists countries where malaria cases have been increasing.[174] However, as incidence has been approximately stable, this curiously neglects the countries with dramatic decreases in malaria, such as the world's largest country, China, where incidence has decreased 90–99 percent since the early 1980s.[175]

Sometimes the numbers are also just plain wrong, as when Pimentel claims that "in Thailand the prevalence of HIV infections in males increased from 1 percent to 40 percent between 1988 and 1992."[176] Not even the so-called commercial sex workers have ever had 40 percent prevalence since measuring started in 1989.[177] Even male STD patients measured since 1989, habitually with the highest rates, have "only" reached 8–9 percent.[178] UNAIDS estimates the adult population prevalence at 2.15 percent, with young males a bit lower.[179]

Also, Pimentel claims that "although the use of lead in US gasoline has declined since 1985, yearly emissions of lead into the atmosphere from other sources remain near 2 billion kg."[180] However, the total emissions from the US have declined by 83 percent since 1985 and now constitute 3,600 tons, or more than 500 times less than claimed.[181] It turns out that the reference (from 1985, no less) is referring to the entire world emission at that time.[182]

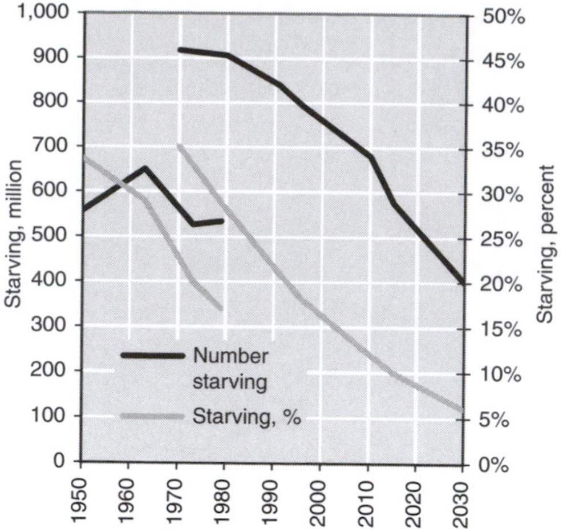

Figure 7 People undernourished, 1949–2030, in numbers (million) and percentage (of developing world). Prediction for 1998–2030. Estimates for 1949–79 count as undernourished individuals with less than 20 percent above physical minimum (1.2BMR), whereas estimates for 1970–2030 use a somewhat more inclusive definition of 55 percent above physical minimum (1.55BMR). Source: Grigg 1993:50, WFS 1996:1:Table 3, FAO 1999:29, 2000c:27, 2000d:20.

Reality: Pimentel and global health II

We have looked at a lot of low-quality, individual claims. But the reason we take time to go through them is to point out how they are used to buttress the central arguments.

The reason Pimentel gives us all these – sometimes incorrect – claims is to show us that the prevalence of human disease is increasing.[183] The cause is more humans, causing an "unprecedented increase in air, water and soil pollutants, including organic and chemical wastes" as well as malnutrition.[184] And Pimentel finds that now more than 3 billion people are malnourished, "the largest number and the highest rate in history."[185] And he finds that 40 percent of all deaths are caused by "various environmental factors, especially organic and chemical pollutants."[186] The consequence of more malnutrition and more pollution then is more disease and more infectious disease.[187] Surprisingly, *all* these central points in Pimentel's paper are wrong and/or seriously misleading.

Let us look at the intermediate findings first. Pimentel maintains that malnutrition has become ever worse: "In 1950, 500 million people (20 percent of the world population) were considered malnourished. Today more than 3 billion people (one-half of the world population) suffer from malnutrition, the largest number and the highest rate in history."[188] This is the entire argument, and Pimentel has repeated it as late as in 2000, adding that the number of malnourished "increases every year."[189] The source for the 1950 figure is *The World Food Problem* by David Grigg (1993), whereas the 1996 figure comes from a press release of the WHO.

However, these two sources are using dramatically different definitions of lacking food. Grigg uses the most common definition, calories. If a person gets less than 20 percent above physical minimum, she is counted as undernourished or starving. The development is shown in Figure 7 from 1949 to 1979. The number of undernourished first goes up from 550 million to 650 million, and then declines to 534 million. Because the developing world increased by more than 1.6 billion people from 1949 to 1979, this implies that many more people in the Third World were well nourished, or that the percentage of starving people dropped from 34 percent to 17 percent.

Since 1970, the UN FAO has produced a similar statistic, only using a more inclusive definition of 55 percent above physical minimum, making the numbers higher. Thus, the number of undernourished has declined from 917 million in 1970 to 792 million in 1997, and is expected to hit 680 million in 2010 and 401 million in 2030. Again because the developing world has increased by some 1.9 billion people since 1970, this means that the percentage of starving people has dropped even faster, from 35 percent to 18 percent in 1996, and further down to 12 percent in 2010 and 6 percent in 2030. Thus, if we want to compare the entire interval, we can imagine pushing the left-hand side of Figure 7 up to align with the right-hand side. This shows that the number of starving people has declined, and the percentage of starving people has dropped dramatically.

Grigg also looks at two other ways of measuring malnutrition, finding that "between 1950 and 1980 available food supply per [person] rose in the world as a whole, in the developed world, in the developing world, and in all the major regions."[190]

The press release from WHO talks about micronutrient malnutrition. This is primarily lack of iodine, iron and vitamin A.[191] While the two are about equally important measured in human death,[192] they are two entirely different measures. Solving the micronutrient problems is generally much cheaper than producing more calories, because all it takes is basically information and supplements either in the food or in a vitamin pill.[193] Since there has only been attention to the micronutrient question within the past decade, we mainly have information for this past decade.[194] Here there has been a 40 percent decline in the prevalence of vitamin A deficiency, and likewise more than 60 percent of all salt is now fortified with iodine.[195]

Thus, it is simply wrong when Pimentel compares the 500 million undernourished with 3 billion lacking micronutrients. Moreover, it is wrong to say that there are more and more malnourished. Actually, both indicators show great improvement since records began.

Equally, Pimentel's article contends from the outset that "we have calculated that an estimated 40 percent of world deaths can be attributed to various environmental factors, especially organic and chemical pollutants."[196] This has become the most cited point of the paper, because it so clearly seems to support that pollution is killing us.[197] Actually, in one citation from the Centers for Disease Control newsletter, the article is summed up in a single bullet-point: The increasing pollution "points to one inescapable conclusion: life on Earth is killing us."[198]

Using an estimate of 50 million deaths a year (the article does not even make an estimate), 40 percent means that Pimentel expects 20 million deaths from pollution.[199] But strangely, the 40 percent calculation is never made explicit. It is all the stranger because WHO estimates that the total deaths from outdoor air pollution, which constitutes by far the most dangerous public pollution, is a little more than half a million per annum.[200] However, on the next page, Pimentel almost repeats his point: "Based on the increase in air, water, and soil pollutants worldwide, we estimate that 40 percent of human deaths each year result from exposure to environmental pollutants and malnutrition."[201] Surprisingly, the 40 percent is now caused not only by pollutants but also by malnutrition. Finally, in the conclusion, all the factors are included: "Currently, 40 percent of deaths result from diverse environmental factors, including chemical pollutants, tobacco, and malnutrition."[202] In an interview, Pimentel makes it clear that tobacco is really "smoke from various sources such as tobacco and wood fuels."[203]

According to Pimentel's own references,

malnutrition costs 6–14 million lives, fuelwood cooking smoke in the Third World costs 4 million lives, and smoking costs 3 million lives.[204] Since the estimate for malnutrition is more likely to be close to the high end of 14 million lives,[205] this means that those three issues alone account for the entire 40 percent. Thus, while the presentation of the data is so nebulous that it is hard to claim that they are absolutely false, it is clear that the much quoted 40 percent deaths caused by pollution is at least seriously misleading.

Finally, we get to Pimentel's central claim that infections have increased and will continue to increase. Both of these are false. The reason Pimentel tells us all these (sometimes incorrect) stories and gives examples of many and new diseases is to make us feel that disease frequency must be increasing. After all, with so many names of diseases, it must be true, no? It is an argument that several other debaters have used.[206] We must, however, wonder how life expectancy can be going up and up if we keep getting more and more sick? (We will look into the discussion of life expectancy and illness in Part II.) And would it not be easier to look at the actual, total disease rates?

Pimentel claims that

> the growth in diseases is expected to continue, and according to Murray and Lopez (1996), disease prevalence is projected to increase 77 percent during the period from 1990 to 2020. Infectious diseases, which cause 37 percent of all deaths throughout the world, are also expected to rise. Deaths in the United States from infectious diseases increased 58 percent between 1980 and 1992, and this trend is projected to continue.[207]

It is not true, that diseases will increase. Actually, deaths will decrease from 862 per 100,000 in 1990 to 764 per 100,000 in 2020, according to Murray and Lopez.[208] And if we more correctly adjust for an aging population, the disease prevalence will decline even more steeply from 862 to 599 per 100,000.[209] When

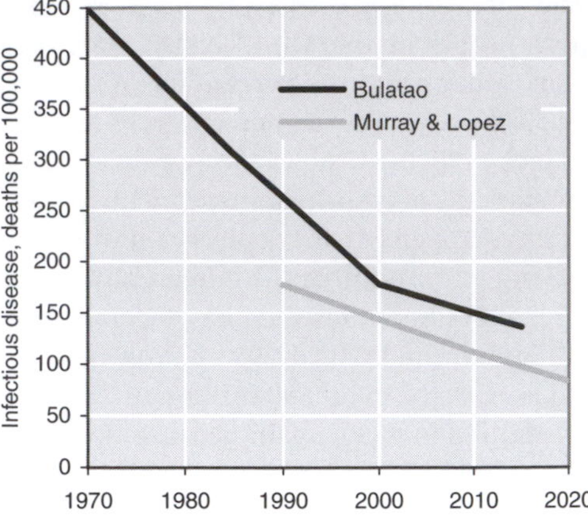

Figure 8 Infectious disease death rates, 1970–2020. Source: Bulatao 1993:50, Murray and Lopez 1996:465, 648, 720, 792.

Pimentel can tell us that disease should increase 77 percent it is because he has misread the book (neglecting infectious disease and only counting non-infectious diseases, which will increase because we get ever older, dying of old-age diseases) and counting diseases in absolute numbers (which of course will increase, since the world population will grow by about 2.5 billion).[210]

The claim about increasing infectious disease is downright wrong, as can be seen in Figure 8. Infectious diseases have been decreasing since 1970 and probably much longer, though we only have evidence from some countries (in Figure 20, p. 56, you can see US infectious disease prevalence over the twentieth century).[211] Likewise infectious disease is expected to decrease in the future, at least until 2020. Even in absolute numbers, infectious deaths are expected to drop from 9.3 million to 6.5 million.[212]

And the final claim for the US is also wrong. It only works because Pimentel chooses 1980 as the absolute bottom, and because most of the increase is due to rising age and increasing pneumonia. If we correct this for aging, the death risk was similar in 1980 and 1997.[213]

Pimentel concludes, "to prevent diseases,

poverty, and malnutrition from worsening" we need population control and "effective environmental management programs." Otherwise, "disease prevalence will continue its rapid rise throughout the world and will diminish the quality of life for all humans."[214]

Of course, Pimentel has not even discussed whether poverty would be increasing. In Figure 33 (p. 72) you will see that poverty incidence has actually been decreasing. Likewise, we have seen that both diseases, especially infectious diseases, and malnutrition have – contrary to Pimentel's claims – been decreasing.

Thus, while some effective environmental programs may constitute good policy decisions, they should certainly not be based on such recitations of a Litany of incorrect information.

Reality versus rhetoric and poor predictions

When we present an argument, there is never enough space or time to state all assumptions, include all data and make all deductions. Thus, to a certain extent all argument relies on metaphors and rhetorical shortcuts. However, we must always be very careful not to let rhetoric cloud reality.

One of the main rhetorical figures of the environmental movement is to pass off a temporary truism as an important indicator of decline. Try to see what your immediate experience is of the following quote from the Worldwatch Institute: "As a fixed area of arable land is divided among ever more people, it eventually shrinks to the point where people can no longer feed themselves."[215] This statements sounds like a correct prediction of problems to come. And yes, it is evidently true – there is a level (certainly a square inch or a speck of soil) below which we could not survive. However, the important piece of information is entirely lacking because we are not told what this level is, how close we are to it, and when we expect to cross it.[216] Most people would probably be surprised to know that, with artificial light, each person can survive on a plot of 36 m^2 (a 6 m square), and that companies produce commercially viable hydroponic food with even less space.[217] Moreover, FAO finds in its newest analysis for food production to 2030 that "land for food production is seen to have become less scarce, not scarcer."[218] Thus, the argument as stated is merely a rhetorical trick to make us think, "oh yes, things must be getting worse."

This rhetorical figure has been used a lot by Worldwatch Institute. Talking about increasing grain yields (which we will discuss in Part III), Lester Brown tells us that "there will eventually come a point in each country, with each grain, when the farmers will not be able to sustain the rise in yields."[219] Again, this is obviously true, but the question is *how far away is the limit?* This question remains unanswered, while Brown goes on to conclude the somewhat unimaginative rerun of the metaphor: "Eventually the rise in grain yields will level off everywhere, but exactly when this will occur in each country is difficult to anticipate."[220] Likewise, Lester Brown tells us that "if environmental degradation proceeds far enough, it will translate into economic instability in the form of rising food prices, which in turn will lead to political instability."[221] Again, the sequence is probably correct, but it hinges on the untold *if* – is environmental degradation taking place and has it actually proceeded that far? That information is never demonstrated.

Greenpeace, in its assessment of the Gulf War, used the same rhetorical figure: "Any environment consists of many complex dynamic interactions, but the system will gradually, sometimes almost imperceptibly, break down once a threshold of damage has been passed. Whether this has happened in the Gulf only time will tell."[222] Certainly it sounds ominous, but the important information of whether that threshold has been crossed, or is close to being crossed, is left out. In Part IV, you will see that the ecosystem of the Gulf, despite the largest oil spill in history, is almost fully restored.

Other rhetorical figures are often employed. In one of the background documents for the UN assessment on water, the authors see two "particularly discomforting" alternatives for the arid, poor countries: "Either by suffering when the needs for water and water-dependent food cannot be met, manifested as famines, diseases and catastrophes. Or, in the opposite case, by adapting the demand to the available resources by importing food in exchange for other, less water-dependent products."[223] Now that sounds like a choice between the plague and cholera, until you think about it – they are essentially asking whether an arid country should choose starvation or partake in the global economy.

Worldwatch Institute wants us to change to renewable energy sources, as we have already described. Some of these arguments are entirely powered by rhetoric, as when they tell us: "From a millennial perspective, today's hydrocarbon-based civilization is but a brief interlude in human history."[224] This is obviously true. A thousand years ago we did not use oil, and a thousand years from now we will probably be using solar, fusion or other technologies we have not yet thought of. The problem is that this does not really narrow down the time when we have to change energy supply – now, in 50 years or in 200 years? When seen from a millennial perspective, many things become brief interludes, such as the Hundred Years War, the Renaissance, the twentieth century and indeed our own lives.

Likewise, when we argue about the consequences of ecosystem changes it is easy to think of and mention only all the negative consequences. This is perhaps most evident when we discuss global warming and global climate change. Take for instance this description of climate change from *Newsweek*:

> There are ominous signs that the Earth's weather patterns have begun to change dramatically and that these changes may portend a drastic decline in food production – with serious political implications for just about every nation on Earth. The drop in food output could begin quite soon, perhaps only 10 years from now.
>
> The evidence in support of these predictions has now begun to accumulate so massively that meteorologists are hard-pressed to keep up with it. In England, farmers have seen their growing season decline by about two weeks since 1950, with a resultant overall loss in grain production estimated at up to 100,000 tons annually. During the same time, the average temperature around the equator has risen by a fraction of a degree – a fraction that in some areas can mean drought and desolation. Last April, in the most devastating outbreak of tornadoes ever recorded, 148 twisters killed more than 300 people and caused half a billion dollars' worth of damage in 13 U.S. states.
>
> To scientists, these seemingly disparate incidents represent the advance signs of fundamental changes in the world's weather. Meteorologists disagree about the cause and extent of the trend, as well as over its specific impact on local weather conditions. But they are almost unanimous in the view that the trend will reduce agricultural productivity.[225]

While this sounds surprisingly familiar with the greenhouse worries we hear today, it is actually a story from 1975 entitled "The Cooling World" – from a time when we all worried about global *cooling*. Of course, today there are better arguments and more credible models underpinning our worry about global warming (which we will discuss in Part V), and since our societies are adjusted to the present temperature, either cooling or warming will entail large costs.

But notice how the description conspicuously leaves out any positive consequences of cooling. Today, we worry that global warming will increase the outreach of malaria – consequently, a world believing in cooling should have appreciated the reduction of infected areas. Equally, if we worried about a shortening of growing seasons with a cooling world, we should be glad that global warming will lengthen the growing season.[226] Obviously, more heat in the US or the UK will cause more heat deaths, but it is seldom pointed out that this will be greatly outweighed by fewer cold deaths, which in the US are about twice as frequent.[227] Notice, this argument does not challenge that total costs, certainly worldwide, will outweigh total benefits from global warming, but if we are to make an informed decision we need to include *both* costs and benefits. If we rhetorically focus only on the costs, it will lead to inefficient and biased decisions.

Another recurrent environmental metaphor is the likening of our current situation with that of Easter Island. A small island situated in the Pacific Ocean more than 3,200 km west of Chile, Easter Island is most well know for its more than 800 gigantic heads cut in volcanic stone, set all over the island.[228] Archaeological evidence indicates that a thriving culture, while producing the stunning statues, also began reducing the forests around 900 CE, using the trees for rolling the statues, as firewood and as building materials. In 1400 the palm forest was entirely gone; food production declined, statue production ceased in 1500, and apparently warfare and hunger reduced the population by 80 percent before an impoverished society was discovered in 1722 by Dutch ships.

Since then, Easter Island has been an irresistible image for the environmentalists, showcasing a society surpassing its limits and crashing devastatingly. A popular book on the environment uses Easter Island as its repeated starting point, even on the front cover.[229] Worldwatch Institute tells us in its millennium edition:

> As an isolated territory that could not turn elsewhere for sustenance once its own resources ran out, Easter Island presents a particularly stark picture of what can happen when a human economy expands in the face of limited resources. With the final closing of the remaining frontiers and the creation of a fully interconnected global economy, the human race as a whole has reached the kind of turning point that the Easter Islanders reached in the sixteenth century.[230]

Isaac Asimov merely tells us that "if we haven't done as badly as the extinct Easter Islanders, it is mainly because we have had more trees to destroy in the first place."[231]

Again, the problem with this rhetorical figure is that it only indicates that crashing is indeed possible, but it makes no effort to explain why such crashing should be likely. It is worth realizing that of the 10,000 Pacific islands, only 12, including Easter Island, seem to have undergone declines or crashes, whereas most societies in the Pacific have indeed been prosperous.[232] Moreover, a model of Easter Island seems to indicate that its unique trajectory was due to a dependence on a particularly slow-growing palm tree, the Chilean Wine palm, which takes 40 to 60 years to mature.[233] This sets Easter Island apart from all the other Polynesian islands, where fast-growing coconut and Fiji fan palms make declines unlikely.

Moreover, the models predicting an ecological collapse need increasing populations with increasing demands on resources to produce an overshoot. But in the modern world, such a scenario seems very unlikely, precisely because increased wealth has caused a fertility decline (we will discuss this so-called demographic transition in Part II).[234] And finally, it is worth pointing out that today's world is much less vulnerable, precisely because trade and transport effectively act to reduce local risks.

The consequences of relying on rhetoric instead of sound analysis are many, primarily poor forecasts and consequent biased decisions. Perhaps the most famous set of predictions came from the 1972 global best-seller *Limits to Growth*, that claimed we would run out of most resources. Indeed, gold was predicted to run out in 1981, silver and mercury in 1985, and zinc in 1990,[235] though as we shall see in Part III, most resources actually have become *more* abundant. Needless to say, gold, silver, mercury and zinc are still here too.

Throughout this book, we will see a lot of poor predictions, often based on little more than rhetorically pleasing arguments. So, let us just end this section with two examples from one of America's foremost environmentalists, Professor Paul Ehrlich, a prolific writer and discussant, whom we shall meet again later.

In 1970, as the first Earth Day approached, Paul Ehrlich wrote an article in *The Progressive* as a fictitious report to the US President, looking back from the year 2000.[236] The ostensible report underlines how environmental scientists in the 1960s and 1970s had "repeatedly pointed out" that overcrowding, hunger and environmental deterioration would lead to "environmental and public health disasters."[237] Unfortunately, people had not heeded the warnings, and Ehrlich tells us of a US that is almost unrecognizable, with a severely decimated population at 22.6 million (8 percent of current population) with a diet of 2,400 daily calories per person (less than the current African average).[238] As an almost ironic glimmer of hope, Ehrlich does not expect that the US is faced with any immediate limits-to-growth threat of running out of resources, because of the "small population size and continued availability of salvageable materials in Los Angeles and other cities which have not been reoccupied."[239]

This view was fleshed out in the book *The End of Affluence* from 1974, written by Ehrlich with his wife Anne.[240] Here they worried about how global cooling would diminish agricultural output[241] (which has since increased 53 percent; see Figure 51, p. 95) and forecast trouble with the fisheries, because the global catch had reached its maximum[242] (since then the global catch has increased by 55 percent, as you can see in Figure 57, p. 107). They saw a society which was driven by deluded economists "entrapped in their own unnatural love for a growing gross national product."[243] The ultimate consequence was clear: "It seems certain that energy shortages will be with us for the rest of the century, and that before 1985 mankind will enter a genuine age of scarcity in which many things besides energy will be in short supply . . . Such diverse commodities as food, fresh water, copper, and paper will become increasingly difficult to obtain and thus much more expensive . . . Starvation among people will be accompanied by starvation of industries for the materials they require."[244]

Though rhetorically eloquent, time has not been kind to these predictions. Thus, when we evaluate the data on the state of the world, it is important not to be swayed merely by rhetoric or simplistic models, but to use and present the best indicators and the best models.

Reality

Matter-of-fact discussion of the environment can be very difficult because everybody has such strong feelings on the issue. But at the same time even as environmentalists it is absolutely vital for us to be able to prioritize our efforts in many different fields, e.g. health, education, infrastructure and defense, as well as the environment.

In the course of the last few decades we have developed a clear impression that the Litany is an adequate and true description of the world. We *know* that the environment is not in good shape. This is also why it has been possible for people to make erroneous claims, such as those we have seen above, without needing to provide the evidence to authenticate them. For that reason we also tend to be extremely skeptical towards anyone who says that the environment is not in such a bad state. To me this indicates a natural and healthy reaction. This is also why I have gone to great lengths to *document* my claims.

This means that this book has an unusually large number of notes. At the same time, however, I have endeavored to enable readers to enjoy the book without necessarily having to read the notes, so as to achieve reading fluency in the knowledge that you can always check my information if you feel that something sounds a little too hard to believe.

The book also has more than 1,800 references. However, I have tried to source as much of the information from the Internet as possible. If people are to check what I write, it is unreasonable to expect them to have a research library at their disposal. Instead it is often sufficient to go on to the Internet and download the relevant text to see from where I have retrieved my data and how I interpret that information. Of course there will always be books and articles central to the relevant literature which are not available on the net. In addition, the Internet has made it possible for me to bring the book right up to date, with data accessed and updated up to May 2001.

But for me the most important thing is that there is no doubt about the credibility of my sources. For this reason most of the statistics I use come from official sources, which are widely accepted by the majority of people involved in the environment debate. This includes our foremost global organization, the United Nations, and all its subsidiary organizations: the FAO (food), the WHO (health), the UNDP (development) and the UNEP (environment). Furthermore, I use figures published by international organizations such as the World Bank and the IMF, which primarily collate economic indicators.

Two organizations work to collect many of the available statistics; the World Resources Institute, together with the UNEP, the UNDP and the World Bank, publishes every other year an overview of many of the world's most important data. The Worldwatch Institute also prepares large amounts of statistical material every year. In many fields the American authorities gather information from all over the world, relating for example to the environment, energy, agriculture, resources and population. These include the EPA (environment), USDA (agriculture), USGS (geological survey) and the US Census Bureau. Finally, the OECD and EU often compile global and regional figures which will also be used here. As for national statistics, I attempt to use figures from the relevant countries' ministries and other public authorities.

Just because figures come from the UNEP does not of course mean that they are free from errors – these figures will often come from other publications which are less "official" in nature. It is therefore still possible to be critical of the sources of these data, but one does not need to worry to the same degree about the extent to which I simply present some selected results which are extremely debatable and which deviate from generally accepted knowledge. At the same time, focusing on official sources also means that I avoid one of the big problems of the Internet, i.e. that on this highly decentralized network you can find *practically anything*.

So when you are reading this book and you find yourself thinking "That can't be true," it is important to remember that the statistical material I present is usually identical to that used by the WWF, Greenpeace and the Worldwatch Institute. People often ask where the figures used by "the others" are, but there *are* no other figures. The figures used in this book are the official figures everybody uses.

When Lester Brown and I met in a TV debate on the State of the World one of the things we discussed was whether overall forest cover had increased or decreased since 1950.[245] Brown's first reaction was that we should get hold of the FAO's *Production Yearbook*, which is the only work to have calculated the area of forest cover from 1949 up to 1994. This is the same book I had used as a reference and so we agreed on the standard. In reality we were merely discussing who could look up a number correctly.

Lester Brown believed there was less forest whereas I thought there was more. I offered Lester Brown a bet, which he reluctantly declined. He would also have lost.

In 1950, FAO estimated that the world had 40.24 million km^2 of forest, while in 1994 it had 43.04 million km^2 (as you can see in Figure 60, p. 111).[246]

Reality and morality

Finally we ought to touch on the moral aspects of the environment debate.

In the same way as you can only be *for* peace and freedom and *against* hunger and destruction, it is impossible to be anything but *for* the environment. But this has given the environment debate a peculiar status. Over the past few decades there has been an increasing fusion of truth and good intentions in the environmental debate.[247] Not only are we familiar with the Litany, and *know* it to be true. We also *know* that anyone who claims anything else must have disturbingly evil intentions.[248]

It is therefore not surprising, albeit a little depressing, that several environmental pundits, and indeed the Danish Secretary of the Environment, have tried to claim that I am probably just a right-wing radical – or at least a messenger boy for the right.[249] But of course such argument is blatantly irrelevant. My claim is that things are *improving* and this is necessarily a discussion which has to be based on facts.

My motives for writing this book are neither evil nor covert. My understanding, in all simplicity, is that democracy functions better if everyone has access to the best possible information. It cannot be in the interest of our society for debate about such a vital issue as the environment to be based more on myth than on truth.

Many people have pointed out at lectures that although I may be right in claiming that things are not as bad as we thought they were, such arguments should not be voiced in public as they might cause us to take things a bit too easy. Although one can argue such a position, it is important to understand how antidemocratic such an attitude really is: we (the few and initiated) know the truth, but because general knowledge of the truth will cause people to behave "incorrectly" we should refrain from broadcasting it. Moreover, such a course of argument will also be harmful to the environmental movement in the long run, since it will erode its most valuable asset, its credibility. I think that, in general, pretty strong arguments have to be presented for it to be permissible to withhold the truth for the sake of some elitist, general good.

This does not mean that I am a demonic little free-market individualist. I believe that there are many circumstances in which environmental intervention is necessary if we are to prevent unnecessary pollution and avoid people shunning their responsibilities. However, we should only intervene if it is reasonable to do so, not simply because myth and worries lead us to believe that things are going downhill.

Often we will hear that environmental worry is an important reason why the environment gets cleaned up – essentially that many of the graphs in this book go in the right direction exactly because people worried in earlier times. However, this is often misleading or even incorrect. Air pollution in London has declined since the late nineteenth century (see Figure 86, p. 165), but for the greater part of the twentieth century this has been due to a change in infrastructure and fuel use and only slightly, if at all, connected to environmental worries expressed in concrete policy changes. Moreover, even to the extent that worries have mattered in policy decisions, as they undoubtedly have during the past 30 years in, say, air pollution, this does not assure us that our resources could not have been put to better use.[250] To the extent that worries have prodded us to spend more money on the environment than we would have done with merely the best available information, the argument for environmental worries is a replay of the democratic dilemma above. Although kindling public concern clearly makes people choose more "correctly" as seen from an environmental viewpoint, it leads to an "incorrect" prioritization as seen from a democratic viewpoint, as it skews the unbiased choice of the electorate.

In general we need to confront our myth of the economy undercutting the environment.[251] We have grown to believe that we are

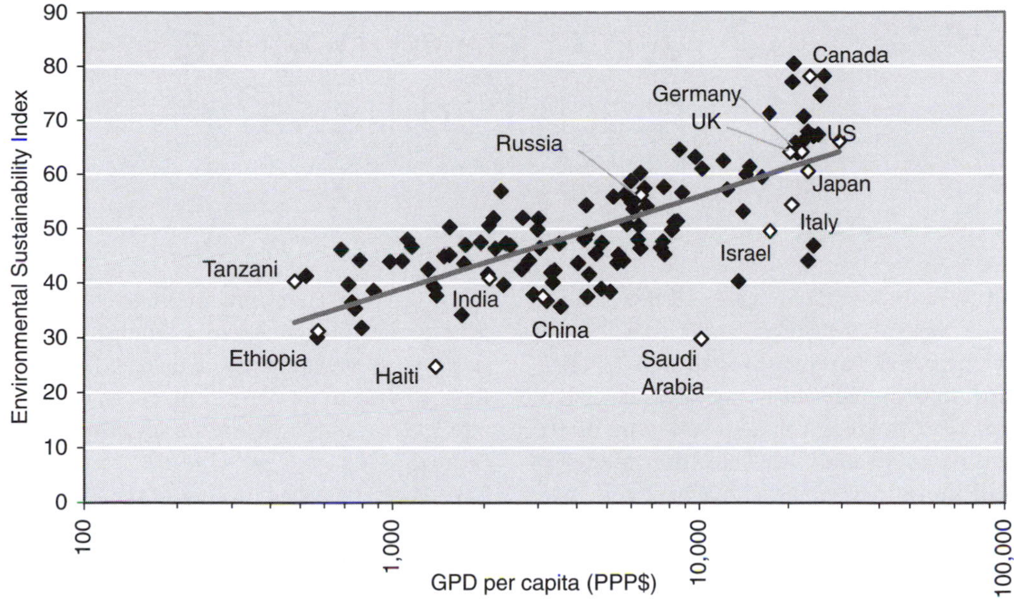

Figure 9 The connection for 117 nations between GDP per capita (current 1998 PPP$) and the 2001 Environmental Sustainability Index, measuring 22 environmental dimensions on 67 variables.[254] A best-fit line is displayed and various nations have been marked out. Source: WEF 2001a&b, World Bank 2000c.

faced with an inescapable choice between higher economic welfare and a greener environment.[252] But surprisingly and as will be documented throughout this book, environmental development often stems from economic development – only when we get sufficiently rich can we afford the relative luxury of caring about the environment. On its most general level, this conclusion is evident in Figure 9, where higher income in general is correlated with *higher* environmental sustainability.[253]

This also has implications for our discussions on prioritization. Many people love to say that we should have a pollution-free environment. Of course this is a delightful thought. It would likewise be nice to have a country with no disease, or the best possible education for all its young people. The reason why this does not happen in real life is that the cost of getting rid of the final disease or educating the slowest student will always be ridiculously high. We invariably choose to prioritize in using our limited resources.

One American economist pointed out that when we do the dishes we are aiming not to get them *clean* but to dilute the dirt to an acceptable degree.[255] If we put a washed plate under an electron microscope we are bound to see lots of particles and greasy remnants. But we have better things to do than spend the whole day making sure that our plates are a little cleaner (and besides, we will never get them *completely* clean). We prioritize and choose to live with some specks of grease. Just how many specks we will accept depends on an individual evaluation of the advantages of using more time doing dishes versus having more leisure time. But the point is that we – in the real world – never ask for 100 percent.

Similarly, we have to find a level at which there is sufficiently little pollution, such that our money, effort and time is better spent solving other problems. This calls for access to the best possible and least myth-based knowledge, which is the whole purpose of this book.

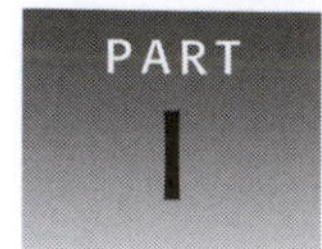

2 Why do we hear so much bad news?

In 1992 a large-scale opinion poll *Health of the Planet* was carried out in many countries.[256] The intention was to investigate people's attitudes to the environment and to what extent fears for the environment only manifest themselves in the rich countries. Many of those consulted expressed fears for the environment. In 16 out of the 24 countries involved in the survey, the environment was named as one of the three most important problems.[257] In the vast majority of nations, both developing and industrialized, more than 50 percent of all people were concerned about problems with environment.[258] But then the interviewees were asked for their opinion about the environment locally, nationally and globally. Their answers can be seen in Figure 10.

Notice that in the vast majority of countries surveyed, the impression of its citizens is that the global environment is in the worst shape, the national environment is a little better, and finally, their local environment is in the best shape of the three, although we can see some tangible, concrete problems in for example the transitional economies of Russia and Poland.

On the face of it, this general evaluation seems reasonable enough – and both Americans and the British follow the pattern by believing their local environment to be better than the national average, which again is much better than the messy world. But look at a typical country like Germany. Here, 22 percent believe that the local environment is in bad shape while almost twice as many – 42 percent – believe that the environment of the country as a whole is in a bad state. Can it be reasonable, though, for people to believe that their own local environment is better than the average for the country as a whole? That the grass is greener on one's own side of the fence? Of course this cannot apply to everyone, precisely because the survey covers all of Germany. It is not possible for everyone to have a better local environment then the average of all the local environments.

We are actually familiar with a similar phenomenon in psychology. Interviews with motorists consistently show that between 70 percent and 90 percent claim that they drive better than the average.[259] Likewise, in the early 1990s 70 percent or more Americans claimed that the American public was not worried enough about the environment – although these 70 percent clearly should be sufficiently worried.[260]

So people have a lopsided view of their environment. The point repeats itself in most of the countries in the survey. Most respondents believe that the environment is worse "elsewhere" in the country than where they themselves live. Having a global survey to refer to enables us to see the same logic applying at a global level. In the vast majority of nations people believe that the environment is worse "somewhere elsewhere'" than in their own country.

Other possible explanations of this connection naturally exist. It is not unthinkable that the environmental problems we experience at a national and international level either are not localized or occur in sparsely populated areas. But it still points to the fact that our knowledge of things close to us, which is derived from our own experiences, is not the primary source of our fears for the environ-

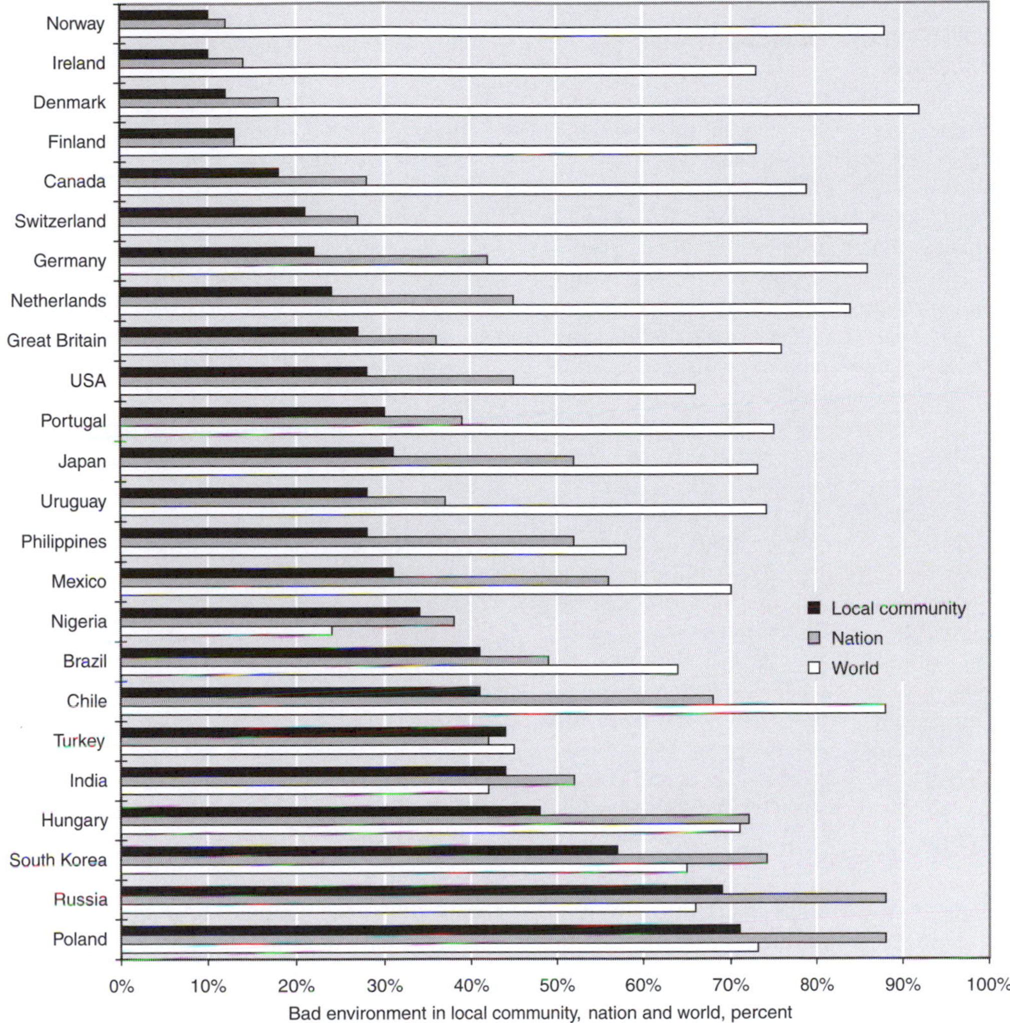

Figure 10 Percentage of respondents who evaluate the environmental quality of their local community, their nation and the world as very or fairly bad. Source: Dunlap *et al.* 1993:12.

ment. On the contrary, we seem more worried about conditions *the further away from us they are,* both physically and mentally.

This points to the fact that our fears for the environment are to a high degree communicated, and here I will look at three of the most important communicators: researchers, the organizations and the media. I will argue that there is good reason to believe that all three communicators will present us with a preponderance of negative tidings. Finally, comment should be passed on our own willingness to listen to and believe bad news.

Research

Research is basically a question of revealing truths about ourselves and our surroundings, be these man-made or natural. But research does not simply come about of its own accord, it has to be financed. This means that the

THE FILE DRAWER AND DATA MASSAGE

An annoying but not unusual problem for researchers occurs when they have spent a long time investigating a problem but have found no important connections. Then what do you do? They may be able to get their results published as they stand ("it is also interesting that there was no connection"), but most editors are pretty negative in this sort of situation and many investigations of this kind end up in a file drawer.

While it is entirely understandable for an editor to reject articles without "good connections," their doing so leads to an imbalance in the overall presentation of science. Suppose, for example, that numerous researchers have investigated the connection between weak electric and magnetic fields from electrical power transmission lines and human cancer.[261] Most of them have found no relationship, but nor have their investigations been published. However, the first study that finds a (perhaps purely coincidental) relationship will be published and probably create quite a stir. It is not until this happens that a study without a connection is considered to be interesting. This phenomenon is known as the file drawer problem – first we get the scare connection, then we find out that other studies with no connection undercut the initial scare.[262]

It is also possible to gather so much material that at least some of the figures will show a connection. When a study of the connections between pesticides and cancer in French farmers finds a link between pesticide use and brain cancer, we may become rather suspicious as to why they particularly asked about this type and not other types of cancer.[263] If they have actually asked about 30 different types of cancer they will probably find at least one connection – the brain cancer connection – although it may be purely coincidental.[264] This way of producing a find is often referred to as *data massage* – torturing the data till they speak.[265] And since everyone wants to publish interesting connections, there is at least a moderate incentive to squeeze the data just a little harder.

The point here is that we must be careful not to put complete faith in all research stories, because some unpublished study in someone's file drawer might be able to disprove them.

problems to be investigated are influenced, to some degree, by the interests of those who finance the research.

In our modern society, much of the research done is publicly funded, which means there will be certain expectations as to the relevance of the research to society.[266] There is nothing at all suspicious about this, as we probably expect to get a reasonable return on our tax money, but it does have consequences for the characteristics of the research.

Research basically has built-in lopsidedness. If a scientist says that she has investigated her field and not found any general problems, we as a society need do no more. If on the other hand the scientist investigates her field and finds a potentially momentous problem, it would be common sense to take action and at least research the field more thoroughly. This means that, other things being equal, we have research which tends to investigate areas where problems can arise.

At the same time, another imperfection also exists. It is not always easy to identify exactly what constitutes a problem. If there have always been periodic oxygen shortages in the Gulf of Mexico then the phenomenon is probably not a problem. If on the other hand occurrences have become more frequent because of an excess of nutrients then the problem could well be serious. Identification of a problem depends on the theory by means of which we interpret what we observe in the world.

In this connection a simple, easily comprehensible theory is fundamental: a theory which links human action (how we damage nature) and a clearly identifiable problem. At the same time most environmental problems are incredibly complex and it can be difficult to accept or reject a theory within a short period of time. Global warming, the eradication of species and oxygen depletion are problems the causes and connections of which can only be determined over a long period and at great cost.

A situation with a potential problem and an easily explained theory will therefore attract sizeable grants for more research, and we can expect this research to continue over long periods of time. *There is nothing wrong with this situation per se.* In reality it is an indication of a well-functioning society: many researchers look into many different problems, thereby providing us with the knowledge we need to make sure that only very few problems ever develop into big ones.

We must expect that efficient research will provide information about many potential future problems. But the fact that we hear so many stories should not necessarily be taken as an indication that doomsday is nigh. On the contrary.

Acid rain (which we will investigate later in the book) is a good example. In the late 1970s and early 1980s there was a considerable loss of foliage in the forests of Central Europe. This alone would probably have triggered considerable interest among researchers in the affected countries. However, German scientists also believed that they were able to link foliage loss to industrial pollution. They predicted that all forests exposed to acid rain would suffer substantial damage.[267] This led to fears on a much wider scale and national research programs were initiated throughout most of the Western world. This also presented the potential for a whole series of research projects. Some of Norway's foremost acid rain scientists wrote that "the possibility for reduced forest growth was the main reason why it was possible to get large funding for research on the effects of acidic rain."[268] Ten years later all fears had evaporated – acid rain only damages trees under very rare conditions – but during these ten years we heard an incredible number of theories, partial research results and popular, primarily negative, explanations.

All the same, it was still a good idea to have investigated the connections. Had an unambiguous explanation been found it would have provided us with the best premise for handling the potential problems. But it also means that during the period we ought to have prepared ourselves for hearing many a negative story which would not necessarily turn out to be true.

Organizations

At the same time as further funding comes on tap, research also becomes a veritable industry. Researchers begin to investigate subsidiary fields and special cases within the original problem field without necessarily having an interest in or any breadth of view of the field as a whole.

Although the field naturally retains its professional integrity it will gradually become increasingly difficult to challenge the consolidating problem. For one thing, a natural tendency to secure funding for their own special field will encourage scientists not to criticize the overall field of research. For another, many participants only investigate problems *within* the field and will not challenge the premises of the field. In this way, the field achieves a certain degree of independence and begins to define its own reality.

One critic of such institutionalization is retired professor Aksel Wiin-Nielsen, former Secretary-General of the UN World Meteorological Organization. On the question of global warming he commented: "The most important explanation as to why so much extensive theoretical work in the development of climate models has been done during the last ten years is that the development of models sustains funding and secures jobs at research institutions."[269] Of course, criticism as far-reaching as this is extremely difficult to substantiate adequately, and the UN

Intergovernmental Panel on Climate Change (IPCC) has also criticized Wiin-Nielsen for his lack of documentary evidence.[270] My point is simply to stress that in important fields of research it can also be difficult to present information which goes against institutional interests.

One researcher has argued in the esteemed journal *Energy Policy* that it was actually the climate researchers, together with for example the windmill manufacturers and environment bureaucracies, who were the primary political initiators of the climate negotiations.[271] The point is that it was institutionalized interests and not, as you may have thought, the prospect of possible global warming that was behind the tremendous support for CO_2 restrictions included in the Kyoto Protocol of December 1997 (we will discuss this much more thoroughly in Part V).

But there are also other, more politically oriented organizations which disseminate environmental research. Such organizations include the obvious environmental movements such as Greenpeace, WWF and Worldwatch Institute, but also organizations like the National Federation of Independent Business and the American Farm Bureau in the US[272] or Confederation of British Industry and National Farmers Union in the UK. All these organizations have vested interests in the political consequences and decisions which result from research. The NFIB and the AFB have an interest in protecting their members and they work to promote decisions which are to the advantage of their members. In exactly the same way, environmental organizations base their activities on a desire to promote decisions which are good for their members.

The difference is that while the traditional organizations usually fight for traditional values such as the distribution of time and money, the environmental organizations fight for such things as bigger forests, diversity of species, restoration of natural environments and strict regulations of chemicals. We may nevertheless argue that the environmental organizations are fighting for the interests of their members because in the last analysis they are only able to do what their members, sympathizers and supporters believe is good and necessary – because without their backing the organizations' campaigns would be more or less worthless. The organizations may present themselves as the patrons of the penguins and the pine trees, to use the expression from the previous chapter, but they are dependent on people who sympathize with their points of view and contribute money, prestige and influence, if nothing else, through their democratic vote and pressure on the politicians.

Most people seem to be perfectly aware that when the NFIB tells us that an environmental regulation of industry is unnecessary, they may have good and sensible arguments, but they certainly also have a clear interest in avoiding such regulation. Many people tend to view NFIB's arguments with a certain natural skepticism because they know that the argument could also be a cover for ulterior motives. This considered, it seems amazing that many people are not equally aware that the environmental organizations also have an interest in environmental regulation.[273] It may be that the environmental organizations have better arguments for regulation (but of course their arguments may also be poorer), but it ought to be obvious that they, too, have an interest in arguing towards a particular end.

Thus as the industry and farming organizations have an obvious interest in portraying the environment as just-fine and no-need-to-do-anything, the environmental organizations also have a clear interest in telling us that the environment is in a bad state, and that we need to act now. And the worse they can make this state appear, the easier it is for them to convince us we need to spend more money on the environment rather than on hospitals, kindergartens, etc. Of course, if we were equally skeptical of both sorts of organization there would be less of a problem. But since we tend to treat environmental organizations with much less skepticism, this might cause a grave bias in our understanding of the state of the world.

Note, however, that this is only a theoretical argument as to the environmental organizations having an interest in portraying the world as gloom and doom. The extent to which they actually do so is very much the theme of the rest of this book.[274]

The media

Finally, it is the media that pass on the results of research, possibly helped along by the organizations. The media play a central role in this connection because the world has become so complex that we can no longer rely primarily on our own experiences. Instead, the mass media provide much of our understanding of reality.

But their particular way of providing us with news profoundly influences our view of the world. There is of course rarely much doubt that facts reported in an article or a news report are generally true. In that sense, the media simply reflect the world as it is. What is interesting, however, is the long and winding path between an event taking place in the world and its possible appearance and placement in the media. Looking at news reporting in this way shows how the media systematically present us with a lopsided version of reality: a picture of reality which is incoherent and sporadic, though at the same time reassuringly predictable and familiar: A picture where problems fill every column, and the emphasis is on drama and conflict. As an editor-in-chief has put it: "Producing a paper is a question of distorting proportions."[275]

This media-based reality has numerous consequences. First, the incoherent information we are given provides us with too little knowledge of concrete problems to enable us to take part in a democratic decision-making process. Second, we feel sufficiently comfortable that we believe we actually do have sufficient knowledge to partake in the debate and to make valid decisions. Third, we will often get a far too negative and distorted impression of the problems.

Lopsided reality: sporadic but predictable

The basic job of the news media is to report individual, unrelated events from many different parts of the world.[276] By definition, news also has to be new. This limits what we can actually call news to events which occurred within the last production cycle, often seven days, 24 hours or even less. This means that items which take a long time to develop will have considerably less news value than here-and-now events. Hunger in Africa is nowhere near as good news as a plane crash. Rather characteristically, the Ethiopian hunger tragedy of 1984 only actually became news because a team of BBC journalists stayed overnight in Addis Ababa on their way to another job and sent home shocking pictures of children literally dying in front of their cameras.[277]

At the same time there is a strong tendency to focus on individual stories. The role of the media in liberal Western democracies has in historical terms primarily been to report events and to a much lesser degree describe possible future events or to put events into perspective. For this reason the news consists primarily of *incidents*, rather than predictions, explanations or background material.[278] The reasons for this predominant focus on events are also technical: it has to be possible to film, photograph or describe news in relatively simple terms. For this reason we only get background information when "newsworthy" people or institutions produce a report of their own which predicts or explains other news. The report thus becomes the peg on which to base the story.[279]

Thus, the world as we see it through news

broadcasts appears to be fragmented and to consist of individual incidents.

When we nevertheless feel it is possible to get a general impression of what is going on in the world it is because ordinary news coverage is subject to a rigid framework giving the news broadcast consistency and a feel of reassuring predictability. It is amazing how an apparently unpredictable universe of news events can be shoehorned into 20 minutes of TV news or 12–16 pages of a newspaper, day after day.[280] This is done through hefty editing of the incoming news stream. A typical editorial office actually edits out more than 75 percent of all incoming news.[281]

News broadcasts typically start, for example, with a major incident to attract viewers' attention, and interest is maintained through a varied offering of news and human interest stories. Withholding popular information (sport and the weather) until the end of the broadcast sends the viewer away with a light touch at the close.[282] This helps to give us the impression that we have gained a global overview and are in control.

Slightly surprisingly one might say, as the media researcher Park pointed out as early as 1940: news is predictable. It is not the entirely unexpected which appears in the newspapers, but the same kinds of events and accidents which have been news before.[283]

Lopsided reality: bad news

The media cannot survive without an audience. Since the arrival of the commercial newspaper in the middle of the nineteenth century the mass media have had to concentrate to a large extent on satisfying the interests of a mass public. With the ease of channel surfing this focus on customers is even stronger with the TV medium.

This means that it is extremely important for news to be *interesting*. And *interesting* usually means packed with serious events, problems and accidents. "A good story is usually bad news," writes a textbook for journalists.[284] Although it is not easy to explain why, we all seem to be curious about and fascinated by bad news, and this sells newspapers. The tabloid papers are forced to focus more on sensation because they depend on their readers finding them exciting enough to buy them every day. Indeed, a recent study showed how the use of the word "fear" has increased in American media, actually doubling in headlines.[285]

We are all perfectly familiar with bad news about the environment. Perhaps the most obvious was the US encounter with the 1997/8 El Niño which eventually was linked to any weather event. Even Worldwatch Institute pointed out, slightly exasperatedly, that "as early 1998 progressed, it became difficult to find a weather-related story that did not mention El Niño's influence."[286] We were told how cities were "bracing for the climate event of the century."[287] We got informed of the "weird weather" and endless lists of problems:

> Experts are saying that this El Niño is one of the most intense on record. San Francisco has had its wettest winter since 1867. Damage from storms and mud slides is expected to cost California more than $300 million, and has caused at least 10 deaths. In Florida, more than 300 homes were destroyed and more than three dozen people were killed by a series of powerful tornadoes. "This shows that El Niño is very dangerous for Florida" said Scott Spratt, a meteorologist for the National Weather Service.[288]

In fact, El Niño got blamed for anything from wrecking tourism,[289] causing more allergies,[290] melting the ski-slopes,[291] and yet dumping snow in Ohio, causing 22 deaths.[292] Perhaps the most surprising statement was Disney's accusation that El Niño had caused its shares to fall.[293] And even when El Niño did have a positive effect, this was powerfully ignored, as in *Time* magazine: "Large parts of the eastern and north-central U.S. continued to bask in the warmest winter in years, one that brought cherry blossoms to Washington in the first week of January. That might sound like the opposite of a disaster, but every weather anomaly has its dark side."[294] And then the journalist went on to tell us about the problems of warmer weather.

However, a recent research article in *Bulletin of the American Meteorological Society* tried to count up all the problems and all the benefits from El Niño.[295] And while all the bad occurrences of Californian storms, crop damage, government relief costs, and human and economic losses from tornadoes were true, they were only one side of the story. At the same time, higher winter temperatures meant about 850 fewer human cold deaths, much diminished heating costs, less spring flood damage and savings in highway-based and airline transportation. Moreover, a well-documented connection between El Niño and fewer Atlantic hurricanes was well expressed in 1998 – the US actually experienced no major Atlantic hurricanes and thus avoided huge losses.

The total damages were estimated at $4 billion, whereas the total benefits were estimated at $19 billion.[296] But given the wide media coverage of all the bad news, that El Niño was overall beneficial for the US was not the impression left with the average reader or viewer.

Lopsided reality: conflict and guilt

In the hunt for good news, conflict is also brought into focus. A conflict has that gripping dramatic element familiar from fairy tales and other literature, a battle between good and evil which the audience must follow to the bitter end to find out what happens. Journalists are actually taught how to tailor their stories to patterns from fairy tales.[297]

Closely related to the story of conflict is the question of guilt.[298] It is not uncommon for one of the involved parties to be given the blame for the conflict, which helps to give the news a more human touch. We have seen examples of this in the US, where efforts to do something about garbage dumps is given far higher priority compared to combating radioactive radon, even though combating radon would be far more effective. Why? Because a garbage dump provides "good pictures" and because garbage dumps are "somebody's fault."[299]

It is generally important to journalists that their stories are "close" to the reader. This is often a question of involving people in a story and being able to explain what is going on in simple terms.

Finally, a story has to be new and exciting. A story about a new problem or new conflict is potentially far more interesting than describing an already familiar, traditional problem.

The consequences

One consequence of the demand for rapid news delivery is that our view of the world becomes fragmented. Our demand for interesting and sensational news means that our picture of the world becomes distorted and negative. Coupled with the finely tuned PR units of the environmental organizations and problem-oriented research, this can provide serious bias towards a negative appraisal of the state of the world.

Note, however, that it is not anybody's "fault." We get primarily negative news not because the journalists have evil intentions, but because the news media are placed in an incentive structure that makes it profitable to focus on negative occurrences. The environmental organizations are interest groups like all others, and they argue in favor of their own cause. The fact that we primarily believe their negative news is not their fault, but ours, because we are only skeptical of the American Farm Bureau arguments and not of those from the environmental lobby. Research is mainly concerned with potential problems. This is socially beneficial, because it gives us the best opportunity to handle problems in the future, but it means that we are continuously faced with news of potential disasters.

The point is that we cannot change this negative lopsidedness. Instead, we must get to grips with the fact that the stream of information we receive is inherently lopsided and compensate for it. Unfortunately, this may be very difficult because we inherently tend to think that things were better in the old days and that everything is going in the wrong direction. The Scottish philosopher David Hume wrote in 1754 that "the humour of blaming the present, and admiring the past, is strongly rooted in human nature, and has an influence even on persons endued with the profoundest judgment and most extensive learning."[300]

Sal Baron wrote in his book about the history of the Jews that prophets who made optimistic predictions were automatically considered to be false prophets.[301] An Assyrian stone tablet, many thousands of years old, tells us of the obstinate feeling of decline: "Our earth is degenerate in these latter days; bribery and corruption are common; children no longer obey their parents; every man wants to write a book, and the end of the world is evidently approaching."[302] Moreover, it has been suggested that the spirit of ascetic Calvinism still hovers over Western civilization.[303] In a sense, when we have done so very well, maybe we ought to be punished? In that light, the worry over global warming could be seen as a search for a nemesis, to punish our overconsumption, a penalty for our playing the Sorcerer's Apprentice.

These observations seem to suggest that historically and perhaps biologically we are disposed to welcome negative news. But if we are to have a rational political decision-making process and choose the best means to the right objectives, we must bear in mind that the stream of information we are receiving is unbalanced. We hear many negative and problematic stories every day that should not necessarily be taken at face value. TV tries to attract attention, the environmental organizations argue for their causes, and research science is already examining a variety of solutions to cover us if and when the problem occurs.

Of course this does not mean that we can just sit back and ignore all problems. But it does imply that we must view the world with a healthy portion of skepticism and take on the challenges, because we know that we are systematically being confronted with a negative surplus of news.

And most of all, it means that we must start searching for the facts to measure the real state of the world. And here we will start by looking at the human endeavor so far.

Human welfare

PART II

3 Measuring human welfare

In this chapter we shall look at the state of human welfare. First, of course, we have to define what the term implies. Welfare is obviously not a discussion confined to money, but one about the whole human's potential to develop.[304]

According to the UN, "the real objective of development should be to create an enabling environment for people to enjoy long, healthy and creative lives. Though this may appear to be a simple truth, it is often forgotten in the immediate concern with the accumulation of commodities and wealth."[305] But how do we measure human welfare? There are many ways of investigating to what extent mankind has been given better surroundings in which their lives can unfold.

The UN introduced the so-called *Human Development Index* for this very purpose. The index attempts to elucidate what kind of surroundings people have in which to make a good life for themselves. The intention is to measure how *long* people can expect to live, how much *knowledge* they can acquire, and how high a *living standard* they can achieve. In practical terms it measures life expectancy, the proportion of illiterates, school attendance in years, and income. The World Bank endeavors in a similar way to evaluate people's quality of life on the basis of life expectancy, malnutrition, access to clean water and sanitation, illiteracy and energy consumption.[306]

It goes without saying that elegant words such as "long, healthy and creative lives" end up sounding a little less spiritual when converted into sterile statistics. Nonetheless, these figures do give us a good idea as to the state of human welfare in different parts of the world. But why only these three or six components? The UN writes that "the ideal would be to reflect all aspects of human experience,"[307] but that the lack of data imposes some limits on this.

That is, however, no reason for not trying. It is true that not enough data are available in order for us to rank all the nations in the world in all sorts of different ways, which is what the UN wants to do. But if all we want to do is to get a general overview of the state of mankind, we can investigate quite a few more indicators. In this part of the book we will look at human welfare from a variety of angles. Of course we cannot hope to approach every single possible aspect, but I have tried to look at the most important ones. In the course of the following pages we will investigate life expectancy and health, food and hunger, income, inequality, education and security – in the industrialized nations and the developing nations, for the young and the old, men and women.

How many people on earth?

The number of people on earth increases every day, and in 1999 we passed the 6 billion mark.[308] As you can see in Figure 11, the massive growth in the world's population began around 1950 and will probably end around 2050.[309] The increase in the population is mainly due to a dramatic fall in the death rate as a result of improved access to food, medicine, clean water and sanitation.[310] The increase is *not*, on the other hand, due to

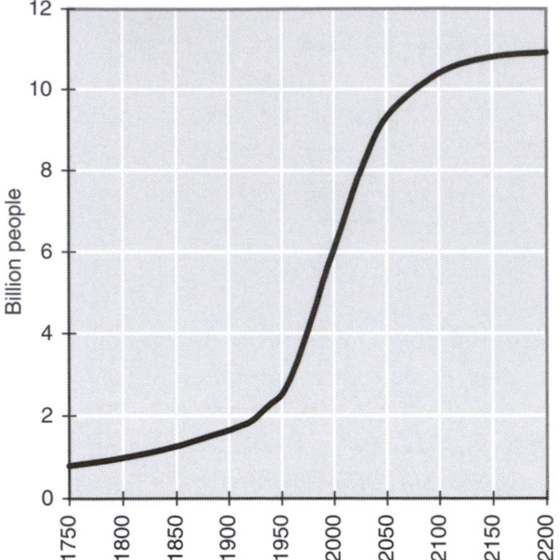

Figure 11 World population 1750–2200, the UN's medium variant forecast from 2000. Source: UNPD 2001b:27; 1998b:37, 1998c.[311]

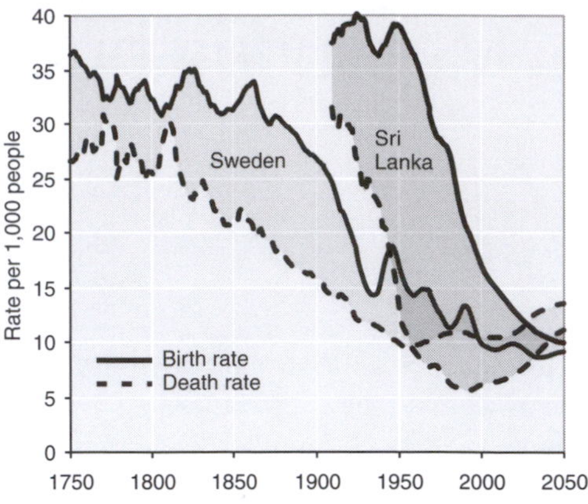

Figure 12 The demographic transition showing birth and death rates in Sweden (1750–2050) and Sri Lanka (1910–2050), forecast for 1999–2050. Notice, how first the death rate declines, and then the birth rate. As the population begins to age, the death rate rises slightly. Source: Mitchell 1975, 1995, World Bank 2000c, USBC 2001a.

people in developing countries having more and more children. In the early 1950s women in developing countries gave birth to an average of more than six children – compared to an average of around three today.[312] As one UN consultant put it, rather bluntly: "It's not that people suddenly started breeding like rabbits; it's just that they stopped dying like flies."[313]

In historical terms we are familiar with this development as "the demographic transition," seen in Figure 12.[314] In a traditional agricultural society, income is low and mortality high. However, children working and providing for their parents in old age generally supply greater benefits than their cost, and therefore the birth rate is high. With improved living conditions, medicine, sanitation and general economic prosperity, the death rate falls. The transition towards a more urban and developed economy makes children more likely to survive while they start to cost more than they contribute, needing more education, working less and transferring the care of their parents to nursing homes. Consequently, the birth rate drops.[315] In the gap between the falling death rate and birth rate, the population grows. In the case of Sweden, it quintupled during this process.[316]

We see a similar trend today in developing countries, where the death rate has fallen drastically and the birth rate is beginning to fall. For Sri Lanka, this development is evident in Figure 12, where its population is expected to somewhat less than sextuple before stabilizing around 2030.[317] The UN estimates that women in the developing countries will achieve an average of 2.1 children, which constitutes a stable reproduction,[318] by 2045–50.[319] At present, the reproduction in the developing world is 3.1 children or already below that of the US and Australia in the early 1960s or Denmark in the early 1920s.[320]

All the same, the world's population will continue to increase for some time beyond 2035 because population figures have a built-in "momentum." Even when the birth rate has fallen to the replacement level of 2.1 children per woman there will be more young people in the population than old. They will in turn bring 2.1 children into the world, which will

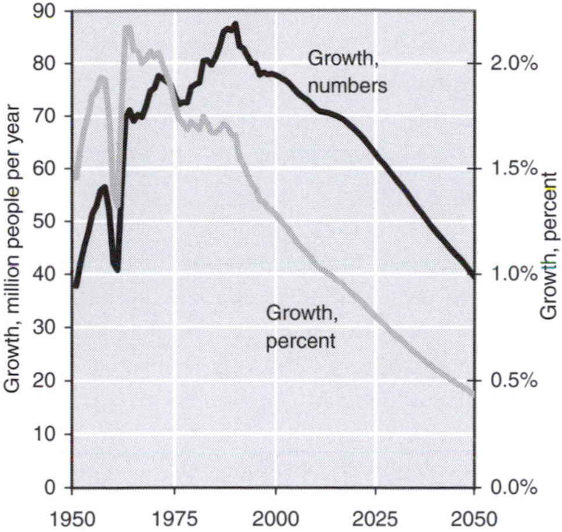

Figure 13 Increase in the Earth's population in absolute figures and as a percentage, 1950–2050. The dramatic fall in 1959–62 was due to China's Great Leap Forward, which led to catastrophic starvation and cost almost 30 million people their lives (WFS 1996:3:3.15). Forecast from 2001. Source: USCB 2001a.

also lead to a slight preponderance of young people, etc. This momentum is already today the primary cause of population growth – we expect world population to increase by 3.3 billion over the next 50 years, but even if world fertility instantly dropped to replacement level, the increase would still be about 2.3 billion.[321]

As demonstrated in Figure 13, the growth of the global population peaked in the early 1960s at just over 2 percent a year. It has since fallen to 1.26 percent and is expected to fall further, to 0.46 percent, by 2050. Even so, the absolute growth of the population did not peak until 1990, when almost 87 million people were added to world population. Today growth is around 76 million per year and will have fallen to approximately 43 million by 2050.[322]

The UN continuously calculates how many of us live on Earth now and will in the future. These figures have been adjusted downward by 1.5 billion for 1994, 1996 and 1998 and upwards again by half a billion for 2000, because of changes in the speed with which the fertility falls in different countries.[323] The latest long-term forecast from 2000 can be seen in Figure 11.[324] It shows that there will be almost 8 billion people on Earth by 2025 and about 9.3 billion by 2050. It is estimated that the world's population will stabilize just short of 11 billion in the year 2200.[325]

The changing demographics

Sixty percent of the population growth comes from just twelve countries. India, Pakistan and China are at the top of the list, respectively adding 563, 203, and 187 million more people in the next 50 years.[326] India has one of the oldest family planning programs in the world but fertility there is only falling very slowly. In both China and India in the early 1950s women gave birth to an average of six children. However, whereas the number in China has fallen to 1.8 it is still at 3.23 in India.[327] For this reason India also has many more young people and will probably overtake China as the world's largest country before 2050, with 1.57 billion inhabitants, compared to China's 1.46 billion. Though Pakistan is only the world's seventh largest country it will nevertheless add the second-most to the global population, and likewise numbers four and seven on the list, Nigeria and Ethiopia, are the world's tenth and twenty-first largest.[328] In the 100 years from 1950 China's population will have increased 160 percent, India's will have quadrupled, and the populations of Pakistan and Nigeria will have increased ninefold.[329]

The industrial nations' share of the world population will continue to fall. Having increased throughout the past centuries, their share of the total has fallen from 32 percent in 1950 to 20 percent today, and will fall still further to just 13 percent in 2050.[330]

As far as Europe is concerned, the change will be even more pronounced. From accounting for 22 percent of the world population in 1950, the continent now only accounts for 13 percent. Africa on the other hand has increased from 9 percent to the same 13 percent. Today both Europe and Africa each make up one eighth of the world's population. However, by 2050 Europe's share will shrink to below 7 percent, while Africa's will grow to 22 percent, i.e. Africa and Europe will have changed places as regards relative population size.[331]

One inevitable consequence of increased life expectancy and the falling birth rate is that there will be far more older people. In 2025 the world's baby-boomers will be between 65 and 75 years old. Compared to just 5 percent over-65s in 1950, the world will have 16 percent in 2050. Growth of the 80+ age group will be even steeper, from about 0.5 percent in 1950 and 1 percent today to almost 10 percent in 2150. The number of centenarians will increase 14-fold over the next 50 years. Today there are three times more children than old people – in 2050 the two groups will be equally large. Globally, our average age will have increased from 27 years in 1950 to almost 33 years in 2020.[332]

Because China has been so successful in restricting the number of children, the age phenomenon will be particularly pronounced in this part of the world. Here the number of centenarians will increase 40-fold. While there are five children for each two old people today, the old will outnumber the young two to one in 2050. The average age will increase from 23 to more than 37 in 2020.[333]

As a matter of curiosity, I can point out that by calculating backwards it is possible to work out how many people have lived on Earth since the beginning of time. The result is somewhere between 50 and 100 billion, which is to say that the 6.1 billion people alive today make up between 6 percent and 12 percent of all those who ever lived.[334]

Overpopulation

We often hear about overpopulation of the Earth. We most often see overpopulation illustrated by large glossy color pictures of tightly packed masses or overcrowded underground stations.[335]

The famous population biologist Paul Ehrlich in his best-seller on the population explosion wrote:

> Psychologically, the population explosion first sunk in on a stinking hot night in Delhi. The streets were alive with people. People eating, people washing themselves, people sleeping, people working, arguing and screaming. People reaching their hands in through taxi windows to beg. People shitting, people pissing. People hanging off buses. People driving animals through the streets. People, people, people.[336]

The point is, however, that the number of people is not the problem. Many of the most densely populated countries are in Europe. The most densely populated region, Southeast Asia, has the same number of people per square km as the United Kingdom. The Netherlands, Belgium and Japan are far more densely populated than India, and Ohio and Denmark are more densely populated than Indonesia.[337]

Today, Ehrlich and others also agree on this. Nevertheless, two other interpretations of overpopulation have come to the fore. One of them conjures up images of starving families; wretched, cramped conditions and premature death.[338] Such images are real enough but are actually the result of poverty rather than population density. We shall discuss poverty below.

Another interpretation of overpopulation, which Ehrlich employs these days, focuses on the population density being *sustainable*. If a nation's present population cannot sustain itself in the long term then the nation is overpopulated.[339] But to put it mildly, it seems bizarre to insist that a population should be able to support itself from the specific land on which it lives. The whole idea of a trading economy is that production does not necessarily have to take place at the physical location of demand, but where it is most efficient.[340]

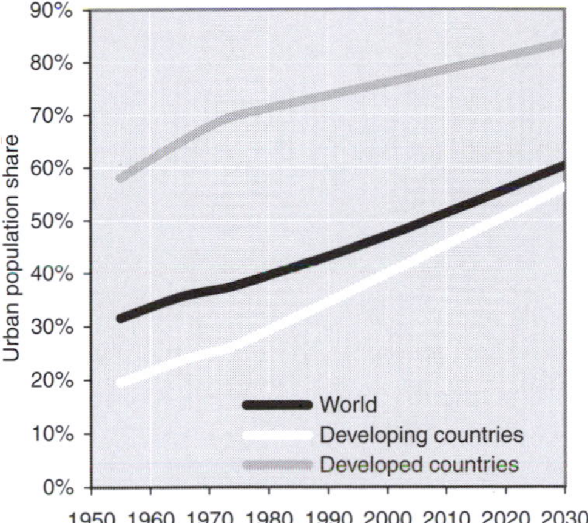

Figure 14 Percentage of urban population in developing and developed countries and the world, 1950–2030, forecast from 2000. Source: WRI 1998a, UNPD 1998b:2.

In connection with overpopulation it is important to point out that most of the Earth's landmass will not become more densely populated than it is today. This is because most population growth from now on will be in the cities. Over the next 30 years the global rural population will stay almost unchanged, and in fact 97 percent of Europe will become *less densely* populated by 2025.[341]

In 2007 more people will live in urban areas than in rural areas for the first time in history, as is seen in Figure 14.[342] In 1950 New York was the only so-called megacity with more than 10 million inhabitants, and London was a close runner-up with 8.7 million.[343] Today we have 19 megacities and the UN predicts 23 in 2015, where Tokyo and Bombay will lead the list with 26.4 and 26.1 million inhabitants respectively.[344] Nineteen of the 23 megacities will be located in the less developed regions.

Urban growth will be distinctly stronger in developing countries, but in reality this is only following the trend of the developed world towards ever-increasing urbanization. Both in the US and in the industrialized world on average, urban population already constitutes about 75 percent.[345] While the proportion of people living in urban areas in the West will increase to 83.5 percent in 2030 the increase in developing countries will only be from 40 percent to 56 percent.

It is often said that urban living mars people's quality of life. One standard textbook on the environment says that "in both the rich and poor nations of the world, large populations cannot be comfortably accommodated. People live in deplorable conditions without adequate water and sanitation."[346] This is a classic example of a mistaken argument. It is quite right that by Western standards many people live poor lives in shanty-towns, but the fact is that even shanty-town dwellers live *better* lives than they would in rural areas.[347]

In more densely populated areas, the most serious infectious diseases such as malaria and sleeping sickness become less of a problem the closer the buildings are together, because less space is left for the swampy areas where mosquitoes and flies can breed. Moreover, water supplies, sewage systems and health services are considerably *better* in urban areas than in rural ones.[348] Education is much easier to come by in the city – in most developing countries there is more than ten percentage points difference between the education of rural and urban areas – and city-dwellers are on average better fed and less malnourished.[349]

Actually, rural regions by far dominate the problem of global poverty.[350] Towns and cities, on the other hand, are power centers which provide greater economic growth. Urban areas in developing countries produce 60 percent of GDP with just one third of the population. The World Resources Institute clearly concludes that "cities are growing because they provide, on average, greater social and economic benefits than do rural areas."[351]

4 Life expectancy and health

One of the basic necessities for human welfare is, of course, life itself. Life expectancy is therefore an essential aspect of any welfare measure. However, living longer does not necessarily mean living better, if that extra time is simply spent suffering more. It is therefore also important to consider whether we live healthier lives and spend less time being ill.

The main point of this chapter is to show how our lives and our health have improved dramatically over the past couple of hundred years. We live longer, and we are more healthy. This is one of the great miracles of our civilization.

Life expectancy

Until around the year 1400, human life expectancy was amazingly short – a newborn child could on average only expect to live 20–30 years.[352] This was mainly due to the fact that infant mortality was incredibly high. Only every other child survived beyond its fifth birthday.[353]

For the early part of human history we have little or no precise statistics to rely on, so the figures must be based on the examination of skeletons and on mathematical population-growth models. Some of the most definitive surveys of Stone Age skeletons from North Africa show a life expectancy of just 21 years. We know from the examination of gravestones, mummies and skeletons that an average citizen of Imperial Rome lived only 22 years.[354]

In Figure 15 we see the development of life expectancy in England over most of the second millennium. The broad picture shows an average life span of 30-something years from 1200–1800, with the most noticeable deviation being the Black Death in the fourteenth-century, bringing the newborn life expectancy down to just 18 years.[355] Notice, however, that the statistics from 1200–1450 are based on male landowners, which probably somewhat overestimate the longevity of the average population.[356]

From 1541 we have much better information on a national level for both sexes, based on large samples of parish registers. Here the average life span was around 35, falling slightly until 1700 and then increasing slightly up to 1850. These short-term fluctuations were due to temporary food shortages, infectious disease and an ineffective food distribution network.[357] After 1850, life expectancy soared. Over the 150 years that followed, the increase in life expectancy was astounding. It almost doubled.

The sequence of events was similar in most industrialized countries. In France, life expectancy in 1800 was about 30.[358] In Denmark it was around 44 in 1845.[359] All have ended up with a life expectancy in the seventies, with an average of 77 years for developed countries.[360] On the other hand, life expectancy in the rest of the world was very low until the beginning of the twentieth century. It is traditionally estimated that the life expectancy of the whole world in 1900 was still around 30.[361] In 1950 people lived for an average of 46.5 years and in 1998 for as long as 67 years.[362] So life expectancy has more than doubled within the last hundred years.

This is in all earnestness an astounding

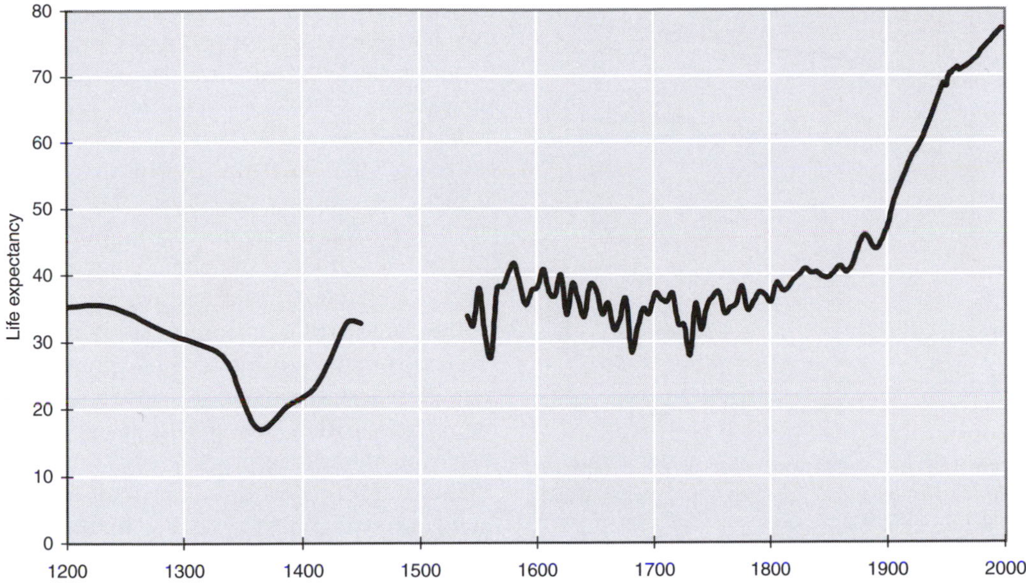

Figure 15 Life expectancy at birth for male landholders in England 1200–1450 and for both sexes in England and Wales or the UK, 1541–1998.[363] Source: Russell 1978:47, Wrigley and Schofield 1981:230, Keyfitz and Flieger 1968; Flora *et al.* 1987:108, World Bank 1999a, 2000c. Life expectancy in the US 1849–1998 is very similar, USBC 1975:56, World Bank 1999a, 2000c.

achievement. By far the largest improvement in our life expectancy has been achieved over the last hundred years.

Life expectancy in the developing world

But what of the developing world? At the beginning of the twentieth century many developing countries were at a life expectancy level reminiscent of the Stone Age. In 1906 life expectancy in India was about 25. In China in 1930, people only lived an average of 24 years. Even in Chile, which at that time was one of the most advanced developing countries, life expectancy was only 31 years in 1909.[364] Overall, the average in developing countries was still well below 30 years.

In 1950 life expectancy in the developing world had reached 41 and in 1998 it was as high as 65.[365] This is a fantastic improvement. This is the equivalent of all people in developing countries being able to expect to live as long as the average British or American in the late 1940s. For the one fifth of the world's population who live in China, development has been even more rapid. From being expected to die by age 24 in 1930, the average Chinese can now expect to live to age 70 – an almost threefold increase in two generations.

Figure 16 shows just how startling the increase in life expectancy in the developing world has been. This trend is expected to continue to improve, so that the developing world can break through the 70-year barrier in 2020 and continue to shorten the lead held by the industrialized nations.

Of course, the average figure may well conceal considerable imbalances in the developing world. The distribution of life expectancy for individual nations can be seen in Figure 17. Here you can see that 4.7 percent of all people in the world live in nations where life

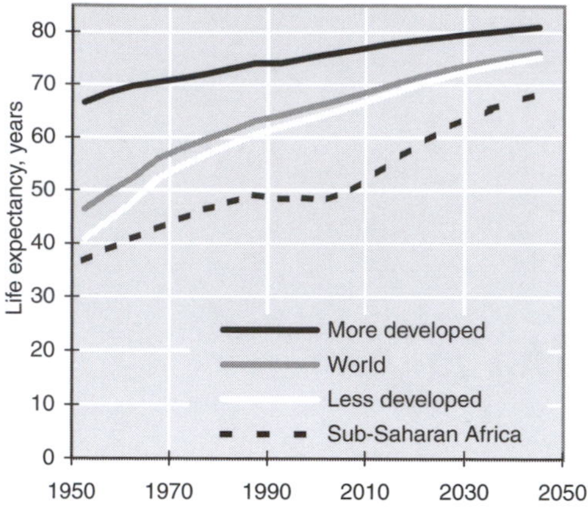

Figure 16 Life expectancy for industrialized countries, developing countries, sub-Saharan Africa, and the entire world 1950–2050, prognosis from 2000, also incorporating the effects of HVI/AIDS. Source: UNPD 1999:4, 8–12, 18.[366]

expectancy is below 50. Right at the bottom of the list is Sierra Leone, where life expectancy is a mere 39 years. Apart from Afghanistan and East Timor, all the other 25 countries at the lower end of the list are African, including Mozambique, Rwanda, Uganda, Zambia, Somalia and Ethiopia.

To a large extent these low life expectancies are caused by the AIDS epidemic that has struck especially hard in sub-Saharan Africa, home to 70 percent of all HIV cases. Here 23 million people, or 3.6 percent of the population, are HIV infected, and since AIDS most often hits young adults or children, many years of life are lost, leading to significant decreases in life expectancies.[367] For some of the hardest-hit countries in the eastern part of the continent, declines of 10–20 years are estimated,[368] and Zimbabwe has by some estimates lost 26 years compared to a situation without AIDS.[369] For sub-Saharan Africa as a whole, the loss amounts to about nine years at present, and may increase to almost 17 years in 2010, and will still be about eight years in 2025, compared to the prediction without AIDS.[370]

This does not mean that life expectancy for sub-Saharan Africa declines however, only that it does not increase as fast as it could and should have, as is evident in Figure 16. From 37 years in 1950, life expectancy had only increased to around 49 years in 1990 where it is expected to stagnate until 2010, after which it picks up, crossing the 60-year line around 2025. The effect on the developing world as a whole is in 2010 a loss of about 2.8 years and in 2025 a bit more than a year lost.[371]

The ironic twist to this tragic loss of life and welfare is that a large part of HIV prevention requires not so much huge expense but rather more information and a change in sexual behavior towards protected sex. However, shame and blame continue to engulf AIDS in many countries, making testing, information and political action hard to come by.[372] In the long run, massive AIDS prevention programs such as Uganda's show the way, having dramatically lowered prevalence rates.[373]

Looking at the rest of Figure 17, we see that people in the next 26 countries or 10.3 percent of the globe expect to live between 50 and 60 years. Many of these countries are African, with Congo at 51 and Nigeria and South Africa at 52, but Nepal and Bangladesh at 59 also belong to this group. This also means that 85 percent of all the world's inhabitants can look forward to living at least to the age of 60. India with 63, Russia and Indonesia with 66 and Brazil with 68 are all in this group. Similarly, more than 45 percent of the world's population can expect to live to 70 or longer. People in such dissimilar countries as China, Ecuador, Thailand and Jordan can expect to live to 70.

People in the last group on the list can expect to live to age 75 or longer. The group includes 15 percent of all the world's inhabitants and consists in the main of OECD countries, such as the US with 77 and the UK with 78 years. Here Japan comes out on top with a life expectancy of 81 years.

A lot still needs to be done to improve conditions in Africa, not only in the context of AIDS prevention but also for food availability and

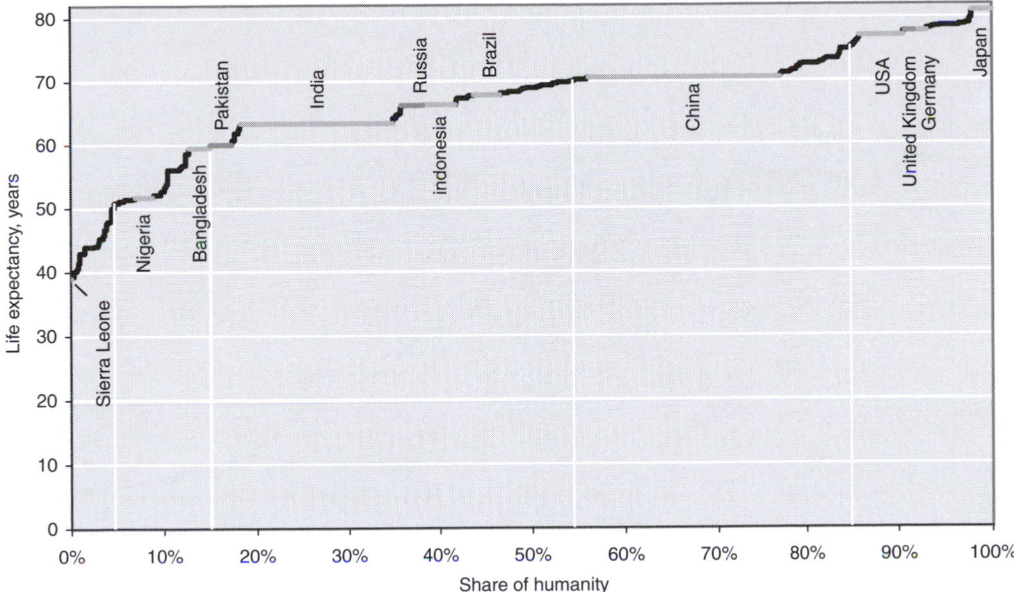

Figure 17 Percentage of humanity with their maximum life expectancy in 2000. Source: UNPD 2001c.[374]

economic production, as will be discussed below. But the important thing is to stress that more than 85 percent of all the world's inhabitants can expect to live for at least 60 years – more than twice as long as people were expected to live on average just a hundred years ago. Incredible progress.

Infant mortality

The improvement in life expectancy is largely due to a dramatic fall in infant mortality. The main reason for our living much longer than we did a hundred years ago is not because we all *live longer*, but because far fewer people *die early*. From 1900 to the present day, the life expectancy of new-born American girls has increased by almost 32 years (from 48 to almost 80 years) while that of a 60 year-old is up by a more modest 7.8 years.[375]

We can use a brief example to explain this phenomenon. Imagine that ten babies are born on a small island. Five of them die within the first year, while the others live on to age 70. Life expectancy will be 35 years. The next year, ten babies are also born, but now a doctor has arrived on the island who can treat the children, so only one of them dies. The other nine live to the age of 70. Life expectancy suddenly increases to 63.

At a global level, the reduction in infant mortality has been amazing. From studies of hunter-gatherer societies we know that around half of all children die within the first five years. From the examination of skeletons and statistical models it is assumed that until about the year 1400, a mortality rate of about 500 out of 1000 live births was also the norm in Europe.[376] For the sixteenth century we have figures for the English nobility, who lived under far better conditions than most of the population. These show a general reduction from 250 deaths per 1000 live-born babies in 1550 to about 100 per thousand in 1850.[377]

Sweden was the first country to collect statistics at a national level. The percentage of children who died there within the first year of birth can be seen from Figure 18. At the end of the eighteenth century, about one child in

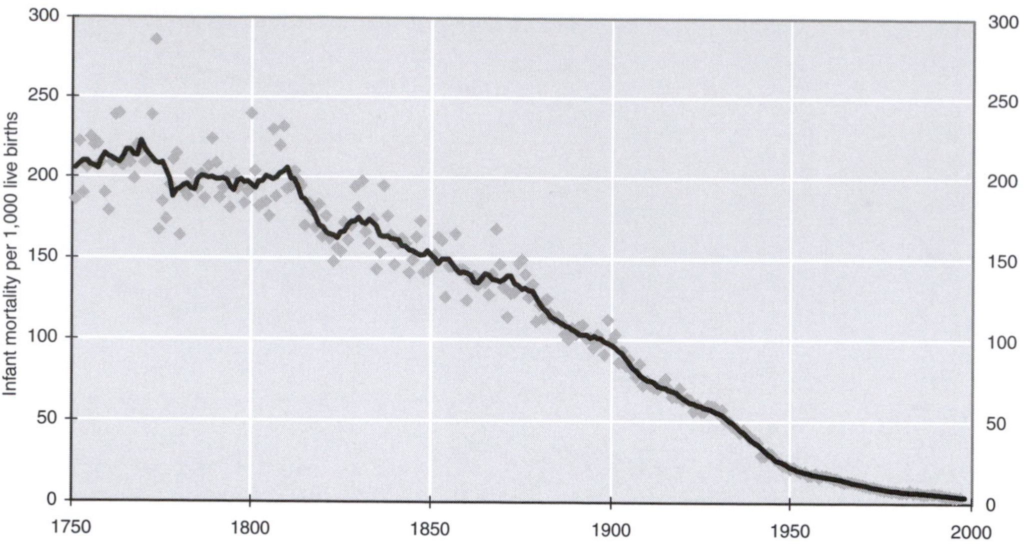

Figure 18 Infant mortality per 1000 live births in Sweden 1750–1998, with 9-year smoothed trend. Source: Mitchell 1975:127–32, World Bank 1999a, 2000c.

every five died before its first birthday and there were substantial fluctuations from year to year caused by hunger and disease.[378] But from 1800 onwards, infant mortality fell drastically and in 1998 the figure is less than four per 1000 or one child in 280.[379] Infant mortality in Sweden has fallen more than 50-fold over the past 200 years.

As regards the developing countries the data are less well documented. In rural China in the 1920s, more than one in three children died before the age of five. In Chile conditions were worse, with two out of five children dying before the age of five in 1920, and in Gambia even higher rates were reported as late as the 1950s.[380]

Figure 19 shows the reduction in infant mortality in the world as a whole, in both developing and industrialized nations, since 1950. Here we can see an overwhelming reduction in infant mortality in the developing world. In 1950, 18 percent or almost every fifth child died; in 1995 only 6 percent died – a fall to just one third. Even for sub-Saharan Africa, infant mortality is steadily declining despite the AIDS epidemic, although the decline is not as fast as it could otherwise have been.[381]

Infant mortality has also continued to fall in the industrialized nations. In 1950 almost 6 percent of all newborns did not survive, compared to less than 1 percent in 2000. Notice that the developing countries have the same infant mortality rate today as the industrialized nations had in 1950. For both categories of countries it is projected that the fall will continue and that the risk in the developing world will be halved yet again by 2020.

Illness

We live longer, but have we only been given more time in which to be ill? The answer has to be: absolutely not. We have generally become much healthier during the past centuries.

We often have a quite mistaken impression of what it was like to live in times past. This impression frequently comes from films, which often portray people who, although dressed in dirty clothes, are beautiful and live

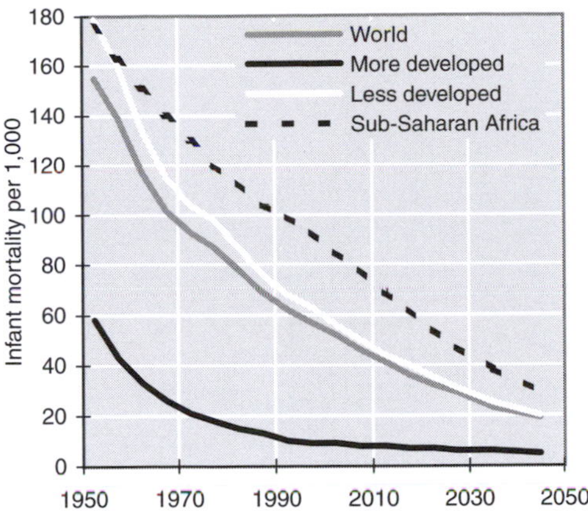

Figure 19 Infant mortality per 1000 live births; world, industrial, developing and sub-Saharan African nations. Prediction from 2000. Including the effects of HIV/AIDS. Source: UNPD 1999:4, 8–12, 18.

in harmony with nature. Unfortunately, reality in the eighteenth century was quite different, as the reputable Princeton historian Lawrence Stone explains:

> The almost total ignorance of both personal and public hygiene meant that contaminated food and water was a constant hazard . . .
>
> The result of these primitive sanitary conditions was constant outbursts of bacterial stomach infections, the most fearful of all being dysentery, which swept away many victims of both sexes and of all ages within a few hours or days. Stomach disorders of one kind or another were chronic, due to poorly balanced diet among the rich, and the consumption of rotten and insufficient food among the poor. The prevalence of intestinal worms . . . were a slow, disgusting and debilitating disease that caused a vast amount of human misery and ill health . . . In the many poorly drained marshy areas, recurrent malarial fevers were common and debilitating diseases . . . [and] perhaps even more heartbreaking was the slow, inexorable, destructive power of tuberculosis . . . For women, childbirth was a very dangerous experience . . . [and finally] there was the constant threat of accidental death from neglect or carelessness or association with animals like horses – which seem to have been at least as dangerous as automobiles – or elements like water . . .
>
> Another fact of Early Modern life which is easy to forget is that only a relatively small proportion of the adult population at any given time was both healthy and attractive, quite apart from the normal features of smell and dirt . . .. Both sexes must very often have had bad breath from the rotting teeth and constant stomach disorders which can be documented from many sources, while suppurating ulcers, eczema, scabs, running sores and other nauseating skin diseases were extremely common and often lasted for years.[382]

In the ever present struggle between health and death, we can identify some of the pivotal events reducing death rates. First, rising standards of living from the late eighteenth century afforded better food, clothing and housing and consequently higher disease resistance. At the same time these changes in living conditions, for example people living closer together, forced an evolutionary change in the pathogens, often towards a lower virulence.[383] Second, improved public hygiene, better water supplies and sewers, hygiene education and quarantine measures from the late nineteenth century helped suppress infections.[384] Finally, better medical therapy in the twentieth century provided a vast array of new technologies to combat illness.[385] Over the last couple of hundred years, we have consequently experienced a substantial decline in death rates and an increase in life expectancy.

To a large degree this is because we have managed to control and defeat the incidence of infectious diseases. Towards the end of the eighteenth century, smallpox, which had been Europe's leading killer causing more than 10 percent of all deaths, proved avoidable through vaccination or inoculation, and in 1891 diphtheria could be cured using antitoxin.[386] The plague pandemic that had ravaged the world, costing a 100 million lives in the late sixth century and 25 million in the Black Death of the late fourteenth, was brought under control by public proscriptions such as quarantine, rat control, better sewers and higher housing standards.[387] Measles and

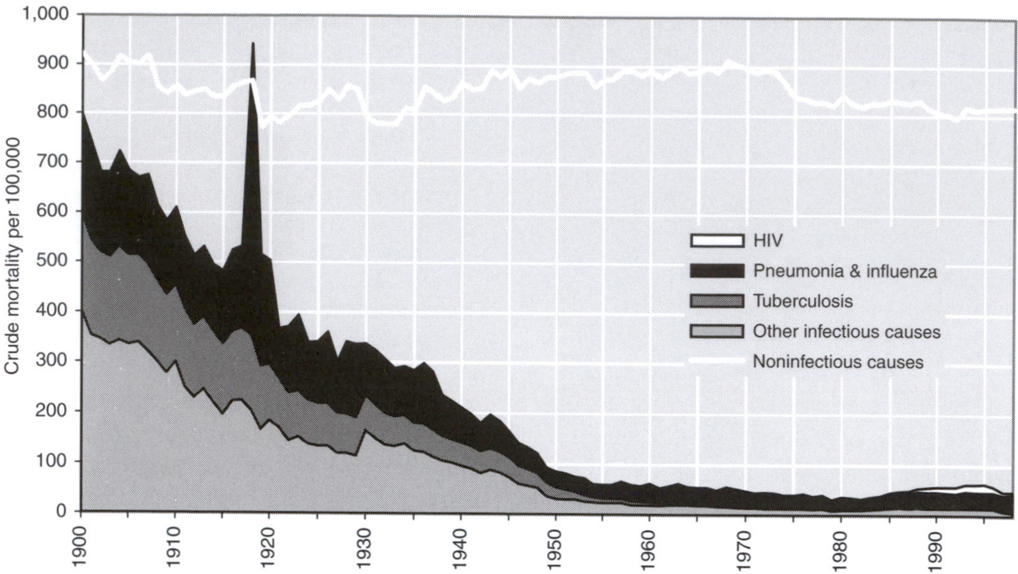

Figure 20 The prevalence of infectious and noninfectious diseases in the US 1900–98, crude mortality rate per 100,000. Infectious diseases split into pneumonia and influenza, tuberculosis, HIV and other infections. The pronounced spike in 1918 marks the so-called Spanish flu pandemic that killed 20 million people worldwide, including half a million in the US. Source: Armstrong *et al.* 1999, Martin *et al.* 1999:27–8, CDC 1999a:622.

chickenpox were rendered harmless because the increase in population density effectively domesticated the pathogens and reduced them to typical infant diseases.[388] Cholera was brought under control by improving the quality of the water supplies.[389] In the first half of the twentieth century sulfa drugs and antibiotics finally made strong inroads against infections such as pneumonia, syphilis, gonorrhea, meningococcal infections, and later typhoid and enteric fevers.

This victory over infectious diseases is clearly demonstrated in Figure 20. The important killers, pneumonia and tuberculosis, have decreased dramatically over the past century in the US, and total mortality from infections per 100,000 has dropped from 800 to 50, compared to the stable non-infection rate of about 800. Figures from the UK and other industrialized nations show similar declines in infectious diseases.[390] The increase since the mid-1980s is due to two factors. First, about two-thirds of the 1980 infection rate is caused by pneumonia. However, pneumonia is deadly almost exclusively in very old age, and an almost doubling in pneumonia since 1980 is caused by an aging population.[391] If we correct for aging, the death risk was similar in 1980 and 1997.[392]

Second, the increase since 1980 is caused by the rise of HIV, where the all-time high of 16.4 in 1995 was comparable to the death rates of syphilis in the beginning of the century.[393] Thanks to the new combination drugs, AIDS-related deaths have now declined to just 4.9 per 100,000 in 1998, and the figure for 1999 is even lower.[394]

As medicine, hygiene and higher living standards in the Western world defeated infectious disease, people began to live longer and better. For this reason we die much more frequently of old-age and lifestyle-related diseases, such as cancer and cardiovascular disease.[395] In 1900 the leading causes of death in the US were pneumonia, tuberculosis, diarrhea and enteritis, causing about one third of all deaths, whereas heart disease and cancers were responsible for just 12.5 percent. In 1997, heart disease and cancers accounted for 55 percent of all deaths, with just 4.5 percent attributable to infectious diseases.[396]

When the cancer mortality rate has kept rising in the UK and the US until the early 1990s, it is not because we are being more "exposed" to cancer, as we shall see in the section on our chemical fears (see also Figure 117, p. 217).[397] Cancer occurs more frequently the older people get, and for this reason alone we would expect more people to die of it, the older we get. In actual fact it turns out that if statistics are corrected for old age and smoking (i.e. we look at identical age groups, with smokers and non-smokers grouped separately), *fewer* of us die of cancer – not more.[398] Where lung cancer rates, even corrected for aging, have been rising in the US from 4.9 in 1930 to 75.6 in 1990, it is largely due to the intensive smoking that took place decades ago. However, smoking is decreasing (in 1965, approximately 42 percent of all Americans smoked, compared to just 25 percent in 1997[399]) and the lung cancer rate for men has actually begun declining in the 1990s. Nevertheless, it is estimated that the death of 25 percent of all men and 14 percent of all women can be blamed on tobacco.[400]

But although we survive longer, and have overcome a large proportion of illnesses not the least from infection, we still have to ask if we are – all in all – more or less sick. This turns out to be a tricky question to answer directly.

Typically, health experts have claimed that the reduced death rates almost by definition mean that we have got less seriously ill, since most of our present illnesses carry less danger of death. Many have proposed that as we survive longer and longer, we have squeezed the lion's share of illness into old age, a phenomena which has also become known as the "compression of morbidity."[401]

However, we could also try to look at the actual rates of illness – particularly how often we are so ill that we stay home from work or otherwise restrict our activity.[402] Researchers have looked at local groups of British workers from 1779 to 1929, and at health surveys in the UK, the US, Japan and Hungary. Fairly consistently, it turns out that as we live ever longer, we also get sick less often – pretty much as we might expect – but the surprising result is that at the same time each sickness period lasts much longer. This not only cancels the effect of lower sickness frequency but on average it actually makes us sick more of the time. Thus, the surprising outcome from this line of research has been to stress the "failure of success," that as we have increasingly fought death we have only achieved more non-lethal disease.[403]

The basic claim of intuition behind this surprising result is twofold. First, after we have won the war against infectious diseases most of the gains in life expectancy come from making non-infectious diseases ever less lethal. However, these chronic diseases are seldom cured but more often just handled through disease management, such that long periods of time would be spent in convalescence – hence on average making us ill more of the time.[404] Second, the people who would have died in earlier periods are now living longer, because of better treatment. We know, however, that these "new survivors" are, on average, much more likely to experience renewed health problems, and thus they also contribute to driving up the average rate of illness.[405]

Not surprisingly, this statistic has been thoroughly challenged.[406] Basically, the question is whether the concept of illness has remained constant throughout long periods of time. While it is pretty obvious what constitutes death and while statistics on mortality are therefore fairly objective, being ill is only meaningful in comparison to an idealized state of health – and although we may think that our sore throat is adequate reason to stay home from work, this attitude may not have been shared by our predecessors.

There is much evidence that we have become much more aware of illness, and that the medical profession has gone on to specify many new (particularly emotional) maladies that people of previous eras would never even have thought of. At the same time we have become more well off and better insured, making it financially easier to bear an illness, such that our threshold for taking sick undoubtedly has diminished.

Actually, the question here is rather simple – does it make sense to believe that we can really be more sick nowadays than the eighteenth-century people with "suppurating ulcers, eczema, scabs, running sores and other nauseating skin diseases" described above by Lawrence Stone? While it is virtually impossible to determine the answer by looking at the sickness rate over time, since the cultural definition of sickness has changed dramatically, we can address the question in a different manner by looking at the rates of illness in different parts of the world with widely differing life expectancies. Here we get a clue to the problems involved in merely asking people whether they are sick or not – it turns out that for a long list of chronic illnesses even young people in the US report *higher* incidence than the poorest rural areas of India.[407]

More systematically, the World Health Organization and the World Bank have tried to evaluate exactly the distribution of illness in the form of disability over different parts of the world with their *Global Burden of Disease* study.[408] The result in Figure 21 shows overwhelming support for the idea that we have become less and less ill as we live ever longer. Having the shortest life expectancy of 50 years, the people of sub-Saharan Africa simultaneously have to endure that more than 15 percent of their life is spent in disability, whereas the 77 years life expectancy of the established market economies only has a corresponding 8 percent of a life spent in disability. Even in absolute terms a sub-Saharan African has on average to contend with 7.5 years of disability during a short life span, compared to the European spending just 6.25 years of disability over a much longer life.

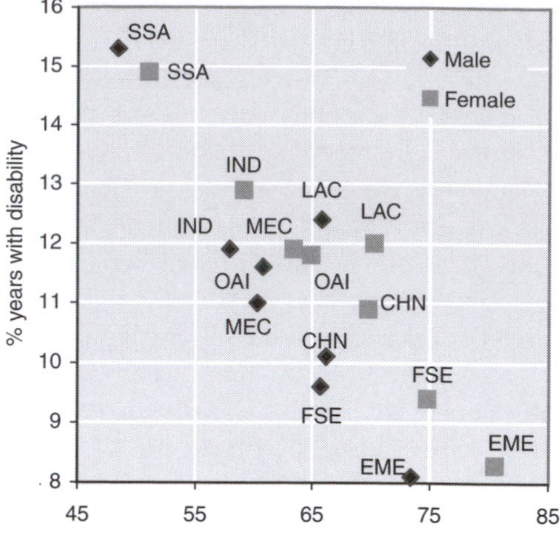

Figure 21 The relationship between life expectancy and percentage of life spent with disability. EME=established market economies; FSE=formerly socialist economies of Europe; IND=India; CHN=China; OAI=other Asia and islands; SSA=sub-Saharan Africa; LAC=Latin America and the Caribbean; MEC=middle eastern crescent. Source: Murray and Lopez 1997b.

These statistics clearly indicate that the trend we see across the regions of today is likely to be the same trend that we have experienced over time – as in both the developed and the developing world we have increased our life expectancy we have also become more and more healthy.[409]

Another indicator of the health of a population is the average height of its citizens. Height is closely linked to health and adequate nutrition from embryo to adulthood, and taller citizens are therefore an indication of better general standards of health. Tall people also have a relatively lower mortality rate (albeit only up to the height of about 192 cm, 6ft 4in!).[410] Again, if we look at Figure 22 we will see that we have got taller and taller over the past couple of hundred years.[411]

Conclusion

All in all, it must be said that mankind's health situation has improved dramatically

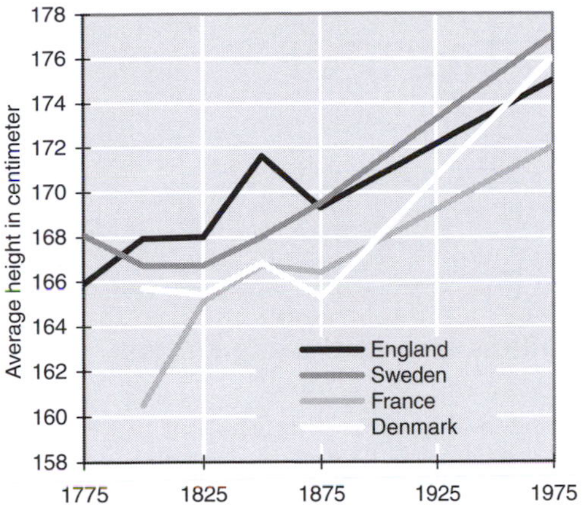

Figure 22 Average height of adult men from 1775 to 1975. Source: Fogel 1989:50, Burnette and Mokyr 1995: 144.

over the past couple of hundred years. We live to more than twice the age we did just a hundred years ago, and the improvement applies to both the industrialized and the developing world. Infant mortality has fallen in both developed and developing countries by far more than 50 percent. Finally, we are much less sick than we used to be, not vice versa.

This should not lead us to forget the problems still outstanding – the AIDS epidemic in southern Africa and the significant improvements that are still possible for the developing world. But basically, life and health on this planet have vastly improved.

5 Food and hunger

"The battle to feed humanity is over. In the course of the 1970s the world will experience starvation of tragic proportions – hundreds of millions of people will starve to death."[412] This was the introduction to one of the most influential books on hunger, Paul Ehrlich's *The Population Bomb* published in 1968. More than 3 million copies of the book have been sold.

Ehrlich runs down what he calls the "professional optimists": "They say, for instance, that India in the next eight years can increase its agricultural output to feed some 120 million more people than they cannot after all feed today. To put such fantasy into perspective one need consider only . . ." [413], and Ehrlich presented a whole list of reasons why this could not be achieved. And sure enough, it turned out that the figure of 120 million did not hold water. Eight years later India produced enough food for 144 million more people. And since the population had grown by 'only' 104 million, this meant there was more food to go round.[414]

From the same quarter Lester Brown, who later became president of the Worldwatch Institute, wrote in 1965 that "the food problem emerging in the less-developing regions may be one of the most nearly insoluble problems facing man over the next few decades."[415]

They were both mistaken. Although there are now twice as many of us as there were in 1961,[416] each of us has *more* to eat, in both developed and developing countries. Fewer people are starving. Food is far cheaper these days and food-wise the world is quite simply a better place for far more people.

Malthus and everlasting hunger

It seems so obvious, though, that there being more people on the Earth should mean less food for each individual. This simple theory was formulated in 1798 by Reverend Thomas Malthus, an English economist and demographer. The argument was made remarkably popular in the 1970s by the best-seller *Limits to Growth*.[417]

Malthus' theory was that the population grows by a certain percentage a year – i.e. exponentially. The Earth's population currently stands to double in about 40 years. So in 80 years' time there will be four times as many of us and in 120 years eight times as many, etc. Food production grows more slowly – its growth is linear. It may double within 40 years but in 80 years it will only be three times the present level, and in 120 years only four times. The population will grow ever more rapidly while the growth in food supplies will remain constant. So in the long term, food production will lose its race against the population. Many people will starve and die.

Malthus' theory is so simple and attractive that many reputable scientists have fallen for it. But the evidence does not seem to support the theory. The population rarely grows exponentially, as we saw in the introductory section (Figure 11). Likewise, the quantity of food seldom grows linearly. In actual fact the world's agricultural production has more than doubled since 1961, and in developing countries it has more than tripled. This means that there has been a steady growth in the amount of food available for each member of the population. According to the UN we

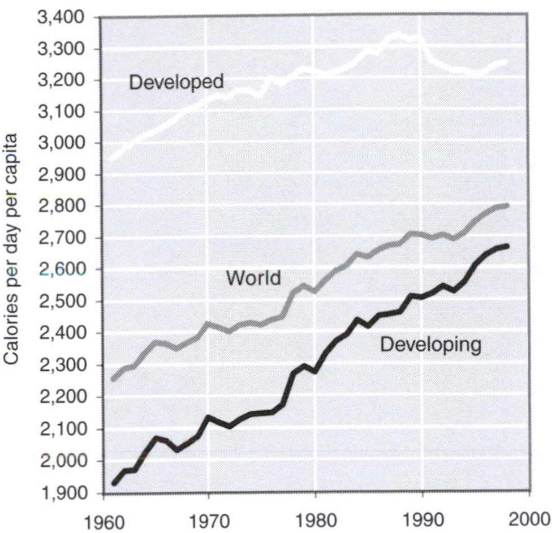

Figure 23 Daily intake of calories per capita in the industrial and developing countries and world. 1961–98. For prediction to 2030, see Figure 58 (p. 109). Source: FAO 2001a.

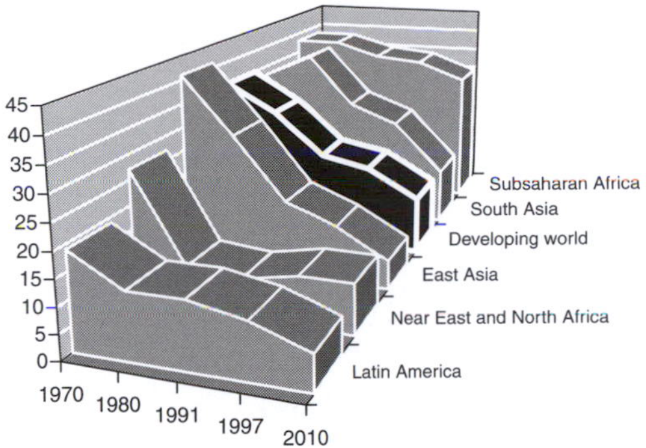

Figure 24 Proportion of starving in percent, developing world by region, for 1970, 1980, 1991, 1997 and estimates 2010. Note the slightly irregular intervals. Source: WFS 1996:1: Table 3, FAO 2000c:27.

produce 23 percent more food per capita than we did in 1961, and the growth in agricultural crops per person in developing countries has grown by as much as 52 percent.[418] Equivalently, meat per person has grown by 122 percent from 17.2 kg in 1950 to 38.4 kg in 2000.[419] In spite of this dramatic increase in demand the price of food fell by more than two-thirds from 1957 to early 2001.[420]

More food than ever

Basically, we now have far more food per person than we used to, even though the population has doubled since 1961. It can be seen from Figure 23 that our calorie intake has increased by 24 percent on a global basis, and that developing countries have experienced a dramatic increase of 38 percent.

The calorie figure is, nonetheless, an average. It is not unthinkable that the figure conceals the fact that some people live better lives while increasing numbers of others just manage or even starve. But here, as elsewhere, things are improving.

According to the UN's definition, a person is starving if he or she does not get sufficient food to perform light physical activity.[421] Figure 24 shows the percentage of people starving in developing countries. Globally, the proportion of people starving has fallen from 35 percent to 18 percent and is expected to fall further to 12 percent in 2010 (see also chapter 9 in Part III).[422] This should be compared to an estimated 45 percent of developing country people starving in 1949.[423]

The proportion of children in the developing world considered to be undernourished has fallen from 40 percent to 30 percent over the past 15 years, and it is expected to fall further to 24 percent in 2020.[424] Since 1970, the proportion of starving people has fallen in all regions, and it is set to fall even further for almost all regions.[425]

It is remarkable that the fall in the proportion of people starving in the world should have come at the same time as the population of developing countries doubled. What is more astounding is that the actual *number* of people starving in the Third World has fallen. While in 1971 almost 920 million people were starving, the total fell to below 792 million in 1997 (see Figure 7). In 2010 it is expected to fall to 680 million.[426] These figures are, of course, still frighteningly high, but it is important to

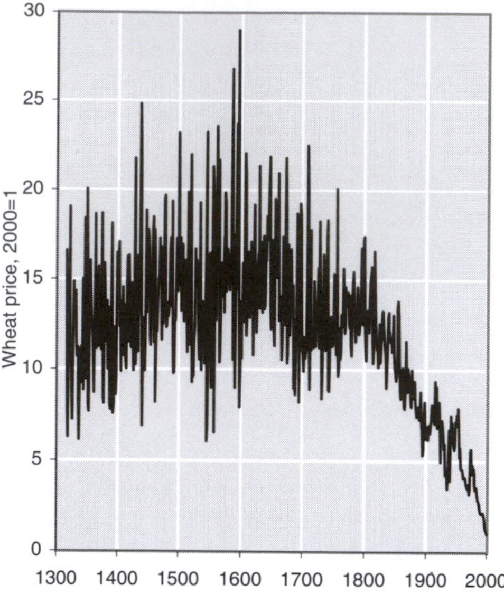

Figure 25 Wheat price index, England 1316–2000 (Exeter 1316–1820, England and Wales 1771–1980, United Kingdom 1966–99). Source: Mitchell 1988:752–8, MAFF 2000:5:4, 2001: 30, FAO 2000, UK CPI 2000, 2001.

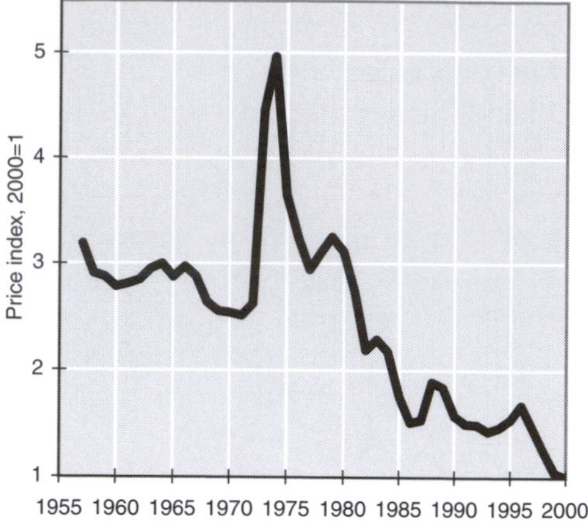

Figure 26 World Bank price index for foodstuffs. 1957–2000, 2000 = 1. Source: IMF 2001a.

emphasize that today more than 2 billion more people are *not* starving.[427]

The improvement in absolute figures has, however, primarily been in Asia and is largely a consequence of China's amazing ability to produce food.

Lower prices than ever

At the same time as the Earth accommodates ever more people, who are making demands for ever more food, food prices have fallen dramatically. In 2000 food cost less than a third of its price in 1957. This fall in food prices has been vital for many people in the developing world, especially the many poverty-stricken city dwellers.[428]

The fall in the price of food is a genuine long-term tendency. The price of wheat has had a downwards trend ever since 1800, and wheat is now more than ten times cheaper than the price charged throughout the previous 500 years (Figure 25). The fall in prices was particularly marked in the post-war period and applied to more or less all major types of food (Figure 26). The only break in the fall in prices was in the 1970s, when the oil crisis led to heavy price increases in the short term. The increase in the price of oil meant that artificial fertilizers became more expensive and that the Soviet Union, a major oil exporter, was able to buy cereals for its domestic meat production.[429]

Since prices reflect the scarcity of a product, foodstuffs have actually become less scarce during this century despite the fact that the population has more than tripled and demand increased by even more.[430]

The Green Revolution

One cannot help asking oneself how development can possibly have been so good. The answer is to be found in a number of technologies which are collectively known as The Green Revolution.[431]

The Revolution consisted primarily of

- High-yield crops
- Irrigation and controlled water supply
- Fertilizers and pesticides
- Farmers' management skills.

The secret of the Green Revolution was to get more food out of each and every hectare of soil. The vision was that of Norman Borlaug, who later received the Nobel Peace Prize for his work on high-yield varieties of crops. In his laboratories in Mexico attention was focused in particular on the major types of cereals: rice, corn and wheat. Characteristic of these modern varieties is that they germinate earlier in the year, grow faster and are more resistant to disease and drought. They often have shorter stems than the old varieties so that most of the plants' sustenance ends up in the grains.

The fact that the plants germinate earlier and grow more quickly means that in many parts of the world it is possible to harvest two or three crops a year. Rice no longer takes 150 days to mature and many varieties can do so in as little as 90 days.[432] At the same time, it is possible to cultivate crops in large areas where climate conditions are less favorable. For example, modern corn can be grown in an 800 km wider belt around the Earth, which has been a boon to countries like Canada, Russia, China and Argentina.[433] Wheat has become resistant to most diseases, such as mildew and rust, which means a lot in developing countries where farmers often cannot afford pesticides.[434] The new varieties of wheat now account for almost 90 percent of production in developing countries.[435]

Since 1960, the new varieties have led to a 30 percent plus increase in maximum yields and are responsible for 20–50 percent of the total, increased productivity.[436] For farmers in the developing world this also means more money – new varieties are estimated to give farmers an additional income of almost four billion dollars each year.[437]

In fact it is not only varieties of grain that have been improved. Chickens and pigs produce more than twice as much meat as they did 60 years ago and cows produce twice the amount of milk. With genetic enhancement and modern fish farming, the Norwegian salmon has since the early 1970s also become twice as productive.[438]

Irrigation and water control (e.g. building dams) have become more widespread, the proportion of irrigated fields having almost doubled from 10.5 percent in 1961 to over 18 percent in 1997.[442] Irrigation renders the soil far more fertile – it has enabled the Egyptians to get almost twice the wheat yield of the average developing country.[443] Irrigation also makes it possible to harvest two or three times a year. This is why irrigated land contributes as much as 40 percent of the Earth's food – even though it only accounts for 18 percent of the total agricultural land mass.[444] The growth in the use of irrigation has been constant in absolute hectares but is, therefore, slightly declining relatively, partly because of an incipient water scarcity in many regions (see chapter 13) and partly because of a general fall-off in the demand for food.

Finally, the increased use of fertilizers and pesticides has made it possible to improve plant growth and not lose such a large proportion of crops to disease and insects. Almost a third of the Asian rice harvest was eaten by insects in 1960![445] The use of fertilizer has increased almost nine-fold since 1950 (see Figure 3, and Figure 106), and although there has been a slight reduction in global consumption because of the Soviet Union's agricultural reforms and later collapse, important countries like China and India still use more fertilizers.[446]

The Green Revolution represents a milestone in the history of mankind. The ensuing fantastic increase in food production has made it possible to feed far more people. Overall, the Green Revolution has meant a tremendous increase in production per hectare as

RELATIVE OR ABSOLUTE IMPROVEMENT?

When we look at a problem such as hunger or a shortage of pure drinking water, the question often arises as to whether we should use absolute or relative figures.

It is naturally a good thing for the number of people starving to have fallen both in absolute figures and as a percentage. Similarly, it would certainly be bad if both the number and the percentage had increased. But what if one figure increases and the other decreases?

My way of understanding this problem in *moral* terms involves setting up an ideal, moral choice situation.[439] The idea is to imagine the problem from the point of view of an individual who must choose in which society he or she wants to live. The point is that the individual does not know his or her position in society (a sort of "veil of ignorance"). This ensures the universality of the moral evaluation.[440]

For the sake of argument, let us say that there are only two types of people – those who die of starvation and those who survive.[441] We can thus describe society A and society B:

A. A world in which 500,000 die of starvation out of a population of 1,000,000.
B. A world in which 750,000 die of starvation out of a population of 2,000,000.

In society B, the absolute figure has increased but the relative figure has fallen. To me the obvious choice in this situation is that society B is better than society A (although a society without death would naturally be preferable). My risk of dying (of hunger) in society B is 37.5 percent, against 50 percent in society A. My argument, then, is that the relative figure is the more important in a comparison, in which the absolute and relative figures point in opposing directions.

One can naturally criticize this choice on moral grounds, and argue that the society with the lowest absolute figure is the best (i.e. that A is better than B). But a view such as this meets a significant challenge in the form of yet another hypothetical society:

C. A world in which 499,999 people die of starvation out of a population of 500,000.

In this situation the absolute point of view has the substantial weakness that it would also prefer society C to society A. Very few people are likely to see this as the right choice.

Therefore, when the absolute and the relative figures each points in its own direction, the relative figure will probably be the more morally relevant way to evaluate whether mankind's lot has improved or deteriorated.

regards all traditional crops. From Figure 27 it can be seen how the developing countries have experienced an increase in productivity as regards the three most important crops: rice, wheat and corn. Rice production has increased by 122 percent, corn by 159 percent and wheat by a whopping 229 percent. And they still have quite a way to go before they reach the same levels as the industrialized world.[447]

One sometimes hears that the use of pesticides and intensive farming methods are harmful to the environment. But what alternative do we have, with more than 6 billion people on Earth? If we abandoned intensive cultivation and the use of pesticides, farmers would either need *far more space* to grow the same quantities or end up producing *far less food*.[448] So they would either have to take over more of the surrounding countryside[449] or we would end up with more hungry souls among us. Yet, this discussion of risks from fertilizer and pesticides is clearly important, and we will look into it in much more detail in chapters 19 and 22.

Finally, the new "designer" varieties of crops offer greater resistance to disease, thereby reducing pesticide consumption, while at the same time having improved uptake of nutrients, thus reducing the overapplication of fertilizer.[450]

Regional distribution: Africa

Improvements in the provision of food per capita have not been evenly distributed throughout all regions of the world. We can see from Figure 28 that there has been a solid increase in Latin America, while Asia and the Near East have experienced fantastic increases of 42 percent and 51 percent, respectively.

Unfortunately, this improvement has not been shared by sub-Saharan Africa. Although some progress has been detectable in recent years, basic development has not been forthcoming. What is going wrong in Africa? What can we do?[451]

In the early 1960s most of the countries in sub-Saharan Africa were at the same level of development as Asia or even higher. Over the last 30 years, however, Asia has achieved an astounding improvement in productivity, whereas sub-Saharan Africa has been marking time. Today Asia uses an average of 129 kg of fertilizer per hectare, while in sub-Saharan Africa only 11 kg per hectare are being spread on the land. Actually, even the present agricultural production in Africa is depleting more than 30 kg of nutrients each year, because of a lack of chemical fertilizer.[452] Irrigation is used on 37 percent of cultivated areas in Asia compared to only 5 percent in sub-Saharan Africa.[453]

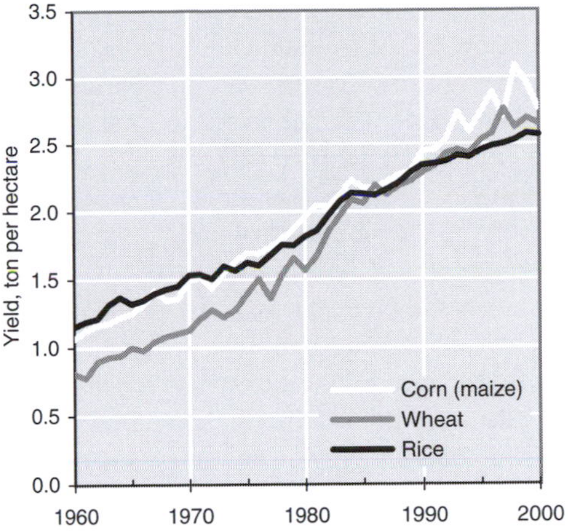

Figure 27 Yield in tons per hectare of rice, corn and wheat in developing countries, 1960–2000. Source: USDA 1998, 2000a, 2001, FAO 2000.

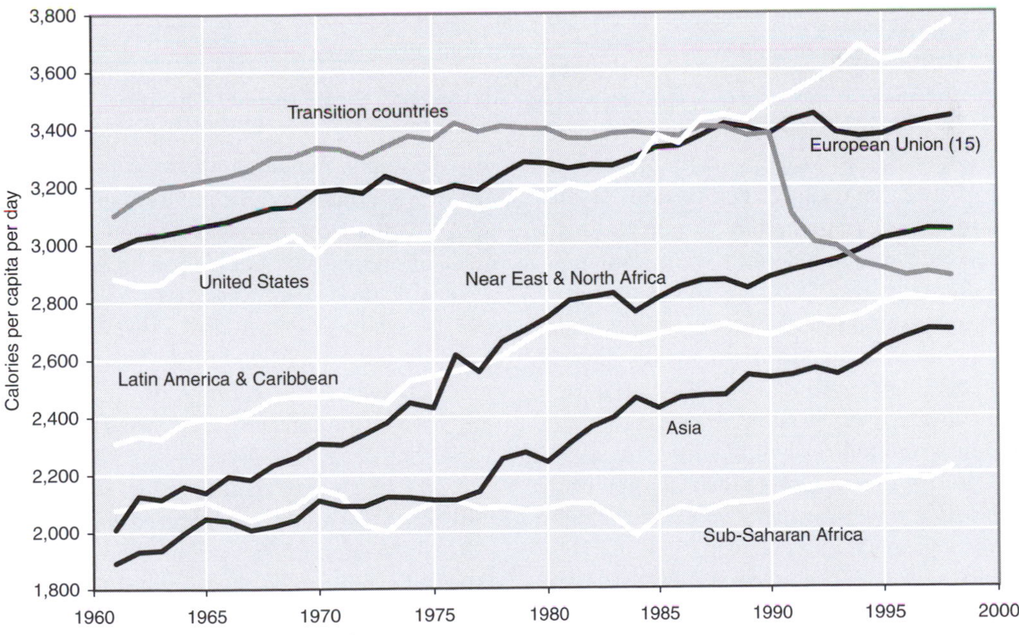

Figure 28 Calories per capita per day for various regions, 1961–98. Source: FAO 2001a.

These are some of the reasons for the food situation in Asia today being considerably better than that in sub-Saharan Africa. But at the same time it is important to note that, by increasing its use of fertilizer and irrigation, sub-Saharan Africa has great potential for increasing the amount of food it produces. Numerous local farming schemes run by the FAO have shown that it is also possible in practice to increase agricultural production substantially in sub-Saharan Africa. A scheme in Eritrea, a country still suffering from widespread food shortage after 30 years of civil war, has succeeded in doubling production with the help of improved seed grain, the correct use of fertilizers and improved irrigation.[454] This has helped local peasants to become self-sufficient.

Similarly, countries like Burkina Faso have managed to break out of stagnation and achieve 25 percent growth in calories per inhabitant in just ten years. Despite the country's exposed position, this has been achieved by carrying out reforms aimed at boosting investments in agriculture and removing price ceilings, which deter peasants from producing more.[455]

Africa's peasant farmers have great potential to produce far more food. According to the FAO, "it is entirely possible to reverse the production trends and safeguard the food security of the increasing population of the region."[456] Why, then, has this not already happened? In a surprisingly frank statement the UN states that "it is not the resources or the economic solutions that are lacking – it is the political momentum to tackle poverty head-on."[457] According to the UN, an improvement in the food situation depends first and foremost on political obligations to secure and protect the economic, social and political rights of the poor. Securing land and the right to own property, access to money markets, effective health authorities and better education are therefore the most important ingredients in the fight against starvation and poverty.

However, since decolonization in the late 1950s, sub-Saharan Africa has been plagued by political and economic instability, where civil and ethnic conflict have been more the rule than the exception.[458] Added to this, the region has been plagued by corruption, inadequate infrastructure, poor education and politically fixed farm prices, all of which have hampered agricultural development. The result of this is the difficult food situation in which sub-Saharan Africa finds itself today. It is therefore vital for sub-Saharan Africa that we actively support policies which secure economic and political reform, thereby enabling the region to start feeding its own population. It does now look as though sub-Saharan Africa is pulling its way out of long-term stagnation. In 1998, after 15 years of growth lower than the rate of increase in the population, the economies of sub-Saharan Africa saw their fourth consecutive year of growth above the population increase, and with further acceleration in growth in 2000 after a slowdown due to the Asian crisis, it is now clear that this was the result of sensible economic and political initiatives.[459]

Regional distribution: China

Nutritionally, the development in the world's most populous state, China, has been fantastic.[460] China now manages to feed over one fifth of the world's population from one fifteenth of the world's farmland. After it took over power in 1949 the Communist Party initiated a massive industrialization process based on cheap labor, price ceilings for the peasants, and food rationing. This policy posed problems for agriculture, and between 1959 and 1962 China experienced catastrophic starvation and almost 30 million people died (Figure 13).

This encouraged the country to join the Green Revolution with a vengeance. High-yield crops, irrigation and fertilization were introduced. Despite this effort the Chinese did not experience any noticeable improvement in prosperity. The problem was that farm productivity remained low because collective organization did not give people the incentive to work.

The crucial change occurred when the Chinese leadership initiated economic reforms in the late 1970s. These paved the way for higher prices and greater flexibility. Equally significant was the fact that they now allowed people to own property and sell goods: China's production potential was set free and it experienced a drastic increase in production.[461] While the population grew by 1.3 percent a year from 1979 to 1984, agricultural production increased annually by as much as 11.8 percent. The FAO estimates that at least half this growth can be accredited to private plots of land. Since 1978 the value of farm production has doubled, a great benefit to China's more than 800 million peasants: rural incomes increased by a good 15 percent a year and the proportion of poor people has fallen from 33 percent to 12 percent. At the same time the number of people employed in agriculture has fallen from almost four out of five to just every other person.[462] As a result, the population now has far more to eat. The proportion of people who face starvation has fallen by three-quarters and Chinese children are today taller and weigh more, a clear indicator of improving nutritional standards.[463] Most impressive perhaps is that China, from having a regular starvation-level diet of around 1,500 calories per capita in the early 1960s has experienced an almost doubling to 2,973 calories per capita in 1998.[464]

Conclusion

"The battle to feed mankind is over." The food problem in the developing world represents a "nearly insoluble problem." We have been told for ages that it will end in disaster. That we can't feed the world. But the doomsday vision has nothing to do with reality. On practically *every* count, humankind is now *better* nourished. The Green Revolution has been victorious. Production in the developing countries has tripled. The calorie intake per capita has here increased by 38 percent. The proportion of starving people has fallen from 35 percent to 18 percent and today more than 2 billion more people do not go hungry.

There is, however, still a lot to be done in the future. Africa needs to get back on its feet and to produce far more food. But as we have seen, this is possible for agriculture; the problems primarily lie with stifling political and economic conditions. We have an obligation to ensure that these conditions are improved by means of international cooperation. China is a good example of how this can be done. From being a poor, backward country in the 1950s, China has, by investing in modern production and privatization, achieved fabulous growth – from a state of hunger and malnutrition to comfortably feeding a fifth of the world's population.

However, before 2050 the world will have 3.3 billion more mouths to feed. Will it be possible to secure them all enough to eat? Both Ehrlich and Brown keep on telling us that food production is going down the tubes – *now* we will see the onset of disaster. Lester Brown tells us that food production now "is experiencing a massive loss of momentum."[465] In Part III we shall see that they are still mistaken.

IS INFLATION-ADJUSTED GDP A REASONABLE MEASURE OF WEALTH?

Getting a general view of the wealth of a nation poses a number of problems. The most frequently used tool for its measurement is GNP, the gross national product, or GDP, the gross domestic product, because these figures are easily obtainable in most countries and for long periods of time.[466] Pedantic economists might tell you that one ought to use slightly different figures,[467] but in reality there is little difference.

It leaves out moonlighting and the work of women

Even so, using GDP as a measure of wealth presents us with some fundamental problems. First, GDP does not include production which takes place outside the formal marketplace. If we build our own carport or repair the gutters on our house, this is not registered in the national accounts. Most of the work outside the market is done by women because, particularly in the Third World, they cook and take care of the children and the home without this production being registered anywhere. The UN estimates that as much as one-third of the global production is informal, and that women are responsible for more than two-thirds of it.[468] Similarly, GDP does not take into consideration the underground economy. When people moonlight this does not get included in the national accounts. By definition the shadow economy cannot be measured precisely, but estimates indicate it constitutes about 9 percent for the US, 13 percent for the UK, and 17 percent for the entire OECD. The figures for the developing countries are much higher – the shadow economy in Nigeria is approximately three-quarters the size of the official GDP.[469] At the same time GDP includes all measurable costs. This means that it also takes into account costs which definitely do not make us wealthier: the treatment of accident victims and disease, commuting costs from increasing distances between home and work, and taking care of environmental problems.[470] GDP automatically gets higher in cold countries, because people spend more money on heating than they do in warmer climates.[471]

These problems obviously make it more difficult to use GDP as a measurement of actual wealth. One can argue, nonetheless, that GDP is a reasonable indicator of wealth. A Danish survey attempted to use a more accurate indicator, but the result differed only slightly from the national statistics.[472] Furthermore, GDP is normally used not for the sake of the actual figure, but to enable comparison with other GDP figures for earlier periods or other nations.[473] In fact the same Danish study also attempted to compare development over the past 20 years, and once again it could be seen that the result obtained using the more accurate wealth indicator differed only slightly from traditional consumption figures.[474]

Problems over an extended period

Even so, problems do arise when using GDP as an expression of wealth over an extended period, because with development the size of both the hidden and the illicit economies is gradually declining. As women join the labor market, more and more of their tasks become part of the formal economy and are therefore registered as part of the GDP figure. The fact that our children are now looked after by paid nursery assistants and our homes are cleaned by commercial service companies gives the statistical impression that we have become richer than we actually have.

For this reason one must expect that GDP accounting will tend to overestimate growth. But there is also an opposing tendency to underestimate growth, a topic greatly discussed in recent years. When we compare the amount of money earned during different periods, the figures must be corrected to account for inflation. This is frequently done using a so-called consumer price index (CPI), which tells us, for example, how much a dollar in the past is worth today. A dollar in 1913 could purchase what $17 can today.[475]

So when the average American made $511 in 1913, the consumer price index tells us that in 2000 terms this would be equivalent to $8,887.[476] The problem is, however, that this price index is extremely difficult to calculate correctly since goods do not simply get more expensive because of inflation or cheaper because of industrialization and mass production. The *same* article also gets *better*, something it is extremely difficult to compensate for in an economy that changes rapidly.[477] VCRs, microwave ovens and personal computers have got cheaper and better, and offer far greater functionality, but they were first included in the index a decade or more after they had penetrated the market and fallen 80 percent or more in price.[478] Consequently, the CPI will tend to underestimate the improvement in VCRs and thus to overestimate inflation.[479]

However, actually *measuring* how much better VCRs and other goods have become has proved to be an almost impossible task. Yale economics professor William Nordhaus has tried to estimate the decline of the actual cost of light from prehistoric fire to Babylonian lamps to town gas, and electric lamps to the new fluorescent light bulbs, while comparing it to the CPI estimates. Over the last 200 years, the CPI index seems to have missed a large part of the quality improvements, to the extent that today's CPI-adjusted light price is more than 1,000 times higher than the true price.[480] Nordhaus argues that this result holds true not just for lighting but for a large number of other revolutionary goods and services, making up about 30–70 percent of all income. Thus, a traditional CPI analysis of American income over the past 200 years has possibly underestimated the true income improvements by anywhere from 300 to 1,500 percent.[481] The American Boskin Commission has estimated that the CPI has overestimated inflation by a little over 1 percent a year, or approximately 30 percent over the last 25 years.[482]

Thus, we found earlier that GDP over time tends systematically to overestimate wealth, due to the progressive inclusion of the informal and illicit economy. Now we also see that growth measured in terms of GDP is systematically and *substantially* underestimated when corrected for inflation. This allows us to conclude that GDP measurement probably provides a reasonable impression of wealth and will over a period of time be not over-optimistic, but rather the contrary.

6 Prosperity

During the last couple of hundred years we have become much richer than in all previous history. This can be measured in many ways (and we shall look at some of these below), but the most obvious of these is to look at the available production per capita. This provides us with a measurement of how much an average individual can buy.[483] Figure 29 gives an estimate of the global development in GDP per capita over the last 2,000 years. After an almost constant $400 throughout most of human history, we passed the $700 line in 1800, and 200 years later we were on average more than eight times richer.[484]

If we look at Figure 30 we can see that there has been a 36-fold increase in per capita American production since 1789,[485] and a similar 20-fold British increase since 1756. In 2000 the US economy produced goods and services for an average American at the value of $36,200; at the end of the eighteenth century, an American would have made just 996 present-day dollars.[486] The average Briton had £15,700 in 2000 compared to just 792 present-day pounds in 1756.

This development is not unique to the US or the UK. In Figure 31 we can see that all regions of the world have experienced substantial per capita growth although it has not been equally pronounced throughout: Western Europe has seen a 13-fold

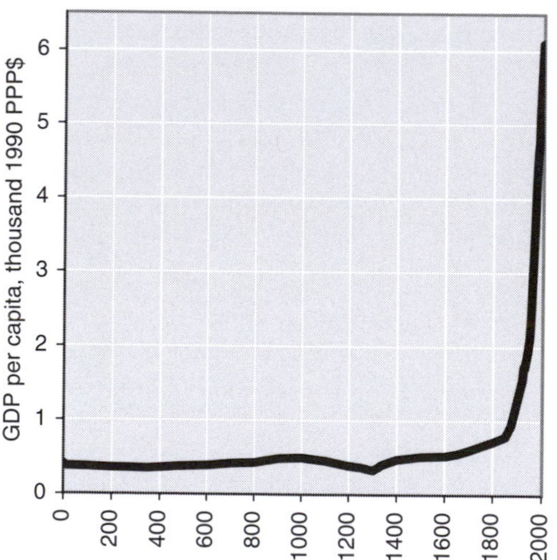

Figure 29 Estimated global GDP per capita 0–2000 CE. The estimate also extends backwards (with very little change) to 1,000,000 BCE. The little break is the 1930s depression. Source: DeLong 2000a.

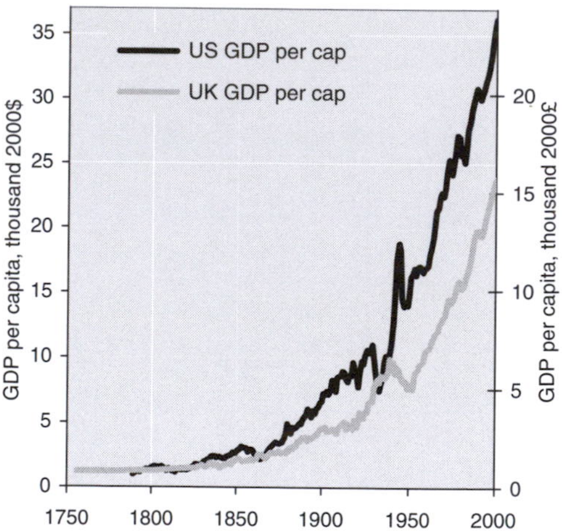

Figure 30 UK (1756–2000) and US (1789–2000) GDP per capita in constant 2000$ and 2000£ at the 2000 exchange rate (£/$=1.52, HM Treasury 2001:16). Source: UK: 1756–1846: Floud and Harris 1996:55, 1830–1975: Flora *et al.* 1983:366–9, 1960–97 World Bank 1999a, 1975–99: HM Treasury 2000:4, 2001:4, ONS 2001d, UK CPI 2001. US: 1789–1988: Mitchell 1993: 748, 749, 753, 761, BEA 2000, 2001, CPI 2001.

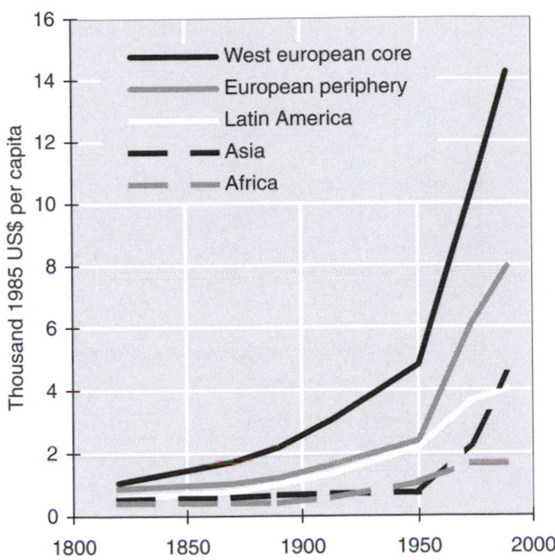

Figure 31 GDP per capita 1985 US$ for regions of the world, 1820–1989. West European Core includes the central capitalist countries such as Britain, Germany, France and the USA. European Periphery encompasses countries such as Greece, Ireland, Spain and the Soviet Union. Source: Maddison 1994:22–3.

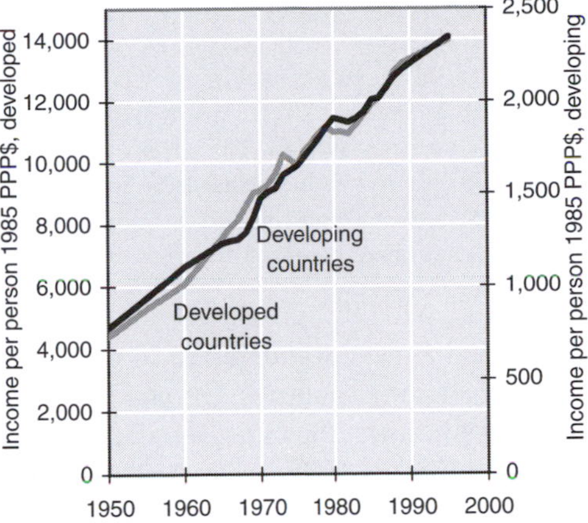

Figure 32 GDP per capita for the developed and developing world in 1985 PPP$, 1950–95. Note the differing values on the axes. Source: Summers and Heston 1991, 1995, World Bank 1997.

improvement, the European Periphery ninefold, Latin America sevenfold, Asia eightfold and Africa fourfold.

Development got a head-start in the Western world and so is that much farther ahead.[487] But both industrial and developing countries experienced fantastic, uniform improvements in income per capita in the post-war years. Throughout the entire period the inhabitants of the industrialized world earned around six times as much as their counterparts in developing countries.[488] Figure 32 shows, that from 1950 to 1995, average incomes in the industrialized countries increased by 218 percent while those in developing countries rose by 201 percent.

During the period as a whole, developing countries have seen annual growth rates of 4.2 percent whereas industrialized countries have had just 3.2 percent. The developing countries did not, however, start to catch up on the industrialized world because their populations at the same time grew at a higher rate.

Poverty and distribution

We often believe life in the developing world is deteriorating and that the proportion of poor people is increasing, but the evidence clearly shows the opposite. In fact the UN writes in its 1997 report on poverty and inequality: "Few people realize the great advances already made. In the past 50 years poverty has fallen more than in the previous 500. And it has been reduced in some respects in almost all countries."[489] Similarly, the World Bank wrote in 1998:

> Fantastic progress has been made in reducing poverty in developing countries. During the last four decades the social indicators have improved in all regions. In the past two decades, poverty has been drastically reduced in East Asia: from six out of ten living on under a $1 a day in the mid-1970s, to two out of ten in the mid-1990s. there has also been a reduction in poverty during the last few years throughout most of southern Asia and parts of the Middle East, North Africa and Latin America.[490]

The UN emphasizes that this progress has been general:

> The accelerated progress in reducing poverty in the 20th-century began in Europe and North America in the 19th-century – in what can now be seen as the first Great Ascent from poverty and human deprivation. The ascent started in the foothills of the Industrial Revolution, with rising incomes, improvements in public health and education and eventually programs of social security . . .

The second Great Ascent started in the 1950s in the developing countries. The end of colonialism was followed by improvements in education and health and accelerated economic development that led to dramatic declines in poverty. By the end of the twentieth-century some 3–4 billion of the world's people will have experienced substantial improvements in their standard of living, and about 4–5 billion will have access to basic education and health care.[491]

It is important not to forget that the developing countries' situation has *much improved*. They have become much more affluent, tripling their real per capita income.

However, both the World Bank and the UN emphasize that there is still a long way to go: "Despite this progress, however, much remains to be done."[492] In 1987, 1.18 billion people lived on less than one 1985-dollar a day (565 current dollars a year), which is the World Bank's poverty line.[493] This number increased in the early 1990s to 1.3 billion, only to decline again towards the end of the decade – in 1998 the number of poor people was again down to 1.2 billion. Because of the concurrent population increase, the percentage of poor in the Third World has declined from 28.3 percent in 1987 to 24 percent in 1998.[494] These data are presented in Figure 33, alongside historical estimates from 1950. Here it is evident that although the total number of poor has remained at about the same number (1.2 billion), the proportion of poor people has been more than halved from around 50 percent in 1950.[495] Thus, over the past 50 years, some 3.4 billion more people have become not-poor.[496]

The question, of course, is what it actually takes to achieve growth, and what consequences growth will have for the distribution of wealth. Generally speaking, research has shown that the best way to secure long-term growth lies in large-scale investment in physical capital (e.g. machinery) and people (education). In addition to this, it is necessary to have an open economy in order to facilitate international trade, investment and economic freedom, because this encourages the exchange of technology and administration. Finally, reasonable stability, both economic and political, is also a prerequisite.[497]

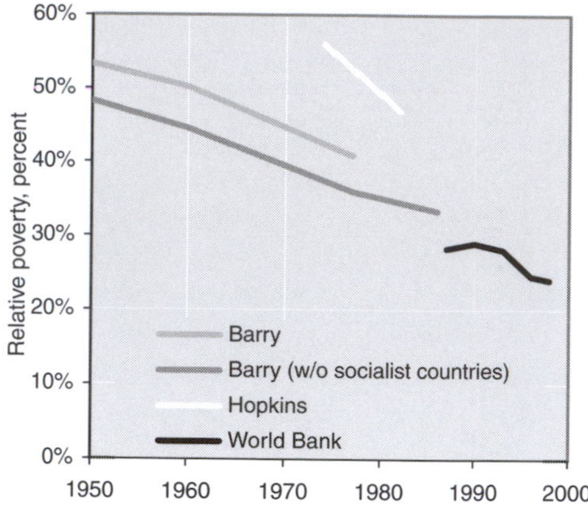

Figure 33 Proportion of people in poverty, 1950–98, with various definitions of poverty and inclusiveness.[502] Sources: World Bank 1999b:5, 2001a:23, Barry *et al.* 1983:341, 1991:73, 77, Grigg 1985:69.

It has often been pointed out that the historic consequence of economic growth seems to have been that inequality initially increased, then stabilized, later to fall as the country gradually got richer. This pattern is know as the Kuznets curve.[498] One of the reasons for this sequence of events was that industrialization, the driving force of growth, also led to the advent of large cities, where inequality is often greater than in rural areas.

In terms of the Kuznets curve, it is development that gives rise to inequality. However, new research seems rather to indicate that it is inequality that has a negative effect on development and growth.[499] A typical example of this is found in Korea and the Philippines, which in 1965 shared more or less the same GDP per capita, population, degree of urbanization, education, etc. However, inequality was substantially more extreme in the Philippines. Subsequent growth in Korea was far greater: 6 percent annually compared with the Philippines' 2 percent.[500] This view is also supported by the UN, according to which the countries that have achieved the highest growth have "emphasized not just the extent of growth but also its quality. They have secured their citizens a degree of justice and improved health, education and work."[501]

Ever greater inequality?

The UN Development Programme (UNDP) emphasizes that inequality has increased globally.[503] Inequality is usually measured in terms of what is known as the gini coefficient. When the coefficient is close to zero, almost everyone has just as much as each other; if the coefficient is close to one, then practically everything is owned by just a few. The gini coefficient tells us something about how much the very rich have compared to the very poor.

The UNDP has presented a simple gini coefficient, which investigates the relationship between the richest 20 percent of all nations in the world and the poorest 20 percent. In terms of GDP per capita the ratio in the 1960s was around 30:1, i.e. the richest 20 percent earned 30 times as much as the poorest 20 percent. By 1991 the ratio had increased to 61:1, and in 1994 to 78:1. This widely quoted statistic is interpreted as "the global chasm between the rich and the poor widens day by day."[504]

The problem with the UNDP figures, however, lies in using international exchange rates as a means of comparing different nations' GDP. Economists have long known that as countries get ever richer they tend to have ever higher price levels.[505] The reason is that economic growth is primarily fueled by productivity increases in manufacture and not in service – over a decade, we can easily imagine producing twice as many gadgets per hour of labor, while it is hard to imagine, say, a butler becoming twice as productive per hour. When productivity in manufacture increases, so does pay, and this forces up wages in the service sector, although this has not become more productive. Since manufacture makes up the greatest part of international trade, the wage increases in the non-traded service sector do not much affect exchange rates.

Thus, while the wage increases in manufacture adequately reflect a country's increased wealth, the wage increase in service does not. So if we try to compare the wealth of an American with the wealth of an Ethiopian, translating everything into dollars, we measure both that Americans produce more gadgets (true wealth) but also that butlers cost much more (illusory wealth from an inflated price level). The upshot is that the comparison tends to overestimate hugely the relative wealth of Americans to Ethiopians.

To put it differently, when you translate the Ethiopian *birr* into dollars it says something about what an Ethiopian can buy in the US, but this comparison is seldom relevant. What is far more important is how much an Ethiopian can buy in Ethiopia. To measure this, the UN initiated a research program to establish an index of Purchasing Power Parity, or PPP, i.e. measuring what people's money can actually buy locally.[506] In a light-hearted vein, the weekly news magazine *The Economist* has tested the PPP index by producing its own Big Mac index. This shows how much a standardized product such as a Big Mac costs in different countries and the result is actually surprisingly close to the PPP index.[507] To an Ethiopian, the difference is enormous: a traditional exchange rate calculation says that he earns US$100 a year, whereas the PPP-calculation estimates his income at $450.[508] If we are interested in knowing the

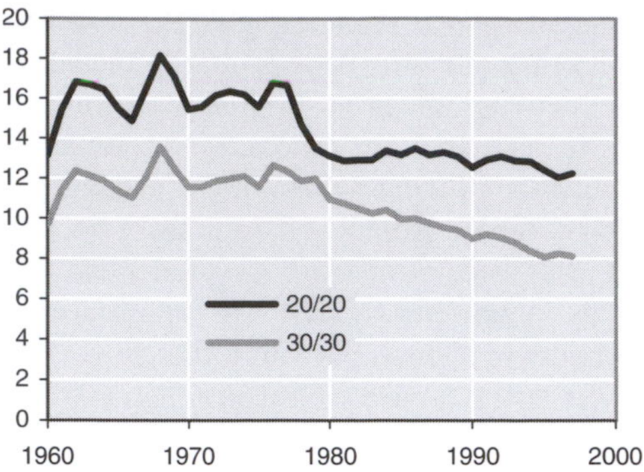

Figure 34 Relationship between the richest and poorest 20 percent and 30 percent in the world in terms of per capita GDP in PPP$, 1960–97. Source: Summers and Heston 1991, 1995, World Bank 1999a.[509]

actual wealth of the Ethiopian it seems much more reasonable to say that he earns $450 in terms of his own local purchasing power.

The PPP measure is now generally seen as superior to exchange rate comparisons by most international agencies, and economists see its use as a "substantial improvement" and as setting a new "industry standard."[510] Actually, UNDP has made great efforts in the rest of their program to use PPP$ in evaluating the per capita incomes of individual countries.[511] Thus it seems remarkable that, when UNDP estimates inequality, it has chosen exchange rate based wealth, when this is known to make for unreliable comparisons that will greatly exaggerate inequality. However, if you measure the true inequality in PPP$ (how much an Ethiopian can buy in Ethiopia versus how much an American can buy in the US), you get Figure 34. This shows that the relative gap between the richest and poorest 20 percent or richest and poorest 30 percent has not doubled or even increased but rather been slightly decreasing. This finding is broadly consistent with other studies of PPP$ inequality.[512] This is a convincing sign of robust development on the part of even the weakest part of the world towards greater material prosperity.

On a longer time scale Figure 35 shows the development in inequality from 1820 to 2100. Inequality increased dramatically from a little more than two (people in the developed countries having just slightly more than twice the income of people in the developing countries) in 1820 to an all-time high in the 1960s of almost 7. This increase was primarily caused by the rapid increase in per capita income from the industrial revolution in the developed world, whereas income only increased slowly in the developing world.[513] Basically, the industrial revolution boosted growth rates, and rising inequality happened because the developing world was left behind.[514]

From the 1950s onwards the developing world increasingly caught up with high economic growth, and from 1970 to 1992 the growth per capita actually outpaced the developed world, making inequality decrease from almost 7 to less than 6.[515] As in Figure 34, this find also indicates that globally we now see a tendency towards less inequality.[516]

It is naturally difficult to predict precisely the future of inequality. We can, however, get a feel for the anticipated development by looking at the scenarios from the UN Climate Panel, which explicitly try to cover a wide range of key future characteristics for the rest of the twenty-first century.[517] In Figure 35 we see that *all* six main scenarios show a market decline in global inequality; the most pessimistic scenario show an almost halving of the inequality from a little less than 6 in 1990 to a little more than 3 in 2100, whereas the most optimistic scenarios show an almost eradication of inequality down to 1.4 (where people in the developed world earn just 40 percent more than people in the developing world). Thus, not only has inequality been decreasing over the past three decades but there is good reason to expect that this tendency will continue throughout much of the century.[518]

Finally, in discussing inequality, we should mention how Worldwatch Institute and UNICEF, to name but two, like to point out that the difference in dollar terms between

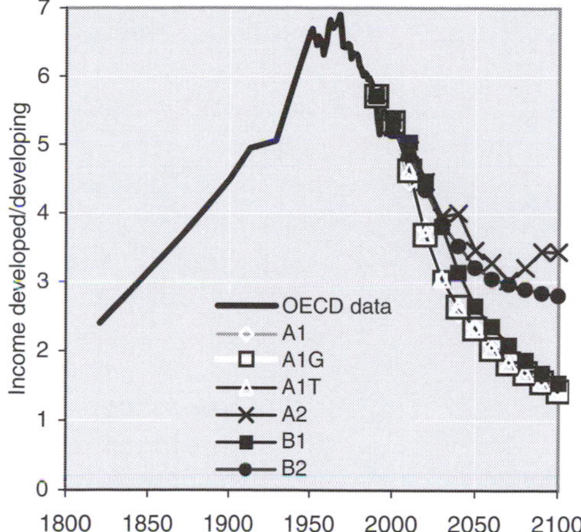

Figure 35 Ratio of per capita income in developed to developing world, 1820–2100, in PPP$. Actual OECD data for 1820–1992, predictions for 1990–2100 based on the six main scenarios from the UN Climate Panel. Source: Maddison 1995a:226–7, IPCC 2000b.[519]

rich and poor has been increasing.[520] But this is a mathematical necessity. When the rich and the poor by definition start out from different levels of wealth and when the improvement per year in percent has been almost identical (as we saw above in Figure 32), then the absolute difference between rich and poor has, of course, increased. The ratio in per capita income between the top 20 percent and the bottom 20 percent has been more or less constant since 1960. If we nevertheless want to follow the Worldwatch Institute in measuring absolute income and say that disparity has increased dramatically then we should contemplate whether we would say the same about the distribution of incomes in, say, the UK or the US.

In 1800 the distribution of income in the UK was probably more skewed than it is today.[521] Back then the poorest 20 percent were at most making 300 present-day pounds a year, compared to the 20 percent richest's £1,650.[522] Today the poor make about £5,500 and the rich £30,000. Now the ratio of rich to poor has declined slightly, and economists would say that inequality has diminished.[523] However, using the Worldwatch argument, inequality has increased more than 18-fold from £1,350 to £24,500. Does this make sense? Would we really believe that the poor are 18 times worse off today? Or to put it differently, even if the distribution in the UK today was the extremely level £14,000 for the poor and £16,000 for the rich, would we still seriously claim that inequality had increased (from £1,350 to £2,000)?[524]

Thus the general conclusion remains, that most people in both the industrialized and the developing worlds have experienced considerable growth in their real incomes, averaging a tripling over the last 45 years, and that inequality peaked in the 1960s, has been decreasing since then and is likely to continue to decrease dramatically for the coming century.

A question remains, though. Has everybody actually benefited from this growth?

Poorer still?

The most recent and much discussed growth crisis took place in East Asia in 1997/8, where high capital inflows combined with weak private and public sector governance created a vulnerable economic environment, which was then triggered by external shocks and spread through the strong capital linkages in the region.[525] Likened to the Latin American debt crisis of the 1980s, it nevertheless proved short-lived;[526] in the words of the International Monetary Fund, October 2000: "The slowdown in global activity in 1998 was shallower than previous troughs and has been followed by a rapid recovery. . . . The rebound from the crisis of 1997–98 is continuing in Asia, with growth projected to rise from 6 percent in 1999 to more than 6½ percent in 2000 and 2001."[527] Of the five worst-affected nations, Korea and the Philippines had already returned to their pre-crisis GDP levels in 1999, and it is projected that Malaysia will do so in 2000, and Thailand in 2001, whereas the hardest-hit Indonesia might take until 2003.[528] Thus, while the financial crisis certainly had serious costs, it did not permanently reverse growth.[529]

In a more serious vein, the UNDP stated in its 1996 development report that almost 1.5 billion people are living in countries where the average income is lower in the nineties then it was in at least one previous decade.[530] This is, of course, serious, as it means that large segments of the developing world are not enjoying the benefits of global growth. It is, however, important to note that many of these countries have recently experienced economic or political crises, or even been in a state of war. So perhaps it is not quite so surprising that the current economic situation in some of these countries seems worse.

There are four primary problem regions among the many countries singled out by the UNDP. The first group is the 200+ million population of the former Soviet Union (now CIS), with the Russian Federation as its leading member.[531] Since the beginning of "the shock reforms" in 1992, Russian industrial production has fallen by almost 50 percent and income by 40 percent, and prices have increased by over 2,500 percent. Because of tight state finances, the social safety net has been substantially weakened – 44 percent of the population live below the local poverty line of only PPP$4 a day.[532] After slight GDP growth in 1997 – the first since 1990 – Russia was hit by another crisis in August 1998, causing yet another drop in production, and only in 1999 has growth returned at 3.2 percent.[533] Although much of this growth was achieved through high prices on energy exports and low imports, real increases in production are now prevalent, with growth at 7 percent in 2000 and a forecast 4 percent for 2001.[534] Growth for the coming decade of the CIS area is estimated by the World Bank at an annual 2.6 percent.[535] Nevertheless, such long term growth depends on a Russia which still needs to tackle its fiscal and structural problems, and with its weak political showing so far, only limited progress has been made.

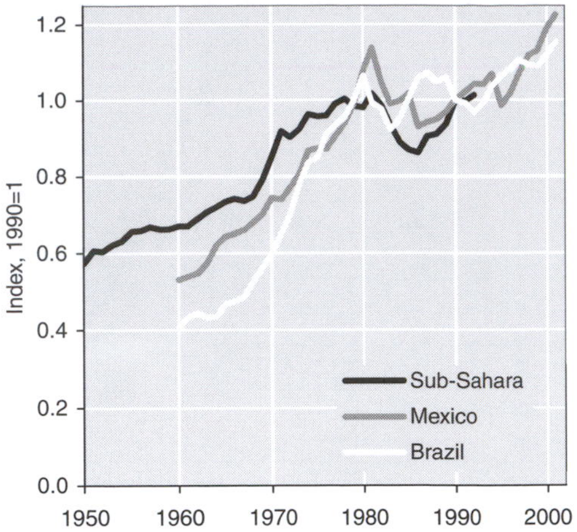

Figure 36 Per capita real local currency GDP in Brazil and Mexico, 1960–2001, per capita GDP in real PPP$ for sub-Saharan Africa, 1950–92. Index=1 at 1990. Source: World Bank 1999a, IMF 2000e, WRI 1996.

The second group is made up of the Latin American countries (with the exception of Chile). Brazil, with a population of 174 million,[536] is a good example. With double-figure growth figures, Brazil was a "miracle economy" in the 1960s. However, because of poor administration of the country's public finances and a tradition of powerful political intervention in the economy, a substantial government deficit has developed. At the same time, indexation of wages and tight controls on currency exchange contributed to extreme inflation, reaching 5,000 percent in early 1994. After introduction of the new currency, the *real*, and tight monetary policy, there now seems to be a potential for more stable development. Although growth is still sluggish, GDP per capita in the late 1990s has consistently exceeded earlier output, as is evident in Figure 36.[537]

Mexico, with a population of 101 million,[538] is a similar example.[539] A large financial deficit, high interest rates to keep inflation under control plus a revolt in the Chiapas region in 1994 led to the collapse of the *peso* and tighter financial and monetary policy. Mexico seems, however, to have made it, with per capita growth rates of 2–5 percent in 1999–2001.[540] Mexico has also been strengthened by its reforms and the country has opened up to competition. In 2000, the real per capita income was again higher than the previous maximum in 1981 (Figure 36).

The third group consists of the many oil-producing nations, which between the onset of the oil crisis and the mid-eighties earned a lot of money on the high price of crude oil. Unfortunately, most of the revenue was spent on consumption and now with much lower oil prices (the latest increase from 1999 notwithstanding) many of these countries have experienced large income drops.[541]

The final, large group consists of the countries south of the Sahara, most of which have experienced extremely low or even negative growth. Together, these nations have shown negative growth of 0.2 percent a year since 1965.[542] We have previously looked into why sub-Saharan Africa has not been able to get into its stride, and again the explanation lies primarily with the political and ethnic struggle. This naturally poses a considerable problem when it comes to global development. Part of the explanation, however, is that production has been measured in terms of exchange rate. This systematically skews the picture, as mentioned above, since the exchange rate only measures the development of tradable goods.

Again, the value of a dollar in Ethiopia is not particularly relevant for most of the country's population, and it is much more a question of what they can buy with their *birr*. For this reason we should look at the situation in terms of PPP-dollars, which produces quite a different result. In Figure 36 we can see how sub-Saharan Africa experienced almost a doubling of its real per capita income from 1950 to 1992, even though the 1980s brought them little improvement.[543]

The UNDP emphasizes that 1.5 billion people live in countries that have had higher average incomes in the past. Their use of language is quite punchy: "Growth has failed for more than a quarter of the world's people."[544] However, as far as sub-Saharan Africa is concerned it does not seem reasonable to make a comparison based primarily on the American dollar. The region has actually experienced a 75 percent increase in PPP income over the last 42 years. Moreover, the "failure of growth" does not apply to Mexico or Brazil, boasting a doubling and almost a tripling of income, respectively, over the past forty years, both experiencing new heights in per capita income. So at most the UN can claim that growth has failed one tenth of the world's population.

This tenth lives primarily in nations of the former Soviet Union and in the oil-rich Arab states. Common to most of these nations were that they had *structural* problems with their economies, and that the readjustment necessary as a result of political and economic instability unfortunately included a sharp decline in income. It is not clear, however, whether this readjustment would not have been necessary in any case in these countries given the history of their local political decisions and their position in the world economy.[545] It certainly seems bold to suggest that growth has failed these countries. There seems to be no reason to assume that they will not once again begin to see substantial growth in income per capita, an income that will eventually exceed their previous maximum.

This should not be interpreted in the sense that the decline in the economy of these and other countries is not serious. It is, however, necessary to preserve an overall view of the situation. More than 85 percent of the population of developing countries (and 90 percent of the entire world) have experienced growth to the extent that they have never been as rich as they are now.

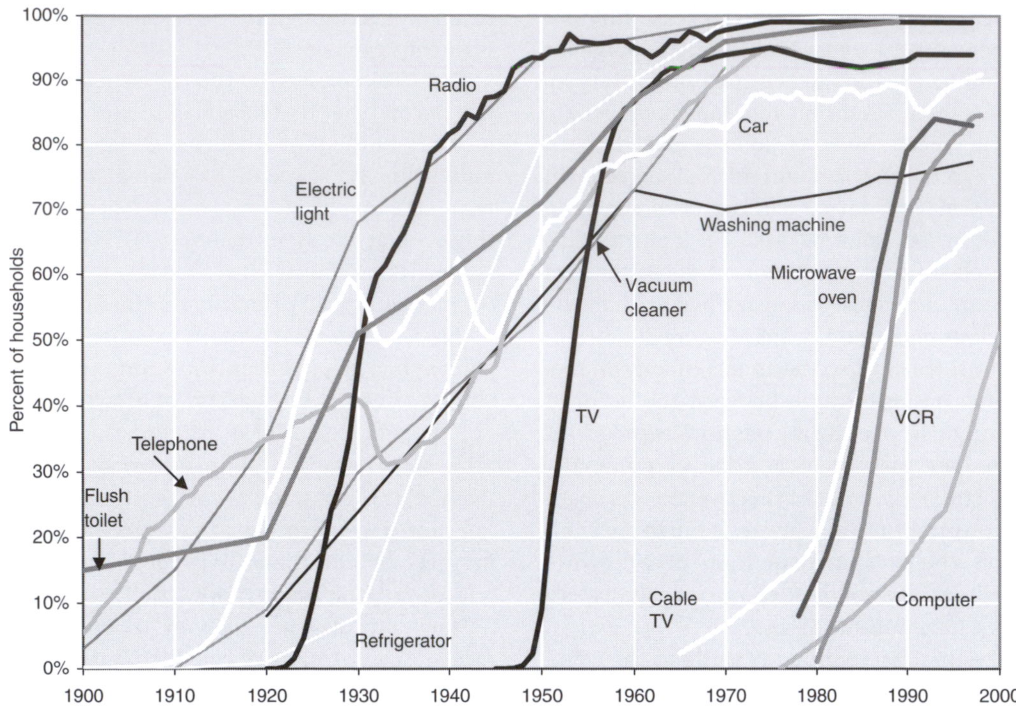

Figure 37 Percentage of households with various consumer goods in the US throughout the twentieth century. Number of households: USBC 1975:41, 1999:60, 2000a. Washing machine, vacuum cleaner, electrical light, refrigerator: Lebergott 1993:113, EIA 1999. Flush toilet: Lebergott 1993:102. Radio, TV: USBC 1975:796, 1999:885. Telephone: USBC 1975:783, 1999:885. Car: FHWA 1996–9, Lebergott 1976:289–90, USBC 1999:878. Cable, VCR: USBC 1999:885, 581. Computer: EIA 1999:14, Kominski and Newburger 1999:15, NTIA 1999:10, 2000:30.

More consumer goods

We can also appraise the development of wealth by investigating more specific markers – for example, how many people own various consumer goods. The results of such a compilation for the US can be seen in Figure 37, which shows the massive increase in many important goods, and how conditions over the past century have vastly improved, even if by now we have come to take many of the conveniences for granted.

In the decade of the 1980s almost all acquired a microwave and a VCR, and almost 70 percent of all families have got cable over the past 30 years. In the 1950s, Americans put TVs into their homes at an almost unbelievable rate, from 0.4 percent in 1948 to 87 percent in 1960, and from 1970 to 1990 these TVs were almost all replaced with color TVs.[546] Since the advent of the first PC in 1976, an increasing number of American families have acquired computers – and between 1990 and 2000 the share tripled to 51 percent.

From a humble presence in 5 percent of all homes at the beginning of the twentieth century, the telephone has become almost ubiquitous, providing instant communication with family and friends. Cellular phones have risen even faster, with a 13-fold increase from 1990 to 1998, putting a cellular in the hands of every fourth American.[547] The mobile phone gives us a new freedom: to communicate whenever we want to.[548] The telephone and the cellular phone give us the possibility not just to arrange a visit to the local cinema, but also to keep in contact with all the people we meet as we travel ever more widely throughout the world.

Americans traveling internationally with American airlines have increased more than sixfold from about 1.5 percent of the population per annum in 1960 to almost 10 percent in 1999, a tendency that applies throughout the world, where the percentage of tourists has increased almost sixfold since 1960, and seems set to increase by another 35 percent by 2010.[549] Globally, air traffic has increased 40-fold since 1950, with passengers flying the equivalent of 442 km per inhabitant of the planet in 1998.[550]

We have also acquired far greater mobility with cars. From virtually no cars in 1900, car ownership in the US soared to almost 60 percent of all families in 1929. After the turbulent years of the Depression and World War II, ownership again increased to almost 80 percent in 1960, inching its way up above 90 percent by 1998. Globally, car ownership has more than quadrupled from 1950 with just one car for every 48 people, to 1999 with less than 12 people to a car.[552]

If we take the comparisons even further back, the advantages become even more obvious. Today, we have stopped heating our homes with coal, and instead use gas- or oil-fired central heating or district heating. We no longer have to clean the coal dust in our carpets, furniture, curtains and bedclothes, or have to shovel six tons of coal into the furnace each heating season – work which we spent on average six hours performing each week.[553] Two thirds of us now have a washing machine; almost everyone has a fridge. The washing machine has been of immense benefit, especially for women. The historical economist Stanley Lebergott wrote only semi-jokingly: "From 1620 to 1920 the American washing machine was a housewife."[554] In 1900 a housewife spent seven hours a week laundering, carrying 200 gallons of water into the house and using a scrub board.[555] In 1985 she and her husband together spent less than three hours doing the laundry.[556] The fridge has allowed us to do more shopping at a time and to buy more ready-to-cook food, which is part of the reason we have more free time. It has also allowed us to avoid rotten food and to eat a more healthy diet of fruit and vegetables.[557] Our higher incomes mean we can afford to eat out more often, enjoy new experiences and save even more time that used to be spent on tedious chores.[558]

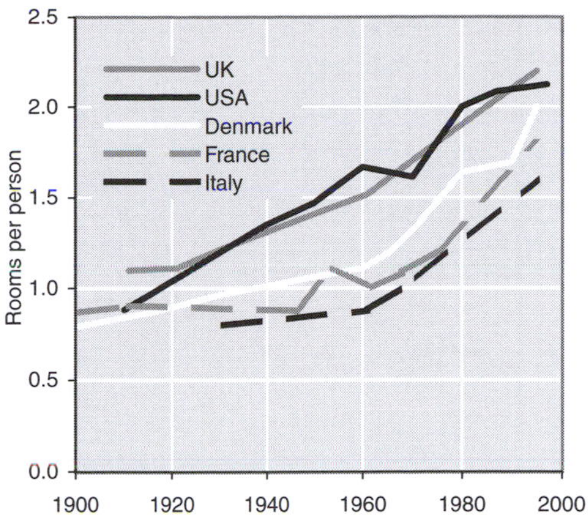

Figure 38 Rooms per person, 1900–98 for the UK, US, Denmark, France and Italy. Source: Flora *et al.* 1987:295, 302, 311, 324, Lebergott 1976:258, Rector 1995:242–3, EIA 1995a, 1999, USBC 1999:873.[551]

At the same time, the relative cost of living has become progressively lower, both because we earn more and because food prices have dropped two-thirds since 1957.[559] In 1900 Americans spent 36 percent of their income on food and other necessities, compared to 21 percent in 1950 and only 11 percent in 1997.[560] American homes have improved to an amazing extent, although the amount spent has remained a constant 15 percent of income.[561] Today, everyone has running water and a lavatory, although at the turn of the century these prized possessions were only available to 25 percent and 15 percent of the population,

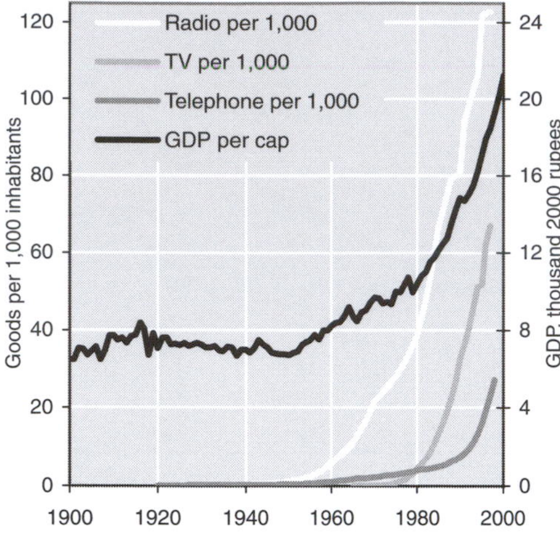

Figure 39 Welfare indicators for India throughout the twentieth century: GDP per capita in constant 2000 rupees, number of radios, TVs and telephones per 1,000 inhabitants. Source: Michel 1995: 1002–5, 799, 791–2, 55, 58–61, World Bank 1999b, 2000c, IMF 2000e, UNESCO 2000.

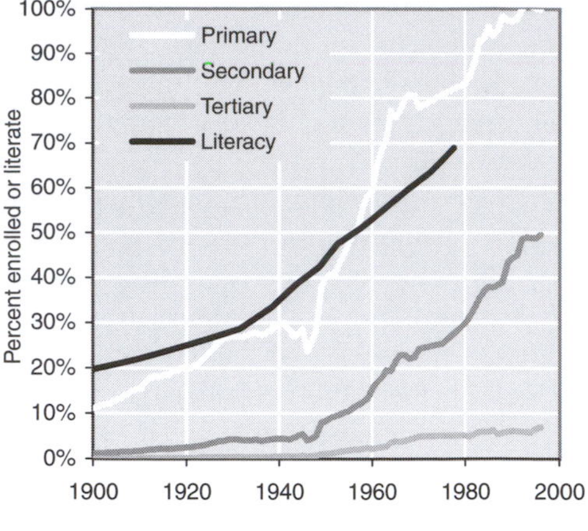

Figure 40 Welfare indicators for India throughout the twentieth century: percent enrolled in primary, secondary and tertiary education (Gross Enrollment Ratio) and percent literate according to birth year. Source: Mitchell 1995:977–9, 956–62, UNESCO 1990:78, 2000.

respectively.[562] The proportion of air conditioners has risen from 56 percent in 1978 to 73 percent in 1997.[563] The space available per person has more than doubled. In 1910 there was somewhat less than one room per person in an American house, whereas in 1997 there were more than two.[564] The same trend has been observable in a great many nations (Figure 38). And also the surroundings have improved. In Danish urban areas, open green areas doubled between 1976 and 1996,[565] and since 1990 the traffic-noise problem for flat dwellers has been greatly reduced.[566] Likewise, 7 million people in the US were exposed to significant airport noise in 1975, whereas the figure now has dropped below half a million.[567]

These developments have been paralleled throughout most of the industrialized world. It is also the case that the developing countries have higher incomes and more goods (for India, see Figures 39 and 40).[568] However, the developing countries generally have some far more basic and important problems to deal with. They need clean water, education and improved infrastructure. They have already made great progress in this direction. Far more people in the developing world now have access to clean drinking water (see Figure 5, p. 22). In countries with the lowest incomes, only 40 percent had access to clean drinking water in 1975; in 1990 the figure had increased to 62 percent. Similarly, the proportion of people having access to proper sanitation has almost doubled.[569] Both these initiatives are incredibly important because a lack of sewerage leads to contamination of the drinking water. Clean drinking water is fundamental to human health. It is estimated that polluted drinking water and lack of proper sanitation annually leads to the death of more than 2 million people from diarrhea, for example, and to more than half a billion people becoming seriously ill.[570] The developing countries have also been given access to more energy per capita and telecommunications capacity has doubled.[571] Finally, the developing world now has better roads, which

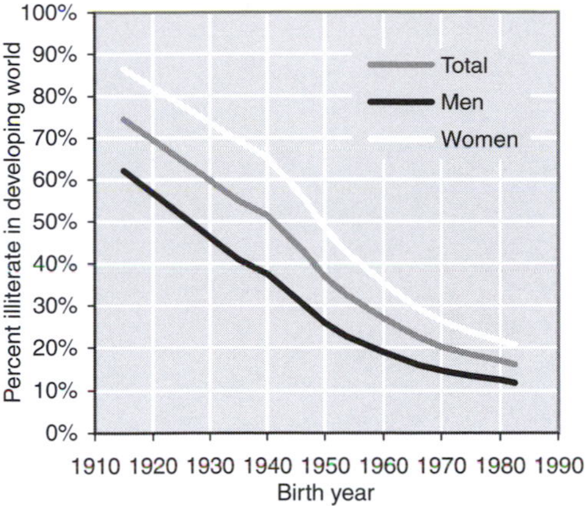

Figure 41 Illiteracy in the developing world according to year of birth, 1915–82, for men, women and total. Source: UNESCO 1990:8.

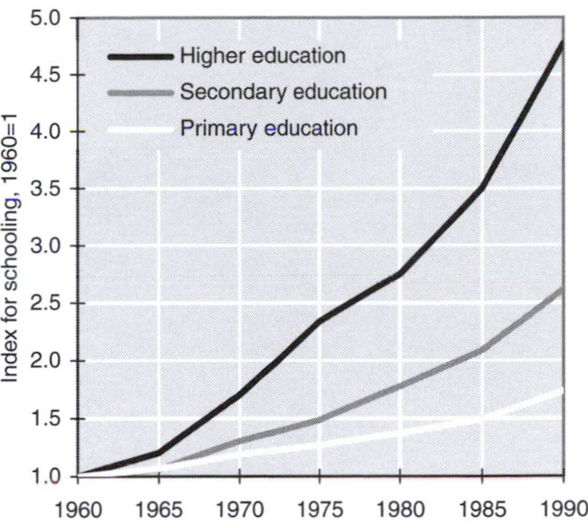

Figure 42 Index for average education per capita in developing countries; primary, secondary and higher education 1960–90, 1960 = 1. Source: Barrio and Lee 1996.

make it much easier to get food aid out to distant, distressed areas, and at the same time give peasant farmers a better chance to sell their produce in the towns and cities.

More education

Generally speaking the world has become a much better educated place. As can be seen from Figure 41, illiteracy in the developing world has fallen from about 75 percent for the people born in the early part of the 1900s to below 20 percent among the young of today.[572] However, women still do not have the same access to education, and this is also reflected in the higher illiteracy rate, which at 21 percent is almost double that of men at 12 percent. Both at home and at school women are frequently held back by a traditional attitude to gender roles, which focuses on education for boys. For example young women in Africa can only expect to attend school for 5.5 years, compared to the boys' 6.5 years. On the other hand, girls have a better chance when they actually get into the school system and spend almost as long there as do boys.[573]

Looking at the number of years of schooling, both industrialized and developing nations have seen a dramatic increase in the number of person-years spent in education. The average number of years spent in school in developing countries has almost doubled over 30 years, from 2.2 in 1960 to 4.2 in 1990. In comparison, people in the Western world spent an average of seven years at school in 1960 and 9.5 years in 1990. Figure 42 shows how the populations of developing countries now spend far more time at primary school, at secondary school and in higher education. On average, they spend almost twice as long at primary school, more than twice as long in high schools and almost five times as much time attending higher education. This improvement has meant that the developing world has partly caught up with the industrialized world. In 1960, people in developing countries only spent one third as long in education as their counterparts in the industrialized countries, while in 1990 they spent almost half as long.[574]

This improvement in schooling is also evident for India (see Figure 40), with an almost universal primary, 50 percent secondary and 7 percent tertiary enrolment. In comparison, college attendance in the US has gone from 50

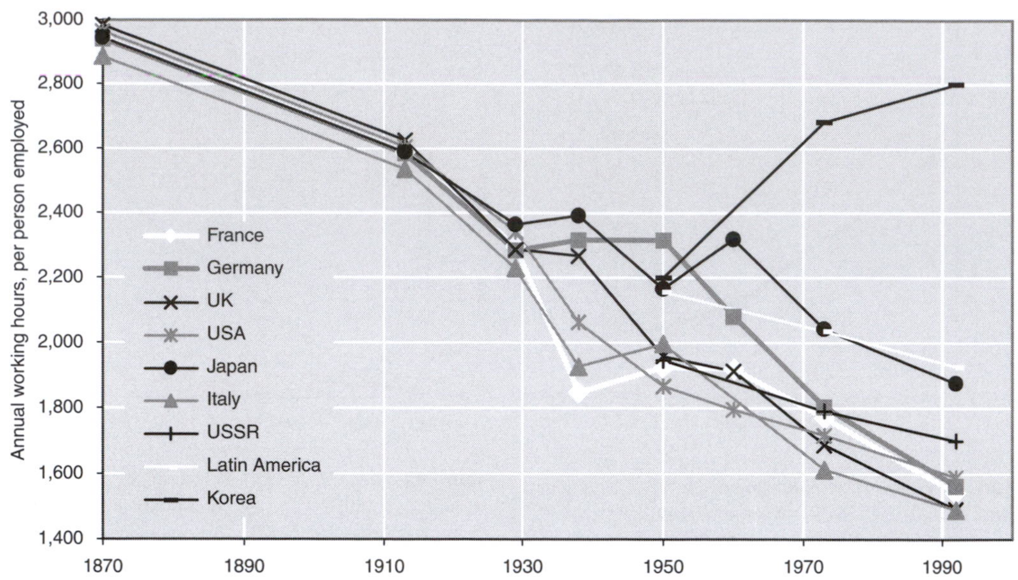

Figure 43 Annual working hours per person employed, selected countries 1870–1992. Source: Maddison 1995a:248.

percent in 1970 to more than 80 percent, and in the UK from 15 percent to 52 percent.[575]

More leisure time

Owing to lack of data we will here only look at leisure trends for the Western world, and the conclusion is quite clear.[576] Despite what we may think (or feel), we have more and more free time at our disposal.

Yearly working hours in the Western world have fallen drastically since the end of the nineteenth century, as can be seen from Figure 43. In most countries we only work about half as much today as we did 122 years ago.[577] Japan, however, seems to have resisted the general reduction in working hours between 1930 and 1960; the hours Japanese work are several decades behind compared to other industrialized countries, with Japanese people working about 400 more hours than workers in other OECD countries.

That we work only half as much per year is due not only to shorter working weeks but also to more vacation. However, even that is not the whole story, because although we live much longer we do not have longer careers. Some of the best long-term data we have come from the UK. They show that in 1870, a typical British man worked from the age of 10 until he died – in all about 47 years.[578] Since on average people died before the age of 60, there was not much need for pensions. As the average age increased, people's working careers gradually got longer, until the 1930s when the average British man worked for 52 years. Since then, improvements in education and a lower retirement age have meant the average length of career in the early 1980s was once again about 47 years.

A fairly stable work career combined with a steady decrease in yearly work hours means less work over a lifetime. Also, we live much longer. The average Briton lived just 41 years in 1870 compared to almost 75 years in 1987 (see Figure 15), giving us an increase in available time. Working less and having more time

Table 1 Trends in work, personal and free time, US 1965-95 (hours per week, age 18-64, sums to 168 hours, apart from rounding error). Source: Robinson and Godbey 1999:326-41.

	Women				Men			
	1965	1975	1985	1995	1965	1975	1985	1995
Housework	40.3	32.9	30.7	27.4	11.3	12.3	15.7	15.6
Work and commute	19.1	19.4	22.5	28.3	47.8	41.4	37.4	38.6
Total Work	59.4	52.3	53.2	55.7	59.1	53.7	53.1	54.2
Sleep	55.7	58.8	56.5	57.8	54.8	56.2	55.5	55.0
Eat	8.7	8.8	8.7	7.2	10.6	10.4	9.3	7.5
Groom	10.1	9.5	10.8	8.9	7.9	8.4	9.4	7.2
Total Personal Care	74.5	77.1	76.0	73.9	73.3	75.0	74.2	69.7
TV	9.3	14.2	14.5	15.0	11.9	15.8	15.6	17.3
Read/Stereo	3.8	3.7	3.3	3.0	4.8	3.6	3.1	2.8
Social Capital	11.2	9.9	9.0	8.3	9.5	8.7	8.2	8.6
Recreation	9.7	10.5	12.1	12.4	9.5	11.1	13.5	14.9
Total Free Time	34.0	38.3	38.9	38.7	35.7	39.2	40.4	43.6

means that our total, free (non-work) time has increased dramatically.

Figure 44 shows the development in the categories of overall useful time (roughly the 14 hours a day during which we are neither sleeping, eating nor washing ourselves) over the last 125 years. We spent 124,000 hours of our lives working in 1856 compared to only 69,000 hours today, whereas the time we spend not working has increased from 118,000 hours to 287,000 hours.[579] Figure 44 shows us that while in 1856 men spent about 50 percent of their life working, they spend about 20 percent today. At the same time the proportion of non-work has increased from around 30 percent to almost 60 percent.

While there is no doubt about the long-term downwards trend in working hours, as outlined in Figure 43, the average hours in a workweek seems to have stabilized over the past decades.[580] The stable workweek for women, however, masks the fact that female participation since 1965 has increased from about 40 percent to 60 percent, and that all women thus on average work more. Arguably, a fairer way of showing the distribution of work and free time over the past decades would be to average it on all women and all men, as in Table 1.[581] Here it is clear that men on average have experienced a substantial decline in work and commuting time, both because employment participation has

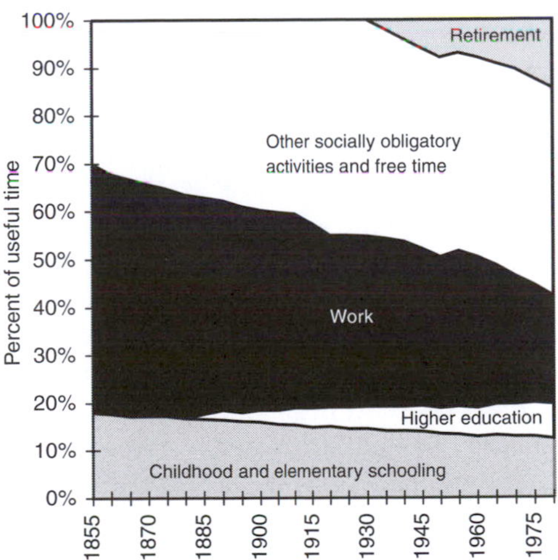

Figure 44 Proportion of useful time (the 14 hours a day not used for sleeping, eating, personal hygiene). Various activities, British men, 1856–1981. Source: Ausubel and Grübler 1995.

dropped and because those employed work four hours less.[582] On the other hand, women's average work hours have gone up dramatically, not because of increased work hours for the employed but because so many more are working. However, we find the opposite trend for housework (housekeeping, children, shopping), where women's share has dropped and men's increased. They are still nowhere equal, but men no longer supply one-fifth of the housework but more than one-third.[583] Total housework has gone down, both because the average person has fewer children and because he or she spends less time being married.[584]

The consequence is that total work time over the past thirty years has decreased by four hours for women and five for men. As men have also cut their eating and grooming time their total free time has increased by almost eight hours. Women sleep and groom somewhat more and have cut less, such that their 4.5 hours increase in free time mainly comes from the reduced workload. A large part of the free time has gone into extra TV watching. Meanwhile, social capital activities (socializing, participating in organizations, and religious practice) have declined and recreation (especially sports and adult education) has increased.

The increase we have seen in American free time is very similar to the general trend in Western countries. If we take the available time series data from nineteen countries (Europe, US and Canada) we find the general trend depicted in Figure 45. Here we see that women have two to three hours less free time than do men (although some of this is likely to be due to disparity in grooming time), and that generally, we have increased our free time by six or seven hours over the last 30 years.

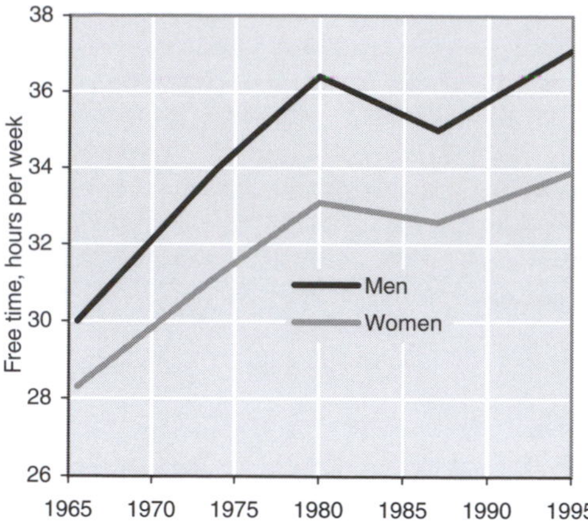

Figure 45 Average trend in free time for 19 countries (Europe, US and Canada) for men and women 1965–95. Source: Bittman 1999.

More safety and security

In almost every society the worst crime anyone can commit is to kill another human being. For this very reason we have pretty good murder statistics. The conclusion, however surprising it may be, is that in Western countries the murder rate has been falling for a very long period of time, although it has increased again in the twentieth century, slightly for most countries but significantly for the US.

We often tend to think that prehistoric societies were gentle and nonviolent. Of course, we have little or no records left, but comparing with the anthropological record, we now suspect this to be a gross idealization – for most band or tribal societies studied in the twentieth century, murder actually turned out to be a leading cause of death.[585]

The oldest statistical material we have comes from England and shows that in the thirteenth century there were more than 20 murders per 100,000 inhabitants. This rate fell steadily until the middle of the twentieth century, when the rate reached 0.5 per 100,000. Since then it has increased slightly.[586] The figures also tally with the violent picture historians paint of the previous centuries:

> Such personal correspondence and diaries as survive suggest that social relations from the 15th

> to the 17th-century tended to be cool, even unfriendly. The extraordinary amount of casual inter-personal physical and verbal violence, as recorded in legal and other records, shows clearly that at all levels men and women were extremely short-tempered. The most trivial disagreements tended to lead rapidly to blows, and most people carried a potential weapon, if only a knife to cut their meat . . . The correspondence of the day was filled with accounts of brutal assault at the dinner-table or in taverns, often leading to death . . .
>
> Casual violence from strangers was also a daily threat. Brutal and unprovoked assaults by gangs of idle youths from respectable families, such as the Mohawks, were a frequent occurrence in eighteenth-century London streets.[587]

Development was similar in Sweden – at the end of the nineteenth century the murder rate stood at 2, falling to around 0.8 in 1960, since when it has increased slightly to 1. Italy (with the exception of the end of the two world wars) had a corresponding fall from 5 to 1.3. The US, with a murder rate of around 10, is the only exception to this general trend.

Generally speaking, the picture for suicide has been the opposite. In traditional societies the suicide rate has been quite low.[588] However, with increasing urbanization the suicide rate has grown dramatically – often from about 1 per 100,000 to 10–25. In 1980 Denmark held the world record for suicide at 32. This has now fallen to around 20 while Russia has experienced a drastic increase in its suicide rate to almost 42, followed by Hungary at 33.[589]

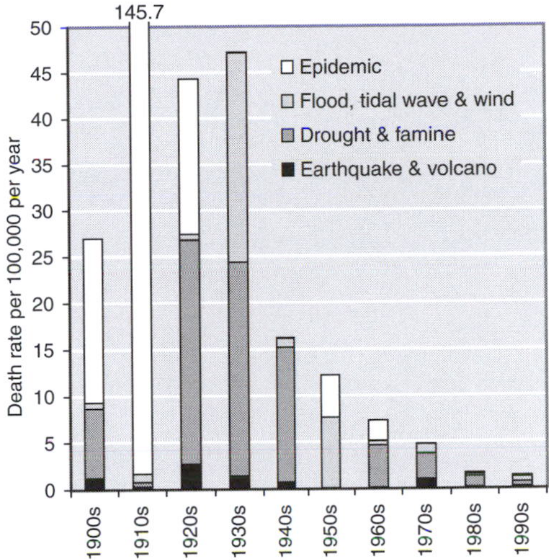

Figure 46 Annual death rate from catastrophes, 1900–99, per decade, for natural disasters: epidemics, floods, tidal waves and wind storms (tornadoes, cyclones, hurricanes etc.), droughts, famines, earthquakes and volcanoes. The high epidemic rate in the 1910s stems from the 1918 global "Spanish flu" pandemic, killing some 20–25 million, making the entire natural disaster death rate reach 145.7. Source: EM-DAT 2000.

Fewer catastrophes and accidents

Catastrophes and accidents make excellent headlines, but in fact we have managed to reduce the number of deaths resulting from both during the past century.

In Figure 46 we see how the death rate from natural disasters has declined dramatically since the early part of the twentieth century.[590] The death rate from 1900 to 1939 was 66 per 100,000 compared to a total death rate of about 2,000–3,000.[591] In the 1990s the disaster death rate was 1.4 compared to a total death rate of 927.[592] The absolute decline has been almost 98 percent, and even compared to the decline in the general death rate, the decline has been more than 94 percent.[593] Despite more than a tripling of the global population, the number of dead has dropped from an average of 1.2 million per year in the early part of the century compared to 77,000 in the 1990s. The sustained decline since the 1930s is due to many factors, including improved medicine, improved warning, improved ability to handle disasters and less vulnerable societies. For instance, the number of dead from cyclones has dropped markedly in Bangladesh, thanks both to a Cyclone Preparedness Program run by the Bangladesh Government and the Bangladesh Red Crescent

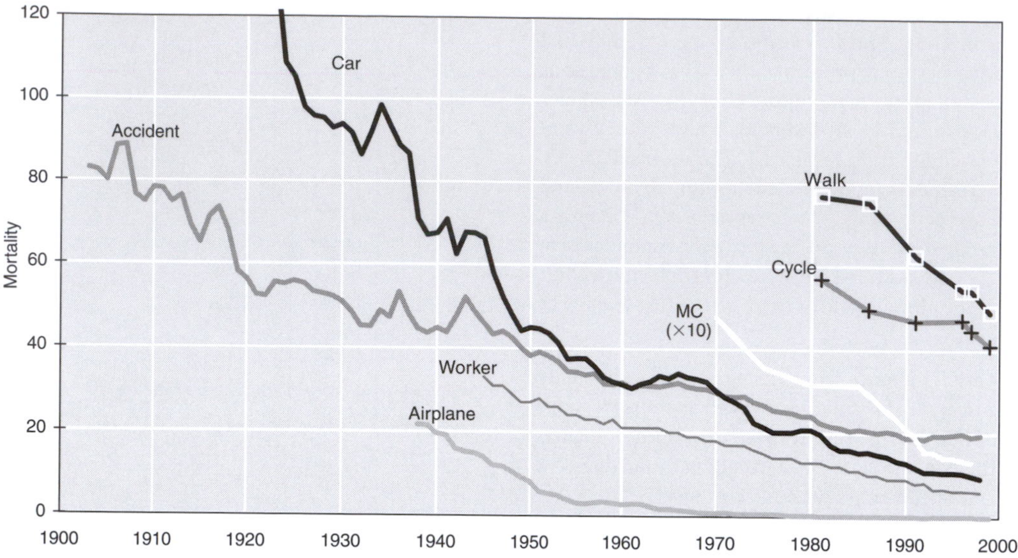

Figure 47 Accident death rate trends of the twentieth century. Work (per 100,000 workers), accidents (excluding car accidents, per 100,000 inhabitants), car (per billion vehicle km), airplane (US Airlines per billion passenger km),[594] motor cycle (per 100 million vehicle km, i.e. 10 times lower than all others), pedal cycle and walk (per billion km). Car death rates in the first decades lie around 150–250. Data for the US, except for cycle and walk for Great Britain. Source: NSC 1990:29–30, 37, 72–3, 1999:36–7, 49, HHS 1997:59, 111, 165, NCHS 1999a:199, USBC 1999c, FHWA 1996, ONS 1999:204, 2000a:205, 2001a:220, ATA 2001b, DOT 1999:1–28, 3–1.

Society and to the existence of cyclone shelters, built in the 1970s.[595]

The decrease in global deaths from natural disasters is also reflected in the decrease in accidents in the US and the UK, presented in Figure 47, showing how all significant accident arenas have become safer. The death rate due to accidents has declined fourfold over the century, reflecting an improvement in the safety of everyday products. Lethal working accidents have diminished by more than 85 percent as a direct result of safer equipment, improved training and better work practices.[596] It is estimated that without this substantial risk reduction, 40,000 additional workers would die each year in the US. Similarly, the number of fatal accidents per billion vehicle kilometers traveled by road has also fallen dramatically, particularly because vehicle construction and safety equipment have improved, and this trend is replicated in all industrialized countries.[597] Most impressive, the air transport risk has dropped more than 150-fold from 1940, such that the risk of flying a billion kilometers is now just 0.13 (on average you have to fly 7.5 billion km or some 200,000 times round the world to die).[598]

If we want to compare risks, we have to measure all risks in km per person. Since the US car today on average hold 1.6 people, the risk per person is about 40 percent lower than the vehicle risk denoted in Figure 47.[599] Thus, on average a car is about 45 times more risky per km than flying,[600] whereas it is 7 times safer than cycling, 8 times safer than walking, and an astounding 22 times safer than traveling the same distance on a motor cycle.

7 Conclusion to Part II: unprecedented human prosperity

We have experienced fantastic progress in all important areas of human activity. We have never lived longer – life expectancy has more than doubled during the past hundred years – and the improvement has been even more pronounced in the developing world. Infant mortality has fallen drastically. As recently as 1950 one in five infants died in the developing countries, whereas only one in 18 dies today – this is the same proportion as in the industrialized world just 50 years ago. We are taller and healthier and get fewer infections. There are far more of us, not because we have "started breeding like rabbits, but because we have stopped dying like flies."

At the same time we have more to eat. The proportion of people starving in the world has fallen from 35 percent in 1970 to 18 percent today and is expected to fall further to 12 percent by the year 2010. More than 2 billion more people get enough to eat and the average calorie intake in the developing world has increased by 38 percent.

Incomes in both industrialized and developing nations have at the same time tripled over the past 50 years and poverty incidence has decreased. The distribution of wealth between the world's richest and poorest has decreased slightly and it is likely to be reduced dramatically over the century.

We now also have numerous consumer goods that improve our lives and make them much easier. People in the developed world have refrigerators, better housing, cars, telephones, computers and VCRs. The developing world has also experienced increases in these goods, but it is much more important that far more people have access to clean water, sanitation, energy and infrastructure.

The number of hours we work has been halved during the last 120 years, and because we live ever longer than we used to, we have more than twice as much leisure time to enjoy.

The murder rate has fallen considerably, although this has been offset by an increase in the suicide rate. There are also far fewer fatal accidents today than in days gone by.

On average, we have become much better educated, and the developing world is catching up with the industrialized world in this respect. The number of people getting a university education in developing countries has almost quintupled. All in all, pretty incredible progress.

This is not to say that there are no problems. There are. Africa stands out as the prime problem area, where African people have experienced much less growth over the past century than people in most other countries, an AIDS epidemic has engulfed parts of southeast Africa, and because of war and ethnic and political division the outlook is not rosy. But even Africa is still better off than it was at the beginning of the twentieth century, with better nutrition, higher incomes and better schooling. Things are not everywhere *good*, but they are *better* than they used to be.

The world at large, the developing countries in particular and even the troubled areas of Africa have all experienced progress. The question we shall investigate in Part III is whether this progress really can be maintained and improved.

Can human prosperity continue?

8 Are we living on borrowed time?

In Part II we saw that by and large all measurable indicators of human welfare show improvement. Indeed, it is difficult to contest these indicators. But maybe we are living on borrowed time.

This is the typical objection we hear from organizations such as Worldwatch Institute:

> The twentieth century has been extraordinarily successful for the human species – perhaps too successful. As our population has grown from one billion to 6 billion and the economy has exploded to more than 20 times its size in 1900, we have overwhelmed the natural systems from which we emerged and created the dangerous illusion that we no longer depend on a healthy environment.[601]

In other words, it may be true that things have been going well. But actually, things have been going *too* well. This development cannot continue. The natural foundations will collapse. With an oft-repeated metaphor, we are told: "Just as a continuously growing cancer eventually destroys its life-support systems by destroying its host, a continuously expanding global economy is slowly destroying its host – the Earth's ecosystem."[602]

Professor Ehrlich reiterates the same basic idea: economists are fond of pointing out that GDP and food availability per capita grow and grow. "But there is a fatal flaw in this argument: it is roughly equivalent to bragging about one's ability to write a bigger check each month, while paying no attention to the balance in the account."[603]

The key concept at the core of much of this criticism is the question of whether or not our current development is *sustainable*. This concept was first raised by the UN *Brundtland Report* in 1987, and sustainable development simply means that humanity ensures "that it meets the needs of the present without compromising the ability of future generations to meet their own needs."[604] Actually, this is an obvious point.[605] We need to act such that our descendants will be at least as well off as we are now. The question, of course, is whether our present society is already sustainable. Most environmentalists vigorously maintain that our current society is unsustainable. "In effect, we are behaving as though we have no children, as though there will not be a next generation," says Worldwatch Institute.[606] The biologist David Ehrenfeld argues that if our ancestors had left us the ecological devastation we are leaving our descendants, our options for enjoyment – perhaps even for survival – today would be quite limited.[607]

The biologist Daniel Chiras is more specific: our society is not sustainable because we pollute too much and because we use our resources much too fast.[608] This claim we will examine in the coming chapters and parts.

Resources – the foundation for welfare

It is absolutely decisive for our continued existence that we have access to a large number of the Earth's resources. Some of these resources are naturally and continuously re-created, for example solar energy, water, air, plants and animals. These resources are *renewable*.

Other resources, such as the Earth's raw materials and minerals are not renewed (at least not in the human time scale of hundreds to thousands of years) and exist in a fixed quantity.

These two kinds of resources differ in their associated problems, as we shall see below. However, to assess the sustainability of our current development we need to look at our use of all resources, renewable and non-renewable.

9 Will we have enough food?

Food is perhaps the most important single resource for humanity, since our very existence depends on it. It is a renewable resource, but still a scarce resource, potentially under pressure from the increasing population.

Lester Brown from Worldwatch Institute has throughout the last 30 years of population increase claimed that agricultural production could no longer keep up and that *now* prices would start increasing.[609] As we have seen in the preceding chapter, this has not happened. In the 1998 edition of *The State of the World*, Figure 48 was produced as evidence. Most people would probably see a general downwards tendency undermining the previous predictions of crises and price hikes. But instead the data are used to prove that prices are turning and *now* on their way up:

> The long-term decline in the real price of wheat, the world's leading food staple, that has been under way since mid-century may have bottomed out during the 1990s. After dropping to a recent low of $3.97 per bushel in 1993, the price increased in each of the next three years, reaching $5.54 per bushel in 1996, a rise of 39 percent. While future year-to-year price changes will sometimes be down, as may be the case in 1997, this analysis indicates that the long-term trend is likely to be up.[610]

In the summary chapter these data are then used to tell us of the much wider implications:

> Rising world grain prices may be the first global economic indicator to tell us that the world is on an economic and demographic path that is environmentally unsustainable.[611]

But the decline in wheat price is not just something that has been underway since mid-century, but at least from 1800 onwards, as was obvious in Figure 25. Moreover, the price hike on which Brown bases his analysis was a passing chimera. As one of the large food research institutions, IFPRI, writes with a barely hidden message for Worldwatch Institute: "the rising cereal prices of 1995–96 were a short run phenomenon and not the beginning of a permanent upswing in prices or the forerunner to another world food crisis as feared by some."[612] At the time of writing, with prices to February 2001, wheat has yet again fallen to its lowest recorded price ever, as can be seen in Figure 49.

At least grain per capita is declining

But if you want to show that there is a problem with food production which data can you

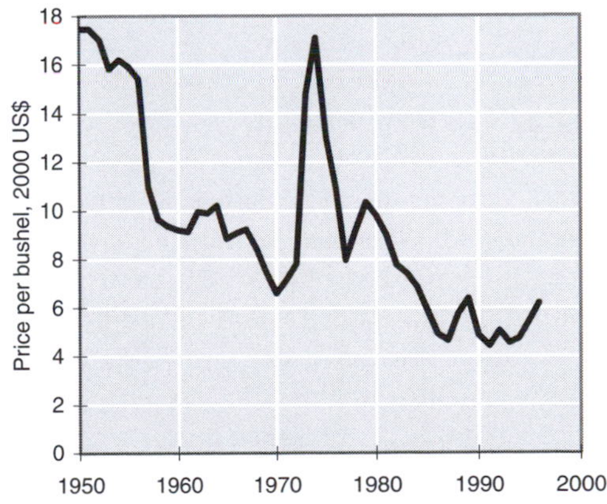

Figure 48 Lester Brown's figure, WI 1998:92. World market price for wheat in 2000 US$ per bushel, 1950–96.[613] Source: IMF 2001, CPI 2001a.

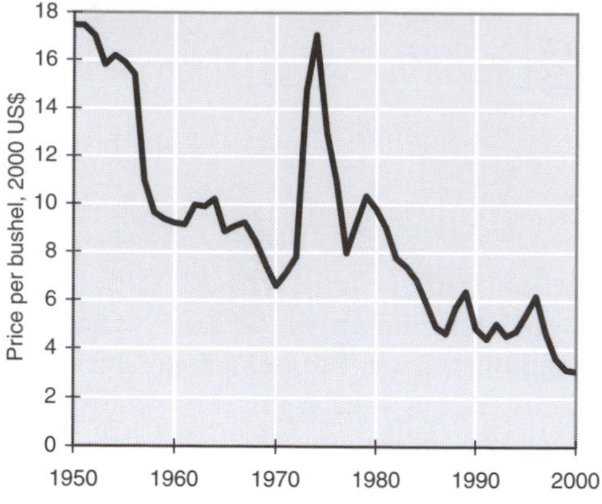

Figure 49 World market price for wheat in 2000 US$ per bushel, 1950–2000. Source: IMF 2001a, CPI 2001.

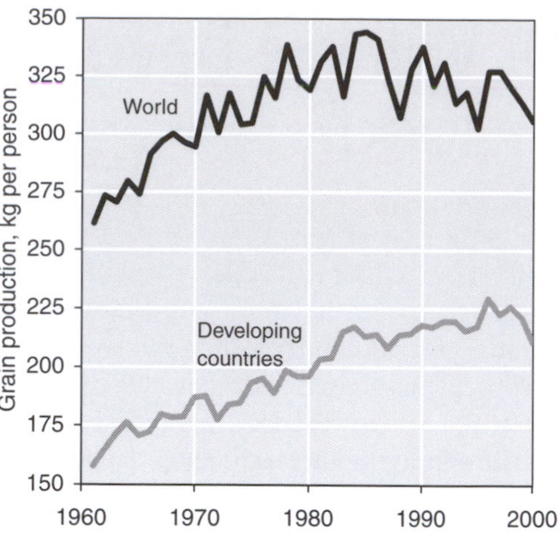

Figure 50 The grain production, kg per capita for the world and the developing world, 1961–2000. Source: FAO 2001.

actually use? We have seen that agriculture has produced *more and more* food and calories per capita in both the developed and the developing world since 1961.

For a number of years now, there has been another set of data that indeed does seem to indicate that food production is falling behind population growth. These data have been presented extensively by the Worldwatch Institute, and are illustrated in Figure 50.[614] We are here shown how the average amount of grain per inhabitant in the world grew until 1984[615] – indicating that the Green Revolution did work – but also how it has dropped by 11 percent thereafter. However, when Worldwatch Institute shows us these figures, they only reproduce the upper graph for the world. This world trend has been extremely effective and it has been reproduced and referenced in numerous places.[616] In an ecologist manifesto from 2000, it was listed as the most important indicator of decline.[617] Production is experiencing a "dramatic loss of momentum" is the way Lester Brown puts it.[618]

But this selective figure gives the wrong impression and is guided by a faulty logic, as is demonstrated when we also plot the grain production of the developing world. It is true that global grain production per capita peaked in 1984 with 344 kg and since then has dropped to 306 kg. But this is mainly due to a statistical finesse. In the industrialized countries production of grain steadily increased from the 1950s to the 1980s, stabilizing around 650 kg per inhabitant, essentially because we just cannot eat any more. Actually, we can only consume so much grain because a large part is fed to animals whose meat we then eat. In the developing countries, however, production has *kept growing* – from 157 kg in 1961 to 211 kg in 2000.[619] An astounding 34 percent. When we nevertheless see that the global average declines, it is because there are more and more people in the developing countries. When more and more people produce about 200 kg, and a constant number of people in the industrialized world produce 650 kg, the global average will have to fall.[620] (Notice, though, that production in 2000 was exceptionally low, primarily because of very low prices and bad weather in China,[621] causing the unusual drop in the average grain even for developing countries. For the other developing countries the average did not decrease significantly in 2000.[622])

Thus, only showing the global decline merely masks the fact that ever more people in the developing world get more and more food. Actually, FAO specifically state that the global grain decline is "no cause for general alarm."[623] FAO expects the per capita food grain production in the developing countries to continue to increase to 2010.[624] And actually, FAO projects that even world grain production per capita will reverse and expand to about 340 kg in 2030, destroying Brown's nice graph.[625]

Thus, a careful examination of the available evidence shows that food production has not lost its momentum.

Declining productivity

It is often argued that the Green Revolution is running out of steam. In yet another variation, Worldwatch Institute argues that we are beginning to experience "a massive loss of momentum."[626] Growth is slowing and "either levels off or shows signs of doing so."[627] Surprisingly, when Lester Brown tries to document this leveling off he uses the figures for the annual growth of the total world grain production.[628] These, of course, are not really the important figures, since we primarily care about individuals, and consequently we would rather look at production per capita. At the same time there is made no correction for the fact that the early 1990s were pretty bad for grain production. This was due both to the former planned economies and to the European Union. The collapse of the former Soviet Union and the other centrally planned economies has caused a drop in production from 1990 to 2000 of almost 40 percent, from supplying almost 17 percent of the world's grain to less than 10 percent. The EU has restructured its Common Agricultural Policy to rely less on subsidy and to avoid overproduction, which has also led to a fall in the EU's grain production of more than 5 percent.[629] Moreover, the EU has increased its environmental farmland set-aside, and low world market prices also depress production.[630]

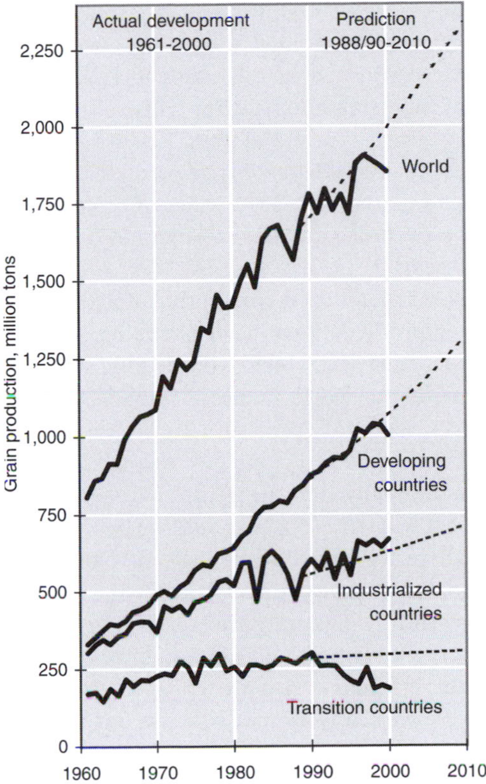

Figure 51 Grain production, prediction from FAO 1989–2010, and actual 1961–2000. Source: Alexandratos 1997, 1998, FAO 2001.

But neither the Soviet breakdown nor the EU's agricultural restructuring matters compared to the question of how much we *can* produce. Here FAO has predicted that grain production will continue to rise as far into the future as can be seen – as is also evident in the official 2010 prediction depicted in Figure 51.

Lester Brown has accused FAO and the World Bank of consistently being too optimistic about grain production in the 1990s. He claims that their totals have been out by almost 14 percent. But these accusations have been shown to rest primarily on simple calculation errors and incorrect data.[631] Figure 51 shows the development of grain production and the FAO prediction, and generally the global production has not been far off.[632] The total deviation mainly stems from the former command economies that have drastically underperformed in the 1990s. It is expected that this production decline will eventually be reversed.[633] The developing countries, however, have closely traced the predicted growth (again, except for 2000, where China due to very low prices and bad weather has underperformed).[634]

Nevertheless, it is correct that global growth rates in yields have been declining for rice, wheat and corn, which make up almost 50 percent of the world's calorie intake.[635] In the 1970s rice yield grew annually by 2.1, percent whereas yield growth is now down to 1.5 percent annually, and the figures look similar for wheat and corn.[636] But should we be worried?

There are three lines of answers to this question. First, we have to ask whether the reduced growth in yields indicates that we are reaching the biological and physiological limits of plant efficiency. Are we close to the point where we really cannot squeeze out any further services from our plants? Second, we have to ask whether it really is the top yield that is restricting production or whether most of the Third World farmers are growing well below maximum yields. Third, whether we should worry depends on whether humanity really needs the high growth rates any more. The population is growing more and more slowly, we have become better nourished, and there is an upper limit to how many calories we can eat.

Limits to yields?

Are we reaching the limits of what can be squeezed out of plants? Lester Brown argues exactly this point with Figure 52, showing the development of yield for some of the top-producing countries in the world – Japanese rice and American wheat. Again, the unsuspecting reader may just see a yield getting better and better. But Brown asks us to consider the American wheat yield in 1983 (marked in the figure). At that time America produced 2.65 tons per hectare, but "since then, however, there has been no further rise."[637] Likewise, Brown asks us to look at Japan's rice yields in 1984, of 4.7 tons per hectare. "Since then, it

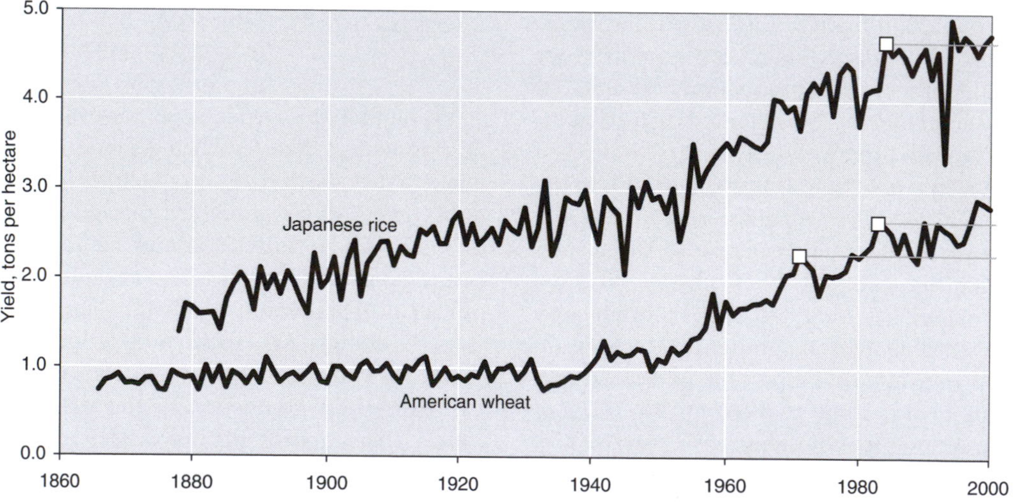

Figure 52 Yields for 1860s–2000 in tons per hectare of wheat from the US and rice from Japan. Identical to Worldwatch Institute figure 5–2 (WI 1998:82), with yields from 1998–2000 added. Previous top points noted out by Worldwatch Institute (1971 and 1984 wheat and 1983 rice) marked. Source: WI 1998b, USDA 2001a, FAO 2001a.

has plateaued."[638] "Farmers in the two countries appear to have 'hit the wall' at about the same time. Is this plateauing in two of the most agriculturally advanced countries temporary? Or does it signal a future leveling off in other countries, as farmers exhaust the known means of profitably increasing yields?"[639]

Lester Brown answers this latter question in the affirmative. We must start "facing biological reality."[640] It does seem likely that "more countries 'hit the wall' in the years immediately ahead," and "eventually the rise in grain yields will level off everywhere."[641] We are told that "the world moves into an age of scarcity"[642] with price increases on grain.[643] This will create "unprecedented political instability in Third World cities," affecting progress and setting the entire monetary system at risk.[644] Although Brown is aware that the UN and the World Bank strongly disagree with his predictions, he finds comfort in a Japanese study referred to in the *Kyoto News* from 1995 which backs him up.[645]

But notice how these data points have been chosen with great care. Only if one chooses *exactly* 1983 as a starting point for the American wheat yield would it be possible to claim that no growth has taken place since then. Likewise for Japan it is *necessary* to pick 1984 to be able to substantiate the claim of plateauing. If – for consistency – Brown had picked 1983, we would have seen a dramatic productivity increase. Ironically, the very year that these statements were made, the wheat yield in the US broke through "the wall," as is evident in Figure 52, up almost 10 percent over 1983.

Lester Brown has actually made this type of argument before. In 1981 he claimed that *now* American wheat yields had reached the limit. As he pointed out, the American yield had *dropped* by 6 percent from 1972 to 1977.[646] And yes, 1971–2 was exactly the moment when yields reached their previous maximum (Figure 52). Also, and this is ironic, the very year Brown made his statement, wheat yields broke through the previous wall, and have since then been *above* the "maximum" every single year save one.

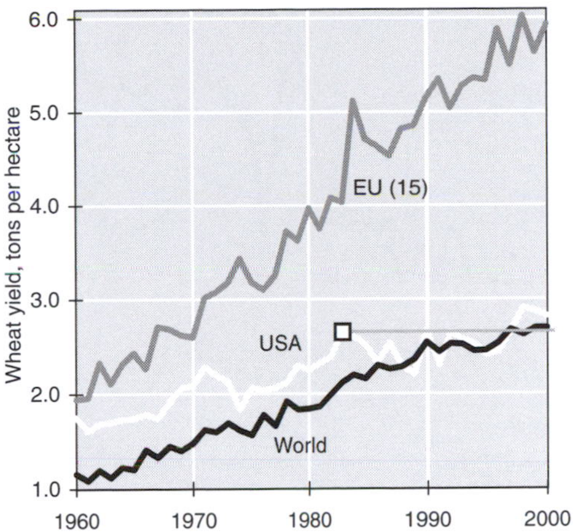

Figure 53 Wheat yield for 1960–2000, tons per hectare, for the US, EU and the World. Source: USDA 1998, 2001a.

The US produces 11 percent of the world's wheat. The EU produces about 15 percent, and we can see both wheat yields in Figure 53. It is clear that the EU produces more than twice the amount of wheat per hectare than the US. This is primarily because the EU farms much more intensively because it has much less farmland. But the first important message from Figure 53 is that the EU has not experienced Lester Brown's "wall." There has been continued growth in yield per hectare. This seems to indicate that Brown's arguments are untenable with respect to wheat. The second message – and perhaps more devastating for Lester Brown – is that while the US presumably was hitting a wall, not only did the US itself break it in 1998–9 but so did the world in 1997 and 1999, as can be seen in Figure 53. For neither the EU, the US nor the world at large do data seem to support the hypothesis of a "wall."

The same pattern is true for Lester Brown's other example, Japanese rice yields (Figure 54). Japan grows rice very intensively on tiny plots

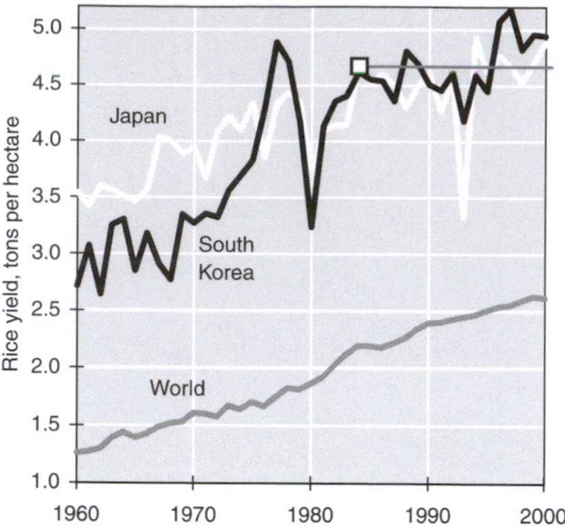

Figure 54 Rice yield for 1960–2000, tons per hectare for Japan, South Korea and the world. Source: USDA 1998, 2001a.

of land, and consequently there are not many countries that have higher yields.[647] Japan also heavily subsidizes its peasants, and according to USDA this implies that there is seldom any economic gain to increasing yields and consequently peasants rather attempt to limit their workload.[648] To save time, increasing numbers of Japanese peasants actually plant their rice from a helicopter![649] Needless to say, we should not expect such an incentive structure to encourage yield gains.

But the development of other intensive rice producers, such as the US and the NICs (Newly Industrialized Countries, e.g. South Korea), clearly shows a steady increase in yields. The "wall" Brown has found for Japanese rice yields seems to be caused by a deliberately misleading example. The development for world yields underscores this, as here we also see a steady yield increase.

But Lester Brown points out that his yield wall also has a theoretical underpinning. He tells us that we are rapidly reaching the biological and physiological limits for yield increases. "Once [the yield] is pushed close to its limit, the remaining options tend to be relatively small." Sooner or later, "there will . . . come a point in each country, with each grain, when farmers will not be able to sustain the rise in yields."[661] However, we have not reached a theoretical "wall" either. The newest studies from CIMMYT, the organization that together with Norman Borlaug started the Green Revolution, remain confident that further, stable increases are still plausible. "We believe that the 'pessimistic' or Malthusian analysts who see disaster looming in recent lower rates of yield growth in cereals are incorrect."[662] The recent, lower growth rates of production are more likely attributable to the declines in real prices.[663]

Actually, the growth rates of top wheat production have in all likelihood not decelerated but remained constant at about 1 percent over the past 30 years, with many opportunities for further yield improvements.[664] Productivity increases for corn are seen as readily achievable, and Lester Brown admits that "corn yields do not yet appear to be leveling off."[665] Finally, the outlook for rice is dramatically optimistic – medium-term increases of 20 percent are within sight, and researchers expect a long-term increase of 50 percent.[666]

At the same time, the new cereal strains have featured improved pest resistance and grain quality, while reducing crop duration and water and nutrient requirements.[667] Furthermore, large productivity increases are possible (and perhaps more likely) by increasing the use of pesticides and fertilizers as well as improving labor management and knowledge.[668]

Of course, actually shifting the productivity of cereals will not come automatically – it requires investment in research by companies and governments, and with the forecast of ever lower grain prices and consequently lower research profits, swift yield increases may only come about through sustained public funding. However, this is a question of policy priority and not a basic problem of limits to food production. There seem to be no "walls" for top yields ahead.

BIOMASS

In 1986 a team of researchers headed by the Ehrlichs examined how much of the Earth's net primary production (NPP) is actually consumed by man.[650] Briefly, solar energy is the only real contributor to growth on our globe through photosynthesis, and consequently the researchers wanted to know how much of the growth in biomass or "green stuff" mankind exploits.

The answer was that man directly, or indirectly through animals, uses about 3.9 percent of the terrestrial biomass production – a figure that does not sound terrifyingly large.[651] The researchers also investigated not only how much humans eat but also the amount of plant growth wasted in production (e.g. straw), how much plant growth our way of life precludes (the biomass growth that no longer can take place where we have put our parking lots, houses, roads and shopping malls), how much less our fields produce (harvesting once a year instead of natural, longer-lived or perennial plant growth), how much more biomass forests could have produced had they not been turned into pasture, and how much desertification has reduced biomass growth.

The oft-quoted result is that man consumes, co-opts or forgoes 38.9 percent of the terrestrial net biomass growth. While this figure may tickle our curiosity, it is perhaps not particularly relevant.

However, it has given rise to a very common interpretation, which sounds ominous but is simply wrong. As some distinguished Danish scientists put it: "Today human activity appropriates 40 percent of all land-based photosynthesis. A doubling of the population implies an appropriation of 80 percent. A 100 percent appropriation is both ecologically as well as socially impossible."[652]

Although the original research team was careful not to make this mistaken claim, the Ehrlichs have since then not been equally cautious: "the human share of . . . NPP reaches almost 40 percent . . . Most demographers project that *Homo sapiens* will double its population within the next century of so. This implies a belief that our species can safely commandeer upwards of 80 percent of terrestrial NPP, a preposterous notion to ecologists who already see the deadly impacts of today's level of human activities. Optimists who suppose that the human population can double its size again need to contemplate where the basic food resource will be obtained."[653] The well-known environmental economist Herman Daly commits the same logical error, which is similarly replicated by a host of other environmental writers.[654]

Naturally, the statement of "from 40 percent to 80 percent with a population doubling" sounds sensible, but it is downright wrong.[655] Presumably, the authors of such statements have reached for the simple interpretation of the 40 percent figure without reading or understanding the background material.

As we have seen earlier, the UN expects the world population to level off at about twice the present-day population. Of course this means that we shall have to produce at least twice the amount of food. But this will *not* require anywhere near twice the arable land, since by far the largest production growth will come from increased yields. The International Food Policy Research Institute estimates that production from 1993 to 2020 will increase by 41 percent but that arable land will only increase by 5.5 percent.[656] The remaining increase in production for yield increases will not cost extra biomass since we merely redirect energy from the straw to the grain and increase growth through irrigation and fertilization.[657]

Agriculture currently appropriates just 10 percent of the potential terrestrial photosynthesis, and a doubling of the agricultural production implies a maximum increase in the appropriation to 12 percent.[658] The other large factors in the 40 percent figure are pastures (6.5 percent), regular land clearing (5.8 percent), and biomass loss for agricultural production instead of forests (7.0 percent), all of which have a significantly smaller than unitary connection with the number of humans.[659]

Consequently the total appropriation will not increase by anywhere near 80 percent but perhaps rather around 50 percent, owing to a doubling of the human population. In the long run and with increased wealth the share will perhaps even decline again when most countries – like at present most OECD countries – commence reforestation, recreation of meadows, and the phasing out of marginal lands for agriculture.[660]

What about ordinary peasants?

At the same time – and potentially much more serious – Lester Brown fails to discuss the situation of ordinary peasants. By far the majority of the peasants in the developing countries achieve much lower yields than even the best local producers. It is estimated that most peasants achieve less than half the maximally attainable yield.[669] In Andhra Pradesh in India, research stations regularly attain yields five to ten times the yields experienced by traditional peasants.[670] Thus, there is still much room for improvement. For example Syria – in antiquity the bread basket of the Middle East – had finally become self-sufficient in wheat again in 1991. Through a focused effort of higher-yield strains, irrigation, fertilization and education, production has been quadrupled since 1950.

The FAO has specifically examined growth in yields in the developing countries. "For the developing countries as a whole, the growth rates of per capita agricultural production (all products) have not been generally lower in recent eight-year moving periods compared with earlier ones."[671] This is also true for those countries that are less dependent on agricultural production. Particularly, it turns out that the growth rate in yields has been slightly increasing for those developing countries that are the most dependent on agriculture. Therefore the FAO points out, with a clear hint to Lester Brown, that "in the light of this evidence, it is difficult to accept a position that developments in recent years have marked a turning point for the worse."[672]

In other words, there are good reasons to presume that the development, particularly in the Third World, will continue with ever higher yields and consequently an ever larger agricultural production.

Do we still need the high growth?

We do not have to fear the development of new, high-yield strains reaching a "wall," and there is good reason to presume that particularly the developing countries will produce ever more. Nonetheless, it is true that the growth in production is declining. We do produce more food per capita each year, but this extra growth is diminishing both in yields and in total production.

But this is *not* a problem. The fact that growth in yield for rice has declined from 2.1 percent to 1.5 percent could seem troublesome. But at the same time population growth has also dropped from over 2 percent in the early 1970s to less than 1.26 percent today, and it will further drop below 0.5 percent within the next 50 years. In fact, most of the previous agricultural production growth was necessitated by increasing population, whereas increasing income will have much less impact on demand.[673] Consequently, a *smaller* growth in production today can actually give *more* to each individual than a considerably larger growth could in the 1970s.

Equally, a much larger fraction of the Earth's inhabitants get sufficient food. The proportion of starving has dropped from 35 percent to 18 percent. In 1961 inhabitants in the developing countries on average received 1,932 calories, whereas in 1998 they received 2,663 – an increase of 38 percent. In the 1960s and the 1970s the world needed a large growth in production not only to keep pace with population growth but also to ensure more food to each individual. Today we need less growth because we only have to keep up with a smaller population growth and because fewer individuals need more food. Consequently, the FAO projections only expect global demand to increase by about 1.5 percent throughout the next 30 years, compared to more than 2 percent throughout the past 30 years.[674]

In summary, the FAO states that that there is no need to worry about the diminished growth in agricultural production. Basically it "reflects some positive developments in the world demographic and development scenes": the world population grows ever more slowly, and inhabitants in more and more countries are reaching a level of food consumption where they cannot eat much more.[675]

Nevertheless there is a moral problem in that the growth rate in the world's agricultural production is diminishing while there are still people starving. This, however, is caused not by a fundamental problem of production but rather by the fact that these people do not have the money to demand more food. In the FAO's words: "It is now well recognized that failure to alleviate poverty is the main reason why undernutrition persists."[676]

Therefore, as discussed in the last chapter, the road ahead for the starving in the poorest countries is larger economic growth such that these individuals will also be allowed a decent existence.

Grain stocks are dropping!

Worldwatch Institute has also raised concerns about the size of the world grain carryover stocks. Grain stocks are the amount of grain left over just before the new harvest. "In many ways, carryover stocks of grain are the most sensitive food security indicator," it is claimed.[677] As can be seen in Figure 55, grain stocks in 2000 are about 62 days of consumption, just below the FAO's 64-day recommendation.[678]

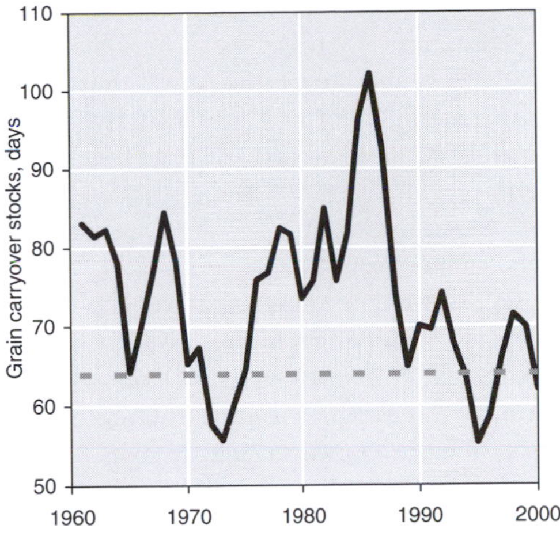

Figure 55 Grain carryover stocks, 1961–2000; number of days of consumption just before the next harvest. Dashed line indicates FAO's 64-day recommendation. Source: USDA 1998, 2001a.

But there are several reasons why this is primarily a propaganda figure. First, grain stocks have diminished particularly in the US and the EU because the financial incentives for large surplus stocks have been cut.[679] Second and more importantly, grain stocks follow the general tendency towards smaller stocks because world trade has become much more flexible. Today better infrastructure, better-organized trade and better information make it easier to get food where it is needed. The world has become more integrated and it is no longer necessary for each and every government to store large stocks to secure its own food supply. Today, we collectively ensure each other and this security is much more efficient.[680]

Studies from the US Department of Agriculture show that the supply of grain has actually become more stable over time, which protects consumers especially in the developing countries against insecurity from single bad harvests.[681] This increased security is due not only to more extensive international trading but also to the so-called feedgrain buffer. A bad harvest means that grain for human consumption gets scarcer. But when world market prices increase as a response, less grain will be used to feed livestock, thus partly compensating for the initial scarcity. When the grain supply dropped and prices increased dramatically in 1972–4, the reduction in US feed consumption was as large as the total global production shortfall.[682]

Food security is not particularly dependent on the number of days in the grain stocks.[683] It is much more important that a smooth international trade makes it possible to minimize grain stocks – and consequently costs – while supplies actually have become more stable. Indeed, although stocks are expected to be falling for the third year in a row, the USDA finds that exporters will be able to fulfil demand at unchanged prices and actually that a bigger concern is how existing, large stocks are straining storage facilities.[684]

Nor does food security simply imply security from starvation in moments of crisis, as is often taken as the implication of Figure 55. It also means security in everyday life: the security of everyday food availability.[685] And here the amazing drop in food prices has made it possible for many more families to get sufficient food and to allow them to spend more of their limited resources on other important and life quality improving targets.

Greater internationalization has allowed food production to move to the most productive places on Earth. This has given us cheaper food and larger economic growth, and has increased the opportunities of choice for each family.[686]

What about China?

Lester Brown has also focused heavily on the possible threat to food security from China in his 1995 book: *Who Will Feed China: A Wake-up Call for a Small Planet*. Point one, China is the world's biggest country with about 20 percent of its inhabitants. Point two, China has had an astounding yearly growth rate of almost 10 percent over the last 20 years.[687] Brown's idea is that when China in 2030 has added another half billion inhabitants and concurrently experienced a rapid economic development, this will imply a drastically higher demand for food.

Of special importance is the development in demand for meat. Today, the Chinese consume very little meat and all experience indicates that increasing income will cause an increase in the consumption of meat and dairy products. Meat is very "expensive" in the sense that 1 kg of edible beef costs 16 kg of grain, where the other 15 kg are used to support the animal's activities and parts we cannot eat.[688] If all meat could be produced by livestock on pastures this would of course not be a problem, but China does not have enough farmland to do so. Lester Brown estimates that on a yearly basis the Chinese will go from eating approximately 35 kg of meat per capita today (close to the present-day Japanese consumption of 40 kg) to the Taiwanese consumption of 75 kg. All in all, Brown finds that this will imply an increase in demand for grain of almost 300 million tons or about 15 percent of the present world grain production. Will this be possible? Lester Brown thinks not: "China may soon emerge as an importer of massive quantities of grain – quantities so large, that they could trigger unprecedented rises in world food prices."[689] Actually, he thinks that "China is teaching us that the western industrial model is not viable, simply because there are not enough resources."[690]

Brown points out that the total agricultural area will drop by about 50 percent, since the land will be used for roads, buildings and other purposes. This pattern we have seen already in Japan, South Korea and Taiwan. Moreover, Brown notes that China already has high yields and consequently cannot expect dramatic improvements. Fertilizer use is already high in China and even higher fertilization is unlikely to increase yields much in the years ahead. Moreover, reports seem to indicate that both water and wind erosion are high, further reducing the probability of productivity increases. China also has a high degree of air pollution, assumed to reduce yields by 5–10 percent. Finally Lester Brown points out that it will not be possible for the world market to cover the staggering needs of China's future imports. Consequently, we can expect to see large price increases on grain and a world economy in crisis. "For the first time in history, the environmental collision between expanding human demand for food and some of the earth's natural limits will have an economic effect that will be felt around the world."[691]

But many of Brown's assumptions have turned out to be very tenuous indeed. Brown overestimates the number of future Chinese in 2030. He assumes there will be more than 1.6 billion, where the UN estimates 1.462, and the US Census Bureau estimates 1.483 billion.[692]

Alexandratos, who has been in charge of the FAO's 2010 world food prognosis, and Crook from the US Department of Agriculture have set Brown straight on a number of issues.[693] They point out that the figures Brown uses to estimate agricultural area are seriously underreported, because peasants evade registration in order to pay less in land taxes, something which Brown is aware of but inexplicably ignores.[694] Several reports and USDA have indicated that the real agricultural area is 40 percent larger, a number which was finally acknowledged by China in late 1999.[695]

Both his critics find that Lester Brown has not argued properly for his assumed dramatic decline in agricultural area. Brown has actually just used the change from 1990 to 1994 – a four-year data period – to predict the change over the next 35 years. Recalling Brown's arguments with yields, it is not surprising that the choice of period is fitted such that the overall low point lies in 1994 and 1990 is almost the peak year.[696] As one agricultural expert points out, Brown's comparison of the land use experience of Japan, South Korea and Taiwan with China "can only be described as audacious and seriously misleading."[697] One authority summarizes in a 2000 assessment of China's agriculture: "Urbanization and other non-agricultural construction have taken only negligible shares of China's land."[698]

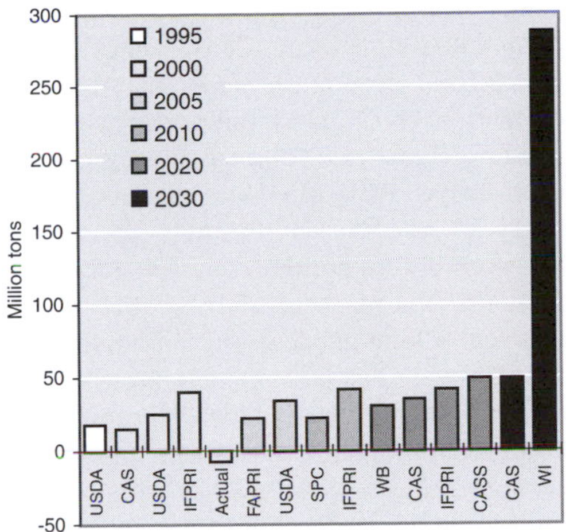

Figure 56 China's future grain import as estimated by different agencies and the actual demand in 1999/2000 (ERS 2000:10). USDA= US Department of Agriculture, CAS= China's Academy of Science, IFPRI=International Food Policy Research Institute, FAPRI=Food and Agricultural Policy Research Institute, SPC=China, State Planning Commision, WB=World Bank, CASS=Chinese Academy of Social Science, WI=Worldwatch Institute. Source: ERS 1996:1, World Bank 1997d, USDA 2000b.

Finally, Brown assumes that China's yields are very high and that they consequently cannot get much higher. But since the area is underreported, it means that the actual yield is much lower than the official estimate, leaving much more room for improvement. Also, Brown himself assumes that China's yields will grow 54 percent over the coming 30 years.

All this means that Lester Brown is the only one to predict that China's grain demand will cause the global food market to tumble. Figure 56 shows that all research organizations agree that China will buy more grain on the international market, but all except Worldwatch Institute make *much lower* demand predictions. The difference is more than 400–500 percent. Consequently, most agricultural economists agree that Brown's evaluation of China is way too pessimistic. IFPRI concludes that "China is already a significant player in world food markets and is likely to become increasingly important. However, it does not represent a major threat to world food markets."[699] In a review of the different China models, the authors found that there are two basic models: Brown's (and a very similar model), which ignores prices and technological advances, and some advanced, multi-sector models with varying degrees of sophistication. Their conclusion states that Brown's, and its sister model, "are really worst case scenarios that suggest what would happen if all other things fail to respond to changes in the economic environment. These studies should not, therefore, be taken seriously, especially in the formulation and evaluation of policies to direct the course of future food balances."[700] Instead the other models give "remarkably consistent projections for production, demand and trade," all predicting imports of 15–25 million tons in 2010–20.[701]

This understanding was supported by a report from the World Bank in September 1997, which concluded that "China can remain food secure over the next two or three decades and domestic food production will largely keep pace with population growth."[702] The total estimated import for 2020 was in line with the estimates from the other research organizations – with a self-reliance strategy the import need would be 30 million tons.[703] Again, far below the estimate of Lester Brown. Likewise, in 1999 the International Institute of Applied Systems Analysis concluded its China analysis with a loud: "Yes, China can feed itself!" pointing out the necessary policy steps to be taken.[704]

Today, we can also evaluate the first five years of Brown's predictions. Land area, which Brown estimates will shrink by 1.58 percent a year, should have declined by more than 15 percent from 1990 to 1999. Actually, the area has *increased* slightly.[705] Brown's dramatic land reduction seems to have vanished thus far.

Equally, Brown assumed a yield increase of 1.09 percent per year, and this is only confirmed due to a very good year in 1990 and the very poor harvest in 2000 – the average yield increase from 1990 to 1999 has been more than 40 percent higher at 1.56 percent.[706]

The latest figures for imports show not only that China has belied Brown's estimates but that imports have been lower than the most moderate estimates. In 1999/2000 China was "awash in grain" as USDA put it, with stocks at "record levels."[707] China will import 4.2 million tons of grain, while exporting 11.4 million tons, making a net *export* of 7.2 million tons.[708] Now, USDA is assuming a total import in 2009/10 of just 2.66 million tons.[709]

Overall, Brown has predicted that China's grain production should be down to 315 million tons in 1999. The actual output was 395.1 million tons, right within the estimates of IFPRI and the World Bank, but some 25 percent above what Brown had predicted.[710]

Should we worry about erosion?

Another common worry that has featured in the literature is "the degradation and depletion of an environmental resource, for example, the erosion of cropland."[711] This fear is based on the fact that when earth erodes owing to the effects of rain and wind, it loses its nutrients and is rendered less capable of retaining water, consequently leading to smaller yields. Lester Brown estimated in 1984 that worldwide we lose 25.4 billion tons of topsoil annually.[712] In 1995, Pimentel from Cornell University (whom we met discussing global health in the introduction) estimated the global erosion at 75 billion tons of lost topsoil annually.[713]

However, there are two serious problems with these figures on erosion. First, they are based on very few and uncertain estimates, primarily stemming from the US. Pimentel found in 1974 that the US lost 30 tons of topsoil per hectare, whereas we now know that the true figure was 12 tons per hectare.[714] His estimate of 17 tons per hectare for all of Europe has turned out to stem – via a string of articles, each slightly inaccurately referring to its predecessor – from a single study of a 0.11 hectare plot of sloping Belgian farmland; the author himself warns against generalization from this.[715] The 75 billion tons figure comes from an environmental atlas by Myers.[716] IFPRI concludes that "the early, high estimates of soil degradation have not been substantiated."[717] One of the few studies actually to have looked at long-term measurements in China and Indonesia (making up 15 percent of the globally eroded area) has found very little support for these high estimates.[718] Indeed, as regards topsoil, the study shows that "the topsoil layer probably did not grow significantly thinner between the 1930s and the 1980s in either China or Indonesia."[719]

Second and more importantly, Pimentel neglects to discuss the two primary erosion studies, of which one has been sponsored by the UN. The studies seem to indicate that the effect on agricultural production is vastly overstated.

There is no doubt that over the last couple of hundred years we have lost more topsoil than has been created, and that the absolute loss is increasing, primarily because we have had increasing agriculture.[720] Nor is there any doubt, that there has been soil erosion ever since the beginning of agriculture and that writers of the classical era were already worrying about the phenomenon.[721]

But the important point here is of course the effect of erosion on agricultural productivity. Here it turns out that there is no clear connection between erosion and yield. FAO, the Food and Agricultural Organization of the UN, puts it thus: the impact of erosion "on crop yields or production has not been well established in physical terms though there have been many attempts to do so. The relationship between erosion and productivity loss is more complex than previously thought."[722] The FAO adds that much of the disappearing soil is simply deposited further down the slope, valley or plain, and that the yield loss in the eroded area could be compensated by yield gains elsewhere. It turns out that only very little eroded topsoil moves very far – the last two hundred years of water erosion in Piedmont, US, has moved only 5 percent of the eroded soil all the way into a river.[723] A comprehensive study on China shows that the total consequence of the ups and downs in all the different soil characteristics shows "no net soil degradation."[724]

The two primary global studies of the effect of erosion on productivity have gone down different paths. One study has drawn on data from FAO to estimate the spatial extent and productivity effects of land degradation in the world's dry areas which constitute the most vulnerable lands. The annual drop in productivity is estimated at 0.3 percent per year.[725] The other study, which has been co-sponsored by the UN environmental organization UNEP, has asked almost 200 soil experts for their expert assessment on the extent and severity of land degradation in their respective areas, information that has been compiled into a large World Soil Degradation Map.[726] About 17 percent of all land is degraded to some extent while only 0.07 percent is strongly degraded.[727] For agricultural land, some 38 percent is affected, 20 percent moderately and 6 percent strongly.[728] In total, this erosion has cost a cumulative loss of 5 percent of agricultural production over the 45 years from the end of World War II, or about 0.1 percent per year.[729]

The question of soil erosion has to be seen in the light of the annual productivity increase of 1–2 percent, stemming from higher-yield varieties, better farming practices and greater use of irrigation, pesticides and fertilization. Compared to this productivity increase, the effect of soil erosion is so small that it often cannot justify an extra effort to combat it.

Clearly, many resources are used each year by farmers to safeguard their lands against serious erosion, simply because they depend upon the land for their livelihood. This safeguarding is for instance achieved by fertilizing to avoid nutrient depletion, by creating terraces to hold water and soil, and by contour plowing and strip-farming.[730] The problem here is primarily with poor peasants who cannot afford to think of tomorrow and consequently overexploit their land today.[731] However, today it is actually possible to maintain the content and composition of soil indefinitely under proper agricultural management.[732] Moreover, the FAO gives several examples of formerly abandoned or heavily degraded lands that have been rehabilitated at modest cost, and IFPRI points out that waiting for higher food prices before rehabilitating land often makes good sense.[733]

For the US it is estimated that the total effect of soil erosion over the next hundred years will be about 3 percent. "By comparison with yield gains expected from advances in technology, the 3 percent erosion-induced loss is trivial."[734] Consequently, soil erosion may be a local problem and will often be a consequence of poverty, but the present evidence does not seem to indicate that soil erosion will to any significant degree affect our global food production, since its effects both up till now have been and in the future are expected to be heavily outweighed by the vast increase in food productivity.[735]

What about fish?

Lester Brown tells us that "the world's farmers are struggling to feed more than 80 million more people each year, good weather or bad. And now, for the first time in history, they can no longer count on fishing fleets to help them expand the food supply."[736]

As we have seen above, agriculture is not particularly in need of help. But more importantly, a slightly increased fishery would not make much difference anyway. Despite Brown's claim that "humanity . . . depends heavily on the oceans for food,"[737] fish constitutes a vanishingly small part of our total calorie consumption – less than 1 percent[738] – and only 6 percent of our protein intake stems from fish.[739]

Nevertheless, Lester Brown is very interested in the fisheries, because here things are just not progressing. The annual *State of the World* practically outbids itself in describing the deplorable state of the "collapsing fisheries." "If fishing continues, the fishery eventually collapses," and "oceanic fisheries have collapsed not just off the coast of developing countries . . . but also off those of industrial countries," and it can be expected that these problems will lead to "mounting social disruption, economic pressures, and the threat of violence."[740] Worldwatch Institute concludes that the per capita fish catch is down by 7.5 percent since 1988 and that it is expected to decline even further.[741]

But as is often the case, this does not tell the whole story.

The global fish catch has in the 1990s not increased as much as earlier, as is evident in Figure 57. This is primarily because the world's fishing fleets have a general tendency to over-fish particular stocks. It is estimated that about 35 percent of the fish catch is obtained from stocks showing declining yields.[742] This is due to a mechanism with which we are all familiar: everyone's responsibility is nobody's responsibility. When the inhabitants in an apartment block share a garden they all want it to look good. The problem is, however, that everyone hopes somebody else will do the cleaning and weeding.

The phenomenon was first named by Garrett Hardin, describing a particular problem in sixteenth-century England. Here large open areas, the so-called commons, were free for all to use as pasture. The poor put out livestock on these commons and obtained a much-needed supplement to their meager income. It was advantageous for each to put

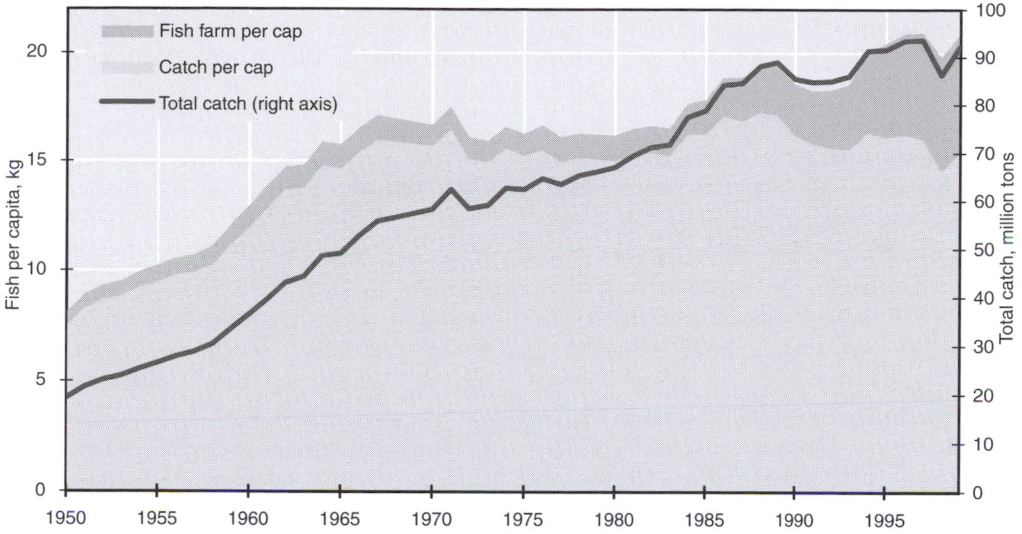

Figure 57 Marine catch and fish farm production per capita and the total marine catch, 1950–99 (1999 data are preliminary). Source: WI 1998b, USBC 2000, FAO 2000b, 2001b .

out more and more livestock, but the social consequence was far more livestock than the commons could handle – damaging the outcome for everyone. Hardin named this phenomenon *Tragedy of the Commons*.[743] Fisheries share much of the same dynamics. Since the oceans belong to everyone they are no one's responsibility. Consequently, for the individual fisherman the name of the game is to fish as much as possible, no matter what the others do. The consequence is that everyone over-fishes.

If all fishermen refrained from fishing they would make no money, but if all fishermen were to fish up the entire ocean, they would make no future money either (because the oceans would have been emptied). It is possible to show that there is an optimal level of fishing in between these two extremes. Here many fish are caught (which means much money now), but at the same time sufficient quantities of fish are left (to breed the fish for the coming years).[744]

The trouble is that the optimal level can only be attained if some sort of ownership can be established over the fish.[745] When, for instance, a state expands its sea territory to 200 nautical miles, and thereby owns all fish within this border, the state can (through permits, for example) make sure only the optimal amount of fish is caught. But often it is hard or impossible to own fish because many species such as tuna and salmon cover long distances, migrating beyond the 200 nautical miles (allowing other states to catch them). Moreover, states – particularly in the Third World – often have a hard time regulating and especially reducing the number of fishermen. Finally, ownership rights cannot easily be allocated over the many fish living in the oceans.

When a state or an international convention cannot secure an optimal exploitation, we are left with everyone battling against everyone else. Here fishermen will over-invest in expensive equipment, so that they can over-fish the oceans fastest and most efficiently. The only limit to the investment is when the sea becomes so empty that further fishery is no longer profitable. Consequently, the world's fishery today is a mixture of control and optimal utilization on the one side, and over-fishing and a gold-digger attitude on the other.

The oceans could produce about 100 million tons of fish a year, which we can harvest "for free" (in the sense that we do not have to feed them). Right now we only catch about 90 million tons, the missing 10 million tons being the price we pay for over-fishing the seas.[746] Of course, we would love to be able to get hold of that extra 10 million tons, but this in no way decides the outcome of food availability, despite Lester Brown's statements quoted above. Even if the world's fisheries could be perfectly orchestrated such that we were able permanently to catch the extra 10 million tons, this addition would be the equivalent to the increase in the rest of the world's agricultural production over the next 19 days, measured in calories.[747] Thus, *not* catching the extra 10 million tons is inefficient but in effect equivalent to just putting the world food development back a bit less than three weeks.

We cannot significantly expand our production of fish catch beyond the 100 million tons, precisely because this harvest comes to us for free. Instead, we have started focusing on *growing* fish on fish farms, particularly in China. This production has quintupled since 1984.[748] The consequence has been that even though fish catches have not been able to keep pace with the population growth, the total fish production has increased so much that the fish per capita in the late 1990s once again exceeded all previous years (Figure 57).[749]

When Lester Brown generally finds that we get less fish per capita it is because he does not include fish farm production. This decision seems somewhat odd, since in getting the calories or protein, it appears of minor importance whether the consumer's salmon stems from the Atlantic Ocean or a fish farm.

Looking forward, the FAO expects that fish consumption will increase dramatically – per person by more than 23 percent till 2030.[750] This will mean that fish farm production will exceed the catch from traditional fisheries.[751] However, it is also likely that prices will be higher because increasing income in the developing countries will lead to higher demand for fish.[752]

Conclusion

Lester Brown has worried about food production since the beginning of the 1970s. Countless times he has predicted that *now* food production would go down and prices up. In 1974 he wrote, "throughout most of the period since World War II, the world food economy has been plagued by chronic excess capacity, surplus stocks, and low food prices. But emerging conditions suggest that this era is ending and is being replaced by a period of more or less constant scarcity and higher prices."[753] He made the same statement in 1996, just updating the years: "Clearly, we are entering a new era. An age of relative food abundance is being replaced by one of scarcity."[754] But both statements were wrong. By early 2001 wheat was cheaper than ever. The IMF's food price index had dropped to the lowest value ever.

Again, in 1981 Lester Brown wrote that the future growth in yields "may be much less than has been assumed in all official projections of world food supply. The post-war trend of rising yields per hectare has been arrested or reversed in the United States, France, and China."[755] All three countries went on to experience annual yield growth rates between 2.3 percent and 5 percent.[756]

We have here studied the best arguments and data that Lester Brown has been able to put forth to vindicate the argument that population growth would outpace food production. However, they do not seem to carry much weight. Prices are still declining. There is no "wall" for maximum yields in sight. At the same time, a large proportion of the world's peasants can achieve a dramatic improvement in yield simply by approaching the yields that are obtained by the best 20 percent of today's producers. The FAO expects that production will still increase by 1.6 percent annually in the developing world over the next 15 years.[757]

The grain stocks are not particularly low, and anyway there is no particular reason to worry about them. Actually, food security is today better exactly because of enlarged international trade. And the "feedgrain buffer" will secure human food supply even in the case of a catastrophic harvest.

There is no reason to believe that China in any decisive way will shake the world's food market. Up till now, Brown has been dramatically wrong on all his predictions concerning China. And finally, since fisheries only supply about 1 percent of the world's food, its future is less decisive for human nutrition, and even here production per capita in the late 1990s have exceeded all previous years.

Consequently, the FAO predicts that there will be *more* food for *more* people, both in 2010, 2015 and 2030.[758] It is expected that there will be fewer malnourished people, and that all regions will experience increasing available calories per capita – the forecast till 2030 is shown in Figure 58. The same general conclusion is reached by IFPRI, USDA and the World Bank – and all three predict ever lower prices.[759]

The development will, however, be unevenly distributed for the individual regions, and sub-Saharan Africa will still do less well than the other regions, with only a slight improvement in nutrition and small growth in the economy. Also, it will become necessary for some developing countries to

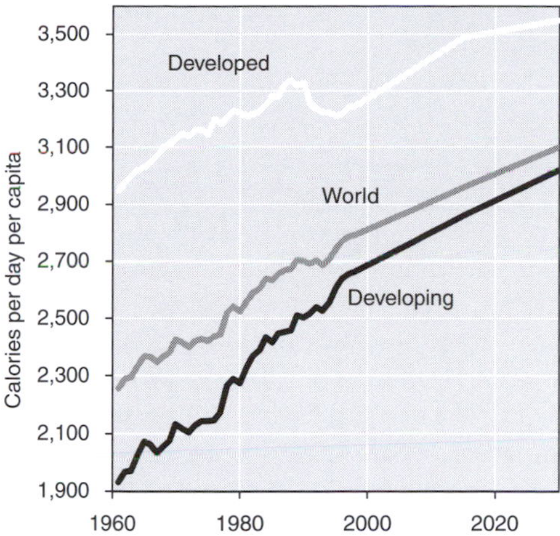

Figure 58 Daily intake of calories per capita in the industrial and developing countries and world, 1961–2030. Forecast from 1998. Source: FAO 2000d:23, 2001a.

import more food, and while this will not be a problem for the resourceful regions in Asia it will cause more hardship for the economically shaky regions of Africa. As mentioned earlier this is primarily a problem of poverty, which again is best handled by strong economic growth.

But the main conclusion remains: all the studies from FAO, IFPRI, USDA and the World Bank show that there is no imminent agricultural crisis or any approaching scarcity of food. Food will get cheaper and ever more people will be able to consume more and better food.

PART III

10 Forests – are we losing them?

The forests are another form of renewable resource we may be overexploiting. Many people have a strong feeling that the forests are simply disappearing. A *Time* magazine environmental survey carried the headline: "Forests: the global chainsaw massacre."[760] The World Resources Institute simply calls it: "Deforestation: the global assault continues."[761] The WWF has disseminated a similar message on its website. The forest front page that greeted the visitor until April 1998 can be seen in Figure 59. "We must ACT NOW to preserve the last remaining forests on Earth," it says. Elsewhere, WWF claims that, "The world's forests are disappearing at an alarming rate."[762] This is in keeping with a statement by the WWF's international president Claude Martin, who in 1997 called a press conference named Eleventh Hour for World's Forests. Here he said: "I implore the leaders of the world to pledge to save their country's remaining forests now – at the eleventh hour for the world's forests."[763] Equally, he claimed that "the area and quality of the world's forests have continued to decline at a rapid rate."[764] Worldwatch Institute even claims that "deforestation has been accelerating in the last 30 years."[765] But there are no grounds for making such claims. Globally, the overall area covered by forest has not changed much since 1950, as can be seen in Figure 60.[766] Estimates of the possible future for global forests for the

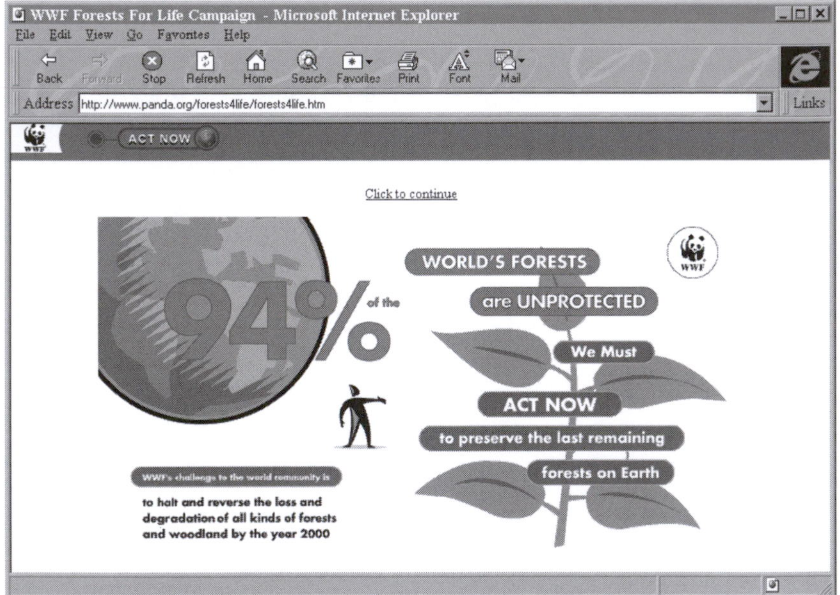

Figure 59 "We must ACT NOW to preserve the last remaining forests on Earth." The WWF's forests web homepage until April 1998. Source: http:www.panda.org/forests4life/

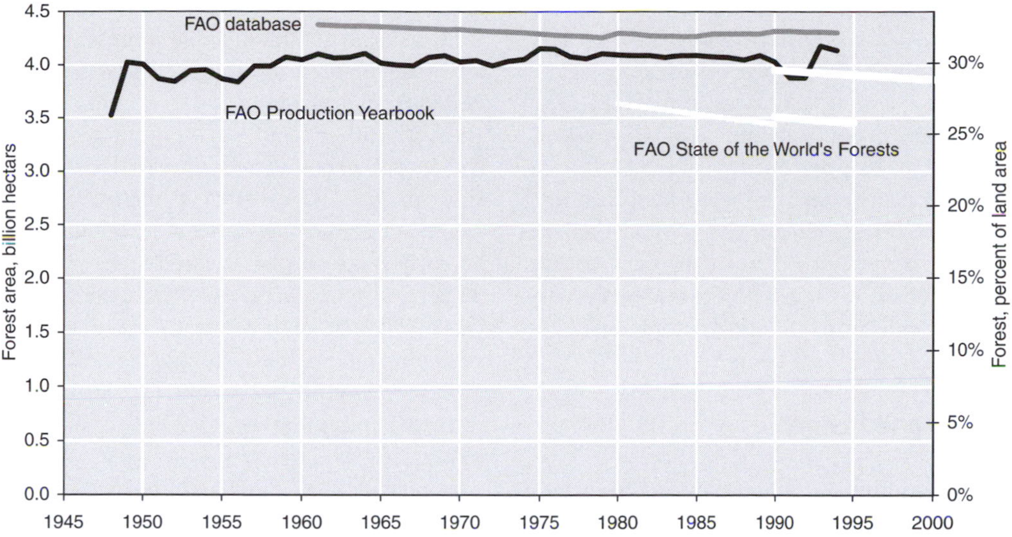

Figure 60 Different UN global forest cover estimates, of forest and woodland, 1948–94 and 1961–94, the more restrictive closed forest for 1980–95 and the new unified forest definition 1990–2000, all from FAO. Source: FAO Production Yearbooks 1949–95, FAO 2000, 1995a, 1997c, 2001c:34. Data availability is poor but by far the best available.[767]

rest of the century is depicted in Figure 150, p. 283, where the very pessimistic estimates show a 20 percent decline, but most scenarios show a constant or even somewhat increasing forest area till 2100.

Of course, it is difficult to determine what actually constitutes forest, because there is a gradual transition from dense rainforest to savanna to bush steppe, in the same way as trees become less tall and stand further apart as one approaches the tree line. It is also extremely difficult to compare Brazilian rainforest with Danish beech woodland or an American plantation. If we nevertheless want to attempt such a comparison, Figure 60 contains the best information on the global forest area. It is, however, important to stress that it only provides a general impression of the situation.

Globally, forest cover has remained remarkably stable over the second half of the twentieth century. With the longest data series, global forest cover increased from 30.04 percent of the global land area in 1950 to 30.89 percent in 1994, or an increase of 0.85 percentage points over 44 years.[768] With the somewhat shorter data series from 1961, global forest cover is estimated to have fallen from 32.66 percent to 32.22 percent. That is to say, it has fallen by 0.44 percentage points over the last 35 years or so. The UN carried out two global forest surveys in 1995 and 1997 and evaluated a more limited definition of forest area for the period 1980–90 and 1990–5. The survey found that the area covered by forest had shrunk from 27.15 percent to 25.8 percent, or by 1.35 percentage points, although these figures are vitiated by considerable uncertainty. For example, an upwards revision of the 1990 forest area was larger than the entire global decline in 1990–5 (or to put it differently – had the 1990 forest area not been revised, the period 1990–5 would have seen an *increase* in forested area).[769] Moreover, Russia, which has the world's largest forest cover, was not included in the survey. Thus, with these considerable short-term uncertainties it seems necessary to focus on the longest possible time periods. Those interested are referred to a longer discussion in the footnotes.[770] In the newest forest study from 2001, the FAO has changed the definitions of forest once again and made a new estimate of forested area from 1990–2000, showing a small decline from 29.5 to 28.8 percent.[771]

Most forest by far is concentrated in a few countries. Russia, Brazil, the US and Canada together have more than 50 percent of the world's forest.[772] Globally there is about two to three times as much forests as cropland.[773]

Forests and history

Since beginning farming, man has been felling woodland to get more land for cultivation. Plato wrote of the Attica heights outside Athens that they resembled "the skeleton of a body wasted by disease" as a result of deforestation.[774]

Europe has lost 50–70 percent of its original forest.[775] Much of the continent's forest was felled in the early Middle Ages, to provide either more agricultural land or firewood. Half of France's forest disappeared between 1000 and 1300.[776] The Black Death wiped out one-third of Europe's population in the middle of the fourteenth century, relieving pressure on the forests, which in many cases grew back again.[777] It was not until the 1500s and 1600s that an ever increasing number of people again put the forests under pressure, and more large areas of it were felled. By 1700, France's forests had been reduced in size by more than 70 percent compared to 1000 CE.[778] In the eighteenth century, however, people became aware of the fact that the forests were a limited resource and that they were important for naval shipbuilding purposes. For this reason forest area in Europe only fell by about 8 percent from 1700 onward.[779]

The US has only lost approximately 30 percent of its original forest area, most of this happening in the nineteenth century.[780] The loss has not been higher mainly because population pressure has never been as great there as in Europe. The doubling of US farmland from 1880 to 1920 happened almost without affecting the total forest area as most was converted from grasslands.[781]

On the other hand, many other regions of the world experienced increased deforestation in the nineteenth century.[782] Latin America became part of the world economy at an early stage and has cleared approximately 20 percent of its forest cover over the last 300 years.[783] Much of it went to make way for sugar and later coffee although a gold and diamond fever, which started in 1690, also helped to clear approximately 2 percent of the forest in Brazil.[784]

Asia, which has long had intensive farming, joined the world economy relatively late. It was not until the American Civil War and the opening of the Suez Canal in 1869 that India began to export cotton on a large scale.[785] All in all, southern Asia and China have lost about 50 percent of their forest cover since 1700.[786] Southeast Asia, on the other hand, has only lost 7 percent over the last 300 years, while Africa and Russia have each lost a little under 20 percent.[787]

Globally it is estimated that we have lost a total of about 20 percent of the original forest cover since the dawn of agriculture.[788] This figure is far smaller than the one so often bandied about by the various organizations. The WWF, for example, claims that we have lost two-thirds of all forests since agriculture was introduced, as mentioned in the introduction, although there is no evidence to support this claim.[789]

Deforestation: a general view

The forests have many advantages to offer. The most obvious of these come from an estimated 5,000 commercial products, mainly construction timber, furniture, paper and firewood.[790] It is estimated that, at the global level, forestry contributes some 2 percent of world GDP, or more than US$600 billion.[791]

In addition to this, the forests offer recreation for urban-dwellers, they help to prevent soil erosion, which silts up rivers and reservoirs, and they reduce flooding.[792] Finally, the forest is home to many species of animals, especially the rainforest, as will be discussed in the section on biodiversity.

The temperate forests, most of which are in North America, Europe and Russia, have expanded over the last 40 years. On the other hand, quite a lot of tropical forest is disappearing. Tropical forests are home to by far the majority of animal and plant species and by far the largest biomass on the planet.[793] In the tropical rainforest, which is the wet part of the tropical forest, one will often find several hundred species of tree within just a few hundred square kilometers.[794] This is in stark contrast to the boreal forests – in Canada's more than 1,000 square kilometers of boreal forest there are only about 20 different tree species.[795]

In the late 1970s it was feared that half or more of the rainforests would disappear within the next few decades. President Carter's environment report, *Global 2000*, estimated an annual tropical forest loss of between 2.3 percent and 4.8 percent.[796] The well-known biologist Norman Myers estimated as recently as the early nineties that 2 percent of all forest was being destroyed every year and believed that by the year 2000 – in just nine years at the time of his prediction – we would have lost about a third of the tropical forest area.[797] Actually, he claimed that "in just another few decades, we could witness the virtual elimination of tropical forests."[798] Estimates in the same range of 1.5–2 percent were common among biologists.[799] Today we know that these estimates went way over the mark. The usual FAO estimates put net deforestation in the tropics in the 1980s at 0.8 percent a year, falling to 0.7 percent in the 1990s.[800] With FAO's new 2001-study, based on accurate satellite imagery, the estimate of the net tropical deforestation has declined even further to 0.46 percent.[801]

These figures are still high though, and there are three main reasons for this. For one thing, the tropical forests often have either no or poorly administered property rights. In reality, the problem resembles the situation of world fishing, described earlier. If the rainforest is everybody's property, it will be nobody's responsibility. Pioneers will simply clear an area, try to farm it and probably ruin the soil in the course of a few years before moving on to a new area.[802] Often the problem of poor regulation is not tackled politically, because the alternative for the local government is an increasing number of poor and unemployed citizens – and therefore more potential political unrest – in the big cities.

For another thing, the tropical forests are extremely valuable in terms of the timber they provide. Trade with large lumber companies is often a quick and easy way out for economically distressed developing nations. In Surinam, timber conglomerates have offered the country investments of a size similar to its GDP for the right to log trees in one-third of the country's forests.[803] With inflation at 500 percent and unemployment on the increase, an offer like this can be almost irresistible. The cost in the first instance would be borne by the small population of Indians who live in the forests. In the long term, though, they are selling the family silver. Over time, Surinam would be able to administer its forests much better and get much more for the produce they offer if the country were under less economic pressure.

Finally, collecting fuelwood is a major reason for deforestation in the developing world. Although wood only provides 1 percent of the world's energy, it accounts for 25 percent of the energy consumption in the developing world as a whole and as much as 50 percent in Africa.[804] Used primarily for cooking and heating, the wood is gathered by the poorest families, who cannot afford other and cleaner fuels such as kerosene. This contributes to local deforestation and desertification. In many African cities, there is no firewood to be found within a radius of 50 kilometers, and women and children spend between 100 and 300 days a year just scavenging for it.[805] There are many quick-growing alternatives to ordinary wood which could be planted in selected areas with poor soil to provide fuel. Also, the traditional three-stone fire only exploits about 6 percent of the energy emitted, whereas cheap metal stoves can double the efficiency and locally made ceramic stoves quadruple the efficiency, reducing indoor pollution and saving up to 20 percent on household fuel costs.[806]

All the three above problems of deforestation can be characterized as bad management. The three causes actually have their roots in other problems faced by the developing world. Unregulated deforestation is largely due to the presence of large groups of poor and landless, and overexploitation of wood fuel is basically due to low income.[807] At the heart of both problems lies the task of reducing poverty and achieving increased growth.

Similarly, the lumber problem frequently arises because countries are caught in a debt trap and are forced to think short-term and thus more easily fall victim to bad deals.[808] If the industrialized countries want to focus on tropical deforestation, then they should pay the developing countries for the preservation of the forests. This happened in the first debt-for-nature swap in Bolivia, where an American bank consortium purchased part of Bolivia's national debt in return for a promise that 1.5 million hectares of tropical forest were converted to a biological reserve. Unfortunately, Bolivia did not keep its promise, and the area is still not legally protected.[809] The idea has, however, been adopted by Ecuador, Costa Rica and the Philippines.[810] Most analysts basically agree that tropical timber can be harvested in a biologically viable fashion, but that stricter rules need to apply.[811]

Deforestation: how much?

However, in order to evaluate the entire extent of this problem, it is necessary to look at how much tropical forest has actually disappeared. Although precise figures are not available, the Conservation Union World, the IUCN, estimates that 80 percent of the original forest cover is still in place. Within historical times, then, just about 20 percent of all tropical forests has disappeared.[812] Compared with the developed world, where we have cleared almost half of our forest, this is a relatively small figure.

Countries such as Nigeria and Madagascar have admittedly lost well over half their original rainforest, and Central America may have lost 50–70 percent.[813] But overall, they are only home to about 5 percent of the world's tropical forest. Most of it by far is in the Brazilian Amazon.[814] The Brazilian forests make up a third of the world's tropical forest. In comparison, Indonesia – the second largest tropical forest area – "only" has 6 percent of the global total.

In 1988, scientists at Brazil's space agency (INPE) announced that its satellites had located as many as 7,000 fires, and that Brazil was now cutting down 8 million hectares of its forests – some 2 percent – a year.[815] These figures attracted extensive criticism of Brazil for its destruction of irreplaceable nature. It later transpired, however, that these figures had been grossly overstated, and the official preliminary estimate for 1999 was about 1.7 million hectares a year, or just below 0.5 percent a year. In actual fact, overall Amazonian deforestation has only been about 14 percent since man arrived, as can be seen in Figure 61.[816] At least some 3 percent of this 14 percent has since been replaced by new forest.[817]

Obviously, Figure 61 doesn't look that bad. There is in fact reason to believe that 70 percent of the Amazon forest will remain intact, and in April 1998 the Brazilian government promised that protection orders would be slapped on a further 25 million hectares.[818]

The WWF, however, told us in 1996 that deforestation had increased by 34 percent since 1992. They did not tell us a year later

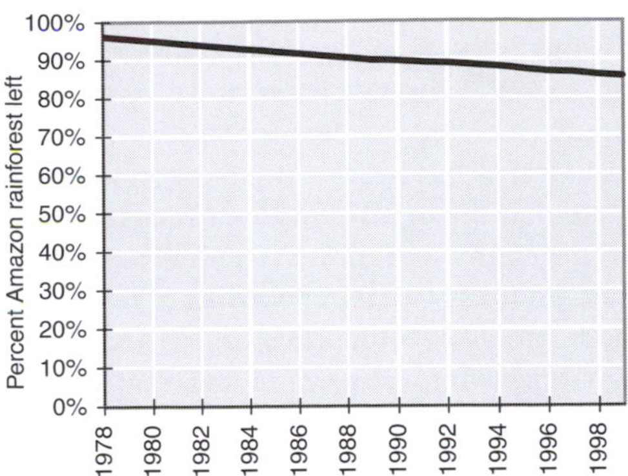

Figure 61 Remaining forest in the Amazon, which accounts for one third of the world's tropical forest, 1978–99. Source: INPE 2000:7; Brown and Brown 1992:121.

that the 1997 rate had fallen by over 50 percent, the second lowest amount since monitoring began.

How much forest?

If a considered political decision is to be made about how much forest we want to have in the world, it is crucial for us to have a comprehensive view of the arguments for and against exploitation of the forests.

There are two primary reasons for viewing the tropical forests as a vital resource. In the 1970s we were told that rainforests were the lungs of the Earth. Even in July 2000, WWF argued for saving the Brazilian Amazon since "the Amazon region has been called the lungs of the world."[819] But this is a myth.[820] True enough, plants produce oxygen by means of photosynthesis, but when they die and decompose, precisely the same amount of oxygen is consumed. Therefore, forests in equilibrium (where trees grow but old trees fall over, keeping the total biomass approximately constant) neither produce nor consume oxygen in net terms. Even if all plants, on land as well as at sea, were killed off and then decomposed, the process would consume less than 1 percent of the atmosphere's oxygen.[821]

The other argument in favor of preserving the forests is to conserve the globe's profusion of species, or the biodiversity. We will look into this argument in chapter 23. In short it can be said that over the next 50 years we will not lose 50 percent of all species as claimed by many, but more like 0.7 percent. One cannot generally argue that these species constitute an actual economic resource (along the lines that they may constitute new and potentially vital medicines) but we may well hold moral reasons for their preservation.

At the same time, numerous false impressions exist regarding the condition of our forests. Most people believe that over the last 50 years we have wiped out large swathes of rainforest, and perhaps temperate forest as well. Statements such as the one from the WWF quoted above naturally help to cement this idea. But as we have pointed out, there has not been a fall in global forest area during this period. On the other hand, Europe got rid of a large proportion of its forest by the end of the Middle Ages in order to make room for farming and bigger populations.

Many people also worry that our paper consumption and the use of printed advertising is laying the forests to waste. The Worldwatch Institute wrote in 1998 that "the dramatically increasing demand for paper and other wood products . . . [is] turning local forest destruction into a global catastrophe."[822] But in actual fact, our entire consumption of wood and paper can be catered for by the tree *growth* of just 5 percent of the current forest area.[823]

Similarly, many allege that although forest cover has remained constant, this is because we have less natural forest and more plantations. The old natural forest has a wealth of species, while plantations consist of genetically identical trees which support very few other plant and animal species.[824] This, of course, is an offshoot from the general biodiversity argument. But for one thing it is not obvious that plantations reduce overall biodiversity. Certainly, they do have fewer species locally, but precisely because the purpose of plantations is to produce masses of wood, they reduce the economic pressure on other natural forests. As a result, these forests are better shielded, can support higher biodiversity or become better recreational areas for humans;[825] 60 percent of Argentina's wood is produced in plantations which constitute just 2.2 percent of the total Argentinean forest area, thus relieving the other 97.8 percent of the forests.[826] For another thing, plantations are typically claimed to be huge. WWF states that plantations "make up large tracts of current forest area."[827] Of course, words such as "large tracts" are vague, but according to the FAO, plantations make up just 3 percent of the world's forest area.[828]

Finally, we heard a great deal about the forest fires in Indonesia in 1997, which for months laid a thick layer of smog over all of Southeast Asia from Thailand to the Philippines. The fires constituted a genuine health problem and with a total cost of almost 2 percent of GDP had appreciable economic impact.[829] However, they were also exploited as a means to focus attention on deforestation. The WWF proclaimed 1997 as "the year the world caught fire" and their president, Claude Martin, stated unequivocally that "this is not just an emergency, it is a planetary disaster."[830] Summing up, WWF maintained that, "in 1997, fire burned more forests than at any other time in history."[831]

This is not the case, however. In their report, the WWF estimated that the fires in Indonesia involved 2 million hectares, despite the fact that this is *higher* than any other estimate cited in the report. Although the 2 million hectares are mentioned constantly, it is only well into the text that it becomes apparent that the figure comprises both forest and "non-forest" areas.[832] The official Indonesian estimate was about 165,000–219,000 hectares.[833] Later, satellite-aided counting has indicated that upwards of 1.3 million hectares of forests and timber areas may have burnt.[834] The independent fire expert Johann Goldammer said that "there is no indication at all that 1997 was an extraordinary fire year for Indonesia or the world at large."[835]

The WWF also estimates that forest fires in Brazil are "on as great a scale as those in Indonesia," but provide no references.[836] They state that the number of forest fires increased in 1997, although they do later tell us that the vast majority of fires involved land that had already been cleared.[837] The Brazil Environment Agency estimates that 94 percent of all fires are on land that has already been burnt, and Brazil's Institute for Environmental Research in the Amazon estimates about 72 percent.[838]

The WWF report fails to sum up the extent of the various other fires, typically about 5,000 hectares in Tanzania and 40,000 in Colombia.

Altogether, however, the WWF's figures are nowhere near the 2.4–3.6 million hectares of forests that burned on just the Indonesian part of Borneo in 1983–4, and the figure is well below the 13 million hectares that burned in China and the former USSR in 1987.[839] In fact, it is estimated that fires each year burn some 10–15 million hectares of boreal and temperate forest, 20–40 million hectares of tropical forests, and up to 500 million hectares of tropical and subtropical savannas, woodlands and open forests.[840] Russian forest fires alone are estimated at about 12 million hectares each year.[841] In conclusion, 1997 was in no way the year in which fire burned more forests than at any other time in history.

What is more, the assessment of forest fires presents other problems. For one thing, only a small portion of the burned areas actually affects original forest. The WWF estimates that "only" approximately 100,000 hectares of primary forest were destroyed in 1997 – less than one-thousandth of the Indonesian forest area.[842] Most forest burning by far takes place on soil already exploited as part of the annual sugar cane harvest, in order to secure fields and grassland, and because it is believed to be good for the soil.[843]

For another thing, fire has been utilized by man since time immemorial. Investigations suggest that simultaneously with man's arrival in Australia, the vegetation became fire-resistant.[844] In global terms it is estimated that overall burning of biomass has only grown by 50 percent at the most since 1880, despite the rapid population increase and an associated increase in the use of slash-and-burn agriculture.[845]

Conclusion

Generally speaking one has to ask what foundation we actually have for our indignation about tropical deforestation, considering our own deforestation of Europe and the US. It seems hypocritical to accept that we have benefited tremendously from felling large sections of our own forests but not to allow developing countries to harvest the same advantages.

However, we can still point to two facts. First, people in developing countries often exploit their forests in a short-term, unnecessarily injudicious fashion – a policy that will harm them in the long run. Exploitation is due both to individual poverty and to poor government finances. Both problems are really rooted in poor economic conditions, and solutions therefore need to include solid, economic growth, in order to ensure that, in future, developing countries will be able to afford the resources to establish a broader perspective on forest development.

Second, we ought to put our money where our mouths are, if we seriously mean what we say about our desire to inhibit the reduction of biodiversity. If we do not want the developing countries to exploit their forest reserves in the same way as we did ours, we should compensate them for it. This could be achieved in several ways. We have already mentioned debt-for-nature swaps, under which Western companies or nations redeem debts in return for the protection of significant natural areas. It would also be possible to achieve better protection of developing nations' forests by implementing a global certification system. Briefly, this involves using a specific international label to inform consumers that timber products come from forests which are cultivated viably and responsibly.[846] Again this solution involves linking problems to the market so as to make it profitable for developing countries to exploit their forests in a responsible fashion.

Basically, however, our forests are not under threat. In a historical perspective, about 20 percent of all forest has been lost, while about a third of the world's land mass is still covered by forest, and since World War II this area has not changed much. Tropical forests are being deforested, though on levels much below the feared 1.5–4.6 percent per year – the newest data from the FAO indicate an annual rate of 0.46 percent. In developing countries, forests are sometimes managed in a thoughtless and irresponsible fashion, but the primary solution to this will be higher growth and a better economic foundation so as to secure the countries concerned the resources to think long-term. On moral grounds, we can aspire to reduce tropical deforestation with the aim of limiting the reduction in biodiversity, although we must also realize that biodiversity is being reduced to a much lesser extent than originally thought.

Finally, the world's demand for paper can be permanently satisfied by the wood production of just 5 percent of the current forest cover. Plantations do not account for much of the overall forest area, and they actually help relieve pressure on natural forest, which still-dominate more than 95 percent of the world's forests.

11 Energy

We will soon run out of oil. Again.

As *E magazine* wrote in July 2000:

> Here's the scenario: Sticker shock at the gas pumps, with prices nearly doubling overnight. Long lines at the few stations that are open. Crude cardboard signs reading "out of gas" blocking incoming traffic at the ones that are closed. Huge sales on "full-sized" vehicles. Long waiting lists for econoboxes. Nineteen seventy three? Nineteen seventy nine? How about 2007?[847]

We have heard it all before.[848] And we probably haven't heard it for the last time. But the argument seems not to be based on the facts. There are good reasons to believe that we will not have dramatic price increases, and that we will actually be able to handle our future energy needs.

We are a civilization built on energy

Each and every one of our actions demands energy. Our own body supplies energy equivalent to a 100 watt bulb,[849] but already early in history man attempted to gain control over more energy, primarily through the use of animals and slaves. Not long after we also learned through technical prowess to use nature's energy: sails for ships as well as wind and water mills. Nevertheless, it was only with Watts' invention of the steam engine in 1769 that it became possible for man to produce large amounts of energy on demand. The steam engine laid the foundation for the Industrial Revolution, which in England over the next hundred years changed production from being based almost exclusively on human labor to obtaining its primary energy input from fossil fuel.

But at the same time it became obvious that production was no longer able to rely on wood for energy supply. England was quickly becoming deforested. Increasingly coal was being used in both England and the US (Figure 62), partly because it was a better energy source than wood, partly because it was available in much larger quantity. This process repeated itself in all industrialized countries and cemented our dependence on energy and non-renewable resources. In this century coal has been replaced by oil, because it is easier to transport, store and use.

Coal, oil and natural gas are all the breakdown products of plants millions of years old. Consequently, they are collectively known as fossil fuels. Most of our coal is the remains of land plants that lived 300–400 million years ago and decomposed in vast swamps. First they were transformed into peat, then later into coal when sufficient pressure and temperature squeezed out the remaining water.[850] Oil and natural gas, however, are composed primarily of plankton which dropped to the seafloor some 2–140 million years ago. The ratio and quality of oil and gas depends on pressure and temperature – perhaps surprisingly most gas is produced where pressure is highest.[851] Crude oil consists of many different chemical elements, and it has to be refined before we can obtain products such as gasoline, diesel fuel, heating oil, and the substances used for asphalt.

Today, our civilization is heavily dependent on the adequate supply of energy. By the end

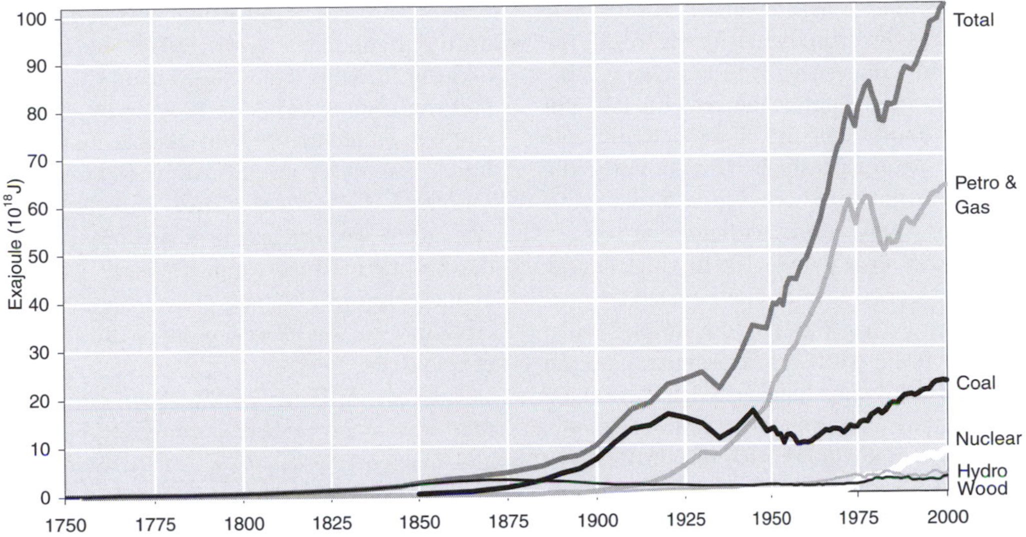

Figure 62 The US energy consumption 1750–2000 of fuel wood, coal, petroleum and gas, hydropower and nuclear power, in exajoule (10^{18} J, approximately 167 million barrels of oil or 37 million tons of coal). Source: EIA 2000d:349–50, 2001a:1.[852]

of the nineteenth century human labor made up 94 percent of all industrial work in the US. Today, it constitutes only 8 percent.[853]

If we think for a moment of the energy we use in terms of "servants," each with the same work power as a human being, each person in Western Europe has access to 150 servants, in the US about 300, and even in India each person has 15 servants to help along.[854] It is indeed unpleasant to imagine what it would be like to live without these helpers.

Do we have enough energy to go on?

The main question is whether this dependency is sustainable. The surprising answer is that we will not run out of fossil fuel within the foreseeable future.

But what do we do in the long run? Our present-day energy supply is based on coal and oil, created over millions of years. Many have pointed out the apparent problem that – to uphold our civilization – we consume millions of years' resources in just a few hundred years. Rather, we should use our resources sustainably, such that our consumption does not prevent future generations from also making use of these resources. But even if this argument sounds quite reasonable, it is impossible to use isolated, non-renewable resources such that future generations can also be assured of their use.[855] Even if the world used just one barrel of oil a year this would still imply that some future generation would be left with no oil at all.[856]

However, this way of framing the question is far too simple. According to the economics Nobel laureate Robert Solow, the question of how much we can allow ourselves to use of this or that resource is a "damagingly narrow way to pose the question."[857] The issue is not that we should secure all specific resources for all future generations – for this is indeed impossible – but that we should leave the future generations with knowledge and capital, such that they can obtain a quality of life at least as good as ours, *all in all.*

This is actually a surprisingly important insight. Let us look at it in connection with oil.

Sooner or later it will no longer be profitable to use oil as the primary fuel for the world. The price of oil will eventually increase and/or the price the other energy sources will fall. But societies do not demand oil as such, only the energy this oil can supply. Consequently, the question is not whether we leave a society for the coming generations with more or less oil, but whether we leave a society in which energy can be produced cheaply or expensively.

Let us put this slightly more simplistically. If our society – while it has been using up the coal and oil – simultaneously has developed an amazing amount of technical goods, knowledge and capital, such that this society now can use other energy sources more cheaply, then this is *a better* society than if it had left the fossil fuel in the ground but also neglected to develop the society.

Asking whether we will run out of oil in the long run is actually a strange question. Of course, in the long run we will undoubtedly rely on other energy sources. The reason why the question nevertheless makes us shudder is because it conjures images of energy crises and economic depression. However, in this chapter (as well as the next on raw materials) we will see that there are sufficient resources for the long-term future and that there are good reasons to expect that when the transition happens it will happen because it actually makes us even better off.

As Sheik Yamani, Saudi Arabia's former oil minister and a founding architect of OPEC, has pointed out: "the Stone Age came to an end not for a lack of stones, and the oil age will end, but not for a lack of oil."[858] We stopped using stone because bronze and iron were superior materials, and likewise we will stop using oil, when other energy technologies provide superior benefits.[859]

The oil crisis

What actually happened to the oil crisis? We were told over and over that oil was getting scarcer and that *now* it would run dry. But it didn't happen. The oil crisis happened because the OPEC countries during the 1970s and the beginning of the 1980s were able to cut back on production and squeeze up prices. But it was never an indication of an actual scarcity. There was – and still is – oil enough.[860] Nevertheless, ever since we started depending on fuel we have been worried about running out. For many, the first oil crisis in 1973 was exactly proof of the scarcity of resources.

One year earlier a book had been published that was to prove both immensely popular and influential – *Limits to Growth*. Using the new concepts of systems analysis and computer simulation, the book served as a focal point for analyses of our overconsumption and our course towards disaster in the 1970s. From seemingly endless scrolls of computer output the book showed us a variety of scenarios leading to catastrophe and breakdown. The book was based on two simple and basic arguments, that even today often seem to be the starting point for most resource discussions. Both points refer back to Malthus and questions of agricultural production, but they can be formulated quite generally. The first point supposes that many processes in social expansion grow; the second assumes that there are limits to this growth.

When you place a single bacterium in a jar with lots of nutrients it will quickly multiply. Suppose it can double each hour. After one hour the glass contains 2 bacteria, after two hours 4 bacteria, then 8, 16, 32, etc. This is an example of exponential growth. A doubling takes place for each time interval. This exponential growth constitutes the first assumption. Many human phenomena seem to have this character. Draw a graph of the number of people on Earth over time, and it will seem exponential. Money in the bank with a 5 percent interest rate will grow exponentially, doubling every fourteenth year. Actually *everything* that has stable growth rates constitutes exponential growth. The economy, the

GDP, society's capital, the demand for goods, etc.

Limits constitute the second assumption. That Earth only contains a limited amount of resources is really just an obvious consequence of the fact that Earth is a sphere. This is why this idea is so enchanting. There is simply a limit to what the Earth can contain. If we use some of the resources there will be less left over for the next year, and sooner or later we will run out. There are, indeed, limits to consumption.

With the assumptions of exponential growth and limited resources we can easily make a doomsday prophecy. Exponential growth means that demand goes up and up, faster and faster, while limited resources set a sharp upper limit for the cumulative supply. And a doomsday prophecy was exactly what we got from *Limits to Growth*. Along with numerous other resources, *Limits to Growth* showed us that we would have run out of oil before 1992.[861] As we know, that did not happen. Ehrlich told us in 1987 that the oil crisis would return in the 1990s.[862] That did not happen either.

One might have thought that history would have made us wiser. But 1992 saw the publication of *Beyond the Limits*, the revised edition of *Limits to Growth*. Here, once again, we were told that our resources would soon run out.[863] Perhaps the first edition had been somewhat mistaken in the exact prediction of the year of resource exhaustion, but *now* we would soon see the problems cropping up. *Beyond the Limits* predicts once again that we will run out of oil (2031) and gas (2050). We might be able to postpone the pain somewhat, but gas consumption grows by 3.5 percent a year, i.e. consumption doubles every 20 years.[864] Thus, every twentieth year we have to find as much new gas as our entire cumulated consumption up till now. "Thus is the nature of exponential growth," as the book puts it.

How much oil left?

Throughout most of history petroleum has been scorned as a sticky, foul-smelling material. Among the few known uses was the fabled Tower of Babel, built to a height of 90 meters with bricks cemented with the petroleum product bitumen.[865] Tar was used to waterproof boats like Noah's Ark.

Until the middle of the nineteenth century the demand for lubricants and illuminants was serviced by vegetable and animal oils, especially whale oil. But through the invention of various distillation processes oil suddenly became an interesting commodity. During the next 50 years the commercial production of oil expanded rapidly, and since the first large discoveries in the Middle East at the beginning of the twentieth century there has been a virtual explosion in production after World War II (Figure 63).

Constituting 1.6 percent of global GDP, oil is today the most important and most valuable commodity of international trade.[866] Oil can be found all around the world, but the largest resources by far are to be found in the Middle East – it is estimated that somewhere between 50 and 65 percent of the global reserves are found here.[867] Consequently, it is also imperative for our future energy supply that this region remains reasonably peaceful.[868]

Oil is the most versatile of the three primary fossil fuels. Oil has high-energy content, it is relatively compact, and it is easy to transport. Conversely, coal is heavier, more bulky and pollutes more. Gas is clean, but very bulky and requires pipelines for transportation.[869] This is reflected in the relative prices as seen in Figure 64, where oil is the most expensive per energy unit, and coal the cheapest. That gas has become more expensive than coal over time is precisely due to the fact that many nations have installed pipelines to exploit this cleaner energy source.

We have long been told that we were running out of oil. In 1914 the US Bureau of Mines estimated that there would be oil left over for

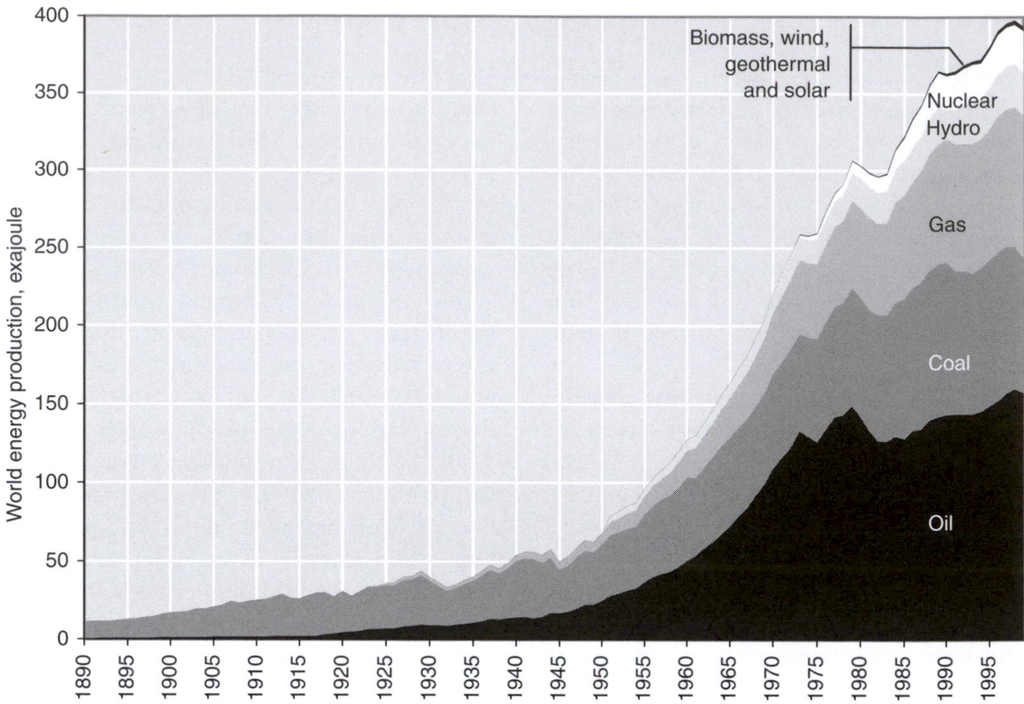

Figure 63 World energy production 1890–1999 in exajoule, distributed by fuel source. Source: Simon *et al.* 1994, WRI 1996a, WI 1999b, EIA 2000:39–40, 269. Note: This figure only represents the energy distributed in a market. It is estimated that about a fourth of all energy in the developing countries derives from wood; Botkin and Keller 1998:264. Including traditional, non-commercial energy sources would add about 7 percent to the commercial production; WRI 1998:332.

only ten years' consumption. In 1939 the Department of the Interior projected that oil would last only 13 more years, and again in 1951 it was again projected that oil would run out 13 years later.[870] As Professor Frank Notestein of Princeton said in his later years: "We've been running out of oil ever since I've been a boy."[871]

How should scarcity be measured? Even if we were to run out of oil, this would not mean that oil was unavailable, only that it would be very, very expensive. If we want to examine whether oil is getting more and more scarce we have to look at whether oil is getting more and more expensive.[872] Figure 65 shows that the price of oil has not had any long-term upward trend.

The oil price hike from 1973 to the mid-80s was caused by an artificial scarcity, as OPEC achieved a consistent restraint to production.[873] Likewise, the present high oil price is caused by sustained adherence to OPEC agreed production cutbacks in the late 1990s.[874] Thus, it is also expected that the oil price will once again decline from $27 to the low $20s until 2020.[875] This prediction lies well in the middle of the $17–$30 stemming from eight other recent international forecasts.[876]

The reason why it is unlikely that the long term trend will deviate much from this price is that high real prices deter consumption and encourage the development of other sources of oil and non-oil energy supplies. Likewise, persistently low prices will have the opposite effects.[877]

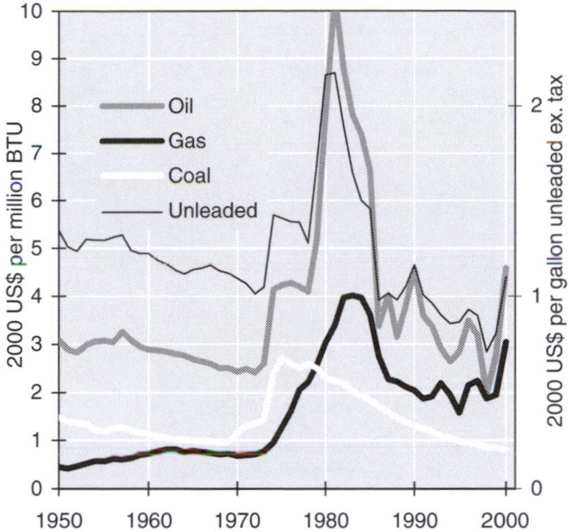

Figure 64 US price per energy unit for oil, gas and coal, and price of gasoline per gallon at the pump (excluding tax and adjusted to regular unleaded price) in 2000 US$, 1950–2000. A million BTU is equivalent to about 30 liters (8 gallons) of oil. Source: EIA 1999c:63, 159–61, 2000c:117, 129, 131, 2001a:129, 131, CPI 2001, DOT 2000:2–9.[878]

In fact, if we look at the real price of gas at the pump (the consumer price) excluding tax, it stands at $1.10, on a par with the lowest prices before the oil crisis (Figure 64). This is because most of the gas price consists of refining and transportation, both of which have experienced huge efficiency increases.[879]

At the same time Figure 66 demonstrates that we have more reserves than ever before. This is truly astounding. Common sense would tell us that if we have 35 years' consumption left in 1955, then we should have 34 years' supply left the year after.[880] Yes, actually we should probably rather have 33 years' worth left because we consumed more oil in 1956 than in 1955. But Figure 66 shows that in 1956 – contrary to what common sense would indicate – there were *more* years of reserves even at a *higher* annual consumption.[881] Nor when we look at remaining years of supply does oil seem to be getting scarcer.

Notice how Figure 65 seems to indicate that oil consumption steadily increases (with the

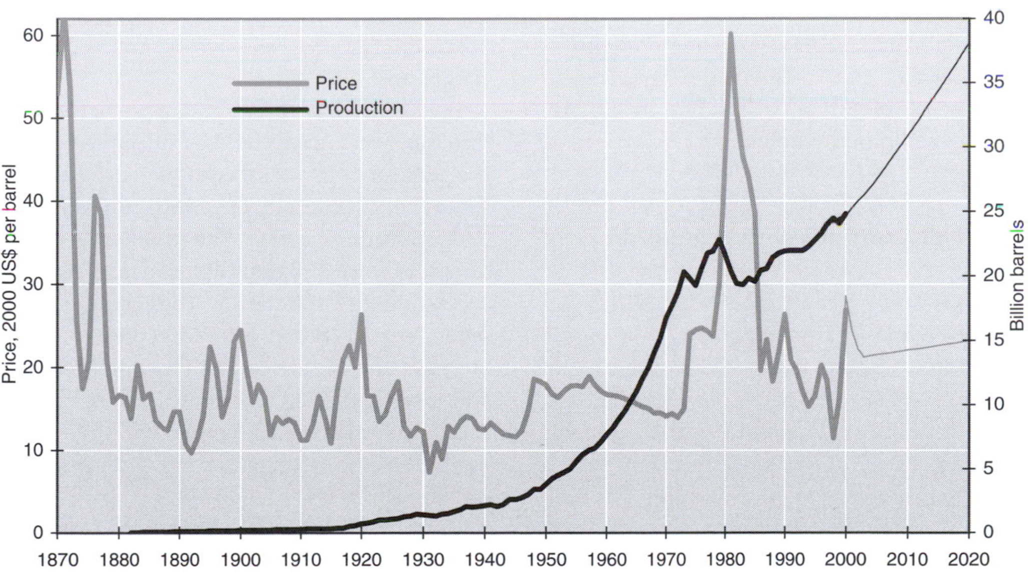

Figure 65 Oil price 1871–2020 in 2000 US$, and world production 1882–2020, US Energy Information Agency prediction for 2001–20. Source: Simon *et al.* 1994, EIA 1999c:63, 273, 2000e:127, 153, 2001a:117, 137, 2001c:13, CPI 2001.

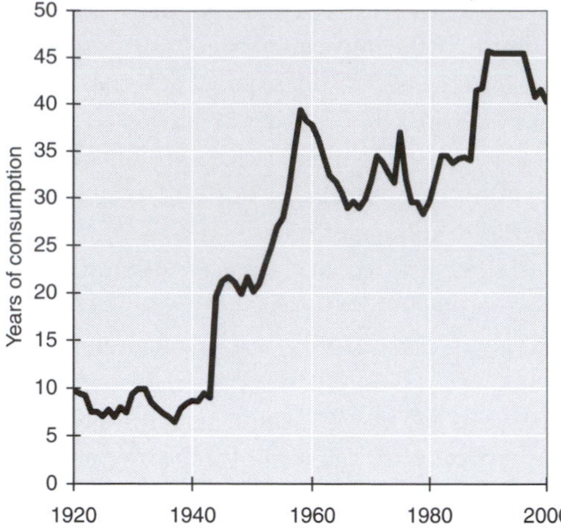

Figure 66 Years-of-consumption: world oil reserves compared to the annual production, 1920–2000. Source: Simon *et al.* 1994, EIA 1997b:Table 11.3, 11.5, 1999c:271, 2000d:277, 2000a:109, 2000c:136, 2001a:137, 2001b:113. Total reserves until 1944 are only American, since 1944 for the entire world.

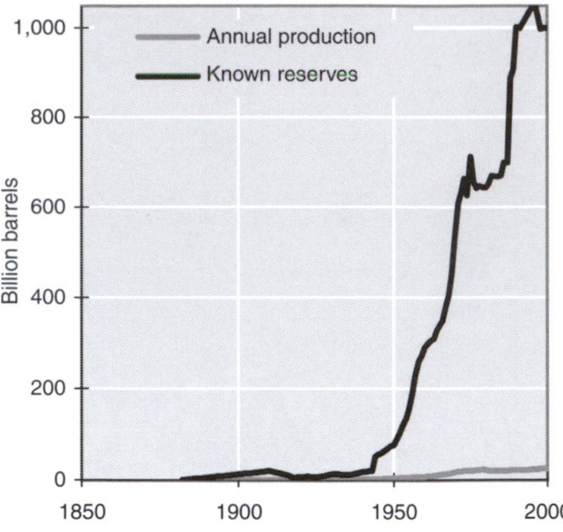

Figure 67 The world's known oil reserves and world oil production, 1920–2000. Source: As Figure 66.

exception of the 1970s) just as predicted by the doomsayers: consumption is headed towards a breakdown. But look at Figure 67, where demand is depicted in the same diagram as the collected, known reserves. Here it is clear that the development in reserves by far outpaces development in demand.

Optimists and pessimists arguing

Why is it that we continuously believe oil will run out, when it is not happening?

In 1865 Stanley Jevons, who was one of Europe's most highly esteemed scientists, wrote a book on England's coal use. In his analysis, the Industrial Revolution saw a relentless increase in the demand for coal, which inevitably would cause the exhaustion of England's coal reserves and grind its industry to a halt. "It will appear that there is no reasonable prospect of any release from future want of the main agent of industry."[882] His arguments were not unlike those expounded in the *Limits to Growth*. But what he did not realize was that when the price of coal increased it would also increase the incentive to search for more effective ways to use coal, to search for new coal reserves, to find cheaper ways of transporting coal, and to search for other energy sources such as oil.[883] Jevons' crisis never took place.

That we can both use resources better and find more and more could be subsumed under the idea of human ingenuity. True, Earth is spherical and limited, but this is not necessarily a relevant objection. The problem is rather how large are the deposits that are actually accessible for exploitation. These deposits can seem limited, but if *price* increases this will increase the incentive to find more deposits and develop better techniques for extracting these deposits. Consequently, the price increase actually increases our total reserves, causing the price to fall again.

Actually, the question of whether resources are becoming more scarce or more abundant is staked on these two approaches: doomsayers claiming that resources are physically limited and consequently *must* grow scarcer and cornucopians focusing on human ingenuity and the empirical evidence of the data. Whether the one or the other is right is in truth an empirical question.[884]

Ever more oil available

Looking at Figure 65 it is clear that the price of oil has not had any long term increase and that oil has not been getting scarcer. Looking at Figure 66, it is clear that we have more and more oil left, not less and less. But it still seems odd. How can we have used ever more and still have even more left?

The answers to this question point to the three central arguments against the limited resources approach.

1. "Known resources" is not a finite entity. It is not that we *know* all the places with oil, and now just need to pump it up. We explore new areas and find new oil. But since searching costs money, new searches will not be initiated too far in advance of production. Consequently, new oil fields will be continuously added as demand rises. This is part of the reason why we see years of consumption increasing and not decreasing.

Actually, it is rather odd that anyone could have thought that known resources pretty much represent what is left, and therefore predict dire problems when these have run out. It is a little bit akin to glancing into my refrigerator and saying: "Oh, you've only got food for three days. In four days you will die of starvation." No, in two days I will go to the supermarket and buy some more food. The point is that oil will come not only from the sources we already know but also from many other sources which we still do not know.[885] US Geological Surveys have regularly been making assessments of the total undiscovered resources of oil and gas, and writing in March 2000 they state: "Since 1981, each of the last four of these assessments has shown a slight increase in the combined volume of identified reserves and undiscovered resources."[886]

2. We become better at exploiting resources. We use new technology to be able to extract more oil from known oil fields, we become better at finding new oil fields, and we can start exploiting oil fields that previously were too expensive and/or difficult to exploit. An initial drilling typically exploits only 20 percent of the oil in the reservoir. Even with present-day, advanced techniques, using water, steam or chemical flooding to squeeze out extra oil, more than half the resource commonly remains in the ground unexploited. It is estimated that the ten largest oil fields in the United States will still contain 63 percent of their original oil when production closes down.[887] Consequently, there is still much to be reaped in this area. In the latest US Geological Survey assessment, such technical improvement is expected to yield more than a 50 percent increase of identified reserves.[888]

At the same time we have become better at exploiting each liter of oil. The average US car has improved its mileage by 60 percent since 1973.[889] Likewise, home heating in Europe and the US has improved by 24–43 percent.[890] Many appliances have become much more efficient – the dishwasher and the washing machine have cut about 50 percent of their energy use.[891]

Still, efficiency has much potential to be increased. It is estimated that 43 percent of American energy use is wasted.[892] The US Department of Energy estimates that we could save anywhere from 50 percent to 94 percent of our home energy consumption.[893] We know today that it is possible to produce safe cars getting more than 50–100 km per liter (120–240 mpg).[894] Of course, while such efficiency gains have often been documented, the reason why they have not all been utilized is simply because it does not pay at the current energy price and level of technology.[895]

Most nations actually exploit energy better and better: we use less and less energy to produce each dollar, euro or yen in our national product. Figure 68 shows how the US has produced ever more goods with the same amount of energy since 1800, and this holds true for

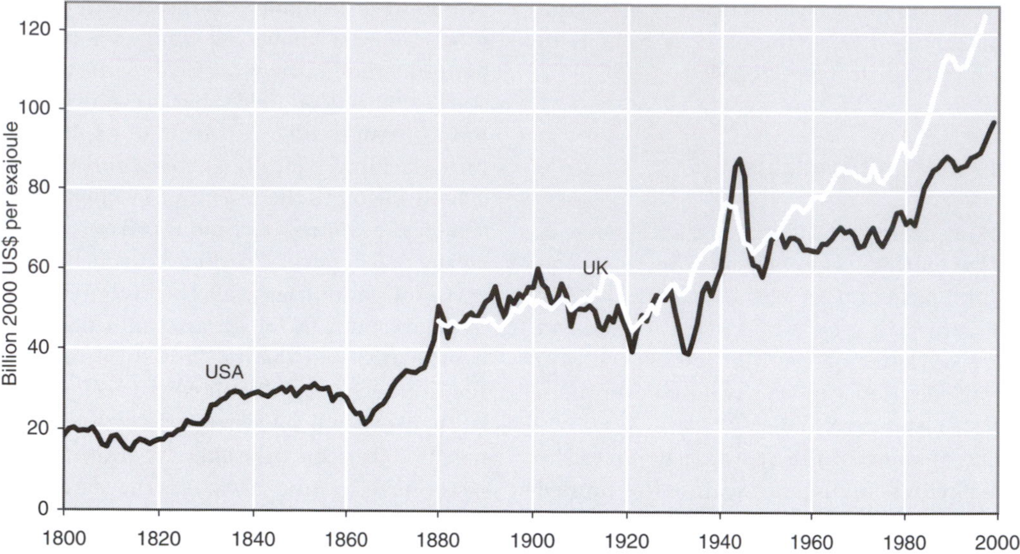

Figure 68 Energy efficiency for the US, 1800–1999 and the UK, 1880–1997. Shows how 1 EJ of energy could produce just 19 billion 2000 US$ in 1800, whereas the same amount of energy could produce more than $90 billion in 1999. Source: As in Figure 30, Figure 62, and Fouquet and Pearson 1998.[896]

the UK since 1880 and the EU and Japan from 1973.[897] For the world at large, almost twice the amount of wealth was produced in 1992 per energy unit compared to 1971.[898] Over the same period Denmark actually went even further and "delinked" the connection between a higher GDP and higher energy consumption: in total Denmark used *less* energy in 1989 than in 1970 despite the GDP growing by 48 percent during that time.[899]

3. We can substitute. We do not demand oil as such but rather the services it can provide. Most often we want heating, energy or fuel, and this we can obtain from other sources. Therefore we can swap to other energy sources if they show themselves to be better or cheaper. In England around the year 1600 wood became increasingly expensive (because of local deforestation and bad infrastructure) and this prompted a gradual switch over to coal, a similar movement to the one in the US, depicted in Figure 62.[900] During the latter part of the nineteenth century a similar substitution took place from coal to oil.

In the short run, it would be most obvious to substitute oil with the other commonly known fossil fuels such as gas and coal. In the longer run, however, it is quite possible that we will cover a large part of our energy consumption using nuclear power, wind and solar power, biomass and shale oil.

Other fossil energy sources

Gas is a clean and cheap energy source, requiring, however, a large pipeline distribution system. Gas has had the largest growth of all the fossil energy sources since World War II – production has increased more than 12-fold since 1950 as is evident in Figure 69. While gas only constituted about 10 percent of the global energy in 1950, today it constitutes 23 percent.[901] Gas releases much less carbon dioxide per energy unit than the other fossil fuels, where coal in particular is the big culprit.[902]

Despite the dramatic increase in production, gas has become *more* abundant over time,

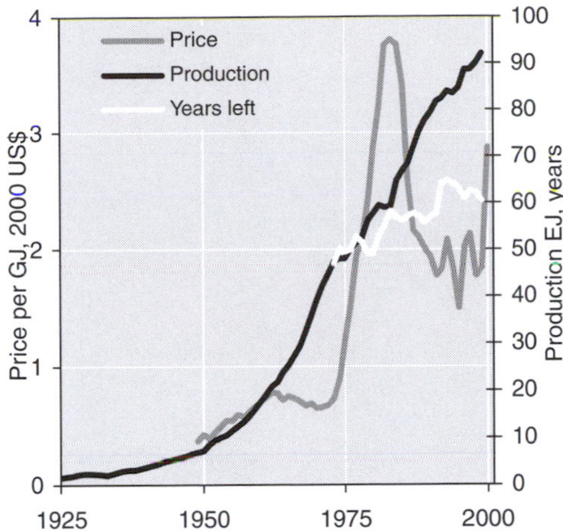

Figure 69 World gas production, price and years of consumption. Production in exajoule, 1925–1999, price in 2000 US$ per gigajoule, 1949–2000, and years of consumption, 1975–1999. Source: WI 1999c, EIA 1999c:63, 269, 2000a:109, 131, 2001b:42, CPI 2001, BP 1998, 1999.[903]

just like oil. But given the arguments above, this should not surprise us. Today, our gas reserves have more than doubled since 1973. Despite using ever more gas each year the gas reserves will last ever more years. In 1973 we had enough gas for the next 47 years given 1973 consumption. In 1999 we had gas for 60 years, despite consumption having shot up more than 90 percent.[904]

Historically, coal has been the most important fossil fuel, but in the post-war period it has been partially displaced by oil. Only with the energy crisis in the 1970s did coal again become an interesting energy source, although it is heavy and bulky and consequently costly to transport.[905] Therefore most coal is consumed close to its source – only 10 percent of all coal is exported compared to 60 percent of all oil.[906] In Denmark, coal replaced a large part of our oil consumption after the initial 1973 oil shock, and only slowly has gas begun to replace coal. This tendency has been widespread throughout Europe since gas is cleaner and because local coal in Germany and England has become too expensive.[907]

Typically, coal pollutes quite a lot, but in developed economies switches to low-sulfur coal, scrubbers and other air-pollution control devices have today removed the vast part of sulfur dioxide and nitrogen dioxide emissions.[908] Coal, however, is still a cause of considerable pollution globally, and it is estimated that many more than 10,000 people die each year because of coal, partly from pollution and partly because coal extraction even today is quite dangerous.[909]

But coal can supply us with energy for a long time to come. As with oil and gas, coal reserves have increased with time. Since 1975 the total coal reserves have grown by 38 percent. In 1975 we had sufficient coal to cover the next 218 years at 1975 levels, but despite a 31 percent increase in consumption since then, we had in 1999 coal reserves sufficient for the next 230 years. The main reason why years-of-consumption have not been increasing more is due to reduced prices.[910] The total coal resources are estimated to be much larger – it is presumed that there is sufficient coal for well beyond the next 1,500 years.[911] Production has increased almost tenfold over the last hundred years, but, as can be seen in Figure 70, this has not led to any permanent increase in price (beyond the oil crisis price hike). Actually, the price of coal in 1999 was close to the previous low of 1969.

At the same time there are several other discoveries that have expanded the fossil fuel resources considerably. First, we have now begun to be able to exploit methane gas in coal beds. Earlier, miners would fear seeping methane gas that could cause explosions and make the mine collapse. Today, this gas can be exploited. The precise recoverable amounts of coal bed methane are not known, but are estimated to exceed the current reserves of natural gas and could be double the size.[912] This discovery alone gives us gas for at least another 60 years.

An increasing amount of attention has been given to tar sands and shale oil. Both contain oil which unfortunately is much harder to

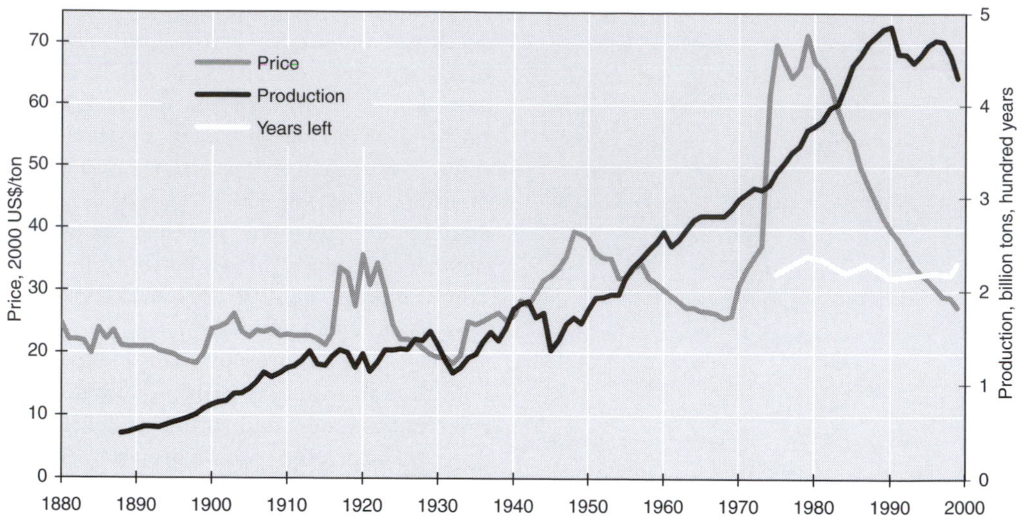

Figure 70 World coal production, price and years of consumption. Production in billion tons, 1888–1999, price in 2000 US$ per ton, 1880–1999, and years of consumption, 1975–1999 in hundreds of years (right axis). Source: Simon *et al.* 1994, EIA 1997b:Table 3.2, 11.15, EIA 1999c:63, 2000a:23, 2000d:205, 2001b:25, 295, Freme and Hong 2000:5, CPI 2001, BP 1998, 1999.[913]

extract and consequently more expensive to exploit. In Canada, oil has been extracted from tar sands since 1978 and here the costs have dropped from $28 per barrel to just $11.[914] For comparison the price of a barrel of oil was $27 in 2000.

The US Energy Information Agency estimates that today it will be possible to produce about 550 billion barrels of oil from tar sands and shale oil at a price below $30, i.e. that it is possible to increase the present global oil reserves by 50 percent.[915] And it is estimated that within 25 years we can commercially exploit twice as much in oil reserves as the world's present oil reserves. Should the oil price increase to $40 per barrel we will probably be able to exploit about five times the present reserves.

The total size of shale oil resources is quite numbing. It is estimated that globally there is about *242 times more* shale oil than the conventional petroleum resources. There is more than eight times more energy in shale oil than in all other energy resources combined – oil, gas, coal, peat and tar sands.[916] This stunning amount of energy is the equivalent of our present *total* energy consumption for more than 5,000 years.[917]

Consequently, there is no need for any immediate worry about running out of fossil fuels. A proportion of the fossil fuels, however, is probably only accessible at a higher price. Still, there is good reason to believe that the total energy share of our budget – even if we continue to depend solely on fossil fuels – will be dropping. Today the global price for energy constitutes less than 2 percent of the global GDP, and yet if we assume only a moderate continued growth in GDP this share will in all likelihood continue to drop. Even assuming truly dramatic price increases on energy of 100 percent, by the year 2030 the share of income spent on energy will have dropped slightly.[918]

Nuclear energy

Nuclear energy constitutes 6 percent of global energy production and 20 percent in the countries that have nuclear power.[919] Despite growth in Asia, the prospects for this sector spell stagnation until 2010 and a minor recession after that. This recession is mainly caused by perceived problems of security as stressed by the accidents at Three Mile Island and Chernobyl which undermined many people's confidence in this energy source.[920]

Ordinary nuclear power exploits the energy of fission by cleaving the molecules of uranium-235 and reaping the heat energy. The energy of one gram of uranium-235 is equivalent to almost three tons of coal.[921] Nuclear power is also a very clean energy source which, during normal operation, almost does not pollute. It produces no carbon dioxide and radioactive emissions are actually *lower* than the radioactivity caused by coal-fueled power plants.[922]

At the same time nuclear power also produces waste materials that remain radioactive for many years to come (some beyond 100,000 years). This has given rise to great political debates on waste deposit placement and the reasonableness of leaving future generations such an inheritance. Additionally, waste from civilian nuclear reactors can be used to produce plutonium for nuclear weapons. Consequently, the use of nuclear power in many countries also poses a potential security problem.

For the moment there is enough uranium-235 for about 100 years.[923] However, a special type of reactor – the so-called *fast-breeder reactor* – can use the much more common uranium-238 which constitutes over 99 percent of all uranium. The idea is that while uranium-238 cannot be used directly in energy production it can be placed in the same reactor core with uranium-235. The uranium-235 produces energy as in ordinary reactors, while the radiation transforms uranium-238 to plutonium-239 which can then be used as new fuel for the reactor.[924] It sounds a bit like magic, but fast-breeder reactors can actually produce more fuel than they consume. Thus it is estimated that with these reactors there will be sufficient uranium for up to 14,000 years.[925] Unfortunately these reactors are more technologically vulnerable and they produce large amounts of plutonium that can be used for nuclear weapons production, thus adding to the security concerns.[926]

Nuclear power, however, has barely been efficient in the production of energy and this is probably the major reason why its use has not been more widespread.[927] It is difficult to find unequivocal estimates of the total costs since there are so many different variables that can affect the calculations, but typically the price hovers around 11–13 cents for one kilowatt-hour (kWh) in 1999 prices.[928] This should be compared with an average energy price for fossil fuels of 6.23 cents.[929]

In the longer run, the primary focus is no longer on fission energy but rather on fusion energy. This technology aims at fusing two hydrogen atoms into a single atom of helium. A single gram of fuel can develop the same energy as 45 barrels of oil.[930] Fuel comes basically from ordinary sea water and thus supply is virtually infinite. Moreover, there will be very little radioactive waste or emissions. However, fusion demands astronomical temperatures and despite investments above $20 billion we have still only managed to achieve 10 percent of the laser power necessary for producing energy.[931] Consequently it is supposed that fusion energy will be commercially available only after 2030 or perhaps only well into the twenty-second century.[932]

Renewable energy

Renewable energy sources, unlike fossil fuels, can be used without ever being used up.[933] These are typically sources such as sun, wind, water and Earth's internal heat. Up until a few years ago these energy sources were considered somewhat "alternative" – pet projects for "bearded vegetarians in sandals" as *The Economist* puts it.[934] But this picture is changing.

There are great advantages in using renewable energy. It pollutes less, makes a country less dependent on imported fuel, requires less foreign currency, and has almost no carbon dioxide emission.[935] Moreover many of the technologies are cheap, easy to repair and easy to transport, ideally suited for developing countries and remote regions.

Looking at Figure 71 it is clear that renewable energy sources constitute only 13.6 percent of the global energy production. Here, the two important constituents are hydroelectric power and traditional fuels. Water power makes up 6.6 percent of global energy production. The traditional fuels consist of fuel wood, charcoal, bagasse (fibrous cane residue left over from sugar production), and animal and vegetal wastes. These make up 6.4 percent of the world's energy production and constitute more than 25 percent of the energy consumption in the developing countries.[936]

The other, more well-known renewable energy sources such as biomass, geothermal energy, wind and solar power make up the last 0.6 percent of global energy production, or the top, thin slice in Figure 71. Of this slice, the greater part is made up by the 0.4 percent of biomass – burning wood and agricultural waste for energy, but also energy production from municipal waste incineration.[937] The rest consists mainly of 0.12 percent from geothermal energy, made with the heat from the earth's interior.

The best-known renewables, wind and solar power, supplied in 1998 just 0.05 percent of all energy produced, wind dominating with almost 0.04 percent and solar energy putting in a mere 0.009 percent.[938] Even for electricity alone, wind power makes up just 0.09 percent and solar energy 0.02 percent.[939] In the progressive EU only 5.6 percent of the consumed energy is renewable, with most being supplied from biomass (3.7 percent) and hydropower (1.8 percent), whereas wind makes just 0.04 percent and solar 0.02 percent.[940]

Virtually every year, Lester Brown makes much of the fact that the use of renewable energy sources grows much faster than that of oil:

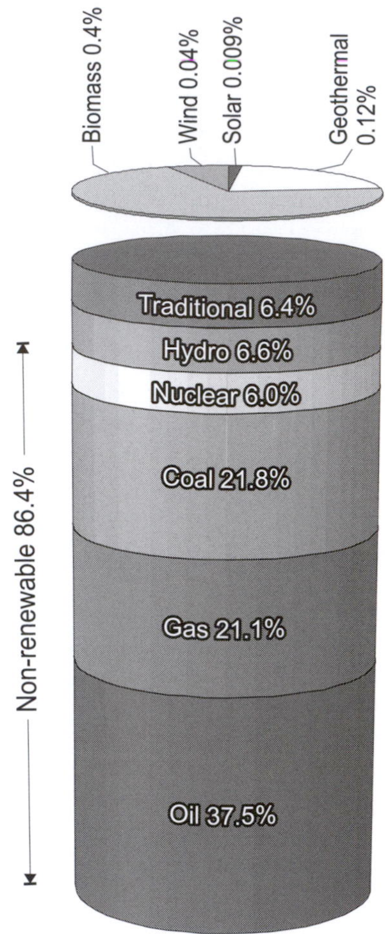

Figure 71 Share of global energy production by different sources, 1998, in total 428 EJ. Non-renewables like oil, gas, coal and nuclear power make up 86.4 percent. Renewables consist primarily of hydroelectric power generation and traditional fuels, such as fuelwood and charcoal primarily used in the Third World. Finally, in the thin slice on top, comes the well-known renewable sources, 0.6 percent in total, with biomass, geothermal, wind and solar power. Source: EIA 2000a:201ff, WRI 1998b.[941]

> In earlier years, the discussion on energy centered on what the new economy would look like. Now we can actually see it emerging. It can be seen in the solar cell rooftops of Japan and

> Germany, in the wind farms of Spain and Iowa, and in the widely varying growth rates of the various energy sources. While wind use was expanding at 22 percent a year from 1990 to 1998 and photovoltaics at 16 percent per year, the use of oil was growing at less than 2 percent and that of coal was not increasing at all.[942]

But such growth rate comparisons are misleading because, with wind making up just 0.05 percent, double-digit growth rates are not all that hard to achieve. In 1998, the amount of energy in the 2 percent oil increase was still 323 times bigger than the 22 percent increase in wind energy.[943] Even in the unlikely event that the wind power growth rate could continue, it would take 46 consecutive years of 22 percent growth for wind to outgrow oil.[944]

Put simply, this low share of renewable sources in global energy production is simply a consequence of the sources not yet being competitive compared to fossil fuels.[945] Up till now most renewable energy projects have been completed with public funding and tax rebates.[946] But as is clear from Figure 72, price has been rapidly declining, and it is expected that this decline will continue.

Hydroelectric power is important for many nations – it supplies more than 50 percent of the electricity production in 63 countries and at least 90 percent in 23 countries.[947] Hydropower has been competitive for quite some time but it is also quite well developed and there are few substantial opportunities for expansion in Europe.[948] Moreover, hydropower also has several downsides: partly because it often has negative consequences for the environment,[949] and partly because most dams silt up within 20 to 50 years. It is expected that Egypt's Aswan High Dam will be at least half silted by 2025.[950]

Geothermal energy from tapping the Earth's internal heat can also be competitive, but only a few places in the world are just right, for example locations in the Philippines and Indonesia.[951]

Presently the most competitive renewable energy source with a wide applicability is

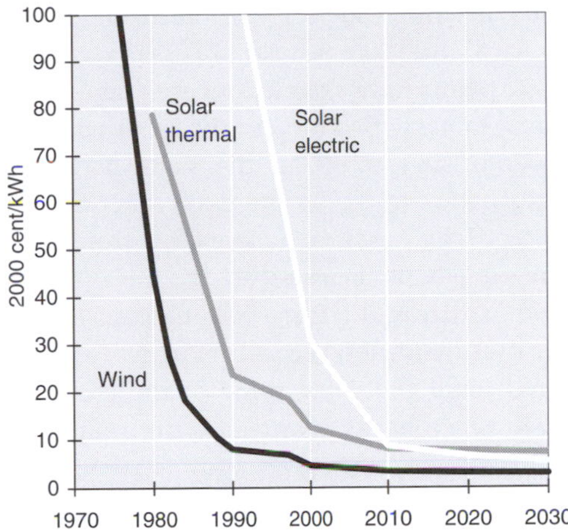

Figure 72 Price per kWh for different renewable energy sources, 1975–2030. Primary source: DOE 1997, CPI 2001.[952]

wind power. The price today is around 5–6.4 cents per kWh, and although this is more than ten times cheaper than the price 20 years ago, it is still somewhat more expensive than energy derived from fossil fuels.[953] Though the price is expected to decline further, it is expected still to be about 50 percent higher than the cheapest electricity production from gas-fired generating plants in 2005, and some 20 percent higher in 2020.[954]

Many people are often surprised that renewable energy is not cheaper than fossil energy. After all, the fuel is free. True, but there are several reasons why this is not the main issue. First, the price of the actual fuel only makes up a fairly small part of the total energy cost – in 1995 the fossil fuel price accounted only for 16 percent of the total cost of electricity.[955] Second, fossil fuels have a solid lead in research and development, since they have been around much longer and have had much larger shares of the national research budgets. Finally, the use of fossil fuels also gets much more efficient over time. New research has made capital costs fall by 2.5 percent with each doubling of new capacity. Concurrently more competition and better management mean that coal-fired power plants needing 250 people in 1982 could make do with just 200 people in 1995. Gas-fired power plants have experienced even larger efficiency gains, with a drop in the required manpower of 28 percent in the same period.[956] Deregulation of the oil and gas market as well as electricity has also made energy from non-renewable fuels cheaper.[957]

Nevertheless, it is important to focus on the fact that the difference in cost between traditional fossil fuels and some of the cheapest renewable energy sources is so relatively slight. Moreover, these economic costs do not include the negative social cost of fossil fuel use on the environment. Energy from a coal-fired power plant may still be 20–50 percent cheaper than the energy produced by a windmill, but if the effects on environment and humans from coal pollution and waste products exceed the price difference then society ought to choose wind energy.[958]

Recently, one European and two American large-scale projects have attempted to examine *all* costs associated with electricity production, all the way from the mortal risks of mining coal, the traffic hazards of transportation and occupational hazards of production including consequences of acid rain, particles, sulfur dioxide, nitrogen oxides and ozone on lakes, crops, buildings, children and old people and up to the consequences of tax codes and occupation plus a long, long list of similar considerations and costs.[959] Altogether these studies find that the extra social cost of new coal-fired power plants is around 0.16–0.59 cents per kWh.[960] None of the three studies, however, quantifies the costs of carbon dioxide which probably means an additional 0.64 cents per kWh (cf. the chapter on global warming).[961]

Consequently renewable energy actually has to drop somewhat in price before it will be competitive, even including social costs. Nevertheless, it is estimated that the price of renewable energy will fall faster than the price for conventional energy. It should however also be added that there is still quite a bit of uncertainty about the predictions of such prices, not the least because early predictions in hindsight have seemed rather optimistic – in 1991 the Union of Concerned Scientists predicted that solar power today would drop below 10 cents per kWh, but unfortunately it has still only dropped to about 50 cents per kWh.[962]

Thus, it is unclear whether it is necessary to support renewable energy with subsidies and tax exemptions. In Denmark this subsidy is as much as 5 cents per kWh for wind energy,[963] and in the US, subsidy for wind power is estimated at about 1.5 cents per kWh.[964] It would still be much more effective to tax energy such that its actual price would adequately reflect the social costs in production and emissions.

The underlying argument is often that we should support renewable energy because the market will discover only too late that we are running out of fossil fuels. But as we have seen above there is no risk of running out of fossil fuels anytime soon, even if some sources might be getting more expensive. Consequently, the assumption should still be that the market will invest the optimal amount of renewable energy if taxes reflect social costs.[965] However, in the chapter on global warming, we will look at whether society might prefer to invest more heavily in *research* into making renewable energy cheaper more quickly.

Nevertheless, the most important point in this section on energy is to stress not only that there are ample reserves of fossil fuels but also that the potentially unlimited renewable energy resources definitely are within economic reach.

Solar energy

By far the largest part of the energy on Earth comes from the sun. Only a small part comes from radioactive processes within the Earth itself. The sun gives off so much energy that it is equivalent to a 180-watt bulb perpetually lighting up every single square meter on Earth. Of course energy is not distributed equally – the tropics receive more than 250 watts whereas the polar regions get only about 100 watts.[966]

The solar energy influx is equivalent to about 7,000 times our present global energy consumption.[967] The scale of these relationships is depicted in Figure 73, where it is also clearly illustrated that the yearly solar energy by far exceeds any other energy resource. Or put in a different way: even with our relatively ineffective solar cells, a square area in the tropics 469 km (291 miles) on each side – 0.15 percent of Earth's land mass – could supply all our current energy requirements.[968] In principle this area could be placed in the Sahara Desert (of which it would take up 2.6 percent) or at sea.[969] In reality, of course, one would not build a single, central power plant, but the example underscores partly how little space really is necessary to cover our energy needs, partly that the area can be placed somewhere of little or no biological or commercial value.

The cheapest photovoltaic cells have become three times as effective since 1978, and prices have dropped by a factor of 50 since the early 1970s.[970] Solar cells are not quite competitive yet, but it is predicted that the price will drop further and it is expected that by 2030 it will drop to 5.1 cents per kWh. Particularly in areas that are far from cities and established grids, solar cells are already now commercially viable.

The remote Indonesian village of Sukatani was changed literally overnight when solar cells were installed in 1989. The equatorial nights, which last 12 hours all year round, previously left little to do. But today, children can do their homework after supper, the village sports a new motorized well pump providing a steady supply of water for better sanitation, and now some of the local *warung* (shops) are open after sunset and television sets provide entertainment and a window on the wider world.[971]

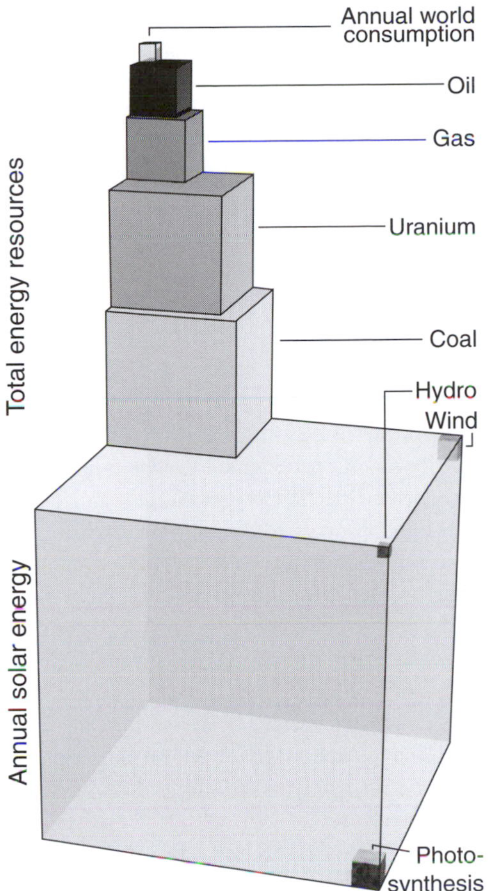

Figure 73 Energy contents in the *annual* solar radiation (2,895,000EJ), compared to the *total* resources of non-renewables (oil 8,690EJ; gas 17,280EJ; uranium 114,000EJ and coal 185,330EJ), and the global, annual energy consumption (400EJ). The potential of the other big renewables are indicated; hydro power can maximally provide 90EJ and wind power 630EJ. For comparison, plant photosynthesis takes up about 1260EJ. All resources and potentials are best guesses and only to be taken as order of magnitude.[972] Source: Craig *et al.* 1996:159, 163, 181, 193, Cunningham and Saigo 1997:505.

Solar energy can also be exploited directly through heating and indirectly by growing plants, later to be burnt (biomass). In Denmark it is estimated that direct solar energy can provide about 10–12 percent of our energy.[973] In the US also, biomass is predicted to have substantial growth. The trouble is, the green plants only poorly exploit sunlight, as is evident from Figure 73. It is unlikely that biomass will be able to provide a major part of global energy consumption – the total agricultural biomass production from stalks and straw, making up half the world's harvests in mass, only constitutes about 65 EJ or about 16 percent of the current consumption.[974] Green plants exploit on average 1–3 percent of solar energy, compared to solar cells' 15–20 percent energy efficiency.[975] Thus, solar cells only use one-thirtieth of the area required by plants – and they need not use good agricultural soil.[976] At the same time biomass gives rise to a slew of other pollution problems, e.g. suspended particles, sulfur, nickel, cadmium and lead.[977] Although biomass today still is not competitive it is cheaper than solar cells.[978]

For many developing countries biomass would also have to compete with food production for access to agricultural land. For some places in the world, however, growing biomass may turn out to be sensible, since production can take place on poor soils, help prevent erosion, and even help recreate more productive soil.[979]

The US Energy Information Agency estimates that solar energy could cover the entire American energy requirements more than 3.5 times over.[980] But for this to become reality a lot of ingenuity is required.

Japan has started integrating solar cells in building materials, letting them become part of roofs and walls.[981] Others have produced watertight thin-film ceramic solar cells to replace typical roofing materials. In Wales an experimental center open to visitors has chosen solar cells not only to supply the building with electricity, but also because it can save costs for traditional roofing.[982]

Wind energy

Wind energy has been exploited through millennia. Long before the Current Era, ancient civilizations in China, India and Persia used wind to pump up water and to mill grain.[983] Already in early medieval times windmills were a known technology throughout Europe, and the windmill remained the primary energy source till the arrival of the steam engine. In countries such as Denmark that did not have their own coal supply, the windmill continued to have a central position. In 1916 alone Denmark built more than 1,300 new windmills.

The oil crisis spurred a new research interest in windmills and since then fantastic results and progress have been achieved. Since 1975 prices have dropped by a whopping 94 percent, and productivity has increased by 5 percent every year since 1980.[984] Globally it is estimated that windmills *can* cover upwards of half of all energy consumption, but this would require in the region of 100 million windmills.[985] Being the world leader in wind power, windmills in Denmark still produced only about 9 percent of all Danish electricity in 1998.[986] In the US, windmills produced just 0.1 percent of the total electricity production in 1998.[987]

But problems will arise if a significant part of a nation's electricity requirements are to be met by wind power. Close to inhabited areas windmill noise can be a nuisance. Moreover, to be effective, windmills need to be placed in open environments, and here they easily mar the scenery. The only long-term solution is placing windmills far out to sea. Not only will there be few if any esthetic problems but windmills are typically 50 percent more effective here.[988]

Critics of windmills often point out that they are still not profitable, that they require much energy to produce, and that they kill birds.[989] As we saw above, windmills are still not fully competitive, although they are probably no more than 30–50 percent more expensive, and even less when including the social and environmental costs of continued use of fossil fuels. In the longer run, they will undoubtedly be competitive or even cheaper.

It is also objected that windmills themselves

demand quite a bit of energy to be produced: the steel has to be mined, smelted and rolled, and the windmill itself has to be transported and in the end disposed of. However, going over the extended energy account, it turns out that a modern windmill can produce the energy used for its own production within just three months.[990]

It is true that windmills kill birds, although the problem will be much smaller at sea. In Denmark it is estimated that about 30,000 birds die in collisions with windmills each year.[991] In the US, the number is about 70,000.[992] While this may seem a large number, it is fairly trivial compared to the loss of birds elsewhere.[993] In Danish traffic alone it is estimated that far more than 1 million birds die each year, and in Holland about 2–8 million.[994] In the US, cars are estimated to kill about 57 million birds every year, and more than 97.5 million birds die colliding with plate glass.[995] In Britain, it is estimated that domestic cats annually kill some 200 million mammals, 55 million birds and 10 million reptiles and amphibians.[996]

Storage and mobile consumption

Both solar power and wind energy have a timing problem: the sun does not necessarily shine and the wind does not necessarily blow when humans need energy the most. Thus it is necessary to be able to store energy.

If the power grid is hooked to dams, these can be used for storage. Essentially, we use wind power when the wind blows, and store water power by letting water accumulate behind the dams. When there's no wind, water power can produce the necessary electricity.

However, this implies that both wind power and water power require a sizeable excess capacity, since both need to be able to meet peak demand. The solution also depends on relatively easy access to large amounts of hydroelectric power.

Generally speaking it is therefore necessary to secure a larger diversification of production. Biomass and geothermal energy can be used at all times. Moreover energy can be stored in hydrogen by catalyzing water.[997] The hydrogen can later be used in electricity production or as a general substitute for petrol in cars.[998] Costs here are still about twice those of ordinary gas, but hydrogen would be an exceedingly environmentally friendly fuel, since its combustion only leaves behind water.

Conclusion

The evidence clearly shows that we are *not* headed for a major energy crisis. There is plenty of energy.

We have seen that although we use more and more fossil energy we have found even more. Our reserves – even measured in years of consumption – of oil, coal and gas have increased. Today we have oil for at least 40 years at present consumption, at least 60 years' worth of gas, and 230 years' worth of coal.

At $40 a barrel (less than one-third above the current world price), shale oil can supply oil for the next 250 years at current consumption. And all in all there is oil enough to cover our total energy consumption for the next 5,000 years. There is uranium for the next 14,000 years. Our current energy costs make up less than 2 percent of the global GDP, so even if we were to see large price increases it would still not have significant welfare impact – in all likelihood the budget share for energy would still be falling.

Moreover there are many options using renewable energy sources. Today, they make up a vanishingly small part of the global energy production, but this can and probably will change. The cost of both solar energy and wind energy has dropped by 94–98 percent over the last 20 years such that they have come much closer to being strictly profitable. Renewable energy resources are almost incomprehensibly large. The sun leaves us with about 7,000 times our own energy consumption – for example, covering just 2.6 percent of the Sahara Desert with solar cells could supply our entire global energy consumption. It is estimated that wind energy realistically could cover upwards of half of our total energy consumption.

Notice that all of these facts do not contest that fossil fuels which today supply most of our energy are non-renewable – if technology remained constant and we kept on using just fossil fuels, we would some day run out of energy. But the point is that technology does not remain constant and fossil fuels are not our only or main long-term energy source. First, the historical evidence shows that we have become constantly better able to find, extract and utilize fossil fuels, outpacing even our increased consumption. Second, we know that the available solar energy far exceeds our energy needs and it will probably be available at competitive prices within 50 years.

Consequently, it is surprising that over and over again we hear the stories that *now* we will run out of energy. The data show us that this is not plausible. As the US Energy Information Agency wrote in the *International Energy Outlook 1999*: "bleak pictures painted of the world's remaining oil resource potential are based on current estimates of proven reserves and their decline in a [typical, theoretical] manner. When undiscovered oil, efficiency improvements, and the exploitation of unconventional crude oil resources are taken into account, it is difficult not to be optimistic about the long-term prospects for oil as a viable energy source well into the future."[999]

In the longer run, it is likely that we will change our energy needs from fossil fuels towards other and cheaper energy sources – maybe renewables, maybe fusion, maybe some as-of-now unimagined technology. Thus, just as the stone age did not end for lack of stone, the oil age will eventually end but not for lack of oil. Rather, it will end because of the eventual availability of superior alternatives.

PART III

12 Non-energy resources

The concern about running out of resources applies not only to energy but also to the vast number of other non-renewable resources that we use today. And the arguments are eerily similar to the arguments in the chapter on energy.

Actually, we have always worried about running out of resources. In antiquity grave concerns were voiced about running out of copper and tin. And the best-seller *Limits to Growth* from 1972 picked up on the old worry, claiming that we would run out of most resources. Gold would run out in 1981, silver and mercury in 1985, and zinc in 1990.[1000] But, of course, this hasn't happened yet.

The pessimists bet on resources running out – and lost

Although economists have long acknowledged that the fear of running out of resources is erroneous, it had an almost magical grip on intellectuals in the 1970s and 1980s. Even today most discussions seem to be played out against a backdrop of arguments pointing back to the logic of *Limits to Growth.*

Frustrated with the incessant claims that the Earth would run out of oil, food and raw materials, the economist Julian Simon in 1980 challenged the established beliefs with a bet. He offered to bet $10,000 that any given raw material – to be picked by his opponents – would have dropped in price at least one year later. The environmentalists Ehrlich, Harte and Holdren, all of Stanford University, accepted the challenge, stating that "the lure of easy money can be irresistible."[1002] The environmentalists staked their bets on chromium, copper, nickel, tin and tungsten, and they picked a time frame of ten years. The bet was to be determined ten years later, assessing whether the real (inflation-adjusted) prices had gone up or down. In September 1990 not only had the total basket of raw materials but also each individual raw material dropped in price. Chromium had dropped 5 percent, tin a whopping 74 percent. The doomsayers had lost.

Truth is they *could not* have won. Ehrlich and Co. would have lost no matter whether they had staked their money on petroleum, foodstuffs, sugar, coffee, cotton, wool, minerals or phosphates. They had all become cheaper.[1003]

Falling prices

Prices of the vast majority of industrial products have been dropping over the past 150 years. Figure 74 shows how the prices of industrial items have fallen by almost 80 percent since 1845. Equally, the World Bank has made an index for the world's 24 top-selling non-energy products (such as aluminum, bananas and wool). Over the past century prices have been reduced to a third.[1004] The same picture repeats itself for metals. The IMF index in Figure 75 shows how prices since 1957 have dropped approximately 50 percent.

Altogether raw materials make up at most 1.1 percent of the global GDP.[1005] Moreover, a rather limited number of raw materials constitute the vast majority of this expense. Table 2 shows the 24 commercially most important raw materials, together accounting for more

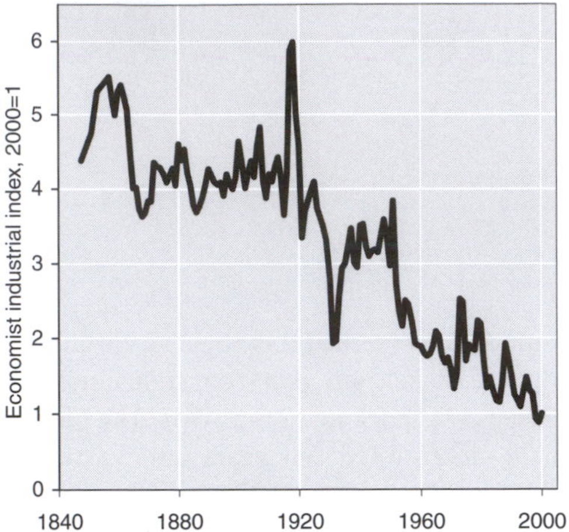

Figure 74 *The Economist*'s industrial price index, 1845–2000, inflation adjusted, with 1845–50=100. The index covers prices of industrial items such as cotton, timber, hides, rubber, aluminum and copper.[1006] Source: Anon. 1999h:147, *Economist*, all issues in 2000, CPI 2001.

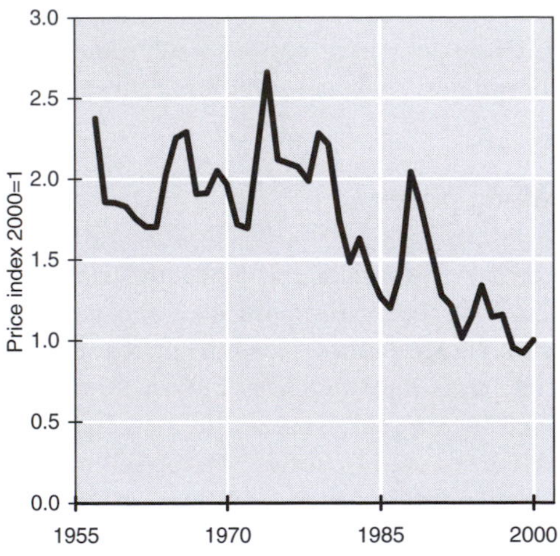

Figure 75 Price index in US$ for metals, 1957–2000, with 2000=1. Source: IMF 2001a, CPI 2001.

than 95 percent of the total, global turnover of raw materials.[1007] The cost of the remaining approximately 70 raw materials is less than 0.05 percent of our income. So, even if the price of some of these raw materials should rise – even dramatically – the consequences for our economic welfare would be negligible.

Cement

Each year we spend $111 billion on cement. Thus, the cost of cement constitutes 34 percent of our total expenditure on raw materials, making it the largest single entry in our raw material budget – not because cement is expensive, but because we use such an overwhelming amount of it.[1008]

Cement is a chemical binder made mainly from limestone, and when mixed with sand or gravel it produces mortar or concrete. Both the Greeks and the Romans knew how to make cement, and the Romans used it to build the Pantheon and the Coliseum. The knowledge of making cement was forgotten during the Middle Ages and only rediscovered in 1756. With the development of a standardized Portland cement type in 1824, cement became the basis of modern construction and is today by far the most used construction material in the world. In fact, twice as much concrete is used as all the other structural materials combined.[1009]

Although we use more than 1.5 billion tons of cement a year, "the materials to make cement are available in many parts of the world in virtually unlimited quantities," with reserves for far more than 1,000 years at present levels of consumption.[1010] However cement production also contributes about 3 percent of the global carbon dioxide emissions, as we will see in the section on global warming.[1011]

Aluminum

Aluminum constitutes 12 percent of our raw material expenditure and it has become more and more important in our economy, because it is light, is easy to handle, has a high conductivity, and is highly resistant to weathering.[1012] Typically this light material is used for cans,

... materials, making up more than 95 percent of the global raw material turnover. Source: USGS 1998a. Note: Some of the raw material categories are somewhat overlapping. Prices and quantities are very volatile. It has been attempted to attain the information as of 1997, but this has not always been possible. Moreover, the categories displayed here involve different degrees of processing. Consequently, the table merely shows the general tendencies for raw materials and gives a maximum limit for our resource expenditure. Here, the value of cement, aluminum, iron, copper, gold, nitrogen, and zinc constitute almost 80 percent of the global resource production. Mt – million tons; Gt – gigatons.

Share of global GDP 1997 (percent)	Cumulative share of global GDP 1997 (percent)	Raw material	Total price in billion US$ 1997	Cumulative price in billion US$ 1997	Amount produced	Price per kilo	Reserve	Reserve base	Years of consumption at stable 1997 consumption[1001]
0.376	1.10	Cement	111.8	327.4	1.5 Gt	¢7.45	Sufficient		
0.118	0.73	Aluminum	35.1	215.7	21.2 Mt	$1.65	23 Gt (Bauxite)		243
0.105	0.61	Iron ore	31.3	180.6	1.03 Gt	¢3.04	240 Gt		228
0.089	0.50	Copper	26.4	149.3	11.3 Mt	$2.34	320 Mt	630 Mt	56
0.089	0.41	Gold	26.4	122.9	2300 t	$11,464	45,000 t	72,000 t	31
0.062	0.32	Nitrogen	18.4	96.5	96 Mt	¢19.20	Sufficient		
0.045	0.26	Zinc	13.4	78.1	7.8 Mt	$1.72	190 Mt	430 Mt	55
0.030	0.22	Gemstones	9.0	64.7	350,000 t				
0.025	0.19	Nickel	7.5	55.7	1.08 Mt	$6.93	40 Mt	140 Mt	130
0.024	0.16	Crushed stone	7.2	48.2	1.33 Gt	¢0.54	Sufficient		
0.015	0.14	Mica, sheet	4.4	41.0	3.7 Mt	$1.20	Large		
0.014	0.12	Sand and gravel for construction, US only	4.3	36.6	961 Mt	¢0.45	Large		
0.011	0.11	Phosphate rock	3.2	32.3	136 Mt	¢2.37	11 Gt	33 Gt	243
0.008	0.10	Silver	2.3	29.0	15.300 t	$148.55	280,000 t	420,000 t	28
0.007	0.09	Sand and gravel for industry, US only	2.1	26.8	115 Mt	¢1.81	Large		
0.007	0.08	Sulfur	2.1	24.7	54 Mt	¢3.80	1.4 Gt	3.5 Gt	65
0.005	0.08	Cobalt	1.4	22.6	27.000 t	$50.71	4 Mt	9 Mt	333
0.004	0.07	Tin	1.3	21.3	201,000 t	$6.61	7.7 Mt	12 Mt	60
0.004	0.07	Chromium	1.2	19.9	12 Mt	¢10	3.6 Gt	7.5 Gt	625
0.004	0.06	Asbestos	1.1	18.7	2.26 Mt	¢50.60	200 Mt	250 Mt	108
0.004	0.06	Lime	1.1	17.6	124 Mt	¢0.90	Sufficient		
0.004	0.06	Molybdenum	1.1	16.5	131,000 t	$8.50	5.5 Mt	12 Mt	92
0.004	0.05	Boron	1.1	15.4	3.25 Mt	¢34	170 Mt	470 Mt	145
0.003	0.05	Talc and pyrophyllite	1.0	14.3	8.27 Mt	¢12.2	30 Mt		36

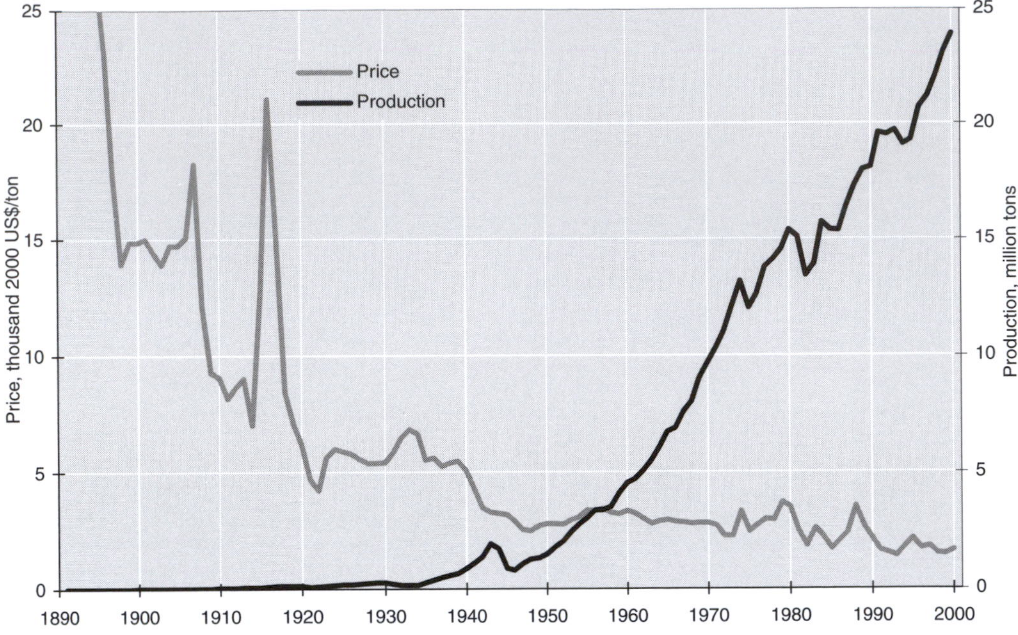

Figure 76 Aluminum, price in 2000 US$, 1895–2000, and production, 1891–2000. Source: Simon *et al.* 1994, USGS 2001a, CPI 2001.

and in cars and airplanes. Additionally, aluminum is used in almost all high power-transmission lines because it is both lighter and stronger than copper.

Aluminum was first discovered in 1827, and since it was exceedingly difficult to extract, it was very expensive. Napoleon III had aluminum forks and spoons produced for himself and honored guests while lesser visitors had to make do with gold utensils.[1013] Aluminum production and price is displayed in Figure 76. Despite the fact that production and consumption have increased more than 3,000-fold since the turn of the century, the price has dropped to a mere one-ninth.

Aluminum is the second most abundant metallic element after silicon – it makes up 8.2 percent of the Earth's crust. It is estimated that with the current identified reserves there is sufficient aluminum for 276 years of consumption at the present level.[1014] But as we have seen with oil, gas and coal, this does not necessarily mean that the number of years left will reduce as time passes, even if we use more and more, because we get better at exploiting resources and finding more of them.

In Figure 77 we see that for the four most frequently used metals there is no sign of falling years of consumption; indeed, there is a slight upward trend. And this is despite the fact that we use ever more of the four raw materials. Aluminum consumption is today more than 16 times higher than in 1950, and yet the remaining years of consumption have increased from 171 years to 276 years.

Iron

We spend annually $31 billion on iron ore or about 11 percent of our raw material budget.

Iron has been used throughout history, because it is surprisingly common and easily accessible, because it is relatively easy to smelt

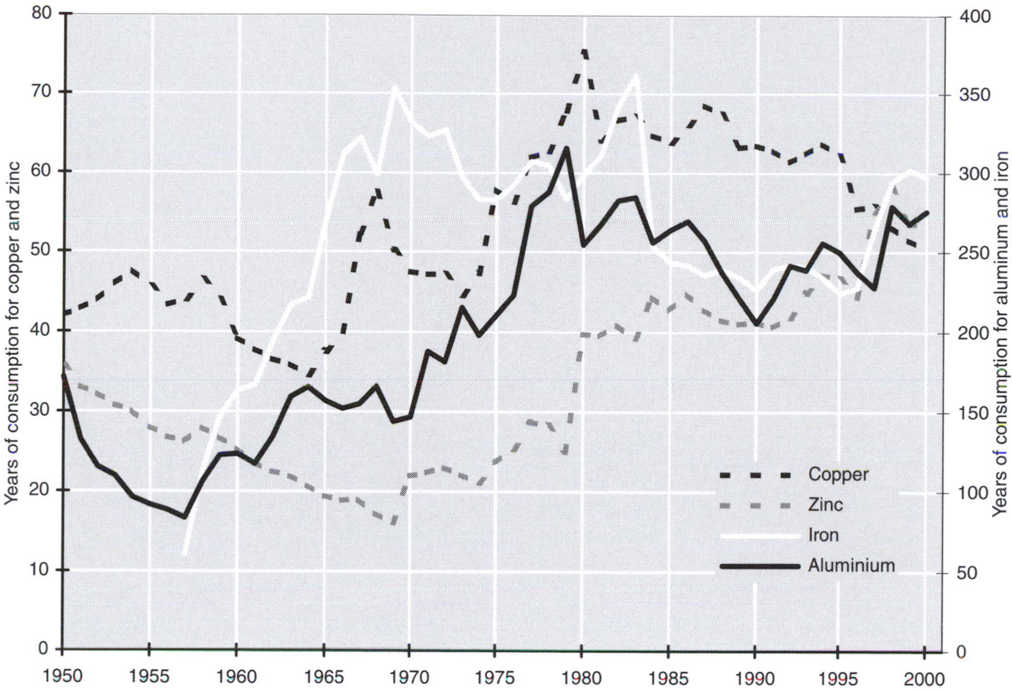

Figure 77 Years of consumption of the four most used metals, 1950–2000 (iron 1957–2000). Source: Simon *et al.* 1994, USGS 2001a.

and shape, and because it is so exceptionally strong and durable.[1015] The first iron objects were hammered pieces of iron meteorites that did not need smelting. But the Iron Age had already begun around 1200 BCE when knowledge of iron smelting and shaping spread across the Middle East.[1016]

Today, more than two-thirds of all iron is used to make steel, an alloy of iron and other metals such as aluminum, chromium or nickel.[1017] Ever since the Industrial Revolution iron and steel have constituted the backbone of our industry and accounted for more than 95 percent of our total metal consumption by weight.[1018] Figure 78 shows how consumption across the twentieth century has increased significantly without this being reflected in any price increase. The price of iron was strongly affected by the oil crisis since its production is very energy consuming, but today the price is at its lowest in the twentieth century.

Iron is the third most abundant metal on Earth – 5.6 percent of the Earth's crust consists of it.[1019] Nevertheless fear has often been expressed that we might soon run out of iron. Andrew Carnegie, a pioneer of the American steel industry, worried about the impending depletion of the richer ores, consisting mainly of iron. In his address to the Conference of Governors at the White House in 1908 he said:

> I have for many years been impressed with the steady depletion of our iron ore supply. It is staggering to learn that our once-supposed ample supply of rich ores can hardly outlast the generation now appearing, leaving only the leaner ores for the later years of the century. It is my judgment, as a practical man accustomed to dealing with those material factors on which our national prosperity is based, that it is time to take thought for the morrow.[1020]

But again, technology has expanded such that today we can exploit ore with just 30–40 percent iron. It is estimated that the currently

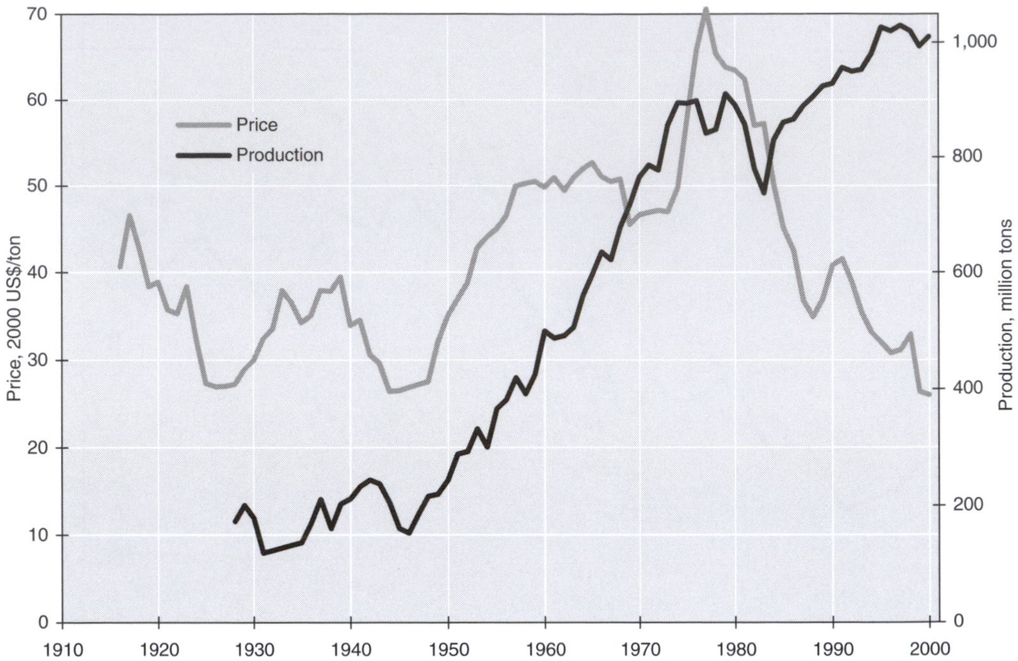

Figure 78 Iron, price in 2000 US$, 1916–2000, and production, 1928–2000. Source: Simon *et al.* 1994, USGS 2001a, CPI 2001.

identified reserves leave us with 297 years of consumption at present levels. As we can see in Figure 77, there were actually *many more* years of consumption left in 2000 than in 1957, despite the fact that annual production has more than doubled. Actually, since the US Geological Service in 1957 estimated the world resource at 25 billion tons, we have used 35 billion tons, and now the reserve base estimate is at some 300 billion tons.

Copper

Copper costs more than $26 billion yearly and makes up 8 percent of our raw material consumption. Copper has been used since prehistoric times both because of its malleability and because copper and its main alloys, bronze and brass, are attractive, durable and relatively corrosion resistant.

In the nineteenth century the demand for copper exploded as it was used to carry electricity, not only because it has a high electrical conductivity but also because it provides transmission wires which are flexible and easily soldered.[1021] As seen in Figure 79, yearly world production at the beginning of the nineteenth century was about 15,000 tons; today we produce more than twice that amount *each day*. Nevertheless, the price has dropped to about a quarter.

Copper is not anywhere as abundant as aluminum and iron. It only makes up 0.0058 percent of the Earth's crust.[1022] Although this is enough for 83 million years of consumption such a figure is rather fictitious, since we will never be able to extract all the copper in the Earth's crust.[1023] With our present reserves we have enough copper left for 50 years at present rates of consumption. This, however, is still *more* than in 1950 when we had copper left for just 42 years, despite the fact that our consumption has quintupled. In 1950, the

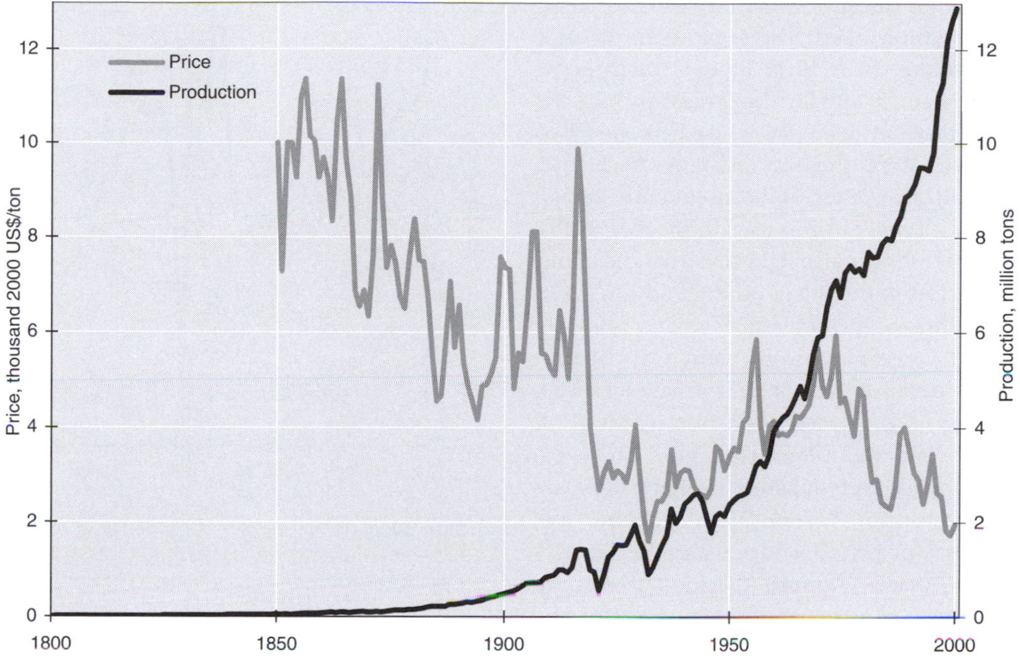

Figure 79 Copper, price in 2000 US$, 1850–2000, and production , 1800–2000. Source: Simon *et al.* 1994, USGS 2001a, CPI 2001.

World reserve base was estimated at 100 million tons, and yet we have since then produced about 338 million tons. Now the reserve base is estimated at 650 million tons. Once again, this shows that we discover and increase our ability to exploit faster than our consumption increases – since 1946, copper has actually been found faster than it has been consumed.[1024]

Moreover, the Earth's crust does not even constitute the most important part of the copper resources. In many places in the deep oceans the seafloor is scattered with small nodules about 5–10 cm in diameter containing manganese, iron, nickel, copper, cobalt and zinc. It is estimated that the total resources in recoverable nodules are in excess of 1 billion tons of copper, or more than our total on-land resources.[1025] Consequently, there is sufficient copper for at least a century or more.

Gold and silver

Gold and silver are the most well known of the precious metals, and they have been used since antiquity. Gold is soft and malleable, but also so durable and corrosion resistant that 85 percent of the gold ever extracted is probably still in use.[1026] The total amount of gold in the world that has been quarried till today is estimated at about 100,000 tons – a cube just 17 meters (56 feet) on each side.[1027] About 35,000 tons comprises official stocks held by central banks, while the rest is privately held as bullion, coins and jewelry.[1028]

Because gold is both rare and durable it early on became a medium of exchange, and eventually it became an accepted measure of value around the world. Today, however, about half of the world's gold production is used in electronic products, aerospace applications, special alloys and dentistry.[1029]

Through the ages, silver has also been used as a medium of exchange, particularly after the Romans made it the basis of their monetary system.[1030] By far the largest part of the silver production today is used for just two purposes. It has the least resistance to electricity of all the metals, and consequently 25 percent of all new silver is used in the electronics industry.[1031] It is also light sensitive and about 50 percent of our silver production is used in the photographic industry.[1032]

Gold and silver are in many ways special metals because their price is driven by speculation, and this price was driven up after the dollar was delinked from gold in 1967. Nevertheless, as is apparent in Figure 80, years of consumption have not been declining over the post-war period, and actually the 32 years left in 2000 are among the highest, despite production that has more than doubled over the past 50 years. Likewise, years of consumption for silver is about 27 years, but it is expected that demand for silver will decrease significantly, as digital photography takes over a large part of the photographic market.[1033]

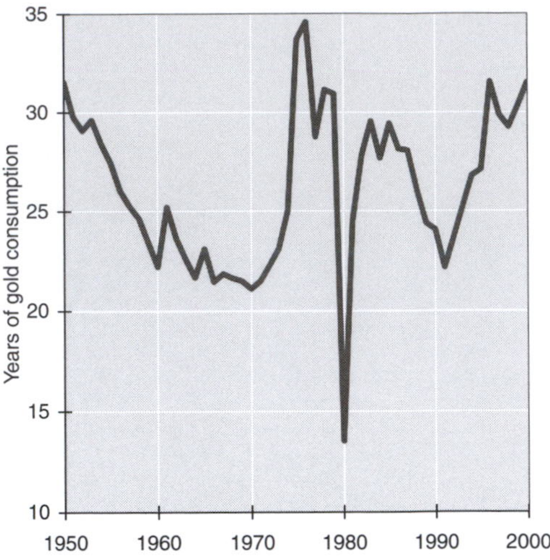

Figure 80 Remaining years of consumption of gold, 1950–2000. Source: Simon *et al.* 1994, USGS 2001a.

Nitrogen, phosphorus and potassium

Food production is crucially dependent on three resources – soil, water and fertilizer. The essential fertilizers are nitrogen, phosphorus and potassium, and until the last century these were mainly provided by manure.

Today, about 6 percent of our raw material expenditure is used on nitrogen. Nitrogen is absolutely essential for food production, since it is an integral part of the chlorophyll molecule, making plants green and enabling them to transform sunlight to starch through photosynthesis. But today nitrogen is almost exclusively synthesized from air, and since air contains about 78 percent nitrogen there are no limits to consumption.[1034]

Phosphorus is a constituent of DNA and consequently indispensable for all forms of life. Often, the amount of phosphorus available sets the limit of biological activity in natural systems. Phosphorus makes up about 1 percent of our raw material expenditure. The phosphorus reserves stand at about 90 years at current consumption, but because phosphate rocks look like ordinary shales and limestones, even to experts, we can anticipate discoveries of new, large deposits in the future. Recently, the US Geological Survey announced the finding of phosphatic crusts and nodules in the offshore continental shelf of Florida containing very large deposits, single-handedly doubling the phosphorus reserves to about 180 years. Consequently, it is not expected that the availability of phosphorus will become a limitation to food production.[1035]

Potassium is the eighth most abundant element in the Earth's crust, and there is no cause for concern for this important fertilizer. We spend about 0.1 percent of our raw material budget on potassium. It is estimated that there are at least 357 years of consumption left at current levels, and total accessible reserves indicate sufficient potassium for more than 700 years.[1036]

As is evident in Figure 81, prices of fertilizer

have dropped about 50 percent in the post-war period. This is a further indication that fertilizer is getting not more scarce but rather more abundant.

Zinc

Zinc makes up 5 percent of our raw material consumption, and it is mainly used to galvanize steel and iron to prevent rust. Zinc, like copper, is relatively rare – it constitutes only 0.0082 percent of the Earth's crust,[1037] which theoretically is equivalent to 169 million years of consumption, although we could never mine all of it.[1038] Nevertheless, we have continuously found much more zinc than has been used, and the number of years of consumption have grown since 1950 from 36 to 54 years (Figure 77).

As with copper, production has increased dramatically, quadrupling since 1950, as seen in Figure 82. In 1950, the remaining world reserve was estimated at 70 million tons, but since then we have used more than three times that, and now the reserve base is estimated at 430 million tons. All the while, the price has not increased but rather has experienced a slight decrease.

Other resources

It should be abundantly clear that we are far from exhausting our raw material resources. After the 3 percent of our raw material budget we spend on precious gems, nickel and crushed stone are the only raw materials costing more than 1 percent of the raw material budget, and we cannot run out of stone. Nickel is mainly used in alloys to make stainless steel, and it is estimated that the identified reserves can last approximately 50 years at current levels of consumption. But it is also estimated that deep-sea nodules contain enough nickel for at least another thousand years.[1039]

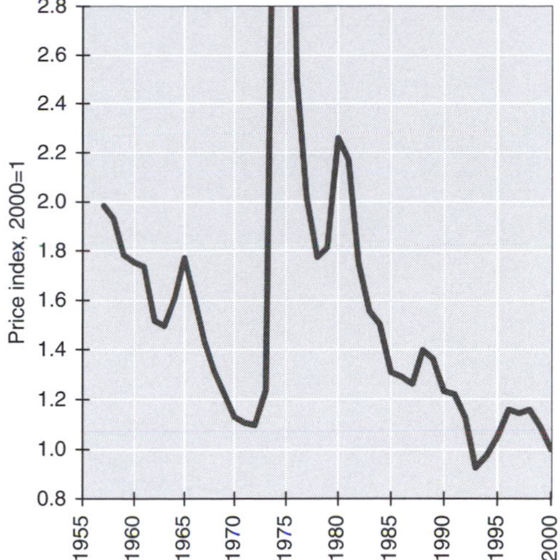

Figure 81 Price index of fertilizer, 1957–2000; 2000=1. The years 1974–5 were 4.3, and 5.0. Source: IMF 2001a, CPI 2001.

Reviewing the 47 elements known to have advanced materials applications, studies from the late 1980s showed that only 11 seemed to have potentially insufficient reserves. These 11 elements are listed in Table 3. It turns out that for all but three the reserves have got *bigger* and not smaller since 1988. The total cost of these last three elements is about three-millionths of our global GDP. Tantalum is used in the aerospace industry, for high-tech alloys and in electronics. We will undoubtedly have to substitute parts of our tantalum use, and replacements will be either more expensive or less effective, but all in all this will constitute a very small cost.[1040] The drop in mercury reserves is primarily caused by the fact that we use it still less – since 1971 global consumption has dropped to less than one-third – and consequently there is no commercial interest in finding new resources. It is estimated that with the present identified reserves there is mercury for more than 100 years.[1041] Cadmium constitutes an even smaller problem. Cadmium is primarily used for rechargeable batteries, and technologically it can be

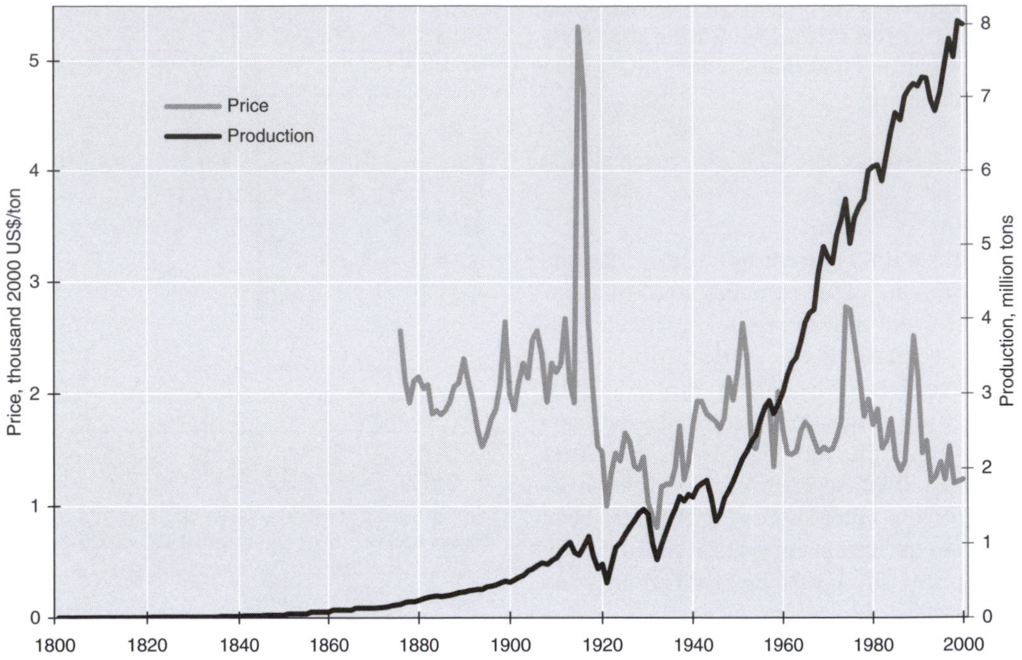

Figure 82 Zinc, price in 2000 US$, 1876–2000, and production , 1800–2000. Source: Simon *et al.* 1994, USGS 2001a, CPI 2001.

replaced by many other – and often better – alternatives. However, the US Geological Survey estimates that "existing resources of cadmium should be adequate to meet demand far into the 21st century."[1042]

And the remaining elements have been getting more abundant, not less. This is why the classical college textbook on natural resource economics, Pearce and Turner, can conclude that the overwhelming evidence suggests that "physical scarcity is unlikely to be a significant problem for most of the materials currently in use."[1043]

Why do we have ever more resources?

How come we do not run out of resources? The explanations look a lot like the explanations for why we do not run out of oil, gas and coal.

First, "known reserves" is still not a fixed measure. We can and do continuously find new deposits. This has been evident in Figure 77, where the most important raw materials have *increased* their number of years of consumption, despite a 2–15 times increase in annual consumption. When we do not find even more deposits even faster it is because searching costs money, and consequently they are discovered only within a reasonable time frame before their use.

Second, we get better at extracting resources and using them more effectively. Today, your car contains only half as much metal as a car produced in 1970. Super-thin optical fibers carry the same number of telephone calls as 625 copper wires did just 20 years ago – and with better quality.[1044] Newspapers can be printed on ever thinner paper because paper production has been much improved. Bridges contain much less steel, both because steel has become stronger and because we can calculate specifications more accurately. Many tools have become

Table 3 The 11 elements with potentially insufficient measured reserves, of 47 studied. Source: Fraser *et al.* 1988:9; cf. Pearce and Turner 1990:295; USGS 1998a.

Share of global GDP 1997 (percent)		Reserve 1997 1988=100
0.000084	Tantalum	51
0.000088	Mercury	94
0.000145	Cadmium	97
0.000065	Thallium	100
0.088656	Gold	113
0.007642	Silver	117
0.000090	Bismuth	122
0.000239	Indium	153
0.004470	Tin	257
0.000067	Arsenic	860
0.000375	Barium	1012

more durable and consequently we need to replace them less often.[1045] Moreover, information technology has changed our consumption – relatively we buy fewer things and more bits. Programs worth several hundred dollars will fit on a CD-ROM worth only 2 cents in plastic.[1046] Despite Americans becoming 30 percent more wealthy over the last 20 years their consumption of wood, metal and plastic has been declining.[1047]

Third, we can recycle metals and thereby further increase the reserves. It is perhaps important to point out that metals, in contrast to energy, do not perish but only change form and location with use. At present about one-third of the global steel production is recycled, while the figures are 25–30 percent for aluminum, 25 percent for nickel, 45–50 percent for silver and lead, 15–20 percent for tin, 35–40 percent for copper and 20–25 percent for zinc.[1048] There are, however, some barriers to recycling. Part of the metals is lost to corrosion, and some products are constructed such that it is only partially possible or even impossible to recycle the constituents. Actually, increased efficiency and recycling imply that it is *theoretically* possible never to run out of a limited resource, even with continued use. If we have a raw material with 100 years of consumption left with a 1 percent yearly increase in demand, and a 2 percent increase in recycling and/or efficiency, it is possible – without ever finding more resources – never to run out. This is simply because recycling or efficiency improvement – our ingenuity – compensates for both consumption and increases in consumption.[1049]

Fourth, we can often substitute one material for another. When Zaire, because of internal political problems, limited the supply of cobalt by 30 percent in 1978, this led to strong price hikes. But newly developed ceramic magnets soon replaced cobalt alloy magnets, and similarly cobalt-based paints were substituted with manganese-based paints, and cobalt prices quickly fell back.[1050] A study of US copper usage showed this substitution mechanism at work. Assuming that cheap copper would run out in 2070, leaving only very expensive rock mining, the total cost would nevertheless be fairly small (less than 0.5 percent of income), because most copper uses would be substituted.[1051]

Similarly, information technology has caused a substitution away from a number of traditional raw materials. When today we use much less mercury, it is partly because we increasingly use digital thermometers. As mentioned above, digital photography is likely to cut the consumption of silver by up to 50 percent. Actually, the vast majority of raw materials can be replaced by others, although only at a price (because otherwise they would already have been substituted).

Finally, demand for minerals has not grown exponentially as was feared by the doomsayers, but rather it has increased linearly:[1052] yet another reason not to worry excessively about the future supply of resources.

Conclusion

All indicators seem to suggest that we are not likely to experience any significant scarcity of raw materials in the future. The prices of nearly all resources have been declining over the last century, and despite an astounding increase in production of a large number of important raw materials they today have more years of consumption left than they did previously.

The total economic expense for raw materials is 1.1 percent of global GDP, and 60 percent of our expenses concern raw materials with more than 200 years of consumption left. An analysis of all the important raw materials shows that the reserves of only three minerals have dropped, and this drop is serious for only one element, namely tantalum. The total cost of tantalum is below one-millionth of global GDP, and the element can be substituted.

We have often feared that we will run out of raw materials. But gold, silver, tin and mercury are still all here, and with good reason.

As with the chapter on fossil fuels, these facts do not contest that non-energy resources are non-renewable – if we continued to use resources with no change in technology, we would eventually run out. But the fact that this chapter can conclude that significant scarcities are unlikely is because we continuously find new resources, use them more efficiently, and are able to recycle them and to substitute them.

13 Water

There is a resource which we often take for granted but which increasingly has been touted as a harbinger of future trouble. Water.

Ever more people live on Earth and they use ever more water. Our water consumption has almost quadrupled since 1940.[1054] The obvious argument runs that "this cannot go on." This has caused government agencies to worry that "a threatening water crisis awaits just around the corner."[1055] The UN environmental report *GEO 2000* claims that the water shortage constitutes a "full-scale emergency," where "the world water cycle seems unlikely to be able to cope with the demands that will be made of it in the coming decades. Severe water shortages already hamper development in many parts of the world, and the situation is deteriorating."[1056]

The same basic argument is invoked when WWF states that "freshwater is essential to human health, agriculture, industry, and natural ecosystems, but is now running scarce in many regions of the world."[1057] *Population Reports* states unequivocally that "freshwater is emerging as one of the most critical natural resource issues facing humanity."[1058] Environmental discussions are replete with buzz words like "water crisis" and "time bomb: water shortages," and *Time* magazine summarizes the global water outlook with the title "Wells running dry."[1059] The UN organizations for meteorology and education simply refers to the problem as "a world running out of water."[1060]

The water shortages are also supposed to increase the likelihood of conflicts over the last drops – and scores of articles are written about the coming "water wars."[1061] Worldwatch Institute sums up the worries nicely, claiming that "water scarcity may be to the nineties what the oil price shocks were to the seventies – a source of international conflicts and major shifts in national economies."[1062]

But these headlines are misleading. True, there may be *regional* and *logistic* problems with water. We will need to get better at using it. But basically we have sufficient water.

How much water in the world?

Water is absolutely decisive for human survival, and the Earth is called the Blue Planet precisely because most of it is covered by water: 71 percent of the Earth's surface is covered by water, and the total amount is estimated at the unfathomably large 13.6 billion cubic kilometers.[1063] Of all this water, oceans make up 97.2 percent and the polar ice contains 2.15 percent. Unfortunately sea water is too saline for direct human consumption, and while polar ice contains potable water it is hardly within easy reach. Consequently, humans are primarily dependent on the last 0.65 percent water, of which 0.62 percent is groundwater.

Fresh water in the groundwater often takes centuries or millennia to build up – it has been estimated that it would require 150 years to recharge all of the groundwater in the United States totally to a depth of 750 meters if it were all removed. Thus, thoughtlessly exploiting the groundwater could be compared to mining any other non-renewable natural resource.[1064] But groundwater is continuously replenished by the constant movement of water through oceans, air, soil, rivers, and lakes in the so-called hydrological cycle. The sun makes water from the oceans evaporate, the wind moves parts of the vapor as clouds over land, where the water is released as rain and snow. The precipitated water then either evaporates again, flows back into the sea through rivers and lakes, or finds its way into the groundwater.[1065]

The total amount of precipitation on land is about 113,000 km^3, and taking into account an evaporation of 72,000 km^3 we are left with a net fresh water influx of 41,000 km^3 each year or the equivalent of 30 cm (1 foot) of water across the entire land mass.[1066] Since part of this water falls in rather remote areas, such as the basins of the Amazon, the Congo, and the remote North American and Eurasian rivers, a more reasonable, geographically accessible estimate of water is 32,900 km^3.[1067] Moreover, a large part of this water comes within short periods of time. In Asia, typically 80 percent of the runoff occurs from May to October, and globally the flood runoff is estimated at about three-quarters of the total runoff.[1068] This leaves about 9,000 km^3 to be captured. Dams capture an additional 3,500 km^3 from floods, bringing the total accessible runoff to 12,500 km^3.[1069] This is equivalent to about 5,700 liters of water for every single person on Earth *every single day*. For comparison, the average citizen in the EU uses about 566 liters of water per day.[1070] This is about 10 percent of the global level of available water and some 5 percent of the available EU water.[1071] An American, however, uses about three times as much water, or 1,442 liters every day.[1072]

Looking at global water consumption, as seen in Figure 83, it is important to distinguish between water withdrawal and water use. Water withdrawal is the amount of water physically removed, but this concept is less useful in a discussion of limits on the total amount of water, since much of the withdrawn water is later returned to the water cycle.[1073] In the EU and the US, about 46 percent of the withdrawn water is used merely as cooling water for power generation and is immediately released for further use downstream.[1075] Likewise, most industrial uses return 80–90 percent of the water, and even in irrigation 30–70 percent of the water runs back into lakes and rivers or percolates into aquifers, whence it can be reused.[1076] Thus, a more useful measure of water consumption is the amount of water this consumption causes to be irretrievably lost through evaporation or transpiration from plants. This is called water use.

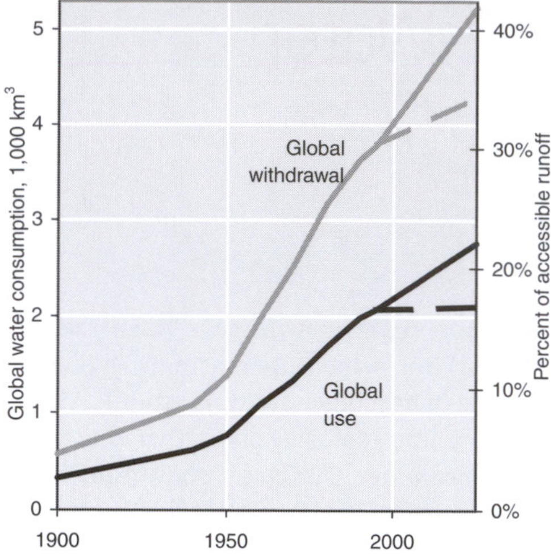

Figure 83 Global, annual water withdrawal and use, in thousand km^3 and percentage of accessible runoff,[1074] 1900–95, and predictions for 2025. Source: Shiklomanov 2000:22 (high prediction), World Water Council 2000:26 (low prediction).

Over the twentieth century, Earth's water use has grown from about 330 km^3 to about 2,100 km^3. As can be seen from Figure 83 there is some uncertainty about the future use and withdrawal (mainly depending on the development of irrigation), but until now most predictions have tended to overestimate the actual water consumption by up to 100 percent.[1077] Nevertheless, total use is still less than 17 percent of the accessible water and even with the high prediction it will require just 22 percent of the readily accessible, annually renewed water in 2025.

At the same time, we have gained access to

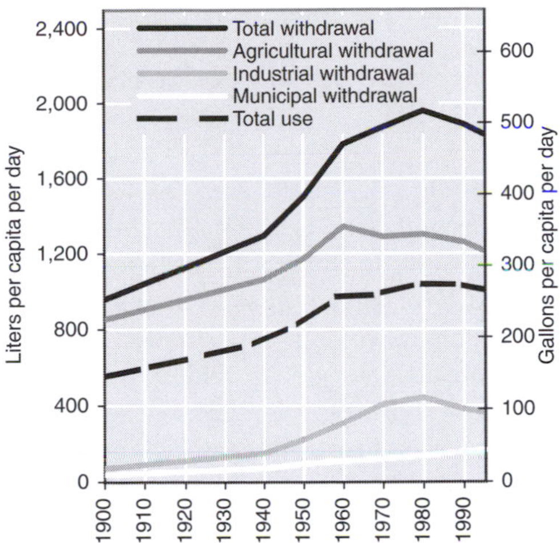

Figure 84 Global withdrawal of water for agriculture, industry and municipal use, and total use, in liters and gallons per capita per day, 1900–95. Source: Shiklomanov 2000:24.

more and more water, as indicated in Figure 84.[1078] Per person we have gone from using about 1,000 liters per day to almost 2,000 liters over the past 100 years. Particularly, this is due to an approximately 50 percent increase in water use in agriculture, allowing irrigated farms to feed us better and to decrease the number of starving people. Agricultural water usage seems, however, to have stabilized below 2,000 liters per capita, mainly owing to higher efficiency and less water consumption in agriculture since 1980. This pattern is also found in the EU and the US, where consumption has increased dramatically over the twentieth century, but is now leveling off.[1079] At the same time, personal consumption (approximated by the municipal withdrawal) has more than quadrupled over the century, reflecting an increase in welfare with more easily accessible water. In developing countries, this is in large part a question of health – avoiding sickness through better access to clean drinking water and sanitation (see Figure 5), whereas in developed countries higher water use is an indication of an increased number of domestic amenities such as dishwashers and better-looking lawns.

So, if the global use is less than 17 percent of the readily accessible and renewable water and the increased use has brought us more food, less starvation, more health and increased wealth, why do we worry?

The three central problems

There are three decisive problems. First, precipitation is by no means equally distributed all over the globe. This means that not all have equal access to water resources and that some countries have much less accessible water than the global average would seem to indicate. The question is whether water shortages are already severe in some places today. Second, there will be more and more people on Earth. Since precipitation levels will remain more or less constant this will mean fewer water resources for each person. The question is whether we will see more severe shortages in the future. Third, many countries receive a large part of their water resources from rivers; 261 river systems, draining just less than half of the planet's land area, are shared by two or more countries,[1080] and at least ten rivers flow through half a dozen or more countries. Most Middle Eastern countries share aquifers.[1081] This means that the water question also has an international perspective and – if cooperation breaks down – an international conflict potential.

Beyond these three problems there are two others issues, which are often articulated in connection with the water shortage problem, but which are really conceptually quite separate. One is the worry about water pollution, particularly of potable water.[1082] While it is of course important to avoid water pollution in part because pollution restricts the presently available amount of freshwater, it is not related to the problem of water shortage *per se*. Consequently, we will look at this problem in the chapter on potable water and pesticides.

Available water, liters per capita per day	2000	2025	2050
Kuwait	30	20	17
United Arab Emirates	174	129	116
Libya	275	136	92
Saudi Arabia	325	166	118
Jordan	381	203	145
Singapore	471	401	403
Yemen	665	304	197
Israel	969	738	644
Oman	1,077	448	268
Tunisia	1,147	834	709
Algeria	1,239	827	664
Burundi	1,496	845	616
Egypt	2,343	1,667	1,382
Rwanda	2,642	1,562	1,197
Kenya	2,725	1,647	1,252
Morocco	2,932	2,129	1,798
South Africa	2,959	1,911	1,497
Somalia	3,206	1,562	1,015
Lebanon	3,996	2,971	2,533
Haiti	3,997	2,497	1,783
Burkina Faso	4,202	2,160	1,430
Zimbabwe	4,408	2,830	2,199
Peru	4,416	3,191	2,680
Malawi	4,656	2,508	1,715
Ethiopia	4,849	2,354	1,508
Iran, Islamic Rep.	4,926	2,935	2,211
Nigeria	5,952	3,216	2,265
Eritrea	6,325	3,704	2,735
Lesotho	6,556	3,731	2,665
Togo	7,026	3,750	2,596
Uganda	8,046	4,017	2,725
Niger	8,235	3,975	2,573
Percent people with chronic scarcity	3.7%	8.6%	17.8%
United Kingdom	3,337	3,270	3,315
India	5,670	4,291	3,724
China	6,108	5,266	5,140
Italy	7,994	8,836	10,862
United States	24,420	20,405	19,521
Botswana	24,859	15,624	12,122
Indonesia	33,540	25,902	22,401
Bangladesh	50,293	35,855	29,576
Australia	50,913	40,077	37,930
Russian Federation	84,235	93,724	107,725
Iceland	1,660,502	1,393,635	1,289,976

Table 4 Countries with chronic water scarcity (below 2,740 liters per capita per day) in 2000, 2025, and 2050, compared to a number of other countries. Source: WRI 1998a.[1053]

The second issue is about the shortage of *access* to water in the Third World, a problem that we have already looked at (pp. 19–21). This problem, while getting smaller, is still a major obstacle for global welfare. In discussing water shortage, reference to the lack of universal access to drinking water and sanitation is often thrown in for good measure,[1083] but of course this issue is entirely separate from the question of shortages. First, the cause is *not* lack of water (since human requirements constitute just 50–100 liters a day which any country but Kuwait can deliver, cf. Table 4)[1084] but rather a lack of investment in infrastructure. Second, the solution lies not in cutting back on existing consumption but actually in increasing future consumption.

Finally, we should just mention global warming (discussed below in Part V, chapter 24) and its connection to water use. Intuitively, we might be tempted to think that a warmer world would mean more evaporation, less water, more problems. But more evaporation also means more precipitation. Essentially, global climate models seem to change *where* water shortages appear (pushing some countries above or below the threshold) but the total changes are small (1–5 percent) and go both ways.[1085]

Not enough water?

Precipitation is not distributed equally. Some countries such as Iceland have almost 2 million liters of water for each inhabitant every day, whereas Kuwait must make do with just 30 liters.[1086] The question, of course, is when does a country not have *enough* water.

It is estimated that a human being needs about 2 liters of water a day, so clearly this is not the restrictive requirement.[1087] The most common approach is to use the so-called *water stress index* proposed by the hydrologist Malin Falkenmark. This index tries to establish an approximate minimum level of water per capita to maintain an adequate quality of life in a moderately developed country in an arid zone. This approach has been used by many organizations including the World Bank, in the standard literature on environmental science, and in the water scarcity discussion in *World Resources*.[1088] With this index, human beings are assessed to need about 100 liters per day for drinking, household needs and personal hygiene, and an additional 500–2,000 liters for agriculture, industry and energy production.[1089] Since water is often most needed in the dry season, the water stress level is then set even higher – if a country has less than 4,660 liters per person available it is expected to experience periodic or regular water stress. Should the accessible runoff drop to less than 2,740 liters the country is said to experience chronic water scarcity. Below 1,370 liters, the country experiences absolute water scarcity, outright shortages and acute scarcity.[1090]

Table 4 shows the 15 countries comprising 3.7 percent of humanity in 2000 suffering chronic water scarcity according to the above definition.[1091] Many of these countries probably come as no surprise. But the question is whether we are facing a serious problem.

How does Kuwait actually get by with just 30 liters per day? The point is, it doesn't. Kuwait, Libya and Saudi Arabia all cover a large part of their water demand by exploiting the largest water resource of all – through desalination of sea water.[1092] Kuwait in fact covers more than half its total use through desalination.[1093] Desalting requires a large amount of energy (through either freezing or evaporating water), but all of these countries also have great energy resources. The price today to desalt sea water is down to 50–80 ¢/m^3 and just 20–35 ¢/m^3 for brackish water, which makes desalted water a more expensive resource than fresh water, but definitely not out of reach.[1094]

This shows two things. First, we can have sufficient water, if we can pay for it. Once again, this underscores that *poverty* and not the environment is the primary limitation for solutions to our problems. Second, desalination puts an upper boundary on the degree of water problems in the world. In principle, we could produce the Earth's entire present water consumption with a single desalination facility in the Sahara, powered by solar cells. The total area needed for the solar cells would take up less than 0.3 percent of the Sahara.[1095]

Today, desalted water makes up just 0.2 percent of all water or 2.4 percent of municipal water.[1096] Making desalination cover the total municipal water withdrawal would cost about 0.5 percent of the global GDP.[1097] This would definitely be a waste of resources, since most areas have abundant water supplies and all areas have some access to water, but it underscores the upper boundary of the water problem.

Also, there's a fundamental problem when you only look at the total water resources and yet try to answer whether there are sufficient supplies of water. The trouble is that we do not necessarily know *how* and *how wisely* the water is used. Many countries get by just fine with very limited water resources because these resources are exploited very effectively. Israel is a prime example of efficient water use. It achieves a high degree of efficiency in its agriculture, partly because it uses the very efficient drip irrigation system to green the desert, and partly because it recycles household wastewater for irrigation.[1098] Nevertheless, with just 969 liters per person per day, Israel should according to the classification be experiencing absolute water scarcity. Consequently, one of the authors in a background report for the 1997 UN document on water points out that the 2,740 liters water bench-mark is "misguidedly considered by some authorities as a critical minimum amount of water for the survival of a modern society."[1099]

Of course, the problem of faulty classification increases, the higher the limit is set. The European Environmental Agency in its 1998 assessment somewhat incredibly suggested that countries below 13,690 liters per person per day should be classified as "low availability," making not only more than half the EU low on water but indeed more than 70 percent of the globe.[1100] Denmark receives 6,750 liters of fresh water per day and is one of the many countries well below this suggested limit and actually close to EEA's "very low" limit. Nevertheless, national withdrawal is just 11 percent of the available water, and it is estimated that the consumption could be almost doubled without negative environmental consequences.[1101] The director of the Danish EPA has stated that, "from the hand of nature, Denmark has access to good and clean groundwater far in excess of what we actually use."[1102]

By far the largest part of all water is used for agriculture – globally, agriculture uses 69 percent, compared to 23 percent for industry and 8 percent for households.[1103] Consequently, the greatest gains in water use come from cutting down on agricultural use. Many of the countries with low water availability therefore compensate by importing a large amount of their grain.[1104] Since a ton of grain uses about 1,000 tons of water, this is in effect a very efficient way of importing water.[1105] Israel imports about 87 percent of its grain consumption, Jordan 91 percent, Saudi Arabia 50 percent.[1106]

Summing up, more than 96 percent of all nations have at present sufficient water resources. On all continents, water accessibility has *increased* per person, and at the same time an ever higher proportion of people have gained access to clean drinking water and sanitation. While water accessibility has been getting *better* this is not to deny that there are still widespread shortages and limitations of basic services, such as access to clean drinking water, and that local and regional scarcities occur. But these problems are primarily related not to physical water scarcity but to a lack of proper water management and in the end often to lack of money – money to desalt sea water or to increase cereal imports, thereby freeing up domestic water resources.

Will it get worse in the future?

The concerns for the water supply are very much concerns that the current problems will become worse over time. As world population grows, and as precipitation remains constant, there will be less water per person, and using Falkenmark's water stress criterion, there will be more nations experiencing water scarcity. In Figure 85 it is clear that the proportion of people in water stressed nations will increase from 3.7 percent in 2000 to 8.6 percent in 2025 and 17.8 percent in 2050.

It is typically pointed out that although more people by definition means more water stress, such "projections are neither forecasts nor predictions."[1107] Indeed, the projections merely mean that if we do not improve our handling of water resources, water will become more scarce. But it is unlikely that we will not become better at utilizing and distributing water. Since agriculture takes up the largest part of water consumption, it is also here that the largest opportunities for improving efficiency are to be found. It is estimated that many irrigation systems waste 60–80 percent of all water.[1108] Following the example of Israel, drip irrigation in countries as diverse as India, Jordan, Spain and the US has consistently been shown to cut water use by 30–70 percent while increasing yields by 20–90 percent.[1109] Several studies have also indicated that industry almost without additional costs could save anywhere from 30 to 90 percent of its water consumption.[1110] Even in domestic distribution there is great potential for water savings. EEA estimates that the leakage rates in Europe vary from 10 percent in Austria and Denmark up to 28 percent in the UK and 33 percent in the Czech Republic.[1111]

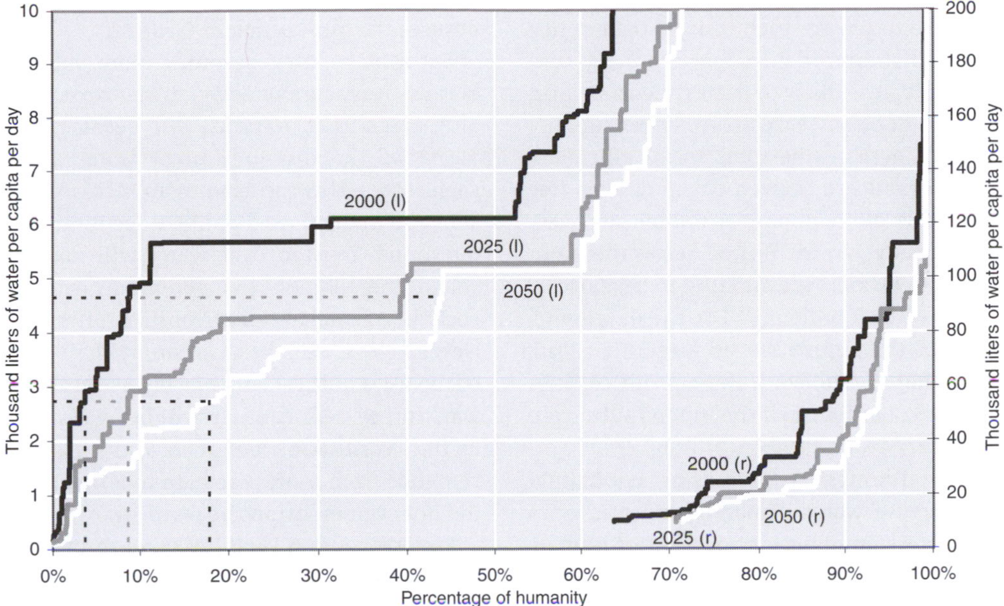

Figure 85 Share of humanity with maximum water availability in the year 2000, 2025, and 2050, using UN medium variant population data. The left side uses the left axis, the right side the right axis. Source: WRI 1998a.

The problem of water waste occurs because water in many places is not well priced. The great majority of the world's irrigation systems are based on an annual flat rate, and not on charges according to the amount of water consumed.[1112] The obvious effect is that participants are not forced to consider whether all in all it pays to use the last liter of water – when you have first paid to be in, water is free. So even if there is only very little private utility from the last liter of water, it is still used because it is free. This is yet another example of The Tragedy of the Commons, as we saw it described in the section on fisheries.

This is particularly a problem for the poor countries. The poorest countries use 90 percent of their water for irrigation compared to just 37 percent in the rich countries.[1113] Consequently, it will be necessary to redistribute water from agriculture to industry and households, and this will probably involve a minor decline in the potential agricultural production (i.e. a diminished increase in the actual production). The World Bank estimates that this reduction will be very limited and that water redistribution definitely will be profitable for the countries involved.[1114] Of course, this will mean increased imports of grain by the most water stressed countries, but a study from the International Water Management Institute indicates that it should be possible to cover these extra imports by extra production in the water abundant countries, particularly the US.[1115]

At the same time there are also large advantages to be reaped by focusing on more efficient household water consumption. In Manila 58 percent of all water disappears (lost in distribution or stolen), and in Latin America the figure is about 40 percent. And on average households in the Third World pay only 35 percent of the actual price of water.[1116] Naturally, this encourages overconsumption. We know that pricing and metering reduces demand, and that consumers use less water if they have to pay for each unit instead of just paying a flat rate.[1117]

Actually, it is likely that more sensible pricing will not only secure future water supplies but also increase the total social efficiency. When agriculture is given cheap or even free water, this often implies a hidden and very large subsidy – in the United States the water subsidy to farmers is estimated to be above 90 percent or $3.5 billion.[1118] For the developing countries this figure is even larger: it is estimated that the hidden water subsidy to cities is about $22 billion, and the hidden subsidy to agriculture around $20–25 billion.[1119]

Thus, although an increasing population will increase water demands and put extra water stress on almost 20 percent of humanity, it is likely that this scarcity can be solved. Part of the solution will come from higher water prices, which will cut down on inefficient water use. Increased cereal imports will form another part of the solution, freeing up agricultural water to be used in more valuable areas of industry or domestic consumption. Finally, desalting will again constitute a backstop process which can produce virtually unlimited amounts of drinking water given sufficient financial backing.

Will we see increased conflict?

Adequate pricing actually turns out to be the main issue for water problems. When water is a free resource – as it typically has been throughout the ages – we consume as much as we possibly can (given our private costs). As we become richer and can use more and more water, and as we support more and more people on this planet, we begin to experience limits. To act as if water is free gives rise to problems. Thus we have to start prioritizing the uses of this resource. Should we use more water to produce extra food, or should we use more water in the cities and force agriculture to become more efficient? Pricing water ensures the most efficient trade-off.

But when water becomes more valuable, because it is acknowledged to be scarce, it will also mean that nations will become more aware of the distribution of water among themselves. This can lead to an increased tension and an increased political focus on water questions. Tension over water will make up yet another element in a potentially explosive cocktail of international conflicts of interest. Nevertheless, this does not imply that "many of the wars of this century were about oil, but wars in the next century will be over water," as the World Bank put it in a much quoted sentence from a press release to a report that did not even mention the word "war."[1120]

Professor Aaron Wolf has gone through the entire international crisis dataset, and of the 412 crises in the period 1918–94, only seven had water as even a partial cause.[1121] In three of these, not a single shot was fired, and none was violent enough to qualify as an actual war.[1122] Wolf concluded: "As we see, the actual history of armed water conflict is somewhat less dramatic than the water wars literature would lead one to believe . . . As near as we can find, *there has never been a single war fought over water*."[1123] The lack of actual water war examples should be compared to the more than 3,600 treaties concerning international water resources that were registered in the centuries between 805 CE and 1984. Within the last hundred years alone, more than 149 treaties have been signed.[1124]

There is actually good reason why we should expect the water war argument to be seriously overstated. First, waging a war for water simply makes very little strategic sense. What would be the goal? Only downstream, strong states have the motivation and ability, but they are forever vulnerable to retribution from upstream states intentionally polluting the water source. So a war would require not just a simple power demonstration but a permanent occupation and possible depopulation of the entire watershed.[1125] Second, such a war would be extremely costly, especially compared to the price of desalination. As an Israeli Defense Forces analyst pointed out: "Why go to war over water? For the price of one week's fighting, you could build five desalination plants. No loss of life, no international pressure, and a reliable supply you don't have to defend in hostile territory."[1126] Third, states often share interests in water, with upstream states getting hydropower from dams and downstream states getting better-managed water for agriculture.[1127] Finally, water cooperation is highly resilient – the Mekong Committee on water functioned throughout the Vietnam war, Israel and Jordan held secret water talks throughout 30 years of formal war, and the Indus River Commission survived two wars between India and Pakistan.[1128]

Actually, a number of quarrels have been solved exactly because the problems surrounding water have gained more attention recently. Ever since independence India and Bangladesh have bitterly disputed the rights to water from the Ganges, which is controlled by India but is essential to Bangladesh's agriculture. After 50 years of India asserting the right to take as much water from the river as it needed, the government signed a treaty in 1996, providing both countries with a guaranteed flow of water in the crucial spring months of March, April and May.[1129]

Thus, while water will get more valuable, there is little reason to expect this to escalate the number of wars, simply because war makes little strategic or economic sense. Rather, it is to be expected that increased water value will help increase the focus and attention needed to solve the remaining, substantial water issues.

Conclusion

Much hype has surrounded the issue of water, perhaps best summarized with the passionate title of a 1995 academic paper: "Global water crisis: the major issue of the 21st century, a growing and explosive problem."[1130] However, the data do not support this view of a mammoth problem. Our wells are not drying up; we are not facing insurmountable shortages. Rather, the water challenges emphasize that we need to manage water more carefully, price it realistically and accept a movement away from self-reliance in food production in the arid parts of the world.

This is also the conclusion of all the important water reports. In 1997, the UN produced its latest *Comprehensive Assessment of the Freshwater Resources of the World*. In its opening statement it says that the increasing water stress occurs "largely as a result of poor water allocation, wasteful use of the resource, and lack of adequate management action."[1131] The global *World Water Vision* report from the World Water Council stated it even more clearly in its summary: "There is a water crisis today. But the crisis is not about having too little water to satisfy our needs. It is a crisis of managing water so badly that billions of people – and the environment – suffer badly."[1132]

We have sufficient water, but we need to manage it better. We need to learn from past mistakes. When the Soviet Union diverted the waters of the Amudarya and Syrdarya rivers from the Aral Sea in order to green the Kara Kum Desert, it destroyed the world's fourth largest lake. Today, we have learnt the lesson, exemplified by the Mono Lake project in eastern California, where diverted water was returned in the mid-1990s.[1133]

We need to stop mining groundwater, estimated globally at about 160 km^3 annually.[1134] In the projection for 2025 from the International Water Management Institute it is assumed that we will need an additional 600 km^3 to increase agricultural production in the future.[1135] Acquiring the extra 760 km^3 should be within reach as it is projected that additional dams alone will produce another 1,200 km^3 in accessible runoff.[1136]

Moreover, we know that large inefficiencies in agriculture, industry and water distribution exist, and adequate pricing will make it possible to produce more crop per drop. At the same time, it is reasonable to expect that the most water-scarce nations will shift their production away from agriculture and towards more valuable output in services and industry. Finally, desalting acts as a back-stop technology that enables us to produce sufficient water at a price. Actually, there is good reason to believe that the coming efficiency improvement will be good both for the economy by removing inefficient subsidies and for the environment, since it will remove the economic pressures from the most vulnerable areas.[1137]

The outcome from the International Water Management Institute projection is a market increase in total food production, from an average of less than 2,800 calories per day per capita in 1995, to more than 3,000 in 2025. At the same time, it is reasonable to expect that an even higher share of the developing world will have access to clean drinking water and sanitation.

It is an often heard cry: "Global water crisis: the major issue of the twenty-first century." But it is needlessly rhetorical and intimidating. It is unreasonable to expect that the world's wells are going to run dry. We need better water management, pricing and import substitution. In return, this will bring more food, less starvation, better health, more environmental development and increased wealth.

14 Conclusion to Part III: continued prosperity

We are not overexploiting our renewable resources. Worldwatch Institute tells us that food scarcity is likely to be the first indication of environmental breakdown.[1138] However, as we have seen in chapter 9, food will in all likelihood continue to get cheaper and more available, while we will be able to feed still more and more people.

The forests have not been eradicated, and since World War II the global forest coverage has been almost constant. Although rainforests are still being cut at 0.5 percent a year and some countries have chosen to use their forest resources unwisely and shortsightedly, about 80 percent of the original rainforest is still intact.

Water is a plentiful and renewable resource, though it can be scarce, partly because it has not sooner been treated as a limited and valuable resource. In many places this has given rise to very wasteful water practices. Basically, the problem is a question of better management, where water pricing can secure a reasonable and entirely sufficient amount of water for all purposes.

Perhaps more surprising, there do not seem to be any serious problems with the non-renewable resources, such as energy and raw materials. In general, we have found so much more of these resources that, despite large increases in consumption, the years of supply still remaining have been increasing and not decreasing, for both energy and raw materials.[1139] While non-renewable resources are in principle exhaustible, more than 60 percent of our consumption consists of resources with reserves of 200 years or more. With sufficient energy we will have the opportunity to exploit much lower grade deposits than today, yet again increasing the exhaustion times substantially and in principle towards millions of years.[1140]

We have many energy resources that can last far into the future. At the same time we have access to renewable energy resources which are getting ever cheaper, and these renewables can potentially supply us with much larger amounts of energy than are used today. We could produce the entire energy consumption of the world with present-day solar cell technology placed on just 2.6 percent of the Sahara Desert, and we have good reason to expect that these energy sources will be near-profitable or even underbid conventional energy production within the next 50 years.

Our consumption of the essential resources such as food, forests, water, raw materials and energy seem to have such characteristics that it will leave the coming generations not with fewer options, but rather with *ever more* options. Our future society will probably be able to produce much more food per capita, while not threatening the forests – or perhaps even allowing us to allocate more space and money to reforest the Earth to achieve higher living standards. Our energy consumption is not limited, in either the short run or the long run, when the almost unlimited source of solar energy can be harnessed. The evidence does not seem to point to tight limits on resources such as water and raw materials, and with sufficient energy in the long run both can be available in the necessary amounts. Consequently, there does not seem to be any foundation for the worried pessimism which claims that our society only survives by writing out ever larger checks without coverage.

The World Bank defines sustainable development as "development that lasts."[1141] In this respect our society certainly seems to be sustainable.

But although we not only uphold but also are likely to improve our immediate welfare, this is not enough to make society better for our children. It is possible that we pollute so much that we are in fact undercutting our life, our long-term welfare and the opportunities for our future generations. To this problem we shall turn next.

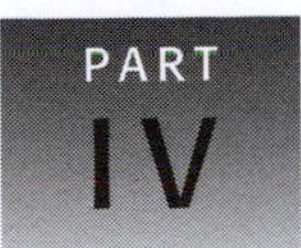
PART IV

Pollution: does it undercut human prosperity?

15 Air pollution

Of all the different types of pollution affecting human health, by far the most important is air pollution (both outdoor and indoor). Of all the major EPA statute areas (air, water, pesticides, conservation, drinking water, toxic control, liability), and even by the agency's own reckoning, 86–96 percent of all social benefits stem from the regulation of air pollution.[1142] Equally, in a 1999 consolidation of 39 regional, state and local comparative risk analysis studies, air pollution almost invariably came out as the most important environmental problem for human health.[1143] We shall therefore start by looking at the problem of air pollution.

We often assume that air pollution is a modern phenomenon, and that it has got worse and worse in recent times. However, as will become clear, the air of the Western world has not been as clean as it is now for a long time. Moreover, there is good reason to assume that air pollution in the developing world will also improve with time.

Air pollution in times past

Air pollution from lead can be documented as far back as 6,000 years ago, reaching its first maximum in the time of the Greeks and Romans. As long ago as 500 BCE, the lead content of the air above Greenland was four times higher than before the European civilizations began smelting metals.[1144] In ancient Rome, the statesman Seneca complained about "the stink, soot and heavy air" in the city.[1145]

In 1257, when the Queen of England visited Nottingham, she found the stench of smoke from coal burning so intolerable that she left for fear of her life.[1146] In 1285, London's air was so polluted that King Edward I established the world's first air pollution commission, and 22 years later the king made it illegal to burn coal – a ban that didn't stick, though.[1147]

As early as the fourteenth century, attempts were made to avoid refuse being thrown into the River Thames and the streets of the city with a resulting foul smell,[1148] but to no avail. In 1661 John Evelyn was still able to assert that "most Londoners breathe nothing but an impure and thick mist, accompanied by a fuliginous and filthy vapour, corrupting the lungs."[1149] In the eighteenth century, the cities were indescribably dirty. Lawrence Stone tells us that:

> the city ditches, now often filled with stagnant water, were commonly used as latrines; butchers killed animals in their shops and threw the offal of the carcasses into the streets; dead animals were left to decay and fester where they lay; latrine pits were dug close to wells, thus contaminating the water supply. Decomposing bodies of the rich in burial vaults beneath the church often stank out parson and congregation . . ..[1150]

In 1742 Dr Johnson described London as a city "which abounds with such heaps of filth as a savage would look on with amazement." There is corroborative evidence that indeed great quantities of human excrement were "cast into the streets at night time when the inhabitants shut up their houses." It was then dumped on the surrounding highways and ditches so that visitors to or from the city "are forced to stop their noses to avoid the ill smell occasioned by it."[1151]

The city was so polluted that the poet Shelley wrote: "Hell must be much like London, a smoky and populous city."[1152]

Much of the pollution was due to cheap coal with a high sulfur content beginning to replace more expensive wood and charcoal for industrial use in the early thirteenth century. Because of deforestation in the London area wood was getting ever more expensive, and from the beginning of the seventeenth century, private households began to burn coal to an increasing extent, causing a 20-fold increase in consumption over the next hundred years.[1153]

Deteriorating air quality led to much protest towards the end of the seventeenth century. Many people observed that buildings became pitted and iron structures corroded much more quickly and complaints were heard of there being fewer anemones, and other plants not growing as well.[1154] Even before restoration of St. Paul's Cathedral was complete, the building was beginning to get dirty again.[1155] The heavy smoke caused house paint to lose its luster so fast, many leases stipulated that facades had to be repainted tri-annually.[1156]

London has been renowned for centuries for its thick fog, the infamous London smog. One contemporary observed:

> By reason likewise of the Smoak it is, that the Air of the City, especially in the Winter time, is rendered very unwholesome: For in case there be no Wind, and especially in Frosty Weather, the City is cover'd with a thick *Brovillard* or Cloud, which the force of the Winter-Sun is not able to scatter; so that the Inhabitants thereby suffer under a dead benumming Cold, being in a manner totally depriv'd of the warmths and comforts of the Day . . . when yet to them who are but a Mile out of Town, the Air is sharp, clear, and healthy, and the Sun most comfortable and reviving.[1157]

The consequences were many. Whereas throughout the eighteenth century London was foggy 20 days a year, this had increased to almost 60 days by the end of the nineteenth century.[1158] Not surprisingly this meant that London got 40 percent less sunshine than the surrounding towns.[1159] Equally, thunderstorms had doubled in London from the early eighteenth to the late nineteenth century.[1160]

The severe pollution led to an inordinately high loss of human life, as we shall see later. Nevertheless, even at the time people were beginning to become aware of a certain connection between the pollution and sicknesses. Not coincidentally, bronchitis was initially known as the "British disease."[1161] The last severe smog of December 1952 still killed about 4,000 Londoners in just seven days.[1162]

The British environmental scientist Peter Brimblecombe has produced a model to estimate air pollution in London from as far back as 1585. On the basis of coal imports, he has estimated the concentrations of sulfur dioxide and smoke (particles or soot) in the air, and the result, updated and adjusted to measurement data from the 1920s till today, can be seen in Figure 86. This shows how levels of smoke pollution increased dramatically over the 300 years from 1585, reaching a maximum in the late nineteenth century, only to have dropped even faster ever since, such that the levels of the 1980s–1990s are *below* the levels of the late sixteenth century. Below, we shall see that smoke or particles are probably by far the most dangerous pollutant. In other words, with respect to the worst pollutant the London air has not been as clean as it is today since the Middle Ages. Almost all of the modern period has been *more* polluted with smoke than it is today. Air pollution is not a new phenomenon that has got worse and worse – it is an old phenomenon, that has been getting better and better, leaving London cleaner than it has been since medieval times.

Equally, Figure 86 shows us how the concentration of sulfur dioxide increased dramatically from 1585, reaching a very high plateau – worse than most Third World megacities of today – from 1700 to 1900, and then dropped fast, such that again the levels of the 1980s–1990s are *below* the levels of the late sixteenth century. So with respect to sulfur diox-

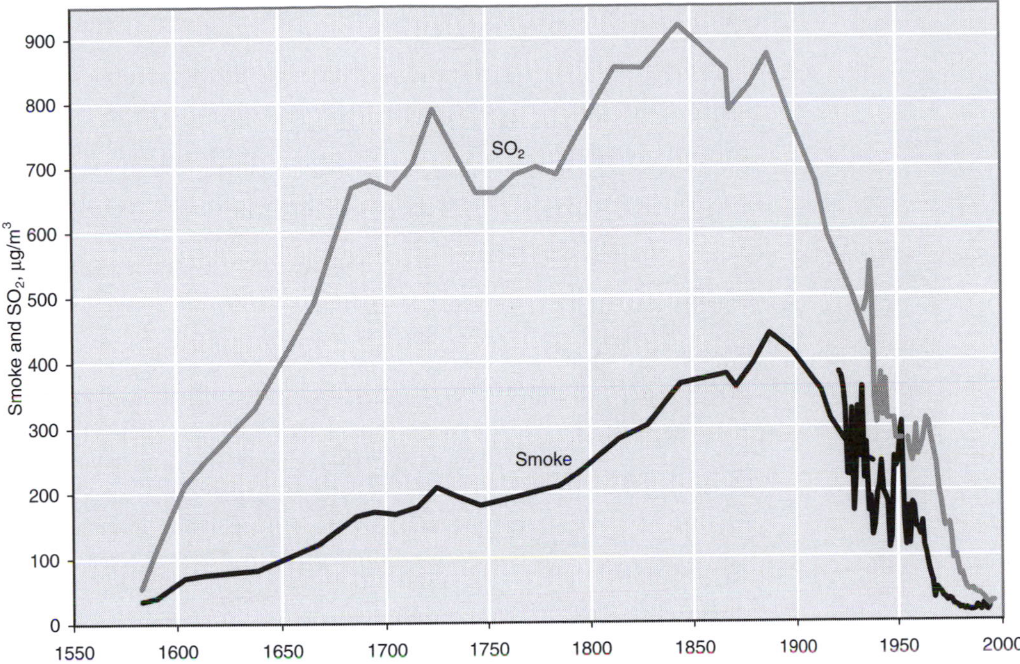

Figure 86 Average concentrations of SO_2 and smoke in London, 1585–1994/5. Data for 1585–1935 are estimated from coal imports and have been adjusted to the average of the measured data.[1163] Source: Brimblecombe 1977:1161, Elsom 1995:477, QUARG 1996:75, EPAQS 1995:Figure 3, Laxen and Thompson 1987:106, OECD 1985a:28, 1987:31, 1999:57.

ide also, the London air has not been cleaner than today since the Middle Ages. To repeat, air pollution is not a new problem getting worse, but an old problem getting ever better.

What is dangerous?

There are many forms of air pollution, but the six most important ones are:

- Particles (smoke and soot)
- Sulfur dioxide (SO_2)
- Ozone (O_3)
- Lead
- Nitrogen oxides (NO and NO_2, together NO_x) and
- Carbon monoxide (CO)

These six substances constitute the so-called criteria pollutants, the only air pollutants for which the US EPA has established National Air Quality Standards.[1164] These are the typically regulated and documented air pollutants; they are used by the World Bank, OECD and numerous other agencies to describe air quality, and both the EU and WHO have established standards and limits for them.[1165] But not all six are equally dangerous.

It is exceptionally difficult to determine exactly how dangerous a substance is. This is both because our knowledge is often inadequate and because the substances have so many and different consequences. Even so, one can try to calculate the overall cost of any pollutant – from more coughs to lowered intelligence to early death.

Although this economic approach may seem somewhat offensive, it does have the advantage of giving us a broad idea of which problems are the most serious. In connection

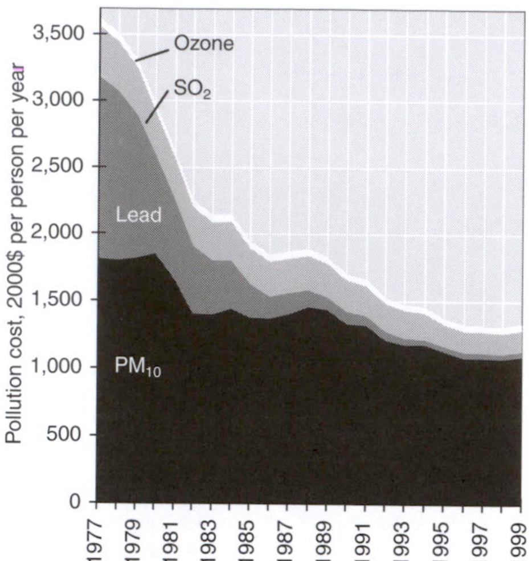

Figure 87 Average cost of PM_{10} (smoke of small-sized particles), lead, SO_2 and ozone pollutants at the measured American pollution level, 1977–99, expressed in annual cost per person in 2000 US$. Extending the cost estimates backwards to 1960, using lead emissions, indicates a total cost of $4,000–4,500 per person in the 1960s. Note, the economic estimates are uncertain and should only be considered rough estimates. Source: EPA 1997b:88, 2000:119, 2000e, 2000f:4, CPI 2001, Krupnick and Burtraw 1996:46–8, Burtraw and Krupnick 1996:462–3.[1166]

with three of the largest new studies of environmental pollution – one by the European Commission, one by the US Department of Energy and one by the New York State Energy Research and Development Authority – attempts were made to map out the overall human cost of different pollutants. In general, it was found that by far the largest proportion of total air pollution costs stem from their health effects, especially mortality.[1167]

Figure 87 shows the overall annual cost per person of pollution from 1977 to 1999 in the US. The harmful effects of NO_x and carbon monoxide have not been calculated, but are probably lower than either SO_2 or ozone.[1168] The UK government has in several publications made estimates of the total UK pollution costs, which are broadly similar.[1169]

Figure 87 shows us two things. First, the overall problems are much less serious today than they were just 22 years ago. Average air pollution costs have dropped almost two-thirds, from $3,600 to $1,300. If we go even further back to the 1960s, using lead emissions to estimate the lead pollution load, the costs seem to have been around $4,000–$4,500, indicating an even more dramatic 70 percent drop in air pollution over the past 39 years.[1170] Also the costs of the individual air pollutants have dropped over the past 22 years, by 27 percent for ozone, 40 percent for particles, 60 percent for SO_2 and 97 percent for lead. Second, there is a considerable difference between substances as to their threat to human health. The most serious air pollution problem is clearly particles, making up 82 percent of the present-day cost. In the 1970s lead also posed a serious problem, making up some 40 percent of the total costs.

Of course, there are many other substances we could also have investigated, such as VOCs (Volatile Organic Compounds), dioxins and heavy metals, but for one thing far fewer data are available on these, and for another they probably pose less of a danger to humans.[1171]

The EPA has begun to monitor many of the toxic pollutants such as benzene, formaldehyde and styrene. By far the worst concentrations of pollutants are found in urban areas.[1172] Within urban areas in the period 1993–8 (a rather short period unfortunately, but the longest available), "the results generally reveal downward trends for most monitored Hazardous Air Pollutants."[1173] In general, for every monitoring station showing a statistically valid upward trend in toxic air pollutants, more than six monitoring stations showed statistically valid downward trends.[1174] The state of California has the largest and longest running air toxins program, and of the six major pollutants discussed by EPA, all have seen declines of 35–70 percent.[1175] For the UK, measurements of six metal concentrations in the London air from 1976 to 1993 all show decreasing concentrations, from 50 percent reductions in chromium and copper, 66 percent in cadmium and zinc, to 75 percent in nickel and 87 percent in lead.[1176]

Particles

It is only within the last decade that we have realized how dangerous airborne particles actually are.

It has long been known that soot, particles and sulfur dioxide contribute to coughing and respiratory disease. With situations such as the one in London in 1952, where 4,000 people died in seven days, it became obvious that there was a connection between extremely high levels of pollution and day-to-day excessive mortality.[1177] But it was not until very large-scale statistical surveys were made in the late 1980s and early 1990s that it became clear that air pollution could also have substantial long-term effects.[1178]

There have been two main problems. For one thing, it has been extremely difficult to differentiate between the effects of the various forms of pollution. When a scientist discovers that the mortality rate is a little higher in a place where the air is polluted by particles, it is tempting to believe that the particles are the cause. However, in places with high concentrations of particles, concentrations of SO_2, lead, O_3, NO_x and CO will typically also be high – so which of them is actually to blame?

From the statistical point of view, researchers try to solve the problem by investigating whether the mortality rate is lower in areas with high concentrations of SO_2 for example, but with low particle pollution. If this were the case, it would suggest that particles are the guilty party. Unfortunately, this kind of connection is extremely complex and the best we can say right now is that it *seems* that particles are the primary cause of mortality due to pollution.[1179] It was also for this reason that the US EPA, in its large-scale 1997 report on the pros and cons of regulating air pollution, decided almost entirely to investigate deaths caused by particles. It was considered that the effect of particles more or less accounted for the entire risk of death from air pollution.[1180]

But this emphasizes the second problem. We still do not know *how and why* particles cause people to die.[1181] It is thought that particles, when breathed in, enter the lungs and gain a foothold. They then cause change in the normal function of the lungs, irritate the bronchi and alter the pH-value of the lungs.[1182] This has led to considerable interest in the question of the size of particles. Whereas large particles are caught in the nose and throat, extremely small particles can find their way into the innermost part of the lungs, the alveoli.[1183] Increasingly, the evidence seems to point to the smallest particles posing the greatest risk to human health.

Until the middle of the 1980s all particles were measured and classified as soot or smoke. Only in the late 1980s when researchers started to become aware of the effect of small particles did the US EPA begin to measure the small particles, less than ten-millionths of a meter across (10μm, or PM_{10}). Most recently, the EPA has begun to measure and set limits for the extremely small particles of just 2.5μm ($PM_{2.5}$). It is assumed that these particles are the actual culprits because they are so small that they can force their way into the very part of the lungs where oxygen is absorbed. Outside the US, there are still few systematic measurements for PM_{10}.

The smallest particles, $PM_{2.5}$, come from combustion in motor vehicle engines, power stations and industry as well as from fireplaces and wood-burning stoves, whereas the slightly larger PM_{10} come from dust and mechanical wear and tear.[1184] Although only 10 percent of all particles are man-made they are by far the most common in our urban environment.[1185]

And what do particles do to our health? Evaluated on the basis of the best international surveys, particle pollution in the US can be estimated to cause roughly 135,000 premature deaths or almost 6 percent of all deaths each year.[1186] By way of comparison, 42,400 people died in US road accidents in 1997.[1187] In the UK, a similar number of excess deaths from particle pollution can be estimated at about 64,000.[1188] Again, this number is surprisingly much higher than road accidents, which cost 3,581 lives in 1998.[1189]

But who is it who actually dies? Or to put it more cynically, how much of their lifetime do these people miss out on?

On 30 May 1998 the world media reported that a heat wave in New Delhi had killed 500 people.[1190] But we often forget to ask *who died.* As a rule it is the elderly and extremely vulnerable individuals who die under such extreme weather conditions, and medical research shows that many would have died within a few days even if the weather had been better.[1191] The medics therefore refer, rather sardonically, to weather conditions such as these having a *harvesting effect.*[1192] If, on the other hand, primarily young and healthy Indians had succumbed to the heat wave, then we might have expected that they would otherwise have lived on to the normal average age of 62 – or about another 35 years. Therefore, it may be bad enough that 500 old people, who might have lived a few days longer, die during a heat wave, but the death of 500 young people is far more awful when they could have lived for another 35 years.

It is estimated that particle pollution mainly kills older people (because they have been living longest with the pollution), but that the average life lost is still 14 years.[1194] This means that the 135,000 Americans who die annually from particulate pollution lose an average of 14 years of their lives. For the entire urban population this means that in the UK on average people lose more than one year of their expected life, and in the US almost two-thirds of a year.[1195] In addition, the present-day US particle pollution causes about 8 million acute cases of bronchitis in children each year, and causes the loss of more than 20 million working days.[1196]

It is not clear whether it will be possible to remove the small particles totally, but figures show that this may be an important priority, depending on how much it costs to reduce discharges. However, as we shall see, we have already improved the quality of our air to an amazing extent.

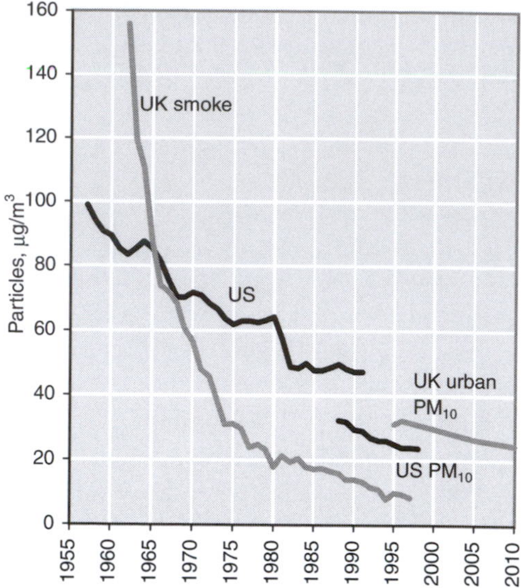

Figure 88 Particle concentration levels for the US (1957–99) and the UK (1962–97) and predictions for the urban UK (1995–2010). The US time series measures TSP (Total Suspended Particles) and from 1988 particles below 10µm (PM_{10}). The UK time series measures black smoke, using a different method, and, at least for the 1990s, the UK smoke should be multiplied by 3.5 to compare it with the US PM_{10} (QUARG 1996:84). The urban UK prediction is PM_{10}. Source: CEQ 1972:214, 1974:263, 1981:168, 1982:243, 1989:351, 1993:337, EPA 1997b:88, 2000e:119, 2000f:4, Ludwig *et al.* 1970:473, Bailey 2000:293, NETC 1999, QUARG 1996:77, Stedman 1998:Table 2.3&4.[1193]

Figure 88 shows American and British particle pollution from the 1960s till today. The crucial point is that particle pollution has fallen dramatically: since 1957 particulate pollution has fallen by 62 percent in the US, and smoke has declined by almost 95 percent in the UK. The more dangerous, small particles (PM_{10}) have only been consistently monitored in the US since 1988, but over the measured

12-year period this pollution has shown a 25 percent decline. Although it is not clear how the number of extremely small particles has changed since the 1960s, it is likely to have fallen dramatically. If we – very cautiously – assume that the extremely small particles ($PM_{2.5}$) have fallen at least by half, the lower particle pollution saves some 135,000 lives each year in the US and some 64,000 lives in the UK, adding 0.7 years to the average American's life and 1.35 years to the average British life. If the real decline in $PM_{2.5}$ has been bigger, as is very plausible, the improvement has been proportionally even greater.[1197] All in all, we have achieved an amazing improvement in the standard of health.

Moreover, this development is not limited to the graphs of Figure 88. Looking at London in Figure 86, the particle pollution has decreased 22-fold since the late nineteenth century. During the last smog in London in December 1952 smoke levels above 6,000$\mu g/m^3$ were recorded – more than 300 times the present-day level in London.[1198] Similarly, in Pittsburgh, downtown dustfall has seen an eightfold decrease since the 1920s, and a concurrent decline in smoky days from about 360 to almost nil.[1199]

Also, it is likely that this trend will continue into the future, as is apparent in Figure 88 and Figure 89. Not only have PM_{10} road traffic emissions been declining in the US since 1960 and urban traffic emissions in the UK since 1990, but the decline is projected to continue to 2010. Despite increasing traffic, emissions will over the next ten years decrease by 20 percent in the US and 30 percent in the UK.[1200] Moreover, this PM_{10} emission decline is not only relevant for road traffic emissions. In the US, total PM_{10} emissions have fallen 42 percent since 1990, and in the UK 47 percent.[1201] Recent studies of PM_{10} concentrations in the major city areas in the UK actually project a 24 percent decrease from 1996 to 2010, as can be seen in Figure 88. Other countries have experienced similar declines. Since 1980, the particle pollution in Japan has declined 14 percent, in Canada 46 percent and in Germany 48.5 percent.[1202] Athens has witnessed a 43 percent decline since 1985, and Spain a 34 percent decline since 1986.[1203] Paris has experienced a dramatic 66 percent decline since 1970.[1204]

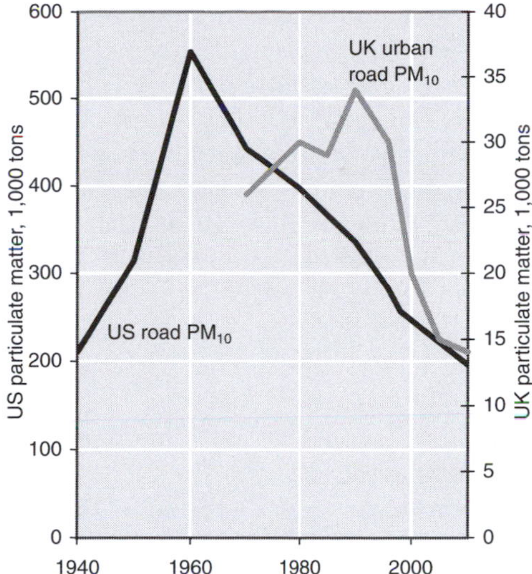

Figure 89 Emission of vehicle PM_{10} in the US (1940–2010) and urban vehicle PM_{10} in the UK (1970–2010). Predictions for 2000–2010. Source: EPA 2000d:3–13, 1999e:12, QUARG 1996:49.

The reason for the dramatic fall in particle levels is partly that the emission of SO_2 causing much of the particle pollution has fallen dramatically – in the EU by about 50 percent since 1980 and in the US by about 37 percent since 1970.[1205] This has been achieved by reducing consumption of fossil fuels, especially high-sulfur coal, by using smoke scrubbing equipment on power plant smokestacks and by increasing energy efficiency.

The political decision to limit sulfur emissions is closely linked to the question of acid rain, which was very much on people's minds in the 1980s. The fear of acid rain, which we will look into later, proved to be grossly exaggerated, although the SO_2 reduction efforts did turn out to be reasonable because they helped reduce the particle pollution.[1206]

However, reductions in urban areas have

several other causes. Historically, a move away from siting power plants in urban areas and the use of taller smokestacks were two of the primary causes of pollution reduction.[1207] At the same time we no longer use coke ovens and we have reduced our dependence on oil central heating, having instead changed to natural gas and district heating.[1208] Finally, cars pollute much less than they used to, partly because of catalytic converters but also because diesel vehicles now use low-sulfur diesel oil.[1209] However, compared to gasoline cars, diesel cars pollute much more in terms of particulate matter – in the UK, although diesel cars make up only 6 percent of the total car park, they contribute 92 percent of all vehicle emissions.[1210] Thus, a marked increase in the use of diesel cars could slow the decline in particulate emissions[1211]

Specialist literature has contained a lot of discussion about the degree to which legislation has been crucial, or at least important, to the reduction of air pollution. Many studies have – perhaps surprisingly – not been able to document any noteworthy effect.[1212] Analysis of the British *Clean Air Act* of 1956 shows that while pollution has, of course, fallen, the difference between the rate of fall before and after 1956, or the difference between cities that did or did not have pollution plans, is not discernible. "It seems likely that in the absence of the Clean Air Act of 1956 substantial improvements in air quality would have occurred anyway."[1213] The explanation is to a high degree to be found in improved products and technology for industry and the home.

In a study of three US cities, it was found that the mandated pollution control had an effect, but that the effects of regulatory control "generally have been overshadowed by the effects of economic changes, weather, and other factors."[1214] Generally it is probably fair to say that regulation is one of the reasons for the reduction of pollution but that other, technological factors also play a major role.

In conclusion, it is worth emphasizing that particle pollution in terms of cost to humanity is by far the most important air pollutant and consequently (since air pollution makes up about 96 percent of all social benefits stemming from EPA regulation) by far the most important pollutant of all. And here the conclusion is unambiguously clear. Our most substantial pollution problem has been drastically reduced.

Lead

Lead was widely used even in antiquity because it was so easy to shape or mould into vessels and pipes. The Romans used a lot of lead in their water supply systems, and women used pulverized lead as makeup.[1215] Throughout the Middle Ages, lead was also widely used, mostly as an additive to make sour wine drinkable – often with painful, sometimes even fatal after-effects.[1216] In modern times, lead has proven an extremely useful metal in crystal glass, ceramic glazing, white paints, ammunition and printer's type. When the motor car came on to the scene, lead batteries provided electrical power, and lead was added to petrol to increase its octane rating.[1217]

Unfortunately, lead is also extremely toxic. Several scientists believe that the Roman upper class, who drank water from lead pipes and used lead-based mugs, vessels and beauty creams, suffered from permanent lead poisoning. This would have led to birth defects and widespread physical impairment that may have contributed to the fall of the Roman Empire.[1218]

It has been known for a long time that high concentrations of lead in the bloodstream can cause cramps, coma and death.[1219] But only within the last 20 years have we become clearly aware of some of the serious consequences stemming from even very small intakes of lead. Unborn children are particularly exposed. Studies have shown a rise in miscarriages if either or both partners have been exposed to lead in their workplaces. Lead can reduce men's fertility and doubles the risk of women giving birth to retarded children.[1220] In the USA, some 12,000–16,000 children each year are admitted to hospital with lead poisoning; 200 of them die and 30 percent of the survivors suffer permanent injury, becoming mentally retarded or paralyzed.[1221]

Large-scale studies of children with varying concentrations of lead in their blood have shown that it has a substantial effect on their IQ – children with high concentrations are quite simply less intelligent, do not concentrate as well and are more restless than children with low concentrations of lead.[1222] Lead can also cause hypertension in adult men.[1223] Children's intake of lead often comes from ingesting flakes of old, lead-based paint, that was banned back in 1940 – children from old houses in Youngstown, Ohio had more than twice the serum level of lead compared to children from new houses.[1224]

Globally about 90 percent of lead emissions comes from lead added to petrol, even though leaded petrol now only represents 2.2 percent of total lead consumption.[1225] The US started phasing out lead in gasoline in 1973, essentially completing the task in 1986.[1226] In the UK, a reduction was started in 1981 and in 1985 the allowed lead contents in gasoline had been reduced by two-thirds.[1227] Today, all US gasoline is unleaded, and likewise more than 75 percent of the gasoline sold in the UK.[1228] The consequence for lead concentrations has been enormous. It can be seen from Figure 90 that the lead concentration in UK air has fallen by 85 percent. In the US the effect has been even more pronounced – since 1977 the lead concentration has dropped more than 97 percent, coming close to the threshold of what is measurable.[1229] And the result can also be measured in people. Over the same period the lead content of Americans' blood fell some 80 percent from 14.5 to 2.8μg/dl. The number of infants with blood-lead concentrations of over 10μg/dl fell from 85 percent to 6 percent in whites and from 98 percent to 21 percent in blacks.[1230]

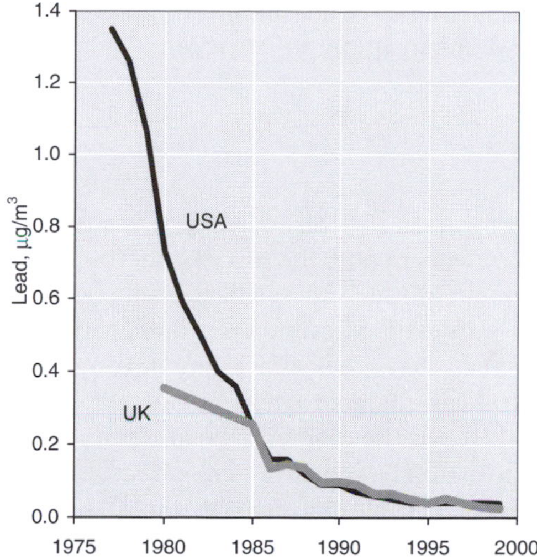

Figure 90 Lead concentration in the US (1977–99) and the UK (1980–96). The US data measure highest quarterly average of 122 monitoring stations until 1986 and 208 thereafter. The UK data measure the annual average over 9 monitoring stations. Source: EPA 1997b:88, 2000e:118, 2000f:4, DETR 1998a:Table 2.18.[1231]

The US EPA estimates considerable benefits from this dramatic decline in lead pollution. It is estimated that about 22,000 deaths are avoided every year, which is about 1 percent of all deaths.[1232] Because many of those who would have died were children the average extra lifetime involved is as much as 38 years.[1233] This is actually the equivalent of one-quarter life-year for every single inhabitant of the USA.[1234] In societies with a comparable lead pollution load, such as the UK, a complete phase-out of lead should lead to roughly identical life expectancy gains. It is also estimated that in the US, children will on average avoid losing up to three IQ-points with lower lead levels and that 45,000 fewer retarded children will be born. Finally, about 12 million fewer men will get hypertension.[1235]

These figures are surprisingly large and demonstrate the amazing air pollution improvement that has taken place. For the second-worst air pollutant, the last 15–20 years have seen lead concentration levels falling dramatically by 80–97 percent.

SO_2

The regulation of SO_2 emissions was primarily a consequence of the anxiety in the 1980s about acid rain and its effect on forests and lakes in exposed areas. Even though it later proved that the effect on forests was extremely slight or even non-existent (as we shall see in the chapter on acid rain), regulation had the positive side-effect that it reduced particle emissions. When SO_2 is emitted during combustion, part of the gas will oxidize and condense around tiny, unburned condensation nuclei to form particles.[1236] It is in avoiding these particles that by far the greatest advantage of SO_2 emission reductions lies.

In addition, SO_2 damages buildings and cultural objects such as statues. Metal corrodes much faster, and marble and sandstone in particular are damaged because SO_2 is converted into sulfuric acid which gradually eats away the stone.[1237] The overall effect, however, was found in the major US study to be relatively minor, whereas British and EU studies indicate much higher costs.[1238] Sulfur dioxide can also reduce visibility, either as a light mist or as a dense gray smog just like the one once familiar to Londoners.[1239] The cost of the reduced visibility in 1990 can be estimated at roughly $12 per person in the US.[1240]

Finally, when SO_2 is deposited it actually makes a free contribution to the fertilization of forests and agricultural crops in particular, estimated to be worth some $500 million annually in the US.[1241] Likewise, when sulfur pollution was at its highest in Denmark, crops needing lots of sulfur, such as oilseed rape and cabbage, had their requirements covered through pollution, whereas it is today necessary to give these crops extra sulfur.[1242]

In 1979 the Long-Range Transboundary Air Pollution convention was adopted in Helsinki,

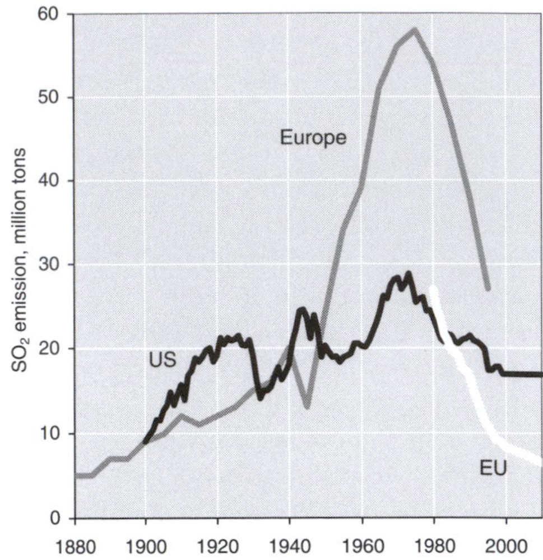

Figure 91 Emission of SO_2 in Europe (1880–1995), the US (1900–2010) and the EU (1980–2010). Predictions for 2000–10. Source: NERI 1998a:49, EPA 1998d:25, 1999e:12, 2000d:3–12, EEA 2000, EMEP 2000.

coming into force in 1983. First, in 1985 a strict protocol was signed, obliging European governments to reduce their emissions by 30 percent by 1993.[1243] But as can be seen from Figure 91, European emissions had already been on the decrease since 1975. The reduction has been achieved by changing to other sources of energy, using less sulfurous coal and the general use of smoke cleansing.[1244] European Union emissions have been declining steadily since 1980 and are expected to decline even further, to a total reduction of more than 75 percent by 2010. In the US similar regulations were introduced by the Clean Air Act Amendment in 1990, cutting emissions from power plants by about 50 percent.[1245] Again, total US emissions had been declining since the early 1970s. Here the SO_2 emissions are also expected to decline further, reaching a total reduction by 2010 of 26 percent. The consequence has been a dramatic reduction in sulfur dioxide pollution in both Europe and the US (Figure 92). In the UK, SO_2 concentrations that Britons have to breathe

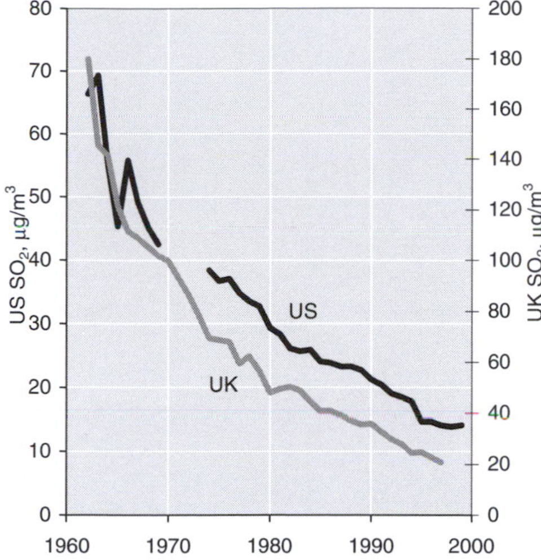

Figure 92 Annual average concentration of SO_2 in the US (1962–99) and the UK (1962–97). Source: CEQ 1972:214, 1981:167, 1989:351, 1993:337, EPA 1997b:88, 2000e:119, 2000f:4, Ludwig *et al.* 1970:474, Bailey 2000:297, NETC 1999.[1246]

each day have fallen from 180µg/m³ in 1962 to just 21µg/m³ today, or a decline of 88 percent. The even steeper SO_2 reduction in the London air is obvious in Figure 86, where concentrations have dropped more than 96 percent over the past hundred years.[1247] Equally, in the US, concentrations of SO_2 have fallen by almost 80 percent since 1962, as can be seen in Figure 92. In a large-scale study from 1995, the EPA estimated that reductions in SO_2 concentrations since 1990 save more than 2,500 human lives a year in 1997.[1248] The lives saved could, however, be attributable solely to reduced particle pollution.[1249] It is expected when the full force of the Clean Air Act Amendment has made its mark in 2010 that about 9,600 lives will be saved every year.

Ozone

Ozone forms a vital layer in the stratosphere which protects us against ultraviolet rays from the sun. The "hole in the ozone layer" will be discussed later (p. 273ff). However, close to the earth ozone is harmful to humans and affects plant growth. Ozone irritates the respiratory organs, causes rubber to disintegrate and negatively affects plant growth.[1250] Ozone is a secondary pollutant, because it is primarily created in a complex interplay between NO_x and hydrocarbons.[1251] Ozone and the NO_x are the major players in the formation of brown (photochemical) smog of the kind familiar in Los Angeles and seen today in many cities in the developing world.[1252]

Ozone is not believed to have any actual life-threatening effect.[1253] The UK Expert Panel on Air Quality Standards "found no evidence that exposure to the levels of ozone that are encountered in the United Kingdom are likely to lead to long term damage to the respiratory system."[1254] On the other hand, it has a substantial impact on agriculture and horticulture: it is believed that the most significant economic damage from pollution is experienced by these industries, and in the US the cost has been valued at several billion dollars.[1255] Ozone can, however, also reduce the risk and effect of fungal attacks.[1256]

Ozone pollution is generally measured in peak concentrations, because these matter the most for health and vegetation effects.[1257] In the US, maximal ozone concentrations have declined since 1977 by almost 30 percent, as can be seen in Figure 93. Ozone levels have not been consistently monitored at the national level in the UK. In the 1997 UK ozone review, it was concluded that there was clear evidence of a reduction in peak concentrations,[1258] and as Figure 93 indicates, London peak data show a fall of 56 percent from 1976 till today.

For agriculture, it is estimated that all 15 countries in the EU will experience a decrease in crop ozone exposure. On average, the exposure level will have decreased from 1990 to 2010 by about 25 percent.[1259]

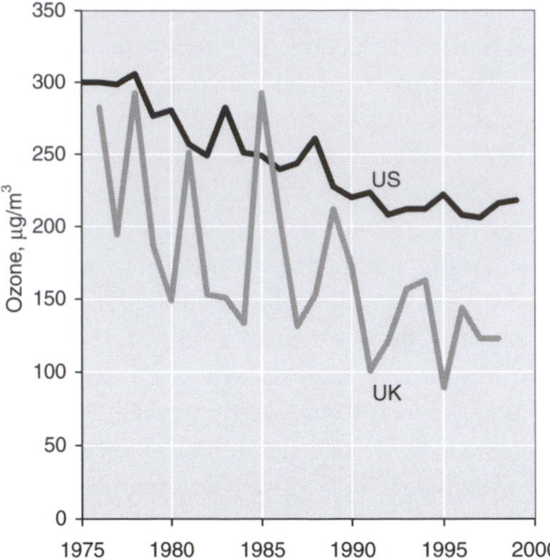

Figure 93 Ozone levels in the US (1975–99) and London, UK (1976–98). The US time series measures the cross country average of the annual second-highest one-hour ozone value (2nd max. 1-hr), while data from London measure the maximum hourly average. Source: CEQ 1993:337, EPA 1997b:88, 2000e:119, 2000f:4, DETR 2000.[1260]

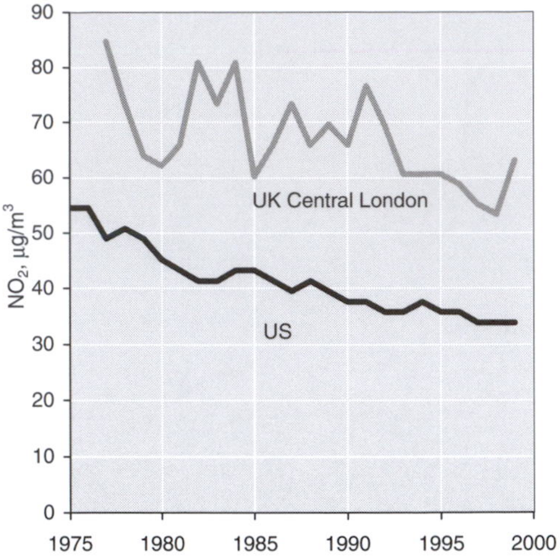

Figure 94 Annual average NO_2 concentrations in the US (1975–99) and in central London, UK (1976–98). The American measurements are based on 238 monitoring stations up to and including 1986, and 600 thereafter. Source: EPA 1997b:88, 2000e:118, 2000f:4, DETR 2000.[1264]

NO_x

Nitrogen oxides come primarily from motor vehicles and power stations. Together with ozone they form the main component of brown Los Angeles smog. Together with SO_2, they contribute to acid rain, and in addition to that they can cause respiratory problems and lung infections in children and other vulnerable groups such as asthmatics.[1261] NO_x is, however, far less dangerous to humans than particles, lead and SO_2, and it has not been possible to link it with any tendency towards excessive mortality.[1262]

NO_x also functions as fertilizer when it is introduced into the soil or water. It can also have a negative effect such as when seas and inland waterways get overfertilized, causing algae to flourish. In late summer this can also increase the risk of oxygen depletion and fish death (this problem will be discussed in chapter 19).[1263] The effect can also be positive when NO_xs are deposited on crops and in principle function as free fertilizer, although the overall amounts involved are probably quite low.[1265]

In the US, NO_x pollution has gradually been reduced. This is evident in Figure 94, where the concentration has fallen some 38 percent since 1975. Although there are no national long-term measures of NO_x in the UK, London data indicate a fall of more than 40 percent since 1976. The emissions of NO_x in the UK have decreased since 1990 and are expected to have fallen around 55 percent before 2010.[1266] Equally, Germany has seen a 15 percent decrease in NO_2 since 1985, Spain a 17 percent decrease since 1987, and Canada a 32 percent decrease since 1980.[1267] Much of the reduction can be credited to catalytic converters, although the reason why the reduction is not even greater is that the formation of NO_2 is also dependent on available ozone, quantities of which were already limited.[1268]

CO

Carbon monoxide can be dangerous in extremely high doses – people are able to commit suicide with their cars idling in a garage precisely because CO is absorbed by the blood instead of oxygen and asphyxiates them.[1269] But CO in common out-door concentrations is not lethal and is probably less dangerous than most of the other pollutants discussed here.[1270] In the words of the Copenhagen Air Monitoring Unit: "The level of carbon monoxide on its own is not considered to entail effects on health."[1271]

The main source of CO for many people is cigarettes – it is estimated that smokers will have 50–700 percent higher CO levels than people exposed to extreme CO pollution.[1272] In cities, by far the majority of CO comes from incomplete combustion in petrol-driven engines.[1273] Catalytic converters reduce CO emissions approximately by a factor of 8.[1274]

Figure 95 shows the dramatic fall in American carbon monoxide concentrations of almost 75 percent since 1970. Carbon monoxide levels have not been monitored at the national level in the UK, but the London data displayed in Figure 95 indicate a fall of 80 percent since 1976. Since the London site is just one measurement station, the year-to-year differences are much larger.

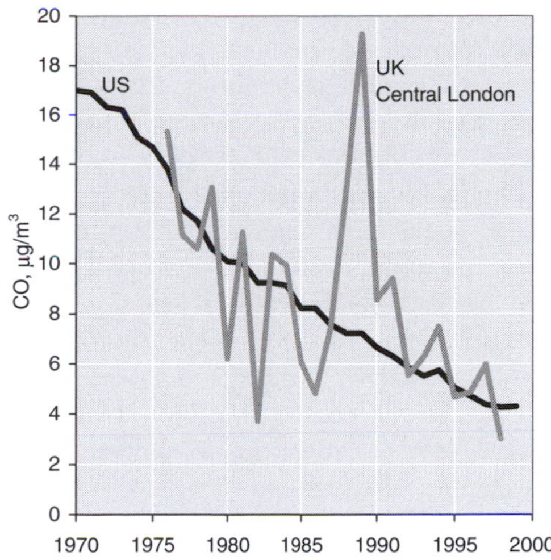

Figure 95 Annual average CO concentrations in the US (1970–99) and in central London, UK (1976–98). The US is measured as the second largest 8-hour maximum and London as the maximum running 8-hour mean. The American figures are from 91 monitoring stations up to and including 1976, 168 from then until 1986 and 345 thereafter. Source: CEQ 1982:243, EPA 1997b:88, 2000e:118, 2000f:4, DETR 2000.[1276]

And the developing world? Both growth and environment

As we have seen above, air quality has vastly improved as far as the main parameters are concerned: particles, lead, SO_2, O_3, NO_x and CO. And this is true not just in the UK and the US – it applies in most parts of the Western world. "Air quality in OECD countries is vastly improved," concludes the World Bank.[1275]

However, the good news does not apply to many developing countries. Today, some of the most polluted places in the world are found in the megacities of the developing world such as Beijing, New Delhi and Mexico City. All three have particle levels of around 400µg/m³ – more than eight times as polluted as American or British air and far in excess of the World Health Organization's recommended threshold of 50–100µg/m³.[1277] Thirteen of the 15 most polluted cities in the world today are in Asia.[1278] The same goes for SO_2, where levels in these cities are at least twice the maximum recommended by the WHO. The World Bank estimates that in Beijing at least 4,000 people lose their lives every year because of SO_2 pollution, and the number is rising.[1279]

But let us consider for a moment what exactly happened in the Western world. Over a period of 100–300 years the West saw increasing incomes and ever increasing pollution. In the 1930s and 1940s, London was even more polluted than Beijing, New Delhi and Mexico City are today. In general, it was not until the last 40 to 100 years that the developed countries de-coupled economic growth from the growth in pollution. The explanation, according to the World Bank, is that with increasing affluence the Western world has gradually become better able to afford to pay for a cleaner environment and at the same time has found a polluted environment less and less acceptable. Political decisions have then followed and a cleaner environment has been achieved.[1280] But if this de-coupling has been achieved in the Western world why should we not expect this to happen in the developing countries as they, too, get ever richer? Will they not want a better environment as well?

The World Bank set about investigating whether there was a general tendency first for growth to act to the *detriment* of the environment, then for growth actually to *promote* positive environmental development and to support it. They tried comparing all the countries in the world for which figures for economic development and pollution were available. The result can be seen in Figure 96. Along the horizontal axis are the countries according to their wealth, and up the vertical axis their levels of pollution. For 1972 the conclusion is perfectly clear: in the first phase of growth, during which countries develop from extreme poverty to medium income, they will pollute more and more, but after this their pollution levels actually fall – to the level they had before they started developing.[1281] So it seems that it is possible to achieve high standards of living and still have an ever better environment (this was also the general point in Figure 9, p. 33).

It is probably even more surprising when we look at how the connection between income and pollution changes from 1972 to 1986. In 1986 we still see the basic pattern of growth and first more then less pollution. But notice that pollution has fallen for all nations at all levels of wealth. This is due to continuing technological development, which makes it possible to produce the same amount of goods while imposing less of a burden on the environment (e.g. more dollars with less energy, Figure 68). The analysis shows that the particle pollution falls about 2 percent each year. Thus, the developing countries can not only achieve both economic growth and a better environment, but over time will get even better environment for a given amount of wealth. This is because developing countries can buy progressively cheaper, cleaner technology from the West. The key factor here is that technology makes it possible to achieve growth as well as a better environment. This may sound paradoxical, because we are accustomed to thinking of growth and the environment as opposites, but this is a misconception rooted in the early Western Industrial Revolution.

Even so, it seems like magic: growth as well as a clean environment? In reality, the explanation is simple. So long as we do not sensibly price our natural resources such as pure water, clean air and human health, it will be easy for producers to exploit them. And so long as most people only want material progress, or are too weak politically to wish for anything else, production continues to pollute ever more. However, as the Western countries to an increasing degree have begun to focus on better quality of life through a cleaner environment, the political decision has been made that pollution should be costly. By means of bans, regulations and taxes, we have changed the market to ensure that production has automatically become far more efficient and less polluting. It is no coincidence that the connection between income and air pollution looks much like the pollution trend for London from 1585 that we saw in Figure 86. There are no decisive reasons to assume that the same development will not happen in the Third World which today faces serious environmental problems equivalent to those we faced 50–80 years ago.

Figure 96 showed us the relationship between income and particles. Figure 97 shows an equivalent unambiguous connec-

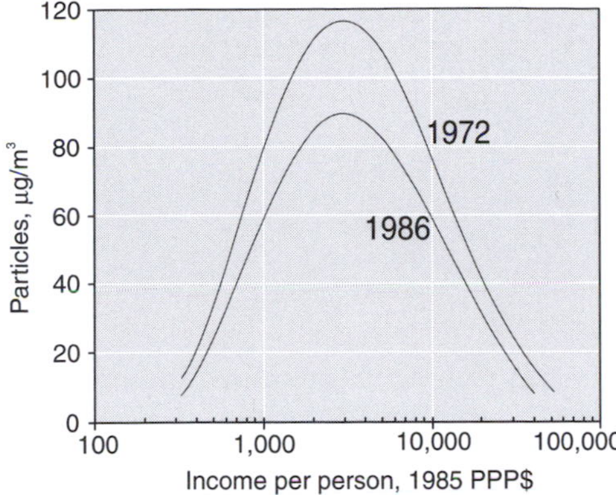

Figure 96 The connection between GDP per capita and particle pollution in 48 cities in 31 countries, 1972 and 1986. Source: World Bank 1992:41, Shafik 1994:764.

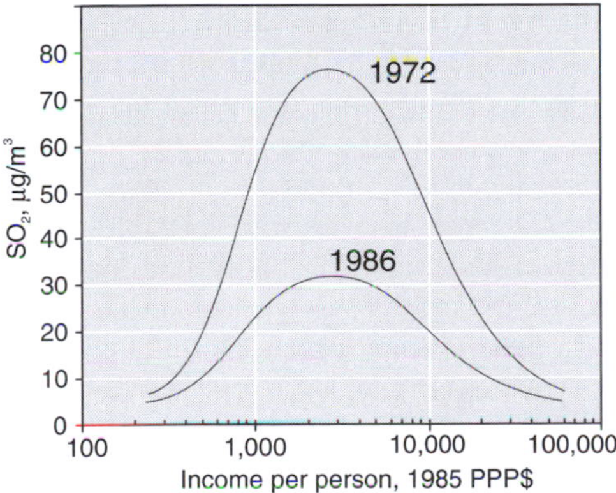

Figure 97 The connection between GDP per capita and SO_2 pollution in 47 cities in 31 countries, 1972 and 1986. Source: World Bank 1992:41, Shafik 1994:764.

tion between income and SO_2 pollution. In this case the reduction between 1972 and 1986 is even greater – the analysis indicates an annual fall of 5 percent.

Conclusion

The achievement of dramatically decreasing concentrations of the major air pollutants in the Western world, as demonstrated in this chapter, is amazing by itself. But it is all the more impressive that it has been attained while the economy and the potential polluters have increased dramatically – in the US, the total number of car miles traveled has more than doubled over the past 30 years. The economy has likewise more than doubled, and the population has increased by more than a third.[1282] Nevertheless, over the same period emissions have decreased by a third and concentrations much more.[1283] This is why it is reasonable to be optimistic about the challenge from air pollution. Not only have we seen that air pollution can be – and historically has been – combated in the developed world. There is also good reason to believe that the developing world, following our pattern, in the long run likewise will bring down its air pollution.

As emphasized by the World Bank, growth and environment are not opposites – they complement each other. Without adequate protection of the environment, growth is undermined; but without growth it is not possible to support environmental protection.[1284] The World Bank points out: "The key is not to produce less, but to produce differently."[1285] This is precisely what new technology has allowed the developed world to do. And it is precisely what it is increasingly allowing the developing world to do also.

16 Acid rain and forest death

Acid rain was the great horror of the 1980s. We saw the sick and dying trees on the TV news and were told that acid rain was killing our forests. Looking at publications from the 1980s one will see that they did not spare their readers when it came to descriptions. Acid rain was the "invisible plague"[1286] which was creating an "ecological Hiroshima."[1287] The UN Brundtland report stated flat out that "in Europe, acid precipitation kills forests."[1288] Several present-day ecology books repeat the charge.[1289]

A popular book published in 1989 with the title *Acid Rain: Threats to Life* told us:

> An acid plague is sweeping the Earth. The rain, snow, fog, and mist have become acid because of pollution from factories and cars all over the world, and it has been converted to *acid rain*.
>
> Acid rain destroys our buildings and statues but it is also threatens the natural environment.
>
> One third of the German forests have been attacked, so the trees are either dead or dying.
>
> 4000 Swedish lakes are dead and 14,000 are in the process of dying . . .
>
> In cities all over the Earth, people are being suffocated – or dying – because the smoke cannot escape . . .
>
> Acid rain has become one of the most serious threats to life here on Earth.[1290]

Apart from the fact that big-city pollution has nothing to do with acid rain, the above was probably a bit shrill even at the time it was written. Today we know that acid rain was nothing like the problem it was made out to be in the 1980s.

"Acid rain" has typically been used as a collective term for damage to forests, lakes and buildings believed to be caused by emissions of NO_x or SO_2.[1291] In fact all rain, even before industrialization, has been naturally acidic, so the expression acid rain has been associated with the extra acid that could arise when NO_x or SO_2 reacted with water to create sulfuric or nitric acid.

In the late seventies and early eighties, areas of central Europe were observed to be suffering extreme forest death. The hardest hit areas in Bavaria had up to 40 percent sick and dying trees.[1292] A group of German scientists predicted that Europe's forests were threatened by acid rain and as many as 10 percent of all trees were at risk.[1293] Despite fierce criticism from other scientists, the images of the sick and dying trees reached all round the world, sowing anxiety both in other European countries and in the US.[1294]

The fear of and assertions about acid rain led to numerous scientific investigations. The official American acid rain project, the National Acid Precipitation Assessment Program (NAPAP), became the world's biggest, longest and most expensive; it spanned most of a decade, involved about 700 scientists, and cost half a billion dollars. A whole series of questions were looked into in order to expose links between acid rain and forests, lakes and buildings.

Figure 98 shows the results of one of NAPAP's long-term controlled experiments, in which seedlings from three species of trees were exposed to various concentrations of acid rain over a period of almost three years. The trees were cultivated in relatively poor soil in order to maximize any negative effects of the acid rain. As the figure shows, no acid

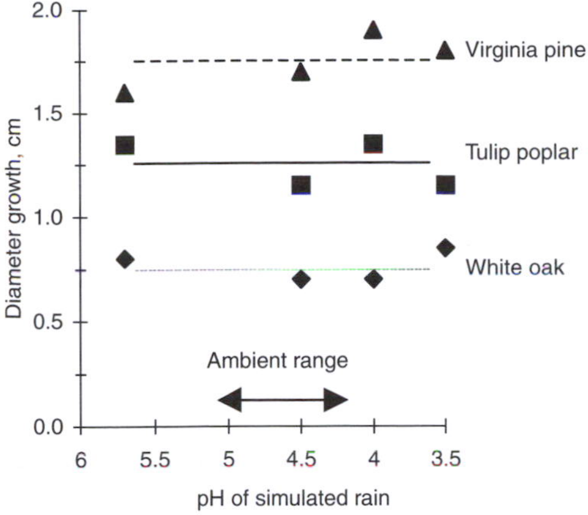

Figure 98 NAPAP experiment showing growth in diameter of 2- to 5-year-old seedlings exposed to various levels of simulated acid rain. (Lower pH-value means more acidic rain.) Source: Kulp 1995:529.

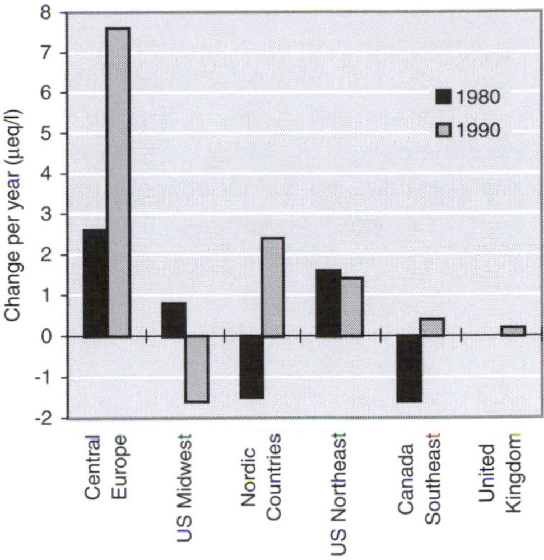

Figure 99 Annual change in acidity of lakes in the 1980s and 1990s. Positive means less acidic. Source: NERI 1998a:52, EEA 1998:75.

rain effect was detected on any of the three species of tree. Even with precipitation almost ten times as acidic as the average acid rain in the eastern US (pH 4.2) the trees grew just as fast. In fact many of the NAPAP's studies showed that trees exposed to moderate acid rain grew *faster*.[1295] Some even longer controlled experiments were carried out in Norway, and here too the conclusion was that the predicted negative effects of acid rain "could not be demonstrated."[1296] For this reason NAPAP's conclusion was that "the vast majority of forests in the U.S. and Canada are not effected by decline . . . Moreover there is no case of forest decline in which acidic deposition is known to be a predominant cause."[1297]

NAPAP also evaluated the consequences of acid rain on lakes and buildings. As far as lakes are concerned, it concluded that in even the most acid-sensitive regions, acidification problems affected only 4 percent of lakes and 8 percent of water courses.[1298] The mountainous regions in the West and the southeastern highlands largely face no problems. Here, less than 1 percent is acidified.[1299] On the other hand there is no doubt that this 1 percent of the lakes have actually lost fish as well as benthic fauna and flora.

As far as lakes in Europe are concerned, Norway and the other Scandinavian countries have been hit hardest. In 27 percent of all lakes in Norway the sulfur deposition exceeds the critical load. In Finland it is 10 percent, in Sweden and Denmark 9 percent.[1300] Within the last decade, however, the lakes in most countries in Europe, including Scandinavia, have become less acidic, as can be seen from Figure 99, primarily because of reductions in SO_2 emissions.

Finally, NAPAP investigated the extent to which acid rain actually damages buildings and monuments. It turned out that if the acid content was increased by 20 percent, the time at which restoration would be necessary was only brought forward by 2–5 percent.[1301] Even if acid content was reduced by 50 percent, restoration would only be delayed by 10–15 percent.[1302] Thus, by reducing acidity by 50 percent it would be necessary to restore facades not every 50 years but only every 56 years.

As regards forestry, European research drew the same conclusions as NAPAP. Thus the annual report on the state of forests published by the UN and the European Commission in 1996 concluded that "Only in a few cases has air pollution been identified as a cause of [forest] damage."[1303] Equally, the UN concluded in its review of the world's forests in 1997 that "the widespread death of European forests due to air pollution which was predicted by many in the 1980's did not occur."[1304]

It has turned out that forest death never actually affected more than 0.5 percent at most of the overall European forest area.[1305] It also turns out that the substantial local forest death in Bavaria, Poland and the Czech Republic was due not to acid rain but to local pollution – that smoke directly from the sources of pollution damaged the trees.[1306] Localized pollution such as this can be, and has been, regulated locally, unlike acid rain which crosses national boundaries. SO_2 emissions have been reduced 30 percent in Germany and 50 percent in both Poland and the Czech Republic, and local SO_2 concentrations decreased 50–70 percent over just seven years from 1989.[1307]

If we look at the growth of European forest, it has not been reduced, as the theories about acid rain had predicted.[1308] In fact, "during the past few decades, forest growth has strongly increased over large parts of Europe," concludes a Dutch study.[1309] That is to say that since the 1950s trees have begun to grow faster and faster, and this is due, as mentioned in connection with rapeseed and cabbage above, to the fact that part of the trees' fertilization requirement is provided for by nitrogen pollution.[1310]

These days, large-scale reports are being prepared about the health of various species of trees in Europe. What is mainly done is to measure the proportion of trees with heavy foliage loss and the proportion of discolored trees. This proportion grew dramatically from the first reports in 1983 and led, understandably enough, to panic. Today we know, however, that this was purely due to a change in the method of calculation.[1311]

Even so, the proportion of trees showing heavy foliage loss today is over 25 percent, which has urged many people to claim that our forests are still in a bad state.[1312] One theory frequently advanced is that pollution does not directly cause damage to the trees (as was assumed by the acid rain theory), but that it weakens the trees' resistance, making them more susceptible to insect attack, frost and drought.[1313] This theory is not easy to put to the test, especially as it is often claimed that the effect can be indirect and delayed. However, it does seem striking that in comparing the various areas' pollution with forest death, there is very little or no correlation.[1314]

This is also why the European Environment Agency concludes that "a causal connection cannot . . . be established between an input of acid deposition . . . and observed foliage reduction."[1315] Actually, the EEA finds that monitoring results show an ever increasing defoliation, despite SO_2 emission reductions, and that the cause may instead be due to the aging of the monitored tree stands.[1316]

In the same vein, a German scientist has analyzed photographs of forest areas taken 30–60 years ago and found that the proportion of damaged trees was just as great then as it is today.[1317] Foliage loss is in reality simply a non-specific expression that applies to numerous specific, familiar diseases, and the reason why we have started worrying about it is that we have started monitoring this loss.[1318]

As mentioned in the section on SO_2, it was probably reasonable to reduce SO_2 emissions from the point of view of health, because the side effect was fewer particles. But acid rain was simply not the terrible threat we were told it was in the 1980s. The anticipated, large-scale forest death never took place.

Unfortunately the myth lives on in many places. In a long litany of worries, published in the *American Journal of Public Health* in 1999, it is stated quite casually how personal health problems are turning into public environmental issues, "as communities discover toxic waste dumps, polychlorinated biphenyls (PCBs) in their rivers, and acid rain destroying their forests."[1319] Likewise, the Danish daily *Politiken* recently wrote, briefly and to the point: "Sulfur in the atmosphere produces acid rain. And acid rain kills forests."[1320]

Simple. But not borne out by the evidence.

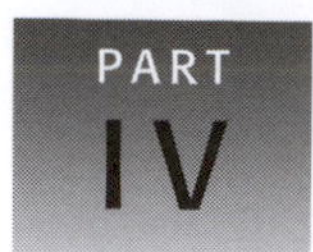

17 Indoor air pollution

When we think of air pollution, what immediately comes to mind is smoke and car exhaust fumes – outdoor pollution. But although this is dangerous, at a global level indoor pollution actually poses a far greater health risk.[1321] The latest estimate from WHO, as depicted in Figure 100, shows that indoor air pollution costs about 14 times more deaths than outdoor air pollution. Moreover, both in developing and developed urban areas, the death toll from it is far greater. In total, indoor air pollution is estimated to cost 2.8 million lives each year.

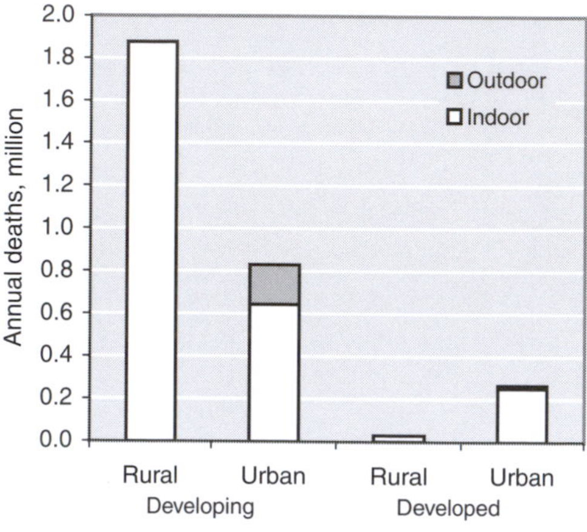

Figure 100 Estimated global annual deaths from indoor and outdoor pollution. Source: WHO 1997:17.

Indoor air pollution in the developing world

Indoor pollution is especially a problem in the Third World. Here, about 3.5 billion people – more than half the population of the globe – depend on traditional fuels such as firewood, charcoal, dried dung and agricultural wastes to cook and heat their homes.[1322] These fuels all develop far more soot, particles, carbon monoxide and toxic chemicals than more modern fuels such as gas and kerosene.

When particles and carbon monoxide in particular are released in large quantities in small homes, they subject the residents to far higher contamination levels than they would meet in even the most highly polluted city. Several WHO studies have shown that average daily indoor air pollution in developing countries is 1,000–2,000 percent or more above the recommended maximum threshold.[1323] So indoors, one finds air that on average is 3–37 times as polluted as the outdoor air in the most polluted megacities such as Beijing, New Delhi and Mexico City.[1324]

Extra fuel is of course burnt when people are making food and already incredibly high pollution levels can be increased by a further 500 percent (i.e. totaling anywhere between 5,000–10,000 percent above the WHO recommended maximum level).[1325] In particular the women who are doing the cooking, as well as their children, are exposed to this indoor atmospheric pollution. Smoke contributes to acute respiratory infections, which on a global basis kill more than 4 million children and infants a year.[1326] It is estimated that children exposed to high levels of indoor atmospheric pollution are between twice and six times as likely to contract serious respiratory infections.[1327] For women, atmospheric pollution means a far higher risk of getting chronic pneumonia or cancer and experiencing problems with childbirth.[1328] A study in Mexico showed that women who had been exposed to wood smoke for many years were 75 times more likely to get chronic pneumonia. Likewise, women in the Xuan Wei country in China cook using traditional fuels. When the US EPA investigated the risk of non-smoking women in the province getting lung cancer, the figure they arrived at was 125.6 per 100,000 compared to the Chinese national average of just 3.2. Analyses of blood and indoor air indicated that fuel burning inside the house was the primary cause of lung cancer.[1329]

The WHO estimates 2.8 million annual deaths from indoor air pollution, making it one of the largest single mortality factors in the world – 5.5 percent of all deaths.[1330] This is an extremely large figure and backs the World Bank's decision to name indoor air pollution as one of the world's four most crucial environmental problems.[1331]

One of the most important contributions to the solution of the indoor air pollution problem will materialize when generally improving wealth in the developing world makes it possible for people to change from cheap but dirty to more expensive but cleaner fuels such as kerosene and gas.[1332] Also for this reason it is vital to focus on increased growth in Third World income per capita.

Indoor air pollution in the developed world

One of the paradoxical consequences of the dramatic and welcome reduction in outdoor air pollution is that the relative impact of air pollution indoors is now greater than it is outdoors.[1333] This is mainly because we spend by far most of our time indoors and because our homes have become more tightly sealed since the oil crisis because we insulate them better. At the same time, indoor air pollution represents a considerable challenge because the level of pollution is much more difficult to monitor, regulate and reduce. As a matter of curiosity it is worth noting that green plants do not help to improve indoor air to any measurable extent.[1334]

According to the US EPA, the four most dangerous substances are not the major outdoor criteria pollutants, but radon gas, cigarette smoke, formaldehyde and asbestos.[1335] Radon is an invisible, radioactive gas which seeps up into buildings through the earth. It is a breakdown product from uranium-238, which occurs naturally in the subsoil and is quite harmless when it is released, spreads and breaks down in fresh air. Inside our homes, however, the gas and its decay products build up to considerable levels and when inhaled can cause lung cancer.[1336]

Radon accounts for about 55 percent of the overall radiation to which humans are exposed under normal conditions.[1337] Although its effects are still disputed, it is estimated that radon seeping into homes causes between 15,000 and 22,000 of the 157,000 lung cancer deaths in the US.[1338] In the EU the mortality figure is estimated to be around 10,000 or about 1 percent of all cancer deaths.[1339]

It is a small proportion of houses that account for most of the radon problem. In the US it is estimated that some 6 percent of all houses are above the threshold value of 148 Bq/m^3 (Becquerel per cubic meter)[1340] and reducing levels in these homes would reduce the incidence of radon-related lung cancer by a third.[1341] In order to reduce these concentrations it is necessary to place an airtight membrane under the carpets or provide some form of ventilation.[1342]

Cigarette smoke causes an very high mortality among smokers, but non-smokers are also affected through passive smoking. The particle pollution (PM_{10}) is two or three times higher in houses with smokers than in other houses.[1343] It is estimated that some 3,000 deaths a year in the US are due to passive smoking and that between 180,000 and 300,000 children a year get pneumonia or bronchitis because of it.[1344] In Denmark, more than 66 percent of all children are subjected to passive smoking either at home or in day-care.[1345]

Formaldehyde in homes comes primarily from the adhesives in pressed wood products like particleboard, hardwood paneling and medium density fiberboard, and it can cause nausea and watery eyes. Higher doses may cause breathing difficulties and trigger asthma attacks, and formaldehyde is also suspected of being carcinogenic.[1346]

Asbestos is a mineral consisting of microscopic fibers which, when breathed in, can cause lung cancer or asbestosis (scar tissue from fiber damage). Asbestos is cheap, fireproof and a good insulator, and it was therefore used in a multitude of products such as pipe and furnace materials, millboards, textured paints, and floor tiles.[1347] Only later was the elevated risk to asbestos workers documented, and the material was banned for interior use in the US in 1974.[1348]

Asbestos is typically encapsulated, for example in ceiling tiles, and in this form it is probably not dangerous.[1349] It has still not been determined whether it is actually a good idea to remove asbestos or whether it should remain in place, just as it is not clear how risky the low-level effect of asbestos actually is.[1350]

Generally speaking it is difficult to determine the relative importance of indoor versus outdoor air pollution in the developed world. The WHO estimates in Figure 100 clearly seem to indicate that even in the developed world the number of deaths from indoor air pollution is far the greater of the two, but the WHO's modeling efforts have primarily focused on indoor pollution, and the estimate on outdoor air pollution seems much too small, given the discussion on particulate pollution above. A more likely estimate is that the two are somewhat equivalent – in the US, indoor air pollution is estimated to cause between 85,000 and 150,000 deaths a year compared to between 65,000 and 200,000 deaths caused by outdoor air pollution.[1351]

As regards the four major indoor air pollutants it can be noted that little has been done about radon and that its effect has probably been aggravated over the last 20 years because better-insulated homes have increasingly poor ventilation. The proportion of the population that smokes, however, has fallen drastically in the USA, from 42 percent in 1965 to only 25 percent in 1997.[1352] As far as formaldehyde and asbestos are concerned, products containing the dangerous substances have been gradually phased out or better regulated, and this has probably increased safety in the long term.

All in all, the number of deaths is undoubtedly considerably lower in the developed world than those caused by indoor air pollution problems in the Third World.

18 Allergies and asthma

We often hear that allergies are becoming much more common and that in some way or other this is linked to the fact that the environment is continually deteriorating.[1353] But how much do we know about allergies and asthma and their connections to our surroundings? On the whole it can be said that, despite considerable research efforts, we are unsure on several essential points as to what causes allergy and asthma and even whether they actually are becoming more common.

To be allergic means that one is hypersensitive to specific substances (allergens); that one gets a powerful immune reaction even at concentrations which do not bother other people.[1354] There are many kinds of allergies: hay fever, asthma, food allergies, nettle rash, anaphylactic shock[1355] and eczema. It is estimated that in Europe around 10–30 percent of people have some form of allergy, by far most common being hay fever and nickel allergy.[1356] In the US, about 35 percent describe themselves as being allergic, whereas official estimates run at about 18.5 percent.[1357] Allergy is the sixth leading cause of chronic disease in the US.[1358]

Globally, asthma is one of the most serious allergies. Just under 6 percent or 15 million Americans have it,[1359] whereas more than 30 percent or 18 million Britons have asthmatic symptoms.[1360] Asthma causes the air passages to narrow. Unlike chronic bronchitis, for example, this narrowing is generally temporary and stops either spontaneously or after treatment.[1361]

Virtually all studies from around the world show that the incidence of asthma has been on the increase, as can be seen from Figure

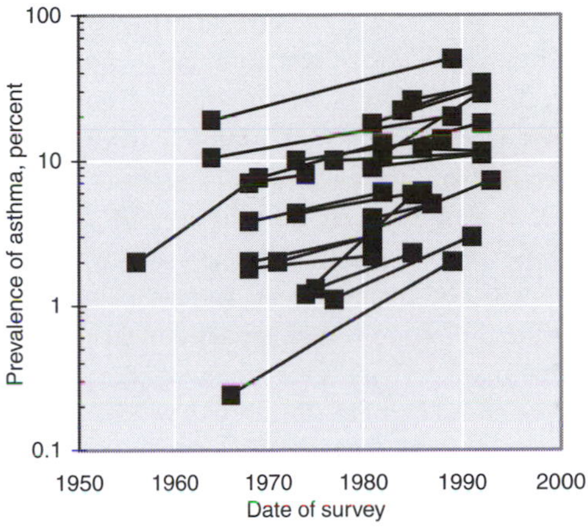

Figure 101 Changes in prevalence of asthma and wheeze, according to surveys conducted 1956–93. Notice, the graph is here reproduced as published in *British Medical Journal*, using a logarithmic second axis. If depicted in actual percent, the increase would look even more dramatic. Source: Jarvis and Burney 1998:607.

101. The rate of increase has been around 5 percent a year in the UK and figures of the same magnitude have been found in Sweden, Switzerland, Norway, the US, Australia, New Zealand and Taiwan.[1362] But the question is, of course, whether this is due to actual increase, or whether it is purely evidence of increased public and medical awareness of the illness. An interpretation of this kind is not as amazing as it may seem. For one thing, diagnosing asthma is far from straightforward. For example, the WHO, the American College of Chest Physicians/American Thoracic Society, and the National Asthma Education Programme

Expert Panel Report use different definitions when identifying asthma.[1363] Consequently, measuring the incidence is not merely a counting problem.[1364]

In addition to this, our own knowledge influences to a large degree our classification of our ailments. Many people today have become aware of allergies related to food and typically about 20 percent of the population believe they have a food allergy. Clinical studies show, however, that only about 1.4 percent of all adults actually suffer from food-related allergies.[1365] Equally, there is an increased public awareness of asthma. Thus, there is a distinct risk that if we had asked a sample of the public 20 years ago whether they suffered from asthma, and asked another sample today, we would get a much larger percentage of affirmations today even if there had been no change.

Unfortunately, there are very few studies that employ robust monitoring of asthma over time so as to provide a reasonable comparison. A recent meta-study (a study of many other investigations) in the *British Medical Journal* concluded that, despite the massive number of scientific studies, "the evidence for increased prevalences of asthma and wheezing is weak because the measures used are susceptible to systematic errors."[1366] Nevertheless, most doctors believe that the massive increases in registered incidence do indeed indicate some actual – though smaller – increase.[1367]

At the same time there has also been a small increase in mortality from asthma. This can be interpreted as objective proof that the number of cases is increasing.[1368] There are, however, certainly other explanations. It was not until the sixties that mortality from asthma increased dramatically for a time in many countries. However, today the increase is believed to have been caused by exaggerated or erroneous use of so-called non-selective β agonists.[1369] A slight increase in mortality over the past 20 years is assumed primarily to have been caused by poor treatment, especially of disadvantaged groups such as blacks and the poor.[1370] Mortality in England and Wales fell during the late eighties and early nineties, and is now at its lowest level since monitoring began in 1969.[1371]

Although it may still not be clear whether asthma is strongly on the advance, the intense growth in *acknowledged* asthma is causing an increasing burden on the public health budget. In the US, the overall cost of asthma is estimated at about $7 billion, and in the EU the total direct and indirect costs are estimated at $29 billion.[1372] Today at least 10 percent of children and 5 percent of adults in the Western world suffer from it.[1373]

Consequently, it is also important to find out what causes asthma. It is to a large extent genetic – because our genes partly decide whether we have a "sensitive" or "thick-skinned" immune defense system.[1374] Studies of twins have shown that between 40 and 60 percent of asthma incidence is hereditary.[1375] However, genetics can probably not explain the large discrepancies there are between the nations (see e.g. Figure 101), where symptoms of asthma are more common in New Zealand, Australia, the USA and UK than in the rest of Europe. Children are also more prone to it – boys more so than girls.[1376] Those children who suffer from a mild form typically grow out of it, whereas those who have a more serious form are burdened with it for the rest of their lives.[1377]

The other major cause of asthma comes from our surroundings. There generally seems to be more in towns and cities than in the countryside.[1378] This could, of course, just be caused by factors such as wealth, nutrition and stress. However, many migrants to urban areas have been examined and it was found that the migrants faced a far higher risk of getting asthma than those who stayed behind.[1379]

Now it would be tempting to believe that the increase is caused by air pollution, but as we have seen, air pollution has been falling in the Western world over the past 20–30 years. It turns out that although pollution can make things worse for asthma sufferers, it cannot in itself cause the disease.[1380] Actually, not even the heavy smoke from the oil fires started by retreating Iraqi forces in the Gulf War aftermath could be registered in the Kuwaiti asthma rates.[1381] In fact, the official British committee set up to investigate the medical aspects of outdoor air pollution drew the somewhat surprising conclusion: "As regards the initiation of asthma, most of the available evidence does not support a causative role for outdoor air pollution . . . Asthma has increased in the UK over the past thirty years but this is unlikely to be the result of changes in air pollution."[1382]

This conclusion is reinforced by the fact that asthma is often most common in industrialized countries, where air pollution has been on the decline, and not in the developing world where it is increasing.[1383] The only obvious external air pollution causes are biological pollutants, known allergens such as pollen and fungal spores.

The causes of asthma are more likely to be found in our homes. The children of smokers face double the risk of getting asthma, and smoke aggravates pre-existing asthma.[1384] It is estimated that around 380,000 asthma cases in the US are caused by parental smoking.[1385] By far the majority of asthmatic patients are also hypersensitive to dust mites, which thrive in our northerly, damp air, where there are generally more asthma sufferers.[1386] When bed sheets, which often come to contain large numbers of dust mites, were introduced among some tribes in New Guinea, the incidence of asthma increased dramatically.[1387] In addition to this, cats, cockroaches and fungal spores also contribute considerably to allergic reactions, but unfortunately no one has yet investigated whether the increase in the number of asthma cases could be caused by the fact that, for example, more people now keep cats.[1388]

On the other hand, we do know that since the energy crisis we have dramatically increased the insulation of our homes in order to cut the heating bill. Today, the indoor air in our homes is replaced on average 10 times less frequently than it was 30 years ago.[1389] This has led to a marked increase in atmospheric humidity, in concentrations of dust mites and other allergens.[1390] In addition to this we now have far more soft furnishings and wall to wall carpets, in which dust mites thrive.[1391]

Finally, we spend much more time indoors. We do not go out nearly as much as we used to, to pursue sports or take part in outdoor events. Instead, we spend our time playing computer games, watching TV and videos, what some researchers have called Indoor Entertainment Culture.[1392] It is estimated that we now spend about 90 percent of our time indoors – 65 percent of this in our own homes.[1393] This means that we are to an ever higher degree exposed to increasingly concentrated doses of allergens, which may be one of the main explanations for the large proportion of asthma cases.

Unfortunately, asthma still has many unknown factors to it. A new explanation which is gaining momentum is the so-called "hygiene hypothesis."[1394] Basically it suggests that as we have stamped out all the major infectious diseases, using antibiotics and vaccinations, we have essentially left our immune system with nothing to do, lacking practice fighting bacteria and viruses. Popularly speaking, this leaves the immune system to run amok when encountering otherwise harmless microbes or substances. Many findings seem to support such an interpretation. Children who suffer many infections (and get their immune system exercised) apparently face a smaller risk of getting asthma. The youngest children in large families face a smaller risk of getting asthma because their older siblings have passed many infections on to them.[1395] More direct confirmation for the hygiene hypothesis comes from a new Italian study. It showed that men heavily exposed to microbes were less likely to experience respiratory allergy.[1396] Several other studies have also shown that exposure to measles, parasites and tuberculosis seems to reduce the risk of getting asthma.[1397] Equally, it has been observed that children receiving oral antibiotics by the age of 2 were more susceptible to allergies than children who had no antibiotics.[1398] A new British study shows that children with early and repeated viral infections seem to have a reduced risk of developing asthma.[1399]

At the same time one can also see a connection between eating habits (e.g. fast food and salty food) and asthma, although it has not yet been determined whether it is a cause.[1400] A connection can also be seen between premature babies and their later development of asthma, and the higher survival rate of premature babies may also be part of the explanation of a larger proportion of asthma cases.[1401]Finally, obesity seems to give a predisposition to asthma, and as more and more people get overweight, that may also explain part of the asthma increase.[1402]

This is why, as time goes by, many researchers agree that developing asthma is probably caused by a whole series of changes in our lifestyle.[1403] The main thing to point out here, however, is that there is no reason to assume that it is due to a deterioration of our environment, but rather because we have sealed up our homes, spend more time indoors and have more soft objects around the home.

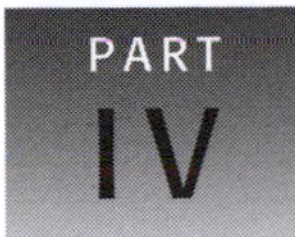

19 Water pollution

About 71 percent of the Earth is covered by the salt water of the oceans. Lakes constitute scarcely half a percent of the surface of the Earth. Half of these are freshwater lakes, and the rivers in turn constitute only 0.2 percent of the area of freshwater lakes.[1404]

Obviously, coastal waters, rivers and lakes are far more important to people than the oceans – primarily because we live much closer to them – but it still illustrates how enormous the oceans are in comparison to the bodies of water we are used to dealing with.[1405]

Oil pollution in the oceans

On the subject of ocean pollution, it is traditional to quote Thor Heyerdahl. In 1947 he traversed the Pacific on his Kon Tiki expedition, without catching sight of people, ships or rubbish for weeks. On his second expedition in 1970, on the other hand, when he crossed the Atlantic with his boat the *Ra II*, he saw "far more oil lumps than fish." Heyerdahl concluded: "It became clear to all of us that mankind really was in the process of polluting its most vital well-spring, our planet's indispensable filtration plant, the ocean."[1406]

But the oceans are so incredibly big that our impact on them has been astoundingly insignificant – the oceans contain more than 1,000 billion billion liters of water.[1407] The UN's overall evaluation of the oceans concludes: "The open sea is still relatively clean. Low levels of lead, synthetic organic compounds and artificial radionuclides, though widely detectable, are biologically insignificant. Oil slicks and litter are common along sea lanes, but are, at present, a minor consequence to communities of organisms living in open-ocean waters."[1408] It actually turns out that the very lumps of oil that Heyerdahl was so worried about are now much fewer in number. It is estimated that in 1985 about 60 percent of the marine sources of oil pollution came from the routine tanker transport operation, while 20 percent came from regular oil spills of the kind we see on TV, and about 15 percent come from natural oil seepage at the bottom of the sea and from sediment erosion.[1409]

Routine oil pollution is due to the fact that tankers use sea water in their tanks as ballast when they sail without oil. This means that oil remnants get mixed into the ballast water, which on arrival gets flushed out into the harbor. Several international agreements have regulated and to a large degree reduced the extent of routine oil pollution, demanding by law new techniques for the handling of ballast water, e.g. exploiting the fact that water and oil separate (ensuring that only the bottom layer of water is poured out on arrival), removing the last remnants of oil in the tanks (by cleaning the tanks with oil instead of water), improving waste facilities in port, and finally demanding separate water ballast tanks.[1410]

Natural oil spills originate from cracks in the bottom of the sea above oil reserves. It may come as a surprise, but mankind's exploitation of oil has relieved the pressure on many of these oil pockets and presumably reduced the natural leak of oil.[1411] However, neither of these two sources of oil pollution has been particularly well documented over time.

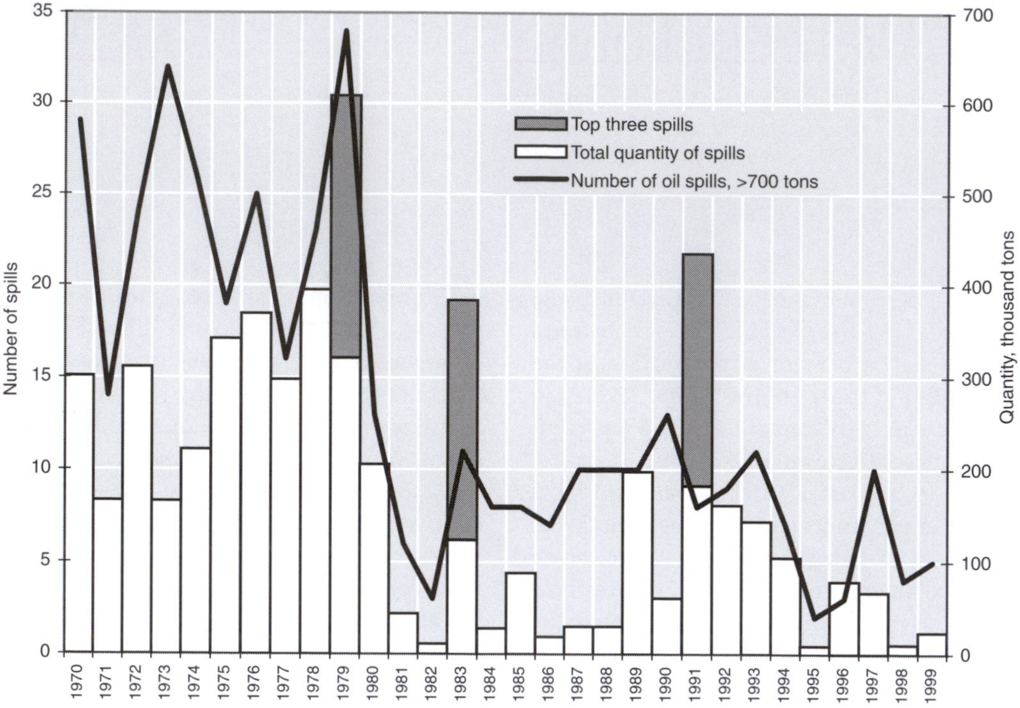

Figure 102 Worldwide number of large oil spills (black line, more than 700 tons spilt) and total quantity of oil spilt (bars), 1970–99. The three largest spills (*Atlantic Empress* in 1979, *Castillo de Bellver* in 1983 and *ABT Summer* in 1991) are marked. Notice that the *Exxon Valdez* oil spill in 1989 was only the 20th worst oil spill, one-eighth of *Atlantic Empress* (see also text below). Source: ITOPF 2000.

We are well aware on the other hand, from international statistics, what has happened over time when it comes to accidental oil spills. Figure 102 shows both the number of major tanker accidents and the overall quantity of oil spilt. Well over 80 percent of the spilt oil originates from major accidents.[1412] It is quite clear that the number of accidental spills has been reduced over time: whereas there were about 24 major accidents a year before 1980 there were about nine a year in the 1980s and just eight in the 1990s. Similarly, the quantity of oil spilt fell from about 318,000 tons a year in the 1970s to just 110,000 tons in the 1990s.[1413] The same reduction in the quantity of oil spilt shows up for the US, as is clear in Figure 103. Here, the average annual oil spill was 14.3 million gallons in the 1970s, compared to just 2.6 million gallons in the 1990s.[1414]

All the same, most tanker accidents occur close to land and the large spills affect the local fauna and flora. We are all familiar with the typical TV news scenario: oil-laden birds expiring before our eyes on the evening news, black-coated seals, the frantic cleanup efforts to avoid ecological catastrophe, and afterwards the massive bill.[1415] Several reports are, however, beginning to question whether these efforts are worth the hefty price tag.

A report carried out for the US Congress investigated two accidents on drilling rigs and four tanker accidents. It showed that although the marine animals affected were hard-hit to begin with, the "recovery of species populations in almost every case studied has been

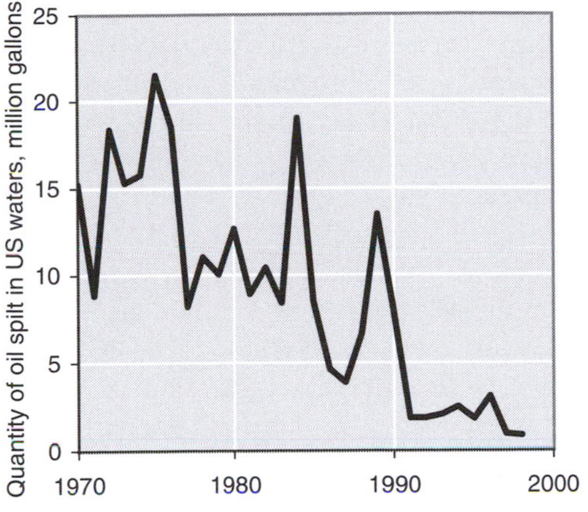

Figure 103 Quantity of oil spilt in US waters, 1970–98. Source: CEQ 1993:421, USCG 1999.[1416]

swift."[1417] Ecological and economic consequences have been "relatively modest, and, as far as can be determined, of relatively short duration."[1418]

The report points out that oil is a naturally occurring substance and, given a little time, most of the oil will evaporate, degrade biologically and chemically, or form relatively harmless lumps of tar.[1419] This is also what has been found in follow-up analyses of the British oil spill from *Braer* in 1993, where the official monitoring program found that "by 1994 the [contamination] levels had fallen to those observed at sites remote from contamination."[1420] In connection with publication of the Congressional report, the esteemed publication *Science* asked several scientists for their opinion; because of the controversial nature of the problem at hand, they were not willing to have their names published, although they did agree with the main message of the report: that there is a good deal of overreaction in connection with oil spills and that the money spent cleaning up often could have been made better use of elsewhere.[1421]

We find the same picture in two of the places to be hardest hit by oil pollution: the Arabian Gulf after the Gulf War and Prince William Sound after the Exxon Valdez accident.

Oil in the Gulf

During his retreat in the Gulf War in 1991, Saddam Hussein ordered a refinery in Kuwait to release between 6 and 8 million tons of oil into the Gulf, leaving it with the world's biggest ever case of marine oil pollution.[1422] In their 1992 Gulf report, Greenpeace claimed it to be "an unprecedented disaster" and described how "there has been considerable damage to the shallow coastal areas of Saudi Arabia and southern Kuwait . . . The flora and fauna in these areas are vital to the survival of the shallow Gulf ecosystem. Disruption at this fundamental level will have repercussions through the whole system that will be seen only after a period of time and possibly at some distance from the immediate areas."[1423] This "devastating blow wreaked on the environment will increase the impact on human life for a long time to come," and yet the events are only indicators of the coming "long-term problems."[1424]

Other initial reports similarly suggested large-scale marine extinction and gave pessimistic prognoses of the future recovery of the Gulf.[1425] Bahrain's Health Minister claimed that the oil slicks were "the biggest environmental crisis in modern times," and that it could spell "the potential end of wildlife in this area."[1426] Consequently, a task force of 70 marine scientists, together with the EU and the Saudi Arabian environment commission, carried out extensive studies in order to chart the damage and evaluate the situation.[1427]

The mid-term report came in 1994 and was basically positive in its conclusions. Animal life in the sea itself was "in much better shape than even the most optimistic of pundits could have predicted."[1428] On the other hand, the coastal areas had been harder hit, but had now "largely recovered".[1429] The upper section of the tidal stretch had been very hard hit and there was still much less animal life than in other comparable areas. There was in general, however, "a trend towards recovery with species diversity and population densities increasing."[1430]

The same conclusion was reached by the IAEA marine biology laboratory in 1992, which had investigated the Gulf for traces of oil and found that in just four months "the spilt oil had to a high degree been degraded." In addition they found when analyzing the water that it did not contain larger quantities of oil residues than on other coastal stretches in the US and the UK, and there was less than in the Baltic.[1431] These findings have been replicated in later studies.[1432]

The latest reviews ending in 1995 also showed firm biological recovery. While the lower-shore biota had suffered 15–80 percent diversity reduction and the upper-shore biota almost 100 percent reduction by the end of 1991, the lower shores were back to 100 percent and the upper shores back to 71–100 percent. The top shores were equally back to 83–100 percent of equal, unpolluted shores in 1995.[1433]

Despite the fact that the oil pollution in the Gulf was the most extensive the world had ever seen and cost many animals their lives, it did not become the long-term ecological catastrophe people had feared and expected.

Exxon Valdez: still a catastrophe?

Four minutes past midnight on 24 March 1989, the oil tanker *Exxon Valdez* ran aground in Prince William Sound in Alaska with more than a million barrels of oil on board. The ship leaked a total of 266,000 barrels of oil, making the accident the twentieth most serious of its kind – an accident about 25 times smaller than the Gulf incident.[1434] The accident has become the symbol of the big greedy company that without consideration for the environment triggers an ecological catastrophe. According to an American poll of young people, the *Exxon Valdez* "symbolizes their biggest worry – the livability of the planet."[1435] Ten years later most Americans still remember the *Exxon Valdez* name, and 66 percent believe that the beaches and waters are still polluted.[1436]

Exxon has paid out about $3.5 billion in connection with the accident: $2.1 billion for the cleanup operation, about a billion for restoration, and a quarter of a billion to the local fishermen, while a 1994 class action suit awarding $5 billion dollars in punitive damages is still wrangling its way through appeals.[1437]

Because of the large sum of money involved, both Exxon and the government authorities have carried out their own scientific investigations.[1438] A so-called Trustee Council of civil servants administered $900 million for the restoration process.[1439] Since they get $100 million more if they find more damage caused by the oil by 2006 it is unlikely that their report would be the most optimistic one.[1440] The Trustee Council's 2000 annual report examined the losses and future prospects.

The oil spill caused heavy oiling of some 200 miles of coastline and light oiling of some additional 1,100 miles of the 9,000 miles of total coastline in the spill region.[1441] It is estimated that the oil spill cost the lives of 300 harbor seals, 2,800 sea otters, 250,000 sea birds, 250 bald eagles and possibly 22 killer whales.[1442] While this is naturally an awful toll, we also need to put this death into perspective – the total 250,000 dead birds from the Exxon Valdez disaster is still less that the number of birds which die on a single day in the US, colliding with plate glass, or the number of birds that are killed by domestic cats in Britain in two days.[1443]

The report also examines the status of the individual species, and it becomes obvious that ecological collapse is a long way off. The river otters have essentially recovered.[1444] For the sea otters, "it is clear that recovery is underway."[1445] Some 13 percent of the harbor seals died as a result of the spill, and their decline in numbers, which began in 1973 –

long before Exxon Valdez – has continued.[1446] The bald eagle has "recovered." A pod of 36 killer whales lost 13 members in the two years following the oil spill, and though the overall Gulf of Alaska population has increased since 1989, the Trustee Council has categorized the killer whales as "not recovering" since the pod has only been increased by two members since 1996 and since "it is expected to take many years for natural reproduction to make up for those losses."[1447]

Pacific herring stocks remained strong until 1992, after which they collapsed. This led to intense charges that the collapse was the result of the oil spill.[1448] Today we know that it was caused by a virus and a fungal infection. This, however, may have been because the fish were weakened by stress, which in turn could have links with the *Exxon Valdez*.[1449]

Several other species were also examined, that are doing better or worse, but the general impression is that not much damage has been done. The report refrains from reaching any conclusion, but *Scientific American* interviewed several of the scientists from the Trustee Council about the restoration process. Ernie Piper of the Alaskan environment department said: "In terms of the ecology, that, in many ways, it appears to me, is a lot more resilient than we deserve. At the same time, there are lots of effects from the spill and the cleanup that are not going to go away." The Trustee fund's senior scientist, Robert Spies, says: "I think it is an improved picture. But it is still variable, depending on what resource you are talking about."[1450]

The US National Oceanic and Atmospheric Administration (NOAA), which has been deeply involved in the cleanup effort, made a ten-year summary, asking themselves whether the Prince William Sound had in fact recovered: "That answer is a definite, 'Yes and no.' On the one hand . . . our work in the field, laboratory, and on the frontlines of statistical theory indicate that, yes, by many criteria, a number of the intertidal communities we study can be considered recovered. Does that mean all traces of the largest spill in U.S. history are gone and the Sound is recovered? No, not necessarily." Yet, they are "impressed by the degree to which Prince William Sound has rebounded from the spill and its aftermath," and conclude that "we consider Prince William Sound to be well along the road to recovery – but not yet recovered."[1451]

Other scientists do not beat about the bush so much. John Wiens of Colorado State University says that it is "apparent that seabird populations were not devastated by the spill" and that "it now appears that the spill had few persistent or devastating long-term effects on seabirds."[1452] Edward Gilfillan, who carried out the large-scale scientific investigation for Exxon, says that as early as "1990 between 73 and 91 percent of the area had recovered."[1453]

Perhaps the clearest statement from the Trustee Council came in 1999, when the executive director, Molly McCammon, stated: "The ecosystem is well on its way to recovery, but the long-term impacts on individual populations may take decades to fully heal."[1454]

Perhaps more surprising, official NOAA investigations have shown that the original cleanup has probably done more harm than good. It is estimated that about 20 percent of the original oil evaporated, 50 percent was broken down, 12 percent is lying in lumps on the bottom and about 3 percent is still on the beaches in non-toxic lumps.[1455] In addition, 8 percent was removed from the surface of the water and 6 percent from the beaches. Pressure-washing the coast, however, killed much of the marine life. By way of experiment, some stretches of beach were left uncleaned, and it transpired that life there returned after just 18 months, whereas it did not do so to the cleaned beaches for three to four years.[1456] The oil experts had said this would be the case time and time again during the first few months of the cleanup – but in vain, as this did not harmonize with the public view of things, i.e. that a cleanup had to be better for the animals.[1457] As *Scientific*

American wrote, "the public wants the animals saved – at $80,000 per otter and $10,000 per eagle – even if the stress of their salvation kills them."[1458]

The conclusion is that although the immediate biological loss in Alaska was high, it was roughly the equivalent of one day of plate glass death to birds in the US or two days of domestic cat kill in Britain. Another thought-provoking comparison is that the overall pollution was less than 2 percent of pollution caused by powerboats in the US every year.[1459] And finally, that all actors agree that the sound has almost fully recovered or will do so within decades.

The price of the cleanup totaled more than $2 billion, and it probably did more to harm the natural environment than it did to repair it. Just a few years after the accident most of the area was teeming with life once again. Or as Jesse Walker puts it in *Reason*: "To the extent that the sound has recovered, it has done so almost entirely through natural processes; the human cleanup has been a money pit and little else."[1460]

This does not of course mean that the oil spill was not a very unfortunate accident, but it does emphasize the question which Congress also put: could we not have put the $2.1 billion to better use?

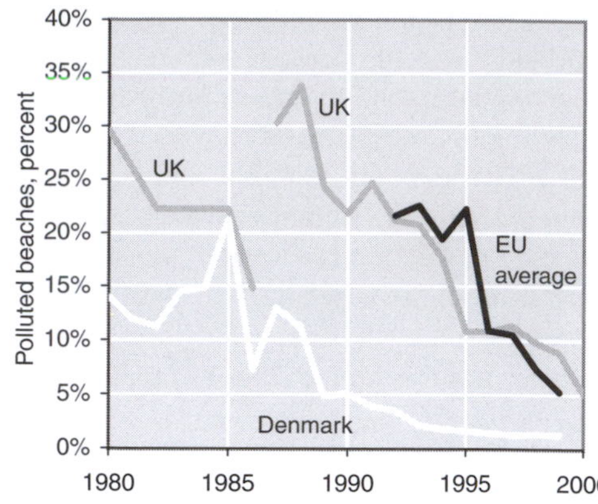

Figure 104 Percentage of beaches not complying with local or EU regulations for the UK (1980–2000), Denmark (1980–99) and an average of the EU (1992–9). The UK changed the number of surveyed beaches dramatically from 1986 (27 beaches) to 1987 (360–463 beaches), effectively making a new index. The Danish index is only based on fecal coliform (and thus lower), whereas the UK and the EU average is based on the EU bathing water directive (measuring also enteroviruses and salmonellae, EU 1975). Source: UK EA 2000, EU 2000b, DK EPA 1994:66, 1996b:67, 1997b:67, 1999, 2000.[1462]

Pollution in coastal waters

As far as people are concerned, one of the most relevant indicators of quality when it comes to sea water is how much of a health risk it is. Water contaminated with bacteria, viruses, protozoans, fungi and parasites can cause ear or skin infections on contact, and inhalation of contaminated water can cause respiratory diseases.[1461] These pathogens typically live in the intestines of warm-blooded animals and are shed in their feces.

Since it is often extraordinarily difficult to analyze the presence of the many possible pathogens, most regulations use concentrations of easily analyzed fecal bacteria (including fecal coliform, enterococci and *Eschericha coli*) as indicators of contaminated water. Earlier, contaminated water most often came from unregulated sewers, whereas today, with well-regulated sewage treatment, most contamination happens because of sewage overflows and polluted stormwater runoff.[1463]

Generally, the sea water picture is one of rapid improvement (Figure 104). In 1987 the UK had 30 percent polluted beaches, whereas in 2000 the share was down to just 5 percent. For Denmark, 14 percent of all beaches violated the health standards in 1980, whereas in 1999 the share was down to just 1.3 percent. For the European Union on average, the share has fallen even faster – in 1992 more than 21 percent of all European beaches were polluted, whereas in 1999 only 5 percent were polluted. For humans this means that it is now safe to bathe from most beaches in the

UK, Denmark and most other countries in the Community.

Similar figures for beach pollution are unfortunately not available for the US, since measuring standards are set locally.[1464] The National Resources Defense Council has since 1988 asked an ever increasing number of states for the number of beach closings. The number has increased from 484 in 1988 to 7,236 in 1998.[1465] This has been taken by many as an indication that ever more beaches have been polluted, e.g. the Council of Environmental Quality.[1466] However, the data do not warrant such a conclusion, since the National Resources Defense Council have asked ever more states for data – seven in 1988 and 23 in 1998 – and since monitoring and closings are locally decided and inconsistently practiced over time.[1467] This is also pointed out by the National Resources Defense Council in their caution: "It is impossible to make direct comparisons between states or to assess trends over time based on this closure data."[1468]

At the same time, the sea is also a source of food, primarily fish and shellfish. We have already discussed the issue of fishing, but the quality of marine produce is also vital. Figure 105 shows how concentrations of harmful substances such as DDT, PCB, dieldrin and cadmium have fallen drastically in coastal seas. In Denmark this has resulted in declines of DDT and PCB in saltwater fish of more than 90 percent since 1973. The UK, unfortunately, has only just embarked on a project to establish long-term pollution trends, and these are only expected to be ready in 2002.[1469] Analysis of shorter series of DDT and PCB in UK cod liver show similar trends to the Danish ones.[1470]

The US has through its Mussel Watch Project tried to assess marine environmental quality.[1471] It makes sense to measure pollutants in mollusks because they are stationary and easy to collect and their pollutant concentrations are proportional with the ambient concentrations.[1472] Unfortunately, this program has only been functional since 1986. Nevertheless, we see large decreases over the past nine years: 28 percent for cadmium, 36 percent DDT, 48 percent polychlorinated biphenyl (PCB), 56 percent dieldrin, 62 percent polycyclic aromatic hydrocarbons (PAH) and 86 percent butyl tin. The latest US *State of the Coastal Environment* concludes that most pollutant concentrations are decreasing and none is increasing.[1473]

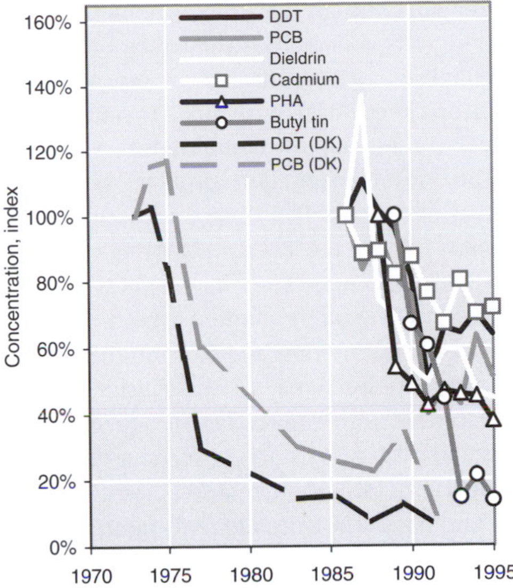

Figure 105 Concentrations of coastal pollutants in fish and shellfish, index for Denmark (1973–92) and the US (1986–95). The Danish data document the average concentrations of DDT and PCB in cod liver (1973=100 percent), the US data shows the median concentrations of DDT, PCB, dieldrin, PAH (1986=100 percent), butyl tin (1988=100 percent) and cadmium (1989=100 percent) in mussels. Source: DK VFA 1994:78, NOAA 1998.

Suffocation in coastal waters

Of course, coastal waters are also the habitat for large populations of flora and fauna, and the welfare of these organisms might also be worth considering on its own. Here we are not thinking in terms of marine life for protein, or water for human amusement, but we are deliberately considering the welfare of plants and animals for themselves or our appreciation of their immediate luxury value – the effect of their "simply being there."

The most conspicuous problem is oxygen depletion – so-called hypoxia – and algae blooms that have been occurring in many parts of the world. They have appeared from New York State's Long Island Sound, California's San Francisco Bay and the Gulf of Mexico off Louisiana, to the Baltic Sea, the Black Sea and the coast of Queensland, Australia.[1474] Apparently, excessive amounts of nutrients run off farmland and into estuaries and bays, allowing algae to flourish, thus causing oxygen depletion as they decay, a condition referred to by biologists as eutrophication.[1475] This condition was described as the UN's main worry about coasts in the world:[1476]

> The rate of introduction of nutrients, chiefly nitrates but sometimes also phosphates, is increasing, and areas of eutrophication are expanding, along with enhanced frequency and scale of unusual plankton blooms and excessive seaweed growth. Two major sources of nutrients to coastal waters are sewage disposal and agricultural run-off from fertilizer-treated fields and from intensive stock raising.[1477]

The problem is often stated to be growing "exponentially"[1478] and was touted – somewhat incredibly – in the UN *Global Environment Outlook 2000* as a problem on a par with global warming.[1479] Thus, while there certainly is a nitrogen problem, it is important to get a feel for its magnitude and importance. This will require a brief detour around the global nitrogen cycle, blue babies and some of nitrogen's other consequences.

Nitrogen is crucially important to life, as it comprises 16 percent of protein, and is a vital component in DNA, enzymes and plant chlorophyll.[1480] Although nitrogen is abundant in the air, N_2 comprising 78 percent, its atmospheric form is unexploitable for plants. They are instead almost exclusively dependent on bacteria that can fix nitrogen in a way that is chemically accessible.[1481] Since this is a rather slow process that has to replace the nitrogen removed by each harvest, nitrogen effectively sets a strict upper limit to yields and thus to food production.[1482]

In the 1800s, European imports of Chilean nitrate and Peruvian guano lifted this production limit slightly. However, it was only when the German Fritz Haber in 1908 synthesized ammonia and Karl Borch in 1914 completed the industrial production process, that it became possible to apply nitrogen fertilizer and increase yields dramatically.[1483] As technical innovation cut electricity requirements by 90 percent,[1484] cheap fertilizer cleared the path for the Green Revolution. The consequence was a sevenfold increase in fertilizer use from 1960 to 1998, as is evident in Figure 106.

However, it is also important to notice that fertilizer use has not continued to grow exponentially, as feared – the growth rates for the US and Western Europe document how total fertilizer consumption has plateaued, as is typical for mature technologies.[1485] And for the developing countries, which still have an expanding population to feed, the growth rate is still positive but has been declining, from 15 percent to just 5 percent a year.

Besides fertilizer, increased biomass production (fields now being sown with soybeans, peas, alfalfa, and other leguminous crops that fix much more nitrogen from the atmosphere than the previous vegetation) and the use of fossil fuels also add to the load on the nitrogen cycle. Fertilizer makes up the main part (about 57 percent) of the extra nitrogen release, increased biomass some 29 percent and fossil fuels the remaining 14 percent.[1486] In all, this nitrogen release is of approximately the same magnitude as the natural nitrogen fixation, thus effectively doubling the globally available nitrogen.[1487]

Synthetic fertilizer has allowed a vast increase in food production, and this was the reasoning of the Swedish Academy of Sciences

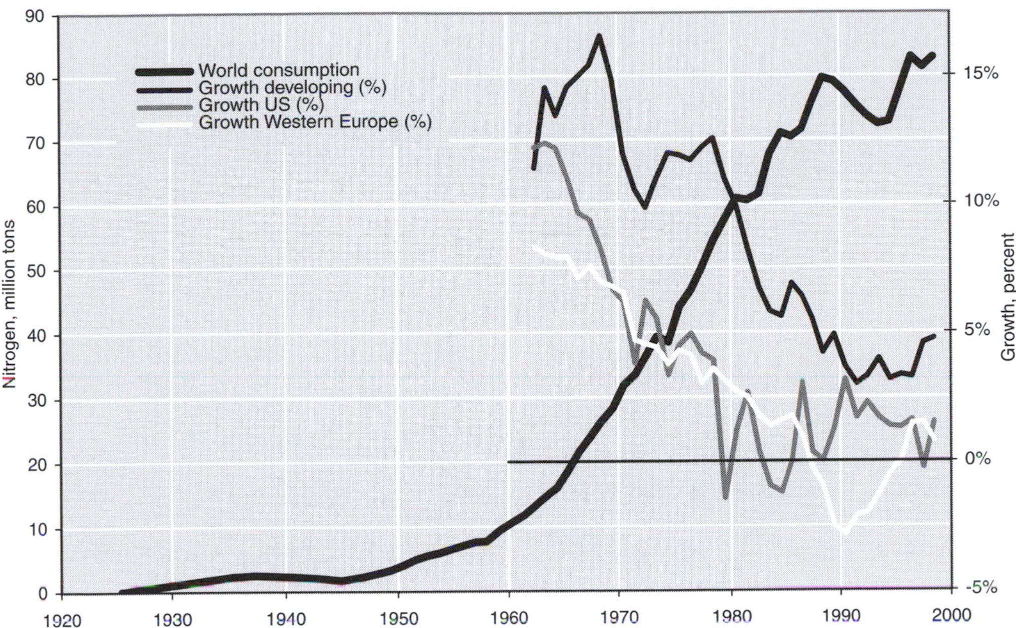

Figure 106 Global fertilizer use 1920–99, and growth in fertilizer use for the US, Western Europe and developing countries 1961–99.[1488] Source: Smil 1990:426, IFA 2000.

when they awarded the Nobel Prize for Chemistry to Fritz Haber in 1919. They argued that Haber had created "an exceedingly important means of improving the standards of agriculture and the well-being of mankind."[1489]

Today, it is estimated that 40 percent of all crop nitrogen comes from synthetic fertilizer, and about one-third of human protein consumption depends on synthetic fertilizer.[1490] Moreover, fertilizer allows us to produce more food on less farmland. This is one of the reasons why the global population could double from 1960 to 2000 *and* get better fed, although farmland area only increased 12 percent.[1491]

This should be compared with the quadrupling of farmland from 1700 to 1960 which of course came from the conversion of large tracts of forests and grasslands.[1492] Essentially, the extraordinary increase in fertilizer availability from 1960 onwards has made it possible to avoid a dramatic increase in human pressure on other natural habitats. Had fertilizer use remained at the 1960 level, we would need at least 50 percent more farmland than the present-day use[1493] – the equivalent of converting almost a quarter of the global forests.[1494] Over the coming decades to 2070, were we to forsake fertilizer, the need for farmland to feed 10 billion people better would place ever higher demands on the globe – one study puts the farmland requirement at an impossible 210 percent of the land surface area.[1495] Thus, synthetic fertilizer has been and especially will be crucially important in feeding the world while leaving sufficient space for other species. However, the doubling of globally available nitrogen has also caused problems.

The most frequently cited nitrogen problem is the above-mentioned problem of oxygen depletion and eutrophication, and this problem is entirely real. In 1997, EPA formed a task force to investigate the causes and consequences of the hypoxia and to indicate possible actions. Led by NOAA and the White House Office of Science and Technology

Policy, many academic, federal and state scientists have completed the *Hypoxia Assessment* – a weighty, six-volume assessment plus an integrated summary.[1496] Much of the following discussion comes from these volumes.

Around the world many areas of low oxygen or hypoxia have been identified.[1497] This naturally affects the local benthic and demersal communities. As oxygen levels fall, the organisms capable of swimming leave the area (fish, crabs and shrimp), whereas the ones left over are severely stressed or die.[1498] Low-oxygen waters have occurred throughout time, but their frequency seems to have increased over the past 50–100 years.[1499] The likely cause is eutrophication – the increased discharge of nitrogen from human activities.[1500]

The largest single zone of low-oxygen coastal waters around the United States, and indeed in the entire western Atlantic Ocean, is the northern Gulf of Mexico off Louisiana.[1501] Since measurements began in 1985, almost every summer has seen an area of about 10,000 km^2 – the size of New Jersey – turn hypoxic.[1502] Although systematic measurements do not exist for before 1985 and there are even fewer observations from the early 1970s, the data seem to suggest that some degree of oxygen depletion has been present throughout the century.[1503] However, when looking at a large number of oxygen indicators from sediment samples, it also seems reasonable to assume that hypoxia has increased, especially since 1950.[1504]

The consequence of oxygen depletion is obviously that some or all of the bottom-dwelling organisms die.[1505] This also causes a shift in species composition away from large, long-lived organisms to small and short-cycled ones – since there is an increased risk of dying, you had better get your business done while there is still oxygen.[1506] This also means a shift towards more microbes, fewer invertebrates and often a decreased species diversity.[1507] However, since shrimp feed heavily on short-lived species, they may actually benefit from a shift to smaller, fast-cycled organisms.

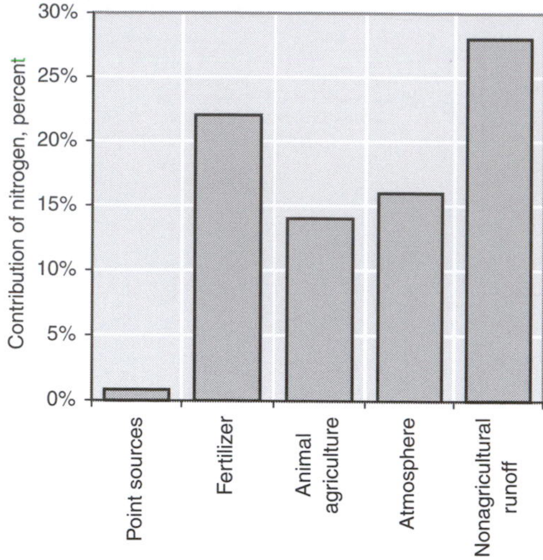

Figure 107 The in-stream contribution of nitrogen from various sources in the coterminous US, median value. Note, these values vary considerably from region to region. Since they are median values they do not sum to 100 percent. Source: Smith and Alexander 2000:7.

Most important to humans, it turned out that there is apparently no connection between fish and shrimp landings and oxygen depletion.[1508] Moreover, the *Hypoxia Assessment* was not able to determine whether the total biomass had increased (because of the nutrient increase) or decreased (because of seasonal kill-off).[1509] Actually, the report notes indications that to a certain extent increased nutrients may increase fishery stocks.[1510]

Figure 107 shows the typical contribution of nitrogen in the watersheds of the US.[1511] The largest contribution of 28 percent comes from runoffs from non-agricultural lands, such as wetlands and urban, forested and barren lands. Fertilizer contributes about 22 percent to the total nitrogen load, and animal agriculture another 14 percent. Atmospheric deposition adds 16 percent, whereas point sources such as municipal sewage treatment plants generally contribute a mere 0.8 percent.[1512] However, the distribution is highly regionally dependent, and when looking at the Gulf of

Mexico, it turns out that atmospheric deposition is slight and the nutrient enrichment comes primarily from the Mississippi river system.[1513] Here fertilizer contributes about 50 percent of the total nitrogen load, other basin runoff contributes 23 percent, animal farming 15 percent and point sources some 11 percent.[1514] Thus, the major part of the eutrophication is caused by fertilizer from agriculture.[1515]

If nothing is done to reduce the nitrogen load, it is expected that the present situation in the Gulf of Mexico will continue.[1516] Since fertilizer application and other nitrogen sources seem to have plateaued from 1980, it is to be expected that the present level of oxygen depletion will continue unabated. In order to restore the Gulf of Mexico to its pre-1950 level of nitrogen load, it is necessary to reduce the nitrogen flow by 40 percent.[1517] This will not mean no more hypoxia in the Gulf, because, as we saw, occasional oxygen depletion is natural, but it would make hypoxia markedly more infrequent. Models show that less ambitious reductions of 20 percent would make less impact but still improve oxygen levels by about 15–50 percent, thus reducing hypoxia but not to the natural background level.[1518]

The *Hypoxia Assessment* identifies two main options to reduce the nitrogen load. First, fertilizer usage on agricultural lands could be reduced, both by a general reduction and through better fertilizer application and management, alternative crops and wider spacing of drains.[1519] Second, the creation of riparian zones and wetlands would diminish the nitrogen load, because when water and nitrogen compounds flow through these areas, several microbiological processes turn significant amounts of the compounds back into N_2, effectively making it unavailable for further plant use.[1520]

However, if we wish to reduce the nitrogen load 20 percent it is not enough to cut 20 percent of fertilizer use. A 20 percent cut will induce farmers to farm differently – to shift to crops using less fertilizer and to grow more nitrogen-fixing legume crops. Thus, a cut of 20 percent will only lead to a nitrogen load reduction of 10.3 percent.[1521] Actually, an effective 20 percent reduction needs a 45 percent cut in fertilizer use.[1522] This will give price rises of 28 percent on corn and 12–14 percent on barley, oats and wheat.[1523] At the same time, these price increases will make farmers elsewhere in the US produce more, thus increasing nitrogen leaching in those regions by 7.6 percent. Moreover, it turns out that soil erosion will increase both within and outside the Mississippi basin.[1524] The total cost, mainly paid by the US consumer through higher food prices, will be about $2.9 billion each year.

The *Hypoxia Assessment* also looks at a so-called mixed policy, with a 20 percent fertilizer reduction and 5 million acres of wetland.[1525] This solution will cut the effective nitrogen load by about 20 percent.[1526] However, it will also lead to higher food prices, from 4–10 percent, while causing a slight increase in the nitrogen load elsewhere and in erosion everywhere.[1527] The main problem is the annual cost of $4.8 billion, both from higher food prices and from the cost of wetlands.[1528] The *Hypoxia Assessment* estimates that the fivefold increase in the Wetland Reserve Program will confer additional benefits on the population in the Mississippi basin through recreational fishing and knowing-it-is-there value of $2.8 billion annually.[1529] Summing up, this means that the mixed policy of a 20 percent reduction plus 5 million acres of wetlands comes with a slightly cheaper annual price tag of $2 billion.

The question is, then, what we get for the proposed annual expenditure of $2–2.8 billion. Of course it cuts the nitrogen load by about 20 percent, meaning that the returning hypoxia in the Gulf will ease though not subside to natural levels.[1530] It is concluded that it will make no noticeable difference to fisheries: "The direct benefits to Gulf fisheries of reducing nitrogen loads from the Mississippi

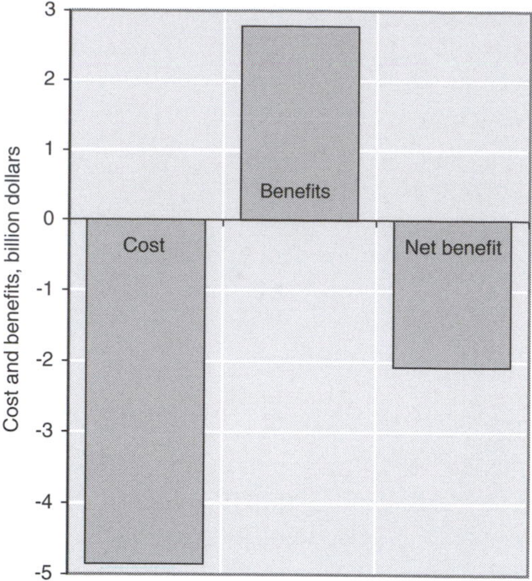

Figure 108 The cost and benefit and net benefit (negative) of the mixed policy option to reduce the nitrogen load in the Gulf of Mexico. Source: Doering *et al.* 1999:133.

River basin are very limited at best."[1531] Two other benefits remain.[1532] First, it is possible that less hypoxia would increase the opportunities for recreational fishing in the Gulf itself. However, this seems unlikely, given the lack of effect on commercial fisheries. Second, we have the knowing-it-is-there benefit of less vulnerable marine bottom organisms for the coast off Louisiana. In effect, the cost of saving these organisms is a little more than $2 billion a year, as is indicated in Figure 108. The obvious, democratic question when considering whether or not to act on the hypoxia in the Gulf of Mexico is whether one can imagine spending the $2 billion better elsewhere.

Of course, we are accustomed to thinking that if there is something wrong, for instance when our usage of fertilizer leaves millions or billions of organisms dead in the Gulf, we should do something about it. And this is an honorable attitude. However, we must also remind ourselves that there are a large number of issues where our acts affects others and decisive action could help – and we should consider where we can do the most good, because we cannot do it all.

Yes, a lot of organisms die prematurely each year in the Gulf, and they will continue to die prematurely if we do not reduce the nitrogen load. The question is whether saving them is worth $2 billion annually. In the end, such a question relies on a political prioritization, but to give a sense of magnitude, it is perhaps worth pointing out that premature death also follows from other human endeavors which we would hardly be willing to change. An estimated 100 million birds die annually in the US colliding with plate glass and 60 million birds die in US traffic each year.[1533] Likewise billions of insects are deliberately killed each year in fields by pesticides. But do we want to spend $2 billion to save birds from plate glass and traffic or prohibit the killing of pests? Finally, if we want to do good with our $2 billion, we might consider that we could save about 30 million people each year in the Third World for the same amount.[1534]

Moreover, why is it that we worry about the organisms that die each year because of enhanced levels of nutrients without considering all the other organisms of at least equal biomass that live precisely because of these nutrients? When *Scientific American* described the eutrophication of the Gulf of Mexico they inadvertently underscored this problem: "Environmentalists have dubbed the region the 'dead zone,' a label that overlooks the fact that life is certainly present – but life of the wrong sort."[1535] Why are some living beings "of the wrong sort"? Likewise UNEP worries about "excessive plant growth."[1536] Such worries run somewhat counter to the other basic concern for reduced biomass, as discussed on pp. 99–100.

Nevertheless, the *Hypoxia Assessment* shows that we can solve eutrophication if we choose to use our resources to do so. The basic question is whether this is a good use of resources.

Summing up, there is good evidence that oxygen depletion in shallow coastal waters is caused by increased agricultural fertilization, and it is likely that this condition has increased around the world. It is also likely that since population will almost double before 2200, fertilizer use will increase further. One study expects an increase of almost 70 percent, mainly in the developing countries, by 2030.[1537] This probably means more, and more pervasive eutrophication.

However, while it is right to be concerned, we must also maintain a sense of proportion. While fertilizer and consequent eutrophication costs the lives of certain organisms in local marine habitats (and provides life to others), it has also made it possible to grow much more food on the same agricultural land. This has saved about 25 percent of today's forests and will save much more in the future. In this respect, eutrophication is the price we let some marine organisms pay for our success in feeding humanity, while maintaining large, forested habitats.[1538]

Of course, to a certain extent we can use our fertilizer better and in the developed part of the world pay our way to avoid eutrophication, but we also need to ask whether this is the best allocation of our scarce resources.

Health effects from fertilizer

Apart from eutrophication, there are a number of other concerns connected to the nitrogen cycle.

The two global nitrogen problems are nitrous oxide (N_2O) contributing to global warming and ozone depletion, which we will look at in chapter 24.[1539] However, N_2O's contribution to global warming is only about one-tenth that of CO_2, and the latest nitrogen review concluded that "both fossil fuel burning and the direct impact of agricultural fertilization have been considered and rejected as the major source" of N_2O.[1540]

Of regional and local problems, nitrogen oxides (NO_x) act as local air pollutants, but as we have seen, this problem is diminishing. NO_xs also contribute to acid deposition, which has been declining, though mainly because of sharply reduced SO_2 emissions, as discussed in the chapter on acid rain.[1541]

Finally, the major nitrogen worry besides eutrophication is the claim that nitrate in drinking water can be a health threat. This has been the motivation behind setting binding nitrate levels, in the EU since 1980 at 50 mg/l and in the US at a lower level of 44 mg/l.[1542]

In the 1980s nitrates in the groundwater came very much into focus.[1543] The Danish environment minister, Christian Christensen, stated flatly that nitrate pollution had serious consequences because:

> a clear relationship has been established between stomach cancer and high levels of nitrates in drinking water. And many infants are in direct danger because they get much of their water from their food. This can result in slow asphyxiation because excessive nitrate inhibits the blood's absorption of oxygen. Internal organs can also break down so that the children become ill or have difficulty concentrating. For this reason I do not dare to drink nitrate-polluted water and I will not allow my child to do so either.[1544]

Although such scare-stories were widely repeated, they were very far from a reasonable assessment of the facts, even at the time when they were put forth.

Most of the nitrates we consume come from vegetables, especially beets, celery, lettuce and spinach, which can give us between 75 and 100 mg of nitrates a day – vegetarians get more than 250 mg.[1545] The main reason why nitrate is dangerous is that it can be converted by bacteria into nitrite which then oxidizes the blood's hemoglobin, impeding the transport of oxygen.[1546] This oxidation is called methemoglobinemia. Nitrates are, however, generally harmless because the offending bacteria are killed when they reach the stomach acid. Infants under six months are at risk, though, because their stomach acid is weaker and because they do not possess the enzyme system to reverse the oxidation of hemoglobin.

Drastic reduction of oxygenation is known as cyanosis and turns the skin blue, thus the name "blue baby" syndrome. At worst this can lead to death, although this has not happened in Western Europe in recent times.[1547] Incidence of "blue baby" syndrome is limited to a few places such as Hungary, Slovakia, Romania and Albania and at very low rates.[1548] Moreover, clinical observations seem to suggest that the main cause of methemoglobinemia is poor hygiene in infant feeding bottles, allowing bacteria to build up dangerous levels of nitrite prior to intake.[1549] This is backed up by several experiments involving infants that have shown that as long as the water is clean, cyanosis does not occur even when the nitrate concentration is as high as 150 mg/l.[1550]

On the other hand, water with a high content of bacteria helps to break down the nitrate and some infants have got cyanosis from drinking water contaminated with between 50 and 100 mg/l. For this reason the WHO has set the global limit value for nitrates at 50 mg/l, precisely because it has the desired effect in the developing world where the groundwater is often contaminated by bacteria. But as is pointed out by Poul Bonnevie, a former professor of environmental medicine, who helped set the WHO's nitrate limit, bacteria pollution was the only reason for setting such a low limit value. In actual fact "the limit value has lost its medical basis in many countries, including [Denmark]."[1551]

The other human health worry is that higher nitrate levels could be correlated with higher incidences of cancer, typically of the stomach. The latest meta-study points out that despite a clear connection between nitrate in water and nitrate in blood and saliva, and despite "extensive population exposure, there is little direct epidemiologic evidence of elevated risk among human populations exposed to nitrate in drinking water."[1552] The study concludes that "the epidemiologic data are not yet sufficient to draw a conclusion."[1553]

No other effects from nitrate have been found, and particularly no indications that nitrates should be able to "cause organs to break down" as stated by the Danish environmental minister.[1554] Moreover, the case for methemoglobinemia and cancer is at best very weak.[1555]

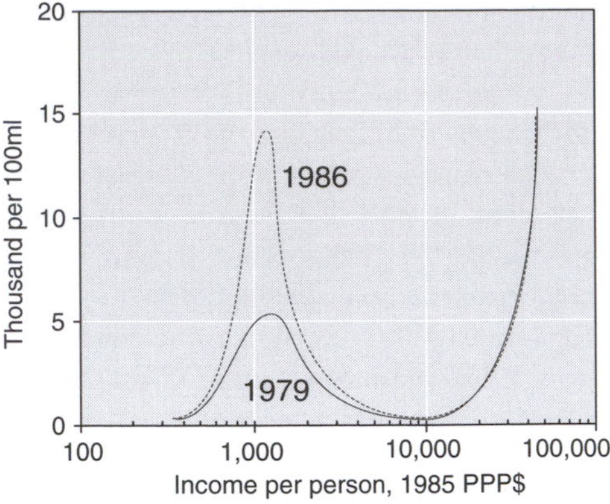

Figure 109 Fecal coliform bacteria in rivers for different levels of per capita income, in 1979 and 1986. Source: World Bank 1992, Shafik 1994:764.

Consequently, the concern over nitrogen health effects seems ill-founded.

Pollution in rivers

From a global point of view, rivers are important because they are major suppliers of water for drinking, personal hygiene purposes, industry and agriculture.[1556] In as far as water is used to drink, it is absolutely vital that it does not contain too many coli bacteria, because this would indicate the presence of other, more serious bacteria and viruses.

Using data from 52 rivers in 25 countries, the World Bank has demonstrated a more complex correlation between income and fecal coliform bacteria, as can be seen in Figure 109. Not surprisingly, and just as with air pollution, fecal pollution first gets worse up to an income of about $1,375, after which rivers get cleaner. However, unlike the air pollution curves, data seem to indicate that when income exceeds $11,500, the fecal pollution starts to increase again. Apparently, this is not due to problems with data, because rivers in Australia, Japan and the US all have fairly high coliform pollution levels.[1557] The explanation seems to be that we see a general downwards trend in fecal pollution *so long as people are dependent on river water.* However, when countries get rich enough they use groundwater to a much greater extent, which diminishes the urgency and political inclination to push for ever lower fecal pollution levels. Nevertheless, for the large majority of countries that depend on rivers for drinking water the conclusion remains: at the outset richer means more polluted rivers, but beyond a fairly low level, richer actually implies less fecal pollution in the rivers.

Biologically speaking, however, the level of oxygen is a much more important measure of water quality than fecal coliform. Dissolved oxygen is absolutely essential for the survival of all aquatic organisms – not only fish but also invertebrates such as crabs, clams, zooplankton, etc. Moreover, oxygen affects a vast number of other water indicators, not only biochemical but esthetic ones like odor, clarity and taste. Consequently, oxygen is perhaps the most well-established indicator of water quality.[1558]

Economic analyses seem to indicate that higher levels of income tend to improve oxygen levels.[1559] This is also the overall picture in Figure 110. Here we see how oxygen levels for some of the major rivers have returned to their previous high levels after decades of low levels. This has consequences for both marine organisms and humans. The increased oxygen levels in these rivers have improved the possibilities of life – in the Rhine, the biodiversity has increased sixfold since 1971, and for the Thames, the number of fish species has increased a phenomenal 20-fold since 1964.[1560] Equally, the improved oxygen levels in New York Harbor have made fishing and bathing possible again.[1561] From levels in the early 1970s when fish could not survive, New York Harbor has witnessed

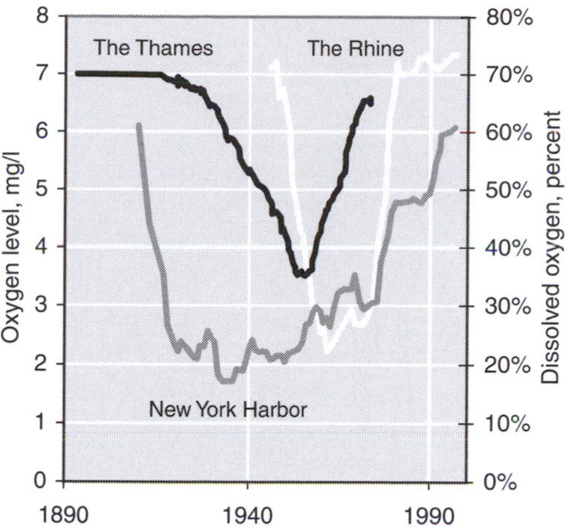

Figure 110 Oxygen levels in the Thames (1890–1974, right axis), the Rhine (1945–97, left axis), and New York Harbor (1910–97, left axis). Note that the oxygen content cannot be directly compared between the rivers, since many other factors determine the natural level of oxygen. Source: Goudie 1993:224, EEA 1994:49, OECD 1999:85, DEP 1997:38.[1562]

record numbers of shortnose sturgeon and the reestablishment of peregrine falcons, herons, egrets, and possibly the first productive bald eagles.[1563] The improvements have taken place because untreated river discharges have been curtailed. In New York, untreated sewage has been cut by 99.9 percent since 1930, and in London, total discharges have been cut by 88 percent from 1950 to 1980.[1564]

The picture of improved water quality is also confirmed if we look at the European oxygen levels. Here, rivers have been exposed to ever increasing pollution since World War II, and this has resulted in severe oxygen depletion as in the Rhine. However, within the last 15–20 years, biological treatment of domestic and industrial wastewaters has increased, such that the EEA finds Europe-wide general "improvement in oxygen conditions and river quality," with the result that "many rivers are now well oxygenated."[1565] For Europe's rivers, an EEA summary of the organic pollution that uses up oxygen (leaving

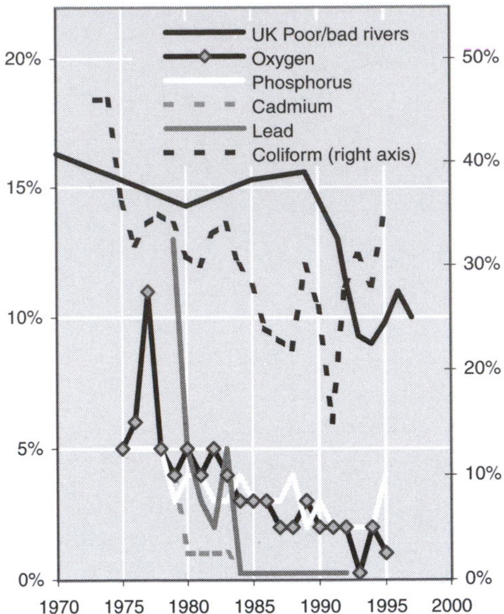

Figure 111 Porportion of low-quality UK and US rivers. For the UK, proportion of poor/bad rivers (1970–97). For the US, proportion of rivers violating EPA standards, fecal coliform (1973–95, right axis), and oxygen, phosphorus, cadmium and lead (1975–95). Source: UK EA 2000, CEQ 1997:299, Simon 1996:251.

less for aquatic organisms) showed deterioration in 27 percent of all rivers (more pollution leaving less oxygen) but improvement in the vast majority of 73 percent.[1566]

If we look at the larger picture for river quality in the UK and the US, we also see a general improvement. In the UK, different and ever more objective systems have been devised by the National Water Council and the National Rivers Authority to classify the nation's rivers as good, fair, poor or bad.[1567] Although the quality classification has changed four times since 1970, the fraction of poor and bad rivers is broadly comparable across the changes as depicted in Figure 111. The overall result is that fewer rivers are of low quality – from a little more than 16 percent in 1970, the fraction of poor and bad rivers is down to 10 percent in 1997. The worst rivers ("bad") have decreased even faster over the past decade, from 2.6 percent to just 0.7 percent. Equally, the share of good and very good rivers has increased from 37 percent in 1989 to 59.2 percent in 1997 – a remarkable increase in less than a decade. Moreover, the very best rivers (with the label "very good") have almost doubled from 17.7 percent to 27.6 percent. In the sparse conclusion of a recent government report: "Water quality in the United Kingdom has improved."[1568]

The same picture is evident for the US. The latest report on national river quality from USGS covering the 1980s concluded that several of the traditional water pollutants "decreased during the 1980's and, collectively, provide evidence of progress in pollution control during the decade."[1569] Looking at violation rates, we see only a slight downward trend – if any – in fecal coliform bacteria. This supports the conclusion from Figure 109, that rich countries not dependent on rivers for drinking water are not particularly motivated to decrease the coliform level. However, the other indicators – oxygen, phosphorus, cadmium and lead – all show substantial reductions in the rate of violation, clearly indicating an improving river quality for aquatic organisms.[1570]

Until now, we have only looked at typical pollution indicators, such as coliforms and oxygen. But equally important, we may want to look at the aquatic levels of chemical pollution. Here we see the same pattern as in the coastal areas. In the US, a National Contaminant Biomonitoring Program has examined the presence of long-lived toxic contaminants in the aquatic environment through analysis of fish. Fish were selected because they tend to accumulate pesticides and the European starling was chosen because of its varied diet and wide geographic distribution.[1571] Figure 112 shows how the US national contamination of DDE (a break-down product of DDT) dropped 82 percent from 1969 to 1986, and over the same period, PCBs fell 83 percent.[1572]

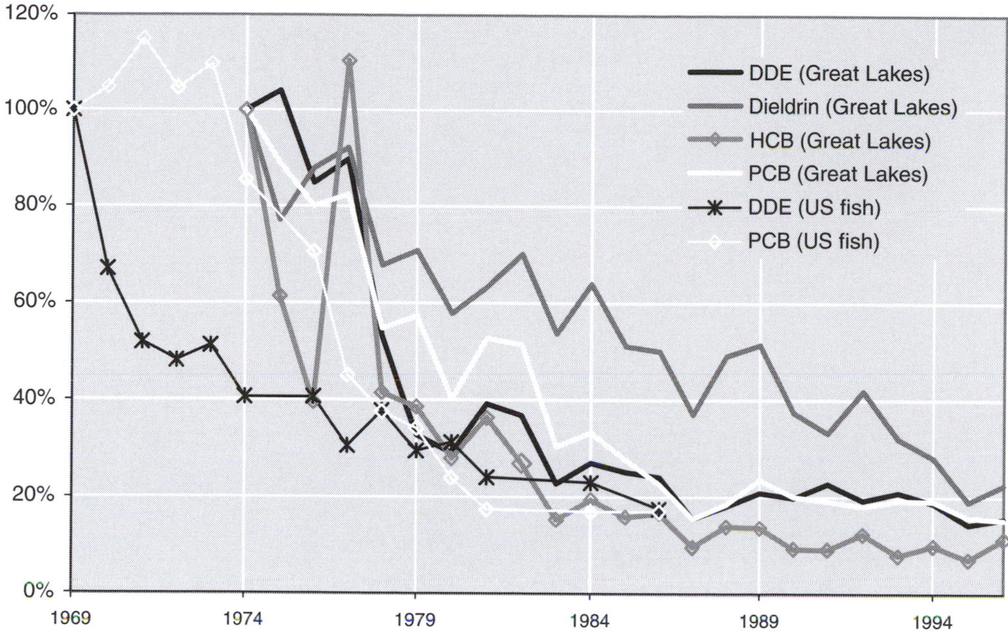

Figure 112 Levels of persistent pollutants in US freshwater fish (1969–86) and in the US/Canada Great Lakes herring gull eggs (1974–96), as indexed from first year. Source: NCBP 2000, CEQ 1997:334–8.[1573]

Figure 112 also shows chemical pollution for the US/Canada Great Lakes. These lakes make up 20 percent of all the fresh surface water on Earth, with an American/Canadian surrounding population of more than 32 million.[1574] Here, measurements are made on herring gull eggs as convenient markers for other, low-level pollution.[1575] Again, we see the same picture – a dramatic decline of 80–90 percent since 1974 of both DDE, PCBs, HCB and dieldrin.[1576]

Summing up, rivers probably experience better water quality as income increases. Certainly, we have seen dramatic increases in the oxygen levels of the Rhine, the Thames and New York Harbor. This tendency towards improved oxygen levels has also been confirmed when analyzing more than 200 European rivers. Moreover, general quality measures for both the UK and the US show better river water quality. Persistent pollutants in fresh waters have been decreasing dramatically. When measured nationally through fish in the US or through herring gull eggs in the Great Lakes, pollutant concentrations have declined 80–90 percent.

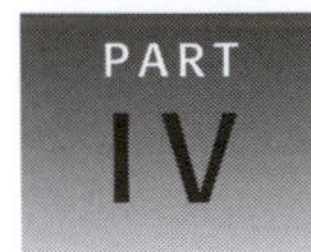

20 Waste: running out of space?

We often worry about all the waste piling up, wondering where it all can go. We feel that the "throwaway society" and its industrial foundation is undermining the environment. This fear is perhaps expressed most clearly by former vice president Al Gore, who is disturbed by "the floodtide of garbage spilling out of our cities and factories."[1577] "As landfills overflow, incinerators foul the air, and neighboring communities and states attempt to dump their overflow problems on us," we are now finally realizing that we are "running out of ways to dispose of our waste in a manner that keeps it out of either sight or mind."[1578] The problem is that we have assumed "there would always be a hole wide enough and deep enough to take care of all our trash. But like so many other assumptions about the earth's infinite capacity to absorb the impact of human civilization, this one too was wrong."[1579] Equally, Isaac Asimov in his environmental book tells us that "almost all the existing landfills are reaching their maximum capacity, and we are running out of places to put new ones."[1580]

It is true that waste generation does increase with GDP. The richer we get the more garbage we produce. This can be seen from the World Bank's analysis of waste per capita in relation to income, shown in Figure 113. The question is, of course, whether this is actually a problem. We may believe that garbage production is spiraling out of control and that landfill garbage is piling up to the extent that soon there will be room for no more, but that is simply not the case.

A waste expert points out that reality has turned out very differently from our fears of just a decade ago: "Images from the nightly news of more and more garbage with no place to go struck fear in the hearts of mayors and public works directors everywhere. Children were taught that the best way to stave off the invasion of sea gulls hovering at landfills was by washing out bottles and stacking old newspapers. But the anticipated crisis did not occur."[1581]

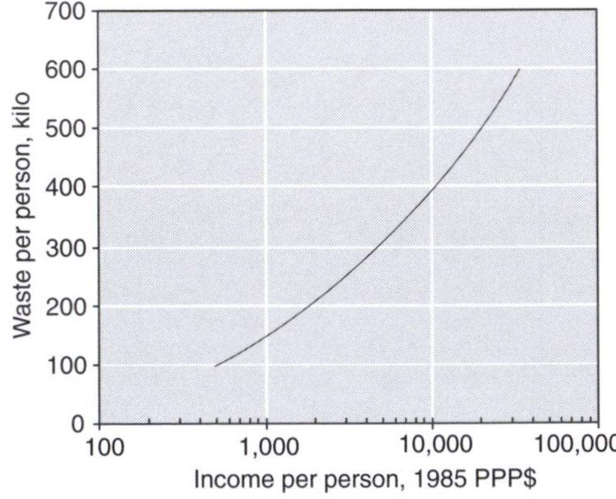

Figure 113 Connection between income and waste production per capita, based on 39 countries in 1985. Source: World Bank 1992, Shafik 1994:764.

Each American produces about 4.5 pounds of waste per person each day – all in all some 200 million tons of municipal waste each year.[1582] Not only does that sound like a lot, but the annual amount has doubled since 1966, as can be seen in Figure 114. However, the growth in waste that actually ends on the landfill has stopped growing since the 1980s, and currently Americans ship off less waste to the landfill than they did in 1979. The main reason is that more and more waste gets incin-

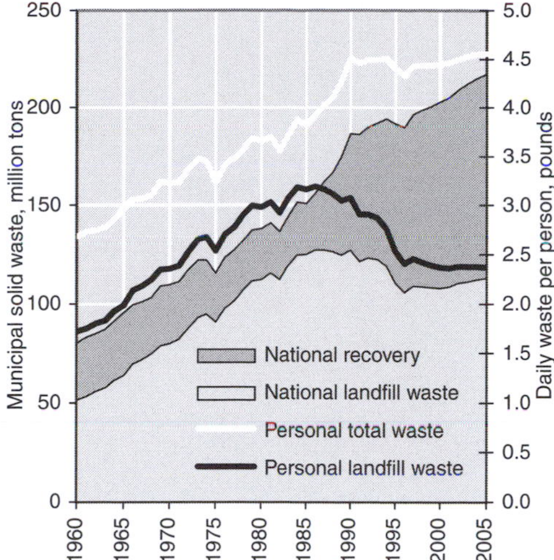

Figure 114 Waste production in the US, national and per person, for landfill and for recovery and combustion, 1960–2005. Forecast from 1998. Source: EPA 1999b:133, USBC 2000d.

erated, recycled or composted. Moreover, a part of the reason why the US produces more waste is more people – per person, total waste has only increased 45 percent since 1966. And looking at the waste that will end up in a landfill, each person only produces 13 percent more waste than in 1966.

EPA's data only go back to 1960, but consumption patterns have changed radically over longer periods. At the beginning of the twentieth century, an American home each day produced in addition to the ordinary waste some 4 pounds of coal ash, making it likely that landfill production has not increased dramatically over the century.[1583]

Nevertheless, it seems likely Americans will continue producing at least 110 million tons of garbage every year, destined for the landfill. Natural intuition, as pointed out by Al Gore above, tells us that this cannot go on for ever. If we envisage that the US will continue to produce 110 million tons of landfill waste every year for the rest of this century, from 2001 to 2100, how much space would it occupy? Let us suppose we placed all the waste in a single landfill – surely not a smart idea, but just for the purpose of illustration – and filled it up to 100 feet. That height is still lower than the Fresh Kills landfill on Staten Island, within the New York City boundaries.[1584] Then the total landfill waste of the US over the entire century would take up just a square 14 miles on each side.[1585]

Now, surely, assuming a stable waste production for the next century is an unreasonably optimistic assumption. Not only will economic growth increase the amount of garbage (as we see in Figure 113), but according to the Census Bureau, the US is expected to more than double its population before 2100.[1586] Thus, let us assume the growth in total, personal waste production as we have seen since 1990 and expect till 2005 will continue till 2100. Moreover, let us adjust the waste production to the ever increasing number of Americans, each producing ever more garbage. Once again, sum up the entire waste mass and pile it to 100 feet. Surprisingly, we will only need a slightly larger area – it will still fit within a square, less than 18 miles on each side.[1587]

In Figure 115 this landfill area is illustrated as being placed in Woodward County, Oklahoma. All the American waste of the entire twenty-first century will fit into a single landfill, using just 26 percent of the Woodward County area.[1588] Of the state of Oklahoma, the landfill would use up less than half a percent[1589] Of the entire US landmass, the landfill would take up about one-12,000th – less than 0.009 percent.[1590] Equivalently, one could imagine that each state would handle its own garbage – for argument's sake, let us just say one-fiftieth each. Then, in order to handle all the waste production of the twenty-first century, each state merely needs to find space for a single, square landfill, 2.5 miles on each side.[1591]

Moreover, the scenario with ever increasing amounts of waste is probably rather exaggerated, especially considering that most economic growth will be in the service industries

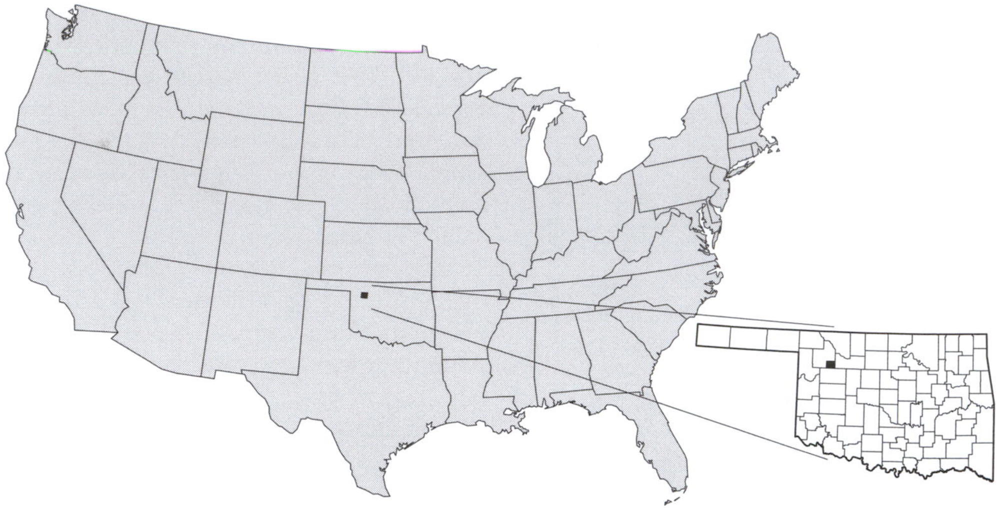

Figure 115 The extent of the necessary landfill area to handle all waste from the US throughout the entire twenty-first century: a square less than 18 miles (28 km) on the side. It is here illustrated as placed in Woodward County, Oklahoma, using 26 percent of its area, or less than 0.009 percent of the US area.

and information technology, as we noted in the chapter on raw materials. Even in material production the general trend is towards the use of fewer materials – a sort of dematerialization of the economy.[1592] The car is an excellent example, representing a full basket of products from an industrialized economy, with metals, plastics, electronic materials, rubber, and glass. Since the early 1970s, carbon steel has been replaced with high-tech steel, plastics and composites, with the new materials substituting the old at a rate of one to three, making the car ever lighter without compromising structural integrity.[1593]

Even so, the main point here is that we will not be inundated with garbage. Garbage is something we can deal with. It is a management problem.

This does not, however, imply that landfills will be easy to site. Nobody wants to be neighbor to a landfill – a phenomenon so familiar that it has even been given a name: NIMBY, or Not In My Back Yard.[1594] Thus, garbage may be a *political* problem, but it is not a problem of lack of physical space.

It is perhaps worth mentioning that landfills today are very safe for the groundwater. The EPA estimates that current environmental regulations governing the US's 6,000 landfills ensure that over the next 300 years they will only cause 5.7 cancer-related deaths, or just one every 50 years.[1595] This should be seen in the light of the fact that cancer kills 563,000 people each year in the US, with about 2,000 deaths caused merely by using spices in food.[1596]

For other nations, waste rates seem to be slightly increasing (as predicted in Figure 113), but at much lower levels than the US. At 1.1 kg/day for Japan and 1.3 kg/day for France, both have seen slow increases, but they are still way below the American production of 2 kg/day. As a result of strict policies, German waste production of 1.2 kg/day has actually decreased 29 percent since 1980.[1597] The UK has very poor waste statistics, but seemingly the trend is slightly upwards, with a daily production on a par with France.[1598] If UK waste production increases at the same rate as the American (surely an overestimate, since the UK population does not increase with nearly the same speed), the total landfill area needed for the twenty-first-century UK waste would be a square 8 miles on the side – an area equivalent to 28 percent of the Isle of Man[1599]

Finally, we should mention recycling. In the US paper, glass, metals and plastics are recovered.[1600] We tend to believe that recycling is a rather new phenomenon, but actually the US has recycled about 20–30 percent of all paper throughout the century, and recycling is still below the levels of the 1930s and 1940s.[1601] However, materials like copper and lead have increasingly been reused, rising steadily through the century from 5–10 percent to more than 50 percent and 70 percent respectively.[1602]

Moreover, we tend to believe that all recycling is good, both because it saves resources and because it avoids waste.[1603] Of course, as chapter 12 showed us, we may not necessarily need to worry so much about raw materials, especially common ones such as stone, sand and gravel, but neither should we worry about wood and paper, because both are renewable resources.

Equally, if the entire US twenty-first-century waste can be contained within a single landfill in part of Woodward County, Oklahoma, we must also consider whether recycling to avoid waste is a good investment of resources. Possibly, we may be able to save more resources by burning old paper at incineration plants, making use of the heat produced and felling more trees, instead of using energy to collect the old paper to be sorted, prepared and filtered. New studies seem to indicate that it actually costs more to recycle paper than to produce new paper.[1604]

Societal-based analyses typically show that recycling does not pay from a private economic point of view, although it is in the balance as far as society as a whole is concerned.[1605] This can be seen as evidence that the current recycling level is reasonable, but that we perhaps should not aim to recycle much more.[1606]

21 Conclusion to Part IV: the pollution burden has diminished

Pollution is not in the process of undermining our well-being. On the contrary, the pollution burden has diminished dramatically in the developed world. As regards air pollution, the improvement has been unequivocal. Human health has benefited phenomenally from reductions in lead and particle concentrations. Contrary to common intuition, London has not been as clean as it is now since 1585.

Indoor air pollution, on the other hand, has remained more or less constant, although it much more depends on individual responsibility – most markedly in relation to smoking. Asthma frequency has increased, but this is primarily because we have sealed our homes so effectively and spend much more time indoors; the increase has had nothing to do with air pollution.

Air pollution has got worse in the developing world, mainly because of the strong economic growth. However, the developing countries are really just making the same tradeoffs as the developed countries made 100–200 years ago. It turns out that when we look at the problems over time, the environment and economic prosperity are not opposing concepts, but rather complementary entities: without adequate environmental protection, growth is undermined, but environmental protection is unaffordable without growth. It is thus reasonable to expect that as the developing countries of the world achieve higher levels of income, they will – as we in the developed world have done – opt for and be able to afford an ever cleaner environment.

On the other hand, numerous serious environmental issues have proven to be unproblematic. Acid rain, which was supposed to have killed the forests in the 1980s, turned out to have little effect on forest growth, although it did damage to vulnerable lakes. The oceans have not been harmed to any significant degree, and the Gulf War and Exxon Valdez accident have probably not caused lasting damage.

The quality of coastal waters in human terms has definitely increased. However, many coastal and marine areas around the world are getting higher inputs of nutrients, which has contributed to an increase in the frequency of oxygen depletion or hypoxia, detrimental to aquatic organisms. The main part of this problem stems from the ready access to fertilizer which has given us the Green Revolution, the ability to feed the world on much less land, and consequently a dramatic reduction of pressure on forests and other natural habitats. In this view, nutrient overload is the price we let the marine organisms pay for our success in feeding humanity, while maintaining large forest habitats.

With sufficient resources we can certainly decrease the oxygen depletion, but the question remains whether this constitutes our wisest use of limited resources. In the Gulf of Mexico, we can diminish hypoxia and save many bottom-dwelling life forms, but at a price tag of more than $2 billion a year. If we want to do good with our $2 billion, we might consider that we could save at least 30 million people in the Third World for the same amount.

Rivers have generally improved for almost all indicators. We saw the Rhine, the Thames and New York Harbor showing increased oxygen content, supporting a much wider flora and

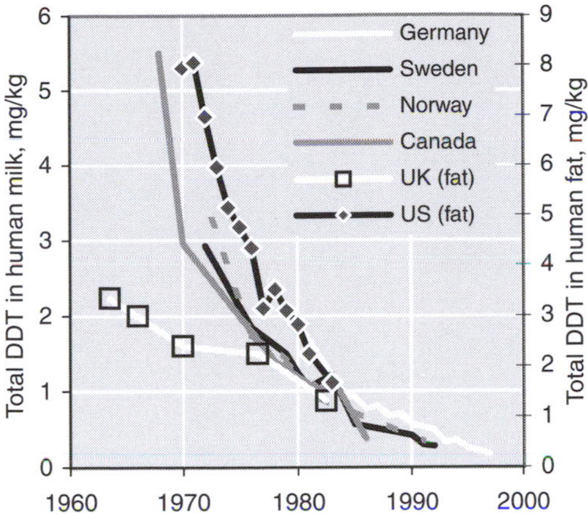

Figure 116 Concentration of total DDT in human milk and fat for various countries, 1963–97. Source: Smith 1999a, Schade and Heinzow 1998, CEQ 1989:417, Bernstam 1995:510, HSDB 2000.[1607]

fauna than 20–40 years ago. Finally, the "waste disposal crisis" was a chimera of the 1980s. Even if waste production continues to increase and the American population doubles over the next hundred years, a single square landfill of less than 18 miles on the side can contain the entire twenty-first-century US waste – just 26 percent of Woodward County, Oklahoma.

The pollution load on humans has been declining in the cities (lower air pollution) and from the sea, land and rivers. As one of many indicators, this has caused a decline in the DDT concentrations in human fat and milk. In Figure 116 we see how levels have declined at least 60 percent and in some cases even more than 93 percent in total DDT, and the fall has been backed up by many other indicators, among them PCB and HCB.[1608] The share of Americans with PCB in their fat fell from 68 percent in 1972 to just 9 percent in 1983.[1609] This is important, as a new survey seems to suggest that large concentrations of PCB in a mother's milk can result in her offspring having learning difficulties and a lower IQ.[1610] Equally, the level of dioxin is falling. In the latest EU report, it is found that "exposure to dioxins within EU Member States has decreased by between 9 percent and 12 percent per year" while concentrations in breast milk have dropped 8 percent a year, and in blood as much as 12 percent a year.[1611]

We have seen how human progress has been phenomenal. We have seen that whether we are talking about food, raw materials or energy, no shortages of resources seem to be forthcoming, no serious problems for the continued growth of production and welfare are in the offing. In Part IV we have seen that problems with pollution do not give us reason to believe that economic growth is in the process of destroying the Earth – rather the contrary. As far as the vast majority of significant areas are concerned, we have reduced pollution and increased environmental quality. On this front too, the world has become a better place in which to live.

However, we also need to look at some of the large environmental problems which have been debated over the past years. Could it be that climate change from global warming, the increasing chemical load, the hole in the ozone layer and the loss of biodiversity will seriously challenge and endanger human prosperity?

Tomorrow's problems

22 Our chemical fears

Rachel Carson, named by *Time* Magazine one of the 100 most influential people of the twentieth century,[1612] kick-started popular environmental awareness with her 1962 book *Silent Spring*.[1613] Here she told us how pesticides like DDT were spoiling the Earth, potentially leaving us with a silent spring, devoid of singing birds. In her vision of the future,

> a strange blight crept over the area and everything began to change. Some evil spell had settled on the community: mysterious maladies swept the flocks of chickens; the cattle and sheep sickened and died. Everywhere was a shadow of death. The farmers spoke of much illness among their families. In the town the doctors had become more and more puzzled by new kinds of sickness appearing among their patients. There had been several sudden and unexplained deaths, not only among adults but even among children, who would be stricken suddenly while at play and die within a few hours.[1614]

The shadow of death, the evil spell, was the onset of the chemical age: "For the first time in the history of the world, every human being is now subjected to contact with dangerous chemicals, from the moment of conception until death."[1615]

This claim of chemical cataclysm in the making became a runaway best-seller, spreading its message far beyond the US.[1616] And the message was not only that chemicals could harm birds and bees but – as is evident from the quote above – that chemicals could kill us and our children. This message has been the legacy of Carson and has remained one of the major underpinnings of the environmental movement: our fear of chemicals.[1617]

Her preoccupation with chemicals and particularly pesticides – which she colorfully termed "elixirs of death"[1618] – set the background for the long trail of chemical frights that have hit the front pages since then.[1619] Some of the most notorious worries, such as Love Canal and Times Beach, have gone on to become popular icons, even if their scientific credentials later turned out to be somewhat jaded.[1620]

Carson described how the chemicals affected animals and humans in a variety of ways, but above all stood cancer, killing "one in every four," as the chapter on the final consequences was named.[1621] Pointing out the possible connection between increasing pesticide use and rising cancer rates, Carson put the cancer issue at the forefront of public attention. This focus, combined with a flurry of new cancer studies and a newly started EPA, struggling for bureaucratic independence, also made cancer one of the main arenas for environmental regulation.[1622]

This has caused the curious fusion of "environment," "cancer" and "pesticides" that remains to this day. In the League of Conservation Voters Education Fund poll of US environmental attitudes from February 2000, three of the five top environmental priorities were focused on toxic control: drinking water, toxic waste and pesticides.[1623] And of the other two, clean air and clean waterways, certainly clean air is somewhat connected through its focus on cancer mortality. The recurrent Gallup polls have similarly found throughout the 1990s that toxic waste and air and water pollution are the key environmental issues.[1624]

The consequences are intertwined and feed on each other. As we hear of ever more cancer studies telling us this and that can give us cancer, and hear about ever increasing cancer rates, we are inclined to believe that cancer pervades our modern world. Consequently, we are also inclined to believe more and more firmly that the environment is deteriorating. And the other way round; as our background knowledge of the Litany tells us that the environment is going downhill with serious health effects on our lives, cancer stories get ever more real.

The media are awash in claims of a cancer epidemic.[1625] *Total Health* tells us that the public needs to be rescued from "the current cancer epidemic."[1626] In an article in the *American Journal of Public Health*, the authors state unequivocally that although the exposures are many and the statistics difficult to decipher, "we know that there is a cancer epidemic in the United States."[1627] Even the World Health Organization Director-General Dr. Gro Harlem Brundtland could not help pointing out that her organization ought to have more money because of "the emerging tide of non-communicable diseases such as cancer."[1628] And *MidLife Woman* almost yells in our faces, how "the cancer epidemic continues to rage around the world."[1629]

And the cancer epidemic is caused by the increased pesticide pollution in the environment. The *Sierra Club* asks the question and answers it straight off: "Why are so many people getting cancer? One reason may be the legal release of millions of pounds of cancer-causing chemicals into our air and waterways."[1630] *MidLife Woman* confidently tells us that "these rising rates of cancer, infections and immune system dysfunctions (asthma, allergies and lupus) are a function of our increasingly polluted environment."[1631] The *Environmental Magazine* tells us that organically grown foods are great not only because they have double the mineral content of those grown conventionally (though this is wrong[1632]). "They're also free from pesticides, ranked the number three cancer risk by the Environmental Protection Agency (EPA)"[1633] (which is also wrong, as we shall see below).

The idea of pesticides-make-cancer-epidemic is perhaps most clearly encapsulated in the famous article from Professor Pimentel of Cornell, which we have already discussed in Part I. In the opening line, neglecting the overwhelming contribution of tobacco and malnutrition to his figures, he confidently states: "We have calculated that an estimated 40 percent of world deaths can be attributed to various environmental factors, especially organic and chemical pollutants."[1634] In *Psychology Today* the study's message is repeated even more simply, showing us "that 40 percent of deaths worldwide are caused by pollution and other environmental factors."[1635] And in the newsletter of the Centers for Disease Control, Pimentel's article is summed up in a single bullet-point: the increasing pollution "points to one inescapable conclusion: life on Earth is killing us."[1636]

Not surprisingly, this information barrage has made us believe that possibly the most important health determinant is not our own acts but influences from the environment. In a poll from 1990, Americans were given two health categories and asked which was the most serious "in terms of causing health problems for people": "Things in the environment, such as air pollution, water pollution, chemical waste disposal, etc." or "personal habits, such as the kinds of food people eat, smoking, drinking, stress, etc.";[1637] 44 percent thought that the environment was the more important, whereas only 34 percent picked personal habits.[1638] Moreover, the number of people believing the environment was the primary health determinant had increased from 38 percent since 1985.[1639]

We know that the environment has perhaps the most important influence on our health. We believe that cancer is on an epidemic rise. We realize that this is in a large part caused by the very chemicals that pollute our environment.

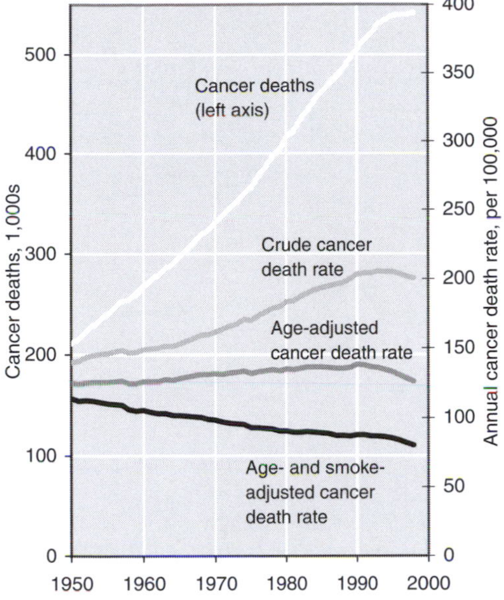

Figure 117 US cancer mortality 1950–98, expressed as total number of deaths, crude cancer death rate, age-adjusted death rate and death rate adjusted for age and smoking. All cancers; age adjusted to standard world population. Source: WHO 2000d, CDC 2001a, HHS 1997:77, 140, Peto *et al.* 1992, 1994.

But the evidence absolutely does not support these myths of the Litany.

Cancer: death

Cancer is probably the disease Western society dreads the most.[1640] It therefore comes as no surprise that cancer is shrouded in many myths. The most pervasive myth is the idea of a cancer epidemic.

The problem with the cancer debate is that it is very easy to pick out numbers that sound alarming. In Figure 117 we see several different ways of describing US cancer mortality. First, we might look at the total number of people dying – in 1950, about 211,000 people died of all cancers, whereas more than 540,000 died of it in 1998. An increase of more than 150 percent. But of course, the US population has increased dramatically over the same period[1641] – and if the population doubles, we would naturally expect twice as many cancer deaths, without this in any way being alarming.

Thus, the cancer problem is more correctly expressed as a rate, typically the number of cancer deaths per 100,000 people. In Figure 117 we can see how this rate has increased from 140 in 1950 to 200 today. Thus, for every 100,000 people, we have 60 more cancer deaths every year in 1998 than we did in 1950. An increase in cancer frequency of 43 percent.

Actually, back in 1900, only 64 of 100,000 people would die from cancer, such that we today are experiencing 136 more deaths per 100,000 every year – an increase of 213 percent.[1642] But before this makes us conclude that the twentieth century has offered us an explosion of cancer, we have to consider what else has happened during this period.

Cancer is almost exclusively a disease of old age. The risk of cancer is roughly four (of 100,000) in the first 25 years of life. Then over the next ten years, the rate triples to 12. Then it roughly triples again every ten years, leaving a rate of 400 around age 50, tripling again over the next 20 years to 1,350.[1643] Thus, when the population ages, it will die more of cancer. Really, it is not all that surprising. In 1900, young people were dying of tuberculosis, influenza, pneumonia and other infectious diseases (see Figure 20, p. 56). Today, when we have got much older exactly because we do not die from these infections, and since we have to die of something sooner or later, we have to die more of heart disease and cancer. In 1900 the US average age was 26; in 1998 the average was 36.[1644]

Thus, as a population ages, more frequent cancer may be not an indication of any higher risk, but merely a consequence of more people having survived infections and moved up into more cancer-risky age groups. This problem is corrected by adjusting the cancer rates for age – essentially asking what the cancer rate would have been if the age distribution in the population had not changed. Typically, a standard like the US 1970 population or the world population (which makes it easier to compare between countries) is chosen. In Figure 117 we see the age-adjusted cancer rate which is the cancer rate the US would have had throughout the period if its population distribution had looked like the typical age distribution of the world. Here we see only a slight increase in age-adjusted cancer rates, from 125 up to 136 in 1983, and back to 126 in 1998, or an increase of 9 percent and now just 1 percent. But still, of course, cancer has actually increased – after correcting for age, there are still 1 percent more people who die from cancer every year.

However, the overwhelming reason for the slight rise in age-adjusted cancer rates is a rapid increase in lung cancer, and this we know is almost exclusively caused by increased smoking.[1645] WHO has used the non-smokers' cancer rates to estimate the number of lung cancers and other cancers attributable to smoking. Today, by far the largest part of lung cancer is due to smoking (about 91 percent)[1646] and the smoking-related lung cancers make up about 70 percent of all smoking-related cancers.[1647] Thus, if we take the age-adjusted cancer rates and remove the cancers attributable to smoking, we get a cancer rate both adjusted for the aging of the population and adjusted for past smoking patterns. This final rate is presented in Figure 117, representing the US cancer rate if the population was not aging and if no one was smoking. The result is a marked decline of almost 30 percent in cancer mortality from 1950 to 1998.

At the same we also die less of other causes, particularly vascular diseases. This is the reason why the average life expectancy goes up. In the US, the age-adjusted risk from dying of everything but cancer has gone down by 40 percent from 1955 to 1995 for men, and 45 percent for women.[1648] For the entire developed world, the drop in non-cancer death rates has been about 37 percent for men and 47 percent for women.[1649]

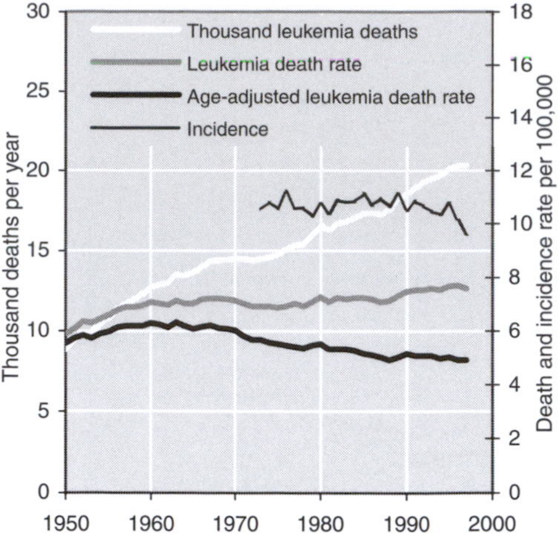

Figure 118 US leukemia mortality and incidence (onset of cancer), 1950–97, expressed as total number of deaths, crude cancer death rate, age-adjusted death rate and incidence. Age adjusted to standard world population for death rate, US 1970 population for incidence. Source: WHO 2000d, SEER 2000b.

Taken together, the evidence consistently shows that non-smokers have experienced decreasing overall cancer death risks as well as ever declining death rates from other diseases. No real cancer epidemic.

Thus, it is important that a cancer scare is not based merely on the wrong indicators such as absolute numbers or unadjusted rates. However, this was exactly what became the standard as Rachel Carson worried about the "disturbing rise" in leukemia from 1950 to 1960.[1650] Here essentially she compared the 8,845 deaths in 1950 to the 12,725 deaths in 1960 – an increase of 43 percent.[1651] This is also depicted in Figure 118. Her point was that we were seeing the absolute numbers of deaths increase by 4–5 percent annually (the increase was actually 3.7 percent). Rhetorically, she asked "what does it mean? To what lethal agent or agents, new to our environment, are people now exposed with increasing frequency?"[1652]

To support her position, she also stated the

crude death rate estimate, again showing an increase of 20 percent from 1950 to 1960. Of course, she should have presented the argument using age-adjusted death rates, which sounds much less worrisome at an increase of 13 percent. If we look further (which Carson naturally could not have done), the death rate for leukemia was back down at its 1950 level in 1974, and decreased a further 11 percent by 1997. Actually, since monitoring began in 1973, incidence (onset of cancer) has declined some 9 percent.

Although the causes of leukemia are still somewhat unclear it seems likely that Carson's singular focus on synthetic chemical killers was off track.[1653] Instead, it seems as though it is a two-step process. First, a rare chromosome recombination takes place in the womb. This can be caused by interfering chemicals, but many of them are of quite natural origin – resins used to treat genital warts, Chinese herbal medicines, genestein from soy sauce, flavors from red wine, onions and other foods, along with synthetics such as benzene and quinoline antibiotics.[1654] Moreover, metabolites of alcohol seem to be able to initiate the chromosome recombination, explaining the observed link between alcohol intake during pregnancy and leukemia.

However, another triggering factor is necessary, and here many studies have shown that rare infections play a part. In areas of higher population density, leukemia is more frequent.[1655] Moreover, many places with higher population mixing have seen increasing leukemia – a famous study showed that during the Second World War in the UK, where the city populations were offered rural places for evacuation, rural leukemia rates were higher the more city people stayed (supposedly increasing infection opportunity).[1656] Thus, Carson's increase in leukemia from 1950 to 1960 may have been nothing more than the increased urbanization of the US – from 64 percent to 70 percent urban in the decade from 1950.[1657]

If we look at the major cancers in the US in Figure 119, the most obvious is the heavy occurrence of lung cancer, particularly male lung cancer. For men, lung cancer has been the predominant cause of cancer since 1953, and for women it surpassed breast cancer in 1986. The growth in lung cancer is strongly linked to smoking. We know from the two largest cancer studies in the world, each involving more than a million people, that non-smokers have a very low and stable lung cancer rate.[1658] Actually, smokers on average have a tenfold increase in the risk of lung cancer, and lung cancer mortality is 23 times higher for smoking men compared to male never-smokers, while 13 times higher for women smokers compared to female never-smokers.[1659]

At the same time, smoking increased dramatically over the first part of the century. The consumption of cigarettes grew from 54 per person per year in 1900 to 4,345 in the 1960s, and has decreased since then to 2,261 in 1998 (the same as in 1942).[1660] The proportion of smokers has declined from 42 percent in 1965 to 25 percent in 1997 – the share of men smoking has declined steadily from 54 percent in 1955 to 28 percent in 1997, whereas women increased their smoking proportion from 24 percent in 1955 to 35 percent in 1965, decreasing since then to 22 percent in 1997.[1661]

This information has been used to make a crude measure of the US cigarette consumption for men and women, depicted in Figure 120. Seen together with the cancer mortality curves, it illustrates the massive effect of smoking. Men started smoking early in this century, peaking around 1960 with an average of more than 16 cigarettes per day (averaged over all men including male non-smokers). The male lung cancer rate equally increased from about five to its peak of 75 in 1991, declining thereafter (also including non-smokers). Women have never smoked on the same scale as men, peaking in the mid-1970s at nine cigarettes and decreasing thereafter. The female lung cancer rate has increased

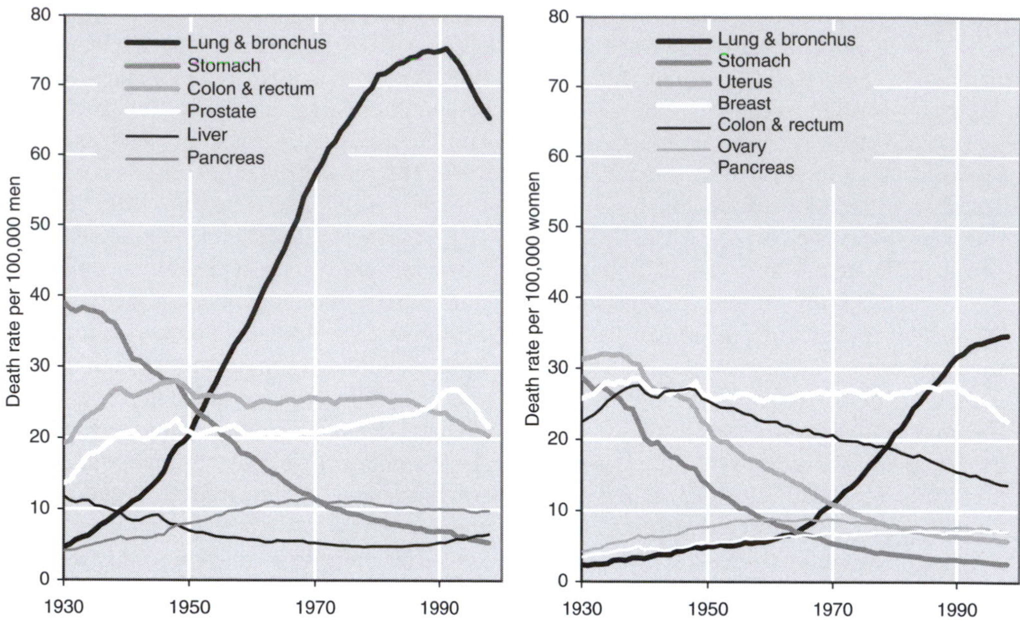

Figure 119 US age-adjusted cancer death rates for men and women, 1930–98. Age adjusted to US 1970 population. Source: ACS 1999, CDC 2000b, 2001a.

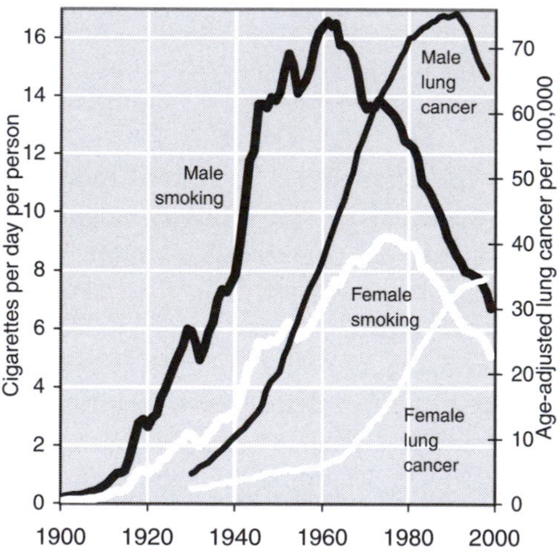

Figure 120 US cigarette consumption for all adult men and women, 1900–9, and lung and bronchus cancer, 1930–98, for men and women.[1662] Source: CDC 1997b:6–7, 8, 21, 35, 2000b, 2001a, ERS 2000a:4, ACS 1999.

from 2.3 in 1950 to more than 34, and it has still not leveled out, although it seems likely to do so soon.

The second most important cancer for women is breast cancer. Again, there is a widespread myth that breast cancer deaths are exploding – one popular article tells us "breast cancer and all reproductive tract cancers are up 300 percent."[1663] However, there is no evidence to support this statement even in absolute numbers: from 1950 to 1998 the annual number of breast cancers increased from 19,000 to 42,000 or an increase of 120 percent.[1664] However, as we know, this is not a very informative way of looking at the numbers, partly because the US has 58 percent more women now than in 1950, and partly because the population has aged and breast cancer risks increase dramatically with age.[1665]

If we look at the age-adjusted breast cancer

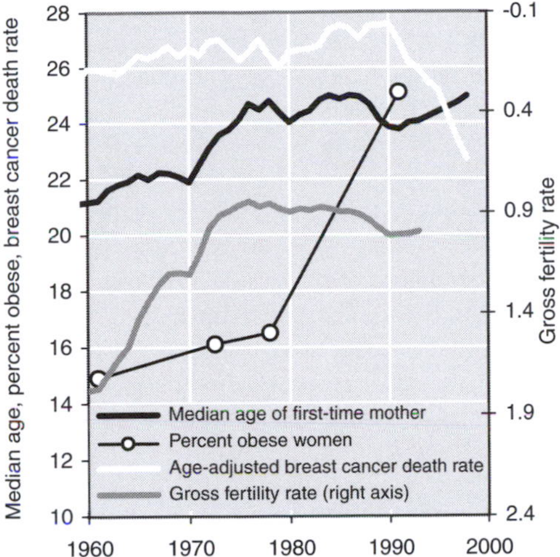

Figure 121 Risk factors for breast cancer, 1960–98: median age of a woman first birth, gross fertility rate (number of females born by the average mother) and percent obesity in population, with age-adjusted breast cancer rate. Source: NCHS 1999a:223, 1999b:13, 6, Ventura *et al.* 1998:12, 2000:26, ACS 1999, CDC 2000b, 2001a.

death rate in Figure 119, there is clearly no explosion – rather the death rate is almost stable at 25–27 all through to 1990 (we will look at incidence in a moment). Nevertheless, from 1960 to 1990 there was a slight increase in mortality, some 6 percent, as can be seen in the enlargement in Figure 121. This should not be surprising, since many other risk factors besides age are known.[1666] One of the most important is having children late and having few children. A woman with a first full-term pregnancy after 30 or a woman who has never borne a child has a risk two to three times greater than a woman with a completed pregnancy before the age of 20.[1667] And since 1960, the median age of first-time mothers has increased from 21.15 years to almost 25 years, because of ever more women delaying their children for education and career.[1668]

Beyond late first birth, it also seems that the risk of breast cancer is increased the fewer children a woman has. And from 1960 to 1975, the average number of children per woman has declined, as can be seen in Figure 121 (notice that the axis is turned upside down). The number of female babies to the average mother (gross fertility rate) dropped from 1.8 in 1960 down to just 0.85 in 1976 and has stayed around the stable 1 woman per woman since then.

Finally, breast cancer risk increases with body weight,[1669] and the share of American women who are obese has increased dramatically. In the first National Health Examination Survey in 1960–2, only 14.9 percent of all women were considered obese, whereas in the fourth examination in 1988–94 the share had increased to 25.1 percent.[1670]

Other risk factors, such as alcohol, probably increase breast cancer risks, but the evidence of increasing usage is vague and conflicting.[1671] Stress seems not to increase breast cancer.[1672] Possibly, prematurely born women seem to be more at risk, and since more premature births survive, this would also drive up the breast cancer rates.[1673] Also, genetics play a part (having both a sister and a mother with breast cancer increases your risks up to sixfold),[1674] but genetics only explains about 5–10 percent and there is no reason to expect that changing genetics should have been able to change the breast cancer risk over the past 40 years.

In sum, the very slight death rate increase to 1990 is amply explained by delayed childbearing, fewer children and more obese women. And these are all factors relating to personal decisions and not some lethal chemical agents in the environment. Since the mid-1980s, regular screening for breast tumors in combination with tamoxifen therapy has been instituted in the US, the UK and Canada, everywhere leading to significant declines in the breast cancer death rate.[1675] A new overview study concludes that the recent decrease in breast cancer mortality will continue.[1676]

The last of the major cancer risks in Figure 119 to increase is male prostate cancer, having increased some 8 percent since 1950. Prostate cancer is primarily a disease of old age – the median age for diagnosis is 72 years.[1677] Many different causes seem to be significant, and research seems particularly to indicate a fairly stable connection between higher intake of animal fat and higher risk of prostate cancer.[1678] Although not yet settled, an NIH overview states that "the evidence for an important role of diet in prostate cancer development has increased over the last decade."[1679]

Moreover, a new testing method, the prostate-specific antigen (PSA) test, has been rapidly adopted since its introduction in 1987. This test has led to the discovery of many latent prostate cancers and consequently has created a much greater pool from which to misattribute the cause of death. A 1999 study from the National Cancer Institute indicates that this may be a major cause of the recent rise and fall of the death rate,[1680] while the PSA in the longer run is likely to decrease further the prostate cancer death rate.[1681]

The mortality rate of the remaining major cancers is generally declining, some even dramatically and sustained over the almost 70 years of coverage, as is evident in Figure 119. For men, cancer in the colon and rectum has declined by 26 percent since 1948, while the reduction for women has been about 51 percent. Moreover, women have experienced a decline in cancers of the uterus by 81 percent. Most dramatically, stomach cancer has declined for both sexes, 84 percent for men and 91 percent for women. This is most likely related to improvements in diet, including the higher availability of fresh fruits and vegetables, better food preservation through refrigeration, and fewer *Helicobacter pylori* infections.[1682]

Thus, the age- and smoking-adjusted death rate from cancer is declining; the few sites where the rate increases are fairly well understood and by now the vast majority of leading sites are declining.[1683] This understanding is very far removed from the typical press stories of the cancer explosion. As the lead author from the WHO study on smoking concludes:

> The common belief that there is an epidemic of death from cancer in developed countries is a myth, except for the effects of tobacco. In many countries cancer deaths from tobacco are going up, and in some they are at last coming down. But, if we take away the cancer deaths that are attributed to smoking then the cancer death rates that remain are, if anything, declining. This is reassuringly true in Western Europe, Eastern Europe and North America – and, in the "West", the death rates from other diseases are falling rapidly. For most non-smokers, the health benefits of modern society outweigh the new hazards. Apart from tobacco (and in places, HIV), the Western world is a remarkably healthy place to live.[1684]

Cancer death rates are declining and the most important factors determining their trends beyond health care are not environmental but related to personal choice of lifestyle.

Cancer: incidence

Nevertheless, there are two other types of strategies to worry about with cancer – two ways to use cancer statistics to restate Carson's question concerning to what "lethal agent or agents, new to our environment, are people now exposed with increasing frequency?"[1685] The first is to look at the incidence or onset of cancer, the other is to look at rare cancers or special groups.

Let us first look at incidence. In the US, the national SEER cancer surveillance program started in 1973, covering about 10–14 percent of the US population.[1686] Since 1973, incidence has increased dramatically for some of the main incidence sites, such as prostate, breast and female genital.[1687] Figure 122 shows the development of the five top sites accounting for more than 60 percent of all incidences.[1688] Here, both breast and prostate cancer incidence has clearly been increasing over the past 25 years. Lung and bronchial cancer as well as female genital cancer have shown a smaller degree of increase, while colon and rectum cancer have decreased slightly.

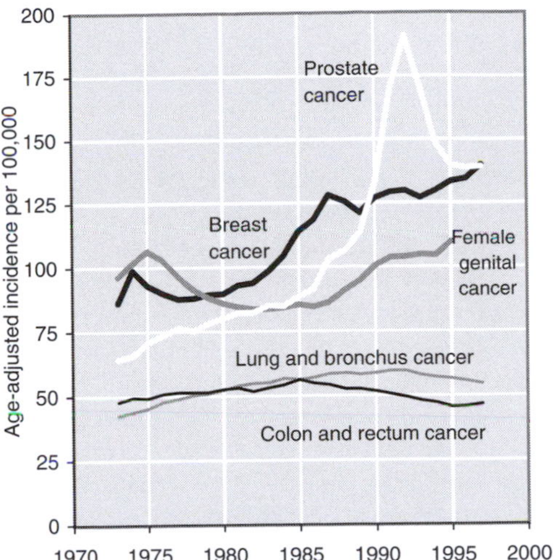

Figure 122 Age-adjusted incidence risks of top sites, 1973–97. Female breast cancer, female genital cancer, male prostate cancer, both sexes lung and bronchus cancer, and colon and rectum cancer. Source: SEER 2000b.[1689]

Does this indicate a worrying trend? As an example, let us take a closer look at breast cancer. Incidence has increased 62 percent since 1973, whereas death rates have decreased more than 13 percent – why? As the American Cancer Society points out, most of the incidence increase occurred from 1982 to 1988, where the annual growth rate was about 4 percent.[1690] This large increase is generally attributed to the rapid increase in mammography screening – in the early eighties screening had reached only 10–20 percent of women over 40, whereas in 1992 at least 60–70 percent of all women over 40 had had a mammogram.[1691]

During this period the incidence of small tumors (<2 cm) more than doubled, while larger tumors (>3 cm) decreased 27 percent, indicating ever earlier detection.[1692] A very large part of the rise also comes from *in situ* cancer (early cancer that has not spread to neighboring tissue) – the rise from 1973 would be 22 percentage points lower without *in situ* cancer.[1693] Most of these cancers are so-called *ductal carcinoma in situ* (DCIS), which are almost only detectable by mammography.[1694] In the judgment of the American Cancer Society this "reflects a shift in the stage of disease at diagnosis toward earlier, more curable cancers rather than a true increase in occurrence."[1695]

We often worry about stories like 1-in-8 women will get breast cancer (see box), but this is not the main story. Because of an increase in early detection and increasing detection of breast lumps that are technically cancerous but benign,[1696] we see a total increase in incidence. Nevertheless, this is exactly the reason why more cancers can be treated in time, causing death rates to decline.

Equally, the increase in prostate cancer of

1-IN-8 AND OTHER LIFETIME RISKS

Perhaps one of the best publicized risks is the "1-in-8 women will get breast cancer," a statistic that has been published by the American Cancer Society since the early 1970s (when it was 1-in-16).[1697] This statistic is technically correct, but when stated alone and without explanation it is difficult to relate to one's own life and it is often taken as overly worrying. The statement that one in eight women will get breast cancer means that if we follow eight women from birth to death, on average one will be diagnosed with breast cancer. (Notice, that we assume all women to go through the current death, accident and disease risks of the relevant age groups.) Sometimes it is stated that this 1-in-8 only applies if the women survive all other deaths,[1698] but this is wrong – of course, other deaths have been taken into account.[1699]

So, the statistic is correct, but there are two things to be noticed. First, the 1-in-8 talks about *incidence*, not *death*. Second, the 1-in-8 is a *lifetime* risk, but is often taken as a risk *right now*.[1700]

Looking at death instead of incidence, a

woman's lifetime risk of dying from breast cancer is "only" 3.29 percent or 1-in-30.[1701] And looking at the risk right now, it depends greatly on age: the risk of a women developing breast cancer before the age of 50 is less than 2 percent (1-in-50) and even before the age of 60, the risk is still just 4.24 percent.[1702] Her total risk of death before 65 years is 1.5 percent (1-in-65).[1703]

Nevertheless, the 1-in-8 statistic has entirely focused women's fears on breast cancer. In a recent survey of 1000 women between the ages 45 and 64, 61 percent feared cancer and particularly breast cancer most, while only 8 percent feared the disease most likely to kill them – heart disease.[1704] Going through all 59 articles on breast cancer in four popular women's magazines, researches found that 20 used the 1-in-8 statistics, but only 6 explained it.[1705] Moreover, the typical age of the women featured in the articles was 41 years, way younger than the US typical age of onset of breast cancer – 65 years.[1706]

Comparing the 1-in-8 number with other risk estimates may be useful to gain a feel for what is dangerous and what is not. Roughly four out of ten people will get cancer, and about two will die – women a little less than men. However, the risks of getting coronary heart disease is roughly similar to cancer while the death risk is much higher.

While breast cancer for women and prostate cancer for men make up more than a third of all cancer incidences, they only make up about one-seventh of all cancer deaths. Lung and bronchus cancer is still the most likely cancer to kill both men and women. Over a lifetime, it is more likely to get involved in a motor vehicle accident with disabling injury than to experience cancer. Also, it is perhaps worth mentioning that the total lifetime death risk is 100 percent – the question is not whether we die but from what and when.

Of course, the timing of different risks is not very well captured by lifetime risks, and likewise behavior can substantially change risks (if you do not smoke, your lifetime lung cancer death risk is far smaller that what is stated in Table 5).

Table 5 Lifetime risks of selected incidences and deaths in percent. Notice, that numbers come from many different sources, years, and computational methods, and are only roughly comparable. Sources: SEER 2000:I.17-18, Merrill et al. 1999:188, Preboth 2000, Walsh & Devlin 1998, Lloyd-Jones et al. 1999, Quinn 1995, Lawrie et al. 1999, NSC 1999:30, 80, USBC 1999:14, NCHS 1999:151.[1707]

	Men		Women	
Lifetime risks (in percent)	Incidence	Death	Incidence	Death
Cancer	42.8	23.94	37.56	20.53
Lung and Bronchus	7.82	7.62	5.66	4.74
Breast	0.12	0.03	14.96	3.29
Prostate	15.65	3.29	–	–
Colon & Rectum	5.76	2.45	5.5	2.43
Skin cancer	1.66	0.34	1.19	0.20
Motor vehicle accidents	48.02	1.69	38.95	0.87
Suicide		1.67		0.41
Homicide, US		0.60		0.21
Homicide, Canada		0.25		0.13
Major depression or dysthymia			20	
Eating disorder			3	
Coronary heart disease	48.6	30.9	31.7	31.9
Parkinson's disease	2.5		2.5	
Schizophrenia	1		1	

116 percent is mostly caused by an increase in early detection. Partly, there are more operations for benign prostate disease, where asymptomatic prostatic tumors are found incidentally.[1708] Partly, new diagnostic techniques such as transrectal ultrasound guided needle biopsy, computer tomography, and the above-mentioned serum testing for prostate-specific antigen (PSA) have increased the detection rate.[1709] Actually, when examining the prostates of men who had died at 70 from completely unrelated causes and with no clinical history of prostate cancer, researchers found that 25 percent had prostate cancer – indicating that there is a very large pool of possible – and potentially harmless – prostate cancers waiting to be discovered.[1710] Nevertheless, the very increase in detection has generally caused prostate cancer to be discovered earlier, consequently giving treatment a better chance and making death rates decline, as is seen in Figure 119.

The other three cancers in Figure 122 are less likely to evoke fear. The 28 percent increase in lung and bronchus incidence is hardly surprising, given the long increase in male and continued increase in female lung and bronchus cancer mortality from smoking. The incidence of colon and rectal cancer has declined some 3 percent, and incidence of female genital cancer has remained stable with a decline in malignant cancer rates.[1711]

Another strategy to evoke problems with cancer statistics is to look at very infrequent cancers or special groups, where increasing rates are likely to be found, even if just by chance. In September 1997, the US EPA held the first-ever national conference to explore possible links between childhood cancer and environmental causes, "spurred by the concerns that childhood cancer rates may be increasing."[1712] With a clear hint from Rachel Carson, EPA administrator Carol M. Browner pointed out at the conference: "The world that our children are born into now includes tens of thousands of new chemicals that simply were not around just a few decades ago – substances that are present in our air, in our water, in our homes, on our foods."[1713]

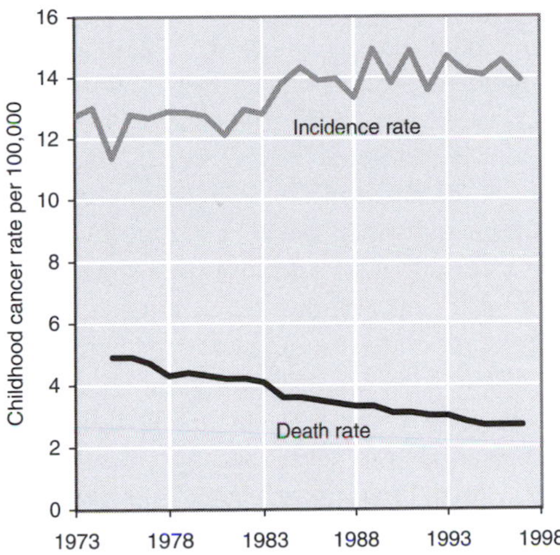

Figure 123 Age-adjusted incidence and death rates for childhood cancers, 0–14 years old, 1973–97. Source: SEER 2000:27, 2000a.

But is there any reason to worry here? Figure 123 shows how childhood cancer incidence rates have increased by 9 percent while death rates have declined by 45 percent. In the latest review from the National Cancer Institute, the researchers have looked at the issue of childhood cancer exactly because of public concern stemming from media reports that incidence may be increasing because of environmental impacts.[1714] The conclusion was that:

> there was no substantial change in incidence for the major pediatric cancers, and rates have remained relatively stable since the mid-1980s. The modest increases that were observed . . . were confined to the mid-1980s. The patterns suggest that the increases likely reflected diagnostic improvements or reporting changes. Dramatic declines in childhood cancer mortality represent treatment-related improvements in survival.[1715]

Likewise with skin cancer. Here there has been an increase in both incidence and death rate, with an impressive-sounding death rate increase of 38 percent. However, making the same point in actual rates is perhaps less impressive – skin cancer death rates have increased from 1.6 per 100,000 in 1973 to 2.2 in 1997.[1716] Lifetime risk is but 0.2–0.34 percent as indicated in Table 5. And the reason is quite prosaic – the increase is mainly due to the fact that we spend more time sunbathing and wear fewer clothes when outside.[1717] (Its very slight relationship to the ozone-layer will be discussed in chapter 24, p. 273.)

Overall, there seems to be no indication of a cancer epidemic, apart perhaps from smoking-related lung cancer. Age- and smoking-adjusted death rates are declining, and when incidence rates are going up, it is mainly an indication of more and earlier screening being part of the cause of declining death rates.

There seems to be no reason to suspect that the chemical "elixirs of death" are causing ever more cancers – rather the opposite.

In its cancer overview, the National Cancer Institute concludes:

> Increasing exposure to general environmental hazards seems unlikely to have had a major impact on the overall trends in cancer rates, in agreement with the conclusion reached in a recent investigation of mortality trends in England and Wales, although rising rates for certain tumors have been clearly influenced by changing exposures to tobacco smoking, HIV infection, and sunlight exposure.[1718]

The fear of pesticides

So, what is the effect of the environment on cancers? How important are chemical pollutants to the formation of cancer?

Several considerations lead us here to look particularly at the effects of the chemical group of pesticides. First, pesticides are well recognized and feared both in the EU and the US. The European Environment Agency named pesticides in drinking water one of the "dominant health issues in Europe" in its evaluation of the European environment at the turn of the century.[1719] Equally, pesticides came at the high end of US environmental concerns, with 75 percent of all Americans being extremely or very concerned about pesticides.[1720]

Second, pesticides are well studied, which

ESTABLISHING THRESHOLDS THROUGH RISK ANALYSIS

The substances we consume via food and water are thoroughly regulated by global (UN), American (FDA, EPA) and European (EU) rules, primarily by means of limit values which, in the words of the UN, achieve an "adequate margin of safety to reduce to a minimum any hazard to health in all groups of consumers."[1721]

Briefly what happens is this. Through experiments on animals, a threshold is set where the substance has no harmful effects such as being toxic, causing irritation, or having consequences for reproduction.[1722] This limit value is known as NOEL (No Observed Effect Level) or more recently NOAEL (No Observed Adverse Effect Level).[1723] This level is then further reduced to achieve a limit-value for humans, the so-called ADI (Acceptable Daily Intake).

In order to make allowances for possible differences in human and animal biological sensitivity, the NAOEL is usually reduced to one-tenth.[1724] To make allowances for differences between various population groups (children, the elderly, etc.) it is further reduced to one-tenth. If various conditions are present such as a lack of information or uncertainty, the limit can be reduced still further. The usual ADI limit is therefore between 100 and 10,000 times lower than the NOAEL.[1725]

Thus, if experiments show that rats can consume substance X in a dose of 100 mg per kilo body-weight per day without adverse effects (NOAEL), and a typical safety factor of 100 is applied, then the Acceptable Daily Intake (ADI) will be set at 1 mg per kilo body-weight per day.[1726]

makes it easier to discuss and document the different costs and benefits. Finally, in 1999 the Danish government completed possibly the biggest study of the societal consequences of phasing out pesticides, which gives us a better background against which to evaluate our various policy options.

Surprisingly, both the EU and the US worry mostly about pesticides in the water. In the EU, pesticides are typically mentioned in connection with groundwater.[1727] Equally, in a study of American attitudes towards pesticides, 71 percent were somewhat or very concerned about pesticides in the water supply.[1728]

This worry is perhaps best expressed in the EU drinking water policy: here pesticides are regulated not because they are dangerous *per se* but simply because we do not want them. The limit value for pesticides was set at 0.1μg/l because this was how much was measurable back in 1980 when the limit was set.[1729] "If one only considered the amount of pesticides permitted in water for reasons of health, then the limit values – depending on the pesticide in question – would with today's knowledge probably be considerably higher," explains the director of the Danish Environment Agency, Erik Lindegaard.[1730] His civil servants are even more blunt: "If health-related limit values were to be set for pesticides they would be far higher than the current political ones."[1731]

Owing to ever better detection methods, pesticides are found in the drinking water all over Europe. As the EEA points out: "Many pesticides are not found in groundwater simply because they are not looked for. Once a pesticide is looked for, it is often found, although the concentration may be below the maximum admissible concentration of 0.1μg/l."[1732] And as member states have started looking, pesticides have been found violating the limit of 0.1μg/l in upwards of 50 percent of all sampling sites.[1733] As far as fruit and vegetables are concerned, around 1 percent exceed the limit values for pesticide content, both in the EU and the US.[1734] But in this case, the limit

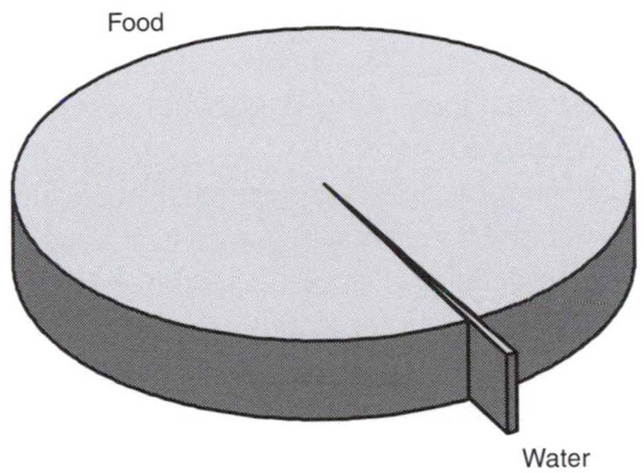

Figure 124 The amount of pesticides from food (45μg/day or 99.6 percent) and water (0.2 μg/day or 0.4 percent), even if one drinks two liters of water a day from sources containing pesticides at EU limit values. Source: Ames *et al.* 1987:272.

values are set according to a health-related evaluation and are around 500 and 50,000 times higher than in drinking water (see box on establishing thresholds).

The average American consumes 295 pounds of fruit and 416 pounds of vegetables a year.[1735] A rough calculation shows that he therefore consumes about 24 mg of pesticide each year.[1736] Even if one drinks 2 liters of water a day for a whole year from a well with a pesticide concentration exactly at the EU limit (which would be a maximally pessimistic scenario), one would absorb about 300 times less pesticide from the water than from fruit and vegetables. This quick-and-dirty estimate is also backed up by much more accurate research, demonstrating that Americans would consume 225 times as much pesticide through food as through water if their entire fluid intake came from a water source polluted with pesticides at the EU limit values (see Figure 124).[1737]

This means, of course, that *if* we are to fear pesticides at all then we have to fear getting them from our food and not our water.[1738]

Pesticides and cancer

Let us try to gauge how dangerous pesticides are to human health.

The fear of pesticides primarily concerns their long-term effects. In contrast, it is much easier to decide whether a substance is actually toxic, or whether it irritates the eyes and skin, and there is relatively broad agreement as to the consequences of various doses.[1739] With the legacy of Carson, the long-term effects concerned have primarily been cancer. In the same way, most official regulation of pesticides has focused on the risk of getting cancer as a result of constant contact with low concentrations of pesticides.[1740] In recent years a new fear has developed, that of pesticides' possible hormonal effects on humans. We shall discuss both problems, starting with cancer.

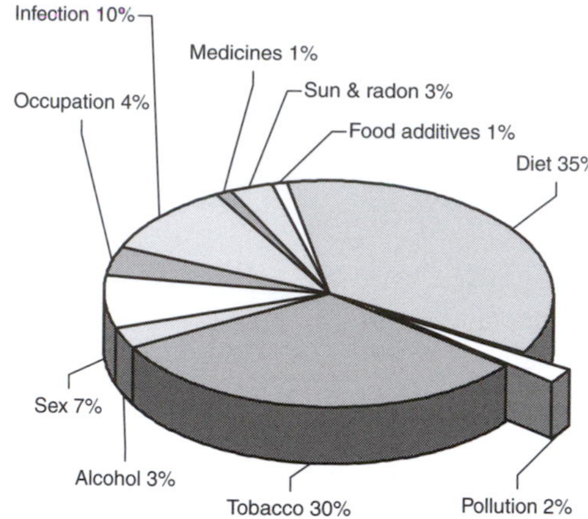

Figure 125 Proportions of cancer attributed to different causes in the US. Pesticides account for a minuscule share of pollution's contribution to cancer. Source: Doll and Peto 1981:1256.[1746]

Cancer is responsible for around 23 percent of all deaths in the Western world, measured in terms of both life-years lost and the number of lives.[1741] Two of the world's leading cancer researchers, Sir Richard Doll and Richard Peto, have carried out one of the largest studies of the relative importance of various causes of cancer in the US.[1742] The conclusions of the important and unimportant causes, as seen in Figure 125, often come as a surprise.

Tobacco is the cause of around 30 percent of all cancer deaths and since the number of smokers increased between 1960 and 1980, an increasing number of people in the Western world will die of cancer caused by tobacco smoking. Tobacco smoking is also the cause of numerous cardiovascular diseases. Today, around 20 percent of *all* deaths are caused by tobacco and it is to be expected that this proportion will increase.[1743]

Diet is the cause of about 35 percent of all cancer-related deaths.[1744] We know from numerous studies, especially those of migrants, that our eating habits affect our cancer risk.[1745] Examples of this are colon and breast cancer, which are among the most common forms in the US, rare in Japan but common among American Japanese.[1747] The food we eat has changed considerably since industrialization: we eat more processed food, far more sugar, meat, dairy products and fat.[1748] Increasing the amount of fat, salt, low-fiber and meat-based food we eat increases our risk of getting cancer. Similarly, obesity and a higher intake of calories also increases the risk of our developing cancer.[1749] On the other hand, eating both fruit and vegetables reduces our risk of getting cancer.[1750] It is believed that changing our diet so as to avoid fat, meat and obesity and focusing on fruit, green vegetables and fibers would get rid of all or almost all food-related occurrences of cancer, i.e. reduce the frequency of cancer in the West by as much as 35 percent![1751]

The fact that infections cause 10 percent of all occurrences of cancer does not mean that cancer is contagious but that some viruses, bacteria and parasites can trigger cancer.[1752] In the same way, sex and childbirth account for some 7 percent of all cancer cases, primarily because of cervical cancer (increasing with the number of sex partners) and cancer of the breasts and ovaries (increasing with later first-time birth).[1753] Spending more time in the sun also results in more cancer (an increase of 50 percent over the last 14 years) and radioactive radon seeping from underground also causes it.[1754] Together, these cause about 3 percent of all cancer deaths.

Alcohol is carcinogenic, causing about 3 percent of all cancer-related deaths. And consumption of it is increasing, in step with higher incomes and urbanization.[1755] Medicines and x-ray examination are estimated to cause around 1 percent of all cancer-related deaths.[1756] Additives such as spices, preservatives and artificial sweeteners may contribute to cancer, but Doll and Peto also believe that because they improve food safety and reduce obesity, they may in fact also have a preventive effect on the disease. Doll and Peto's best estimate is that food additives cause less than 1 percent of all cancer deaths, although this could be as low as minus 5 percent (avoiding 5 percent extra deaths).

Finally, there is pollution. This includes atmospheric pollution, water pollution and food contamination, which together account for about 2 percent of all cancer-related deaths. Of these factors, air pollution is the main cause of cancer, whereas water pollution is considered "relatively less important."[1757]

We finally come to pesticides, and how much they contribute to cancer. Doll and Peto conclude that "the occurrence of pesticides as dietary pollutants seems unimportant."[1758] This conclusion then, equates very poorly with our fear of pesticides. *Virtually no one dies of cancer caused by pesticides.*

We pointed out above that Americans believe most cancer risks to be caused by "things in the environment, such as air pollution, water pollution, chemical waste disposal, etc.," rather than personal choices such as food, smoking and drinking.[1759] However, if we count the categories in Figure 125, at least 75 percent of the cancer risk stems from personal choices, whereas less than 7 percent comes from without, and this is even including the work environment's 4 percent as involuntary. The pesticide scare, causing 75 percent of all Americans to be extremely or very concerned about pesticides, is seemingly without foundation.[1760]

One could of course assume that Doll and Peto – despite their internationally acclaimed reputation – are alone in their assertions. But this is not the case. Many others have tried to evaluate both the general cancer risk and the specific pesticide risk, finding estimates in the same range. An earlier 1977 attempt to attribute cancer to specific causes found very similar estimates to Doll and Peto.[1761] Here, almost all factors were found to be due to individual behavior whereas pollution although considered was not even included in the final attribution. Occupation was found to be the only non-individual cause, explaining 2–5 percent of all cancers.[1762] A later and much quoted 1993 study in the *Journal of the American Medical Association* attempted to attribute not just cancer but all deaths to some cause.[1763] At least 80 percent of the explained deaths are based on individual behavior, whereas just 6 percent of the explained deaths stem from toxic agents, covering both occupational hazards, environmental pollutants, contaminants of food and water supplies, and components of commercial products.[1764] The main environmental effects come from asbestos exposure, from occupational hazard and again about 2 percent from pollution.[1765]

Actually, the US EPA 1987 estimates of environmentally caused cancers are surprisingly similar to Doll and Peto. EPA estimates that pollution contributes 1–3 percent (compared to Doll and Peto's 2 percent), sun and radon 3–6 percent (Doll and Peto: 3 percent), occupation 0.5–4 percent (4 percent) and consumer products less than 1 percent (1 percent).[1766] In a review of EPA's toxicological method and Doll and Peto's epidemiological method it is concluded that "the agreement between Doll and Peto's and EPA's estimates may be seen as buttressing the conclusion that cancer risks from environmental exposures are a relatively small percentage of total cancer risk."[1767]

In the EPA risk estimate is included an evaluation of the overall risk of pesticides in food. Here, EPA found *by far the highest* risk of all studies. The overall risk was estimated to constitute between 0.5 percent and 1 percent of all cancer-related deaths or 3,000–6,000 annual deaths. The EPA acknowledges that this is a worst-case figure, and that the correct figure could be much lower and perhaps close to zero.[1768]

However, three new comprehensive studies have shown that the true figure is probably very small. In 1996, the US National Research Council, part of the National Academy of Sciences, produced a 500-page report on carcinogens in food, sponsored by, among others, the EPA. Its main conclusion was that "the great majority of individual naturally occurring and synthetic chemicals in the diet appear to be present at levels below which any significant adverse biologic effect is likely, and so low that they are unlikely to pose an appreciable cancer risk."[1769]

Once again, this challenges our usual view of pesticides. However, the National Research Council was not alone in its evaluation. In 1997, the World Cancer Research Fund and the American Institute of Cancer Research, with the help of the WHO, the National Cancer Institute, the FAO and the International Agency for Research on Cancer (IARC) scrutinized more than 4,500 studies in order to investigate the effect of foods on the development of cancer. The 650-page report also discusses the problem of pesticides and concludes that:

> There is no convincing evidence that any food contaminant [including pesticides] modifies the risk of any cancer, nor is there evidence of any probable causal relationship. Indeed, there is currently little epidemiological evidence that chemical contamination [pesticides] of food and drink, resulting from properly regulated use, significantly affects cancer risk.[1770]

It also says that "it is commonly thought by the public that chemical contamination [pesticides] of food and drink is a significant cause of human cancer" but that "experts . . . have generally come to the view that residues are relatively unimportant factors."[1771]

Finally, in 1997 the Canadian Cancer Society produced a major report on the very topic of pesticides. The evaluation was that "there has been a growing concern on the part of many Canadians that exposure to pesticides, either in food residues or when applied to lawns and gardens, may be a major cause of cancers."[1772] The conclusion is, however, that they still share Doll and Peto's assessment of pesticides and that "the general population, through food residues, is not exposed to any appreciable risk."[1773]

The conclusion of all the recent studies is that we got it wrong. We worry about a minute or non-existing threat. Extremely few people – if any – die of cancer because of pesticide residues in foods and in drinking water under present conditions.

On the other hand, several studies have shown that farmers, who are far more exposed to pesticides than most, do face a greater risk of getting cancer. For example, a study of French wine growers shows that they face a 25 percent greater risk of developing brain cancer.[1774] The problem with the studies, which are often reported in the media, is that it is impossible to know what other types of cancer have been tested. This is the "file drawer" problem mentioned in chapter 2 – it is possible (and as far as this survey is concerned it even seems probable) that the authors have collected information about 20 or 30 types of cancer and have then found one that is different as far as farmers are concerned and reported it, while the ones that were not of interest were left to languish in the file drawer.[1775] This means that we cannot be sure that finds such as this one, of the connection between pesticides and cancer in the brains of French wine growers, are examples of true and causal connections.[1776]

On the other hand, several teams of scientists have made a whole series of studies of farmers in an attempt to correct the file drawer problem. The latest, most comprehensive study from 1998 examines 37 other studies and finds that "cancer of the lips is the only form of cancer which is obviously more common in farmers."[1777] Cancer of the lips is in all likelihood related to the fact that farmers face greater exposure to the sun as they work outdoors. The farming discussion does not appear to provide support for the argument that pesticides should to any substantial degree contribute to cancer.

Cancer in animal experiments

So do pesticides cause cancer at all? It is difficult to say. The basic problem is that when we consider such small cancer risks as those which apply to most pesticides, we simply cannot see any increased occurrence of cancer in the population because too many other factors get in the way. This is what statisticians call noise. Sometimes one can look at individual professional groups who have worked with heavy concentrations of a substance for years. For instance, studies investigating miners exposed to intense levels of radon have formed the primary background material to deduce the carcinogenic effects of radon in ordinary homes, as discussed in chapter 17.[1778] A very few pesticides such as arsenic, benzene and chromium have been confirmed as carcinogenic in humans, but then naturally these have also been regulated and banned.[1779]

We therefore find ourselves in the situation today that, to the extent to which current pesticides produce cancer, the risk to the individual is so small that it would be very difficult to see any increased cancer risk, even among such exposed groups as farmers.[1780] Of course, this does not necessarily mean that the overall risk to society may not be serious.

This is why scientists instead investigate whether pesticides cause cancer in rats and mice. The trouble is that standard animal experiments with only 50 animals in each group are so small-scale that it is not possible statistically to detect differences of less than about 10 percent.[1781] If one divides the mice into two groups and gives one group pesticides throughout their lives, and discovers that four mice develop cancer, whereas only three do so in the toxin-free control group, no conclusion can be drawn because the difference could just as well be a matter of chance. The difference has to be at least five mice before statistical significance can be achieved.

One could, of course, simply give the substance to far more mice, but even the standard 50 animal per group experiment costs around US$400,000 and it will generally be necessary to carry out at least two experiments on different species.[1782] Instead experts have chosen to investigate cancer risk by giving the laboratory animals extremely high, close to harmful doses, so as to be sure of getting a high cancer frequency.[1783] On evaluation, the question then arises as to what the cancer risk to mice on a high dose means to human beings at low intake levels. The question is whether one can transfer conclusions drawn from mice to humans, and from high doses to low ones.

The short answer is: we do not know.[1784] But to be on the safe side the EPA uses data from the most sensitive species of animals and assumes that there is a direct correlation from high to low dose.[1785] The Acceptable Daily Intake (ADI) is then set such that the lifetime risk of getting cancer from this particular chemical is less than 1 to 1,000,000.[1786]

Particularly contestable is the direct correlation between high and low doses. How are we to interpret a typical experiment, as shown here in Figure 126, on ETU, a well-known by-product of a fungicide? There is statistically no doubt that 500 ppm of ETU will give rats thyroid cancer. And at 0 ppm, ETU obviously cannot cause cancer (the 2 percent apparently being the background cancer level – thyroid cancers from other causes). It actually seems that ETU does not increase the cancer risk at levels below 125 ppm, and that the cancer risk only increases above this level. It is possible

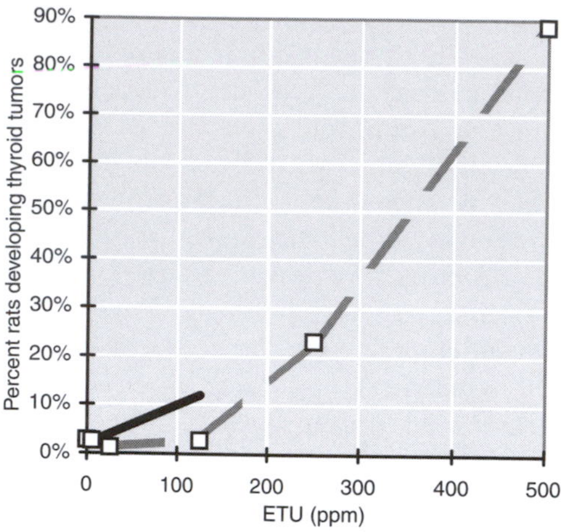

Figure 126 Rat study of carcinogenity of ethylene thiourea (ETU). Daily dose (in parts per million) against percentage of rats (approx. 70 in each group) which at the end of the experiment had developed thyroid tumors. The straight black line illustrates the EPA's general evaluation of risk correlation at low doses. Source: Rodricks 1992:133, EPA 1996c:117.

that the 125 ppm represents a threshold value – that ETU levels below 125 ppm are harmless, while those above cause cancer. This interpretation is equivalent to the oft-quoted insight from the founder of pharmacology, Paracelsus (1493–1541), who said that "all substances are poisons; there is none which is not a poison. The right dose differentiates a poison and a remedy."[1787]

Even so, statistically we can not exclude the possibility of a minimal risk still existing between 0 and 100 ppm, and that we just cannot discern this risk using only 70 rats. Many different, complicated models have been proposed as a means of estimating the correlation for small doses.[1788] The EPA estimates that the risk steadily decreases as the line in Figure 126 shows.[1789] Almost everyone (the EPA included) agrees that this straight-line risk estimation is a worst-case approach and possibly leads to a drastic overestimation of the risk.[1790]

This is the crux of the dispute – whether carcinogens have threshold values beneath which they are not dangerous or whether they simply become less and less dangerous right down to zero. And it will probably be extremely difficult to settle this dispute using normal methods of measurement because the figures involved are so incredibly small.[1791]

Natural and synthetic pesticides

Professor Bruce Ames of the University of California, Berkeley, has for some years been proposing a radical new point of view to the threshold/no-threshold discussion.[1792] Bruce Ames is one of the world's most highly respected microbiologists and cancer researchers, who invented and gave his name to one of the most frequently used tests for cancer.[1793] His point of view was recently backed up by the US National Research Council.[1794]

Ames has repeatedly pointed out that we have almost exclusively worried about artificial pesticides, even though many pesticides are natural. This often seems to come as a surprise to people, but when you think about it, it is actually obvious: plants – unlike animals – cannot run away, which is why one of their most important evolutionary survival strategies is to become poisonous, and thus inedible.

But with Rachel Carson the early environmental movements focused virtually exclusively on man-made pesticides, which is what formed the basis of our fear of, and focus on, synthetic chemicals.[1795] Carson set out the environmental objective with her famous quote: "For the first time in the history of the world, every human being is now subjected to contact with dangerous chemicals, from the moment of conception until death."[1796] Ames points out the basic misconception: "This statement is wrong: the vast bulk of the chemicals humans are exposed to are natural, and for every chemical some amount is dangerous."[1797]

Chemically there seems to be no basis for

distinguishing between natural and synthetic pesticides.[1798] Arsenic has been used as a weed-killer and is a naturally occurring mineral. Aflatoxin is the most carcinogenic pesticide known to man. It occurs naturally in a fungus that infects, among other things, peanuts, grain and maize.[1799] Pyrethrum is an insecticide which occurs naturally in the chrysanthemum family, just as nicotine is a natural pesticide which the tobacco plant uses to protect itself.[1800]

It turns out that we consume far more natural pesticides than synthetic ones. Typically, natural pesticides make up 5–10 percent of a plant's dry weight.[1801] It is estimated that by weight 99.99 percent of the pesticides we consume are natural, while only 0.01 percent are synthetic.[1802] Reference is frequently made to the 99.99 percent figure, although it is not relevant in itself since we also need to know whether synthetic pesticides are more or less carcinogenic than natural ones.[1803]

Ames, together with several colleagues from Berkeley, has evaluated the various things we eat and drink. Coffee, for example, contains around 1,000 chemicals, of which only 30 have so far been tested for cancer in mice and rats. Twenty-one of the tested chemicals are carcinogenic to rodents.[1804]

In order to evaluate how serious a cancer threat these substances constitute one can compare the intake per kilo of body weight with the dose which gives 50 percent of mice or rats cancer from life-long consumption (known as TD_{50} – about 350 ppm in Figure 126).[1805] If one drinks a cup of coffee made from 4 g of ground coffee, one is consuming 7.2 mg of caffeic acid or about 0.1 mg/kg bodyweight.[1806] Half a group of rodents will develop cancer from a daily lifetime intake of around 285 mg/kg of caffeic acid (the TD_{50}). Thus, one cup of coffee every day subjects a human being to 0.1/285 = 0.035 percent, known as 0.035 percent HERP (Human Exposure dose/Rodent Potency dose).[1807] This risk only applies on two important conditions: *if* it is possible to transfer results from rodents to humans, and *if* the EPA's linear, no-threshold method is relevant.

Unless it is possible to transfer results directly from mice to humans (something which obviously poses big problems), the figures cannot be used as absolutes. But one can still compare the *relative* risk, because this rests purely on the no-threshold assumption. So using no-threshold we can compare the relative cancer risk of a whole series of the things we eat – both food and pesticide residues. Since the no-threshold assumption gives a worst case estimate for very small intakes our comparison will also ensure that if anything we will *over*estimate the danger of synthetic pesticides.

If we take a look at Figure 127 we can see that drinking three cups of coffee (the American average) represents a risk of around 0.1 percent, whereas the 14.9 g of lettuce eaten by the average American represents a risk of 0.04 percent, both owing to their content of caffeic acid.[1808] The average intake of a little less than one glass of orange juice also represents a risk of 0.03 percent from d-limonene, and 2.55 g or one-sixth of a mushroom produces a risk of 0.02 percent due to hydrazines. Only after the average intake of apple, cinnamon, carrot, potato, celery, white bread and nutmeg do we come to the first pesticide – Ethylene thiourea from Figure 126. The risk from the American daily intake of ETU is 0.002 percent. This is equivalent to the cancer risk posed by pre-1972 DDT intake (DDT was banned in the US in 1972) – today the risk for DDT is about 0.00008 percent. The risk from consuming the American average of apple juice with Alar in 1988 was 0.001 percent – less than the risk from caffeic acid in the American daily average intake of one-tenth of a pear.[1809]

Although only 79 of the roughly 10,000 known natural pesticides have been tested for their carcinogenicity, with our intake they are clearly at the top of the risk list.[1810]

The consequence of these figures is that many of our perfectly ordinary foods would

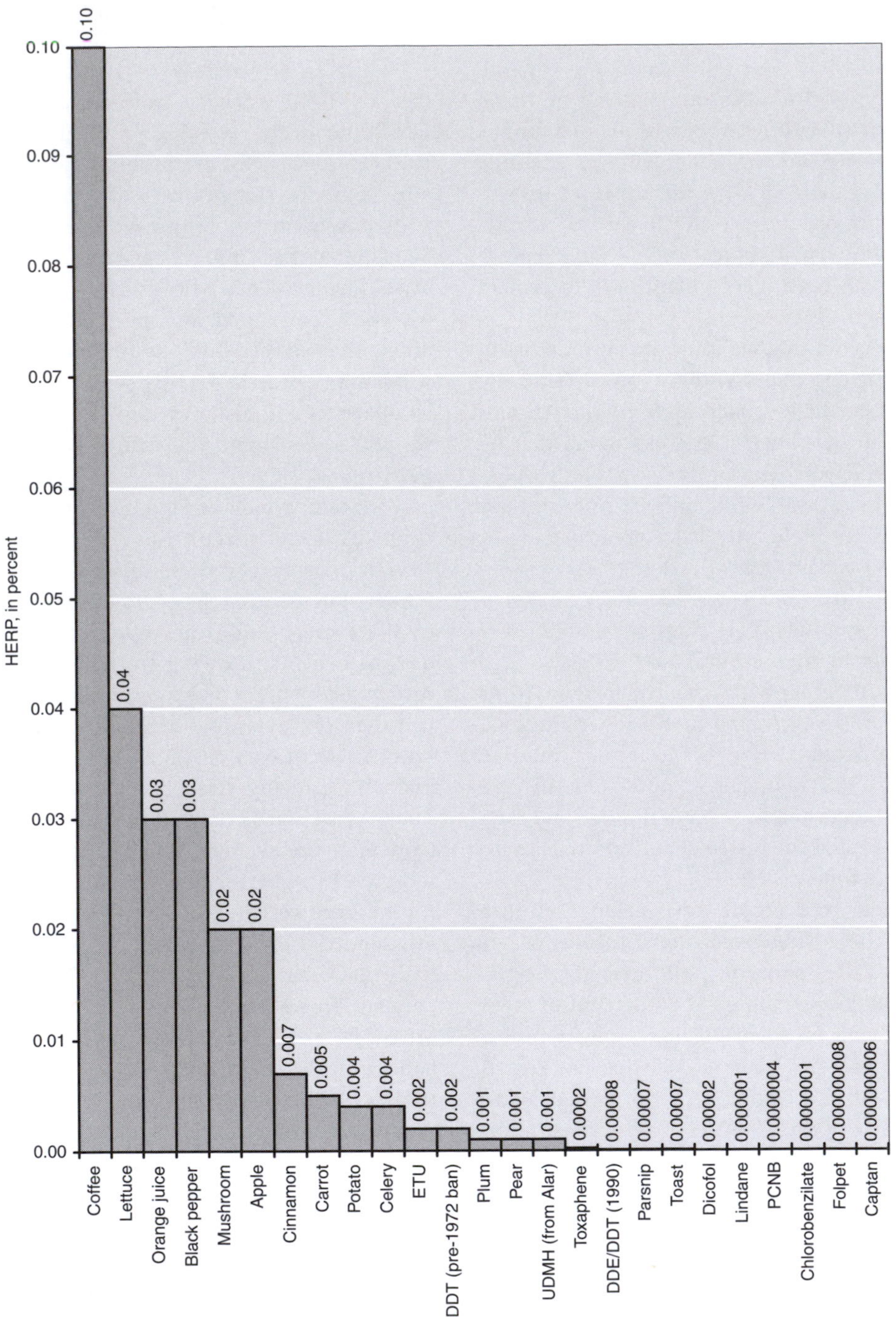

Figure 127 Comparison of relative cancer risk (HERP) of the average American daily intake of various foods and synthetic pesticides. The alcohol intake of the average adult American is equivalent to 1.7 beers or a HERP of 3.6 percent, i.e. 36 times greater than coffee. Note that UDMH-intake from Alar is the average from 1988. Source: Ames and Gold 1998:214–15, Gold *et al.* 1992:264.

not pass the regulatory criteria we use for synthetic chemicals.[1811] Our intake of coffee is about 50 times more carcinogenic than our intake of DDT before it was banned, more than 1,200 times more carcinogenic than our present DDT intake, and more than 66 times more carcinogenic than the most dangerous present-day pesticide intake, ETU.[1812]

What we cannot see in Figure 127 (because we do not know the average daily intake) is that 1 g a day of basil, with its content of estragole, is just as risky as three cups of coffee and 66 times more dangerous than our intake of ETU.[1813] Equally, the indoor air inside the average American, conventional (non-mobile) home contains formaldehyde as discussed in the indoor air pollution section, such that the risk of staying inside 14 hours a day is 0.4 percent or some 260 times the risk from ETU.

Alcohol is way outside the bounds of the diagram. The average American consumes alcohol at the equivalent of 1.7 beers a day,[1814] or a HERP risk of 3.6 percent and more than 2,100 times more risky than the most dangerous pesticide, ETU.[1815] Put differently, consuming the average quantity of ETU every day throughout a lifetime is just as dangerous as drinking 13 beers once in a lifetime. Or with a different comparison, the average intake of ETU throughout a lifetime is as risky as staying indoors in an average American home for a little more than two months – once.

This analysis suggests either that we should worry much more about coffee, basil and lettuce than about synthetic pesticides, or that the assumption of the non-threshold value is mistaken. The large-scale World Cancer Research Fund study found that the possibility cannot be excluded of coffee causing cancer of the bladder, although there exists "uncertainty about the relationship" and the association under any circumstances "was not clinically important."[1816]

In Professor Ames' opinion, it is more likely that typical animal cancer tests present a misleading picture.[1817] Feeding animals with extremely high doses of substances such as caffeic acid, estragole or synthetic pesticides can cause chronic cell death simply because of a localized overload, e.g. of the stomach.[1818] Cancer occurs precisely because of the high doses involved. This is supported by the fact that approximately half of all the synthetic pesticides that have been tested were found to be carcinogenic, *but that similarly half of all natural pesticides were carcinogenic.*[1819] An extremely high proportion of all the substances in the world would probably test positive in a cancer test, which suggests that we are in fact measuring something entirely different, namely localized overloading.

However many people have wondered whether evolution may have developed defense mechanisms against natural pesticides because these have been with us for quite some time, unlike their synthetic counterparts.[1820] Several facts make such a view implausible.[1821]

First, man's cancer defenses (typically DNA repair) are of a general nature and effective against both natural and synthetic pesticides.[1822] Second, there are still many natural pesticides (e.g. aflatoxin from fungus in peanuts) which we have not yet learned to deal with. Equally, many common elements are carcinogenic to humans, e.g., salts of cadmium, beryllium, nickel, chromium and arsenic, despite their presence throughout our evolution.[1823]

Third, it is often claimed that humans have developed a "toxic harmony" with their dietary plants, but not with our new chemicals.[1824] However, only a very small proportion of our present diet has been with us throughout our evolutionary process: most of us eat many things unknown to our forefathers, such as coffee, cocoa, tea, potatoes, tomatoes, sweet corn, avocado, mango, olives and kiwi fruit.[1825]

Fourth, it is not only synthetic pesticides such as DDT that can accumulate in the food chain; the natural, neurotoxic pesticides solanine and chaconine from potatoes can accumulate in human fatty tissues.[1826] These toxins have been shown to cause birth defects in rodents.[1827] Finally, it is not reasonable to expect, from an evolutionary point of view, that the human body should develop defences against naturally carcinogenic pesticides, since cancer is a disease of old age and does not usually occur until *after* propagation.[1828]

In other words, it can be said that the risk posed by synthetic pesticides above has proven to be quite small in comparison with the already imperceptibly tiny risk posed by some of the healthy things we consume such as lettuce, fruit juice, apples and celery.[1829] Depending on how much faith one has in the EPA's maximum-evaluation that synthetic pesticides cost 3,000–6,000 lives a year, the evidence indicates that the natural pesticides in lettuce, fruit juice, apples and celery actually cost far more lives. However, it is much more likely that animal cancer tests do not indicate true risks but give us extreme worst-case risk assessments, with enormous safety factors built in.[1830] Thus, there is good reason to assume that the cancer risks from both natural and synthetic pesticides are indeed very small.

It is difficult to find anyone willing to venture a concrete estimate of these two extremely small risks – most of the large-scale cancer evaluations simply and cautiously describe the risk posed by synthetic pesticides as "infinitesimal" and "insignificant," because it is incredibly difficult to determine the precise magnitude. The head of the Food and Drug Administration's Office of Toxicology, Dr Robert Scheuplein, has, however, proffered his idea of the general conception of magnitude in the profession.[1831] He estimates that the most probable distribution of food-related cancers is:[1832] 98.79 percent from traditional food (red meat, poultry, grains, potatoes, sugar, cocoa, salt, etc.), about 1 percent from spices and natural flavorings (mustard, pepper, cinnamon, vanilla, etc.), 0.2 percent from indirect additives (remnant substances from factories, such as lubricants, surface residues, packaging migrants, etc.), 0.01 percent from pesticides (insecticides, herbicides, fungicides, PCB, DDE, dioxin, aflatoxin, etc.), 0.01 percent from animal drug residues (antibiotics, growth hormones, etc.) and 0.01 percent from preparation (fermentation, frying, boiling, etc.).

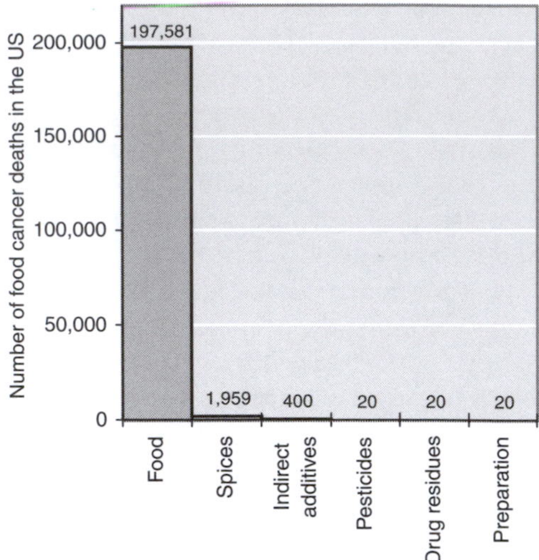

Figure 128 Number of deaths from cancer related to foodstuffs in the US, according to cause. Total 200,000. Source: Scheuplein 1991.

If we take the number of cancer-related deaths in the US (around 563,000 in 1999[1833]), using Doll and Peto's estimate which says that about 35 percent are caused by foods (200,000), and distribute them according to Dr Scheuplein, the result can be seen in Figure 128. Consequently, a more realistic estimate is that pesticides probably cost about twenty statistical deaths a year in the US.

Synthetic estrogens

A new, major anxiety has begun to proliferate, that of synthetic chemicals mimicking human and animal hormones, particularly since publication of the popular scientific book *Our Stolen Future*.[1834] In the overview section of the millennium edition of *State of the World*, Worldwatch Institute specifically links the 1962 worry of Rachel Carson with this "growing concern" over hormonally active "synthetic chemicals associated with pesticides and plastics."[1835]

It turns out that even mild hormonal influences during pregnancy can have significant consequences – it has been shown that if a female mouse fetus lies between two male fetuses in the womb she will be more "aggressive" and less attractive, simply because her brothers' hormones influenced her fetal development.[1836]

The problem is that certain substances, especially DDT and the industrial compound PCB, have proven able to imitate our hormones, particularly the female hormone estrogen.[1837] From the late 1940s to 1971 the estrogen-like substance DES was widely used for the prevention of abortion and pregnancy complications. In total, about 5 million women used the substance.[1838] DES unfortunately proved itself not only unable to prevent abortion but in fact to increase the rate of abortion and at the same time cause an increasing frequency of a rare type of cancer in the vaginas of young girls whose mothers had taken DES during pregnancy. Sons of high-dose DES-mothers also had markedly lower sperm counts.[1839]

Similarly in animals exposed to DDT and PCB, altered sex ratios (fewer males and more females) and small penises and testicles have been observed.[1840] Just as in the mouse offspring mentioned above, DES, DDT, PCB and their breakdown products have had an estrogen-like effect, and at specific junctures in the fetal stage have altered the development, feminizing or changing the sex of some males. DES was banned in 1971, DDT in many industrial countries in the early 1970s and PCB in the late 1970s. Concentrations in the environment of both DDT and PCB have fallen dramatically since then (e.g. Figure 112 and Figure 116).[1841]

So why do we start to worry now? Well, there are a number of other substances which show a mild estrogen-like effect. This effect is many thousand times weaker than estrogen, although it is unclear exactly how strong they are because synthetic estrogens are not, like natural estrogen, blocked by the body's other proteins.[1842]

Many plants also contain natural estrogens for the same reason that they contain natural pesticides: they are among the plants' many ways of defending themselves. If they can destroy the natural hormone balance in the animals that eat them, these will not fare so well in the evolutionary process, which will alleviate pressure on the plant species.[1843] Sheep, for example, will experience reproductive disorders if they eat red clover, which has a high content of the estrogen-like substance genistein.[1844]

Scientists have found natural estrogens in numerous common foodstuffs, including rye, wheat, cabbage, spinach, barley, rice, soybeans, potatoes, carrots, peas, beans, alfalfa sprouts, apples, cherries, plums, coffee, whisky, parsley, sage and garlic.[1845] In terms of weight we generally consume far more natural estrogens than synthetic ones. But once again, what is most important is the effect and not just the weight. Several studies have shown that exposure to plant estrogens early in life can undermine the ability of rat pups to reproduce when they reach adulthood.[1846] Soy protein has an extremely high estrogen content and there is evidence that it can influence the menstrual cycle of women.[1847] Scientists also point out the problem of feeding babies soy milk without having investigated how this major type of estrogen can influence body functions.[1848]

Many researchers have pointed out that the synthetic chemicals' hormonal effects are far weaker than those of naturally occurring hormones and that exposure to them is not significant enough to represent any real danger – one report shows that our overall intake of synthetic estrogens calculated in estrogen equivalents is more than 40 million times lower than the average intake of natural plant estrogens.[1849] If we compare the intake of synthetic estrogens with the average daily birth control pill, they are more than 6 billion times weaker. This, of course, makes the entire worry sound a bit like the worry about pesticides – an effect far lower than the natural background effects.

Here is the authors' response to these calculations in *Our Stolen Future*: "Such assertions are not supported by the evidence. When one surveys the available information and scientific literature, one quickly discovers that there are far too many blank spaces and missing pieces to provide even a rough picture of how much humans might be taking in or to allow for definitive conclusions."[1850] In short, although simple estrogen counts may show that synthetic estrogen constitutes a vanishing fraction of the total estrogenic impact, we simply know too little about the field. The same argument is made in one of the major estrogen papers in *Environmental Health Perspectives Supplements*, which concludes that much more research is necessary.[1851]

However, accepting that we know little about the consequences let alone the causes also means that the main argument for the estrogenic worry as presented in books like *Our Stolen Future* relies on the stories and examples of possible estrogenic consequences. Here we shall take a look at the three most well known and noteworthy of these.

Synthetic estrogens: a fall in sperm quality

In the major surveys of the effects of estrogen, the discussion about sperm quality is the most important: "The most fundamental change has been the striking fall in the sperm count in men's ejaculations."[1852] In *Our Stolen Future*, the authors write: "The most dramatic and troubling sign that hormone disrupters may already have taken a major toll comes from reports that human male sperm counts have plummeted over the past half century"[1853] The alleged fall is also typically used as a primary argument for organic farming.[1854]

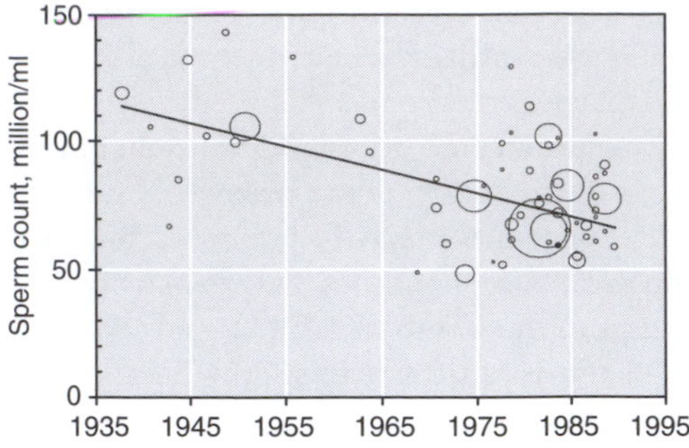

Figure 129 Average sperm count in 61 studies from 1938 to 1990 (the area of the circle indicates the number of men in each study). Source: Carlsen *et al.* 1992:610.[1855]

In 1992 a group of Danish scientists, led by Professor Niels Skakkebæk of Copenhagen University Hospital, published a report which showed that the number of sperm cells in men's semen had fallen from 113 to only 66 million per milliliter from 1938 to 1990 (see Figure 129).[1856] The article concluded by pointing out that it was yet to be established whether this reduction was due to estrogen-like substances or other to causes.[1857]

The story appeared in the media all over the world and inspired Greenpeace to produce a rather quick-witted advert. A picture of a man, mid-thirties, with an exceedingly small penis, under the caption: "You're not half the man your father was."[1858] Quite a dig at male pride.

Together with professor Richard Sharpe of the British Medical Research Council, Skakkebæk sketched out a hypothesis of the correlation between the fall in sperm quality and the effect of estrogen in *The Lancet* the year after.[1859] They also estimated that the deterioration of sperm quality could be linked to the significant documented increase in testicular cancer incidence over the last 30–50 years.[1860] In the article they listed seven different ways in which we may have become exposed to more estrogens; they noted among other things that:

- a low-fiber diet seems to increase "recycling" of estrogens in women
- obesity increases bioavailable estrogen
- changes in diet (e.g. soy) can increase estrogen intake
- drinking more milk increases the estrogen intake and
- perhaps we are becoming more exposed to synthetic estrogens.

Synthetic estrogens, then, only constitute a subset (and one of the most uncertain) of all the possible explanations, but it was this story the media chose to circulate.

All the same, the primary question remains as to whether it really is correct that the sperm count has halved over the last 50 years. The 1992 article has led to numerous critical responses and new studies which have shown both deterioration and stable sperm counts.[1861] Sperm counts in Paris have fallen, while in Toulouse the count remained stable.[1862] Sperm counts in Scotland have fallen, whereas those in Finland remained constant or increased slightly.[1863] Studies in Belgium and parts of London showed a fall in the count, whereas those in the US, in New York, Los Angeles, Minnesota as well as Seattle were constant.[1864]

Our Stolen Future only mentions the surveys which showed a fall in the sperm count.[1865] It is also mentioned that the surveys are still viewed with a certain skepticism by some in the medical profession. But we are somewhat arrogantly told that "this skepticism recalls similar disbelief at the first news in 1985 that a dramatic hole had developed in the Earth's protective ozone layer over Antarctica."[1866]

The problem is basically that we lack information on sperm count prior to 1970 – in spite of its great efforts, the Skakkebæk team only managed to dig out 13 relevant surveys. Of the 1,780 men from the 13 pre-1970 surveys, 84 percent come from just five large-scale studies (the large circles in Figure 129), and they are all from the US.[1867] In actual fact the first four large-scale studies (for 1938–51) are from a single city, New York.[1868] This is important because New York is one of the cities in the world to have the highest sperm count, at around 130 million/ml.[1869] It is not known exactly why New York is so much higher, although, for example, the sperm count is temperature-dependent and is much higher in winter – Finnish men have an equally high sperm count of about 130 million/ml.[1870]

If New York has far more men with a high sperm count than the other cities in Europe and the rest of the world, this obviously produces more noise (the sperm counts hop up and down more in Figure 129 because some of the circles are from New York while others are not). This weakens the analysis but does not render it useless. But when one looks at the geography after 1970 it turns out that only 20 percent of the large-scale studies are from the US and only 7 percent from New York. So New York is heavily represented early in the survey (93 percent) and only slightly at the end (11 percent).[1871] Moreover we know from a study just of New York that there has *not* been a decline in sperm count from 1972 to 1994.[1872] It is, therefore, perhaps reasonable to remove the five New York studies. If one does so, the sperm counts no longer fall by 40 percent – in actual fact, a fall can no longer be statistically detected.[1873] Surprisingly, Skakkebæk has never publicly commented on these facts.[1874]

This leads to an even more important point. The period after 1970 is by far the best documented, with by far the most information available (79 percent in studies and 89 percent in people). This information shows that since 1970 *no change in sperm count can be demonstrated*.[1875] In fact a slight increase is discernible but it is not statistically significant.[1876] Moreover, a reanalysis of the American data for New York and the rest of the US showed that there has been "no significant change in sperm counts in the U.S. during the last 60 years."[1877]

Even so, our point of departure must be the information we have available. It is a problem that we primarily have New York data in the early years and data from everywhere later, but as the question of the possible fall in sperm count is important we have to do the best we can with the available data.[1878] Here it seems as though there was a slight fall in sperm count, especially from 1942 to 1970. There does seem, however, to be yet another problem.[1879]

We know that the shorter the time since a man ejaculated, the lower his sperm count will be.[1880] This means that if men have been having more sex over the last 50 years (with or without a partner) this would decrease the sperm count and risk an incorrect interpretation of declining sperm quality. Of course, attempts are made to get around this problem, typically by asking donors to abstain from ejaculation for a specific number of days, but – not surprisingly – this turns out to be something quite difficult to check or enforce.[1881]

On the other hand, Skakkebæk claims that "to our knowledge there are no data to indicate a change in masturbation or coital frequency since the 1930s."[1882] Even superficially, this is a surprising statement, considering that in the meantime we have undergone a sexual revolution and gained access to the contraceptive pill. But actually, we do have some pretty good statistics in this field. From the early 1940s to the early 1970s the masturbation rate grew from about 30 times a year to 60 times a year for unmarried 30-year-olds, whereas for married 30-year-olds it rose from about 6 to 24 times a year.[1883] As regards intercourse, "the data show that there has been an important, even historic, increase in the typical (median) frequency of marital coitus throughout the population."[1884] For married 30-year-olds the frequency has gone up from 1.9 to 3.0 times a week.[1885]

One naturally has to be careful when simply taking people's own statements at their face value, but these figures equate pretty well with the other information we have, including a large-scale survey in 1983 of American couples. It shows that 45 percent of all relatively newly married couples have sex more than three times a week.[1886] Similarly, probably the biggest representative study, involving more than 4,500 women from 1965 and 1970, showed an increase in the frequency of intercourse of at least 17 percent in just five years, not least because of the much wider availability of contraceptives.[1887] A follow-up survey in 1975 showed that intercourse frequency had increased still further.[1888] A Swedish survey showed that the period of abstinence fell from 7.5 days to 4.4 days between 1956 and 1986, equivalent to an increase in frequency of around 70 percent.[1889]

The data thus seem to suggest that men had far more sex and twice as many ejaculations a week in 1970 as they did in 1940.

We know that if men abstain from ejaculation for ten days rather than three, their sperm concentration increases by about 60 percent.[1890] In other words, this means that reducing the period of abstinence by one day reduces the number of sperm cells by about 13 million.[1891] Skakkebæk's discovery (including the problematic New York findings) of a fall of 47 million sperm cells/ml over a period of 50 years is thus the equivalent of the reduction in the abstinence period of 3.6 days.[1892] As we saw above, the abstinence period in Sweden has fallen by 3.1 days in just 30 years.

ORGANIC FARMERS

We ought to mention two Danish surveys[1893] that were quoted world-wide and showed that organic farmers and ecologists had better semen quality than other groups of workers.[1894]

It is, of course, tempting to believe that improved sperm quality would correlate with better organic food (as was strongly pointed out in e.g. the book *Eco Living*),[1895] but even when the study was published this was just one of the many possible explanations.

Ecologists are definitely to a high degree different from the "ordinary man in the street" in more way than one – particularly in that far more of them live outside the capital and can be assumed to lead much less stressful lives.[1896]

A survey by the Danish EPA later showed that traditional (non-organic) greenhouse gardeners also had better quality sperm than numerous other professional groups.[1897]

Finally, in 1999, a large study of 171 traditional and 85 organic farmers settled the issue.[1898] Of 15 different sperm quality parameters, 14 were indistinguishable. On the last, the organic farmers had significantly more normal spermatozoa. Another analysis showed, however, that for five pesticides, *higher* intake correlated significantly with fewer dead sperm cells. The conclusion was: "The estimated dietary intake of 40 pesticides did not entail a risk of impaired semen quality."[1899]

In an early evaluation of the declining sperm quality, Professor James writes that if the apparent fall from 1942 to 1980 of around 40 million sperm cells/ml was to be explained by more frequent sex it would demand that we have sex about twice as often as we did before.[1900] And that is precisely what we see. There is thus every indication that more sex can be yet another part of the explanation.

All in all, it seems obvious that there is a problem with using New York statistics. If we do not include New York, the drop in the sperm count disappears. Analyses of the last 20 years have shown that there has been no general fall, and perhaps even an increase instead.[1901]

Moreover, another obvious way to assess the quality of semen shows no decline – male fertility. In the US, rates of infertility have remained constant at about 8–11 percent over the past three decades, and male infertility has accounted for approximately one-third of cases.[1902] In the UK, the newest study from 2000 shows that male fertility has actually *increased* since 1961.[1903]

The question of sperm quality is, of course, vital nonetheless. Even when we try to correct the figures for methodological problems such as New York, Skakkebæk's survey probably shows that there has been some reduction in sperm quality. Of course this is not a problem if it is simply due to the fact that we have more sex. It seems obvious that at least part of the remaining sperm quality decline is explained by the massive increase in frequency of intercourse over the past 50 years.

However, we are still confronted with contradictory data and can see that sperm quality is falling in places such as Paris and Scotland. Although we also know that these statistics fluctuate quite a lot and are highly dependent on the point in time at which data collection starts and finishes, it is of course essential to investigate these conditions further.[1904]

It is, however, even more essential to point out that today we now know for certain that the scary vision of the general, overriding reduction in sperm quality was mistaken. Sperm quality has remained constant throughout the last 20–25 years in numerous places such as Toulouse, New York, Los Angeles, Minnesota, Seattle and Finland.[1905] If there has been a reduction at all it has not been global.

Synthetic estrogens: the "cocktail" effect

One of the reasons we perhaps need not worry so much about the effects of synthetic estrogens is that they are several thousand times weaker than natural estrogen and DES.[1906] However, in 1996, a number of well-known estrogen scientists from Tulane, led by John McLachlan, published an article in *Science* in which they described how a combination of two estrogens could amplify their effect by between 160 and 1,600 times – often called the cocktail or synergy effect.[1907] So one plus one was no longer just two but more like a thousand.[1908]

Since most natural occurrences come in

combinations, this was a discovery that could potentially change many extremely weak estrogens into a combined, strong and threatening one. The story quickly spread around the world. Professor Stephen Safe, one of the estrogen skeptics, obviously felt extremely awkward in an interview and had to acknowledge that the results could well be extremely important: "It is extremely interesting and could have environmental significance."[1909]

The result could mean a radical departure from everything that had been learned to date about toxicology, and the fear of a cocktail effect frequently cropped up in the debate.[1910]

In June 1997, the many scientists who had tried to repeat McLachlan's experiment met at the official Estrogens in the Environment conference in New Orleans. They had no option but to conclude that none of the many studies had succeeded in finding any synergy effect. One plus one was still only two.[1911] Even the team behind McLachlan was unable to reproduce its original results. That same week they therefore withdrew their article from *Science*.[1912] According to Poul Bjerregaard, professor of eco-toxicology at Odense University, Denmark, all scientists agree today that estrogen-like substances have no synergy effect.[1913]

Nonetheless, the American environment administration is still convinced of the value of the study: "Even if the specific synergy hypothesis raised by the Tulane study cannot be reproduced, it does not negate the possibility of synergy through other mechanisms. As such, the Tulane study remains important in that it raised awareness of synergy to the forefront of scientific investigation."[1914]

So, even though all the facts currently suggest that estrogens have no cocktail effect, it is apparently a good thing that we were made aware of the phantom-problem.

Synthetic estrogens: breast cancer

One of the best-selling points of the estrogenic fear has been the position that synthetic estrogens could be the explanation for the alleged breast cancer explosion.

In 1993, a group of scientists announced that they had found a link between breast cancer and the estrogenic substance DDE in 58 women.[1915] The authors wrote that since estrogenic pesticides were so common in the environment and in our food, "the implications are far-reaching for public health intervention worldwide."[1916] This was the kick-off for a substantial research effort and much has since been written about breast cancer.[1917]

In the accompanying editorial in the *Journal of the National Cancer Institute*, the title harked back to Rachel Carson and restated our chemical fears: "Pesticide residues and breast cancer: the harvest of a Silent spring?" Though the editorial was sound and balanced, the message from a title like this was not lost on the media: through rampant breast cancer women worldwide were now paying the dues of an irresponsible, chemically obsessed society.

Time magazine told us about the "relentless DDT" triggering breast cancer.[1918] Greenpeace released a study claiming that "chemical pollutants are a major cause of rapidly rising breast cancer rates worldwide."[1919] An article in *Scientific American* told us that although the synthetic estrogen/breast cancer link was still speculative, "evidence in its favor is accruing steadily."[1920]

Dr. Marion Moses, director of the Pesticide Education Center in San Francisco, explained the connection in the *Nation*: "When you think about all that toxic stuff stored in the breast . . . you may not be surprised that a woman today has a one-in-eight chance of getting breast cancer. And given that organochlorines have been part of our world only since World War II . . . it's also not surprising a woman today has twice the chance of getting breast cancer that her mother had."[1921] Dr. Mary Wolff, one of the researchers from the 1993 study, exclaimed: "The numbers are terrifying, really. I still can't believe the risk is that high."[1922]

Our Stolen Future hinges a large part of its argument on this connection, ominously claiming that "by far the most alarming health trend for women is the rising rate of breast cancer, the most common female cancer."[1923] The link to pesticides is made very clear: "Since 1940, when the chemical age was dawning, breast cancer deaths have risen steadily by one percent per year in the United States, and similar increases have been reported in other industrial countries," and they are very careful to point out that this is for age-adjusted rates.[1924] This, of course, is incorrect, as is obvious in Figure 119 and as we pointed out earlier – at the time of writing *Our Stolen Future*, the age-adjusted death rate had actually *dropped* some 9 percent since 1940; the latest figures for 1998 indicate a drop of 18 percent.[1925]

Nevertheless, the real issue of course is whether synthetic estrogens can be causing breast cancer. Generally, it is correct that the total amount of estrogen a woman is exposed to during a lifetime contributes to cancer.[1926] Typically, this hormonal exposure comes from the woman's own body (greater effect due to later first births, earlier menarche, etc.) and from oral contraceptives.[1927] The connection between pesticides and breast cancer is thus theoretically based on the idea that some of these pesticides can mimic estrogens, increase the female estrogenic load and cause excess cancer. However, there are several problems with this interpretation.[1928] For one thing, DDT, DDE and PCB are weak estrogens and it is known that they can have both a boosting and an inhibiting effect on cancer in animals.[1929] For another, high occupational exposure of PCBs and other organochlorines to women does not seem connected to any increase in breast cancer frequency.[1930] Third, the incidence of breast cancer has been *increasing* while concentrations of DDT, DDE and PCB in the environment have *fallen*.[1931] In the words of the National Research Council: "It seems unlikely that a declining exposure would be responsible for an increasing incidence of cancer."[1932]

Moreover, a study from the National Cancer Institute of breast cancer incidences for different regions of the US for blacks and whites showed a surprising result. Whereas the white women of the Northeast have higher relative breast cancer mortality rates, the rates for black women in this region is not higher than in other regions. This indicates that "widespread environmental exposures are unlikely to explain the higher relative breast cancer mortality rates observed for U.S. white women in the Northeast."[1933]

Already in 1994, a meta-study of the five small, available studies on breast cancer and synthetic estrogens concluded that "the data do not support the hypothesis that exposure to DDE and PCBs increases risk of breast cancer."[1934] The National Research Council in its latest review reached the same conclusion.[1935]

Since then, seven large studies (with more than 100 women) and four smaller studies have been published.[1936] In 1999, the British advisory committee on carcinogenicity of chemicals to the UK Department of Health published its conclusions, based on the available studies on breast cancer and synthetic estrogens. For DDT, it found that only two, relatively small studies had found an association, whereas one large study had found a *reverse* association (more DDT, less breast cancer).[1937] Thus, in conclusion, the committee stated that "overall, there is no convincing evidence from epidemiological studies for an elevated relative risk of breast cancer in association with DDT."[1938]

For dieldrin, only two studies had tested the connection, one finding no relationship, the other finding a positive association. However, the study in question had tested 46 different associations, making it plausible that the single, statistical find was a "chance finding."[1939] Moreover, in studies of rats and mice, it has not been possible to show any estrogenic activity of dieldrin.[1940] Finally, occupational studies of dieldrin show no excess cancers.[1941] Consequently, the committee finds that "there is no convincing evidence from epidemiological studies for an elevated relative risk of breast cancer associated with dieldrin."[1942]

Of the three studies that have examined β-HCH and lindane, none has found evidence for an association with increased risk of breast cancer for either compound.[1943]

In 1999 the National Research Council of the American Academy of Sciences, sponsored by the US EPA among others, examined the evidence for synthetic estrogens' effect on cancer risks.[1944] Its summary conclusion on breast cancer sounded much like the British verdict: "An evaluation of the available studies conducted to date does not support an association between adult exposure to DDT, DDE, TCDD, and PCBs and cancer of the breast."[1945]

We now have the data, and they supply no evidence as to synthetic chemicals causing breast cancer.

Synthetic estrogens: should we worry?

Our latest chemical fear of pesticides seems surprisingly unfounded. The reduction in sperm quality is for the most part likely to be a result of using New York statistics and the fact that we have more sex – at worst it is a decline that is only partial and local. It is not backed up by fertility studies.

The cocktail effect simply did not hold up.

With regards to breast cancer, the two newest summaries on all the available evidence show that synthetic estrogens do not cause breast cancer. Actually, the National Research Council focused not only on breast cancer but also on endometrial, prostate and testicular cancers, since these cancers arise in hormonally sensitive tissues, and any synthetic estrogenic effect should therefore be most readily observable here.[1946] And the NRC did not find any connection here either.

Take the case of testicular cancer. Here, the NRC observes that while incidence has been increasing for white men over the past 40 years, it has been decreasing for black men, although they have much higher blood concentrations of PCBs, DDE and DDT.[1947] Moreover, levels of DDT and its breakdown components have been declining in both blood and breast milk over the past 40 years. The committee therefore concludes that "increasing testicular cancer incidence rates in northern European countries and in North America are unlikely to be related to environmental DDT."[1948]

Looking at all the studies available, the general conclusion is that, "individually and as a group, these studies do not support an association between DDE and PCBs and cancer in humans."[1949]

In 1998 the US EPA Science Policy Council stated its interim position on synthetic estrogens in a lengthy report.[1950] The report looks into a whole series of problems and, with regard to the hypothesis about the fall in sperm quality, it says that Skakkebæk's data are geographically diffuse, that the pre-1970 data are inadequate, and that "a systematic decrease in abstinence interval could explain much of the purported decrease in sperm concentration and semen volume."[1951] The EPA concludes that Skakkebæk's conclusions should therefore be considered "tenuous."[1952]

In its overall evaluation of the estrogen problems, the EPA writes, "with few exceptions (e.g., DES) a causal relationship between exposure to a specific environmental agent and an adverse effect on human health operating via an endocrine disruption mechanism has not been established."[1953]

This does not of course mean that we should not do research in these areas to expand our knowledge, but it does mean that we must be more cautious of using scary slogans like "our stolen future."

We did not see another "harvest of a Silent Spring" with the estrogenic effects of pesticides. And as documented earlier, we did not see a silent spring from pesticides causing cancer either. This, of course, raises the question whether phasing out pesticides really is such a good idea.

Conclusion: should we use pesticides?

In 1989, the US had its most spectacular example yet of pesticide worries versus risk facts, when *60 minutes* had the nation worrying about the apple pesticide Alar. Supposedly the "most dangerous chemical residue," the risk was later found to be grossly overstated and was adjusted downwards by a factor of 20.[1954] Compared with other natural and synthetic pesticides, the average intake in 1988 was still about 100 times less risky than drinking three cups of coffee each day, as can be seen in Figure 127.[1955] But the public outcry and worry stopped the use of Alar.[1956] Was this a good move? Should we ban more or maybe all pesticides?

Many people and organizations would be inclined to answer yes – we should stop using pesticides. Al Meyerhoff from Natural Resources Defense Council argued that many forms of cancer were on the rise, not least in children, and claimed that "mounting evidence suggests a strong correlation between pesticide exposure and the development of cancer in humans."[1957] The problem is pesticides. "Exposure to these deadly chemicals can cause cancer, birth defects, and neurological damage." The conclusion? "We must get rid of pesticides in the food supply."

Similar claims were made at the World Breast Cancer Conference in Ottawa in 1999. Here Elizabeth May, Executive Director of Sierra Club of Canada, pointed out that increases in breast cancer rates are parallel and linked with the increased presence of pesticides in the environment.[1958] Peggy Land, the Director of the pesticides campaign for the Sierra Club, added that "we need to put our health ahead of the bank accounts of pesticides companies, and to reclaim our right to live without these poisons."[1959] The solution? "We need a moratorium on these toxic chemicals until we have established their safety through improved testing-standards."

These attitudes are also reflected in national surveys, where 45 percent of all Americans find that pesticide use is unsafe, even when applied according to approved directions.[1960] 62 percent actually found that the "dangers to human health posed by pesticides outweigh their benefits."[1961]

But as we have seen throughout this section, the fear of cancer and the fear of the estrogenic effects from pesticides are pretty groundless. We have no reason to assume that pesticides affect our hormonal balance to any appreciable degree. And at the same time, pesticides contribute astoundingly little to deaths caused by cancer. If we employ a no-threshold model, pesticides cause a maximum of 1 percent of all cancer-related deaths, although this estimate is probably far too high for a variety of reasons. All six studies reviewed and the three largest and most recent studies of the causes of cancer concur that pesticides' contribution to cancer is vanishingly small.

We possess only extremely limited knowledge from studies involving humans, and by far the majority of our evaluations of carcinogenic pesticides are based on laboratory experiments on animals.[1962] The studies show us, however, that three daily cups of coffee or one gram of basil a day is more than 60 times as risky as the most toxic pesticide at current levels of intake. This emphasizes that our fear of pesticides causing cancer is quite exaggerated, and that the overall cancer effect of pesticides is negligible, even when estimated from animal experiments. A plausible estimate for the excess annual cancer mortality due to pesticides in the US is probably close to 20 extra cancer deaths out of 560,000. For comparison, about 300 Americans die each year drowning in their bathtub.[1963]

Even so, one could maintain that the argument above has quite rightly shown that pesticides cause very few cancer deaths but if just one person dies then this should be reason enough for us to reduce seriously or even phase out pesticides. Even if we only *assume* that the excess cancer possibility might exist, we ought for reasons of caution to refrain from using pesticides.

Obviously we should, for reasons of caution, minimize individuals' intake of pesticides as long as doing so does not have other, more costly consequences. But the problem with the above desire to avoid or to completely ban the use of pesticides so as to avoid a minuscule excess cancer load is that it does not take into account far more major side-effects.

There are great advantages to pesticide use. Even one of pesticides' most ardent critics, Professor David Pimentel, found that the net social value of pesticides in the US is about $4 billion annually, even though he used a method that systematically skews the results against pesticides.[1964]

More relevant is to measure the total cost to society from a partial or complete phase-out of pesticides.[1965] The most recent US estimate of phasing out a particular group of pesticides – the so-called organophosphates and carbamates, constituting about half of all US pesticides – finds that the total cost would be about $17 billion annually.[1966]

Of course, in different political settings around the world, different attitudes to pesticides make across-the-board bans more or less plausible. Certainly, in the US there is no widespread political support for banning all pesticides, though the complete banning of organophosphates and carbamates was included in the debate around the implementation of the 1996 Food Quality Protection Act.[1967] In many European debates, however, the mood is somewhat more radical, and in Denmark the option to reduce drastically or completely phase out all pesticides has been voiced by a parliamentary majority.[1968]

Consequently, the Danish Parliament unanimously established a national committee to conduct a two-year study of all effects from pesticides, and to evaluate the overall consequences of a partial or complete ban on pesticide use in Denmark.[1969] Unlike some of the American economic estimates which have been criticized for conflicts of interest,[1970] this is a consensus committee with appointed chairmen from the Danish EPA and members from conventional and organic agricultural organizations, academia, green organizations and consumers' organizations.[1971] The conclusions were published in 1999, over a thousand pages, spanning seven volumes and building on approximately ten times the amount of commissioned background papers.[1972]

The conclusion was that a limited optimization of pesticide use was possible at a cost of 2–3 percent to the farmer, and the cost to society was considered insignificant, though not modeled.[1973] The estimate required total information on weather and damage impacts, which in some areas were considered hard or impossible to obtain at present, making this a somewhat best-case estimate.[1974] The total pesticide reduction, calculated in crop treatment frequency, would amount to 29 percent.[1975]

For further reductions in pesticide use, the committee looked at a scenario with limited use of pesticides, where pesticides would only be allowed to treat significant pests.[1976] The pesticide reduction in this scenario is about 76 percent.[1977] The total social cost was estimated at 0.4 percent of GNP, about $500 million annually, or the value of about 9 percent of total agricultural output.[1978] Translated to the US, the loss from limited use of pesticides would be roughly equivalent to a yearly $11–37 billion, an estimate roughly comparable to the above-mentioned $17 billion from banning organophosphates and carbamates.[1979]

Finally, the complete phase-out of pesticides was estimated to carry a social price tag of 0.8 percent of GNP or about $1 billion annually.[1980] A rough translation to the US is about $23–74 billion per year.[1981] However, since EU legislation prohibits member countries from restricting imports of agricultural products produced with pesticides, this cost only reflects less marketable produce, whereas produce import is assumed to be upheld and probably increased substantially.[1982] Thus, animal production will still be using imported, pesticide-grown grains.

The committee also evaluated the total cost

of transition to an organic society, where all animal feed is also produced without pesticides. Here, the social costs for Denmark are about 3 percent of GNP or $3.5 billion,[1983] roughly equivalent to $93–277 billion per year in the US.[1984]

Thus, to the extent that it is possible to reduce pesticide use at a low cost, it seems prudent to do so.[1985] However, a more substantial reduction in pesticide use will incur major costs to society.

One might, of course, still believe a more comprehensive pesticide reduction to be a good investment. After all, the US is a rich country and could afford to spend about $20–300 billion every year to save upwards of twenty people a year from dying of cancer. This works out at a minimum $1 billion per saved life. Our initial reaction may be to say that we should save lives, no matter the cost. However, such an argument has to consider whether such an amount of money could not have been spent better. We saw in the section on indoor air pollution how radioactive radon gas, naturally seeping from underground, costs about 15,000 lives in the US. With a regulatory program to identify, test and mitigate radon, we could save about 800 lives at a cost of a little less than $1 million per life.[1986] Thus, for the same amount of money, say $1 billion, we could save about one person (and quite plausibly less) through pesticide reductions or we could save 1000 persons through radon reductions. Should we then not spend the money where it does the most good?

What is more serious, however, is that not only does it cost money to phase out pesticides, it will also cause a lot of deaths from cancer.[1987]

Pesticides help to make fruit and vegetables cheaper because they improve crop yields. In the Danish scenarios, a total ban on pesticides would reduce yields by 16–84 percent, causing price increases of 30–120 percent.[1988] First, this scenario would take up more countryside because it would be necessary to cultivate more soil, which would probably also be less fertile.[1989] Second, it would mean that people would eat less fruit and fewer vegetables because these would become more expensive. The share of income spent on food would increase substantially. It is estimated that limitations on the use of pesticides would increase costs by around 10 percent; a comprehensive ban would perhaps double the proportion a North American or European family spends on food from the 8 to 20 percent today.[1990] We know that the less money they have to spend, the less fruit and fewer vegetables people eat.[1991] Instead low-income families will buy more primary starch, more meats and consume more fat.[1992] In addition it can be expected that the quality of foodstuffs would fall and less would be available during the winter months.[1993]

The consequences in terms of cancer frequency could be significant. The World Cancer Research Fund study estimates that increasing the intake of fruit and vegetables from an average of about 250 g/day to 400 g/day would reduce the *overall* frequency of cancer by around 23 percent.[1994] The American average intake of fruit and vegetables is about 297 g/day.[1995] Thus, a decrease of just 10 percent in fruit and vegetable consumption in the US because of higher prices would cause an increase in cancer of about 4.6 percent of the total number of cancers or some 26,000 surplus cancer deaths in the US.[1996] Moreover, other studies seem to indicate that death rates from non-cancer diseases such as ischaemic heart disease and cerebrovascular disease would also be substantially increased.[1997]

The World Cancer Research Fund study emphasizes that increasing people's intake of fruit and vegetables is absolutely vital if cancer frequency is to be reduced – but no mention is made of how this can be achieved.[1998] The objective of increasing consumption of fruit and vegetables is backed by the National Research Council study, but once again the discussion focuses on the medical aspects and does not suggest how increased consumption can be achieved.[1999] The Canadian Cancer

Society, on the other hand, emphasizes the necessity of looking at both economy and health when policy is being made. "The Panel does not believe that any increase in intake of pesticide residues associated with increased intake of fruits and vegetables poses any increased risk of cancer and, in any case, believes that any risks, however small, are outweighed greatly by the benefits of such a diet."[2000] At the same time, "the Panel recognizes the importance of pesticide use toward enhanced crop production and food quality and the associated impact on declining costs of fruits and vegetables, concomitant increase in consumption, and resulting positive effect on declining cancer risks."[2001]

The respected journal *Science* is more blunt:

> Fruit and vegetables are subject to attack by pests that include hundreds of species of fungi. If the number of permissible fungicides is reduced so that few are available, fungi will destroy crops. Were synthetic fungicides not available, experts have said that production of apples would be reduced 40 percent; grapes 33 percent, peaches 49 percent, and strawberries 38 percent. Production of most vegetables also would be decreased. Prices would rise. Low-income people would be victims.[2002]

Astounding as it may seem, the choice is fairly clear. If we choose to remove pesticides from agricultural production we will get food and water without these substances. It will probably also mean that we can avoid some twenty deaths a year. The cost, on the other hand, would be at least $20 billion a year, putting more of the countryside under the plow and allowing perhaps 26,000 more people to die of cancer a year.[2003]

23 Biodiversity[2004]

We lose something in the region of 40,000 species every year, 109 a day. One species will be extinct before you have finished reading this chapter.

This was what we were told 22 years ago when Norman Myers first published his book *The Sinking Ark* in 1979.[2005] The message was relayed to the world at large in the official US environment report *Global 2000*.[2006] After this it became part of our shared consciousness: Former US vice-president Al Gore repeats the figure of 40,000 species in his *Earth in the Balance*,[2007] the popular science magazine *Discover* tells us that half the species we know today will be extinct within the next 100 years,[2008] and the famous Harvard biologist E. O. Wilson points out that we are losing between 27,000 and 100,000 species a year.[2009] Not to be outdone, professor Paul Ehrlich even estimated in 1981 that we lose some 250,000 species every year, with half of the Earth's species gone by the year 2000 and all gone by 2010–25.[2010]

Although these assertions of massive extinction of species have been repeated everywhere you look, they simply do not equate with the available evidence.[2011]

The story is important, because it shows how figures regarding the extinction of 25–100 percent of all the species on Earth within our lifetime provide the political punch to put conservation of endangered species high on the agenda. Punch which the more realistic figure of 0.7 percent over the next 50 years would not achieve to the same degree.

How many species are there?

Since life on Earth began with the first bacteria 3.5 billion years ago, species getting blotted out has been part and parcel of evolution. Those species which could not survive became extinct. Extinction is the ultimate destiny of every living species.[2012]

However, the rate at which species have become extinct has fluctuated over the various periods, and the number of species has generally increased up to our time, as can be seen in Figure 130. Never before have there been so many species as there are now. The growth in the number of families and species can be accredited to a process of specialization which is both due to the fact that the Earth's physical surroundings have become more diverse and a result of all other species becoming more specialized.[2013] Even so, there have

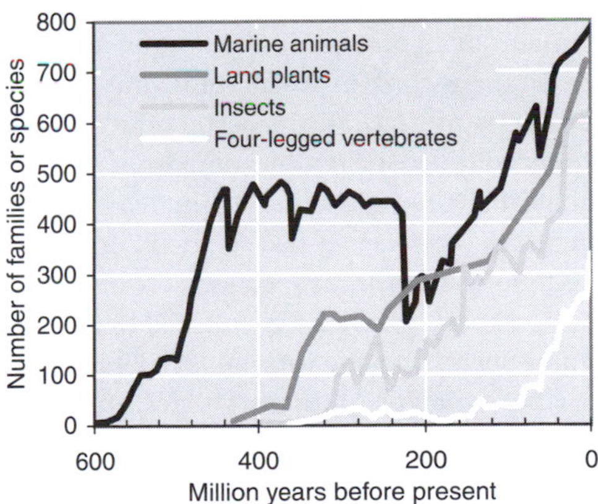

Figure 130 Number of families of marine animals, insects and four-legged vertebrates, and species of land plants, from 600 million years ago to the present. Source: UNEP 1995:204, 206, 207.

Table 6 Number of species and documented extinctions from the year 1600 to the present day. Note that because of the severe requirements for documenting extinctions these figures certainly underestimate their true number. Source: Baillie and Groombridge 1997; Walter and Gillett 1998; May et al. 1995:11; Reid 1992:56.

Taxa	Approximate number of species	Total extinctions since 1600
Vertebrates	47,000	321
Mammals	4,500	110
Birds	9,500	103
Reptiles	6,300	21
Amphibians	4,200	5
Fish	24,000	82
Mollusks	100,000	235
Crustaceans	4,000	9
Insects	> 1,000,000	98
Vascular Plants	250,000	396
Total	Approx. 1,600,000	1,033

been several major occurrences of extinction – the best known of these is probably the last break in the curve 65 million years ago when most of the dinosaurs became extinct, but the most serious one occurred 245 million years ago when around half of all marine animals and four-legged vertebrates and two-thirds of all insects were wiped out.[2014]

The information on past extinctions and number of species is based purely on the uncertain record of fossil finds, but in this respect we are actually no better off today. We do not know the true number of species inhabiting the Earth. The estimated number fluctuates between a paltry 2 million and a prodigious 80 million species. Only about 1.6 million species have been counted to date, as can be seen from the estimates in Table 6. By far the majority of these species are to be found among the insects, such as beetles, ants, flies, as well as worms, fungi, bacteria and viruses. We have already found most of the mammals and birds – they are large and easy to recognize. On the other hand, our knowledge of the many small creatures can hardly be anything but fragmentary, and describing them is, of course, nowhere near as prestigious.

The attempt to find out how many species exist has given rise to some pretty ingenious methods. The biologist Erwin sprayed insecticide in the upper foliage of the rainforest so as to count the number of species that fell out of the trees.[2015] By comparing the number of overlapping species from the various areas, one can obtain a rough estimate of the number of new species per square meter. This can be used to produce estimates for larger areas and ultimately the entire globe.

Researchers have also made use of the observation that the larger animals are, the fewer the number of species (there are very few species the size of elephants but masses the size of beetles).[2016] Both the Erwin extrapolation and the size–number extrapolations give us the currently best estimates of 10–80 million species.

Because of the considerable variations in the estimated number of species, it is therefore best to discuss extinction in terms of percentage loss per decade.

Is biodiversity important?

It is necessary to ask the somewhat irreverent question why there is any reason at all to worry about the loss of species. Many reasons can be given.

The first of these is human-centered: we are fond of wild animals and plants because they make it a pleasure for us to exist on a fascinating, living planet. However, the species we are thinking of are probably "large species" such as tigers, whales, albatrosses, parrot fish and teak trees.[2017] It is most unlikely to be the millions of black beetles, flies and fungus spores. So this argument for preservation is pretty selective.

One frequently hears the idea that the rainforest functions as a medicine stockpile.[2018] It is true that many medicines used to originate in plants – aspirin from willow trees, heart medicine from foxgloves – although most of this medicine is now produced synthetically. The problem is that most of the time we do not know where to start looking.[2019] For this reason, indigenous natural medicine is investigated in the search for leads. This is one argument for conserving plants (if necessary in botanical gardens) that have been noted as potential sources of medicine. But so long as we do not even have any practical means of analyzing even a fraction of those plants already known to us, this cannot be used as a general argument for the protection of all species, for example in the rainforest.

Pimentel and other researches have tried to evaluate the total worth of biodiversity. When counting up the many human uses of nature (for ecotourism, waste disposal, pollination, crop breeding, etc.) this results in some remarkably large annual values from $3–33 trillion or 11–127 percent of the world economy.[2020] These high values have then been used as general arguments as to the importance of biodiversity.[2021] While such estimates have been criticized largely because many of the ecosystem services have no market,[2022] the main problem with regard to biodiversity is that the relevant cost is not that of the whole ecosystem – no one is suggesting or expecting that we remove all species or ecosystems – but the value of losing the last beetle of a million species of beetles. Here, several analyses show that the human value of the final species of plants or animals for medicine is extremely low – mainly because we have either found what we were looking for long before getting to the end of the line, or because to search all the way through all species would have been fantastically expensive.[2023]

Genetic diversity is crucial to the survival of our crops. This argument is true since our main crops (wheat, maize, rice, yams, etc.) are cultivated from just a few, extremely high-yielding strains. The standard example is stripe rust, which threatened the world's wheat harvest in the late 1960s. The disease was dealt with by using genetic material from a wild strain of wheat from Turkey.[2024] Today we have extensive gene libraries in which many of these species are stored: the US Agricultural Research Service National Small Grains Collection in Aberdeen, Idaho, holds some 43,000 specimens.[2025] Again, the question is not whether it is a good idea to preserve the gene pool of our crops but whether this can be used as a reasonable argument for preserving all sorts of other species.

How many go extinct?

In the natural environment species are constantly dying in competition with other species. It is estimated that more than 95 percent of all species that have ever existed are now extinct.[2026] A species typically survives 1–10 million years.[2027] Translated to the case of our described 1.6 million species, we must reckon with a natural extinction of around two species every decade.[2028] Table 6 shows that about 25 species have become extinct every decade since 1600. Thus, what we see is clearly not just natural extinction. Actually, mankind has long been a major cause of extinction. Around the time of the last ice age, about 33 major families of mammals and birds were eradicated – an extremely large number, considering only 13 families had become extinct within the 1.5 million years prior to that.[2029] It is presumed that Stone Age man hunted these 33 families to extinction.

The Polynesians have colonized most of the 800 or so islands in the Pacific over the last 12,000 years. Because the birds on these islands had developed without much competition they were extremely easy to catch and were therefore frequently hunted to extinction. By studying bones from archaeological excavations it has been estimated that the Polynesians in total have eradicated around 2,000 species of birds, or more than 20 percent of all current bird species.[2030]

Mankind, then, has long been a cause of an increase in the extinction rate. But when we look at the last 400 years, there are other things to consider as far as extinction is concerned. For one thing, in order to document extinction, one must have looked for the species for several years wherever it may exist.[2031] A task of this magnitude requires a lot of resources, which reduces the number of documented cases of extinction to a minimum. For another thing, there is much greater focus on mammals and birds than on the other groups.

Thus, when discussing the extinction of species the best-documented rates come from mammals and birds. In their case, the documented rate has been increasing over the last 150 years from one species every four years to one a year.[2032] Some of this increase could be explained by an increase in the number of professional biologists, interested ornithologists, and animal lovers to observe any examples of extinction that may occur, but there has undoubtedly been an increase in extinction.

The point is, however, that there is still an awfully long way to go to 40,000 species every year.

The claim of 40,000 species

The original estimate of 40,000 species lost every year came from Myers in 1979.[2033] His arguments make astonishing reading. He states, as above – though without references – that until the year 1900, one species became extinct every four years and after that one species every year. Then Myers quotes a conference in 1974, which "hazarded a guess" that the extinction rate had now reached 100 species a year.[2034] This figure does not just cover mammals and birds, but is an "overall extinction rate among all species, whether known to science or not,"[2035] and is not surprisingly, therefore, much larger. The crucial part of the argument is this:

> Yet even this figure seems low ... Let us suppose that, as a consequence of this man-handling of natural environments [the clearing of tropical forest], the final one-quarter of this century witnesses the elimination of 1 million species – a far from unlikely prospect. This would work out, during the course of 25 years, at an average extinction rate of 40,000 species per year, or rather over 100 species per day.[2036]

This is Myers' argument in its entirety. If we assume that 1 million species will become extinct in 25 years, that makes 40,000 a year. A perfectly circular argument. If you assume 40,000, then you get 40,000. One naturally refuses to believe that this can be the only argument, but Myers' book provides no other references or argumentation. Note the massive deviation between the observed rate of one quarter, one and perhaps 100 per year and Myers' estimate of 40,000. This assertion is 40,000 times greater than his own *data*, 10,000 times the latest *observed* rate and 400 times the maximum *guess* as seen in Figure 131.

It was, however, the figure of 40,000 that reached millions of people the world over.

A model backup

In 1980, an extremely influential environment report entitled *Global 2000*, was published at the request of the American President Jimmy Carter. Among many other issues, the report looked into the extinction of species. Here, the WWF biologist Thomas Lovejoy repeated Myers' assertion that 15–20 percent of all species would be lost by the year 2000.[2037] At the same time, however, Lovejoy constructed a model to back up Myers' controversial figure of 40,000. Lovejoy's model is in reality attractively simple. A large part of all species are found in the tropical rainforests. If we simply allow the rainforests to remain in place nothing will happen. If we cut down all the rainforest, practically all the species will disappear. Lovejoy then assumes that if half the forest is cut down, a third of the species will disappear.[2038]

And there you have it. With an estimated 50

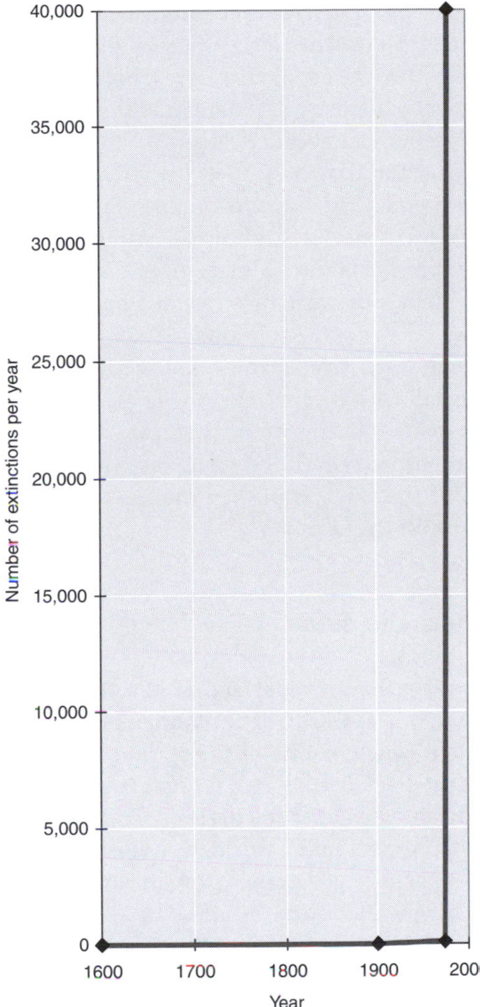

Figure 131 Estimate of extinction rates from 1600 to 1974, plus Myers' estimate for 1980. Source: Myers 1979:5.

percent to 67 percent reduction in rainforest in 20 years we get a localized reduction in the number of species of 33–50 percent. Lovejoy estimates that this will lead to an overall reduction in the number of species in the world of approximately 20 percent.[2039]

What do we lose?

To the Western world, this contribution cemented the significance of the rainforests. If we ignore the brief flirtation with the rainforests as "lungs of the Earth" (which was a false story),[2040] biodiversity is now the primary reason for our wanting to save the rainforest.

But what exactly is it claimed will die out? Many people believe that it is a question of elephants, gray whales and the broad-leaved mahogany. But no, far more than 95 percent of the species consist of beetles, ants, flies, microscopic worms and fungi, as well as bacteria, algae and viruses.[2041] It is not clear how much political backing the rainforest lobby could have attracted if the biologists had emphasized that what would be lost would primarily be insects, bacteria and viruses.[2042]

But the most important thing, of course, is whether the simple correlation between cleared rainforest and species loss actually holds water.

Models and reality

The correlation between the number of species and area was formulated by the biologist E. O. Wilson in the 1960s.[2043] The model seem appealingly intuitive.[2044] Its logic is that the more space there is, the more species can exist. The theory was launched in order to explain the number of species on islands, and it works well in this context. Wilson formulated a rule of thumb: if the area is reduced by 90 percent, then the number of species will be halved.[2045] But the question is, of course, whether the theory for islands can be used on large and forested areas such as rainforests. If islands get smaller, there is nowhere to escape. If, on the other hand, one tract of rainforest is cut down, many animals and plants can go on living in the surrounding areas.

One obvious thing to do would be to look at our own experiment, the one carried out in Europe and North America. In both places, primary forest was reduced by approximately 98–99 percent. In the US, the eastern forests were reduced over two centuries to fragments totaling just 1–2 percent of their original area, but nonetheless this resulted in the extinction of only one forest bird.[2046]

The largest tropical study of the correlation between rainforest and the extinction of species was carried out in Puerto Rico by Ariel Lugo of the United States Department of Agriculture. He found that the primary forest had been reduced by 99 percent over a period of 400 years. "Only" seven out of 60 species of birds had become extinct although the island today is home to 97 species of birds.[2047] This indicates a serious problem with Wilson's rule of thumb. And what is perhaps more astonishing is that even though the area of primary forest on Puerto Rico was reduced by 99 percent they ended up with *more* species of birds![2048]

We get some idea of how to understand the situation when we are told that the overall forest area of Puerto Rico never fell below 10–15 percent. Our mistake is to believe that all cleared rainforest is simply razed and left barren. In fact, FAO figures show that about half of all tropical forest that is cut down is converted to secondary forest.[2049]

The biologists' reaction

The issue of biodiversity resembles the classic battle between model and reality. The biologists acknowledge that there is a problem when it comes to the figures. Myers says that "we have no way of knowing the actual extinction rate in the tropical forests, let alone an approximate guess."[2050] Colinvaux admits in *Scientific American* that the rate is "incalculable."[2051] Even so, E. O. Wilson attempts to put a lid on the problem with the weight of his authority: "Believe me, species become extinct. We're easily eliminating a hundred thousand a year."[2052] His figures are "absolutely undeniable" and based on "literally hundreds of anecdotal reports."[2053]

One prominent conservationist admitted in *Science* that "the lack of data does worry me."[2054] Worried about the reaction from the other biologists, he demanded to remain anonymous, because "they'll kill me for saying this," as he put it. Although "kill" is presumably intended to be taken in the metaphorical sense, it does rather emphasize that the biologists have a clear opinion of where the debate between figures and models should end. There are many grants at stake.

Similarly, Ariel Lugo explains that "no credible effort" has yet been made to pin down the scientific assumptions behind the mega-extinction scenario.[2055] "But," he adds, "if you point this out, people say you are collaborating with the devil."[2056]

Check the data

In 1990, the IUCN decided to join this discussion.[2057] The IUCN is the World Conservation Union which maintains the official Red List of threatened animals, and it organizes the BCIS, which is the largest biodiversity and conservation program in the world. Its American members include government organizations such as NOAA, USAID, USDA, the Fish and Wildlife Service, and the National Park Service, as well as green organizations such as the Natural Resources Defense Council, the Environmental Defense Fund, and the US World Wide Fund for Nature.

The result can be read in the book by Whitmore and Sayer published in 1992 – and its conclusions do not exactly make boring reading. Heywood and Stuart point out that the recorded extinction figures for mammals and birds (see Table 6) are "very small."[2058] If the extinction rates are similar for other species and if we assume 30 million species, we get an annual extinction rate of 2,300 or 0.08 percent a decade.[2059] Since the area of the rainforest has been reduced by approximately 20 percent since the 1830s, "it must be assumed that during this contraction, very large numbers of species have been lost in some areas. Yet surprisingly *there is no clear-cut evidence for this*."[2060]

One of the few examples of extinction appears in a paper by Gentry, who reported that 90 species had become extinct when a ridge in the foothills of the Ecuadorian Andes had been cleared.[2061] The biologists often mention this story as a fine example of documented extinctions.[2062] Wilson counts it as a valuable anecdotal report: "One of the famous examples is a mountain ridge in Ecuador. In a relatively small ridge of a few square kilometers, they found something like 90 species of plants found nowhere else. Between 1978 and 1986, farmers cleared the ridge and extinguished most of the species in one shot."[2063] In two brief return visits six years later, Gentry refound at least 17 of the previously assumed lost species.[2064]

As we saw above in the chapter on forests, about 86 percent of the Brazilian Amazon rainforest is still intact.[2065] On the other hand, Brazil's Atlantic rainforest had been almost entirely cleared in the nineteenth century, with only 12 percent extremely fragmented forest left. According to Wilson's rule of thumb, one ought to expect half of all the species to have become extinct. However, when members of the Brazilian Society of Zoology analyzed all 171 known Atlantic forest animals, the group "could not find *a single known animal species which could be properly declared as extinct, in spite of the massive reduction in area and fragmentation of their habitat*."[2066] And 120 animals in a secondary list "show no species considered extinct."[2067] Similarly no species of plants was reported to have become extinct.[2068] The zoologists allege that "closer examination of the existing data . . . supports the affirmation that little or no species extinction has yet occurred (though some may be in very fragile persistence) in the Atlantic forests. Indeed, an appreciable number of species considered extinct 20 years ago, including several birds and six butterflies, have been rediscovered more recently."[2069]

Several scientists have investigated asserted extinction rates of 15 percent for birds up until 2015. Heywood and Stuart write that after thorough research on 1,000 birds that have been claimed to become extinct, they have been able to ascertain that – primarily because of conservation efforts – "relatively few of these species are likely to become extinct by 2015."[2070]

Despite the fact that the IUCN predicts higher extinction rates it is concluded that "actual extinctions remain low."[2071] Holden points out in the preface that calculations and observations simply do not match up: "The coastal forests of Brazil have been reduced in area as severely as any tropical forest type in the world. According to calculation, this should have led to considerable species loss. Yet no known species of its old, largely endemic, fauna can be regarded as extinct."[2072]

In fact, the latest model calculations seem to back the observations. Biologists Mawdsley and Stork have shown, on the basis of information from Great Britain, that there is a fairly constant relationship between the rates of extinction of different species. If this model is used it is actually possible to estimate the number of extinct birds from the number of extinct insects and, amazingly, these figures fit very well.[2073] Using this model it is possible to show that since 1600, 0.14 percent of all insects have died out, or 0.0047 percent per decade. But as we saw above, the extinction rate is on its way up. For this reason – and for safety's sake – Mawdsley and Stork use an extremely high estimate by Professor Smith which says that the extinction rate will increase 12- to 55-fold over the next 300 years.[2074] This still means that the extinction rate for all animals will remain below 0.208 percent per decade and probably be about 0.7 percent per 50 years.[2075]

An extinction rate of 0.7 percent over the next 50 years is not trivial. It is a rate about 1,500 times higher than the natural background extinction.[2076] However, it is a *much smaller* figure than the typically advanced 10–100 percent over the next 50 years (equal to some 20,000 to 200,000 times the background rate).[2077] Moreover, to assess the long-term impact, we must ask ourselves whether it is likely that this extinction rate will continue for many hundreds of years (accumulating serious damage) or more likely will be alleviated as population growth decelerates and the developing world gets rich enough to afford to help the environment, reforest and set aside parks (see development in forest area till 2100, Figure 150, p. 283).[2078]

This estimate of 0.7 percent per 50 years also concurs with the estimate from the UN *Global Biodiversity Assessment*. Here, the authors are very careful, stating that "the rate at which species are likely to become extinct in the near future is very uncertain," and taking note of "the discrepancy between field knowledge and predictions."[2079] The final summary does not state actual extinction rates but only expresses them relatively in that "the rate of extinction today is hundreds, if not thousands, of times higher than the natural background rate."[2080] This translates into an extinction rate of 0.1–1 percent per 50 years.[2081]

The biologists' response

Unfortunately, when it comes to the crunch, observations do not seem to satisfy most biologists. Wilson continues to say "believe me." As late as 1999 Myers actually reaffirmed his estimate of about 40,000 species, telling us that "we are into the opening stages of a human-caused biotic holocaust."[2082]

The summary article of Western and Pearl's *Conservation for the Twenty-First Century* repeats the assertion of 15–25 percent extinction by the year 2000. They point out that "while the figures and the impact of such extinctions are debatable, the more pervasive impact to our planet is not."[2083]

According to Professor Ehrlich, we do not know just how many species are becoming extinct each year. Yet, "biologists don't need to know how many species there are, how they are related to one another, or how many disappear annually to recognize that Earth's biota is entering a gigantic spasm of extinction."[2084] This is a most surprising statement. Apparently it alleviates scientists of the need to demonstrate the amount of losses as long as they can *feel* they are right. Such a statement seems to abandon the ordinarily assumed duty of scientists to objectively gather evidence to help society make real, well-informed choices.

Jared Diamond, a professor at UCLA and the author of well-known books such as *The Third Chimpanzee* and the Pulitzer Prize winner *Guns, Germs and Steel*, actually develops Ehrlich's idea. He emphasizes that we can only know something about the familiar species in the developed part of the world (where practically no extinction has taken place). For this reason we ought to reverse the burden of proof and assume that all species are extinct unless their existence can be proven.[2085] "We biologists should not bear the burden of proof to convince economists advocating unlimited human population growth [overconfident economists] that the extinction crisis is real. Instead, it should be left to those economists to fund research in the jungles that would positively support their implausible claim of a healthy biological world."[2086]

Having the attitude that in scientific discourse on species extinction it is unnecessary to provide evidence is, of course, problematic. The biologists seriously argue that any skeptic should himself go to the jungle and carry out the biologists' research, because the biologists already *know* that things are going askew. In reality, of course, they are asking society for a blank check to prevent something which is claimed to be a catastrophe (50 percent over the next 50 years) but which is not supported by data (indicating a problem in the region of 0.7 percent over the next 50 years).

Conclusion: what are the consequences of seriously overstating the extinctions?

Taking the biologists' warnings about the extinction of species has consequences for our priorities. We accepted the biodiversity convention signed in Rio in 1992, partly because the "species extinction caused by human activities continues at an alarming rate."[2087] It obliges us to introduce the conservation of species into the national political process.[2088]

We demand that the developing countries stop chopping down their rainforest even though we have eradicated about 99 percent of our own primary forest.

A 1993 article in *Science* on the cost of biodiversity reported that "scientific luminaries such as Edward O. Wilson of Harvard and Paul Ehrlich of Stanford" were endorsing the principles behind the Wildlands Project, a hugely ambitious plan to protect biodiversity in North America, which called for "a network of wilderness reserves, human buffer zones, and wildlife corridors stretching across huge tracts of land" amounting to as much as half of the continent. In the words of the *Science* article the long-term goal of the project amounted to "no less than a transformation of America from a place where 4.7% of the land is wilderness to an archipelago of human-inhabited islands surrounded by natural areas." Inevitably, the implementation of such a scheme would involve mass movements of people.[2089]

Why sign the biodiversity convention? Why save the rainforest? Why require millions of Americans to move to city islands with severely restricted access to neighbouring countryside? The answer has always been: in order to save 40,000 species from becoming extinct every year.[2090]

It is a "common knowledge" argument that has entered our political vocabulary. The Brundtland report states that "over the longer term, at least one-quarter, possibly one-third, and conceivably a still larger share of species existing today could be lost."[2091] The well-publicized internet site Web of Life tells us that 50,000 species die every year.[2092] Worldwatch Institute warns us of economic development: we may grow richer, but we should consider if we really have gained if we "also wipe out half of the world's plant and animal species."[2093]

The dramatic loss of biodiversity, expressed in the 40,000 species a year, is a dramatic figure, created by models. It is a figure which with monotonous regularity has been repeated everywhere until in the end we all believed it. It has become part of our environmental Litany. But it is also a figure which conflicts with both observation and careful modeling.

Of course, losing 25–100 percent of all species would be a catastrophe by any standards. However, losing 0.7 percent per 50 years over a limited time span is not a catastrophe but a problem – one of many that mankind still needs to solve. Facing these facts is important when we have to make tough choices where to do the most good with our limited resources.

PART V

24 Global warming

Climate change and especially global warming[2094] has become the overriding environmental concern since the 1990s.[2095] Most discussions about the environment end up pointing out that, despite all other indicators that may show us doing better and better, we still have to change our current lifestyle dramatically because our way of life is now changing the climate and causing global warming.

In the words of the President's Council on Sustainable Development: "The risk of accelerated climate change in the next century has emerged as one of the most important issues we will face as we seek to achieve our sustainable development goals."[2096] In their 2000 edition, Worldwatch Institute concludes that stabilizing the climate along with stabilizing the population growth are the two "overriding challenges facing our global civilization as the new century begins."[2097] Likewise, UNDP sees global warming as one of the two crises that nudge humanity ever closer to "the outer limits of what earth can stand."[2098] Global warming is, according to former President Clinton, "one of the two or three major issues facing the world over the next 30 years."[2099] Head of the George W. Bush EPA, Christine Todd Whitman, has called global warming "one of the greatest environmental challenges we face, if not the greatest."[2100] And the opening remark on their homepage proclaims that "Greenpeace has identified global climate change as one of the greatest threats to the planet."[2101]

The consequence is that we must change our industrial ways. Worldwatch Institute tells us that "the only feasible alternative is a solar/hydrogen-based economy."[2102] Greenpeace equivalently tells us that although we may have lots of oil (see also chapter 11), global warming prevents us from using it – "we are in a second world oil crisis. But in the 1970s the problem was a shortage of oil. This time round the problem is that we have too much."[2103] The only solution is choosing "a fundamentally new energy direction based on clean renewable energy, like wind or solar power."[2104]

In this way, climate change has become the environmental trump card – possibly we are not running out of raw materials, possibly we are actually doing better and better on almost any objective indicator, but if global warming demands a change, all other arguments will be of lesser import. Worldwatch Institute actually envisions how in the twenty-first century "the climate battle may assume the kind of strategic importance that wars – both hot and cold – have had during" the twentieth century.[2105] Backed up by a number of leading scientists writing in *Nature*, Worldwatch Institute asserts that to develop the necessary technologies to combat climate change will require a monumental research effort, conducted with the urgency of the Manhattan Project or the Apollo space program.[2106]

These drastic efforts are justified by a general understanding of the severe consequences of global warming. In many people's view, climate change is linked to drastic increases in temperature and catastrophic climatic shifts. We fear that global warming could result in the destruction of our ecosystems, widespread famine, more and more powerful hurricanes, the melting of the ice caps and the oceans flooding the Maldives, Bangladesh and other low-lying areas on Earth.

This is no wonder, given the constant media barrage of possible greenhouse related catastrophes. Almost any weather event is now linked to climate change.[2107] In Leonardo DiCaprio's March 2000 interview of the President, Clinton told us that if we do not change our ways, what will happen is,

> the polar ice caps will melt more rapidly; sea levels will rise; you will have the danger of flooding in places like the precious Florida Everglades or the sugarcane fields of Louisiana; island nations could literally be buried. The whole climate of the United States, for example, could be changed where you would have more flooding, more heat waves, more storms, more extreme weather events generally.
>
> And then you'll have some public health consequences. For example, we're already seeing in Africa, for example, malaria being found at higher and higher altitudes where it used to be too cool for the mosquitoes.
>
> So there will be a lot of very bad, more dramatic weather events. There will be a shift in the patterns of agricultural production. There will be flooding that will be quite bad, and there will be more public health crises.[2108]

In this chapter, we will try to look at these dire claims and go through both the technical and the economic side of the arguments. This will enable us to separate the hyperbole from the real problems and allow us to plot the best course of action for the future. This chapter accepts the reality of man-made global warming but questions the way in which future scenarios have been arrived at and finds that forecasts of climate change of 6 degrees by the end of the century are not plausible. I shall argue that the limitations of computer modeling, the unrealistic nature of the basic assumptions made about future technological change and political value judgements have distorted the scenarios being presented to the public. I shall further argue that an economic analysis of the costs and benefits of an immediate reduction in CO_2 emissions clearly shows that the world as a whole would benefit more from investing in tackling problems of poverty in the developing world and in research and development of renewable energy than in policies focused on climate change.

In the following I shall – unless otherwise stated – use the figures and computer models from the official reports of the UN climate panel, the IPCC.[2109] The IPCC's reports are the foundation for most public policy on climate change and the basis for most of the arguments put forth by the environmental organizations.

The basic greenhouse effect

The main concern of climate change is global warming and the predicted warming is based on the so-called greenhouse effect. The fundamental principle of the greenhouse effect is really quite simple and entirely uncontroversial.[2110] Several types of gases can reflect or trap heat, including water vapor, carbon dioxide (CO_2), methane (CH_4), laughing gas (N_2O), CFC gases and ozone (see also the box on the ozone layer). Together they are known as greenhouse gases. In this chapter we will primarily discuss CO_2 since it makes up 60 percent of the present extra heat-trapping gases and is expected to constitute an even larger part in the future (see Figure 132).[2111]

The greenhouse gases trap some of the heat emitted by the Earth, rather like having a

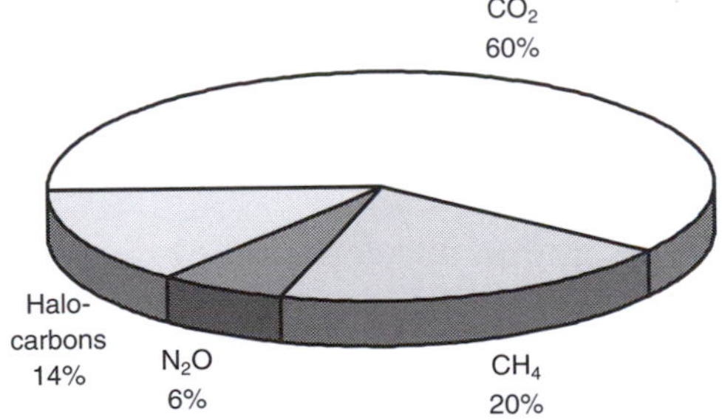

Figure 132 Relative influence of the manmade greenhouse gases on temperature change. Total change in forcing from 1750 to 1998 is 2.43W/m^2. Source: IPCC 2001a:table 6.1.

blanket wrapped around the globe. The basic greenhouse effect is good – if the atmosphere did not contain greenhouse gases the average temperature on the Earth would be approximately 33°C (59°F) colder and it is unlikely that life as we know it would be able to exist.[2112]

The problem is that man has increased the quantity of greenhouse gases, CO_2 in particular, in the atmosphere. About 80 percent of the extra CO_2 comes from the combustion of oil, coal and gas whereas the other 20 percent comes from deforestation and other land changes in the tropics.[2113] About 55 percent of the released CO_2 is absorbed again by the oceans, by northern forest regrowth, and generally by increased plant growth (plants use CO_2 as fertilizer),[2114] but the rest is added to the atmosphere, such that the concentration of CO_2 has increased by 31 percent from pre-industrial times to the present day.[2115] Both the increasing emission of CO_2 and the increasing concentration can be seen in Figure 133.

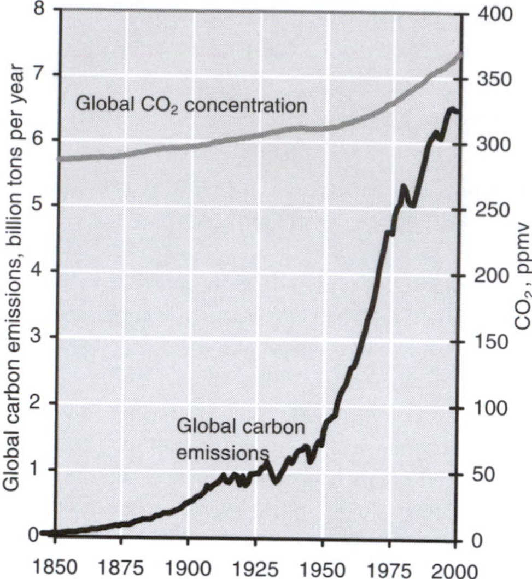

Figure 133 Annual, global emissions of carbon from fossil fuels and cement production, 1850–1999, and concentration of CO_2 in the atmosphere (ppmv: parts per million volume), 1850–2000. Source: Marland *et al.* 1999, Etheridge *et al.* 1998, Hansen and Sato 2000, Keeling and Whorf 1999, WI 2000a:67, pers. comm. P. Tans, Climate Monitoring and Diagnostics Laboratory, National Oceanic and Atmospheric Administration, USA.

The logic then is that if the extra greenhouse gases, and among them CO_2, reflect heat then more greenhouse gases in the atmosphere will (everything else being equal) lead to an increase in the temperature on Earth. This is the so-called anthropogenic greenhouse effect, the extra, man-made greenhouse effect. Since this effect is our main interest, we will in the following just call it the greenhouse effect. That there should be some sort of anthropogenic greenhouse effect is also fairly uncontroversial.

The long-term development of the climate

In order to understand what will happen with the global temperature, it is necessary first to look at what has happened. We have only used thermometers systematically and globally over the past century and a half (the world's longest record in Central England only goes back to 1659)[2116] so if we want to know about the long-term development of the climate, we have to look for other ways of measuring temperature.

We can get a grip on the development of temperature by studying how it has affected other objects that we can measure today – the so-called proxy indicators. For instance, temperature has in many ways affected the ice that has accumulated in polar regions, so when we drill out an ice core, we can count the layers backwards in time and measure the fraction of melted ice, the concentration of salts and acids, the load of pollen or trace gases trapped in air bubbles.[2117] Equally, we can estimate temperature by looking at tree rings (because trees grow wider rings in warm weather), corals (measuring growth rings or trace elements), lake and ocean sediments, boreholes etc.[2118]

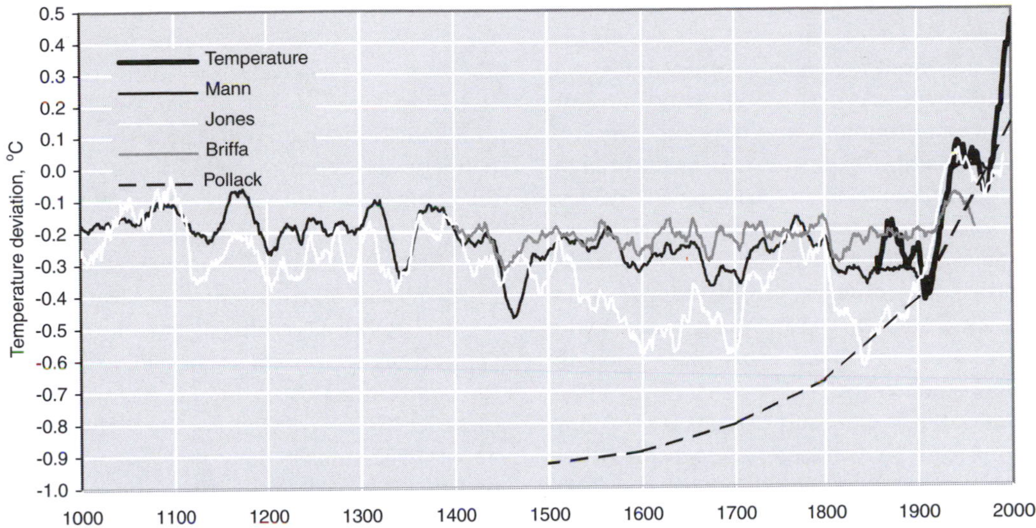

Figure 134 Temperature over the past millennium for the Northern Hemisphere. Mann *et al.*, annual 1000–1980, use many proxies, although early data rely almost exclusively on North American tree rings. Jones *et al.*, warm season 1000–1991, also use many proxies, but again only 3–4 remain before 1400. Briffa *et al.*, warm season 1400–1960, only rely on tree rings. Pollack and Huang, centennial 1500–2000, measure temperature directly from 616 individual boreholes. Instrumental temperature, annual Northern Hemisphere 1856–2000, is shown for reference. Mann, Jones and Briffa smoothed by running 21-year averages, instrumental temperature by running 11-year averages. All temperatures adjusted to instrumental mean of 1961–90. Sources: Mann *et al.* 1999a&b, Jones *et al.* 1998b&c, 1999b, 2000, 2001, Briffa *et al.* 1998a&b, Huang *et al.* 2000, Pollack & Huang 2001.

Throughout the past 1 million years there has occurred a series of eight glacial/interglacial cycles, driven by the changes in earth's orbit around the sun.[2119] The last interglacial period – the Holocene, which we still live in – began about 10,000 years ago. The melting ice caused the sea to rise some 120m (400ft)[2120] while the early temperatures were generally warmer than the twentieth century.[2121] The records seem to indicate substantial temperature swings throughout the Holocene on a millennial scale, and some indicators even show changes of 5 to 8°C over 1,500 years.[2122] Yet, when looking over the long 400,000 years of ice cores, the Holocene appears by far the longest warm and stable period, which has naturally had profound implications for the development of civilization.[2123]

It is only when we get to the last millennium that we have several attempts to construct a global or hemispherical temperature data series as seen in Figure 134. By far the most popular record is the one by Mann *et al.* which is presented in the IPCC summary for policy-makers[2124] and is typically used as a strong visual argument for global warming.[2125]

Basically, the Mann temperature shows a weak declining temperature trend from 1000–1900, possibly caused by an astronomical trend towards an new ice age,[2126] followed by a rapid temperature increase in the twentieth century. This graph allows IPCC to conclude that not only was the last century the warmest in the millennium but the 1990s the warmest decade and 1998 the warmest year of the millennium for the Northern Hemisphere.[2127]

Basically, there is no disagreement that the centuries before 1900 were much colder. This phenomenon is well known in history as the "Little Ice Age," broadly stretching from

1400–1900.[2128] Evidence from a wide range of sources shows colder continents where glaciers advanced rapidly in Greenland, Iceland, Scandinavia, and the Alps.[2129] Many European springs and summers were outstandingly cold and wet, and crop practices changed throughout Europe to adapt to a shortened and less reliable growing season, causing recurrent famines.[2130] Likewise in China, warm weather crops, such as oranges, were abandoned in the Kiangsi Province, and in North America the early European settlers reported exceptionally severe winters.[2131]

Indeed, it is more surprising that the Mann data do not show a larger temperature drop. Such a drop is, however, suggested by the Jones temperature and definitely by the Polack borehole measurements.

Likewise, the early part of the Mann data indicates a slightly warmer climate, some periods of which could even be on par with the mean twentieth century temperature.[2132] Again, there is no disagreement that the early part of the second millennium was warmer, a period known in history as the "Medieval Warm Period."[2133] Here, 2–3°C warmer climates made possible the colonization of the otherwise inhospitable Greenland and Vinland (Newfoundland) by the Vikings.[2134] Likewise, the Japanese cherry blossoms returned to early blooming in the 12th century and the snow line in the Rocky Mountains was about 300 meters higher than today.[2135]

Again, the surprising part of the Mann data seems to be that the early temperature is not higher. Usually, the temperature for the 900s–1100s has been estimated to be much warmer, including by the IPCC in its first 1990 report.[2136] However, such estimates have been very dependent on individual temperature series and thus it is not unlikely that the Medieval Warm Period could have been a more local phenomenon, primarily restricted to the North Atlantic, as it is argued in the 2001 IPPC report.[2137]

But the basis for the long-term temperature data in Mann is also problematic, especially for the years 1000–1400. First, the data are almost exclusively based on North American tree ring data.[2138] This, of course, severely limits the claim of presenting a hemispherical temperature series. Second, tree ring data (like almost all proxies) are naturally limited to land data, which means they do not describe temperature of the more than 70 percent of the Earth's surface covered by oceans.[2139] Third, growth of trees are dependent on many other factors besides temperature, and while it is essential to have such disturbances removed, it is not altogether clear how that should be done without matching tree ring data with other, better temperature records, which naturally begs the question.[2140] Fourth, trees mainly grow in the summer and during the day-time, which means that they do not reliably measure full, annual temperature.[2141]

Thus, the available estimates in Figure 134 seem to indicate that there is considerable disagreement about the actual development in temperature. The Jones temperature shows a much more marked temperature decline throughout the fifteenth and seventeenth centuries, whereas the Briffa temperature essentially shows no change from 1400–1960.[2142] The only data estimated from direct measurements of temperatures come from boreholes and these show a dramatic rebound from the Little Ice Age.

Consequently, a recent status report concludes that "at present, it is debatable whether there is enough temperature proxy data to be representative of hemispheric, let alone global, climate changes given the lack of large spatial scale coherence in the data."[2143] Moreover, data seem to indicate that there has been regular recurrence of episodes like the Little Ice Age and the Medieval Warm Period in a roughly 1500-year climatic cycle over the past 140,000 years,[2144] which would indicate that the 1000-year period is too short to reveal the relevant climatic pattern. Finally, many studies point to a climate system with large, natural temperature changes, which are not apparent in the Mann data.[2145]

Summing up, there is no doubt that the temperature of the late twentieth century is greater than many previous centuries, but this cannot be taken as a simple indication of overwhelming global warming as we are also coming out of a Little Ice Age. The claim that the temperature is higher now than at any time throughout the past 1000 years seems less well substantiated, as the data essentially exclude ocean temperatures, night temperatures and winter temperatures and moreover are based almost exclusively on North American data. Finally, the Mann data impart an impression of an almost stable climate system which has only been severely disturbed in the past century, although this impression of stability is almost certainly incorrect.

The climate, 1856–2100

The development in the instrumental global temperature record from 1856–2000 is shown in Figure 135.[2146] On the whole, the temperature since then has increased by 0.4–0.8°C.[2147] Closer inspection reveals that all of the twentieth century's temperature increase has occurred abruptly within two time periods, from 1910 to 1945 and again from 1975 till today.[2148] While the second period fits well with the greenhouse concern, the temperature increase from 1910 to 1945 is harder to align with the human emission of greenhouse gases, since the concentration and increase in the early part of the last century was slight (Figure 133).[2149] The IPCC finds that some of the increase can be explained by a substantial and natural increase in solar irradiation from 1700 onwards, which however is still only poorly quantified.[2150]

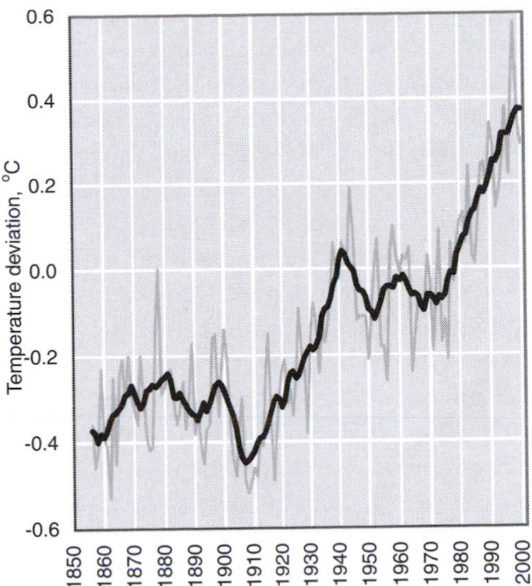

Figure 135 Global temperature, 1856–2000, expressed as deviations (anomalies) from the average of the period 1961–90. Temperature is a weighted average of land air and sea surface temperatures. Light lines, actual yearly measurements; black heavy line, moving 9-year average. To obtain absolute global temperature add 14.0°C (57.2°F). Source: Jones *et al.* 2000, 2001.

The crucial question is what the temperature development will be in the future. In the first analysis, this depends on how much more CO_2 and other greenhouse gases we will put into the atmosphere. This again requires a forecast of the future greenhouse gas emissions.

The first IPCC report from 1990 presented a primary scenario which assumed a future where few or no steps would be taken to limit greenhouse gas emissions – the so-called business-as-usual scenario.[2151] The climate consequences from this scenario could then be contrasted to the consequences of three other scenarios, with differing degrees of greenhouse gas controls. In 1992 the scenarios were updated and more scenarios were added, reflecting the substantial uncertainty about how the future would evolve.[2152] Nevertheless, one remained the primary and *de facto* business-as-usual scenario, named the IS92a.

The scenarios were once again updated in 2000 for the third IPCC assessment. However, this time the uncertainty was placed squarely in the center as any business-as-usual approach was scrapped and four so-called storylines were used to create a bewildering 40 scenarios, with none considered more plausible than others.[2153] While such an approach laudably maintains the inherent uncertainty of the long future, it also makes any discussion and comparison between different policies numbingly complex. The six scenarios presented here constitute the smallest subset recommended by the IPCC.[2154]

Fundamentally, the scenarios are distinguished on two dimensions.[2155] One primary dimension is whether the future will be most focused on *economic* or *environmental* development. The four scenarios that focus on the economic development are denoted *A* whereas the other two scenarios concerned about environmental sustainability are denoted *B*. The other primary dimension describes the degree of *global* or *regional* orientation. The four global scenarios get the number *1* whereas the two more regionally motivated scenarios get the number *2*.

With these two dimensions, we should just have four scenarios, but the economic/global scenario (A1) is further divided into three separate scenarios. One is fossil fuel *intensive* (A1FI), one is *balanced* between fossil and non-fossil fuels (A1B) and one will eventually make a *transition* to non-fossil fuels (A1T).[2156]

As a final quirk, the IPCC has required that all the scenarios explicitly *do not* envisage reductions in greenhouse gas emissions due to worries about global warming or even reductions that would be due to already signed treaties.[2157] This makes all the scenarios somewhat artificial and certainly worst-case. The modeling teams reasonably complained that it was quite difficult to imagine a society focused on stringent environmental policies but without any climate policies whatsoever.[2158]

We will discuss how reasonable the scenarios are below, but here we will just look at the actual emission suggested by the new scenarios in Figure 136. Basically, they show very different possible futures affecting the climate,

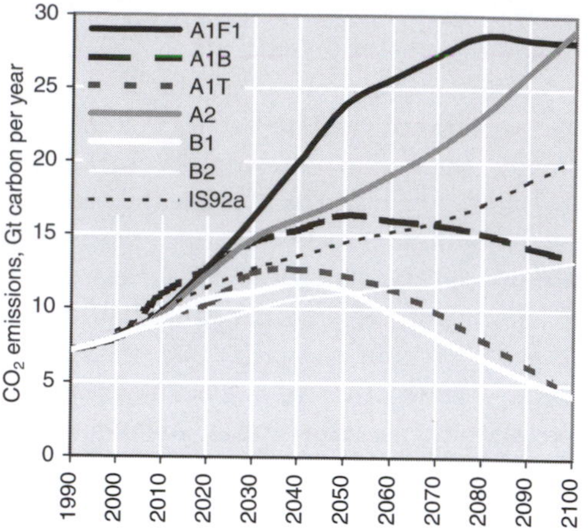

Figure 136 The six new CO_2 emission scenarios, 1990–2100, with the old IS92a business-as-usual emission scenario added for reference. Scenarios are focused on the economy (A) or the environment (B), and oriented globally (1) or regionally (2), as explained in the text. Measured in billion ton (Gt) carbon per year. Source: IPCC 2001b, 2001a:table II.1.1, 1992:91.

even though none of the scenarios are at all concerned about climate change. Moreover, it is perhaps worth noting that the three A1-scenarios span almost the entire spectrum of CO_2 emissions (from 4.3 to 28.2Gt C in 2100) – essentially rendering the two primary dimensions making up the 40 scenarios unnecessary.

The IPCC estimates of the climate consequences of these emission scenarios are then depicted in Figure 137. What they show are significant temperatures increases, in the range of 2–4.5°C (3.6–8.1°F) in 2100. This is considerably higher than the estimate from the previous IPCC assessment, where the IS92a can be seen near the low end at 2.38°C in 2100, and the range was approximately 1.3–3.2°C.[2159] This much-quoted increase in expected temperature is mainly due to lower levels of particle pollution and higher emission scenarios, which we will discuss below.

Equivalently, the total sea level rise over the century is expected to be about 31–49 cm (12.2–19.3 in). Despite the higher expected temperature, this is slightly lower than the

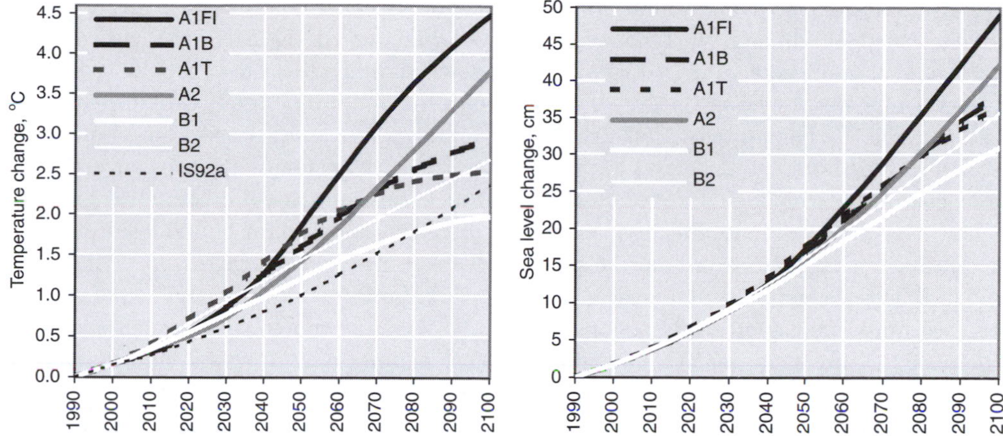

Figure 137 The predicted temperature and total sea level increase, 1990–2100, with the six new scenarios, using a simple climate model tuned to seven complex model results. (Note, this simple model seems to overestimate warming by about 20 percent, see text below.) IS92a is added in temperature graph for reference. The estimated total sea level rise from IS92a was 49 cm (IPCC 2001a:table 11.13, 1996a:383). Source: IPCC 2001a:figure 9.14, figure 11.12 and appendix, table II:4&5.

previously estimated increase of 38–55 cm,[2160] primarily because of better models.

Both the temperature and the sea level increase are important and have potentially serious consequences. However, if we are to react sensibly to the challenge of global warming there are at least six important – and controversial – questions we need ask ourselves:

1. *How much effect does CO_2 have on the temperature?* The important question is not *whether* the climate is affected by human CO_2, but *how much*. If the effect on the climate of an increased amount of CO_2 in the atmosphere is slight, global warming may not be particularly important.
2. *Could there be other causes behind the increasing temperature?* If the temperature increase we have been able to observe until now is not due solely to global warming, this also means that global warming is less important.
3. *Are the greenhouse scenarios reasonable?* When we are being told what will happen, we must ask if these predictions are based on reasonable assumptions.
4. *What are the consequences of a possible temperature increase?* If any temperature increase does not imply catastrophic consequences as described in the introduction to this chapter, then the problem – CO_2 or no – is perhaps not as great as we have been told.
5. *What are the costs of curbing versus not curbing CO_2 emissions?* If we are to make an informed decision on global warming we need to know the costs of not acting but also the costs of acting.
6. *How should we choose what to do?* What considerations should we employ to decide between costs of action and costs of inaction?

How much does CO_2 affect the temperature?

It is quite odd that so much of the argument on global warming has been on whether or not a human influence could be seen. The most quoted sentence from the previous 1996 IPCC report was that "the balance of evidence suggests that there is a discernible human influence on global climate."[2161] The new 2001 report tells us more categorically that "most of the warming observed over the last 50 years is attributable to human activities."[2162] (See also discussion on this quote below.)

However, even with lots of countervailing (negative feedback) climate effects, it would seem unlikely that there would not be some form of warming coming from increased CO_2. Thus, the important question is not *whether* man-made CO_2 increases global temperature, but *how much* – whether this effect will be negligible, significant or even devastating. This question turns out to be very tricky.

Essentially, answering the question about temperature increase from CO_2 means predicting the global temperature over the coming centuries – no mean feat, given that Earth's climate is an incredibly complex system. It is basically controlled by the Earth's exchange of energy with the sun and outer space. The calculations comprise five important basic elements: the atmosphere, the oceans, the land surface, the ice sheets and the Earth's biosphere.[2163]

The interaction between these five basic elements is enormously complicated, and crucial mechanisms are still unknown or extremely sparsely documented in the scientific literature. The complexity of the climate has meant that climate scientists have had to rely on simulating the climate on supercomputers with so-called Atmosphere-Ocean General Circulation Models (AOGCMs or sometimes just GCMs).

Inside these models, the Earth's atmosphere is typically divided into grids, 250 km on the side and 1 km high, whereas the ocean is sliced slightly thinner.[2164] The model of the atmosphere then calculates the evolution of momentum, heat, and moisture within each grid, while similar equations are solved for the ocean grids. These equations are solved for every half-hour of model time which again runs over several hundred model years.

But faithfully modeling all the important factors in the climatic system involves representing everything from the entire planet down to individual dust particles, which our current computers simply cannot manage.[2165] Some of the most important climate processes, such as clouds or ocean convection, are much smaller than the computer grid, and therefore they cannot be modeled explicitly. Instead they are roughly approximated on average effects from the larger-scale variables – a technique known as parameterization.[2166]

It is important to point out that *all* the IPCC's predictions are based on such climatic computer model simulations.[2167] In principle there is nothing suspicious about using computer simulations to describe complex systems. This technique is widely used in natural science and economics for example. It is important to realize, however, that the result of simulations depends entirely on the parameters and algorithms with which the computer is fed. Computers are number-crunchers and not crystal balls.

The three most difficult problems for the climate simulations are modeling the cooling effects of particles, fitting the water vapor feedback and handling clouds.[2168] Moreover, obtaining reasonable models for all three are crucial for making sensible predictions of the future climate.

How much does CO_2 affect the temperature? Particles

The first issue of the cooling effect of particles (the so-called aerosols) has turned out to be absolutely essential in the IPCC predictions. The problem was that the original computer models used in the 1990 IPPC report and well into the nineties just did not match up with the data: they predicted way too much warming from CO_2 and other greenhouse gases. This is evident in Figure 138, where the simulation only with greenhouse gases predicts a temperature for 2000 of about 0.91 °C or almost half a degree higher than observed. The IPCC admit-

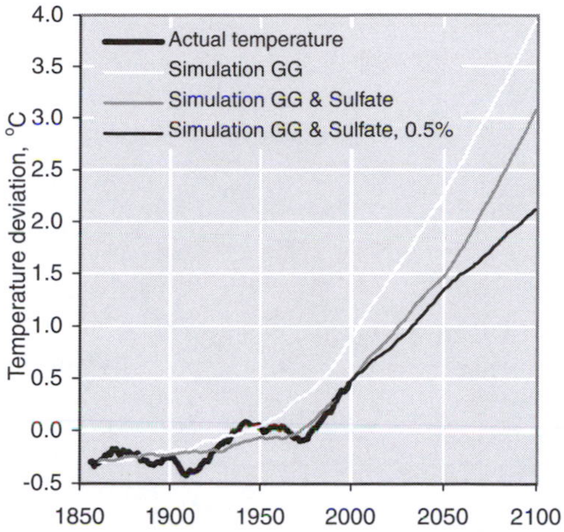

Figure 138 Global average temperature simulations from the Hadley Centre GCM (CM2), for just greenhouse gases (GG) and for greenhouse gases plus sulfate aerosols with standard IPCC assumptions (historic CO_2 and SO_x from 1861–1989, 1 percent annual CO_2 equivalent increase and IS92a SO_x emissions 1990–2099), 1861–2099. Extra simulation for 1990–2099 with more realistic emissions of greenhouse gases and sulfate aerosols (0.5 percent annual CO_2 equivalent increase and IS92d for 1990–2099). Actual temperature 1856–1999 for reference. All simulations average of 4 runs, smoothed by 19 year running means and forced to average of instrumental temperature record, 1861–99, as in Wigley *et al* (1997:8317). Sources: IPCC/DDC 2000, 2000a, Johns *et al.* 1997, Jones *et al.* 2000.

ted this much in their 1996 report in one of their surprisingly overlooked statements:

> When increases in greenhouse gases only are taken into account in simulating climate change over the last century, most GCMs . . . produce a greater warming than that observed to date, unless a lower climate sensitivity than that found in most GCMs is used.
>
> . . . There is growing evidence that increases in sulphate aerosols are partially counteracting the [warming] due to increases in greenhouse gases.[2169]

The IPCC basically tells us that previous models got it wrong – either it is not going to warm as much as previously claimed or something is hiding the warming. This could very well be sulfur particles from fossil fuel burning and other particles from volcanoes, biomass burning and land change, some of which reflect solar energy and thus have a cooling effect.[2170]

Incorporating sulfate particles in the simulations has gone some way towards producing a temperature development more closely resembling the observations.[2171] In Figure 138 this is demonstrated when the predicted general warming signal is tracking the latter part of the twentieth century fairly well, although the rapid temperature increase from 1910 to 1945 is still left unexplained.[2172]

Basically, the aerosols in the IPCC models are posited to hide a strong warming from CO_2, but this hinges on the claim that particles overall have a large cooling effect. However, as is apparent in Figure 139 this estimate is *very* uncertain. There are a large number of different effects from aerosols, both positive and negative, and all have very large uncertainties. Sulphate particles have a significant cooling effect but with an uncertainty factor of two – the actual cooling could be half or twice as great. Aerosols from biomass also have a smaller cooling effect with an uncertainty factor of three (3x). Particles from fossil fuels both make black carbon with a warming effect (2x uncertainty) and organic carbon with a cooling effect (3x uncertainty). For mineral dust it is not even certain whether they significantly cool or warm the climate. Moreover, aerosols also indirectly affect the climate by making more water drops (1st indirect effect) and by decreasing precipitation (2nd indirect effect).[2173] The first indirect effect could be zero or massively cooling – we don't know yet. The second indirect effect is virtually unknown but seems to amplify the first.[2174] The level of scientific understanding for all the effects is judged to be "very low" except for the direct sulphate aerosols, where it is judged to be low. In summary, the IPCC states that "the effect of the increasing

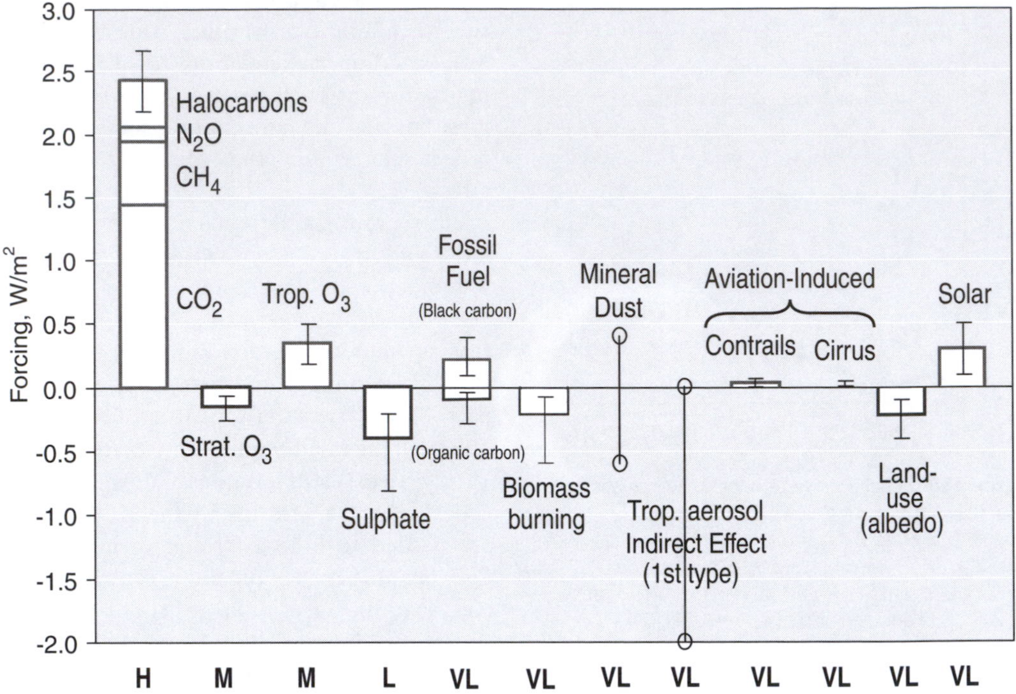

Figure 139 Global mean radiative forcing and uncertainties due to a number of agents, net changes from pre-industrial (1750) till today (late 1990s–2000). Basically, the figure shows the incoming extra energy to Earth due to changes over the past 250 years of a total of about 2.35W/m². As a rough approximation, one extra W/m² means a temperature increase of about 0.5–1°C.[2175] The total effect of the well-mixed greenhouse gases (CO_2, CH_4, N_2O and halocarbons) is a warming of about 2.43W/m² (as shown in Figure 132), with an uncertainty of 10 percent. Changes in stratospheric ozone cools (the "hole in the ozone layer") whereas ozone in the troposphere warms (ozone pollution). Sulfate, biomass and organic carbon aerosols from fossil fuels cool, whereas black carbon from fossil fuels warms. Mineral dust has no central estimate, only an uncertainty between +.4 and -.6W/m². Tropospheric aerosol, first indirect effect making more water drops, is poorly understood and with no central estimate and an uncertainty between 0 and -2W/m². Second indirect effect is not even estimated. Aviation effects from contrails and extra cirrus clouds indicated. Changes in land use have cooled the Earth slightly, whereas the solar irradiance has increased. Below is indicated the IPCC index of "Level of Scientific Understanding" ranging from High, over Medium to Low and Very Low. Source: IPCC 2001: table 6.11, figure 6.6.[2176]

amount of aerosols on the radiative forcing is complex and not yet well known."[2177]

Yet almost all AOGCMs only include the direct sulfate effect.[2178] While such a decision makes sense for modelers trying to limit the number of uncertain factors, picking just one cooling effect of many cooling and warming effects essentially allows one to better fit the output with reality without needing to change the predicted CO_2 warming.[2179] The nagging question is whether it is sulfate particles that are temporarily cooling an otherwise relentless CO_2 warming, or whether the climate sensitivity to CO_2 truly is smaller than previously expected.[2180] As pointed out in a recent overview, this leaves models less robust than is often claimed.[2181] For instance, studies making optimistic conclusions such as the one by the IPCC that there for temperature is a "large-scale consistency between models and observations"[2182] is problematic: the conclusion "would be significantly modified if, for example, the additional negative forcing due to the indirect effect of sulphate aerosols had been included; these studies may have, fortuitously, obtained an approximately correct net forcing when including only the well-mixed greenhouse gases and direct sulfate forcings."[2183]

Moreover, recent estimates seem to indicate that the direct cooling effect from particles may be much smaller than previously expected.[2184] The newest study in *Nature* 2001 shows that using better mixing models the total forcing is actually 0.55W/m^2 or much higher than expected in Figure 139. The result is that "the warming effect from black carbon may nearly balance the net cooling effect of other anthropogenic aerosol constituents."[2185] This would mean that the climate models are back to overestimating the actual warming (as in Figure 138), indicating that the estimate of total warming from CO_2 needs to be lowered.

How much does CO_2 affect the temperature? Water vapor

The second modeling issue deals with atmospheric water vapor. The water vapor feedback is the main reason why our emissions of CO_2 would cause a significant warming.[2186] It is estimated that the direct effect of doubling the atmosphere's CO_2 concentration (in 2070 or later)[2187] would be a temperature increase of about 1–1.2°C.[2188] But at the same time, the atmosphere has a built-in amplification mechanism, because as the Earth heats up, more water will evaporate and the water vapor will trap ever more heat.[2189] The IPCC therefore estimate that the effective warming that would result from a doubling of CO_2 in the atmosphere would be 1.5–4.5°C (the so-called climate sensitivity).[2190]

However, a strong water vapor feedback is not primarily dependent on the surface temperature but especially on the temperature in the troposphere, the lowest part of the atmosphere, stretching from the ground up to the stratosphere, some 10–13 km up. Basically, the feedback only works effectively if the entire lower atmosphere warms up, making the troposphere able to hold more water – otherwise the water vapor feedback will be much weaker.[2191] It is estimated that the troposphere accounts for about 90 percent of the water vapor feedback.[2192]

All AOGCMs predict that the temperature in the troposphere increases as fast or faster than that of the surface, as can be seen with the NASA/Goddard simulation in Figure 140.[2193]

Since 1979, a series of NOAA satellites have made very precise measurements of the tropospheric temperatures from all regions of the world (passing 80 percent of the globe every 24 hours, covering 100 percent within three or four days), including remote deserts, rainforests and oceans where reliable temperature data are often hard or impossible to obtain.[2194] The problem arises when we look at the temperature graph of the troposphere from 1979, seen in Figure 140. The observed tropospheric temperature essentially shows no trend. Whereas the model expects a warming of about 0.224°C/decade, the data show a warming of only 0.034°C/decade, almost all of which is attributable to the 1997–8 El Niño – a warming less than a sixth of the expected amount. This is truly important for our long-term warming prediction. Little or no temperature increase in the troposphere means much less water feedback and a much smaller warming estimate.[2195]

Numerous studies have tried to identify the causes of the difference between surface and tropospheric temperature, and quite a few have tried to identify errors in the satellite data.[2196] One study correctly identified a problem with the satellite algorithm, a problem which has now been corrected (the corrected data are used here).[2197]

However, there is a more obvious way to approach the satellite measurements. Weather balloons have regularly been measuring the temperature of the entire lower troposphere, and the data since 1958 have been

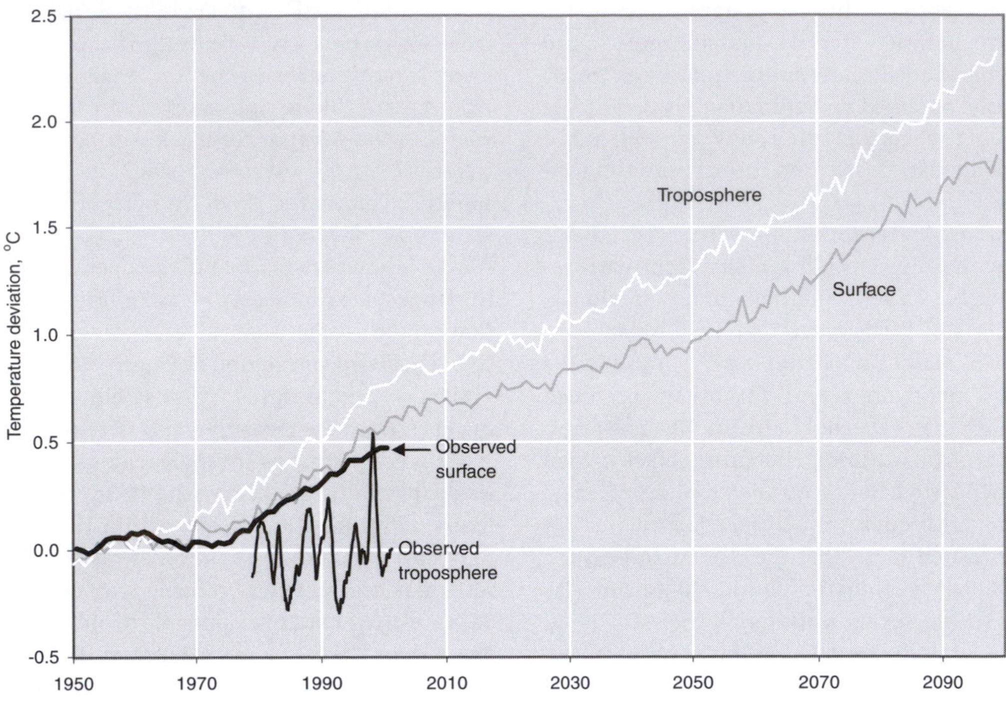

Figure 140 Temperature deviations of the NASA/Goddard AOGCM for the surface and the troposphere, 1950–2099. Averages of two runs, anomalies for 1950–60 mean, with CO_2 observed concentrations till 1990 and 0.5 percent compounded annual increase thereafter; sulfate aerosols from Mitchell *et al.* 1995. The troposphere temperature is an average of anomalies from 200, 500 and 850mb. Observed surface temperature 1856–1999, observed troposphere from satellite-based microwave sounding units (MSU 2LT), 1979–April 2001. Source: NASA/GISS 2000, Jones *et al.* 2000, Christy *et al.* 2000, 2000a, 2001.

averaged globally. If we compare the two independent measurements, they line up almost perfectly, as seen in Figure 141. They both show very little warming (0.034°C/decade for satellites and 0.029°C/decade for weather balloons) compared to the surface warming (0.17°C/decade) and especially to the AOGCMs expectation (0.22°C/decade). Consequently, most commentators, the IPCC and a 2000 study from the National Research Council now confirm that there seems to be a genuine difference in the two trends[2198] – a difference which if persistent should lower the water feedback and consequently lower the CO_2 warming.

How much does CO_2 affect the temperature? Clouds

The third modeling issue is clouds. Clouds can both cool and warm the climate, depending on cloud height and thickness as well as the distribution of water vapor, water drops, ice particles and atmospheric aerosols. Since clouds fall below the computer model grid they are parameterized, but this makes models extremely sensitive to cloud assumptions.[2199] In 1995 one of the leading climate models – developed at the Hadley Centre in England – predicted a temperature increase of 5.2°C if the CO_2 concentration was doubled. The programmers then improved the cloud parameterization in two places, and the

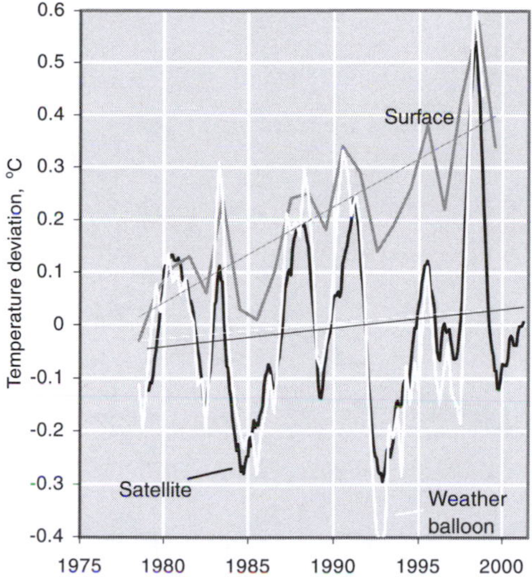

Figure 141 Temperature deviation in the troposphere, measured by weather balloons (1978–99, white line) and satellites (1979–April 2001, black line). Surface temperature inset for reference (1978–2000). Source: Angell 1999, Christy *et al.* 2000, 2000a, 2001, Jones *et al.* 2000.

model reacted by reducing its temperature estimate from 5.2°C to 1.9°C.[2200]

The IPCC frankly admit that

> probably the greatest uncertainty in future projections of climate arises from clouds and their interactions with radiation. . . . Clouds represent a significant source of potential error in climate simulations. . . . The sign of the net cloud feedback is still a matter of uncertainty, and the various models exhibit a large spread. Further uncertainties arise from precipitation processes and the difficulty in correctly simulating the diurnal cycle and precipitation amounts and frequencies.[2201]

This basically means that better cloud models potentially could throw off the IPCC temperature predictions – the cloud feedback is currently about half the size of the entire twenty-first century CO_2 temperature effect, but there is still no agreement on whether it will actually cool or warm the climate.[2202] We will look at the much discussed connections between clouds and cosmic radiation below.

However, here we will describe another model which might seriously change the IPCC temperature relationship. This new and potentially revolutionary research was published in March 2001 in *Bulletin of the American Meteorological Society*.[2203] Data show that a higher sea surface temperature of cloudy regions is strongly linked to fewer clouds – a one degree Celsius increase seems to cause 22 percent fewer upper-level clouds.[2204] Basically, such a mechanism opens up and closes down regions free of upper-level clouds,[2205] which more effectively permit infrared cooling, in such a manner as to resist changes in tropical surface temperature.[2206] This behavior the authors liken to a global iris; it is similar to the way an eye's iris opens and closes in response to changing light levels.[2207] Examining several of the important AOGCMs, none seemed to replicate this negative feedback, indicating that present models seriously overestimate CO_2-induced warming.[2208] Using the typical climate sensitivity of 1.5–4.5°C, the authors show that the negative cloud feedback by itself would diminish this sensitivity to the much lower range of 0.64–1.6°C.[2209]

Summing up, this section asked how much CO_2 affects the temperature. The answer both depends on the climate models and on the representation of crucial areas, such as aerosols, water vapor feedback and clouds.

The basic IPCC prediction of climate sensitivity of 1.5–4.5°C has remained constant throughout all the IPCC reports from 1990 to 2001 and indeed has remained constant in the scientific literature since the 1970s.[2210] This means that throughout the past 25 years the basic range of estimates of global warming from CO_2 has *not* improved. Instead when we have been presented with changes in predictions, this has primarily been due to changes in the scenarios. In 1990, the IPCC expected a 3.3°C increase over the next 100 years.[2211] In 1996, the IPCC reported a smaller expected warming at 2°C, with the range between 1.0

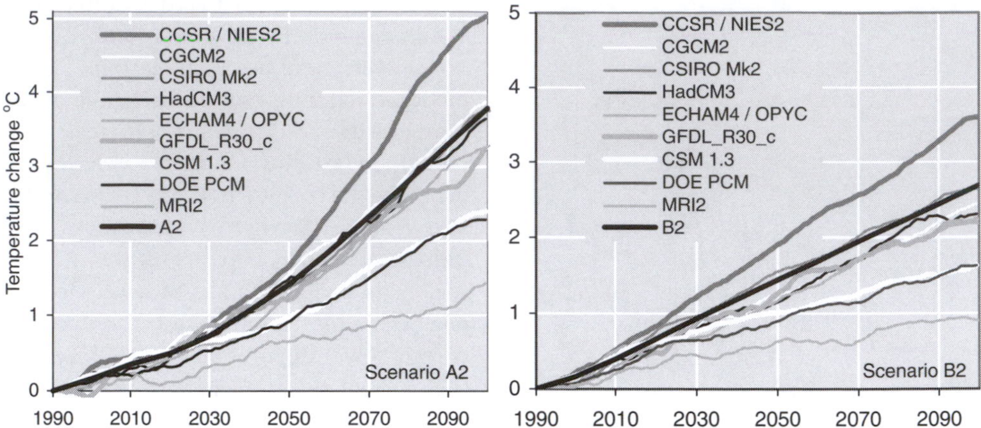

Figure 142 Temperature, 1990–2100, from 9 AOGCMs running the scenarios A2 (to the left) and B2 (to the right). Simple IPCC model for A2 and B2 (as in Figure 137) inserted for reference. Adjusted to zero in 1990 and presented with moving 9-year average. The models derive from the Japanese Centre for Climate System Research (CCSR) and the Japanese National Institute of Environmental Studies (NIES), the Australian Commonwealth Scientific and Industrial Research Organisation (CSIRO), the Canadian Centre for Climate Modelling and Analysis (CGCM), the UK Hadley Centre for Climate Prediction and Research (HadCM3), the German Climate Research Centre (ECHAM), US Geophysical Fluid Dynamics Laboratory (GFDL), Climate and Global Dynamics Division at the National Center for Atmospheric Research (CSM, DOE), the Japanese Climate Research Department, Meteorological Research Institute (MRI). Source: IPCC 2001a:figures 9.6a and 9.14.

and 3.5°C.[2212] The primary cause was that the scenarios now included dramatically higher emissions of particles, that would cool the climate.[2213] Again, when the IPCC now predicts a higher temperature range of 1.4–5.8°C,[2214] the cause is not that we have found the climate to be more affected by CO_2. Instead the new scenarios partly envision a marked reduction in the particle emissions (less cooling) and the most intensive CO_2 scenario now emit some 25 percent more carbon compared to the older scenarios (more warming).[2215]

That the basic climate sensitivity has remained at 1.5–4.5°C also means that we have very little ability to determine whether doubling the CO_2 concentrations will mean a rather small (1.5°C) or a dramatic (4.5°C) temperature increase. Actually, if we look at the 9 AOGCMs which ran the A2 and B2 scenario (the only scenarios the IPCC had time to run)[2216] in Figure 142 it becomes obvious that the temperature prediction for A2 is predominantly dependent on the choice of computer model – the span between the lowest 1.43°C and the highest 5.04°C is actually *bigger* than the entire temperature span of the marker scenarios in Figure 137. This basically means that the noise from the models is bigger than the signal we are supposed to formulate policy from. Discouraging but honest, the IPCC concludes that "the choice of model makes a bigger difference to the simulated response than the choice of scenario."[2217]

Moreover, it should be noted that for both scenarios, the IPCC seems to have chosen a rather pessimistic simple model description, as can also be seen Figure 142.[2218] For the A2, the average temperature increase for the computer models from 1990 to 2100 is 3.21°C whereas the IPCC simple model estimates the increase at 3.79°C. For the B2, the computer models indicate an average temperature increase of 2.17°C, where the IPCC expects 2.69°C. As the A2 and the B2 were the only scenarios run by several AOGCMs,[2219] this indicates that the IPCC simple model systematically overestimates the warming and consequently that the much-quoted range of

1.4–5.8°C would be more likely to be 1.2–4.8°C.[2220]

Answering how much CO_2 affects the temperature also hinges on the reasonable representation of crucial areas such as aerosols, water vapor feedback and clouds. As we have seen, the inclusion of certain aerosols makes the simulations look more realistic, but the models may not be robust and new research seems to indicate that they disguise a lower climate sensitivity. Likewise, the water vapor feedback requires a strong tropospheric warming which has been absent since the beginning of satellite measurements, again indicating a smaller climate sensitivity. The cloud simulations are fraught with uncertainty and new research seems to indicate a strong, negative cloud feedback which would lower the climate sensitivity dramatically.

Basically we have to conclude that the present models are complicated, but far from complicated enough to capture all the essential aspects of the global climate. The basic uncertainty of climate sensitivity still makes the models more noisy than the climate response. Consequently, most modelers still believe that accurate models are a decade away.[2221] Moreover, the simplistic models used by the IPCC appear to overestimate the climate sensitivity.

At the same time, the representation of aerosols, water vapor feedback and clouds also seems to indicate that climate sensitivity is overestimated. Generally, this points towards a smaller but definitely not negligible effect of CO_2 on the climate.

THE OZONE HOLE

Following the publication of an article in the reputable British science journal *Nature* in 1985 a new environmental problem was suddenly on everybody's lips – there was a hole in the ozone layer above the Antarctic.[2222] At ground level, ozone is a pollutant (as discussed in chapter 15), but in the upper atmosphere (the stratosphere) a thin ozone layer[2223] protects people, animals and plants by filtering out the sun's harmful ultraviolet (UV-B) rays.[2224] Ozone depletion is also linked in several ways to climate change, but the links are fairly weak and can be disregarded here.[2225]

Although the ozone hole of 1985 appeared over an essentially uninhabited area, its finding marked a crucial turning point in public awareness, because observations for the first time confirmed what had until then only been theoretical speculations.[2226] Since then, it has been unequivocally corroborated that the ozone layer over the inhabited mid-latitudes also has declined – in 1998 by about 3–6 percent below 1979 levels.[2227] This is important since a thinner ozone layer lets more UV-B rays through,[2228] increasing eye diseases (cataracts), skin cancer and photoaging (wrinkling and premature aging of skin).[2229]

The ozone depletion was caused by man.[2230] Already in 1974, two researchers at the University of California, Irvine, who later earned a Nobel prize for their work, had suggested that the so-called chlorofluorocarbons (CFCs) could be breaking down the ozone layer.[2231] Much research has later confirmed this basic link.[2232] CFCs had become ubiquitous since the 1930s, because they were cheap, chemically stable and completely non-toxic. During the 1960s the use of CFCs exploded (Figure 143); they were used among other things in refrigerators, spray cans and air-conditioners and as foam blowing agents and solvents. CFCs are mixed into the atmosphere, some reaching the stratosphere, where they are broken down by high-energy solar ultraviolet radiation into free chlorine. Through complex interactions, these chlorine atoms react with ozone, essentially breaking down thousands of ozone molecules for each chlorine atom.[2233]

The shocking prospect of increasing skin cancer and cataracts caused politicians to react quickly. The Montreal protocol was signed in 1987, followed by the London (1990), Copenhagen (1992), Vienna (1995),

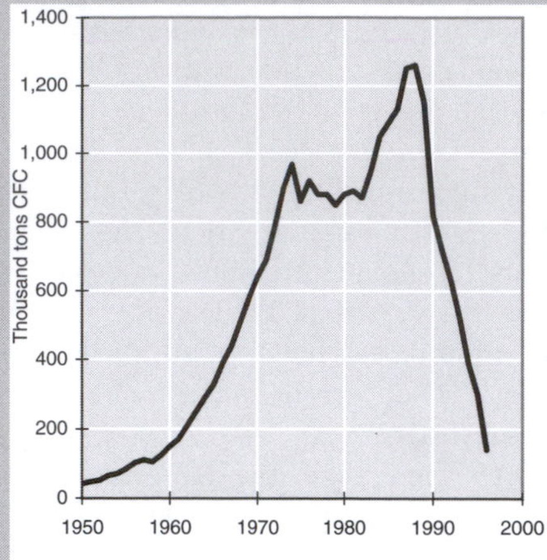

Figure 143 The annual global production of CFC gases, 1950–96, measured in tons weighted by ozone depletion potential. Source: Blackmore 1996:120, WI 1999b.[2234]

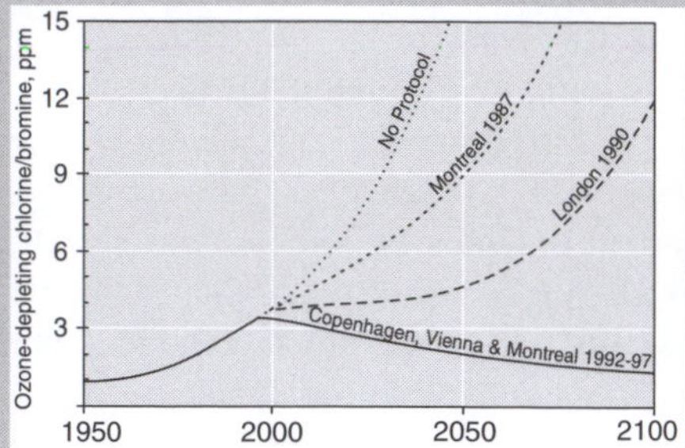

Figure 144 Concentration of ozone-depleting stratospheric chlorine/bromine, 1950–2100, without a protocol, with the Montreal (1987), London (1990), Copenhagen (1992), Vienna (1995) and Montreal (1997) protocols, assuming full compliance. Source: UNEP 1999a:5, WMO/UNEP 1994.

another Montreal (1997) and Beijing (1999) protocols. The aim of these international agreements was initially to halve the consumption of the five main CFC gases in relation to 1986 figures and later to ban them almost entirely.[2235] The expected result of the agreements can be seen in Figure 144.

The international cooperation has rapidly borne fruit: as can be seen in Figure 143, total production in 1996 was down below the production in 1960. At the same time, the total combined abundance of ozone-depleting compounds in the lower atmosphere peaked in about 1994 and is now slowly declining – actually faster than was predicted by the UN just four years earlier.[2236] The concentration of the ozone-depleting chlorine and bromine was predicted to peak in the stratosphere before the year 2000.[2237] The latest synthesis report of the UNEP ozone assessment predicts that "the ozone layer will slowly recover over the next 50 years."[2238] Likewise, the Antarctic ozone hole will slowly recover.[2239] Thus, today we have pretty much done what we can,[2240] ozone depletion is at its maximum and it will recover within the next 50 years.

The case of the depleted ozone layer and the solution through restrictive protocols is seen as a success story, in which the world community finally pulled itself together and put the environment before money. For this reason among others the ozone story is often quoted as a successful application of the principle of caution[2241] and of environmental awareness in general. However, it is worth pointing out that the implementation of the CFC ban was strictly profitable. It was actually relatively cheap to find substitutes for CFC (e.g. in refrigerators and spray cans[2242]) and at the same time the advantages were quite clear-cut.

In a report for Environment Canada, the Canadian EPA, it was estimated that the overall global cost until 2060 of the implementation of the CFC protocols was about 235 billion 1997 US dollars.[2243] By way of comparison, the overall advantage, stemming from avoided damages to fisheries, agriculture and outdoor materials was estimated to amount to some 459 billion 1997 US dollars, not even including about 333,500 fewer skin cancer deaths.[2244]

However, these are global figures accumulated over the next 63 years, which because of both the long time and the number of people easily get very large. While they clearly show that global intervention was justified, it is also important to get a feel for the actual, *personal* consequences of the thinning

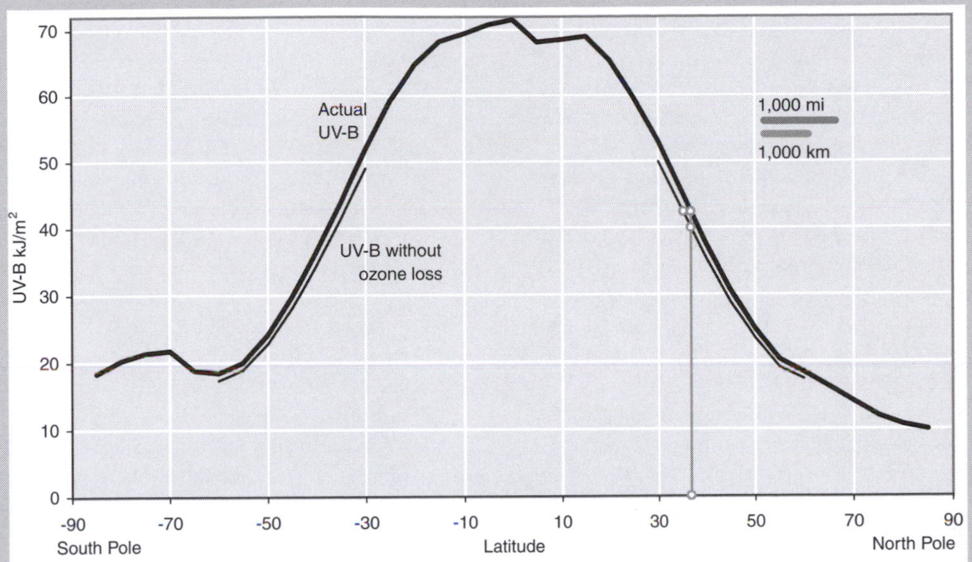

Figure 145 Average annual UV-B radiation with clouds and aerosols, depending on latitude.[2245] The ozone hole at Antarctica is evident to the far left. In mid-latitudes, a theoretical value of the UV-B radiation, had the ozone layer not been thinned.[2246] Source: Sabziparvar 1997, Sabziparvar *et al.* 1999, see also Newton and Ferlay 1996.

of the ozone layer. As a sociological study of the ozone debate points out, almost everyone "knows" that "the ozone layer is thinning, more sunlight is getting through, we're all going to get skin cancer, so you have to stay out of the sun."[2247] This is in no small part because the media will tell us about the "frightening" increases in skin cancer, "linked to increased UV levels penetrating Earth's depleted ozone layer."[2248] Indeed, in a study of the environmental concerns of British young people, the "loss of the ozone layer" was found to be the most worrying.[2249]

Although the skin cancer rate has increased dramatically over the twentieth century, the long latency period means that the increases we see today are due to much more mundane causes. As concluded in a recent study: "The skin cancer increase must be attributed to harmful solar UV-B levels existing even in the 1960s, accentuated later not by ozone depletion (which started only much later, by 1979) but by other causes, such as a longer human life span, better medical screening, increasing tendencies of sunbathing at beaches, etc., in affluent societies."[2250] However, the present-day thinning of the ozone layer and the concomitant rise in UV-B will cause more skin cancer in the future. Had the Montreal and consecutive protocols not been implemented, skin cancer would have more than tripled by 2100, but now it will cause a very much smaller excess of skin cancer.[2251]

About 95 percent of skin cancers today consist of the highly curable basal and squamous cell cancers, whereas the last 5 percent consist of the much more lethal melanoma skin cancer.[2252] In total, the US experiences about 50,000 new melanoma cases each year and about a million new basal and squamous cell cancers, with almost all mortality stemming from the melanomas.[2253] Assuming no change in behavior (sun exposure, etc.) and full compliance with the CFC protocols, it is estimated that the current ozone minimum will lead to more cancers in the future, reaching a maximum in 2060 of 27,000 extra annual skin cancers in the US, or an increase in total skin cancer of about 3 percent.[2254]

Since the vast majority of extra cancers will be the almost entirely curable skin cancers, the maximum extra deaths in 2060 in the US are estimated at about 350 or about 5 percent of all skin cancer deaths.

Thus, even at ozone depletion's greatest impact, it will cause a relatively slight increase in the cancer incidence and death rate. This can also be seen in a different light. Since more ozone is present at high latitudes and the sun has to penetrate a longer column of ozone, UV-B is much more intense at the equator than at high latitudes, as is evident in Figure 145. For the mid-latitudes and disregarding differences in local weather, a move from Edinburgh (55°N) to Madrid (40°N) would approximately double the average annual UV-B exposure, as would a move from Seattle (47°N) to New Orleans (30°N) or from the Falklands (52°S) to Buenos Aires (34°S).

If we look at a city on 36°53′N where the line starts on Figure 145 – this could be Fresno, California – there is an annual UV-B radiation of 42.4 kJ/m². Had the ozone layer not been depleted, the radiation would only have been 40 kJ/m² (the thin line below). The thinning of the ozone layer adds about 6 percent to the UV-B radiation.[2255] Now, the question is, how far south would you have to move in order to receive the same extra amount of UV-B radiation? The answer, as can be seen in Figure 145, is that 42.4 kJ/m² would have occurred in an ozone-full world at 35°17′N, or close to Bakersfield, California, some 179 km (111 miles) south of Fresno.[2256] This gives us a feel for how much more dangerous the world has become as a result of the ozone depletion.

That the ozone layer has been damaged and now is at its lowest level, allowing in more UV-B radiation, is equivalent on the mid-latitudes[2257] to moving approximately 200 km (124 miles) closer to the equator – a move smaller than that from Manchester to London, Chicago to Indianapolis, Albany to New York, Lyons to Marseilles, Trento to Florence, Stuttgart to Düsseldorf or Christchurch to Wellington.[2258]

Are there other causes?

With the publication of Nigel Calder's *The Manic Sun* in 1997 a renewed focus was brought on the sun as another important factor in the explication of increasing global temperatures. At times, the ensuing debate has had a tendency to assume either that only the greenhouse gases mattered or that only the sun determines the temperature. However, it is much more likely that both can be seen as partial causes of global warming. Since IPCC mentions solar influences only briefly and incorporates only the smaller direct forcing,[2259] it is probable that including indirect solar activity will also lead to a lowering of the estimates of the CO_2 warming effect.

It has been known for a long time that there is a correlation between solar activity and temperature. Probably, solar brightness has increased about 0.4 percent over the past 200–300 years, causing an increase of about 0.4°C (see solar irradiance in Figure 139), and the trend over the last decades is equivalent to another 0.4°C to 2100.[2260] A recent AOCGM study showed that the increase in direct solar irradiation over the past 30 years is responsible for about 40 percent of the observed global warming.[2261]

However, an even more intriguing solar connection, and the one that Nigel Calder pointed to, is the indirect effect, established through research at the Danish Meteorological Institute. Here, two researchers, Eigil Friis-Christensen and Knud Lassen, pointed out a clear correlation between the duration of the solar sunspot cycle and the Earth's average temperature.[2262] Figure 146 shows the correlation between measured average temperature and the sunspot cycle duration for the period for which accurate temperature measurements exist, but the researchers have actu-

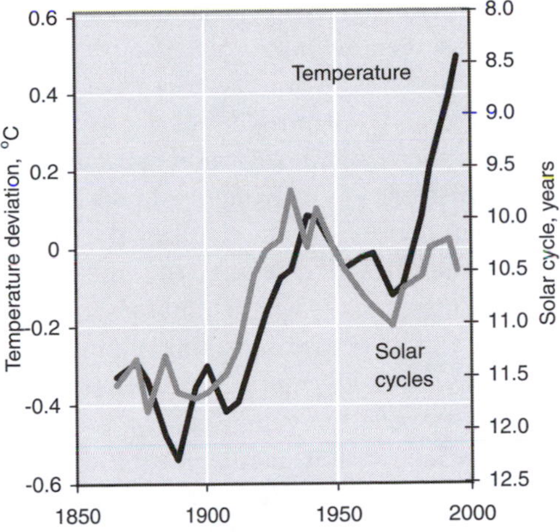

Figure 146 The correlation between sunspot period and Northern Hemisphere average temperature change, 1865–1995. Update of Friis-Christensen and Lassen 1991:699. In order to use the newest data with few assumptions, a smaller smoothing filter has been chosen, giving a poorer fit over the rest of the graph, resulting in a gap between solar cycle decrease and temperature increase for 1900–40. Source: Thejll and Lassen 2000.

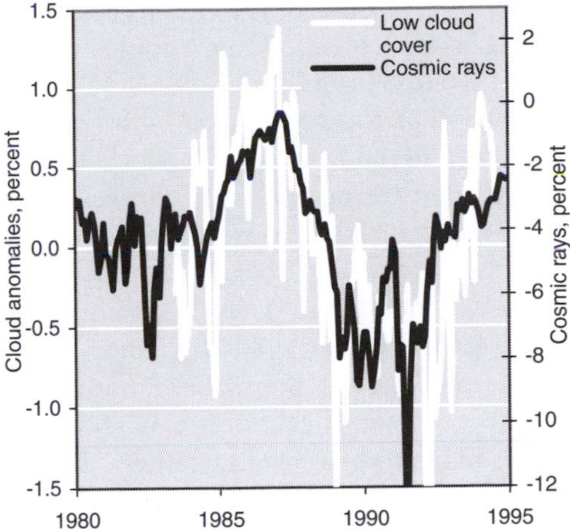

Figure 147 The relationship between the change in global low-level cloud cover (>680hPa) and the change of incoming cosmic radiation. Source: Marsh and Svensmark 2000.

ally achieved an impressive correlation going back as far as 1550.[2263] Moreover, other researchers have found similar connections going further back and using different temperature measures.[2264]

One long-standing criticism of the theory has been that there was no clear causal correlation between the two curves in Figure 146. How should sunspot cycle duration be able to affect the temperature? However, new research seems to have found the connection, which not only explains the link between the sunspot cycle and temperature, but also brings the problematic though decisive clouds back into the picture. Today, about 65 percent[2265] of the Earth is covered with clouds, an extremely significant factor when determining the warming effect of CO_2. This is because the clouds help to keep the Earth cool by reflecting the sun's rays, while at the same time warming it by keeping in the heat. The overall effect for low-level clouds is a cooling of the Earth, so that more low-level clouds mean lower temperatures.[2266]

But Svensmark, along with several others, has shown that there seems to be a clear connection between global low-level cloud cover and incoming cosmic radiation, as can be seen in Figure 147.[2267] The explanation is probably that cosmic rays produce ions, which together with small particles in the atmosphere can create the basis for the development of low-level clouds.[2268] And more cosmic radiation is the result of lower solar activity, which in turn correlates with longer sunspot cycle duration.[2269]

A number of unanswered questions and unsolved scientific problems still remain in these theoretical relationships.[2270] But the point is that the sunspot theory has created a possible correlation in that a shorter sunspot cycle duration, such as the one we are experiencing now, means more intense solar activity, less cosmic radiation, fewer low-level clouds, and therefore higher temperatures. This theory also has the tremendous advantage, compared to the greenhouse theory, that it can explain the temperature changes from

1860 to 1950, which the rest of the climate scientists with a shrug of the shoulders have accredited to "natural variation."

Notice that the connection between temperature and the sunspot cycle seems to have deteriorated during the last 10–30 years, with temperatures outpacing sunspot activity in Figure 146. Most likely we are instead seeing an increasing signal, probably from greenhouse gases like CO_2. Such a find exactly underscores that neither solar variation nor greenhouse gases can alone explain the entire temperature record. Rather, the fact that the emerging greenhouse gas signal only appears now seems to indicate once again that the estimated CO_2 warming effect needs to be lowered. One such IPPC-loyal study finds that the solar hypothesis explains about 57 percent of the temperature deviations and that the data suggest a climate sensitivity of 1.7°C, a 33 percent reduction of the IPPC best estimate.[2271]

Are the scenarios realistic?

Forecasting a century into the future is a business fraught with pitfalls, as we can easily tell from past forecasts.[2272] Some predictions turned out to be spectacularly wrong and some surprisingly prescient, but of course the problem is telling one from the other without the advantage of hindsight.[2273] Perhaps the greatest danger in prognoses is that we tend to underestimate how technical innovations can make the original worry moot. In the words of one modeler:

> One hundred years ago icebergs were a major climatic threat impeding travel between North America and Europe. 1,513 lives ended when the British liner Titanic collided with one on 14 April 1912. 50 years later jets overflew liners. Anticipating the solution to the iceberg danger required understanding not only the rates and paths on which icebergs travel but the ways humans travel, too.[2274]

Yet, with climate change spanning centuries, we must somehow make a sensible attempt to predict the areas of our behavior most important to global warming.[2275] By far the most important variable in this respect is our long-term emissions of CO_2 from fossil fuels.[2276]

We will first look at the traditional IPCC scenarios, then the 40 new scenarios and finally we will come back to what ought to be the central issue of all scenario-making – how much CO_2 will we actually emit. To remain with the metaphor above, it seems that the scenarios are more concerned about plotting a better course for Titanic than investigating the likeliness of alternative means of travel.

To standardize the global climate forecasts, IPCC in 1992 formulated six scenarios (named IS92a–f) of future population and economic growth, deforestation rates, energy supplies, environmental efforts, etc.[2277] The IS92a, in particular, is still important, as most predictions until now have been based on this business-as-usual scenario – what will happen if we do not change our behavior towards reducing greenhouse gas emissions.[2278] However, some of the important factors in IS92a have been clearly off target.[2279] For instance, the IS92a expects 8.4 billion people in 2025[2280] which is almost half a billion beyond what the UN expects today (see Figure 11) and some 11.3 billion in 2100, or just about a billion beyond the current expectation.[2281] Equivalently, they somewhat surprisingly expect more than 82 percent of all tropical forests to have been cleared by 2100.[2282]

The IS92a also expects the concentration of the greenhouse gas methane (CH_4) to continue to increase.[2283] (Surprisingly, the new scenarios make the same assumption.)[2284] Yet the growth rate of methane has been declining and seems to approach a steady state.[2285] This would lead to an overestimate of warming in 2100 by at least 5 percent.[2286]

The most important problem comes with the IS92a CO_2 scenario and its typical use in climate simulations. Here, the IPCC have assumed that the CO_2 concentration will grow

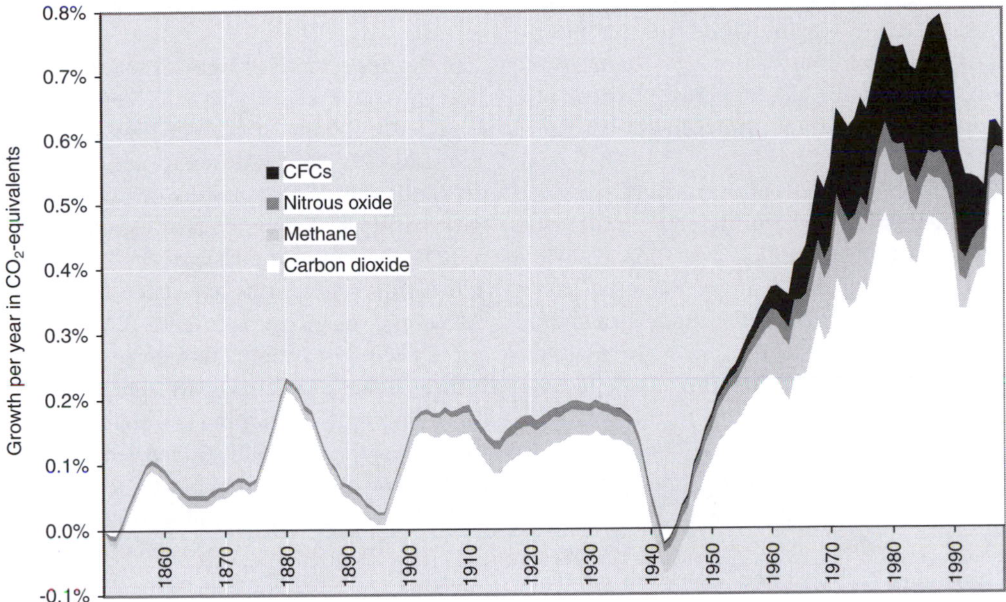

Figure 148 Growth per year in greenhouse gases, 1851–1998, measured in CO_2 equivalent growth rate. 5-year averages. Source: Hansen and Sato 2000, IPCC 1996:92–3.

by 0.64 percent per year, from 1990 to 2100.[2287] However, this is much higher than the observed growth rate. In the 1980s, CO_2 concentration grew by 0.47 percent, in the 1990s by just 0.43 percent.[2288] Focusing on such small percentages is not merely pedantic; since these are cumulative growth rates, the IPCC estimate means that CO_2 concentration will double in 109 years, whereas a sustained growth at the observed rate means a CO_2 doubling in 154 years.[2289]

Nevertheless, focusing on CO_2 alone is not particularly sensible, since *all* greenhouse gases contribute to global warming. Consequently, the impact from other gases is often translated into CO_2, such that we only need to think about one greenhouse gas.[2290] Counting in CH_4, N_2O and the CFCs, the IPCC finds that the equivalent growth rate of CO_2 alone would be 0.85 percent.[2291] This is also way above the current measured rate.

In Figure 148 you can see the growth since 1851 expressed in CO_2 equivalent growth rate. In the 1980s the growth rate peaked at 0.76 percent, but since 1990 it has been down to just 0.58 percent.[2292] And again, this is not just pedantic, since an increase of 0.85 percent doubles the effective CO_2 in just 82 years, compared with the 120 years needed by the measured current growth rate.[2293]

Yet most standard computer simulations use an even higher value for CO_2 increase, namely 1 percent.[2294] This is done for simplicity and convenience, though the IPCC admits this is "arbitrary" and "on the high side."[2295] Again, this makes the doubling time CO_2 just below 70 years, compared to the empirical estimate of 120 years. It is truly hard to understand why modelers programming amazingly complex computer models, with millions of carefully assembled data points from every part of the world, from the surface to the stratosphere, running for weeks and months on expensive supercomputers, nevertheless have chosen to model *the* central point in question – the accumulation of the most important greenhouse gases – with an arbitrary, round figure like 1.0 percent instead of the more accurate and much lower 0.6 percent.[2296]

The consequence is that the models run way too fast, predicting warming coming almost twice as fast (70 versus 120 years) or, equivalently, predicting much more warming in a given time.[2297] Typically, the models that we are presented with in the press are exactly these sorts of models that run much faster than the IPCC scenario, itself running faster than the observations. Thus, *Scientific American* shows us the 1 percent CO_2 increase in the Hadley model from Figure 138, and informs us that we should see about a 3°C temperature increase by 2100, without mentioning the unrealistic assumption of the 1 percent increase itself.[2298]

Are the scenarios realistic? The 40 new scenarios

Turning to the 40 new IPCC scenarios, the modelers have explicitly abandoned the idea of predicting the future and instead talk about projections and possible futures.[2299] As one of the modeling groups fairly honestly point out, the IPCC scenarios are "an attempt at 'computer-aided storytelling.'"[2300]

Some of the interesting trends in the six marker/illustrative scenarios are depicted in Figure 149 and Figure 150. First, note that all of the IPCC scenarios were set from the beginning to fit two quantitative targets, population and wealth.[2301] Thus, the population and total wealth are *not* the outcome of a model but the result of an initial choice.[2302]

With regards to population development, we see in Figure 149 how IPCC has chosen to let B2 follow the UN medium variant (as in Figure 11), whereas A2 approximately follows the high variant and the other scenarios[2303] the low variant.[2304]

In the upper right of Figure 149, we see how the emissions of SO_2 in all scenarios are expected to be much smaller than originally assumed in IS92a.[2305] Although there has been no doubt that SO_2 emissions would go down with sufficient affluence (see e.g. Figure 97, p. 177)[2306] a closer analysis of the speed with which sulfur emissions have been reduced in the EU and the US (see Figure 91, p. 172)[2307] has led to the reassessment. To a large extent the future reductions in SO_2 are due to restrictions placed by developing countries in order to decrease local air pollution. A recent World Bank report pointed out that the costs of air pollution in China are about 8 percent of GDP whereas the abatement costs would be 1–2.5 percent of GDP.[2308] Thus, it is no surprise that policies to cut down SO_2 are already being implemented.

The SO_2 emissions are important, because sulfur aerosols cool the climate. Thus, if emissions are cut sooner, we will be unable to postpone as much of the warming as under IS92a. These new, lower emission scenarios are therefore the primary reason why the 2001 IPCC high temperature prediction for 2100 has increased.[2309] This problem we will deal with below. However, since outdoor air pollution is a major killer and was expected by the IS92a to increase even further in importance, it is also important to point out that the dramatic reduction in SO_2 emissions are a great boon to human health and furthermore an important improvement to vulnerable ecosystems.

The income per person generated in developing and developed countries is shown in the lower part of Figure 149. Generally, we see that all scenarios describe futures that are more affluent than today, both in the developed and the developing world.[2310] Moreover, income inequality is dramatically lowered, and even faster than in IS92a, from 6:1 today to a range of 3:1 to 1.4:1, as described in Figure 35, p. 75. Finally, it is perhaps worth noting

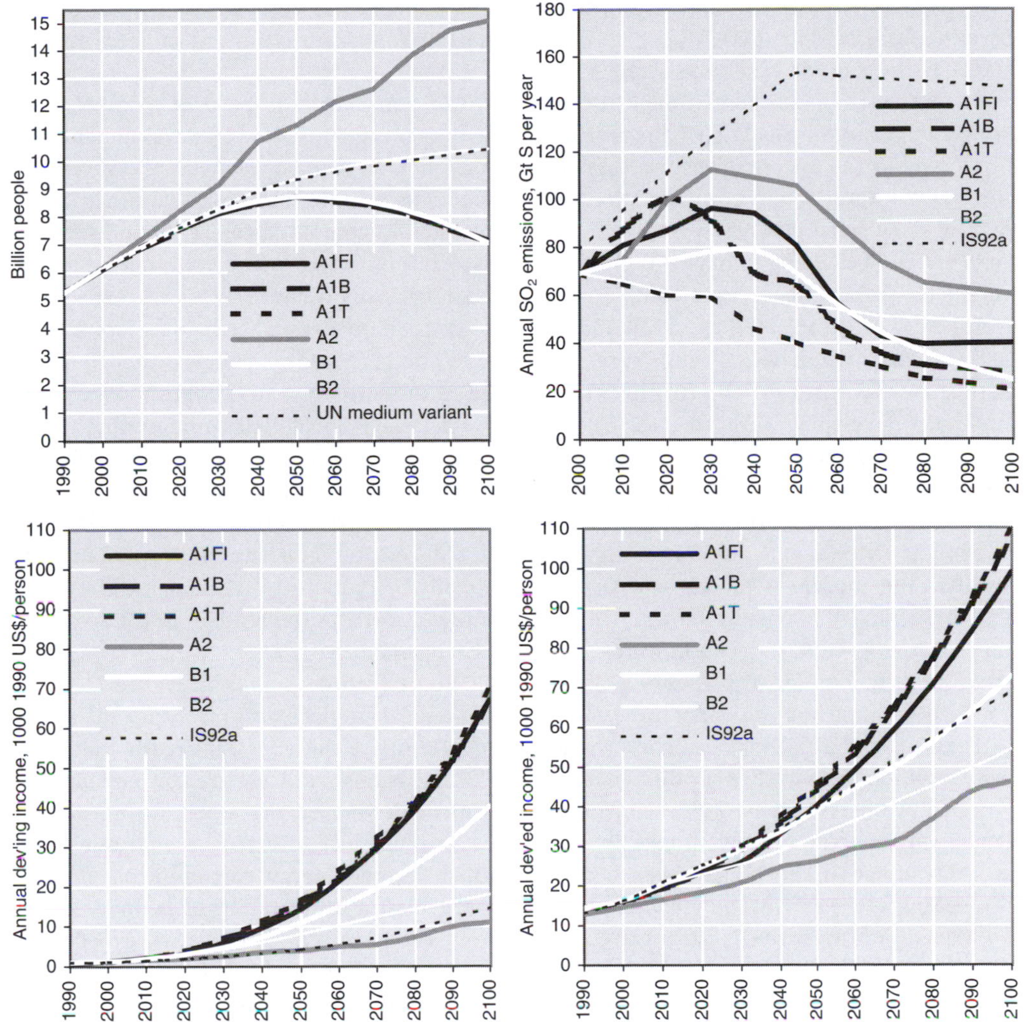

Figure 149 IPCC scenarios, 1990–2100. Population in billion, with UN medium variant for reference. Annual SO_2 emissions in billion tons, 2000–2100, with IS92a for reference. Annual income for developing and developed countries, 1990 US$ per person, 1990–2100, with IS92a for reference. Note that as these studies come from six very different modeling teams, one should be careful not to compare small differences.[2311] Source: IPCC 2000b, 2001a:table II.1.8, IPCC/DDC 2001 and data from Figure 11.

that even for the most pessimistic of scenarios, at the end of the century the average person in the developing world will be almost as well off as the average person in the industrialized world is today, and in all other scenarios *much* richer. This provides a reassuring background for the quote of Julian Simon, opening this book: "Within a century or two, all nations and most of humanity will be at or above today's Western living standards."[2312]

There is an exceptional economic difference between the A1-scenarios and all other scenarios. (Although the A1FI seems to do slightly worse for the industrialized countries, this is merely due to slightly varying assumptions between models – the A1FI for the same models as the A1T, do exactly as well.)[2313] To the extent that this is an expression of true differences in economic capability[2314] it reminds us that we have to ask ourselves whether the marginally improved environment that we get from B1 instead of A1 is worth so much that we would be willing to have our children give up 50 percent more in income in the developed world ($73,000 vs. $110,000 in 2100).[2315] And we have to ask ourselves whether it is worth it for the future inhabitants in the developing world to give up some 75 percent more income to live in a B1-world ($40,000 vs. $70,000).

Remarkably, the scenario authors, without any explicit criteria, rank the four scenarios, giving B1 the top grade "good" whereas A1 only gets a "fair."[2316] Considering that the difference for the world in economic terms is some $7,000 trillion (or in present-day value some $107 trillion – more than three times the present global GDP)[2317] such a hand-waving opinion seems rather cavalier. In order to reach a prudent judgement of scenario, we have to consider both the advantages but also the disadvantages in choosing B1 over, say, A1, both looking at the environment *and* the economy. We will return to this issue at the end of this chapter, as it is central to the entire question of dealing with global warming.

Since the scenarios need to make predictions for all greenhouse gas emissions, they also incorporate estimates of forest area (causing CO_2 emission when cut down or sequestration when extended). Thus, looking at Figure 150, top left, we can see the plausible development of forest area over the 150 years from 1950. This shows for all but the A2 scenario a *larger* forest area in 2100 than in 2000. Since the A2 marker scenario had no forest data, the other two A2 scenarios are shown – also indicating the amount of variability within the individual storylines. A2 MiniCAM shows a significant decline of world forests (about 17 percent reduction), in line with a relatively poor and populous world, whereas the A2 AIM scenario actually shows a slight increase of forest area.[2318]

The remarkable 35 percent forest increase in B1 is primarily driven by developments that may not appear so realistic, however. The modelers assume that despite a much higher population compared to e.g. A1 in 2100 (10.4 vs. 7 billion) there will be less need for cropland, basically because yields are expected to more than quadruple in the developing countries and because it is believed that there will be a dramatic consumer shift away from Western style meat consumption, due to both health and environmental concerns.[2319] All in all, it is assumed that from 2050 to 2100, cropland can be reduced by 27 percent.[2320] Thanks to reduced animal production, grasslands will equally be reduced by 32 percent.[2321] We will return shortly to the realism in the scenario's driving assumptions.

The final three graphs in Figure 150 show the crucial energy assumptions for the scenarios. These are the ones that really matter for CO_2 emissions and they are consequently the central drivers of the warming predictions (shown in Figure 137). Most scenarios expect a much higher energy consumption – for A1 more than a quintupling of primary energy over the century. Only B1 is expected to reduce its energy need from mid-century, bringing the total consumption at the end of the century back down to its present level.

The two central drivers determining the CO_2 emissions are total energy consumption and share of energy from fossil fuels. The first really depends on how much can be produced by one unit of energy. As we saw in Figure 68 (p. 126), the energy efficiency for both the US and the UK has been steadily increasing, and the past 50 years of US development are shown in the top right graph in Figure 150. Since the first oil crisis, US energy efficiency has increased so as to double every 50 years.[2322] All scenarios assume that efficiency will continue to increase but at very different rates – whereas A2 will stumble along with

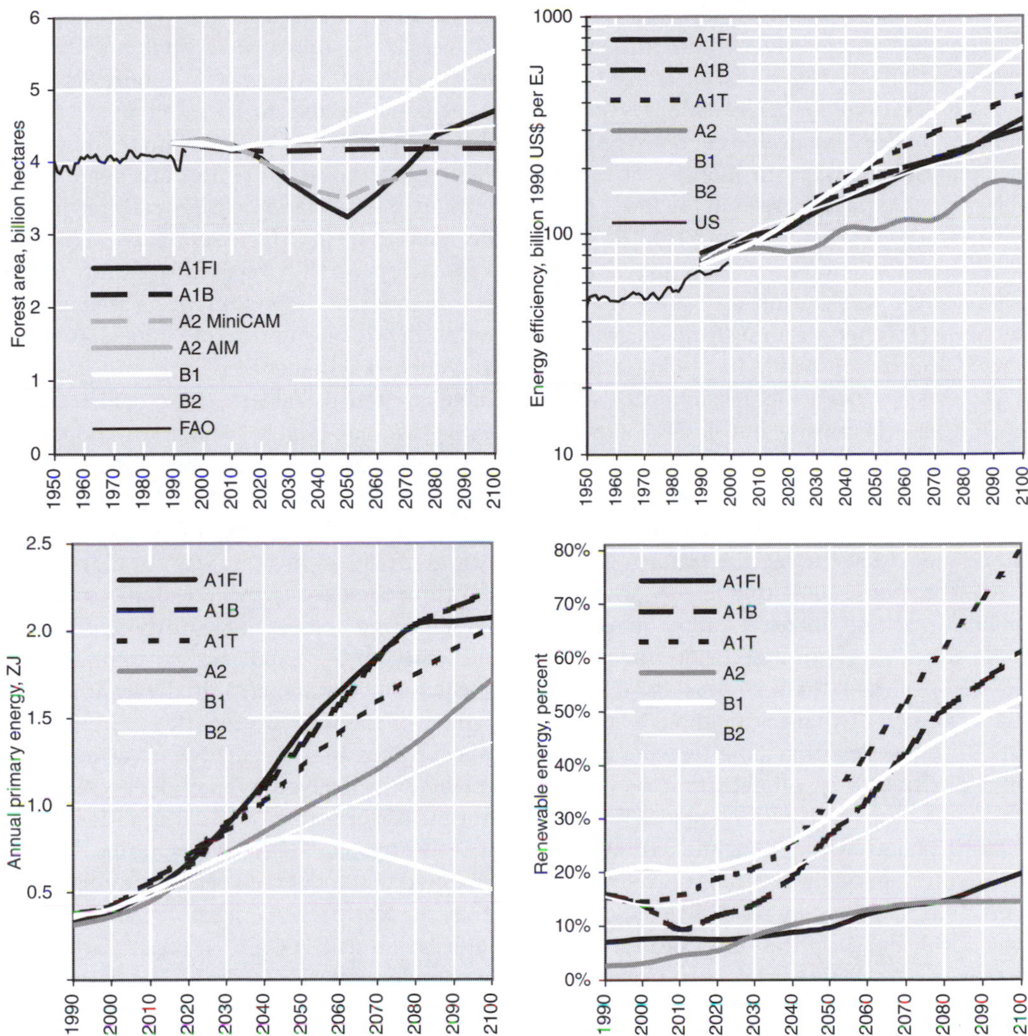

Figure 150 IPCC scenarios, 1990–2100. Forest area in billion hectares, with FAO statistic from 1950–94 for reference. Note that the A2 marker scenario has no forest data; the two other A2 scenarios are shown here. Energy efficiency, billion 1990 US$ per exajoule, 1990–2100, with US energy efficiency for reference. Annual primary energy in zetajoule (1,000 EJ) , 1990–2100. Percentage of energy from renewable sources, 1990–2100. Note that as these studies come from six very different modeling teams, one should be careful not to compare small differences. Source: IPCC 2000b, and data from Figs. 11, 60, and 68.

little improvement over the century (doubling every 94 years), B1 assumes a high improvement in efficiency, equivalent to a doubling every 32 years.[2323] Which will be the correct magnitude of improvement[2324] hinges to a large part on the cost of energy – if energy is cheap, there is little incentive to increase efficiency, whereas costly energy will speed up efficiency improvements.[2325] Yet, for both coal, oil and gas, prices are expected to be *lower* in B1 than in A1, primarily because the higher energy consumption in A1 will drive up energy prices.[2326] This would indicate that *ceteris paribus* energy efficiency improvements should actually be *higher*, not lower in A1.

The other driver for CO_2 emissions is the use of fossil fuels vs. renewable energy.[2327] Again, all scenarios envisage an increase of renewables in percentage, as seen in the lower right of Figure 150.[2328] However, the A2 and the A1FI only slightly increase their percentage, whereas A1T will end up with more than 80 percent of its energy coming from renewables. This is the reason why A1T despite a much higher energy use will curb total CO_2 emissions from mid-century and closely follow B1, as seen in Figure 136. Again, the question is, why does the substitution happen. Again, the relative price of different energy sources would seem to be the decisive factor.

All scenarios assume that energy prices for oil and gas will increase rather markedly, some suggesting a tripling before the end of the century, and the scenarios also assume that coal prices will increase, though less rapidly.[2329] Likewise, all assume that the energy price of renewables will decline, as we saw in the energy chapter (Figure 72, p. 131).[2330]

Most models assume that the cost of solar and wind energy will drop to 2–5¢/kWh, which "makes them increasingly competitive as coal, oil, and gas prices continue to rise."[2331] Yet, as the fossil fuel price only makes up a smaller part of the total electricity cost,[2332] and as fossil fuel efficiency increases also continue to reduce costs,[2333] the substitution from fossil fuels to renewables really hinges on whether prices of renewables will decrease so fast as to outcompete ever cheaper fossil fuel energy.

Thus, when deciding the future CO_2 emissions, the two most important factors seem to be to what extent energy efficiency will increase faster or slower and to what extent renewables will get cheaper than fossil fuels. However, this was not the primary approach for the IPCC scenario modelers, especially for the B-scenarios. Here, it is not technical progress and economic reasons that limit the use of fossil fuels but rather "environmental concerns."[2334] The modelers tell us straight out that when coal loses out to renewables in B1 it could be due to its being perceived as dirty or it could be because of increasing costs – but "such processes are not considered explicitly in this scenario."[2335] Basically, it is just decided that in B1, renewables win. This approach is actually repeated for most of the major decisions in the scenarios, based mainly on a surprising number of somewhat naïve and clichéd statements.[2336] Summing up, the modelers tell us that the B1 scenario is not value-free, but largely "depict situations and conditions as one would hope they would emerge."[2337]

Likewise, the basic decision of the level of energy efficiency increase was merely made to adjust to the basic storyline – doing "parameter adjusting to meet the key driving forces of the storylines."[2338] But instead of choosing such crucial parameters initially from the storylines of the various scenarios it would possibly be more useful to analyze to what extent it is actually likely that renewables will or will not outperform fossil fuels. The difference is well illustrated in the A1-scenarios. If it is assumed that fossil fuels retain the edge, as in A1FI, the world will be rich but go on emitting large amounts of CO_2.[2339] If rapid technological development is assumed as in A1T, where the solar power cost could drop to less than 0.8¢/kWh, we would get a world which will be just as rich but emit little CO_2.[2340]

Thus, what we need to know is which world is the more likely – A1FI or A1T – and what we should do, if we want to steer more towards a scenario as in A1T?[2341] Although this is arguably the single most important problem for the scenario discussion concerning global warming, this issue is never addressed, because of the modelers' original intention of regarding *all* scenarios as likely.

But it seems patently implausible that most of the scenarios are likely. As we saw in the chapter on energy, there is sufficient fossil fuel, especially coal, to cover many centuries.

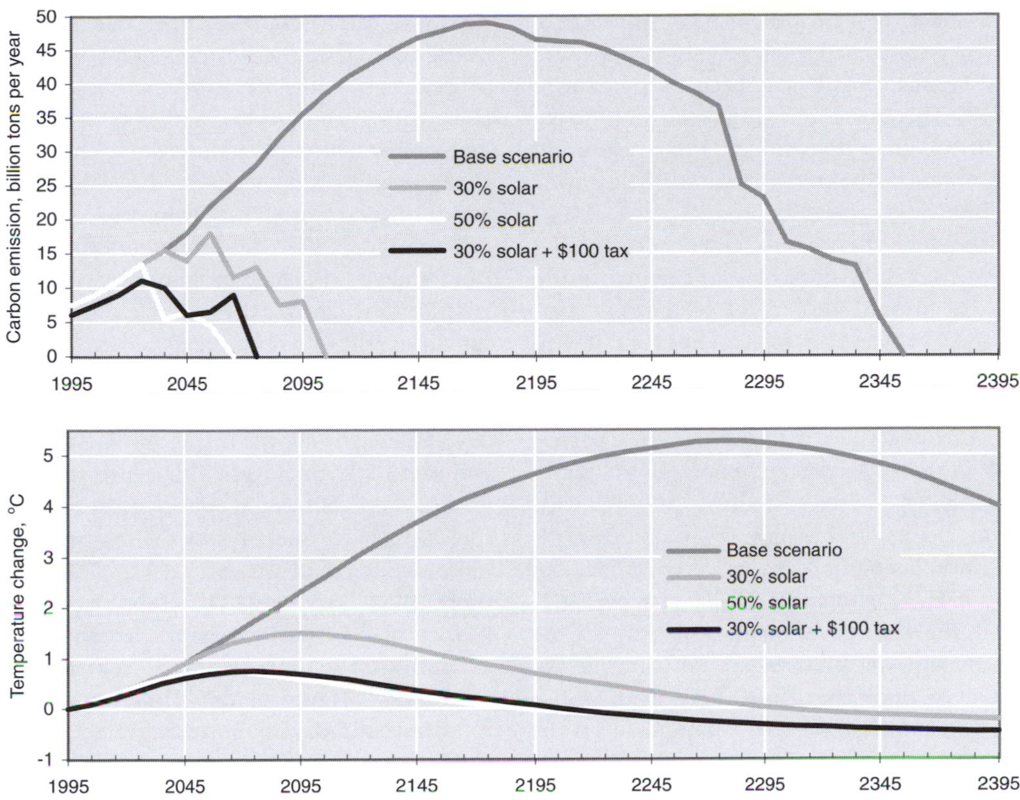

Figure 151 Top panel: Global carbon emission, 1995–2395, with four scenarios. A base scenario with no substitution towards renewables, two scenarios with solar power price declining by the current 50 percent per decade and a more conservative 30 percent per decade, with a 2/kWh lower bound, and finally a 30 percent solar power decline per decade with a US$100 carbon tax. Lower panel: Change in global mean temperature, with the same four scenarios. Source: Chakravorty *et al.* 1997: 1222–3, Ahmed 1994.

However, we also found that renewable sources such as wind and solar energy are decreasing rapidly in price, with wind almost competitive and solar energy competitive within two or three decades.[2342] Actually, the price for solar energy estimated in A1FI to be reached at the end of the century is by most analyses placed just a few decades away.[2343] Thus, it seems plausible that renewable energy will by itself or with fairly little "nudging" be competitive before mid-century.

Researchers in the *Journal of Political Economy* addressed exactly this issue with a major model to investigate the consequences of more expensive fossil fuels and ever cheaper renewable fuels.[2344] For simplicity, they only looked at coal, gas and oil as the fossil fuels, and solar electricity as a currently expensive but potentially unlimited source of energy (see Figure 73).[2345] Any other energy source we might dream up in the future – an obvious example would be hydrogen fusion, which incidentally the IPCC also leaves out of consideration[2346] – could equally be modeled and would make the model even more compelling.[2347] Their findings are depicted in Figure 151. In the top panel we see the base-line scenario with no technological advances in solar power production. This will mean very little substitution to renewables fuels. With no price change on solar power, most of the energy production will eventually move to coal, and it will take the world 370 years to move completely to solar energy, and then only because fossil fuels become too expensive.[2348] This causes the carbon emissions to be slightly higher than the A1FI, because even this scenario expects a slight cost improvement in renewables.[2349]

However, the model more realistically shows that if the price of solar energy continues its present decline of 50 percent per decade, as it has been forecast by many, it will become competitive by 2030–40.[2350] This, of course, will bring about a massive substitution of fossil fuels with solar energy, beginning in the 2030s and ending in the 2060s.[2351] Actually, 98.5 percent of all coal reserves will never be used, because solar power will become cheaper.[2352] The underlying idea is that if solar energy gets ever cheaper and fossil fuels get ever more expensive, it is plainly unlikely that we would continue to use large amounts of fossil fuels in the long run. (Of course, in the short run – and even on a 20–30-year scale – huge investments in fossil energy technology, such as power plants and gasoline cars, makes the transition "sticky" in that local transition only happens when the worn-out technology gets replaced.)[2353] Fundamentally, this model shows that the A1FI seems fairly implausible and that the carbon emissions future is much more likely to follow the A1T, the B1 or even a lower trajectory.

The model also shows a conservative price decline estimate of just 30 percent per decade for solar power. This means later competitiveness and later substitution. Nevertheless, solar power use will begin to be used in the 2040s, increasing throughout the rest of the century, taking over all sectors by 2105.[2354] Here the emissions scenario still looks like something between A1T and A1B, and even here, 92 percent of all coal reserves will never be used.[2355] Finally, the model includes a scenario where the price decline is still 30 percent per decade but a (global) tax on carbon emissions of US$100 per ton is included. Such a tax will naturally cause less fossil fuel consumption (more about that effect later) and it will make solar power relatively cheaper, causing earlier substitution. The effect is that the total carbon emission will be of the same order as the more rapid price decline scenario (i.e. below B1). However, and not shown here, this tax will also cause a great deal of economic disruption, and we will come back to this issue, discussing to what extent it will be worthwhile for the world to pay that extra price for less CO_2 emissions.

The consequence for global temperature development is shown in the lower panel of Figure 151. With no price decrease in solar power, the world would continue using fossil fuels for a long time, causing the temperature to rise more than 2°C by 2100 and peak at more than 5°C in 2275 before declining. (Notice that these temperature estimates are generally lower than the IPCC central estimates, as in Figure 137.)[2356] However, with a more realistic development for solar power, the temperature will increase only by 0.7°C over the next 50 years and then decline. Even for the more pessimistic solar scenario, the temperature increase will be just 1.5°C over the next 100 years, and decline from there, reaching the 1995 temperature in 2195.[2357]

This more realistic model contains several key points. First, it shows that global warming is not an ever worsening problem. In fact, under any reasonable scenario of technological change and without policy intervention, carbon emissions will not reach the levels of A1FI and they will decline towards the end of the century, as we move towards ever cheaper renewable energy sources.[2358] Second, temperatures will increase much less than the maximum estimates from IPCC – it is likely that the temperature will be at or below the B1 estimate (less than 2°C in 2100) and the temperature will certainly not increase even further into the twenty-second century. Third, and perhaps most importantly, this suggests that we have been looking the wrong way when trying to handle global warming. Most political discussions and certainly the international agreement in Kyoto, which we will discuss below, focus on *limiting* carbon emissions, through taxes, quotas or bans. While this will lower present-day emissions, it also carries a huge price tag in lower economic growth, of the order of 1–2 percent of our GDP.

However, what matters much more in the coming transition to a non-fossil fuel future is the relative cost of solar power, wind power and fusion compared to carbon-based energy sources.[2359] Thus, the truly important point is to make sure these renewable energy sources rapidly decrease in price, and this again requires substantially increased funding for much more research.[2360] Moreover, the cost of such energy research would be orders of magnitude cheaper than the cost of limiting carbon emissions. The current US research and development cost for renewable energy is about $200 million per year.[2361] Even a tenfold increase to $2 billion a year would pale beside the cost of even a small-scale carbon intervention (a cost of 1 percent GDP would for the US be about $80 billion a year) and a $100 carbon tax would generate about $200 billion a year.[2362]

To sum up, the previous IPCC business-as-usual scenario and its usage as background for a 1 percent CO_2 increase lead to overestimates in the speed of global warming.

Furthermore, the IPCC decision to treat all scenarios as likely means that a scenario such as A1FI is plausible: although fossil fuel prices soar and solar power price plummets, we will still predominantly use fossil fuel at the end of the century. Yet, such a scenario is unlikely under reasonable technological assumptions. Rather, more plausible assumptions point towards almost complete fossil fuel substitution over the twenty-first century, drastically limiting global carbon emissions, and restricting temperature increases at or below the B1 temperature. This more realistic understanding also makes us focus on what may be needed to nudge the future towards a more A1T-like development – the need to make renewable energy competitive through intensified research.

What seems necessary is to understand that we will undoubtedly still use fossil fuels for many years to come. In order to handle global warming, we need not necessarily phase out fossil fuels rapidly. Instead we need to make sure that, through sufficient research funding, sun, wind and fusion will become competitive energy sources before or by mid-century. This will cost much less and give rise to only a smaller temperature increase.

Consequences: agriculture

We also need to discuss the consequences of global warming. Here, let us leave the discussion about the IPCC scenarios, theories and alternative causes and instead make the conservative assumption that the IPCC predictions are generally correct. With this – conservative – proviso we will investigate the consequences of global warming and how they are best handled.

The first issue we will look at is the question of agriculture. When Isaac Asimov and Frederik Pohl looked at global warming, they found it would cut agricultural productivity drastically.[2363] Continuing their sinister tone, they pointed out that "this could well imply famines, even some quite large-scale ones."[2364] However, this question has been thoroughly investigated by the IPPC. They have studied the agricultural impacts by imagining a world with a doubled CO_2 level. With the models the IPCC uses for agricultural production, this means a 4.0–5.2°C temperature increase – thus at the high end or even beyond the marker scenario outcomes.[2365] Moreover, the IPCC imagines this world to take place in 2060, when we would expect temperatures to have increased even less. Consequently, this study should be considered to be a worst-case scenario.

The result can be seen in Table 7.[2366] First, the IPCC investigated the effect of the

Table 7 Change in percentage of cereal production in the event of an equilibrium doubling of CO_2 in 2060 (causing 2.5–5.2°C temperature increase) compared to a world without warming. Intervals from three different climate models, and results from four degrees of realism. Source: IPCC 1996b:451, from Rosenzweig and Parry 1994:136.

Scenario	World	Industrial countries	Developing countries
Temperature increase only	−11 to −20	−4 to −24	−14 to −16
+ CO_2 fertilizer effect	−1 to −8	−4 to +11	−9 to −11
+ light adaptation	0 to −5	+2 to +11	−9 to −13
+ moderate adaptation	−2 to +1	+4 to +14	−6 to −7

temperature increase itself. A temperature increase will produce both winners and losers, but because the computer models still have difficulty producing reliable regional predictions it is difficult to define the effects as regards individual countries.[2367] It is assumed, however, that there will be an overall increase in rainfall of between 10 and 15 percent.[2368] All in all, if all that happens is a drastic temperature increase, a slight precipitation increase and yet farmers go on as if nothing had happened, it is no wonder that the world's cereal production would be reduced by 11 to 20 percent (the first row of Table 7).[2369]

This hypothetical situation would have an equally drastic effect on both industrialized and developing countries, although the industrial countries would experience a higher degree of variation. It is, however, important to comment on these two percentages: since even the most pessimistic evaluation from the UK Met Office expects that cereal production will grow dramatically over the next 50 years, these falls do not mean that overall production will fall. A 1999 study using the Met Office model estimates that in 2080 production might be not 94 percent greater than today but only 90 percent greater.[2379]

Most plants (especially wheat and rice) grow considerably better when there is more CO_2 in the atmosphere – CO_2 actually works as a fertilizer.[2371] Moreover, a higher temperature usually further enhances the CO_2 fertilizing effect.[2372] Average productivity will increase by about 30 percent although the variations can be between −10 percent and as much as +80 percent.[2373] Naturally, if this effect is taken into account, production declines will be smaller, and this is reflected in the second row in Table 7.

The light adjustment refers to the fact that individual farmers might adjust the planting date and perhaps change to another variety of the same crop. The moderate adjustment refers to changing the planting date by more than a month, changing to a different crop or perhaps extending irrigation.[2374] Both changes are clearly sensible to expect as responses over a 50–100 year period.[2375]

Thus, looking at the global outcome in the bottom row of Table 7, it is clear that even a rather high temperature increase will not be particularly damaging in terms of agricultural production. In fact, the 2001 IPCC report finds that the effects "of climate change on agriculture after adaptation are estimated to result in small percentage changes in global income, and these changes tend to be *positive* for a moderate global warming, especially when the effects of CO_2 fertilization are taken into account."[2376]

There is, however, a relatively large difference between the relative outcome of global warming for the industrialized world and the developing world. Generally speaking, the industrialized countries will gain both the advantage of a longer growing season and a CO_2 fertilizer effect. The developing countries, on the other hand, may also benefit from the fertilizer effect but the temperature increase will, all in all, have a negative effect. Furthermore, it is assumed that the industrial countries, with their greater economic resources and better infrastructure, will find it easier to secure the necessary changes in farming methods to counteract the effect of a temperature increase.[2377]

As far as agriculture is concerned, global warming will be tough on the developing countries while probably being advantageous to the industrialized world.[2378] However, since these changes will be gradual and in all likelihood not make their mark until the middle of the twenty-first century, it is also highly probable that many developing countries will by that time be considerably richer and better developed and therefore be more capable of handling the problems of the future than is suggested in the current IPCC analyses, based as they are on access to current resources.[2379]

Finally, it is important to point out that IPCC in its evaluations apparently does not consider the fact that over time new varieties of crops will be developed which are better able to exploit higher temperatures and higher CO_2 concentrations. Along with the somewhat unrealistic assumption of a 4.0–5.2°C temperature increase in 2060 and the assumption of present-day resources for the developing world, this also tends to indicate that the figures in Table 7 should be seen as a worst-case estimate.[2380]

Consequences: sea level rise

In the popular press and in statements from many politicians it has become standard to claim that global warming will lead to increased storms, hurricanes, El Niños and pretty much any kind of extreme weather. Tellingly, *Newsweek*'s 1996 cover on global warming featured a man lost in a blinding blizzard with the claim: "THE HOT ZONE: blizzards, floods & dead butterflies: blame it all on global warming."[2381] Reporting on the new IPCC report, the cover story of *U.S. News & World Report* told its readers in February 2001 how "global warming could cause droughts, disease, and political upheaval" and other "nasty effects, from pestilence and famine to wars and refugee movement."[2382] In the US, the consequences could be dire: "By midcentury, the chic Art Deco hotels that now line Miami's South Beach could stand waterlogged and abandoned. Malaria could be a public health threat in Vermont. Nebraska farmers could abandon their fields for lack of water."[2383] Let us try briefly to look at a number of these claims, and more closely at the most important, namely the worry over increased meteorological catastrophes.

First, global warming has often been connected to oceans that will rise several meters and polar ice caps that begin to melt.[2384] An article in the *UNESCO Courier* showed us a picture of a large iceberg detaching, asking us: "Will global warming melt the polar ice caps?"[2385]

There are, however, no grounds for these worries. It is right that the first models predicted extreme sea level increases but these predictions have since been falling constantly.[2386] The global water level has risen between 10 and 25 cm over the last hundred years and as can be seen in Figure 137, it is envisaged that it will rise by a further 31–49 cm (12–19 in) over the next hundred.[2387] About three-fourths of this rise is due to the fact that the water has got warmer and therefore expanded, and only one-fourth comes from changes in glaciers and increased runoff from ice caps.[2388] Yet, Greenland contributes virtually nothing over the coming century (2.5 cm or 1 in) and Antarctica actually decreases sea level with about 8 cm (3 in).[2389]

The increase is predicted, however, to make more people exposed to recurrent flooding.[2390] The IPCC assess that given a 40 cm sea level increase, the number of people at risk of annual flooding will – depending on adaptive responses – increase by 75 to 200 million in the 2080s, compared to no sea level increase.[2391] Yet, if we look at the model behind these figures, it shows us several things. First, it looks at the number of people at risk, with constant protection and no sea level rise. Since population increases, this also means increasing populations in risk areas, and consequently, the number of people at risk increases from 10 million today to 36 million in the 2080s.[2392] However, since the world also gets much richer, it can afford more protection, and consequently, the model shows that increased protection will make the total number at risk in the 2080s only 13 million.[2393]

Now, the model looks at a 40 cm rise and constant protection, which gives 237 million people at risk in the 2080s – some 200 million more people, as quoted by the IPCC.[2394] But surely, it is unreasonable to assume that a much richer world will make no improvement in sea protection, so this number seems rather irrelevant even to include in the IPCC *Summary for Policymakers*. Thus, finally the model looks at a 40 cm rise and evolving protection, showing 93 million people at risk in the 2080s – 70 million more than with no sea level rise.[2395] This figure, however, is still unrealistic, because the model explicitly assumes that "evolving protection only includes measures that would be implemented without sea-level rise."[2396] It seems plainly unreasonable to assume that in a much richer world, where developing countries will be at least as well off as the industrialized countries are today (Figure 149), responses would be made only to protect against a sea level 80 years ago and not against the *actual* sea level rise. Moreover, the total cost of protection is fairly low, estimated at 0.1 percent of GDP for most nations, though it might be as high as several percent for small island states.[2397]

Consequently, it seems likely that rich countries (as almost all countries will be by the end of this century) will protect their citizens at such a low price that virtually no one will be exposed to annual sea flooding. This does not mean that sea level rising is not costly – we would rather live in a world without having to pay such a cost, and below we will discuss how to incorporate sea level costs along with many other costs from global warming to assess the total magnitude of the problem.

Likewise, when the IPCC tells us in the *Summary for Policymakers* how "potential damages to infrastructure in coastal areas from sea level rise have been projected to be tens of billions of dollars for individual countries, for example Egypt, Poland, and Vietnam,"[2398] they neglect to tell us that these losses *will not occur*. For Egypt, the $35 billion estimate comes from simply allowing 30 percent of Egypt's second largest city, Alexandria, to be inundated, without the government taking action.[2399] Unfortunately the analysis makes no attempt to estimate the cost of avoiding such loss. For Poland, the estimate of $28–46 billion[2400] equally comes from allowing cities and farmland to be flooded by an extreme 100 cm sea level increase. The Polish analysis, however, shows that even a *full* protection against the extreme flooding will cost the much lower amount of $6.1 billion[2401] and with a more likely sea level increase of 30 cm, the full protection cost will be $2.3 billion and a partial protection just $1.2 billion.[2402] Again, the implication is that relatively cheap measures will be taken to avert costly inundation.

Summing up, we have to constantly keep focus on the fact that humanity has dealt with and overcome problems all through history. We have actually already experienced a significant sea level increase over the past century, and we have handled that. As the IPCC writes in the executive summary, "human settlements are expected to be among the sectors that could be most easily adapted to climate change, given appropriate planning and foresight and appropriate technical, institutional, and political capacity."[2403] This is why it is plainly implausible, as *U.S. News & World Report* let us believe, that "by midcentury, the chic Art Deco hotels that now line Miami's South Beach could stand waterlogged and abandoned."[2404] Sea level change in 2050 will be no more than the change we already *have* experienced over the past 100 years (Figure 137)[2405] or indeed pretty much the change the Art Deco hotels from the 1920s and 1930s have already experienced.[2406] Moreover, with sea level changes occurring slowly throughout the century, economically rational foresight will make sure that protection will be afforded only to property that is worth more than the protection costs and settlements will be avoided where costs will outweigh benefits.[2407] Thus, the IPCC cite the total cost for the US national protection *and* property abandonment for a 1 meter sea level rise (more than twice what is expected in 2100) at about \$5–6 billion over the century.[2408] Considering that the adequate protection costs for Miami would be just a tiny fraction of this cost spread over the century, given that the property value for Miami Beach in 1998 was close to \$7 billion,[2409] and that the Art Deco Historic District is the second tourist magnet in Florida after Disney, contributing over \$11 billion annually to the economy,[2410] 16 cm (6 in) will simply not leave Miami Beach hotels waterlogged and abandoned.

Consequences: human health

It is often assumed that global warming will put human health under greater pressure.[2411] The IPCC finds that higher temperatures will cause an increase in death and illness, especially among the old and the urban poor, with limited access to air conditioning.[2412] The IPCC does not discuss the fact that a much richer world will be far more able to afford most people access to air-conditioning. Moreover, reporting on human health often leaves out that in a warming world, there would also be fewer people dying from cold weather. Generally, there is no doubt that more people die from cold weather – some 15–20 percent higher death rates in winter compared to summer.[2413] Twice as many people die in the US from cold as from heat, and it is estimated that about 9,000 fewer people would die in the United Kingdom each winter if there were greenhouse warming.[2414] However, since the winter-associated mortality is less strongly associated with temperature, it is unclear whether a warming world will all in all experience fewer or more deaths.[2415]

A recent study of many different regions in Europe showed that the populations have adjusted successfully to mean summer temperatures ranging from 13.5°C to 24.1°C, and while heat-related mortality started around 17.3°C in north Finland, it first set in at 22.3°C in London, and at 25.7°C in Athens.[2416] Heat-related deaths occur not beyond a certain fixed temperature, but somewhat beyond the *usual* temperature. This clearly shows that local populations can successfully adjust to protect themselves from heat stress. The authors conclude that this also indicates that populations are likely to be able to successfully adjust to increased temperatures from global warming, "with little increase in heat related mortality."[2417] At the same time, all populations showed much greater deaths in winter time, and thus even a small decrease in winter deaths would greatly outweigh a small heat death increase.[2418]

Likewise, it is often pointed out that with increasing temperatures the potential area of tropical diseases such as malaria will increase, because the mosquitoes that transmit malaria ordinarily need winter temperatures above 16–18°C to survive.[2419] However, this point ignores the many species that can hibernate in sheltered sites, and it ignores the fact that throughout the Little Ice Age, malaria was a major epidemic disease in Europe and far into the Arctic Circle.[2420] It was only in the late 1800s that England began to rid itself of malaria, through better building techniques and cheaper medicine.[2421] Malaria was still endemic in Finland, Poland and Russia, and in the countries bordering the Black Sea and the eastern Mediterranean till after World War II, and at that time malaria in the US was still endemic in 36 states, including Washington, Oregon, Idaho, Montana, North Dakota,

Minnesota, Wisconsin, Iowa, Illinois, Michigan, Indiana, Ohio, New York, Pennsylvania and New Jersey.[2422] Thus, although the *potential* area of malaria could be expanded by global warming, the experience from Europe and the US shows that combating malaria is primarily a question of development and resources – development to ensure efficient monitoring of the disease, resources to secure a strong effort to eradicate the mosquitoes and their breeding grounds.[2423] In one – otherwise very pessimistic – summary of US health risks, it is found that reestablishment of malaria due to a warming climate "seems unlikely" as long as the current infrastructure and health care systems are maintained.[2424] Thus, the *U.S. News & World Report* worry for malaria as a "public health threat in Vermont"[2425] seems unfounded.

Mathematical models, merely mapping out suitable temperature zones for mosquitoes, show that global warming in the 2080s could increase the number of people *potentially* exposed to malaria by 2–4 percent (260–320 million people of 8 billion at risk.)[2426] Yet, the IPCC points out that most of the additionally exposed would come from middle- or high-income countries, where a well functioning health sector and developed infrastructure makes actual malaria unlikely.[2427] Thus, the global study of *actual* malaria transmission shows "remarkably few changes, even under the most extreme scenarios."[2428]

Consequences: extreme weather

One of the most repeated claims of global warming is that is causes extreme weather, for instance that it intensifies El Niño. Al Gore has claimed that "we know that as a result of global warming, there is more heat in the climate system, and it is heat that drives El Niño . . . Unless we act we can expect more extreme weather in the years ahead."[2429] Likewise, the National Wildlife Federation issued in 1999 a report with the title "El Niño and wildlife: you can't fool Mother Nature."[2430] Here they predicted increasing numbers of extreme weather events like El Niño, which could spell the end of threatened and endangered species, such as the salmon of the Pacific Northwest, the brown pelican in California, and South America's Galapagos and Humboldt penguins.

The El Niño phenomenon is naturally recurring every 3–5 years, changing the weather patterns in the south Pacific, much as the weaker Atlantic oscillation affects the European weather.[2431] Essentially, El Niño relaxes or reverses the trade winds, bringing heat and heavy rains to Ecuador and Peru, whereas the flip-side La Niña strengthens the trade winds, bringing heavy rains to the far western tropical Pacific.[2432]

The driving forces behind the fluctuation are not yet clearly understood, but El Niño/La Niña has occurred regularly over the last 5,000 years.[2433] Nevertheless, the two most intense El Niño episodes in the twentieth century occurred within the past two decades, in 1982 and 1997.[2434] Obviously, a lot of speculation has gone into whether this is caused by global warming. Several historical studies seem to indicate that this need not be so. In the words of one *Nature* article, several El Niño "events that occurred before 1880 had effects at least as intense and wide-ranging as those associated with the current event."[2435] And a study in *Science* using archaeological and palaeontological evidence documented how El Niño had not been active in the early mid-Holocene (8,000–5,000 years ago), when global and regional climate was 1–2°C warmer than it is now.[2436] This could be seen to imply that a warmer climate would if anything turn El Niño off. Also, evidence indicates that there is a large-scale pattern over the century, making El Niños stronger and weaker, and that since 1977 it has been in the stronger mode.[2437]

Computer models of future El Niños in a warmer world have given inconclusive results. Some have predicted increasing frequency, whereas others have found no change within the next couple of hundred years.[2438] In the newest 2000 review in *Nature*, these models are generally characterized as failing to be realistic. In conclusion, it is found that several "projections have been made and yield results that differ from one another. At this time, it is impossible to decide which, if any, are correct."[2439] Likewise, the IPCC finds that "the confidence in models and understanding is inadequate to make firm projections."[2440]

As a curiosity it is perhaps worth pointing out that in years with El Niño the US experiences the *least* hurricane damage. Strong statistical results show that in El Niño years, the risk of two or more landfalling hurricanes is just 28 percent as opposed to the normal 48 percent.[2441] Actually, the most danger comes in La Niña years, where the risk of two or more landfalling hurricanes increases to 63 percent.

Possibly the most common claim in the popular press and in statements from many politicians is that global warming will lead to increased frequency of storms, hurricanes and general extreme weather.[2442] The main thrust of *Newsweek*'s 1996 cover story on global warming was one of possible "catastrophic global warming" with "more floods, worse hurricanes."[2443] The US experience was summed up in this way: "The weather is always capricious, but last year gave new meaning to the term. Floods, hurricanes, droughts – the only plague missing was frogs. The pattern of extremes fit scientists' forecasts of what a warmer world would be like."[2444] Likewise, in a story on the political choices in global warming, *Congressional Quarterly* told us how since the signing of the Kyoto Protocol "the weather has intensified . . . It was a time of killer storms, such as Hurricane Mitch, raging wildfires in Florida and stifling drought in Texas. Floods in China displaced an estimated 56 million people."[2445] In their summer 2000 cover story, the *Earth Island Journal* even told us how extreme weather is linked to global warming and will give us "higher (and lower) temperatures, fiercer winds, deadlier floods, longer droughts, and an increased frequency of dust storms, tsunamis, storm surges, tornadoes, hurricanes and cyclones."[2446] The *Global Environmental Outlook 2000* also claims that "global warming models indicate that rising global temperatures are likely to affect many atmospheric parameters including precipitation and wind velocity, and raise the incidence of extreme weather events, including storms and heavy rainfall, cyclones and drought."[2447]

These many confident statements are surprising and conflict clearly with the 1996 findings of the IPCC, which set aside an entire section to discuss the question: "Has the climate become more variable or extreme?"[2448] In conclusion, the IPCC found:

> Overall, there is no evidence that extreme weather events, or climate variability, has increased, in a global sense, through the twentieth century, although data and analyses are poor and not comprehensive. On regional scales there is clear evidence of changes in some extremes and climate variability indicators. Some of these changes have been toward greater variability; some have been toward lower variability.[2449]

In the new 2001 report, IPCC has *only* found that there has been an increase in precipitation and in heavy and extreme precipitation (see below).[2450] However, for tropical and extratropical storms, "intensity and frequency are dominated by interdecadal to multidecadal variations, with no long-term trends evident."[2451] Moreover, no systematic changes in the frequency of tornadoes, thunder days, or hail are evident in the limited areas analyzed."[2452]

This lack of evidence was made even clearer in an overview article in *Science* by one of the main GCM modelers:

> There are a number of statements in informal writings that are not supported by climate science or projections with high-quality climate models. Some of these statements may appear to be physically plausible, but the evidence for their validity is weak, and some are just wrong. There are assertions that the number of tropical

> storms, hurricanes, and typhoons per year will increase. That is possible, but there appears to be no credible evidence to substantiate such assertions. Assertions that winds in midlatitude (versus tropical) cyclones will become more intense do not appear to have credible scientific support.[2453]

Theoretically, several models have looked especially at tropical cyclones (aka tropical storms, hurricanes or typhoons, depending on origin) because these globally are by far the deadliest and costliest natural weather disasters.[2454] The IPCC concluded in 1996 that "it is not possible to say whether the frequency, area of occurrence, time of occurrence, mean intensity or maximum intensity of tropical cyclones will change."[2455] Some climate models show an increasing number of cyclones while others show decreasing trends.[2456] Equally, for extratropical storms, GCMs have found both increasing, stable and decreasing trends.[2457] However, these GCMs are consistently poor at recreating past patterns[2458] and poor at predictions,[2459] and they cannot generally simulate cyclone activity.[2460]

Thomas Karl from the NOAA along with several other members of the IPCC wrote an overview in *Scientific American*, where the conclusion was that "overall, it seems unlikely that tropical cyclones will increase significantly on a global scale."[2461] In 1998, the UN World Meteorological Organization produced a post-IPCC assessment of tropical cyclones and global climate change. Their conclusion was that "the very modest available evidence points to an expectation of little or no change in global frequency."[2462] The 2001 IPCC still finds the issue unresolved: "there is no general agreement yet among models concerning future changes in midlatitude storms (intensity and frequency) and variability,"[2463] and "there is some evidence that shows only small changes in the frequency of tropical cyclones."[2464]

The observed evidence also counts against the idea of increased frequency of tropical cyclones. Generally, it has been impossible to establish a reliable global record of variability of tropical cyclones through the twentieth century because of changing observing systems and population changes in tropical areas.[2465] Based on relatively short time series, the Northwest Pacific basin has shown an increase in tropical cyclones since 1980, preceded by an almost identical decrease in frequency from about 1960 to 1980. Since the 1960s, the Northeast Pacific has experienced a significant upward trend in tropical cyclone frequency, the North Indian Ocean a significant downward trend, and no appreciable long-term variation was observed in the Southwest Indian Ocean and Southwest Pacific. Finally, the numbers of tropical cyclones occurring in the Australian region have decreased since the mid-1980s.[2466]

However, the North Atlantic has good cyclone data because weather aircraft have reconnoitered there since the 1940s.[2467] Here, it turns out that although there are great decadal variations, the trends are generally declining, with a noticeable quiet period in the 1970s and 1980s.[2468] Particularly, it turns out that the number of intense cyclones (those that cause the greatest damage)[2469] has been declining, as has the number of cyclone days. Equally, and as shown in Figure 152, the average wind of an Atlantic cyclone has been decreasing over the past half-century. Moreover, the record of US cyclone landfall goes back to 1899 and shows no increase either in total or split into East Coast or Gulf Coast landfalls (actually all three show a small, statistically insignificant decline).[2470]

Despite this rather overwhelming theoretical and observed evidence against popular, sweeping statements of increased storms and hurricanes, they are nevertheless often made. Cavalier statements abound, as when Worldwatch Institute tells us how global warming causes higher temperatures, where the result is that "storm systems are more intense, more frequent, and more destructive."[2471]

Meteorologically unsubstantiated claims of

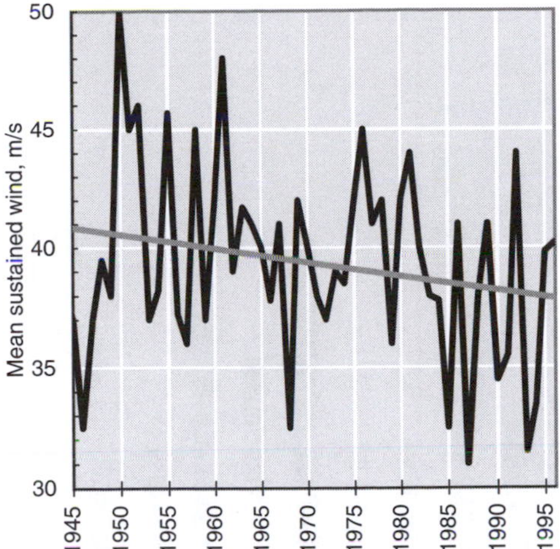

Figure 152 The mean annual maximum sustained wind speed for Atlantic basin cyclones 1945–96. Source: Landsea *et al.* 1999:108, updated from IPCC 1996:170, Landsea *et al.* 1996.

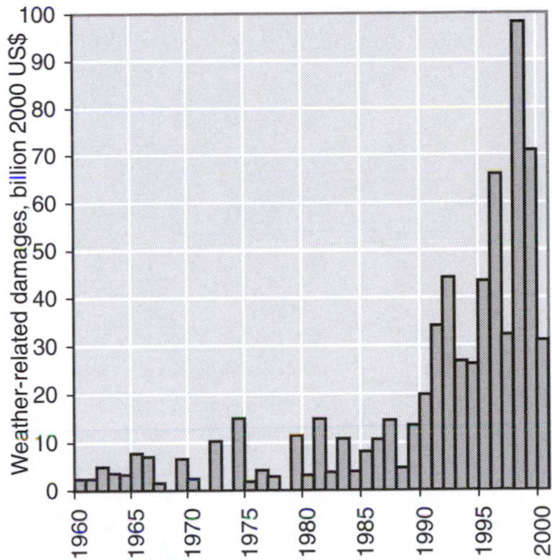

Figure 153 Economic losses from weather-related natural disasters, 1960–2000, in constant 2000 US$. Source: WI 1999b, 2000a:77, Munich Re 2001:8, CPI 2001.

more extreme weather are often backed up by the economic observation of ever increasing weather-related costs. Worldwatch Institute tells us in their 2000 overview of the world how "some of the expected effects of climate change, such as more destructive storms . . . are now becoming evident. Weather-related damage in 1999 totaled $67 billion worldwide, the second highest after the 1998 figure of $93 billion. Weather-related damage world-wide during the 1990s was more than five times the figure during the 1980s."[2472] Both Worldwatch Institute and many others have presented these increasing weather-related costs (Figure 153) as testimony to a world at the peril of ever more extreme weather.[2473]

However, it is unclear if a direct comparison of costs, even in constant dollars,[2474] is reasonable. Comparing costs over long periods of time ignores the change in population patterns and demography as well as economic prosperity. World-wide, there are twice as many people today as in 1960, each is more than twice as rich, most probably have more than doubled their physical wealth, and many have migrated to low-lying and coastal, risk-prone areas.[2475] Thus, there are many more people, residing in much more vulnerable areas, with many more assets to lose. In the US today, the two coastal South Florida counties, Dade and Broward, are home to more people than the number of people who lived in 1930 in *all* 109 coastal counties stretching from Texas through Virginia, along the Gulf and Atlantic coasts.[2476] While the US population has quadrupled over the century, the Florida coastal population has increased more than 50-fold.[2477]

Moreover, in taking the entire weather-related cost of the world, as in Figure 153, we include flooding, which is a disaster only weakly connected to climate itself. Rather, in an Office of Technology Assessment report, it was pointed out that flooding is caused primarily by increasing populations, development and conversion of flood-moderating wetlands as well as lack of information and clear policies.[2478] In the record year of 1998, almost half the costs came from flooding disasters.[2479] Actually, $30 billion or one-third of the total

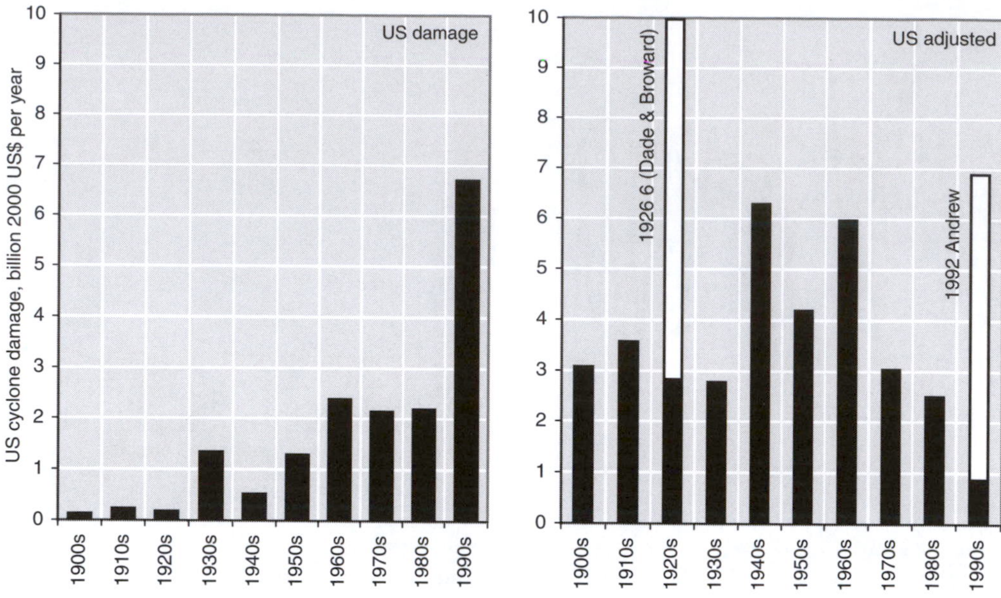

Figure 154 US hurricane damage, 1900–95. Left panel shows the actual economic cost in 2000$, right panel shows the cost, if the hurricanes had hit today, with the contribution of the two costliest hurricanes singled out. Note, annual, average values of decadal costs, except the 1990s only covering the first 6 years. Also, damage for 1900–25 is underestimated and more uncertain due to poor data availability. Source: Pielke and Landsea 1998, CPI 2001.

loss came from a single catastrophic summer flooding of the Yangtze and Songhua areas in China, and here Worldwatch Institute itself points out that the catastrophe was in large measure caused by clear-cutting forests on the upstream slopes, causing more rapid runoff.[2480]

Let us instead try to look at one of the best long-term, clearly weather-related loss records, namely hurricane damage in the US. Here we see a pattern of inflation-adjusted hurricane cost in the left part of Figure 154, much like the global one in Figure 153. What we see are small costs through the earlier part of the century, escalating towards very high costs in the 1990s, with the 1992 Hurricane Andrew as the all-time high at 30 billion 1999$.[2481] Two researchers from NOAA and NCAR wondered whether the reason why the early part of the century got off so much more cheaply was because there were fewer people and fewer assets to be harmed. Thus, they asked the hypothetical question: what would the damage have been, if all hurricanes throughout the century had hit a US like the one today?[2482] The answer can be seen in the right part of Figure 154. Suddenly, an unnamed category 4 hurricane in 1926, hitting just north of where Hurricane Andrew hit in 1992, would have created the most damage ever at an estimated cost of $69 billion – more than twice the cost of Andrew.[2483] The important point, of course, is that when we look at hurricane damage and have taken out the variability from increased wealth and increased concentration of people in coastal areas, the tendency towards ever greater meteorological damage disappears.[2484] The 1990s look like the 1920s, 1940s or 1960s.

We get the same conclusion from several other places.[2485] Munich Re, the world's largest re-insurer company, provided the weather-related loss estimates used by Worldwatch Institute and in Figure 153. In Munich Re's annual catastrophe review they point out how natural catastrophes have tripled and inflation-adjusted costs increased ninefold.[2486] This statement is repeated almost verbatim by Worldwatch, but without Munich Re's ensuing paragraph.[2487] Here, Munich Re explains why we see the increase:

> The main reasons for this dramatic increase are the concentration of population and values in a constantly growing number of larger and larger cities often located in high-risk zones, the greater susceptibility of modern industrial societies to catastrophes, the accelerating deterioration of natural environmental conditions and also, as far as insured losses are concerned, the increasing insurance density in the sector of natural hazards.[2488]

No mention of global warming. Though Munich Re and their lead scientist, Dr. Gerhard Berz,[2489] worry about global warming, Berz has also pointed out in several papers that the main causes of increasing weather-related costs are human:[2490]

> In the last few decades, the international insurance industry has bean confronted with a drastic increase in the scope and frequency of great natural disasters. The trend is primarily attributable to the continuing steady growth of the world population and the increasing concentration of people and economic values in urban areas. An additional factor is the global migration of populations and industries into areas such as coastal regions, which are particularly exposed to natural hazards. The natural hazards themselves, on the other hand, have not yet shown a significant trend, in spite of a number of indications.[2491]

Berz was also co-author on the post-IPCC assessment mentioned above, where they found "little or no change" in tropical cyclones.[2492] And Munich Re's competitor, the second largest reinsurer, Swiss Re, has reached the same conclusion on catastrophes:

> Since 1970 the extent of natural and man-made catastrophes covered by [Swiss Re] has increased. This reflects bigger potential losses due to:
> - higher population densities
> - more insured valuables in endangered areas
> - higher concentration of values in industrialised countries[2493]

In conclusion, a 1999 American damage study of not only hurricanes but also floods and tornadoes "did not show an increase during the 1990s, revealing that weather changes were not the principal cause of more catastrophes."[2494] All in all, "the high losses and numerous catastrophes of the 1990s were largely the result of societal changes and not major weather changes."[2495] These findings have been backed up by several other, new studies.[2496]

Consequences: present and future weather

But after looking at all the claims that *cannot* be made on behalf of global warming, then what actually has happened and what can we expect to happen with the climate? Again, we will conservatively dispense with all the other reservations about scenarios, alternative models, sensitivity and data problems, and merely assume that the GCMs give us a reasonable picture of the future.

When answering questions about global warming, the most obvious point is that the temperature has increased some 0.6°C over the past century (Figure 135).[2497] However, it turns out that the global temperature increase does not mean that everything has just got a bit warmer. Actually, there is a general strong trend that it is the cold temperatures that have warmed the most.[2498]

Globally, minimum (night) temperatures have increased much more than maximum (day) temperatures. This characteristic is evident for all seasons and both hemispheres in Figure 155. From 1950–1993, the global trend

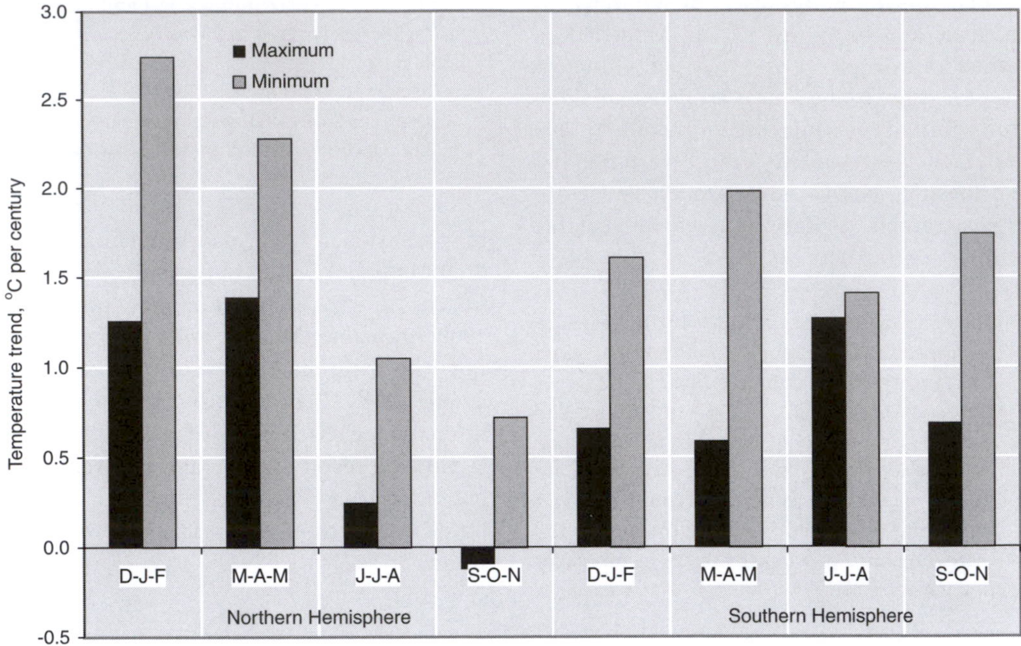

Figure 155 Seasonal trends from 1950 to 1993 of maximum and minimum temperatures for the Northern and Southern Hemispheres, in °C per century. The statistics cover 54 percent of the total global land area and are calculated from non-urban stations only. Source: Easterling *et al.* 1997.

has been just 0.1 °C/decade for maximum temperatures whereas the minimum temperatures have increased by 0.2°C/decade.[2499] The tendency has also been observed individually for the US, China, England, and Northern and Central Europe.[2500] At the same time, more warming has taken place during the winter than during the summer,[2501] which is also clear for the northern hemisphere in Figure 155, where the temperature increase has been strongest in winter and spring.[2502] Finally, winter temperatures have been warming the most in colder locations – actually, more than three-quarters of the winter warming in the northern hemisphere has been confined to the very cold high-pressure systems of Siberia and northwestern North America.[2503]

Not surprisingly, this has meant that both the US, Northern and Central Europe, China, Australia and New Zealand have experienced fewer frost days.[2504] However, since most of the warming has happened to cold temperatures, only Australia and New Zealand have had their maximum temperature go up.[2505] For the US, the maximum temperatures show no trend and for China the maximum has even declined.[2506] For the Central England Temperature series, the longest temperature record in the world, going back to 1659, there has been a clear reduction in the number of cold days, but no increase in the number of hot days.[2507]

Generally speaking, it is much better that warming happens when it is cold than when it is warm. It means that cold-related stresses (e.g. influenza, strokes and heart attacks)[2508] are alleviated without heat-related stresses (e.g. heat strokes)[2509] setting in. Actually, an argument could be made that overall such warming would be beneficial. For the US, it turns out that despite much regional and temporal variation the number of days with extreme high temperatures has been declining slightly over the past century.[2510]

Also, less cold and no more heat means relatively more agricultural output. This is especially true when we attempt to estimate the long-term consequences of global warming.[2511] In the IPCC study on the agricultural impact of global warming (Table 7), the models did not take into account that warming would generally take place for colder temperatures.[2512] However, a recent study using four different GCMs shows that when allowing for most of the temperature increase to take place at night, increases in yields are 0–16 percent, with most crops around 7–8 percent.[2513] For this reason also, it is reasonable to expect that Table 7 is a worst-case estimate.

It is also likely that warming will cause more precipitation.[2514] Already now, most of the places surveyed show more rain, for example the US, western Russia, southern Canada, coastal eastern Australia and South Africa, whereas Japan, northeastern China, Ethiopia, western Kenya and Thailand show less rain.[2515] Moreover, it seems that with more rain, there will typically also be more heavy rain.[2516] Thus it is shown for the US that there has been an increase in days with heavy rain, and these increases are responsible for about half the total precipitation increase.[2517] While increasing heavy rain, everything else being equal, will increase the risk of flooding, it is important to realize that physical planning, as mentioned above (conserving flood-moderating wetlands, decreasing upstream runoff, maintaining dams and levees, better information, etc.),[2518] is probably more important in determining the extent of a possible disaster.[2519] Moreover, a USGS study of 395 undisturbed streamflows showed less drought but no increase in flooding.[2520]

Perhaps more surprisingly, it seems that although precipitation generally is increasing, drought has not been decreasing as much, at least since the late 1970s.[2521] In some areas, mainly the US and Europe, both drought and moisture surplus have been increasing over the past 20 years. Although this is still a rather short time span and the changes are within the limits of natural variation over the century, they also could point towards a climate of greater extremes of precipitation.[2522]

Finally, the combined increase in temperature, CO_2 and precipitation will make the Earth greener. Over the millennia and centuries, human activities have changed the vegetation, mainly through fire and conversion from forests to fields. Through carbon budgets, it is estimated that humans have reduced the total live vegetation mass over the past 6,000 years some 30 percent, 20 percent alone within the last 300 years.[2523] However, with continued fossil fuel use, increasing CO_2 concentrations will fertilize the globe. A test of six different vegetation models using the IS92a scenario shows that global biomass will increase more than 40 percent over the century, almost back to prehistoric levels, as can be seen in Figure 156.[2524]

Equally, Earth's food resource or the Net Primary Production (NPP) is estimated to increase by some 80 percent (Figure 156). We discussed NPP in relation to the worry of Professor Ehrlich and others that humans appropriate or forgo 40 percent, or 58.1 billion tons, of the natural production (p. 99).[2525] It is worth noting that the expected increase in NPP from increased CO_2 is about 90 billion tons or about 50 percent *more* than the entire human appropriation.

Summing up, it is *not* true that global warming has made us experience or will make us experience great increases in hurricanes and storms, and likewise the claim of an unprecedented and ever stronger El Niño seems weak and theoretically unsubstantiated. However, it is true that the temperature has increased, although mainly at night, in the winter, and in cold places. Such reduction in cold extremes without increasing heat extremes has in many respects been beneficial, but if the warming continues, eventually heat extremes will also start to take their toll. Likewise, although increased precipitation is

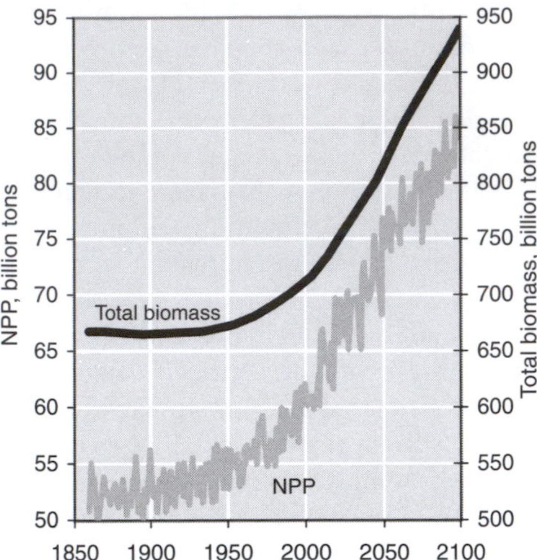

Figure 156 Simulated increase in biomass and Net Primary Production (NPP) for increasing temperature and CO_2, 1850–2100. IPCC business-as-usual scenario, Hadley GCM (HadGCM2), average of 6 different Dynamic Global Vegetation Models, measured in weight of dry organic matter.[2526] Source: Cramer *et al.* 2000, cf. White *et al.* 1999:S24, S26.

not necessarily bad – and for some indeed it will be good – a sustained increase would increase flood risks. Equally, increasing temperature has caused water levels to rise some 10–25 cm, with a prediction of 31–49 cm for the century. While this will probably not increase coastal flooding risk (due to increased protection) it will increase protection cost. Moreover, higher temperatures might increase evaporation and thereby increase the risk of drought.[2527]

Thus, while global warming may not produce the immediately nasty and costly weather catastrophes that much of the rhetoric has claimed, some weather trends are already less desirable and a sustained warming will increase a number of these unwanted trends.

The cost of warming

If the global temperature continues to increase over the coming century, it will have a whole series of effects, both positive and negative, though mostly negative. We have mentioned some of the most important effects above but the second volume of both the IPCC's 1996 and 2001 report describes 800+ pages of possible changes. The question really is what the *overall* consequences of the myriad of individual warming effects will be.

This problem is typically addressed by looking at the total *cost* – in essence, aggregating all the positive and negative effects of global warming will give us an overall measure of the impact of global warming. Such cost estimates have been made by many models, but since the new IPCC scenarios were only released in mid-2000, the estimates have been made using either the old IS92a business-as-usual scenario or a so-called $2xCO_2$ scenario. These latter scenarios, mainly used by IPCC, look at a rather hypothetical world, where CO_2 levels are instantly doubled and then stabilized (which implies a temperature increase of approximately 2.5°C).[2528] This means that the cost is undoubtedly overstated, because it is estimated as if the 2.5°C increase comes *now*, and not gradually in the future so that adaptations can be made slowly and smoothly.[2529]

The new IPCC scenarios cause a much wider temperature range (1.4–5.8°C).[2530] Nevertheless, as discussed above, the high end of this range seems somewhat unlikely, both due to overestimates in the IPCC's simple model and because of reasonable expectation that renewables will become cheaper than fossil fuels before mid-century, which makes a scenario like A1T the most likely (with a total expected temperature increase of about 2.5°C),[2531] much like the 1996 IPCC expected temperature from IS92a or $2xCO_2$. Moreover, as we will see below, the physical effect of a marginal curbing of carbon emissions is primarily to postpone warming for some years, which means that cost-benefit models are primarily affected by the *timing* of costs and benefits whereas they are very robust to different absolute costs. Consequently and in line with available models, we will in the following use the IS92a or 2xCO_2 costs and effects, and at the end address the issue of how the new IPCC scenarios may change these results.

Unfortunately, a 1998 policy decision by the IPCC government representatives[2532] decided that the IPCC should no longer look at the economics of climate change but rather on how to curb further greenhouse gas emissions.[2533] This means that the third IPPC 2001 report has little new information about the costs and benefits of global warming and generally less information about the social costs and benefits of controlling greenhouse gas emissions. In the following, we will therefore mainly look at the previous IPCC report and the independent research results that have been published since then.

In assessing the total costs of global warming, the IPCC listed a whole series of consequences of a doubling of atmospheric carbon dioxide. It includes the cost to agriculture, as we saw above, and also looks at forestry, fisheries, energy, water supply, infrastructure, hurricane damage, drought damage, coast protection, land loss (caused by a rise in sea level, e.g. as in Holland), loss of wetlands, forest loss, loss of species, loss of human life, pollution and migration.[2534] This naturally involves many uncertainties, and considering the extremely comprehensive nature of IPCC studies, not all areas have been investigated equally thoroughly.[2535] The most important areas may well be included, but some – such as the transport sector and the question of political instability – have still not been addressed.

Costs are expressed as the sum of two quantities: the costs of adaptation (building dams, changing to other crops, etc.) and the costs we must incur from the remaining non-adapted consequences (not all land is saved by building dams, production may fall despite the introduction of new crops, etc.).[2536]

The total annual cost of all the considered global warming problems is estimated to be around 1.5–2 percent of the current global GDP, i.e. between 480 and 640 billion dollars.[2537] In absolute figures, the cost is divided more or less equally between the industrial and the developing countries, around 280 billion dollars each.[2538] However, since the developed world is about five times richer than the developing world, the cost in relative terms is unevenly distributed. The cost to the industrial world will be around 1–1.5 percent of their GDP, whereas the cost to the developing world will be between 2 and 9 percent.[2539]

The IPCC 2001 report did not further elaborate these cost estimates. However, it further stressed the unequal costs of global warming. In the *Summary for Policymakers*, it was pointed out:[2540]

> Published estimates indicate that increases in global mean temperature would produce net economic losses in many developing countries for all magnitudes of warming studied, and that the losses would be greater in magnitude the higher the level of warming. In many developed countries, net economic gains are projected for global mean temperature increases up to roughly 2°C. Mixed or neutral net effects are projected in developed countries for temperature increases in the approximate range of 2 to 3°C, and net losses for larger temperature increases. The projected distribution of economic impacts is such that it would increase the disparity in well being between developed countries and developing countries, with the disparity growing with higher temperatures. The more damaging impacts estimated for developing countries reflects, in part, their lesser adaptive capacity.[2541]

This sends us two messages. First, global warming will be costly – on the scale of half a trillion dollars annually. Second, developing countries will be hit much harder by global warming, partly because they are much poorer and consequently have less adaptive capacity.[2542]

Such costs and such unequal distribution should naturally urge us to consider changing course. The solution here is quite simple.[2543] If we want to avoid (some of) the temperature increase associated with global warming, we must reduce our emissions of greenhouse gases, especially CO_2.[2544] This was the background to the Kyoto Protocol of December 1997, which was the first attempt to reach a binding agreement on reduction of CO_2 emissions. It was decided that the so-called Annex I countries (essentially the industrial nations) should reduce their overall emissions of CO_2 in the period 2008–12 such that they would be 5.2 percent below emissions in 1990.[2545] But this does not mean that global warming will be entirely avoided – far from it, in fact, because Kyoto did not impose any limit on emissions by developing countries.[2546] As a matter of fact we can see that the effect of the Kyoto Protocol will be marginal – even if we assume that the Kyoto emission ceilings will be kept in place indefinitely, an issue which has not been addressed by the protocol.[2547] Several models have calculated that the consequence of Kyoto will be a temperature increase by 2100 of around 0.15°C less than if nothing had been done, as can be seen in Figure 157.[2548] Equivalently, the permanent Kyoto curbs on carbon emissions would result in a sea level rise in 2100 which will be just 2.5 cm (1 in) less.[2549]

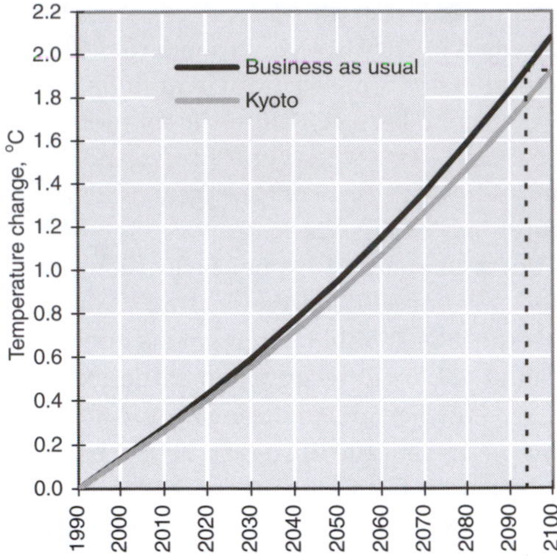

Figure 157 The expected increase in temperature with business-as-usual (IS92a) and with the Kyoto restrictions extended forever. Broken line shows that the temperature for the business-as-usual scenario in 2094 is the same as the Kyoto temperature in 2100 (1.92°C). Source: Wigley 1998.

As one of the chief negotiators of the Montreal agreement on ozone reductions, Richard Benedick, says: "The Kyoto outcome will have an inconsequential impact on the climate system."[2550] Similarly, *Science* tells us that "climate scientists say, however, that it will be miraculous indeed if the Kyoto pact ... even temporarily slows the accumulation of warming gases in the atmosphere."[2551] Actually, looking at Figure 157 it is clear that the reduction in temperature corresponds to a mere six years' difference – the temperature that we would have reached in 2094 (1.92°C) without a deal, Kyoto has now postponed to 2100.[2552]

This of course also means that Kyoto is only a first step. The Danish secretary of the environment wrote a week after returning from Japan: "The decision in Kyoto was just the first of many future decisions, necessary for solving global warming ... In Kyoto it was emphasized once again that the development can only really be reversed if far greater greenhouse gas reductions are made."[2553]

Jerry Mahlman of Princeton University added that "it might take another 30 Kyotos over the next century" to control warming.[2554]

The cost of cutting CO_2

So how much will Kyoto cost? This very much depends on how the Kyoto Protocol will actually be implemented. As signed, the protocol specifies clear targets for each participant – the US must cut 7 percent, the EU 8 percent, Canada 6 percent, etc.[2555] However, the protocol also establishes the possibility of *trading* the rights for CO_2 emissions.[2556]

The basic idea is that, for the climate, it is

unimportant who emits a ton of CO_2, because no matter its origin it will get completely mixed in the atmosphere. Thus, if a country (A) can cut its CO_2 emissions at a much lower cost than another (B), it would make economic sense if A cuts even more that it is supposed to, and B cuts less. In practice, states would be given allowances to emit CO_2, which they could then use themselves or sell to others. In this case, B would be willing to buy emission allowances from A at a higher price than the emission would be worth for A itself, leaving both better off. Of course, such a statement is nothing but the classic argument for the advantages of free trade.

The trading question was hoped to be settled in further meetings in Berlin, Buenos Aires and the Hague, but is at the time of writing still unresolved.[2557] The US essentially is pressing for a large degree of trade, whereas the EU wants most of the promised cuts to be made by the individual states.[2558] The possible outcome may be no trade at all; some sort of split deal where the EU partners will trade among themselves and the others will trade among themselves (the so-called double bubble), trade among all Annex I countries or global trade.

In 1999, economists representing 13 different models were assembled by the Stanford Energy Modeling Forum to evaluate the Kyoto Protocol, by far the largest effort to look into the costs of Kyoto.[2559] Half the models were American, half were from Europe, Japan and Australia. Since these models of course have different assumptions about future growth, energy consumption, alternative costs, etc., their findings often diverge by a factor of 2–4. However, they generally found much the same picture in relative terms. Moreover, since each scenario was estimated by many models, the figures reported here are the averages – representing neither the most optimistic nor the most pessimistic model.[2560]

The cost of the Kyoto Protocol is depicted in Figure 158. If no trade is allowed the cost is estimated at \$346 billion a year around 2010.

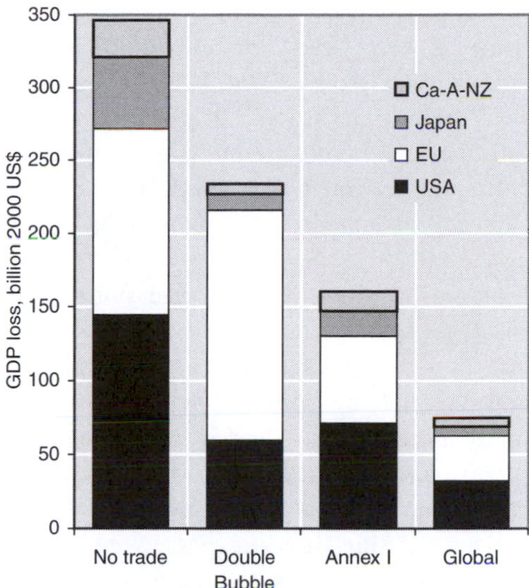

Figure 158 The cost of the Kyoto Protocol in 2010 (billion 2000 US\$) for the US, EU, Japan and Canada/Australia/New Zealand under four different trading assumptions: No trade, trade in two blocks of Annex I – inside and outside of EU (Double Bubble), trade in all of Annex I, and global trade. Average typically of 6–8 models. Source: Weyant and Hill 1999:xxxiii–xxxiv, BEA 2001b–c.

That is equivalent to about 1.5 percent of the region's present GDP.[2561] If trade is allowed within the Annex I countries, the cost drops to \$161 billion annually. If trade is only allowed within two blocks of Annex I (EU and the others), then the cost increases to \$234 billion. However, a large share of the cost is borne by the EU, since it is cutting itself off from the benefits of trade, whereas the US, Japan and the others will actually fulfil their Kyoto targets more cheaply, because they will not have to compete with the EU in buying emission permits. Finally, if global trade were an option (a problematic assumption, as we will see shortly), the cost could be cut even further to \$75 billion.

It might seem strange that a cut of just 5.2 percent CO_2 should cost so much, but this is because the percentage is stated as 5.2 percent of *1990 emissions*. Since emissions would otherwise have increased with a growing economy (although not as fast as the economy, because the economy gets ever more efficient in energy use (Figure 68) and because we switch away from high-CO_2 coal to low-CO_2 gas), it is estimated that compared to the "natural" CO_2 emissions in the OECD in 2010, the Kyoto Protocol actually demands a cut of 28 percent by then.[2562]

Moreover, since the CO_2 emissions of the OECD countries would otherwise have continuously increased, keeping the Kyoto promise and staying 5.2 percent below 1990 levels will really mean making deeper and deeper cuts, such that in 2050 the entire OECD must have cut its "natural" emissions by more than 50 percent.[2563] Since it is cheapest to cut the first few percent whereas the next get progressively more expensive, this also means that the cost of Kyoto will increase over time from the price in Figure 158. The OECD estimates that the cost in 2050 will be around 2 percent of the OECD countries' GDP, and around 4 percent of GDP in 2100.[2564] The actual cost in 2050 will be in the order of more than $900 billion annually.[2565]

This means that the cost to the OECD countries of complying with Kyoto will – each year – by 2050 cost about as much as global warming will cost in 2100 (that is, about 2 percent of present GDP).[2566] And almost the entire cost of global warming in 2100 must nevertheless be paid, because the Kyoto emissions reduction will only delay the temperature increase about six years in 2100, as was evident in Figure 157. Put very simplistically, the world ends up paying for the trouble from global warming twice over – first, every year from 2050 we pay 2 percent of GDP for cutting CO_2, and when reaching 2100 we pay 2 percent more because of higher temperatures which are almost unaffected by the Kyoto Protocol.

The problem is due partly to the fact that the developing countries' emissions are not restricted by the Kyoto Protocol. So while the developed world puts the brakes on its emissions, the developing countries are predicted not only to overtake but to heavily increase their own CO_2 emissions as part of their economic development (Figure 159). Moreover, it is likely that much of the carbon-intensive production will merely move to the developing countries, undermining the intent of Kyoto.[2567]

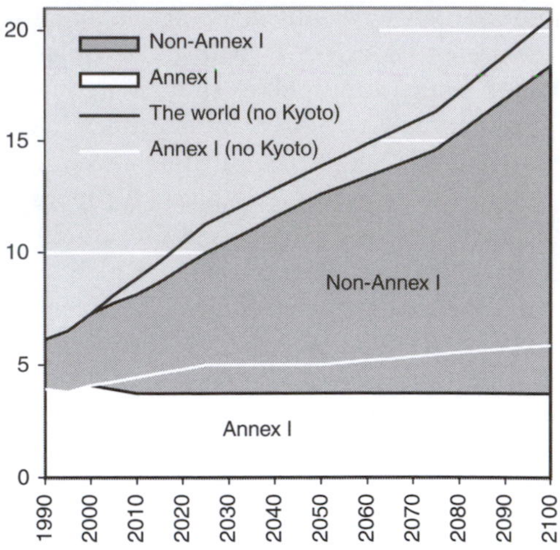

Figure 159 Projected global CO_2 emissions in billion tons carbon, if the Annex I countries stabilize their emissions slightly below the 1990-level in 2010, as envisaged in the Kyoto Protocol. Non-Annex I countries are expected to emit ever more (following emissions in IS92a). Thin black lines indicate the level of Annex I and world emissions without Kyoto. Source: Wigley 1998:2,286, cf. OECD 1994:44.

This seems to indicate that in order to achieve any long-term goal of CO_2 reduction, the developing world must in one way or another be obliged to introduce restrictions. This has also been the position of the US Senate, which in a 95–0 resolution stated that exemption of the developing countries is "inconsistent with the need for global action" and that the US should not sign a treaty without specific commitments for the developing countries.[2568] However, achieving such a goal will be hard or maybe even impossible. First, many developing countries feel that global warming is caused by the rich countries and will mostly harm the developing world. Consequently, reducing greenhouse gas emissions should be the responsibility of the developed world. Of course, this would still be technically possible with an extended Kyoto agreement which gave the developing countries emission permits for the business-as-usual scenario, which the developed world could then buy (this is how the cost of Kyoto with global trade in Figure 158 was calculated).

However, this underlines the second problem. The value of the total rights to CO_2 emissions are staggering, but this will also make the initial assignment of emission rights very hard. As the economist Thomas Schelling expresses it: "Global emissions trading is an elegant idea, but I cannot seriously envision national representatives sitting down to divide up rights in perpetuity worth a trillion dollars."[2569] This would also involve a major redistribution from developed to developing countries. And even if the distribution of rights could be decided, a huge hurdle would persist in ensuring compliance among countries with weak administrations and the possibility of future abandonment of present commitments.[2570]

Then what should we do?

The effects of global warming will be costly, but it will also be expensive to cut CO_2. Together these two pieces of information give us no clear idea as to what we should do. If we focus on how extensive the damage from global warming will be, we will be inclined to intervene now and in a big way – but this approach ignores the cost of such intervention.[2571] On the other hand, if we focus on the high cost of reducing CO_2 emissions then we are inclined just to let things take their course – but this approach ignores the ever increasing damages from warming. So the question is in reality how best to act.

We could, of course, achieve almost instantaneous stabilization of the atmosphere's CO_2 content and achieve a slow stabilization of the climate by banning all use of fossil fuels right now, but at the same time doing so would practically bring the world to a standstill. This would have incalculable consequences, both economic, health-related and environmental.[2572] We could also choose to let things take their course, continue our ever increasing emissions of CO_2 and then pay the costs by adapting society in 2100 and later by building dikes, moving island populations, changing farming methods, etc.

In between these two extremes, of course, we have the option of reducing CO_2 emissions somewhat and accepting some greenhouse warming. There are also a whole series of further considerations to be made as regards *when* prospective cuts should be made,[2573] but basically it is a choice as to the degree we want to reduce CO_2 emissions and pay up now, and the degree we are willing to live with higher temperatures at a later date. So the question is whether between stabilization of the climate and business-as-usual there can be found a solution that does not upset present society too much but does not result in too high climatic costs in the future either. This issue was investigated in the IPCC's 1996 report and the research has since been continued using the so-called integrated assessment models.[2574]

One of the most important model-builders in this field is the professor of economics William Nordhaus of Yale University. He produced the first computer model, the Dynamic Integrated Climate-Economy model (DICE) in order to evaluate the pros and cons of different political choices.[2575] The other modelers have all been inspired by DICE, and according to the IPCC they have all produced more or less the same results.[2576] This model has undergone extensive development and enlargement over the 1990s, now incorporating 13 economic regions in the Regional Integrated Climate-Economy (RICE) model.[2577] What is unique about the DICE and RICE models is that they include both a climate system and an economic system, with costs to the economic system stemming from both climate changes and greenhouse gas emission

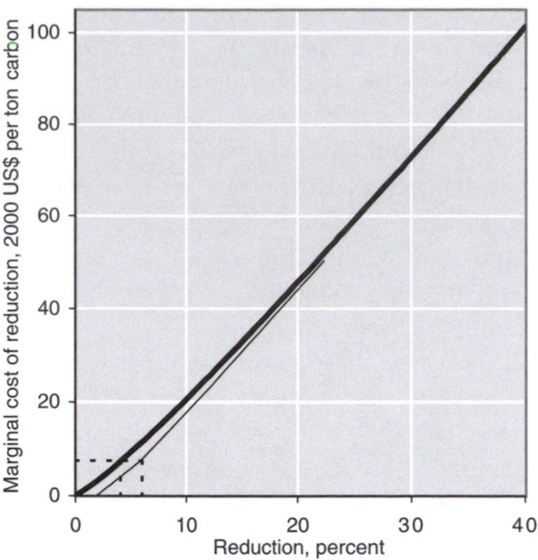

Figure 160 The cost of the last ton of carbon emitted for various levels of carbon reduction in 1995 (expressed in 2000 US$). Price of $7.5/ton carbon gives a reduction of 4 percent. If adjusting for extra environmental benefits that come from regulating CO_2, the actual cost curve is reduced slightly at low regulations.[2578] Source: DICE 1999, Burtraw *et al.* 1999:7–8, BEA 2001b–c.

restrictions. It is crucially important to point out, that while the presentation below will rely on the RICE model, this model gives the same qualitative conclusions as *all* other integrated assessment models.[2579]

The advantage to these models is that they take into account both the costs and benefits of business-as-usual and compare them to the costs and benefits of, say, heroic CO_2 cuts. As far as costs are concerned, the point is that the more CO_2 we try to cut, the more expensive it becomes, as we also saw above with the increasing Kyoto costs. Estimates show that the cost of cutting the first ton of carbon is almost nil, whereas when cutting back 40 percent the last ton will cost about $100, as shown in Figure 160.[2580] Next, the question is to establish what kind of damage the emitted CO_2 will have on society, through global warming, on into the twenty-fourth century. The model takes into account damage from global warming to agriculture, energy, forestry and water, the damages from sea level rise on settlements, human health and life, water quality, time use and catastrophic damages from a large range of studies.[2581] Converted to their present value, the total and long-term damages from emitting an extra ton of carbon today is the equivalent of $7.5.[2582] In other words, it would be well worth society reducing CO_2 emissions until the cost of cutting back an extra ton of carbon is equal to the advantage – which is equivalent to a 4 percent reduction for 1995, as can be seen in Figure 160. However, these calculations do not take account of the fact that reducing CO_2 emissions, depending on geographic location and fuel type, can also mean reduced pollution, which will make the social cost lower. The new 2001 IPCC report points out that these so-called ancillary benefits could make a difference,[2583] but one of their primary sources puts this extra benefit at maximally $3.8/tC around a $10 tax, and falling to just $1.6/tC at $50.[2584] This extra effect is also marked as the thin line in Figure 160, and it shows that the reduction could be slightly larger at maximally 6 percent.[2585] Notice also that these ancillary benefits decrease rapidly, so as to make almost no difference beyond 20 percent reductions. Moreover, the ancillary benefit evaluations are not designed to capture the costs of changing to other renewables, such as biomass, with the resultant added pollution of particles, sulfur, nickel, cadmium and lead.[2586] Finally, since the RICE model was consistently in the low end of Stanford Energy Modeling Forum cost reduction estimates,[2587] this will further counter the left-out ancillary benefits because the model will tend to estimate somewhat higher CO_2 emission cuts.[2588]

Thus, in the model, the 4 percent cut in 1995 is the optimal carbon reduction for the globe. If an attempt is made on one hand to cut back more than 4 percent, it will be a net *cost* to society, because cutting back the final tons above 4 percent costs more than the long-

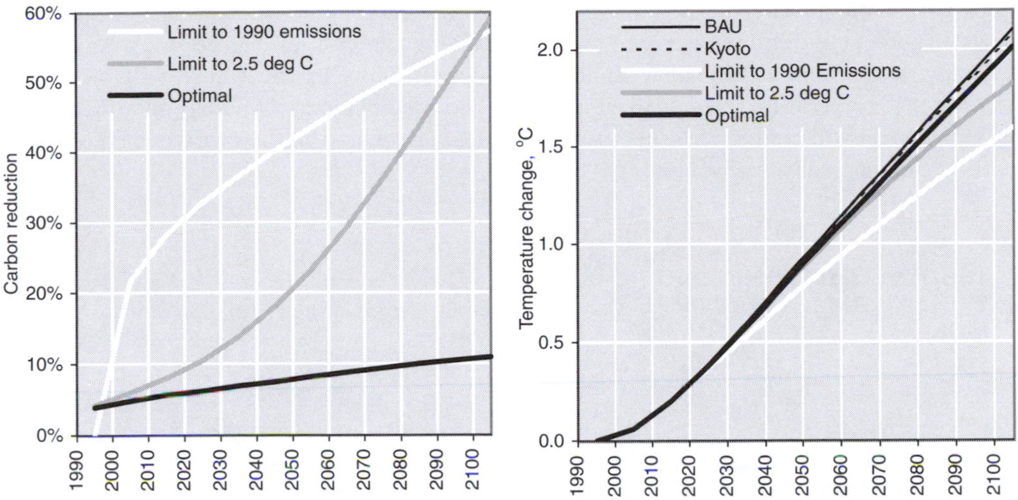

Figure 161 Left: Reduction of CO_2 emissions, 1995–2105, compared to business-as-usual; stabilize global emissions at 1990 levels; limit temperature increases to 2.5°C and to achieve the socially optimal outcome. Right: Temperature change, 1995–2105, for business-as-usual (BAU) and the other scenarios, plus Kyoto (with trading among all Annex I countries). Source: Nordhaus and Boyer 2000:7:29, 31, 8:24.

term advantage gained from having a marginally lower temperature. On the other hand, a reduction of less than 4 percent will also be a net *cost* to society in the long run because the little money saved from not making cheap cuts in CO_2 emissions are outweighed by the forgone advantages from a slightly less warm future.

Over time, the cost of carbon emissions will increase, because the model indicates that higher temperatures will mean much greater damage. Essentially, a 1°C change in today's temperatures will be a lesser cost to society, compared to the marginal cost of a change from 3°C to 4°C. This change will be much more costly, not the least because of an increased risk from catastrophic impacts.[2589] At the same time, costs from cutting back a ton of carbon will decrease, because of better technology, lesser CO_2 contents per dollar produced and higher fossil fuel prices.[2590] The optimal path of carbon emissions cuts is given in the left part of Figure 161, climbing from 4 percent to 11 percent in 2100.

Notice that finding the optimal scenario does not mean that there will not be an enormous number of practical problems tied up with achieving a global warming solution. It is not presented merely as "we-found-the-solution-and-now-we-go-home." However, identifying this optimal solution gives us a clear standard with which to compare alternative policy approaches and judge their relative efficiency or inefficiency.[2591]

Let us take a look at the other two possibilities often proposed in connection with greenhouse effect intervention. One of these is a Kyoto-like proposal to stabilize global CO_2 emissions at the 1990 level. As Nordhaus points out, such a proposal has no particular scientific or economic significance – because stabilizing CO_2 emissions does not mean stabilizing the atmospheric CO_2 concentration, the temperature or the damage, which is what interests most decision-makers – but the proposal has the virtue of simplicity.[2592] We can see the result in the left part of Figure 161: because a steadily growing world economy would have emitted ever more CO_2, stabilization means cutting progressively more and more CO_2, with global cuts at mid-century above 40 percent and still increasing.

Finally, let us look at the policy choice of limiting the temperature increase to 2.5°C. In order to do so it will eventually be necessary to cut CO_2 emissions drastically, although much of the cuts should be placed as far out as possible (left part of Figure 161). This is so, because cuts in the future will be cheaper because of better technology and higher fossil fuel prices, and because we will be richer then.

THE DOUBLE DIVIDEND: IMPROVE THE ENVIRONMENT *AND* MAKE MONEY?

In the 1990s an academic discussion on the efficiency of taxes was suddenly turned towards dealing with the emerging concern for global warming.[2593] Since the cost of curbing CO_2 was clearly going to be great, some environmental economists suggested that new environmental taxes, whose revenues are used to lower existing, distortionary taxes on capital or labor, could actually achieve what was called the strong double dividend: the first dividend would be the improved environmental quality, and the second dividend was a net economic benefit.[2594] Such a marvelous "win-win" property meant that you no longer had to show that environmental damage was sufficiently great to justify the economic cost of taxing it away – instead, if you could just show that it was bad, the double dividend would secure that taxing it would be a net benefit to society.[2595]

This sounded almost too good to be true, and indeed, it was too good – much academic analysis over the last decade has conclusively demonstrated that the strong double dividend is incorrect.[2596] However, the discussion has focused attention on the three distinct effects of a tax on economic welfare: the "primary welfare gain," a "revenue-recycling effect," and a "tax-interaction effect."[2597] The primary welfare gain comes from regulating pollution – if the cost of an extra ton of carbon in the atmosphere is \$7.5, we should tax carbon emissions by \$7.5.[2598] This will make carbon polluters cut back on carbon till its emission is worth \$7.5, and since the first tons costs almost nothing to eliminate (the first percent in Figure 160 is almost free to cut) but still would have made about \$7.5 in damage, society is now better off. The collected tax was normally assumed to be recycled in a lump sum to society.

The double dividend point was that if the tax was not just recycled through a lump sum but used to alleviate other, already distortionary taxes (labor taxes in Europe, perhaps capital taxes in the US),[2599] this could create an additional benefit for society in the form of higher employment and higher welfare. This is indeed correct, and hence, there is a second source of welfare gain: the revenue-recycling effect.

However, if we look at one distortion, we need to look at all distortions. And the new environmental tax itself is distortionary as it discourages work effort by reducing the real household wage. This tax-interaction effect reduces welfare. It is the *sum* of these three effects that determine the overall economic welfare of an environmental tax. Unfortunately, most analytical and computable models show that the tax-interaction effect is *bigger* than the revenue-recycling effect.[2600] The consequence is that taxing carbon in the above example at \$7.5 is actually *too much*.

In Figure 162 you can see how a \$40 environmental damage would normally have been thought to require a \$40 environmental tax. Taking all distortions into account, we see that even using a high revenue-recycling by lowering personal income taxes, we should only tax by \$31, simply because higher taxes will all in all lead to lower welfare. And should we instead make a lump sum replacement, there is no revenue-recycling to outweigh the negative tax-interaction and – perhaps surprisingly – we should not tax at all. Though this may feel "wrong"

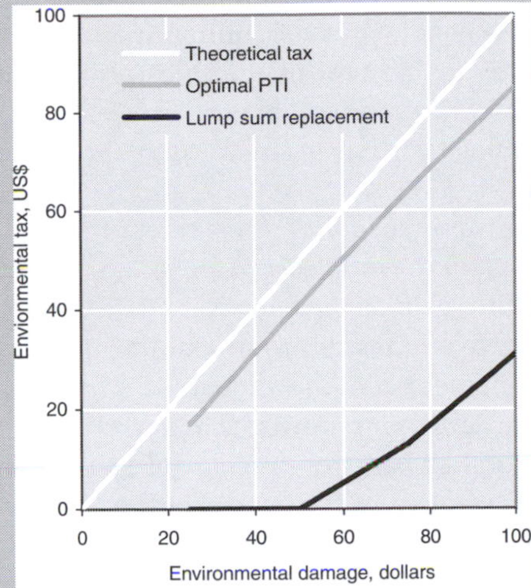

Figure 162 Environmental damage and environmental tax. The theoretical tax shows the simple, first-best argument ("if the environmental damage is $40, the polluter should pay $40"). The other curves show the optimal tax levels as calculated by economic models. If we manage to recycle the tax as reductions in personal income tax (PIT), we should use the optimal PTI curve ("if the environmental damage is $40, the polluter should pay $31") whereas if the tax is just recycled as a lump sum, which is the norm, we should follow the lump sum replacement curve ("if the environmental damage is $40, the polluter should pay nothing"). Source: Parry and Oates 1998:7.

what the model shows is that any tax would actually lead to even lower total welfare (including the environmental damage).

In 1996 the IPCC did mention that a double dividend might partially offset or even more than offset the costs of a carbon tax, although the point was not much stressed.[2601] In its 2001 report, the IPCC has chosen to put a great deal more focus on the double dividend, with somewhat conflicting statements of what it really means.[2602] The IPCC generally accepts that there is no strong double dividend,[2603] yet its *Summary for Policymakers* suggests that it might hold.[2604]

It is important to state that today we know that the strong double dividend cannot be supported in general: "the double-dividend hypothesis is typically invalid."[2605] However, the discussion has taught us that tax recycling is very important if only to make environmental taxes almost as good as we thought they were before the whole discussion started.[2606] This insight is crucial, because empirically, most carbon taxes have specifically *not* been recycled as reductions in the most distorting taxes but rather been earmarked to particular spending programs, which needlessly increases welfare losses.[2607]

Thus, for the present discussion, the double dividend does not mean that we should tax carbon higher, but actually lower (as in Figure 162). Moreover, unless we are very careful to recycle the tax revenue by reducing very distortionary taxes – and until now, we have not done so – the correct tax should in fact be much lower.

The impact on temperature will be slight, no matter what action we take, as can be seen in the right part of Figure 161. This is partly because the time-lag in the climate system is very large and partly because even if we stabilize global emissions at the 1990 level, we will still be putting out large amounts of CO_2, increasing the global CO_2 concentration. Indeed, should we want to limit the temperature increase to 1.5°C, this would require a complete cessation of all carbon emission by 2035,[2608] essentially shutting down the world as we know it.

It is perhaps worth noting that the Kyoto reductions in the Nordhaus and Boyer model will cause a surprisingly small reduction in temperature (0.03°C) in 2100, partly because the developing countries will increase their CO_2 emissions compared to the business-as-usual model.[2609] Actually, the optimal path will reduce the temperature more than Kyoto.

But what will be the overall cost of these

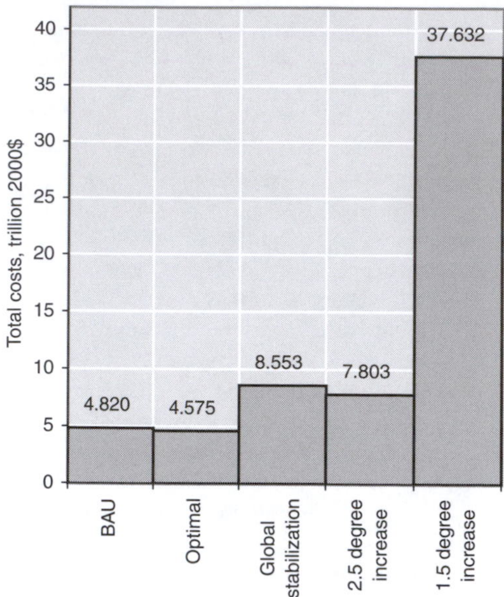

Figure 163 The total, present-value cost (in 2000 US$) of business-as-usual (just global warming); the optimal reduction; global stabilization of emissions at 1990-level; limiting the temperature increase to 2.5 and 1.5°C. All from the RICE-99 model. Source: Nordhaus and Boyer 2000:7:25, BEA 2001b–c.

interventions? Figure 163 shows the cost of the various types of intervention, with the baseline being a situation with no global warming. It shows that business-as-usual will present society with a total, one-time cost of $4,820 billion.[2610] This cost can also be seen as the cost of the anthropogenic greenhouse effect as such – if it should prove that our CO_2 emissions have no effect on the climate it would mean a gain of a little less than 5 trillion dollars.

Of course we would prefer to be without the anthropogenic greenhouse effect, but the phenomenon is not something we can simply wish away. If global warming is coming we must pay the bill – and then the central question is just how small we can keep this bill. It turns out, as we have already argued above, that the optimal policy costs a little less. The total cost in this case is $4,575 billion, or $245 billion cheaper than taking no action. These total savings of $245 billion pertain to a slightly higher cost in the short term of controlling CO_2, offset by the rather greater advantage of slightly less warming in the long run.

The optimal policy thus saves us about 5 percent of the total cost of global warming. To put this gain in perspective, $245 billion is about five times the total amount of official development aid the industrial world gives to the developing world each year.[2611] Equally, the total global warming cost of $5 trillion is the equivalent of total world output for about two months.[2612]

Global stabilization of CO_2 emissions, on the other hand, is far more costly. In this case the cost will be about $8.5 trillion, or almost twice the cost of global warming itself. The cost of limiting the temperature increase to 2.5°C is almost as costly at $7.8 trillion, and the cost of limiting the temperature increase to 1.5°C is an almost unimaginable $38 trillion.

We can also compare the cost of different ways of implementing the Kyoto Protocol, shown in Figure 164. For reference, the $245 billion in savings from the optimal path is shown. If the protocol ends up with no trade or just trade among the OECD countries, the cost will be a significant loss of $550–900 billion. If trade within the entire Annex I is achieved, Kyoto will still be a drawback all in all, but less so at $150 billion. Only if global trading is somehow negotiated will the Kyoto pact actually bring a net benefit at $61 billion, though this is still less than what could be achieved with the optimal path.

This tendency towards lower costs with more trade was also the picture we saw in the total cost overview in Figure 158. Now, however, we can take into account both this cost and the benefit from a Kyoto emissions cut. The clear message is that without global trade, Kyoto is actually a net detriment to the world.

If we get global trade, what we have really done is to make world emissions grow slightly

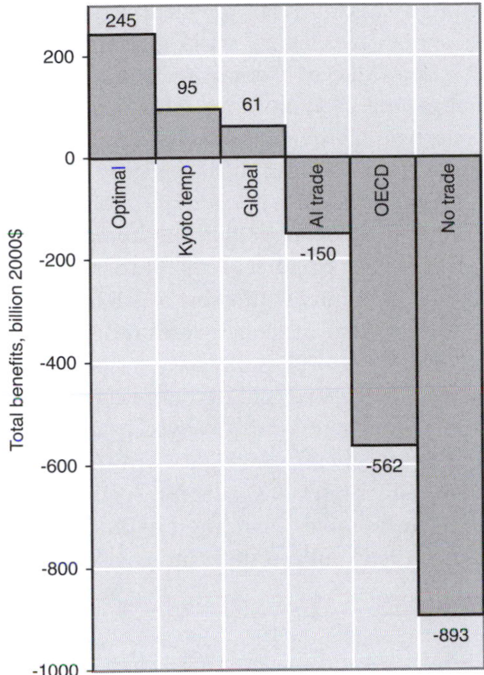

Figure 164 The present value (in 2000 US$) from a business-as-usual baseline of a number of scenarios: the optimal reduction; achieving the same temperature decrease as Kyoto; implementing Kyoto with global trade; Annex I trade; trade only within OECD and no trade. Source: Nordhaus and Boyer 2000:8:28, BEA 2001b–c.

more slowly than they otherwise would have done. But we could actually do better than that, because Kyoto inefficiently focuses on emissions instead of the temperature, which is what harms us. If we instead focused on getting the same temperature curve as Kyoto from 2100 onwards, we could start emission cuts later but more harshly, all in all being slightly cheaper, thus giving the slightly higher net benefit of $95 billion saved.

Nevertheless, a policy aimed at achieving the optimal policy could attain an even better outcome of $245 billion saved. It is important to point out that Kyoto with global trade limits the emissions in much the same way as the optimal path, although the optimal path later on limits emissions more (the temperature reduction from the optimal path is also greater, right in Figure 161). Thus, if a global trade regime could be established, including limits on the developing world emissions (if only at their business-as-usual level), this could be the first step towards achieving the best possible outcome.

This does not mean that the outcome is great. Global warming will still cost us about $5 trillion compared to a hypothetical world without the anthropogenic greenhouse effect.[2613] But the optimal path is the best we can do. If we fail to implement at least global trading within the Kyoto Protocol, our honorable intentions of helping the world by curbing CO_2 emissions would actually end up incurring a net cost to the world. Should we only achieve OECD trading or no trade, the costs inflicted could grow substantially. And even more ambitious plans suggested by many concerned environmentalists to secure a global stabilization of emissions or stringent limits on the temperature would involve immense costs to the world.

However, such an analysis is typically met by the three objections to be looked into in more detail in the accompanying box. In short it is claimed that CO_2 emissions can be reduced far more cheaply or even entirely without cost. Most economists are very skeptical of such arguments – if it was already privately profitable to reduce CO_2 emissions, it seems surprising that this is not already being done. Several analyses suggest that the acclaimed tremendous reduction potentials are mirages, essentially kept alive by a whole series of costs being overlooked.

The assertion has also been made that if efforts to combat global warming are not worthwhile, this is because everything is calculated with an interest rate of at least 5 percent, and that the distant future therefore almost vanishes. In short, if we have to pay now to cut CO_2, and the advantages are only slowly revealed over the coming centuries, it is no wonder that with a 5 percent interest rate, the money is worth more in our own pockets. This approach is often claimed to be immoral and an expression of indifference to coming generations. In fact, however, a sensible investment with a good yield will leave our descendants and future generations of poor people with far greater resources, and this is probably a far better way of looking after their interests than investing in low-yielding greenhouse gas reductions. Moreover, the present faces far more pressing issues than redistribution of wealth among far richer nations in a hundred years' time – such as securing access to clean water and sanitation for everyone on the planet.

Finally, it is asserted that the efforts to combat global warming are an insurance policy against extreme events. When included in the computer models, these do not alter the results appreciably, but the insurance mentality *can* be justified by those who harbor an intense dislike of risk-taking. This does not change the fact, however, that the investments would probably be far better made elsewhere, for example in the developing world.

The point in this case is that with the best intentions of doing something about global warming, we could end up burdening the global community with a cost much higher or even twice that of global warming alone. As the Kyoto Protocol is unlikely to be implemented with global trading, simply because of the staggering amounts involved in distributing the initial emission rights and the consequent redistribution, Kyoto represents a waste of global resources. If we want to do good, we have to spend our resources more wisely.

OBJECTIONS: CUT CO_2 AND MAKE MONEY

One frequently heard assertion is that the price of reducing carbon dioxide emissions is considerably lower than the predictions made by the many economic models illustrated in Figure 158 above. Some of the IPCC authors believe there is a category of so-called "no regret" options constituting between 10 percent and 30 percent of CO_2 emissions. These options involve changes to our energy structure which are actually worth implementing regardless of global warming.[2614] Many of these no regret policies consist of energy savings, technological improvements and a move to electricity/district heating production.[2615] It is assumed that within our existing energy system there are important areas in which private companies, consumers and public authorities could make tremendous savings but apparently do not for a variety of reasons.[2616]

In the IPCC studies, Denmark is singled out as one of the countries where major reductions of CO_2 emissions could be had for free or even at a profit.[2617] Although it may seem rather surprising that such profit opportunities should routinely be ignored, the argument typically carries a lot of weight in the international greenhouse discussion, so we will take a good look at Denmark's case.

The Danish energy plan counts on the possibility of reducing national carbon dioxide emissions by 20 percent and still expects to make a profit by it.[2618] It is also considered possible to reduce carbon dioxide emissions by as much as 65 percent at a cost of just $1 billion, or 0.5 percent of GNP, by 2030.[2619] This result is arrived at partly by evaluating how much energy can be saved by various sectors.[2620] It is estimated that better insulation can reduce heat requirements by 40 percent,[2621] that behavioral changes can make for savings of up to 10–20 percent,[2622] that new electrical appliances can save 70–80 percent,[2623] and that the transport sector can save some 65 percent.[2624]

The fundamental problem is that the overall cost of such savings is not included in the calculation,[2625] even though the plan is painfully aware that cuts of this magnitude require a "massive technical and behavioral effort."[2626] We have already seen that reduced ventilation in connection with ever more efficient insulation of our homes is probably one of the main reasons for the increasing incidence of asthma and allergies. However, the discussion about new, more tightly sealed homes does not include consideration of such costs. At the same time, behavioral change is not without cost to the individual: savings can only be achieved by "reducing the temperature in rooms that are not used, by careful airing and more thrifty use of hot water for personal hygiene purposes."[2627]

New appliances do save energy, but "some of the biggest savings require the development and marketing of new energy-saving technologies such as vacuum insulation, new washing machine technology employing a vacuum in the drum or ultrasound."[2628] The costs of such new technology are not included in the calculation.

As regards transport, it is assumed that new cars with fuel consumption of more than 33 km/l (more than 77 mpg) will hit the market in around 2000; unfortunately, for this to happen it would be necessary to introduce "strict norms and higher fuel prices." The cost of such incentives is not included in the accounts, nor is the cost of limiting the joy of driving if greater fuel economy means sacrificing horsepower.[2629] The plan also requires that private and goods vehicles be electric in the future, covering 30 percent of all transport by the year 2030.[2630] And yet, the cost of such vehicles is not included: "Higher investments in the transport sector are disregarded in this study."[2631] Nor does the plan take into consideration that electric vehicles will probably have to be subsidized.[2632]

Finally, no welfare economic evaluation is made of the cost of the consequent doubling of energy prices,[2633] the increased cost of gas, the required purchase of energy-saving consumer durables and the increased personal time expenditure. The argument is that the reductions will lead to "greater shifts and structural changes in Danish society which it would be difficult to work into the calculations. It is difficult to project how changing private transport from more or less 0 percent electric cars today to 30 percent in 2030 will influence the sectors in society."[2634] It is certainly correct that it is difficult to carry out such evaluations, but then this probably applies to all the decisions we will need to make as to what our society should look like in 20, 50 or 100 years from now.

Most economists are therefore extremely skeptical towards assertions of such improvements in efficiency which can be implemented at no cost or even produce a profit, among other things because these calculations, as we have seen above, often omit important items of expenditure. For this reason, economists also argue that if it really is possible to implement profitable restructuring then it would be reasonable to expect that the possibility would already have been exploited.[2635]

One typical economist's expression is that "there is no such thing as a free lunch" – that costs are bound to occur somewhere along the line. Nordhaus expresses the problem of the possible, profitable carbon dioxide emissions reductions thus: "In the colloquialism of economics, this analysis suggests not only that there are free lunches, but that in some restaurants you can get paid to eat!"[2636]

A new study also seems to suggest that these "no regret" possibilities are much more limited than normally assumed; it turns out that they can probably only reduce consumption by a couple of percent and could possibly be pushed to providing 5 percent.[2637] Equally, a study of monthly electricity bills showed that the engineers' estimates of huge savings from attic insulation fell far short of real payoffs, which were closer to what economists would have expected.[2638]

The first objection to low optimal CO_2 reduction therefore seems rather feeble.

OBJECTIONS: THE PRICE OF THE FUTURE

The second objection relates to the use of discounting.[2639] This is a vast and technically complicated field, but in short the subject has to do with evaluating costs and incomes which first materialize in the future. Normally, economists choose to discount all future costs and benefits at a certain so-called discount rate. The idea is that if I am to pay $1,000 40 years from now I want to know what this obligation is worth today. If I can invest my money in bonds with a 5 percent annual yield, economists will say that the current value of the loan is $142 – if I bought bonds today worth $142 which paid an annual dividend of 5 percent then I would have exactly $1,000 in 40 years. (In this and the following examples we have ignored inflation, which with a little extra trouble could be included in the calculation, without any effect on the logic.)[2640]

These considerations are absolutely vital precisely because global warming is all about costs and benefits over the next hundreds of years and the question is how we "do the sums." Almost all evaluations of the costs and advantages of global warming make use of discounting and the debate lies in how large this discount rate should be.[2641] If the rate is high it means that amounts due well into the future are of very little importance today. If on the other hand the rate is (close to) zero, this means that money in the future will be worth (virtually) the same as it is today. Many environmentalists have argued that high rates of interest are morally reprehensible; one environmental economics textbook expresses this belief rather starkly: "A high rate of interest means saying to hell with our own future – not to mention that of our children and our grandchildren."[2642]

It is therefore tempting to suggest that future generations should be given as much consideration as our generation, and that the discount rate should be zero or almost zero. This seems like the nice and ethically just way to go. However, this apparently sound assumption leads to a grim surprise. If the welfare of future generations means just as much (or almost as much) to us as our own, then we ought to spend an extremely large share of our income on investment in the future, because the dividend payable on investments will be much greater in the future.[2643] If I were given the choice between spending $142 now or leaving $1,000 to my children in 40 years, I ought to choose in favor of my children, because they matter almost as much as me and because their gain is much greater than mine. With a discount rate of zero, I should actually choose $1,000 to my kids over $999 today. Even if we ourselves should have to scrape our way through life, then future generations will be able to live extremely well as a result of our investments. (Perhaps it is worth pointing out that these future generations will probably also only think of the future and save up even more for their future generations, etc.)

But this is where reality gets into a pickle, because we don't behave like that. When we weigh up our own situation and that of future generations, we usually choose to give priority to our own desires and let the future fend for itself.[2644] This is something we may find morally lamentable, but it ought not to get in the way of a realistic analysis of how the wealth distribution in society functions.

In choosing to give the present higher priority than the future, we do so not only because we are impatient or egotistical. It is also because we know that future generations will have more money to spend. Because of growth we are actually the poor generation, and future generations will be richer than us (as in Figure 149). We expect that in 2035 the average American will be twice as rich as she is now.[2645] For this reason it is perhaps not entirely unreasonable that society expects richer, later generations to pay more towards the cost of global warming – in exactly the same way as high income groups in our society pay higher taxes.[2646]

Both these arguments indicate that it is probably reasonable to have a discount rate of at least 4–6 percent. But it does not mean, as the quote above suggested, that we are saying to hell with future generations. It actually means that we are making sure we administer our investments sensibly so that future generations can choose for themselves what they do – and do not – want.[2647] If we chose an artificially low discount rate of 2 percent (so as to make more greenhouse gas cuts profitable) we would leave investments to future generations that were only worth 2 percent. If on the other hand our discount rate was set at 5 percent, we would spend the money on projects that make a profit of more than 5 percent.[2648] The difference between the two investments over 100 years is 18-fold. Unless our investment rate increases drastically – and there is no empirical reason why it should do so – then it means that although the 2 percent investments were more future oriented, they would all in all probably leave our children and grandchildren with far fewer resources.

Finally, it is also worth noting that the argument in favor of doing something about global warming is often that we do it for the sake of the developing world, which will be hardest hit.[2649] However, this collides with attempts to keep the discount rate low, since as a rule developing countries have amazingly high domestic interest rates. An overview study by the World Bank estimated the average rate of return in the developing world to be around 16 percent.[2650] The IPCC finds the rate to be at least 10–12 percent or even higher.[2651] So the large amounts we will end up investing in global warming could be far more efficiently investing in the developing world. Imagine that investing an amount no larger than a single year's cost of stabilizing the CO_2 emissions in the developing world could grow in 60 years to the equivalent of more than twice the world's current output.[2652] An absolutely phenomenal sum.

Similarly, the cost of the Kyoto Protocol for the US alone, even with Annex I trading, would more than amply cover the *entire* expense for providing the whole of mankind with clean drinking water and sanitation.[2653] It is estimated that this would avoid several million deaths every year and prevent half a billion people becoming seriously ill each year.[2654] This would probably be a far better help for the developing countries than a temperature reduction from Kyoto of some 0.15°C in 2100.

So the objection that the optimal reduction is so small only because 'economists don't give a damn about the future' is also mistaken. A reasonable discount rate will probably in the long term mean a far better utilization of society's resources, for our descendants too.

OBJECTIONS: THE FEAR OF CATASTROPHE

The final objection to optimal investment in global warming is that we may want to pay more in order to reduce the risk of an eventual catastrophe.

It is actually possible that global warming will lead to other dramatic and chaotic changes in the climate system.[2655] Worries have long been expressed about melting the polar ice caps, and especially the West Antarctic Ice Sheet (WAIS) because it could slide into the sea and cause a general 6-meter rise in sea level.[2656] Despite worried media reports,[2657] the IPCC has found that "no significant trends of Antarctic sea-ice extent are apparent over the period of systematic satellite measurements (since the 1970s)."[2658] Although the WAIS, as observed over centuries, has been retreating, this is a process that started in the early Holocene, due to a still on-going readjustment from the last glacial, and a process which is entirely unrelated to global warming.[2659] Moreover a WAIS breakup is considered in the 2001 IPCC report "very unlikely during the 21st century."[2660] Throughout the millennium, it is estimated that the WAIS "will contribute no more than 3 mm/yr to sea-level rise over the next thousand years, even if significant changes were to occur in the ice shelves."[2661]

New Scientist ran a story after having seen the IPCC 2001 draft, entitled: "Washed off the map: Better get that ark ready, because the sea levels are gonna rise."[2662] Here it was suggested that sea levels could rise some 10 meters (33 ft) over the coming millennium, primarily due to 7 meters coming from a complete dissolution of the Greenland ice sheet. This would be enough to "drown immense areas of land and many major cities" with a "total area larger than the US, with a population of more than a billion people and most of the world's most fertile farmland."[2663] In its *Summary for Policymakers*, the IPCC likewise cautioned that "ice sheet models project that a local warming of larger than 3°C, if sustained for millennia, would lead to virtually a complete melting of the Greenland ice sheet with a resulting sea level rise of about 7 meters."[2664]

However, the question is whether any models would envisage a sustained warming over the entire millennium – certainly most of the IPCC scenarios would not, and as we saw above, a A1T-like scenario with renewables becoming competitive before mid-century would already see temperatures decline in the early part of the 22nd century. Even by 2200, the model referred to by IPCC does not show much melt-off from Greenland, and thus makes this entire scenario very hypothetical.[2665]

Another concern is that the thermohaline circulation (THC) that drives the Gulf Stream could weaken or completely terminate, leading to a temperature drop of several degrees Celsius in Europe.[2666] Most models show some weakening of the THC which will mean a reduction of heat transport into Northwest Europe.[2667] Yet, even with the weakened THC, models still show a net warming also over Northwest Europe.[2668] IPCC conclude that "the current projections using climate models do not exhibit a complete shut down of the thermohaline circulation by 2100" but point out that it could completely, and possibly irreversibly, shut down "if the change in radiative forcing is large enough and applied long enough."[2669] Generally, it is extremely difficult to evaluate the risk of these extreme occurrences coming about.[2670] It is generally clear, as the economist Schelling also points out, that we ought to spend more effort looking into the likelihood of such occurrences than on improving our mean prognosis, since it is the extreme occurrences that are truly costly.[2671] One should be aware all the same that, although the consequences of a weakening or breakdown of the Gulf Stream would be serious indeed, it would not be catastrophic – Western European society would face substantially greater expense, but temperatures and climate would "only" fall into line with Canada.[2672] Moreover, the currently available (but very conjectural) evidence does not seem to suggest that the current Gulf Stream circulation has been weakened by global warming.[2673] Finally, some of the newest models also challenge the modeling behind the weakening of the TCH.[2674]

An estimate of the risks from such damage are of course included in the RICE/DICE models and many others (explaining why Europe wants to go further in cutting CO_2 emissions). Likewise, other models have also tried to take into consideration uncertainty about the fate of the Gulf Stream, but this does not alter the fundamental outcome of the above analysis – stabilizing global CO_2 emissions is still a poor use of resources.[2675]

Nonetheless it can be argued that we are scared enough about the thought of a potential catastrophe to want a reduction of more than the optimal 11 percent – that we are willing to buy a little extra insurance, so to speak.[2676] This argument is logically feasible, but as I see it there are two important points to be made in connection with it.

For one thing, we ought to be skeptical about spending almost 2 percent of our global GDP every year on a partial insurance (2 percent will not stop the rising temperature, just slow it down), against a risk, the extent of which we know very little about. If one favors insurance against these chaotic dangers on the basis of current knowledge, there are probably quite a few other threats one should also invest against; for instance it seems quite reasonable to argue that one should favor spending 2 percent or more to implement monitoring the destructive capability of incoming meteors, especially considering their potentially devastating impact. In addition to that, we still do not know the actual cost of a breakdown of the Gulf Stream.

For another thing we need to be crucially aware of the fact that we could probably spend this insurance money far more sensibly on other projects which have a far greater chance of success. There are masses of high-yield, crucial investments to be made, particularly in the developing world. We know that the developing countries would be able to achieve a real rate of return of 26 percent on primary education.[2677] In this connection it seems unreasonable to me to spend the equivalent of 2 percent of the world's production on highly theoretical problems with as yet quite large uncertainties. Nevertheless, it is obvious that we ought to do more research into such problems and that new knowledge thus gained should guide our future investment decisions.

Therefore it may be possible to sustain the third objection to optimal investment in global warming, although it still seems unreasonable to spend such large sums of money on such uncertain events when at the same time we have far more obvious, certain and significant projects in which to invest our money.

Summing up

Global warming has become the great environmental worry of our day. There is no doubt that mankind has influenced and is still increasing atmospheric concentrations of CO_2 and that this will influence temperature. Yet, we need to separate hyperbole from realities in order to chose our future optimally. Temperatures have increased 0.6°C over the past century (Figure 135) and it is unlikely that this is not in part due to an anthropogenic greenhouse effect, although the impression of a dramatic divergence from previous centuries is almost surely misleading (Figure 134). The central climate sensitivity of 1.5–4.5°C has not changed over the past 25 years, indicating a fundamental lack of model adequacy, because we still do not know whether we live in a world where doubling the CO_2 concentrations will mean a rather small (1.5°C) or a dramatic (4.5°C) temperature increase. All the IPCC predictions are based on GCMs, but there is still crucial problems with the representation of aerosols, water vapor feedback and clouds. In all three areas, research points towards a smaller climate sensitivity.

With the forty new scenarios the IPCC has explicitly rejected making predictions about the future, but instead gives us "computer-aided storytelling,"[2678] basing the development of crucial variables on initial choice[2679] and depicting normative scenarios "as one would hope they would emerge."[2680] While the spread of scenario profiles are wide, three scenarios of the A1-group (A1T, A1B, and A1FI) stand out as securing a much richer world – in the industrialized world about 50 percent more per capita income in 2100 than the closest scenario, and 75 percent more for the developing world (Figure 149). The total extra benefit is above \$107 trillion, which is more than 20 times more than the total cost of global warming. For comparison, we spend 1–2 percent of GDP today on the environment.[2681] If we continued to spend the high end of 2 percent of an ever increasing GDP, we would end up spending about \$18 trillion on the environment throughout the twenty-first century.[2682] In this perspective, materializing an A1 scenario would secure extra resources almost six times bigger than the total environmental costs of this entire century. Yet, the spread of global warming effects under A1 ranges from the almost lowest (A1T) to the highest (A1FI). Thus, the important decision really lies between these two A1 scenarios.

Reasonable analysis suggest that renewables – and especially solar power – will be competitive or even outcompete fossil fuels by mid-century, and this means that the A1FI seems fairly implausible and that carbon emissions are much more likely to follow the much lower A1T, causing a warming of about 2–2.5°C.

Global warming will not decrease food production, it will probably not increase storminess or the frequency of hurricanes, it will not increase the impact of malaria or indeed cause more deaths. It is even unlikely that it will cause more flood victims, because a much richer world will protect itself better. However, global warming will have serious costs – the total cost is about \$5 trillion.

Moreover, the consequences of global warming will hit the developing countries hardest, whereas the industrialized countries may actually benefit from a warming lower than 2–3 °C.[2683] The developing countries are harder hit primarily because they are poor – giving them less adaptive capacity.

Despite our intuition that we naturally need to do something drastic about such a costly global warming, economic analyses clearly show that it will be far more expensive to cut CO_2 emissions radically than to pay the costs of adaptation to the increased temperatures.

The economic analysis indicates that unless Kyoto is implemented with global trading, thus also ensuring a commitment from the developing countries, it will actually constitute a net loss of welfare. Moreover, the effect of Kyoto on the climate will be minuscule – in the order of 0.15 °C in 2100, or the equivalent of putting off the temperature increase just six years. In the longer run, a Kyoto Protocol with global trading will be less efficient than the more stringent optimal policy described above, but even that policy will only cut 11 percent of the CO_2 emissions and only diminish the temperature increase slightly.

If on the other hand Kyoto is implemented without global trading – even if it ends up allowing trade among all Annex I countries – it will not only be almost inconsequential for the climate, but it will also be a poor use of resources. The cost of such a Kyoto pact, just for the US, will be higher than the cost of providing the entire world with clean drinking water and sanitation. It is estimated that the latter would avoid 2 million deaths every year and prevent half a billion people becoming seriously ill each year. If no trading mechanism is implemented for Kyoto, the costs could approach $1 trillion, or almost five times the cost of world-wide water and sanitation coverage.

If we were to go forward as many have suggested, seeking to curb emissions to the global 1990 level, the net cost to society would seriously escalate to about $4 trillion – comparable almost to the cost of global warming itself. Likewise, a temperature increase limit would cost anywhere from $3 to $33 trillion extra.

This emphasizes that we need to be very careful in our willingness to act on global warming. If we do not ensure global trading, the world will lose. If we go much beyond an 11 percent global CO_2 reduction, the world will lose. And this conclusion does not just come from the output from a single model. Almost all the major computer models agree that even when chaotic consequences have been taken into consideration "it is striking that the optimal policy involves little emissions reduction below uncontrolled rates until the middle of the next century at the earliest."[2684] Equally, another study concluded that "the message of this admittedly simple model seems to be that it matters little whether carbon emissions are cut or not, only that protocols to stabilize emissions or concentrations are avoided."[2685] A recent overview concluded that the first insight gained from these models was that "all appear to demonstrate that large near-term abatement is not justified."[2686] A central conclusion from a meeting of all economic modelers was: "Current assessments determine that the 'optimal' policy calls for a relatively modest level of control of CO_2."[2687]

More than meets the eye

Global warming is important. Its total costs could be about $5 trillion. Yet, our choices in dealing with global warming are also important, with few, carefully chosen actions shaving some hundred billion dollars off the global warming price but with many actions which could cost the world trillions and even tens of trillion dollars over and above the global warming cost.

Is it not curious, then, that the typical reporting on global warming tells us all the bad things that could happen from CO_2 emissions, but few or none of the bad things that could come from overly zealous regulation of such emissions? And this is not just a question of the media's penchant for bad news, as discussed in chapter 2, because both could make excellent bad news.[2688] Indeed, why is it that global warming is not discussed with an open attitude, carefully attuned to avoid making big and costly mistakes to be paid for by our descendants, but rather with a fervor more fitting for preachers of opposing religions?

This is an indication that the discussion of global warming is not just a question of choosing the optimal economic path for humanity, but has much deeper, political roots as to what kind of future society we would like.

When the three IPCC *Summary for Policymakers* were approved, they were also rewritten by government-appointed scientists. From the previous IPCC report, it was well known that the most important statement would be about the human culpability in global warming: "the balance of evidence suggests that there is a discernible human influence on global climate."[2689] Consequently, there was considerable discussion over the formulation in the new report. In April 2000, the text was supposed to read "there has been a discernible human influence on global climate."[2690] In the October 2000 draft, it was stated that "it is likely that increasing concentrations of anthropogenic greenhouse gases have contributed substantially to the observed warming over the last 50 years."[2691] Yet, in the official summary, the language was further toughened up to say that "most of the observed warming over the last 50 years is likely to have been due to the increase in greenhouse gas concentrations."[2692] When asked about the scientific background for this change by *New Scientist*, the spokesman for the UN Environment Program, Tim Higham, responded very honestly: "There was no new science, but the scientists wanted to present a clear and strong message to policy makers."[2693]

Likewise, when discussing the costs and benefits of global warming, the October 2000 draft stated (in accordance with the background documents and as cited earlier here), that "in many developed countries, net economic gains are projected for global mean temperature increases up to roughly 2°C. Mixed or neutral net effects are projected in developed countries for temperature increases in the approximate range of 2 to 3°C, and net losses for larger temperature increases."[2694] Such a statement of net benefits from moderate global warming would naturally have been much quoted. However, the statement in the final *Summary* was changed to: "an increase in global mean temperature of up to a few degrees C would produce a mixture of economic gains and losses in developed countries, with economic losses for larger temperature increases."[2695]

As noted above, a political decision stopped IPCC from looking at the total cost-benefit of global warming and made it focus instead on how to curb further greenhouse gas emissions.[2696] This means that the crucial discussion above on assessing the costs of our policy choices – potentially incurring trillions of dollars of extra costs – are no longer made within the IPCC reports.[2697] Instead, some of main IPCC analyses have begun to link climate policy with all other policy areas:

> Future emissions will be determined not just by climate policy, but also and more importantly by the "world" in which we will live. Decisions about technology, investment, trade, poverty, biodiversity, community rights, social policies, or governance, which may seem unrelated to climate policy, may have profound impacts upon emissions, the extent of mitigation required, and the cost and benefits that result. Conversely, climate policies that implicitly address social, environmental, economic, and security issues may turn out to be important levers for creating a sustainable world.[2698]

Thus, climate policy may be used as a tool and a justification for charting an alternative course of development.[2699] However, "against the background of environmental scarcities" this course has to focus on eco-efficiency, industrial ecology, eco-efficient consumption etc.[2700] Basically, the IPCC conclude that it will be necessary to decouple wellbeing from production.[2701] Indeed, it will be necessary to make people understand that the performance of things cannot keep improving, for the sake of the environment.

For instance, ever "higher speed in transportation are (efficiency gains notwithstanding) unlikely to be environmentally sustainable in the long run."[2702] But this is okay, since "it is doubtful that this trend really enhances the quality of life."[2703] Instead, the IPCC suggests that we should build cars and trains with lower top speeds, and extol the qualities of sails on ships, biomass (which "has been the renewable resource base for humankind since time immemorial") and bicycles.[2704] Likewise, it is suggested that in order to avoid demand for transport, we should obtain a regionalized economy.[2705]

Essentially, what the IPCC suggests – and openly admits – is that we need to change individual lifestyles, and move away from consumption.[2706] We must focus on sharing resources (e.g. through co-ownership), choosing free time instead of wealth, quality instead of quantity, and "increase freedom while containing consumption."[2707] Because of climate change we have to remodel our world, and find more "appropriate lifestyles."[2708]

The problem is, that "the conditions of public acceptance of such options are not often present at the requisite large scale."[2709] Indeed, it is even "difficult to convince local actors of the significance of climate change and the need for corrective action."[2710] The IPCC goes as far as suggesting that the reason why we are unwilling to accept slower (or no) cars and regionalized economies with bicycles but no international travel, is that we have been indoctrinated by the media, where we see the TV characters as reference points for our own lives, shaping our values and identities.[2711] Consequently, IPCC finds that the media could also help form the path towards a more sustainable world: "Raising awareness among media professionals of the need for greenhouse gas mitigation and the role of the media in shaping lifestyles and aspirations could be an effective way to encourage a wider cultural shift."[2712]

When we think we want more goods, it is just because we have been conditioned that way.[2713] As the IPCC tells us, we do not need more consumption – research shows that "there is no clear link between level of GNP and quality of life (or satisfaction) beyond certain thresholds."[2714] The argument is based on a study showing that "although consumption in the USA has doubled since 1957, it is reported that the average US citizen considers his or her happiness to have decreased since then."[2715] However, the study is incorrectly referred,[2716] such studies are notoriously difficult to compare over time,[2717] and most of all it is now incorrect – for the only comparable data series since 1957, happiness has shown no marked tendency and it actually exceeded the 1957 result in 1988 and 1990.[2718] Moreover, the claimed absence of a link between income and happiness is incorrect – it is true that there is *less* more satisfaction, the richer you get, but there is still more.[2719]

Nevertheless, this exposition clearly show that global warming is not just about CO_2 quotas, measuring temperatures and choosing the path leaving the richest world for our descendants. The IPCC has entered the fray in telling us that climate deliberations is not only climate policy but "a wide range of issues, including development, equity, sustainability, and sustainable development."[2720]

Likewise, the environmental movement has an interest in greenhouse gas curbs which goes far beyond the narrow concerns of global warming. Perhaps the best illustration comes from an episode back in March 1989, when electrochemists B. Stanley Pons and Martin Fleischmann shocked the world, announcing that they had achieved fusion at room temperature.[2721] As other researchers tried and failed to replicate cold fusion, it led to skepticism and today most researchers dismiss cold fusion as a grand illusion.[2722] Nevertheless, for a some short months, it was actually possible to believe that we had cold fusion within reach – essentially giving humanity access to clean, cheap and unlimited power.

In April 1989 the *Los Angeles Times* interviewed a number of top-environmentalists about their view on cold fusion.[2723] With the assumption that the technology would be cheap and clean, Jeremy Rifkin nevertheless thought

> "it's the worst thing that could happen to our planet." Inexhaustible power, he argues only gives man an infinite ability to exhaust the planet's resources, to destroy its fragile balance and create unimaginable human and industrial waste.[2724]

UC Berkeley physicist John Holdren pointed out that "clean-burning, non-polluting, hydrogen-using bulldozers still could knock down trees or build housing developments on farmland."

UC Berkley anthropologist Laura Nader told us that

> many people just assume that cheaper, more abundant energy will mean that mankind is better off, but there is no evidence for that. Between 1950 and 1970 there was a doubling of energy use while at the same time quality of life indicators all declined.[2725]

Stanford biologist Paul Ehrlich was cautious. While cheap, clean, inexhaustible power *could* be a boon for mankind, the problem was that "industrialized societies, so far, have not used power wisely," but caused massive pollution. In summary, Ehrlich said that cold fusion, even if clean and cheap, would be "like giving a machine gun to an idiot child."[2726]

Finally, Barry Commoner, Center for Biology of Natural Systems, pointed out that "fusion power could prove to be a dangerous distraction from existing energy sources. It does not make sense, he says, to jump on an unproven, possibly dangerous technology like fusion when a safe, proven and decentralized technology like solar power is there for the asking."[2727]

What these statements of opposition to an almost ideal energy source show is that the relevant agenda is not about energy or the economics of energy. Indeed this could not be the case, since the question from the *Los Angeles Times* was originally formulated "what *if* cold fusion would be cheap and clean?" Instead the opposition is based on a different agenda, focused on the potentially damaging consequences from using cold fusion. Essentially, the criticism points to other values, arguing for a change to a decentralized society which is less resource oriented, less industrialized, less commercialized, less production-oriented. Such an agenda is entirely valid, but it is important to realize that the discussion is no longer primarily about energy.

So this is the answer as to why the global warming discussion sounds like the clash of two religions. The argument I have presented above is one way to look at the world. It attempts to deal with the basic problem of global warming, and tries to identify the best possible policy to deal with it. But it does not ask of its solutions that they should also help fundamentally change the fabric of society.

The other approach, using global warming as a springboard for other wider policy goals is entirely legitimate, but in all honesty these goals should naturally be made explicit. When the scenario modelers tell us that the B1 scenario is "best," they really tell us that they prefer a society with less wealth but also with less climate change.[2728] However, I think they really have to explicate this choice, given a difference in wealth of $107 trillion and a climate cost of "just" $5 trillion. Likewise, will B1 really be better for the developing countries, loosing out on some 75 percent personal income?

When the IPCC tells us that we do not need more money to be happy and that bicycles and sailing ships would work fine in a decentralized world with a regionalized economy, this is indeed a legitimate argument. But this is not the story that has reached the news headlines.[2729] Rather, the IPCC has tightened the description of human culpability in global warming – "to present a clear and strong message to policy makers."[2730] And this message was clearly captured, as in this headline: "We are all guilty! It's official, people are to blame for global warming."[2731]

Many scientists in the IPCC are undoubtedly professional, academically committed and clearheaded, but the IPCC works in a minefield of policy, and it has to take political responsibility for its seemingly scientific decisions, if they cause obvious biases in reporting. When the IPCC used scenarios that were presented as far-ranging "stories," the choice of many extremes nevertheless had political implications. In the reporting from the major media, such as CNN, CBS, *The Times*, and *Time*, it was found that *all* used the high estimate of 5.8°C warming, and yet *none* mentioned the low estimate of 1.4°C.[2732]

Conclusion: scares and sound policy

The important lesson of the global warming debate is threefold. First, we have to realize what we are arguing about – do we want to handle global warming in the most efficient way or do we want to use global warming as a stepping stone to other political projects. Before we make this clear to ourselves and others, the debate will continue to be muddled. Personally, I believe that in order to think clearly we should try to the utmost to separate issues, not least because trying to solve all problems at one go may probably result in making bad solutions for all areas. Thus, I here try to address just the issue of global warming.

Second, we should not spend vast amounts of money to cut a tiny slice of the global temperature increase when this constitutes a poor use of resources and when we could probably use these funds far more effectively in the developing world. This connection between resource use on global warming and aiding the Third World actually goes much deeper, because, as we saw above, the developing world will experience by far the most damage from global warming. Thus, when we spend resources to mitigate global warming we are in fact and to a large extent helping future inhabitants in the developing world.[2733] However, if we spend the same money directly in the Third World we would be helping present inhabitants in the developing world, and through them also their descendants. Since the inhabitants of the Third World are likely to be much richer in the future, and since we have shown that the return on investments in the developing countries is much higher than those on global warming, the question really boils down to: Do we want to help more well-off inhabitants in the Third World a hundred years from now a little or do we want to help poorer inhabitants in the present Third World more? To give a feel for the size of the problem – the Kyoto Protocol will likely cost at least $150 billion a year, and possibly much more (Figure 164). UNICEF estimates that just $70–80 billion a year could give all Third World inhabitants access to the basics like health, education, water and sanitation.[2734] More important still is the fact that if we could muster such a massive investment in the present-day developing countries this would also give them a much better future position in terms of resources and infrastructure from which to manage a future global warming.

Third, we should realize that the cost of global warming will be substantial – about $5 trillion. Since cutting back CO_2 emissions quickly becomes very costly, and easily counterproductive, we should focus more of our effort at finding ways of easing the emission of greenhouse gases over the long run. Partly, this means that we need to invest much more in research and development of solar power, fusion and other likely power sources of the future. Given a current US investment in renewable energy R&D of just $200 million, a considerable increase would seem a promising investment to achieve a possible conversion to renewable energy towards the latter part of the century. Partly, this also means that we should be much more open towards other techno-fixes (so-called geoengineering). These suggestions range from fertilizing the ocean (making more algae bind carbon when they die and fall to the ocean floor) and putting sulfur particles into the stratosphere (cooling the earth) to capturing CO_2 from fossil fuel use and returning it to storage in geological formations.[2735] Again, if one of these approaches could indeed mitigate (part of) CO_2 emissions or global warming, this would be of tremendous value to the world.

Finally, we ought to have a look at the cost of global warming in relation to the total world economy. If we implement Kyoto poorly or engage in more inclusive mitigation like stabilization, the price will easily be 2 percent or more of world GDP per year towards the middle of the century.

Now, can 2 percent of world production be described as a lot of money when it comes to combating global warming?[2736] That all depends on how we look at it. In a sense, 2 percent annually of world production is naturally a massive amount – almost the same as is spent annually on the military globally.[2737]

At the same time, the world economy is expected to grow by around 2–3 percent throughout the twenty-first century. So one could also argue that the total cost of managing global warming *ad infinitum* would be the same as deferring the growth curve by less than a year. In other words we would have to wait until 2051 to enjoy the prosperity we would otherwise have enjoyed in 2050. And by that time the average citizen of the world will have become twice as wealthy as she is now.

This is not to make light of $5,000 or $10,000 billion. Far from it. I still believe that we should use it as sensibly as we can. But

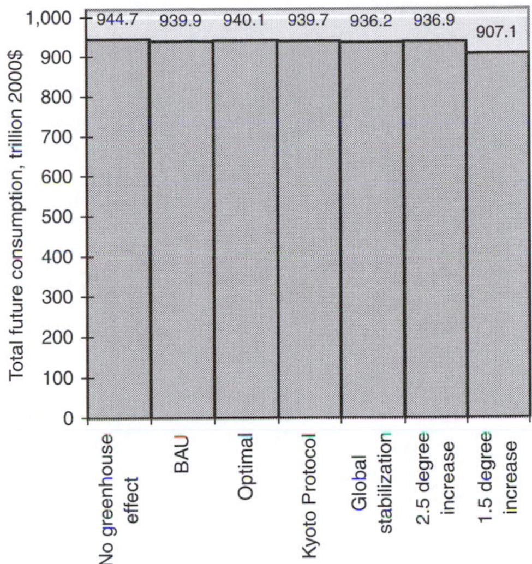

Figure 165 Total future consumption in trillion 2000 US$, for business-as-usual, five scenarios and the value if global warming was not happening. Source: Nordhaus 1992:1317, Nordhaus and Boyer 2000:7:26, 8:28, BEA 2001b–c.

there is no way that the cost will send us to the poorhouse. Global warming is in this respect still a limited and manageable problem.

Figure 165 shows the total cost of applying the various policies to total future consumption. Global warming will cost us approximately 0.5 percent of our overall consumption. Even stabilization of emissions will "only" cost 0.4 percent more of our overall wealth compared to choosing the optimal solution to global warming.

This total future consumption also underscores that *global warming is not anywhere near the most important problem facing the world.* What matters is making the developing countries rich and giving the citizens of developed countries even greater opportunities. In Figure 166 we see the total income over the coming century for the four main scenarios in the IPCC. If we choose a world focused on economic development within a global setting, the total income will be some $900 trillion. However, should we go down a path focusing on the environment, even if we

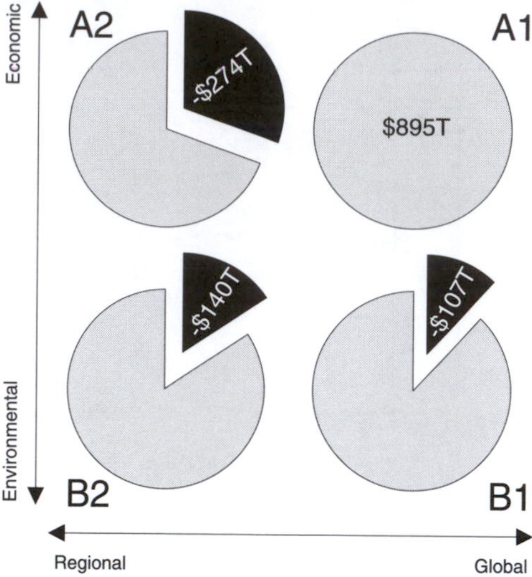

Figure 166 The four main scenarios in IPCC, along the dimension Global–Regional and the dimension Economic–Environmental. The total worth of income over the century 2000–2100 is estimated at $895 trillion in A1, the global economically focused scenario.[2738] The cost of focusing on the environment in a global setting is $107 trillion (B1), the cost of focusing on the economy but in a regionalized setting is $274 trillion (A2) and the cost of focusing on the environment in a regionalized economy is $140 trillion (B2). For comparison, the total cost of global warming is estimated at 4.8 trillion, or 0.5 percent of the A1 scenario. All amounts in 2000 US$. Source: IPCC 2000b, BEA 2001b–c.

stay within a global setting, humanity will lose some $107 trillion, or 12 percent of the total, potential income. And should we choose a more regional approach to solving the problems of the twenty-first century, we would stand to lose $140–274 trillion or even more than a quarter of the potential income. Moreover, the loss will mainly be to the detriment of the developing countries – switching from A1 to B1 would cost the developing world a quarter of its total income.[2739]

Again, this should be seen in the light of a total cost of global warming at about $5 trillion and a cost of all other environmental policies throughout the twenty-first century of $18 trillion. What this illustrates is that if we want to leave a planet with the most possibilities for our descendants, in both the developing and the developed world, it is imperative that we focus primarily on the economy and solving our problems in a global context rather than focusing – in the IPCC lingo – on the environment in a regionalized context. Basically, this puts the spotlight on securing economic growth, especially in the third world, while ensuring a global economy, both tasks which the world has set itself within the framework of the World Trade Organization (WTO). If we succeed here, we could increase world income with $107–274 trillion, whereas even if we achieve the absolutely most efficient global warming policies, we can increase wealth with just $0.245 trillion (Figure 164). To put it squarely, what matters to our and our children's future is not primarily decided within the IPCC framework but within the WTO framework.

Yet, one could be tempted to suggest that we are actually so rich that we can afford both to pay a partial insurance premium against global warming (at 2–4 percent of GDP), and to help the developing world (a further 2 percent), because doing so would only offset growth by about 2–3 years. And that is true. I am still not convinced that there is any point in spending 2–4 percent on a pretty insignificant insurance policy, when we and our descendants could benefit far more from the same investment placed elsewhere. But it is correct that we are actually wealthy enough to do so.

And this is one of the main points of this book.

The Real State of the World

PART 6

25 Predicament or progress?

Throughout this book I have tried to present all the facts, to give us a rounded feel of the real state of the world, and I have tried to compare and contrast it to our current understanding, stemming from the recurrent incantations of the Litany. In this concluding chapter I want to sum up the problems and consequences of our biased view of the world. However, I will also allow myself to be more free to point out what I think are the great remaining challenges for humanity.

On the global level, it seems obvious to me that the major problems remain with hunger and poverty. Although we have witnessed great improvements both in feeding ever more people, ever better, and bringing ever more people out of poverty, and although these positive trends are likely to continue into the future, there still remain some 800 million hungry people and some 1.2 billion poor people in this world. In terms of securing a long-term improvement of the environmental quality of the developing world, securing growth so as to lift these people out of hunger and poverty is of the utmost importance, since our historical experience tells us that only when we are sufficiently rich can we start to think about, worry about and deal with environmental problems.

As regards the developed world, we have seen great improvements overall and also within the environmental area. These positive developments do not imply that we need do no more for the environment. On the contrary, in many areas and over time it will make good sense to invest even more in sound environmental management: as the discussion on air pollution pointed out, although particle pollution is probably lower now than at any time since the 1500s, lowering emissions even further will probably be a wise use of resources. However, we have to realize that investing in an ever better environment is only one of the many ways we can invest in a better world, and that we must prioritize the environment as against better education, more health care, and better infrastructure as well as improving conditions in the Third World.

The central point here remains: if we are to make the best decisions for our future, we should base our prioritizations not on fear but on facts. Thus, we need to confront our fears; we need to challenge the Litany.

The Great Fable of the Litany

We have been told for a long time the story of the Litany, that doomsday is nigh. Lester Brown and an entire army of environmental organizations, pundits and politicians have warned us of the impending débâcle. This message has had enormous social and political impact. Former vice-president Al Gore's *Earth in the Balance* is an excellent example of the mood. The opening paragraph of its conclusion states plainly: "Modern industrial civilization as presently organized, is colliding violently with our planet's ecological system."[2740]

And this is not all, Gore insists. For sure, the deterioration of the world's rainforests, of fertile agricultural land, of the ozone layer and of the climate balance is terrible, but Gore actually informs us that these calamities are "only the first of a steady stream of progressively more serious ecological catastrophes that will be repeatedly proffered to us."[2741]

At the same time he insists that the loss is not only in the environment but also within ourselves. We have lost our natural contact with the Earth and become strangers to our own existence. "The pursuit of happiness and comfort is paramount," and we have ended up concentrating on "the consumption of an endless stream of shiny new products."[2742] We have constructed "a false world of plastic flowers and Astroturf, air-conditioning and fluorescent lights, windows that don't open and background music that never stops . . . sleepy hearts jump-started with caffeine, alcohol, drugs and illusions." We have forgotten our "direct experience with real life."[2743] Our civilization has achieved not only the destruction of the world but of ourselves. This is, indeed, "a dysfunctional civilization."[2744]

And consequently, Gore sees this civilization as the new antagonist, just as Nazi Germany and communist totalitarianism were for the previous generation. "It is not merely in the service of analogy that I have referred so often to the struggles against Nazi and communist totalitarianism, because I believe that the emerging effort to save the environment is a continuation of these struggles."[2745] And this is the reason why "we must make the rescue of the environment the central organizing principle for civilization."[2746]

The Real State of the World

But this vision and its political consequences are borne on the myth of the Litany. Gore's Litany about "a dysfunctional civilization" and the loss of a "direct experience with real life" reveals both a scary idealization of our past and an abysmal arrogance towards the developing countries of the world.

The fact is, as we have seen, that this civilization has over the last 400 years brought us fantastic and continued progress. Through most of the couple of million years we have been on the planet we had a life expectancy of about 20–30 years. During the course of the past century we have more than doubled our life expectancy, to 67 years.

Infants no longer die like flies – it is no longer every other child that dies but one in twenty, and the mortality rate is still falling. We are no longer almost chronically ill, our breaths stinking of rotting teeth, with festering sores, eczema, scabs, and suppurating boils. We have far more food to eat – despite the fact that the Earth is home to far more people: the average inhabitant in the Third World now has 38 percent more calories. The proportion of people starving has fallen dramatically from 35 percent to 18 percent, and by the year 2010 this share will probably have fallen further to 12 percent. By that time, we will feed more than 3 billion more people adequately.

We have experienced unprecedented growth in human prosperity. In the course of the last 40 years, everyone – in the developed as well as the developing world – has become more than three times richer. Seen in a longer perspective this growth has been quite overwhelming. Americans have become 36 times richer over the past 200 years.

We have gained access to far more amenities, from clean drinking water to telephones, computers and cars. We are better educated; in the Third World, illiteracy has fallen from 75 percent to less than 20 percent, and the standard of education in the developing and the developed world has increased tremendously – as regards university education in the developing countries by almost 400 percent in 30 years.

We have more leisure time, greater security and fewer accidents, more education, more amenities, higher incomes, fewer starving, more food and a healthier and longer life. This is the fantastic story of mankind, and to call such a civilization "dysfunctional" is quite simply immoral. In the developing world there are still many who lack the basic necessities and for whom growth and development are not an inconsequential experience of plastic flowers, microwaved food, alcohol and drugs, but a chance to live a decent life with the possibilities of choices, reaching beyond the concerns of getting enough to eat.

For the industrialized world, growth and progress have given us a life that is so much better that we at last have enough time and resources to consider how we want to make the most of life. Ironically, Al Gore's dressing-down of our society is only possible because growth has liberated us (and him) sufficiently from our physical limitations to give us the possibility to choose – even if this choice is to turn one's back on present-day society.

In so far as Gore simply wants us to consider whether we would not be happier shopping less and living more (leave the mall and visit friends, go for a hike in the wilderness, take up painting, etc.), his commentary is naturally sympathetic and serves as a reasonable reminder. But Gore goes much further and tells us that we live superficial and phony lives, that our civilization and our parents' generation have indoctrinated us into living this dysfunctional life and that we cannot see the prison walls that surround us.[2747] We are repressed without being aware of it. This kind of supercilious attitude is a challenge to our democratic freedom and contests our basic right to decide for ourselves how we lead our lives, so long as doing so does not bring us into collision with others.

But for both Al Gore and Lester Brown the argument goes much deeper. Because the actual justification of their criticism of civilization is not that we are doing better, but that we are doing better to an increasing extent at the cost of Earth's ecosystem. This is why in reality we should put a stop to the insane collision with Earth's limits.

Al Gore thus joins the long list of cultural pessimists who have experienced the modern world but have also seen the seeds of its destruction.[2748] From Frankenstein to Jurassic Park, our technical ingenuity is seen as catastrophically exceeding our expectations, creating a world that has spun out of control.

Ironically, Al Gore believes that the way to escape this dysfunctionality is by means of "the harsh light of truth."[2749] And as we have seen throughout the book, the light of truth does have a harsh edge, especially on the core myths of the Litany.

Because our food production will continue to give more people more and cheaper food. We will not lose our forests; we will not run out of energy, raw materials or water. We have reduced atmospheric pollution in the cities of the developed world and have good reason to believe that this will also be achieved in the developing world. Our oceans have not been defiled, our rivers have become cleaner and support more life, and although the nutrient influx has increased in many coastal waters like the Gulf of Mexico, this does not constitute a major problem – in fact, benefits generally outweigh costs. Nor is waste a particularly big problem. The total US waste throughout the twenty-first century could be deposited in a single square landfill, less than 18 miles on the side – or 26 percent of Woodward County, Oklahoma.

Acid rain did not kill off our forests, our species are not dying out as many have claimed, with half of them disappearing over the next 50 years – the figure is likely to be about 0.7 percent. The problem of the ozone layer has been more or less solved. The current outlook on the development of global warming does not indicate a catastrophe – rather, there is good reason to believe that our energy consumption will change towards renewable energy sources way before the end of the century. Indeed, the catastrophe seems rather in spending our resources unwisely on curbing present carbon emissions at high costs instead of helping the developing countries and increasing non-fossil fuel research. And finally, our chemical worries and fear of pesticides are misplaced and counterproductive. First, phasing out pesticides will probably waste resources and actually cause more cancer. Second, the main causes of cancer are not chemicals but our own lifestyle.

The Litany is based on myths, although many of these myths may be propagated by well-meaning, compassionate people. And one can of course choose to believe that these myths may represent "only the first of a steady stream of progressively more serious ecological catastrophes." But it is essential to point out that this is purely a matter of conviction. We know of no other substantial problems looming on the horizon.

It is difficult not to get the impression that the criticism leveled by Brown and Gore of a "dysfunctional civilization" is simply an expression of our Calvinistic sense of guilt.[2751] We have done so well that some actually feel rather ashamed. We may really believe that we have deserved global warming.

But such a conclusion is quite unnecessary. We ought not to punish ourselves in shame. We ought to be pleased that we have thrown off so many of humanity's yokes and made possible fantastic progress in terms of prosperity. And we ought to face the facts – that on the whole we have no reason to expect that this progress will not continue.

This is the real state of the world.

Yet we worry ever more

Of course this does not mean that everything is hunky dory and that we face no problems at all. Humanity still has a whole series of challenges to tackle, now and in the future. Things are *better* now, but they are still not *good enough*.

However, being presented with the real state of the world makes us realize that, given our past record, it is likely that by humanity's creativity and collected efforts we can handle and find solutions to these problems. Consequently we can approach the remaining problems with confidence and inspiration to create an even better world.

And honestly, we are perfectly aware of the true challenges for our globe. There are still 800 million people who starve. While the number of starving people has decreased and the percentage has decreased rapidly since 1950, this is still far too many. Equally, there are still 1.2 billion poor people. While the share of poverty has declined rapidly since 1950, this is also still far too many.

We need to set these challenges as top priorities, and this entails helping the developing countries with structural changes and committing them to the path of democracy and the rule-of-law, while fulfilling our UN pledge of donating 0.7 percent of the GNP, which currently only Denmark, Norway, the Netherlands and Sweden fulfill.[2752] But it also entails allowing the developing countries into the global economy, letting them compete precisely in the areas where they have the competitive advantage. This means we need to lift restrictions and cut subsidies on labor-intensive products such as agriculture and textiles, two of the areas most protected by the developed countries.

As far as the Western world is concerned, we also know the challenges. Many people still die needlessly because of air pollution. While air pollution has decreased dramatically over the past 30 years, it is still too high, especially with regard to particulate pollution. Thus, stringent pollution restrictions in areas where benefits outweigh costs will still be a necessary goal. Beyond that, we need to quit smoking, avoid fatty foods, get more exercise, and as a society we need to achieve a whole series of social and educational improvements. However, these areas are unfortunately not quite as sexy as focusing on pesticides, oxygen depletion, global warming, forests, wind power, biodiversity, etc. – issues which are more clearly someone else's fault.

One of the most serious consequences of the Litany of Brown, Gore and the entire environmentally worried elite is that it undermines our confidence in our ability to solve our remaining problems. It gives us a feeling of being under siege, constantly having to act with our backs to the wall, and this means that we will often implement unwise decisions based on emotional gut reactions. The Litany gets to modern man and impacts us directly: the Litany frightens us.

The social scientist Aaron Wildavsky pondered this paradox: "How extraordinary! The richest, longest lived, best protected, most resourceful civilization, with the highest degree of insight into its own technology, is on its way to becoming the most frightened."[2753]

This fear becomes evident when people are interviewed. We are afraid. We fear the future. In the *Health of the Planet* survey, people were asked how much they believed environmental problems affected their health ten years ago and now, and how it would affect their children 25 years from now. As can be seen in Figure 167, the respondents were – overwhelmingly – frightened. The respondents believe that the environmental problems of the future will consistently affect our health much more in the future than it did in the past. This is – at least as far as the industrialized world is concerned – astonishing: we *know* that atmospheric pollution, which accounts for more than half the incidences of environment-related cancer, has been drastically reduced.[2754] But we still *believe* that it has become worse and worse.

This feeling is in large part caused by the Litany. It is due to the steady flow of information about the terrible state of the environment. But how is it possible to believe that things are getting worse when objective figures show the exact opposite? This apparent paradox seems to be a consequence of prosperity often described by the expression: "No food, one problem. Much food, many problems."[2755] We are now so well off in so many different respects that we have time to worry about a whole series of other minor problems.

Some sociologists see this as an expression of modern society having begun systematically to produce risks which are invisible (e.g. pesticides and radioactivity) and about which we can thus only be informed by experts.[2756] However, this argument seems misplaced. In times past, our society produced large numbers of invisible risks – tuberculosis, the plague and smallpox could not be seen by the naked eye and seemed to strike at random. These risks were far greater, as is reflected by much shorter life expectancy.[2757] It seems more plausible that our society has changed character because it has begun to produce far more *information about risks*.[2758]

This was the point made in the introduction. Our fear is due to a high degree to the fact that we are given ever more negative information by scientists, the organizations and the media. We are being made aware of things we had no idea we needed worry about.

More research is being conducted than ever before. One obvious consequence is that we find ever more causal connections. Many of these connections are extremely marginal. And given the statistical nature of most of the studies, some of them will later prove to be wrong. There is nothing improper in that, since this is the way science works, but it does mean that there are ever more bits of accessible information about things which are not necessarily either relevant or even correct. We are familiar with this tendency from the world of medicine and the continuous bombardment of information about dos and don'ts: now salt is good for you, now it is bad for you; now estrogens cause breast cancer, now they don't.

At the same time both the organizations and the media have an ever-increasing need to profile themselves in the struggle for attention and market segments. The environmental organizations fight for the environment, and as we pointed out in the introduction, they therefore also have an obvious interest in presenting a specific image of the world: that the environment is in an awful state and getting poorer. The worse they can portray the environment, the easier it is for them to convince us that we need to spend more money on the environment rather than on hospitals, child day care, etc. The organizations are keen to tell us when the deforestation rate in the

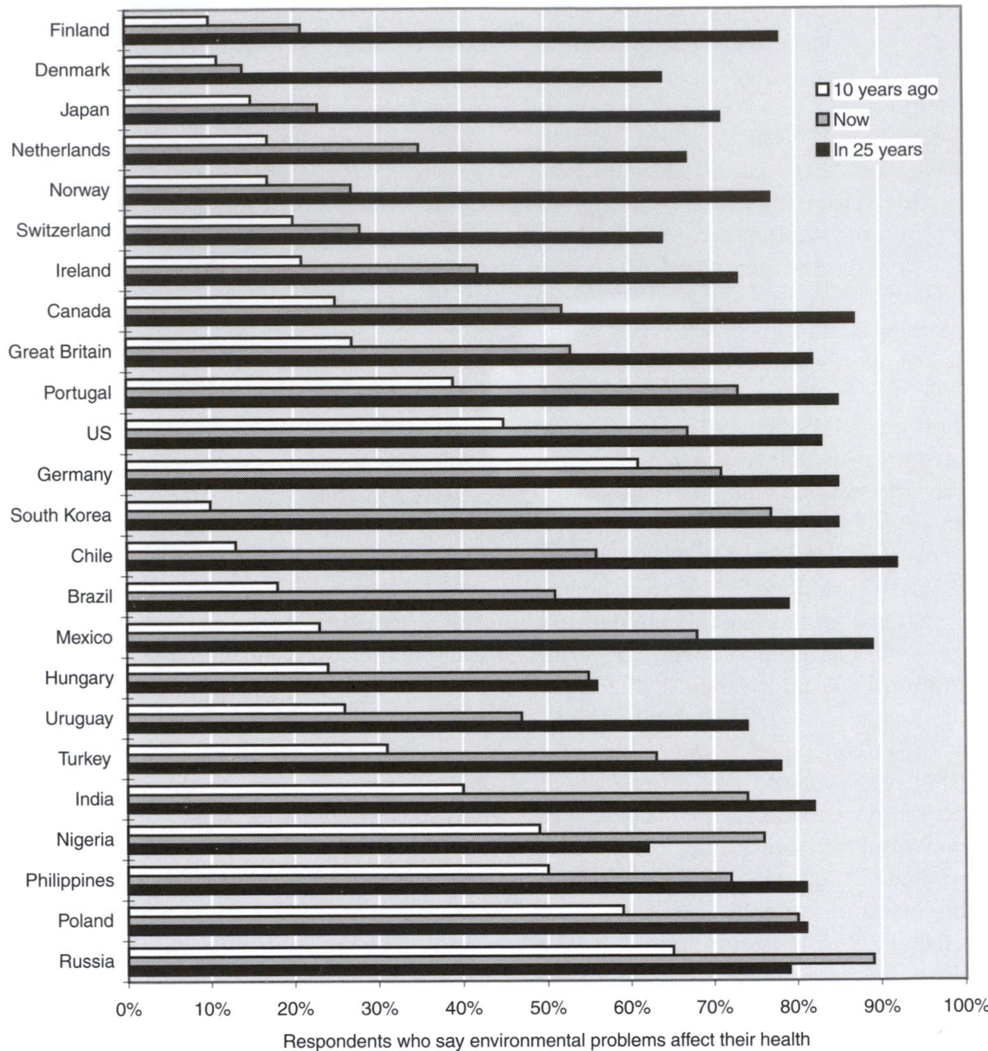

Figure 167 The percentage of respondents who say that environmental problems affect their health "a great deal" or "a fair amount," 10 years ago, now and 25 years in the future.[2750] Source: Dunlap *et al.* 1993:14.

Amazon has gone up, but not when it has dropped.[2759]

The media look for interesting and sensational news but often end up focusing on the negative aspects and giving us yet more worries to consider. When the harvest is good we hear about how low prices will be bad for the farmers; however, when the harvest is bad we hear how the consumers will suffer from high prices. When in February 1992 NASA predicted that a hole might open in the ozone layer above the US, the story hit the front page of *Time* magazine. NASA's withdrawal of the story two months later was only given four lines inside the magazine.[2760] Unless readers are extremely observant they would in both situations be left with the distinct impression that the state of the world had deteriorated.

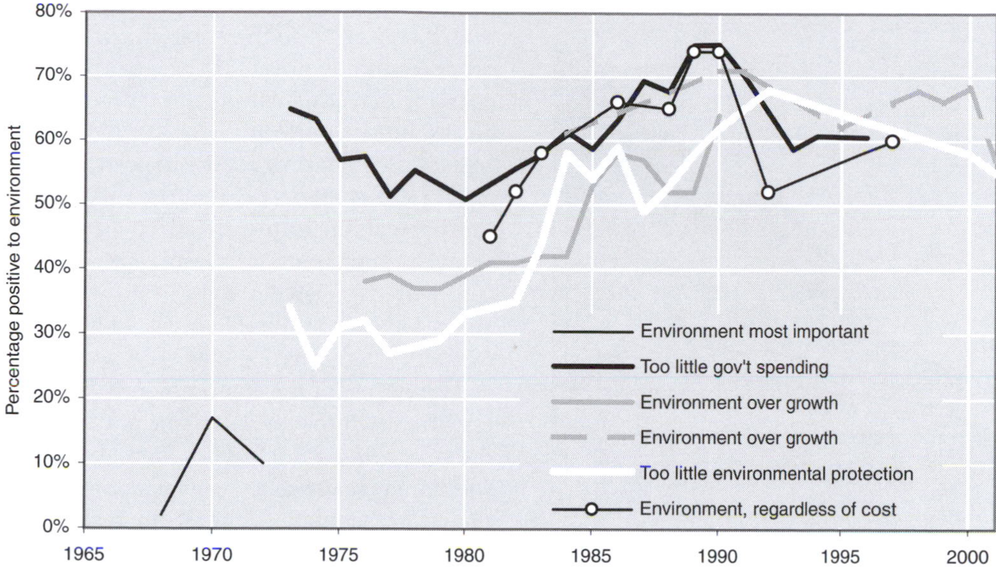

Figure 168 Trends in public opinion about the importance of the environment, 1968–2001.[2761] Source: Dunlap 1991b:291, 294, 300, 1991a:13, GSS 2000, Gallup 2000, Saad & Dunlap 2000, Dunlap & Saad 2001, Anon. 1997b.

Setting priorities and risks

The fear created by the Litany is effectively communicated by organizations and the media, which again (and for a variety of reasons) selectively use some of science's many results to confirm our concerns. This fear is absolutely decisive because it paralyses our reasoned judgment. Thus, it is imperative that we regain our ability to prioritize the many different worthy causes.

We all care for the environment. In Figure 168, we can see how environmental consciousness was ignited around the first Earth Day in 1970 (unfortunately we only have very poor poll data before 1973), when 17 percent of Americans mentioned it as one of the most important problems. Since then, however, the environment has never really been *the* most important problem, which is more likely to be the economy, employment, the deficit, crime, drugs or healthcare – even today, the environment seldom rises above 2 percent in most-important-problem polls.[2762]

But there is a basic goodwill towards the environment, with 50 percent of all Americans describing themselves as environmentalists.[2763] Actually, during the Reagan years, the belief that too little was done for the environment increased as did the will to set environmental protection over economic growth. In the 1990s the support may have slipped slightly, but the basic support for tougher environmental policies has remained.

In all liberal democracies, voters have displayed ever increasing and broadening expectations for public services, which has put the squeeze on public funding throughout most of the Western world. Many worthy causes, not just environmental ones but also issues of health, education, infrastructure and care make ever increasing demands on our time, attention and not least money. The US expenditure on the environment has increased sevenfold since 1962 (Figure 169), significantly outpacing the GDP, which has increased only a little more than threefold. In 1999, expenditure on the environment was $227 billion or

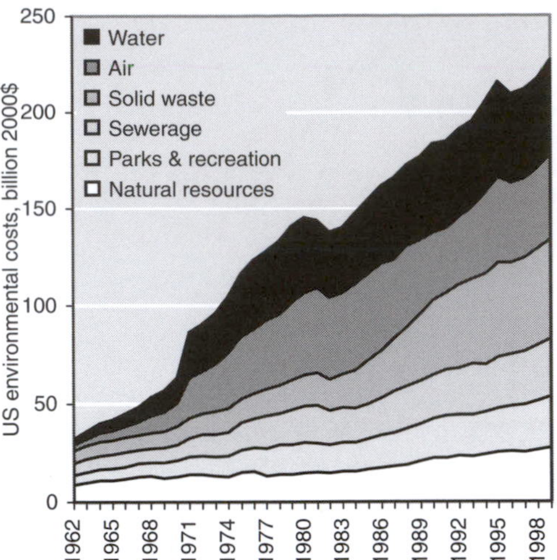

Figure 169 Expenditure on the US environment, 1962–99, in 2000$. Not all costs are included and some years have been estimated.[2764] Source: CEQ 1997:249–50, EPA 2000a:013.txt, USBC 1999d, OMB 2000b:Table 3.2, BEA 2001b–c.

about 2.4 percent of GDP. Furthermore, there is no reason to assume that the number of good and deserving environmental projects will not grow in the future as well.[2765] For this reason it will be ever more crucial for us to be able to prioritize between the many different causes, each of them worthy. To use the idiom of the introduction, it is necessary for us to learn to do the dishes until they are clean *enough*, and not continue washing them when they are already 99.9999 percent clean.

This problem of prioritization, of course, is conspicuous in Figure 168, where 50–60 percent of all American voters declare themselves in agreement with the statement: "Protecting the environment is so important that requirements and standards cannot be too high, and continuing environmental improvements must be made regardless of cost."[2766] Such an understanding is problematic in at least two ways. First, it prevents prioritizing between environmental problems, so that we handle the most important ones first, essentially claiming that *all* environmental problems are of the utmost importance. Second, it hinders prioritizing between the environment and all other essential areas of society, basically claiming that any environmental problem has an absolute first priority.

Such statements of dislike of prioritization have grave consequences. Of course, in real life popular majorities of 50–60 percent of voters are not translated into approved budgets with 100 percent for the environment and 0 percent for all other areas. But because so many voters have claimed that "we should do everything for the environment" they have essentially left the difficult issue as to *which* of the many important environmental projects we should choose to the persons or organizations that shout the loudest. In reality, the expressed dislike of prioritization does not mean that we will not end up prioritizing, only that our choices will be worse. Against this, I will try to argue that if we want the best possible solutions for society, we have to tackle prioritization head on. Using the title of a recent book, we really do have to do *worst things first*.[2767]

In the following I shall take a good look at death risks. This does not mean that other essential yardsticks do not exist (such as the risk of illness and the threat to ecosystems), but for one thing the risk of death is essential and often overshadows other considerations as far as the individual voter is concerned, and for another it has been the typical focal point of much environmental regulation.

First of all, therefore, we must ask ourselves how significant pollution actually is to human life. Figure 170 shows the proportion of deaths caused by ten of the most important risk factors. We have to weigh up how this distribution of risks tallies with our preconceived idea of where the problems lie. Do these figures reflect our political aims and areas of effort?

What we see in Figure 170 is that by far the most of the years of life lost (YLL) in the developing world are caused by hunger, by the lack of access to clean drinking water and sanita-

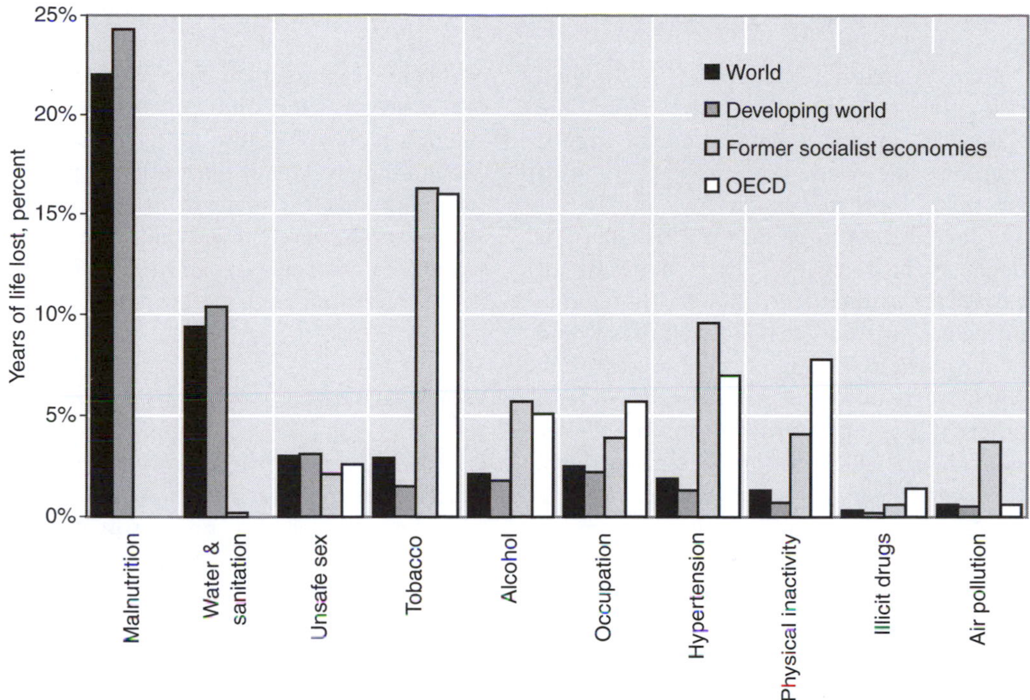

Figure 170 The WHO estimate of the distribution of Years of Life Lost (YLL) caused by ten important risk factors, for the world, the developing countries, the former socialist countries of Europe (incl. Russia) and the OECD.[2768] The figures only add up to approximately 46 percent because it must be possible to attribute death to individual risk factors. Source: Murray and Lopez 1996a:311–15.

tion, and by poor hygiene, as we discussed in Part II. These problems have practically disappeared in the developing countries. Of course, since we eventually have to die, we now face numerous other risks. Our years of life lost stem primarily from use of tobacco, alcohol and drugs, a lack of exercise, hypertension and risks faced at work (e.g. accidents and asbestos). Notice that within the OECD, lack of exercise actually leads to the loss of more life-years than hypertension. Unsafe sex covers both HIV and hepatitis B infections as well as the group of cervical cancers attributable to infections. Also included are the deaths caused by unwanted pregnancies as well as from abortions.

Air pollution is indeed a significant health threat in the former socialist economies, where decades of inefficient production and unregulated pollution still takes its toll. Nevertheless, apart from the risk of unsafe sex and illicit drugs, even here the pollution risk of 3.5 percent YLL is the smallest of the industrialized world risks. And when we look at the OECD-area, it becomes obvious that at 0.6 percent the environmental risk from air pollution is by far the smallest of all OECD risks. For the OECD, air pollution simply accounts for a very small share of the overall life-years loss. This result corresponds to the finds of Doll and Peto from the chapter on chemicals and pesticides, where we saw that pollution contributed about 2 percent to cancer. Here we find once again that only a tiny proportion of the overall loss of life-years is attributable to pollution. *The fact that the figure is only 0.6 percent does not mean that we can just ignore pollution or should dismiss political action, but it does indicate the degree of worry we should attach to pollution.*

There is a clear tendency to wish away all risk. We saw how Al Meyerhoff from the Natural Resources Defense Council argued that pesticides cause cancer. Thus, "we must get rid of pesticides in the food supply."[2769] The logic seems to be that if a risk exists it ought to be removed. This is naturally an extremely sympathetic though thoroughly unrealistic attitude. To remove all risks would be impossible.[2770] And far more essential: when we remove one risk we cause several others to pop up. We saw during the discussion on pesticides that if we remove them, then we will naturally avoid (some time in the future) having any pesticides in our drinking water. But at the same time we will get a decrease in agricultural production and higher fruit and vegetable prices, with a resulting increase in the cancer rate. Simply presenting the direct, advantageous consequences of removing pesticides without contemplating the secondary and considerable disadvantages leaves us with a poor basis on which to make decisions.

We must get used to the idea that *all* decisions are in reality a trade-off of various risks. When we choose between chlorinated and unchlorinated water we choose between the slight risk of getting cancer from chlorine and the many diseases unchlorinated water can spread.[2771] When we take an aspirin to relieve a headache we also risk irritation of the stomach lining, and with prolonged use perhaps even an ulcer.[2772] In effect, we choose between the certainty of a headache and the possibility of an irritated stomach. If we go to the bakery, we really choose a Danish pastry at the expense of an (extremely small) risk of getting killed on the road to or from the baker. And if we eat the Danish pastry we give greater priority to our sweet tooth than to the risk of getting a circulatory disease.

It is tempting to wish for an end to all these risks. With enough money we could secure everybody pure water supplies without chlorine and subsidize the use of ibuprofen, which does not have the side-effects of aspirin; we could build safer roads and reduce the wait for heart surgery. But the crucial words are 'enough money.' Because we will never have enough money. Money must also be spent on hip operations, roundabouts, public libraries and overseas development aid. The list of sound, worthy causes is practically endless, and this forces us to choose.

Weighing risks

Prioritizing is made harder by two tendencies which supplement each other. Psychologically we have a tendency to underestimate large risks and to overestimate small ones.[2773] At the same time the media have a tendency to focus on dramatic rather than everyday risks. This is a dangerous cocktail.

For the very purpose of attracting public interest the media present us with far more about tragedies and sudden accidents than one ought to expect if the media simply reflected the mortality statistics. The scientists Combs and Slovic carried out a survey of the newspapers' mention of various causes of death compared to actual mortality figures from statistical reports. They found very little connection.[2774] People die a thousand times more often from ordinary diseases but murders appear three times as frequently in the papers.[2775] Plane crashes are overrepresented by almost 12,000 times compared to deaths caused by smoking.[2776]

The media rarely present us with information about actual risks. In a survey of 26 American newspapers a group of scientists asked for the papers' best articles on environmental risks. As many as 68 percent of the returned articles did not contain *any* information on risk.[2777] So newspapers and television only give us an indirect impression of the danger of different phenomena by reason of their frequency. It transpires that we overestimate the risks we read a lot about and under-

Table 8 Actions which increase the risk of dying by 0.000001, and their cause. Source: Wilson 1979:45.

Actions increasing the risk of death by one-millionth	Cause
Drinking 0.5 liter (1 pint) of wine	Cirrhosis of the liver
Living 2 days in New York or Boston	Air pollution
Travelling 16 km (10 miles) by bicycle	Accident
Travelling 480 km (300 miles) by car	Accident
Flying 1,600 km (1,000 miles) by jet	Accident
Flying 10,000 km (6,000 miles) by jet	Cancer caused by cosmic radiation
Living 2 months in average stone or brick building	Cancer caused by natural radioactivity
One chest X-ray taken in a good hospital	Cancer caused by radiation
Living 2 months with a cigarette smoker	Cancer, heart disease
Drinking 30 350 ml (12 oz) cans of diet soda	Cancer caused by saccharin
Living 150 years within 30 km (20 miles) of a nuclear power plant	Cancer caused by radiation
Eating 100 charcoal broiled steaks	Cancer from benzopyrene
Living 2 months in Denver on vacation from NY	Cancer caused by cosmic radiation
Eating 40 tablespoons of peanut butter	Liver cancer caused by aflatoxin B
Drinking Miami drinking water for 1 year	Cancer caused by chloroform
Smoking 1.4 cigarettes	Cancer, heart disease
Spending 3 hours in a coal mine	Accident

estimate the risks overlooked by the media.[2778]

At the same time there is a well-documented tendency to underrate sizeable risks while overrating minor, dramatic ones.[2779] It seems we generally believe that we are fairly immune to the large risks such as cancer from smoking and heart attacks.[2780] Coupled to the media's focus on things sensational, this means that we overrate dramatic causes of death such as accidents, killings, botulism and tornadoes while at the same time underrating "boring problems" such as diabetes and asthma.[2781]

Finally, we have great difficulty handling extremely small risks. The problem appears to be that if we think about the small risks they have already become much bigger – simply because we have thought about them.[2782] Most readers will be familiar with the feeling when sitting in an airplane: as soon as you have thought "what was that noise?" then the very thinking has made the risk grow much larger, as our mind's eye sees a desperate pilot in a smoke-filled cockpit.

Psychologically, therefore, we handle small risks either by making them significant enough to think about, or by making them so insignificant that there is good reason to ignore them. This presents problems, for example in connection with chemical substances, because their safety levels are set at the magically low limit of one to one million, i.e. if one million people are subjected to a substance it should result in a maximum of one person's death in the course of a lifetime.[2783]

How in the world is one to handle a risk as small as 1:1,000,000? The answer is that we either ignore it or choose to focus on it, thus making it psychologically much greater. Both solutions are poor ones. We will have to judge the risks to which we are exposed in a reasonable fashion if we are to prioritize. Table 8 shows some examples of what increases a lifetime risk by 1:1,000,000.

With the media and the organizations focusing so strongly on pesticides, for example, it is only natural that we start thinking about them and make them psychologically that much more significant. But the risk posed by pesticides in drinking water is probably a good deal lower than 1:1,000,000.[2784] If we drink water which contains pesticides at the EU limit value for a *whole lifetime*, we face the same death risk as if we smoke 1.4 cigarettes, cycle 15 km, live two months in a brick building *or* drink a half liter of wine – *just once*. If the pesticide content is below such limit value, do pesticides represent any substantial problem?

Many people would argue that risk is not the only factor to be considered in this question of priorities. It is also significant whether the risk was accepted voluntarily or thrust upon the person involuntarily.[2785] Investigations have shown that people are often willing to take on a risk that is a 1,000 times greater so long as they do so of their own free will.[2786] The obvious example is choosing to skydive or to go off-piste skiing but still resenting the much smaller risks from pesticides or food preservatives, risks that are seen as unavoidable and therefore involuntary.[2787] True, involuntary risks make it impossible for the individual to choose optimally. Presumably skydivers find that the thrills of a free fall outweigh the risks of the free fall extending all the way to the ground, while others would be terrified at the prospect of jumping out of a plane from 10,000 feet. Thus, a society based on forced skydiving would make some people happy but leave lots of people intensely worried.

However, it is important to realize how many of the risks that we ordinarily claim to be voluntary are not, and vice versa. Although driving a car is fairly dangerous (see Table 5, p. 224), the lack of risk concern is typically explained in terms of its being voluntary.[2788] Yet for many people, travelling by car is not really a voluntary choice, given the need to go to work and go shopping at some distance from available housing. Moreover, some of the most important auto risks are clearly not voluntary – the obvious examples being drunk drivers, who kill many people besides themselves, and highway design, which has strong and well-documented effects on crash risks.[2789]

Likewise, urban air pollution is described as an involuntary risk, since we have to breathe. But of course, choosing to locate ourselves (or choosing not to relocate) within a city is the result of an overall trade-off on many different parameters – since housing in less polluted areas generally costs more, we are in effect making a trade-off between living in a larger house or breathing cleaner air. This problem is clear in the often heard claim that poor or black Americans are more likely to live close to toxic waste dumps and other environmental hazards.[2790] Although the connection is true, it is more correctly seen as a problem of poverty, because poor and black Americans are not just environmentally disadvantaged but also more likely to live in areas afflicted with high crime, noise, bad infrastructure, etc.

Thus, in the following we shall look at both voluntary and involuntary risks over a wide assortment of different areas and demonstrate that the extreme focus on environmental risks means that other and larger risks are routinely ignored.[2791]

The costs of the Litany

The Harvard University Center for Risk Analysis has carried out the largest survey of life-saving public initiatives (so-called interventions) in the US for which there are publicly available economic analyses.[2792] In total, 587 different interventions were analyzed. By using an extremely detailed evaluation procedure, at least two researchers out of 11 have computed the cost evaluations and the number of life-years saved and rendered the figures comparable. All the costs pertain to society as a whole, so no consideration has been made for possible distributional consequences.

The areas investigated cover health care, as well as residential, transportation, occupational and environmental aspects of society. The aim was to evaluate the individual areas' efficiency when it comes to saving human lives. It is important to point out that *only* interventions that have as the primary stated political goal to save human lives are included. Thus, the many environmental interventions which have little or no intention to save human lives are not considered here. We only compare those environmental interventions whose primary goal it is save human lives (as in toxin control) with life-saving interventions from other areas. Thus, all the interventions have similar intent and are therefore comparable.

The results revealed an astounding variation in the efficiency of the various interventions, as can be seen in Table 9. Some of the initiatives cost nothing or actually save money. These include, for example, informing black women not to smoke during pregnancy as this will give fewer birth complications – the net savings for society is about $72 million.[2793] For $182,000 a year it is possible to screen black new-borns for sickle cell anemia and save 769 life-years: a cost of just $236 per life-year.[2794] By spending $253 million on heart transplants, an extra 1,600 life-years can be saved at a cost of $158,000 per life-year. Equipping all school buses with passenger safety belts would cost around $53 million, but because this would only save much less than one child a year, the cost would be $2.8 million per life-year. Regulating radionuclide emission at elemental phosphorus plants (refining mined phosphorus before it goes to other uses) would cost $2.8 million, but would only save at most one life per decade. This gives an estimated cost of $9.2 million per life-year.

The decision as to how much money should be spent on saving a life-year is naturally a political one, and one could of course conceive of both refining the yardstick (possibly children's life-years should count more or less) and challenging some of the figures (the price may be twice as high, or half as much). The point here, however, is to look at typical prices in the various areas, as shown in Figure 171. Here it is quite obvious that there are tremendous differences in the price to be paid for extra life-years by means of typical interventions: the health service is quite low-priced at $19,000, and the environment field stands out with a staggeringly high cost of $4.2 million.

Similarly, one can look at costs for different government agencies where this is possible, as shown in Figure 172. Again, it transpires that the EPA is astonishingly more expensive.

Although the prices are still only typical (median values), we can look finally at the distribution of costs in medicine as against toxin control shown in Figure 173. Here we can see that both areas have a group of socioeconomically free or almost free interventions, although the health sector has far more free interventions. However, it is clear that while the health sector has more projects in the below $20,000 category, most environmental chemical regulation schemes cost above $1,000,000 per life-year. Thus, the extremely high typical cost of $7.6 million for the EPA area is fairly representative of the cost of saving life by means of toxin control.

The advantage of this method of accounting is that it is possible to see the overall effectiveness of the American public effort to save human life. Information exists about the actual cost of 185 programs that account for the annual spending of $21.4 billion which saves around 592,000 life-years. An analysis of the data showed, however, that there was no connection between efficiency and implementation. It was not that the most efficient programs were fully implemented and the least efficient ones had not been implemented or only just begun. It is therefore also possible to ascertain, rather surprisingly, that the number of life-years saved could have been much higher. Spending almost $3 million to control radionuclide emissions from phosphorus plants to save only one life per decade is a poor way of saving lives. If one really wants to save the maximum possible number of human lives, it would be a much better idea to implement the most efficient programs first

Table 9 Cost efficiency in saving life for selected interventions, with cost per life year saved, in 1993$. Source: Tengs *et al.* 1995.

Intervention	Cost per life-year
Federal law requiring smoke detectors in homes	< $0
Fire detectors in homes	< $0
Flammability standard for children's sleepwear size 0–6x	< $0
Reduced lead content of gasoline from 1.1 g to 0.1 g per leaded gallon	< $0
Measles, mumps and rubella immunization for children	< $0
SO_2 controls by installation of capacity to desulphurize residual fuel oil	< $0
Mandatory seat belt use laws	$69
Sickle cell anemia screening for Black new-borns	$240
Influenza vaccination for high-risk people	$570
Mammography for women age 50	$810
Pneumonia vaccination for people age 65+	$2,000
Cervical cancer scanning every 2 (versus 3) years for women age 30–39	$2,300
Chlorination of drinking water	$3,100
Selective traffic enforcement programs at high-risk times and locations	$5,200
Smoking cessation advice for people who smoke more than one pack a day	$9,800
Annual mammography and breast exam for women age 35–49	$10,000
Heart transplants for patients age 50 with terminal heart disease	$10,000
Screening blood donors for HIV	$14,000
Low-cholesterol diet for men age 30	$19,000
Improve basic driver training	$20,000
Ban asbestos in brake blocks	$29,000
Smoke detectors in airplane lavatories	$30,000
Regular leisure time physical activity, such as jogging, in men age 35	$38,000
Child-resistant cigarette lighters	$42,000
Flashing lights and gates at rail–highway crossings	$45,000
Child restraint systems in cars	$73,000
Pedestrian and bicycle visibility enhancement programs	$73,000
Benzene exposure standard of 1 (versus 10) ppm in rubber and tire industry	$76,000
National (versus state and local) 55 mph. speed limit	$89,000
Annual mammography for women age 55–64	$110,000
Air bags (versus manual lap belts) in cars	$120,000
First aid training for drivers	$180,000
Front disk (versus drum) brakes in cars	$240,000
Seat belts for passengers in school buses	$2,800,000
Dioxin emission standard of 5 lb/air dried ton at pulp	$4,500,000
Radionuclide emission control at elemental phosphorous plants	$9,200,000
Strengthen buildings in earthquake-prone areas	$18,000,000
Arsenic emission control at glass manufacturing plants	$51,000,000
Radiation emission standard for nuclear power plants	$180,000,000
Benzene emission control at rubber tire manufacturing plants	$20,000,000,000

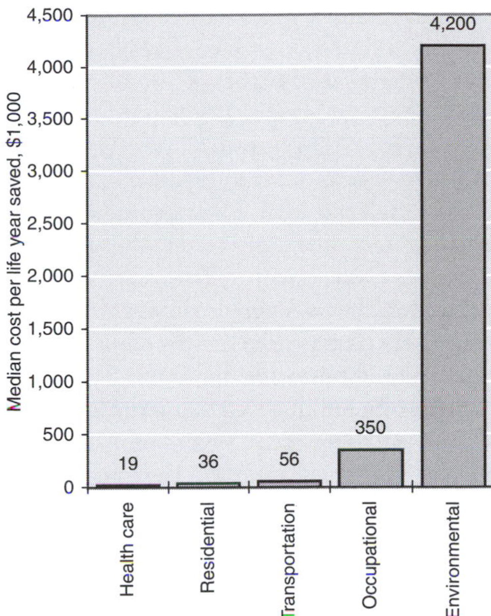

Figure 171 Median cost[2795] per life-year saved for different sectors of society in 1993$. Number of interventions for each sector is 310, 30, 87, 36, and 124 respectively. Source: Tengs *et al.* 1995:371.

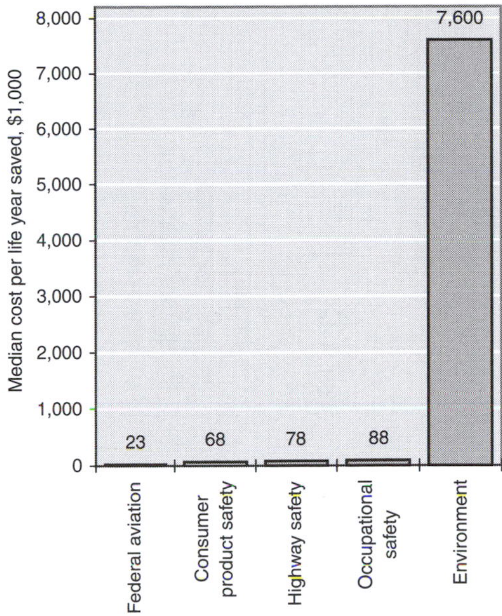

Figure 172 Median cost per life-year saved for different government sectors in 1993$. Agencies are Federal Aviation Administration, Consumer Product Safety Commission, National Highway Traffic Safety Administration, Occupational Safety and Health Administration, and Environmental Protection Agency. Number of interventions for each sector is 4, 11, 31, 16, and 89 respectively. Source: Tengs *et al.* 1995:371.

and then to continue with less and less efficient programs for as long as funds were available (of course weighing the issues in relation to other policy areas).

The Harvard study did make such calculations and discovered that instead of saving 592,000 life-years, 1,230,000 life-years could have been saved for the same money.[2796] *Without further costs it would have been possible to save around 600,000 more life-years or 60,000 more human lives.*[2797]

Of course it is probably impossible to redistribute all public spending to saving human lives on the basis of this relatively simple analysis – not least because there can be considerations of equality between various population groups which will affect some of the results.

Even so, the results are so unambiguous and so forceful that they are impossible to ignore. Moreover, considering our concern about voluntary and involuntary risks discussed above, it is clear that most of the areas covered (outside occupation, which could be said to be voluntary) aim at preventing death which is involuntary (fire regulations for children's sleepwear, speed monitoring to reduce road accidents, HIV screening of blood donors, mammography screening, and radiation emission standards for nuclear power plants). Thus, even when taking the dimension of involuntary risks into account, all of these issues are broadly comparable.

As a society we use vast amounts of resources to regulate both health risks and environmental risks such as toxins. We have also seen above that pesticides, for example, probably result in very few deaths. But because the media attention is so great, many people think that pesticides are rather dangerous. The consequence of the constantly

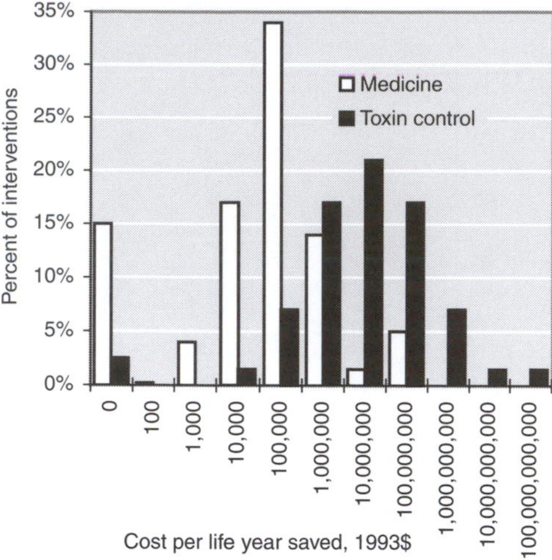

Figure 173 Distribution of cost per life-year saved for medicine and toxin control in 1993$. Number of interventions is 310 for medicine and 144 for toxin control. Source: Graham 1995.[2798]

repeated Litany is that we thoroughly regulate and phase out toxins but leave alone other areas where the same resources could do much more good, saving many more people from dying from involuntary risks. If the Litany makes us demand regulation of particular areas of the environment while we fail to consider how the money could otherwise have been spent, we actually create a societal structure in which fewer people survive.

To use a harsh – albeit fitting – metaphor, we could say that when we ignore the cost of our environmental decisions on the lesser regulations in other areas, we are in reality committing statistical murder. And the Harvard study gives us an indication that, with greater concern for efficiency than with the Litany, we could save 60,000 more Americans each year – for free.

GENETICALLY MODIFIED FOODS – THE ENCAPSULATION OF THE LITANY

Another environmental controversy has been brewing for some years now, the question of genetically modified (GM) foods or, as they have successfully been named by their opponents, the so-called Frankenfoods.[2799] In many ways the discussion tends to be a replay of the Litany vs. evidence, as described in this book. However, unlike most of the other issues this debate has in no way been concluded and consequently the analysis of the GM issue will necessarily be preliminary and rely more on an examination of concrete examples.

Here we will talk about genetic modification used not in medical production but in agriculture, since this is where most of the controversy has been centered.[2800] From 1996 to 2000, the area of GM production has steadily increased from 1.7 Mha to 44.2 Mha, or an increase from 0.1 percent to 2.9 percent of the global crop area.[2801] Four nations grow almost all GM crops, with the US growing 30.3 Mha (16.9 percent of its crop area), Argentina growing 10 Mha (36.8 percent), Canada 3 Mha (6.6 percent) and China 0.5 Mha (0.4 percent).[2802] Nevertheless, by now all six continents grow GM crops commercially.[2803] The four top GM crops are soybean, corn, cotton, and canola (rapeseed), at a total estimated value of US$3 billion.[2804]

The promise of GM food is huge but so are its potential problems. Let us look at both, starting with the benefits.

GM foods will contribute – possibly greatly – to the world's food supply.[2805] Models indicate that over the next 20 years, food prices will decline 10–15 percent more due to GM foods than they would otherwise. Equivalently, of course, the cost of delaying GM foods for just a decade are prices that will have fallen 10–15 percent *less*, hurting especially the third world poor.[2806]

There are possibilities of countering malnutrition by increasing the nutritional value of staple foods. A typical example is the *golden rice* which will supply extra vitamin A which could help combat the millions of cases of blindness and other diseases stemming from vitamin A deficiency[2807] – though such an approach can not by itself totally eradicate the deficiencies.[2808]

For the industrialized world, GM crops can help reduce the need for intensive use of chemical fertilizers, pesticides, herbicides and fungicides.[2809] Whereas most present GM crops have features such as pesticide resistance (which may be interesting for the farmer but hardly for the consumer), the coming decade will see far more useful products. In foods we will see more nutritious cereals, potatoes that absorb less fat in frying, reduced calorie sugar beets and oilseeds with more healthy reduced-saturates.[2810] For non-food, we should see cotton and flax with improved fiber quality, better ingredients for personal hygiene and flowers with stronger color and longer vase life.[2811]

Yet, for all its promise, there is a marked difference in the consumer perception of GMs in the EU and the US.[2812] In the EU, 59 percent of the consumers view GM foods as risky and consistent majorities reject their usefulness and find them morally unacceptable and to be discouraged.[2813] In the US, 60 percent are positive about food biotechnology, and in a survey of consumer food safety concerns, GM came in last, after biological contamination, pesticides, nutritional quality and artificial preservatives.[2814] The difference is often ascribed to the bad European experiences with food safety (e.g. BSE, bacterially contaminated meat and dioxin in poultry, pork, beef, chickens, eggs and Belgian chocolate).[2815]

Moreover, both the EU and the US have seen eroding trust in GM foods over the past years.[2816] This coincides with the global mobilization against GM foods that has been led by international NGOs such as Greenpeace and Friends of the Earth.[2817]

Owing to the very dispersed and network-oriented opposition, there is no single source that will encapsulate all worries, yet the primary two concerns from Friends of the Earth,[2818] have been at the center of the GM controversy and are replicated in many other lists.[2819] These two issues are "health concerns" and "environmental concerns."[2820] The health concern is further related to GM foods possibly being both toxic and allergenic.[2821]

These three concerns have each been backed primarily with a widely publicized story. We will look at each of these stories and see that all three seem to have been severely skewed.

Health – toxic potatoes

On August 10, 1998, Dr. Arpad Pusztai appeared on Granada's TV show *World in Action* and declared that GM potatoes had stunted growth and suppressed immunity in rats that had eaten them for 110 days.[2822] These findings, Pusztai said, raised grave questions about the safety of GM foods for humans, and personally, he would not eat GM foods.[2823] Naturally, the statements made a splash. They immediately prompted members of the House of Commons to urge a moratorium or even a outright ban on GM foods.[2824]

Dr. Pusztai was suspended from the Rowett Research Institute, which in an audit report concluded that "the existing data do not support any suggestion that [GM potatoes] . . . has an effect on growth, organ development or the immune function."[2825] This caused 20 independent scientists, shocked by the harsh treatment of Pusztai by the Rowett, to review the data and publish a memorandum, finding that the GM potatoes were different from the control potatoes and that the reduction in growth and immune function was real.[2826] The Royal Society in 1999 published its own review of the GM potato data, finding that the study was flawed and thus "the data reviewed provide no reliable or convincing evidence of adverse (or beneficial) effects."[2827]

Finally, Pusztai published his findings in *The Lancet* in 1999.[2828] Now the data did not show changes in growth or immune system, but variable effects on different parts of the rat's gastrointestinal tract, which could have been caused by the genetic modification. In the same issue of *Lancet*, three other researchers again found that the experiments were incomplete, and thus did not allow a conclusion on the risks of GM foods.[2829]

The entire course of events naturally left the public wondering whether truth was being distorted by the government or the biotech industry[2830] and with the story of Pusztai, NGOs have claimed that we have all "become involuntary guinea pigs in a vast genetic experiment."[2831]

It is important to point out what this study can actually say. Originally, Pusztai had used a potato line, genetically modified with a gene coding for lectin from the common snowdrop (Galanthus nivalis agglutinin or GNA). Such lectins are widely known to be toxic[2832] – in fact, another lectin (ricin) was the poison used on an umbrella tip to kill Bulgarian dissident Georgi Markov in 1978.[2833] Consequently, it is no surprise that potatoes expressing this lectin equally could cause damage to growth, organs and the immune system.[2834] Even Pusztai acknowledges that the lectins cause primary damage.[2835] As Iain Cubitt, chief executive of Axis Genetics in Oxford, pointed out, everyone know that lectins are toxic:[2836] "so if you put this in a potato and it ends up toxic, why is that such a surprise?"[2837] This quote is actually made the central argument of one of the co-authors of the memorandum.[2838]

Thus, the potato is toxic, but that is due to the choice of a toxic gene, not the GM technology. However – and this was the new Pusztai argument – the experiments also revealed effects on the small intestine and caecum, that did not come from the GNA but only occurred with the GM potato.[2839] Yes, the potato was toxic, but the genetic modification also could have caused other effects.[2840] (Notice, these effects were not consistent, rather sometimes good, sometimes bad.)[2841]

The code word here is *could*. The problem with the Pusztai experiment was that the GM and non-GM potato were so different – they even had very different contents of starch and protein.[2842] Thus, what could be a difference between GM and non-GM could also just be a difference attributable to natural variations in potato lines.[2843] Actually, since the GM potato had less protein, the rats had to be feed protein supplements, and this supplement could equally well explain the differences.[2844] These problems were to a large part the reason why the Pusztai experiment got such statistical criticism.

Naturally, making a new line of, say, potato, can result in unrecognized and unwanted characteristics. This has happened many times before in conventional breeding, whereas we have no knowledge of such occurrences with commercial GM crops.[2845] Moreover, the National Academy of Sciences in their latest GM report notes that such bad crops would probably be *more* likely to come out of conventional breeding.[2846]

Thus, the GM potato was *not* toxic, the subtle effects could probably have been produced by natural variation, and this variation might actually be a bigger problem for conventional breeding. But note, until the Pusztai experiment has been repeated many times, we cannot know for sure.

Health – allergenic beans

This is how the Organic Consumers Organization puts the worry over allergic beans: "In 1996 a major GE food disaster was narrowly averted when Nebraska researchers learned that a Brazil nut gene spliced into soybeans could induce potentially fatal allergies in people sensitive to Brazil nuts."[2847] Almost all those concerned about GM foods mention this story.[2848] Friends of the Earth asks us: "will we know what is in our food and if we're allergic to it?"[2849]

However, the story is actually one of a fairly well-functioning food system. Back in the 1980s, a small biotech firm in California wanted to help combat third world malnutrition, focusing on the health problems of a diet predominantly based on beans.[2850] While beans are generally nutritious, they lack the two crucial sulfur-containing amino acids, methionine and cysteine. On the other hand, nuts – and especially the Brazil nut – store a high concentration of these two amino acids.[2851] Thus, the thinking was that if one took the gene for methionine and cysteine and spliced it into beans, this could at low or no cost eradicate their potential health problems. Yet before the actual GM bean was even made, the scientists themselves pointed out the folly of transferring a gene from a known allergenic source into a major food crop, and the project was stopped.

Later, the work was revived by Pioneer Hi-Breed. This time the idea was not meant for humans but to improve soy-based animal feeds. Ordinarily, these feeds are supplemented with methionine (which can be converted to cysteine) to promote optimal growth, but naturally it would be cheaper to have the sulfur-containing amino acids built in. During this work, Pioneer themselves conducted allergenicity studies, since it had not previously been conclusively shown that the particular Brazil nut gene was responsible for the allergic response. When it turned out it was, Pioneer killed the project and – to their credit – published the results.[2852]

Thus, it would seem that the brazil nut case was a demonstration of a food system that actually works. As is pointed out in a recent review in *British Medical Journal*: "The point that is usually not emphasized in coverage of this case is that the problem was identified because safety checks were, and continue to be, in place to identify the unintended introduction of an allergen into a genetically modified crop."[2853]

This, however, does not mean that there are no risks. First, we rely on the food producer to act responsibly, and test and if necessary withdraw the product – as we do with all other food production.[2854] Second, whereas testing is mandatory when using a known allergen, there are currently no clear procedure for using foods that are rarely allergenic or non-food organisms with unknown allergenicity.[2855]

These concerns are real, although about 90 percent of all US food allergies are caused by a few well-known substances, namely cow's milk, eggs, fish and shellfish, tree nuts, wheat, and legumes, all of which are tested.[2856] Moreover, the FDA states that new allergenic cases can happen from both GM and traditional breeding.[2857] Indeed, it is ironic that the fear of allergenicity should be an argument against GM foods, when in reality the new technology offers a promising way to breed out this undesirable trait from plants which produce allergens naturally.[2858]

Environment – GM foods killing butterflies

Of the many environmental worries, by far the most referred has been the fear that GM foods would harm the ecosystem,[2859] and especially the story that GM corn kills Monarch butterflies.[2860]

The GM corn carries a gene to manufacture the so-called Bt toxin family, which comes from the soil bacterium *Bacillus thuringiensis*.[2861] Because Bt toxins (about 130 in all)[2862] are naturally occurring, biodegradable and harmless to humans and non-target groups, they are extensively used by organic farmers.[2863] Actually, Rachel Carson specifically suggested that Bt sprays, along with biological control, would be the way forward for agriculture.[2864]

One of the main pests for corn is the European corn borer, which in the US can infest 24 Mha (75 percent) of the total area and cause a crop loss of up to 20 percent.[2865] Large amounts of pesticide (around $20–30 million) are spent each year controlling the pest, but this is difficult since it spends much of its life-cycle inside the plant.[2866] Bt is toxic to lepidopteran insects, of which the European corn borer is one.[2867] Thus, it seemed an obvious idea to try to incorporate the gene for Bt toxin into corn, making it impervious to the corn borer, and indeed, the GM corn has been very successful, being the second largest GM crop in 2000.[2868]

In 1999, researchers from Cornell University tried to assess the effect of the GM corn on the Monarch catarpillar.[2869] Milkweed is the only food monarch caterpillars eat to survive. Since corn is pollinated by wind, its pollen often lands on milkweed growing by the cornfields.[2870] So, the Cornell scientists dusted ordinary and Bt corn pollen onto milkweed leaves in amounts that roughly reproduced the appearance of leaves around cornfields and fed it to caterpillars in the lab. Almost half the caterpillars eating Bt-sprinkled milkweed died after 4 days of feeding, whereas all the caterpillars consuming milkweed with ordinary corn pollen lived.[2871]

This set off the alarms. Though the Monarch is not an endangered species, it was pointed out that the half of all its caterpillars hatch in the US corn belt,[2872] and although the caterpillars need not get far away from the corn to avoid the GM pollen, one entomologist explained: "if you're a Monarch, odds are you're going to be close to a cornfield."[2873] *Time* asked itself whether this new threat to the Monarch could "happen in cornfields across the Midwest?"[2874] And *Discovery* claimed (incorrectly) that the Monarchs had been poisoned irreversibly.[2875] A coalition of 60 environmental groups and organic farmers, with Greenpeace in front, even prepared to sue the EPA for failing to protect the Monarch by approving GM corn,[2876] and in Europe, the Monarch story caused the European Commission to delay approval of a GM corn from Pioneer.[2877]

Yet, it was not really surprising Monarchs died from Bt. Bt is a natural insecticide, toxic to lepidopteran insects, and yes, Monarchs are lepidopteran insects.[2878] And the original Cornell University report specifically states, that "all of the mortality . . . seems to be due to the effects of the Bt toxin."[2879] Thus, the story is *not* about GM but about Bt. Unfortunately, the study was not repeated with ordinary corn pollen dusted on milkweed and spiked with organic Bt, but it is unlikely that this would not also have caused high mortality.[2880] As with the Pusztai experiment, the GM feature was the hook of the story but unrelated to the main issue which was that natural toxins (lectin or Bt) are toxic. The question, of course, is whether a story about butterflies dying from the usage of organic Bt sprays would have made headlines.

Moreover, as one of the caterpillar researchers points out, it is impossible to imagine that we can grow food and only affect the targeted pests: using pesticides would have non-target effects and indeed "plowing has non-target effects."[2881] Nevertheless, it is of course important to look at the consequences of large-scale use of Bt toxins.

EPA published in October 2000 its preliminary risks and benefits evaluation of Bt GM crops.[2882] Summing up on extensive field testing, they found that the actual level of Bt encountered by the caterpillars ranged from "relatively low" to "very low," and that there was very little time overlap between monarch breeding and pollen shedding.[2883] In conclusion, the EPA found "a low probability for adverse effects of Bt corn on monarch larvae," and that there is no reason to have "undue concern of widespread risks to monarch butterflies at this time."[2884]

In fact, in its conclusion EPA noted that since these GM crops need much less pesticide, some authors even predict "that the widespread cultivation of Bt Crops may have huge benefits for Monarch butterfly survival."[2885]

GM foods – disaster or blessing?

GM foods have been claimed to be a potential disaster[2886] or something we should outright love.[2887] Why this wide gap in judgment? No doubt, part of the reason is caused by a lack of information.

In the latest survey, Europeans were asked whether it was true or false that "ordinary tomatoes do not contain genes, while genetically modified tomatoes do."[2888] Half – correctly – said this was false, but the other half thought it true.[2889] These people actually believe that the good-old food was gene-free, whereas the new GM foods shoves foreign genes down their throat. Moreover, only 42 percent knew that ingesting genes from GM foods would not modify their own genes.[2890] And other surveys show that Americans know no better.[2891] No wonder there is widespread worry over GMs.

And yes, as we have seen, the most exploited scare stories of toxic potatoes, allergenic beans and dead Monarchs were based on myths.[2892]

Nevertheless, there are also real problems to be considered. Our exposure of the myths showed us some of the problematic areas. We know by far the most important human allergens, but we do not know the consequence of using genes from non-food organisms.[2893] We should make allergenicity tests for these, but since we do not know what we are looking for we can never be absolutely sure to find everything.

There is also rightly a concern for antibiotic resistance.[2894] Spliced genes have often conveniently been marked with genes coding for resistance to specific antibiotics.[2895] This has led to concerns that the resistance gene might be transferred to human pathogens in the gut, which would make them impervious to useful antibiotics. It is important to avoid such a situation.

Equally, there is anxiety that GM crops may spread their pesticide resistance to weeds.[2896] Such superweeds would lessen the value of the pesticide and make pest control much harder. We know the problems of superweeds – from the Johnson grass choking crops in fields, to kudzu blanketing trees, to melaleuca trees invading the Everglades.[2897]

These are concerns that should be addressed. Yet we also have to remember that while GM could potentially risk incorporating new allergens, the technique also holds the promise of removing many of the most common allergens and thus of significantly reducing the troubles of present-day sufferers.[2898] While the early GM technology potentially could cause selective antibiotic resistance, this risk is "very small" compared to normal pathways of antibiotic resistance,[2899] and new technologies are increasingly becoming available.[2900] Finally, while pesticide resistant weeds would be a nuisance, many have pointed out that it is unlikely that such resistance could confer any advantage in a natural environment.[2901] New research actually shows that when untended by people, GM crops tend to do worse than ordinary crops.[2902] This indicates that the risks of superweeds may be smaller than otherwise thought.

Moreover, we need to realize that traditionally bred varieties equally can turn out allergenic or toxic. [2903] A new, conventionally bred, insect-resistant celery was loved by the organic movement, but it turned out that people who handled the celery developed rashes after subsequent exposure to sunlight, due to very high levels of the carcinogenic and mutagenic psoralens.[2904] Likewise, a new conventional potato, developed at the cost of millions of dollars, had to be withdrawn from the market because it was acutely toxic to humans when grown under particular soil conditions.[2905]

Many crops have been given pesticide resistance through conventional breeding techniques, and the spread of resistance to pests could equally well originate from these crops.[2906] Actually, most of our superweeds come not from advanced crops but alien plants (e.g. the above-mentioned kudzu or the Japanese knotweed, resistant to virtually all pesticides).[2907]

The unifying theme is that the problems stem not from a particular technique (GM or conventional) but from particular products.[2908] Rapeseed (GM or conventional) is by nature promiscuous and will attempt aggressively to infiltrate natural wildlife areas – thus, rapeseed with special features (achieved through GM or conventionally) should arguably only be grown in areas such as Australia, Argentina and Canada with huge open farmlands.[2909] On the other hand, wheat is almost completely self-pollinating, and thus constitutes much less of a risk.[2910]

This is why the British House of Lords in their recommendation tells us, "We need to look at the product, not the process."[2911] Likewise, this is why the US National Research Council in their overview state that "the potential hazards and risks associated with the organisms produced by conventional and transgenic [GM] methods fall into the same general categories."[2912]

This also ties in nicely with the other typical concern of collusion and potential monopoly on GM foods stemming from ever fewer life science corporations. The concern is not that companies could patent existing varieties (patent law requires innovation). Thus, farmers can easily go on sowing these varieties at their present cost. However, if biotech innovations are more productive (which makes them more profitable for the farmer), a near monopoly could reap almost the entire economic surplus from such improvement. This of course argues for a strong anti-trust regulation. But such issues are *not* related to GM technology but to the basic regulation of a well-functioning market economy, just as for example the case against Microsoft is not an argument against computers.

Thus the basic argument, both from biology and economics is that the focus should be on making the best possible regulatory system. But we also need to realize that no system can provide absolute certainty.[2913] Science cannot *prove* that something is not dangerous. Technology cannot provide absolutely risk-free products. The products we have today are not risk-free and neither will this be the case for the products of tomorrow.

The difference is that we feel comfortable with the products of today whereas we mainly see the problems in tomorrow's products. Yet, the promises of the new and improved products are also alluring. Which we choose depends on our averseness to risk and our historical experience in overcoming past problems.[2914]

Thus, choosing sensibly in the GM debate requires us to see the risks but also compare them thoughtfully with all other risks. We need to know how we have handled past problems. We must be able to dispose of the many myths but also face the true challenges. It is only with this information that we can weigh the risks and the benefits in order to make the most informed decision.

In this way, the GM debate truly is a replay of the *Litany* vs. facts, and in a certain way a replay of this book. Most of the risks are very low, and many are unrelated or only vaguely related to GM technology. As a human species we have not lived without creating problems but overall we have solved more, and more important, problems than we have created. Some of the absolutely central arguments against GM are based mainly on myths. Yet there are definitely real problems to be handled.

Weighing the risks and the benefits it seems obvious that the substantive benefits GM foods can deliver both for the developed and the developing world far outweigh the manageable risks, which, however, suggest the need for a strong regulatory system.

Caution when invoking the principle

This book has shown that many of our deeply ingrained beliefs from the Litany are not supported by the facts. Conditions in the world are not getting worse and worse. As mentioned earlier, we have more leisure time, greater security and fewer accidents, better education, more amenities, higher incomes, fewer starving, more food, and healthier and longer lives. There is no ecological catastrophe looming around the corner to punish us.

Consequently, we must stop giving our environmental thinking a Doomsday perspective. It is imperative for us to see the environment as an important – but only *one* important – part of the many challenges we must handle to create an even better world and the most progress for the rest of the century.

Prioritization is absolutely essential if we are to achieve the best possible distribution of resources in society. The environment must participate in this social prioritization on equal terms with all other areas. Environmental initiatives must present sound arguments and be evaluated on the basis of their advantages and disadvantages, in precisely the same way as proposals to boost Medicaid, increase funding to the arts or cut taxes.

However, this necessitates that the precautionary principle be strictly circumscribed. This principle has become enshrined in many different international treaties, as in the 1992 Rio Declaration, where it is pointed out: "Where there are threats of serious or irreversible damage, lack of full scientific certainty shall not be used as a reason for postponing cost-effective measures to prevent environmental degradation."[2915]

In this formulation, the principle merely informs us that since we can never prove anything absolutely, scientific uncertainty ought not to be used merely as a political strategy to avoid environmental action. The most obvious example is global warming, where the mere fact of scientific uncertainty is not in itself an argument against (or for that matter, for) action. Rather, as we discussed in the chapter on global warming, we need to look at the level of uncertainty, the direction of that uncertainty, and then particularly at the likely costs and benefits of different levels of action.

However, this understanding of the precautionary principle is very Anglo-Saxon, whereas a much more radical interpretation comes from the German version (the so-called *Vorsorgeprinzip*), the more common interpretation on the Continent.[2916] This principle in essence suggests building "a margin of safety into all decision making."[2917] In the Danish interpretation it becomes "giving nature and the environment the benefit of the doubt."[2918]

But this is a rather problematic argument. In essence it argues "better safe than sorry," which of course sounds eminently agreeable. However, such an approach ignores the fundamental insight from the Harvard study, namely that if we try to become more safe in some areas, we spend resources that cannot be used doing good in other areas. Thus, saving extra lives at great cost – just to be sure – quite possibly means forgoing the chance to save many more lives more cheaply in other areas.

Often it is pointed out that the challenges in the environmental area are special compared to other areas on a number of points.[2919] Some environmental decisions are hard to change – when we have once paved over a bog or plowed the moor, it is expensive to reverse (and sometimes, as with species die-off, impossible). Some environmental decisions have consequences that reach far into the future – nuclear power plants leave waste products that will remain radioactive for millennia, affecting the decisions of many future generations. Some environmental processes have momentous effects – as we saw earlier, global warming will have many and diverse effects, costing 1–9 percent of GDP.

All of these points are relevant and need to be included in the social prioritization among the many different proposals. But *none of these points is in fact particular to the environment.* Most of our more significant political decisions are hard or impossible to reverse. Moral and political decisions such as the abolition of slavery in the US, the adoption of human rights in France, the legalization of abortion throughout most of the Western world in the 1970s, the stages in the construction of the European Union, are all examples of decisions which would be exceedingly difficult or even impossible to reverse. Equally significant, if smaller in impact, decisions on the placement of airports, bridges and other large infrastructure investments are examples of almost irreversible initiatives, as are zoning decisions, placements of schools, roads, parks, etc.

Moreover, many of these decisions have important impacts that stretch far into the future. All such information needs, of course, to be included in our final prioritization, but the decision needs to be taken on the basis of this information and not by reference to yet another principle of precaution.

Two further differences are often pointed out. First, the precautionary principle should emphasize our concern for the future and our unwillingness to hazard the future of our children. Essentially this argument says that we are unwilling to gamble that new products or inventions will improve life, if there is an even much smaller chance that it will harm life – in other words, that we are risk averse. Again, this sounds eminently congenial, but this risk averseness cannot only be applied to environmental problems. Of course, introducing a new chemical with high promises for the future may nevertheless have a small probability of causing more bad than good.[2920] But equally, so may any other invention – maybe the development of, say, the computer and the internet will end up making personal contacts superfluous?[2921] It is not likely, but it is conceivable. So if we are risk averse in the one case, then we need also to be so in all other cases. (See also the box on GM foods.)

Second, it is pointed out how the precautionary principle is especially relevant when science is unable to give us sufficient information on the consequences of our actions. But again, this uncertainty is in no way unique to the environmental area. We have very sparse information as to the social consequences of using computers and the internet; international relations theory gives us little firm knowledge of the consequences of various foreign policies; we know little of the economic consequences of the Euro or NAFTA, etc. Actually, it is hard to imagine any policy area of significant import where the full consequences are known with any reasonable degree of scientific certainty.

Thus, any significant prioritization in our society is evaluated against a background of uncertain knowledge and our propensity to be risk averse, and with the realization that the decision will be hard to reverse, and have momentous consequences, both for many people and far into the future. This still makes the environmental proposals just one example among many.

That the environmental area has been able to monopolize the precautionary principle is in essence due to the Litany and our fear of doomsday. Of course, if large-scale ecological catastrophes were looming on the horizon we might be more inclined to afford the extra margin of safety just for the environment. But as is documented in this book, such a general conception is built on a myth.

The whole point of prioritization is to use our resources as well as possible, on the basis of all the information available. For this reason, the precautionary principle should not be used to tip the scales a bit more in favor of the environment, because the distribution would by definition no longer be the best possible.[2922] In this way, the precautionary principle is actually all about making *worse* decisions than we need to.[2923]

And if we want to back off from making prioritizations all together, because it seems "narrow minded" or "cold,"[2924] this still does not prevent a distribution of resources from taking place; only now it is no longer considered and well-argued, but random and irrational.[2925] Avoiding prioritization simply means that we abandon the opportunity of doing the best we can. A lack of prioritization, backed by however many good intentions, can in the final analysis result in the statistical murder of thousands of people.

Continued progress

If we do not make considered, rational decisions but base our resolution on the Litany, that typical feeling that the world is in decline, we will make poor and counterproductive choices. In Peru, the authorities refrained from chlorinating the drinking water because they were afraid of the risk of cancer.[2926] Today, it is considered to have been one of the main reasons for the cholera epidemic that broke out again with such vehemence in 1991.[2927] Had they known how low the risk of using chlorine actually was, the epidemic probably never would have occurred.

In 1967 Paul Ehrlich predicted that the world was headed for massive starvation. In order to limit the extent of this, he believed – reasonably enough given his point of view – that aid should only be given to those countries that would have a chance to make it through. According to Ehrlich, India was not among them. We must "announce that we will no longer send emergency aid to countries such as India where sober analysis shows a hopeless imbalance between food production and population . . . Our inadequate aid ought to be reserved for those which can survive."[2928] Ehrlich was basically saying that India should be left to paddle its own canoe. India, however, has today lived through a green revolution. In 1967, when Ehrlich wrote those words, the average Indian consumed 1,875 calories a day. Even though the population had almost doubled, in 1998 the average Indian got 2,466 calories a day.[2929] Had we paid more notice to Ehrlich and less to Borlaug and the incredible willpower and inspiration that surrounded the green revolution, things might have looked quite worse.

As far as the Western world is concerned, I hope that this book can lead to an appreciable change in *attitude* to environmental problems. We can forget about our fear of imminent breakdown. We can see that the world is basically headed in the right direction and that we can help to steer this development process by focusing on and insisting on reasonable prioritization.

When we fear for our environment, we seem easily to fall victim to a short-term feel-good solution which spends money on relatively trifling issues and thus holds back resources from far more important ones. We need to be rational and make well-considered decisions in our use of resources when it comes to the aquatic environment, pesticides and global warming. This does not mean that rational environmental management and environmental investment is not often a good idea – only that we should compare the costs and benefits of such investments to similar investments in all the other important areas of human endeavor.

On the whole I believe it is important to emphasize that being overly optimistic is not without costs, *but that being too pessimistic also carries a hefty price tag*. If we do not believe in the future we will become more apathetic, indifferent and scared – hiding within ourselves. And even if we choose to fight for the planet it will very probably be as part of a project that is born not of reasonable analysis but of increasing fear.

Of course we cannot simply *choose* to believe in the future. But the documentation and the arguments in this book can have a considerable effect because they can free us of our unproductive worries. They can give us new faith in the fact that we are involved in creating a better world by taking part in society's production of assets, tangible as well as intangible.

We encounter the same considerations when it is often pointed out that things have only gone as well as they have because we have worried. No, things have gone so well because we have worked hard to improve our situation. In some circumstances this has happened almost automatically, as in the continued growth of economic wealth. We have become richer and richer primarily because of our fundamental organization in a market economy and not because we have worried. Some of the most significant recent progress in the area of pollution has been achieved through regulation, but the regulation has been right to the extent that it represented a reasonable prioritization and not because it was founded on a general worry.

More food is available in the world not because we have worried but because visionary individuals and organizations created a Green Revolution. It is not because we have worried that we have more leisure time, greater safety, higher incomes and better education, but because we have tackled the problems.

We must take care of the problems, prioritize reasonably, but not worry unduly.

We are actually leaving the world a better place than when we got it and this is the really fantastic point about the real state of the world: that mankind's lot has vastly improved in every significant measurable field and that it is likely to continue to do so.

Think about it. When would you prefer to have been born? Many people are still stuck with the Litany and have a mental image of children growing up with a shortage of food and water, and with pollution, acid rain and global warming.[2930] But the image is a mixture of our own prejudices and a lack of analysis.

Thus, this is the very message of the book:

children born today – in both the industrialized world and developing countries – will live longer and be healthier, they will get more food, a better education, a higher standard of living, more leisure time and far more possibilities – without the global environment being destroyed.

And that is a beautiful world.

Notes

1. Quoted in: Mark Twain, Autobiography, chapter 29 (ed. by Charles Neider, 1959).

2. Also, a few fields have their own favorite standards, as oil is often measured in barrels and energy in BTU (British Thermal Unit). Following convention, these are often used, but typically introduced with a description of their equivalents. See efunda 2001.

3. efunda 2001.

4. Lester Brown was president for Worldwatch Institute till 2000, and now chairman of the board and senior researcher.

5. Of course many other environmental papers and reports are available which are better from an *academic* point of view (e.g. the many reports by the UN, WRI and EPA, as well as all the fundamental research, much of which is used in this book and can be found in the bibliography).

6. Hertsgaard 2000.

7. Scott 1994:137.

8. Linden 2000.

9. *New Scientist* 2001:1.

10. The term "the Litany" as well as the following description is from Regis (1997).

11. I often hear it claimed that no one would make these statements anymore, but an almost identical description was the backbone of *Time* magazine's presentation of the state of nature in their special edition for 2001: "Throughout the past century humanity did everything in its power to dominate nature. We dammed earth's rivers, chopped down the forests and depleted the soils. Burning up fossil fuels that had been created over eons, we pumped billions of tons of greenhouse gases into the air, altering atmospheric chemistry and appreciably warming the planet in just a few decades. And as our population began the year 2000 above the 6 billion mark, still spreading across the continents, dozens of animal and plant species were going extinct every day, including the first primate to disappear in more than 100 years, Miss Waldron's red colobus.

"At the start of the 21st century there were unmistakable signs that exploitation of the planet was reaching its limit-that nature was beginning to take its revenge. Melting ice in the polar regions suggested that the climate was changing rapidly. Weather was even more erratic than usual, giving some places too little rain and others too much. Fires raced across the parched American West last summer, and recent storms spread devastation from Britain to Taiwan. No specific event could be directly blamed on global warming, but scientists say that in a greenhouse world, deluges and droughts will be more frequent and severe. Already the hotter climate has increased the range of tropical diseases such as malaria and yellow fever. Other ominous signals from an overburdened planet include falling grain and fish harvests and fiercer competition for scarce water supplies." Anon. 2001b.

12. Perhaps the most concentrated statement exemplifying all the Litany comes from Isaac Asimov and Frederik Pohl's book on *Our Angry Earth* (1991:ix): "It is already too late to save our planet from harm. Too much has happened already: farms have turned into deserts, forests have been clear-cut to wasteland, lakes have been poisoned, the air is filled with harmful gases. It is even too late to save ourselves from the effects of other harmful processes, for they have already been set in motion, and will inevitably take their course. The global temperature will rise. The ozone layer will continue to fray. Pollution will sicken or kill more and more living creatures. All those things have already gone so far that they must now inevitably get worse before they can get better. The only choice left to us is to decide how *much* worse we are willing to let things get."

13. It is impossible to cover *all* important areas, but I believe that this book covers most of them, and the Scandinavian debate has not suggested significant new areas. New suggestions, of course, are always welcome.

14. This and the following claims are documented in the individual chapters below.

15. Strictly speaking this is not true, since *better and better* also has ethical connotations (what is *better?*), but this will usually be quite uncontroversial, e.g. is it better for an infant to have an improved chance of survival? The difference between "is" and "ought" presented here stems originally from David Hume (1740:468–9).

16. WFS 1996: I, table 3; FAO 1999c :29.

17. Brundtland 1997:457.

18. The following argument relies on Simon 1995:4ff.

19. Simon 1995:6.

20. WRI 1996a:105.

21. E.g. Easterlin 2000.

22. UNEP 2000:52ff.

23. WFS 1996:I:table 3; FAO 1999c:29.

24. UNEP 2000:55.

25. Scotney, D. M. and F.H. Djikhuis 1989: "Recent changes in the fertility status of South African soils." Soil and Irrigation Research Institute, Pretoria, South Africa. Despite several attempts, I was unable to get hold of this publication.

26. IFPRI 1999:14, and FAO 1995b:86–7. Notice, FAO does not split up food production increase into yield and area increase (expecting a total annual increase of 3.4 percent, cf. IFPRI 2.9 percent, of which 1.7 percent comes from yield increases).

27. The annual yield growth has been 0.37 percent since 1990, the total production 20.7 percent (FAO 2000a).

28. Pimentel *et al.* 1995a.

29. Boardman 1998.

30. Technically speaking, the error is known as selecting on the dependent variable: we tend to choose the examples according to the result we desire (remembering only grandfathers who smoked and lived long lives) and then quote a long series of them – without achieving the desired power of argumentation.

31. Of course checks should also be made for a whole series of other factors, e.g. whether there is a difference between smokers and non-smokers in terms of social class, income, geography, education, sex, etc.

32. From 2,007 to just 1,579 calories per day per capita (FAO 2000a).

33. From 1,711 to 2,170 calories per day per capita, 1988–98 (FAO 2000a).

34. Of course, one should also take into account that the countries are of very different sizes.

35. FAO 2000a.

36. WI 1984:18.

37. WI 2000c.

38. Notice that data and graph for exports in Worldwatch Institute *Vital Signs 2000* (2000b:74–75) is incorrect, compared to previous editions (1998b:69, 1999b:77, and the electronic database (2000c), and also when compared to goods and services in constant 1995$ from World Bank (2000c).

39. E.g. Brown and Kane 1994:138.

40. Brown and Kane 1994:142.

41. Asimov and Pohl 1991:45. The ellipsis is in the original text. I have left out an obvious repetition: "The twenty-three years from 1947 to 1969 averaged about 8.5 days of very violent Atlantic hurricanes *from 1947 to 1969*, while. . ."

42. Landsea 1993:figure 8, see http://www.aoml.noaa.gov/hrd/Landsea/climo/Fig8.html.

43. Landsea 1993.

44. Landsea *et al.* 1999:108.

45. WWF 1997a:18.

46. INPE 2000:9.

47. WWF 1997a:18.

48. A football pitch 70 m × 110 m occupies 0.77 ha. So 1,489,600 ha/year is the equivalent of 1.9 million football pitches, or 220 football pitches an hour. The Amazon occupies approximately 343 million ha, or about 445 million football pitches. Does that make us any the wiser?

49. INPE 2000:7; Brown and Brown 1992:121.

50. Anon. 2000a:5; see also http://www.recycline.com/.

51. Hudson 2000.

52. Stiefel 1997.

53. Notice, in the article, the estimate is in pounds, probably because it sounds better at 100 million pounds. Anon. 2000a:5, http://www.recycline.com/recinfo.html.

54. EPA 2000c:table 1.

55. EPA 1999b:5 (table ES-1) for 1997, with 267.645 million inhabitants and 100 million pounds of annual toothbrush waste (Anon. 2000a:5).

56. WI 1995:7.

57. WI (2000b:46): "Perhaps the most dramatic and unexpected change was the precipitous decline in fertilizer use in the Soviet Union after the economic decline that began a decade ago."

58. In the environmental science area, this is known as "problem solution by displacement" (Weale 1992:22).

59. Asimov and Pohl 1991:76.

60. Asimov and Pohl 1991:78.

61. Gore 1992:82.

62. E.g. Andersen 1998. Al Gore also points out that scrubbers cause the release of 6 percent more CO_2 (1992:82), though the modern estimate is less than 1 percent (Anon. 1995b).

63. Elsom 1995:480; see also the section on pollution in Part IV.

64. See the calculations in note 1188 from particle pollution in Part IV.

65. Goodstein 1995 cites EPA as saying that groundwater pollution from the over 6,000 US landfill sites is estimated to cause 5.7 cancer incidents every 300 years, or a little less than one every 50 years. Since the number of landfills is smaller in the UK and scrubber slurry is only a minor constituent of the landfill, this risk is a maximum estimate.

66. I do not generally buy the argument that animals should have *equal* rights, cf. Singer 1977.

67. Although I refrain from using more radical interpretations, this formulation was naturally inspired by Baxter 1974. A view of life like this is known as *objectification*, and is the dominant view (Agger 1997:64ff).

68. I strongly feel that animals and plants have the right not to be damaged or to die unnecessarily (I am a vegetarian for that very reason), but the crucial word here is "unnecessary." When is something sufficiently necessary for a human to justify the death of a cow?

69. But the choice is rarely unambiguous: virgin forests naturally also provide humans with recreational facilities, while the fields give life to a lot of corn.

70. Although we will see counter-examples, as in Pimentel *et al.* (1998), below.

71. WI 1998a:4.

72. The rest of the Worldwatch Institute's books naturally contain many *examples* of these claims, but as mentioned above, such singular examples are practically useless in terms of global evaluation.

73. WI 1998a:22. They continue in the following sentence with, "As noted earlier, almost half the forests that once blanketed the Earth are gone." Despite the fact that this estimate is extremely exaggerated (Goudie [1993:43] estimates 20 percent and Richards [1990:164] 19 percent during the last 300 years), it suggests an unreasonable comparison between a trend over a couple of decades and a trend over a couple of millennia.

74. It seems obvious that the 1949 estimate was off and would cause an even more optimistic conclusion than the one reported here.

75. WI 1998a:22.

76. 11.26 million ha/yr (FAO 1997c:17).

77. WI 1998a:9.

78. 873,000a ha in the latest assessed period 1990–5 (FAO 1997c:189).

79. WI 2000a:xvii.

80. WI 2000a:xvii.

81. World Bank 2000c, 2000e:I:188. Incidentally, this is also the trend (for 1984–98) presented in another Worldwatch Institute publication (WI 2000b:73).

82. EEA 2000.

83. Measured in constant 2000 US$; IMF 2001a; data from Figure 65.

84. EIA 2000e:127, 153.

85. USBC 2000a.

86. WI 2000a:xvii.

87. WI 2000a:4; cf. WI 1998a:xvii, quoted in the opening of Part II.

88. WI 2000a:4.

89. WI 2000a:4.

90. WI 2000a:15.

91. Caldwell 2000.

92. Ainsworth and Teokul 2000.

93. Worldwatch Institute return to the AIDS example again in their introduction (WI 2000a:14–15).

94. WI 2000a:13.

95. WI 2000a:12.

96. WI 2000a:12.

97. WI 1998b:15.

98. WWF 1997b, 1997d, 1998c.

99. WWF 1997b, title and p. 1.

100. See references in the section on forests.

101. WWF 1997e.

102. WWF 1997a, 1997e.

103. Goudie (1993:43) estimates 20 percent, probably from Matthews 1983. We do not have other estimates going back to pre-agricultural times, but several estimates from the last centuries, where deforestation has been by far the most intense. Thus, these estimates should be just slight underestimates of the entire pre-agricultural deforestation. Here Williams (1994:104) estimates 7.5 percent and Richards (1990:164) 19 percent loss during the last 300 years. IPCC also estimate a global forest area reduction of 20 percent from 1850 to 1990 (2001a:3.2.2.2).

104. A problem of definition which could be applied to as much as 33 percent of the currently forested area – this is unclear from provisional descriptions, although the Northern forests cover 1.2 billion ha (Stocks 1991:197). Aldrich was not

aware of other historical accounts of forest loss and was happy to receive a copy of the references in note 102.

105. WWF 1997e.

106. In the period 1980–95 the world lost 180 million ha (FAO 1997c:16), for 1990–5, 56.3 million ha (p. 17) which is the total forested area at 3,454 million ha (p. 10). For the 1980s (in million ha): 3,634(1–0.346 percent) 10 = 3510.3 and for 1990–5 (in million ha): 3510.3(1–0.32 percent)5 = 3,454. When I told Mark Aldrich at the WCMC about the claims of increasing deforestation, he said candidly "Well, that sounds like the WWF."

107. http://www.panda.org/forests4life/news/10897.htm.

108. FAO 1997c:189, 18.

109. WWF 1997d; 1998c:36; 1999:27, with WWF forest cover for 1990 being 3,410 million ha, compared to FAO's 3,454 + 56.3 = 3,510.3 million ha in 1990 (FAO 1997c:10, 17).

110. 1–3,410/6,793 = 49.8 percent instead of 1–3,044/8,080 = 62.3 percent.

111. Fairhead and Leach 1998; Leach and Fairhead 1999.

112. Leach and Fairhead 1999:1. You can also see this forest reduction claim on the color map in WWF 1998d:7, available on the internet.

113. Fairhead and Leach 1998:xix.

114. Fairhead and Leach 1998:183.

115. WWF 1999:1.

116. FAO 1997c:13, table 2.

117. WWF 1998a:6.

118. "Only about 3 percent of the world's forests are forest plantations" (FAO 1999a:1). Compare, however, to a FAO estimate in 1997: plantations in the industrialized world total approx. 80–100 Mha, in the developing world 81.2 Mha out of a total forest area of 3,454 million ha, i.e. 5.2 percent (FAO 1997c:10, 14, and WWF 1998a:36).

119. Costanza *et al.* 1997; WWF 1998a:24.

120. WWF 1998a:24.

121. This claim was not made in the new WWF 1999.

122. WI 1999b:77.

123. "The two hard data (the critique of the 40,000 species dying each year and that the species extinction rate is now at 0.7 percent) Greenpeace and most others have accepted long ago." *Politiken*, 13 February 1998.

124. Greenpeace, *Protecting Biodiversity*: http://www.greenpeace.org/~comms/cbio/bdfact.html. This link has now been removed because of my criticism.

125. From the Norwegian newspaper *Verdens Gang*, 19 March 1998.

126. *Verdens Gang*, 19 March 1998.

127. Colborn *et al.* 1996.

128. Colborn *et al.* 1996:182. It is ironic and insupportable, when reading the book, to believe Theo Colborn's assertion, that "we wrote into our book that I thought it was a very weak, very poor connection [between environmental contaminants and breast cancer]" (PBS Frontline 1998).

129. Colborn *et al.* 1996:182.

130. 175 percent=1.01^(1996–1940).

131. ACS 1999, CDC 2001a.

132. UNEP 2000:41ff.

133. UNEP 2000:42, http://www.grida.no/geo2000/english/0046.htm.

134. WHO 1998: "In 1997, there were 10 million deaths among children under 5." 10.466 million, Murray and Lopez 1996c:648.

135. UNEP 2000:148, http://www.grida.no/geo2000/english/0099.htm.

136. ECQ 1997. As is unfortunately common in the environmental literature, GEO 2000 only refers to the *entire* book without a page reference, making it exceedingly (and unreasonably) hard to locate a single argument in a 300+ page book.

137. WI 1999b:16–17, cf. p. 48, 54; 1997b:54; 2000a:17.

138. 22 percent of 0.045 EJ versus 2 percent of 159.7 EJ.

139. 0.045EJ*1.22^45.7=159.7EJ*1.02^45.7.

140. Hohmeyer 1993.

141. Krupnick and Burtraw 1996. The three studies are: US Department of Energy (Oak Ridge National Laboratories/Resources for the Future, Lee *et al.* 1995), EU (DG XII 1995) and Empire State Electric and NY State Energy Research and Development Authority (1995).

142. Krupnick and Burtraw 1996:24.

143. WI 1999a:28.

144. WI 1999a:39.

145. WI 1999a:39.

146. WI 1999a:18. Notice that although it sounds as if reducing CO_2 emissions is going to be cheap or even profitable (and this is certainly the way the quote is intended by Worldwatch Institute), Casten may just be very honest, stating that he doesn't care about the absolute costs to society, but only that companies like his will stand to make an enormous profit in supplying the means to do so.

147. WI 1999a:35.

148. WI 1999a:35; Hoffert *et al.* 1998: 884.

149. Miller 1998:494. It is added that "in most of these countries the problem is not a shortage of water but the wasteful and unsustainable use of normally available supplies." However, it does not seem aware that most of the 40 percent comes from *lack* of access to water.

150. Miller 1998:494; Engelmann and LeRoy 1993: http://www.cnie.org/pop/pai/water-11.html.

151. World Bank 1995b.

152. Serageldin 1995:2.

153. Estimate by USAID and WHO; World Bank 1992:49.

154. About 1.1 billion people do not have access to clean drinking water today (Annan 2000:5) and the World Bank estimates that it would cost some $150 per person for water systems, or $165 billion to provide clean water supplies for everyone (World Bank 1994:11). Equally, about 2.5 billion do not have access to sanitation (Annan 2000:5), and this is estimated to cost less than $50 per household (World Bank 1994:83), or some $30 billion (assuming four per household). Thus the total cost of providing full coverage of water and sanitation is less than $200 billion. OECD (2000:270) estimates a total official development assistance of US$50 billion in 1998.

155. The figures for sewerage have been extremely heavily discussed because China claims to have provided facilities for almost its entire population (81 percent in 1990, World Bank 1994:146), but most people doubt this statistic (24 percent in 1990–5, UNDP 1996a:144).

156. Today we know that the figure will be around 764 million because the birth rate has fallen more rapidly than expected (USBC 1996:A-3).

157. Engelman and LeRoy 1993; see http://www.cnie.org/pop/pai/image4.html;http://wwwcatsic.ucsc.edu/~eart80e/SpecTopics/Water/water1.html. It is important, however, to point out that it actually does not look as though the provision of water and sewerage facilities will show such rapid progress, and that we see both an absolute and a relative increase from 1992 to 1994 (Wright 1997:3).

158. The logistic line has a slightly higher explanatory power and a better basic model.

159. These estimates are reproduced in Gleick 1998a:262, 264.

160. Gleick (1998a:261, 263): "WHO utilized the current and most stringent definition of access in each country to estimate what access *would have been* in 1990 if this *current* definition had been used."

161. The depressing 1990–94 numbers are also presented in *Global Environment Outlook 2000* (UNEP 2000:35), estimating an even larger increase in sanitation unserved by the year 2000. This prediction turned out to be incorrect, as the text explains (Annan 2000:5).

162. Gleick 1998a:262, 264.

163. Gleick 1998b.

164. Annan 2000:5.

165. Pimentel *et al.* 1995a; Pimentel and Pimentel 1995.

166. Pimentel *et al.* 1998.

167. Anon. 1999d; Gifford 2000; Anon. 1998b.

168. Pimentel *et al.* 1998:822–3.

169. WHO 2000b:164; Murray and Lopez 1996c:465, 648.

170. Pimentel *et al.* 1998:823.

171. USBC 2000d.

172. From 0.7 to 0.4; Armstrong *et al.* 1999; Martin *et al.* 1999:27.

173. Pimentel *et al.* 1998:818. This connection is especially clear in Anon. 1998b: "Of the 80,000 pesticides and other chemicals in use today, 10 percent are recognized as carcinogens. Cancer-related deaths in the United States increased from 331,000 in 1970 to 521,000 in 1992, with an estimated 30,000 deaths attributed to chemical exposure."

174. Pimentel *et al.* 1998:819.

175. WHO 1999a:269.

176. Pimentel *et al.* 1998:824.

177. Peaking at 32 percent in 1994 (Tangcharoensathien *et al.* 2000:802).

178. Tangcharoensathien *et al.* 2000:802.

179. UNAIDS 2000:128–9.

180. Pimentel *et al.* 1998:820.

181. EPA 2000d:3–19, 3–20.

182. Again, Pimentel *et al.* do not use page numbers, but the reference is OECD 1985a:38. Anon. (1998b) also report this as US emissions: "Although the use of lead in U.S. gasoline declined since 1985, other sources inject about 2 billion kilograms of lead into the atmosphere in this country each year. An estimated 1.7 million children in the United States have unacceptably high levels of lead in their blood."

183. Pimentel *et al.* 1998:817.

184. Pimentel *et al.* 1998:824.

185. Pimentel *et al.* 1998:822.

186. Pimentel *et al.* 1998:817.

187. Pimentel *et al.* 1998:824.

188. Pimentel *et al.* 1998:822.

189. Henderson 2000.

190. Grigg 1993:48.

191. WHO 2000c.

192. World Bank (1993:76) estimate that direct and indirect lost Disability Adjusted Life Years are 73.1 million DALYs for undernourishment, and 72.1 million DALYs for micronutrient deficiencies.

193. World Bank 1993:82; Underwood and Smitasiri 1999:312ff.

194. Underwood and Smitasiri 1999:304.

195. Darnton-Hill 1999.

196. Pimentel *et al.* 1998:817.

197. Anon. 1999d; Gifford 2000.

198. Anon. 1998b.

199. The 50 million is a round figure, from the early 1990s, where most of the data from Pimentel *et al.* (1998) come from; WRI 1998a:12.

200. 567,000 deaths (Murray and Lopez 1996a:315).

201. Pimentel *et al.* 1998:818.

202. Pimentel *et al.* 1998:824.

203. Henderson 2000.

204. Pimentel *et al.* 1998:822, 820, 820.

205. Because the estimate stems from Murray and Lopez 1996a, which only attributes about 40 percent of all causes, and only estimates the death burden for children (1996a:305).

206. Dobson and Carper 1996. McMichael (1999) is a good example: "Infectious diseases receded in western countries throughout the latter 19th and most of the 20th centuries. The receding tide may have turned within the last quarter of this century, however. An unusually large number of new or newly discovered infectious diseases have been recorded in the past 25 years, including rotavirus, cryptosporidiosis, legionellosis, the Ebola virus, Lyme disease, hepatitis C, HIV/AIDS, Hantavirus pulmonary syndrome, Escherichia coli 0157, cholera 0139, toxic shock syndrome (staphylococcal), and others." The argument seems to be, if you can name *that* many, frequency must be increasing.

207. Pimentel *et al.* 1998:824.

208. Murray and Lopez 1996c:465–6, 648–9, 720–1, 792–3.

209. Calculated from the age groups in Murray and Lopez 1996c:465–6, 648–9, 720–1, 792–3.

210. He has no page reference, but the 77 percent comes from Murray and Lopez 1996b:358.

211. This fact is known as the "epidemiological transition," where increased health care has cut infectious disease early on, leaving more noncommunicable disease for later (NAS 1993). WHO shows evidence for changes away from infectious diseases in Chile 1909–99 (1999a:13).

212. Murray and Lopez 1996c:465, 792.

213. NCHS 1999a:142.

214. Pimentel *et al.* 1998:824.

215. WI 2000a:7.

216. We will here ignore the fact that the whole metaphor is biased towards stationarity, while it is likely that as we get to be ever more people, we will also develop ever better grains, making the minimum area smaller and smaller.

217. Simon 1996:100–1.

218. FAO 2000d:108.

219. WI 1998a:89.

220. WI 1998a:90.

221. Brown 1996b:199–200.

222. Greenpeace 1992:8.1.

223. Falkenmark and Lundqvist 1997:8.

224. WI 1999a:23.

225. Gwynne 1975.

226. Of course, this also includes a distributional issue – if England has a longer and more agreeable growing season, Ethiopia may get more stifling heat, but then under the cooling scenario when England got colder climates, Ethiopia must have benefited.

227. 4,131 deaths from excessive cold versus 2,114 deaths from excessive heat, 1987–9 and 1994–6 (NSC 1990:10; 1999:16). For the UK, Subak *et al.* (2000:19) find: "a warmer climate would lead to additional deaths in extreme summer heat waves but these would be more than offset by the decrease in winter mortality." See Moore (1998) for other considerations of heat benefits.

228. The following builds on Brander and Taylor 1998.

229. Gonick and Outwater 1996.

230. WI 1999a:11.

231. Asimov and Pohl 1991:140–1.

232. Brander and Taylor 1998:122; Encyclopedia Britannica estimates about 10,000 islands.

233. Brander and Taylor 1998:129.

234. Brander and Taylor 1998:135.

235. Meadows *et al.* 1972:56ff.

236. Ehrlich 1970.

237. Ehrlich 1970:25.

238. Each African had 2,439.4 calories/day in 1998 (FAO 2000a).

239. Ehrlich 1970:24. *New Scientist* (2001) equally worries that pollution and limits to growth will lead

to a "Great Depopulation," leaving just 2 billion in 2100.

240. Ehrlich and Ehrlich 1974.

241. Ehrlich and Ehrlich 1974:28.

242. Ehrlich and Ehrlich 1974:30: "Marine biologists seem to agree that the global catch is now about at its maximum."

243. Ehrlich and Ehrlich 1974:158.

244. Ehrlich and Ehrlich 1974:33. They also predict a stock market crash for 1985 (p.176).

245. Danish TV news, DR1, 18.30, 4 February 1998.

246. It should be pointed out that these small fluctuations up or down are not really decisive, given the great uncertainties and model estimates inherent in the data. The best one can say about the forests is probably that they have neither declined nor increased significantly since 1950.

247. This was the point in Poulsen 1998.

248. A prime example is Al Gore categorizing anyone not entirely convinced of the supremacy of the environmental question with Nazism (e.g. Gore 1992:272ff).

249. Auken 1998. Poulsen (1998) was able to tell readers of *Politiken* that I actually am a "sandal-wearing leftie," and although this is closer to the mark than the characterization by the Secretary of the Environment, I would prefer not to state my political position because I believe my strength lies in *arguing on the basis of fact* and not in how to use these facts to pursue policy.

250. Although of course I would like to document the (in)efficiency of past decisions, such evaluations are rarely ever available. Apparently, making a cost-benefit analysis of a decision already made and effected would be somewhat pointless as it could make no difference.

251. This myth is invoked by e.g. Worldwatch Institute: "Just as a continuously growing cancer eventually destroys its life-support systems by destroying its host, a continuously expanding global economy is slowly destroying its host – the Earth's ecosystem." WI 1998a:4, cf. WI 2001a:12. It stems originally from the 1973 Ehrlich claim of negative environmental impact being determined multiplicatively by population size, affluence and technology (sometimes written I = PAT, see Common 1996). Consequently, this relationship by definition makes affluence affect the environment negatively (although its impact can be temporarily tempered by technological progress).

252. Conspicuously, this trade-off is central to the new IPCC scenarios, where a choice between the economy and the environment is one of the two main dimensions, IPCC 2000:28.

253. Notice, though, that there is no *determination* in this relationship – only that richer nations in general are more likely to care more for the environment.

254. This index is "a function of five phenomena: (1) the state of the environmental systems, such as air, soil, ecosystems and water; (2) the stresses on those systems, in the form of pollution and exploitation levels; (3) the human vulnerability to environmental change in the form of loss of food resources or exposure to environmental diseases; (4) the social and institutional capacity to cope with environmental challenges; and finally (5) the ability to respond to the demands of global stewardship by cooperating in collective efforts to conserve international environmental resources such as the atmosphere. We define environmental sustainability as the ability to produce high levels of performance on each of these dimensions in a lasting manner" (WEF 2001:9).

255. Simon 1996:226–7.

256. Dunlap *et al.* 1993.

257. Dunlap *et al.* 1993:10.

258. Percentage saying they are concerned a "great deal" or a "fair deal" (Dunlap *et al.* 1993:11).

259. Svenson 1981. One sees similar behavior in a systematic, overoptimistic evaluation of people's own chances in life, cf. Weinstein 1980.

260. Saad 1999.

261. Electric and magnetic fields are known as EMF. In the latest report on the matter, the National Institute of Environmental Health Sciences concluded that "the scientific evidence suggesting that extremely low frequency EMF exposures pose any health risk is weak," (NIEHS 1999:ii).

262. Ashworth *et al.* 1992.

263. Viel *et al.* 1998.

264. This is for instance the judgement of Høyer *et al.* 1998 by both COC (1999:5) and NRC (1999:257–8), see also the discussion of pesticides vs. breast cancer in Part V.

265. In metastudies of cancer, studies have been excluded which do not involve at least three different types of cancer, precisely in order to avoid this type of data massage; Acquavella *et al.* 1998:65.

266. Not all research, of course. However, basic research generally does not generate any public awareness, and if it should do so there is no reason to suppose that it will systematically do so in a

positive way, negating the following mechanism of negative lopsidedness.

267. Abrahamsen *et al.* 1994c:298.

268. Abrahamsen *et al.* 1994c:298.

269. *Ingeniøren* (The Engineer), no. 26–7, 1996, p.14.

270. *Ingeniøren*, no. 28–9, 1996, p.8.

271. Boehmer-Christiansen 1997.

272. Named the 2nd and the 21st most powerful lobbies in Washington by *Fortune* (Birnbaum and Graves 1999). See also critical discussion of AFB as lobbyists in Rauber and McManus 1994.

273. Polls show that people have much more trust in the environmental groups to protect the environment than in business (78 percent versus 38 percent) or even the EPA (72 percent) (Dunlap 2000).

274. The Danish president of WWF, Kim Carstensen, wrote in *Politiken*, "we in the WWF are greatly looking forward to seeing [Lomborg's] 'facts' about how the species are not being wiped out and that the global warming worries can be cancelled. We will jump for joy if he is right." *Politiken*, 22 January 1998. But really, we can decode this writing – it is not obvious that the WWF would jump for joy, because after all, then what would be the *raison d'être* of the organization?

275. Bent Falbert, quoted in Meilby 1996:53

276. McQuail 1994:268.

277. Singer and Endreny 1993:36.

278. Singer and Endreny 1993:21.

279. Singer and Endreny 1993:22, note 1.

280. McQuail 1983:145.

281. McCombs 1994:4.

282. McQuail 1994:272.

283. Quoted in McQuail 1994:268.

284. Meilby 1996:58. This focus on negative news has been analyzed by among others the Glasgow Media Group 1997, 1990; Zillman and Bryant 1994:452ff.

285. Altheide and Michalowski 1999.

286. Dunn 1998.

287. Ridnouer 1998.

288. Anon. 1998c.

289. Brady 1998.

290. Gorman 1998.

291. Griffith 1998.

292. Nash and Horsburgh 1998.

293. Because of Disney's lower theme park attendance (Anon. 1998a).

294. Nash and Horsburgh 1998.

295. Changnon 1999.

296. Notice, these are US figures. The cost of El Niño for other parts of the world would undoubtedly be very different.

297. The Actant model in Thorsen and Møller 1995.

298. Singer and Endreny 1993:103ff.

299. Finkel 1996.

300. Hume 1754:464.

301. Quoted in Simon 1995a.

302. Quoted in Simon 1996:17. However, the original quote has no reference, so this may be apocryphal.

303. Knudsen 1997.

304. Although this is not always the case (UNDP 1996a:5), simple wealth figures such as GDP per capita are often surprisingly closely tied to indicators such as life expectancy, infant mortality and illiteracy as well as political and civil rights (Dasgupta and Weale 1992; Pritchett and Summers 1996).

305. UNDP 1998.

306. World Bank 1998b: table 1.2.

307. UNDP 1998.

308. The UN set the crossing mark at October 12 1999 (UNFPR 1999), although this of course is way too precise – when uncertainties of the population of, say, Nigeria are still in the order of tens of millions people (Okolo 1999).

309. Most estimates are taken from the UN's 2000 review of world population development (UNPD 2001a-c). The UN operates with several different assumptions as regards development in fertility, an optimistic (low), a pessimistic (high), and an "in between" (the so-called *medium variant*). In keeping with most of the literature I here refer to the *medium variant* figures.

310. Chiras 1998:131.

311. Notice that the long-range prediction (UNPD 1998b) is based on the 1996 revision (UNPD 1998a) which is more like the new 2000 revision (UNPD 2001a).

312. The figures represented here are for total fertility, or how many children a woman would give birth to in her lifetime if she followed the current birth pattern. For a stable population this demands a total fertility of just over two (because some of the children will die before they can have their own children). This is measured in Total Fertility Rate, TFR (Heilig 1996). In 1950 TFR in the developing countries was 6.16; for the period 1995–2000 it is estimated at 3.00 and for 2000–2005 at 2.80 (UNPD 1999:I:12).

313. UN consultant Peter Adamson, quoted in Miller 1998:293.

314. E.g. Berry *et al.* 1993: 57ff.

315. The drop in fertility has many other causes, chief among them the increased independence of women due to better education and legislation, making them forsake burdensome excess births for careers or more free time. See Dasgupta 1995 and Gallagher and Stokes 1996.

316. From 1.781 million in 1750 (Mitchell 1975: 23) to 8.910 million in 2000 (UNPD 1999:I:386). In an analysis of Swedish fertility over the last 250 years, Eckstein (1999:164) " found that wage increases and reductions in child mortality could account for a large part of the fertility decline in Sweden."

317. From 4.1 million in 1911 (Mitchell 1995) to 23 million in 2030 (USBC 2001a).

318. The stable rate needs slightly more than 2 children per couple, because some of these children will not themselves get children (either from choice or because they die before reaching maturity).

319. UNPD 2001a:2.

320. TFR for developing countries, UNPD 2001a:4, for the US 3.314 in 1960–65, for Australia 3.27; UNPD 1999:I:418, 84, and Denmark had a TFR of 3.3 in 1920 (Statistics Denmark 1995: 8).

321. UNPD 2001a:1, 1999a:xi, 10.

322. Growth culminated in 1964 at 2.167 percent for the Earth as a whole and 2.624 percent for the developing world (USBC 2000).

323. For the year 2050, the forecast figure has been: 9,833 million (1994 revision) to 9,366 million (1996 revision), 8,909 million (1998 revision) and now 9,322 million (WRI 1996a, WRI 1998a, UNPD 1999a:I:8, 2001a:1).

324. Unfortunately, there is a tendency to only show the development of ever more people up till 2000, giving the impression of a population increase out of control, e.g. Gore 1992:32–3, Burne 1999:104.

325. Again, using the long-range projection of 1998, which is based on the 1996 revision, which looks much like the 2000 revision, UNPD 1998b.

326. UNPD 2001c, cf. 1999a:I:2, 228, 138.

327. China had a TFR of 6.22 in 1950–55, and India a TFR of 5.97 (UNPD 1999a:I:138, 228). Present day numbers from 1995–2000, from UNPD 2001c.

328. UNPD 2001c.

329. UNPD 2001c.

330. UNPD 2001a:1, cf. Bailey 1995: 12. USBC 2000.

331. Based on 1998 revison, UNPD 1999a.

332. Heilig 1996, UNPD 1999a, Keyfitz and Flieger 1990:105. Equivalently, the median age – the age that divides the population into two equal halves – will increase from 23.6 years in 1950 over 26.5 in 2000 to 36.2 in 2050, UNPD 2001a:14.

333. UNPD 1999a:I:, 1999a:II:, Heilig 1996. UNPD 1999a, Keyfitz and Flieger 1990:213.

334. 50 billion estimated in Botkin and Keller 1998:81 (using Dumond 1975, although it is not clear where he should state this number), 77 billion in Desmond 1975, 80.3 billion in Bourgeois-Pichat 1989:90, between 80–100 billion in Hammel 1998: Table 3.

335. E.g. Porrit 1991: 116, Time 1997: 31.

336. Ehrlich 1968:16.

337. The top scorers are Hong Kong with 5952 people/km^2 and Singapore with 4817. The first country as such is Bangladesh with 832. After Mauritius and Korea comes Holland no. 6 with 414, Belgium no. 8 with 332, no. 9: Japan 331, no. 10: India 283. Southern Asia has 242 people /km^2, while the UK has 239, Denmark has 121, Ohio has 106 (273 per square mile), and Indonesia has 101 (World Bank 1997:table 1, USBC 1999:29). Although no causal effect should be read into this, it turns out that a regression analysis of the entire data set shows a positive, not a negative connection between population density and GDP/per capita.

338. Bailey 1995:15.

339. Ehrlich and Ehrlich 1996:70–1. Sustainability should, however, certainly be globally defined, i.e. trade in various goods which can be sustainably produced in different places is acceptable.

340. The US Mid-West is extremely fertile, but the vast majority of Americans choose to live by the coast. A country's economy can manage this, but for some inexplicable reason Ehrlich claims that everyone should live where the food is.

341. Globally, the rural population will grow by just 1.7 percent from 3.20 billion in 2000 to 3.25 billion in 2030, while the urban population will grow by 77 percent from 2.89 billion to 5.12 billion. In Europe, the rural population, which inhabits 97 percent of land area, will be reduced by 36 percent from 183 million to 118 million, while the cities will grow by 4.5 percent to 571 million (UNPD 1998a:96–9, 104–7).

342. UNPD 1998b:3.

343. UNPD 1998a:140. And London had itself gone from a village of 100,000 in 1801 to 2.5 million in 1850 (Floud and Harris 1996:5).

344. UNPD 1998b:8, cf. UNPD 1998a:23–4.

345. Data for the US give 75.2 percent from the last 1990 census, http://www.census.gov/population/censusdata/table-4.pdf.

346. Chiras 1998:133. He continues: "Social problems run rampant. Crowding in urban centers has been implicated in a variety of social, mental, and physical diseases. Many social psychologists assert that divorce, mental illness, drug and alcohol abuse, and social unrest result, in part, from stress caused by overcrowding . . . Research on animals supports the contention that crowding is not a healthy condition." (For a similar argument, see Cunningham and Saigo 1997:129–30.) Subjective crowding lowers psychological well-being (e.g. Fuller *et al.* 1996), but this does not primarily depend on the physical number of people in a city but rather on wealth expressed in the *number of rooms per person*, which we will see has been increasing over time (Figure 38). Second, these studies tend systematically to focus on problems rather than opportunities within the city (e.g. Verheij 1996; Simon 1996:464; for a clear example, see UNFPA 1996: chapter 2).

347. Miller 1998:313: "Despite joblessness, squalor, overcrowding, environmental hazards, and rampant disease, most squatter and slum residents are better off than the rural poor." Of course, shanty-town newcomers may not compare favorably with the *average* rural population, but presumably many left the countryside because they were worse off than the average, see e.g. Siwar and Kasim 1997:1,532 for a partly unsuccessful test.

348. 89 percent in the cities have access to safe water, compared to just 62 percent in rural areas, and for sanitation, the figures are 79 percent versus 25 percent (UNICEF 2000:95; cf. World Bank 1994:6, 27). For less equal access to health services in rural areas, see World Bank 1999c:26.

349. More than two-thirds of 44 countries investigated showed more than ten percentage points difference (UNICEF 1997:39). For cities less malnourished, see Haddad *et al.* 1999:21.

350. Naylor and Falcon 1995:507; see also Haddad *et al.* 1999:18.

351. WRI 1996a:10, cf. *The Economist*, 31 December 1999:27ff.

352. Preston 1995:30; Acsadi and Nemeskeri 1970.

353. Infant mortality lay between 440 and 600 per 1,000 live births (Hill 1995:38).

354. The figure applies to a one-year-old Roman, so life expectancy for a newborn would be even lower. However, because it was uncommon to raise memorial stones for dead infants in Roman times (Russell 1978:45), estimating life expectancy for newborns is very difficult. The data were collected during the first 400 years CE (Botkin and Keller 1998:91).

355. Statistically speaking, the plague mainly affected the young – the life expectancy of 30-year-olds remained constant at about 22 further years throughout the epoch (Russell 1978:47, 56). The low life expectancy of the fourteenth century is also corroborated by painstakingly kept records of Benedictine monks in Canterbury, which showed them to live only an average of 28 years, although the conditions they lived under were far better than those faced by the rest of the population. If we convert this to a life expectancy for the population as a whole we are left with 22 years from birth (for e20=28, e0=22; Hatcher 1986:28, 32). This conversion should be reasonable, since although the monks were better nourished, and enjoyed better sanitation and protection, they did also live much closer together, which could have caused more disease among them.

356. Not so much because they were landowners, as the upper class diet and living conditions were little better than that of the peasants (Russell 1978:44), but because they were men – females having considerably shorter lives owing to the risks from childbirth and heavy field work (Russell 1978:45).

357. Fogel (1989) points out that only 5–15 percent of excessive mortality is due to a general lack of food – by far the most significant factor is poor distribution, which makes it difficult to get food from places which have a surplus to those with a shortage.

358. Preston 1995:31.

359. Statistics Denmark 1995.

360. Japan has even reached 80 (World Bank 1997a:table 1).

361. Preston 1976:ix.

362. Keyfitz and Flieger 1990:105; World Bank 2000a:233, 2000c.

363. The difference in life expectancy between England and Wales and the entire UK is very small (0.2 years lower for the UK in 1998, ONS 2000b:60.

364. Japan did have a life expectancy of 43 in 1899. Chile from Preston *et al.* 1972:144–6. China from Barclay *et al.* 1976. India from Preston 1995:33.

365. Keyfitz and Flieger 1990:107; UNDP 2000b:160, cf. World Bank 2000a:233.

366. Notice, the latest data from the 2000 revision (UNPD 2001a-c) show only very slight differences with the 1998 revision, where the Sub-Saharan figures are also available.

367. UNAIDS 1999:6; USBC 1999a:62. Of the hardest hit 26 countries, 21 are in Africa (USBC 1999:B-7).

368. Annan 1999:19; Olshansky *et al.* 1997.

369. USBC 1999a:62, although these estimates are somewhat more extreme than the UN equivalents, see UNPD 1999a:I, 438.

370. From 1998, 2010: weighted averages from USBC 1999a:56–7, maximal estimates, since the modeled areas only constitute about 70 percent of sub-Saharan Africa; for 2010 also UNAIDS 1999:5. For 2025: Cf. USBC 1999b:49 estimate of 57 years to pre-AIDS estimate of somewhat less than 65 years (Keyfitz and Flieger 1990:109, for 2022.5 but including 18 percent higher life expectancy area of North Africa). UNPD sets the loss of all 35 affected African countries at the somewhat lower 6.5 years loss in 1995–2000, 8.9 years in 2000–2005, and 8.8 years in 2010–2015 (2001a:9).

371. Assuming that sub-Saharan Africa is approximately one-sixth of the developing world. The indicated long-range figures depend, however, also on the future development of HIV in Asia, e.g. USBC 1999a:66.

372. UNAIDS 1998.

373. USBC 1999a:66; see also description of the policies of the southern Indian state of Tamil Nadu in UNAIDS 1999:12.

374. Life expectancy in 2000 taken as average of life expectancy in 1995–2000 and 2000–2005.

375. 48.3 years in 1900 (USBC 1975:I, 55); 79.7 years for 2000 (USBC 1999a:93). For the 60–year-old, the difference is calculated for a white woman with an additional life expectancy of 15.2 years in 1900 and of 23.0 in 2000 (USBC 1975:I, 56, 1999a:94).

376. Hill 1995:38.

377. The figures apply to mortality before age 5 (Hill 1995:40).

378. Sharpe 1987:49.

379. The trend for the US is best documented for Massachusetts, where infant mortality has declined from around 150 in the middle of the nineteenth century to 5.1 in 1998 (USBC 1975:57, MDPH 2000:33.

380. Hill 1995:45.

381. USBC 1998:58.

382. Quotes from Stone 1979:62–4, 306.

383. Haines 1995:58

384. CDC 1999b.

385. Haines 1995:58; Porter 1997:426.

386. Riley 1992; Porter 1997:274ff, 438–9.

387. Reisner 1996:153; Haines 1995:57.

388. Porter 1997:24–5. It became obvious that these were dangerous to adults who had not been infected with the diseases during childhood in the New World when the Spanish arrived in large numbers in the early sixteenth century (Porter 1997:27).

389. Porter 1997:412–13.

390. Preston *et al.* 1972; Haines 1995:56.

391. USBC 1999a:101.

392. NCHS 1999a:142.

393. Armstrong 1999:64.

394. Data for 1999 not ready from NCHS. Due to different methods of registration, CDC HIV/AIDS Surveillance gives higher incidence rates of 19.25 in 1995, declining to 6.6 in 1998 and to 6.0 in 1999, CDC 2000c:35, USBC 2000c.

395. The so-called theory of epidemiological transition, from an era of pestilence and famine to an era of old-age diseases (Armstrong *et al.* 1999:61).

396. CDC 1999a:622–3; Botkin and Keller 1998:87.

397. Unadjusted mortality rate from WHO 2000d; see also http://www.cancer.org/statistics/index.html, for an age-adjusted mortality rate for the US.

398. Peto *et al.* 1992:1,273.

399. CDC 1999d:986.

400. About 19.5 percent for both sexes for 1990–4 (CDC 1997a). Cf. Denmark with 30 percent of all male deaths related to smoking, and 15 percent of female deaths (Middelevetidsudvalget 1994a:74), not the least because the female smoking rate is still high (Engeland *et al.* 1995:146–7).

401. Fries 1980, 1988, 2000.

402. There is a large literature on this subject: Riley 1990, 1997; Riley and Alter 1996; Alter and Riley 1998; Crimmins *et al.* 1989; Crimmins and Ingegneri 1995. Notice some of the newest work does seem to suggest that the health of older people is improving, e.g. Jarvis and Tinker 1999.

403. Gruenberg 1977; Kramer 1980; Feldman 1983.

404. Riley 1990:424.

405. Riley 1990:424–5.

406. Johansson 1991, 1992; Riley 1992; Murray and Chen 1992, 1993; Riley 1993, Murray and Lopez 1997.

407. Murray and Chen 1992:484–5, where they also demonstrate that residents of Ghana report *higher* incidence of illness with *higher* income, p. 492.

408. Murray and Lopez 1996a, 1996c, 1997a–d.

409. In order to negate this argument one has to contend that the Europeans several centuries ago with much lower life expectancies essentially were *dramatically more* healthy than are the equivalent inhabitants of the developing countries today, despite the outstanding increase in medical knowledge and technology available in these countries today.

410. Fogel 1995:66.

411. Although in much earlier times we were somewhat taller, and closer to the present-day height. For London, male height is estimated at 170 cm in prehistory, 169 cm in Roman times, 173 cm in Saxon times, 172 cm in the medieval, Tudor and Stuart periods, with height dropping to 171 cm in Georgian and 166 cm in Victorian times and only now up to 175cm (Werner 1998:108).

412. Ehrlich 1968:xi.

413. Ehrlich 1967:653.

414. India produced 28 percent more food from 1967 to 1975 (FAO agricultural production index from 48.9 to 62.5). The population increased from 518.5 million to 622.7 million, and calorie consumption from 1,871 to 1,939. The current value is 2,496 (1997). FAO 2000a.

415. Brown 1965.

416. The world's population grew from 3,080 million in 1961 to 6,157 million in 2001, or by 99.9 percent (USBC 2001a).

417. Meadows *et al.* 1972.

418. FAO's production index, 1961–99, entire world: from 49.8 to 118.6; developing world: from 40.1 to 135.4. The increase per capita for entire world: from 85.0 to 104.5; for developing world: from 76.6 to 116.3. The Production Index is price weighted and can therefore be distorted, especially in countries plagued by inflation where price and consumption patterns change substantially over time (WRI 1996a:246).

419. FAO 2001a, WI 2000b:39.

420. World Bank food index, IMF 2001a, CPI 2001.

421. This depends on climate, weight, sex and age. It is estimated from the Basic Metabolic Rate (BMR), which is the amount of energy necessary to maintain life in a relaxed state (or in bed). This is usually between 1,300 and 1,700 calories. Light physical activity is assumed to require 55 percent more energy, which brings the total requirement to 1,720–1,960 calories (WFS 1996:1, box 1). The number of people existing below this limit is estimated on the basis of the distribution of energy intake in individual countries (FAO 1995:37ff).

422. Data are from WFS 1996:1, table 3, an improvement on FAO 1995b, and FAO 1999c:29, 2000c:27.

423. This is estimated from Figure 7, assuming a roughly constant relationship between starvation at 1.2 BRM and at 1.55 BRM, throughout the entire period 1949–79. Empirically, this seems true for the period 1970–9.

424. Data for underweight children 0–5 years old (UNDP 1996a:149). The fall applies to all regions except sub-Saharan Africa (UNICEF 1998:15). UNICEF, however, also emphasizes that the absolute number of malnourished children has increased (1998:10). (UNICEF also employs underweight as a measure of malnutrition, 1998:18.) Unfortunately, UNICEF does not provide a figure for the number of malnourished souls, although the increase cannot be that great. Children aged 0–5 years account for 13.36 percent of the population of developing nations, a proportion which is falling slightly (because we are getting older and the birth rate is falling) (Keyfitz and Flieger 1990:107). Therefore, 40 percent of people starving in 1975 must be at least 159.5 million, whereas the figure for 1985–90 should be 163.8 million at the most (156.9 million according to UNDP 1996a:147) (cf. however, statistical warning from UNICEF 1996, http://www.unicef.org/pon96/nutale.htm). IFPRI estimates that the number of malnourished children under 5 will fall from 160 million to 135 million of 557 million (IFPRI 1999:18; UNPD 1999a:II, 19). The proportion of stunted (low height-for-age) children has dropped from 47.1 percent in 1980 to 32.5 percent today, and is predicted at 29 percent in 2005 (ACC/SCN 2000:8).

425. The proportion of starving people in the Near East and North Africa will grow slightly from 8 percent in 1991, to 9 percent in 1996, and 10 percent in 2010. Notice, that Worldwatch Institute incorrectly states that the share of starving people in Africa has increased since 1980 (WI 2001:44) – the share has decreased in North Africa from 8 to 4 percent and in sub-Saharan Africa from 37 to 33 percent (FAO 1999c:29). The Worldwatch Institute reference (ACC/SCN 2000) never mentions the development of the African share of hunger.

426. WFS 1996:1, table 3.

427. In 1971 the developing world had 2.771 billion inhabitants and 1.851 non-starving. In 2000 it had 4.891 billion inhabitants, 4.099 non-starving cit-

izens (USBC 2000a), meaning that an extra 2.248 billion were actually fed beyond the starvation threshold.

428. WFS 1996:VI, 4.4.

429. Bailey 1995:420.

430. The UN climate panel, IPCC (which we will discuss much more in chapter 24), clearly state: "prices are the best indicator of the balance between global food supply and demand," IPCC 2001b:5.3.6.

431. WFS 1996:VI, 4.

432. Heinrichs 1998.

433. Avery 1995:382.

434. Bailey 1995:64; Reeves *et al.* 1999:10. The new varieties of wheat are resistant to mildew; CGIAR newsletter 1; http://www.worldbank.org/html/cgiar/newsletter/Oct94/WheatBrd.html.

435. Reeves *et al.* 1999:23: CIMMYT 1999:1.

436. About 1 percent annual increase since 1960 (Pingali 1999:3; cf. Bell *et al.* 1995; Oram 1995, http://www.worldbank.org/html/CGIAR/25years/gains.html).

437. Tenenbaum 1995.

438. WFS 1996:VI, Figure.

439. The following discussion was inspired by an original contract situation involving a veil of ignorance as discussed in Rawls (1972). This formulation made it possible to take into account all forms of risk-aversion (e.g. I don't want to risk my life, so I will choose a precautionary decision principle [maxmin]).

440. If people knew that they would be privileged in an otherwise awful society or rejected by one that was otherwise good, a good number of them would be tempted to choose the former.

441. This simplification can be omitted but this makes the expected value more complex without changing the basic point.

442. 139 M ha of an overall agricultural area of 1,330 M ha in 1961, versus 268 M ha of an overall area of 1,466 M ha in 1997/1994 (FAO 2000a; ERS 1995; WRI 1998a:298).

443. Egypt produces 5 t/ha (FAO 1995b:13); the wheat yield for developing countries was 3.15 t/ha in 1997 (USDA 1998).

444. WI 1999b:44.

445. Heinrichs 1998.

446. WI 1997a:38. Growth in the use of fertilizer per capita of the population has "only" quadrupled.

447. Rice, wheat and corn make up 24 percent of the world's energy intake (FAO 1996b:98, 107). The increase for the developing world was 39 percent, 144 percent and 84 percent respectively. In the UK, Germany and Denmark the wheat harvest produces more than 7.2 t/ha. Italy, France and Chile harvest more than 9 t/ha of corn, and Australia produces more than 6 t/ha of rice. (USDA 1998.)

448. FAO 2000d:70.

449. Goklany (1998) estimates about twice the area since 1961; Bailey (1995:71–2) estimates that about three times as much space would have to be used.

450. Pingali 1999:8–13.

451. This is also the question of Collier and Gunning 1999, whose argument infuses the following text. See also IMF 1999a:VI.

452. Henao and Baanante 1999.

453. FAO 1996b:I.

454. FAO 1997d.

455. FAO 1996b:2:3.4ff and 2000a; Burkina Faso improved its daily calorie intake from approx. 1,800 in the period 1961–85 to 2,250 in 1995.

456. FAO

457. UNDP 1997.

458. One of the latest famines in the Sudan, spring of 1998, threatened 250,000 people. It was described by Dan Effie, the spokesman of a major Norwegian aid organization, as "purely and simply a man-made catastrophe." http://cnn.com/WORLD/africa/9804/10/africa.drought. The UN's Secretary General Kofi Annan is pretty direct in his report on Africa that the lack of development is primarily due not to the colonial period but to the desire of Africa's own leaders for wealth and power (Annan 1998:12).

459. "Evidence continues to confirm the link between good policies and good economic performance, especially in the poorer African countries." World Bank 1997c:37; 1999d:30–1, 2000f:46.

460. The following is based on WFS 1996:II, 3.13ff, and FAO 2000a.

461. Hu and Kahn 1997.

462. Hu and Kahn 1997:5.

463. WFS 1996: I, 1:table 3 estimates 41 percent undernourished in East Asia in 1970, compared to 13 percent in China 1996 (FAO 1999c:29).

464. WFS 1996:II, 3.13, FAO 2000a.

465. WI 1994:177; 1998a:93. Ehrlich: "Most of the readily available opportunities for substantial increases in food production have already been taken, and agriculture is now faced with a series of hurdles and potential difficulties that will not be easily surmounted. No obvious new set of

technologies is at hand (as the newly developed high-yielding grain varieties were in 1950) that could be used to create another miraculous 'green revolution'" (Ehrlich *et al.* 1995:21–2).

466. GDP measures the value of goods and services entirely within a nation (e.g. the US), whereas GNP measures the value of goods and services produced by a nation's citizens (e.g. US residents), regardless of whether they are in the US or abroad.

467. Such as NNP, net national product, or NDP, net domestic product. In comparison over time and different nations, however, the differences are not that great.

468. The UNDP estimated in 1995 that the value of unpaid and underpaid work was $5,000 and $11,000 billion for men and women (UNDP 1995). In comparison, world GDP in 1995 was $26,900 billion (WI 1997b:67).

469. Schneider and Enste 2000: 100; see also "Black hole," *The Economist* 28 August 1999, 352(8,134):59–60.

470. Statistics Denmark 1995:22.

471. World Bank 1994:230.

472. Jensen 1995. The welfare indicator deviated only 3–4 percent from the consumer figures.

473. Comparing the size of GDP between various currencies produces another problem. Should one use the rate of exchange or purchasing power? This problem will be investigated in connection with the possibly increasing inequality in the developing countries.

474. It was discovered that consumption in the period 1970–90 had increased by 40.3 percent, whereas the welfare indicator had increased by 40.7 percent. Only if the value of leisure time was included in the equation (it was almost constant throughout the period) was the increase substantially lower (23.4 percent). However, this was purely because including the value of leisure time makes us wealthier, therefore rendering any increasing income less notable. In other words – if it is assumed that the pleasure people get from life is great enough, economic growth can be accorded as little significance as you like.

475. $17.39, CPI 2001.

476. See Figure 30.

477. It is naturally not impossible *in principle* to produce a correct index (e.g. by using hedonistic regression models). The problem is, however, that it would take a lot of effort to handle the many changes rapidly enough. This seems to be the thrust of the apology in Armknecht *et al.* 1997.

478. Boskin *et al.* 1997:79.

479. Similarly, cellular phones have since their introduction in 1983 significantly affected the Western lifestyle, but they were first included in the American CPI in 1998. It is estimated that their exclusion has led the CPI for telecommunications to overestimate inflation between 0.8 percent and 1.9 percent per year (Hausman 1999).

480. Nordhaus 1997b:47.

481. Nordhaus 1997b:63. This is likely to be somewhat of an overestimate, however, since parts of lighting come with a package that cannot be changed – the utility of lighting may double with the first doubling in light bulb lumen, but further doubling does not double the utility again, since what we need is light in *different* places, not just one, very luminous bulb in the center of the house, cf. Hulten 1997.

482. Boskin Commission 1996; Boskin and Jorgensen 1997; Boskin *et al.* 1998. The issue became a political one because the Federal Government could save money if it could be concluded that the index overestimated price developments. However, Janet Norwood, former chairman of Labor Statistics which prepares the CPI, was more or less in agreement; see Norwood 1995.

483. Both directly and through public sector spending.

484. DeLong also shows that with the Nordhaus new-goods correction, mentioned in the box above (Nordhaus 1997b), the GPD per capita has grown about 33-fold over the past 200 years.

485. Compare this to a total estimated 57-fold increase over the past 1000 years, Anon. 1999h:147.

486. Comparisons over such a long period of time should be taken with certain reservations. Price indexing is based on specific "baskets" of goods, which by their very nature cannot remain even reasonably constant throughout the period.

487. This is why inequality has indeed grown over the last 120 years (Pritchett 1997; Crafts 2000; IMF 2000b), whereas it has not within the last 40–50 years, measured in PPP$ (see below). The causes for the different starting points are outlined in Landes 1998.

488. The ratio fluctuates between 5.5 and 6.5.

489. UNDP 1997.

490. World Bank 1998a:vii.

491. UNDP 1997.

492. World Bank 1998a:vii

493. Using CPI 2000.

494. Notice, that especially because of problematic poverty measurements from India, the true poverty rate could actually have been falling even faster, World Bank 2001a:26.

495. Since the 50 percent estimate in Figure 23 is based on the total world population and the World Bank 24 percent estimate only on the developing and transitional world, the World Bank estimate would be about 20 percent of total world population, and thus the 50 percent has been more than halved.

496. 1.2 billion poor in 1950 (Barry *et al.* [1991:73] estimate 1.178–1.297 billion poor people) means 1.36 billion not-poor; 1.2 billion in 1998 means 4.72 billion not-poor, i.e. an increase of 3.36 billion not-poor.

497. Frankel 1997.

498. Lindert and Williamson 1995.

499. Persson and Tabellini 1994.

500. Frankel 1997:7.1–2; cf. UNDP 1996a:66ff.

501. UNDP 1996a.

502. World Bank figures from 1987–98 use poverty definition to be persons with less than $1 1985–PPP a day (see explanation of PPP below). Percentage is calculated on developing countries and transitional economies. Estimates from Barry *et al.* are based on consumption (GDP estimates give approximately the same development, though lower estimates). Poverty is defined as less than US 1970$ 200 per year (Barry *et al.*:70). The estimate for 1950–78 includes almost all countries and the percentage is of the whole world. For the estimate without socialist countries 1950–1986, only the rest of the world is used. Regarding Hopkins, poverty definition is not indicated, China is not included, and percentage seems to be world population without China.

503. UNDP 1996a:13; 1999a:38.

504. UNDP 1996a; cf. Korzeniewicz and Moran 1997, also using exchange rate comparisons. The inequality statement has been repeated in countless places; e.g. UNICEF 2000:22; World Bank 2000a:14. UNDP 1999a:39 takes inequality back even further to 1820, but does not try to keep constant the percentage of people compared – actually it seems that the number of poor people covered from 1820 to 1992 declines significantly, thus making it a comparison between, say, top 10 percent/bottom 10 percent and top 10 percent/bottom 2 percent, which definitely skews the result. It is, however, true that inequality has grown over the past 120 years, since this was when the industrializing countries took off (or equivalently, this was when much of the rest of the world was turned into the developing world). See Pritchett 1997; IMF 2000b.

505. The so-called Balassa-Samuelson hypothesis, Balassa 1964; Kravis *et al.* 1978:219–20; see Rogoff 1996: "Overall, there is substantial empirical support for the Balassa-Samuelson hypothesis, especially in comparisons between very poor and very rich countries."

506. *The International Comparison Program*; see e.g. WRI 1996a:162–3.

507. "Big Mac Currencies," *The Economist*, 3 April 1999, 351(8113):66; Annaert and de Ceuster 1997.

508. World Bank 1997a: table 1.

509. This graph is based on estimating the income of the 20–30 percent of the people in the poorest (richest) nations of the world, similar to Dunghyun (1997, 1999) and consistent with log variance estimates on PPP income by Schultz (1998).

510 Heston and Summers 1996: "After considerable resistance, international agencies now seem to be persuaded that PPP-based estimates of GDP are superior to exchange-rate-based ones for most if not all of their purposes." Dowrick and Quiggin 1997: "Constant international price measures of per capita GDP, based on the International Comparison Project (ICP) and the Penn World Tables (PWT) have now replaced exchange-rate comparisons as the industry standard in cross-country studies of economic performance. This change in method represents a substantial improvement in that constant price measures discount those differences in nominal expenditures which are due simply to differences in the relative prices of traded and nontraded goods." World Bank 1999a:230: using exchange rate instead of PPP "tends to undervalue real consumption in economies with relatively low prices and to overvalue consumption in countries with high prices." Schultz 1998:310: "The general concept of purchasing power parity is the appropriate one for [studying inequality]."

511. UNDP uses PPP in its Human Development Index; see UNDP 2000.

512. This approach is also used by Dunghyun (1997, 1999) with broadly similar results, and it is consistent with log variance estimates on PPP income by Schultz (1998). Inexplicably leaving out China and Indonesia, however, Sarkar (1999) finds

an increase in inequality 1950–92 in PPP$. Chotikapahich *et al.* (1997) find some evidence of catch-up and convergence between regions. Note also that the relationship of top 10 percent/bottom 10 percent shows a slight *increase* from 20 to about 25 in the 1990s (Dunghyun 1999). Also, as everyone in a country is implicitly assigned the national average, inequality *within* countries is not estimated, not least because of scarcity of data. However, Korzeniewicz and Moran (1997) estimate inequality within and between countries (using exchange rate). They find that inequality between countries is much more important in shaping global inequality and that inequality within countries has actually decreased, thus making the present inter-country comparison probably overestimating inequality.

513. Per capita income increased from 1820–1950 376 percent for the developed world and only 71.5 percent for the developing world.

514. Of course, the very definition of developed/developing world rests in large parts on whether these nations made it into the industrial revolution. Thus, we should also be aware that showing the inequality over such a long period could hide other, emerging groupings which might show higher inequality.

515. From 1970 to 1992 per capita income increased 38 percent for the developed world and a whopping 72 percent for the developing world.

516. When IMF (2000b:59ff) finds that inequality has risen, it is mainly because they only compare 1900 to 2000, which we can see in Figure 35 would be somewhat misleading.

517. IPCC 2000a:4. We will look more at these scenarios in chapter 24.

518. The actual income can be seen in Figure 149, p. 281. Notice, that whereas the world GDP was fixed from the outset of the scenario-making, the income inequality was endogenously determinated.

519. Maddison measure from 1820–1992 in Geary-Khamis PPP$, based on weighted per capita income from 199 countries (with developed countries being Western Europe, Western Offshoots, Southern and Eastern Europe and the developing countries being Latin America, Asia and Oceania and Africa), adjusted to the level in 1990 at 5.72 from IPCC 2000b (corresponding to the level in Figure 32). IPCC covers all main scenarios from MESSAGE, which has made PPP$ GDP estimates for developed and developing world. Notice, the sharp drop in inequality from 1990–92 is due to the breakdown of the Soviet/Russian economy.

520. E.g. in WI 1997a:116; UNICEF 2000:20.

521. Top 20 percent making 55 percent of all income, declining to 43 percent in 1970 and back up to about 50 percent now (Lindert 2000a:179).

522. This is *only* a back-of-an-envelope argument, estimated with the inequality percentages in World Bank 2000a:239, the income per capita from Fig. 29, and rounded.

523. From 5.5 to 5.45.

524. We have less information to estimate the American inequality, but it is probably correct to say that inequality today is in the same general ballpark as the 1789 inequality (see e.g. Shammas 1993:420). Thus, with an inequality of about 14 (USBC 1999b:xiv), the poorest 20 percent made 180 present-day dollars in 1789, compared to the 20 percent richest's $2,500. Today, these groups make $9,200 and $128,000. Has inequality increased from $2,320 to $117,800 and has the US become approximately 50-fold more unequal over the last 211 years? Would we accept the argument, that even if the wage distribution today was $36,000 and $39,000, inequality had gone up from $2,320 to $3,000?

525. Stone and Kochar 1998.

526. "Growth for most of the East Asia and Pacific region in 1999, as anticipated earlier this year, will revive from the deep crisis-induced recessions of 1998. The turnaround has been much stronger than initially anticipated." World Bank 1999e:9; 2000b:133.

527. IMF 2000d:1, 24.

528. World Bank 2000b:133, estimated with p.134.

529. IMF 1999a:64–7 gives an estimate of the total, social costs.

530. UNDP 1996a:3. The UN also argues that "economic gains have benefited greatly a few countries, at the expense of many"; http://www.undp.org/news/hdr96pr1.htm. This argument is not without its problems, since it is not possible to apportion a country moral status. About half the inhabitants of the developing world live in China and India alone. It is, therefore, naturally crucial to the developing world that these two countries have both achieved substantial growth (of 8.3 percent and 3.2 percent respectively). From a moral point of view it is meaningless to say that growth in a hundred small countries is better than heavy growth in two big ones if

the two have more inhabitants. (One could just divide China and India up into 100 small countries each. Could it then seriously be argued that things had improved?) This is why the question is being dealt with purely as that of 1.5 billion people.

531. Based on UNDP 1996b, 1999b. World Bank 1995a, 2000a; US State Department 1998, 2000; IMF 1998:110, 145; De Broeck and Koen 2000.

532. IMF 1998:110, 2000d:100.

533. IMF 2000d:207.

534. IMF 2000d:30.

535. World Bank 2000b:138, including all the CIS area.

536. USBC 2001a.

537. World Bank 1995a, 1999b, 2000a; US State Department 1998, 2000.

538. USBC 2001a.

539. World Bank 1995a, 1999b, 2000a; US State Department 1998, 2000.

540. As indicated in Figure 36.

541. UNDP 1996a:2.

542. World Bank 1998b:table 1.4.

543. Notice, that by February 2001, the Summers and Heston constant-PPP data-set (1995), ending in 1992, had still not been updated.

544. UNDP 1996a:3.

545. It is clear that if other – and wiser – policies had been pursued by these nations, many of their worst problems could have been avoided. Such an argument as this is, however, often easier to make in retrospect.

546. USBC 1999a:581.

547. USBC 1999a:584.

548. Of course, as with so many other types of technology, we must get used to using them: i.e. learn to switch them off when we want to be left alone.

549. The number of international passengers enplaned (assuming that they also go back) to the total number of Americans, ATA 2001a, USBC 2000d. The total number of Americans transported by American airlines increased from 3.2 million in 1940 to 635.4 in 1999 (USBC 1999a:885, ATA 2001a). World Tourism Organization estimates the total number of tourists in 1960 at 69 million, in 1999 at 657 million and at 1,006 million in 2010, or 2.3 percent in 1960, 10.9 percent in 1999 and 14.7 percent in 2010, ITA 1999, WI 2000b:83, USBC 2001a.

550. WI 2000b:87, 1999a:87; WRI 1998a:244, USBC 2001a.

551. Figures for other countries can be retrieved at http://www.un.org/Depts/unsd/social/housing.htm.

552. WI 1999b:83; WRI 1998a:244.

553. Lebergott 1995:152–3

554. Lebergott 1993:112.

555. Lebergott 1993:112–13.

556. Robinson and Godbey 1997:321, 12 minutes "clothes care" per day.

557. Lebergott 1995:155.

558. In 1960 Americans spent only 20 percent of their food budget away from home; in 1997 the share was up to 38 percent. (USBC 1999a:876).

559. IMF 2001a, see Figure 26.

560. Lebergott 1993:148; USBC 1999a:876. In 1929 the percentage was 23.9 percent, cf. Putnam and Allshouse 1999.

561. USBC 1999a:880; important, since Americans spend some 70 percent of their lives in and around their homes (Lebergott 1993:95).

562. Lebergott 1993:100, 102.

563. EIA 1999a:12.

564. The average space was 631 ft2 or 58.6 m^2 (EIA 1999a:135 and 2.63 people per household); cf. Danish average of 49.5 m^2, and just 32 m^2 in 1950 (Ågerup 1998:48).

565. An increase from 14 m^2 to 30 m^2 per person (NERI 1998A:62).

566. Danish Transport Ministry 1993:27ff.

567. DOT 1997:25.

568. In 1960 one in 40 people had TV in the developing world – in 1994, this applied to one in six (UNESCO 1997:6–7). http://unescostat.unesco.org/statsen/statistics/yearbook/tables/CultAndCom/Table_IV_S_3.html.

569. Provision of sanitation has improved in the poorest countries from 23 percent to 42 percent (World Bank 1994:26). See also UNDP 1996a:149, which it states that access to clean drinking water was 40 percent in 1975 and 68 percent in 1990.

570. This is the number of people who would not get sick or die if water supply and sewerage facilities were improved globally, according to WHO and USAID (WHO 1992:30; World Bank 1992:49).

571. In 1990 there were 396 km of road per person compared to 308 km in 1975. Energy production has increased from 41 to 53 Wh per individual from 1975 to 1990. Telecommunications are measured in trunk lines per 1,000 people; the value was 3 in 1975, 6 in 1990 (World Bank 1994: 26).

572. UNESCO estimates that the total number of

illiterates is 872 million in the developing world (29.6 percent) (UNESCO 1998:table 2).

573. 9.3 to 9.9 years (UNESCO 1998:table 9).

574. The data come from Barro and Lee's dataset (1996).

575. Gross enrollment rate, UNESCO 2000.

576. Crafts 1998 and Maddison 1995a give indications as to similar patterns for much of Asia.

577. See also Simon and Boggs 1995:216.

578. Ausubel and Grübler in 1995:117.

579. These are averages for men and women (Ausubel and Grübler in 1995:122). For men, the transition has been from 150,000 hours of work to just 88,000, and in non-work from 91,000 to 256,000; for women, the reduction in work has been from 63,000 hours to 40,000, with non-work up from 182,000 to 334,000.

580. Different statistics show somewhat different trends. The UN International Labor Organization estimates that average hours of work per week in the US have dropped from 43.0 in 1969 to 40.6 in 1998. However, a large part of this fall is caused by ever more women and fewer men in the workforce, since women typically work fewer hours (ILO 2000; the female participation in the workforce has almost doubled from 1950 to 1998 [33.9 percent to 59.8 percent], while the male participation has dropped somewhat [86.4 percent to 74.9 percent] [Fullerton 1999:4]. The UK hourly workweek was 40.4 in 1986 and 40.2 in 1998.) Similarly, the US Current Employment Statistics with numbers based on actual payroll data indicate a steady decline from 40 hours in 1947 to just 34.5 hours in 1990 and a stable workweek in the 1990s, but the data do not cover all employers (CES 2000). However, the Labor Force Statistics based on national surveys indicate that the average workweek over the past two decades has increased about an hour for women and about 12 minutes for men (Rones *et al.* 1997:4), and this has led several commentators to complain about the "overworked American" (Schor 1991). The problem with the latter statistics is though that it relies on *asking* people how long they work, which may not lead to accurate estimates.

By comparison, most time studies use the more precise diary method, where people have to account for every 15 minutes of their lives. When diary data are compared to self-reported working hours it turns out that hardworking people have a tendency to exaggerate their workload. (Robinson and Godbey 1994, 1997:87ff. However, little-working people have a tendency to *underreport* their work.) If people claim to work 75 hours a week, on average they overestimate their effort by a good 25 hours. Moreover, the diary studies show that respondents have been giving progressively more exaggerated estimates of hours worked over time (for a critical view, which however does not seem to be able to account for the substantial overreporting, see Jacobs 1998).

The reasons are many: more flexible jobs with no fixed schedule make it harder to peg the specific working hours on recall; an increasing blending of work and non-work time may dilute the effective hours compared to hours-on-the-job. Essentially, the impression of being rushed makes us more prone to report how many hours our work *felt* like rather than how many we may actually have performed.

The diary method shows that employed American men have gone from 46.5 hours in 1965 to 42.3 hours in 1995, whereas women have gone from 36.8 hours to 37.3 (Robinson and Godbey 1999:326). This also accords with Danish findings of 2.6 hours less work from 1964 to 1987, making allowances for the fact that the composition of society has also changed (Körmendi 1990:57).

581. It is important to point out that these figures are average values for working weeks, i.e. they do not consider the fact that we have more holiday these days. These weekly and annual figures can therefore not be directly compared.

582. From 82 percent to 75 percent (Fullerton 1999:4; Robinson and Godbey 1999:326).

583. This is broadly equivalent with the Danish figures: in 1964, women were responsible for 90 percent of unpaid housework, while in 1987 they were "only" responsible for 65 percent. On the other hand, women still only contribute 38 percent (up from 24 percent) of paid work (Jensen 1991:71). See also Haslebo 1982:31ff.

584. Robinson and Godbey 1997:104; 1999:328.

585. Diamond 1999:277.

586. Chesnais 1995:96.

587. Stone 1979:77. Stone also points out that 92 percent of violence was directed away from the family (unlike today, where 50 percent of it occurs within the family).

588. Measuring suicide rates also presents some quite general problems in traditional societies, because these do not accept or acknowledge suicide. Again, England has some very good data going right back to the seventeenth century.

589. USBC 1997:834

590. Notice that there are other ways to measure the severity of disasters, mainly the number of people affected, which has increased over the century – however, number of dead has been recorded much more consistently than numbers affected, since this latter concept is exceedingly vague and many different definitions exist (Red Cross 1998:136). The downwards trend is further strengthened since the data have become better recorded over time, which by itself induces an upwards trend (Lidstone 1997: the data "before 1960 are largely anecdotal and are incomplete").

591. This is a rough estimate, given the assumption of an average life expectancy of 30 years in 1900 (Preston 1976:ix). The crude death rate in 1950 was 1,968 (Keyfitz and Flieger 1990:105).

592. Keyfitz and Flieger 1990:105.

593. In the early part of the 1900s, disasters made up about 2.64 percent of all deaths, compared to 0.15 percent in the 1990s.

594. Air death rate smoothed by moving seven-year average.

595. Lidstone 1997.

596. CDC 1999f.

597. Tessmer 1999; CDC 1999e.

598. Notice, though, since most accidents from flying happen at take-off and landing, measuring the risk in km is only reasonable if the mix of short- and long-haul flights remains the same over time.

599. DOT 1999:1–28, 1–30. However, Figure 47 was not updated to measure person km, since the average occupancy has changed over the century and data are lacking for the early part. In 1960 almost two was the average occupancy.

600 Again, since air risks mainly occur at take-off and landing, a car is generally safer for trips of less than 300 km (Laudan 1994:58).

601. WI 1998a:xviii. Emphasis in original.

602. WI 1998a:4.

603. Ehrlich 1997:131. Surprisingly, Ehrlich also insists that the development in GDP and food production up till now tells us *nothing* about what happens to the Earth's resources. This seems unlikely and is at least at odds with Ehrlich's oft-made claim that many other indicators show negative trends (which consequently should also be unrelated to the measurement of the Earth's future resources).

604. WCED 1987:8.

605. Naturally, this is a moral judgment, but one that the vast majority (the present writer included) finds obviously true.

606. WI 1998a:19.

607. Quoted in Miller 1998:752.

608. Chiras 1998:40.

609. See detailed documentation in Crosson 1997b.

610. WI 1998a:91, cf. p.17. Actually WI (1997b:19) goes as far as claiming that the price of wheat went up to an all-time high in the spring of 1996, which is seriously misleading since it is only true if not corrected for inflation.

611. WI 1998a:16. Brown recognizes that "three years do not make a new long-term trend," but continues to set the figures as a confirmation of his worst fears. Somewhat dishonest, Brown announces this short-term effect, saying: "An early hint of the shift to an economy of scarcity came in late April 1996, when wheat prices on the Chicago Board of Trade soared above $7 a bushel, the highest level in history and more than double the price a year earlier." Apparently he forgets to correct for inflation, whereas in real terms the 1996 price hike was nowhere near the maximum, as his own figures also tell us. See http://www.worldwatch.org/pubs/ea/tc.html.

612. IFPRI 1997:16.

613. As shown in WI 1998:92, the graph is in 1995$ and has no source for inflation adjustment. Figure 48 reproduced here, however, looks almost identical.

614. WI 1994:188; 1997a:25, 44; 1999a:119, 2001a:46.

615. Brown uses data from USDA where my data are from FAO. Owing to slight differences in accounting and periodization, FAO's numbers reach a maximum in 1985, but the general picture is the same.

616. Miller 1998:601; Botkin and Keller 1998:93; Chiras 1998:164; Pimentel *et al.* 1995a:1,118.

617. Costanza *et al.* 2000.

618. WI 1997a:26.

619. The last four years have been below the top 1996 production of 230 kg, but this is normal for such statistics with large, natural variability. Notice how 2000 production was adversly affected by conditions in China, as discussed in the text.

620. WFS 1996:I, 4.12.

621. ERS 2000c:12, FAO 2000e:6, 2000f:1.3.

622. FAO 2001a.

623. FAO 1995b:7.

624. FAO 1995b:8.

625. Alexandratos 1999:5,911, FAO 2000d:49.

626. WI 1994:177.

627. WI 1998a:88.

628. WI 1998a:88–9.

629. FAO 2000d:50, WFS 1996:I, 2.15, and CGIAR 1996.

630. ERS 1999b:8–9; IFPRI 1999:21ff.

631. Alexandratos 1997.

632. Alexandratos 1997, 1998.

633. Alexandratos 1999:5,911.

634. ERS 2000c:12, FAO 2000e:6.

635. Rice constitutes 22 percent, wheat 19.5 percent and corn 6.1 percent (FAO 1995b:107).

636. From the period 1963–83 to the period 1983–93 growth rates in yield decreased for wheat from 3.6 percent per year to 2.1 percent and for corn from 2.9 percent to 2.5 percent (WFS 1996:Box 1 VI).

637. WI 1998a:82.

638. WI 1998a:81.

639. WI 1998a:82.

640. WI 1998a:88.

641. WI 1998a:90. While this last sentence is strictly logically true – necessarily any increase will level off, if we stay around for long enough – it is also uninteresting. The question is, of course, *when* the leveling off will take place – before or after the population increase and food demand increase has ended?

642. WI 1998a:93.

643. WI 1998a:91, 94.

644. WI 1998a:17.

645. WI 1998a:94 note 63. Unfortunately, this article has been impossible to retrieve, and after several requests it turns out that Worldwatch Institute cannot find it in their archives either.

646. Brown 1981:78.

647. Only countries like Australia, Korea, Spain, Greece and the US. Of these, only Korea and the US have a large output.

648. Personal correspondence 29 March 1998 from John H. Dyck, Japan rice expert from USDA. He also points out that South Korea deliberately refrained from achieving a large increase in yields with a new rice variety, since the population did not like it.

649. Personal correspondence 29 March 1998 from John H. Dyck, Japan rice expert from USDA.

650. Vitousek *et al.* 1986.

651. Terrestrial figure, otherwise the number is 3.2 percent (Vitousek *et al.* 1986:369).

652. Agger *et al.* 1997:114.

653. Ehrlich 1988.

654. Daly (1996:79, 231), Gonick and Outwater (1996:135–6) and Miller (1998:113) come preciously close to making the same mistake.

655. Sagoff 1995.

656. IFPRI 1997:10, 11, cf. FAO (2000d:11) expects only 20 percent of production increase to come from land expansion, whereas the remainder will come from increased production intensity.

657. An increase in production on agricultural lands due to the way the percentage is formed makes it seem as if man is exploiting more photosynthesis, but this makes the percentage dependent on the output and no longer an indicator of a natural limit to productivity (Sagoff 1995; Vitousek *et al.* 1986:372). Notice that this definition of the percentage also makes it seem possible that we could cultivate a much smaller area than today but do it very, very effectively, and consequently – at least theoretically – exploit more than 100 percent of the natural, potential production. Neither seems like a reasonable measure for limits to production.

658. If 41 percent increase requires 5.5 percent more land, a 100 percent increase will require about 13.4 percent. Thus the total appropriation will increase from 10 to 11.3 percent.

659. 9.8 Pg, 8.5 Pg, and 10.4 Pg of 149.6 Pg (Vitousek *et al.* 1986:370, 371, 372, 372). The loss from agricultural production will likewise increase 13 percent or 0.91 percentage points to 9.91 percent while pasture is an estimate for all of human history (and since its area has dropped just 1 percent over the last 300 years it is unlikely that it will grow significantly [Richards 1990:164]). The regular land clearing will probably continue at about the same level as now. Notice that the argument hinges on all pasture and arable land having been forests and consequently deforestation should not be counted as anything but increased pasture or agriculture.

660. Sagoff 1995, FAO 2000d:207.

661. WI 1998a:93. Notice how Lester Brown often expresses himself in conditional sentences, such that they are technically correct: "*Once*" and "*there will eventually come a point.*" Both statements are logically correct (*once* we've reached limit yields, there are clearly few further options left), but it is clearly not the conditional idea that Brown conveys. Instead, he makes it sound as if we indeed *have* reached the limit, and that the point *is* coming up.

662. Rejesus *et al.* 1999:38.

663. Rejesus *et al.* 1999:38.

664. Rejesus *et al.* 1999:31; Pingali and Heisey 1999:23–4.

665. Pingali and Heisey 1999:24; WI 1998a:91.

666. Pingali and Heisey 1999:22.

667. Pingali and Heisey 1999:22.

668. Pingali and Heisey 1999:26.

669. WFS 1996:VI, 5.1.

670. WFS 1996:VI, Box 2.

671. FAO 1995b:44.

672. FAO 1995b:44. Particularly, the growth will come from low- and middle-yield countries (WFS 1996:I, 5.12).

673. Gale Johnson 1999.

674. FAO 2000d:45.

675. FAO 1995b:5; WFS 1996:I, 4.6–7.

676. FAO 1995b:2, 5; WFS 1996:I, 4.6–7. This is now also the position of Worldwatch Institute (WI 2001a:44).

677. WI 1997a:25.

678. WFS 1996:XII, 2.12. Worldwatch Institute seem somewhat unsure of what they really find to be a necessary level of food security: in 1991 they claim 60 days, in 1998 they say 70 (WI 1991:15; 1998a:17).

679. WFS 1996:XII, 3.14. Editorial from CGIAR: http://www.worldbank.org/html/cgiar/newsletter/Mar96/4edit.htm.

680. Donald Winkelmann, CGIAR, in http://www.worldbank.org/html/cgiar/newsletter/Mar96/4edit.htm.

681. Quoted in WFS 1996:XII, 3.13.

682. WFS 1996:XII, 3.13. That the feedgrain buffer can mean so much is exactly because we have much more food and do not live on the edge of starvation

683. Actually, a simple calculation shows that since 1960 there has not been a single year where we have needed more than 70 percent of the grain stocks, even assuming away the feedgrain buffer and an uninterrupted growth in demand of 2.35 percent as the growth has been historically.

684. ERS 2000c:12.

685. WFS 1996:XII, 3.1.

686. WFS 1996:XII, 3.6, 3.22.

687. IMF 1997:155.

688. Cunningham and Saigo 1997:212. Poultry is somewhat cheaper in energy consumption (ERS 1996:6).

689. Brown 1995:24.

690. WI 1998a:13.

691. Brown 1995:24.

692. Brown (1995:36) gives only a graph, but states 1990 population plus 490 million, which would be 1.645 billion. UN/USBC estimates: UNPD 2001b:27, USBC 2000a.

693. A good overview is Crosson 1996.

694. Brown 1995:77–8.

695. ERS 1996:10; USDA 2000a:97.

696. FAO 2000a.

697. Johnson quoted in Crosson 1996b.

698. Lindert 2000b:17.

699. IFPRI 1997:19.

700. Fan and Agcaoili-Sombilla 1997:24.

701. Fan and Agcaoili-Sombilla 1997:7.

702. World Bank 1997:1; cf. http://www.worldbank.org/html/extdr/extme/ampr_005.htm.

703. World Bank 1997a:36, although the World Bank estimates that it will be cheaper to import 60 million tons, which "the major grain-exporting countries could readily supply."

704. Heilig 1999.

705. 1.58 percent from Fan and Agcaoili-Sombilla 1997:12 – agricultural land was 93,555,602 ha in 1990, 93,623,783 ha in 1999 (FAO 2000a). From 1994 the agricultural area increased 6.5 percent or 1.27 percent a year on average.

706. From 3.76 tons/ha in 1990, 4.35 in 1999 and 4.13 in 2000, USDA 2001a. Indeed, if we take the period 1991–9, increase is almost twice Brown's at 1.98 percent, or for 1991–8 it is 2.49 percent (FAO 2000a).

707. The actual size is treated as a state secret (ERS 2000a:8).

708. ERS 2000a:10. This is to a large extent due to a political decision of more self-reliance.

709. USDA 2000b:131–5, grain estimate (wheat, rice and coarse grains).

710. The 315 million tons comes from WI 1999c. However, this datasheet seems riddled with errors – it assumes that China starts off with 325 million tons in 1990 although the right figure was 343 (USDA 2000a, and even Brown states 341 [Brown 1995:95]), and it estimates the production in 1995 to be 328, although the right number was 356 (poorly estimated by Brown as 337 [1995:95]). Moreover, it estimates a production in 2030 of 230 million, although Brown states 272 (1995:95). Even if we allow for a more reasonable and data-driven development (see Fan and Agcaoili-Sombilla 1997:5), Brown would have estimated 344.6 million tons for 1999 (linear interpolation), making his error 14.6 percent.

711. Percival and Homer-Dixon 1998:280.

712. Brown and Wolf 1984:21–2.

713. Crosson 1996a, 1997d; Pimentel *et al.* 1995a.

714. Goudie 1993:161–2. Pimentel *et al.* (1995a:1,117) put it at 17, but the newest estimate from his own source (USDA) shows just 12 (Crosson 1995:462).

715. Boardman 1998.

716. Consult the involved critique of Pimentel by Crosson in Pimentel *et al.* 1995a, 1995b; Pimentel 1997; Crosson 1995, 1996a, 1997c, 1997d; Boardman 1998.

717. Scherr 1999:3.

718. Lindert 1999, 2000b.

719. Lindert 2000b:16. It should be noted that the author finds that other forms of erosion are probably more important in determining erosion effects on yields, but also here he finds that the net erosion has been "not negative" (p.18).

720. Rozanov *et al.* 1990:205.

721. Goudie 1993:374; Oldeman *et al.* 1991:4–5.

722. FAO 1995b:357.

723. Crosson 1997d.

724. Lindert 2000b:18.

725. Crosson 1996a, 1997d.

726. Oldeman *et al.* 1990, 1991; Buol 1994:218ff.

727. UNEP 1993:162.

728. Oldeman 1994:115–16. However, other more careful studies have indicated that at least in South and Southeast Asia the actual extent of erosion is less serious than indicated by the World Soil Degradation Map (van Lynden and Oldeman 1997:16).

729. Crosson 1996a, 1997d. Oldeman finds a similar impact of 4.8–8.9 percent (Scherr 1999:20).

730. Cunningham and Saigo 1997:240–2.

731. WFS 1996:VI, 14ff. There are many other explanations, but FAO underscores the importance of securing ownership (and clear rights/duties in the commons) and to secure access to fertilizer.

732. Rozanov *et al.* 1990:212.

733. Alexandratos 1995:356; Scherr 1999:9.

734. Crosson quoted in FAO 1995b:119.

735. IFPRI makes the slightly more cautious conclusion: "Degradation appears not to threaten aggregate global food supply by 2020, though world commodity prices and malnutrition may rise" (Scherr 1999:3).

736. WI 1997a:34.

737. WI 2000a:8.

738. Berry *et al.* 1993:126.

739. FAO 1996b:101. The equivalent numbers for the developing world are 0.8 percent calories from fish (23 of 2,650) and 5.5 percent of protein (3.7 g of 67 g) or 23 percent of animal protein (19.2 g) (FAO 2000a).

740. WI 2000a:5; 1998a:4, 18, 59.

741. WI 1997a:32.

742. FAO 1997a:22. FAO (2001b:part 3) find that 28 percent of the total stocks are either overfished, depleted or slowly recovering.

743. Hardin 1968.

744. E.g. Pearce and Turner 1990:241ff; Tietenberg 2000:307–9.

745. FAO 2000d:178.

746. FAO 1997b:25–6. And FAO warns that if we do not become better at coordinating our fisheries, catches could drop another 10 million tons, p. 27.

747. FAO 2000a. Global annual caloric production is currently 5.9e15 (1997), increasing over the past 10 years by 1.95 percent yearly. Fish contribute 59e12 (or 1 percent), and an additional 10 percent (10 million tons) would be 5.9e12, or 19/365 of 1998 growth (115e12=1.95%*5.9e15). For protein, fish is equivalent to 107 days, for animal production, calories is 100 days and protein 252 days.

748. From 6.7 million tons in 1984 to 32.9 million tons in 1999 (WI 1998b; FAO 2001b).

749. The dip in marine catches of more than 9 percent in 1998 was due mainly to El Niño, especially affecting the landings from the Southeast Pacific, FAO 2001b:part 1.

750. FAO (2000d:189) expects an increase in average human consumption (a more restrictive measure than total production used in Figure 57) will increase from 15.8 kg to 19–20 kg.

751. FAO 2001b:part 4.

752. FAO 1997b:27ff.

753. Quoted in Crosson 1997b. Notice how Lester Brown manages to make *both* situations equally appalling, both "plagued by chronic excess" and "constant scarcity."

754. Brown 1996b.

755. Brown 1981:86.

756. Crosson 1997b.

757. FAO 2000d:49.

758. WFS 1996:Table 3, 1; WI 1998a:98; FAO 2000d:23.

759. IFPRI 1997, 1999; ERS 1997:4; USDA 2000b; Mitchell *et al.* 1997. Strangely, Brown quotes FAO to the effect that they expect food prices to fall (when they clearly state they will not forecast prices WI

[1998a:94; FAO 1995b:119; Alexandratos 1997]) instead of focusing on IFPRI, USDA and the World Bank, all making this prediction.

760. *Time* 1997:7.

761. WRI 2000a.

762. WWF 1998b.

763. WWF 1997c and 1997a:6.

764. WWF 1997c.

765. WI 1998d.

766. After I expressed my criticism, the Danish branch of WWF convinced the international organization to change its web page as well.

767. The two long time-series of forest area depicted are *Forests and Woodland*, which was discontinued from 1995 onwards, whereas the new estimates are for closed forest, i.e. with tree canopy cover of more than 20 percent of forest cover in the industrialized world and 10 percent in the developing world (FAO 1997c:173–4). The new 1990–2000 estimate is based on a common definition of 10 percent forest (more than 0.5 ha, with a tree canopy cover of more than 10 percent, which are not primarily under agricultural or urban land use, FAO 2001c:23). Notice that FAO 1999a does not contribute new data (p.1, note 1). According to figures in the FAO database, overall forest cover in 1961 was 4.375086e9 ha or 32.66 percent of the world's land area. In 1991 the figure was 4.316746e9 ha or 32.22 percent of total land area. In 1994 (the last available year) forest cover constituted 4.172401e9 or only 31.15 percent, although the entire fall of one percentage point relates to the fact that the report in connection with the change from USSR to SNG falls from (a stable) 9.41530e8 ha in 1991 to (a stable) 8.11689e8 ha in 1992. This must be a data error, since it is also reported that forest cover in Russia has increased sharply because of the economic downturn (e.g. WRI 1996a:206–7). This has therefore been corrected here.

768. It seems obvious that the 1948 estimate was off and would cause a too optimistic conclusion.

769. The global area of 1990 was estimated at 3.442 Mha in FAO 1995a, but at 3.510 Mha in FAO 1997c:189, estimating 1995 at 3.454 Mha (FAO 1997c:189).

770. The discussion of what constitutes the "correct" definition of forest is a long one. The FAO has three definitions (see e.g. WRI 1996a:222–3; FAO 1999b): "Forest," "forest and woodland" and "forest and other wooded land." "Forest" comprises only enclosed forest with 10–20 percent tree crown cover (20 percent in developed nations, 10 percent in developing nations). This applies to about 26 percent of the world. "Forest and woodland" counts everything with regular tree trunks and accounts for about 32 percent of the world. "Forest and wooded land" also covers forest fallows and shrubs, accounting for about 40 percent of the world.

The discussion is related to the way forest is measured. Measurement of global forest areas is notoriously inaccurate, as has been pointed out by many (Williams 1990; WRI 2000b: "The Food and Agriculture Organization of the United Nations [FAO] and the United Nations Economic Commission for Europe [ECE] recently published reports on the conditions of tropical and temperate forests with data on change in forest cover from 1980 to 1990. Such data are notoriously inaccurate and often recycled between reports simply because better data is not available.") The reason for this inaccuracy is primarily that the data are generated by models (often based on population figures) and based on scant, out of date and inadequate raw data.

This inaccuracy is pretty obvious when one examines FAO's data. "Forest and woodland" has been used for almost 50 years, but even so, global reckoning for the same year has fluctuated by as much as 2 percent! (E.g. 1976, where "forest and woodland" was estimated in the 1987 FAO Production Yearbook at 4,150 Mha, and in 1992 at 4,231 Mha). If one looks at the figures for 1990, FAO believed in 1995 that forest accounted for 3.442368e9 ha (FAO 1995a), and in 1997 they believed that the figure was 3.510728e9 ha (FAO 1997c:189). A change of 1.9 percent or a little more than the overall reduction found for 1990–5 with FAO 1997 figures of 1.6 percent. Had they used the old 1990 figures, the world's overall forest area would have increased by about 0.3 percent for 1990 to 1995! On top of this, they failed to include Russia (FAO 1997c:17, table 4, note a), which has 20 percent of the world's forest, and where there has actually been growth (se e.g. WRI 1996a:206–7).

Using short time-span series actually risks losing the general tendency in noise created by the individual adjustments. It has therefore been important to employ the longest time-span series available, and FAO's long series from 1950 is the only one available. Unfortunately, the FAO database only provides access to figures from 1961 onward. Overall, it seems reasonable to consider all land with regular tree trunks as forest, and considering the above-mentioned problems with the accuracy of data, I find that the best description of the earth's forest development can be achieved using FAO's "forest and woodland" figures. Even if one uses FAO's narrow "forest" definition, which has only been calculated three times beginning in 1980 and has the above-mentioned data problems, one reaches the conclusion that closed forest area fell from 1980 to 1995 from 27.15 percent to 25.8 percent of the earth's land surface area, i.e. 1.35 percentage points.

771. FAO 2001c:35.

772. FAO 1997c:12.

773. 1,451 Mha cropland compared to 3,442 Mha enclosed forest or 5,120 Mha forest and other wooded land (WRI 1996a:216–18).

774. Plato 1961:111b–c;1,216.

775. WRI 1996a:201 estimates more than 50 percent and 60 percent; Chiras 1998:212 gives 70 percent. Because most of Europe's forest cover was cleared so early on, considerable doubt exists about the figures. Furthermore, different figures have been derived from different definitions of forest, as discussed above.

776. UNECE 1996:19.

777. Williams 1990:180, 181; UNECE 1996:1.

778. UNECE 1996:19.

779. Richards 1990:164.

780. UNECE 1996:59.

781. CEQ 1997:32.

782. Williams 1990:table 11–1.

783. Richards 1990:164.

784. Williams 1990:183.

785. Williams 1990:188–9.

786. Richards 1990:164.

787. Richards 1990:164.

788. Goudie estimates 20 percent (1993:43); Richards estimates the overall loss over the last 300 years to be 19 percent (1990:164). Williams (1994:104) estimates 7.5 percent. IPCC also estimate a global forest area reduction of 20 percent from 1850 to 1990 (2001a:3.2.2.2).

789. WWF 1997e. In later publications, WWF has, however, lowered its estimates to about 50 percent, WWF 1997d

790. Chiras 1998:211.

791. FAO (1997c:36) estimate 2 percent of global GDP, which was about $32.000 billion (IMF 2000b:113).

792. Chiras 1998:211.

793. Cunningham and Saigo 1997:297.

794. Botkin and Keller 1998:179.

795. Botkin and Keller 1998:175–6.

796. Barney 1980:II, 134 and 331. The 2.3 percent is referred to as mildly optimistic (equivalent to 40 percent in 22 years), whereas the 4.8 percent is equivalent to 66 percent in 22 years.

797. Myers cited in Goudie 1993:46. 33 percent in Myers 1991:52–3, where he predicts a 17 percent reduction in forest cover, which has already been halved, that is to say the third of the current cover.

798. Myers 1991:47.

799. E.g. Raven and Prance 1991:71.

800. FAO 1997c:12, table 1, and 18, table 5. Note that the reduction in forest clearance is actually greater, because the 0.7 percent is based on an area slightly smaller. Also, Miller recounts a satellite-based estimate which shows deforestation of about 20 percent of FAO's figure (1998:342).

801. The loss of tropical forests is 9.2 Mha in the 1980s and 8.6 Mha in the 1990s (FAO 2001c:9). The total tropical forest area is 1810 Mha in 2000 (FAO 2001c:19), and using these deforestation figures to backcast total forest area, taking averages, gives 0.4689 percent for the 1980s and 0.4592 percent for the 1990s.

802. Sedjo and Clawson 1995:342.

803. WRI 1996a:208–9.

804. Botkin and Keller 1998:264; Cunningham and Saigo 1997:295–6.

805. Williams 1990:194–5; Goudie 1993:58. By way of comparison, a lumberjack in the US in the year 1800 would have to have spent between 13 and 20 percent of his working life chopping firewood (Williams 1990:182).

806. Miller 1998:356; Cunningham and Saigo 1997:296–7.

807. Miller 1998:351; Williams 1990:194; WWF/IUCN 1996:14.

808. Chiras 1998:213.

809. Miller 1998:353.

810. Chiras 1998:200.

811. Miller 1998:352. If one wants to exploit the forests in order to expand the area available for agriculture it is vital to secure a far greater knowledge of deforestation, so that local populations do not, for example, remove forest from steep slopes, which are bound to be hit by erosion (e.g. Williamson *et al.* 1997). At the same time it is crucial to allow farmers access to fertilizer, etc. (Miller 1998:351).

812. Reid 1992:60. Several sources state that we should have lost more than 50 percent of the rainforest (Miller 1998:342; WWF: *A Future for Forests?* http://www.panda.org/forest4life/news/f4f.html). Unfortunately, there are no references.

813. Nigeria has lost 85–90 percent, Madagascar 60–85 percent (WCMC 1998). Reference to Central America from Williams 1990:191–2.

814. Notice, that Brazil's Atlantic rainforest has been reduced by some 88 percent, almost all of which was cleared before the end of the nineteenth century (Brown and Brown 1992:122).

815. Cunningham and Saigo 1997:297–8. See a general criticism of the many erroneous guesstimates in Glantz *et al.* 1997.

816. As several researchers have pointed out, the figure of 13 percent could mean that much more forest has been disturbed, as the forest next door to a cleared area is also affected – a so-called edge effect – (Botkin and Keller 1998:283). The original article by Skole and Tucker (1993) showed that 6 percent clearance of the Amazon led to an edge-effect of 15 percent. The problem is that the edge-effect is simply assumed to be one kilometer (also because of satellite resolution); had the edge-effect only been 100 m, the area concerned would not have been much larger than the 6 percent.

817. More than 100.000 km^2 has returned to forest since 1960 (Faminow 1997). See also Fearnside 1991:93.

818. 70 percent (Brown and Brown 1992:122). 25 million ha (WWF.http://www.panda.org/forests4life/news/allirel.htm).

819. Quote from WWF chief executive officer Mohamed El-Ashry, cited in Anon. 2000b. Note equivalent quotes: from an academic text dealing with how to teach our children about the environmental problems: "We need to protect the forests, the precious 'lungs' of the Earth, that are being destroyed at a growing pace to obtain wood, agricultural land, mineral resources" (Camino and Calcagno 1995). Greaves and Stanisstreet (1993) state that 42 percent of all children incorrectly believe and voluntarily expressed this story.

820. Broecker 1970.

821. Broecker 1970:1,538; Ehrlich and Ehrlich 1987:138.

822. WI 1998d.

823. Bailey 1995:180. The world uses 1,55e9 m^3 of wood for timber and paper (WRI 1996a:220); forest such as that in Denmark has a net growth rate of approx. 7.5 m^3/ha (EEA 1995:474). At this rate of growth, total world demand would call for 2E8 ha, or about 4.95 percent of the Earth's forest cover of 4,168E9 ha.

824. WI 1998a:23; WWF 1998a:6.

825. Myers 1991:54.

826. FAO 1997c:13, table 2.

827. WWF 1998a:6.

828. "Only about 3 percent of the world's forests are forest plantations" (FAO 1999a:1). Compare, however, to a FAO estimate in 1997: Plantations in the industrialized world total some 80–100 Mha, in the developing world 81.2 Mha out of a total forest area of 3,454 Mha, i.e. 5.2 percent (FAO 1997c:10, 14).

829. Estimate of fire, health and tourism costs of US$ 3.8 billion, EEPSEA/WWF 1998; of an annual GDP of US$ 198 billion, WRI 1998a:237.

830. WWF 1997b, title and p.1.

831. WWF 1997b, 1997d, 1998c.

832. WWF 1997b:7.

833. WWF 1997b:7; Woodard 1998; UNEP 1999a:8.

834. UNEP (1999a:40) reports 4.56 Mha burnt, of which 28.58 percent is forests and timber areas.

835. Goldammer is a scientist at the Max Planck Chemistry Institute and a participant in the Biomass Burning project with the National Center for Atmospheric Research, the US Forest Service NASA. http://asd-www.larc.nasa.gov/biomass_burn/biomass_burn.html. Personal communication and Woodard 1998.

836. WWF 1997b:17. They also tell us several times that "thousands of fires are burning across 10,000 miles of the Amazon rainforest," although 10,000 miles stretches around more than one-third of the globe (WWF 1997b:4, 17).

837. WWF 1997b:18.

838. WWF 1997b:18; LaFranchi 1997; IPAM 1998.

839. UNEP 1999a:40; Golddammer 1991:84; Levine *et al.* 1995. In May alone more than 4.7 Mha burned (Cahoon *et al.* 1991:66).

840. UNEP 1999a:4.

841. Conard and Ivanova 1997:308.

842. Indonesia has 109 Mha of forest (FAO 1997c:183). This is in accordance with the UNEP estimate (1999a:41) of 4.58 percent protected areas of forests, or about 208,000 ha.

843. Andreae 1991:5, 7; WWF 1997b:18.

844. Andreae 1991:4.

845. Levine 1991:xxviii.

846. The WWF itself is involved in a certification process of this kind (Sedjo and Clawson 1995:343). Obviously, since so small a share of the world's forests are actually used in wood and paper production, this practice is not enough in itself.

847. Motavalli 2000.

848. See e.g. CNN from 1996, Mattingly 1996.

849. Craig *et al.* 1996:103.

850. Craig *et al.* 1996:111–14.

851. Craig *et al.* 1996:125–8.

852. The year 2000 is estimated from its first ten months. There is a discontinuity in the wood figures between 1945 and 1949 (1949 being 22 percent higher than 1945) due to changes in definitions. Data through 1945 are for fuelwood only, while thereafter include wood-derived fuel and wood byproducts burned as fuel, such as cord wood, limb wood, spent pulping liquor, pulp waste, wood sludge, hogged fuel, peat, railroad ties, sawdust, wood chips, bark, forest residues, and charcoal, EIA 2000d:349.

853. Barry *et al.* 1993:131.

854. Craig *et al.* 1996:103.

855. Unless we also include a certain probability that the civilization dies out.

856. "One barrel" should be taken as a metaphor for a tiny fraction of the present day oil consumption. Since oil is created on a million-year time scale, we can actually use a small amount each year (the oil that was created during this period), and still leave the coming generations with their own supply. A back-of-an-envelope calculation would seem to indicate that this amount is less than 50,000 barrels per year or what is equivalent to one minute of today's oil consumption.

857. Solow 1986:142.

858. Greider 2000, although, as with all popular phrases, more people seem to claim ownership, Anon. 1999g, 2001a.

859. Likewise, when *The Economist* asked in early 2001: "Will The Oil Run Out?" their answer was: "Eventually, yes; but by then it might no longer matter" (Anon. 2001a).

860. Even Ehrlich agrees on this: Ehrlich and Ehrlich 1991:46–7.

861. Meadows *et al.* 1972:58.

862. Ehrlich and Ehrlich 1987:222.

863. Meadows *et al.* 1992:74 *et passim*.

864. Meadows *et al.* 1992:74.

865. Craig *et al.* 1996:123.

866. Craig *et al.* 1996:135. In 1996 the total oil production was 64 million barrels a day (EIA 1997b:table 11.5), each valued at about $20 (BP 1998). All in all $467 billion, or 1.58 percent of the global GDP of $29,609 billion (IMF 1997:147).

867. EIA 1997b:table 11.3.

868. One of the background reasons for the Gulf War (CRS 1995b).

869. Barry *et al.* 1993:135–6.

870. Simon 1996:165.

871. Simon *et al.* 1994:325.

872. Simon 1996:24ff.

873. Greene 1997. Although it is often claimed that OPEC is a monopoly, oligopoly or a cartel, there is actually obvious evidence against this – 1) OPEC lacks the clout since non-OPEC production constitutes the majority of the world output, 2) only since 1983 has OPEC attempted to set production quotas and it has never agreed on price, and 3) OPEC has no mechanism for punishing members for defecting from any OPEC agreement. Instead, empirical evidence seems to point to Saudi Arabia as the dominant producer, with its production *negatively* correlated to the rest of OPEC, allowing the price to increase beyond the competitive price (Alhajji and Huettner 2000).

874. IEA 2000b:25.

875. EIA 2000e:58.

876. EIA 2000e:102.

877. EIA 2000b:26.

878. Price of unleaded spliced with price of leaded from 1950s to 1970s; tax information for the 1950s from http://www.eia.doe.gov/oiaf/issues98/gastax.html.

879. Adelman 1995:287; cf. EIA 1997b:table 3.3, when measured in real prices, table D1.

880. This argument is used in, e.g., Ehrlich and Ehrlich 1974:48.

881. Be aware that part of the increase in the reserve estimates for the OPEC countries in the late 1980s could be caused by the fact that these figures are also used in negotiations for OPEC quotas. This is suggested by CRS (1995b) and Ivanhoe (1995:82). Nevertheless, it is generally estimated that reserves did go up, also in the 1980s (USGS 1997a).

882. Quoted in Simon 1996:165.

883. Simon 1996:164–5.

884. E.g. Nordhaus 1992b:16.

885. It should be added that more advanced models like the Hubbert curve try to predict future discoveries, but although these models have been successful with countries like the US, using up its resources early, it is not at all clear whether these models will work with the much bigger and more important oilfields. It is still possible that the low rates of new discoveries primarily are reflections of low prices and very high oil reserves. See Campbell 1997 and Ivanhoe 1995.

886. USGS 2000b.

887. Craig *et al.* 1996:134. In Denmark it was esti-

mated that less than 20 percent of the oil is exploited, *JyllandsPosten*, 15 May 1998:E5.

888. USGS 2000b.

889. From 13.4 mpg to 21.4 (EIA 2000c:17).

890. Europe uses 24 percent less energy per square meter in 1992 than in 1973; the US uses 43 percent less (Schipper *et al.* 1996:184).

891. Schipper *et al.* 1996:187. In Denmark electric home appliances have become 20–45 percent more effective over the last ten years (NERI 1998a:238).

892. "Unnecessarily" meaning that the waste could have been avoided. A further 41 percent is wasted in transforming fossil fuels to electricity, and this waste is not (easily) avoidable (Miller 1998:398).

893. Cunningham and Saigo 1997:494–5.

894. Miller 1998:404. See also *Time* 1997:48–9.

895. See the discussion in Wirl 2000, but this is a protracted debate, which we will discuss in chapter 24.

896. There are data for Japan and the EU back to 1960 (which is where the World Bank 1999b data start) and it shows a slight U-curve. However, this is misleading, since this does not take into account the use of non-traded energy and that the energy efficiency of Japan improves dramatically before 1960 (Grubler *et al.* 1996:245; cf. CIA 1997, http://www.odci.gov/cia/publications/hies97/f/fig18.jpg). For similar reasons, the UK energy efficiency is not extended back before 1880, since non-traded energy is not estimated (unlike for the US) but becomes ever more important when going back in time.

897. That Japan and the EU can produce more with the same amount of energy is strongly related to higher average energy prices than in the US (Moisan *et al.* 1996:54–5).

898. World Bank 1994:171; see also EU 2000a:36.

899. Turner *et al.* 1994:45–6. This also holds true for the time span 1970 to 1994 per capita (Statistics Denmark 1997a:128). Jespersen and Brendstrup note, however, that part of this effect is due to better insulation, which is pretty much a one-time gain; consequently they estimate the true energy efficiency to have increased by 22 percent rather than 33 percent (1994:66).

900. Hausman 1995.

901. WRI 1996b.

902. 40 percent less CO_2 than coal (NERI 1998A:169).

903. Other reserve years from a graph of reserves for 1973–98 (BP 1999; http://www.bpamoco.com/worldenergy/naturalgas/page_01.htm#).

904. Measured at the current rate of consumption for each quoted year. Gas reserves have increased to 252 percent (BP 1999).

905. WRI 1996a:276; Botkin and Keller 1998:336.

906. Hargreaves *et al.* 1994:373.

907. EIA 1997c:67.

908. Jespersen and Brendstrup 1994:58–9; NERI 1998A:169.

909. Cohen 1995:579. In the US more than 50 miners die each year in coal extraction related accidents (Craig *et al.* 1996:119). The total death toll seems to be very uncertain, as we will see in the chapters on pollution: Cunningham and Saigo (1997:468–9) estimate excess deaths in the US to be close to 5,000; Miller (1998:441) suggests 65,000–200,000 extra annual deaths. In comparison, the World Bank estimates an annual 300,000–700,000 extra deaths in the developing world, where pollution is much higher (with 1.3 billion people, this estimate is much lower than Miller) (World Bank 1992:52).

910. WEC 2000:chapter 1.

911. Craig *et al.* (1996:159) estimate global resources at 7.8e12 tons. EIA (1995a:8) estimate that the US resources alone are approximately 4e12 tons.

912. Methane gas reserves are estimated by the US Geological Survey to be somewhere between 85 and 262e12 m^3, compared to natural gas at 119e12 m^3 (Craig *et al.* 1996:150; USGS 1997d).

913. Additional resource data from *International Energy Annuals*, personal communication, Harriet McLaine, EIA. Price of Bituminous Coal FOB Mines.

914. Notice, though, that this is also due to production facilities having been written off (EIA 1997c:37).

915. EIA 1997c:37. See also USGS 1997b.

916. Craig *et al.* 1996:159. Notice that this is from a resource and not a reserve view – coal resources are here estimated at around 7.8e9 tons, or more than 1,700 years at present consumption.

917. The total energy in shale oil is estimated at 2.11e24J, while we consumed 4e20J in 1999 (see Figure 63).

918. World's yearly non-renewable energy consumption of 3.25e20J in 1993, or about 3.09e17 BTU, at a 1996 average price of $1.85 per million BTU (EIA 1997b:table 3.1), or approximately $570 billion, or 1.9 percent of the global GDP at $29.609 billion (IMF 1997:147). With an annual growth of 2.7 percent

from 1998 to 2030 (IFPRI's assumption to the year 2020, 1997:10), global GDP will have grown to about 2.35 times the present size. If the price of energy is doubled in real terms, this will imply an energy share in 2030 of 1.6 percent. Historically, this share has been declining too (Simon 1996:31).

919. EIA 1997c:75.

920. 30 percent of all new nuclear reactors are placed in Asia (EIA 1997d:13). Stagnation (EIA 1997d:5). From 1975 to 1986 the attitude in the US changed from 65 percent in favor to just 20 percent, whereas opposition exploded from 19 percent to 78 percent (Cunningham and Saigo 1997:482; Craig *et al.* 1996:172–3).

921. Craig *et al.* 1996:164.

922. Because coal has trace amounts of radioactive materials, released during combustion (Chiras 1998:266; Cunningham and Saigo 1997:467; USGS 1997c).

923. This is very dependent on the price of uranium (WEC 2000:chapter 6). Nuclear power produced 2.266e12 kWh (EIA 2000a:93) or 8.16e18J. It is assumed that with conventional U-235 about 8e20J is producible, i.e. 100 years (Craig *et al.* 1996:181).

924. See e.g. Craig *et al.* 1996:170.

925. All in all about 1140e20J (Craig *et al.* 1996:181).

926. Cunningham and Saigo 1997:477–9.

927. Miller 1998:452.

928. The median price in the year 2000 is 7.7¢ in 1987 prices (=10.99¢) cited by a pro-nuclear writer (Cohen 1995:table 29.2), while it is 13.5¢ cited by an opponent (Miller 1998:452).

929. Average price is 6.63¢ in 1999 in 1999$ (EIA 2000c:128). In the commercial price is included the price of distribution, which should be subtracted before comparing with the nuclear power price – typically around 0.4¢ (EIA 1996:108).

930. Using the two isotopes of hydrogen – deuterium and tritium. Deuterium can be extracted economically from ocean water, and tritium from reactions with lithium in the fusion process (Botkin and Keller 1998:371).

931. Cunningham and Saigo 1997:484.

932. Miller 1998:454.

933. CRS 1998.

934. Anon. 1998d.

935. EIA 1993:1.

936. WRI 1996a:286; Botkin and Keller 1998:264.

937. Biomass is the extraction of energy from wood, wood waste, wood liquors, peat, railroad ties, wood sludge, spent sulfite liquors, agricultural waste, straw, tires, fish oils, tall oil, sludge waste, waste alcohol, municipal solid waste, landfill gases, other waste, and ethanol blended into motor gasoline (EIA 1999a:249, see also EIA 1998c).

938. This can also be estimated independently. The global sold wind power is estimated at 10,153 MW (http://www.windpower.dk/stat/tab19.htm, accessed 23 April 2000) yielding an annual, maximal production of 8.9e10 kWh. In California with 20 percent of all wind power, it is estimated that the actual power production is about 21 percent of the maximal figure (26 percent for windmills after 1985, CEC 1995:12) because the wind does not always blow. With 26 percent efficiency, the global production is maximally 2.3e10 kWh, or about 83.3 PJ. The global energy production in 1998 was about 400 EJ, and with wind counting in fossil-fuels-avoided of a factor 3, this makes about 0.062 percent. The total, shipped solar cell capacity is 960.7 MW (WI 1999a:55), which is a maximum estimate of installed capacity. If these solar cells operate at 100 percent efficiency 12 hours a day, this is equivalent to 15.2 PJ annually, or 0.011 percent of the total energy production.

939. The global electricity production is 48 EJ (or about 144 EJ in fossil-fuel-avoided, EIA 2000a:93), where wind makes up 0.045 EJ and solar 0.01 EJ.

940. From 1997 in actual energy and not on fossil-fuel-avoided basis, EU 2000a:21, 64.

941. Data broken down into net electricity generation from biomass, geothermal, solar and wind electric power in 1998 provided by Michael Grillot, EIA, personal correspondence, from Energy Information Administration, International Energy Database, December 1999. Data for nuclear, hydro, biomass, geothermal, solar and wind electric power is measured by fossil-fuel-avoided energy. Since 1 kWh produced would take about three times that energy in, say, oil to produce, these are about three times higher than their direct energy production (65.6 percent in USA, EIA 1997b:diagram 5). Outside the US, only energy from biomass, geothermal, solar and wind used for electricity generation is counted. Data for traditional fuels are from 1995, projected on past increases to 1998. The total generated electricity from geothermal, solar and wind is 56.8 TWh, which compares well with the IEA estimate of 57.6 TWh (IEA 1999:II, 18. Notice, when WRI finds geothermal energy ten times bigger (2000:292), it is because they assume not only the 10 percent electri-

cal energy is exploited but also the other 90 percent heat, p347).

942. WI 1999b:16–17, cf. p. 48, 54; 1997b:54; 2000a:17.

943. 22 percent of 0.045 EJ versus 2 percent of 159.7 EJ.

944. .045EJ*1.22^45.7=159.7EJ*1.02^45.7.

945. EIA 1997c:85.

946. In the US, subsidy for wind power is about 1.5 ¢/kWh (CRS 1998), and in Denmark the Center for Biomass Technology under the Department of Agriculture states quite honestly: "When the Centre for Biomass Technology hosts foreign visit groups a major question is always: how can you have so many plants and techniques in your small country? The answer is: it pays off! And the reason that it pays off is the subsidies for investment and subsidies for electricity production, which improve the situation for biomass, and the taxes on fossil fuels, which make these more expensive" (CBT 2000).

947. WEC 2000:chapter 7.

948. EIA 1997c:88.

949. Hille 1995:193.

950. Craig *et al.* 1996:191.

951. DOE 1997:3–1ff.

952. Primary figures and estimates are summarized in DOE 1997:7–3. For wind energy (at 5.8 m/s wind) also: EIA 1997c:85; 1993:11; 1996:55. For solar thermal generation EIA 1993:11; Ahmed 1994:39. For photovoltaic systems, Ahmed 1994:77. A number of other sources give somewhat non-comparable prices, among these DOE 1995:9; WI 1991:27; 1995:70; EU 1994b; DOE 1996:11; Andersen 1998; Greenpeace (http://www.greenpeace.org/~comms/no.nukes/nenstcc.html); Cunningham and Saigo 1997:496.

953. DOE 1997:7–3.

954. EIA (2000e:75) estimates that wind power will cost 6 ¢/kWh in 2005 and 4.5 ¢/kWh in 2020, still more expensive than power from coal (4.3 and 4.2 ¢/kWh) and gas-fired combined cycle (4.2 and 3.8 ¢/kW). Notice, that due to very different ways of calculating total cost, including different capital recovery time spans, it is difficult to compare prices across studies.

955. EIA 1996:108.

956. EIA 1997a:53.

957. McVeigh 2000:237–8.

958. Hohmeyer 1993. Of course, we should also include any social costs from wind mills in the calculation, but these will probably be small.

959. Krupnick and Burtraw 1996. The three studies are: US Department of Energy (Oak Ridge National Laboratories/Resources for the Future, Lee *et al.* 1995), EU (DG XII 1995) and Empire State Electric and NY State Energy Research and Development Authority (1995).

960. Krupnick and Burtraw 1996:24. It is here relevant to disregard the EU estimate for SO_2, since we want a cost estimate on the *present* social price (i.e. what it costs with the present technology to replace a part of the present electricity consumption). EU's own estimate is 1.56 ¢/kWh.

961. Krupnick and Burtraw 1996:38. Taking into account not only the detrimental effects of CO_2 but also the benevolent consequences on employment and tax revenues, coal turns out to be *better* than gas, for example, and has a *positive* social value.

962. Cunningham and Saigo 1997:496; cf. McVeigh *et al.* 2000.

963. This is the result of a direct subsidy of 10 and 17 ører (8 ører to the cent), and an indirect subsidy through tax exemption of somewhere between 12.2 and 22 ører per kWh (Ministries of Finance *et al.* 1995:35, 51).

964. CRS 1998.

965. This also means that it is problematic when people like Lovins (in Miller 1998:426–7) argue that we should conserve energy, since much energy is used for "bad energy." Lovins finds that we should not use electricity to heat and cool buildings, because this is very expensive – we should rather insulate more, use superwindows, plant trees, etc. But the point is that if the consumer – after including social cost – still would prefer to use electricity instead of extra-thick windows, then it is dangerous to argue that the social planner would know better than the consumer what would give the highest mix of utilities. See discussion in Wirl 2000.

966. Craig *et al.* 1996:183.

967. 180 W/m^2 on the Earth's 5.1e8 km^2 gives an annual energy of 2,895e24 J or 6,951 times the energy consumption in 1997.

968. With an average influx of 300 W/m^2 and an efficiency at 20 percent, 21,9961 km^2 would exactly produce an annual 416 EJ. 21,9961 km^2 is 0.147 percent of the Earth's land area of 1.495e8 km^2.

969. The Sahara Desert takes up about 8.6e6 km^2, "Sahara," *Encyclopædia Britannica Online*, http://www.britannica.com/bcom/eb/article/5/0,5716,66425+1+64749,00.html?query=sahara.

970. EIA 1993:13; Ahmed 1994:80.

971. Cunningham and Saigo 1997:487–8.

972. For alternative estimates, see IPCC 2000a:134, 136. Here 'recoverable with technological progress' is estimated for oil to be 9ZJ, gas 20ZJ, coal 80ZJ, and nuclear >11ZJ. For renewables, annual 'long-term technical potentials' are estimated at >130EJ for hydro, >130EJ for wind, >2,600EJ for solar, and >1,300 for biomass.

973. *Danmarks Energifremtider* 1995:137.

974. Smil 1999.

975. Ahmed 1994:10–11.

976. 20 percent efficiency at 100 W/m² on 27,746 ha gives an annual energy production of 175 PJ.

977. Radetzki 1997:552–3.

978. DOE 1997:7–3 estimates 8.7 ¢/kWh for biomass and 49.1 ¢/kWh for solar cells.

979. Miller 1998:420.

980. EIA 1993:3.

981. IEA/OECD 1996.

982. IEA/OECD 1998.

983. The following is based on Andersen 1998.

984. http: // www.windpower.dk / present / produke. pdf.

985. Hille 1995:195–6.

986. http://www.windpower.dk/stat/tab14.htm, accessed 26 April 2000; cf. Windpower Note 1998a:7

987. EIA 2000a:211.

988. 51 percent more efficient (Windpower Note 1997:11). Price is estimated at 49 øre (about 7 cents)/kWh (http://www.caddet-re.org/html/article2 .htm).

989. E.g. Bradley 1997.

990. Windpower Note 1997:8 estimates that a windmill earns the energy used to produce it 80 times through its 20 years of service, meaning that its own energy is paid back after 91 average days.

991. Andersen 1998 (calculating with 4,000 turbines, where the correct number for 1997 is 4,700 [Windpower Note 1998a:7]).

992. The average Danish turbine has a nameplate capacity of 276 kWh (Windpower Note 1998a). Assuming approximately similar setup for the US, with total nameplate capacity of 2,500 MWh (AWEA 2000b), and using 30,000 birds per 4,000 turbines (Andersen 1998), gives 67,000 birds annually. Notice, that when AWEA (2000a:2) claim only 500 birds lost in California, this is incorrect – the 500 refers *only* to raptors, not all birds (Kenetech 1994:3).

993. NERI 1995.

994. Andersen 1998; NWCC 1994:appendix 2.

995. Kenetech 1994:3; AWEA 2000a.

996. The total number of domestic cats are estimated at 9 million (the survey did not measure the kills of the approximately 800,000 stay cats), making each cat catch some 30 animals per year, Mammal Society 2001a&b, Wark 2001.

997. See e.g. DOE 1997:appendix 1.

998. Miller 1998:423ff.

999. EIA 1999d:23.

1000. Meadows *et al.* 1972:56ff.

1001. The calculated years of consumption are primarily based on present production divided by reserve base.

1002. Simon 1996:35–6.

1003. WRI 1996a:170

1004. Leon and Soto 1995:16 (index from 1900–92) finds that 15 out of 24 products have declined in price, six have remained stable and only three have become more expensive.

1005. This is calculated with prices and quantities for 93 raw materials from US Geological Survey the first 24 listed in Table 2. It is equivalent to the 1.2 percent, mentioned in Goeller and Zucker 1984:457. Since parts of the raw materials listed overlap, this is undoubtedly a maximal estimate.

1006. Anon. 2000c. The industrials price index consists of Metals and Nfas (non-food agricultural commodities), each weighted with the following percentages, now based on the value of world imports in 1994–96. Metals: Aluminum 47.0 Copper 32.4 Nickel 8.2 Zinc 6.7 Tin 2.9 Lead 2.8. Nfas: Cotton 30.7 Timber 19.4 Hides 15.4 Rubber 15.4 Wool 64s 6.5 Wool 48s 6.5 Palm oil 2.9 Coconut oil 1.5.

1007. Surprisingly, previous analyses have focused on *weight* of the raw materials, a decision which does not seem quite obvious (Ågerup 1998:83; Simon 1996:48; Kahn *et al.* 1976:101ff).

1008. Notice that this assumes the entire world paying the American price for Portland cement, which is definitely a maximal assumption.

1009. Craig *et al.* 1996:339.

1010. Craig *et al.* 1996:340; Hille 1995:299.

1011. WRI 1998a:344.

1012. Craig *et al.* 1996:232ff.

1013. Craig *et al.*. 1996:43.

1014. Measured in 1999 reserve base/world production of bauxite.

1015. Craig *et al.* 1996:212.

1016. Craig *et al.* 1996:221.

1017. The price of this steel production is probably around $200–270 billion, depending on choice of prices. (All in all, about 773 million tons of steel is produced. With a price of $352.2 [World Bank steel rods 1998: http://www.worldbank.org/html/ieccp/pkjan98.html] this gives $272 billion; with World Metals Information Network sheet price of $250 [http://www.amm.com/inside/wsdanal/ws012998.htm] we get $193 billion.) When we look at the iron ore price here, it is because this is the price that might rise with scarcity (notwithstanding energy prices, which were discussed earlier).

1018. Craig *et al.* 1996:212.

1019. Craig *et al.* 1996:210.

1020. Quoted in Craig *et al.* 1996:221.

1021. Craig *et al.* 1996:266.

1022. Since copper's share of the Earth's crust is calculated from chemical analyses of thousands of samples and weighted by their relative frequency, the occurrence should be seen as a weight percentage and not a volume percentage (this goes for zinc as well).

1023. Craig *et al.* 1996:266; Hille 1995:279.

1024. Craig *et al.* 1996:273.

1025. Craig *et al.* 1996:273.

1026. Amey 1996:1.

1027. Craig *et al.* 1996:284; Amey 1996:1. Gold weighs 19 kg/dm^3.

1028. Amey 1996:1.

1029. Craig *et al.* 1996:280.

1030. Craig *et al.* 1996:287.

1031. Craig *et al.* 1996:288.

1032. Craig *et al.* 1996:288.

1033. Craig *et al.* 1996:291.

1034. Craig *et al.* 1996:304–5. Exactly because nitrogen can be synthesized from air, it has not been necessary to find new nitrogen reserves. Consequently, the present reserves constitute only consumption for about half a year.

1035. Craig *et al.* 1996:307–10.

1036. USGS 1998a. http://minerals.er.usgs.gov/minerals/pubs/commodity/potash/560398.pdf.

1037. Since zinc's share of the Earth's crust is calculated from chemical analyses of thousands of samples and weighted by their relative frequency, the occurrence should be seen as a weight percentage and not a volume percentage (this goes for copper as well).

1038. Hille 1995:279.

1039. The deep-sea nodules contain more nickel than copper, and the copper content is estimated at more than 1 billion tons (Craig *et al.* 1996:231, 273). Since we use 1 million tons of nickel yearly, this means that there is nickel for at least a thousand years.

1040. "Substitution for tantalum is made at either performance or economic penalty in most applications" (http://minerals.er.usgs.gov/minerals/pubs/commodity/niobium/230496.pdf, p1).

1041. http://minerals.er.usgs.gov/minerals/pubs/commodity/mercury/430398.pdf.

1042. Kuck and Platchy 1996:6.

1043. Pearce and Turner 1990:293–4.

1044. Meadows *et al.* 1992:83.

1045. Hille 1995:329–30.

1046. Ausubel (1996) points out, how a few compact discs now can contain all the phone numbers of all U.S. homes and businesses, an amount of information in telephone books which formerly weighed five tons.

1047. In 1972 income per capita was $13,747 whereas in 1992 it was $17,945 in real 1985 PPP$ (WRI 1996a). Consumption of wood, metal and plastic down, CEQ 1996:75.

1048. Hille 1995:322.

1049. Baumol 1986. This is clearly a model assumption – no one would believe that it is possible forever to increase efficiency by, say, 2 percent, but in practical terms it is possible for a long period and this means that it is possible to stretch the resources much further than ordinarily assumed.

1050. Goeller and Zucker 1984:456–7.

1051. Tietenberg 2000:326.

1052. Meadows *et al.* 1992:82.

1053. Available water including river inflow. Population is UN 1996 revision, which is fairly compatible with the new 2000 revision.

1054. WRI 1996a:301.

1055. GEUS 1997b:4.

1056. UNEP 2000:362, http://www.grida.no/geo2000/english/0236.htm.

1057. WWF 1998a:18.

1058. Population Reports 1998:3

1059. Couzin 1998; Johnson 1998; Time 1997:17. "A water crisis looms closer, it seems, every day" (UNESCO Courier 1999).

1060. WMO/UNESCO 2000:20.

1061. E.g. Bridgland 1999.

1062.http://www.worldwatch.org/pubs/ea/lo.html; see also Engelman and LeRoy 1993.

1063. Craig *et al.* 1996:366ff.

1064. Craig *et al.* 1996:374.

1065. Craig *et al.* 1996:366–7.

1066. There are several estimates, ranging from 37,400 km^3 to 47,000 km^3 (see Shiklomanov 1993 and Gleick 1993b:120–1).

1067. Postel *et al.* 1996:786.

1068. Postel *et al.* 1996:786. In India, the bulk of a year's rainfall comes during some 100 hours of heavy downpour (Shah 2000:9).

1069. Postel *et al.* 1996:786.

1070. EEA (1999:159) states that the EU uses 77 km^3/year, and the EU has 372 million citizens (Krinner *et al.* 1999:21).

1071. EEA 1999:157; a withdrawal rate of 16 percent. This is found to be sustainable (Krinner *et al.* 1999).

1072. USGS (1998b:63) estimates about 100e9 gallons a day as consumer use from freshwater sources.

1073. IWMI 2000:24.

1074. With the percentage axis, accessible runoff is assumed constant, which is not true; it is determined from 9,000 km^3 plus dam storage which has changed throughout the century, from about nil, to 2,500 km^3 today, to about 3,700 km^3 in 2025 (Postel *et al.* 1996:787). However, the error is not great – in 1900 global use was not 2.6 percent but 3.7 percent, and the high use in 2025 will be not 22 percent but 20.2 percent.

1075. EEA 1999:158–9; USGS 1998b:63; 190/402 billion gallons = 47 percent.

1076. IWMI 2000:24.

1077. Projections from 1967 till the early 1990s expected water withdrawal at the year 2000 as 4,300–8,400 km^3 compared to 1995 withdrawal of 3,788 km^3 (Gleick 1999b). Shiklomanov (1993:20) estimated the global withdrawal in 2000 at 5,190 km^3. Cf. Rasking *et al.* 1997:21.

1078. Here consumption is measured in withdrawal, since the utility derived from the water stems from the actual amount consumed (withdrawn) and not whatever amount happens to be used irretrievably.

1079. Shiklomanov 2000:22; EEA 1999:161; USGS 1998b.

1080. Wolf 1999:251.

1081. World Bank 1992:48; Wallensteen and Swain 1997:9–12; Engelman and LeRoy 1993; http://www.cnie.org/pop/pai/water-25.html.

1082. World Water Council 2000:xxvii; CSD 1997:8.

1083. Stated as the *first* problem in World Water Council 2000:xx. CSD 1997:100.

1084. "Billions of people lack access to even a basic water requirement of 50 [liters per capita per day], though . . . absolute water *availability* is not the problem" (Gleick 1999b:9).

1085. Arnell 1999:S43–4.

1086. WRI 1996a:306.

1087. Craig *et al.* 1996:387; Gleick 1999b.

1088. Engelman and LeRoy 1993; Gardner-Outlaw and Engelman 1997; GEUS 1997b; WRI 1996a:301ff; Miller 1998:494; Serageldin 1995:1–2; Wallensteen and Swain 1997:8; Chaibi 2000.

1089. Engelman and LeRoy 1993, http://www.cnie.org/pop/pai/water-12.html; Gardner-Outlaw and Engelman 1997:5. Both refer to Falkenmark and Widstrand 1992:14, which does not mention these limits beyond the 100 liters, and neither does Falkenmark and Lindh 1993.

1090. Equivalent to 1,700 m^3/year, 1,000 m^3/year and 500 m^3/year (Wallensteen and Swain 1997:8).

1091. Notice that this is less than the 20 countries Engelman and LeRoy present themselves in 1990 (WRI 1996a:302); the figures from WRI are quite a lot higher, because the influx from rivers quite sensibly has been included in the total water resources. These figures have also later been used by Engelman himself (Gardner-Outlaw and Engelman 1997).

1092. Craig *et al.* 1996:396–8; Al-Rashed and Sherif 2000.

1093. Gleick 1993b:381.

1094. Semiat 2000:54, 62.

1095. We can today desalinate close to 6 kWh/m^3 (with a theoretical lower limit of 0.78 kWh/m^3) (Hille 1995:242; Gleick 1993b:372; Aly 1999). Consequently, the world's water use of 2,073 km^3 could be covered by $6 \cdot 3{,}6e6 J/m^3 \cdot 2073e9 m^3$ = 45EJ, or about 11 percent of the present energy consumption. This could be covered by solar cells covering 0.27 percent of the Sahara Desert, with a 300 W influx and a 20 percent efficiency. Obviously, it would be ridiculous to make such a single facility, owing to transportation of water among other things, but it serves here as an illustration.

1096. 22.735 million m^3/day in 1998, http://www.ida.bm/html/inventory.htm, cf. Semiat 2000:61, or 8.3 km^3 annually, compared to 3,788 km^3 total and 344 km^3 municipal water.

1097. At 50 ¢/m^3 and a consumption of 344 km^3 this makes $172 billion, or 0.5 percent of the global $32,110 billion GDP (IMF 2000a:113).

1098. WI 1993:28.

1099. Shuval 1997:37.

1100. EEA 1998b:182–3.

1101. Teknologirådet 1997.

1102. Lindegaard 1998.

1103. WRI 1996a:306.

1104. Postel 1999:130.

1105. Postel 1998:table 1; Shuval 1997:38.

1106. Postel 1999:130.

1107. Engelman and LeRoy 1993; http://www.cnie.org/pop/pai/water-29.html.

1108. WRI 1996a:303; Falkenmark and Widstrand 1992:15. IWMI (2000:23–4) cautions, however, that since part of this waste runs off into aquifers or freshwater bodies to be reused, utilizing the water 60 percent more efficiently does not actually mean saving all 60 percent.

1109. Postel 1999:174.

1110. WI 1993:34.

1111. EEA 1999:160

1112. Dinar *et al.* 1997:12.

1113. World Bank 1992:16.

1114. World Bank 1992:16.

1115. IWMI 2000.

1116. World Bank 1992:16; 1994:47.

1117. Anderson 1995:430; Krinner *et al.* 1999: 68–70; water use in the UK was reduced by 10 percent through metering, p. 71. This has probably also been the case in Denmark, where ever higher water taxes have been accompanied by ever less consumption, e.g. Danish Ministry of Finance 1997:19. The fact that the connection is not quite clear is because the fall had already commenced in 1987, whereas taxes first kicked in 1993.

1118. Dinar *et al.* 1997:20; Cunningham and Saigo 1997:431.

1119. World Bank 1994:121–2; de Moor 1998:chapter 5.

1120. Anon. 1995c; World Bank 1995b; MEWREW 1995.

1121. Wolf 1999:255. The International Crisis Behavior dataset (Brecher and Wilkenfeld 1997) only identified four disputes, and these were supplemented by three others.

1122. Wolf 1999.

1123. Wolf 1999:256, italics in original.

1124. Wolf 1999:256–7. Compare how Wallensteen and Swain (1997:12) find that although US intelligence in the mid-1980s pointed out at least ten places in the world where war could break out over water, "as of yet serious conflicts have not yet arisen."

1125. Wolf 1999:259–60.

1126. Quoted in Wolf 1999:261.

1127. Wolf 1999:260.

1128. Wolf 1999:261.

1129. Gardner-Outlaw and Engelman 1997:7; Wallensteen and Swain 1997:20–2.

1130. Saeijs and van Berkel 1995.

1131. CSD 1997:1.

1132. World Water Council 2000:xix.

1133. Craig *et al.* 1996:416.

1134. Postel 1999:80, although for Saudi Arabia the size of the aquifer may be so large that it is reasonable to mine parts of it, cf. Al-Rashed and Sherif 2000:66.

1135. IWMI 2000:8.

1136. Postel *et al.* 1996:787.

1137. Anderson 1995:432.

1138. WI 1998a:14.

1139. This was also the point of the UN Secretary General's comments to the Commission on Sustainable Development: "During the 1970s, predictions abounded that the world would shortly 'run out' of fossil fuels and other essential raw materials. Since then, however, rising demand has generally been matched by discoveries of new reserves and substitution between resources, in response to the operation of market forces and technological advance. Concerns have shifted away from resource depletion to a wider and more complicated package of issues relating to the provision of adequate energy supplies in developing countries and the environmental and health impacts resulting from conventional patterns of energy and materials use" (Annan 1997:42–3). This shift in worry is what we shall look at in Part IV.

1140. Hille 1995:279; Goeller and Weinberg 1976.

1141. World Bank 1992:34.

1142. Major areas, e.g. Luken 1990:7. Based on EPA estimates, Hahn finds that the benefit from the Clean Air Act is $280.6 billion out of a total benefit of all EPA regulation estimated at $325.1 billion or 86 percent (Hahn 1996a:222). Based on the new and updated EPA analyses (especially EPA 1997d), the Office of Management and Budget finds that environmental benefits make up $1,450 billion of the total EPA benefits of $1510 billion, or 96 percent (OMB 2000:11; similar ranges in OMB 1997, 1999). Notice that estimating benefits gives the better view, since they indicate the absolute size of pollution costs, irrespective of the regulatory approach to redressing the problem. However, it is only indicative, since many areas are not under EPA purview or could not reasonably be regulated (like indoor air pollution).

1143. "Indoor air pollution and outdoor air pollution repeatedly emerge as the environmental problem categories most frequently cited as presenting the most significant risks to human health" (Konisky 1999:21).

1144. Measured in ice cores (Weiss *et al.* 1999:264).

1145. Miller 1998:466.

1146. Brimblecombe 1977:1,158; Elsom 1995:476.

1147. Brimblecombe 1987:9. One Londoner was actually executed for burning coal shortly after the year 1300 (Baumol and Oates 1995:447).

1148. "Royal Proclamation against the Pollution of the Thames," Henry Thomas Riley (ed.) 1,868:367–8, *Memorials of London and London Life in the XIIIth, XIVth and XVth Centuries, being a Series of Extracts, Local Social and Political, from the Early Archives of the City of London*, London: Longmans, Green and Co., cited here from Baumol and Oates 1995:447–8.

1149. Cited in Elsom 1995:476.

1150. Stone 1979:62.

1151. Stone 1979:62–3.

1152. Miller 1998:466.

1153. Brimblecombe 1977:1,158; Elsom 1995:476.

1154. Brimblecombe 1977:1,158.

1155. Brimblecombe 1987:64, cf. quote from Baumol and Oates 1995:448: "the glorious Fabrick of St. Paul's now in building, so Stately and Beautiful as it is, will after an Age or Two, look old and discolour'd before 'tis finish'd, and may suffer perhaps as much damage by the Smoak, as the former Temple did by the Fire."

1156. Brimblecombe 1977:1,162.

1157. Quoted in Baumol and Oates 1995:448. Compare this with the similar observation on Copenhagen in 1861: "When the wind is not blowing very hard [the city] is still full of smoke, and over it hangs a massive layer of smoke best seen when approaching the city from the land or sea side . . . Altogether, conditions are such as to be intolerable from time to time and they will gradually get worse." In 1908, the physician Poul Hertz commented: "If one looks out over Copenhagen on a quiet summer afternoon from Brønshøj Hill, the city is covered with a grayish cloud which blurs the contours and restricts one's field of vision. It is the coal smoke which has been added to the air, virtually exclusively from factories at this time of year, and the sources of the fog loom like veils of smoke from the numerous high chimneys, these slender minarets characteristic of the modern-day town" (quoted from Jensen 1996:171). Jes Fenger of the Danish National Environmental Research Institute estimates that the sulfur dioxide content of the air in Copenhagen was around ten times as high between 1850 and 1970 as it is today: "Pitcoal clouds (Stenkulsskyer)," feature article in the daily *Politiken*, 9 May 1995.

1158. Brimblecombe 1977:1,159.

1159. Elsom 1995:480.

1160. Brimblecombe 1977:1,159.

1161. Elsom 1995:477.

1162. Botkin and Keller 1998:466.

1163. This necessitates an upwards adjustment of Brimblecombe's data by approximately a factor of 4. However, since Brimblecombe's model data are averages for London as a whole, it must be assumed that central London was much more polluted, in line with the actual measurements (Brimblecombe 1977:1,159; Elsom 1995:477). Also, it must be expected that the decline towards the end of the curve is presumably slightly exaggerated because the model is based only on coal, whereas over the centuries many other sources of pollution appeared. Finally, the model also has difficulty defining urban boundaries (Brimblecombe 1977:1,161). The SO_2 data for 1933–80 come from Laxen and Thompson (1987:106), using concentrations at County Hall in London. Note that the data are from different time series using various methods of measurement.

1164. EPA 1998c:7ff.

1165. World Bank 1992; OECD 1999; WHO 1999b; EU 1994a; HLU 1997:128ff.

1166. This graph requires several estimates. Since PM_{10} was not measured systematically before 1988 in the US, the 1982 figure is estimated from TPS which typically is about 50 percent higher (data comparison; personal communication with Kåre Kemp, National Environmental Research Institute of Denmark, 10 June 98). Since ozone is measured as the fourth-highest daily maximum eight-hour average, the annual average has been determined from all sampling units with more than 90 percent sampling rate from EPA 2000b for sample years and estimated for the others. The reported concentration of lead is taken as annual average, although it is the maximal quarterly average.

1167. Krupnick and Burtraw 1996:22. Health related costs make up 99.3 percent of the total air pollution costs (EPA 1997d:52–3) and mortality alone accounts for 81 percent ("Perhaps the most important health effect that is examined in this analysis is mortality" [EPA 1997d:D-16]). In comparison, the total costs of non-health in the US are "only" about \$30 or in the UK about £10 per person, annually (EPA 1997d:52; IGCB 1999:table 5.6).

1168. It is estimated that the mortality effect for NO_x per ton is around 15 percent of SO_2, \$463 versus \$3,102 (Burtraw *et al.* 1997:14–15). "CO, while obviously fatal at high concentrations, has much more limited health effects (primarily related to cardiovascular systems) at ambient exposure levels normally encountered" (Burtraw and Toman 1997:3); cf. the EU conclusion (AEA 1999:18): "it appears probable that the major cause of [CO problems] is not exposure to ambient CO levels, but exposure to CO through smoking or faulty domestic appliances, or the health effects of poor diet, or other factors unrelated to air quality. Under these circumstances the effect of exposure to ambient CO may simply be to advance hospital admissions or death by a few days."

1169. COMEAP 1998; Stedman *et al.* 1999; IGCB 1999. The greatest mortality stems from PM_{10}, followed by SO_2 and ozone (unless assuming a no-threshold) (COMEAP 1998:table 1.2). However, the studies only look at acute deaths, whereas it is estimated that long-term mortality from studies in the US "suggest that the overall impacts may be substantially greater than those that we have as yet been able to quantify" (COMEAP 1998:1.14). This makes the studies somewhat less interesting in assessing total health costs.

1170. The estimates of lead concentration 1960–76 are based on estimated lead emissions from EPA 2000d:3-19–20 and Graney 1995:1,722.

1171. The effect is obviously relative: the less serious the criteria pollutant problems are, the more serious those that remain will become, relatively speaking.

1172. EPA 2000e:73.

1173. EPA 2000e:78.

1174. EPA 2000e:77.

1175. EPA 2000e:85.

1176. UK EA 2000:http://www.environment-agency.gov.uk/s-enviro/viewpoints/3compliance/1air-quality/3-1j.html.

1177. EPA 1996a:1.12.

1178. In particular the 1993 Six Cities Study by Dockery *et al.* (1993) which examined 8,111 adults over 14 years of age in six eastern US cities, and the American Cancer Society Study by Pope *et al.* (1995), which examined 550,000 people in 151 cities and towns in 1982–9 in the US (EPA 1996b:V, 14–15).

1179. EPA (1996b:V-47ff) documents the many studies registering for several sources of pollution. The general result seems to be that parameter estimates for the other pollutants are often insignificant when studying for particles: "while consistent associations between PM and health effects are observed across the different studies, the reported association between health effects and SO_2 can vary widely" (p. 49). For ozone: particles are "a stronger predictor of mortality than O_3" (p. 50). The same is concluded for CO (p. 51–2), and for NO_x EPA finds: "while the association between NO and health effects in these studies is inconsistent, the association between PM and health effects remains positive and consistent, both across study areas with varying levels of NO_x and after controlling for NO_x in the model" (p. 53).

1180. EPA 1997d:34. This choice has also been made because uncertainty still exists regarding the causal pathway and it was therefore decided to use particles as "a surrogate for a mix of criteria pollutants" (p. 34, note 48).

1181. EPA 1996a:1–21: "Epidemiological studies show consistent positive associations of exposure to ambient PM with health effects, including mortality and morbidity . . . However, a clear understanding of specific biologic mechanisms remains to be established." One possible explanation comes from the University of Texas, where scientists have shown that repressive macrophages – which protect against excessively powerful immune reactions – die under the influence of man-made pollutant particles, whereas stimulant macrophages survive. This could imply that the lungs become "overprotected" against pollution and consequently suffer inflammatory lung injury (Raloff 1998).

1182. Fenger 1985:167ff: Cunningham and Saigo 1997:397ff.

1183. EPA 1996b:V-4; Fenger 1985:167. Furthermore, more water-soluble particles would more often be dissolved in the nose, mouth and throat, whereas less water-soluble ones more easily reach further down (Fenger 1985:166).

1184. EPA 1997b:34.

1185. EPA 1997b:32. Actually, by far the majority of these particles originate from volcanic eruptions, forest fires, sandstorms and wind-blown sea spray. Sea spray consists of tiny bubbles of air at the surface of the sea which burst and release tiny droplets which rapidly dry to sea salt and are carried away by the wind (Brimblecombe 1996:59–61; Fenger and Tjell 1994:55).

1186. This figure is very much a ballpark estimate, based on a series of rough calculations.

Current particle pollution in the US is 23.7 μg/m³ (PM10, EPA 2000e:119), and 56 percent of this typically consist of $PM_{2.5}$ (EPA 1997d:D-16; cf. 60 percent in the UK, QUARG 1996:82), i.e. about 13.3 μg/m³. It is estimated that a reduction of $PM_{2.5}$ by 25 μg/m³ will result in a 14.5 percent reduction in mortality (or conversely, a relative increase of 17 percent [EPA 1996b:VI-12]; this assumes that mortality is primarily an effect of average and not peak load). If it is assumed that mortality is linear and there is no threshold effect (this is still not certain and could have a profound effect on the result – it is possible that the lower limit for damage lies around the present-day level [EPA 1996b:VI-18]), this means that removing 13.3 μg/m³ would produce a relative decrease in mortality of 7.7 percent. Since about 2.3 million people die each year in the US (USBC 1999a:75), and of these about 76 percent live (and die) in urban areas (UNPD 1998a:87), this implies an excess mortality of about 134,596. This is comparable with the 184,000 EPA finds would have died if the particular pollution level had been slightly more than twice as high as the somewhat higher level in 1990 (EPA 1997d:37, D-45, "just over half" p. 23).

1187. USBC 1999a:99.

1188. Current UK smoke pollution in 1997–8 was 9.4 μg/m³ (Loader *et al.* 1999:4.3). In PM2.5 this is equivalent to about 19.6 μg/m³ (QUARG 1996:84). With a linear, no threshold effect, this would mean a mortality decrease of 11.35 percent. Since 632,500 die each year in the UK, and 89 percent live in urban areas (UNPD 1998a:85), this implies an excess mortality of 63,892. For Denmark, the estimate runs about 50 μg/m³ (TSP), 33 μg/m³ (PM10) and 18.5 μg/m³ (PM2.5), producing a relative decrease in mortality of 10.7 percent. Since about 60,000 people die every year in Denmark, and of these about half live (and die) in urban areas, this implies an excessive mortality of around 3,210 (cf. Larsen *et al.*'s assessment that reducing particle levels to a third would mean an annual fall in mortality of 300–400 urban dwellers [1997:11]).

1189. EC-ET 2000:87; 3,137 in GB, DETR 1998c:18.

1190. http: // cnn.com / world / asiapcf / 9805 / 29/ AP000628.ap.html.

1191. EPA 1996b:V-18.

1192. EPA 1996b:V-19.

1193. Note the US data series is collected and adjusted from several data series with varying numbers of monitoring stations (80–2,350), either purely urban or mixed urban/rural. The UK data series is the National Survey for 1962–80 and the Basic Urban Network for 1981–97.

1194. EPA 1997d:37. In the *Criteria* and *Staff Document*, the EPA had otherwise found that "it is not possible to confidently estimate quantitatively the number of years lost" (EPA 1996b:V-20). The figure is plausibly slightly under that of a Dutch investigation, which showed that the life-year loss among young Dutchmen is around 1.11 years per 10 μg/m³ $PM_{2.5}$ reduction (Larsen *et al.* 1997:11; EPA 1997d:D-17). This is because it is based on a slightly higher risk evaluation factor, an average of Pope's 7 percent and Dockery's 14 percent (which the EPA avoids since Pope is based on far more data).

1195. For the US: 135,000 people a year lose 14.24 years, each over an average life span of 76.7 years for 214 million urban people. This means 0.69 years lost for everyone. For the UK, 64,000 people lose 14.24 years of 77.1 years for 52 million urbanites, or 1.35 years. This calculation demands that the reduction in pollution maintains its mortality distribution across all age groups.

1196. These figures are based on EPA 1997d:38 with no threshold and linearity, and the estimate of slightly more particle pollution avoided than left over in 1998 (EPA 1997d:23).

1197. These estimates naturally require linearity over a pretty large range, although it no longer requires a no-threshold assumption, since these calculations are way inside the Pope data material. It should however be noted that in the 1960s there were fewer urban dwellers in relation to the population as a whole, as well as fewer people altogether.

1198. QUARG 1996:75–6; cf. Fenger and Tjell 1994:206.

1199. Davidson 1979:1,040, 1,037.

1200. DETR 1999:27.

1201. EPA 1999e:14; QUARG 1996:50.

1202. OECD 1985a:28; 1987:31; 1999:57.

1203. OECD 1985a:28; 1987:31; 1999:57.

1204. OECD 1985a:28; 1987:31; 1999:57.

1205. NERI 1998A:49; EPA 2000d:3–19–20.

1206. Burtraw *et al.* 1997, Burtraw and Krupnick 1998 – and not quite as clear-cut, EPA 1995 – show that the overall cost of reducing acid rain is considerably less than the overall advantage of reduction. The advantages are carried to an overwhelming extent by the effect on health. It is, however, important to emphasize that just because sulfur reduction was a good idea (because it happened also to reduce concentrations of airborne particles, which are dangerous) it is possible that particle reduction could have been achieved at a far lower cost had the effort been focused at achieving just that.

1207. QUARG 1996:75.

1208. NERI 1998A:59. District heating systems distribute steam and hot water to multiple buildings. See http://www.energy.rochester.edu/dh.

1209. HLU 1997:120.

1210. QUARG 1993:1.

1211. If the proportion of diesel cars were to be 50 percent in 2005 (a rather unrealistic assumption), emission levels would be only marginally lower than 1993 levels, QUARG 1993:1.

1212. See the literature discussed in Powell 1997.

1213. Auliciems and Burton 1973:1,069.

1214. Powell 1997:15.

1215. Botkin and Keller 1998:286. The English word *plumbing* comes from the Latin for lead, *plumbum*.

1216. Eisinger 1996.

1217. Craig *et al.* 1996:274. The octane rating is increased to avoid premature ignition or *knocking* (Fenger 1985:116). In reality lead is not added to the petrol but an organic lead compound (tetraethyl lead or tetramethyl lead).

1218. Chiras 1998:348.

1219. EPA 1997d:G-1.

1220. Chiras 1998:348; EPA 1997d:G-8.

1221. Miller 1998:585.

1222. Tong *et al.* 1998; EPAQS 1998:23; Chiras 1998:348.

1223. EPA 1997d:G-9.

1224. Gemmel 1995.

1225. WRI 1998a:60. The other sources are food (from pollution) and water (from lead pipes, storage tanks or other fixtures, fittings and solders in pipes) (EPAQS 1998:9; Chiras 1998:349).

1226. Chiras 1998:349; Kitman 2000.

1227. DETR 1998a:2.53.

1228. DETR 1998a:table 2.17.

1229. EPA refers to 0.04 $\mu g/m^3$ as "approaching the minimum detectable level" (EPA 1997b:14).

1230. WRI 1998a:60. 1- to 5-year-old children in the period 1976–92 (Miller 1998:586). For differences in the leaded burden based on income and race, see CEQ 1996:112ff.

1231. It is assumed to be an error when EPA 2000e:118 denotes lead as measured in ppm, when all other comparable data are measured in $\mu g/m^3$, including the NAAQS, the data in EPA 2000e:18 and EPA 1997b:88.

1232. EPA 1997d:37.

1233. EPA 1997d:37.

1234. 22,000 lives of 38 years, on average 77 years over a population of 250 million.

1235. EPA 1997d:38. Up by 3 IQ-points: the US has about 36 million children under age 10 (Keyfitz and Flieger 1990:349), and the EPA estimates that, every year, children lose about 10.4 million IQ points. Over a childhood of 10 years this is therefore around 2.9 IQ points.

1236. The condensation nuclei are often fine mineral particles from coal use or unburned and pyrolyzed fuel from engines (Fenger 1985:59; QUARG 1996:7).

1237. The calcium carbonate of the stone is converted into gypsum, which is either washed off by the rain or falls off in flakes (Fenger 1985:1977–8, 180–1).

1238. The comprehensive survey by NAPAP showed that corrosion problems were "second order" (according to the head of NAPAP, Kulp 1995:531). The overall cost in the US was under 100 million dollars and the cost related to stone and marble was "less than 10 percent of the overall cost" of restoration (NAPAP 1990:Question 1, 3–1). Cf. UK studies finding an annual cost of £800 million in the UK alone (IGCB 1999:table 5.2), and €10–13.5 billion for Europe as a whole (EEA 1995:33; 1999:152).

1239. Haze and gray smog are primarily formed by particles and SO_2, which swell up in damp weather, thus restricting the amount of sun that can get through (Chiras 1998:362; Fenger and Tjell 1994:205; 1985:61). SO_2 is estimated to account for between 15 and 60 percent of light reduction, and in general considerably more than NO_x (NAPAP 1990:Question 1, 4–16).

1240. Burtraw *et al.* (1997:14) find that the benefits of reducing SO_2 substantially from 1990 is about 9 1990$ per person, or about $11.5 today.

1241. $400 million 1990$ (NAPAP 1990:Question 1:2–17; Kulp 1995:533).

1242. Fenger and Tjell 1994:183.

1243. CLTAP 1979; EEA 1995:544–5.

1244. Fenger and Tjell 1994:32.

1245. Burtraw *et al.* 1997; Botkin and Keller 1998:487–8, cutting total emissions by nearly 40 percent (EPA 1995:1–1).

1246. Note that there is a change in the number of American measuring stations: 1962–9: 21; 1974–6: 188; 1977–86: 278; 1987–96: 479.

1247. Cf. EPAQS 1995b:figure 1.

1248. EPA 1995:table S-2. The study is compared with a situation in which there is a weak increase in emissions of SO_2, so the actual human lives saved must be assumed to be a little on the high side. On the other hand, only the eastern 32 states have been modeled.

1249. To what extent SO_2 also has any appreciable independent health-damaging effect is under debate, but by far the greatest effect is due to particle formation.

1250. Chiras 1998:362; HLU 1997:123.

1251. Fenger and Tjell 1994:49.

1252. EPA 1997b:21; Chiras 1998:362; Botkin and Keller 1998:476–7.

1253. EPA 1996b:V-49–51. "While there are some short-term health effects from increases in O_3 concentrations, there is little evidence that ozone is associated with long-term illness or premature mortality for most of the population" (Burtraw and Toman 1997:3).

1254. EPAQS 1994b:15.

1255. Fenger and Tjell 1994:167–8; Burtraw and Toman 1997:3.

1256. Fenger and Tjell 1994:184.

1257. The London graph is composed of the urban background station London Bridge Place 1990–8 adjusted to the urban background station Central London 1976–90.

1258. PORG 1997:ii: "The peak concentrations are associated with human health and vegetation effects."

1259. PORG 1997:53; however, the *averages* for rural sites seem to show a slight increase, p. 52.

1260. The London graph is composed of the urban background station London Bridge Place 1990–8 adjusted to the urban background station Central London 1976–90.

1261. EEA 1999:149.

1262. EPA 1997b:17; Fenger and Tjell 1994:212; 1985:174.

1263. EPA 1996b:V-53; Burtraw *et al.* 1997:11. EPAQS (1996:22) found the issue "unresolved."

1264. NERI 1998A:48, 109–13; EPA 1997b:17.

1265. Fenger and Tjell 1994:183.

1266. DETR 1999:27.

1267. HLU 1997:121.

1268. OECD 1999:58–9.

1269. The London graph is composed of the urban background station London Bridge Place 1990–8 adjusted to the urban background station Central London 1976–90.

1270. EPA 1996b:V-51–2.

1271. HLU 1997:122.

1272. EPAQS 1994a:11: "Non-smokers, exposed at rest to concentrations in the air of 25–50 ppm [29–57_g/m^3] might be expected to show carboxyhaemoglobin levels of 2–3 percent after several hours . . . Smokers may have levels of 4 percent to as high as 15 percent, depending on the numbers of cigarettes smoked."

1273. HLU 1997:122. As much as 95 percent of all CO in towns comes from motor traffic (EPA 1997b:9).

1274. HLU 1997:122.

1275. An OECD study has shown that lead has fallen by almost 100 percent, particles by 60 percent and SO_2 by 38 percent since 1970, while only NO_x levels have increased, around 12 percent, according to estimates by a group of countries consisting of Germany, Italy, the Netherlands, the UK and the US (World Bank 1992:40).

1276. Fenger and Tjell 1994:212.

1277. UNEP and WHO 1992:16, 21, 32.

1278. WRI 1996a:3.

1279. Dasgupta *et al.* 1997:3.

1280. The following argument is based on World Bank 1992:38–41 and on Shafik 1994, who wrote the original background paper for the World Bank. Note, that a number of later studies have discussed and questioned the approach in Shafik, but for local pollution problems like SO_2 and particles, the general inverse-u shape has been reaffirmed (Grossman and Krueger 1995; Torras and Boyce 1998; List and Gallet 1999).

1281. The change happens around $3,280, or about 36 percent more than the present developing world average (Shafik 1994:765, cf. Figure 32).

1282. EPA 1998c:9.

1283. EPA 1998c:9. Equally, in 1987, 102 million people lived in areas where at least one pollutant was above the National Ambient Air Quality Standard. In 1996 the number was just 47 million. CEQ 1997:292.

1284. World Bank 1992:25.

1285. World Bank 1992:25.

1286. Park 1987.

1287. Claudi 1988:249.

1288. WCED 1987:2.

1289. "Forest die-back," Christensen 2000:3; "killing forests," Burne 1999:142.

1290. Albert 1989:4. Many similar books were published in the 1980s; one Norwegian book was titled *If Trees Could Cry* (Roll-Hansen 1994).

1291. Fenger 1985:67; Kulp 1995:523–4.

1292. EU 1983:23.

1293. EU 1983:23; Abrahamsen *et al.* 1994a:298.

1294. Abrahamsen *et al.* 1994a:298.

1295. NAPAP 1990:2–43.

1296. Ulrich's hypotheses about aluminum's damaging properties were particularly in focus for these tests (Abrahamsen *et al.* 1994a:321).

1297. Cited in Kulp 1995:528–9.

1298. NAPAP 1990:Q1, 1–30, 1–65ff.

1299. NAPAP 1990:Q1, 1–1.

1300. EEA 1998b:75.

1301. NAPAP 1990:Q3, 5–1.

1302. NAPAP 1990:Q3, 5–1.

1303. UNECE/EU 1996.

1304. FAO 1997c:21.

1305. Kauppi *et al.* 1992:71.

1306. Gundersen *et al.* 1998.

1307. EEA 1999:143.

1308. NAPAP 1990:Q1, 2–15.

1309. van Dobben 1995:295.

1310. van Dobben 1995:295.

1311. Gundersen *et al.* 1998; Abrahamsen *et al.* 1994a:320.

1312. Less than 75 percent foliage (UNECE/EU 1997:22).

1313. E.g. Gundersen *et al.* 1998; UNECE/EU 1997:104–5.

1314. UNECE/EU 1997:105; Abrahamsen *et al.* 1994a:323.

1315. EEA 1998b:74.

1316. EEA 1998b:74.

1317. Cited in Abrahamsen *et al.* 1994a:322.

1318. Cited in Abrahamsen *et al.* 1994a:322.

1319. Rosner and Markowitz 1999.

1320. *Politiken*, 28 June 1993, section 3, p. 3.

1321. WRI 1998a:65.

1322. WRI 1998a:66; Cunningham and Saigo 1997:391; WHO 2000a:73.

1323. Measurements are still pretty sporadic, so the figures should be considered with reservation; ref. in WRI 1998a:66; World Bank 1992:52; UNEP 1993:103; WHO 2000a:80–1.

1324. WHO has measured average indoor particulate pollution of 1,300–18,400 μg/m^3 (UNEP 1993:103) compared to averages in Beijing of 250–410 μg/m^3 and in Mexico City of 100–500 μg/m^3 (UNEP 1993:26).

1325. WRI 1998a:66.

1326. World Bank 1992:52.

1327. WRI 1998a:67.

1328. WRI 1998a:67.

1329. WRI 1998a:119.

1330. The total annual number of deaths in the world is estimated around 50 million (WRI 1998a:10).

1331. WRI 1998a:66.

1332. WRI 1998a:67.

1333. Ott and Roberts 1998; WHO 2000a:81.

1334. EPA 1994a: "Can plants control indoor air pollution?"

1335. Miller 1998:475.

1336. It is presumed that the breakdown product polonium-218 is the cause of cancer (Botkin and Keller 1998:502–3).

1337. Of the remaining radioactivity,16 percent comes from space and the Earth, 11 percent from our own bodies, 14 percent from medical X-rays, etc., 3 percent from consumer goods and only 1 percent from "other sources" (Miller 1998:267).

1338. Estimated for 1993 (BEIR 1998). The effect is calculated on the basis of large-scale cancer studies on miners (68,000 men) who were exposed to far higher levels of radon and assumes no definitive lower threshold or linearity. Estimating the damage by radon on everyone in the population poses considerable problems, given that most miners were exposed not only to radon, but also to dust; almost all of them smoked and were men.

1339. EEA 1995:303. In Denmark, radon-related deaths account for about 300 of 5,000 lung cancer related deaths (Andersen *et al.* 1997:2; Storm *et al.* 1996:91).

1340. Becquerel is a measure of radioactivity. A SI derived unit for radioactivity named after the French scientist A. H. Becquerel. It is equal to 1 nuclear transition or disintegration per second. (efunda 2001).

1341. NAS 1998.

1342. Andersen *et al.* (1997) look in detail into the various initiatives and the efficiency of same.

1343. WHO 2000a:74.

1344. EPA 1994b.

1345. Tobaksskadesrådet 1993.

1346. EPA 1999c.

1347. EPA 1999a.

1348. Miller 1998:476. It was banned in Denmark in 1980 (Riiskjær 1988:146).

1349. http://www.lungusa.org/air/envasbestos.html.

1350. Miller 1998:476.

1351. Miller 1998:480, unfortunately without reference.

1352. CDC 1999d:994; cf. CDC 1997a:8; 1996:section 8.

1353. WWF links, for example, the deterioration of the environment and, among other things, asthma: "a decline in the environment – urban air quality and asthma, food hygiene and BSE, drinking water quality, the deterioration of our countryside, the loss of garden birds, the destruction of our conservation sites for new roads and so on." http://www.wwf-uk.org/news/news15.htm.

1354. McLoughlin and Nall 1994. See Discover 1998 for an interpretation.

1355. Anaphylactic shock can come about as the result of an allergic reaction to bee or wasp stings, foodstuffs and medicines.

1356. UCB 1999; Watson 1997.

1357. Meggs and Dunn (1996) report that in the US around 35 percent of people describe themselves as being allergic, of whom two-thirds get symptoms once a month or more frequently; 50 million Americans are estimated to suffer from allergic diseases (AAAAI 2000:i), of 270 million (USBC 1999:8).

1358. AAAAI 2000:i.

1359. NCHS (1998:78) reports 5.68 percent chronic asthma, or 14.9 million of 263 million in 1995 (USBC 1999a:8).

1360. UCB 1999.

1361. Taylor 1998. Some people with serious asthma do, however, suffer from chronic narrowing of the air passages, which can only partially be treated even after extensive use of anti-inflammatory drugs.

1362. Jarvis and Burney 1998.

1363. UCB 1999:http://theucbinstituteofallergy.ucb.be/WhitePaper/PageEpidemiology.htm

1364. "Defining asthma in terms of symptoms alone has formed the basis of many epidemiological studies, but this is fraught with difficulty in the absence of objective measurement of airflow limitation and its variability" (NHLBI and WHO 1995:17).

1365. UCB 1999; Bindslev-Jensen 1998. This has, however, to be seen in contrast to children, of whom 5–7 percent have some kind of food allergy.

1366. Magnus and Jaakkola 1997.

1367. Jarvis and Burney 1998:607; Høst 1997.

1368. Bates 1995.

1369. Beasley *et al.* 1998; Jarvis and Burney 1998:607.

1370. NHLBI and WHO 1995:27; Jarvis and Burney 1998:607.

1371. Jarvis and Burney 1998:607; Campbell *et al.* 1997.

1372. The price in the US was estimated at 6.2 billion 1990$ (7.9 billion 1999$, Weiss *et al.*. 1992, cf. NIAID 2000) or 5.8 billion 1994$ (6.5 billion 1999$, Smith *et al.* 1997:789). EU: UCB 1997; Watson 1997. Cf. a price of about SEK 3 billion in Sweden (approx. €500 million, Jacobson *et al.* 2000).

1373. Sears 1997a. More price estimates in Blaiss 1997.

1374. In the following I use Jarvis and Burney 1998 and WRI 1998:31–2, as well as NHLBI and WHO 1995:37–50.

1375. Holgate 1997. Sears (1997b) reports on a Norwegian study involving 5,864 twins, where 75 percent of the asthma propensity was determined by the genes.

1376. Sears 1997b. The fact that boys more frequently get asthma than girls could be due to boys having narrower air passages in their early years (NHLBI and WHO 1995:29).

1377. This was decided on the basis of cohort tests (Sears 1997). Otherwise one might expect this to be evidence of asthma rates increasing (such that those who are adults now were born earlier and are therefore less susceptible to attack) (Jarvis and Burney 1998:609).

1378. Newman-Taylor 1995; Yemaneberhan and Bekele 1997.

1379. Becklake and Ernst 1997.

1380. Newman-Taylor 1995; Becklake and Ernst 1997; Sears 1997b, WRI 1998a:30.

1381. Al-Khalaf 1998; cf. faulty logic in Anon. 1994c.

1382. COMEAP 1995:1.19. This find is also supported by a large-scale 1998 study in the UK of more than 27,000 12–14-year-olds. Here the scientists find very little difference in asthma incidence between rural and urban teenagers. In conclusion, they state that the study "suggests that factors which do vary geographically in Great Britain – such as climate, diet, and outdoor environment – are not the main determinants of prevalence" (Kaur 1998:123).

1383. Sears 1997a.

1384. WRI 1998a:30; Newman-Taylor 1995.

1385. Sears 1997b.

1386. Platts-Mills and Carter 1997.

1387. Newman-Taylor 1995.

1388. Newman-Taylor 1995; Rosenstreich *et al.* 1997; Celedon 1999; Plaschke *et al.* 1999a; 1999b.

1389. Woodcock and Custovic 1998:1,075.

1390. Woodcock and Custovic 1998:1,075.

1391. Woodcock and Custovic 1998:1,075.

1392. Platts-Mills and Woodfolk 1997, cited in WRI 1998a:31.

1393. Woodcock and Custovic 1998; http://www.alaw.org/liscapih.html.

1394. Martinez and Holt 1999; Carpenter 1999.

1395. Jarvis and Burney 1998.

1396. Matricardi *et al.* 2000.

1397. Clark 1998; Anon. 1997e.

1398. Carpenter 1999.

1399. Illi *et al.* 2001.

1400. Becklake and Ernst 1997.

1401. WRI 1998a:31.

1402. Shaheen *et al.* 1999. "Excess pounds may lead to asthma," in *Tufts University Health and Nutrition Letter*, June 1998, 16(4):2.

1403. WRI 1998a:31.

1404. The figures are 70.8 percent, 0.4 percent, 0.24 percent and a maximum of 0.0004 percent for rivers, assuming a minimum average river depth of 1 meter (Shiklomanov 1993:12).

1405. 60 percent of all people live less than 100 km from the sea UNEP 1997: http://www-cger.nies.go.jp/geo1/exsum/ex3.htm). The relationship in volume between oceans and lakes is naturally even greater: lakes account for 0.013 percent of the ocean's volume (Shiklomanov 1993:12). As regards the question of mixing of pollutants it is the volume that counts.

1406. Quoted in *Time* magazine 1997:36; Jickells *et al.* 1990:313; Porritt 1991:143.

1407. 1.338e9 km^3 (Shiklomanov 1993:12; cf. Jickells *et al.* 1990:313).

1408. GESAMP 1990:1, cf. the UK 1998 marine water evaluation: "In broad terms, the biological quality of waters and sediments at intermediate and offshore locations, as revealed by oyster embryo and other bioassays, is generally good" (MPM 1998:24).

1409. About 2.5 percent comes from oil platforms. The figures are characterized by considerable uncertainty (NRC 1985:82). In addition to the approximately 2 million tons of oil a year from the sea are a further 1.2 million tons from municipal and industrial waste and runoff.

1410. These techniques are known as LOT (Load on Top) and COW (Crude Oil Washing) (NRC 1985). See also MARPOL 2000. Load-on-top: "Under this, the oily mixtures resulting from the normal tank cleaning processes are pumped into a special slop tank. During the course of the return voyage to the loading terminal this mixture separates. Oil, being lighter than water, gradually floats to the surface leaving the water at the bottom. This is then pumped into the sea, leaving only crude oil in the tank. At the loading terminal fresh crude oil is then loaded on top of it." Crude oil washing: "Cleaning to be carried out by crude oil washing, rather than water – in other words, the cargo itself. When sprayed onto the sediments clinging to the tank walls, the oil simply dissolves them, turning them back into usable oil that can be pumped off with the rest of the cargo. There is no need for slop tanks to be used since the process leaves virtually no oily wastes." http://www.imo.org/imo/news/197/tankers.htm.

1411. Goudie 1993:232–3.

1412. The statistics ignored oil spills of less than 7 tons. This probably means little or nothing because even with the current statistics, in which about 83 percent (8,688) are under 7 tons, this is the equivalent of a maximum of 60,800 tons or 1.1 percent of overall spills. Similarly, the proportion of spills in the 7–700 ton range accounts for a maximum of 14 percent (and probably somewhat less) of total spills. This is why the focus here is on large spills.

1413. Or not counting the three largest accidents, 289,000 tons down to 88,000 tons.

1414. CEQ 1996:250. For Denmark, the situation is a little less clear-cut. An increase was reported in the early part (1988–91) of the registration period, although the National Environmental Research Institute of Denmark credits this to greater awareness (NERI 1998a:118). Apart from that it can be seen that over time fewer birds die as a result of oil pollution, which could certainly suggest that oil pollution has become less serious (NERI 1998a:119).

1415. Holden 1990.

1416. Note, that DOT (1999) also gives oil spills for 1982–98 (table 4–47), but 1994 is apparently off by a factor of almost 10 from the US Coast Guard numbers.

1417. "Oil in the ocean: the short- and long-term impacts of a spill," 90–356 SPR, from CRS, here cited in Holden 1990.

1418. The consequences have been "relatively modest." CRS, here cited in Holden 1990.

1419. In the Gulf of Fos (France) it was found that,

despite severe overpollution by petroleum wastes, the "sediments from the open sea could be considered to be unpolluted . . . and unaffected by the refinery wastes two years after the end of oil spills."

1420. MPM 1998:25.

1421. Holden 1990.

1422. Abdulaziz and Krupp 1997; cf. with the inland pollution of some 22 million barrels of oil running free from 810 oil wells (Dobson *et al.* 1997).

1423. Greenpeace 1992:9 and 8.

1424. Greenpeace 1992:8.

1425. Jones *et al.* 1998a:472.

1426. Thomas 1991:49.

1427. Jones *et al.* 1998a:472; Abdulaziz and Krupp 1997.

1428. Abdulaziz and Krupp 1997: "The damage to sublittoral benthic habitats was very limited."

1429. Abdulaziz and Krupp 1997: "The lower eulittoral and sublittoral fringe have largely recovered."

1430. Abdulaziz and Krupp 1997.

1431. Measured in terms of the content of PAH (Readman *et al.* 1992:662, 664). See also *Science News* 29 August 1992, 142(9):143.

1432. Readman *et al.* 1996.

1433. Jones *et al.* 1998a:487.

1434. http://www.oilspill.state.ak.us/history/history.htm, ITOPF 2000.

1435. Anon. 1995a.

1436. 62 percent remembered the name, 66 percent did not think the beaches and water were "mostly cleaned up" (Gillespie 1999).

1437. EVOSTC 2000a; Romano 1999.

1438. The spill has in many ways made the Prince William Sound one of the best researched areas (Kaiser 1999).

1439. What is actually understood by the "restoration, rehabilitation and replacement of natural resources" is still unclear, since most money has gone towards scientific investigation, tourist projects and forest acquisitions (Hedges 1993).

1440. Holloway 1996:84: "The Trustees . . . are still watching, waiting for the long-term negative effects they are sure will manifest themselves."

1441. EVOSTC 2000a.

1442. EVOSTC 2000a.

1443. AWEA (2000) estimate that 97.5 million birds die annually, or about 267,000 each day. The Mammal Society estimate that 55 million birds are killed annually, or 300,000 over two days, Mammal Society 2001a&b. Cf. also with about a million birds killed each year in Denmark by traffic alone, Andersen 1998.

1444. EVOSTC 2000b:29.

1445. EVOSTC 2000b:29.

1446. EVOSTC 1997; 2000b:28.

1447. EVOSTC 2000b:28.

1448. Grisanzio 1993:33.

1449. EVOSTC 1997: Recovery Status.

1450. Holloway 1996:84.

1451. http://response.restoration.noaa.gov/bat2/recovery.html.

1452. Wiens 1996; Wiens adds that the research he has done was supported by Exxon but carried out and interpreted independently.

1453. Holloway 1996:84.

1454. Knickerbocker 1999.

1455. Raloff 1993; Holloway 1996:85–6.

1456. Hoke 1991:24; Raloff 1993.

1457. Holloway 1996:85.

1458. Holloway 1996:88.

1459. Anon. 1993a.

1460. Walker 1998.

1461. EPA 1998a:2.

1462. EPA 1997c:2.

1463. EPA 1997a; NRDC 1999.

1464. The EU average is merely the average of the 10–12 relevant states (France did not report in 1999 and is not included in EU 2000b, Sweden and Finland have only participated since 1995, and Austria and Luxembourg have no sea access). The simple average was chosen since the number of sampling stations is not indicative of length of beaches. For the 2000 data for the UK, se http://www.environment-agency.gov.uk/senviro/viewpoints/3compliance/5bathing/3-5a.txt and 3-5.txt.

1465. NRDC 1999.

1466. CEQ 1996:255.

1467. NRDC 1999.

1468. NRDC 1997. However, from 1999, the wording has for unclear reasons been changed to the less clear-cut: "Because of inconsistencies in monitoring and closing practices among states and over time, it is difficult to make comparisons between states or to assess trends over time based on the closing data" (NRDC 1999).

1469. MPM 2000:5, whereas MPM 1998 describes spatial trends.

1470. 72 percent decline of PCBs and 50 percent in total DDT from 1983 to 1996 (DETR 1998a:table 4.18).

1471. NOAA 1998; cf. CEQ 1996:252. These are the

best available, national data (Turgeon and Robertson 1995).

1472. NOAA 1998.

1473. NOAA 1998.

1474. Vitousek *et al.* 1997:11; Smil 1997; Socolow 1999:6,004; Beardsley 1997.

1475. NERI 1998A:109; EEA 1998b:210.

1476. Cf. EEA 1998b:210: "One of the major causes of immediate concern in the marine environment."

1477. GESAMP 1990:2.

1478. Vitousek *et al.* 1997:13.

1479. UNEP 2000:29: "There is a growing consensus among researchers that the scale of disruption to the nitrogen cycle may have global implications comparable to those caused by disruption to the carbon cycle." http://www.grida.no/geo2000/english/0036.htm.

1480. Data for 1920–61 are for production, and growth is expressed as a seven-year moving average, except at edges.

1481. Smil 1990:424.

1482. Frink *et al.* 1999:1,175.

1483. Frink *et al.* 1999:1,175.

1484. Smil 1997.

1485. Frink *et al.* 1999:1,180.

1486. 80 Tg, 40 Tg and 20 Tg respectively; Vitousek *et al.* 1997:5–6.

1487. Vitousek *et al.* 1997.

1488. Cited in Smil 1997.

1489. Smil 1990:423; Frink *et al.* 1999:1,175.

1490. The total protein is lower than the crop total, since about 25 percent of human protein intake comes from fish as well as meat and dairy foodstuffs produced by grazing (Smil 1998).

1491. Goklany 1998. FAO 2000a shows an increase in arable and permanent crop land from 1346 Mha to 1512 Mha from 1961 to 1998.

1492. 265 Mha cropland in 1700 (Richards 1990:164) compared to 1,346 Mha in 1961 (FAO 2000a).

1493. With 40 percent of all crop nitrogen stemming from synthetic fertilizer (Smil 1997) and 1960 using just one-eighth of the present-day nitrogen, 1960 fertilizer level could only produce 65 percent on the present-day area (100 percent-(40 percent*7/8)), needing about 53 percent more area. Cf. calculation in Frink *et al.* 1999:1,179, noting a decrease of 47 percent in production from reliance on air deposition (in line with the above calculation), but when factoring in the need for crop rotation the actual land productivity declines by 80 percent, thus indicating a need for some four times more area.

1494. 50 percent of 1,512 Mha (FAO 2000a) of 3,454 Mha forests (FAO 1997c:10).

1495. Frink *et al.* 1999:1,179.

1496. HWG 1998, http://www.nos.noaa.gov/products/pubs_hypox.html.

1497. Rabalais *et al.* 1999:117ff.

1498. Rabalais *et al.* 1999:1.

1499. Rabalais *et al.* 1999:1, 117ff.

1500. Rabalais *et al.* 1999:xv, 93ff.

1501. Rabalais *et al.* 1999:xiv.

1502. Not 1988, where only 40 km^2 were affected. However, the latest years have reached upwards to 15,000–18,000 km^2 *et al.* 1999:7).

1503. "The sediment geochemistry record indicates that while there was probably some oxygen stress on the Louisiana shelf as early as the turn of the century, there was a striking increase in that stress starting roughly during the 1940s and 1950s" (HWG 1999:19; cf. Rabalais *et al.* 1999:103).

1504. Rabalais *et al.* 1999:106ff. We see the same situation in Denmark. Oxygen depletion has always been a recurring problem in Danish waters. The biggest depletion catastrophe is believed to have hit 900 years ago, when the sea bed off the island of Funen was dead 40 years in succession (Flemming Olsen, Head of Dept of Thermal Material Processes at Denmark's Technical University [DTU], in *Ingeniøren*, 1997(41):12; the reference is from Gerlach, *Nitrogen, Phosphorous, Plankton and Oxygen Deficiency in the German Bight and in Kiel Bay*, Sonderheft, 1990:7. Kieler Meeresforschungen). The lack of oxygen made it extremely difficult to catch enough fish to feed the population, and it managed to give King Oluf the nickname Hunger before he was deposed for the same reason. Records exist which clearly suggest that there was oxygen depletion during the first part of the twentieth century; 1937 and 1947 in particular were years with low counts of life at the bottom of the sea, and vulnerable inlets such as Mariager Fjord, Flensburg Fjord and Aabenraa Fjord were affected by oxygen depletion (Flemming Møhlenberg, chief biologist at the Water Quality Institute, Vandkvalitetsinstitutet, in *Ingeniøren*, 1997(45):10). Unfortunately, no statistics exist from that period. On the other hand, there has been a constant increase in the frequency of oxygen depletion since the early 1980s. This comes as no surprise, though, as monitoring has also increased

(*Ingeniøren*, 1997(45):10). All things considered, however, there is good reason to assume that the oxygen depletion episodes have become more frequent and more widespread over the last 20 years.

1505. Diaz and Solow 1999:8.

1506. Diaz and Solow 1999:28ff.

1507. Diaz and Solow 1999:29.

1508. "The economic assessment based on fisheries data, however, failed to detect effects attributable to hypoxia. Overall, fisheries landings statistics for at least the last few decades have been relatively constant. The failure to identify clear hypoxic effects in the fisheries statistics does not necessarily mean that they are absent" (Diaz and Solow 1999:8–9).

1509. Diaz and Solow 1999:8.

1510. Diaz and Solow 1999:23.

1511. These figures show – more meaningfully – the actual nitrogen load into the water and not how much nitrogen has been used at the source (Smith and Alexander 2000:1).

1512. Other point sources include plastics and nitrogen fertilizer manufacturers, refuse systems, beef cattle feedlots, wet corn milling, steel mills and petroleum refineries (Goolsby *et al.* 1999:52).

1513. The direct atmospheric deposition contributes only about 1 percent (Goolsby *et al.* 1999:15, 77).

1514. Goolsby *et al.* 1999:14–15.

1515. Not surprisingly, the fertilizer industry is somewhat more skeptical of the soundness of these conclusions (Carey *et al.* 1999).

1516. HWG 1999:8.

1517. HWG 1999:8.

1518. Brezonik *et al.* 1999:xv–xvi.

1519. Mitsch *et al.* 1999:xii.

1520. Mitsch *et al.* 1999:27–9.

1521. Doering *et al.* 1999:33.

1522. Doering *et al.* 1999:33 – actually 21.8 percent (p. 114).

1523. Doering *et al.* 1999:112.

1524. Doering *et al.* 1999:33.

1525. Doering *et al.* 1999:40ff.

1526. Actually, 18.8 percent (Doering *et al.* 1999:114).

1527. Doering *et al.* 1999:112, 114, 40.

1528. Doering *et al.* 1999:133.

1529. Doering *et al.* 1999:132, 133. Assuming there is a knowing-it-is-there value (or technically non-use value) is quite reasonable. Tietenberg mentions the example that if the federal government decided to sell Grand Canyon to a chicken farmer to serve as a place to store manure, feathers and chicken entrails, it is easy to imagine that even citizens who have never been, and never plan to go, to Grand Canyon would be outraged (2000:37–8). The question, of course, is how great the non-use value is for more wetland.

1530. Brezonik *et al.* 1999:xv–xvi.

1531. Doering *et al.* 1999:57.

1532. Doering *et al.* 1999:128.

1533. Kenetech 1994:3.

1534. Using the average cost per life-year of $62 (Hahn 1996:236).

1535. Beardsley 1997.

1536. UNEP 2000:363, http://www.grida.no/geo2000/english/0237.htm.

1537. Vitousek and Mooney 1997.

1538. It is perhaps worth pointing out that ecological farming will not lessen the problem of nitrogen leaching, since if anything it leaches more (IFA and UNEP 2000:38). Thus, only by using less fertilizer will leaching be diminished, but this just means that more land needs to be ploughed up. (Of course, this argument requires that municipal sewage treatment plants contribute little nitrogen, as in Figure 107.)

1539. Socolow 1999:6,004.

1540. Socolow 1999:6,004; Vitousek *et al.* 1997:6.

1541. Socolow 1999:6,004.

1542. EU 1980; EU 1999:175. The EU also has a lower guide level of 25 mg/l. The US limit is 10 mg/l, but measured in nitrogen only, approximately equal to 44 mg/l of nitrate (IRIS 1991)

1543. And in some texts, still are, see e.g. Christensen 2000:3.

1544. *Jyllands-Posten*, 9 October 1986, section 1, p. 9.

1545. Wolfson and D'Itri 1993; L'hirondel 1999:120.

1546. This, as well as what follows, is based on EPA documentation and literature (IRIS 1991). Please note that the Americans alternate between two standards of measurement: nitrate and nitrogen-in-nitrate. The WHO limit value is 50 mg/l, which is equivalent to around 11 mg/l. In the US the limit value is 10 mg/l.

1547. Poul Bonnevie, *Jyllands-Posten*, 3 December 1986, section 1, p. 9.

1548. Lack 1999:1,681; reported incidences per 100,000 are 0.26 in Hungary, 0.56 in Slovakia, 0.74 in Romania and 1.26 in Albania.

1549. L'hirondel 1999:124.

1550. IRIS 1991 cites Cornblath and Hartmann (1948), Simon *et al.* (1964) and Toussaint and Selenka (1970).

1551. Poul Bonnevie, *Jyllands-Posten,* 3 December 1986, section 1, p. 9.

1552. Cantor 1997:296.

1553. Cantor 1997:292.

1554. IRIS 1991 reports on a whole series of experiments which show that nitrates have no developmental or reproductive effects even at levels which exceed normal intake a thousandfold.

1555. The EEA also accepts that methemoglobinemia occurs only way above 50 mg/l and that the cancer link is at best "suggestive." Surprisingly, EEA concludes: "Nevertheless, these two factors together totally justify a precautionary approach being taken in the establishment of this parameter" (1999:175). It is perhaps also worth pointing out that a recent study (Yang *et al.* 1997) found that while nitrate was not related to stomach cancer, water hardness was – the less hard the water, the higher the risk of gastric cancer. Should this necessarily make us target water hardness at great cost – or should we try to replicate the study first, and if this does not succeed then maybe attempt to regulate more pressing problems first?

1556. Shiklomanov 1993:15, 18.

1557. The finding is roughly equivalent to Grossman and Krueger 1995:364. Shafik points out, however, that her result may be biased, since possibly only the most polluted rivers are monitored in rich countries, 1994:765.

1558. Smith *et al.* 1993a; DEP 1998:5.

1559. DEP 1998:7 also speaks of a "consistent increase" in dissolved oxygen for 1998, but presents a shorter time-series which differs from DEP 1997:38.

1560. EEA 1999:173; Gillfillan 1995:figure 43.

1561. DEP 1998:7.

1562. DEP 1998:7; 1997:55.

1563. This is the result from Grossman and Krueger (1995:364), and also the finding of Torras and Boyce (1998:157), whereas Shafik (1994:764) saw a declining effect.

1564. DEP 1997:11; Gillfillan 1995:figure 42.

1565. EEA 1995:84; 1999:172.

1566. Measuring organic matter in terms of Biochemical Oxygen Demand or BOD (EEA 1995:87, 82).

1567. UK EA 2000: http://www.environment-agency.gov.uk / s-enviro / viewpoints / 3compliance / 2fwater-qual/3-2-1.html.

1568. DETR 1998b:4.

1569. Smith *et al.* 1993a.

1570. The Rhine has shown similar improvements since 1970 – with 4-fold to 8-fold declines in copper, zinc, cadmium and lead (Scholten *et al.* 1998:832), and the Thames has shown declines of 30–50 percent for Ag, Cd, Cu, Pb and Zn, and 70 percent decrease for Hg (Wiese *et al.* 1997).

1571. Data from NCBP are moving three-year averages; 1987 is not shown because only 17 observations (of 3,839). Data from Great Lakes are an average of all five lakes.

1572. Not shown is dieldrin, falling some 78 percent.

1573. SOLEC 1995.

1574. Schmitt and Bunck 1995:413.

1575. "The value of the Herring Gull as a chemical indicator will remain, and probably increase, as contaminant levels become harder to measure in water, fish or sediments" (SOLEC 1999:18).

1576. A find that it is replicated in the studies of fish (Hesselberg and Gannon 1995).

1577. Gore 1992:145. Gore also talks of "vast mountain ranges of waste" (p. 147).

1578. Gore 1992:145.

1579. Gore 1992:151.

1580. Asimov and Pohl 1991:144. Likewise, *Get a grip on Ecology* tells us about "landfill space running out," (Burne 1999:137).

1581. Chertow 1998.

1582. The data come from EPA 1999b and 2000c.

1583. Simon 1996:277.

1584. Simon 1996:277.

1585. Depositing 110 million metric tons for 100 years yields 1.1e10 tons. Since one ton of garbage occupies approximately 1.43 m^3 (Ågerup 1998:110), this gives us 1.573e10 m^3, close to 30 m x 22,898 m x 22,898 m = 1.573e10 m^3, or a square 14.23 miles on the side, 100 feet deep.

1586. USBC 2000c.

1587. Using the cumulative growth rate of total waste per person for 1990–2005 (0.07 percent) and using the middle population projection from USBC 2000c, yields a total waste production of 1.727e10 tons. With one ton using 1.43 m^3 (Ågerup 1998:110), this gives us 2.469e10 m^3, close to 30 m x28,688 m x 28,688 m = 2.469e10 m^3, or a square 17.83 miles on the side, 100 feet deep.

1588. Woodward County area is 1,242 square

miles (USBC 1998b), making the 17.83 mi x 17.83mi=318 mi^2 constitute 25.6 percent.

1589. 0.45 percent of Oklahoma which is 69,903 mi^2 (USBC 2001b:227).

1590. The US landmass is 3,717,796 mi^2 (USBC 2001b:227).

1591. 318 mi2/50 = 5.36 mi^2, with 2.52 mi x 2.52 mi = 6.35 mi^2.

1592. Wernick *et al.* 1996.

1593. Wernick *et al.* 1996.

1594. Rathje and Murphy 1992:109.

1595. Goodstein 1995.

1596. ACS 1999:4. For spice death, see exposition of Scheuplein (1991), Figure 128, p. 236.

1597. OECD 1999:164.

1598. "Waste statistics for England and Wales are not available readily" (UK EA 2000: http://www.environment-agency.gov.uk//s-enviro / stresses / 5waste-arisings/2disposal/5-2.html; OECD 1999:164).

1599. The UK annual landfill is 21.8e6 tons or 20.185 percent of the American. Thus the total area will be 318 mi^2 x 20.185% = 64 mi^2 or a square 8 miles on each side. The Isle of Man is 227 mi^2 (http://www.gov.im/geography.html).

1600. EPA 1999b:33ff.

1601. Wernick *et al.* 1996:figure 5.

1602. Wernick *et al.* 1996:figure 5.

1603. A Danish mainstream politician claims that "all forms of waste which can be used in one form or another should be considered as resources. For this reason, economics should not dictate whether or not Denmark's refuse and recycling policy should be further developed. This should be determined solely out of consideration for raw materials and the consumption of resources so we are able to protect the air, water, and the earth" (http://www.radikale.dk/meninger/251.html).

1604. Pearce 1997.

1605. E.g. Hanley and Slark 1994; Ackerman 1997. Compare Gore's story of the recyclers, finding no buyers for the material, and wanting public support (1992:159).

1606. We must assume that the best recycling ideas have already been exploited and that yields from further recycling will be lower. If we increase the level of recycling, social profitability will thus decline.

1607. Cf. also to the fall in DDE (a breakdown product of DDT) in the milk of Danish women from 1.05 mg/kg fat in 1982 to 0.2 mg/kg fat in 1993, Hilbert *et al.* 1996:125.

1608. The US National Contaminant Biomonitoring Program also measured starlings all over the country, finding clear and general downwards trends in persistent contaminants like a decline of 75 percent in DDT (CEQ 1982:242; Schmitt and Bunck 1995:413; NCBP 2000b).

1609. PCB>1 ppm (CEQ 1989:417).

1610. Jacobson and Jacobson 1997.

1611. EC-E 1999:Summary report, p. 2.

1612. Anon. 1999e, and a "hero" of that century, too, in Golden 2000.

1613. "She is deservedly hailed as the mother of modern environmentalism" (Golden 2000).

1614. Carson 1962:2.

1615. Carson 1962:15.

1616. Matthiessen 1999.

1617. Actually, Carson is still used as the first reference in the US Geological Survey's latest evaluation of US water quality (1999:59).

1618. Carson 1962:15.

1619. For an easy if somewhat casual overview, see Lieberman and Kwon 1998.

1620. A *Lancet* 1992 editorial described the Love Canal incident thus: "Love Canal served for more than 20 years as a dumping site for organic pesticides, and in the 1950s was developed as a residential area. More than two hundred chemicals have been found at the dump site, including benzene, trichloroethylene, and dioxin, all three being well-established carcinogens in animal experiments. Higher frequencies of low birthweight and growth retardation were found among children born at the dump site but there was no increase in total mortality, mortality for any cancer, or evidence of genetic damage even after 20 years" (Anon. 1992b; cf. Vrijheid 2000). Love Canal became the immediate background for the passing of the Superfund. Similarly, the Times Beach was later repudiated in *New York Times* by the very official who urged the evacuation, Dr. Vernon Houk: "Given what we now know about this chemical's toxicity and its effects on human health, it looks as though the evacuation was unnecessary" and "Times Beach was an overreaction . . . It was based on the best scientific information we had at the time. It turns out we were in error" (Schneider 1991:A1, D23).

1621. Carson 1962:219ff.

1622. Colborn *et al.* 1996:202.

1623. LCVEF 2000:8. These five get 75–81 percent, with a marked drop down to number 6 (ocean/beach protection) at 66 percent.

1624. Gillespie 1999.

1625. *Encyclopedia Britannica* defines an epidemic as "an occurrence of disease that is temporarily of high prevalence." But it also notes that "By the late 20th century the definition of epidemic had been extended to include outbreaks of any chronic disease (e.g., heart disease or cancer) influenced by the environment." http://www.britannica.com/bcom/eb/article/printable/1/0,5722,33361,00.html.

1626. Kidd 2000.

1627. Rosner and Markowitz 1999.

1628. Brundtland 1999.

1629. Anon. 1997d.

1630. Anon. 1999a.

1631. Anon. 1997d.

1632. Baret 1998: "The nutrient content of plants is determined primarily by heredity. Mineral content may be affected by the mineral content of the soil, but this has no significance in the overall diet." Similarly, Ovesen (1995:71) finds no difference in overall contents.

1633. Bogo 1999.

1634. Pimentel *et al.* 1998:817.

1635. Gifford 2000.

1636. Anon. 1998b.

1637. Dunlap 1991b:15.

1638. 21 percent believed the two to be of equal importance.

1639. Dunlap 1991b:15. Notice, though, that although we publicly believe the environment causes health problems and cancer, we seem to be much more clear-headed when confronted with personal cancer – when asked for perceived reasons for an actual cancer, most state heredity, physiology and personal actions, whereas "very few respondents cited environmental factors" (Vernon 1999).

1640. Colborn *et al.* 1998:218.

1641. 79 percent from 151 to 270.5 million (USBC 1999a:8).

1642. USBC 1975:I, 58.

1643. See HHS 1997:136.

1644. USBC 1975:I, 15; 1999a:15, calculated from interval midpoints. The median age has increased from 23 to 35 (USBC 1999a:14).

1645. Peto *et al.* 1992. The same conclusion can be reached by looking at the geographical differences in lung cancer incidence (Devesa *et al.* 1999).

1646. Peto *et al.* 1994:535.

1647. Estimated from Peto *et al.* 1992:1,273. In 1965 smoking-related lung cancers (both sexes) make up 68 percent of all smoking related cancers, standardized to world population, in 1995, 72.3 percent. This corresponds well to the actual number estimates for the US in Peto *et al.* 1994:534–5.

1648. Peto *et al.* 1994:532–3.

1649. Peto *et al.* 1994:232–3, estimating the 1955 all cancer figure.

1650. Carson 1962:227.

1651. Carson vacillates between just leukemia and all lymphatic and haematopoietic diseases, but here, owing to better registration and clearer discussion, the focus is on leukemia.

1652. Carson 1962:227.

1653. Kinlen and John 1994; Stiller and Boyle 1996; Kinlen *et al.* 1995; Ross *et al.* 1999; McCann 1998; Reynolds 1998a.

1654. Reynolds 1998a.

1655. Ross *et al.* 1999.

1656. Kinlen and John 1994; cf. Stiller and Boyle 1996.

1657. UNPD 1998a:94.

1658. Peto *et al.* 1992:1,278.

1659. ACS 1999:1, 12. Lung cancer mortality is 23 times higher for smoking men compared to male never-smokers, and 13 times higher for women smokers compared to female never-smokers (ACS 1999:25).

1660. CDC 1999d:986, 988; 1997a:5.

1661. CDC 1999d:988.

1662. The consumption for men and women was crudely estimated from the difference in smoking ratios. Unfortunately, we do not have figures before 1955 (54 percent men, 24 percent women, CDC 1997a:35), so conservatively, this proportion has been used for 1900–55. Moreover, men smoked about 10 percent more cigarettes than women in 1987–91 (CDC 1997a:21), and this number has – somewhat heroically – been used as an estimate for the entire period.

1663. Anon. 1997d.

1664. From 18,734 to 41,737 in 1998; WHO 2000d, CDC 2001a.

1665. ACS 1999:8; Byrne 2000.

1666. See Fraser and Shavlik 1997.

1667. Byrne 2000.

1668. Byrne 2000.

1669. Byrne 2000. Velie *et al.* (2000) find this for women with no previous history of benign breast disease.

1670. From 1976–80 to 1988–91 the average white female weight increased by 3.9 kg, while the average height only increased by 1 cm (Kuczmarski *et al.* 1994:208). Also the British have become more fat. The percentage of obese adults increased from 7 percent in 1980 to 20 percent in 1998 (Holmes 2000:28).

1671. Byrne 2000. Alcohol consumption has been increasing over time from 1935 to around 1980, decreasing slightly ever since, and mirroring the female increase in share of drinkers (NIAAA 1997:6–7, http://silk.nih.gov/silk/niaaa1/database/dkpat1.txt; Newport 1999).

1672. Protheroe *et al.* 1999.

1673. Ekbom *et al.* 2000.

1674. Byrne 2000.

1675. Chu *et al.* 1996.

1676. Chu *et al.* 1996.

1677. Hayes 2000.

1678. Hayes 2000.

1679. Hayes 2000.

1680. Feuer *et al.* 1999:1,030.

1681. "PSA testing may lead to a sustained decline in prostate cancer mortality" (Hankey *et al.* 1999:1,024).

1682. Devesa *et al.* 1995.

1683. "Cancer death rates were decreasing for all 10 leading cancer mortality sites, except for non-Hodgkin's lymphoma and female lung cancer" (Wingo *et al.* 1999:678).

1684. Cited in Ames and Gold 1998:206.

1685. Carson 1962:227.

1686. Note that *in situ* cervical cancer (part of female genital cancer) drops some 74 percent within the two years 1996–7 after being reasonably stable over 23 years. Since this seems likely to be a coding or data error, these last years have been left out.

1687. Wingo *et al.* 1999:678.

1688. By number of *in situ* and malignant incidences of the five sites over the period 1973–97 (1,566,880) compared to the total registered number of incidences (2,453,706) (SEER 2000b). This percentage (63.9 percent) is about the same as in 1973 (62.6 percent) and in 1997 (63.0 percent).

1689. ACS 2000.

1690. Ries *et al.* 2000.

1691. ACS 2000; Chu *et al.* 1996.

1692. ACS 2000.

1693. SEER 2000b.

1694. ACS 2000.

1695. ACS 2000.

1696. Doll and Peto 1981:1,276.

1697. Walsh 1996:67, Merrill *et al.* 1999:179, 185–86, Feuer *et al.*1993.

1698. See e.g. Walsh 1996:68, Bunker *et al.* 1998:1309.

1699. Feuer *et al.*1993:896.

1700. Anon. 1997a.

1701. SEER 2000:I-18.

1702. Feuer *et al.* 1993:894; Merrill *et al.* 1999:188 has a table, where the percentage for 30-year-old white women most certainly is a typo – it is way higher than the equivalent black rate.

1703. These are data for British women, Bunker *et al.* 1998:1308.

1704. Anon. 1997a.

1705. Marino and Gerlach 1999.

1706. Median years, Marino and Gerlach 1999.

1707. Lifetime risk for injury is estimated from yearly injury rates, and lifetime heart disease death from current death figures.

1708. Devesa *et al.* 1995; Hayes 2000.

1709. Hankey *et al.* 1999; Hayes 2000. "For prostate cancer, striking increases in incidence rates occurred during the late 1980's and early 1990's. These increases occurred along with rising use of prostate specific antigen (PSA) as a screening test. In Connecticut, as in certain other cancer registries, the incidence rates for prostate cancer reached a peak in 1992 and then declined for most age groups" (CTR 1999:3).

1710. Doll and Peto 1981:1,277.

1711. SEER 2000b.

1712. Reynolds 1998a; Cushman 1997.

1713. Cit. in Reynolds 1998b.

1714. Linet *et al.* 1999:1,051.

1715. Linet *et al.* 1999:1,051.

1716. SEER 2000a:XVI, 3.

1717. Devesa *et al.* 1995.

1718. Devesa *et al.* 1995.

1719. EEA 1999:264, 268–9.

1720. LCVEF 2000:8. Equally, the US Geological Survey points out that "Concerns about the unintended effects of pesticides continue to this day" (USGS 1999:59). One of the distinguished cancer experts points out that "public concern regarding the role of environmental pollutants in causing human cancer remains intense, and for no specific class of potential pollutant is concern more intense than for chemical pesticides" (Heath 1997).

1721. Here cited from Larsen 1992:116; see also Cheeseman and Machuga 1997:296.

1722. This is naturally an incredibly brief résumé of something extremely complicated. Experiments on animals have primarily been carried out when human studies were not available (which they usually are not). See Larsen 1992:116ff and EPA 1993.

1723. Benford and Tennant 1997:24ff.

1724. Benford and Tennant 1997:34–6.

1725. See Larsen 1992:117–18; Poulsen 1992:41ff.; EPA 1993:2.1.2. It is, however, also possible, if good human data are available, for the limit to be as high as 1 (i.e. ADI = NOEL).

1726. Notice that the factor 10 does not in itself have any "scientific" foundation – it is just a rough rule-of-thumb (Rodricks 1992:194).

1727. See e.g. EEA 1998b:187–91.

1728. Dunlap and Beus 1992.

1729. "The Danish Environment Agency, the Institute for Food Safety and Toxicology of the Veterinary and Foods Directorate as well as the Danish Toxicology Centre point out that the limit values of pesticides are determined politically at a previous detection limit of 0.1µg/l. If one were to set a health-related limit value for pesticides, it would be far higher than the current political one, according to head of department John Christian Larsen of the Department of Biochemical and Molecular Toxicology of the Institute for Food Safety and Toxicology" (*Ingeniøren*, http://www.ing.dk/arkiv/pesti5.html). See also Poulsen 1992:40–1.

1730. Leading article in *MiljøDanmark*, 1 January 1998; http://mstex03.mst.dk/fagomr/02040000.htm.

1731. *Ingeniøren*, http://www.ing.dk/arkiv/pesti5.html.

1732. EEA 1998b:188.

1733. EEA 1998b:190.

1734. This is a rather conservative estimate. The figures fluctuate between 0.6 percent and 2.9 percent. See DK VFA 1996b:58; 1997:3; CEQ 1997:339.

1735. Putnam and Gerrior 1999:148.

1736. In 1996 there were 14 transgressions totaling 9,528 mg/kg out of 1,273 samples, or approx. 75 µg/kg. For 711 pounds or 322.5 kg fruit and vegetables give 24.19 mg of pesticide per year. This is naturally only a rough estimate – the various pesticides produce widely differing effects for the same weight and part of the pesticide content not consumed since it is contained in the husk. However, it must be taken into account that when only transgressions are included, pesticide intake is simultaneously underestimated. The Danish Veterinary and Food Administration estimates an annual intake of 0–5 mg (DK VFA 1998).

1737. Ames *et al.* (1987:272) give 45 µg/day (plus 105 µg, made up of three non-carcinogenic pesticides), compared to a maximum intake through water of 2 liters per day, and therefore 0.2 µg pesticide per day.

1738. The EPA states that "pesticide levels in drinking water normally result in a much lower exposure than exposure through food or through handling pesticide products" (EPA 1990:6). In 1994 the EPA estimated that drinking water does not constitute an essential share of exposure to pesticides, cited in Ritter 1997. See also Toppari *et al.* 1996:782: "Diet is the major route of exposure for the general population."

1739. It is fairly well accepted that the toxicity of most substances is "sigmoid-shaped". If one plots the dose on one axis and percentage mortality in a population on the other, very small doses will kill close to 0 percent, whereas very high doses will reach saturation point just below 100 percent. This means that less than a very small dose or more than a very high dose has very little effect on mortality (Dragsted 1992:78).

1740. "Cancer has also dominated the scientific research programme exploring possible human health effects from chemical contaminants in the environment" (Colborn *et al.* 1998:202).

1741. 23 percent in the US (Ames and Gold 1997), 25 percent in Denmark (Middellevetidsudvalget 1994b:34) and 21 percent in the Western world, 2.421 million deaths of a total of 11.436 million in 1992 (WHO 1992:29).

1742. Doll and Peto 1981, produced for the US Congress. This study is frequently referred to and is generally accepted as valid. WCRF 1997:75: "This analysis was done with specific reference to the USA but may be taken to apply elsewhere." See also Ritter *et al.* 1997; Rodricks 1992:118.

1743. Peto *et al.* 1992:1,277–8.

1744. There is considerable uncertainty about this figure: Doll and Peto estimate an interval between 10 percent and 70 percent. Willett (1995) sets it at 32 percent.

1745. Despite substantial geographical differences between different types of cancer, immigrants usually adopt the same cancer rate as the population they join within one or two generations (WCRF 1997:75).

1746. Observant readers will notice that the percentage figures only add up to 95 percent, which is due to uncertainty as to the distribution of factors. In addition, a cancer estimate of less than 1 percent of industrial products has also been omitted. Apart from the "best estimate," which has been used here, Doll and Peto also give a range of "acceptable estimates" which will be discussed under the individual factors.

1747. Ames *et al.* 1987:271.

1748. WCRF 1997:24, Mintz 1985:chapter 3.

1749. WCRF 1997:542; Ames and Gold 1997.

1750. WCRF 1997:436; Ames and Gold 1997.

1751. WCRF 1997:540; Doll and Peto 1981:1,235.

1752. Ames and Gold 1997 estimate that chronic infection can cause as much as one-third of all cases of cancer.

1753. Doll and Peto 1981:1,237–8.

1754. Devesa *et al.* 1995:tables 1and 2; Doll and Peto 1981:1,253–4.

1755. Doll and Peto 1981:1,224–5: Ames *et al.* 1987:273; WCRF 1997:398ff.

1756. Doll and Peto 1981:1,252–3.

1757. Doll and Peto 1981:1,249.

1758. Doll and Peto 1981:1,250.

1759. Dunlap 1991b:15.

1760. LCVEF 2000:8.

1761. Wynder and Gori 1977.

1762. Wynder and Gori (1977) assigned 40–60 percent cancer from diet, 9–30 percent from tobacco (9 percent for women, 30 percent for men), 9 percent from radiation, sun and medical, 0.8–5 percent from alcohol, 4 percent for women from estrogenic products, and 2–5 percent from occupation.

1763. McGinnis and Foege 1993. Note, the total percentage of deaths explained is only 50.

1764. McGinnis and Foege 1993:2,208. Since the total percentage of deaths explained is only 50, the individual causes are 40 percentage points (19 percent tobacco, 14 percent diet, 5 percent alcohol, 1 percent motor vehicles). Likewise, McGinnis and Foege only attribute 3 percent to toxic agents, making it 6 percent of the explained deaths.

1765. McGinnis and Foege 1993:2,209.

1766. Gough 1989:929.

1767. Gough 1989:929.

1768. Cited in Gough 1989:928. The EPA states the number of cancer incidences (to 1.03 percent), and mortality from cancer fluctuates between 50 and 100 percent. The EPA adds in its footnote that the risk analysis uses a linear model, in which "the slope value [potency] is an upper bound in the sense that the true value (which is unknown) is not likely to exceed the upper bound and may be much lower, with a lower bound approaching zero" (p. 929).

1769. NRC 1996:5.

1770. WCRF 1997:475.

1771. WCRF 1997:477.

1772. Ritter *et al.* 1997:2,019.

1773. Ritter *et al.* 1997:2,029.

1774. Viel *et al.* 1998.

1775. The file-drawer problem may also occur because many investigations never find anything interesting and are therefore never published.

1776. In statistical terms this is the equivalent of carrying out a whole series of post hoc tests, severely compounding the risk of a Type I error.

1777. Acquavella *et al.* 1998:73. One should be aware that Acquavella is affiliated with a pesticide organization although this study was written together with external people and the paper is peer reviewed. The National Cancer Institute's own statistician Aron Blair believes that the study "obscured the slight excess risk that farmers seem to carry for some cancers besides lip" (Saphir 1998).

1778. See e.g. an overview of carcinogens in Grandjean 1998:45.

1779. EPA 1998b.

1780. Acquavella *et al.* 1998:73, as mentioned above. There is also the question of the extent to which farmers have different lifestyles possibly compensating for extra cancer deaths, which is virtually impossible to control for.

1781. Rodricks 1992:69–70.

1782. Rodricks 1992:70. Almost 40,000 individual tissue samples have to be tested in connection with just a single study (p. 131).

1783. The Maximum Tolerable Dose (MTD) is usually set through shorter, sub-chronic studies (Rodricks 1992:72).

1784. We know that all the substances that have proven to be carcinogenic in humans have also been so in at least one species of animal. It does not, however, follow that all substances which in large quantities cause cancer in some species of animal also do so in low doses in humans (Rodricks 1992:138).

1785. The so-called linear or "no threshold" assumption; see explanation below.

1786. Rodricks 1992:188–9; Grandjean 1998:97.

1787. Rodricks 1992:39.

1788. Rodricks 1992:174ff.; Grandjean 1998:94–6.

1789. In principle you draw a curve through the data, insert the low 95 percent confidence interval and locate the dose which produces tumors at 10 percent extra (12 percent in the figure used as an illustration, at about 125 ppm ETU). Then you draw a straight line down to (0, no effect); EPA 1996c. This increase is still not official, but it is considerably easier to explain as well as producing more or less the same result as a multi-stage model (EPA 1996c:8).

1790. Rodricks 1992:167; Gough 1989:929. The increase is probably incorrect for substances which do not initiate cancer by influencing the DNA (non-genotoxic substances), and inconclusive for genotoxic substances (Rodricks 1992:167–9; Grandjean 1998:46, 97).

1791. Rodricks 1992:166ff.

1792. Ames *et al.* 1987, 1990a, 1990b; Gold *et al.* 1992; Ames *et al.* 1993; Ames and Gold 1990, 1997, 1998, 2000.

1793. Strictly speaking, it is a test for genotoxicity of a chemical (Rodricks 1992:152). Ames also helped to ensure bans on many dangerous synthetic substances in the 1970s (Postrel 1991).

1794. NRC 1996:306ff.

1795. *Silent Spring* by Rachel Carson (1962) "caught the cresting wave of public anxiety and rode it to the top of the best-seller list" (Colborn *et al.* 1998:65; Rodricks 1992:43).

1796. Carson 1962:15.

1797. Ames and Gold 1998:212.

1798. Rodricks 1992:43; NRC 1996:306, 308ff.

1799. Atkins and Norman 1998:260.

1800. Ritter *et al.* 1997:2,021.

1801. Ames *et al.* 1987:272.

1802. Ames *et al.* 1990a; Gold *et al.* 1992:261; Ames and Gold 2000:5.

1803. It is unfortunately an expression of the environmental debate's frequently amazing superficiality that 99.99 percent happens to be the most popular Ames quote among advocates and opponents alike, when it is obvious that this is not his primary message.

1804. And caffeine is still uncertain; Ames and Gold 2000:6. It is also often pointed out that a cup of coffee contains at least 10 mg of natural pesticides, which is more than the total amount of synthetic pesticides the average American consumes in a whole year (Gold *et al.* 1992:262). Once again, this is a good rhetorical point, but an irrelevant one – the crucial thing is to compare their total carcinogenic potency.

1805. Ames *et al.* 1987:272.

1806. Gold *et al.* 1992:263.

1807. Ames *et al.* 1987:272. If data are available for both mice and rats, that from the most sensitive species is used, in accordance with EPA guidelines (Gold *et al.* 1992:263).

1808. Three cups of coffee also contain catechol, furfural and hydroquinone, giving risks of 0.02 percent, 0.02 percent and 0.006 percent (Ames and Gold 1998:214), but only the largest risk has been denoted.

1809. Ames and Gold 1998:214; Gold *et al.* 1992:264.

1810. Ames and Gold 2000:4; Gold *et al.* 1992:262.

1811. Gold *et al.* 1992:264.

1812. Unfortunately, not enough tests have been done for HERP to be indicated for all pesticides.

1813. Ames and Gold 1998:214; Ames *et al.* 1987:273. Notice, calculations with ETU use the true average of 0.0017197 percent.

1814. The average American consumes 2.18 gallons of ethanol a year, or 22.6 ml/day (http://silk.nih.gov/silk/niaaa1/database/consum01.txt).

1815. Ames and Gold 1998:214; Ames *et al.* 1987:273. Alcohol is also verifiably carcinogenic (WCRF 1997:398ff.)

1816. WCRF 1997:469.

1817. Ames *et al.* 1990; Ames and Gold 1997.

1818. This primarily applies to non-mutagens. Similar arguments can be put forward for mutations, which overburden the DNA repair mechanisms, see Ames and Gold 1997.

1819. Ames and Gold 1997.

1820. Ames *et al.* 1990b.

1821. Here I will only deal with the most important ones; the rest can be found in Ames *et al.* 1990b:7,782ff.

1822. Ames *et al.* 1990b:7,782.

1823. Ames and Gold 2000:7.

1824. Ames and Gold 2000:7.

1825. Ames *et al.* 1990b:7,782–3.

1826. Ames *et al.* 1990b:7,783.

1827. Ames and Gold 2000:7.

1828. Ames *et al.* 1987:277.

1829. This refers not to Doll and Peto's 35 percent, primarily focused on fat and meat as well as ice-cream and other low-fiber food, but to individual risks of coffee, basil and lettuce, cf. NRC 1996:309.

1830. Ames and Gold 1998:205.

1831. Scheuplein 1991. It is worth pointing out that these figures are an expression of a general *impression*, based on experience and general scientific understanding, but whether the correct figures are 0.005 percent or 0.02 percent is quite impossible to determine using statistical tools. Nonetheless I believe it is important for the sake of comprehension to have some absolute figures instead of phrases like "minimal" or "worst-case evaluation."

1832. Scheuplein's *Case I* which he refers to as "risk assessment the way the government does it" (Scheuplein 1991).

1833. ACS 1999:4.

1834. Colborn *et al.* 1996.

1835. WI 1999a:14. Cf. "Perhaps the most serious danger posed by chemicals is 'hormone mimicking,'" Christensen 2000:48.

1836. Colborn *et al.* 1996:31–4.

1837. Toppari *et al.* 1996:756ff.

1838. Toppari *et al.* 1996:753.

1839. Toppari *et al.* 1996:753; Golden *et al.* 1998:118–20.

1840. Toppari *et al.* 1996:756–7.

1841. Toppari *et al.* 1996:791, 794.

1842. Colborn *et al.* 1996:73.

1843. Colborn *et al.* 1996:76ff.

1844. Toppari *et al.* 1996:758.

1845. Colborn *et al.* 1996:76; Toppari *et al.* 1996:758.

1846. Colborn *et al.* 1996:79.

1847. Toppari *et al.* 1996:759.

1848. Colborn *et al.* (1996:95) also repeat the discussion as to whether we have been evolutionarily adapted to natural estrogens, although arguments like those above against adaptation to natural pesticides seem to be applicable.

1849. Safe 1995:349; Golden *et al.* 1998.

1850. Colborn *et al.* 1996:136.

1851. Toppari *et al.* 1996:769.

1852. Toppari *et al.* 1996:768.

1853. Colborn *et al.* 1996:172.

1854. Christensen 2000:3.

1855. Studies with 100 or more men (n = 1,500). In all, studies with 100 or more men account for 20 of Carlsen's 61 studies, but more than 90 percent of all observations (Fisch and Goluboff 1996:1,045). In actual fact the US accounts for 94 percent of all observations until 1970 (Fisch *et al.* 1996:1,013).

1856. Carlsen *et al.* 1992:610.

1857. Carlsen *et al.* 1992:612.

1858. Fannin 2000. Skakkebæk and Sharpe publicly objected to the advert (personal communication, Skakkebæk, 8 July 1998).

1859. Sharpe and Skakkebæk 1993.

1860. The increase is substantial and has been particularly drastic in Denmark (having doubled since 1959, Toppari *et al.* 1997:774), but the question has been given nowhere near the same political attention. A link between testicular cancer and sperm quality is possible though not obvious; Olsen *et al.* (1996:452) point out that large increases in the occurrence of testicular cancer were reported between 1970 and 1990, precisely during a period when it was *not* possible to prove a change in sperm counts (see the discussion in the text below). Moreover, the increase in incidence could have many other explanations, e.g. smoking (Clemmesen 1997), lack of iron (Crawford 1998), change towards a more fatty diet (Sigurdson *et al.* 1999), moderate and strenuous recreational activity in the mid-teens (Srivastava and Kreiger 2000). Moreover, there are indications that testicular cancer – like other incidence rates – is also apparently increasing because of earlier detection (Sonneveld *et al.* 1999). Both because of greater political attention and the possibly problematic link, the focus here is on the question of diminishing sperm quality.

1861. Bromwich *et al.* 1994; Sherins 1995; Auger *et al.* 1995; Irvine *et al.* 1996; Paulsen *et al.* 1996; Fisch *et al.* 1996; Fisch and Goluboff 1996; Swan *et al.* 1997.

1862. Auger *et al.* 1995; Bujan *et al.* 1996.

1863. Irvine *et al.* 1996; Suominen and Vierula 1993.

1864. Van Waeleghem *et al.* 1996; Ginsburg and Hardiman 1992; Fisch *et al.* 1996; Paulsen *et al.* 1996.

1865. Colborn *et al.* 1996:174–5. Toppari *et al.* (1996), however, describe all findings.

1866. Colborn *et al.* 1996:173.

1867. Notice that the original figure was misdrawn, but it is here drawn from the tabulated data, equivalent to Toppari *et al.* 1997:742.

1868. Fisch and Goluboff 1996.

1869. Fisch *et al.* 1996:1,011. It is not known why the figure for New York is so high.

1870. Fisch *et al.* 1997; Carlsen *et al.* 1992:612.

1871. New York accounts for 1,400 out of 1,500 before 1970, and 1,300 out of 12,040 after that (Fisch and Goluboff 1996:1,045).

1872. Fisch *et al.* 1996. It seems *completely* incomprehensible to me that the meta-study (Swan *et al.* 1997), rejects the New York problem so nonchalantly (cf. Becker and Berhane 1996). It was ascertained that there may be geographic differences; they then constructed "broad geographic regions," among other things of the *entire* US, and then finally ascertained that the differences between New York (131 million/ml) and California (72 million/ml) are just as great as the whole of Carlsen *et al.*'s fall over a period of 45 years. The fact that they decided not to analyze New York and California individually seems quite simply unreasonable. Skakkebæk states in personal correspondence (8 July 1998), that Carlsen's data include one study for New York, which for 1975 shows a sperm quality of 79 million/ml, and that one should therefore question Fisch's study, which shows 131. This seems surprising in that Skakkebæk sees no problems with the four previous studies from the first part of the period for New York in Carlsen's data, which show 120, 134, 100 and 107 million/ml. Skakkebæk himself uses two studies from England which for the same year (1989) show 91.3 and 64.5 (Carlsen *et al.* 1992:610).

1873. There are still 12,247 men and 56 studies left in the investigation; the weighted regression analysis shows that the sperm figure falls by 20 percent over 50 years but that this is not statistically significant (we cannot reject the hypothesis that the true fall is zero). Skakkebæk has personally informed me that the problem in this case was in reality not the statistical analysis of the data but the fact that I ought instead to investigate who financed Fisch (8 July 1998). Asked directly, Skakkebæk does not himself possess any knowledge that could suggest any question of conflict of interest. Nor does Skakkebæk dispute the factual information in Fisch's articles and he has said that "Fisch's data are very important" (Bauman 1996). Harry Fisch comes from the Columbia-Presbyterian Medical Center in New York. I was unable to find any accusations on the internet as regards Fisch's motives or source of finance; he is supposed to have told the *Wall Street Journal* that he had been surprised by his own findings and had expected to find a fall in semen quality (http://pw2.netcom.com/~malkin1/future.html, accessed 20 July 1998 [no longer accessible] – this is, however, not necessarily a reliable source).

1874. Personal correspondence, 9 July 1998.

1875. Olsen *et al.* 1995.

1876. Keiding and Skakkebæk 1996:450. If one tests Europe solely in the period 1971–90 this shows a clear falling tendency, although this tendency is not significant either.

1877. Saidi *et al.* 1999:460.

1878. This seems to be the essence of Keiding and Skakkebæk 1996.

1879. There are also problems with the method of collection. Several later studies collected semen through masturbation, whereas earlier studies more frequently used other methods (through intercourse), which definitely produces a higher sperm count (Swan *et al.* 1997:1,230). This does not, however, seem to be a serious problem.

1880. Swan *et al.* 1997:1,229.

1881. Swan *et al.* 1997:1,229. Here it is also noted that in a study requesting an abstinence of 3–5 days, only 66 percent complied (and this is by asking – another question is also how many of the 66 percent lied). Carlsen *et al.* state that it was impossible to monitor abstinence (1992:609).

1882. Carlsen *et al.* 1992:611.

1883. Hunt 1974:85, 87; not only did the average increase, but many more men, especially those who are married, masturbate. The average age for sperm donors in Skakkebæk's study is 30.8 years (Carlsen *et al.* 1992:609), which is why the figures used here are for 30-year-olds (even though other groups show the same tendencies).

1884. Hunt 1974:189.

1885. These are median values which are probably of the most consequence in this context. The average value has only increased from 2.5 to 2.8 (Hunt 1974:190).

1886. Blumstein and Schwartz 1983:196; Sprecher and McKinney 1993:70.

1887. Westoff 1974:137. The figure of 17 percent was corrected for a younger group of respondents in 1970 – direct analysis shows an increase of 21 percent.

1888. Sprecher and McKinney 1993:70–1.

1889. Swan *et al.* 1997:1,229. Reference is mistakenly made in the article to Bendvold 1989, the correct reference being to article no. 47 (personal correspondence with Swan, 24 July 1998).

1890. Swan *et al.* 1997:1,229.

1891. James 1980:385.

1892. Carlson *et al.* 1992:610.

1893. E.g. Anon. 1994a, 1994b; BSAEM/BSNM 1995; Gallia and Althoff 1999.

1894. Abell *et al.* 1994; Jensen *et al.* 1996. The ecologists were surprisingly compared to not-so-obviously "ordinary people," namely Danish airline workers.

1895. Christensen 2000:4.

1896. Jensen *et al.* 1996:1,844. Tina Kold Jensen agreed on this evaluation when I spoke to her (3 July 1998). It is nowhere stated in the study, but Tina Kold Jensen also told me that, amazingly, there are no differences between the drinking and smoking habits of the ecologists and the control group, Danish airline workers.

1897. DK EPA 1997b. Greenhouse gardeners did,

however, have a sperm count 20 percent inferior to that of the ecologists.

1898. Juhler *et al.* 1999.

1899. Juhler *et al.* 1999:415.

1900. James 1980:385.

1901. Looking at Europe separately, we see a decline, which, however, is not statistically significant.

1902. Sherins 1995.

1903. Joffe 2000.

1904. Fisch *et al.* 1997. The fall could conceivably be due to even more sex, although this is perhaps not quite as likely as the general sex frequency development we saw from the 1940s to the 1970s.

1905. MacLeod and Wang (1979) also show that the four occurred longer ago, although it is uncertain to what extent generalization is permissible in this study.

1906. This was also Stephen Safe's argument (1995), and it can also be found in Arnold *et al.* 1996:1,489–90.

1907. Arnold *et al.* 1996.

1908. It has often been possible to find synergy effects of 2 to 10 times but the real worry is mainly in the really *big* synergic effects described here (Raloff 1997).

1909. *Ingeniøren*, 30, 1996, section 1, p. 4.

1910. In Denmark, it was one of the fundamental elements of the fear of pesticides and the primary argument behind green movements like *ØkoVandspejlet* in their plans for the total abolition of pesticides (Teknologirådet 1997).

1911. Raloff 1997.

1912. McLachlan 1997.

1913. *Ingeniøren*, 47, 1997; http://www.ing.dk/arkiv/hormon5.html.

1914. Dr. Lynn Goldman, EPA, cited in Online 1997. "The U.S. Environmental Protection Agency (EPA) has indicated that it will not change its research or policy regarding endocrine disruption, despite the recent retraction of an influential Tulane University, New Orleans, Louisiana, study on synergy among estrogenic chemicals" (Key and Marble 1997b).

1915. Wolff *et al.* 1993.

1916. Wolff *et al.* 1993:648.

1917. Congress has earmarked funding for a large-scale breast cancer project in Long Island and northeast USA (Safe 1997b).

1918. Anon. 1993b.

1919. As summarized in Anon. 1993c.

1920. Davis and Bradlow 1995.

1921. Greene and Ratner 1994.

1922. Greene and Ratner 1994.

1923. Colborn *et al.* 1996:182. It is ironic and difficult, when reading the book, to believe Theo Colborn's assertion, that "we wrote into our book that I thought it was a very weak, very poor connection [between environmental contaminants and breast cancer]" (PBS Frontline 1998).

1924. Colborn *et al.* 1996:182. There seems, however, to be a confusion between death rates and incidence rates, all through the discussion of breast cancer.

1925. ACS 1999, CDC 2001a.

1926. Hulka and Stark 1995.

1927. Hulka and Stark 1995.

1928. Safe 1997a, 1998; Davidson and Yager 1997.

1929. NRC 1999:243–4.

1930. NCR 1999:258ff.

1931. See also Crisp *et al.* 1998:23; NRC 1999:263.

1932. NCR 1999:263.

1933. Tarone *et al.* 1997:251.

1934. Krieger *et al.* 1994:589.

1935. "Overall, these studies published prior to 1995 do not support an association between DDT metabolites or PCBs and risk of breast cancer." NCR 1999:250.

1936. Large studies: Lopez-Carrillo *et al.* 1997; Hunter *et al.* 1997; Veer *et al.* 1997; Høyer *et al.* 1998; Olaya-Conteras *et al.* 1998; Moyish *et al.* 1998; Dorgan *et al.* 1999, and small studies: Sutherland *et al.* 1996; Schecter *et al.* 1997; Liljegren *et al.* 1998; Guttes *et al.* 1998; see COC 1999:5; NRC 1999:251–5.

1937. Veer *et al.* 1997; cf. NRC 1999:256.

1938. COC 1999:6.

1939. COC 1999:5, a so-called Type I error. (This was the problem discussed in the file-drawer problem in chapter 1). The NRC (1999:257–8) makes the same observation.

1940. COC 1999:2; NRC 1999:258.

1941. NRC 1999:258.

1942. COC 1999:6.

1943. COC 1999:6.

1944. NRC 1999.

1945. NRC 1999:6.

1946. NRC 1999:272.

1947. NRC 1999:266–8.

1948. NRC 1999:272.

1949. NRC 1999:272.

1950. Crisp *et al.* 1998.

1951. Crisp *et al.* 1998:26.

1952. "Because of the limitations in virtually all of the data, the conclusions should be viewed as tenuous" (Crisp *et al.* 1998:26).

1953. Crisp *et al.* 1998:14.

1954. Marshall 1991:20.

1955. Ames and Gold 1998:214.

1956. Marshall 1991:20.

1957. Meyerhoff 1993.

1958. Anon. 1999c.

1959. Anon. 1999c.

1960. Dunlap and Beus 1992.

1961. Dunlap and Beus 1992.

1962. NRC 1996:303. See also the EPA database, 1998b.

1963. NSC 1999:16.

1964. Pimentel *et al.* (1992) find direct benefits of $16 billion, direct costs of $4 billion (the cost of pesticides) and indirect costs of another $8 billion. While it is relevant to compare the direct costs and benefits *or* to compare total costs and benefits, it produces a skewed picture to compare only direct benefits with all sorts of indirect costs, overall expenses and income; it is not relevant to compare direct income with overall expenditure, which is what Pimentel *et al.* do (they list a whole series of items of indirect expenditure but never estimate indirect benefits, primarily a lower occurrence of cancer when fruit and vegetable prices are lower and consumption higher). Additionally, many of Pimentel *et al.*'s assumptions seem somewhat questionable, like valuing each dead bird at $30, making up about $2 billion of the $8 billion without references to studies of bird valuation.

1965. This procedure only estimates economic costs and benefits (which are thus comparable), but typically does so within a general equilibrium model, thus also accounting for secondary, economic effects.

1966. Knutson and Smith 1999:114; Gray and Hammit 2000. For earlier estimates see Knutson *et al.* 1990a, 1990b, 1994.

1967. Gray and Hammit 2000.

1968. Socialdemokratiet 1996; Det radikale Venstre 2000; SF (Gade 1997); Enhedslisten (Kolstrup 1999).

1969. http://mstex03.mst.dk/fagomr/02050000.htm.

1970. Ayer and Conklin 1990; Smith 1994.

1971. See Bichel Committee 1999a:7.

1972. Bichel Committee 1999a–g.

1973. Cost estimate from model of free best choice and constrained pesticide best choice, Bichel Committee 1999c:78; "insignificant" from Bichel Committee 1999a:134–5.

1974. See e.g. Bichel Committee 1999c:78.

1975. Bichel Committee 1999c:78. Treatment frequency is considered the best indicator of pesticide use. Notice, the main conclusion speaks of reductions of 43 percent (Bichel Committee 1999a:134), but this compares non-optimized present-day production with optimized future production, thus also incorporating the assumed extra benefits of the model telling the farmer which crops would be most efficient – however, if this is possible (and not just a consequence of limited information in the model, making it assume it knows better than the farmer), such information and consequent change of crop choice is separate from pesticide considerations.

1976. Bichel Committee 1999a:132ff.

1977. Bichel Committee 1999c:78.

1978. Bichel Committee 1999a:133, DKK 3.1 billion in 1992 currency; 9 percent comes from the estimate of total agricultural production of DKK 35 billion (Statistics Denmark 1997a:436).

1979. If the pesticide reduction means an equivalent ratio of reduction in agriculture worth $125.2 billion in 1998 (USBC 2001b:452) of 9 percent. If taken as a reduction in total GNP of $9,236 billion (USBC 2001b:456) this comes to $37. Naturally, such an estimate is very much a ballpark figure, given the very big differences in climate, production, markets and technology.

1980. Bichel Committee 1999a:130.

1981. Taken as a percentage of agricultural production, it is $23 billion (18 percent), in GNP it is $74 billion (0.8 percent).

1982. Bichel Committee 1999a:129.

1983. Bichel Committee 1999a:129; 1999g:69.

1984. Taken as a percentage of agricultural production, it is $93 billion (74 percent – notice, this cost of course does not just come from a reduction in agricultural production, but is here used as a proxy), in GNP it is $277 billion (3 percent).

1985. Remembering, though, that the optimization of pesticide use constitute a best-case estimate.

1986. Ford *et al.* 1999.

1987. We will make no analysis here of the consequences of banning pesticides in the Third World which would probably lead to far more serious price increases, political unrest and famine.

1988. Bichel Committee 1999b:155ff.; cf. Knutson *et al.* 1994; Zilberman *et al.* 1991.

1989. Ritter *et al.* 1997:2,027. It is rather ironic that we are often told how birds are more abundant in and around organically cultivated fields (Bichel Committee 1999d:188), because this information is worthless unless they also tell us how much more forest and woodland organic farms need to take over.

1990. Zilberman 1991:520; Ritter *et al.* 1997:2,027. The proportion of Denmark's budget spent on food is around 16 percent and in the US around 8 percent (Meade and Rosen 1996).

1991. Edgerton *et al.* 1996:108–10; Knutson and Smith 1999:109; Lutz and Smallwood 1995. Patterson and Block (1988:284) show that the relative amount of fruit and vegetables people eat increases in step with their income.

1992. Lutz and Smallwood 1995. Notice, the primary starch will also come from a higher consumption of potatoes, but potatoes do not help reduce cancer frequency, WCRF 1997:540.

1993. Ritter *et al.* 1997:2,027.

1994. Best-guess estimate between 7 and 31 percent (WCRF 1997:540).

1995. Composed of 169 g of fruit and 128 g of vegetables (189 g minus potatoes, which are excluded in WCRF 1997:540) (ERS 1998:tables 9–2, 9–3).

1996. Linearity is assumed close to the original estimate, which is what is also suggested in WCRF (1997:540); 4.6 percent of 593,100 (ACS 1999:4). An increase in fruit and vegetable prices would *not* in general lead to higher meat prices, since feedstuffs can still be freely imported (Bichel Committee 1999c:68). Thus, the income effect would probably not lead to reduced consumption of meat and fat. Moreover, such reduced consumption would probably also lead to a reduction in the intake of fiber (Patterson and Block 1988:284).

1997. Gillman 1996.

1998. WCRF 1997:512 *et passim.*

1999. NRC 1996.

2000. Ritter *et al.* 1997:2,030.

2001. Ritter *et al.* 1997:2,030.

2002. Abelson 1994.

2003. Obviously, if we only introduce pesticide restrictions in a single country and do not impose restrictions on imports of fruit and vegetables, we will still be able to buy cheap fruit and vegetables from abroad which have been cultivated using pesticides. This will only increase prices somewhat. (Notice that just a 2 percent vegetable consumption decline would entail almost 2,000 extra American cancer deaths annually). This may mean that we get groundwater less burdened by pesticides while avoiding heavy price increases on fruit and vegetables, but it would, on the other hand, have no positive effect on health since drinking water represents an exceedingly small part of the total pesticide risk (cf. Figure 124). We would end up paying $20 billion for an aesthetic advantage (clean drinking water). It has therefore been assumed in the above that we will choose the total, consistent solution.

2004. In this section I use the number of species as a definition of biodiversity, although the word naturally has other, partially overlapping meanings, e.g. the number of habitats or the amount of genetic variation. See UNEP 1995.

2005. Myers 1979:4–5.

2006. Lovejoy 1980.

2007. Gore 1992:28.

2008. Diamond 1990:55.

2009. Wilson 1992:280; Regis 1997:196; Mann 1991:737.

2010. Using 10 million species, as in Myers. Cited in Stork 1997:62.

2011. In a summary chapter on biodiversity, Ulfstrand cites Myers' asserted reduction by half within 50 years and writes that "Ecologists and evolutionary biologists in general agree with this estimate" (1992:3). If no new nature management is instituted, the Brundtland report states that "over the longer term, at least one-quarter, possibly one-third, and conceivably a still larger share of species existing today could be lost" (WCED 1987:152). The internet site Web of Life tells us that 50,000 species die out every year, http://www.weboflife.co.uk/weboflife/press_centre/pr_0006006.html. The *UN Chronicle* carried an article claiming that "UNEP has predicted that up to 25 per cent of living species may become extinct within a single human lifetime" (Anon. 1992a:52). Greenpeace claimed on their website that "it is expected that half of the Earth's species are likely to disappear within the next seventy-five years." This document was removed at the request of the Danish chairman of Greenpeace, after I criticized it in the Danish daily *Politiken* (18 February 1998, www.greenpeace.org/~comms/cbio/bdfact.html). This chapter is to a large degree based on Simon and Wildawsky 1995.

2012. Botkin and Keller 1998:235.

2013. UNEP 1995:204–5.

2014. UNEP 1995:208.

2015. Stork 1997:50.

2016. Stork 1997:56–8.

2017. This is also the point of Ehrlich (1995:224): "Public opinion on issues related to extinctions is unlikely to be swayed as much by scientific study as by publicizing the declines of charismatic megavertebrates . . . Lay people can relate well to pandas and whales."

2018. E.g. WCED 1987:155ff.

2019. Myers 1983.

2020. Pimentel *et al.* 1997; Costanza *et al.* 1997; note that the Constanza *et al.* reference to 180 percent of world GDP seems to be incorrect: Pearce 1998; IMF 2000a:113.

2021. E.g. Pimentel and Pimentel 1999:423; Janetos 1997. The Brundtland report (WCED 1987:155) claims that "the economic values inherent in the genetic materials of species are alone enough to justify species preservation."

2022. See e.g. Pearce 1998; Pimm 1997; Sagoff 1997.

2023. Simpson and Sedjo 1996; Simpson and Craft 1996. Simpson and Sedjo finds that the value of the final species of 5 million species is just $\$10^{-37}$ – an absurdly tiny figure (1996:24). They therefore conclude that: "the economic incentives for conservation generated by biodiversity prospecting are negligible" (1996:31). Likewise, Simpson and Craft estimate the value for 25 percent of all the world's species at US$ 111 billion or 0.4 percent of the world's annual GDP (1996:16–17).

2024. Kaplan 1998; Cambell 1993. The Brundtland report gives us a similar example of US corn suffering severe setbacks in 1970 from leaf fungus and being saved by genetic materials from stocks of Mexican corn species (WCED 1987:155).

2025. De Quattro 1994.

2026. UNEP 1995:202.

2027. May *et al.* 1995:3.

2028. Ehrlich and Wilson 1991:759.

2029. Botkin and Keller 1998:235–6.

2030. Steadman 1995; cf. Goudie 1993:115ff.

2031. Diamond 1990:56.

2032. Reid 1992:55.

2033. Myers 1979:4–5.

2034. Myers 1979:4 writes 1,000 although it is obvious from his only source that this should be 100: "the world-wide extinction rate up to now is estimated at about 10,000 species per century" (Holden 1974:646).

2035. Myers 1979:4.

2036. Myers 1979:5.

2037. Lovejoy (1980:331) writes 563e3/3e6 = 18,75 percent or 1,875e3/1e7 = 18,75 percent.

2038. Lovejoy 1980:330, using graph D.

2039. This also includes an estimated 8 percent reduction because of "the combined effects of loss of habitat, presence of toxic substances, eutrophication, desertification, simplification of forests in the temperate zones, acid rain, etc." (Lovejoy 1980:331, note E).

2040. As we also saw in the section on forests, cf. Broecker 1970.

2041. See e.g. Stork 1997:57.

2042. Again, recalling Ehrlich (1995:224): "Public opinion on issues related to extinctions is unlikely to be swayed as much by scientific study as by publicizing the declines of charismatic megavertebrates . . . Lay people can relate well to pandas and whales."

2043. E.g. Simberloff 1992.

2044. Somewhat akin to the Laffer diagram, an economic graph drawn for Ronald Reagan on the backside of a napkin in the late 1970s, which became the intellectual backdrop to *reaganomics*.

2045. Mann 1991:737.

2046. Simberloff 1992:85. Simberloff writes here that three species of birds became extinct, but that forest clearance was probably not responsible in two of these cases.

2047. Lugo 1988:66.

2048. Obviously, if one alters the number of niches there will be room for more birds, so this need not come as such a surprise. The most significant finding is that only seven species of birds became extinct.

2049. Lugo 1988:60.

2050. Myers 1979:43.

2051. Colinvaux 1989:68.

2052. Quoted in Mann 1991:737.

2053. Quoted in Mann 1991:736.

2054. Quoted in Mann 1991:736.

2055. Quoted in Mann 1991:736.

2056. Quoted in Mann 1991:736.

2057. International Union for Conservation of Nature and Natural Resources; http://www.iucn.org.

2058. Heywood and Stuart 1992:93.

2059. Heywood and Stuart 1992:94.

2060. Heywood and Stuart 1992:96, italics added.

2061. Gentry 1986.

2062. Diamond 1990:56; Heywood and Stuart 1992:96.

2063. Quoted in Mann 1991:738.

2064. Haywood and Stuart 1992:96.

2065. Brown and Brown 1992:121.

2066. Brown and Brown 1992:127, italics added. Note, however, that the Mitu mitu, a large ground-dwelling frugivore bird, in the last decades only known from a few coastal lowland forest patches in Alagoas, northeastern Brazil, is now probably extinct in the wild, with only a small private, captive population (Baillie and Groombridge 1997, http://www.wcmc.org.uk/species/data/red_note/18610.htm, Fog 1999:133).

2067. Brown and Brown 1992:127.

2068. Brown and Brown 1992:127. Fog reports that since then, 10 plant species have been declared extinct (1999:133).

2069. Brown and Brown 1992:128.

2070. Haywood and Stuart 1992:98.

2071. Heywood and Stuart 1992:102. The question here (of course) is whether we have the necessary empirical material to substantiate the frightening figures, or whether researchers simply fear that these massive extinction rates will materialize in future.

2072. Holden 1992:xvii.

2073. Stork 1997:60–1.

2074. Smith *et al.* 1993.

2075. Stork (1997:61) estimates that between 100,000 and 500,000 of 8 million insects will die out over the next 300 years. This is equivalent to a maximum of 0.208 percent/decade, and an average of 350,000 is equivalent to 0.729 percent every 50 years, the figure mentioned at the beginning of this chapter.

2076. Since invertebrates constitute by far the most species and their average lifespan is estimated at 11e6 years (May *et al.* 1995:3), a rate 1,540 times higher over 50 years would induce 1500*(1/11e6)*50 = 0.7%. It is worth contemplating how most green organizations today have stopped talking about percentages and started talking about multiples of natural extinction, although the latter is much less informative. It seems probable that this shift is due in no small respect to the latter sounding more ominous.

2077. See overview from Stork 1997:62–3.

2078. Sagoff 1995; FAO 2000d:207; Victor and Ausubel 2000.

2079. UNDP 1995:12.

2080. UNDP 1995:244.

2081. Using the invertebrate species lifespan of 11e6 years (May *et al.* 1995:3) and interpreting the quote to be from 200 to 2,000 times the natural background (the "if not thousands" means it *could* be thousands, not all the way up to 9,999): 200*(1/11e6)*50 = 0.09% and 2000*(1/11e6)*50 = 0.9%. The authors are not quite consistent, using a somewhat lower lifespan when comparing 1,000 times the background rate to 2 percent per 50 years (UNDP 1995:235), making the conclusion 0.4–4 percent over the next 50 years.

2082. Setting the extinction rate in tropical forests at "50–150 species per day, and rising" (Myers and Lanting 1999).

2083. Western and Pearl 1989:xi.

2084. Ehrlich and Ehrlich 1996:112–13.

2085. Diamond 1989:41.

2086. Diamond 1989:41.

2087. http: // www.biodiv.org / conv / background.html.

2088. CBD 1992:Article 10.

2089. Mann and Plummer 1993.

2090. One of the Wildlands Project participants exactly pointed out that, while it may seem "nuts," "it is more or less where the science is pointing to" (Mann and Plummer 1993:1868).

2091. WCED 1987:152.

2092. http://www.weboflife.co.uk/weboflife/press_centre/pr_0006006.html.

2093. WI 1999a:19, a statement echoed by Al Gore (1992:92).

2094. Global warming is the concern that the global temperature, due to the greenhouse effect, will increase. The technical term used by IPCC is the more inclusive climate change attributable to human activities (IPCC 2001a:Glossary), which refers to any change in state or variability in any climate variable.

2095. It may seem rather ironic, but just 20–30 years ago practically everyone was worried about an oncoming ice age (Bray 1991).

2096. PCSD 1999:10.

2097. WI 2000a:16.

2098. UNDP 1998b:4.

2099. DiCaprio 2000. Al Gore has called global warming "the most serious problem that our civilization faces," cited in Carrel 1994.

2100. Chumley 2001.

2101. Greenpeace 2000.

2102. WI 2000a:17.

2103. Greenpeace 2000. Cf. IPCC's statement: "Fossil-fuel scarcity, at least at the global level, is therefore not a significant factor in considering climate change mitigation," IPCC 2001c:TS.3.2.

2104. Greenpeace 2000.

2105. WI 1999a:35.

2106. WI 1999a:35; Hoffert *et al.* 1998: 884.

2107. See e.g. Michaels and Balling 2000:7–9.

2108. DiCaprio 2000, very similar to other statements, e.g. Clinton 1999, 2000.

2109. Http://www.ipcc.ch. In this section I will therefore to far less a degree evaluate to what extent the IPCC can be considered to be purveyors of the reviled truth. The IPCC's reports are often referred to in the press as the result of the work of 2,000 scientists, but if you count, there are only some 80 main authors – and only a smaller number of these actually worked on the climate models. It is true enough, however, that the results have been approved – directly or indirectly – by almost 2,000 scientists and officials. But it is important to realize that the scientists concerned are involved in all sorts of more or less peripheral areas of climate research. It is far from self-evident that people can pass qualified judgment on climate models and their predictions merely because they have expert knowledge of prehistoric shells at the bottom of the Atlantic Ocean. It is, however, reasonably certain that it will become more difficult to get research grants for one's own area of specialty if the threat posed by CO_2 to mankind is not maintained to some degree. It takes courage and very powerful conviction to speak out against the results of the IPCC computer models – it is not only one's own research funding that would be at stake, but also that of all the others. (See also Laut 1997:41–2.)

2110. See e.g. Ross and Blackmore 1996; Mahlman 1997; Karl and Trenberth 1999.

2111. In 2100 CO_2 is expected to constitute anywhere from 68 percent of total forcing in scenario A2 to 97 percent in scenario B1, IPCC 2001a:tabel 6.14 (cf. IPCC 1996a:24; 1997a:8).

2112. IPCC 2001a:1.2.1; Ross and Blackmore 1996:135; IPCC 1996a:57.

2113. For the 1980s, IPCC 1996a:79, the figures for the 1990s are still not in, IPCC 2001a:table 3.3.

2114. IPCC 2001a:3.2.2.4, 1996a:79.

2115. IPCC 2001a:3.1.

2116. Met Office 2001.

2117. IPCC 2001a:2.3.2

2118. See the many other indictors at the NOAA Paleoclimatology Program (NOAA 2001).

2119. Jäger and Barry 1990:335.

2120. With rates of about 1cm/year from 15,000 to 6,000 years before present, IPCC 2001a:TS:B4, 11.2.4.1, figure 11.4.

2121. "The early Holocene was generally warmer than the twentieth century," IPCC 2001a:2.4.2, table 2.4; cf. Jäger and Barry 1990:337.

2122. IPCC 2001a:2.4.2.

2123. IPCC 2001a:2.4.2; Petit *et al.* 1999.

2124. IPCC 2001d:figure 1.

2125. E.g. NAST 2000:13; Hileman 1999:16.

2126. Mann *et al.* 1999:762.

2127. IPCC 2001a:2.3.5.

2128. E.g. Kerr 1999.

2129. Reiter (2000), actually notes how the pack ice extended so far south that there are six records of Eskimos landing their kayaks in Scotland.

2130. See also Burroughs 1997:109.

2131. Reiter 2000.

2132. Mann *et al.* 1999:762.

2133. Jäger and Barry 1990:335, *Encyclopedia Britannica*: Holocene Epoch.

2134. Dillin 2000, *Encyclopedia Britannica*: Holocene Epoch.

2135. *Encyclopedia Britannica*: Holocene Epoch.

2136. Jäger and Barry 1990:337; IPCC 1990:202.

2137. IPCC 2001a:2.3.3.

2138. Mann *et al.* 1999:760, 761.

2139. IPCC 2001a:2.3.2.1.

2140. IPCC 2001a:2.3.2.1, Mann *et al.* (1999:760) actually try to remove a possible CO_2 signature from the tree ring data using other data from 1400.

2141. See e.g. review in Barnett *et al.* 1999:2,636.

2142. The reason it lies below twentieth century temperature is because it was adjusted to 1881–1960, which in the instrumental record lies 0.17°C below the temperature of 1961–90.

2143. Barnett *et al.* 1999:2,635.

2144. IPCC 2001a:2.4.2; Kerr 1999; Broecker 2001.

2145. IPCC 2001a:2.4.2; Cowen 1996. Such lack of temperature change could be due to averaging out (that the large temperature changes were exactly regional and happening at different times) but as we have seen, this is indeed not the case for the period 1000–1400, which is primarily based on tree ring data from North America, and for later periods seems to be contradicted by both Jones *et al.* 1998 and Pollack *et al.* 2000.

2146. There has been an extensive discussion about adjustments for urban heat (almost all temperature gauges are close to large cities which have grown ever larger over time and therefore emit and attract more and more heat), which I will not embark upon (see e.g. Burroughs 1997:114), since the margin of error does not seem to be that great. Peterson *et al.* (1999) showed essentially the same global temperature time series for rural stations only. IPCC estimate the error to be less than 0.05°C over the past century (2001a:2.2.2.1).

2147. IPCC 2001a:2.2.2.3.

2148. Barnett *et al.* 1999:2,637, IPCC 2001a:2.2.2.4.

2149. Tett *et al.* (1999) find "attribution of the warming early in the century has proved more elusive," and Delworth and Knutson (2000) find an "unusually large" natural variation is needed to model the temperature curve. Typically, the simulations just simply do not handle the 1910–45 temperature increase; see e.g. Barnett *et al.* 1999:2,634; IPCC 1997c:30. This way of interpreting temperature data has given rise to criticism and wonder. Aksel Wiin-Nielsen, professor emeritus in meteorology and former director-general of the UN World Meteorological Organization, argues that since the early part of the temperature increase was natural, it is implausible that the last temperature increase could not also have natural causes (Christensen and Wiin-Nielsen 1996:58–9).

2150. IPCC 2001a:6.15.1, 12.2.3.1.figure 12.7, 8.6.4. IPCC 2001a:6.11.1.1.2 finds that the level of scientific understanding of past development in irradiance is "very low."

2151. IPCC 1990:xvii-xviii.

2152. IPCC 1992:75; cf. IPCC 1995.

2153. IPCC 2000a&b, 2000a:27.

2154. IPCC 2000a:46, the four marker scenarios and the two illustrative scenarios from A1.

2155. IPCC 2000a:169ff.

2156. Though it is never stated explicitly, such special treatment of one of the scenarios seem to indicate that A1 is indeed the most business-as-usual scenario, although such advantage is quickly lost thanks to the further splitting of the A1 scenario.

2157. IPCC 2000a:3.

2158. IPCC 2000a:46.

2159. IPCC 1996a:323.

2160. IPCC 1996a:364.

2161. IPCC 1996a:5.

2162. IPCC 2001d:6.

2163. For basic description of the dynamics, see IPCC 2001:TS:Box 3, 1997c.

2164. See IPCC 2001:TS:Box 3.

2165. Kerr 1997a.

2166. Parameterization fails to model actual interaction (which can be extremely non-linear) but simply provides a functional connection; see IPCC 1997c:2 *et passim*; Christensen and Wiin-Nielsen 1996:23.

2167. "Future climate is projected using climate models" (IPCC 1996a:31). Cf. computer models are "the only way to measure how human activity affects the climate" (Burroughs 1997:148).

2168. IPCC 2001a:TS:D1, 1.3.1, 7.2.1.

2169. IPCC 1996a:295.

2170. Shine *et al.* 1999:212–13; Hansen *et al.* 1998:12,757–8.

2171. Mitchell *et al.* 1995.

2172. As noted earlier, some of this increase might be explained by increased solar irradiance, although the data are very uncertain, IPCC 2001a:6.15.1, 12.2.3.1, figure 12.7, 8.6.4.

2173. IPCC 2001a:5.4.3.

2174. IPCC 2001a:figure 6.6, 5.executive summary.

2175. IPCC 2001a:1.3.1.

2176. Notice, that some of the boxes and uncertainties (e.g. contrails and cirrus) are larger in figure 6.6 than in table 6.11. In that case, the tabulated values were used.

2177. Hansen *et al.* 2000:9,876.

2178. "Climate change simulations are assessed for the period 1990 to 2100 and based on a range of scenarios for projected changes in greenhouse gas concentrations and sulfate aerosol loadings (direct effect). A few AOGCM simulations include the effects of ozone and/or indirect effects of aerosols (see Table 9.1 for details). Most integrations do not include the less dominant or less well understood forcings such as land use changes, mineral dust, black carbon, etc." IPCC 2001a:9.executive summary, cf. 9.1.2.

2179. Such problems are suggested and discussed in Harvey 2000, Rodhe *et al.* 2000, Weaver and Zwiers 2000:572.

2180. It is true when it is pointed out that most of the large-scale models have begun to produce more consistent results. However, as several modelers have pointed out, this can be due to the fact either that the large-scale models have become more accurate or that these models have all begun to produce the same errors (Kerr 1997).

2181. Shine and Forster 1999:220.

2182. IPCC 2001d:5.

2183. Shine and Forster 1999:220.

2184. Hansen *et al.* 1997.

2185. Jacobson 2001:695; cf. Andreae 2001.

2186. "Water vapour feedback continues to be the most consistently important feedback accounting for the large warming predicted by general circulation models in response to a doubling of CO_2," IPCC 2001a:7.2.1.1.

2187. IPCC 2001a:II.2.1, shows that present CO_2 concentrations of 367ppm would be doubled in 2070 to beyond 2200.

2188. Hall and Manabe 1999:2,333; IPCC 1997c:11–12, 2001a:1.3.1; Ross and Blackmore 1996:137.

2189. 2001a:7.2.1.

2190. IPCC 2001a:9.3.4.1.4.

2191. "What controls the strength of water vapor feedback is the degree to which a surface temperature anomaly penetrates the troposphere. The more it penetrates, the stronger the water vapor feedback" (Hall and Manabe 1999:2,342).

2192. IPCC 2001a:7.2.1.1.

2193. E.g. Bengtsson *et al.* 1999.

2193. NRC 2000:41.

2195. The IPCC acknowledges the problem of diverging troposphere temperatures in models and observations as the first important uncertainty in 2001a:12:executive summary.

2196. Hansen *et al.* 1995; Hurrell and Trenberth 1997. Apparently, the microwave data has also generated quite some irritation – one employee of NASA's Mission to Planet Earth program, which studies climate change, allegedly told the microwave scientist, John Christy: "I'm paying people to come at you with bricks and bats" (Royte and Benson 2001c).

2197. Wentz and Schabel (1998) identified a problem with so-called orbital decay, causing the satellites slowly to drift into ever lower orbits, causing a small, spurious cooling in the data. According to Wentz and Schabel, this would change the temperature trend from -0.05°C/decade to +0.07°C/decade. However, other satellite drifts were also left out (east–west and time-of-day) and are now included, causing the true 1979–96 trend to be -0.01°C/decade, cf. Christy *et al.* 2000a, 2000b.

2198. NRC 2000; Santer *et al.* 2000; Gaffen *et al.* 2000; Parker 2000. IPCC 2001a:2.executive summary: "It is very likely that these differences in trends between the surface and lower troposphere are real and not solely an artifact of measurement bias."

2199. IPCC (2001a:7.2.2.4) describes how a change from a diagnostic prescription of clouds in the NCAR atmospheric GCM to a prognostic cloud liquid water formulation even changed the sign of net cloud forcing in the eastern tropical Pacific and completely altered the nature of the coupled model response to increased greenhouse gases.

2200. The two changes dealt with how fast precipitation fell out of different cloud types and how sunlight and radiant heat interacted with clouds, Kerr 1997a.

2201. IPCC 2001a:TS:D1.

2202. About ±3W/m^2, compared to a CO_2 effect of 4–6.7W/m^2 in 2100, IPCC 2001a:7.2.2.4.1, table II.3.1.

2203. Lindzen *et al.* 2001.

2204. Lindzen *et al.* 2001:figure 5d.

2205. Upper-level clouds lead to a net worming of the earth, Svensmark and Friis-Christensen 1997:1,226.

2206. Such negative feedback mechanism is one of those sought after in the AOGCM review in *Science*: "Looking at global climate evolution from a very long-term perspective, it is surprising that despite major glaciations, an Earth mostly without continental ice sheets, a sun with increasing luminosity, and a 10-fold variation in atmospheric CO_2 content mean surface temperature has remained in comparably narrow bounds of about ±5°C as compared to the present mean. We need to understand the negative feedback that stabilizes climate and thus keeps Earth a living planet," Grassl 2000.

2207. Lindzen *et al.* 2001:417.

2208. Lindzen *et al.* 2001:430.

2209. Lindzen *et al.* 2001:430.

2210. IPCC 1990:135, 1996a:34, 2001a:9.3.4.1.4. Brian Farrell of Harvard University is quoted as saying: "the IPCC left the estimate of the warming from a doubling of carbon dioxide at 1.5 Celsius to 4.5 Celsius, where it has been for 20 years," Kerr 1997a.

2211. There were only one business-as-usual scenario and three CO_2 reduction scenarios, so therefore only the central value for the BaU is reported, IPCC 1990:xxii, 336.

2212. IPCC 1996a:5–6, 289, 324.

2213. IPCC 1996a:324.

2214. IPCC 2001a:9.3.2.1, 2001d:8.

2215. IPCC 2001a:9:executive summary, 2000a:41.

2216. IPCC 2001a:9.3.1.3.

2217. IPCC 2001a:9.3.2.1.

2218. The reason seems to be that the simple model has been calibrated with a different set of

AOGCMs, some of which surprisingly have not even run the new scenarios (e.g. GFDL_R15_a and HadCM2, IPCC 2001a:table 9.A1, table 9.1).

2219. IPCC 2001a:9.3.1.3.

2220. As this range is solely determined by the IPCC simple model and this seems to overestimate the warming for A2 and B2 by about 20 percent (18 and 23 percent, respectively).

2221. Most modelers "today agree that climate models will not be capable of linking global warming to human actions for at least ten years," Kerr 1997a. "In about a decade, coupled atmosphere-ocean-land models (CGCMs) assimilating near-real-time data from the global observing system (including the ocean interior) will . . . allow the attribution of a large part of observed climate variability and change to natural and/or anthropogenic causes," Grassl 2000.

2222. Farman *et al.* 1985.

2223. The ozone layer is not really "thin" in the sense that it is distributed over most of the stratosphere from 15 to 35 km up, but the total column of ozone, if brought to the ground, would only form a layer about 3 mm (0.1 in) thick (Blackmore 1996:72).

2224. Blackmore 1996:106.

2225. "Ozone depletion is not a major cause of climate change" (WMO/UNEP 1998:31), cf. stratospheric ozone in Figure 139.

2226. Cf. UNEP 1999c, which has slightly different measures, and seems to be somewhat inconsistent with the figures in WI 1999c in the last years (1995–6), however pointing perhaps towards a small *increase* of about 5 percent in production for 1996–7, mainly caused by increasing production in China.

2227. WMO/UNEP 1998:18; UNEP 1999b:23.

2228. Since increasing cloud cover and pollution could cancel out the increased UV-B radiation coming through, there has been an interest in showing that UV-B has actually increased over the past ten years. However, this has turned out to be very difficult, owing to poorly calibrated and unstable instruments (UNEP 1999b:99; Madronich *et al.* 1998).

2229. UNEP 1999b:9, 13, 108–9.

2230. A natural part of the ozone equilibrium is mediated by naturally generated N_2O and CH_4, but the *additional* 80 percent of active radicals entering the stratosphere in the 1990s came from human sources (Blackwell 1996:83; WMO/UNEP 1998:25).

2231. Molina and Rowland 1974.

2232. E.g. WMO/UNEP 1998:24.

2233. Blackmore 1996:83–5; WMO/UNEP 1998:23.

2234. Blackmore 1996:92.

2235. The treaty texts are available at http://www.unep.org/ozone/treaties.htm.

2236. UNEP 1999b:11, 90.

2237. UNEP 1999b:11, 23.

2238. UNEP 1999b:24.

2239. UNEP 1999b:103.

2240. "Options to reduce the current and near-term vulnerability to ozone depletion are very limited," and "over the longer term, few policy options are available to enhance the recovery of the ozone layer" (UNEP 1999b:25).

2241. See e.g. Blackmore 1996:115–23.

2242. Smith *et al.* 1997b, http://www.ec.gc.ca/ozone/choices/index_e.html.

2243. Smith *et al.* 1997b, http://www.ec.gc.ca/ozone/choices/sect3_e.html.

2244. Smith *et al.* 1997b, http://www.ec.gc.ca/ozone/choices/sect2_e.html.

2245. Estimated as 1/1.06, where the 6 percent are an average of expected increases in UV-B radiation of 6 percent in the Southern Hemisphere and 4–7 percent in the Northern Hemisphere (UNEP 1999b:23).

2246. Expected increases in UV-B radiation of 6 percent in the Southern Hemisphere and 4–7 percent in the Northern Hemisphere (UNEP 1999b:23; UNEP/WMO 1998:18).

2247. Garvin and Eyles 1997:49; cf. Boyes and Stanisstreet 1998.

2248. Anon. 1997c.

2249. ESRC 1997:3.

2250. Kane 1998.

2251. E.g. Ortonne 1997.

2252. ACS 1999:15, 4.

2253. More than 99 percent of all patients are cured of basal cell cancer and more than 97 percent of squamous cell cancer (de Gruijl 1999:2,004).

2254. Longstreth *et al.* 1998:33; UNEP 1999b:22.

2255. This is an average over all longitudes.

2256. Fresno, CA, 36°47'N, Bakersfield, CA, 35°22'N.

2257. This is true for 30°–75°N and 30°–55°S.

2258. Measured only north–south.

2259. IPCC (2001a:12.2.3.2) concluding that the indirect solar effect "is difficult to assess due to limitations in observed data and the shortness of the correlated timeseries," and that "we conclude that mechanisms for the amplification of solar forcing are not well established" (IPCC 2001a:6.11.2.2); cf. IPCC 1996a:115–17, 424.

2260. IPCC 1996a:117; Wilson 1997. Wilson also estimates that a 1 percent increase in total solar irradiance causes a 1 °C temperature increase.

2261. Cubasch *et al.* 1997:765. Svensmark and Friis-Christensen (1997:1,225) find changes in solar irradiance too small to be of major importance for the climate.

2262. Friis-Christensen and Lassen 1991; Friis-Christensen 1993; Lassen and Friis-Christensen 1995; Svensmark and Friis-Christensen 1997. Description can be retrieved from Calder 1997.

2263. Lassen and Friis-Christensen 1995; notice that this paper had a small problem with joining the two temperature curves, cf. Laut and Gundermann 1998.

2264. Zhou and Butler 1998; Butler and Johnston 1996.

2265. Rossow and Schiffer 1999:2,270.

2266. Although the actual magnitude is still under discussion (Svensmark and Friis-Christensen 1997:1,226).

2267. Notice that an earlier article (Svensmark and Friis-Christensen 1997:128), showing the same basic relationship but over a much shorter timespan, has been criticized, because the correlation did not hold up for high and middle clouds and it used poor data (Kristjansson and Kristiansen 2000). This has been corrected in the presented graph from Marsh and Svensmark 2000. Their cloud data from the International Satellite Cloud Climatology Project are described best in Rossow and Schiffer 1999. Notice that the IPCC still finds that "the evidence for a cosmic ray impact on cloudiness remains unproven," 2001a:6.11.2.2.

2268. Svensmark and Friis-Christensen 1997:1,230.

2269. Svensmark and Friis-Christensen 1997:1,226.

2270. Laut 1997:5, 16–17.

2271. Laut and Gundermann 1998. The title of the critical paper "Solar cycle length hypothesis appears to support the IPCC on global warming" appears ironically ill-suited for its contents.

2272. Walter (1992) presents 74 of America's most noted commentators, predicting the world in a hundred years from the 1893 World's Columbian Exposition. William A. Peffer correctly saw that "men will navigate the air, and smoke will be suppressed" (p. 68), whereas Erastus Wiman worried greatly about food production and soil erosion (p. 118) and thought it likely that the future would mean "taxation reduced to a minimum, without the need of a standing army" (p. 117).

2273. The IPCC scenario modelers highlight how some developments were seen as likely but incorrect (that nuclear power would be "too cheap to meter") and how some developments were hardly considered but turned out to have momentous consequences (the pessimistic market outlook for gasoline-powered cars at the end of the nineteenth century), IPCC 2000a:216.

2274. Ausubel 1995:411.

2275. If we want good predictions to come from the climate models it is, of course, important that we feed them with correct information. Otherwise, it is just garbage-in garbage-out.

2276. "Emissions of CO_2 due to fossil-fuel burning are virtually certain to be the dominant influence on the trends in atmospheric CO_2 concentration during the 21st century," IPCC 2001d:7.

2277. IPCC 1992:chapter A3, especially p. 77.

2278. It is very similar to the original 1990 scenario (SA90), describing a future, where "the energy supply is coal intensive and on the demand side only modest efficiency increases are achieved. Carbon monoxide controls are modest, deforestation continues until the tropical forests are depleted and agricultural emissions of methane and nitrous oxide are uncontrolled," IPCC 1990:xxxiv.

2279. For a general critique of the IS92, see Gray 1998.

2280. IPCC 1992:78.

2281. IPCC 1992:78.

2282. IPCC (1992:80) puts down 1,447 million hectares of cleared tropical forests from 1990 to 2100, compared to a total tropical forest area in 1990 of 1,756 million hectares (FAO 1997c:12). The IPCC claims this is only 73 percent (1992:88).

2283. Methane comes from a wide variety of sources, primarily wetlands, coal mining and use, gas leaks and rice production, with about one fifth from "enteric fermentation" – essentially cows burping, IPCC 1992:91. As indicated in Figure 132, CH_4 makes up about one fifth of the greenhouse warming, and it has more than doubled in the atmosphere since 1850 from 791 ppb to 1752 ppb in 2000. (Hansen and Sato 2000; Dlugokencky *et al.* 1998, and personal communication for updates.) The IPPC IS92a scenario expects that the concentration of CH_4 in 2100 will have more than doubled again, to 3616 ppb, similarly more than doubling the warming potential of methane, IPCC 1996a:97, 321.

2284. All are increasing throughout the first part of the century, and only B1 decreases in the second part, IPCC 2001a:II.2.2.

2285. "The decreasing growth rate in atmospheric methane reflects the approach to a steady state on a timescale comparable to methane's atmospheric lifetime," Dlugokencky *et al.* 1998.

2286. Since the forcing is then 0.6 W/m^2, or 7 percent too high (IPCC 1996a:321).

2287. 0.6388 percent. This is the sustained, cumulative growth rate implied in Figure 2.3 (IPCC 1996a:83), growing from 355 ppmv in 1990 to 710 ppmv in 2100.

2288. Mauna Loa measurements (Marland *et al.* 1999). Over the past 38 years, the annual growth rate has exceeded 0.64 percent in only three years, 1973, 1988 and 1998.

2289. Using the 1980–98 rate of 0.45065 percent. Nevertheless, IPCC seems pretty comfortable with the projections, as they laconically inform us that "it should be noted that recent emissions are low compared to IS92a-projected emissions . . . although the slow-down may be temporary," IPCC 1996a:83.

2290. "The concentration of CO_2 that would cause the same amount of radiative forcing as the given mixture of CO_2 and other green-house gases" (IPCC 1997c:45).

2291. IPCC/DDC 2000c. Notice that IPCC states that 1 percent is 20 percent above this level (i.e. 0.833 percent, IPCC 1996a:297), but also confuses this with an equivalent CO_2 counting in aerosols, making the total equivalent rate 0.7 percent (p. 313). In order to compare this with the present growth rate, however, it would be necessary to subtract the extra cooling from the additional aerosols. Thus, it is easier to compare total CO_2 equivalent to actual CO_2 equivalent.

2292. Actually, just three years have been greater than 0.85 percent, namely 1973, 1988 and 1998 (they do not show up on Figure 148 because it is averaged, and these were extreme years).

2293. Using 1990–8 rate of 0.599 percent.

2294. IPCC/DDC 2000c.

2295. "The forcing scenarios used by the [computer] models do not originate directly from any coherent future view of the world. They are an arbitrary imposition of a 1 percent per annum growth in future greenhouse gas concentrations. In fact, the closest of the IS92 emissions scenarios to this arbitrary forcing is the IS92a scenario (IPCC 1996 calculated the equivalent per annum growth rate in concentrations for IS92a to be about 0.85 percent per annum)" IPCC/DDC 2000c. The 1 percent per year "increase of radiative forcing lies on the high side of the SRES scenarios," IPCC 2001a:9.executive summary.

2296. The relaxed attitude to the realism of the scenarios is traceable to IPCC, which asked itself whether the different CO_2 increase scenarios really mattered. Their somewhat mellow conclusion was that "the difference in model response to IPCC Scenario IS92a . . . and the experiments using a 1 percent/yr increase in CO_2 are likely to be small at the time of doubling," IPCC 1996a:313. IPCC here writes (incorrectly) that IS92a is equivalent to 0.7 percent increase (which here only makes their argument weaker). Essentially, their argument is to compare 4 percent with 0.25 percent, and notice that a factor 16 in CO_2 increase only causes a factor 2 in warming. However, the important question is, of course, what the difference looks like *close* to the actual increase, and here it seems much more linear, cf. IPPC 1996a:figure 6.13, p. 312.)

2297. IPCC has an instructive comparison of the consequences of different doubling times (1996a:312, reproduced in IPCC 1997c:35). Since warming also takes time to reach equilibrium, a 0.5 percent increase is closer to equilibrium than a 1 percent increase, thus at any given time experiencing more than 50 percent of the extra heat, cf. 1 percent and 0.5 percent in Figure 138.

2298. Karl *et al.* 1997:56.

2299. IPCC 2000a:46–7, 2001a:1.3.2.

2300. The IMAGE group, responsible for the B1 marker scenario, de Vries *et al.* 2000:138.

2301. IPCC 2000a:170.

2302. "The major difficulty was the objective lack of data about numeric functional relationships between major emission drivers and underlying parameters that are needed to compute driver values at each time step. Rather than following this route, many models including ASF relied on fixed storyline-specific population, GNP/capita, and energy intensity profiles, which were either determined by consensus or left at the discretion of individual modeling teams," Sankovski *et al.* 2000:285.

2303. The six models are the Asian Pacific Integrated Model (AIM) from the National Institute of Environmental Studies in Japan, the Atmospheric Stabilization Framework Model (ASF) from ICF

Kaiser in the USA, the Integrated Model to Assess the Greenhouse Effect (IMAGE) from RIVM in the Netherlands, the Multiregional Approach for Resource and Industry Allocation (MARIA) from University of Tokyo in Japan, the Model for Energy Supply Strategy Alternatives and their General Environmental Impact (MESSAGE) from IIASA in Austria and the Mini Climate Assessment Model (MiniCAM) from PNNL, in the USA, Kram *et al.* 2000:337.

2304. The decision on what scenario has what population development is presented as a pre-model decision, with no extra information presented.

2305. See IPCC 2000a:149ff.

2306. Although this is measured in concentration, and the first solution to lowering concentration may just be taller smokestacks, actual emissions also decline with structural change (substitution of solids by gas and electricity) and sulfur reduction measures (e.g. scrubbing), IPCC 2000a:150.

2307. Due to the Second European Sulfur Protocol and the Clean Air Act amendments.

2308. Quoted in IPCC 2000a:151.

2309. IPCC 2001a:9:executive summary.

2310. IPCC 2000a:46.

2311. UNPD 2001a:1; cf. IPCC 2000a:114.

2312. "This is my long-run forecast in brief: The material conditions of life will continue to get better for most people, in most countries, most of the time, indefinitely. Within a century or two, all nations and most of humanity will be at or above today's Western living standards," Regis 1997:198. Notice, though, that Simon talks about *all* nations and *most* of humanity whereas the data is only an average of all developing nations. Thus, it is likely that we need the average income to be considerably above the industrialized 2000-level for Simon's quote to be true. Should we be so unlucky that the economic part of scenario A2 would be materialized, it would seem that this level would still be reachable within 150–200 years. For scenarios A1 and B1 it seems likely that Simon's quote would be true already in 2100. (Even in B1, the poorest region, India and South Asia, will be as rich by 2100 as the average US citizen in 2000, de Vries *et al.* 2000:156.)

2313. See A1G (A1FI) by MESSAGE, who made the illustrative A1T, with the exact same income per capita for the OECD, IPCC 2000a:432, 447.

2314. As the global GDP and population was determined exogenously.

2315. Using MESSAGE numbers (from A1T or A1FI) vs. B1.

2316. Kram *et al.* 2000:369. B2 gets a "medium," and it is quite honestly difficult to say, whether that is better or worse than "fair."

2317. This is based on rough 10-year mid-interval approximations, 2000$ and a 7 percent discount factor.

2318. About 0.7 percent from 2000.

2319. de Vries *et al.* 2000:163,141.

2320. With cropland remaining essentially constant at 1,400 Mha from 1990–2050, reduced to 1,038 Mha in 2100, IPCC 2000b, cf. de Vries *et al.* 2000:167.

2321. IPCC 2000b.

2322. Exponential trend from 1975 onwards.

2323. All estimated as exponential trends, 1990–2100.

2324. All indicators seem to show that some energy improvement will happen no matter what – basically because of dematerialization and improved efficiency even at constant energy costs, so the issue is the *level* of efficiency increase.

2325. This is also the problem in Chapman and Khanna (2000:227), when they claim such efficiency increase is unlikely, because they choose to compare world energy efficiency from 1980–1996, where the energy prices went from about the highest to about the lowest, cf. Figure 65.

2326. IPCC 2000a:204; "the B1-ASF scenario has the lowest fuel prices, which is due in part to its low energy demand," Sankovski *et al.* 2000:272.

2327. In no scenarios will nuclear power make up more than 0–15 percent and since it does not change the qualitative message of the graphs, we will here only talk about fossil fuels vs. renewables.

2328. Notice, the large variability in percentage even for 1990 seems to be due to inconsistencies and definitional problems of both total energy and inclusion of renewables for the different scenarios.

2329. Mori 2000:300, de Vries *et al.* 2000:161, IPCC 2000a:204, assuming a cost of about $16/barrel in 2000 (sic!) and some $40 in 2100 (at a conversion of 6.7 barrels per toe, or about 6GJ per barrel, Craig *et al.* 1996, efunda 2001).

2330. IPCC 2000a:138–9, 218, de Vries *et al.* 2000:161.

2331. de Vries *et al.* (2000:161) find 3–5¢/kWh, Sankovski *et al.* (2000:270) finds 2¢/kWh,

2332. In 1995 only 16 percent of the total cost of electricity, EIA 1996:108.

2333. For instance with combined cycle gas turbines, see IPCC 2000a:137.

2334. "When fossil fuel use drops in A1, this is primarily due to technological progress whereas in the B-scenarios this is due to a political sentiment against fossil fuels," Kram *et al.* 2000:364

2335. "The decreasing competitiveness of coal can be related to its perceived inconvenience and dirtiness, in line with strong acid rain abatement strategies. An alternative interpretation could be that clean coal development processes, such as coal desulphurization and liquefaction/gasification, drive up its price as a clean fuel. Such processes are not considered explicitly in this scenario," de Vries *et al.* 2000:161.

2336. The B scenario is summarized to be a "prosperous, fair, and green world," de Vries *et al.* 2000:139. A persistent change in economy stems from "a growing number of people begin organizing their own employment and income. Partly in reaction to globalization trends and the perceived side-effects of increasing unemployment and inequity and overexploitation of the environment, there is increasing support for a citizen's income and Local Exchange Trade Systems," de Vries *et al.* 2000:140. This will lead to peace and reconciliation: "The affluent regions develop consistent and effective ways to support sustainable development in the poor regions, technology transfer agreements being one of the instruments. In the ensuring spiral of mutual trust, most less-developed regions manage to control social and economic tensions; corruption gradually vanishes and local conflicts are resolved by negotiation. In this atmosphere of sincerity on both sides, international organizations gain some of the authority and effectiveness their founders had hoped for," de Vries *et al.* 2000:140. For the economy, "the 'greening' of business gets an unexpected boom," de Vries *et al.* 2000:140. In transportation, "to solve environmental and congestion problems, there is an active policy to invest in infrastructure: subways in large cities, separate lanes for bicycling and electric buses, etc." de Vries *et al.* 2000:141. And for agriculture, there is a move away from meat, as already discussed. Likewise, "the use of fertilizer and other agricultural inputs starts declining because farmers are taught to use inputs more selectively or switch to sustainable agriculture practices altogether. . . The virtues of locally-grown crops and traditional farming practices are rediscovered," de Vries *et al.* 2000:141. Less resource use is tackled thus: "changing activities, values, and lifestyles, the transition to a service- and information-economy, and the inclusion of the informal economy all contribute to a decline in energy- and material-demand per unit of economic output ('dematerialization,' ecological restructuring, 'factor ten' etc.)," de Vries *et al.* 2000:141.

2337. The full quote is "Normative scenarios depict situations and conditions as one would hope they would emerge; exploratory scenarios attempt to describe plausible futures by taking into account constraining and counteracting conditions, possibly starting from a normative scenario. In this sense our scenario is largely normative," de Vries *et al.* 2000:170.

2338. Mori 2000:299; cf. Sankovski *et al.* 2000:266.

2339. In 2100, the cost of integrated coal gassification combined cycle (IGCC) is estimated at 2.77–2.80¢/kWh ($7.7–7.8/GJ) vs. solar voltaic at 5.8–8.5¢/kWh ($16.2–23.6/GJ), IPCC 2000a:218–9, using scenario A1C.

2340. In 2100, the cost of IGCC is estimated at 2.6–2.7¢/kWh ($7.2–7.5/GJ) vs. solar voltaic at 0.5–0.8¢/kWh ($1.4–2.3/GJ), IPCC 2000a:218–19, using scenario A1T.

2341. Asking, of course, both what would be the extra benefits and the extra costs of such a change in course.

2342. This tendency towards ever cheaper renewables and more expensive fossil fuels were also what made the IS92a problematic. The IS92a forecast a quadrupling of energy production and consumption from 1990 (344EJ) to 2100 (1453EJ), IPCC 1992:84. Fossil fuels would make up about 85 percent of the energy production in 2025 (which surprisingly is more than the 80 percent today, see Figure 63) and still some 57 percent in 2100. Since the total energy production will quadruple, this means that fossil fuel production will triple over the century. At the same time, IPCC expected that this fossil fuel consumption will come with a high price tag. A barrel of oil will increase from the present-day US$10–30 to US$55 in 2025 and US$70 in 2100. Finally, IPCC states that "the costs of non-fossil energy supplies are assumed to fall significantly over the next hundred years. For example, solar electricity prices are assumed to fall to US$0.075/kWh in the IS92a . . . Overall, while renewables are not significantly competitive with fossil energy in 1990, their market penetration speeds as unit costs fall and fossil fuel prices increase rapidly around 2025," IPCC 1992:84.

Nevertheless, IPCC expects non-fossil fuels to have a lower market share in 2025, and only a somewhat higher share in 2100, despite the enormous fossil fuel prices. This seems strange.

2343. See Figure 72; Anon. 1999f; Hasek 2000; Bucci 1999; Carts-Powell 1997; Hoagland 1995.

2344. Chakravorty *et al.* 1997.

2345. Notice, we here only discuss the solar power production cost, but naturally there is also a conversion cost (from electrical power to end use, e.g. hydrogen for cars). This part is also included in the presented model (Chakravorty *et al.* 1997:1,218–19).

2346. IPCC 2000a:216.

2347. Chakravorty *et al.* 1997:1,208. For fusion, see Ariza 2000; Yonas 1998.

2348. Chakravorty *et al.* 1997:1,220.

2349. IPCC 2001a:table II.1.1, 2000a:218–19.

2350. Chakravorty *et al.* 1997:1,217.

2351. Chakravorty *et al.* 1997:1,221.

2352. Chakravorty *et al.* 1997:1,224–5.

2353. IPCC 2000a:137.

2354. Chakravorty *et al.* 1997:1,223.

2355. Chakravorty *et al.* 1997:1,224.

2356. This could possibly be due to usage of IS92 sulfur aerosol assumptions. Nevertheless, below we will only use the relative conclusion from Chakravorty *et al.* 1997.

2357. Chakravorty *et al.* 1997:1,223.

2358. Chakravorty *et al.* 1997:1,203.

2359. Actually, Chakravorty *et al.* (1997:1,225–7) show that the impact of an across-the-board reduction in all conversion costs will postpone the solar power transition, simply because fossil fuels get to be very cheap to use.

2360. This is also the conclusion of Tsur and Zemel 2000.

2361. Margolis and Kammen 1999:582.

2362. Chakravorty *et al.* 1997:1,224; Tsur and Zemel 2000:391.

2363. Asimov and Pohl 1991:34.

2364. Asimov and Pohl 1991:34.

2365. Rosenzweig and Parry 1994:133, which is the reference for IPCC 1996b:451.

2366. The basic result presented here is consistent with the most recent studies, cf. Reilly and Schimmelpfennig 1999; Parry *et al.* 1999. Moreover, the IPCC 2001b:5.3.1ff did not summarize better results.

2367. IPCC 1996b:429; Crosson 1997b:1.

2368. Crosson 1997b:1; IPCC 1996a:4–5.

2369. The nearly consistently most pessimistic model is from the UK Met Office (1997).

2370. Production in 2080 is estimated at 4,012 million tons without global warming (Parry *et al.* 1999:S60) and at 100 million tons less with global warming (Parry *et al.* 1999:S62; HadCM3 seems to produce fairly weird conclusions, see below – here about 160 million tons), compared to 2,064 million tons in 1999 (FAO 2000a), cf. Met Office 1997:12–13.

2371. This is a well-known phenomenon and has been documented in countless studies – e.g. the recent review in Rötter and van de Geijn 1999:653ff.

2372. IPCC 2001b:5.3.3.1, though this naturally only works for moderate temperature increases – for rice, other deleterious effects set in above 26°C. See also IPCC 2001b:TS:4.2.

2373. IPCC 1996b:431, 2001b:box 5–4.

2374. Crosson 1997b:2.

2375. While these changes are clearly crucial in determining the agricultural impact of global warming, the IPCC concludes that there has been little progress in modeling such agronomic adaptations since 1996, IPCC 2001b:5.3.4.

2376. IPCC 2001b:executive summary, emphasis added, cf. 2001b:5.3.5: "impacts on aggregate welfare are a small percentage of Gross Domestic Product, and tend to be positive, especially when the effects of CO_2 fertilization are incorporated." Notice that IPCC finds, but with "very low confidence" that food prices may increase if the temperature increases beyond 2.5°C, 2001b:5.3.6.

2377. Crosson 1997b:3; Reilly and Schimmelpfennig 1999:762ff.

2378. IPCC 2001b:5.3.5, also quoting other research showing that "the developing regions are likely to have welfare effects that are less positive or more negative than the more developed regions."

2379. Crosson 1997b:3.

2380. Crosson 1997b:2.

2381. *Newsweek*, 22 January 1996, Kaplan 1996.

2382. Shute *et al.* 2001. Notice that the "water wars" that *U.S. News and World Report* worry about are the exact same ones as discussed in chapter 13. The IPCC also note that while such developments are possible, they only have "low confidence" exactly because of the issues mentioned in chapter 13 (IPCC even refers to a different article by Wolf, 1998, IPCC 2001b:7.2.2.3.).

2383. Shute *et al.* 2001.

2384. Laut 1997:23; World Bank 1992, Box 8.2.

2385. Agarwal and Narian 1998.

2386. Yohe and Neumann 1997:250.

2387. IPCC 1996a:4, 6, 2001a:table 11.10, II.5.1.

2388. IPCC 2001a:table II.5.2&3.

2389. IPCC 2001a:table II.5.4&5.

2390. Met Office 1997:14.

2391. IPCC 2001e:3.6, 2001b:7.2.1.2, using the results from Nicholls *et al.* 1999.

2392. Nicholls *et al.* 1999:S78.

2393. Nicholls *et al.* 1999:S78.

2394. Nicholls *et al.* 1999:S78, IPCC 2001e:3.6.

2395. Nicholls *et al.* 1999:S78.

2396. Nicholls *et al.* 1999:S75.

2397. IPCC 1998:7.

2398. IPCC 2001e:3.6, cf. 2001b:7.2.1.2, referencing El-Raey (1997) and Zeidler (1997).

2399. "Analysis of the results indicate that for sea level rises of 0.5 m, *if no action is taken*, an area of about 30% of the city will be lost due to inundation." El-Raey 1997:31, emphasis added.

2400. Value lost ($28 billion) and at risk ($18 billion), Zeidler 1997:165, as mentioned in IPCC, 2001b:7.2.1.2,

2401. Zeidler 1997:165.

2402. Zeidler 1997:164, 165, using the $1.2 billion for a 30 cm sea level increase in 2030 (SLR2), as a maximal estimate for cost of 30 cm in 2100, which is not monetarized. Also, notice that these costs, when compared to the US costs which include foresight and adaptation, seem much too high, Yohe and Neumann 1997, IPCC 2001b:7.2.1.2.

2403. IPCC 2001b:7.executive summary.

2404. Shute *et al.* 2001.

2405. IPCC estimate 10–20 cm over the past 100 years, 2001a:table 11.10.

2406. Matthews 2000.

2407. IPCC 2001b:7.2.1.2; Yohe and Neumann 1997.

2408. IPCC 2001b:7.2.1.2.

2409. Miami EDD 2001b.

2410. Miami EDD 2001a.

2411. *U.S. News and World Report*: "Cities in the Northern Hemisphere would very likely become hotter, prompting more deaths from heatstroke in cities such as Chicago and Shanghai," Shute *et al.* 2001.

2412. IPCC 1996b:563, 2001b:9.executive summary, 9.4.1.

2413. IPCC 2001b:9.4.2.

2414. NSC 1990:10; 1999:16; IPCC 1996b:570.

2415. IPCC 2001b:9.4.1–2.

2416. Keatinge *et al.* 2000:671.

2417. Keatinge *et al.* 2000:672.

2418. Keatinge *et al.* 2000:673.

2419. IPCC 1996b:571ff.; Martens *et al.* 1999.

2420. IPCC 1996a:571; Reiter 2000:1.

2421. Reiter 2000:9.

2422. Reiter 2000:9.

2423. IPCC 1996b:572; Morgan and Dowlatabadi 1996:357.

2424. Longstreth 1999:172.

2425. Shute *et al.* 2001.

2426. IPCC 2001b:9.7.1.1

2427. IPCC 2001b:9.7.1.1.

2428. Rogers and Randolph 2000, which is cited in IPCC 2001b:9.7.1.1.

2429. Cook 1998.

2430. Anon. 1999e.

2431. Fedorov and Philander 2000:2000; Latif and Grotzner 2000; Elsner and Kocher 2000; Qian *et al.* 2000.

2432. Fedorov and Philander 2000:1,997.

2433. Sandweiss *et al.* 1996.

2434. Fedorov and Philander 2000:1,997.

2435. Grove 1998:318.

2436. Sandweiss *et al.* 1996, see also controversy in DeVries *et al.* 1997; Wells and Noller 1997; Sandweiss *et al.* 1997.

2437. Mantua *et al.* 1997.

2438. Timmermann *et al.* 1999 and Collins 2000 only see an increase of four times CO_2 concentration.

2439. Fedorov and Philander 2000:2,001.

2440. IPCC 2001a:9.3.6.5. The IPCC also finds that the interannual variability differ from model to model, and that there at present are considerable uncertainties due to model limitations, 2001a:9.executive summary.

2441. Bove 1998; Pielke and Landsea 1999.

2442. Such statements have been made by the US Congress among others, ref. in Pielke and Landsea 1998. See also Asimov and Pohl (1991:19): "It is quite likely that a global warming significantly increases the number and intensity of hurricanes and may have already begun to do so."

2443. Kaplan 1996.

2444. Begley and Glick 1996.

2445. Pope 1998.

2446. Smith 2000.

2447. UNEP 2000:31.

2448. IPCC 1996a:168ff. For an on-line overview of cyclones see Landsea 2000 or Swiss Re 1997.

2449. IPCC 1996a:173. Notice that IPCC 1996b:547 conflicts with this statement, pointing out that "many insurers feel that the frequency of extreme events also has increased." While this "feel" argument seems somewhat out of place in a scientific report, it is also contrasted in Henderson-Sellers *et al.* 1998:22, discussed below and we will also show below why this approach is flawed.

2450. IPCC 2001a:2.executive summary.

2451. IPCC2001a:2.executive summary.

2452. IPCC2001a:2.executive summary.

2453. Mahlman 1997.

2454. Landsea 2000; Henderson-Sellers *et al.* 1998:20. E.g. earthquakes are even more costly – the Kobe 1995 earthquake cost more than $100 billion (Munich Re 1998:29, 2000).

2455. IPCC 1996a:334.

2456. Bengtsson *et al.* 1996; Knutson and Tuleya 1999; Druyan *et al.* 1999; Yoshimura 1999 (cited in Meehl 2000:433).

2457. Meehl *et al.* 2000:431.

2458. E.g. Druyan *et al.* 1999.

2459. Henderson-Sellers *et al.* 1998:35.

2460. IPCC 1996a:334.

2461. Karl *et al.* 1997:59. Cf. "little evidence is available to suggest a real increase in damaging winds" (Karl 1999:2).

2462. Henderson-Sellers *et al.* 1998:19.

2463. IPCC 2001a:9.3.6.6, continuing "though there are now a number of studies that have looked at such possible changes and some show fewer weak but greater numbers of deeper midlatitude lows, meaning a reduced total number of cyclones."

2464. IPCC 2001a:9.3.6.6, continuing "though some measures of intensities show increases, and some theoretical and modeling studies suggest that upper limit intensities could increase," which is equivalent to the post-IPCC conclusion that "thermodynamic schemes predict an increase in MPI [maximum potential intensity] of 10%–20% for a doubled CO_2 climate but the known omissions (ocean spray, momentum restriction, and possibly also surface to 300 hPa lapserate changes) all act to reduce these increases," Henderson-Sellers *et al.* 1998:35.

2465. Karl *et al.* 1997:59.

2466. Landsea 2000.

2467. Karl *et al.* 1997:59.

2468. Landsea *et al.* 1996, 1997, 1999:108; Bove *et al.* 1998:1,327. Notice even Smith (1999a), updating to 1998, shows an increase compared to the 1970s, but still below the 1940s and 1950s.

2469. Easterling *et al.* 2000:422

2470. Landsea *et al.* 1999:108.

2471. WI 1997b:17; cf. "rising temperatures lead to more severe storms, floods, and droughts in many regions," writes senior Worldwatch Institute researcher Abramovitz (1999).

2472. WI 2000b:20. Cf. "The upward trend in weather-related disasters has occurred in tandem with a rise in global average surface temperatures" (WI 1999a:74). Worldwatch Institute is in no way alone in making these claims, they have been voiced by Nicholson-Lord (2000) and Unsworth (2000).

2473. In 2000, the cost was about $31 billion. Munich Re, however, goes out of its way to point out that "in spite of the overall balance being favourable in 2000, there is no justification for speaking of a weakening, let alone change, in the trend" (2001:4).

2474. Until 1999, Worldwatch Institute inexplicably used just the dollar amounts without adjusting for inflation (WI 1997b:70–1; 1998b:80–1).

2475. 6.055 billion in 2000 versus 3.022 billion in 1960 (UNPD 1999a:8), average income of $6,757 in 1999 versus $3,262 in 1960 (WI 2000b:71); with increasing income, more wealth can be accumulated, making wealth grow faster than income, moving to coastal areas, see Swiss Re 1999:8; Pielke 1999.

2476. Pielke and Landsea 1998.

2477. Pielke and Landsea 1998:figure 3.

2478. Pielke 1999:419; cf. Munich Re 1997:37–8.

2479. Munich Re 1999:3.

2480. WI 1998b:74; Abramovitz 1999.

2481. Pielke and Landsea 1998.

2482. The adjustment uses information on population then and now, as well as information on the level of wealth available (from Herman 2000:21), Pielke and Landsea 1998.

2483. In Figure 145 the 1926 hurricane cost is distributed over ten years, whereas Andrew's cost is only distributed over six years, which explains why they look almost similar. Moreover, the 1926 hurricane made a second landfall as a category 3 storm on the Florida and Alabama Gulf coasts, causing almost $10 billion extra in damages (Pielke and Landsea 1998).

2484. Pielke and Landsea 1998.

2485. IPCC finds that "part of the observed upward trend in historical disaster losses is linked to socio-economic factors, such as population growth, increased wealth, and urbanisation in vulnerable areas, and some part is linked to climatic factors such as the observed changes in precipitation and flooding events. Precise attribution is complex, and there are differences in the balance of these two causes by region and by type of event" (IPCC 2001b:TS4.6, cf. 8.2.2) Thus, while disaster loss increases may be due to flooding and precipitation (the only ones actually linked to global warming, as we will discuss below), there seems to be very little evidence to support the contention that hurricanes and storms might do more damage. In the IPCC chapter on insurance costs, mention of "tropical and extra-tropical windstorm" merely points out that there is no consensus on the likely future occurrence of tropical and extra-tropical windstorms, but that they have "a very large capacity to cause damage" (IPCC 2001b:8.2.3).

2486. Munich Re 1999:2.

2487. WI 1999b:74.

2488. Munich Re 1999:2. The deterioration of natural environmental conditions seems to refer to increasing flood risks from clear-cutting and conversion of wetlands.

2489. He is credited by name in Worldwatch compilations, e.g. WI 1998b:81.

2490. Berz 1993.

2491. Berz 1997.

2492. Henderson-Sellers *et al.* 1998:19.

2493. Swiss Re 2000:8.

2494. Changnon and Changnon 1999:287.

2495. Changnon and Changnon 1999:287.

2496. Changnon *et al.* 2000, and the conclusion of Kunkel *et al.* (1999:1,094): "In general, the results of the review strongly suggest that the increasing financial losses from weather extremes are primarily due to a variety of societal changes. These include population growth along the coasts and in large cities, an overall increased population, more wealth and expensive holdings subject to damage, and lifestyle and demographic changes exposing lives and property to greater risk."

2497. Easterling *et al.* 1997:364.

2498. Easterling *et al.* 1997, 1999; Balling *et al.* 1998; Michaels *et al.* 1998, 2000; Jones *et al.* 1999a, 1999b; Heino *et al.* 1999; Zhai *et al.* 1999; Gruza *et al.* 1999.

2499. IPCC 2001a:2.2.2.1.

2500. Easterling *et al.* 2000:419; Zhai *et al.* 1999; Jones *et al.* 1999a; Heino *et al.* 1999.

2501. Michaels *et al.* 1998, 2000; Balling *et al.* 1999.

2502. For the Southern Hemisphere, most of the maximal warming has taken place during the winter (June through August).

2503. Michaels *et al.* 2000; Balling *et al.* 1998.

2504. Easterling *et al.* 2000:419.

2505. Plummer *et al.* 1999.

2506. Easterling *et al.* 2000:419.

2507. Jones *et al.* 1999a:137.

2508. Kalkstein and Davis 1989:61.

2509. Kalkstein and Davis 1989:52.

2510. Easterling *et al.* 2000:419–20. Notice this is at variance with the findings of Gaffen and Ross (1998), but this seems to be because in their "apparent temperature" measure they include humidity, which is probably increasing.

2511. There is still some theoretical controversy over whether the day–night temperature difference will continue to diminish, e.g. Hansen *et al.* 1995; IPCC 1996a:6.

2512. Rosenzweig and Parry 1994; Dhakhwa and Campbell 1998:661.

2513. Dhakhwa and Campbell 1998:661–2. Notice, this is a relative increase to the model with equal day–night warming. Since the study does not allow for light or moderate adaptation, many of the modeled yields with differential day–night temperatures are still lower than today's yields.

2514. IPCC 1996a:7.

2515. Easterling *et al.* 2000:422.

2516. Easterling *et al.* 2000:420–1.

2517. Karl *et al.* 1995; Karl and Knight 1998.

2518. Pielke 1999:419.

2519. Kunket *et al.* 1999:1,081.

2520. "Hydrologically, these results indicate that the conterminous U.S. is getting wetter, but less extreme" (Lins and Slack 1999).

2521. Dai *et al.* 1998.

2522. Dai *et al.* 1998:3,367.

2523. Measured in carbon, some 800 Pg in 6000 BP, to 700 Pg in 1850, and 560 Pg in 1985 (Houghton and Skole 1990:404).

2524. All six models are in reasonable agreement on a substantial increase in NPP (Cramer *et al.* 2000). Note that increased CO_2 alone increases biomass whereas increased temperature alone decreases biomass somewhat less. The overall effect of CO_2 and temperature increase is biomass increase (Cramer *et al.* 2000).

2525. Vitousek *et al.* 1986:372.

2526. Converted from carbon weight to dry organic matter through multiplying by 2.2 (Vitousek *et al.* 1986:368; Houghton and Skole 1990:393).

2527. Meehl *et al.* 2000:431.

2528. IPCC 1996c:188; 1996a:34; 1997a:31.

2529. Talking about the 1.5–2 percent of world GDP, "this means that if a doubling of CO_2 occurred now, it would impose this much damage on the world economy now" (IPCC 1996c:183).

2530. IPCC 2001a:9.executive summary.

2531. See Figure 137.

2532. In the so-called IPCC Plenary, Mentzel 1999.

2533. IPCC 2001cTS.1.1: "In 1998, Working Group (WG) III of the Intergovernmental Panel on Climate Change (IPCC) was charged by the IPCC Plenary for the Panel's Third Assessment Report (TAR) to assess the scientific, technical, environmental, economic, and social aspects of the mitigation of climate change. Thus, the mandate of the Working Group was changed from a predominantly disciplinary assessment of the Economic and Social Dimensions on Climate Change (including adaptation) in the Second Assessment Report (SAR), to an interdisciplinary assessment of the options to control the emissions of greenhouse gases (GHGs) and/or enhance their sinks."

2534. IPCC 1996c:189.

2535. IPCC 1996c:184 evaluates their analysis as relatively unsophisticated.

2536. IPCC 1996c:187.

2537. With global GDP at 32,110 billion dollars in 2000 (IMF 2000b:113). It is not at all clear how the cost will scale to 50 or 100 years since some costs will fall, expressed as a percentage, and others increase (IPCC 1996c:189). It must be assumed that many of the major items, especially coast protection and farming as a maximum are sublinearly dependent on the size of the other economies.

2538. Given an approximate distribution between the two as in 1993: $23 trillion to the industrialized world, $5 billion to developing world (WI 1997a:116).

2539. IPCC 1996c:183; 1997a:31. The difference in cost is in part due to the fact that a better infrastructure and more resources will make coping relatively easier.

2540. This quote was later removed in the political approvement process and does not appear in the final *Summary*, but it quite adequately express the background reports, see e.g. IPCC 2001b:TS./.2.4. For a discussion on the political control of IPCC, see below.

2541. IPCC 2001b:Summary for Policymakers, original government draft, 2.6. All statements were assessed to have medium confidence. This statement was changed in the final version to: "Based on a few published estimates, increases in global mean temperature would produce net economic losses in many developing countries for all magnitudes of warming studied (low confidence), and losses would be greater in magnitude the higher the level of warming (medium confidence). In contrast, an increase in global mean temperature of up to a few degrees C would produce a mixture of economic gains and losses in developed countries (low confidence), with economic losses for larger temperature increases (medium confidence). The projected distribution of economic impacts is such that it would increase the disparity in well-being between developed countries and developing countries, with disparity growing for higher projected temperature increases (medium confidence). The more damaging impacts estimated for developing countries reflects, in part, their lesser adaptive capacity relative to developed countries," IPCC 2001e:6.

2542. In the summary words: "Those with the least resources have the least capacity to adapt and are the most vulnerable," IPCC 2001e:5.a

2543. As Hansen *et al.* 2000 points out, reducing black carbon, which also warms (see Figure 139, p. 268), might be a cheaper solution in the medium run. Nevertheless, the primary greenhouse gas will be CO_2 in the long run.

2544. This is also more or less the only solution which the IPCC adduces in addition to planting forests to soak up CO_2; for alternative techno-fixes, see Laut 1997:30–1; Schelling 1996; NAS 1992.

2545. The agreement contains a series of different requirements for various countries (Kyoto 1997), and painstaking conversion procedures translate all emissions of greenhouse gases into CO_2. The figure of 5.2 percent is the overall reduction in CO_2 equivalent greenhouse gas emissions (Masood 1997). Notice that the designation "Annex I" comes from the original UN Framework Convention on Climate Change (FCCC) from 1992, whereas the Kyoto Protocol prescribes emission limitations for a list of countries in a so-called "Annex B" (Weyant and Hill 1999:xi). As both lists include most of the major players (Slovakia, Slovenia, Liechtenstein, and Monaco have been added to Annex B, whereas Belarus and Turkey are left out) only the term "Annex I" will be used here (as in Weyant and Hill 1999:xi).

2546. Masood 1997; Kyoto 1997; IPCC 1997b:19–20.

2547. This is the assumption used in Figure 157, "B-constant" in Wigley 1998.

2548. Different models indicate 0.15°C (Parry *et al.* 1998:286), 0.15°C (WEC 1998), 0.13°C (Nordhaus and Boyer 1999:104).

2549. Wigley 1998:2,288.

2550. Benedick 1998. In the ensuing debate in Denmark, the Greenpeace chairman attacked my credibility because I used Mr. Benedick as a witness to the low impact of Kyoto (*Aktuelt*, 23 October 1998). Conceding the correctness of the quote, the chairman thought it manipulative to use it without stating that Benedick in his article would like to see bigger cuts in the CO_2 emissions. This is correct but beside the point – the debate here is what impact Kyoto will have (a scientific question), not whether it should have been bigger (a value/political question).

2551. *Science*, 19 December 1997, 278:2048.

2552. Actually, the reduction is slightly less than six years, since the temperature in 2094 will be 1.913°C.

2553. *Jyllands-Posten*, 19 December 1997, section 1, p. 10.

2554. *Science*, 19 December 1997, 278:2,048.

2555. Kyoto 1997.

2556. Weyant and Hill 1999:xii, both emission trading and the more obscure clean development mechanism, see Kyoto 1997:Articles 3 and 12.

2557. Weyant and Hill 1999:x.

2558. Gusbin *et al.* 1999:833. There is the whole issue of hot air (Russia and others selling permits to emit CO_2, which they had never intended to use anyway because of the slow economy, cf. Böhringer 2000), which the EU finds it would be wrong to exploit. Although allowing Russia to sell the permits would still mean that the total Kyoto Protocol emissions would be achieved, barring the sale of hot air will make emissions even lower. This actually seems to be the core difference between the US and the EU – the EU wants a harder treaty than does the US.

2559. See Weyant and Hill 1999; Manne and Richels 1999; MacCracken *et al.* 1999; Jacoby and Wing 1999; Nordhaus and Boyer 1999; Tol 1999; Kurosawa *et al.* 1999; Bollen *et al.* 1999; Kainuma *et al.* 1999; Bernstein *et al.* 1999; Tulpule *et al.* 1999; McKibbin *et al.* 1999; Cooper *et al.* 1999; Peck and Teisberg 1999. For an even higher cost estimate for the US, see EIA 1998a. These models are also the ones used by IPCC, 2001c:Table TS.4.

2560. In general, the uncertainty is about a factor 2 – i.e. the true cost could turn out to be twice or half as big. However, the relative findings are much more clear.

2561. Of $23 trillion (World Bank 2000b).

2562. Radetzki 1999:373; cf. OECD 1994:42, 44.

2563. OECD 1994:42, 44.

2564. OECD (1994:45) indicates 1.9 percent for OECD in 2050, and Weyant (1993) indicates *c.* 4 percent for 2100. It is not necessary to evaluate extra damage caused by reduced growth; it is estimated that stabilization at around 1990 levels will do nothing but alter the growth rate from 2.3 percent to 2.25 percent (i.e. only about 5 percent in 100 years) (Gaskins and Weyant 1993:320).

2565. 2 percent of OECD GDP of 32,294 billion 1985 US$ (OECD 1994:38), updated to 1999$, BEA 2001b.

2566. Notice, a lot of these numbers are very vague – the 2 percent was calculated from present GDP and probably need not scale fully with future GDP increase. On the other hand, the 2 percent figure is only from inside-OECD trade, whereas world trade would be cheaper.

2567. Weyant 1993, so-called carbon leaking (Manne and Richels 1999:12ff).

2568. US Senate 1997.

2569. Cited in Sagoff 1999; see also Sagoff 1999 for good arguments along this line.

2570. Nordhaus and Boyer 2000:VIII, 6–7.

2571. Curiously, Munich Re seems to take the extreme view in this case: "Manmade climate change must be curbed at all cost" (2000:4).

2572. Note that initially we are simply deliberating which solution is *globally and collectively* the best. Then we will discuss below the problems of implementing such a solution in the real world, with different governments and various incentives.

2573. It can generally be said that given a certain stabilization, the cheapest solution is to postpone cuts until as far as possible into the future, because this will facilitate the reduction of capital adaptation costs; IPCC 1996c:386–7.

2574. See also Parson and Fisher-Vanden 1997.

2575. Nordhaus 1991d, 1991a–c, 1992a, 1993, 1994.

2576. IPCC 1996c:385.

2577. Nordhaus and Boyer 2000; DICE 1999.

2578. In Europe, it is customary to express the cost in tons of CO_2, which is about four times less or \$28.4; 1 kg C = 3.7 kg CO_2, IPCC 1990:364.

2579. The conclusions of the individual models will be quoted in the final part of this chapter, see Peck and Teisberg 1992, Maddison 1995b:345, Parson and Fisher-Vanden 1997:614, Nordhaus 1998:18, Hamaide and Boland 2000. This is also the conclusion of a very seriously critical essay on the issue: "The economic literature on climate change implies that there is no urgent need for serious climate policy," Chapman and Khanna 2000:225. Notice that the 2001 IPCC report commits a couple of pages to the total costs of stabilization (IPCC 2001c:8.4.1.2), and finds that costs lie from slightly negative (that is a net benefit) to 3 percent reduction of GDP on average. They furthermore describe that averaged over all scenarios and for stabilizing at 450, 550, 650 and 750ppm, they are about 1–1.5 percent over the century. However, these are not integrated assessments, as they do not look at the optimal course, and the economic models seem non-optimized, as at least some models for low-emission scenarios (as A1T) shows *benefits* to further economic restrictions. In the IPCC report it is explained as "apparent positive economic feedbacks of technology development and transfer," IPCC 2001c:8.4.1.2. As described below in the discussion of no-regrets, such features of economic models seem somewhat unrealistic, essentially pointing out that there was unfulfilled optimization potential in the basic scenario, and such an optimization benefit should be included in a proper baseline description of the scenario, not ascribed as a benefit to environmental regulation.

2580. Notice, it would be more proper to *add* the extra environmental benefits to the benefits from avoiding a ton of carbon, but since the functional form is only given for the cost, this gives a clearer picture of the diminishing force of the ancillary benefits.

2581. Nordhaus and Boyer 2000:chapter 4.

2582. Nordhaus and Boyer 2000:VII, 28, in 2000\$; cf. \$7.33; Nordhaus 1991d:927.

2583. IPCC 2001f:7, 2001c:7.3.3, 8.2.3.

2584. Burtraw *et al.* 1999:7–8, both tax and benefits in 1996 US\$, adjusted to 2000 US\$, BEA 2001b-c.

2585. This is a maximal estimate, since the \$3.8/tC is a maximal estimate (could be closer to \$2.6/tC).

2586. IPCC 2001c:8.2.4.4; Radetzki 1997:552–3.

2587. Weyant and Hill 1999:xxxvii–xl.

2588. Notice, although the DICE model costs are provided in Figure 160, all the calculations are based on the RICE model.

2589. In effect, it is assumed that the damages grow quadratically with temperature (Nordhaus and Boyer 2000:IV, 30).

2590. Strangely, Nordhaus and Boyer (2000) decided not to include a backstop like solar power as we discussed above (Chakravorty *et al.* 1997), which means that their carbon emission projections will be worst case.

2591. Nordhaus and Boyer (2000:VII, 7) point out that the optimal solution "is not presented in the belief that an environmental pope will suddenly appear to provide infallible canons of policy that will be scrupulously followed by all. Rather, the optimal policy is provided as a benchmark for policies to determine how efficient or inefficient alternative approaches may be."

2592. Nordhaus 1992a:1317; Nordhaus and Boyer 2000:VII,14; cf. Morgan and Dowlatabadi 1996:349.

2593. Pezzey and Park 1998:541ff; Bovenberg 1999:421–2.

2594. An early example would be Pierce 1991, and it is still repeated today, see e.g. Bernow *et al.* 1998 (emphasis added): "Recent analyses have emphasized that pollution taxes can not only curb pollution, but also fund cuts in other levies, raising the prospect of *benefits to both the economy and the environment*. Recent work on the possibility of such a 'double dividend'. . ."

2595. Pezzey and Park 1998:542.

2596. Bovenberg and de Mooij 1994; Fullerton and Metcalf 1997; Goulder *et al.* 1998; Parry and Oates 1998.

2597. See Parry and Oates 1998:3ff.

2598. This is the so-called first-best analysis, resulting in a so-called Pigouvian tax.

2599. IPCC 2001c:8.2.2.1.2&3.

2600. Bovenberg and de Mooij 1994; Fullerton and Metcalf 1997; Goulder *et al.* 1998; Parry and Oates 1998; Bovenberg 1999.

2601. IPCC 1996c:308–9.

2602. See IPCC 2001f:7, 2001c:7.3.3.1, 8.2.2, 9.2.1.

2603. IPCC 2001c:7.3.3.1, footnote 11: "The term 'strong double dividend' has been used in the literature for cases in which the revenue-recycling effect not only exceeds the interaction effect but also the direct (GDP) costs of reducing emissions, thus making revenue-generating environmental policy costless. A revenue-recycling effect this large presupposes that the original tax structure is seriously inefficient (e.g., that capital is highly overtaxed relative to labor). This in itself calls for a tax reform the benefits of which should not be ascribed to the introduction of a revenue-generating environmental policy, even if the two were made on one and the same occasion." IPCC 2001c:8.2.2.2.5: "In general, however, modeling results show that the sum of the positive revenue-recycling effect and the negative tax-interaction effect of a carbon tax or auctioned emission permits is roughly zero."

2604. IPCC 2001f:7: "under some circumstances, it is possible that the economic benefits may exceed the costs of mitigation."

2605. Parry and Oates 1998:6.

2606. Cf. Pezzey and Park 1998:552: "the double dividend debate has weakened the overall case for further environmental control."

2607. Brett and Keen 2000.

2608. Nordhaus 1992a:1317.

2609. Nordhaus and Boyer 2000:VIII, 9. This effect was not included in the calculations for the Kyoto Protocol in Figure 157.

2610. One should not put too much faith into all these digits, given the numerous assumptions and approximations – it would be more correct to say about $5 trillion. However, the important point is here to compare the outcome with other scenarios, in which case the relative costs are much more robust.

2611. OECD (2000:270) estimates a total official development assistance of US $50 billion in 1998.

2612. IMF (2000b:113) estimates the world output to be $32 trillion in 2000.

2613. This cost could be said to be a consequence of our building a world based on fossil fuels. In advancing such an argument we also have to remember, though, that this world based on fossil fuels in many ways has brought us the quality of life documented in Part II, and it is unclear whether we could have chosen a different path, not using fossil fuels but achieving approximately the same welfare. Moreover, since we indeed did build such a world, an argument pointing the finger at the fossil fuels world would merely have an I-told-you-so quality.

2614. IPCC 1997a:6, or 1997a:47: "measures worth doing anyway."

2615. IPCC 1996c:309–10; Lovins and Lovins 1997.

2616. Denmark has just estimated, in connection with its promised, relatively significant cutback, that there is a high degree of inefficiency (IPCC 1996c:318).

2617. IPCC 1996c:318.

2618. UNEP 1994:II, 22: *Danmarks Energifremtider ("Danish energy futures")* 1995:185

2619. *Danmarks Energifremtider* 1995:184; DK EA 1996:118. *Energi 21* gets an even lower figure because of an estimated increase in energy prices during the period, see *Energi 21*:68–9.

2620. Also includes a substantial stake in renewable energy.

2621. *Danmarks Energifremtider* 1995:70.

2622. *Danmarks Energifremtider* 1995:72.

2623. *Danmarks Energifremtider* 1995:18.

2624. *Danmarks Energifremtider* 1995:20.

2625. *Danmarks Energifremtider* 1995:163. It is put quite directly in the UNEP section on Denmark: "The main question is: How much of this [CO_2 reduction] potential can be realised without substantial increases in costs associated with finding and implementing these options, and without serious welfare losses? None of these costs are included in the following calculations, which are based on the concept of direct costs" (UNEP 1994:II, 21).

2626. *Danmarks Energifremtider* 1995:19.

2627. *Danmarks Energifremtider* 1995:72.

2628. *Danmarks Energifremtider* 1995:18.

2629. *Danmarks Energifremtider* 1995:99.

2630. *Danmarks Energifremtider* 1995:175.

2631. *Danmarks Energifremtider* 1995:166. It is actually known that the transport sector will need extra investments: The transport sector's fuel cuts "must be seen in relation to the extra investments envisaged in the energy-saving scenario. These have not, however, been computed" (*Danmarks Energifremtider* 1995:167).

2632. *Danmarks Energifremtider* 1995:113.

2633. *Energi 21*:64.

2634. DK EPA 1996a:118.

2635. IPCC 1996b:267. Schelling calls it "totally contradictory to econometric estimates" (1992). If there really is large-scale, feasible and profitable restructuring that has not been realized, this is probably due to structural barriers and it is not certain that these can be overcome without considerable ensuing expense. Halsnæs *et al.* (1995:81ff) discuss some of the arguments.

2636. Nordhaus 1991a.

2637. Morgan and Dowlatabadi 1996:359–60.

2638. Metcalf and Hassett 1997.

2639. Read the excellent expositions in IPCC 1996c:chapter 4, 125ff; Nordhaus 1997a; Toman 1998; and Portney and Weyant 1999b.

2640. We also ignore taxes, which is more problematic, since taxes do influence personal behavior. However, as the discounting with regards to climate change is mainly focused on societal costs and benefits, taxes can be ignored for the purpose of exposition.

2641. Portney and Weyant (1999a:6–7) point out that all but one of the contributors suggest it is appropriate and even essential to discount future benefits and costs at some positive rate.

2642. Jespersen and Brendstrup 1994:94. Cf. the rhetorical question from Chapman and Khanna (2000:230): "is our children's happiness and safety really worth less than our own?"

2643. IPCC 1996c:133.

2644. Nordhaus 1997a:317.

2645. E.g. OECD 1994:38.

2646. Nordhaus 1997a:317.

2647. Wildavsky cited in IPCC 1996c:133.

2648. IPCC 1996c:132.

2649. Schelling (1999) argues persuasively that this is the primary distributional conflict.

2650. IPCC 1996c:133.

2651. IPCC 2001c:TS.7.2.3.

2652. This is, of course, a back-of-an-envelope argument which demands the actual availability of investment potential of 16 percent, but the argument is simply intended to support our own intuition; $150 billion at 16 percent for 60 years – discounted to current value this would give about $59 trillion.

2653. About 1.1 billion people do not have access to clean drinking water today (Annan 2000:5) and the World Bank estimates that it would cost some $150 per person for water systems, or $165 billion to provide clean water supplies for everyone (World Bank 1994:11). Equally, about 2.5 billion do not have access to sanitation (Annan 2000:5), and this is estimated to cost less than $50 per household (World Bank 1994:83), or some $30 billion (assuming four per household). Thus the total cost of providing full coverage of water and sanitation is less than $200 billion. The US cost of Kyoto (Annex I trade) is $325 billion (Nordhaus and Boyer 2000:VIII, 27).

2654. Estimate by USAID and WHO (World Bank 1992:49).

2655. IPCC 1996a:42–3.

2656. IPCC 2001a:11.5.4.3.

2657. Woodward 1998b.

2658. IPCC 2001a:TS.B.7.

2659. IPCC 2001a:11.3.1, cf. Conway and Hall 1999: "We suggest that modern grounding-line retreat is part of ongoing recession that has been under way since early to mid-Holocene time. It is not a consequence of anthropogenic warming or recent sea level rise. In other words, the future of the WAIS may have been predetermined when grounding-line retreat was triggered in early Holocene time. Continued recession and perhaps even complete disintegration of the WAIS within the present interglacial period could well be inevitable."

2660. IPCC 2001a:TS.B.7, 11. executive summary: "It is now widely agreed that major loss of grounded ice and accelerated sea-level rise are very unlikely during the 21st century."

2661. IPCC 2001a:11.executive summary, cf. IPCC 1996b:251; Fankhauser 1998.

2662. Pearce 2000.

2663. Pearce 2000:5,

2664. IPCC 2001d:10–1.

2665. IPCC 2001a:Figure 11.16.

2666. Fankhauser 1998; IPCC 1996b:271–2; Broecker 1997, 1999; Perry 2000:64.

2667. IPCC 2001d:10, cf. 2001a:9.3.4.3.

2668. Perry 2000:64; IPCC 2001d:10.

2669. IPCC 2001d:10, where long enough seems to be at least 1 percent CO_2 increase over 100 years (2001a:9.3.2.3), which as discussed earlier is way beyond the 0.6 percent empirical increase (Figure 148). This is important, since the shutting down seems to depend primarily on the *speed of forcing increase* with which the system is affected, and not the long-run resultant temperature increase (ibid.).

2670. Marotzke 2000.

2671. Schelling 1992.

2672. Fankhauser 1998. I have not been able to find any studies that investigate the costs of a potential interruption of the Gulf Stream.

2673. "The mid-latitude Atlantic THC [thermohaline circulation] appears to be quite steady in time" (Marotzke 2000:1,349). Doherty *et al.* 1998 from *US Joint Institute for the Study of Atmosphere and Oceans* in http://www.theatlantic.com/issues/98may/9805lett.htm: "The collective evidence from the scientific literature suggests that an anthropogenically induced climate change has been detected and that this change includes a *strengthening* of the North Atlantic circulating pattern."

2674. Latif *et al.* 2000. In the 2000 *Science* overview

of Coupled GCMs, the new research is described thus: "The strong interest in thermohaline circulation changes in the past arose with the observation in CGCM runs that deep water formation in the high-latitude North Atlantic would shrink or even stop if there were an enhanced greenhouse effect in the atmosphere. However, a mechanism not included in these models may dampen the entire discussion." Grassl 2000.

2675. If one maximizes expected payoff; Fankhauser 1998; Schellnhüber and Yohe 1997: part 3.

2676. Technically speaking, that we have an aversion to risk.

2677. IPCC 1996c:133.

2678. de Vries *et al.* 2000:138.

2679. IPCC 2000a:170, Sankovski *et al.* 2000:285.

2680. The full quote is "Normative scenarios depict situations and conditions as one would hope they would emerge; exploratory scenarios attempt to describe plausible futures by taking into account constraining and counteracting conditions, possibly starting from a normative scenario. In this sense our scenario is largely normative," de Vries *et al.* 2000:170.

2681. IPCC 2001c:SPM.12 estimate that "the current annual environmental expenditure in most developed countries is 1–2 percent of GDP." Notice, this sentence fell out of the final SPM.

2682. Using A1T GDP, all discounted, as was the $107 trillion, by 7 percent.

2683. "Published estimates indicate that increases in global mean temperature would produce net economic losses in many developing countries for all magnitudes of warming studied, and that the losses would be greater in magnitude the higher the level of warming. In many developed countries, net economic gains are projected for global mean temperature increases up to roughly 2°C. Mixed or neutral net effects are projected in developed countries for temperature increases in the approximate range of 2 to 3°C, and net losses for larger temperature increases. The projected distribution of economic impacts is such that it would increase the disparity in well being between developed countries and developing countries, with the disparity growing with higher temperatures. The more damaging impacts estimated for developing countries reflects, in part, their lesser adaptive capacity." IPCC 2001b:Summary for Policymakers, original government draft, 2.6.

2684. Peck and Teisberg 1992.

2685. Maddison 1995b:345.

2686. Parson and Fisher-Vanden 1997:614.

2687. Nordhaus 1998:18.

2688. Although monetary losses from macroeconomic models may be harder to present.

2689. IPCC 1996a:5.

2690. Kerr 2000.

2691. IPCC 2001a:SPM:5.

2692. IPCC 2001d:6.

2693. Pearce 2001:5.

2694. IPCC 2001b:SPM:4.

2695. IPCC 2001e:6. Moreover, the confidence was changed from medium to low.

2696. IPCC 2001c:TS.1.1, see endnote 2531.

2697. Some of the final WGIII analysis comes no further than to express the obvious, as in the chapter on *Towards what Objective should the Response be Targeted? High versus Low Stabilization Levels – Insights on Mitigation*, which concludes: "lower stabilization targets involve exponentially higher mitigation costs and relatively more ambitious near-term emissions reductions, but, as reported by WGII, lower targets induce significantly smaller biological and geophysical impacts and thus induce smaller damages and adaptation costs," IPCC 2001c:10.4.6.

2698. IPCC 2001c:1.4.1.

2699. "Alternative Development Pathways" is the title of IPCC 2001c:1.4.1.

2700. IPCC 2001c:1.4.2.1.

2701. IPCC 2001c:1.4.3.

2702. IPCC 2001c:1.4.3.1.

2703. IPCC 2001c:1.4.3.1.

2704. IPCC 2001c:1.4.3.1.

2705. IPCC 2001c:1.4.3.2.

2706. IPCC 2001c:1.4.3.3.

2707. IPCC 2001c:1.4.3.3.

2708. IPCC 2001c:1.4.3.3; cf. IPCC 2001c:TS.5.2: "Adoption of more sustainable consumption patterns."

2709. IPCC 2001c:1.4.3.

2710. IPCC 2001c:1.5.1.2.

2711. IPCC 2001c:5.3.8.4.

2712. IPCC 2001c:5.3.8.4.

2713. IPCC tells us, lifestyles are "not economically rational, but they are still culturally rational," meaning that our Western consumerism is merely another way of relating ourselves to others (IPCC 2001c:10.3.2.3.1). This we do through consuming, but really we are partaking in "a cultural project the purpose of which is to complete the self" (quoting approvingly McCracken, IPCC 2001c:10.3.2.3.1).

2714. IPCC 2001c:1.4.3.

2715. IPCC 2001c:10.3.2.3.2. There is only a reference to UNDP 1998b, but it comes from page 4.

2716. Even in the cited document, it was not Americans remembering back, when they were happiest: "The percentage of Americans calling themselves happy peaked in 1957 – even though consumption has more than doubled in the meantime," UNDP 1998b:4.

2717. A changed proportion of respondents calling themselves "very happy" could be cause by many other factors apart from happiness. Over time, tendency to reply dishonestly (faking happiness) could decline, the format of the interviews could change etc. see Smith 1979, which is the original reference. Simon noticed a similar decline in the evaluation of the American "situation of the country" since the late 1950s (1995b:6). However, here we have another question to check the answers with, namely the respondent's view of his or her *own life*. Here the average remained constant over time, indicating that the decline in "situation of the country" was not one of absolute decline but of decline in perception.

2718. See Smith 1979:22, where the SRC/GSS showed 34.7 percent "very happy," which were exceeded in 1988 with 36.1 percent and in 1990 with 35.7 (GSS 2001). The 1998 result was 33.3 percent.

2719. For a review, see Argyle 1987:91ff.

2720. IPCC 2001c:1.5.3.

2721. Hartill 1998.

2722. Bishop 1993.

2723. Ciotti 1989.

2724. Ciotti 1989. Summing up, Rifkin thought that "The Age of Progress is really an illusion. Far more people – 800 million – go to bed hungry today than at any time in history." (A statement which is incorrect, as can be seen in Figure 7.)

2725. Ciotti 1989. The sentence runs ". . .mankind is better off, *and* there is . . .," where *and* has been substituted with *but* for meaning.

2726. Ciotti 1989.

2727. Ciotti 1989.

2728. Kram *et al.* 2000:369.

2729. Though IPCC naturally does not control the media, their *Summary for Policymakers* does not exactly make the above mentioned policy points clear (IPCC 2001f).

2730. Pearce 2001:5.

2731. Pearce 2001:5.

2732. CNN.com 2001a, b (notice, these are apparently the first stories from CNN, appearing almost a month after the release of WGI summary), Hawkes 2001, CBSnews.com 2001, Karon 2001.

2733. This is the basic thrust of Schelling's argument (1999).

2734. UNICEF 2000:37.

2735. See NAS 1992; Herzog *et al.* 2000.

2736. Schelling 1992.

2737. Was 700 billion dollars (2.4 percent of global GDP) in 1996; WI 1998b:114–15.

2738. Notice, this is slightly different from the Nordhaus estimate at $945 trillion, because the scenarios have somewhat different assumptions of discount rate and income profile. The discount parameter used here is 7 percent. The calculations are all rough, 10-year average income, discounted at mid-interval discount-parameter, starting in 2005–2095.

2739. From $378 trillion to $291 trillion, IPCC 2000b.

2740. Gore 1992:269.

2741. Gore 1992:273.

2742. Gore 1992:222.

2743. Gore 1992:232.

2744. Gore 1992:232.

2745. Gore 1992:275.

2746. Gore 1992:269.

2747. Gore 1992:230ff.

2748. Herman 1997:400ff.

2749. Gore 1992:236.

2750. The question is: "How much, if at all, do you believe environmental problems (a) now affect your health (b) affected your health in the past – say 10 years ago (c) will affect the health of our children and grandchildren – say over the next 25 years? A great deal, a fair amount, not very much or not at all?"

2751. Knudsen 1997.

2752. At 0.96 percent, 0.87 percent, 0.81 percent and 0.77 percent (WI 1997b:108).

2753. Quoted in Slovic 1987:280.

2754. Doll and Peto (1981:1,246–8) estimate that half of all pollution-related incidences of cancer (1 percent of 2 percent) are due to atmospheric pollution. With the latest evaluations of particle pollution, this can only be adjusted upwards.

2755. Ågerup 1998:14.

2756. Beck 1986; Rasborg 1997.

2757. Adams 1995:179–81. "In terms of basic life security, nonetheless, the risk-reducing elements seem substantially to outweigh the new array of risks" (Giddens 1991:116).

2758. E.g. Zeckhauser and Viscusi 1990.

2759. WWF 1997a:18.

2760. Ågerup 1998:15

2761. "Environment most important" (Dunlap 1991b:291): percentage of individuals volunteering environment as one of the country's "most important problems."

"Too little gov't spending": "Are we spending too much, too little, or about the right amount on improving and protecting the environment?" Measured by the percentage answering too little.

"Environment over growth" full line (Dunlap 1991:294, 300): "Which of these two statements is closer to your opinion: We must be prepared to sacrifice environmental quality for economic growth. We must sacrifice economic growth in order to preserve and protect the environment?" Measured by the percentage choosing second statement.

"Environment over growth" broken line (Gallup 2000a): "Here are two statements which people sometimes make when discussing the environment and economic growth. Which of these statements comes closer to your own point of view? (1) Protection of the environment should be given priority, even at the risk of curbing economic growth or (2) Economic growth should be given priority, even if the environment suffers to some extent." Measured by the percentage choosing statement 2.

"Too little environmental protection" 1973–1980 (Dunlap 1991b:294): "There are also different opinions about how far we've gone with environmental protection laws and regulations. At the present time, do you think environmental protection laws and regulations have gone too far, or not far enough, or have struck about the right balance?" Measured by the percentage choosing "not far enough." 1982–1990 (Dunlap 1991a:13): "In general, do you think there is too much, too little, or about the right amount of government regulation and involvement in the area of environmental protection?" Measured by the percentage answering "too little." 1992–2000 (Saad and Dunlap 2000): "Do you think the U.S. government is doing too much, too little, or about the right amount in terms of protecting the environment?" Measured by the percentage answering "too little."

"Environment, regardless of cost" 1981–1990 (Dunlap 1991b:300): "Do you agree or disagree with the following statement: Protecting the environment is so important that requirements and standards cannot be too high, and continuing environmental improvements must be made regardless of cost." Measured by percentage agreeing. 1992, 1997 (Anon. 1997b, notice this reference is not as trustworthy as the others, since it is a web-page reference to a study of Public Opinion Strategies for the GOP. However, a possible vested interest seems not to be to inflate these numbers): "Environmental protection is so important that requirements and standards cannot be too high, and continuing environmental improvements must be made, regardless of cost." Measured by percentage agreeing.

2762. Gallup 2000b.

2763. Saad 1999.

2764. Costs in Natural resources, Parks and recreation and Sewerage only includes local, state and federal costs, whereas Solid waste, Air and Water also includes private and business costs. Since only federal costs are available throughout the entire period, whereas state and local costs are available for 1955–96 and total costs for 1972–94, these costs are estimated on available trends for 1962–71 and from 1994/6–9. The total cost of the environment data series for 1972–94 was unfortunately discontinued, see Blodgett 1997.

2765. The fact that we spend more on the environment does not mean that environmental problems have got worse, but rather that we have become more aware of them (in the same way, spending more money on health care does not imply that we have become more sick).

2766. Dunlap 1991b:300.

2767. Finkel and Golding 1994.

2768. The WHO uses the term "established market economies," but besides the OECD this only includes small states such as the Vatican, Bermuda, the Channel Islands, etc.

2769. Meyerhoff 1993.

2770. Putnam and Wiener 1995:147.

2771. Putnam and Wiener 1995.

2772. Graham and Wiener 1995:2.

2773. Literature describes numerous examples of illusions of risk to which we yield, and I will here only investigate a few of them. See also Magolis 1996; Slovic 1986, 1990; Zeckhauser and Viscusi 1990; Wilson 1979; Slovic *et al.* 1986, Fischhoff *et al.* 1979; Grandjean 1998:106ff.

2774. Combs and Slovic 1979.

2775. Combs and Slovic 1979:841.

2776. Sandman 1996.

2777. Sandman 1996.

2778. Slovic *et al.* 1979; Singer and Endreny 1993:61ff.

2779. Grandjean 1998:108.

2780. Slovic *et al.* 1986:116.

2781. Slovic *et al.* 1986:116, Combs and Slovic 1979.

2782. Slovic *et al.* 1986:117.

2783. Grandjean 1998:151.

2784. If we expect about 20 deaths a year in the US from pesticides, and only 0.4 percent stem from drinking water (Ames *et al.* 1987:272), this means 5.6 deaths per lifetime (70 years) from drinking water of a population of 270 million, or a lifetime risk of 2 percent of 1:1,000,000 (2e-8). Thus, even with the EPA extreme worst-case assumption of 1,500–3,000 dead, lifetime risk would be 1.5–3 of 1,000,000 (1.5e–6 to 3e–6).

2785. Grandjean 1998:110.

2786. Fischhoff *et al.* 1979:32.

2787. It has also been suggested that resentment is a reasonable evaluation factor: if someone is resentful towards or dislikes a polluter and the social order which permits such pollution, she has the right to demand its removal, even though the objective risk involved is extremely low (described in Grandjean 1998:107). But here we are confronted by a fundamental problem in that if society's resources are used to remove an objectively minimal risk, one is also choosing not to use the same resources to remove other, greater risks. How acceptable the person concerned finds this is naturally a moral question, but as I see it, it simply means they are maintaining that their own (objectively lower) risk is of greater consequence than others' (objectively greater) risk. Or to put it more bluntly: My life is more important than yours. (An imbalance also arises in that such resentment-based evaluation will escalate: it is to my advantage to say that I am *very* resentful of developments on my street and it is to your advantage to say that you are *extremely* resentful of the development of the smoke nuisance from your neighbor's garden. Later on, I ought then to say that I really am *most extremely* resentful . . .)

2788. Margolis 1996:38.

2789. Margolis 1996:38.

2790. Taylor 2000.

2791. In a phrase from Mendeloff (cited in Margolis 1996:161): overregulation (of what gets on the agenda) yields underregulation (of many things consequently left off the agenda.

2792. Tengs *et al.* 1995; Tengs 1997; Tengs and Graham 1996; Graham 1995.

2793. Tengs 1997:table II.

2794. Tengs 1997.

2795. The median cost of all health interventions is the price of the health intervention which splits all the other interventions in two equal parts, where 50 percent are cheaper and 50 percent are more expensive. The advantage of the median is that it is less affected by very atypical (high) prices. Of the cost $5, $10, $70, $100, and $1000, $70 would be the median, whereas the average would be $237, highly affected by the single value of $1000.

2796. Note that medicine and toxic control in Graham 1995 have been mislabeled. They have here been labeled correctly, such that the median, mentioned in Graham's text, agrees with the figure.

2797. Tengs 1997.

2798. Graham 1995; Tengs 1997.

2799. E.g. Greenpeace MTV commercial (2001a) whose *only* written message is the word "frankenfood," with a somewhat ominous feel to it.

2800. GMOs for medical uses generally employ enclosed production and produce life-saving products, and this has made medical GMOs more readily accepted, ESRC 1999:9, Dixon 1999:547. Eurobarometer find 60 percent concerned about the risks associated with GM food, compared with just 40% in the case of the medical applications of biotechnology, EU 2001b:55.

2801. James 1999, 2000. The world crop area is about 1510 Mha, WRI 2000c:272.

2802. James 2000; WRI 2000c272–3.

2803. James 2000.

2804. Anon. 2000d.

2805. Hoisington *et al.* 1999.

2806. Evenson 1999:5,925.

2807. Nash and Robinson 2000.

2808. Greenpeace 2001b.

2809. House of Commons 1999:13.

2810. McHughen 2000:255.

2811. McHughen 2000:255.

2812. Levy and Newell 2000; EU 2001b:50ff. For a long, but possibly biased overview, see CFS 2001.

2813. 57, 63 and 69 percent, respectively. EU 2000d:36–8.

2814. Hennessy 2000.

2815. Anon. 1999i; Margaronis 1999.

2816. EU 2001b:56; 2000d:36–8.

2817. "The opposition to GMOs in Europe has been informed and led by environmental organizations like Greenpeace and Friends of the Earth," Margaronis 1999; EU 2001b:51.

2818. FotE 2001.

2819. Greenpeace 1996; Orogan and Long 2000; OCE 2001; UCS 2001; as well as the answer in AS 2000, House of Lords 1998:73–4, and House of Commons 1999:15–20.

2820. FotE 2001.

2821. First point in Greenpeace (1996) list of concerns: "Toxic or allergenic effects."

2822. Enserink 1999; Reuters 1998.

2823. BBC 1998. Apparently, he also added that he found it "very, very unfair to use our fellow citizens as guineapigs," Anon. 1999j.

2824. Liberal Democrat environment spokesman Norman Baker: "The only proper thing to do now is to ban GM ingredients from all foodstuffs," BBC 1998.

2825. RRI 1998.

2826. "Although some of the results are preliminary, they are sufficient to exonerate Dr. Pusztai," van Driessche and Bøg-Hansen 1999. Again, members of the British House of Commons urged a moratorium on genetically modified food, Enserink 1999.

2827. Royal Society 1999:4.

2828. Ewen and Pusztai 1999.

2829. Kuiper *et al.* 1999.

2830. After the memorandum (van Driessche and Bøg-Hansen 1999) several allegations were made that the government or the biotech industry had a hand in suppressing the data, Enserink 1999.

2831. OCE 2001:2.

2832. "It is well known that lectins may be toxic, and several cases of 'favism' occur every year because people do not cook beans well enough thus leaving the bean lectin active in the uncooked or insufficiently cooked beans." Bøg-Hansen 1999.

2833. Coghlan and Kleiner 1998.

2834. "Potatoes with a transgenic lectin, such as used in the experimental work by Pusztai, would be produced only in order to do such experimental animal research and under the strictest control. I have not heard that such genetically engineered potatoes have ever been intended for human consumption - much less used for human consumption." Bøg-Hansen 1999.

2835. Ewen and Pusztai 1999.

2836. Cubitt was refering specifically to concanavalin A, a lectin from the jack bean gene, as the study originally was presented, Enserink 1998.

2837. Coghlan and Kleiner 1998; cf. McHugen 2000:118.

2838. Bøg-Hansen 1999.

2839. Ewen and Pusztai 1999.

2840. "Other parts of the GM construct, or the transformation, could have contributed to the overall effects." Ewen and Pusztai 1999.

2841. Kuiper *et al.* 1999.

2842. Kuiper *et al.* 1999; Royal Society 1999:3.

2843 NRC 2000b:68, Kuiper *et al.* 1999. Actually, the memorandum finds that the two GM-lines were substantially different, van Driessche and Bøg-Hansen 1999, which lends more credibility to the potato lines not really being stable.

2844. Royal Society 1999:3.

2845. NRC 2000b:68.

2846. NRC 2000b:68.

2847. OCE 2001:2.

2848. Although not all with such drastic description: FotE 2001; Greenpeace 1996; Orogan and Long 2000; Montague 1999; UCS 2001.

2849. FotE 2001.

2850. The following is based on McHughen 2000:119–21.

2851. Nestle 1996.

2852. Nordlee *et al.* 1996.

2853. Jones 1999:583.

2854. This is part of the oft-quoted (e.g. Orogan and Long 2000) "The next case could be less ideal, and the public less fortunate," Nestle 1996.

2855. Nestle 1996; UCS 2001.

2856. McInnis and Sinha 2000.

2857. Jane Henney, commissioner of the FDA, quoted in McInnis and Sinha 2000.

2858. Dixon 1999:547.

2859. Orogan and Long 2000; OCE 2001.

2860. Yoon 1999; BBC 1999.

2861. Milius 1999.

2862. Trewavas 1999:231.

2863. McInnis and Sinha 2000; Nottingham 1998:47.

2864. Nottingham 1998:47.

2865. Nottingham 1998:49; USDA 2001b:4.

2866. Nottingham 1998:49.

2867. McHughen 2000:178.

2868. James 2000.

2869. Losey *et al.* 1999, see also similar results from Hansen and Obrycki 2000.

2870. Guynup 2000.

2871. Losey *et al.* 1999.

2872. Guynup 1999.

2873. Yoon 1999.

2874. Nash and Robinson 2000.

2875. Anon. 2000d.

2876. Anon. 2000e.

2877. Levidow 1999.

2878. McHughen 2000:178. Equally, the *New York Times* writes: "The Bt toxin itself is already known to be lethal to many butterflies and moths," Yoon 1999.

2879. Losey *et al.* 1999.

2880. The argument comes from McHughen 2000:178.

2881. Milius 2000.

2882. EPA 2000g.

2883. EPA 2000g:IIC57.

2884. EPA 2000g:IIC57, 58.

2885. EPA 2000g:IIC57.

2886. Sadar 2000.

2887. Bailey 2001.

2888. EU 2000d:15.

2889. 35 percent said true, 35 percent false, and 30 percent don't know, EU 2000d:25.

2890. "If a person eats a genetically modified fruit, their genes could be modified as a result." 42 percent identified this correctly as false, whereas 24 percent thought it true and 34 percent didn't know, EU 2000d:16, 25.

2891. Freivalds and Natz (1999) reports that 45 percent of all Americans incorrectly thought it true that "ordinary tomatoes do not contain genes while genetically modified tomatoes do."

2892. Not all alleged myths are myths. McHughen (2000:14–16) claims that the story of a fish gene in a tomato is wrong: "'Fish gene in tomato' has all the standard characteristics of an urban myth – it's scary and it sounds 'too good to be real.'" However, the permit to grow such a tomato with the antifreeze gene of the winter flounder was actually granted in 1991, as can be read at the Animal and Plant Health Inspection Service database (APHIS 1991). But this story seems much less pervasive in the debate and has none of the dread and destruction attached to the three main myths discussed here.

2893. FotE 2001.

2894. UCS 2001.

2895. Jones 1999:583–4.

2896. Orogan and Long 2000; Greenpeace 1996.

2897. All examples from UCS 2001.

2898. McHughen 2000:161.

2899. Chair of the UK Advisory Committee on Releases to the Environment, Beringer 1999.

2900. Schiermeier 2000; Jones 1999:584; House of Commons 1999:17.

2901. McHughen 2000:162–3.

2902. Crawley *et al.* (2001:683): "Our results . . . indicate that arable [GM] crops are unlikely to survive for long outside cultivation."

2903. NRC 2000b:68.

2904. Ames and Gold 1993; Zimberoff and Mosely 1991; Edelson 1990.

2905. Ames and Gold 1993.

2906. NRC 2000b:9; McHughen 2000:113.

2907. Trewavas 1999:231.

2908. McHughen 2000:259.

2909. McHughen 2000:162–4.

2910. McHughen 2000:164.

2911. House of Lords 1998:110.

2912. NRC 2000b:6.

2913. House of Commons 1999:12.

2914. As a human race it is probably safe to say that we have mostly progressed by taking risks and not by being better-safe-than-sorry (Esty 1999), but as we get increasingly richer, the trade-off clearly swings to the ever more risk averse.

2915. Cited in EU 2000c:26.

2916. See Weale 1992:79ff.

2917. Lundmark 1997.

2918. DK EPA 1995a: http://www.mem.dk/publikationer/RED/2.htm.

2919. Well illustrated in IPCC 2001c:10.1.2.

2920. E.g. thalidomide, suggested to be a wonder-drug for pregnant women, but which resulted in birth defects such as deafness, blindness, disfigurement, cleft palate, and many other internal disabilities (Muggleton 1999).

2921. Friedman (2000) discusses a "glimpse of the future" from Japan, where teenagers communicate by a so-called DoCoMo, a palm-held phone and internet connection. "As for their social implications" the DoCoMo means that people meet in chat rooms and eventually, when friendships are forged, people will arrange an "offkai" or an offline meeting. "That's right, now meeting online is normal and meeting offline – i.e. in person – has its own term." A teenager says that before she spent a lot of time together around the dinner table. "Now, after we have our meal we go back to our rooms with our own DoCoMo's and Internet, so we have less time to spend with the family. People use their own private links with the world, so they don't look back and depend on their family as much anymore."

A mother is quoted seeing this as deeply concerning: "As a parent, I deeply deplore the situation. My son is 17 and he seems to have a girlfriend, but I'm not sure, because it seems that they don't meet each other so much, they usually communicate over the e-mail. There are so many things you can learn from human physical contact, but this younger generation is losing these interpersonal skills."

2922. That it is often used this way is perhaps best expressed by the Danish chief executive of the Ministry of Environment, who said on the precautionary principle: Within the department "there are not many who are in doubt that it is a correct principle . . . But we haven't had great theoretical discussions about it. We just use it, and we are quite pleased with it" (DK EPA 1998b).

2923. E.g. Tim O'Riordan has suggested that the precautionary principle should apply in the following: "Where there is the possibility of irreversible damage to natural life support functions, precautionary action should be taken *irrespective* of the foregone benefits," (quoted in ESRC 1999:17, italics added). This, of course, means that even though a democratic risk evaluation would show that benefits far outweigh costs (say, paving over a bog, definitely destroying some natural life support functions), the precautionary principle *a priori* excludes such a decision.

2924. As has been suggested by the Danish Environmental High Adviser, Peder Agger (Agger 1997:10).

2925. Or perhaps, more correctly, the agenda will be set and the distribution of resources allocated according to the interests with the loudest and most well-organized lobbyists.

2926. Anderson 1991.

2927. WRI 1998a:22.

2928. Ehrlich 1967:655.

2929. FAO 2001a.

2930. See for instance the opening page in *Time* magazine environmental supplement, describing the morning of an ordinary boy placed in the future where the environment has gone awry: "Child of the future: The young boy awoke on a hot, oppressive morning. It wasn't a school day, so he could afford to lie back for a while with his favorite storybook. That was the one with drawings of the great forests – the woodlands filled with tall trees, wild animals and clear-running streams. The scenes seems so magical that the boy could hardly believe in them, though his parents assured him that such wonders once existed. Closing his book, he saw no joy in the day ahead. He wished the air conditioner weren't broken. He wished there were more food in the refrigerator. He wished he could see the great forests. But there was no use in thinking about that now. It was enough of a struggle just to be alive, especially for a child." Time 1997:1.

Bibliography

AAAAI 2000 *Allergy Report vols. I–III*. The American Academy of Allergy, Asthma and Immunology, in partnership with the National Institute of Allergy and Infectious Diseases (NIAID). http://www.theallergyreport.org/.

Abdulaziz, Abuzinda and Fridhelm Krupp 1997 "What happened to the Gulf: two years after the world's greatest oil-slick." *Arabian Wildlife* 2:1. http://www.arabianwildlife.com/past_arw/vol2.1/oilglf.htm.

Abell, Annette, Erik Ernst and Jens Peter Bonde 1994 "High sperm density among members of organic farmers' association." *The Lancet* 343:1,498.

Abelson, Philip H. 1994 "Editorial: adequate supplies of fruits and vegetables." *Science* 266:1,303.

Abrahamsen, Gunnar, Arne O. Stuames and Bjørn Tveite 1994a "Discussion and synthesis." In Abrahamsen *et al.* 1994c:297–331.

1994b: "Summary and conclusions." In Abrahamsen *et al.* 1994c:332–5.

Abrahamsen, Gunnar, Arne O. Stuames and Bjørn Tveite (eds.) 1994c: *Long-Term Experiments with Acid Rain in Norwegian Forest Ecosystems*. New York: Springer-Verlag.

Abramovitz, Janet N. 1999 "Unnatural disasters." *World Watch* 12(4):30–5.

ACC/SCN 2000 *Fourth Report on the World Nutrition Situation: Nutrition throughout the Life Cycle*. January 2000. United Nations Administrative Committee on Coordination, Sub-Committee on Nutrition, in collaboration with the International Food Policy Research Institute. http://www.unsystem.org/accscn/Publications/4RWNS.html.

Ackerman, Frank 1997 "Recycling: looking beyond the bottom line." *BioCycle* 38(5):67–70.

Acquavella, John, Geary Olsen, Philip Cole, Belinda Ireland, Johan Kaneene, Stanely Schuman and Larry Holden 1998: "Cancer among farmers: a meta-analysis." *Annals of Epidemiology* 8:64–74.

ACS 1999 *Cancer Facts and Figures – 1999*. Atlanta, GA: American Cancer Society.

2000 "How has the occurrence of breast cancer changed over time?" Atlanta, GA: American Cancer Society. http://www.cancer.org/statistics/99bcff/occurrence.html.

Acsadi, George and J. Nemeskeri 1970 *History of Human Life Span and Mortality*. Budapest: Akademiai Kiado.

Adams, John 1995 *Risk*. London: University College London Press.

Adams, W. C. 1986 "Whose lives count? TV coverage of natural disasters." *Journal of Communication* 36(2):113–22.

Adleman, Morris A. 1995 "Trends in the price and supply of oil." In Simon 1995b:287–93.

AEA 1999 *Economic Evaluation of Air Quality Targets for CO and Benzene*. By AEA Technology for European Commission DGXI. http://europa.eu.int/comm/environment/enveco/studies2.htm.

Agarwal, Anil and Sunita Narian 1998 "The greenhouse gas trade." *UNESCO Courier* 10:10–13.

Ågerup, Martin 1998 *Dommedag er aflyst: velstand og fremgang i det 21. Århundrede*. [Doomsday canceled: wealth and prosperity in the twenty-first century.] Copenhagen: Gyldendal.

Agger, Peder, Lennart Emborg and Jørgen S. Nørgård 1997 *Livet i drivhuset – En debatbog om miljø og samfund*. [Life in the greenhouse – a debate book on the environment and the society.] Copenhagen: Mellemfolkeligt Samvirke.

AGU 1995 *U.S. National Report to International Union of Geodesy and Geophysics 1991–1994*. American Geophysical Union, supplement to *Reviews of Geophysic*, 33. http://earth.agu.org/revgeophys/contents.html.

Ahmed, Kulsum 1994 *Renewable Energy Technologies:*

A Review of the Status and Costs of Selected Technologies. Washington, DC: World Bank Technical Paper 240.

Ainsworth, Martha and Waranya Teokul 2000 "Breaking the silence: setting realistic priorities for AIDS control in less-developed countries." *The Lancet* 356(9223):55–60.

Albert, Jørn E. 1989 *Syreregn: trusler mod livet*. [Acid rain: threats against life.] Copenhagen: Forum.

Alexander, Bruce H., Harvey Checkoway, Chris van Netten, Charles H. Muller, Timothy G. Ewers, Joel D. Kaufman, Beth A. Mueller, Thomas L. Vaughan and Elaine M. Faustman 1996 "Semen quality of men employed at a lead smelter." *Occupational and Environmental Medicine* 53:411–16.

Alexandratos, Nikos 1997 "FAO's Cereals Projections to 2010 and Recent Developments: Response to Lester Brown." Chief of Global Perspective Studies Unit, FAO, Rome, unpublished manuscript; received from John Lupien, Director of Food and Nutrition Division.

1998 *World Food and Agriculture: Outlook to 2010*. Downloaded (but no longer available) at http://www.fao.org/waicentfaoinfo/economic/esd/at2010.pdf.

1999 "World food and agriculture: outlook for the medium and longer term." *Proceedings of the National Academy of Sciences* 96:5,908–14. http://www.pnas.org.

Alhajji, A.F. and David Huettner 2000 "OPEC and World Crude Oil Markets from 1973 to 1994: Cartel, Oligopoly, or Competitive?" *Energy Journal* 21(3):31–60.

Al-Khalaf, Bader 1998 "Pilot study: the onset of asthma among the Kuwaiti population during the burning of oil wells after the Gulf War." *Environment International* 24(1–2):221–5.

Allen, Ruth H., Michelle Gottlieb, Eva Clute, Montira J. Pongsiri, Janette Sherman and G. Iris Obrams 1997 "Breast cancer and pesticides in Hawaii: the need for further study." *Environmental Health Perspectives Supplements* 105:679–83.

Al-Rashed, Muhammad F. and Mohsen M. Sherif 2000 "Water resources in the GCC countries: an overview." *Water Resources Management* 14:59–75.

Alter, George and James C. Riley 1998 "Sickness, recovery, and sickness redux: transitions into and out of sickness in nineteenth-century britain." Working Paper 98–2, Department of History, Indiana University. http://www.indiana.edu/~pirt/wp98-2.html.

Altheide, David L. and R. Sam Michalowski 1999 "Fear in the news: a discourse of control." *Sociological Quarterly* 40(3):475–503.

Aly, S. E. 1999 "Gas turbine total energy vapour compression desalination system." *Energy Conversion and Management* 40(7):729–41.

Ames, Bruce N. and Lois Swirsky Gold 1990 "Chemical carcinogenesis: too many rodent carcinogens." *Proceedings of the National Academy of Sciences* 87:7,772–6. http://www.pnas.org.

1993 "Another perspective...nature's way." *Consumers' Research Magazine* 76(8):22–3.

1997 "The causes and prevention of cancer: gaining perspective." *Environmental Health Perspectives Supplements* 105(4):865–73.

1998 "The causes and prevention of cancer: the role of environment." *Biotherapy* 11:205–20.

2000 "Paracelsus to parascience: the environmental cancer distraction." *Mutation Research* 447:3–13. http://socrates.berkeley.edu/mutagen/Paracelsus.pdf.

Ames, Bruce N., Renae Magaw and Lois Swirsky Gold 1987 "Ranking possible carcinogenic hazards." *Science* 236:271–80.

Ames, Bruce N., Margie Profet and Lois Swirsky Gold 1990a "Dietary pesticides (99.99 percent all natural)." *Proceedings of the National Academy of Sciences* 87:7,787–81.

1990b "Nature's chemicals and synthetic chemicals: comparative toxicology." *Proceedings of the National Academy of Sciences* 87:7,782–6.

Ames, Bruce N., Mark K. Shigenaga and Tory M. Hagen 1993 "Oxidants, antioxidants, and the degenerative diseases of aging." *Proceedings of the National Academy of Sciences* 90:7,915–22.

Amey, Earle B. 1996 *Gold*, US Geological Surveys. http://minerals.er.usgs.gov/minerals/pubs/commodity/gold/300496.pdf and *Natural Resources* 4:285–312.

Andersen, Claus E., Niels C. Bergsøe, Jens Brendstrup, Anders Damkjær, Peter Gravesen and Kaare Ulbak 1997 *Radon-95: en undersøgelse af metoder til reduktion af radonkoncentrationen i danske enfamiliehuse*. [Radon-95: an investigation of methods for reduction of the radon concentration in Danish single-family houses.]

Risø-R-979. http://www.risoe.dk/rispubl/NUK/ris-r-979.htm.

Andersen, Mikael Skou 1998 "Lomborgs fejl." [Lomborg's errors]. *Politiken*, 22 February 1998, section 2, p. 1.

Andersen, Per Dannemand 1998 *Review of Historical and Modern Utilization of Wind Power.* http://www.risoe.dk/vea-wind/history.htm.

Anderson, Christopher 1991 "Cholera epidemic traced to risk miscalculation." *Nature* 354:255.

Anderson, Terry L. 1995 "Water, water everywhere but not a drop to sell." In Simon 1995b:425–33.

Andreae, Meinrat O. 1991 "Biomass burning: its history, use and distribution and its impact on environmental quality and global climate." In Levine 1991:3–21.

2001 "The dark side of aerosols." *Nature* 409(6821):671–2.

Angell, J. K. 1999 "Global, hemispheric, and zonal temperature deviations derived from radiosonde records." In *Trends Online: A Compendium of Data on Global Change*. Carbon Dioxide Information Analysis Center, Oak Ridge National Laboratory, US Department of Energy, Oak Ridge, Tennessee. http://cdiac.esd.ornl.gov/trends/temp/angell/angell.html.

Annaert, Jan and Marc J. K. de Ceuster 1997 "The big mac: more than a junk asset allocator?" *International Review of Financial Analysis* 6(3):179–92.

Annan, Kofi 1997 "Global change and sustainable development: critical trends." Report of the Secretary-General to the Commission on Sustainable Development. E/CN.17/1997/3. gopher://gopher.un.org/00/esc/cn17/1997/off/97—3.EN%09% 9%2 B.

1998 *The causes of conflict and the Promotion of Durable Peace and Sustainable Development in Africa.* S/1998/318, 13 April 1998. http://www.un.org/Docs/sc/reports/1998/s1998318.htm.

1999 *Concise report of the Secretary-General on world population monitoring, 2000: population, gender and development.* Commission on Population and Development, 33rd session. E/CN.9/2000/3. http://www.undp.org/popin/unpopcom/33rdsess/official/3e1.pdf.

2000 *Progress Made in Providing Safe Water Supply and Sanitation for all During the 1990s. Report of the Secretary-General.* Economic and Social Council, Commission on Sustainable Development, 8th session. http://www.un.org/esa/sustdev/csd8/wss4rep.pdf.

Anon. 1992a "Biodiversity: variety is the spice of life." *UN Chronicle* 29:52–3.

1992b "Editorial: environmental pollution: it kills trees, but does it kill people?" *The Lancet* 340(8823):821–2.

1993a "Powerboat pollution." *Environment* 35:10:23.

1993b: "Relentless DDT." *Time* 141(18):24–5.

1993c "Breast cancer linked to chlorine." *Earth Island Journal* 8(2):23.

1994a "Farmer sperm count puzzle." *Earth Garden* 89:8.

1994b "Organic farmers have more sperm density." *Nutrition Health Review* 71:6.

1994c "Respiratory ailments linked to Gulf War fires?" *Earth Island Journal* 9(3):18.

1995a "Generation why?" *Psychology Today* 28(1):18.

1995b "Scrubber myths and realities." *Power Engineering* 99:(1):35–8.

1995c "Flowing uphill." *Economist*, 8/12/95, 336(7927):36.

1997a "Assessing the odds." *The Lancet* 350(9091):1563.

1997b "Eye on Washington." The National Grassroots Organization of Republicans for Environmental Protection. http://www.repamerica.org/news/ge3_eye.htm.

1997c "Tan now, pay later." *Earth Island Journal* 12(3):3.

1997d "Turning the tides – creating a cancer-free environment now." *MidLife Woman* 6(1):3–7.

1997e "Asthma epidemic: A link to moving or childhood vaccinations?" *Science News* 151(4):60.

1998a "Disney blames El Niño, ABC for stock fall." *Electronic Media* 17(11):22.

1998b "Pollution and degradation causes 40 percent of deaths worldwide." *Health Letter on the CDC*. 10/12/98, p. 3–4. Can be read at http://www.news.cornell.edu/releases/Sept98/ecodisease.hrs.html (uncredited)

1998c "Weird weather." *Junior Scholastic* 100(15):8.

1998d "When virtue pays a premium." *Economist* 04/18/98, 346(8064):57–8.

1999a "Cancer country." *Sierra* 84(5):17.

1999b "El Niño disasters may typify impact of global warming, NWF says." *International Wildlife* 29(1):6.

1999c "Group calls for moratorium on pesticides to reduce risk of breast cancer." *Natural Life* 69:12.

1999d "Nasty, brutish, and dirty." *Discover* 20(2):30.

1999e "Persons of the century." *Time*. 14 June 1999, 153(23):8.

1999f "Solar ready to compete with fossil fuels." *Natural Life* 70:13.

1999g "Fuel cells meet big business." *Economist* 07/24/99, 352(8129):59–60.

1999h "Indicators: Millenium issue." *Economist* 31/12/99, 353(8151):147–8.

1999i "Food for thought." *Economist*, 06/19/99 351(81):24–42.

1999j "Health risks of genetically modified foods." *Lancet* 353(9167):1,811.

2000a "Recycle your toothbrush." *Environment* 42(4):5.

2000b "Spectrum." *Environment* 42(6):6–9.

2000c "Market indicators." *Economist*, 15/1/00, 354(8153): 89.

2000d "Poisoned monarchs." *Discover* 21(1):62.

2000e "Environmental Coalition to Sue EPA Over Registrations of Bt Crops." *Chemical Market Reporter*, 11/06/2000, 258(19):15.

2000d "GM Crops: More Food, or Thought?" *Chemical Market Reporter*, 3/20/2000, 257(12):FR10-2.

2001a "Will the oil run out?" *Economist* 02/10/2001, 358(8208):special section 13–15.

2001b "The Year in NATURE." Special Edition of Time Magazine, Winter2000/2001, 156(27):58–63.

APHIS 1991 "Permit Number 91–079–01: Tomato; antifreeze gene; staphylococcal Protein A." *Animal and Plant Health Inspection Service*. http://www.nbiap.vt.edu/biomon/relea/9107901r.eaa.

Argyle, Michael 1987 *The Psychology of Happiness*. London: Routledge.

Ariza, Luis Miguel 2000 "Burning times for hot fusion." *Scientific American* 282(3):19–20.

Arkes, Hal R. and Kenneth R. Hammond (eds.) 1986 *Judgment and Decision Making: An Interdisciplinary Reader*. Cambridge: Cambridge University Press.

Armknecht, Paul A., Walter F. Lane and Kenneth J. Stewart 1997 "New products and the U.S. Consumer Price Index." In Bresnahan and Gordon 1997:375–91.

Armstrong, Gregory L., Laura A. Conn and Robert W. Pinner 1999 "Trends in infectious disease mortality in the United States during the 20th century." *Journal of the American Medical Association* 281(1):61–6.

Arnell, Nigel W. 1999 "Climate change and global water resources." *Global Environmental Change* 9:S31–S49.

Arnold, Steven F., Diane M. Klotz, Bridgette M. Collins, Peter M. Vonier, Louis J. Guillette Jr. and John A. McLachlan 1996 "Synergistic activation of estrogen receptor with combinations of environmental chemicals." *Science* 272:1,489–92.

AS 2000 "Transgenic Plants and World Agriculture." Prepared by the Royal Society of London, the US National Academy of Sciences, the Brazilian Academy of Sciences, the Chinese Academy of Sciences, the Indian National Science Academy, the Mexican Academy of Sciences and the Third World Academy of Sciences. http://www.nap.edu/catalog/9889.html.

Ashworth, Steven D., John C. Callender and Kristin A. Boyle 1992 "The effects of unrepresented studies on the robustness of validity generalization results." *Personnel Psychology* 45(2):341–61.

Asimov, Isaac and Frederik Pohl 1991 *Our Angry Earth*. New York: Tom Doherty Associates.

ATA 2001a *Traffic Summary 1960–1999: U.S. Scheduled Airlines Air Transport Data and Statistics*. Air Transport Association. http://www.air-transport.org/public/industry/1624.asp.

2001b *Safety Record of U.S. Airlines*. Air Transport Association. http://www.air-transport.org/public/industry/28.asp.

Atkins, David and Julie Norman 1998 "Mycotoxins and food safety." *Nutrition and Food Science* 5:260–6.

Atkinson, A. B. and F. Bourguignon (eds.) 2000 *Handbook of Income Distribution*. Amsterdam: Elsevier Science.

ATV 1992 *Risk Management and Risk Assessment in Different Sectors in Denmark*. Proceedings from a conference by the Danish Academy of Technical Sciences on "Risk Management, Hazard and Risk Assessment in Connection with the Setting of Limit Values for Chemicals," Lyngby, Denmark: Danish Academy of Technical Sciences.

Auger, Jaques, Jean Marie Kunstmann, Françoise Czyglik and Pierre Jouannet 1995 "Decline in semen quality among fertile men in Paris during the past 20 years." *New England Journal of Medicine* 332(5):281–5.

Auken, Svend 1998 "Planetens sande tilstand?" [The true state of the planet?] *Politiken*, 3 February 1998, section 2, p. 5–6.

Auliciems, Andris and Ian Burton 1973 "Trends in smoke concentrations before and after the Clean Air Act of 1956." *Atmospheric Environment* 7:1,063–70.

Ausubel, Jesse H. 1995 "Technical Progress and Climatic Change." *Energy Policy* 23(4/5):411–6. http://phe.rockefeller.edu/tech_prog.

1996 "Real numbers." *Issues in Science and Technology* 13(2):78–81.

Ausubel, Jesse H. and Arnulf Grübler 1995 "Working less and living longer: long-term trends in working time and time budgets." *Technological Forecasting and Social Change* 50:113–31. http://phe.rockefeller.edu/work_less.

Avery, Dennis 1995 "The world's rising food productivity". In Simon 1995b:376–91.

AWEA 2000a *Facts about Wind Energy and Birds*. American Wind Energy Association. http://www.awea.org/pubs/factsheets/avianfs.pdf http://www.awea.org/pubs/factsheets.html.

AWEA 2000b *Global Wind Energy Market Report*. American Wind Energy Association. http://www.awea.org/faq/global99.html.

Ayer, Harry and Neilson Conklin 1990 "Economics of Ag chemicals." *Choices: The Magazine of Food, Farm and Resource Issues* 5(4):24–7.

Bailey, Ronald (ed.) 1995 *The True State of the Planet*. New York: Free Press.

2000 *Earth Report 2000: Revisiting the True State of the Planet*. New York: McGraw-Hill.

Baillie, Jonathan and Brian Groombridge (eds.) 1997 *1996 IUCN Red List of Threatened Animals*. Compiled by the World Conservation Monitoring Centre. Gland, Switzerland: IUCN – The World Conservation Union. Searchable database at http://www.wcmc.org.uk/species/animals/animal_redlist.html.

Balassa, Bela 1964 "The purchasing-power parity doctrine: a reappraisal." *The Journal of Political Economy*. 72(6):584–96.

Balling, Robert C. Jn., Patrick J. Michaels and Paul C. Knappenberger 1998 "Analysis of winter and summer warming rates in gridded temperature time series." *Climate Research* 9(3):175–82.

Barclay, George, Ansley Coalle, Michael Stoto and James Trussel 1976 "A reassessment of the demography of traditional rural China." *Population Index* 42(4):606–35.

Barnett, T. P., K. Hasselmann, M. Chelliah, T. Delworth, G. Hegerl, P. Jones, E. Rasmusson, E. Roeckner, C. Ropelewski, B. Santer and S. Tett 1999 "Detection and attribution of recent climate change: a status report." *Bulletin of the American Meteorological Society* 80(12):2,631–60. http://ams.allenpress.com.

Barney, Gerald O. (ed.) 1980 *The Global 2000 Report to the President of the U.S.: Entering the twenty-first Century*, vols. I–III. New York: Pergamon Press.

Barrett, Stephen 1998 "The truth about organic certification." *Nutrition Forum* 15(2)9–12.

Barro, Robert J. and Jong-Wha Lee 1996 "International measures of schooling years and schooling quality." *American Economic Review, Papers and Proceedings* 86(2):218–23. Datase from http://www.worldbank.org/research/growth/ddbarle2.htm.

Bates, David V. 1995 "Observations on asthma." *Environmental Health Perspectives Supplements* 103(6):243–8.

Bauman, Norman 1996 "Panic over falling sperm counts may be premature." *New Scientist* 11 May:10.

Baumol, William J. 1986 "On the possibility of continuing expansion of finite resources." *Kyklos* 39:167–79.

Baumol, William J., Richard R. Nelson and Edward N. Wolff 1994 *Convergence of Productivity: Cross-National Studies and Historical Evidence*. Oxford: Oxford University Press.

Baumol, William J. and Wallace E. Oates 1995 "Long-run trends in environmental quality." In Simon 1995b:444–75.

Baxter, William F. 1974 *People or Penguins: The Case for Optimal Pollution*. New York: Columbia University Press.

BBC 1998 "Experiment fuels modified food concern" Monday, August 10, 1998. http://news.bbc.co.uk/hi/english/sci/tech/newsid_148000/148267.stm

1999 "GM pollen 'can kill butterflies'." http://news.bbc.co.uk/hi/english/sci/tech/newsid_347000/347638.stm.

BEA 2000 *National Income and Product Accounts.* Accessed 2000. Bureau of Economic Analysis. http://www.bea.doc.gov/bea/dn/gdplev.htm.

2001 *National Income and Product Accounts.* Accessed 2001. Bureau of Economic Analysis. http://www.bea.doc.gov/bea/dn/gdplev.htm.

2001b *Price Indexes for Gross Domestic Product and Gross Domestic Purchases.* Bureau of Economic Analysis. http://www.bea.doc.gov/bea/dn/st3.csv.

2001c *Selected NIPA Tables showing advance estimates for the fourth quarter of 2000.* Bureau of Economic Analysis. http://www.bea.doc.gov/bea/dn/dpga.txt.

Beardsley, Tim 1997 "Death in the deep: 'dead zone' in the Gulf of Mexico challenges regulators." *Scientific American* 277(5):17–18.

Beasley, R., S. Nishima, N. Pearce and J. Crane 1998 "Beta-agonist therapy and asthma mortality in Japan." *The Lancet* 351(9,113):1,406–7.

Beck, Ulrich 1986 *Risk Society: Towards a New Modernity.* Translation 1992. London: Sage.

Becker, Stan and Kiros Berhane 1996 "A meta-analysis of 61 sperm count studies revisited." *Fertility and Sterility.* 67(6):1,103–8.

Becklake, Maargret R. and Pierre Ernst 1997 "Environmental factors." *The Lancet,* supplement *Asthma,* 350(9,085):10–13.

Begley, Sharon and Daniel Glick 1996 "He's not full of hot air." *Newsweek.* 22 January, 127(4):24–9.

BEIR 1998 *The Health Effects Of Exposure to Indoor Radon.* Biological Effects of Ionizing Radiation (BEIR) VI Report. Executive summary: http://www.epa.gov/iedweb00/radon/beirvi1.html. Public summary: http://www.epa.gov/iedweb00/radon/public.html.

Bell, M. A., R. A. Fischer, D. Byerlee and K. Sayre 1995 "Genetic and agronomic contributions to yield gains: a case study for wheat." *Field Crops Research* 44(2–3):55–65.

Bendvold, Erik 1989 "Semen quality in Norwegian men over a 20-year period." *International Journal of Fertility* 34(6):401–4.

Benedick, Richard 1998:"How workable is the Kyoto Protocol?" *Weathervane.* http://www.weathervane.rff.org/pop/pop5/benedick.html.

Benford, D. J. and D. R. Tennant 1997 "Food chemical risk assessment." In Tennant 1997:21–56.

Bengtsson, L., M. Botzet and M. Esch 1996 "Will greenhouse gas-induced warming over the next 50 years lead to higher frequency and greater intensity of hurricanes? *Tellus* 48A(1):57–73.

Bengtsson, L., E. Roeckner and M. Stendel 1999 "Why is the global warming proceeding much slower than expected?" *Journal of Geophysical Research-Atmospheres* 104(D4):3,865–76.

Beringer, John 1999 "Keeping watch over genetically modified crops and foods." *Lancet* 353(9,153):605–6.

Bernow, Steve, Robert Costanza, Herman Daly, Ralph DeGennaro, Dawn Erlandson, Deeohn Ferris, Paul Hawken, J. Andrew Hoerner, Jill Lancelot, Thomas Marx, Douglas Norland, Irene Peters, David Roodman, Claudine Schneider, Priya Shyamsundar and John Woodwell 1998 "Ecological tax reform." *Bioscience* 48(3):193–6.

Bernstam, Mikhail S. 1995 "Comparative trend in resource use and pollution in market and socialist economies." In Simon 1995b:502–22.

Bernstein, Paul M. and W. David Montgomery 1998 *How Much Could Kyoto Really Cost? A Reconstruction and Reconciliation of Administration Estimates.* Washington, DC: Charles River Associates.

Bernstein, Paul, David Montgomery, Thomas Rutherford and Gui-Fang Yang 1999 "Effects of restrictions on international permit trading: the MS-MRT model." *The Energy Journal,* Kyoto Special Issue:221–56.

Berry, Albert, François Bourguignon and Christian Morrisson 1983 "Changes in the world distribution of income between 1950 and 1977." *The Economic Journal* 93:331–50.

1991: "Global economic inequality and its trends since 1950." In Osberg 1991:60–91.

Berry, Brian J. L., Edgar C. Conkling and D. Michael Ray 1993 *The Global Economy: Resource Use, Locational Choice and International Trade.* Englewood Cliffs, NJ: Prentice Hall.

Berz, Gerhart A. 1993 "Global warming and the insurance industry." *Interdisciplinary Science Reviews* 18(2):120–5.

1997 "Catastrophes and climate change: risks and (re-)actions from the viewpoint of an international reinsurer." *Eclogae Geologicae Helvetiae* 90(3):375–9.

Bichel Committee 1999a *Rapport fra hovedudvalget.* [Main conclusions.] The Committee to evaluate the full consequences of a total or partial phase-out of pesticide use. Copenhagen: Danish Environmental Protection Agency. http://mstex03.mst.dk/199903publikat/87-7909-296-9/Default.htm.

1999b *Rapport fra udvalget om jordbrugsdyrkning*. [Agricultural production consequences.] The Committee to evaluate the full consequences of a total or partial phase-out of pesticide use. Copenhagen: Danish Environmental Protection Agency. http://mstex03.mst.dk/199903publikat/87-7909-289-6/Default.htm.

1999c *Rapport fra underudvalget om produktion, økonomi og beskæftigelse*. [Consequences for production, economy and employment.] The Committee to evaluate the full consequences of a total or partial phase-out of pesticide use. Copenhagen: Danish Environmental Protection Agency. http://mstex03.mst.dk/199903publikat/87-7909-295-0/Default.htm.

1999d *Rapport fra underudvalget for miljø og sundhed*. [Consequences for environment and health.] The Committee to evaluate the full consequences of a total or partial phase-out of pesticide use. Copenhagen: Danish Environmental Protection Agency. http://mstex03.mst.dk/199903publikat/87-7909-291-8/Default.htm.

1999e *Rapport fra underudvalget om lovgivning: juridiske spørgsmål vedrørende afvikling af pesticidanvendelsen i jordbrugserhvervene*. [Legal considerations in pesticide reductions.] The Committee to evaluate the full consequences of a total or partial phase-out of pesticide use. Copenhagen: Danish Environmental Protection Agency. http://mstex03.mst.dk/199903publikat/87-7909-293-4/Default.htm.

1999f *Rapport fra underudvalget om lovgivning: tillægsrapport*. [Legal considerations in pesticide reductions, addendum.] The Committee to evaluate the full consequences of a total or partial phase-out of pesticide use. Copenhagen: Danish Environmental Protection Agency. http://mstex03.mst.dk/199903publikat/87-7909-294-2/Default.htm.

1999g *Rapport fra den tværfaglige økologigruppe: økologiske scenarier for Danmark*. [Organic scenarios for Denmark.] The Committee to evaluate the full consequences of a total or partial phase-out of pesticide use. Copenhagen: Danish Environmental Protection Agency. http://mstex03.mst.dk/199903publikat/87-7909-292-6/Default.htm.

Bindslev-Jensen, Carsten 1998 "Food allergy." *British Medical Journal* 316(7,240):1,299. http://www.bmj.com/cgi/content/full/316/7140/1299.

Birnbaum, Jeffrey H. and Natasha Graves 1999 "How to buy clout in the capital." *Fortune* 140:(11) 207–8.

Bishop, Jerry E. 1993 "It Ain't Over Till It's Over . . . Cold Fusion: The controversial dream of cheap, abundant energy from room-temperature fusion refuses to die." *Popular Science* 243(2):47–52.

Bittman, Michael 1999 "The land of the lost long weekend? Trends in free time among working age Australians, 1974–1992." *Society and Leisure* 21(2):353–79. http://www.sprc.unsw.edu.au/dp/dp083.pdf.

Blackmore, Roger 1996 "Damage to the ozone layer." In Blackmore and Reddish 1996:70–128.

Blackmore, Roger and Alan Reddish 1996 *Global Environmental Issues*. London: Hodder and Stoughton.

Blaiss, Michael S. 1997 "Outcomes analysis in asthma." *Journal of the American Medical Organization* 278:1,874–80. http://www.ama-assn.org/special/asthma/library/readroom/pr7003.htm.

Blodgett, John E. 1997 *Environmental Protection: How Much It Costs and Who Pays*. Congressional Research Service. http://cnie.org/nle/rsk-10.html

Blumstein, Philip and Pepper Schwartz 1983 *American Couples: Money, Work, Sex*. New York: Morrow and Co.

Boardman, Joan 1998 "An average soil erosion rate for Europe: myth or reality?" *Journal of Soil and Water Conservation* 53(1):46–50.

Bobbink, Roland and Jan G. M. Roelofs 1995 "Ecological effects of atmospheric deposition on non-forest ecosystems in Western Europe." In Heij and Erisman 1995.

Bøg-Hansen, Thorkild C. 1999 "Comments to GM food." http://plab.ku.dk/tcbh/RowettvsPusztai.htm.

Bogo, Jennifer 1999 "The diet–cancer connection." *E Magazine: The Environmental Magazine* 10(3):42–3.

Böhringer, Christoph 2000 "Cooling down hot air: a global CGE analysis of post-Kyoto carbon abatement strategies." *Energy Policy*. 28:779–89.

Bollen, Johannes, Arjen Gielen and Hans Timmer 1999 "Clubs, ceilings and CDM: macroeconomics of compliance with the Kyoto Protocol." *The Energy Journal*, Kyoto Special Issue:177–206.

Boskin, Michael J., Ellen R. Dulberger, Robert J. Gordon, Zvi Griliches, and Dale W. Jorgenson 1996 *Toward a More Accurate Measure of the Cost of Living*. Final report to the Senate Finance Committee from the Advisory Commission to Study the Consumer Price Index, 4 December, 1996. http://www.ssa.gov/history/reports/boskinrpt.html.

1997 "The CPI Commission: findings and recommendations." *AEA Papers and Proceedings* 87(2):78–83.

1998 "Consumer prices, the Consumer Price Index, and the cost of living." *Journal of Economic Perspectives* 12(1):3–26.

Boskin, Michael J. and Dale W. Jorgenson 1997 "Implications of overstating inflation for indexing government programs and understanding economic progress." *AEA Papers and Proceedings* 87(2):89–93.

Botkin, Daniel B. and Edward A. Keller 1998 *Environmental Science: Earth is a Living Planet*. New York: John Wiley and Sons.

Bourgeois-Pichat, J. 1989 "From the 20th to the 21st century: Europe and its population after the year 2000." *Population*, English Selection 1:57–90.

Bove, Mark C., James B. Elsner, Chris W. Landsea, Xufeng Niu and James J. O'Brien 1998 "Effect of El Niño on U.S. landfalling hurricanes, revisited." *Bulletin of the American Meteorological Society* 79(11):2,477–82. http://ams.allenpress.com/.

Bove, Mark C., David F. Zierden and James J. O'Brien 1998 "Are gulf landfalling hurricanes getting stronger?" *Bulletin of the American Meteorological Society*. 79(7):1,327–8. http://ams.allenpress.com/.

Bovenberg, A. Lans and Ruud A. de Mooij 1994 "Environmental levies and distortionary taxation." *American Economic Review* 84(4):1,085–9.

Boyd, Helle Buchardt 1998 "Hvor farligt er drikkevand med indhold af miljøfremmede stoffer?" [How dangerous is drinking water with chemical pollutants?] *Vandteknik* 2:62–4.

Boyes, Edward and Martin Stanisstreet 1998 "High school students' perceptions of how major global environmental effects might cause skin cancer." *Journal of Environmental Education* 29(2):31–6.

BP 1998 *BP Statistical Review of World Energy 1997*.

1999 *BP Statistical Review of World Energy 1998* (Latest statistics available at http://www.bp.com/worldenergy/ http://www.bpamoco.com/worldenergy/.)

Bradley, Robert L. Jn., 1997 "Renewable energy: not cheap, not 'green'." *Policy Analysis* 280. http://cato.org/pubs/pas/pa-280.html.

Brady, Stephanie 1998 "El Niño dampens area tourist trade." *Business Journal: Serving Greater Tampa Bay* 18(12):1–2.

Brander, James A. and M. Scott Taylor 1998 "The simple economics of Easter Island: a Ricardo-Malthus model of renewable resource use." *American Economic Review*. 88(1):119–38.

Bray, Anna J. 1991 "The Ice Age cometh." *Policy Review* Fall 82–4

Brecher, Michael and Jonathan Wilkenfeld 1997: *A Study of Crisis*. Ann Arbor: University of Michigan Press.

Bresnahan, Timothy F. and Robert J. Gordon (eds.) 1997 *The Economics of New Goods*. Chicago: University of Chicago Press.

Brett, Craig and Michael Keen 2000 "Political uncertainty and the earmarking of environmental taxes." *Journal of Public Economics* 75:315–40.

Brezonik, Patrick L., Victor J. Bierman, Richard Alexander, James Anderson, John Barko, Mark Dortch, Lorin Hatch, Dennis Keeney, David Mulla, Val Smith, Clive Walker, Terry Whitledge and William Wiseman Jn. 1999 *Gulf of Mexico Hypoxia Assessment: Topic #4. Effects of Reducing Nutrient Loads to Surface Waters within the Mississippi River Basin and the Gulf of Mexico*. Hypoxia Work Group, White House Office of Science and Technology Policy, Committee on Environment and Natural Resources for the EPA Mississippi River/Gulf of Mexico Watershed Nutrient Task Force. NOAA Coastal Ocean Program. http://www.nos.noaa.gov/products/pubs_hypox.html.

Bridgland, Fred 1999 "Looming water wars." *World Press Review*, 46(12):16–17.

Briffa, K. R., P. D. Jones, F. H. Schweingruber and T. J. Osborn 1998a "Influence of volcanic eruptions on northern hemisphere summer temperature over the past 600 years." *Nature* 393(6684):450–5.

1998b *Northern Hemisphere Temperature Reconstructions.* ftp://medias.meteo.fr/paleo/treering/reconstructions/n_hem_temp or ftp://ftp.ngdc.noaa.gov/paleo/treering/reconstructions/n_hem_temp/NHemTemp.data.txt.

Brimblecombe, Peter 1977 "London air pollution, 1500–1900." *Atmospheric Environment* 11:1,157–62.

1987 *The Big Smoke: A History of Air Pollution in London since Medieval Times.* London: Methuen.

1996 *Air Composition and Chemistry.* Second edition. Cambridge: Cambridge University Press.

Brimblecombe, Peter and H. Rodhe 1988 "Air pollution – historical trends." *Durability of Building Materials,* 5:291–308.

Brodersen, Søren 1990 "The historical analysis of the consumption surveys." In Viby Mogensen 1990:291–332.

Broecker, Wallace S. 1970 "Man's oxygen reserves." *Science* 168(3,939):1,537–8.

1997 "Thermohaline circulation, the Achilles heel of our climate system: will man-made CO_2 upset the current balance?" *Science.* 278(5,343):1,582–8.

1999 "What if the conveyor were to shut down? Reflections on a possible outcome of the great global experiment." *GSA Today* 9(1):1–7. http://www.geosociety.org/pubs/gsatoday/gsat9901.htm.

2001 "Was the Medieval Warm Period Global?" *Science* 291(5,508):1497–9.

Bromwich P., J. Cohen, I. Stewart and A. Walker 1994 "Decline in sperm counts: an artefact of changed reference range of 'normal'?" *British Medical Journal* 309:19–22.

Brown, K. S. and G. G. Brown 1992 "Habitat alteration and species loss in Brazilian forests." In Whitmore and Sayer 1992:119–42.

Brown, Lester R. 1965 "Population growth, food needs, and production problems." *World Population and Food Supplies 1980,* ASA special publication 6: 17–20. Madison, WI: American Society of Agronomy.

1981 "The worldwide loss of cropland." In Woods 1981:57–98.

1995 *Who Will Feed China: Wake-up Call for a Small Planet.* London: Earthscan Publications.

1996a *Tough Choices: Facing the Challenge of Food Scarcity.* New York: W. W. Norton and Company.

1996b "Who will feed China?" *Futurist.* 30(1):14–18.

Brown, Lester R. and Hal Kane 1994 *Full House: Reassessing the Earth's Carrying Capacity.* New York: W. W. Norton and Company.

Brown, Lester R. and Edward C. Wolf 1984 *Soil Erosion: Quiet Crisis in the World Economy.* Worldwatch Paper 60. Washington, DC: Worldwatch Institute.

Brundtland, Gro Harlem 1997 "The scientific underpinning of policy." *Science* 277:457.

1999 "Investing in global health." *Presidents and Prime Ministers* 8(6):31–3.

Burne, David 1999 *Get a Grip on ECOLOGY.* London, Weidenfeld and Nicolson.

Bryant, Jennings and Dolf Zillmann 1994 *Media Effects: Advances in Theory and Research.* Hillsdale, NJ: Lawrence Erlbaum Associates.

BSAEM/BSNM 1995 "Evidence of adverse effects of pesticides." British Society for Allergy and Environmental Medicine/British Society for Nutritional Medicine. *Journal of Nutritional and Environmental Medicine* 5(4):352–63.

Bucci, Pete 1999 "Solar energy now in demand as a low-cost power option." *Business First – Columbus* 16(9):49.

Bujan, L., A. Mansat, F. Pontonnier and R. Mieusset 1996 "Time series analysis of sperm concentration in fertile men in Toulouse, France between 1977 and 1992." *British Medical Journal* 312:471–2.

Bulatao, Rodolfo A. 1993 "Mortality by cause, 1970 to 2015." In NAS 1993:42–68.

Bunker, John P., Joan Houghton and Michael Baum 1998 "Putting the risk of breast cancer in perspective." *British Medical Journal* 317:1,307–9.

Buol, S. W. 1994 "Soils." In Meyer and Turner II 1994:211–29.

Burnette, Joyce and Joel Mokyr 1995 "The standard of living through the ages." In Simon 1995b:135–48.

Burroughs, William James 1997 *Does the Weather Really Matter? The Social Implications of Climate Change.* Cambridge: Cambridge University Press.

Burtraw, Dallas and Alan Krupnick 1996 "The social costs of electricity: Do the numbers add up?" *Resource And Energy Economic* 18(4):423–66.

1998 "Costs and benefits of reducing air pollutants related to acid rain." *Contemporary Economic Policy* 16(4):379–400.

Burtraw, Dallas, Alan J. Krupnick, Erin Mansur, David Austin, and Deirdre Farrell 1997 *The Costs and Benefits of Reducing Acid Rain.* Discussion Paper 97–31–REV. Washington, DC: Resources for the Future. http://www.rff.org/disc_papers/summaries/9731.htm.

Burtraw, Dallas and Michael Toman 1997 *The Benefits of Reduced Air Pollutants in the U.S. from Greenhouse Gas Mitigation Policies.* Discussion Paper 98–01–REV. Washington, DC: Resources for the Future. http://www.rff.org/disc_papers/summaries/9801.htm.

Burtraw, Dallas, Alan Krupnick, Karen Palmer, Anthony Paul, Michael Toman and Cary Bloyd 1999 *Ancillary Benefits of Reduced Air Pollution in the U.S. from Moderate Greenhouse Gas Mitigation Policies in the Electricity Sector.* Discussion Paper 99–51. Washington, DC: Resources for the Future. http://www.rff.org/CFDOCS/disc_papers/PDF_files/9951.pdf.

Butler, C. J. and D. J. Johnston 1996 "A provisional long mean air temperature series for Armagh Observatory." *Journal of Atmospheric and Terrestrial Physics* 58(15):1,657–72.

Byrne, Celia 2000 *Risk Factors: Breast.* National Institutes of Health, National Cancer Institute. http://rex.nci.nih.gov/NCI_Pub_Interface/raterisk/risks120.html.

Calder, Nigel 1997 *The Manic Sun.* Yelvertoft Manor, UK: Pilkington Press.

Caldwell, John C. 2000 "Rethinking the African AIDS epidemic." *Population and Development Review.* 26(1):117–35.

Camino, Elena and Carla Calcagno 1995 "An interactive methodology for 'empowering' students to deal with controversial environmental problems." *Environmental Education Research* 1(1):59–64.

Campbell, C. J. 1997 "Depletion patterns show change due for production of conventional oil." *Oil and Gas Journal, OGJ Special,* 29 December 1997:33–7.

Campbell, John 1993 "Setting environmental priorities." *Regional Review* 3(2):6–12.

Campbell, M. J., G. R. Cogman, S. T. Holgate and S. L. Johnston 1997 "Age specific trends in asthma mortality in England and Wales, 1983–95: results of an observational study." *British Medical Journal* 314:1,439. http://www.bmj.com/cgi/content/full/314/7092/1439.

Cantor, Kenneth P. 1997 "Drinking water and cancer." *Cancer Causes and Control* 8:292–308.

Carey, Anne E., Jonathan R. Pennock, John C. Lehrter, W. Berry Lyons, William W. Schroeder and Jean-Claude Bonzongo 1999 *The Role of the Mississippi River in Gulf of Mexico Hypoxia.* Environmental Institute, University of Alabama. Sponsored by the Fertilizer Institute, Washington, DC. http://www.tfi.org/hypoxia%20report.pdf.

Carlsen, Elisabeth, Aleksander Giwercman, Niels Keiding and Niels E. Skakkebæk 1992 "Evidence for decreasing quality of semen during past 50 years." *British Medical Journal* 305:609–13.

1995 "Declining semen quality and increasing incidence of testicular cancer: is there a common cause." *Environmental Health Perspectives Supplements* 103(7):137–9.

Carlsen, E., A. Giwercman and N. E. Skakkebæk 1993: "Decreasing quality of semen [letter]." *British Medical Journal* 306:461.

Carpenter, Siri 1999 "Modern hygiene's dirty tricks." *Science News* 156(7):108–10.

Carpenter, Will D. 1991 "Insignificant risk must be balanced against great benefits." *Chemical and Engineering News* 69 (Jan.7):37–9.

Carrel, Chris 1994 "Greenhouse plan is in trouble." *Earth Island Journal* 9(4):10.

Carson, Rachel 1962 *Silent Spring.* Boston, MA: Houghton Mifflin.

Carts-Powell, Yvonne 1997 "Solar energy closes in on cost-effective electricity." *Laser Focus World.* 33(12):67–74.

CBD 1992 *Convention on Biological Diversity.* http://www.biodiv.org/chm/conv/default.htm.

CBSnews.com 2001: "Double-Digit Global Warming?" January 22nd 2001. http://www.cbsnews.com/now/story/0,1597,266129-412,00.shtml.

CBT 2000 *Subsidies, Taxes and Duties on Energy in Denmark.* Centre for Biomass Technology. Download from http://www.videncenter.dk/samlet2.htm.

CDC 1995 "Summary of notifiable diseases, United States, 1994." *MMWR* 43(53):i–xvi, 1–80. ftp://ftp.cdc.gov/pub/Publications/mmwr/wk/mm4753.pdf.

1996 *1995 National Household Survey on Drug Abuse.*

Centers for Disease Control and Prevention under US Department of health and Human Services. http://www.samhsa.gov/oas/nhsda/ar18ttoc.htm.

1997a "Pespectives in disease prevention and health promotion smoking-attributable mortality and years of potential life lost – United States, 1984." *MMWR*. 46(20):444–51. http://www.cdc.gov/epo/mmwr/preview/mmwrhtml/00047690.htm.

1997b: *Surveillance for Selected Tobacco-Use Behaviors – United States, 1900–1994*. Centers for Disease Control and Prevention under US Department of Health and Human Services. http://www.cdc.gov/epo/mmwr/preview/mmwrhtml/00033881.htm.

1999a "Achievements in public health, 1900–1999: control of infectious diseases." *MMWR* 48(29):621–9. http://www.cdc.gov/epo/mmwr/preview/mmwrhtml/mm4829a1.htm.

1999b "Achievements in public health, 1900–1999: changes in the public health system." *MMWR* 48(50):1,141–7. http://www.cdc.gov/epo/mmwr/preview/mmwrhtml/mm4850a1.htm.

1999c "Achievements in public health, 1900–1999: decline in deaths from heart disease and stroke – United States, 1900–1999." *MMWR* 48(30):649–56. http://www.cdc.gov/epo/mmwr/preview/mmwrhtml/mm4830a1.htm.

1999d "Achievements in public health, 1900–1999: tobacco use – United States, 1900–1999." *MMWR* 48(43):986–93. http://www.cdc.gov/epo/mmwr/preview/mmwrhtml/mm4843a2.htm.

1999e "Achievements in public health, 1900–1999: motor-vehicle safety: a 20th century public health achievement." *MMWR* 48(18):369–74. http://www.cdc.gov/epo/mmwr/preview/mmwrhtml/mm4818a1.htm.

1999f "Achievements in public health, 1900–1999: improvements in workplace safety – United States, 1900–1999." *MMWR*. 48(22):461–9. http://www.cdc.gov/epo/mmwr/preview/mmwrhtml/mm4822a1.htm.

1999g "Summary of notifiable diseases, United States, 1998." *MMWR* 47(53):i–xvi, 1–92. ftp://ftp.cdc.gov/pub/Publications/mmwr/wk/mm4753.pdf.

2000a "Final 1999 Reports of Notifiable Diseases 1999." *MMWR* 49(37):851–8. http://www.cdc.gov/mmwr/PDF/wk/mm4937.pdf.

2000b *Compressed Mortality File*. Accessed in 2000. Office of Analysis and Epidemiology, National Center for Health Statistics, Centers for Disease Control and Prevention. http://wonder.cdc.gov/.

2000c *HIV/AIDS Surveillance Report*. 12(1). http://www.cdc.gov/hiv/stats/hasr1201.htm.

2001a *Compressed Mortality File*. Accessed in 2001. Office of Analysis and Epidemiology, National Center for Health Statistics, Centers for Disease Control and Prevention. http://wonder.cdc.gov/.

CEC 1995 *Wind Project Performance 1995 Summary*. California Energy Commission, Research and Development Office. http://www.energy.ca.gov/wind/wind-html/95_wind_report.html.

Celedon, Juan C., Augusto A. Litonjua, Scott T. Weiss and Diane R. Gold 1999 "Day care attendance in the first year of life and illnesses of the upper and lower respiratory tract in children with a familial history of atopy." *Pediatrics*. 104(3):495–500.

CEQ 1972 *Environmental Quality 1971*. The President's Council on Environmental Quality. Washington, DC: US Government Printing Office.

1975 *Environmental Quality 1974*. The President's Council on Environmental Quality. Washington, DC: US Government Printing Office.

1981 *Environmental Quality 1980*. The President's Council on Environmental Quality. Washington, DC: US Government Printing Office.

1982 *Environmental Quality 1981*. The President's Council on Environmental Quality. Washington, DC: US Government Printing Office.

1989 *Environmental Quality 1987–1988*. The President's Council on Environmental Quality. Washington, DC: US Government Printing Office.

1993 *Environmental Quality 1992*. The President's Council on Environmental Quality. Washington, DC: US Government Printing Office.

1996 *Environmental Quality 1994–1995: 25th Anniversary Report of the Council on Environmental Quality*. The President's Council on Environmental Quality. http://ceq.eh.doe.gov/reports/1994-95/rep_toc.htm.

1997 *Environmental Quality 1996*. The President's Council on Environmental Quality. http://www.whitehouse.gov/CEQ/reports/1996/toc.html.

CES 2000 *Current Employment Statistics*. US Bureau of Labor Statistics. http://www.bls.gov/ceshome.htm.

CFS 2001 *Compilation and Analysis of Public Opinion Polls on Genetically Engineered (GE) Foods*. The Center for Food Safety. http://www.centerforfoodsafety.org/facts&issues/polls.html.

CGIAR 1996 Editorial. *CGIAR News*. 3:1. http://www.worldbank.org/html/cgiar/newsletter/Mar96/4edit.htm.

Chaibi, MT. 2000 "An overview of solar desalination for domestic and agriculture water needs in remote arid areas." *Desalination* 127(2):119–33.

Chakravorty, Ujjayant, James Roumasset and Kinping Tse 1997 "Endogenous substitution among energy resources and global warming." *Journal of Political Economy*. 105(6):1,201–34.

Changnon, David and Stanley A. Changnon Jr. 1998 "Evaluation of weather catastrophe data for use in climate change investigations." *Climatic Change* 38(4):435–45.

Changnon, Stanley A. 1999 "Impacts of 1997–98 El Niño-generated weather in the United States." *Bulletin of the American Meteorological Society* 80(9):1,819–27. http://ams.allenpress.com/.

Changnon, Stanley A. and David Changnon 1999 "Record-high losses for weather disasters in the United States during the 1990s: how excessive and why?" *Natural Hazards* 18(3):287–300.

Changnon, Stanley A., Roger A. Pielke Jr., David Changnon, Richard T. Sylves and Roger Pulwarty 2000 "Human factors explain the increased losses from weather and climate extremes." *Bulletin of the American Meteorological Society* 81(3):437–42. http://ams.allenpress.com/.

Chaoon, Donald R. Jr., Joel S. Levine, Wesley R. Cofer III, James E. Miller, Patrick Minnis, Geoffrey M. Tennille, Tommy W. Yip, Brian J. Stocks and Patrick W. Heck 1991 "The great Chinese fire of 1987: a view from space." In Levine 1991:61–6. See also http://asd-www.larc.nasa.gov/biomass_burn/sat_anal.html.

Chapman, Duane and Neha Khanna 2000 "Crying no wolf: Why economists don't worry about climate change, and should." *Climatic Change* 47(3):225–32.

Cheeseman, M. A. and E. J. Machuga 1997 "Threshold of regulation." In Tennant 1997:296–316.

Chertow, Marian R. 1998 "Waste, industrial ecology, and sustainability." *Social Research*. 65(1):31–53.

Chiras, Daniel D. 1998 *Environmental Science: A Systems Approach to Sustainable Development*. Belmont, CA: Wadsworth Publishing Company.

Chotikapahich, Duangkamon, Rebecca Valenzuela and D. S. Prasada Rao 1997 "Global and regional inequality in the distribution of income: estimation with limited and incomplete data." *Empirical Economics* 22:533–46.

Chrispeels, Maaten J. 1999: "Statement on Pusztai." http://plab.ku.dk/tcbh/Pusztaimjc.htm.

Christensen, Charlotte Wiin and Aksel Wiin-Nielsen 1996 *Klimaproblemer*. [Climate problems.] Copenhagen: Teknisk Forlag.

Christensen, Karen 2000 *Eco Living: A handbook for the 21st Century*. London: Piatkus.

Christy, J. R., R. W. Spencer and W. D. Braswell 2000a *MSU temperature data*. http://vortex.atmos.uah.edu/essl/msu/.

2000b "MSU tropospheric temperatures: dataset construction and radiosonde comparisons." *Journal of Atmospheric and Oceanic Technology* 17:(9) 1153–70(in press).

2001 *MSU temperature data*. http://vortex.atmos.uah.edu/essl/msu/.

Chu, K. C., R. E. Tarone, L. G. Kessler, L. A. Ries, B. F. Hankey, B. A. Miller and B. K. Edwards 1996 "Recent trends in U.S. breast cancer incidence, survival, and mortality rates." *Journal of the National Cancer Institute* 88(21):1,571–9.

Chumley, Cheryl K. 2001 "Evidence Mounts: Bush May Support Global Warming Treaty." *CNS News* March 09, 2001, http://www.cnsnews.com/ViewPolitics.asp?Page=\\Politics\\archive\\200103\\POL20010309a.html.

CIA 1998 *Handbook of International Economic Statistics, 1997*. http://www.odci.gov/cia/publications/hies97/toc.htm.

CIMMYT 1999 *A Sampling of CIMMYT Impacts, 1999: New Global and Regional Studies*. International Maize and Wheat Improvement Center. Mexico City: CIMMYT. http://www.cimmyt.cgiar.org/about/pdf/CIM-Imp99.pdf. (no longer available).

Ciotti, Paul 1989 "Fear of Fusion: What if It Works?" *Los Angeles Times*, April 19, 1989, A5.

Cipolla, Carlo M (ed) 1978 *The Fontana economic history of Europe*. Six volumes. Glasgow: Collins.

Clark, Mike 1997 "Increase in asthma correlates

with less childhood infection." *The Lancet* 349(9,045):107.

Claudi, Erik 1988 *Greenpeace, Bind 1: Regnbuens krigere*. [Greenpeace: The Rainbow Warriors.] Copenhagen: Tiderne Skifter.

Clemmesen, J. 1997 "Is smoking during pregnancy a cause of testicular cancer?" [in Danish]. *Ugeskrift for Læger* 159(46):6,815–19.

Clinton, Bill 1999 "Remarks to the people of New Zealand in Christchurch, New Zealand, September 15, 1999." *Weekly Compilation of Presidential Documents* 35(37):1,744–7.

2000 "Commencement address at Eastern Michigan University in Ypsilanti, Michigan." *Weekly Compilation of Presidential Documents* 36(18):948–53.

CLTAP 1979 *Convention on Long-Range Transboundary Air Pollution*. http://www.unece.org/env/lrtap/welcome.html.

CNN.com 2001a: "Conflicts over global warming theory." February 19th 2001. http://www.cnn.com/2001/WORLD/europe/02/19/environment.report/index.html.

2001b: "Climate report prompts action call." February 19th 2001. http://www.cnn.com/2001/WORLD/europe/02/19/emissions.world/index.html.

COC 1999 *Breast Cancer Risk and Exposure to Organochlorine Insecticides: Consideration of the Epidemiology Data on Dieldrin, DDT and Certain Hexachlorocyclohexane Isomers*. Committee on the Carcinogenicity of Chemicals in Food, Consumer Products and the Environment. Advisory Committee of the UK Department of Health. http://www.doh.gov.uk/pub/docs/doh/ocbreast.pdf.

Coghlan, Andy and Kurt Kleiner 1998 "Spud U dislike." *New Scientist* 159(2,147):5. http://www.newscientist.com/ns/980815/nspuds.html.

Cohen, Bernard L. 1995 "The hazards of nuclear power." In Simon 1995b:576–87.

Colborn, Theo, Dianne Dumanoski and John Peterson Myers 1996 *Our Stolen Future: Are We Threatening Our Fertility, Intelligence, and Survival? – A Scientific Detective Story*. New York: Dutton.

Colinvaux, Paul Alain. 1989 "The past and future Amazon." *Scientific American*, May 1989:102–8.

Collier, Paul and Jan Willem Gunning 1999: "Why has Africa grown slowly?" *Journal of Economic Perspectives* 13(3): 3–22.

Collins, M. 2000 "The El Nino-Southern Oscillation in the second Hadley Centre coupled model and its response to greenhouse warming." *Journal of Climate* 13(7):1,299–1,312.

Combs, B. and P. Slovic 1979 "Newspaper coverage of causes of death." *Journalism Quarterly* 56:837–43.

COMEAP 1995 *Asthma and Outdoor Air Pollution*. Department of Health, Committee on the Medical Effects of Air Pollutants. London: HMSO. http://www.doh.gov.uk/hef/airpol/airpol2.htm

1998: *The Quantification of the Effects of Air Pollution on Health in the United Kingdom*. Department of Health, Committee on the Medical Effects of Air Pollutants. London: HMSO. http://www.doh.gov.uk/hef/airpol/airpol7.htm

Common, Michael 1996 "Background Paper." *Consumption and the Environment*. Department of the Enviornment, Sport and Territories. http://www.environment.gov.au/epcg/eeu/consumption/bgpaper.htm.

Conard, Susan G. and Galina A. Ivanova 1997 "Wildfire in Russian boreal forests – potential impacts of fire regime characteristics on emissions and global carbon balance estimates." *Environmental Pollution* 98(3):305–13.

Conway, Gordon 2000 "Food for all in the 21st century." *Environment* 42:1–18.

Conway, H. and B. L. Hall 1999 "Past and future grounding-line retreat of the west Antarctic ice sheet." *Science* 286(5,438):280–3.

Cook, William J. 1998 "The force of El Niño." *U.S. News and World Report* 124(24):58.

Cooper, Adrian, S. Livermore, V. Rossi, A. Wilson and J. Walker 1999 "The economic implications of reducing carbon emissions: a cross-country quantitative investigation using the oxford global macroeconomic and energy model." *The Energy Journal*, Kyoto Special Issue:335–66.

Costanza, Robert, Herman Daly, Carl Folke, Paul Hawken, C. S. Holling, Anthony J. McMichael, David Pimentel and David Rapport 2000 "Managing our environmental portfolio." *Bioscience* 50(2):149–55.

Costanza, Robert, Ralph d'Arge, Rudolf de Groot, Stephen Farber, Monica Grasso, Bruce Hannon, Karin Limburg, Shahid Naeem, Robert V. O'Neill, José Paruelo, Robert G. Raskin, Paul Sutton and Marjan van den Belt 1997 "The value of the world's ecosystem services and natural capital." *Nature* 387(6,630):253–60.

Couzin, Jennifer 1998 "Forecast for global water shortage." *Science* 281(5,384):1,795.

Cowen, Robert C. 1996 "Is earth still gripped by little Ice Age?" *Christian Science Monitor* 88(147):12.

Cowling. Ellis B. 1995 "Lessons learned in acidification research: implications for future environmental research and assessements." In Heij and Erisman 1995: 307–19.

CPI 2000 *Consumer Price Index 1913–May 2000*; Washington, DC: Bureau of Labor. ftp://ftp.bls.gov/pub/special.requests/cpi/cpiai.txt.

CPI 2001 *Consumer Price Index 1913–February 2001*; Washington, DC: Bureau of Labor. ftp://ftp.bls.gov/pub/special.requests/cpi/cpiai.txt.

Crafts, Nicholas 1998 *East Asian Growth before and after the Crisis*. IMF Working Paper WP/98/137. http://www.imf.org/external/pubs/ft/wp/wp98137.pdf.

2000 *Globalization and Growth in the Twentieth Century*. IMF Working Paper WP/00/44. http://www.imf.org/external/pubs/ft/wp/2000/wp0044.pdf.

Craig, James R., David J. Vaughan and Brian J. Skinner 1996 *Resources of the Earth: Origin, Use and Environmental Impact*. Upper Saddle River, NJ: Prentice Hall.

Cramer, Wolfgang, Alberte Bondeau, F. Ian Woodward, I. Colin Prentice, Richard A. Betts, Victor Brovkin, Peter M. Cox, Veronica Fisher, Jonathan A. Foley, Andrew D. Friend, Chris Kucharik, Mark R. Lomas, Navin Ramankutty, Stephen Sitch, Benjamin Smith, Andrew White and Christine Young-Molling 2000 "Global response of terrestrial ecosystem structure and function to CO_2 and climate change: results from six dynamic global vegetation models." *Global Change Biology* (in press).

Crawford, R. D. 1998 "The case for iron repletion as a promoter in testicular cancer." *Medical Hypotheses* 51(2):129–32.

Crawley, M. J., S. L. Brown, R. S. Hails, D. D. Kohn and M. Rees 2001 "Biotechnology: Transgenic crops in natural habitats." *Nature* 409(6,821):682–3.

Crimmins, Eileen M. and Dominique G. Ingegneri 1995 "Trends in health of the US population: 1957–89." In Simon 1995b:72–84.

Crimmins, Eileen M., Yasuhiko Saito and Dominique Ingegneri 1989 "Changes in life expectancy and disability-free life expectancy in the United States." *Population and Development Review* 15(2):235–67.

Crisp, Thoman M., Eric D. Clegg, Ralph L. Cooper, Willian P. Wood, David G. Anderson, Karl P. Baetcke, Jennifer L. Hoffmann, Melba S. Morrow, Donald J. Rodier, John E. Schaeffer, Leslie W. Touart, Maurice G. Zeeman and Yogendra M. Patel 1998 "Environmental endocrine disruption: an effects assessment and analysis." *Environmental Health Perspectives Supplement* 106(1):11–56.

Crosson, Pierre 1995 "Soil erosion estimates and costs." *Science* 269:461–4.

1996 *Who Will Feed China*. Federation of American Scientists; Long-Term Global Food Project; Issue 2, Spring 1996.

1996a *Resource Degradation*. Federation of American Scientists; Long-Term Global Food Project; Issue 3, Summer 1996.

1997a *Impacts of Climate Change on Agriculture*. Washington, DC: Resources for the Future. http://www.rff.org/issue_briefs/PDF_files/ccbrf4.pdf.

1997b *Lester Brown*. Federation of American Scientists; Long-Term Global Food Project; Issue 3, Fall 1997. http://www.fas.org/cusp/food/fall97.htm.

1997c "Soil erosion." [Comment on Pimentel 1997.] *Environment* 39(10):5.

1997d "Will erosion threaten agricultural productivity?" *Environment* 39(8):4–12.

CRS 1992 *The Delaney Clause: The Dilemma of Regulating Health Risk for Pesticide Residues*. Donna U. Vogt, Analyst in Life Sciences, Science Policy Research Division. Congressional Research Service, Report for Congress. http://www.cnie.org/nle/pest-3.html.

1995a *The Delaney Clause Effects on Pesticide Policy*. Donna U. Vogt, Analyst in Life Sciences, Science Policy Research Division. Congressional Research Service, Report for Congress. http://www.cnie.org/nle/pest-1.html.

1995b *World Oil Production after Year 2000: Business as Usual or Crises?* Joseph P. Riva, Jn., Specialist in Earth Sciences, Science Policy Research Division, 18 August, 1995. Congressional Research Service, Report for Congress. http://www.cnie.org/nle/eng-3.html.

1998 *Renewable Energy: Key to Sustainable Energy Supply*. Fred Sissine, Science Policy Research

Division, 7 January 1998. Congressional Research Service, Report for Congress. http://www.cnie.org/nle/eng-29.html.

CSD 1997 *Comprehensive Assessment of the Freshwater Resources of the World*. Report (E/CN.17/1997/9) prepared for the UN Commission for Sustainable Development by UN/DPCSD, FAO, UNEP, WMO, UNESCO, WHO, UNDP, UNIDO, the World Bank, and Stockholm Environment Institute. http://www.un.org/esa/sustdev/freshwat.htm or gopher://gopher.un.org/00/esc/cn17/1997/off/97—9.EN.

CTR 1999 *Cancer Incidence in Connecticut 1980–1996*. State of Connecticut, Department of Public Health, Connecticut Tumor Registry. http://www.state.ct.us/dph/OPPE/hptr.htm.

Cubasch, U., R. Voss, G. C. Hegerl, J. Waszkewitz and T. J. Crowley 1997 "Simulation of the influence of solar radiation variations on the global climate with an ocean-atmosphere general circulation model." *Climate Dynamics* Vol 13(11):757–67.

Cunningham, William P. and Barbara Woodworth Saigo 1997 *Environmental Science: A Global Concern*. Dubuque, IA: Wm C. Brown Publishers.

Cushman, John H. Jn 1997 "US reshaping cancer strategy as incidence in children rises: increase may be tied to new chemicals in environment." *New York Times*, 29 September 1997, 148:A1, A14.

Dai, Aiguo, Kevin E. Trenberth and Thomas R. Karl 1998 "Global variations in droughts and wet spells: 1900–1995." *Geophysical Research Letters* 25(17):3,367–70. http://www.agu.org/GRL/articles/98GL52511/GL382W01.pdf.

Daly, Herman 1996 *Beyond Growth: The Economics of Sustainable Development*. Boston, MA: Beacon Press.

Danish Ministry of Finance 1997 *Miljøvurdering af finanslovforslaget for 1998*. [Environmental evaluation of the budget 1998.] Copenhagen: Finansministeriet.

Danish Transport Ministry 1993 *Kortlægning af vejtrafikstøj i Danmark*. [Survey on road traffic noise in Denmark.] Copenhagen: Trafikministeriet.

Danmarks Energifremtider 1995. [Danish energy futures.] Published by the Ministry of Environment and Energy, December 1995. Obtainable at http://www.ens.dk/pub/enspub.htm.

Darnton-Hill, I. 1999 "The challenge to eliminate micronutrient malnutrition." *Australian and New Zealand Journal of Public Health* 23(3):309–14.

Dasgupta, Partha 1995 "The population problem: theory and evidence." *Journal of Economic Literature*. 33(4):1,879–1,902.

Dasgupta, Partha and Martin Weale 1992 "On measuring the quality of life." *World Development* 20:119–31.

Dasgupta, Susmita, Hua Wang and David Wheeler 1997 *Surviving Success: Policy Reform and the Future of Industrial Pollution in China*. Policy Research Working Paper 1,856, World Bank Development Group, November 1997.

Davidson, Cliff I. 1979 "Air pollution in Pittsburgh: a historical perspective." *Journal of the Air Pollution Control Association* 29(10):1,035–41.

Davidson, Nancy E. and James D. Yager 1997 "Pesticides and breast cancer: fact or fad?" *Journal of the National Cancer Institute* 89(23):1,743–5.

Davis, Devra Lee and H. Leon Bradlow 1995 "Can environmental estrogens cause breast cancer?" *Scientific American* 273(4):166–71.

De Broeck, Mark and Vincent R. Koen 2000 *The Great Contractions in Russia, the Baltics and the Other Countries of the Former Soviet Union – a View from the Supply Side*. International Monetary Fund, Working Paper WP/00/32. http://www.imf.org/external/pubs/ft/wp/2000/wp0032.pdf.

de Gruijl, F. R. 1999 "Skin cancer and solar UV radiation." *European Journal of Cancer Part A*. Vol.35(14):2,003–9.

de Moor, A. P. G. 1998 *Perverse Incentives. Subsidies and Sustainable Development: Key Issues and Reform Strategies* http://www.ecouncil.ac.cr/rio/focus/report/english/subsidies/.

De Quattro, Jim 1994 "With soybeans and wheat – good breeding has made all the difference." *Agricultural Research* 42(10):12–13.

De Vries, W., E. E. J. M Leeters, C.M.A. Hendriks, H. van Dobben, J. van den Brug and L. J. M. Boumans 1995 "Large scale impacts of acid deposition on forest and forest soils in the Netherlands." In Heij and Erisman 1995:261–77.

de Vries, Bert, Johannes Bollen, Lex Bouwman, Michel den Elzen, Marco Janssen and Eric

Kreileman 2000 "Greenhouse Gas Emissions in an Equity-, Environment- and Service-Oriented World: An IMAGE-Based Scenario for the 21st Century." *Technological Forecasting and Social Change* 63:137–74.

DeLong, J. Bradford 2000a "Estimating world GDP, one million B.C. – Present." http://econ161.berkeley.edu/tceh/2000/world_gdp/estimating_world_gdp.html.

2000b "The Economic History of the Twenty-First Century." http://econ161.berkeley.edu/Econ_Articles/21st/EH_21st_century.html.

Delworth, T. L. and T. R. Knutson 2000 "Simulation of early 20th century global warming." *Science* 287(5,461):2,246–50.

DEP 1997 *1997 New York Harbor Water Quality Survey*. New York City, Department of Environmental Protection. Bureau of Wastewater Pollution Control, Marine Sciences Section. http://www.ci.nyc.ny.us/html/dep/html/news/hwqs1997.html.

1998 *1998 New York Harbor Water Quality Survey*. New York City, Department of Environmental Protection. Bureau of Wastewater Pollution Control, Marine Sciences Section. http://www.ci.nyc.ny.us/html/dep/pdf/hwqs1998.pdf.

Desmond, Anabelle 1975 "How many people have ever lived on Earth?" *Population Bulletin* 18:1–19. Reprinted in Kenneth C. W. Kammeyer (ed). 1975, *Population Studies: Selected Essays and Research*, p. 18–32 Chicago: Rand McNally.

Det radikale Venstre 2000 *Målsætninger for miljø og udvikling*. [Goals for environment and development.] http://www.radikale.dk/program/miljø.html

DETR 1998a *Digest of Environmental Statistics*. No. 20. Department of the Environment, Transport and the Regions. http://www.detr.gov.uk/environment/des20/index.htm.

1998b *Economic Instruments for Water Pollution*. Department of the Environment, Transport and the Regions. http://www.environment.detr.gov.uk/wqd/eiwp/eiwp01.htm.

1998c *Highways Economics Note No.1: 1998*. Department of the Environment, Transport and the Regions. http://www.detr.gov.uk/roads/roadsafety/hen198/index.htm.

1999 *The Environmental Impacts of Road Vehicles in Use Air Quality, Climate Change and Noise Pollution*. The Cleaner Vehicles Task Force. Department of the Environment, Transport and the Regions. http://www.detr.gov.uk/roads/cvtf/impact/index.htm.

2000 *The UK National Air Quality Information Archive*. http://www.aeat.co.uk/netcen/airqual/.

Devesa, Susan S., William J. Blot, B. J. Stone, B. A. Miller, R. E. Tarone and J. F. Fraumeni, Jn 1995 "Recent cancer trends in the United States." *Journal of the National Cancer Institute* 87(3):175–82.

Devesa, Susan S., Dan J. Grauman, William J. Blot and Joseph F. Fraumeni, Jr. 1999 "Cancer surveillance series: changing geographic patterns of lung cancer mortality in the United States, 1950 through 1994." *Journal of the National Cancer Institute* 91(12):1,040–50.

DeVries, T. J., L. Ortlieb and A. Diaz 1997 "Determining the early history of El Niño." *Science* 276:965–6.

Dhakhwa, Gyanendra B. and C. Lee Campbell 1998 "Potential effects of differential day–night warming in global climate change on crop production." *Climatic Change*. 40(3–4):647–67.

Diamond, Jared 1989 "Overview of recent extinctions." In Western and Pearl 1989:37–41.

1990 "Playing dice with megadeath." *Discover* April:54–9.

1999 *Guns, Germs, and Steel: The Fates of Human Societies*. Paperback edition. New York: W. W. Norton.

Diaz, Robert and Andrew Solow 1999 *Gulf of Mexico Hypoxia Assessment: Topic #2. Ecological and Economic Consequences of Hypoxia*. Hypoxia Work Group, White House Office of Science and Technology Policy, Committee on Environment and Natural Resources for the EPA Mississippi River/Gulf of Mexico Watershed Nutrient Task Force. NOAA Coastal Ocean Program. http://www.nos.noaa.gov/products/pubs_hypox.html.

DiCaprio, Leonardo 2000 "Interview with Bill Clinton for ABC News' *Planet Earth 2000*." *Weekly Compilation of Presidential Documents* 36(17):907–12.

DICE 1999 *Dynamic Integrated Climate-Economy*. Model can be downloaded as a spreadsheet from http://www.econ.yale.edu/~nordhaus/homepage/dicemodels.htm.

Dillin, John 2000 "Global cooling – mini-ice age." *Christian Science Monitor* 92(191):16.

Dinar, Ariel, Mark W. Rosegrant and Ruth Meinzen-Dick 1997 *Water Allocation Mechanisms: Principles and Examples*. World Bank and International Food Policy Research Institute. http://www.worldbank.org/html/dec/Publications/Workpapers/wps1700series/wps1779/wps1779.pdf.

Discover 1998 "Allergy and immunity." Special supplement for *Discover* 19(3):8–10.

Dixon, Bernard 1999 "The paradoxes of genetically modified foods: A climate of mistrust is obscuring the many different facets of genetic modification." *British Medical Journal* 318(7183):547–8.

DK EA 1995 *Klimaproblemer og drivhuseffekten*. [Problems of the climate and the greenhouse effect.] Danish Energy Agency. Copenhagen: Miljø- og Energiministeriet, Energistyrelsen.

DK EPA 1994 *Tal om Natur og Miljø 1994*. [Statistics on nature and environment 1994.] Danish Environmental Protection Agency. Publiceret sammen med Statistics Denmark. Copenhagen: Statistics Denmark.

1995a *Natur og Miljøredegørelsen*. [Nature and Environment Status Report.] Danish Environmental Protection Agency. Copenhagen: Miljø- og Energiministeriet. http://www.mem.dk/publikationer/RED/index.htm.

1995b *Vandmiljø-95: Grundvandets miljøtilstand samt status for det øvrige vandmiljøs tilstand i 1994*. [Water environments – 95: the groundwater's and other water environment's status in 1994.] Danish Environment Agency. Redegørelse fra Miljøstyrelsen 3. Copenhagen: Miljø- og Energiministeriet.

1996a *Drivhuseffekt og klimaændringer: Betydningen for Danmark set i lyset af IPCC's 1996–rapporter*. [Greenhouse effect and climate changes: the impact for Denmark in the light of IPCC's 1996 reports.] Danish Environment Agency. Jes Fenger, Anne Mette K. Jørgensen and Kristen Halsnæs (eds.). Copenhagen: Miljø- og Energiministeriet, Miljøstyrelsen.

1996b *Miljøindikatorer 1995*. [Environmental indications 1995.] Danish Environmental Protection Agency. Copenhagen: Miljø- og Energiministeriet.

1996c *Energi 21: Regeringens energihandlingsplan 1996*: Copenhagen: Miljø- og Energiministeriet 1996. http://www.ens.dk/e21/e21dk/energi21.pdf.

1997a *Bekæmpelsesmiddelforskning fra Miljøstyrelsen: Sædkvalitet og kromosomskader hos pesticideksponerede væksthusgartnere*. [Pesticide research at the DK EPA: semen quality and chromosome damage of greenhouse gardeners exposed to pesticides.] Danish Environment Agency. Annette Abell, Jens Peter Bonde, Erik Ernst, Flemming Lander, Lisbeth Ehlert Knudsen and Hannu Norppa. Copenhagen: Miljø- og Energiministeriet, Miljøstyrelsen.

1997b *Miljøindikatorer 1996*. [Environmental indicators 1996.] Danish Environmental Protection Agency. http://www.mem.dk/publikationer/indikatorer96/indhold.htm.

1998a *Drikkevandsudvalgets betænkning*. [Comments from the Committee on Drinking Water.] Danish Environment Agency. Betænkning fra Miljøstyrelsen 1. Copenhagen: Miljø- og Energiministeriet.

1998b *Forsigtighedsprincippet. Udskrift og resumé fra Miljøstyrelsens konference om forsigtighedsprincippet*. [The precautionary principle. Text from the Danish Envionment Agency's conference on the precautionary principle.] http://www.mst.dk/199811publikat/87-7909-088-5/helepubl.htm.

1998c *Miljøindikatorer 1997*. [Environmental indicators 1997.] Danish Environmental Protection Agency. http://www.sns.dk/U&U/N&M97/indhold.htm (no longer available).

1998d *Energy Statistics 1998*. Copenhagen: Miljø- og Energiminster: et. http://www.ens.dk/statistik/98.

1999 *Badevandskort 1999*. [Bathing water map 1999.] Danish Environmental Protection Agency. http://www.mst.dk/fagomr/03020000.htm.

2000 *Badevandskort 2000*. [Bathing water map 2000.] Danish Environmental Protection Agency. http://www.mst.dk/fagomr/03050100.htm.

DK VFA 1994 *Pesticidrester i danske levnedsmidler 1993*. [Pesticide residues in Danish food 1993.] The Danish Veterinary and Food Administration. Copenhagen.

1996a *Danskernes kostvaner 1995: Hovedresultater*. [Eating habits of Danes 1995: main conclusions.] The Danish Veterinary and Food Administration. Copenhagen.

1996b *Pesticidrester i danske levnedsmidler 1995*. [Pesticide residues in Danish food 1995.] The Danish Veterinary and Food Administration. Copenhagen.

1997 *Pesticidrester i danske levnedsmidler 1996*. [Pesticide residues in Danish food 1996.] The

Danish Veterinary and Food Administration. Copenhagen.

1998 *Forureninger i Maden: Pesticidrester*. [Contamination of food: pesticide residues.] Danish Veterinary and Food Administration. Copenhagen. http://1st.min.dk/publikationer/publikationer/pjecer/pesticid2.htm.

Dlugokencky, E. J., K. A. Masarie, P. M. Lang and P. P. Tans 1998 "Continuing decline in the growth rate of the atmospheric methane burden." *Nature* 393:447–50.

Dobson, Andrew P. and E. Robin Carper 1996 "Infectious diseases and human population history." *BioScience* 46(2):115–26.

Dobson, M. C.; A. Y. Kwarteng and F. T. Ulaby 1997 "Use of SIR-C/X-SAR to monitor environmental damages of the 1991 Gulf War in Kuwait." *IGARSS'97. 1997 International Geoscience and Remote Sensing Symposium. Remote Sensing – A Scientific Vision for Sustainable Development* (Cat. No. 97CH36042), vol.1. pp. 119–21.

Dockery, D. W., C. A. Pope III, X. Xu, J. D. Spengler, J. H. Ware, M. E. Fay, B. G. Ferris, F. E. Speizer 1993 "An association between air pollution and mortality in six US cities." *New England Journal of Medicine*. 329(24):1,753–9.

DOE 1995 *Photovoltaics: The Power of Choice. The National Photovoltaics Program Plan for 1996–2000*. US Department of Energy. http://www.osti.gov/bridge/home.html.

1996 *Wind Energy Information Guide*. US Department of Energy. http://www.osti.gov/bridge/home.html.

1997 *Renewable Energy Technology Characterizations*. US Department of Energy and Office of Utility Technologies, December 1997. http://www.eren.doe.gov/power/pdfs/techchar.pdf.

Doering, Otto C., Fransisco Diaz-Hermelo, Crystal Howard, Ralph Heimlich, Fred Hitzhusen, Richard Kazmierczak, John Lee, Larry Libby, Walter Milon, Tony Prato and Marc Ribaudo 1999 *Gulf of Mexico Hypoxia Assessment: Topic #6. Evaluation of Economic Costs and Benefits of Methods for Reducing Nutrient Loads to the Gulf Of Mexico*. Hypoxia Work Group, White House Office of Science and Technology Policy, Committee on Environment and Natural Resources for the EPA Mississippi River/Gulf of Mexico Watershed Nutrient Task Force. NOAA Coastal Ocean Program. http://www.nos.noaa.gov/products/pubs_hypox.html.

Doll, Richard and Richard Peto 1981 "The causes of cancer: quantitative estimates of avoidable risks of cancer in the United States today." *Journal of the National Cancer Institute* 66(6):1,191–1,308.

Dorgan, J. F., J. W. Brock, N. Roltman, L. L. Neddleman, R. Miller, H. E. Stephensen Jn, N. Schussler and P. R. Taylor 1999 "Serum organochlorine pesticides and PCBs and breast cancer risk: results from a prospective analysis (USA)." *Cancer Causes and Control* 10(1):1–11.

DOT 1997 *Transportation in the United States: A Review*. US Department of Transportation, Bureau of Transportation Statistics. Washington, DC. http://www.bts.gov/programs/transtu/titus/titus97t.pdf.

1999 *National Transportation Statistics 1999*. US Department of Transportation. http://www.bts.gov/btsprod/nts/.

Dowrick, Steve and John Quiggin 1997 "True measures of GDP and convergence." *American Economic Review* 87(1):41–63.

Dragsted, Lars 1992 "Low dose extrapolation of data from animal bioassays: applied in the setting of limit values in Denmark and internationally." In ATV 1992:77–107.

Druyan, L. M., P. Lonergan and T. Eichler 1999 "A GCM investigation of global warming impacts relevant to tropical cyclone genesis." *International Journal of Climatology* 19(6):607–17.

Dumond, D. E. 1975 "The limitation of human population: a natural history." *Science* 187:713–21.

Dunlap, Riley E. 1991a "Public opinion in the 1980s. Clear consensus, ambiguous commitment." *Environment* 33(8):10–15.

1991b "Trends in public opinion toward environmental issues: 1965–1990." *Society and Natural Resources* 4(3):285–312.

2000 "Americans have positive image of the environmental movement: majorities agree with movement's goals, and trust it to protect the nation's environment." *Gallup Poll Releases* 18 April, 2000. http://www.gallup.com/poll/releases/pr000418.asp.

Dunlap, Riley E. and Curtis E. Beus 1992 "Understanding public concerns about pesticides: an empirical examination." *Journal of Consumer Affairs* 26(2):418–38.

Dunlap, Riley E., George H. Gallup and Alec M. Gallup 1993 "Of Global Concern: Results of the Planetary Survey." *Environment* 35(9):7–39.

Dunlap, Riley E. and Angela G. Mertig 1995 "Global concern for the environment: is affluence a prerequisite?" *Journal of Social Issues* 51(4):121–37.

Dunlap, Riley E. and Lydia Saad 2001 "Only one in four Americans are anxious about the environment." *Gallup Poll Releases* 16 April 2001. http://www.gallup.com/poll/releases/pr010416.asp.

Dunlap, Riley E. and Rik Scarce 1991 "The polls – poll trends. Environmental problems and protection." *Public Opinion Quarterly* 55:651–72.

Dunn, Seth 1998 "Looking past El Niño." *World Watch* 11(5):2.

Easterlin, Richard A. 2000 "The globalization of human development." *Annals of the American Academy of Political and Social Science* 570:32–48.

Easterling, David R., Henry F. Diaz, Arthur V. Douglas, William D. Hogg, Kenneth E. Kunkel, Jeffry C. Rogers and Jaime F. Wilkinson 1999 "Long-term observations for monitoring extremes in the Americas." *Climatic Change* 42(1):285–308.

Easterling, D. R., J. L. Evans, P. Ya. Groisman, T. R. Karl, K. E. Kunkel and P. Ambenje 2000 "Observed variability and trends in extreme climate events: a brief review." *Bulletin of the American Meteorological Society* 81(3):417–25. http://ams.allenpress.com/.

Easterling, David R., Briony Horton, Philip D. Jones, Thomas C. Peterson, Thomas R. Karl, David E. Parker, M. James Salinger, Vyacheslav Razuvayev, Neil Plummer, Paul Jamason and Christopher K. Folland 1997 "Maximum and minimum temperature trends for the globe." *Science*. 277:364–7.

EC-E 1999 *Compilation of EU Dioxin Exposure and Health Data Summary Report*. Report produced for European Commission DG Environment, UK Department of the Environment Transport and the Regions (DETR).

EC-ET 2000 *EU Transport in Figures*. European Commission, Directorate-General for Energy and Transport in co-operation with Eurostat. http://europa.eu.int/en/comm/dg07/tif/index.htm.

Eckstein, Zvi, Pedro Mira and Kenneth I. Wolpin 1999 "A quantitative analysis of Swedish fertility dynamics: 1751–1990." *Review of Economic Dynamics* 2:137–65.

Edelson, E. 1990 "The man who upset the apple cart." *Popular Science* 236(2):64–7.

Edgerton, David L., Bengt Assarsson, Anders Hummelmose, Ilkka P. Laurila, Kyrre Rickertsen and Per Halvor Vale 1996 *The Econometrics of Demand Systems: With Applications to Food Demand in the Nordic Countries*. Advanced Studies in Theoretical and Applied Econometrics. Dordrecht: Kluwer Academic Publishers

EEA 1994 *European Rivers and Lakes: Assessment of their Environmental State*. Peter Kristensen and Hans Ole Hansen (eds.). Copenhagen: European Environment Agency.

1995 *Europe's Environment: The Dobris Assessment*. David Stanners and Philippe Bourdeau (eds.): Copenhagen: European Environment Agency. http://themes.eea.eu.int/fulldoc.php/state/water?fn=92-826-5409-5&l=en.

1998a *Europe's Environment: Statistical Compendium for the Second Assessment*. Copenhagen: European Environment Agency.

1998b *Europe's Environment: The Second Assessment*. Preliminary version for press conference. Copenhagen: European Environment Agency. http://themes.eea.eu.int/fulldoc.php/state/water?fn=92-828-3351-8&l=en.

1999 *Environment in the European Union at the Turn of the Century*. Copenhagen: European Environment Agency. http://themes.eea.eu.int/fulldoc.php/state/water?fn=92-9157-202-0&l=en.

2000: *Data Service*. http://warehouse.eea.eu.int.

EEPSEA/WWF 1998: *The Indonesian Fires and Haze of 1997: The Economic Toll*. Economy and Environment Program for SE Asia and World Wide Fund for Nature. http://www.eepsea.org/specialrept/specreptIndofire.htm (no longer available).

efunda 2001 *Engineering Fundamentals*. www.efunda.com.

Ehrlich, Anne H. and Paul R. Ehrlich 1987 *Earth*. London: Methuen.

Ehrlich, Paul R. 1967 "Paying the piper." *New Scientist* 14, December:652–5.

1968 *The Population Bomb*. New York: Ballantine Books.

1970 "Looking back from 2000 A.D." *The Progressive* April:23–5.

1995 "The scale of the human enterprise and biodiversity loss." In Lawton and May 1995:214–26.

1997 *A World of Wounds: Ecologists and the Human Dilemma*. Oldendorf: Ecology Institute.

Ehrlich, Paul R. and Anne H. Ehrlich 1974 *The End of Affluence: A Blueprint for Your Future*. New York: Ballantine Books.

1991 *Healing the Planet: Strategies for Resolving the Environmental Crisis*. Reading, MA: Addison-Wesley Publishing Company.

1996 *Betrayal of Science and Reason: How Anti-Environmental Rhetoric Threatens Our Future*. Washington, DC: Island Press.

Ehrlich, Paul R., Anne H. Ehrlich and Gretchen C. Daily 1995 *The Stork and the Plow: The Equity Answer to the Human Dilemma*. New York: G. P. Putnam.

Ehrlich, Paul R. and Edward O. Wilson 1991 "Biodiversity studies: science and policy." *Science* 253:758–62.

EIA 1993 *Renewable Resources in the U.S. Electricity Supply*. Energy Information Agency under US Department of Energy. http://www.eia.doe.gov/cneaf/electricity/pub_summaries/renew_es.html.

1995a *Coal Data – A Reference*. Energy Information Agency under US Department of Energy. ftp://ftp.eia.doe.gov/pub/coal/coallast.pdf.

1995b *Housing Characteristics 1993*. Energy Information Agency under US Department of Energy. http://www.eia.doe.gov/emeu/recs/recs2f.html.

1996 *Annual Energy Outlook 1997*. Energy Information Agency under US Department of Energy. http://www.eia.doe.gov/emeu/plugs/plaeo97.html.

1997a *Annual Energy Outlook 1998*. Energy Information Agency under US Department of Energy. http://www.eia.doe.gov/pub/forecasting/aeo98/.

1997b *Annual Energy Review 1996*. Energy Information Agency under US Department of Energy. http://www.eia.doe.gov/emeu/aer/contents.html.

1997c *International Energy Outlook 1997*. Energy Information Agency under US Department of Energy. http://www.eia.doe.gov/oiaf/ieo97/home.html.

1997d *Nuclear Power Generation and Fuel Cycle Report 1997*. Energy Information Agency under US Department of Energy. http://www.eia.doe.gov/cneaf/nuclear/n_pwr_fc/npgfcr97.pdf.

1998a *Impacts of the Kyoto Protocol on U.S. Energy Markets and Economic Activity*. Energy Information Agency under US Department of Energy. SR/OIAF/98–03. http://www.eia.doe.gov/oiaf/kyoto/kyotorpt.html.

1998b *International Energy Annual 1996*. Energy Information Agency under US Department of Energy. Data at http://www.eia.doe.gov/pub/international/iea96/.

1998c *Renewable Energy Annual 1998 with Data For 1997*. Energy Information Agency under US Department of Energy. http://www.eia.doe.gov/cneaf/solar.renewables/rea_data/html/front-1.html.

1999a *A Look at Residential Energy Consumption in 1997*. Energy Information Agency under US Department of Energy. http://www.eia.doe.gov/emeu/recs/.

1999b *Annual Energy Outlook 2000*. Energy Information Agency under US Department of Energy.

1999c *Annual Energy Review 1998*. Energy Information Agency under US Department of Energy. http://www.eia.doe.gov/emeu/aer/contents.html.

1999d *International Energy Outlook 1999*. Energy Information Agency under US Department of Energy.

2000a *International Energy Annual 1998*. Energy Information Agency under US Department of Energy. Data at http://www.eia.doe.gov/pub/international/iea98/.

2000b *International Energy Outlook 2000*. Energy Information Agency under US Department of Energy. http://www.eia.doe.gov/oiaf/ieo/index.html.

2000c *Monthly Energy Review March 2000*. Energy Information Agency under US Department of Energy.

2000d *Annual Energy Review 1999*. Energy Information Agency under US Department of Energy. ftp://ftp.eia.doe.gov/pub/pdf/multi.fuel/038499.pdf.

2000e *Annual Energy Outlook 2001*. Energy Information Agency under US Department of Energy. http://www.eia.doe.gov/oiaf/aeo/pdf/0383(2001).pdf.

2001a *Monthly Energy Review January 2001*. Energy Information Agency under US Department of Energy. http://www.eia.doe.gov/pub/pdf/multi.fuel/00350101.pdf.

2001b *International Energy Annual 1999*. Energy Information Agency under US Department of Energy. http://www.eia.doe.gov/pub/pdf/international/021999.pdf.

2001c *Short-Term Energy Outlook – February 2001*. Energy Information Agency under US Department of Energy. http://www.eia.doe.gov/emeu/steo/pub/pdf/feb01.pdf.

Eisinger, Josef 1996 "Sweet poison." *Natural History* 105(7):48–543.

Ekbom, Anders, Gunnar Erlandsson, Chung-cheng Hsieh, Dimitrios Trichopoulos, Hans-Olov Adami and Sven Cnattingius 2000 "Risk of breast cancer in prematurely born women." *Journal of the National Cancer Institute*. 92(10):840–1.

El-Raey, M. 1997 "Vulnerability assessment of the coastal zone of the Nile delta of Egypt, to the impacts of sea level rise." *Ocean and Coastal Management*.37(1):29–40.

Elsner, J. B. and B. Kocher 2000 "Global tropical cyclone activity: link to the North Atlantic oscillation." *Geophysical Research Letters* 27(1):129–32.

Elsom, Derek M. 1995 "Atmospheric pollution trends in the United Kingdom." In Simon 1995b:476–90.

EM-DAT 2000 *The OFDA/CRED International Disaster Database*. Emergency Events Database by WHO Collaborating Centre for Research on the Epidemiology of Disasters (CRED), with the US Committee for Refugees (USCR), the Organisation for Economic Co-operation and Development's (OECD) Development Assistance Committee (DAC), and INTERFAIS, a World Food Programme (WFP) information system. http://www.cred.be/emdat/intro.html.

EMEP 2000 Data on European air pollution emissions. http://www.emep.int/.

Engeland, A., T. Haldorsen, S. Treli, T. Hakulinen, L. G. Hörte, T. Luostarinen, G. Schou, H. Sigvaldason, H. H. Storm, H. Tulinius and P. Vaittinen 1995 "Prediction of cancer mortality in the Nordic countries up to the years 2000 and 2010, on the basis of relative survival analysis: a collaborative study of the five Nordic cancer registries." *APMIS* suppl. 49, 103.

Engelman, Robert and Pamela LeRoy 1993 *Sustaining Water: Population and the Future of Renewable Water Supplies*. Washington, DC: Population Action International. http://www.cnie.org/pop/pai/h2o-toc.html.

Enserink, Martin 1998 "Institute copes with genetic hot potato." *Science* 281(5380):1,124–5.

Enserink, Martin 1999 "Preliminary Data Touch Off Genetic Food Fight." *Science* 283(5405):1094–5.

EPA 1990 *Pesticides in Drinking-Water Wells*. US Environmental Protection Agency, Pesticides and Toxic Substances, H-7506C. http://www.epa.gov/epahome/epadocs/drink1.pdf.

1993 *Reference Dose (RfD): Description and Use in Health Risk Assessments*. Background Document 1A. http://www.epa.gov/ngispgm3/iris/rfd.htm.

1994a *Indoor Air Pollution: An Introduction for Health Professionals*. Co-sponsored by: The American Lung Association (ALA), The Environmental Protection Agency (EPA), The Consumer Product Safety Commission (CPSC), and The American Medical Association (AMA). US Government Printing Office Publication no. 1994–523–217/81322. http://www.epa.gov/iaq/pubs/hpguide.html.

1994b Setting the record straight: secondhand smoke is a preventable health risk. EPA 402–F–94–005. http://www.epa.gov/iaq/pubs/strsfs.html.

1995 *Human Health Benefits from Sulfate Reductions under Title IV of the 1990 Clean Air Act Amendments: Final Report*. US Environmental Protection Agency, EPA Document Number 68–D3–0005 November 10, 1995. http://www.epa.gov/acidrain/effects/healthx.html.

1996a *Air Quality Criteria for Pariculate Matter*. US Environmental Protection Agency. http://www.epa.gov/ttn/caaa/t1cd.html.

1996b *Review of the National Ambient Air Quality Standards for Particulate Matter: Policy Assessment of Scientific and Technical Information*. OAQPS Staff Paper, US Environmental Protection Agency, EPA-452 \ R-96–013, July 1996. http://www.epa.gov/ttn/oarpg/t1sp.html.

1996c "Proposed guidelines for carcinogen risk assessment." *Federal Register* 61:17,959–18,011. http://www.epa.gov/ordntrnt/ORD/WebPubs/carcinogen/index.html.

1997a *Beach Program*. US Environmental Protection Agency, Office of Water, EPA Document Number EPA–820–F–97–002. http://www.epa.gov/OST/beaches/BeachPro.pdf.

1997b *National Air Quality and Emissions Trends Report 1996*. US Environmental Protection Agency, EPA Document Number 454/R–97–013. http://www.epa.gov/oar/aqtrnd96/toc.html

1997c *National Ambient Air Quality Standards for*

Particulate Matter; Final Rule 18/7 1997. US Environmental Protection Agency, 40 CFR Part 50. http://www.epa.gov/ttn/caaa/t1pfpr.html

1997d *The Benefits and Costs of the Clean Air Act, 1970 to 1990*. US Environmental Protection Agency. http://www.epa.gov/oar/sect812/copy.html.

1998a *Bacterial Water Quality Standards Status Report* Standards and Applied Science Division, Office of Science and Technology, Office of Water, US Environmental Protection Agency.

1998b *Pesticidal Chemicals Classified as Known, Probable or Possible Human Carcinogens*. Office of Pesticide Programs, US Environmental Protection Agency. http://www.epa.gov/pesticides/carlist/table.htm (but presently removed).

1998c *National Air Quality and Emissions Trends Report 1997*. US Environmental Protection Agency. http://www.epa.gov/oar/aqtrnd97/.

1998d *National Air Pollutant Emission Trends Update: 1970–1997*. http://www.epa.gov/ttn/chief/trends97/browse.html.

1999a *Asbestos*. Sources of information on indoor air quality. http://www.epa.gov/iaq/asbestos.html.

1999b *Characterization of Municipal Solid Waste in the United States: 1998 Update*. Franklin Associates. http://www.epa.gov/epaoswer/non-hw/muncpl/msw98.htm.

1999c *Formaldehyde*. Sources of information on indoor air quality. http://www.epa.gov/iaq/formalde.html.

1999d *Part 141—National Primary Drinking Water Regulations*. http://www.epa.gov/safewater/regs/cfr141.pdf.

1999e *The Benefits and Costs of the Clean Air Act, 1990 to 2010*. US Environmental Protection Agency. http://www.epa.gov/airprogm/oar/sect812/copy99.html.

2000a *A Guide to Selected National Environmental Statistics in the U.S. Government*. http://www.epa.gov/ceisweb1/ceishome/ceisdocs/usguide/contents.htm.

2000b *AIRS*. Air Quality Database. http://www.epa.gov/airs/aewin/.

2000c *Municipal Solid Waste Generation, Recycling and Disposal in the United States: Facts and Figures for 1998*. EPA530–F–00–024. http://www.epa.gov/epaoswer/non-hw/muncpl/msw99.htm.

2000d *National Air Pollutant Emission Trends: 1900–1998*. http://www.epa.gov/ttn/chief/trends/trends98/http://www.epa.gov/ttn/chief/trends98/emtrnd.html.

2000e *National Air Quality and Emissions Trends Report 1998*. US Environmental Protection Agency. http://www.epa.gov/oar/aqtrnd98/.

2000f *Latest Findings on National Air Quality: 1999 Status and Trends* US Environmental Protection Agency. EPA-454/F-00–002. http://www.epa.gov/oar/aqtrnd99/brochure/brochure.pdf

2000g *Biopesticides Registration Action Document: Preliminary Risks and Benefits Sections: Bacillus thuringiensis Plant-Pesticides*. http://www.epa.gov/scipoly/sap/2000/october.

EPAQS 1994a *Carbon Monoxide*. Expert Panel on Air Quality Standards, Department of the Environment, Transport and the Regions, the Scottish Executive, the National Assembly for Wales, and the Department of the Environment for Northern Ireland. http://www.detr.gov.uk/environment/airq/aqs/co/index.htm.

1994b *Ozone*. Expert Panel on Air Quality Standards, Department of the Environment, Transport and the Regions, the Scottish Executive, the National Assembly for Wales, and the Department of the Environment for Northern Ireland. http://www.detr.gov.uk/environment/airq/aqs/ozone/index.htm.

1995a *Particles*. Expert Panel on Air Quality Standards, Department of the Environment, Transport and the Regions, the Scottish Executive, the National Assembly for Wales, and the Department of the Environment for Northern Ireland. http://www.detr.gov.uk/environment/airq/aqs/particle/index.htm.

1995b *Sulphur Dioxide*. Expert Panel on Air Quality Standards, Department of the Environment, Transport and the Regions, the Scottish Executive, the National Assembly for Wales, and the Department of the Environment for Northern Ireland. http://www.detr.gov.uk/environment/airq/aqs/so2/index.htm.

1996 *Nitrogen Dioxide*. Expert Panel on Air Quality Standards, Department of the Environment, Transport and the Regions, the Scottish Executive, the National Assembly for Wales, and the Department of the Environment for Northern Ireland. http://www.detr.gov.uk/environment/airq/aqs/no2/index.htm.

1998 *Lead*. Expert Panel on Air Quality Standards,

Department of the Environment, Transport and the Regions, the Scottish Executive, the National Assembly for Wales, and the Department of the Environment for Northern Ireland. http://www.detr.gov.uk/environment/airq/aqs/lead/index.htm.

ERS 1995 "World agriculture: trends and indicators." Database from ERS, USDA. World.wk1 from http://usda.mannlib.cornell.edu/data-sets/international/89024/14/ (file world.wk1).

1996 *The Future of China's Grain Market*. Agricultural Economic Report no. 750. Frederick W. Crook and W. Hunter Colby, Economic Research Service, US Department of Agriculture. http://www.ers.usda.gov/epubs/pdf/aib730/index.htm.

1997 *International Agricultural Baseline Projections to 2005*. Economic Research Service under US Department of Agriculture. http://www.ers.usda.gov/epubs/pdf/aer750/.

1998 "Food and nutrient intake by individuals in the United States by sex and age, 1994–96." NFS Report no. 96–2, NTIS Order Number PB99–117251INZ. http://www.barc.usda.gov/bhnrc/foodsurvey/Products9496.html.

1999a *Rice Situation and Outlook Yearbook 1999*. RCS 1999. Economic Research Service, US Department of Agriculture. http://usda.mannlib.cornell.edu/reports/erssor/field/rcs-bby/.

1999b *Wheat Situation and Outlook Yearbook 1999*. WHS 1999. Economic Research Service, US Department of Agriculture. http://usda.mannlib.cornell.edu/reports/erssor/field/whs-bby/.

2000a *International Agriculture and Trade (China)*. WRS-99-4 Economic Research Service, US Department of Agriculture. http://usda.mannlib.cornell.edu/reports/erssor/international/wrs-bb/1999/china/wrs99.pdf.

2000b *Tobacco Situation and Outlook Report*. Market and Trade Economics Division, Economic Research Service, US Department of Agriculture, April 2000, TBS-246. http://usda.mannlib.cornell.edu/reports/erssor/specialty/tbs-bb/2000/tbs246.pdf.

2000c *Agricultural Outlook: August 2000*. Economic Research Service, US Department of Agriculture. http://www.ers.usda.gov/publications/agoutlook/aug2000/contents.htm.

ESRC 1997 *Learning to be Green: the Future of Environmental Education* ESRC Global Environmental Change Programme, Special Briefing No. 2, University of Sussex. http://www.susx.ac.uk/Units/gec/pubs/briefing/sbrief2.pdf.

1999 *The Politics of GM Food: Risk, Science and Public Trust*. ESRC Global Environmental Change Programme, Special Briefing No. 5, University of Sussex. http://www.susx.ac.uk/Units/gec/gecko/gec-gm-f.pdf.

Esty, Dan 1999 "Feeding Frankenstein." *WorldLink*, Sept/Oct99:12–3.

Etheridge, D. M., L. P. Steele, R. L. Langenfelds, R. J. Francey, J.-M. Barnola and V. I. Morgan 1998 "Historical CO_2 records from the Law Dome DE08, DE08–2, and DSS ice cores." In *Trends: A Compendium of Data on Global Change*. Carbon Dioxide Information Analysis Center, Oak Ridge National Laboratory, US Department of Energy, Oak Ridge, Tennesee. http://cdiac.esd.ornl.gov/trends/co2/lawdome.html.

EU 1975 *Council Directive of 8 December 1975 concerning the Quality of Bathing Water*. 76/160/EEC. http://www.europa.eu.int/water/water-bathing/directiv.html.

1980 *Council Directive 80/778/EEC of 15 July 1980 relating to the Quality of Water Intended for Human Consumption*. http://europa.eu.int/eur-lex/en/lif/dat/1980/en_380L0778.html.

1983 *Acid Rain: A Review of the Phenomenon in the EEC and Europe*. London: Graham and Trotman.

1994a *15.10.20.30 – Monitoring of Atmospheric Pollution. Consolidated Legislation*. http://www.europa.eu.int/eur-lex/en/consleg/reg/en_register_15102030.html.

1994b *The European Renewable Energy Study: Prospects for Renewable Energy in the European Community and Eastern Europe up to 2010*. Main Report, Luxembourg: Office for Official Publications of the European Communities.

2000a *1999 Annual Energy Review*. European Union DG 17. http://www.europa.eu.int/en/comm/dg17/aerhome.htm.

2000b *Bathing Water Quality: Annual Report, 1999 Bathing Season*. http://europa.eu.int/water/water-bathing/report.html.

2000c *Communication from the Commission on the Precautionary Principle*. COM (2000) 1. 2/2/2000. http://europa.eu.int/comm/off/com/health_consumer/precaution_en.pdf.

2000d *Eurobarometer 52.1 - The Europeans and*

Biotechnology. http://europa.eu.int/comm/research/pdf/eurobarometer-en.pdf.

2000e *White Paper On Food Safety*. COM (1999) 719 final. http://europa.eu.int/comm/dgs/health_consumer/library/pub/pub06_en.pdf.

2001a *Genetics and the Future of Europe*. http://europa.eu.int/comm/research/quality-of-life/genetics/pdf/genetics_en.pdf.

2001b *Economic Impacts of Genetically Modified Crops on the Agri-Food Sector – a First Review*. http://europa.eu.int/comm/agriculture/publi/gmo/full_en.pdf.

Eurostat 1999 *Yearbook 1998/99: A Statistical Eye on Europe*. Luxemburg: Eurostat.

Evenson, Robert E. 1999 "Global and local implications of biotechnology and climate change for future food supplies." *Proceedings of the National Academy of Sciences* 96:5,921–8.

EVOSTC 1997 *Status Report 1997*. Exxon Valdez Oil Spill Trustee Council.

2000a *Exxon Valdez Oil Spill Trustee Council website*. http://www.oilspill.state.ak.us.

2000b *2000 Status Report*. Exxon Valdez Oil Spill Trustee Council. http://www.oilspill.state.ak.us/publications/2000AnRpt.pdf.

Ewen, Stanley W.B. and Arpad Pusztai 1999 "Effect of diets containing genetically modified potatoes expressing Galanthus nivalis lectin on rat small intestine." *Lancet* 354(9187):1,353–4.

Fairhead, James and Melissa Leach 1998 *Reframing Deforestation: Global Analysis and Local Realities: Studies in West Africa*. London: Routledge.

Falkenmark, Malin and Gunnar Lindh 1993 "Water and economic development." In Gleick 1993b:80–91.

Falmenmark, Malin and Jan Lundqvist 1997 "World freshwater problems – call for a new realism." Background document for CSD 1997. Stockholm: Stockholm Environment Institute.

Falkenmark, Malin and Carl Widstrand 1992 "Population and water resources: a delicate balance." *Population Bulletin* 47(3):2–36.

Faminow, Merle 1997 "The disappearing Amazon rainforest problem." *International Association of Agricultural Economists, Canadian Newsletter*. http://www.oac.uoguelph.ca/www/Agec/IAAE/Art_Faminow01.htm.

Fan, Shenggen and Mercedita Agcaoili-Sombilla 1997 *Why Do Projections on China's Future Food Supply and Demand Differ?* Environment and Production Technology Division discussion paper 22. International Food Policy Research Institute. http://www.cgiar.org/ifpri/divs/eptd /dp/dp22.htm.

Fankhauser, Samuel 1998 *Economic Estimates of Global Environment Facility*. Sustainable Development and Global Climate Change Conference. http://www.gcrio.org/USGCRP/sustain/fankhaus.html.

Fannin, Penny 2000 "Is the duck dangerous?" *The Age* 20 January. http://theage.com.au/news/20000120/A34128-2000Jan19.html.

FAO 1949–95 *FAO Production Yearbook*. Rome: Food and Agriculture Organization of the United Nations.

FAO 1995a *Forest Resources Assessment 1990*. Rome: Food and Agriculture Organization of the United Nations. Data from gopher://faov02.fao.org/00Gopher_root:[fao.worldfo.T34FF]T34FF.TXT (no longer available).

1995b *World Agriculture: Towards 2010. An FAO Study*. Nikos Alexandratos (ed.). Rome: Food and Agriculture Organization of the United Nations. Online version at http://www.fao.org/docrep/v4200e/v4200e00.htm.

1996a *Food Supply Situation and Crop Prospects in Sub-Saharan Africa*. Africa report 2/96. http://www.fao.org/giews/english/eaf/eaf9605/af9605tm.htm.

1996b *The Sixth World Food Survey*. Rome: Food and Agriculture Organization of the United Nations.

1997a *Review of the State of World Fishery Resources: Marine Fisheries*. http://www.fao.org/waicent/faoinfo/fishery/publ/circular/c920/c920-1.htm.

1997b *State of World Fisheries and Aquaculture:1996*. http://www.fao.org/waicent/faoinfo/fishery/publ/sofia/sofiaef.htm.

1997c *State of The World's Forests 1997*. Rome: Food and Agriculture Organization of the United Nations. http://www.fao.org/montes/fo/sofo/SOFO97/97toc-e.stm.

1997d *Telefood Profiles: In Eritrea, 140 Farmers Lead the Way to a Future of Abundant Harvests*. http://www.fao.org/food/tf97/docs/eritre-e.pdf.

1997e *The State of Food and Agriculture*. Rome: Food and Agriculture Organization of the United Nations. Incl. disk database.

1999a *State of The World's Forests 1999*. Rome: Food and Agriculture Organization of the United Nations. http://www.fao.org/forestry/FO/SOFO/SOFO99/sofo99–e.stm.

1999b *The Forest Resources Assessment Programme.* http://www.fao.org/docrep/field/385901.htm.

1999c *The State of Food Insecurity in the World 1999.* Rome: Food and Agriculture Organization of the United Nations. http://www.fao.org/FOCUS/E/SOFI/home-e.htm.

2000a Database, accessed in 2000: http://apps.fao.org/.

2000b Fisheries update. http://www.fao.org/fi/statist/summtab/default.asp.

2000c *The State of Food Insecurity in the World 2000.* Rome: Food and Agriculture Organization of the United Nations. http://www.fao.org/news/2000/001002–e.htm

2000d *Agriculture: Towards 2015/30.* Technical Interim Report, April 2000. Rome: Food and Agriculture Organization of the United Nations. http://www.fao.org/es/esd/at2015/toc-e.htm.

2000e *Food Outlook.* November, No. 5. Global Information and Early Warning System on Food and Agriculture. Rome: Food and Agriculture Organization of the United Nations. http://www.fao.org/giews/english/fo/fotoc.htm.

2000f *The State of Food and Agriculture 2000.* Rome: Food and Agriculture Organization of the United Nations. http://www.fao.org/docrep/x4400e/x4400e00.htm.

2001a Database, accessed in 2001: http://apps.fao.org/.

2001b *The state of world fisheries and aquaculture 2000.* Rome: Food and Agriculture Organization of the United Nations. http://www.fao.org/docrep/003/x8002e/x8002e00.htm.

2001c *The Global Forest Resources Assessment 2000: Summary Report.* Food and Agriculture Organization of the United Nations. ftp://ftp.fao.org/unfao/bodies/cofo/cofo15/X9835e.pdf.

Farman, J. C., B. G. Gardiner and J. D. Shanklin 1985 "Large losses of total ozone in Antarctica reveal seasonal ClO_x/NO_x interaction." *Nature* 315:207–10. http://www.ciesin.org/docs/011–430/011–430.html.

Fearnside, Philip M. 1991 "Greenhouse gas contributions from deforestation in Brazilian Amazonia." In Levine 1991:92–105.

Fedorov, Alexey V. and S. George Philander 2000 "Is El Niño changing?" *Science* 288:1,97–2,002.

Feldman J. 1983 "Work ability of the aged under conditions of improving mortality." *Millbank Memorial Fund Quarterly/Health and Society* 61:430–44.

Fenger, Jes 1985 *Luftforurening – en introduktion.* [Air Pollution – an introduction.] Lyngby: Teknisk Forlag A/S.

Fenger, Jes and Jens Chr. Tjell (eds.) 1994 *Luftforurening.* [Air pollution.] Lyngby: Polyteknisk Forlag.

Feuer, Eric J., Ray M. Merrill and Benjamin F. Hankey 1999 "Cancer surveillance series: interpreting trends in prostate cancer – part II: cause of death misclassification and the recent rise and fall in prostate cancer mortality." *Journal of the National Cancer Institute* 91(12):1,025–32.

Feuer, Eric J., Lap-Ming Wun, Catherine C. Boring, W. Dana Flanders, Marilytl J. Timmel and Tolly Tong 1993 "The lifetime risk of developing breast cancer." *Journal of the National Cancer Institute* 85(11):892–7.

FHWA 1996 *Highway Statistics Summary to 1995.* Federal Highway Administration. http://www.fhwa.dot.gov/ohim/summary95/index.html.

1997 *Highway Statistics 1996.* Federal Highway Administration. http://www.fhwa.dot.gov/ohim/1996/index.html.

1998 *Highway Statistics 1997.* Federal Highway Administration. http://www.fhwa.dot.gov/ohim/hs97/hs97page.htm.

1999 *Highway Statistics 1998.* Federal Highway Administration. http://www.fhwa.dot.gov/ohim/hs98/hs98page.htm.

Ministries of Finance, Agriculture, Fisheries, Environment, Energy, Taxes and General Economics 1995 [Finansministeriet, Landbrugs- og Fiskeriministeriet, Miljø- og Energiministeriet, Skatteministeriet and Økonomiministeriet] 1995 *Budgetanalyse om vedvarende energi.* [Budget analysis of renewable energy.] Copenhagen.

Finkel, Adam M. 1996 "Comparing risks thoughtfully." *Risk: Health, Safety and Environment* 7:325. http://www.fplc.edu/RISK/vol7/fall/finkel.htm.

Finkel, Adam M. and Dominic Golding 1994 *Worst Things First? The Debate over Risk-Based National Environmental Priorities.* Washington, DC: Resources for the Future.

Fisch, Harry, H. Andrews, J. Hendriks, E. T. Gouboff, J. H. Olson and C. A. Olsson 1997 "The relationship of sperm counts to birth rates: a population based study." *Journal of Urology* 157:840–3.

Fisch, Harry and Erik T. Goluboff 1996 "Geographic variations in sperm counts: a potential cause of bias in studies of semen quality." *Fertility and Sterility* 65(5):1,044–6.

Fisch, Harry, Erik T. Goluboff, John H. Olson, Joseph Feldshuh, Stephen J. Broder and David H. Barad 1996 "Semen analyses in 1,283 men from the United States over a 25-year period: no decline in quality." *Fertility and Sterility* 65(5):1,009–14.

Fischhoff, Baruch, Paul Slovic and Sarah Lichtenstein 1979 "Which risks are acceptable?" *Environment* 21(4):17–38.

Flora, Peter, Franz Pfenning Kraus and Jens Winfried Alber 1983 *State, Economy, and Society in Western Europe 1815–1975. 1: The Growth of Mass Democracies and Welfare States.* Frankfurt: Campus Verlag.

1987 *State, Economy, and Society in Western Europe 1815–1975. 2: The Growth of Industrial Societies and Capitalist Economies.* Frankfurt: Campus Verlag.

Floud, Roderick and Bernard Harris 1996 *Health, Height and Welfare: Britain 1700–1980.* NBER Working Paper H0087. http://papers.nber.org/papers/h0087.

Fog, Kåre 1999 "Hvor mange arter uddør der." [How many species go extinct.] Schroll *et al.* 1999:119–42.

Fogel, Robert William 1989 *Second Thoughts on the European Escape from Hunger: Famines, Price Elasticities, Entitlements, Chronic Malnutrition and Mortality Rates.* NBER Working Paper 1 on Historical Factors in Long Run Growth. http://www.nber.org/papers/h0001.pdf.

1995 "The contribution of improved nutrition to the decline in mortality rates in Europe and America." In Simon 1995b:61–71.

Ford, Earl S., Alison E. Kelly, Steven M. Teutsch, Stephen B. Thacker and Paul L. Garbe 1999 "Radon and lung cancer: a cost-effectiveness analysis." *American Journal of Public Health* 89(3):351–7.

Forslund, Janne 1994 *Prices of Drinking Water: The Choice between "Growing" Water and Treating Water.* Revised version of a background paper for EC Conference on Drinking Water, Brussels, 23–24 September 1993, DK EPA.

FotE 2001 "What's wrong with genetic modification?" Friends of the Earth, http://www.foe.co.uk/campaigns/food_and_biotechnology/gm_food.

Fouquet, Roger and Peter J. G. Pearson 1998 "A thousand years of energy use in the United Kingdom." *Energy Journal* 19(4):1–42.

Frankel, Jeffrey A. 1997 *Determinants of Long Term Growth.* Background Paper for the Morning Session of the Meeting of the Asia-Pacific Economic Cooperation of Economic Advisers, Vancouver, Canada. Published as "Why economies grow the way they do." *Canadian Business Economics*, Spring/Summer 1998. http://www.ksg.harvard.edu/fs/jfrankel/Apecgrow.pdf.

Fraser, Gary E. and David Shavlik 1997 "Risk factors, lifetime risk, and age at onset of breast cancer." *Annals of Epidemiology* 7(6):375–82.

Fraser, S. A. Barsotti and D. Rogich 1988 "Sorting out material issues." *Resources Policy*, March:3–20.

Frazão, Elizabeth (ed.) 1999 *America's Eating Habits: Changes and Consequences.* Food and Rural Economics Division, Economic Research Service, US Department of Agriculture. Agriculture Information Bulletin No. 750 (AIB-750). http://www.econ.ag.gov/epubs/pdf/aib750/.

Freivalds, John and Daryl Natz 1999 "Overcoming phood phobia." *Communication World* 16(6):26–8.

Freme F. L. and B. D. Hong 2000 *U.S. Coal Supply and Demand: 1999 Review.* U.S. Energy Information Administration. http://www.eia.doe.gov/cneaf/coal/cia/99_special/coal99.pdf

Friedeman, Thomas L. 2000 "Brave New World." *New York Times* September 22, pA27.

Fries, J. F. 1980 "Aging, natural death, and the compression of morbidity." *New England Journal of Medicine.* 303:130–5.

1988 "Aging, illness and health policy: implications of the compression of morbidity." *Perspectives of Biological Medicine* 31:407–28.

2000 "Compression of morbidity in the elderly." *Vaccine* 18(16):1,584.

Friis-Christensen, Eigil 1993 "Solar activity variations and global temperature." *Energy* 18(12):1,273–84.

Friis-Christensen, E. and K. Lassen 1991 "Length of the solar cycle: an indicator of solar activity closely associated with climate." *Science* 254:698–700.

Frink, Charles R., Paul E. Waggoner and Jesse H. Ausubel 1999 "Nitrogen fertilizer: retrospect and prospect." *Proceedings of the National Academy of Science*. 96:1,175–80. http://www.pnas.org.

Fuller, Theodore D., John N. Edwards, Sairudee Vorakitphokatorn and Santhat Sermsri 1996 "Chronic stress and psychological well-being: evidence from Thailand on household crowding." *Social Science and Medicine* 42(2):265–80.

Fullerton, Don and Gilbert E. Metcalf 1997 *Environmental Taxes and the Double-Dividend Hypothesis: Did You Really Expect Something for Nothing?* NBER Working Paper 6,199. http://papers.nber.org/papers/W6199.

Fullerton Jn., Howard N. 1999 "Labor force participation: 75 years of change, 1950–98 and 1998–2025." *Monthly Labor Review*. 122(12):2–12. http://www.bls.gov/opub/mlr/1999/12/art1full.pdf.

Gade, Steen 1997 "Pesticidfrit Danmark, ja tak." [Pesticide-free Denmark, yes please.] Editorial in *Folkesocialisten*, May 1997. http://www1.hotlips.sf.dk/Alt/Avisartikler/%2326390.

Gaffen, D. and R. Ross 1998 "Increased summertime heat stress in the U.S." *Nature* 396:529–30.

Gaffen, D. J., B. D. Santer, J. S. Boyle, J. R. Christy, N. E. Graham and R. J. Ross 2000 "Multidecadal changes in the vertical temperature structure of the tropical troposphere." *Science* 287(5456):1,242–5.

Gallagher, Sally K. and Randall G. Stokes 1996 "Economic disarticulation and fertility in less developed nations." *Sociological Quarterly* 37(2):227–44.

Gallia, Katherine and Susanne Althoff 1999 "Real men eat organic." *Natural Health* 29(4):31.

Gallup 2000a "Environment." *Gallup Poll Topics: A–Z*. http://www.gallup.com/poll/indicators/indenvironment.asp.

Gallup 2000b "Most important problem." *Gallup Poll Topics: A–Z*. http://www.gallup.com/poll/indicators/indmip.asp.

Gardner-Outlaw, Tom and Robert Engelman 1997 *Sustaining Water, Easing Scarcity: A Second Update*. Revised Data for the Population Action International Report 1993: *Sustaining Water: Population and the Future of Renewable Water Supplies*. Population Action International. http://www.populationaction.org/why_pop/water/water-toc.htm and http://www.populationaction.org/why_pop/water/water97.pdf.

Garvin, Theresa and John Eyles 1997 "The sun safety metanarrative: translating science into public health discourse." *Policy Sciences* 30(2):47–70.

Gaskins, Darius W. Jn. and John P. Weyant 1993 "Model comparisons of the costs of reducing CO_2 emissions." *American Economic Review Papers and Proceedings* 83(2):318–23. http://sedac.ciesin.org/mva/EMF/GW1993.html.

Gatto, Marino and Giulio A. De Leon 2000 "Pricing biodiversity and ecosystem services: the never-ending story." *BioScience* 50(4):347–55.

Geertz, Armin W. 1992 "Høvding Seattle: nutidens håb, urtidens profet?" [Chief Seattle: the future now, prophet earlier?] *Religion* 3:6–19.

Gemmel, D. 1995 "Association of housing age and condition with blood lead levels." In *Proceedings of the 25th Public Health Conference on Records and Statistics*. http://www.cdc.gov/nceh/lead/research/pub/pub.htm.

Gentry, A. H. 1986 "Endemism in tropical versus temperate plant communities." In M. E. Soule (ed.), *Conservation Biology*, Sunderland, MA: Sinauer Associates, pp. 153–81.

GESAMP 1990 *The State of the Marine Environment*. IMO/FAO/UNESCO/WMO/WHO/IAEA/UN/UNEP Joint Group of Experts on the Scientific Aspects of Marine Pollution. Oxford: Blackwell Scientific Publications.

GEUS 1997a *Grundvandsovervågning 1997* [Groundwater surveillance 1997]. Danmarks og Grønlands Geologiske Undersøgelse. Copenhagen: Miljø- og Energiministeriet.

1997b "Vandressourcer: Ferskvand! Det 21. århundredes hovedproblem?" [Water resources: fresh water! The main problem of the twenty-first century.] *Geologi: Nyt fra GEUS*. Danmarks og Grønlands Geologiske Undersøgelse, en forsknings- og rådgivningsinstitution i Miljø- og Energiministeriet 2, October 1997. http://www.geus.dk/publications/geo-nyt-geus/gi97-2.htm.

Giddens, Anthony 1991 *Modernity and Self-Identity*. Cambridge: Polity Press.

Gifford, Robert 2000 "Why we're destroying the Earth." *Psychology Today* 33(2):68–9.

Gillespie, Mark 1999 "U.S. public worries about toxic waste, air and water pollution as key environmental threats." *Gallup Poll Releases*, 25 March 1999. http://www.gallup.com/poll/releases/pr990325.asp.

Gillfillan, Edward S. 1995 *Impacts of Human Activities on Marine Ecosystems*. Bowdoin College. http://www.bowdoin.edu/dept/es/200/guide/.

Gillman, Matthew W. 1996 "Enjoy your fruits and vegetables." *British Medical Journal* 313:765–6.

Ginsburg, J. and P. Hardiman 1992 "Decreasing quality of semen." *British Medical Journal* 305:1,229.

Ginsburg, J., S. Okolo, G. Prelevis and P. Hardiman 1994 "Residence in the London area and sperm density." *The Lancet* 343:230.

Glantz, Michael H., Amara Tandy Brook and Patricia Parisi 1997 *Rates and Processes of Amazon Deforestation*. Environmental and Societal Impacts Group/NCAR. http://www.pik-potsdam.de/mirror/bahc/lba/rates/rates.html.

Glasgow Media Group 1976 *Bad News*. London: Routledge and Kegan Paul.

1980 *More Bad News*. London: Routledge and Kegan Paul.

Gleick, Peter H. 1993a "Water and conflict: fresh water resources and international security." *International Security* 18(1):79–112.

1993b *Water in Crisis: A Guide to the World's Fresh Water Resources*. New York: Oxford University Press.

1998a *The World's Water 1998–1999. The Biennial Report on Freshwater Resources*. Washington, DC: Island Press.

1998b "The world's water." *Issues in Science and Technology* 14(4):80–2.

1999a "The human right to water." *Water Policy* 5(1):487–503. Download workingpaper from http://www.pacinst.org/gleickrw.pdf.

1999b "Water futures: a review of global water resources projections." Study for WWC 2000: *World Water Vision*. http://www.watervision.org/clients/wv/water.nsf/WebAdmin/wUnderConstruction/$file/GlobalWaterResourcesProjections.pdf.

Global Financial Data 2000 *Metal and Commodity Price Data*. http://www.globalfindata.com/freecom.htm.

Goeller, H. E. and Alvin M. Weinberg 1976 "The age of substitutability: what do we do when the mercury runs out?" *Science* 191:683–9.

Goeller, H. E. and A. Zucker 1984 "Infinite resources: the ultimate strategy" *Science* 223:456–62.

Goklany, Indur M. 1998 "Saving habitat and conserving biodiversity on a crowded planet." *BioScience* 48(11):941–52.

Gold, Lois Swirsky, Thomas H. Slone, Bonnie R. Stern, Neela B. Manley and Bruce N. Ames 1992 "Rodent carcinogens: setting priorities." *Science* 258:261–5.

Golddammer, Johann Georg 1991 "Tropical wild-land fires and global changes: prehistoric evidence, present fire regimes, and future trends." In Levine 1991:83–91.

Golden, Frederic 2000 "A century of heroes." *Time* 155(17):54–7.

Golden, Robert J., Kenneth L. Noller, Linda Titus-Ernstoff, Raymond H. Kaufman, Robert Mittendorf, Robert Stillman and Elizabeth A. Reese 1998 "Environmental endocrine modulators and human health: an assessment of the biological evidence." *Critical Reviews in Toxicology* 28(2):109–226.

Gonick, Larry and Alice Outwater 1996 *The Cartoon Guide to the Environment*. New York: HarperPerennial.

Goodstein, Eban 1995 "Benefit-cost analysis at the EPA." *Journal of Socio-Economics* 24(2):375–89.

Goolsby, Donald A., William A. Battaglin, Gregory B. Lawrence, Richard S. Artz, Brent T. Aulenbach, Richard P. Hooper, Dennis R. Keeney and Gary J. Stensland 1999 *Gulf of Mexico Hypoxia Assessment: Topic #3. Flux and Sources of Nutrients in the Mississippi-Atchafalaya River Basin*. Hypoxia Work Group, White House Office of Science and Technology Policy, Committee on Environment and Natural Resources for the EPA Mississippi River/Gulf of Mexico Watershed Nutrient Task Force. NOAA Coastal Ocean Program. http://www.nos.noaa.gov/products/pubs_hypox.html.

Gore, Al 1992 *Earth in the Balance: Ecology and the Human Spirit*. Boston, MA: Houghton Mifflin.

Gorman, Christine 1998 "El Niño's (achoo!) allergies." *Time* 151(11):73.

Goudie, Andrew 1993 *The Human Impact on the Natural Environment*. Oxford: Blackwell.

Gough, Michael 1989 "Estimating cancer mortality: epidemiological and toxicological methods produce similar assessments." *Environmental Science and Technology* 23(8):925–30.

Goulder, Lawrence H., Ian W. H. Perry, Roberton C. Williams III and Dallas Burtraw 1998 *The cost-effectiveness of alternative insturments for environmental protection in a second-best setting.* Resources For the Future, Discussion Paper 98–22.

Graham, John D. 1995 "Comparing opportunities to reduce health risks: toxin control, medicine, and injury prevention." *NCPA Policy Report* 192. http://www.ncpa.org/studies/s192/s192.html.

Graham, John D. and Jonathan Baert Wiener 1997a "Confronting risk tradeoffs." In Graham and Wiener 1997b:1–41.

Graham, John D. and Jonathan Baert Wiener (eds.) 1997b *Risk vs. Risk: Tradeoffs in Proctecting Health and the Environment.* Cambridge, MA: Harvard University Press.

Grandjean, Philippe 1998 *Farlig Forurening.* [Dangerous pollution.] Copenhagen: Nyt Nordisk Forlag Arnold Busck.

Graney, J. R., A. N. Halliday, G. J. Keeler, J. O. Nriagu, J. A. Robbins and S. A. Norton 1995 "Isotopic record of lead pollution in lake sediments from the northeastern United States." *Geochimica et Cosmochimica Acta* 59(9):1,715–28.

Grassl, Hartmut 2000 "Status and improvements of coupled general circulation models." *Science* 288:1,991–7.

Gray, George M. and John D. Graham 1997 "Regulating pesticides." In Graham and Wiener 1997b:173–92.

Gray, George M. and James K. Hammitt 2000 "Risk/risk tradeoffs in pesticide regulation: an exploratory analysis of the public health effects of a ban on organophosphate and carbamate pesticides." Forthcoming in *Risk Analysis.*

Gray, Vincent 1998 "The IPCC future projections: are they plausible?" *Climate Research* 10:155–62.

Greaves, Emma and Martin Stanisstreet 1993 "Children's ideas about rainforests." *Journal of Biological Education* 27(3)189–94.

Greene, David L. 1997 "Economic scarcity. " *Harvard International Review* 19(3):16–21.

Greene, Gayle and Vicki Ratner 1994 "A toxic link to breast cancer?" *Nation* 258(24):866–9.

Greenland, D. J. and I. Szabolcs 1994 *Soil Resilience and Sustainable Land Use.* Wallingford, UK: CAB International.

Greenpeace 1992 *The Environmental Legacy of the Gulf War.* A Greenpeace Report. http://www.greenpeace.org/gopher/campaigns/military/1992/gulfwar3.txt.

1996 *Perils Amid Promises of Genetically Modified Foods.* Dr. Mae-Wan Ho on behalf of Greenpeace International. http://www.greenpeace.org/~geneng/reports/food/food002.htm

1999 *True Cost of Food.* True Food Campaign, Greenpeace, and the Soil Association. http://www.greenpeace.org.uk/Multimedia/Live/FullReport/1141.pdf.

2000 *Greenpeace's International Campaign to Save the Climate.* http://www.greenpeace.org/~climate/.

2001a *Greenpeace MTV spot "Frankenfood."* http://www.tappedintogreenpeace.org/ram/react-apple.ram.

2001b "GE rice is fool's gold." *Press Release* 9 February 2001. http://www.greenpeace.org/%7Egeneng/highlights/food/goldenrice.htm.

Greider, William 2000 "Oil on Political Waters." *Nation*, 10/23/2000 271(12):5–6.

Griffith, Ted 1998 "All downhill." *Boston Business Journal* 18(3):1–2.

Grigg, David 1993 *The World Food Problem 1950–1980.* Oxford: Basil Blackwell.

Grisanzio, James A. 1993 "Exxon Valdez: the oil remains." *Animals* 126(6):33.

Groisman, Pavel Ya., Thomas R. Karl, David R. Easterling, Richard W. Knight, Paul F. Jamason, Kevin J. Hennessy, Ramasamy Suppiah, Cher M. Page, Joanna Wibig, Krzysztof Fortuniak, Vyacheslav N. Razuvaev, Arthur Douglas, Eirik Førland and Pan-Mao Zhai 1999 "Changes in the probability of heavy precipitation: important indicators of climatic change." *Climatic Change* 42(1):243–83.

Grossman, Gene M. and Alan B. Krueger 1995 "Economic growth and the environment." *Quarterly Journal of Economics* 110(2):353–77.

Grove, Richard H. 1998 "Global impact of the 1789–93 El Niño." *Nature* 393:318–19.

Grubler, Arnulf, Michael Jefferson and Nebojsa Nakicenovic 1996 "Global energy perspectives: a summary of the joint study by the International Institute for Applied Systems Analysis and World Energy Council." *Technological Forecasting and Social Change* 51(3):237–64.

Gruenberg, E. M. 1977 "The failures of success." *Millbank Memorial Fund Quarterly/Health and Society* 55:3–24.

Gruza, G., E. Rankova, V. Razuvaev and O. Bulygina 1999 "Indicators of climate change for the Russian Federation." *Climatic Change* 42(1):219–42.

GSS 2000 *US General Social Survey 1972–1996*. Online access to the Cumulative Datafile. http://csa.berkeley.edu:7502/cgi-bin12/hsda?harcsda+gss96.

2001 *US General Social Survey 1972–1996*. Online access to the Cumulative Datafile. http://www.icpsr.umich.edu/GSS.

Gundersen, Per, J. Bo Larsen, Lars Bo Pedersen and Karsten Raulund Rasmussen 1998 "Syreregn er ikke en myte: det er et kompliceret miljø- og formidlingsproblem." [Acid rain is not a myth: it is a complicated environmental and communication problem.] Unpublished paper, partially published in *Jyllands-Posten*, 3 February 1998.

Gusbin, Dominique, Ger Klaassen and Nikos Kouvaritakis 1999 "Costs of a ceiling on Kyoto flexibility." *Energy Policy* 27(14):833–44.

Guttes, S., K. Failing, K. Neumann, J. Kleinstein, S. Georgii and H. Brunn 1998 "Chlorogenic pesticides and polychlorinated biphenyls in breast tissue of women with benign and malignant breast disease." *Archives of Environmental Contamination and Toxicology* 35:140–7.

Guynup, Sharon 1999 "Killer Corn." *Science World* 56(2):4.

Gwynne, Peter 1975 "The cooling world." *Newsweek* 28 April 1975, p. 64.

Haddad, Lawrence, Marie T. Ruel and James L. Garrett 1999 *Are Urban Poverty and Undernutrition Growing? Some Newly Assembled Evidence*. Discussion Paper 63. International Food Policy Research Institute, Food Consumption and Nutrition Division. http://www.cgiar.org/ifpri/divs/fcnd/dp/dp63.htm.

Hahn, Robert W. 1996a "Regulatory reform: what do the government's numbers tell us?" In Hahn 1996b: 208–53.

Hahn, Robert W. (ed.) 1996b *Risks, Costs, and Lives Saved: Getting Better Results form Regulation*. New York: Oxford University Press.

Haines, Michael R. 1995 "Disease and health through the ages." In Simon 1995b:51–60.

Hall, Alex and Syukuro Manabe 1999 "The role of water vapor feedback in unperturbed climate variability and global warming." *Journal of Climate* 12(8):2,327–46.

Halsnæs, Kirsten, Henrik Meyer, Peter Stephensen and Lene Sørensen 1995 *Nordens interesser i principper for internationale drivhusgasaftaler*. [The Nordic interest in the principles for international Greenhouse Gas Agreements.] Risø-R-794(DA). Roskilde: Forskningscenter Risø.

Hamaide, Bertrand and John J. Boland 2000 "Benefits, Costs, and Cooperation in Greenhouse Gas Abatement." *Climatic Change* 47(3):239–58

Hammel, E. A. 1998 *History of Human Population*. http://demog.berkeley.edu/~gene/193/lectures/hpophist.htm (no longer available).

Hankey, Benjamin F., Eric J. Feuer, Limin X. Clegg, Richard B. Hayes, Julie M. Legler, Phillip C. Prorok, Lynn A. Ries, Ray M. Merrill and Richard S. Kaplan 1999 "Cancer surveillance series: interpreting trends in prostate cancer – part I: evidence of the effects of screening in recent prostate cancer incidence, mortality, and survival rates." *Journal of the National Cancer Institute* 91(12):1,017–24.

Hanley, Nick and Rick Slark 1994 "Cost-benefit analysis of paper recycling: a case study and some general points." *Journal of Environmental Planning and Management* 37(2):189–97.

Hanbury-Tenison, Robin 1992 "Tribal peoples: honouring wisdom." In Porritt 1992:137–41.

Hansen, James and Makiko Sato 2000 *Data for Well-Mixed Anthropogenic Greenhouse Gases*. http://www.giss.nasa.gov/data/si99/ghgases/.

Hansen, J., M. Sato and R. Ruedy 1995 "Long-term changes of the diurnal temperature cycle – implications about mechanisms of global climate-change." *Atmospheric Research* 37(1–3):175–209.

1997 "Radiative forcing and climate response." *Journal of Geophysical Research-Atmospheres*. 102(D6):6,831–64.

Hansen, James E., Makiko Sato, Andrew Lacis, Reto Ruedy, Ina Tegen and Elaine Matthews 1998 "Climate forcings in the industrial era." *Proceedings of the National Academy of Sciences* 95:12,753–8. http://www.pnasp.org.

Hansen, James , Makiko Sato, Reto Ruedy, Andrew Lacis and Valdar Oinas 2000a "Global warming in the twenty-first century: An alternative scenario." *Proceedings of the National Academy of Sciences* 97(18):9,875–80. http://www.pnas.org.

Hansen, James, Helene Wilson, Makiko Sato, Reto Ruedy, Kathy Shah and Erik Hansen 1995 "Satellite and surface temperature data at odds?" *Climatic Change* 30:103–17.

Hansen, Jesse, Laura C. and John.J. Obrycki 2000b "Field deposition of Bt transgenic corn pollen: lethal effects on the monarch butterfly." *Oecologia*. http://ecophys.biology.utah.edu/oecologia.html.

Hansen, Larry G. and Frederick S. vom Saal 1998 "Organochlorine residues and breast cancer." *New England Journal of Medicine* 338:14. http://www.nejm.org/content/1998/0338/0014/0988.asp.

Hardin, Garret 1968 "The tragedy of the commons." *Science* 162:1,243–8.

Hargreaves, David, Monica Eden-Green and Joan Devaney 1994 *World Index of Resources and Population*. Aldershot, UK: Dartmouth.

Hartill, Lane 1998 "Cold fusion." *Christian Science Monitor* 90(211):9.

Harvey, L. D. Danny 2000 "Constraining the Aerosol Radiative Forcing and Climate Sensitivity." *Climatic Change* 44:413–8.

Hasek, Glen 2000 "Powering the future." *Industry Week* 249(9):45–8.

Haskins, Jack B. 1981 "The trouble with bad news." *Newspaper Research Journal* 2(2):3–16.

Haslebo, Gitte 1982 *Fordeling af tid og arbejde i velfærdsstaten*. [Distribution of time and work in the Welfare State.] Copenhagen: Miljøministeriet, Planstyrelsen.

Hausman, Jerry 1999 "Cellular telephone, new products and the CPI." *Journal of Business and Economic Statistics* 17(2):188–94. Previous version as National Bureau of Economic Research, Working Paper no. W5982.

Hausman, William J. 1995 "Long-term trends in energy prices." In Simon 1995b:280–6.

Hawkes, Nigel 2001: "Global warming 'will be twice as bad'". The Times.com. January 22nd 2001. http://www.thetimes.co.uk/article/0,,2-71643,00.html.

Hayes, Richard B. 2000 *Risk Factors: Prostate*. National Institutes of Health, National Cancer Institute. http://rex.nci.nih.gov/NCI_Pub_Interface/raterisk/risks185.html.

Heath, Clark W. 1997 "Pesticides and cancer risk." *Cancer* 80:1,887–8.

Hedges, Stephen J. 1993 "The cost of cleaning up." *U.S. News and World Report* 115(9):26–9.

Heij, G. J. and J. W. Erisman (eds.) 1995 *Acid Rain Research: Do We Have Enough Answers?* Amsterdam: Elsevier.

Heilig, Gerhard K. 1996 *World Population Prospects: Analyzing the 1996 UN Population Projections*. Working Paper WP-96-146 IIASA-LUC. http://www.iiasa.ac.at/Research/LUC/Papers/gkh1/index.html.

1999 *Can China Feed Itself? A System for Evaluation of Policy Options*. Online version at International Institute of Applied Systems Analysis, http://www.iiasa.ac.at/Research/LUC/ChinaFood/.

Heino, R., R. Brázdil, E. Førland, H. Tuomenvirta, H. Alexandersson, M. Beniston, C. Pfister, M. Rebetez, G. Rosenhagen, S. Rösner and J. Wibig 1999 "Progress in the study of climatic extremes in Northern and Central Europe." *Climatic Change* 42(1):183–202.

Heinrichs, E. A. 1998 *Management of Rice Insect Pests*. Department of Entomology, University of Nebraska. http://ipmworld.umn.edu/chapters/heinrich.htm.

Henao, Julio and Carlos Baanante 1999 "Nutrient depletion in the agricultural soils of Africa." *2020 Vision Brief* 62. http://www.cgiar.org/ifpri/2020/briefs/number62.htm.

Henderson, C. W. 2000 "Death by global warming? Climate change, pollution, and malnutrition." *World Disease Weekly* 12 March 2000, pp. 13–14. Can be read at http://www.news.cornell.edu/releases/Feb00/AAAS.Pimentel.hrs.html (uncredited).

Henderson-Sellers, A., H. Zhang, G. Berz, K. Emanuel, W. Gray, C. Landsea, G. Holland, J. Lighthill, S.-L. Shieh, P. Webster and K. McGuffie 1998 "Tropical cyclones and global climate change: a post-IPCC assessment." *Bulletin of the American Meteorological Society* 79(1):19–38. http://ams.allenpress.com/.

Hennessy, Terry 2000 "Produce in progress." *Progressive Grocer* 79(12):69–72.

Herman, Arthur, 1997 *The Idea of Decline in Western History*. New York: The Free Press.

Herman, Shelby W. 2000 "Fixed assets and consumer durable goods." *Survey of Current Business* 2000(4):17–30. Bureau of Economic Analysis. http://www.bea.doc.gov/bea/pub/0400cont.htm.

Hertsgaard, Mark 2000 "A global green deal." *Time* 155(17):84–5.

Herzog, Howard, Baldur Eliasson and Olav Kaarstad 2000 "Capturing greenhouse gases." *Scientific American* 282(2):72–9.

Hesselberg, Robert J. and John E. Gannon 1995

"Contaminant trends in Great Lakes fish." In NBS 1995:242–4.

Heston, Alan and Robert Summers 1996 "International price and quantity comparisons: potentials and pitfalls." *AEA Papers and Proceedings* 86(2):20–4.

Heywood, V. H. and S. N. Stuart 1992 "Species extinctions in tropical forests." In Whitmore and Sayer 1992:91–118.

HHS 1997 *Health, United States, 1996–97 and Injury Chartbook*. US Human Health Service, Warner M. Fingerhut (ed.). Hyattsville, MD: National Center for Health Statistics. http://www.cdc.gov/nchswww/releases/97news/97news/hus96rel.htm.

Hilbert, Gudrun, Tommy Cederberg and Arne Büchert 1996 "Time Trend Studies of Chlorinated Pesticides, PCBs and Dioxins in Danish Human Milk." *Organohalogen Compounds* 30:123–6.

Hileman, Bette 1999 "Case Grows for Climate Change: New evidence leads to increasing concern that human-induced global warming from CO_2 emissions is already here." *Chemical and Engineering News* 77(32):16–23.

Hill, Kenneth 1995 "The decline of childhood mortality." In Simon 1995b:37–50.

Hille, John 1995 *Sustainable Norway: Probing the Limits and Equity of Environmental Space*. Oslo: The Project for an Alternative Future.

HLU 1997 *Luftkvalitet i Hovedstadsregionen 1996*. [Air quality in the capital region 1996.] Hovedstadens Luftovervågningsenhed.

HM Treasury 2000 *Pocket Data Bank UK Tables*. http://www.hm-treasury.gov.uk/e_info/overview/pdb160600.pdf.

2001 *Pocket Data Bank*. http://www.hm-treasury.gov.uk/e_info/overview/pdb300101.pdf.

Hoagland, William 1995 "Solar energy." *Scientific American* 273(3):170–3.

Hoffert, M. I., K. Caldeira, A. K. Jain, E. F. Haites, L. D. D. Harvey, S. D. Potter, M. E. Schlesinger, S. H. Schneider, R. G. Watts, T. M. L. Wigley and D. J. Wuebbles 1998 "Energy implications of future stabilization of atmospheric CO_2 content." *Nature* 395(6,705):881–4.

Hohmeyer, Olav 1993 "Renewables and the full costs of energy." Seminar on *External Effects in the Utilisation of Renewable Energy*. Risø National Laboratory, pp. 31–41.

Hoisington, David, Mireille Khairallah,Timothy Reeves,Jean-Marcel Ribaut,Bent Skovmand, Suketoshi Taba and Marilyn Warburton 1999 "Plant genetic resources: What can they contribute toward increased crop productivity?" *Proceedings of the National Academy of Sciences* 96:5,937–43.

Hoke, F. 1991 "Valdez cleanup a washout." *Environment* 33(5):24.

Holden, Constance 1974 "Scientists talk of the need for conservation and an ethic of biotic diversity to slow species extinction." *Science* 184:646–7.

1990 "Spilled oil looks worse on TV." *Science* 250:371.

Holdgate, Martin W. 1992 "Foreword." In Whitmore and Sayer 1992:xv–xix.

Holen, Arlene 1995 "The history of accident rates in the United States." In Simon 1995b:98–105.

Holgate, Stephen T. 1997 "The cellular and mediator basis of asthma in relation to natural history." *The Lancet*, supplement *Asthma* 350:5–9.

Holloway, Marguerite 1996 "Sounding out science: Prince William Sound is recovering, seven years after the Exxon Valdez disaster, but the spill's scientific legacy remains a mess." *Scientific American* 275(4):82–8.

Holmes, Robert 2000 "The obesity bug." *New Scientist* 167:2,250:26–31.

Høst, Arne 1997 "Development of atopy in childhood." *Allergy* 52:695–7.

Houghton, R. A. and David L. Skole 1990 "Carbon." In Turner *et al.* 1990:393–408.

House of Commons 1999 *Science and Technology – First Report*. http://www.parliament.the-stationery-office.co.uk/pa/cm199899/cmselect/cmsctech/286/28602.htm.

House of Lords 1998 *European Communities – Second Report*. http://www.parliament.the-stationery-office.co.uk/pa/ld199899/ldselect/ldeucom/11/8121501.htm.

Høyer, Annette Pernille, Phillippe Grandjean, Torben Jørgensen, John W. Brock and Helle Bøggild Hartvig 1998 "Organochlorine exposure and risk of breast cancer." *The Lancet* 352:1,816–20.

HSDB 2000 *Hazardous Substances Data Bank*. http://toxnet.nlm.nih.gov/cgi-bin/sis/htmlgen?HSDB.

Hu, Zuliu and Mohsin S. Khan 1997 *Why Is China Growing So Fast?* IMF Economic Issues 8.

http://www.imf.org/external/pubs/ft/issues8/issue8.pdf.

Huang, S., H. N. Pollack and P. Y. Shen 2000 "Temperature trends over the past five centuries reconstructed from borehole temperatures." *Nature* 403:756–8.

Hudson, Eric 2000 *Recycling Is Your Business*. http://www.recycline.com/recissue.html.

Hulka, Barbara S. and Azadeh T. Stark 1995 "Breast cancer: cause and prevention." *The Lancet* 346:883–7.

Hulten, Charles R. 1997 "Comment [on Nordhaus 1997a]." In Bresnahan and Gordon 1997:66–70.

Hume, David 1739, 1740 *A Treatise of Human Nature*. L. A. Selby-Bigge and P. H. Nidditch (eds.). Oxford: Oxford University Press.

1754 "Of the populousness of ancient nations." In David Hume, *Essays: Moral, Political and Literary*, 1985. Indianapolis: Liberty Classics.

Hunt, Morton 1974 *Sexual Behavior in the 1970s*. Chicago: Playboy Press.

Hunter, David J., Susan E. Hankinson, Francine Laden, Graham A. Colditz, JoAnn E. Manson, Walter C. Willett, Frank E. Speizer and Mary S. Wolff 1997 "Plasma organochlorine levels and the risk of breast cancer." *New England Journal of Medicine* 337(18):1,253–8.

Hunter, David J. and Karl T. Kelsey 1993 "Pesticide residues and breast cancer: the harvest of a silent spring?" *Journal of the National Cancer Institute* 85(8):598–9.

Hurrell, J. W. and K. E. Trenberth 1997 "Spurious trends in satellite MSU temperatures from merging different satellite records." *Nature* 386:164–7.

HWG 1998 *Gulf of Mexico Hypoxia Assessment Plan*. Hypoxia Work Group and Committee on Environment and Natural Resources, for the Mississippi River/Gulf of Mexico Watershed Nutrient Task Force. http://www.cop.noaa.gov/HypoxiaPlan.html.

1999 *Integrated Assessment of Hypoxia in the Northern Gulf of Mexico. Draft for Public Comment*. Hypoxia Work Group, White House Office of Science and Technology Policy, Committee on Environment and Natural Resources for the EPA Mississippi River/Gulf of Mexico Watershed Nutrient Task Force. NOAA Coastal Ocean Program. http://www.nos.noaa.gov/products/pubs_hypox.html.

IEA 1999 *Energy Balances of Non-OECD Countries, 1996–1997*. Paris: OECD/International Energy Agency.

IEA/OECD 1996 "Integrating PV Modules with Building Materials." *CADDET Renewable Energy* September. http://www.caddet-re.org/html/septart3.htm

IEA/OECD 1998 "Large-scale Photovoltaic-integrated Roof at a Visitor Centre." CADDET Centre for Renewable Energy Technical Brochure No.71. http://www.caddet-re.org/assets/no71.pdf.

IFA 2000 *Fertilizer Statistical Database*. International Fertilizer Industry Association. http://www.fertilizer.org/stats.htm.

IFA and UNEP 2000 *Mineral Fertilizer Use and the Environment*. By K. F. Isherwood, International Fertilizer Industry Association and United Nations Environment Programme. http://www.fertilizer.org/publish/pubenv/fertuse.htm.

IFPRI 1997 *The World Food Situation: Recent Developments, Emerging Issues, and Long-Term Prospects*. By Per Pinstrup-Andersen, Rajul Pandya-Lorch and Mark W. Rosegrant. December. Washington, DC. http://www.cgiar.org/ifpri/pubs/2catalog.htm.

1999 *World Food Prospects: Critical Issues for the Early Twenty-First Century*. By Per Pinstrup-Andersen, Rajul Pandya-Lorch and Mark W. Rosegrant. October. http://www.cgiar.org/ifpri/pubs/2fdpolrp.htm.

IGCB 1999 *An Economic Analysis of the National Air Quality Strategy Objectives: An Interim Report*. Interdepartmental Group on Costs and Benefits, Department of the Environment, Transport and the Regions. http://www.detr.gov.uk/environment/airq/naqs/ea/.

Illi, Sabina, Erika von Mutius, Susanne Lau, Renate Bergmann, Bodo Niggemann, Christine Sommerfeld and Ulrich Wahn 2001 "Early childhood infectious diseases and the development of asthma up to school age: a birth cohort study." *British Medical Journal* 322:390–395.

ILO 2000 *LABORSTA: Labor Statistics Database*. International Labor Organization, Bureau of Statistics. http://laborsta.ilo.org.

IMF 1997 *World Economic Outlook: October 1997*. Washington, DC: International Monetary Fund. http://www.imf.org/external/pubs/ft/weo/weo1097/weocon97.htm.

1998 *World Economic Outlook*. May. Washington,

DC. http://www.imf.org/external/pubs/ft/weo/weo0598/index.htm.
1999a: *World Economic Outlook; October 1999.* Washington, DC: International Monetary Fund. http://www.imf.org/external/pubs/ft/weo/1999/02/index.htm.
1999b *World Economic Outlook Database*, September. http://www.imf.org/external/pubs/ft/weo/1999/02/data/index.htm.
2000a Data from *International Statistical Yearbook*. Updates at http://www.imf.org/external/np/res/commod/index.htm.
2000b *World Economic Outlook; April 2000.* Washington, DC: International Monetary Fund. http://www.imf.org/external/pubs/ft/weo/2000/01/index.htm.
2000c *World Economic Outlook Database*, April. http://www.imf.org/external/pubs/ft/weo/2000/01/data/index.htm.
2000d *World Economic Outlook: Focus on Transition Economies*. October 2000. http://www.imf.org/external/pubs/ft/weo/2000/02/index.htm.
2000e *World Economic Outlook Database*, September. http://www.imf.org/external/pubs/ft/weo/2000/02/data/index.htm.
2001a 2001 updates from *International Statistical Yearbook*. http://www.imf.org/external/np/res/commod/index.htm.
INPE 2000 *Monitoring of the Brazilian Amazonian Forest by Satellite*. The Brazilian National Institute for Space Research. http://www.inpe.br/Informacoes_Eventos/amz1998_1999/PDF/amz1999.pdf.
IPAM 1998 *Fire in the Amazon*. Brazil's Institute for Environmental Research in the Amazon. http://www.ipam.org.br/fogo/fogoen.htm.
IPCC 1990 *Climate Change – The IPCC Scientific Assessment*. Report of IPCC Working Group I. Cambridge: Cambridge University Press.
1992 *Climate Change 1992: The Supplementary Report to the IPCC Scientific Assessment*. Cambridge: Cambridge University Press.
1995 *Climate Change 1994: Radiative Forcing of Climate Change and An Evaluation of the IPCC IS92 Emission Scenarios*. Reports of Working Groups I and III of the Intergovernmental Panel on Climate Change, forming part of the IPCC Special Report to the first session of the Conference of the Parties to the UN Framework Convention on Climate Change. Cambridge: Cambridge University Press.
1996a *Climate Change 1995 – The Science of Climate Change*. Report of IPCC Working Group I. Cambridge: Cambridge University Press.
1996b *Climate Change 1995 – Scientific-Technical Analyses of Impacts, Adaptations and Mitigations of Climate Change*. Report of IPCC Working Group II. Cambridge: Cambridge University Press.
1996c *Climate Change 1995 – The Economic and Social Dimensions of Climate Change*. Report of IPCC Working Group III. Cambridge: Cambridge University Press.
1997a *Stabilization of Atmospheric Greenhouse Gases: Physical, Biological and Socio-economic Implications*. John T. Houghton, L. Gylvan Meira Filho, David J. Griggs and Kathy Maskell (eds.). Technical Paper 3. http://www.ipcc.ch/pub/IPCCTP.III(E).pdf.
1997b *Implications of Proposed CO_2 Emissions Limitations*. Tom M. L. Wigley, Atul K. Jain, Fortunat Joos, Buruhani S. Nyenzi and P. R. Shukla (eds.). Technical Paper 4. http://www.ipcc.ch/pub/IPCCTP.IV(E).pdf.
1997c *An Introduction to Simple Climate Models used in the IPCC Second Assessment Report*. John T. Houghton, L. Gylvan Meira Filho, David J. Griggs and Kathy Maskell (eds.). Technical Paper 2. http://www.ipcc.ch.
1998 *The Regional Impacts of Climate Change: An Assessment of Vulnerability*. A Special Report of IPCC Working group II. R. T. Watson, M. C. Zinyowera, R. H. Moss (eds). Cambridge: Cambridge University Press. Summary at http://www.ipcc.ch/pub/regional(E).pdf.
2000a *Special Report on Emission Scenarios*. A Special Report of Working Group III of the Intergovernmental Panel on Climate Change. http://www.grida.no/climate/ipcc/emission/index.htm, with a summary at http://www.ipcc.ch/pub/SPM_SRES.pdf.
2000b *Emission Scenarios Database*. SRES Scenarios, version 1.1, July 2000. http://sres.ciesin.org/final_data.html
2001a *Climate Change 2001: The Scientific Basis*. Contribution of Working Group I to the Third Assessment Report of the Intergovernmental Panel on Climate Change. J. T. Houghton, Y. Ding, D. J. Griggs, M. Noguer, , P. J. van der Linden and D. Xiaosu (eds.). Cambridge: Cambridge University Press.
2001b *Climate Change 2001: Impacts, Adaptation, and Vulnerability*. Contribution of Working Group II

to the Third Assessment Report of the Intergovernmental Panel on Climate Change. J. J. McCarthy, O. F. Canziani, N. A. Leary, D. J. Dokken and K. S. White (eds.). Cambridge: Cambridge University Press.

2001c *Climate Change 2001: Climate Change 2001: Mitigation.* Contribution of Working Group III to the Third Assessment Report of the Intergovernmental Panel on Climate Change. B. Metz, O. Davidson, R. Swart and J. Pan (eds.). Cambridge: Cambridge University Press.

2001d *Summary for Policymakers.* Working Group I. Shanghai Draft 21–01–2001 20:00. http://www.meto.gov.uk/sec5/CR_div/ipcc/wg1/WGI-SPM.pdf.

2001e *Summary for Policymakers.* Working Group II. Geneva Draft 19–02–2001. http://www.meto.gov.uk/sec5/CR_div/ipcc/wg1/WGII-SPM.pdf.

2001f *Summary for Policymakers.* Working Group III. Accra Draft, 03–03–2001 http://www.meto.gov.uk/sec5/CR_div/ipcc/wg1/WGIII-SPM.pdf

IPCC/DDC 2000a *The Intergovernmental Panel on Climate Change/Data Distribution Centre: Providing Climate Change and Related Scenarios for Impacts Assessments.* http://ipcc-ddc.cru.uea.ac.uk/index.html.

2000b *The IPCC Data Distribution Centre: HadCM2.* http://ipcc-ddc.cru.uea.ac.uk/cru_data/examine/HadCM2_info.html.

2000c *The IPCC Data Distribution Centre: Frequently Asked Questions (FAQs).* http://ipcc-ddc.cru.uea.ac.uk/cru_data/support/faqs.html.

2001 *The IPCC Data Distribution Centre: Emissions Scenarios.* http://ipcc-ddc.cru.uea.ac.uk/cru_data/examine/emissions/emissions.html.

IRIS 1991 *Nitrate.* Integrated Risk Information System, US Environmental Protection Agency, CASRN 14797–55–8. http://www.epa.gov/ngispgm3/iris/subst/0076.htm.

Irvine, Stewart, Elizabeth Cawood, David Richardson, Eileen MacDonald and John Aitken 1996 "Evidence of deteriorating semen quality in the United Kingdom: birth cohort study in 577 men in Scotland over 11 years." *British Medical Journal* 312:467–41.

ITA 1999 *Forecast of International Travel – October 1999.* International Trade Administration and US Department of Commerce. http://tinet.ita.doc.gov/view/f-1999-99-002/index.html.

ITOPF 2000 *Tanker Oil Spill Statistics.* The International Tanker Owners Pollution Federation Limited. http://www.itopf.com/datapack%202000.pdf.

Ivanhoe, L. F. 1995 "Future world oil supplies: there is a finite limit." *World Oil*, October:77–88.

IWMI 2000 *World Water Supply and Demand: 1995 to 2025.* Colombo, Sri Lanka: International Water Management Institute. http://www.cgiar.org/iwmi/pubs/wwvisn/wwsdhtml.htm.

Jacobs, Jerry A. 1998 "Measuring time at work: are self-reports accurate?" *Monthly Labor Review* 121(12)42–53. http://www.bls.gov/opub/mlr/1998/12/art3full.pdf.

Jacobson, Joseph L. and Sandra W. Jacobson 1997 "PCBs and IQs." *Harvard Mental Health Letter* 13(8):7.

Jacobson, L., P. Hertzman, C. G. Lofdahl, B. E. Skoogh and B. Lindgren 2000 "The economic impact of asthma and chronic obstructive pulmonary disease (COPD) in Sweden in 1980 and 1991." *Respiratory Medicine* 94(3):247–55.

Jacobson, Mark Z. 2001 "Strong radiative heating due to the mixing state of black carbon in atmospheric aerosols." *Nature* 409(6821):695–7.

Jacoby, Henry and Ian Sue Wing 1999 "Adjustment time, capital malleability and policy cost." *The Energy Journal*, Kyoto Special Issue:73–92.

Jäger, Jill and Roger G. Barry 1990 "Climate." In Turner *et al.* 1990:335–51.

James, W. H. 1980 "Secular trend in reported sperm counts." *Andrologia* 12(4):381–8.

James, Clive 1999 "Preview: Global Review of Commercialized Transgenic Crops: 1999." The International Service for the Acquisition of Agri-biotech Applications. *ISAAA Briefs* 12–1999.

2000 "Preview: Global Review of Commercialized Transgenic Crops: 2000." The International Service for the Acquisition of Agri-biotech Applications. *ISAAA Briefs* 21–2000.

Janetos, Anthony C. 1997 "Do we still need nature? The importance of biological diversity." *CONSEQUENCES* 3(1). http://www.gcrio.org/CONSEQUENCES/vol3no1/biodiversity.html.

Jarvis, Claire and Anthea Tinker 1999 "Trends in old age morbidity and disability in Britain." *Ageing and Society* 19:603–27.

Jarvis, D. and P. Burney 1998 "The epidemiology of allergic disease." *British Medical 316:607–10.* http://www.bmj.com/cgi/content/full/316/7131/607.

Jensen, Bent 1991 *Danskernes dagligdag: træk of udviklingen I Danmark fra 1960erne til 1990erne.* [Danish everyday life: trends in Denmark from the 1960s to the 1990s.] Copenhagen: Spektrum.

1996 *Træk af miljødebatten i seks danske aviser fra 1870'erne til 1970'erne.* [Outlines of the environmental debate in six Danish newspapers from the 1870s to the 1970s.] Copenhagen: Rockwool Fondens Forskningsenhed.

Jensen, Peter Rørmose 1995 *En velfærdsindikator for Danmark 1970–1990. Forbrug, miljø, husholdningsarbejde og fritid.* [A Welfare Indicator for Denmark, 1970–1990. Consumption, the environment, household work and leisure time.] Rockwool Foundation Research Unit Working Paper 8. Copenhagen: Statistics Denmark.

Jensen, Tina Kold, Alexander Giwercman, Elisabeth Carlsen, Thomas Scheike and Niels E. Skakkebæk 1996 "Semen quality among members of organic food associations in Zealand, Denmark." *The Lancet* 347:1,844.

Jespersen, Jesper and Stefan Brendstrup 1994 *Grøn økonomi: en introduktion til miljø-, ressoruce- og samfundsøkonomi.* [Green economics: an introduction to environment, resource and social economics.] Copenhagen: Jurist- og Økonomforbundets Forlag.

Jickells, Timothy D., Roy Carpenter and Peter S. Liss 1990 "Marine environment." In Turner *et al.* 1990:313–34.

Joffe, Michael 2000 "Time trends in biological fertility in Britain." *The Lancet* 355:1,961–5.

Johansen, Hans Chr. 1985 *Dansk historisk statistik 1814–1980.* [Danish historical statistics 1814–1980.] Copenhagen: Gyldendal.

Johansson, S. Ryan 1991 "The health transition: the cultural inflation of morbidity during the decline of mortality." *Health Transition Review* 1:39–68. http://www-nceph.anu.edu.au/htc/htrall.htm.

1992 "Measuring the cultural inflation of morbidity during the decline of mortality." *Health Transition Review* 2:78–89. http://www-nceph.anu.edu.au/htc/htrall.htm.

Johns, T. C., R. E. Carnell, J. F. Crossley, J. M. Gregory, J. F. B. Mitchell, C. A. Senior, S. F. B. Tett and R. A. Wood 1997 "The second Hadley Centre coupled ocean-atmosphere GCM: model description, spinup and validation." *Climate Dynamics* 13:103–34.

Johnson, D. Gale 1999 "The growth of demand will limit output growth for food over the next quarter century." *Proceedings of the National Academy of Sciences* 96:5,915–20. http://www.pnas.org.

Johnson, Dan 1998 "Environment: averting a water crisis." *The Futurist* 32(2):7.

Jones, D. A., J. Plaza, I. Watt and M. Al Sanei 1998a "Long-term (1991–1995) monitoring of the intertidal biota of Saudi Arabia after the 1991 Gulf War oil spill." *Marine Pollution Bulletin* 36(6):472–89.

Jones, Leighton 1999 "Genetically modified foods." *British Medical Journal* 318(7183):581–4.

Jones, P. D., K. R. Briffa, T. P. Barnett and S. F. B. Tett 1998b "High-resolution palaeoclimatic records for the last millennium: interpretation, integration and comparison with general circulation model control-run temperatures." *The Holocene* 8:455–71.

1998c *Multi-proxy hemispherical temperature data 1000–1991.* ftp://medias.meteo.fr/paleo/contributions_by_author/jones1998 or ftp://ftp.ngdc.noaa.gov/paleo/contributions_by_author/jones1998.

Jones, P. D., E. B. Horton, C. K. Folland, M. Hulme, D. E. Parker and T. A. Basnett 1999a "The use of indices to identify changes in climatic extremes." *Climatic Change* 42(1):131–49.

Jones, P. D., M. New, D. E. Parker, S. Martin and I. G. Rigor 1999b "Surface air temperature and its changes over the past 150 years." *Reviews of Geophysics* 37(2):173–99.

Jones, P. D., D. E. Parker, T. J. Osborn and K. R. Briffa 2000 "Global and hemispheric temperature anomalies – land and marine instrumental records." In *Trends: A Compendium of Data on Global Change.* Carbon Dioxide Information Analysis Center, Oak Ridge National Laboratory, US Department of Energy, Oak Ridge, Tennesee. http://cdiac.esd.ornl.gov/trends/temp/jonescru/jones.html.

2001 "Global and hemispheric temperature anomalies – land and marine instrumental records." http://www.cru.uea.ac.uk/cru/data/temperature/.

Juhler, R. K., S. B. Larsen, O. Meyer, N. D. Jensen, M. Spanò, A. Giwercman and J. P. Bonde 1999

"Human semen quality in relation to dietary pesticide exposure and organic diet." *Archives of Environmental Contamination and Toxicology* 37:415–23.

Kahn, Herman, William Brown and Leon Martel 1976 *The Next 200 Years: A Scenario for America and the World*. New York: William Morrow and Company.

Kainuma, Mikiko, Yuzuru Matsuoka and Tsuneyuki Morita 1999 "Analysis of post-Kyoto scenarios: the Asian-Pacific integrated model." *The Energy Journal*, Kyoto Special Issue:207–20.

Kaiser, Jocelyn 1999 "The Exxon Valdez's scientific gold rush." *Science* 284:247–9.

Kalkstein, Laurence S. and Robert E. Davis 1989 "Weather and human mortality: an evaluation of demographic and interregional responses in the United States." *Annals of the Association of American Geographers* 79(1):44–64.

Kane, R. P. 1998 "Ozone depletion, related UVB changes and increased skin cancer incidence." *International Journal of Climatology* 18(4):457–72.

Kaplan, David A. 1996 "This is global warming?" *Newsweek* 127(4):20–3.

Kaplan, J. Kim 1998 "Conserving the world's plants." *Agricultural Research* 46(9):4–9. http://www.ars.usda.gov/is/AR/archive/sep98/cons0998.htm.

Karl, Thomas R. 1999 "Overview." *Climatic Change* 42:1–2.

Karl, Thomas R. and Richard W. Knight 1998 "Secular trends of precipitation amount, frequency, and intensity in the United States." *Bulletin of the American Meteorological Society* 79(2):231–41. http://ams.allenpress.com/.

Karl, Thomas R., Richard W. Knight and Neil Plummer 1995 "Trends in high-frequency climate variability in the twentieth century." *Nature* 377:217–20.

Karl, Thomas R., Neville Nicholls and Jonathan Gregory 1997 "The coming climate." *Scientific American* 276(5):54–9. http://www.sciam.com/0597issue/0597karl.html.

Karl, Thomas R. and Kevin E. Trenberth 1999 "The human impact on climate." *Scientific American* 281(6):100–5.

Karon, Tony 2001: "Global Warming Challenge for Bush". Time.com. January 22nd 2001. http://www.time.com/time/world/article/0,8599,96299,00.html.

Kauppi, Pekka E., Kari Mielikäinen and Kullervo Kuusela 1992 "Biomass and carbon budget of European forests, 1971 to 1990." *Science* 256:70–4.

Kaur, Balvinder, H. Ross Anderson, Jane Austin, Michael Burr, Leigh S. Harkins, David P. Strachan and John O. Warner 1998 "Prevalence of asthma symptoms, diagnosis, and treatment in 12–14 year old children across Great Britain (international study of asthma and allergies in childhood, ISAAC UK)." *British Medical Journal* 316:118–24. http://www.bmj.com/cgi/content/full/316/7125/118.

Keatinge, W. R., G. C. Donaldson, Elvira Cordioli, M. Martinelli, A. E. Kunst, J. P. Mackenbach, S. Nayha and I. Vuori 2000 "Heat related mortality in warm and cold regions of Europe: observational study." *British Medical Journal*.321(7262):670–3. http://www.bmj.org/cgi/reprint/321/7262/670.pdf.

Keeling, C. D. and T. P. Whorf 1999 "Atmospheric CO_2 records from sites in the SIO air sampling network". In *Trends: A Compendium of Data on Global Change*. Carbon Dioxide Information Analysis Center, Oak Ridge National Laboratory, US Department of Energy, Oak Ridge, Tennesee. http://cdiac.esd.ornl.gov/trends/co2/sio-mlo.htm.

Keiding, N., A. Giwercman, E. Carlsen and N. E. Skakkebæk 1994 "Importance of empirical evidence [commentary]." *British Medical Journal* 309:22.

Keiding, Niels and Niels E. Skakkebæk 1996 "Sperm decline – real or artifact." *Fertility and Sterility* 65(2):450–51.

1998 "To the editor." *Journal of Urology* 159(6):2103.

Keigwin, Lloyd D. 1996 "The Little Ice Age and medieval warm period in the Sargasso Sea." *Science* 274:1,504–8.

Kenetech 1994 *Avian Research Program Update*. Kenetech Windpower, November 1994.

Kerr, Richard A. 1997a "Climate change: greenhouse forecasting still cloudy." *Science* 276:1,040–2.

1997b "Model gets it right – without fudge factors." *Science* 276:1,041.

1999 "The Little Ice Age – Only the Latest Big Chill." *Science* 284(5423):2,069.

2000 "U.N. to blame global warming on humans." *Science Now*, 25 April:1.

Key, Sandra W. and Michelle Marble 1997a "EPA endocrine program unlikely to change despite retraction of synergy study." *Cancer Weekly Plus*, 24 November: 9–11.

1997b "Increased rates in Hawaii may be linked to pesticides." *Cancer Weekly Plus* 18 August:5–6.

Keyfitz, Nathan and Wilhelm Flieger 1968 *World Population: An Analysis of Vital Data*. Chicago: University of Chicago Press.

1990 *World Population Growth and Aging*. Chicago: University of Chicago Press.

Kidd, Parris M. 2000 "At last, a breakthrough against cancer: the Gonzalez-Isaacs program." *Total Health* 22(1):19–21.

Kinlen, L. J., M. Dickson and C. A. Stiller 1995 "Childhood leukaemia and non-Hodgkin's lymphoma near large rural construction sites, with a comparison with Sellafield nuclear site." *British Medical Journal* 310:763–8. http://www.bmj.com/cgi/content/full/310/6982/763.

Kinlen, L. J. and S. M. John 1994 "Wartime evacuation and mortality from childhood leukaemia in England and Wales in 1945–9." *British Medical Journal* 309:1,197–1,202. http://www.bmj.com/cgi/content/full/309/6963/1197.

Kitman, Jamie Lincoln 2000 "The secret history of lead." *Nation* 270(11):11–40.

Knickerbocker, Brad 1999 "The big spill." *Christian Science Monitor* 91(79).

Körmendi, Eszter 1990 "Time use trends in Denmark." In Viby Mogensen 1990:51–74.

Knudsen, Jørgen 1997 "Den store fortælling om synd og straf." [The great story of sin and punishment.] In Agger *et al.* 1997:36–47.

Knutson, Ronald D. 1999 *Economic Impacts of Reduced Pesticide Use in The United States: Measurement of Costs and Benefits*. Agricultural and Food Policy Center, Department of Agricultural Economics, Texas A&M University. AFPC Policy Issues Paper 99-2. http://afpc.tamu.edu/.

Knutson, Ronald D., Charles Hall, Edward G. Smith, Sam Cotner and John W. Miller 1994 "Yield and cost impacts of reduced pesticide use on fruits and vegetables." *Choices: The Magazine of Food, Farm and Resource Issues* 9(1):15–18.

Knutson. Ronald D. and Edward G. Smith 1999 *Impacts of Eliminating Organophosphates and Carbamates from Crop Production*. Agricultural and Food Policy Center, Department of Agricultural Economics, Texas A&M University. AFPC Policy Working Paper 99-2. http://afpc.tamu.edu/.

Knutson, Ronald D., C. Robert Taylor, John B. Penson Jn., Edward G. Smith and Roy B. Davis 1990a "Pesticide-free equals higher food prices." *Consumers' Research Magazine* 73(11):33–5.

Knutson, Ronald D., C. Robert Taylor, John B. Penson Jn. and Edward G. Smith 1990b "Economic impacts of reduced chemical use." *Choices: The Magazine of Food, Farm and Resource Issues* 5(4):25–8.

Knutson, T. R. and R. E. Tuleya 1999 "Increased hurricane intensities with CO_2-induced warming as simulated using the GFDL hurricane prediction system." *Climate Dynamics* 15(7):503–19.

Kolstrup, Søren 1999 *Pesticider skal helt afskaffes*. [Pesticides should be banned entirely.] http://www.enhedslisten.dk/elhp4/12miljoe/pesticid.htm.

Kominski, Robert and Eric Newburger 1999 "Access denied: changes in computer ownership and use: 1984–1997." Population Division, US Census Bureau. http://www.census.gov/population/socdemo/computer/confpap99.pdf.

Konisky, David M. 1999 *Comparative Risk Projects: A Methodology for Cross-Project Analysis of Human Health Risk Rankings*. Discussion Paper 99-46. Resources for the Future. http://www.rff.org/disc_papers/abstracts/9946.htm.

Korzeniewicz, Roberto Patricio and Timothy Patrick Moran 1997 "World-economic trends in the distribution of income, 1965–1992." *American Journal of Sociology* 102(4):1,000–39.

Kram, Tom, Tsuneyuki Morita, Keywan Riahi, R. Alexander Roehrl, Sascha van Rooijen, Alexei Sankovski and Bert de Vries 2000 "Global and Regional Greenhouse Gas Emissions Scenarios." *Technological Forecasting and Social Change* 63:335–71.

Kramer M. 1980 "The rising pandemic of mental disorders and associated chronic diseases and disabilities." *Acta Psychiatrica Scandinavia* 62(suppl. 285):282–97.

Kravis, Irving B., Alan W. Heston and Robert Summers 1978 "Real GDP per capita for more than one hundred countries" *The Economic Journal* 88(350):215–42.

Krieger, Nancy, Mary S. Wolff, Robert A. Hiatt,

Marilyn Rivera, Joseph Vogelman and Norman Orentrich 1994 "Breast cancer and serum organochlorines: a prospective study among white, black, and asian women." *Journal of the International Cancer Institute* 86(8):589–99.

Krinner, W., C. Lallana, T. Estrela, S. Nixon, T. Zabel, L. Laffon, G. Rees and G. Cole 1999 *Sustainable Water Use in Europe, part 1: Sectoral Use of Water*. http://themes.eea.eu.int/binary/e/enviasses01.pdf.

Kristjansson J. E. and J. Kristiansen 2000 "Is there a cosmic ray signal in recent variations in global cloudiness and cloud radiative forcing?" *Journal of Geophysical Research-Atmospheres* 105(D9):11,851–63.

Krupnick, Alan J. and Dallas Burtraw 1996 *The Social Costs of Electricity: Do the Numbers Add Up?* Resources for the Future Discussion Paper 96–30. http://www.rff.org/disc_papers/pdf_files/9630.pdf.

Kuck, Peter H. and Jozef Plachy 1996 *Cadmium*. US Geological Surveys. http://minerals.er.usgs.gov/minerals/pubs/commodity/cadmium/140496.pdf.

Kuczmarski, Robert J., Katherine M. Flegal, Stephen M. Campbell and Clifford L. Johnson 1994 "Increasing prevalence of overweight among US adults." *Journal of the American Medical Association* 272(3):205–11.

Kuiper, Harry A., Hub P. J. M. Noteborn and Ad A. C. M. Peijnenburg 1999: "Adequacy of methods for testing the safety of genetically modified foods." *Lancet* 354(9187):1,315–6.

Kulp, J. Laurence 1995 "Acid rain." In Simon 1995b:523–35.

Kunkel, Kenneth E., Roger A. Pielke Jn. and Stanley A. Changnon 1999 "Temporal fluctuations in weather and climate extremes that cause economic and human health impacts: a review." *Bulletin of the American Meteorological Society* 80(6):1,077–98. http://ams.allenpress.com/.

Kurosawa, Atsushi, H. Yagita, Z. Weisheng, K. Tokimatsu and Y. Yanagisawa 1999 "Analysis of carbon emission stabilization targets and adaptation by integrated assessment model." *The Energy Journal*, Kyoto Special Issue:157–76.

Kyoto 1997 *Kyoto Protocol to the United Nations Framework Convention on Climate Change*. http://www.cnn.com/SPECIALS/1997/global.warming/stories/treaty.

Lack, Tim 1999 "Water and health in Europe: an overview." *British Medical Journal* 318:1,678–82. http://www.bmj.com/cgi/content/full/318/7199/1678.

LaFranchi, Howard 1997 "Is burning of Amazon all smoke?" *Christian Science Monitor* 89:247.

Landes, David 1998 *The Wealth and Poverty of Nations*. London: Abacus.

Landsea, Christopher W. 1993 "A climatology of intense (or major) Atlantic hurricanes." *Monthly Weather Review* 121:1,703–13. http://www.aoml.noaa.gov/hrd/Landsea/climo/index.html.

2000 "Climate variability of tropical cyclones: past, present and future." In Pielke and Pielke 2000:220–41. http://www.aoml.noaa.gov/hrd/Landsea/climvari/index.html.

Landsea, Christopher W., Neville Nicholls, William M. Gray and Lixion A. Avila 1996 "Downward trends in the frequency of intense Atlantic hurricanes during the past five decades." *Geophysical Research Letters* 23:1,697–1,700. http://www.aoml.noaa.gov/hrd/Landsea/downward/index.html.

1997 "Reply to comment on 'Downward trends in the frequency of intense Atlantic hurricanes during the past five decades'." *Geophysical Research Letters* 24:2,205. http://www.aoml.noaa.gov/hrd/Landsea/downtrend/index.html.

Landsea, Christopher W., Roger A. Pielke Jr., Alberto M. Mestas-Nuñez and John A. Knaff 1999 "Atlantic basin hurricanes: indices of climatic changes." *Climatic Change* 42(1):89–129. http://www.aoml.noaa.gov/hrd/Landsea/atlantic/index.html.

Larsen, John Christian 1992 "Food additives, positive list: philosophy, regulation, special conditions." In ATV 1992:109–24.

Larsen, Poul Bo, Steen Solvang Jensen and Jes Fenger 1997 "Sundhedsskader fra små partikler i byluft." [Health damage by small particles in city air.] *Miljø og Sundhed* SMF Formidlingsblad 6, August 1997:7–12.

Lassen, K. and E. Friis-Christensen 1995 "Variability of the solar cycle length during the past five centuries and the apparent association with terrestrial climate." *Journal of Atmospheric and Terrestrial Physics* 57(8):835–45.

Latif, M. and A. Grotzner 2000 "The equatorial Atlantic oscillation and its response to ENSO." *Climate Dynamics* 16(2–3):213–18.

Latif, M., E. Roeckner, U. Mikolajewicz and R. Voss

2000 "Tropical stabilization of the thermohaline circulation in a greenhouse warming simulation." *Journal of Climate* 13(11):1,809–13.

Laudan, Larry 1994 *The Book of Risks*. New York: Wiley.

Laut, Peter 1997 "Drivhuseffekten og globale klimaændringer: Videnskabelig Status Januar 1997." [Greenhouse effect and global climate changes: a scientific status, January 1997.] EFP-961. *Udredningsprojekt: journalnr.* 151/96–0013.

Laut, Peter and Jesper Gundermann 1998 "Solar cycle length hypothesis appears to support the IPCC on global warming." *Journal of Atmospheric and Solar-Terrestrial Physics* 60(18):1,719–28.

Lawrie, S. M., H. Whalley, J. N. Kestelman, S. S. Abukmeil, M. Byrne, A. Hodges, J. E. Rimmington, J. J. Best, D. G. Owens and E. C. Johnstone 1999 "Magnetic resonance imaging of brain in people at high risk of developing schizophrenia." *The Lancet* 353:30–3.

Lawton, John H. and Robert M. May 1995 *Extinction Rates*. Oxford: Oxford University Press.

Laxen, Duncan P. H. and Mark A. Thompson 1987 "Sulphur dioxide in Greater London, 1931–1985." *Environmental Pollution* 43:103–14.

LCVEF 2000 *Environment: Top Tier Voting Issue*. Greenberg Quinlan Research for League of Conservation Voters Education Fund. http://www.lcvedfund.org/poll/index.htm.

Leach, Melissa and James Fairhead 1999 "Challenging environmental orthodoxies: the case of West African deforestation." *Renewable Energy for Development* 11(1):1, 8–10.

Lebergott, Stanley 1976 *The American Economy: Income, Wealth, and Want*. Princeton, NJ: Princeton University Press.

1993 *Pursuing Happiness: American Consumers in the Twentieth Century*. Princeton, NJ: Princeton University Press.

1995 "Long-term trends in the US standard of living." In Simon 1995b:149–60.

Le Dreau, Yveline, Frederic Jacquot, Pierre Doumenq, Michel Guiliano, Jean Claude Bertrand and Gilbert Mille 1997 "Hydrocarbon balance of a site which had been highly and chronically contaminated by petroleum wastes of a refinery (from 1956 to 1992)." *Marine Pollution Bulletin* 34(6):456–68.

Leon, Javier and Raimundo Soto 1995 *Structural Breaks and Long-Run Trends in Commodity Prices*. Policy Research Working Paper. World Bank, January 1995, no. 1,406.

Levidow, Les 1999 "Regulating Bt Maize in the United States and Europe." *Environment* 41(10):10–21.

Levine, Joel S. 1991 *Global Biomass Burning: Atmospheric, Climatic, and Biospheric Implications*. Cambridge, MA: MIT Press.

Levine, Joel S., Wesley R. Cofer III, Donald R. Cahoon Jr. and Edward L. Winstead 1995 "Biomass burning: a driver for global change." *Envionmental Science and Technology*, March 1995. http://asd-www.larc.nasa.gov/biomass_burn/globe_impact.html.

Levy, David L. and Peter Newell 2000 "Oceans Apart?" *Environment* 42(9):8–20., 13p

L'hirondel, Jean-Louis 1999 "Dietary nitrates pose no threat to human health." In Mooney and Bate 1999:119–28.

Lidstone, John 1997 "Global patterns of natural disasters." *Geodate* 10(4):1–4.

Lieberman, Adam J. and Simona C. Kwon 1998 *Facts versus Fears: A Review of the Greatest Unfounded Health Scares of Recent Times*. American Council on Science and Health. http://www.acsh.org/publications/reports/factsfears.html.

Liljegren, G., L. Hardell, G. Lindstrom, P. Dahl and A. Magnuson 1998 "Case-control study on breast cancer and adipose tissue concentrations of congener specific polychlorinated biphenyls, DDE and hexachlorobenzene." *European Journal of Cancer Prevention* 7(2):135–40.

Lindegaard, Erik 1998 "Grundvand og bekæmpelsesmidler. Hvad kan vi forvente af godkendelsesordningen?" [Groundwater and pesticides.] *MiljøDanmark* 1998(1):6.

Linden, Eugene 2000 "Condition critical." *Time* 155(17):18–22.

Lindert, Peter H. 1999 "The bad earth? China's soils and agricultural development since the 1930s." *Economic Development and Cultural Change* 47(4):701–36.

2000a "Three centuries of inequality in Britain and America." In Atkinson and Bourguignon 2000:167–216.

2000b *Shifting Ground: The Changing Agricultural Soils of China and Indonesia*. Cambridge, MA: MIT Press (forthcoming).

Lindert, Peter H. and Jeffrey G. Williamson 1995

"The long-term course of American inequality: 1647–1969." In Simon 1995b:188–95.

Lindzen, Richard S., Ming-Dah Chou and Arthur Y. Hou 2001 "Does the Earth Have an Adaptive Infrared Iris?" *Bulletin of the American Meteorological Society* 82(3):417–32. http://ams.allenpress.com.

Linet, Martha S., Lynn A. G. Ries, Malcolm A. Smith, Robert E. Tarone and Susan S. Devesa 1999 "Cancer surveillance series: recent trends in childhood cancer incidence and mortality in the United States." *Journal of the National Cancer Institute* 91(12):1,051–8. http://jnci.oupjournals.org/cgi/content/full/91/12/1051.

Lins, Harry F. and James R. Slack 1999 "Streamflow trends in the United States." *Geophysical Research Letters* 26:227–30. http://water.usgs.gov/osw/lins/streamflowtrends.html.

List, John A. and Craig A. Gallet 1999 "The environmental Kuznets curve: does one size fit all?" *Ecological Economics* 31:409–23.

Lloyd-Jones, Donald M., Martin G. Larson, A. Beiser and D. Levy 1999 "Lifetime risk of developing coronary heart disease." *The Lancet* 353:89–92.

Loader, A., D. Mooney and R. Lucas 1999 *UK Smoke and Sulphur Dioxide Monitoring Network – Summary Tables for April 1997–March 1998*. Prepared by the National Environmental Technology Centre as part of the Department of the Environment, Transport and the Regions Air Quality Research Programme. http://www.aeat.co.uk/netcen/airqual/reports/smkso2/head.html.

Longstreth, Janice 1999 "Public health consequences of global climate change in the United States – some regions may suffer disproportionately." *Environmental Health Perspectives Supplements* 107(1):169–79.

Longstreth, J., F. R. de Gruijl, M. L. Kripke, S. Abseck, F. Arnold, H. I. Slaper, G. Velders, Y. Takizawa and J. C. van der Leun 1998 "Health risks." *Journal of Photochemistry and Photobiology B: Biology* 46(1–3):20–39.

Lopez-Carrillo, L., A. Blaie, M. Lopez-Cervantes, M. Cebrian, C. Rueda, R. Reyes, A. Mohar and J. Bravo 1997 "Dichlorodiphenyltrichloroethane serum levels and breast cancer risk: a case-control study from Mexico." *Cancer Research* 57:3,728–32.

Losey, J.E., I. S. Rayor and M. E. Carter 1999 "Transgenic pollen harms monarch larvae." *Nature* 399(6,733): 214.

Lovejoy, Thomas E. 1980 "A projection of species extinctions." In Barney 1980:II, 328–31.

Lovins, Amory B. and L. Hunter Lovins 1997 *Climate: Making Sense and Making Money*. Old Snowmass, CO: Rocky Mountain Institute. http://www.rmi.org/images/other/C-ClimateMSMM.pdf.

Ludwig, John H., George B. Morgan and Thomas B. McMullen 1970 "Trends in urban air quality." *Transactions American Geophysical Union* 51(5):468–75.

Lugo, Ariel E. 1988 "Estimating reductions in the diversity of tropical forest species." In Wilson and Peter 1988:58–70.

Luken, Ralph A. 1990 *Efficiency in Environmental Regulation: A Benefit–Cost Analysis of Alternative Approaches*. Boston, MA: Kluwer.

Lundmark, Thomas 1997 "Principles and instruments of German environmental law." *Journal of Environmental Law and Practice* 4(4):43–4.

Lundqvist, J. and P. Gleick 1997 "Sustaining our waters into 21st century." Background document for CSD 1997. Stockholm: Stockholm Environment Institute.

Lutz, Steven M. and David M. Smallwood 1995 "Limited financial resources constrain food choices." *Food Review* 18(1):13–7.

McCann, Jean 1998 "Infections and cancer: viruses are still prime suspects." *Journal of the National Cancer Institute* 90(6):418–20.

McCombs, Maxwell 1994 "News influence on our pictures of the world." In Bryant and Zillmann 1994:1–16.

MacCracken, Christopher, James Edmonds, S. Kim and R. Sands 1999 "The economics of the Kyoto Protocol." *The Energy Journal*, Kyoto Special Issue:25–72.

McGinnis, J. Michael and William H. Foege 1993 "Actual causes of death in the United States." *Journal of the American Medical Association* 270(18):2,207–12.

McHughen, Alan 2000 *A consumer's guide to GM food: From green genes to red herrings*. Oxford: Oxford University Press.

McInnis, Doug and Gunjan Sinha 2000 "Genes." *Popular Science* 256(4):64–8.

McKibbin, W., M. Ross, R. Shakleton and P. Wilcoxen 1999 "Emissions trading, capital flows and the Kyoto Protocol." *The Energy Journal*, Kyoto Special Issue:287–334.

McLachlan, John A. 1997 "Synergistic effect of environmental estrogens: report withdrawn." *Science* 227:462–3.

Macleod, John, and Ying Wang 1979 "Male fertility potential in terms of semen quality: a review of the past, a study of the present." *Fertility and Sterility* 31(2):103–16.

McLoughlin, James A. and Micahel Nall 1994 "Allergies and learning/behavioral disorders." *Intervention in School and Clinic* 29(4):198–207.

McMichael, Anthony J. 1999 "From hazard to habitat: rethinking environment and health." *Epidemiology* 10(4):460–4. http://www.epidem.com/.

McQuail, Denis 1983 *Mass Communication Theory*, 1st edition. London: Sage Publications.

1994 *Mass Communication Theory*, 3rd edition. London: Sage Publications.

McVeigh, James J., Dallas Burtraw, Joel Darmstadter and Karen Palmer 2000 "Winner, loser, or innocent victim? Has renewable energy performed as expected?" *Solar Energy* 68(3):237–55.

Maddison, Angus 1991 *Dynamic Forces in Capitalist Development: A Long-Run Comparative View*. Oxford: Oxford University Press.

1994 "Explaining the economic performance of nations, 1820–1989." In Baumol *et al.* 1994:20–61.

1995a *Monitoring the World Economy 1820–1992*. Development Centre Studies, OECD. Paris: OECD.

Maddison, David 1995b "A cost-benefit analysis of slowing climate change." *Energy Policy* 23(4/5):337–46.

Madronich, S., R. L. McKenzie, L. O. Bjorn and M. M. Caldwell 1998 "Changes in biologically active ultraviolet radiation reaching the Earth's surface." *Journal of Photochemistry and Photobiology B: Biology* 46(1–3):5–19.

MAFF 2000 *Agriculture in the United Kingdom 1999*. London: Ministry of Agriculture, Fisheries and Food. http://www.maff.gov.uk/esg/Work_htm/publications/cf/auk/for_auk99/auk.pdf.

2001 *Agriculture in the United Kingdom 2000*. London: Ministry of Agriculture, Fisheries and Food. http://www.maff.gov.uk/esg/Work_htm/publications/cf/auk/current/complete.pdf.

Magnus, Per and Jouni J. K. Jaakkola 1997 "Secular trend in the occurrence of asthma among children and young adults: critical appaisal of repeated cross sectional surveys." *British Medical Journal* 314:1,795–1,800. http://www.bmj.com/cgi/content/full/314/7097/1795.

Mahlman, J. D. 1997 "Uncertainties in projections of human-caused climate warming." *Science* 278:1,416–17.

Malakoff, David 1997 "Thirty Kyotos needed to control warming." *Science* 278:2,048.

Malthus, Thomas 1798 *An Essay on the Principle of Population*. Harmondsworth: Penguin.

Mammal Society 2001a "Look what the cat's brought in! The survey." http://www.abdn.ac.uk/mammal/catkills1.htm

2001b "Look What the Cat Brought In! Press Release." http://www.abdn.ac.uk/mammal/catspress.htm.

Mann, Charles C. 1991 "Extinction: are ecologists crying wolf?" *Science* 253:736–8.

Mann, Charles C. and Mark L. Plummer 1993 "The high cost of biodiversity." *Science* 260:1,868–71.

Mann, M. E., R. S. Bradley and M. K. Hughes 1998 "Global-scale temperature patterns and climate forcing over the past six centuries." *Science Nature* 392(6,678):779–827. http://www.umass.edu/newsoffice/archive/1998/042298climate.pdf.

1999a "Northern hemisphere temperatures during the past millennium: inferences, uncertainties, and limitations." *Geophysical Research Letters* 26(6):759–62.

1999b Data for northern hemisphere temperatures 1000–1980. http://www.ngdc.noaa.gov/paleo/pubs/mann_99.html or http://medias.meteo.fr/paleo/globalwarming/medieval.html.

Manne, Alan S. and Richard Richels 1999 "The Kyoto Protocol: a cost-effective strategy for meeting environmental objectives?" *The Energy Journal*, Kyoto Special Issue:1–24.

Mantua, Nathan J., Steven R. Hare, Yuan Zhang, John M. Wallace and Robert C. Francis 1997 "A Pacific interdecadal climate oscillation with impacts on salmon production." *Bulletin of the American Meteorological Society* 78(6):1069–79. http://ams.allenpress.com/.

Margaronis, Maria 1999 "The politics of food." *Nation*, 12/27/99, 269(22):11–4.

Margolis, Howard 1996 *Dealing with Risk: Why the Public and the Experts Disagree on Environmental Issues*. Chicago: University of Chicago Press.

Margolis, Robert M. and Daniel M. Kammen 1999 "Evidence of under-investment in energy R&D in the United States and the impact of Federal policy – basic science and technological innovation." *Energy Policy* 27(10):575–84.

Marino, C. and K. K. Gerlach 1999 "An analysis of breast cancer coverage in selected women's magazines, 1987–1995." *American Journal of Health Promotion* 13(3):163–70.

Marland, G., T. A. Boden, R. J. Andres, A. L. Brenkert and C. Johnston 1999 "Global, regional, and national CO_2 emissions." In *Trends: A Compendium of Data on Global Change*. Carbon Dioxide Information Analysis Center, Oak Ridge National Laboratory, US Department of Energy, Oak Ridge, Tennesee. http://cdiac.esd.ornl.gov/trends/emis/tre_glob.htm.

Marotzke, Jochem 2000 "Abrupt climate change and thermohaline circulation: mechanisms and predictability." *Proceedings of the National Academy of Sciences* 97(4):1,347–50. http://www.pnap.org.

MARPOL 2000 *The International Convention for the Prevention of Pollution from Ships*. International Maritime Organization. http://www.imo.org/imo/convent/pollute.htm.

Marsh, Nigel and Henrik Svensmark 2000 "Cosmic rays, clouds, and climate." *Space Science Reviews*. In press.

Marshall, Eliot 1991 "A is for apple, alar, and . . . alarmist?" *Science* 254:20–2.

Martens, P., R. S. Kovats, S. Nijhof, P. de Vries, M. T. J. Livermore, D. J. Bradley, J. Cox and A. J. McMichael 1999 "Climate change and future populations at risk of malaria." *Global Environmental Change* 9:S89–S107.

Martin, A. and F. R. Barber "Two long term air pollution surveys around power stations." *Clean Air* 18(2):61–73.

Martin, Joyce A., Betty L. Smith, T. J. Mathews and Stephanie J. Ventura 1999 "Births and deaths: preliminary data for 1998." *National Vital Statistics Reports* 47:25. Hyattsville, MD: National Center for Health Statistics. http://www.cdc.gov/nchs/data/nvs47_25.pdf.

Martinez, Fernando D. and Patrick G. Holt 1999 "Role of microbial burden in aetiology of allergy and asthma." *The Lancet*. Supplement Paediatrics, 354:supplement II:12–15. http://www.thelancet.com/newlancet/sub/supplements/vol354s2/article3.html.

Mattingly, David 1996 "Future oil crisis: Will demand outrun supply?" *CNN* May 11, 1996. http://www.cnn.com/EARTH/9605/11/oil.supply/index.html

Masood, Ehsan 1997 "Kyoto agreement creates new agenda for climate research." *Nature* 390:649–50.

Matricardi, Paolo M., Francesco Rosmini, Silvia Riondino, Michele Fortini, Luigina Ferrigno, Maria Rapicetta and Sergio Bonini 2000 "Exposure to foodborne and orofecal microbes versus airborne viruses in relation to atopy and allergic asthma: epidemiological study." *British Medical Journal* 320:412–17. http://www.bmj.com/cgi/content/full/320/7232/412.

Matthews, Neal 2000 "The Attack of the Killer Architects." *Travel Holiday* 183(7):80–8.

Matthiessen, Peter 1999 "Rachel Carson." *Time* 29 March 1999, 153(12):187–9.

May, Robert M., John H. Lawton and Nigel E. Stork 1995 "Assessing extinction rates." In Lawton and May 1995:1–24.

MDPH 2000 *Advance Data: Births 1998*. Massachusetts Department of Public Health. http://www.state.ma.us/dph/pdf/birth98d.pdf.

Meade, Birgit and Stacey Rosen 1996 "Income and diet differences greatly affect food spending around the globe." *Food Review* 19(3):39–45.

Meadows, Donella H., Dennis L. Meadows and Jørgen Randers 1992 *Beyond the Limits*. London: Earthscan Publications Limited.

Meadows, Donella H., Dennis L. Meadows, Jørgen Randers and William W. Behrens III 1972 *Limits to Growth*. London: Potomac Associates Book.

Meehl, Gerald A., Francis Zwiers, Jenni Evans, Thomas Knutson, Linda Mearns and Peter Whetton 2000 "Trends in extreme weather and climate events: issues related to modeling extremes in projections of future climate change." *Bulletin of the American Meteorological Society* 81(3):427–36. http://ams.allenpress.com/.

Meggs, William J., Kathleen A. Dunn, Richard M. Bloch, Peggy E. Goodman and Ann L. Davidoff 1996 "Prevalence and nature of allergy and chemical sensitivity in a general population." *Archives of Environmental Health* 51(4):275–82.

Meilby, Mogens 1996 *Journalistikkens grundtrin: fra idé til artikel*. [The basics of journalism.] Aarhus: Forlaget Ajour.

Mentzel, Maarten 1999 "'Climate' for Social

Assessment: Experts, Uncertainty and Policy Development." *Innovation: The European Journal of Social Sciences* 12(2):221–34.

Merrill, Ray M., Larry G. Kessler, Joshua M. Udler, Gloria C. Rasband and Eric J. Feuer 1999 "Comparison of risk estimates for selected diseases and causes of death." *Preventive Medicine* 28:179–93.

Met Office 1997 *Climate Change and Its Impacts: A Global Perspective*. London: Department of the Environment, Transport, and the Regions. http://www.meto.gov.uk/sec5/CR_div/Brochure97/climate.pdf.

2001 *Historical Central England Temperature Data 1659–2001*. http://www.badc.rl.ac.uk/data/cet.

Metcalf, Gilbert E. and Kevin A. Hassett 1997 *Measuring the Energy Savings from Home Improvement Investments: Evidence from Monthly Billing Data*. NBER Working Paper W6074. http://papers.nber.org/papers/W6074.

MEWREW 1995 "Review of Serageldin: 'Water supply, sanitation and environmental sustainability: financing the challenge.'" *Middle East and African Water Review* 4. http://www.soas.ac.uk/Geography/WaterIssues/Reviews/0401.html.

Meyer, William B. and B. L. Turner II (eds.) 1994 *Changes in Land Use and Land Cover: A Global Perspective*. Cambridge: Cambridge University Press.

Meyerhoff, Al 1993 "We must get rid of pesticides in the food supply." *USA Today Magazine* 122(2,582):51–53.

Miami EDD 2001a: "Tourism Overview." *City of Miami Beach Economic Development Division*. http://www.ci.miami-beach.fl.us/newcity/depts/econdev/visitors%20Profile.htm.

2001b: "Real Estate and Development." *City of Miami Beach Economic Development Division*. http://www.ci.miami-beach.fl.us/newcity/depts/econdev/Real%20Estate%20and%20Development.htm.

Michaels, Patrick J. 1995 "The greenhouse effect and global change: review and reappraisal." In Simon 1995b:544–64.

1998 "The consequences of Kyoto." *Policy Analysis*, May 1998, 307. Http://www.cato.org/pubs/pas/pa-307.html.

Michaels, Patrick J. and Robert C. Balling Jr. 2000 *The Satanic Gases: Clearing the Air about Global Warming*. Washington, DC: Cato.

Michaels, Patrick J., Robert C. Balling Jr., Russel S. Vose and Paul C. Knappenberger 1998 "Analysis of trends in the variability of daily and monthly historical temperature measurements." *Climate Research* 10(1):27–34.

Michaels, Patrick J., Paul C. Knappenberger, Robert C. Balling Jr. and Robert E. Davis 2000 "Observed warming in cold anticyclones." *Climate Research* 14(1):1–6.

Middellevetidsudvalget under Sundhedsministeriet [Life Expectancy Committee] 1994a *Udviklingen i selvmordsdødelighed i Danmark 1955–1991*. [Trends in suicide mortality in Denmark 1955–1991.] Copenhagen: Sundhedsministeriet.

1994b *Levetiden i Danmark*. [Life expectancy in Denmark.] Copenhagen: Sundhedsministeriet.

1994c *Hjertesygdom i Danmark*. [Heart disease in Denmark.] Copenhagen: Sundhedsministeriet.

Milius, S. 1999 "New studies clarify monarch worries." *Science News* 156(25/26):391.

2000 "Bt corn variety OK for black swallowtails." *Science News* 157(24):372–3.

Miller, G. Tyler Jr. 1998 *Living in the Environment: Principles, Connections, and Solutions*. Belmont, CA: Wadsworth Publishing Company.

Mintz, Sidney W. 1985 *Sweetness and Power: The Place of Sugar in Modern History*. New York: Penguin.

Mitchell, B. R. 1975 *European Historical Statistics 1750–1970*. London: Macmillan.

1988 *British Historical Statistics*. Cambridge: Cambridge University Press.

1993 *International Historical Statistics: The Americas, 1750–1988*. London: Macmillan.

1995 *International Historical Statistics: Africa, Asia and Oceania 1750–1988*, 2nd rev. edn. New York: Stockton.

Mitchell, Donald O., Merlinda D. Ingco and Ronald C. Duncan 1997 *The World Food Outlook*. Cambridge: Cambridge University Press.

Mitchell, J. F. B., T. C. Johns, J. M. Gregory and S. F. B. Tett 1995 "Climate response to increasing levels of greenhouse gases and sulphate aerosols." *Nature* 376:501–4.

Mitsch, William J., John W. Day Jr., J. Wendell Gilliam, Peter M. Groffman, Donald L. Hey, Gyles W. Randall and Naiming Wang 1999 *Gulf of Mexico Hypoxia Assessment: Topic #5. Reducing Nutrient Loads, Especially Nitrate-Nitrogen, to Surface Water, Groundwater, and the Gulf of Mexico*.

Hypoxia Work Group, White House Office of Science and Technology Policy, Committee on Environment and Natural Resources for the EPA Mississippi River/Gulf of Mexico Watershed Nutrient Task Force. NOAA Coastal Ocean Program. http://www.nos.noaa.gov/products/pubs_hypox.html.

Moisan, François, Didier Bosseboeuf, Bertrand Château and Bruno Lapillonne 1998 *Energy Efficiency Policies and Indicators*. Study for World Energy Council. http://www.worldenergy.org/wec-geis/global/downloads/1998report.pdf.

Molina, Mario J. and F. S. Rowland 1974 "Stratospheric sink for chlorofluoromethanes: chlorine atom-catalyzed destruction of ozone." *Nature* 249:810–12. http://www.unep.org/ozone/pdf/stratopheric.pdf.

Montague, Peter 1999 "Against the Grain." *Rachel's Environment and Health Weekly* #637. Environmental Research Foundation. http://www.biotech-info.net/grain.html.

Mooney, Lorraine and Roger Bate 1999 *Environmental Health: Third World Problems – First World Preoccupations*. Oxford: Butterworth-Heinemann.

Moore, Thomas Gale 1998 "Health and amenity effects of global warming." *Economic Inquiry* 36(3):471–98.

Morgan, M. Granger and Hadi Dowlatabadi 1996 "Learning from integrated assessment of climate change." *Climatic Change* 34:337–68.

Mori, Shunsuke 2000 "The Development of Greenhouse Gas Emissions Scenarios Using an Extension of the MARIA Model for the Assessment of Resource and Energy Technologies." *Technological Forecasting and Social Change* 63:289–311.

Motavalli, Jim 2000 "Running on EMPTY." *E Magazine: The Environmental Magazine* 11(4):34–9.

Moysich, K. B., C. B. Ambrosone, J. E. Vena, P. G. Shields, P. Mendola, P. Kostyniak, H. Greizerstein, S. Graham, J. R. Marshall, E. F. Schisterman and J. L. Freudenheim 1998 "Environmental organochlorine exposure and postmenopausal breast cancer risk." *Cancer Epidemiology, Biomarkers and Prevention* 7(3):181–8.

MPM 1998 *Survey of the Quality of UK Coastal Waters*. Marine Pollution Monitoring, National Monitoring Programme. Aberdeen: Marine Pollution Monitoring Management Group. http://www.marlab.ac.uk/NMPR/NMP.htm.

2000 *Green Book*. Version 5. http://www.marlab.ac.uk/greenbook/GREEN.htm.

Muggleton, Ellis 1999 "Thalidomide – a regret of the past, but a hope for the future?" *Student BMJ* 7:368–9.

Munich Re 1998 *World Map of Natural Hazards*. Order number 2658-V-e. Münchener Rückversicherungs-Gesellschaft.

1999 *Topics: Annual Review of Natural Catastrophes 1998*. Order number 2821-M-e. Münchener Rückversicherungs-Gesellschaft.

2000 "A year, a century, and a millennium of natural catastrophes are all nearing their end – 1999 is completely in line with the catastrophe trend – Munich Re publishes a millennium review." Press release, 20 December 1999. Münchener Rückversicherungs-Gesellschaft. http://www.munichre.com/.

2001 *Topics: Annual Review of Natural Catastrophes 2000*. Münchener Rückversicherungs-Gesellschaft. http://www.munichre.com/.

Murray, Christopher J. L. and Alan D. Lopez 1996a "Quantifying the burden of disease and injury attributable to ten major risk factors." In Murray and Lopez 1996c:295–324.

1996b "Alternative visions of the future: projecting mortality and disability, 1990–2020." In Murray and Lopez 1996c:325–95.

(eds.) 1996c *The Global Burden of Disease: A Comprehensive Assessment of Morality and Disability from Diseases, Injuries, and Risk Factors in 1990 and projected to 2020*. Cambridge, MA: Harvard University Press. Published by Harvard School of Public Health on behalf of the World Health Organization and the World Bank. Summary at http://www.hsph.harvard.edu/organizations/bdu/summary.html (summary).

1997a "Mortality by cause for eight regions of the world: global burden of disease study." *The Lancet* 349:1,269–76.

1997b "Regional patterns of disability-free life expectancy and disability-adjusted life expectancy: global burden of disease study." *The Lancet* 349:1,347–52.

1997c "Global mortality, disability, and the contribution of risk factors: global burden of disease study." *The Lancet* 349:1,436–42. http://www.healthnet.org/programs/procor/gbd3.htm.

1997d "Alternative projections of mortality and

disability by cause 1990–2020: global burden of disease study." *The Lancet* 349:1,498–1,504.

Murray, Christopher J.L. and Lincoln C. Chen 1992 "Understanding morbidity change." *Population and Development Review* 18(3):481–503.

1993 "Understanding morbidity change: reply to Riley." *Population and Development Review* 19(4):812–15.

Myers, John G., Stephen Moore and Julian L. Simon 1995. "Trends in availability of non-fuel minerals." In Simon 1995b:303–12.

Myers, Norman 1979 *The Sinking Ark: A New Look at the Problem of Disappearing Species*. Oxford: Pergamon Press.

1983 *A Wealth of Wild Species: Storehouse for Human Welfare*. Boulder, CO: Westview Press.

1991 "The disappearing forests." In Porritt 1991:46–55.

Myers, Norman and Frans Lanting 1999 "What we must do to counter the biotic holocaust." *International Wildlife* 29(2):30–9.

NAPAP 1990 *Integrated Assessment*, vols. 1–3. The National Acid Precipitation Assessment Program, External Review Draft, August 1990.

NAS 1992 *Policy Implications of Greenhouse Warming: Mitigation, Adaptation, and the Science Base*. National Academy of Sciences, Committee on Science, Engineering, and Public Policy. Washington, DC: National Academy Press. http://www.nap.edu/readingroom/books/greenhouse.

1993 *The Epidemiological Transition: Policy and Planning Implications for Developing Countries*. National Academy of Sciences. Washington, DC: National Academy Press. http://www.nap.edu/books/0309048397/html/.

NASA/GISS 2000 *Atmosphere-Ocean Model Simulations: Future Climate Projections*. NASA and Goddard Institute for Space Studies. http://aom.giss.nasa.gov/.

Nash, J. Madeleine and Simon Robinson 2000 "Grains of Hope." *Time*, 07/31/2000, 156(5):38–46.

Nash, J. Madeleine and Susan Horsburgh 1998 "The fury of El Niño." *Time South Pacific* 2 March 1998, pp. 44–51.

NAST 2000 *Climate Change Impacts on the United States: The Potential Consequences of Climate Variability and Change*. National Assessment Synthesis Team, US Global Change Research Program. http://www.gcrio.org/NationalAssessment.

Naylor, Rosamond L. and Walter P. Falcon 1995 "Is the locus of poverty changing?" *Food Policy* 20(6):501–18.

NBS 1995 *Our Living Resources: A Report to the Nation on the Distribution, Abundance, and Health of U.S. Plants, Animals, and Ecosystems*. Edward T. LaRoe, Gaye S. Farris, Catherine E. Puckett, Peter D. Doran and Michael J. Mac (eds.), National Biological Service, US Department of the Interior. Washington, DC: US Government Printing Office. http://biology.usgs.gov/s+t/index.htm.

NCBP 2000a: *NCBP Fish Database*. National Contaminant Biomonitoring Program. http://www.cerc.usgs.gov/data/ncbp/fish.htm.

2000b: *NCBP Starling Database*. National Contaminant Biomonitoring Program. http://www.cerc.usgs.gov/data/ncbp/starling/starling.htm.

NCHS 1998 *Current Estimates from the National Health Interview Survey, 1995*. Vital and Health Statistics Series 10 no. 199, From the Centers for Disease Control and Prevention/National Center for Health Statistics. http://www.cdc.gov/nchs/data/10_199_1.pdf.

1999a: *Health, United States, 1999, with Health and Aging Chartbook*. US Human Health Service, E. Kramarow, H. Lentzner, R. Rooks, J. Weeks, and Saydah S. Warner (eds). Hyattsville, MD: National Center for Health Statistics. http://www.cdc.gov/nchs/data/hus99.pdf.

1999b: *Vital Statistics of the United States 1993: Volume I – Natality*. Hyattsville, MD: National Center for Health Statistics.

NERI 1995 *Mindmøllers indvirkning på fugle: status over viden og perspektiver*. [The effect of windmills on birds: state of knowledge and perspectives.] Roskilde: National Environmental Research Institute of Denmark, Report no. 147, Ib Calusager and Henning Høhr.

1998a *Natur og Miljø 1997: påvirkninger og tilstand*. [Nature and environment 1997: effects and state.] Roskilde: National Environmental Research Institute of Denmark. http://www.dmu.dk/news/Natur/.

1998b *Air Quality Data*. http://www.dmu.dk/atmosphericenvironment/aq_aar/aovers.htm. (no longer available).

Nestle, Marion 1996 "Allergies to transgenic foods – questions of policy." *New England Journal of Medicine* 334 (11):726–7. http://www.nejm.org/content/1996/0334/0011/0726.asp.

NETC 1999 *UK Air Pollution*. National Environmental Technology Centre on behalf of the UK Department of the Environment, Transport and the Regions. http://www.aeat.co.uk/netcen/airqual/reports/brochure/head.html.

New Scientist 2001 *Judgement Day: There Are Only Angels and Devils*. Global environment supplement to *New Scientist* 170 (2,288).

Newman-Taylor, Anthony 1995 "Environmental determinants of asthma." *The Lancet* 45:296–9.

Newport, Frank, David W. Moore and Lydia Saad 1999 "Long-term gallup poll trends: a portrait of American public opinion through the century." Gallup Poll release, 20 December 1999. http://www.gallup.com/poll/releases/pr991220.asp.

Newton, Robert and Jacques Ferlay 1996 "Effect of ambient solar ultraviolet radiation on incidence of squamous-cell carcinoma of the eye." *The Lancet* 347:,1,450–1.

NHLBI and WHO 1995 *Global Initiative For Asthma: Global Strategy for Asthma Management and Prevention*. NHLBI/WHO Workshop Report; National Institutes of Health; National Heart, Lung and Blood Institute; Publication no. 95–3659. http://www.ginasthma.com/workshop/workshop.pdf.

NIAAA 1997 *U.S. Apparent Consumption of Alcoholic Beverages Based on State Sales, Taxation, or Receipt Data. U.S. Alcohol Epidemiologic Data Reference Manual, Volume 1*. 3rd edn. National Institute on Alcohol Abuse and Alcoholism, NIH Publication no. 97–4263. http://silk.nih.gov/silk/niaaa1/publication/manual.htm.

NIAID 2000 "Asthma and allergy statistics." Fact Sheet. National Institute of Allergy and Infectious Diseases. National Institutes of Health. http://www.niaid.nih.gov/factsheets/allergystat.htm.

Nicholls, Robert J., Frank M.J. Hoozemans and Marcel Marchand 1999 "Increasing flood risk and wetland losses due to global sea-level rise: regional and global analyses." *Global Environmental Change* 9:S69–S87

Nicholson-Lord, David 2000 "The drowning of the Earth." *New Statesman* 129(4,476):8–9.

NIEHS 1999 *Health Effects from Exposure to Power-Line Frequency Electric and Magnetic Fields*. National Institute of Environmental Health Sciences. NIH Publication no. 99–4493. http://www.niehs.nih.gov/emfrapid/.

NOAA 1998 *State of the Coastal Environment: Chemical Contaminants in Oysters and Mussels*. By Tom O'Connor, National Oceanic and Atmospheric Administration. Silver Spring, MD: NOAA. http://state-of-coast.noaa.gov/bulletins/html/ccom_05/ccom.html.

2001 *Paleoclimatology Program*. http://www.ngdc.noaa.gov/paleo.

Nordhaus, William D. 1991a: "The cost of slowing climate change: a survey." *Energy Journal* 12(1):37–65.

1991b "Economic approaches to greenhouse warming." In *Global Warming: Economic Policy Approaches*. R. D. Dornbush and J. M. Poterba (eds.), pp. 33–68. Cambridge, MA: MIT Press.

1991c "A sketch of the greenhouse effect." *Greenhouse Warming* 81(1):146–50.

1991d "To slow or not to slow: the economics of the greenhouse effect." *Economic Journal* 101:920–37.

1992a "An optimal transition path for controlling greenhouse gases." *Science* 258:1,315–19. http://www.econ.yale.edu/~nordhaus/homepage/Optimal.science.1192.pdf.

1992b "Lethal model 2: the limits to growth revisited." *Brookings Papers on Economic Activity* 2:1–43.

1993 "Optimal greenhouse-gas reductions and tax policy in the 'DICE' Model." *Economic Modeling of Greenhouse Warming* 83(2):313–17.

1994 *Managing the Global Commons: The Economics of Climate Change*. Cambridge, MA: MIT Press.

1997a "Discounting in economics and climate change." *Climatic Change* 37:315–28.

1997b "Do real-output and real-wage measures capture reality? The history of lighting suggests not." In Bresnahan and Gordon 1997:29–66.

(ed.) 1998 *Economics and Policy Issues in Climate Change*. Washington, DC: Resources for the Future.

Nordhaus, William and Joseph Boyer 1999 "Requiem for Kyoto: an economic analysis of the Kyoto Protocol." *The Energy Journal*, Kyoto Special Issue:93–130.

2000 *Roll the DICE Again: Economic Models of Global Warming*. Cambridge, MA: MIT Press. In press. http://www.econ.yale.edu/~nordhaus/homepage/web%20table%20of%20contents%20102599.htm.

Nordhaus, William D. and Zili Yang 1996 "A regional dynamic general-equilibrium model of alternative climate-change strategies." *American Economic Review* 86(4):741–65.

Nordlee, Julie A., Steve L. Taylor, Jeffrey A. Townsend, Laurie A. Thomas and Robert K. Bush 1996 "Identification of a Brazil-Nut Allergen in Transgenic Soybeans." *New England Journal of Medicine* 334 (11):688–92.

Norwood, Janet L. 1995 "The consumer price index, the deficit, and politics." *Policy Bites* 22, The Urban Institute. http://www.facsnet.org/cgi-bin/rt_back.cgi?rownumber=5&query=cpi.

Nottingham, Stephen 1998 *Eat Your Genes: How Genetically Modified Foodd is Entering Our Diet*. London: Zed Books.

NRC 1985 *Oil in the Sea: Inputs, Fates, and Effects*. National Research Council. Washington, DC: National Academy Press. http://books.nap.edu/books/0309034795/html/index.html.

1996 *Carcinogens and Anticarcinogens in the Human Diet: A Comparison of Naturally Occurring and Synthetic Substances*. National Research Council. Washington, DC: National Academy Press. http://books.nap.edu/books/0309053919/html/index.html, http://stills.nap.edu/html/diet/summary.html.

1999: *Hormonally Active Agents in the Environment*. Committee on Hormonally Active Agents in the Environment. Board on Environmental Studies and Toxicology, Commission on Life Sciences. National Research Council. Washington, DC: National Academy Press. http://books.nap.edu/html/hormonal_agents/.

2000 *Reconciling Observations of Global Temperature Change*. Washington, DC: National Academy Press. http://www.nap.edu.

2000b *Genetically Modified Pest-Protected Plants: Science and Regulation*. Committee on Genetically Modified Pest-Protected Plants, National Research Council. Washington, DC: National Academy Press. http://www.nap.edu/books/0309069300/html.

NRDC 1997 *Testing the Waters VII: How Does Your Vacation Beach Rate*. Natural Resources Defense Council.

1999 *Testing the Waters – 1999 A Guide to Water Quality at Vacation Beaches*. Natural Resources Defense Council. http://www.nrdc.org/water/oceans/ttw/titinx.asp.

NSC 1990 *Accident Facts, 1990 Edition*. Chicago: National Safety Council.

1999 *Injury Facts, 1999 Edition*. Chicago: National Safety Council.

NSTC 1996 *Interagency Assessment of Potential Health Risks Associated with Oxygenated Gasoline*. National Science and Technology Council; Committee on Environment and Natural Resources; Interagency Oxygenated Fuels Assessment Steering Committee. http://www1.whitehouse.gov/WH/EOP/OSTP/NSTC/html/MTBE/mtbe-top.html.

NTIA 1999 *Falling through the Net: Defining the Digital Divide*. National Telecommunications and Information Administration. http://www.ntia.doc.gov/ntiahome/fttn99/FTTN.pdf.

2000 *Falling Through the Net: Toward Digital Inclusion. A Report on Americans' Access to Technology Tools*. National Telecommunications and Information Administration. http://search.ntia.doc.gov/pdf/fttn00.pdf.

NWCC 1994 *1994 National Avian-Wind Power Planning Meeting Proceedings*. National Wind Coordinating Committee. http://www.nationalwind.org/pubs/avian94/TOC.htm.

OCE 2001 "Hazards of Genetically Engineered Foods and Crops: Why We Need A Global Moratorium." GE-Fact Sheet &Guidelines for Grassroots Action. By Ronnie Cummins, Organic Consumers Association. http://www.purefood.org/ge/gefacts.pdf.

OECD 1985a *OECD Environmental Data Compendium 1985*. Paris: Organization for Economic Co-operation and Development.

1985b *The State of the Environment 1985*. Paris: Organization for Economic Co-operation and Development.

1987 *OECD Environmental Data Compendium 1987*. Paris: Organization for Economic Co-operation and Development.

1994 *The OECD Green Model: An Updated Overview*. By Hiro Lee, Joaquim Oliveira Martins and Dominique van der Mensbrugghe. Technical Paper no. 97. http://www.oecd.org/dev/PUBLICATION/tp/tp97.pdf.

1999 *OECD Environmental Data Compendium 1999*. Paris: Organization for Economic Co-operation and Development.

2000 *Geographical Distribution of Financial Flows to Aid Recipients: Disbursements, Commitments, Country Indicators, 1994–1998*. Paris: Organization For Economic Co-operation and Development.

Okolo, Abraham 1999 "The Nigerian Census: Problems and Prospects." *American Statistician* 53(4):321–4.

Økologisk Jordbrug 1998 *Danske Forbrugeres Informationsadfærd i forbindelse med valg af fødevarer – herunder Økologiske Fødevarer*. [The Danes information habits concerning the choice of food – including ecological food.] Tina V. Møller and Teo Geer.

Olaya-Conteras, P., J. Rodriguez-Villamil, H. J. Posso-Valencia and J. E. Cortez 1998 "Organochlorine exposure and breast cancer risk in Colombian women." *Cad. Saude Publica*, Rio de Janeiro, 14(suppl. 3):125–32.

Oldeman, L. R. 1994 "The global extent of soil degradation." In Greenland and Szabolcs 1994:99–118.

Oldeman, L. R., R. T. A. Hakkeling and W. G. Sombroek 1990 *World Map of the Status of Human-Induced Soil Degradation: An Explanatory Note*. Global Assessment of Soil Degradation; International Soil Reference and Information Centre. Nairobi: UNEP.

1991 *World Map of the Status of Human-Induced Soil Degradation: A Brief Explanatory Note*. Global Assessment of Soil Degradation; International Soil Reference and Information Centre. Nairobi: UNEP.

Olsen, Geary W., Kenneth M. Bodner, Jonathan M. Romlow, Charles E. Ross and Larry I. Lipshultz 1995 "Have sperm counts been reduced 50 percent in 50 years? A statistical model revisited." *Fertility and Sterility* 63(4):887–93.

1996 "Reply of the authors." *Fertility and Sterility* 65(2):451–3. Reply to Keiding and Skakkebæk 1996.

Olshansky S. J., S. Jay, Mark A. Rudeberg, Bruce A. Carnes, Christine K. Cassel and Jacob A. Brody 1991 "Trading off longer life for worsening health: the expansion of morbidity hypothesis." *Journal of Aging Health* 3:194–216.

Olshansky, S. Jay, Bruce Carnes, Richard G. Rogers and Len Smith 1997 *Infectious Diseases – New and Ancient Threats to World Health*. Washington, DC: Population Reference Bureau. http://www.prb.org/pubs/bulletin/bu52-2.htm.

OMB 1997 *Report to Congress on the Costs and Benefits of Federal Regulations*. 30 September 1997, Office of Management and Budget; Office of Information and Regulatory Affairs. http://www.whitehouse.gov/omb/inforeg/rcongress.html.

1999 *Report to Congress on the Costs and Benefits of Federal Regulations 1998*. http://www.whitehouse.gov/omb/inforeg/costbenefitreport1998.pdf.

2000a *Draft Report to Congress on the Costs and Benefits of Federal Regulations 1999*. January 2000. http://www.whitehouse.gov/omb/inforeg/3stevensdraft.pdf.

2000b: *Budget of the United States Government, Fiscal Year 2001: Historical Tables*. Washington, DC: US Government Printing Office. http://w3.access.gpo.gov/usbudget/fy2001/maindown.html.

Online 1997 "Toxic cocktail? Is a toxic mix more deadly than its parts?" Online NewsHour's editors ask. http://www.pbs.org/newshour/forum/april97/toxic3.html.

ONS 1999 *Social Trends 29*. The Office for National Statistics, Jil Matheson and and John Pullinger (eds.). London: The Stationery Office.

2000a: *Social Trends 30*. The Office for National Statistics, Jil Matheson and and John Pullinger (eds.). London: The Stationery Office.

2000b *Population Trends 102 - Winter 2000*. The Office for National Statistics, http://www.statistics.gov.uk/products/p2295.asp.

2001a *Social Trends 31*. The Office for National Statistics, Jil Matheson and Carol Summerfield (eds.). London: The Stationery Office. http://www.statistics.gov.uk/products/p5748.asp

2001b *UK Retail Price Index: index numbers of retail prices 1948 - 2000*. Available on-line, dataset rpi1. http://www.statistics.gov.uk/statbase.

2001c *Population: age and sex, 1971 onwards for the constituent countries of the United Kingdom*. Available on-line, dataset PT10215. http://www.statistics.gov.uk/statbase.

2001d *Gross domestic product. Preliminary estimate - 4th quarter 2000*. 26 January 2001. http://www.statistics.gov.uk/pdfdir/gdpr0101.pdf.

OPP 2000 *USEPA/OPP Pesticide Products Database*. Office of Pesticide Programs, US Environmental Protection Agency. http://www.cdpr.ca.gov/docs/epa/m2.htm.

Oram, Peter 1995 "The potential of technology to meet world food needs in 2020." *2020 Vision Brief* 13. http://www.cgiar.org/ifpri/2020/briefs/number13.htm.

Orogan, John and Cheryl Long 2000 "The Problem with Genetic Engineering." *Organic Gardening* 47(1):42–6.

Ortonne, J.-P. 1997 "The ozone depletion and the skin." *Journal of the European Academy of Dermatology and Venereology* 9 (1,001):S17.

Osberg, Lars (ed.) 1991: *Economic Inequality and Poverty: International Perspectives*. Armonk, NY: M. E. Sharpe.

Ott, Wayne R. and John W. Roberts 1998 "Everyday exposure to toxic pollutants." *Scientific American* 278(2):86–91.

Ovesen, Lars 1995 "Effekten af øget indtagelse af økologiske landbrugsprodukter på folkesundheden." [The effect on national health from increased intake of organic farm products.] from the Danish Veterinary and Food Administration. In SID 1995:61–74.

Park, Chris C. 1987 *Acid Rain – Rhetoric and Reality*. London and New York: Methuen.

Park, Donghyun 1997 "An alternative examination of intercountry income inequality and convergence." *Comparative Economic Studies* 39(3/4):53–65.

1999 "Intercountry income inequality: an expansion and an update." *Comparative Economic Studies* 41(4):103–8.

Parker, David E. 2000 "Temperatures high and low." *Science* 287:1,216–17.

Parry, Ian W. H. and Wallace E. Oates 1998 "Policy Analysis in a Second-Best World." Discussion Paper 98-48. Washington, D.C.: Resources for the Future. http://www.rff.org/CFDOCS/disc_papers/PDF_files/9848.pdf.

Parry, Martin, Nigel Arnell, Mike Hulme, Robert Nicholls and Matthew Livermore 1998 "Buenos Aires and Kyoto targets do little to reduce climate change impacts." *Global Environmental Change* 8(4):285–9.

Parry, Martin, Cynthia Rosenzweig, Ana Iglesias, Günther Fischer and Matthew Livermore 1999 "Climate change and world food security: a new assessment." *Global Environmental Change* 9:S51–S67.

Parry, Martin (ed) 2000 *Assessment of Potential Effects and Adaptations for Climate Change in Europe: The Europe ACACIA Project*. Jackson Environment Institute, University of East Anglia, UK.

Parson, Edward A. and Karen Fisher-Vanden 1997 "Integrated assessment models of global climate change." *Annual Review of Energy and Environment* 22:589–628.

Patterson, Blossom H. and Gladys Block 1988 "Food choices and the cancer guidelines." *American Journal of Public Health* 78(3):282–6.

Paulsen, C. Alvin, Nancy G. Berman and Christina Wang 1996 "Data from men in greater Seattle area reveals no downward trend in semen quality: further evidence that deterioration of semen quality is not geographically uniform." *Fertility and Sterility* 65(5):1,015–20.

PBS Frontline 1998 "Fooling with nature: interview with Theo Colborn." http://www.pbs.org/wgbh/pages/frontline/shows/nature/interviews/colborn.html.

PCSD 1999 *Towards a Sustainable America: Advancing Prosperity, Opportunity, and a Healthy Environment for the 21st Century*. May 1999. President's Council on Sustainable Development. http://www.whitehouse.gov/PCSD/Publications/tsa.pdf (no longer available).

Pearce, David 1991 "The Role of Carbon Taxes in Adjusting to Global Warming." *The Economic Journal* 101(407):938–48.

1998 "Auditing the Earth." *Environment* 40(2):23–9.

Pearce, David W. and R. Kerry Turner 1990 *Economics of Natural Resources and the Environment*. Baltimore: Johns Hopkins University Press.

Pearce, Fred 1997 "Burn me." *New Scientist*, 156(2,109): 22 November. 1997, 2,109:30–4.

2000 "Washed off the map: Better get that ark ready, because the sea levels are gonna rise." *New Scientist* 168(2,266):5. http://www.newscientist.com/news/news.jsp?id=ns22664

2001 "We are all guilty! It's official, people are to blame for global warming." *New Scientist* 169(2275):5. http://archive.newscientist.com/archive.jsp?id=22750300.

Peck, Stephen C. and Thomas J. Teisberg 1992 "CETA: a model for carbon emissions trajectory assessment." *Energy Journal* 13(1):55–77.

1999 "CO_2 emissions control agreements: incentives for regional participation." *The Energy Journal*, Kyoto Special Issue:367–90.

Percival, Val and Thomas Homer-Dixon 1998 "Environmental scarcity and violent conflict: the case of South Africa." *Journal of Peace Research* 35(3):279–98.

Persson, Torsten and Guido Tabellini 1994 "Is

inequality harmful for growth?" *American Economic Review* 84(3):600–20.

Peterson, T. C., K. P. Gallo, J. Lawrimore, T. W. Owen, A. Huang and D. A. McKittrick 1999 "Global rural temperature trends." *Geophysical Research Letters* 26(3):329–32.

Petit, J. R., J. Jouzel, D. Raynaud, N. I. Barkov, J.-M. Barnola, I. Basile, M. Bender, J. Chappellaz, M. Davis, G. Delaygue, M. Delmotte, V. M. Kotlyakov, M. Legrand, V. Y. Lipenkov, C. Lorius, L. Pépin, C. Ritz, E. Saltzman and M. Stievenard 1999 "Climate and atmospheric history of the past 420,000 years from the Vostok ice core, Antarctica." *Nature* 299(6735):429–36.

Peto, Richard, Alan D. Lopez, Jillian Boreham, Michael Thun and Clark Heath Jn. 1992 "Mortality from tobacco in developed countries: indirect estimation from national vital statistics." *The Lancet* 229:1,268–78.

1994 *Mortality from Smoking in Developed Countries 1950–2000*. Oxford: Oxford University Press.

Pezzey, John C.V., and Andrew Park 1998 "Reflections on the Double Dividend Debate: The Importance of Interest Groups and Information Costs." *Environmental and Resource Economics* 11(3–4):539–55.

Pielke, Roger A. 1999 "Nine fallacies of floods." *Climatic Change* 42:413–38.

Pielke, Roger A. Jn. and Christopher W. Landsea 1998 "Normalized hurricane damages in the United States: 1925–1995." *Weather and Forecasting* 13(3):621–31. http://www.aoml.noaa.gov/hrd/Landsea/USdmg/index.html.

1999 "La Niña, El Niño, and Atlantic hurricane damages in the United States." *Bulletin of the American Meteorological Society* 80(10):2,027–33. http://ams.allenpress.com/.

Pielke, R. A. Sn. and R. A Pielke Jn. 2000 *Storms*. New York: Routledge.

Pimentel, David 1997 "Soil erosion." *Environment* 39(10):4–5.

Pimentel, David, H. Acquay, M. Biltonen, P. Rice, M. Silva, J. Nelson, V. Lipner, S. Giordano, A. Horowitz and M. D'Amore 1992 "Environmental and economic costs of pesticide use." *BioScience* 42(10):750–60.

Pimentel, D., C. Harvey, P. Resosudarmo, K. Sinclair, D. Kurtz, M. McNair, S. Crist, L. Spritz, L. Fitton, R. Saffouri and R. Blair 1995a "Environmental and economic costs of soil erosion and conservation benefits." *Science* 267:1,117–23.

1995b: "Response" [to Crosson 1995]. *Science* 269:465–6.

Pimentel, David and Marcia Pimentel 1995 *Land, Energy and Water: The Constraints Governing Ideal U.S. Population Size*. NPG Forum Series. http://www.npg.org/forums/land_energy&water.htm.

1999: "The future: prospects for the global availability of food and ways to increase it." *Social Research* 66(1):417–28.

Pimentel, David, Maria Tort, Linda D'Anna, Anne Krawic, Joshua Berger, Jessica Rossman, Fridah Mugo, Nancy Doon, Michael Shriberg, Erica Howard, Susan Lee and Jonathan Talbot 1998 "Ecology of increasing disease: population growth and environmental degradation." *BioScience* 48(10):817–26.

Pimentel, David, Christa Wilson, Christine McCullum, Rachel Huang, Paulette Dwen, Jessica Flack, Quynh Tran, Tamara Saltman and Barbara Cliff 1997 "Economic and environmental benefits of biodiversity." *BioScience* 47(11):747–57.

Pimm, Stuart L. 1997 "The value of everything." *Nature* 387:231–2.

Pingali, Prabhu L. (ed.) 1999 *CIMMYT 1998–99 World Wheat Facts and Trends. Global Wheat Research in a Changing World: Challenges and Achievements.* International Maize and Wheat Improvement Center. Mexico City: CIMMYT. http://www.cimmyt.cgiar.org/research/Economics/wheatft9899.htm (no longer available).

Pingali, Prabhu L. and Paul W. Heisey 1999 *Cereal Crop Productivity in Developing Countries: Past Trends and Future Prospects*. International Maize and Wheat Improvement Center. Economics Working Paper 99–03. http://www.cimmyt.cgiar.org/Research/Economics/PDFs/EWP%2099_03.pdf (no longer available).

Plaschke, P., C. Janson, B. Balder, O. Lowhagen and B. Jarvholm 1999b "Adult asthmatics sensitized to cats and dogs: symptoms, severity, and bronchial hyperresponsiveness in patients with furred animals at home and patients without these animals." *Allergy* 54(8):843–50.

Plaschke, P., C. Janson, E. Norrman, E. Bjornsson, S. Ellbjar and B. Jarvholm 1999a "Association between atopic sensitization and asthma and bronchial hyperresponsiveness in Swedish adults: pets, and not mites, are the most important allergens." *The Journal of Allergy and Clinical Immunology* 104(1):58–65.

Plato 1961 *The Collected Dialogues*. Princeton, NJ: Princeton University Press.

Platts-Mills, Thomas A. E. and Melody C. Carter 1997 "Asthma and indoor exposure to allergens." *The New England Journal of Medicine* 336(19):1,382–4. http://www.nejm.org/content/1997/0336/0019/1382.asp.

Platts-Mills, Thomas A. E. and Judith A. Woodfolk 1997 "Rise in asthma cases." *Science* 278:1,001.

Pollack, H.N. and S. Huang 2001 "Global Borehole Temperature Database for Climate Reconstruction." ftp://ftp.ngdc.noaa.gov/paleo/borehole/global.composite.txt.

Pope, CA, III, M. J. Thun, M. M. Namboodiri, D. W. Dockery, J. S. Evans, F. E. Speizer and C. W. Heath Jr. 1995 "Particulate air pollution as a predictor of mortality in a prospective study of U.S. adults." *American Journal of Respiratory and Critical Care Medicine* 151:669–74.

Pope, Charles 1998 "A year after Kyoto pact's completion, the political heat is unabated." *CQ Weekly* 56(46):3,175–7.

Population Reports 1998 "The coming water crisis." *Population Reports* 26(1):3–4.

PORG 1997 *Ozone in the United Kingdom: Fourth Report of the Photochemical Oxidants Review Group, 1997*. Prepared at the request of the Air and Environment Quality Division, Department of the Environment, Transport and the Regions. http://www.aeat.co.uk/netcen/airqual/reports/porg/fourth1.html.

Porritt, Jonathon 1991 *Save the Earth*. London: Dorling Kindersley.

Porter, Roy 1997 *The Greatest Benefit to Mankind: A Medical History of Humanity from Antiquity to the Present*. London: Fontana Press.

Portney, Paul R. and John P. Weyant 1999a "Introduction." In Portney and Weyant 1999b:1–11. http://www.rff.org/books/summaries/Discounting%20ch01.pdf.

Portney, Paul R. and John P. Weyant (eds.) 1999b *Discounting and Intergenerational Equity*. Washington, DC: Resources for the Future.

Postel, Sandra L. 1998 "Water for food production: will there be enough in 2025?" *BioScience* 48(8):629–38.

1999 *Pillar of Sand: Can the Irrigation Miracle Last?* New York: Norton.

Postel, Sandra L., Gretchen C. Daily and Paul R. Ehrlich 1996 "Human appropriation of renewable fresh water." *Science* 271:785–8.

Postrel, Virginia 1991 "Of mice and men: an interview with Bruce Ames." *Reason Magazine*. December 1991. http://reason.com/amesint.html.

Poulsen, Emil 1992 "Setting of limit values for chemicals and chemical compounds." In ATV 1992:37–47.

Poulsen, Jørgen 1998 "Dissidentens stemme." [The voice of the dissident.] *Politiken*. 13 March 1998, section 2, pp. 3–4.

Powell, Mark R. 1997 *Three-City Air Study*. Discussion Paper 97–29; Resources for the Future.

Preboth, Monica 2000 "Clinical review of recent findings on the awareness, diagnosis and treatment of depression." *American Family Physician* 61(10):3,158–61.

Preston, Samuel 1976 *Mortality Patterns in National Populations*. New York: Academic Press.

1995 "Human mortality throughout history and prehistory." In Simon 1995b:30–6.

Preston, Samuel H., Nathan Keyfitz and Robert Schoen 1972 *Causes of Death: Life Tables for National Populations*. New York: Seminar Press.

Pritchett, Lant 1997 "Divergence, big time." *Journal of Economic Perspectives* 11(3):3–17.

Pritchett, Lant and Lawrence H. Summers 1996 "Wealthier is healthier." *Journal of Human Resources* 31(4):842–68.

Protheroe, David, Kim Turvey, Kieran Horgan, Eddie Benson, David Bowers and Allan House 1999 "Stressful life events and difficulties and onset of breast cancer: case-control study." *British Medical Journal* 319:1,027–30.

Putman, Susan W. and Jonathan Baert Wiener 1997 "Seeking safe drinking water." In Graham and Wiener 1997:124–48.

Putnam, Judith Jones and Jane E. Allshouse 1999 *Food Consumption, Prices, and Expenditures, 1970–97*. Food and Rural Economics Division, Economic Research Service, US Department of Agriculture. Statistical Bulletin 965. http://www.ers.usda.gov/epubs/pdf/sb965.

Putnam, Judy and Shirley Gerrior 1999 "Trends in the U.S. food supply, 1970–97." In Frazão 1999:133–60.

Qian, B. D., J. Corte-Real and H. Xu 2000 "Is the North Atlantic Oscillation the most important atmospheric pattern for precipitation in

Europe?" *Journal of Geophysical Research – Atmospheres*. 105(D9):11,901–10.

QUARG 1993 *Diesel Vehicle Emissions and Urban Air Quality*. Second Report of the Quality of Urban Air Review Group. http://www.aeat.co.uk/netcen/airqual/reports/quarg/q2intro.html.

1996 *Airborne Particle Matter in the United Kingdom*. Third Report of the Quality of Urban Air Review Group. http://www.aeat.co.uk/netcen/airqual/reports/quarg/q3intro.html.

Quinn, Niall 1995 "Parkinsonism – recognition and differential diagnosis." *British Medical Journal* 310:447–52.

Rabalais, Nancy N., R. Eugene Turner, Dubravko Justić, Quay Dortch and William J. Wiseman Jn. 1999 *Gulf of Mexico Hypoxia Assessment: Topic #1. Characterization of Hypoxia*. Hypoxia Work Group, White House Office of Science and Technology Policy, Committee on Environment and Natural Resources for the EPA Mississippi River/Gulf of Mexico Watershed Nutrient Task Force. NOAA Coastal Ocean Program. http://www.nos.noaa.gov/products/pubs_hypox.html.

Radetzki, Marian 1997 "The economics of biomass in industrialized countries: an overview." *Energy Policy* 25(6):545–54.

1999 "Taxation of greenhouse gases: why Kyoto will not be implemented." *International Journal of Global Energy Issues* 12(7–8):372–6.

Raloff, J. 1993 "Valdez spill leaves lasting oil impacts." *Science News* 143(7):103–4.

1997 "Is synergy of estrogen mimics an illusion?" *Science News* 152(5):69.

1998 "How inhaled dust harms the lungs." *Science News* 153(5):68.

Rasborg, Klaus 1997 "Refleksiv modernisering i risikosamfundet." [Reflexive modernization in the risk society.] *Dansk Sociologi* 2(8):7–20.

Raskin, P., P. Gleick, P. Kirshen, R. G. Pontius Jn. and K. Strzepek 1997 "Water futures: assessment of long-range patterns and problems." Background document for CSD 1997. Stockholm: Stockholm Environment Institute.

Rathje, William and Cullen Murphy 1992 *Rubbish! What Our Garbage Tells Us about Ourselves*. New York: HarperPerennial.

Rauber, Paul and Reed McManus 1994 "Down on the farm bureau." *Sierra* 79(6):32–3.

Rave, Peter and Ghillean Prance 1991 "The richness of life." In Porritt 1991:70–3.

Rawls, John 1972 *A Theory of Justice*. Oxford: Oxford University Press.

Reader, M. C. and G. J. Boer 1998 "The modification of greenhouse gas warming by the direct effect of sulphate aerosols." *Climate Dynamics* 14:593–607.

Readman, J. W., J. Bartocci, I. Tolosa, S. W. Fowler, B. Oregioni and M. Y. Abdulraheem 1996 "Recovery of the coastal marine environment in the Gulf following the 1991 war-related oil spills." *Marine Pollution Bulletin* 32(6):493–8.

Readman, J. W., S. W. Fowler, J.-P. Villeneuve, C. Cattini, B. Orgioni and L. D. Mee 1992 "Oil and combustion-product contamination of the Gulf marine environment following the war." *Nature* 358:662–5.

Reaka-Kudla, Marjorie, Don E. Wilson and Edward O. Wilson (eds.) 1997 *Biodiversity II*. Washington, DC: Joseph Henry Press.

Rector, Robert 1995 "How 'poor' are America's poor?" In Simon 1995b:241–56.

Red Cross 1998 *World Disasters Report*. International Federation of Red Cross and Red Crescent Societies. Oxford: Oxford University Press.

Reeves, Timothy G., Sanjaya Rajaram, Maarten van Ginkel, Richard Trethowan, Hans-Joachim Braun and Kelly Cassaday 1999 *New Wheats for a Secure, Sustainable Future*. Mexico City: CIMMYT. http://www.cimmyt.cgiar.org/about/pdf/New%20Wheats.pdf (no longer available).

Regis, Ed 1997 "The envionment is going to hell, . . ." *Wired* 5(2):136–40, 193–8.

Reid, W. V. 1992 "How many species will there be?" In Whitmore and Sayer 1992:55–74.

Reilly, J. M. and D. Schimmelpfennig 1999 "Agricultural impact assessment, vulnerability, and the scope for adaptation." *Climatic Change* 43(4):745–88.

Reisner, Barbara S. 1996 "Plague – past and present." *Clinical Microbiology Newsletter* 18(20):153–6.

Reiter, Paul 2000 "From Shakepeare to Defoe: malaria in England in the Little Ice Age." *Emerging Infectious Diseases* 6(1):1–10. http://www.cdc.gov/ncidod/eid/vol6no1/reiter.htm.

Rejesus, Roderick M., Paul W. Heisey and Melinda Smale 1999 *Sources of Productivity Growth in Wheat: A Review of Recent Performance and Medium- to Long-Term Prospects*. International Maize and Wheat Improvement Center. Economics Working Paper 99–05. http://www.cimmyt.cgiar.org/Research/

Economics/PDFs/EWP%2099_05.pdf (no longer available).

Reuters 1998 "Altered-gene potatoes hurt rats, report says. Scientist urges more study prior to use by humans." Monday, August 10, 1998. http://www.desnews.com/cgi-bin/libstory_reg?dn98&9808100179.

Reynolds, Tom 1998a "Causes of childhood leukemia beginning to emerge." *Journal of the National Cancer Institute* 90(1):8–10.

Reynolds, Tom 1998b "Researchers hunt for elusive environmental causes of leukemia." *Journal of the National Cancer Institute* 90(2):90–2.

Richards, John F. 1990 "Land transformation." In Turner *et al.* 1990:163–80.

Ridnouer, Nathan M. 1998 "Cities bracing for 'climate event of the century'." *Nation's Cities Weekly* 21(12):14.

Ries, Lynn A. G., Phyllis A. Wingo, Daniel S. Miller, Holly L. Howe, Hannah K. Weir, Harry M. Rosenberg, Sally W. Vernon, Kathleen Cronin and Brenda K. Edwards 2000 "The annual report to the nation on the status of cancer, 1973–1997, with a special section on colorectal cancer." *Cancer* 88(10):2,398–424. http://www3.interscience.wiley.com/cgi-bin/abstract/72502069/START.

Riiskjær, Erik 1988 *Når lofterne drysser i kommunen: en historie fra den lokalpolitiske virkelighed.* [Story of the local politics of asbstos ceilings.] Århus: Politica.

Riley, James C. 1990 "The risk of being sick: morbidity trends in four countries." *Population and Development Review* 16:403–42.

1992 "From a high mortality regime to a high morbidity regime: is culture everything in sickness?" *Health Transition Review* 2:71–8. http://www-nceph.anu.edu.au/htc/htrall.htm.

1993 "Understanding morbidity change: comment on an article by Murray and Chen." *Population and Development Review* 19(4):807–11.

1997 *Why are Morbidity and Mortality Rarely Parallel?* Working Paper 97-10, Department of History, Indiana University. http://www.indiana.edu/~pirt/wp97-10.html.

Riley, James C. and George Alter 1996: "The sick and the well: adult health in Britain during the health transition." *Health Transition Review* Supplement 6:19–44. http://www-nceph.anu.edu.au/htc/htrall.htm.

Ritter, Len, Clark Heath Jn., Elizabeth Kaegi, Howard Morrison and Susan Sieber 1997 "Report of a panel on the relationship between public exposure to pesticides and cancer." *Cancer* 80:2,019–33.

Robinson, John P. 1995 "Trends in free time." In Simon 1995b:224–30.

Robinson, John P. and Ann Bostrom 1994 "The overestimated workweek? What time diary measures suggest." *Monthly Labor Review* 117(8)11–23. http://stats.bls.gov/opub/mlr/1994/08/art2full.pdf.

Robinson, John P. and Geoffrey Godbey 1997 *Time for Life: The Surprising Ways Americans Use Their Time.* University Park: Pennsylvania State University Press.

1999 *Time for Life: The Surprising Ways Americans Use Their Time.* 2nd edn. University Park: Pennsylvania State University Press.

Rodhe, H., R. J. Charlson and T. L. Anderson 2000 "Avoiding Circular Logic in Climate Modeling." *Climatic Change* 44:419–22.

Rodricks, Joseph V. 1992 *Calculated Risks: Understanding the Toxicity and Human Health Risks of Chemicals in Our Environment.* Cambridge: Cambridge University Press.

Rogers, David J. and Sarah E. Randolph 2000 "The Global Spread of Malaria in a Future, Warmer World." *Science* 289(5485):1763–6.

Rogoff, Kenneth 1996 "The purchasing power parity puzzle." *Journal of Economic Literature* 34(2):647–68.

Roll-Hansen, Nils 1994 "Science, politics, and the mass media: on biased communication of environmental issues." *Science, Technology and Human Values* 19(3):324–41.

Romano, Mike 1999 "A questionable verdict." *U.S. News and World Report* 126(19):28.

Rones, Philip L., Randy E. Ilg and Jennifer M. Gardner 1997 "Trends in hours of work since the mid-1970s." *Monthly Labor Review* 120(4):3–14. http://www.bls.gov/opub/mlr/1997/04/art1full.pdf.

Rosenstreich, David L., Peyton Eggleston, Meyer Kattan, Dean Baker, Raymond G. Slavin, Peter Gergen, Herman Mitchell, Kathleen McNiff-Mortimer, Henry Lynn, Dennis Ownby and Floyd Malveaux 1997 "The role of cockroach allergy and exposure to cockroach allergen in causing morbidity among inner-city children with asthma." *The New England Journal of Medicine* 336(19):1,356–63. http://www.nejm.org/content/1997/0336/0019/1356.asp.

Rosenzweig, Cynthia and Martin L. Parry 1994

"Potential impact of climate change on world food supply." *Nature* 367:133–8.

Rosner, David and Gerald Markowitz 1999 "Labor day and the war on workers." *American Journal of Public Health* 89(9):1,319–21.

Ross, Julie A., Max J. Coppes and Leslie L. Robison 1999 "Population density and risk of childhood acute lymphoblastic leukaemia." *The Lancet* 354:532.

Ross, Shelagh and Roger Blackmore 1996 "Atmospheres and climatic change." In Blackmore and Reddish 1996:129–91.

Rossow, William B. and Robert A. Schiffer 1999 "Advances in understanding clouds from ISCCP." *Bulletin of the American Meteorological Society* 80(11):2,261–87. http://ams.allenpress.com.

Rötter, R. and S. C. van de Geijn 1999 "Climate change effects on plant growth, crop yield and livestock." *Climatic Change* 43(4):651–81.

Royal Society 1999 *Review of data on possible toxicity of GM potatoes*. 11/99. http://www.royalsoc.ac.uk/files/statfiles/document-29.pdf.

Royte, Elizabeth and Harry Benson 2001 "The Gospel According to John." *Discover* 22(2):66–73.

Rozanov, Boris G., Viktor Targulian and D. S. Orlov 1990 "Soils." In Turner *et al.* 1990:203–14.

RRI 1998 "Audit Report of Rowett Research on Lectins. Genetically Modified Organisms." Rowett Research Institute. http://www.rri.sari.ac.uk/press/pr04.98.html [no longer available].

Russell, Josiah Cox 1978 "Population in Europe 500–1500." In Cipolla 1978:1:25–71.

Saad, Lydia 1999 "Environmental concern wanes in 1999 Earth Day poll: Americans still care, but more likely to see progress." *Poll Releases*, 22 April 1999. http://www.gallup.com/poll/releases/pr990422.asp.

Saad, Lydia and Riley E. Dunlap 2000 "Americans are environmentally friendly, but issue not seen as urgent problem: concern has dropped somewhat over past decade." *Poll Releases* 17 April 2000. http://www.gallup.com/poll/releases/pr000417.asp.

Sabziparvar, Ali-Akbar 1997 "A model derived surface climatology of surface daily ultraviolet irradiance including an estimate of trends due to changes in atmospheric composition." PhD thesis, University of Reading. Data can be downloaded from http://www.met.rdg.ac.uk/~piers/ali/ali.html (temporarily unavailable).

Sabziparvar, Ali-Akbar, Keith P. Shine and Piers M. de F. Forster 1999 "Environmental photobiology and UVR effects – a model-derived global climatology of UV irradiation at the earth's surface." *Photochemistry and Photobiology* 69(2):193–202.

Sadar, Ziauddin 2000 "Put blame for BSE where it belongs." *New Statesman*, 10/23/2000, p17.

Saeijs, H. L. F. and M. J. van Berkel 1995 "Global water crisis: the major issue of the 21st century, a growing and explosive problem." *European Water Pollution Control* 5(4):26–40.

Safe, Stephen H. 1995 "Environmental and dietary estrogens and human health: is there a problem?" *Environmental Health Perspectives* 103(4):346–51.

1997a "Is there an association between exposure to environmental estrogens and breast cancer." *Environmental Health Perspectives Supplements* 105(3):675–8.

1997b "Xenoestrogens and breast cancer." *New England Journal of Medicine* 337(18):1,303–4.

1998 "Interactions between hormones and chemicals in breast cancer." *Annual Review of Pharmacological Toxicology* 38:121–58.

Sagoff, Mark 1995 "Carrying capacity and ecological economics." *BioScience* 45(9):610–20.

1997 "Can we put a price on nature's services?" *Report from the Institute for Philosophy and Public Policy* 17:3. http://www.puaf.umd.edu/ippp/nature.htm.

1999 "Controlling global climate: the debate over pollution trading." *Report from the Institute for Philosophy and Public Policy* 19:1. http://www.puaf.umd.edu/ippp/winter99/controlling_global_climate.htm.

Sahagian, Dork L., Frank W. Schwartz and David K. Jacobs 1994 "Direct anthropogenic contributions to sea level rise in the twentieth century." *Nature* 367:54–7.

Saidi, James A., David T. Chang, Erik T. Goluboff, Emilia Bagiella, Geary Olsen and Harry Fisch 1999 "Declining sperm counts in the United States? A critical review." *The Journal of Urology* 161:460–2.

Sandman, Peter M. 1996 "Mass media and environmental risk: seven principles" *Risk: Health, Safety and Environment* 5. http://www.fplc.edu/risk/vol5/summer/sandman.htm

Sandweiss, Daniel H., James B. Richardson III, Elizabeth J. Reitz, Harold B. Rollins and Kirk A.

Maasch 1996a "Geoarchaeological evidence from Peru for a 5000 years B.P. onset of El Niño." *Science* 273:1,531–3.

1996b "Determining the early history of El Niño." *Science* 276:966–7.

Sankovski, Alexei, Wiley Barbour and William Pepper 2000 "Quantification of the IS99 Emission Scenario Storylines Using the Atmospheric Stabilization Framework." *Technological Forecasting and Social Change* 63: 263–87.

Santer, B. D., T. M. L. Wigley, D. J. Gaffen, L. Bengtsson, C. Doutriaux, J. S. Boyleft, M. Esch, J. J. Hnilo, P. D. Jones, G. A. Meehl, E. Roeckner, K. E. Taylor and M. F. Wehner 2000 "Interpreting differential temperature trends at the surface and in the lower troposphere." *Science* 287:1,227–32.

Saphir, Ann 1998 "Farmers and cancer: old crop of data gets new scrutiny." *Journal of the National Cancer Institute* 90(9):651–3.

Sarkar, Prabirjit 1999 "Theory of convergence and real income divergence 1950–92." *Economic and Politcal Weekly*, 20 February 1999:500–4.

Schade, G. and B. Heinzow 1998 "Organochlorine pesticides and polychlorinated biphenyls in human milk of mothers living in northern Germany: current extent of contamination, time trend from 1986 to 1997 and factors that influence the levels of contamination." *The Science of the Total Environment* 215(1–2):31–9.

Schecter, A., P. Toniolo, L. C. Dai, L. T. B. Thuy and M. S. Wolff 1997 "Blood levels of DDT and breast cancer risk among women living in the north of Vietnam." *Archives of Environmental Contamination and Toxicology* 33:453–6.

Schelling, Thomas C. 1992 "Some economics of global warming." *American Economic Review* 82(1):1. http://sedac.ciesin.org/mva/iamcc.tg/articles/SC1992/SC1992.html.

1996 "The economic diplomacy of geoengineering." *Climatic Change* 33:303–7.

1999 "Intergenerational Discounting." In Portney and Weyant 1999:99–102.

Schellnhüber, Hans Joachim and Gary Wynn Yohe 1997 *Comprehending the Economic and Social Dimensions of Climate Change by Integrated Assessment*. Potsdam: Potsdam Institute for Climate Impact Research. http://www.pik-potsdam.de/portrait/schellnh/home/hjs_talk/hjs_ge_1.htm.

Scherr, Sara J. 1999 "Soil degradation: a threat to developing-country food security by 2020?" Food, Agriculture, and the Environment Discussion Paper 27, International Food Policy Research Institute. http://www.cgiar.org/ifpri/pubs/catalog.htm#dp.

Scheuplein, Robert 1991 "Do pesticides cause cancer?" *Consumers' Research Magazine* 74(12):30–3.

Schiermeier, Quirin 2000 "Novartis pins hopes for GM seeds on new marker system." *Nature* 406(6,799):924.

Schipper, L. J., R. Haas and C. Sheinbaum 1996 "Recent trends in residential energy use in OECD countries and their impact on carbon dioxide emissions: a comparative analysis of the period 1973–1992." *Mitigation and Adaptation Strategies for Global Change* 1(2):167–96.

Schmitt, C. J. and C. M. Bunck 1995 "Persistent environmental contaminants in fish and wildlife." In NBS 1995:413–16.

Schneider, Friedrich and Dominik Enste 2000 "Shadow economies around the world – size, causes, and consequences." *Journal of Economic Literature* 38(1):77–114. Working Paper can be downloaded from http://www.lrz-muenchen.de/~u5121aw/ceswww/c02.htm.

Schneider, Keith 1991 "U.S. backing away from saying dioxin is a deadly peril: a new assessment begins." *New York Times*, 15 August, 140(48,693):A1, D23.

Scholten, M. C. Th., K. J. M. Kramer and R. W. P. M. Laane 1998 "Trends and variation in concentration of dissolved metals (Cd, Cu, Pb, and Zn) in the North Sea (1980–1989)." *ICES Journal of Marine Science* 55(5):825–34.

Schor, J. 1991 *The Overworked American*. New York: Basic Books.

Schroll, Henning, Kåre Fog, Christian Ege and Jaenne Lind Christiansen (eds.) 1999 *Fremtidens Pris: Talmagi i Miljøpolitikken*. [The Price of the Future: Statistics and Magic in Enviornmental Policy.] Copenhagen: Det Økologiske Råd and Mellemfolkeligt Samvirke.

Schultz, T. Paul 1998 "Inequality in the distribution of personal income in the world: how it is changing and why." *Journal of Population Economics* 11:307–44.

Scott, Michael 1994 *The Young Oxford Book of Ecology*. Oxford: Oxford University Press.

Sears, Malcolm R. 1997a "Descriptive epidemiology

of asthma." *The Lancet*, supplement *Asthma* 350(9,085):1–4.

1997b "Epidemiology of childhood asthma." *The Lancet* 350:9,083:1,015–20.

Sedjo, Roger A. and Marion Clawson 1995 "Global forests revisited." In Simon 1995b:328–45.

SEER 2000a *SEER Cancer Statistics Review, 1973–1997*. NCI (National Cancer Institute) Surveillance, Epidemiology, and End Results program. http://seer.cancer.gov/Publications/CSR1973_1997/

2000b *SEER*Stat 3.0*. Statistical system for the analysis of SEER incidence database, August 1999 submission, 1973–1997 diagnoses. CD-ROM from http://seer.cancer.gov/ScientificSystems/SEERStat/.

Semiat, Raphael 2000 "Desalination: present and future." *Water International* 25(1):54–65.

Serageldin, Ismail 1995 *Toward Sustainable Management of Water Resources*. World Bank, Directions in Development 14,910.

Shafik, Nemat 1994 "Economic development and environmental quality: an econometric analysis." *Oxford Economic Papers* 46:757–73.

Shah, Tushaar, David Molden, R. Sakthivadivel and David Seckler 2000 *The Global Groundwater Situation: Overview of Opportunities and Challenges*. Colombo, Sri Lanka: International Water Management Institute. http://www.cgiar.org/iwmi/pubs/WWVisn/GrWater.pdf.

Shaheen, S. O., J. A. Sterne, S. M. Montgomery and H. Azima 1999 "Birth weight, body mass index and asthma in young adults." *Thorax* 54(5):396–402.

Shammas, Carole 1993 "A new look at long-term trends in wealth inequality in the United States." *The American Historical Review* 98(2):412–31.

Sharma, Dinesh C. 1999 "Alarming amounts of lead found in Indian children." *The Lancet* 353:647.

Sharpe, J. A. 1987 *Early Modern England: A Social History 1550–1760*. London: Arnold.

Sharpe, Richard M. 1995 "On the importance of being Earnest." *Human and Experimental Toxicology* 14:462–6.

Sharpe, Richard M. and Niels E. Skakkebæk 1993 "Are oestrogens involved in falling sperm counts and disorders of the male reproductive tract?" *The Lancet* 341:1,392–5.

Sherins, Richard J. 1995 "Are semen quality and male fertility changing?" *New England Journal of Medicine* 332(5):327–8. http://www.nejm.org/content/1995/0332/0005/0327.asp.

Shiklomanov, Igor A. 1993 "World fresh water resources." In Gleick 1993:13–24.

2000 "Appraisal and assessment of world water resources." *Water International* 25(1):11–32. http://www.iwra.siu.edu/win/win90s.html#251.

Shine, Keith P. and Piers M. de F. Forster 1999 "The effect of human activity on radiative forcing of climate change: a review of recent developments." *Global and Planetary Change* 20:205–25.

Shute, Nancy, Thomas Hayden, Charles W. Petit, Rachel K. Sobel, Kevin Whitelaw and David Whitman 2001 "The Weather Turns Wild." *U.S. News and World Report*, February 5, 130(5):44–50.

Shuval, Hille "Israel: national water resources conservation planning and policies for rapid economic development and conditions of severe scarcity." In Lundqvist and Gleick 1997:37–9.

SID 1995 *Rapport om økologisk jordbrugsreform*. [Report on organic agricultural reform.] Copenhagen: Specialarbejderforbundet i Danmark.

Sigurdson, A. J., S. Chang, J. F. Annegers, C. M. Duphorne, P. C. Pillow, R. J. Amato, L. P. Hutchinson, A. M. Sweeney and S. S. Strom 1999 "A case-control study of diet and testicular carcinoma." *Nutrition and Cancer* 34(1):20–6.

Simberloff, D. 1992 "Do species-area curves predict extinction in fragmented forest?" In Whitmore and Sayer 1992:75–90.

Simon, Julian 1995a "Why do we hear prophecies of doom from every side?" *Futurist* 29(1):19–24.

(ed.) 1995b: *The State of Humanity*. Oxford: Blackwell.

1996 *The Ultimate Resource 2*. Princeton, NJ: Princeton University Press.

Simon, Julian and Rebecca Boggs 1995 "Trends in the quantities of education – USA and elsewhere." In Simon 1995b:208–23.

Simon, Julian L., G. Weinrauch and S. Moore 1994 "The reserves of extracted resources: historical data." *Non-Renewable Resources* 325–40. Text from http://www.inform.umd.edu/EdRes/Colleges/BMGT/.Faculty/JSimon/Articles/RESOURCE.txt.

Simon, Julian L. and Aaron Wildavsky 1995 "Species loss revisited." In Simon 1995b:346–62.

Simons Jn., S. Stoney 1996 "Environmental estrogens: can two 'alrights' make a wrong?" *Science* 272:1,451.

Simpson, David R. and Amy B. Craft 1996 *The Social Value of Using Biodiversity in New Pharmaceutical Product Research.* Discussion Paper 96–23. Washington, DC: Resources for the Future. http://www.rff.org/disc_papers/PDF_files/9633.pdf.

Simpson, David R. and Roger A. Sedjo 1996 *Valuation of Biodiversity for Use in New Product Research in a Model of Sequential Search.* Discussion Paper 96–27. Washington, DC: Resources for the Future. http://www.rff.org/disc_papers/PDF_files/9627.pdf.

Singer, Elanor and Phyllis Endreny 1993 *Reporting on Risk: How the Mass Media Portray Accidents, Diseases, Disasters, and Other Hazards.* New York: Russel Sage Foundation.

Singer, Peter 1977 *Animal Liberation.* New York: Avon Books.

Siwar, Chamhuri and Mohd. Yusof Kasim 1997 "Urban development and urban poverty in Malaysia." *International Journal of Social Economics* 24(12):1,524–35.

Skakkebæk, Niels E. 1997 "Mandlig infertilitet." [Male infertility.] *Ugeskrift for Læger* 159(25):3,922–3.

Skole, David and Compton Tucker 1993 "Tropical deforestation and habitat fragmentation in the Amazon: satellite data from 1978 to 1988." *Science* 260:1,905–10.

Skou Andersen, Michael and Michael W. Hansen 1991 *Vandmiljøplanen: fra symbol til handling.* [The water environment action plan – from symbol to action.] Herlev: Niche.

Slovic, P., B. Fischhoff and S. Lichtenstein 1979 "Weighing the risks." *Environment* 21:14–20, 36–9.

1986 "Informing the public about the risks from ionizing." In Arkes and Hammond 1986:114–26.

Slovik, P. 1987 "Perception of risk." *Science* 236:280–5.

Smil, Vaclav 1990 "Nitrogen and phosphorus." In Turner *et al.* 1990:423–36.

1997 "Global population and the nitrogen cycle." *Scientific American* 277(1):76–81.

1999 "Crop residues: agriculture's largest harvest." *BioScience* 49(4):299–308.

Smith, Daniel 1999a "Worldwide trends in DDT levels in human breast milk." *International Journal of Epidemiology* 28:179–88.

Smith, David H., Daniel C. Malone, Kenneth A. Lawson, Lynn J. Okamoto, Carmelina Battista and William B. Saunders 1997a "A national estimate of the economic costs of asthma." *American Journal of Respiratory and Critical Care Medicine* 156(3):787–93. http://ajrccm.atsjournals.org/cgi/content/full/156/3/787.

Smith, Douglas A., Keith Vodden, Leon Rucker and Rose Cunningham 1997b *Global Benefits and Costs of the Montreal Protocol on Substances that Deplete the Ozone Layer.* Report made for Environment Canada by ARC, Applied Research Consultants. http://www.ec.gc.ca/ozone/choices/index_e.html.

Smith, Eddie 1999b "Atlantic and East Coast hurricanes 1900–98: a frequency and intensity study for the twenty-first century." *Bulletin of the American Meteorological Society* 80(12):2,717–20. http://ams.allenpress.com/.

Smith, F. D. M, R. M. May, R. Pellew, T. H. Johnson and K. R. Walter 1993a "Estimating extinction rates." *Nature* 364:494–6.

Smith, Gar 2000 "W2K: the extreme weather era." *Earth Island Journal* 15(2):36–8.

Smith, Katherine Reich 1994 "Science and social advocacy: a dilemma for policy analysts." *Choices: The Magazine of Food, Farm and Resource Issues* 9(1):19–22.

Smith, Richard A. and Richard B. Alexander 2000 "Sources of nutrients in the nation's watersheds." US Geological Survey. Proceedings from the Natural Resource, Agriculture, and Engineering Service Conference *Managing Nutrients and Pathogens from Animal Agriculture*, 28–30 March 2000, Camp Hill, Pennsylvania. http://water.usgs.gov/nawqa/sparrow/nut_sources/nut_sources.htm.

Smith, Richard A., Richard B. Alexander and Kenneth J. Lanfear 1993b *Stream Water Quality in the Conterminous United States: Status and Trends of Selected Indicators During the 1980's.* US Geological Survey Water Supply Paper 2400. http://water.usgs.gov/nwsum/sal/index.html.

Smith, Tom W. 1979 "Happiness: Time Trends, Seasonal Variations, Intersurvey Differences, and Other Mysteries." *Social Psychology Quarterly* 42(1):18–30.

Socialdemokratiet 1996 *Socialdemokratiets*

arbejdsprogram 1996–2000. [The Social-Democratic Working Program 1996–2000.] http://www.socialdemokratiet.dk/main/om/arbejd.shtml.

Socolow, Robert H. 1999 "Nitrogen management and the future of food: lessons from the management of energy and carbon." *Proceedings of the National Academy of Science* 96:6,001–8. http://www.pnas.org.

SOLEC 1995 *State of the Great Lakes 1995*. State of the Lakes Ecosystem Conference. http://www.on.ec.gc.ca/glimr/data/sogl-final-report/.

1999 *State of the Great Lakes 1999*. State of the Lakes Ecosystem Conference. http://www.on.ec.gc.ca/glimr/data/state-of-the-lakes/99/.

Solenergiudvalget 1998 *Solenergi: Handlingsplan 1998–2000*. [Solar Energy: action plan 1998–2000.] Energistyrelsens Solenergi Udvalg, January 1998.

Solow, Robert M. 1986 "On the intergenerational allocation of natural resources." *Scandinavian Journal of Economics* 88:141–9.

Sonneveld, D. J., H. J. Hoekstra, W. T. Van der Graaf, W. J. Sluiter, H. Schraffordt Koops and D. T. Sleijfer 1999 "The changing distribution of stage in nonseminomatous testicular germ cell tumours, from 1977 to 1996." *BJU International* 84(1):68–74.

Sprecher, Susan and Kathleen McKinney 1993 *Sexuality*. London: Sage Publications.

Srivastava, A. and N. Kreiger 2000 "Relation of physical activity to risk of testicular cancer." *American Journal of Epidemiology* 151(1):78–87.

Statistics Denmark 1975a *Statistisk Årbog 1975*. [Statistical yearbook for Denmark.] Copenhagen: Statistics Denmark.

1975b *Statistisk Tiårsoversigt 1975*. Copenhagen: Statistics Denmark.

1985 *Statistisk Tiårsoversigt 1985*. Copenhagen: Statistics Denmark.

1992 *Statistisk Tiårsoversigt 1992*. Copenhagen: Statistics Denmark.

1995 *50–års Oversigten*. [Denmark through 50 years.] Copenhagen: Statistics Denmark.

1997a *Statistisk Årbog 1997*. Copenhagen: Statistics Denmark.

1997b *Statistisk Tiårsoversigt 1997*. Copenhagen: Statistics Denmark.

Steadman, David W. 1995 "Prehistoric extinctions of Pacific island birds: biodiversity meets zooarchaeology." *Science* 267:1,123–31.

Stedman, John R., Emma Linehan, Sarah Espenhahn, Beth Conlan, Tony Bush and Trevor Davies 1998 *Predicting PM_{10} concentrations in the UK*. AEAT 4630. A report produced for the Department of the Environment, Transport and the Regions. http://www.aeat.co.uk/netcen/airqual/reports/pm10rep/pconts.htm.

Stedman, John R., Emma Linehan and Katie King 1999 *Quantification of the Health Effects of Air Pollution in the UK for the Review of the National Air Quality Strategy*. A report produced for the Department of the Environment, Transport and the Regions. http://www.aeat.co.uk/netcen/airqual/reports/health/health.html.

Stiefel, Chana 1997 "Plastic's brand new spin." *Science World* 54(7):17–19.

Stiller, C. A. and P. J. Boyle 1996 "Effect of population mixing and socioeconomic status in England and Wales, 1979–85, on lymphoblastic leukaemia in children." *British Medical Journal* 313:1,297–1,300. http://www.bmj.com/cgi/content/full/313/7068/1297.

Stocks, Brian J. 1991 "The extent and impact of forest fires in northern circumpolar countries." In Levine 1991:197–202.

Stone, Lawrence 1979 *The Family, Sex and Marriage in England 1500–1800*. London: Penguin.

Stone, Mark and Kalpana Kochar 1998 *The East Asian Crisis: Macroeconomic Developments and Policy Lessons*. International Monetary Fund, Working Paper WP/98/128. http://www.imf.org/external/pubs/ft/wp/wp98128.pdf.

Stork, Nigel E. 1997 "Measuring global biodiversity and its decline." In Reaka-Kudla et al. 1997: 41:68

Storm, H. H., J. Pihl, E. Michelsen and A. L. Nielsen 1996 *Cancer Incidence in Denmark 1993*. Copenhagen: Kræftens Bekæmpelse.

Subak, S., J. P. Palutikof, M. D. Agnew, S. J. Watson, C. G. Bentham, M. G. R. Cannell, M. Hulme, S. McNally, J. E. Thornes, D. Waughray and J. C. Woods 2000 "The impact of the anomalous weather of 1995 on the U.K. economy." *Climatic Change* 44:1–26.

Summers, Robert and Alan Heston 1991 "The Penn World Table (Mark 5): an expanded set of international comparisons, 1950–1988." *The Quarterly Journal of Economics* 106(9):327–68.

1995 *Penn World Tables Version 5.6*. Downloadable at http://datacentre.chass.utoronto.ca/pwt/index.html.

Suominen, Jyrki and Matti Vierula 1993 "Semen quality of Finnish men." *British Medical Journal* 306:1,579.

Sutherland, Ronald J. 2000 "'No Cost' Efforts to Reduce Carbon Emissions in the U.S.: An Economic Perspective." *Energy Journal* 21(3):89–112.

Sutherland, S. E., V. B. Benard, J. E. Keil, H. Austin and D. G. Hoel 1996 "Pesticides and twenty year risk of breast cancer." 29th Annual Meeting of the Society for Epidemiological Research, Boston, MA, 12–15 June 1996. *American Journal of Epidemiology*, SER Abstracts 143(11):133.

Svensmark, Henrik and Eigil Friis-Christensen 1997 "Variation of cosmic ray flux and global cloud coverage – a missing link in solar–climate relationships." *Journal of Atmospheric and Solar-Terrestrial Physics* 59(11):1,225–32.

Svensson, Ola 1981 "Are we all less risky and more skillful than our fellow drivers?" *Acta Psychologica* 47:143–8.

Swan, Shanna H., Eric P. Elkin and Laura Fenster 1997 "Have sperm densities declined? A reanalysis of global trend data." *Environmental Health Perspectives* 105(11):1,228–32.

Swiss Re 1997 *Tropical cyclones*. Swiss Reinsurance Company. http://www.swissre.com.

1999 "Natural catastrophes and man-made disasters 1998: storms, hail and ice cause billion-dollar losses." *Sigma* 1/1999. Swiss Reinsurance Company. http://www.swissre.com/e/publications/publications/sigma1/sigma9901.html.

2000 "Natural catastrophes and man-made disasters 1999: storms and earthquakes lead to the second-highest losses in insurance history." *Sigma* 2/2000. Swiss Reinsurance Company. http://www.swissre.com/e/publications/publications/sigma1/sigma060300.html.

Tangcharoensathien, Viroj, Piya Harnvoravongchai, Siriwan Pitayarangsarit &Vijj Kasemsup 2000 "Health impacts of rapid economic changes in Thailand." *Social Science and Medicine* 51:789–807.

Tarone, Robert E., Kenneth C. Chu and Leslie A. Gaudette 1997 "Birth cohort and calendar period trends in breast cancer mortality in the United States and Canada." *Journal of the National Cancer Institute* 89:251–6.

Taylor, A. J. Newman 1998 "Asthma and allergy definitions and distinctions." *British Medical Journal* 316:997–9.

Taylor, David 1988 *Mastering Economic and Social History*. London: Macmillan.

Taylor, Dorceta E. 2000 "The rise of the environmental justice paradigm." *American Behavioral Scientist* 43(4):508–80.

Teknologirådet 1997 *Drikkevand – rent vand, men hvordan?* [Drinking water – clean water, but how?] The Danish Technology Assessment Council on Drinking Water. http://www.ing.dk/tekraad/udgiv/945/p97drik/p97drik.htm.

Tenenbaum, Dave 1995 "Beyond the green revolution." *World and I* 10(8):168–74.

Tengs, Tammy O. 1997 "Dying too soon: how cost-effectiveness analysis can save lives." *NCPA Policy Report* 204. http://www.public-policy.org/~ncpa/studies/s204/s204.html.

Tengs, Tammy O., Miriam E. Adams, Joseph S. Pliskin, Dana Gelb Safran, Joanna E. Siegel, Milton C. Weinstein and John D. Graham 1995 "Five-hundred life-saving interventions and their cost-effectiveness." *Risk Analysis* 15(3):369–90.

Tengs, Tammy O. and John D. Graham 1996 "The opportunity costs of haphazard social investments in life-saving." In Hahn 1996:167–82.

Tennant, David R. (ed.) 1997 *Food Chemical Risk Analysis*. London: Blackie Academic and Professional.

Tessmer, Joseph M. 1999 "Comparing international crash statistics." *Journal of Transportation and Statistics* 2(2):159–66. http://www.bts.gov/jts/V2N2/05tess.pdf.

Tett, S. F. B., P. A. Stott, M. R. Allen, W. J. Ingram and J. F. B. Mitchell 1999 "Causes of twentieth-century temperature change near the Earth's surface." *Nature* 399:569–72.

Thejll, Peter and Knud Lassen 2000 "Solar forcing of the Northern Hemisphere land air temperature: new data." *Journal of Atmospheric and Solar-Terrestrial Physics*, 62(13):1,207–13..

Thobani, Mateen 1995 *Tradable Property Rights to Water*. Finance and Private Sector Development Note 34. http://www.worldbank.org/html/fpd/notes/34/34summary.html.

Thomas, Randy 1991 "Eco war." *Earth Island Journal* 6(2):49.

Thorsen, Michael and Hans-Georg Møller 1995 *TV-*

journalistik. [TV Journalism.] Copenhagen: Forlaget Ajour.

Tietenberg, Tom 2000 *Environmental and Natural Resource Economics*. 5th edn. Reading, MA: Addison-Wesley.

Time 1997 *Our Precious Planet*. Special issue, supplement to *Time* Magazine, 27 October 1997.

Timmermann, A., J. Oberhuber, A. Bacher, M. Esch, M. Latif and E. Roeckner 1999 "Increased El Niño frequency in a climate model forced by future greenhouse warming." *Nature* 398:694–7.

Tobaksskadesrådet 1993 *Passiv rygning og overfølsomhed*. [Passive smoking and hypersensitivity.] http://www.tobaksskaderaadet.dk/fakta/overf.html.

Tol, Richard 1999 "Kyoto, efficiency, and cost-effectiveness: applications of FUND." *The Energy Journal*, Kyoto Special Issue:131–56.

Toman, Michael 1998 "Research frontiers in the economics of climate change." *Environmental and Resource Economics* 11(3–4):603–21.

Tong, Shilu, Peter A. Baghurst, Michael G. Sawyer, Jane Burns and Anthony J. McMichael 1998 "Declining blood lead levels and changes in cognitive function during childhood: the Port Pirie Cohort study." *Journal of the American Medical Association* 280(22):1,915–19.

Toppari, Jorma, John Chr. Larsen, Peter Christiansen, Aleksander Giwercman, Philippe Grandjean, Louis J. Guillette Jn., Bernard Jégou, Tina K. Jensen, Pierre Jouannet, Niels Keiding, Henrik Leffers, John A. McLachlan, Otto Meyer, Jørn Müller, Ewa Rajpert-De Meyts, Thomas Scheike, Richard Sharpe, John Sumpter and Niels E. Skakkebæk 1996 "Male reproductive health and environmental xenoestrogens" *Environmental Health Perspectives Supplements* 104, Supplement 4:741–803.

Torras, Mariano and James K. Boyce 1998 "Income, inequality, and pollution: a reassessment of the environmental Kuznets Curve." *Ecological Economics* 25:147–60.

Trefil, James 1995 "How the body defends itself from the risky business of living." *Smithsonian* 26(9):42–9.

Trewavas, Anthony 1999 "Much food, many problems." *Nature* 402(6,759):231–2.

Tsur, Yacov and Amos Zemel 2000 "Long-term perspective on the development of solar energy." *Solar Energy* 68(5):379–92.

Tulpule, Vivek, Stephen Brown, J. Lim, C. Polidano, H. Pant and B. Fisher 1999 "The Kyoto Protocol: an economic analysis using GTEM." *The Energy Journal*, Kyoto Special Issue:257–86.

Tummon, Is and David Mortimer 1992 "Decreasing quality of semen." *British Medical Journal* 305:1,228–9.

Turgeon, Donna and Andrew Robertson 1995 "Contaminants in coastal fish and mollusks." In NBS 1995:408–12.

Turner, B. L. and Karl W. Butzer 1992 "The Columbian encounter and land-use change." *Environment* 34(8):16–20, 37–44.

Turner, B. L. II, William C. Clark, Robert W. Kates, John F. Richards, Jessica T. Mathews and William B. Meyer 1990 *The Earth as Transformed by Human Action*. Cambridge: Cambridge University Press.

Turner, R. Kerry, David Pearce and Ian Bateman 1994 *Environmental Economics: An Elementary Introduction*. New York: Harvester/Wheatsheaf.

UCB 1999 *European Allergy White Paper*. Executive summary, http://theucbinstituteofallergy.ucb.be/WhitePaper/WhitePaper.htm.

UCS 1999 "Toxic Pollen Threatens Monarchs." Union of Concerned Scientists. http://www.ucsusa.org/Gene/may99.pollen.html

2001 "Risks of Genetic Engineering." Union of Concerned Scientists. http://www.ucsusa.org/food/gen.risks.html.

UK CPI 2000 *English Consumer Prices, 1264–1999*. Global Financial Data, download at http://www.globalfindata.com/freeinf.htm [no longer available].

2001: *English Consumer Prices, 1900–2000*. Global Financial Data, download at http://www.globalfindata.com/.

UK EA 2000 *State of the Environment*. http://www.environment-agency.gov.uk/state_of_enviro/index3+.html.

Ulfstrand, Staffan 1992 "Biodiversity – how to reduce its decline." *OIKOS* 63(1):3–5.

UNAIDS 1998 *AIDS in Africa*. http://www.unaids.org/publications/documents/epidemiology/determinants/saepap98.html.

1999 *AIDS Epidemic Update: December 1999*. Joint United Nations Programme on HIV/AIDS with World Health Organization. http://www.unaids.org/publications/documents/epidemiology/surveillance/wad1999/embaee.pdf (no longer available).

2000 *Report on the Global HIV/AIDS Epidemic.* http://www.unaids.org/epidemic_update/report/Epi_report.pdf.

Underwood, Barbara A. and Suttilak Smitasiri 1999 "Micronutrient malnutrition: policies and programs for control and their implications." *Annual Reviews Nutrition* 19:303–24.

UNDP 1995 *Human Development Report 1995.* UN Development Program. http://www.undp.org/hdro/95.htm.

1996a *Human Development Report 1996.* UN Development Program. http://www.undp.org/hdro/96.htm.

1996b *Russian Federation Human Development Report 1996.* UN Development Program. http://www.undp.ru/NHDR/summary_1996.htm.

1997 *Human Development Report 1997.* UN Development Program. http://www.undp.org/hdro/97.htm.

1998a *Analytical Tools for Human Development.* http://www.undp.org/hdro/anatools.htm.

1998b *Human Development Report 1999.* UN Development Program. New York: Oxford University Press.

1999a *Human Development Report 1999.* UN Development Program. http://www.undp.org/hdro/99.htm.

1999b *Russian Federation Human Development Report 1999.* UN Development Program. http://www.undp.ru/NHDR/summary_1999.htm.

2000 *Analytical Tools for Human Development.* UN Development Program. http://www.undp.org/hdro/anatools.htm.

2000b *Human Development Report 2000.* UN Development Program. http://www.undp.org/hdr2000/english/HDR2000.html.

UNECE 1996 *Long-Term Historical Changes in the Forest Resource.* United Nations Economic Commision for Europe and FAO, Timber Section, Geneva, Switzerland. Geneva Timber and Forest Study Papers 10, ECE/TIM/SP/10.

UNECE/EU 1996 *Forest Condition in Europa – Result of the 1995 Crown Condition Survey, 1996 Technical Report.* Prepared by Federal Research Centre for Forestry and Forest Products (BFH) for UN Economic Commision for Europe and the European Commision.

1997 *Forest Condition in Europa – Result of the 1996 Crown Condition Survey, 1997 Technical Report.* Prepared by Federal Research Centre for Forestry and Forest Products (BFH) for UN Economic Commision for Europe and the European Commision.

UNEP 1993 *Environmental Data Report 1993–94.* UN Environment Programme. Oxford: Blackwell.

1994 *UNEP Greenhouse Gas Abatement Costing Studies* vols. I–III. Roskilde: Forskningscenter Risø.

1995 *Global Biodiversity Assessment.* V. H. Heywood (ed.). United Nations Environment Programme. Cambridge: Cambridge University Press.

1997 *Global Environment Outlook 1: United Nations Environment Programme Global State of the Environment Report 1997.* http://www-cger.nies.go.jp/geo1/ch/toc.htm.

1999a *Wildland Fires and the Environment: A Global Synthesis.* By J. S. Levine, T. Bobbe, N. Ray, A. Singh, and R. G. Witt. UNEP/DEIAEW/TR.99-1. http://www.grid.unep.ch/fires/htm/wildland.html.

1999b *Synthesis of the Reports of the Scientific, Environmental Effects, and Technology and Economic Assessment Panels of the Montreal Protocol. A Decade of Assessments for Decision Makers Regarding the Protection of the Ozone Layer: 1988–1999.* United Nations Environment Programme, Ozone Secretariat. http://www.unep.org/ozone/pdf/Synthesis-Complete.pdf.

1999c *Production and Consumption of Ozone Depleting Substance, 1986–1998.* United Nations Environment Programme, Ozone Secretariat. http://www.unep.org/ozone/DataReport99.htm.

2000 *Global Environment Outlook 2000.* London: Earthscan Publications. http://www.grida.no/geo2000/english/index.htm.

UNEP and WHO 1992 *Urban Air Pollution in Megacities of the World.* Oxford: Blackwell.

UNESCO 1990 *Compendium of Statistics on Illiteracy – 1990 Edition.* Statistical Reports and Studies 31. Paris: United Nations Educational, Scientific and Cultural Organization, Office of Statistics.

1995 *Compendium of Statistics on Illiteracy – 1995 Edition.* Statistical Reports and Studies 35. Paris: United Nations Educational, Scientific and Cultural Organization, Office of Statistics.

1997 *Statistical Yearbook 1996.* Paris: UNESCO Publishing.

1998 *Gender-Sensitive Education Statistics and Indicators.* http://unescostat.unesco.org/en/pub/pub0.htm.

2000 *On-line Statistics*. Accessed in 2000. http://unescostat.unesco.org/en/stats/stats0.htm.

2001 *On-line Statistics*. Accessed in 2001. http://unescostat.unesco.org/en/stats/stats0.htm.

UNESCO Courier 1999 "What price water?" *UNESCO Courier*, February 1999, 52(2):17.

UNFPA 1996 *The State of World Population 1996: Changing Places: Population, Development and the Urban Future. New York: United Nations Population Fund.* http://www.unfpa.org/swp/1996/SWP96MN.htm.

1996 *The Progress of Nations 1996*. http://www.unicef.org/pon96/contents.htm.

1997 *The Progress of Nations 1997*. http://www.unicef.org/pon97/.

1998 *The State of the World's Children 1998*. http://www.unicef.org/sowc98/pdf.htm.

1999 *12 October 1999: The day of 6 billion*. http://web.unfpa.org/modules/6billion/index.htm.

2000 *The State of the World's Children 2000*. http://www.unicef.org/sowc00/.

UNPD 1998a *World Urbanization Prospects: The 1996 Revision*. United Nations Department of Economic and Social Affairs, Population Division. New York: United Nations Publications.

1998b *World Population Projections to 2150*. United Nations Department of Economic and Social Affairs, Population Division. New York: United Nations Publications. http://www.undp.org/popin/wdtrends/execsum.htm.

1998c *Historic World Population Figures*. United Nations Department of Economic and Social Affairs, Population Division. Gopher://gopher.undp.org/00/ungophers/popin/wdtrends/histor. [No longer available]

1999a *World Population Prospects: The 1998 Revision. Volume I: Comprehensive Tables; Volume II: Sex and Age*. United Nations Department of Economic and Social Affairs, Population Division. New York: United Nations Publications.

1999b *World Urbanization Prospects: The 1999 Revision*. Key findings. http://www.undp.org/popin/wdtrends/urbanization.pdf.

2001a *World Population Prospects: The 2000 Revision. Key findings*. http://www.un.org/esa/population/wpp2000h.pdf.

2001b *World Population Prospects: The 2000 Revision. Annex Tables*. http://www.un.org/esa/population/wpp2000at.pdf.

2001c *World Population Prospects: The 2000 Revision. Additional Data*. http://www.un.org/esa/population/wpp2000at.xls.

Unsworth, Edwin 2000 "Global warming risk rising, speaker says." *Business Insurance* 34(8):39.

US Senate 1997 "A resolution expressing the sense of the Senate regarding the conditions for the United States becoming a signatory to any international agreement on greenhouse gas emissions under the United Nations Framework Convention on Climate Change." 105th Congress, 1st Session, S. RES. 98. http://thomas.loc.gov/cgi-bin/bdquery/z?d105:s.res.00098:.

US State Department 1998a *1997 Country Reports: Brazil*. http://www.state.gov/www/issues/economic/trade_reports/latin_america97/brazil97.html.

1998b *1997 Country Reports: Mexico*. http://www.state.gov/www/issues/economic/trade_reports/latin_america97/mexico97.html.

1998c *1997 Country Reports: Russia*. http://www.state.gov/www/issues/economic/trade_reports/russia_nis97/russia97.html.

2000a *1999 Country Reports: Brazil*. http://www.state.gov/www/issues/economic/trade_reports/1999/brazil.pdf.

2000b *1999 Country Reports: Mexico*. http://www.state.gov/www/issues/economic/trade_reports/1999/mexico.pdf.

2000c *1999 Country Reports: Russia*. http://www.state.gov/www/issues/economic/trade_reports/1999/russia.pdf.

USBC 1975 *Historical Statistics of the United States: Colonial Times to 1970*. Bicentennial edition, two volumes. Washington, DC: US Government Printing Office.

1996 *World Population Profile: 1996*. US Bureau of the Census, Report WP/96 by Thomas M. McDevitt. Washington, DC: US Government Printing Office. http://www.census.gov/ipc/www/wp96.html.

1997 *Statistical Abstract of the United States 1997*. US Bureau of the Census. http://www.census.gov/prod/www/statistical-abstract-us.html.

1998 *World Population Profile: 1998*. US Bureau of the Census, Report WP/98 by Thomas M. McDevitt. Washington, DC: US Government Printing Office. http://www.census.gov/ipc/www/wp98.html.

1998b *USA Counties 1998*. US Bureau of the Census Database. http://tier2.census.gov/usac/index.html-ssi.

1999a *Statistical Abstract of the United States 1999*. US Bureau of the Census. http://www.census.gov/prod/www/statistical-abstract-us.html.

1999b *Money Income in the United States: 1998*. US Bureau of the Census, Current Population Reports, P60–206. Washington, DC: US Government Printing Office. http://www.census.gov/prod/99pubs/p60–206.pdf.

1999c *US Historical National Population Estimates: July 1, 1900 to July 1, 1998*. http://www.census.gov/population/estimates/nation/popclockest.txt.

1999d *State and Local Government Finance Estimates, by State*. http://www.census.gov/govs/www/estimate.html.

2000a *International Data Base*. Accessed in 2000. US Bureau of the Census. http://www.census.gov/ipc/www/idbnew.html.

2000b *Household and Housing Estimates*. http://www.census.gov/population/www/estimates/housing.html.

2000c *National Population Projections*. http://www.census.gov/population/www/projections/natsum-T1.html.

2000d *US Historical National Population Estimates: July 1, 1900 to July 1, 1999*. http://www.census.gov/population/estimates/nation/popclockest.txt.

2001a *International Data Base*. Accessed in 2001. US Bureau of the Census. http://www.census.gov/ipc/www/idbnew.html.

2001b *Statistical Abstract of the United States 2000*. US Bureau of the Census. http://www.census.gov/prod/www/statistical-abstract-us.html.

USCG 1999 *Pollution Incidents in and around US Waters: A Spill/Release Compendium: 1969–1998*. Commandant (G-MOA), Office of Investigations and Analysis, US Coast Guard, Department of Transportation. http://www.uscg.mil/hq/g%2Dm/nmc/response/stats/aa.htm.

USDA 1998 United States Agricultural Department: Production database from March 1998. http://usda.mannlib.cornell.edu/data-sets/international/91017/.

2000a United States Agricultural Department: Production database from March 2000. http://usda.mannlib.cornell.edu/data-sets/international/93002.

2000b *USDA Agricultural Baseline Projections to 2009*. US Department of Agriculture. WAOB-2000–1. Report and data, http://usda.mannlib.cornell.edu/data-sets/baseline/2000/.

2001a United States Agricultural Department: Production database from February 2001. http://usda.mannlib.cornell.edu/data-sets/international/93002.

2001b *Crop Production 2000 Summary*. Agricultural Statistics Board. http://usda.mannlib.cornell.edu/reports/nassr/field/pcp-bban/cropan01.pdf.

USGS 1997a *Changing Perceptions of World Oil and Gas Resources as Shown by Recent USGS Petroleum Assessments*. USGS Fact Sheet FS-145–97. http://greenwood.cr.usgs.gov/pub/fact-sheets/fs-0145–97/fs-0145–97.html.

1997b *Describing Petroleum Reservoirs of the Future*. USGS Fact Sheet FS-020–97. http://energy.usgs.gov/factsheets/Petroleum/reservoir.html.

1997c *Radioactive Elements in Coal and Fly Ash: Abundance, Forms, and Environmental Significance*. USGS Fact Sheet FS-163–97. http://energy.cr.usgs.gov:8080/energy/factshts/163–97/FS-163–97.pdf.

1997d *Coalbed Methane – An Untapped Energy Resource and an Environmental Concern*. USGS Fact Sheet FS-019–97. http://energy.usgs.gov/factsheets/Coalbed/coalmeth.html.

1998a *Database*. 93 minerals, US Geological Survey (accessed 1998).

1998b *Estimated Use of Water in the United States in 1995*. Edited by Wayne B. Solley, Robert R. Pierce and Howard A. Perlman. US Geological Survey Circular 1200. http://water.usgs.gov/watuse/pdf1995/html.

1999 *The Quality of Our Nation's Waters – Nutrients and Pesticides*. US Geological Survey Circular 1,225. Denver, CO: US Geological Survey. http://water.usgs.gov/pubs/circ/circ1225/pdf/index.html.

2000a *Database*. 93 minerals, US Geological Survey, accessed in 2000. http://minerals.er.usgs.gov/minerals.

2000b *USGS World Petroleum Assessment 2000*. http://greenwood.cr.usgs.gov/energy/WorldEnergy/DDS-60/. Download US Geological Survey Fact Sheet 0070–00. http://greenwood.

cr.usgs.gov/pub/fact-sheets/fs-0070-00/ fs-0070-00.pdf., and http://energy.cr.usgs.gov/ energy/WorldEnergy/weptotal.htm.

2001a *Database*. 93 minerals, US Geological Survey, accessed in 2001. http://minerals.er. usgs.gov/minerals.

Van Dobben, H. F. 1995 "Evalution, integration." In Heij and Erisman 1995:293–303.

van Driessche, Edilbert and Thorkild C. Bøg-Hansen 1999: "Memorandum Published On 12 February 1999." http://plab.ku.dk/tcbh/ Pusztaimemorandum.htm.

van Lynden, G. W. J. and L. R. Oldeman 1997 *The Assessment of the Status of Human-Induced Soil Degradation in South and Southeast Asia*. International Soil Reference and Information Centre. http://www.isric.nl/ASSOD.htm.

Van Waeleghem, K., N. De Clercq, L. Vermeulen, F. Schoonjans and F. Comhaire 1996 "Deterioration of sperm quality in young healthy Belgian men." *Human Reproduction* 11:325–9.

Veer, Pieter van't, Irene E. Lobbezoo, José M. Martín-Moreno, Eliseo Guallar, Jorge Gómez-Aracena, Frans J. Kok, Alwine F. M. Kardinaal, Lenore Kohlmeier, Blaise C. Martin, John J. Strain, Michael Thamm, Piet van Zoonen, Bert A. Baumann and Jussi K. Huttunen 1997 "DDT (dicophane) and postmenopausal breast cancer in Europe: case-control study." *British Medical Journal* 315:81–5.

Velie, Ellen, Martin Kulldorff, Catherine Schairer, Gladys Block, Demetrius Albanes and Arthur Schatzkin 2000 "Dietary fat, fat subtypes, and breast cancer in postmenopausal women: a prospective cohort study." *Journal of the National Cancer Institute* 92(10):833–9.

Ventura, Stephanie J., Robert N. Anderson, Joyce A. Martin and Betty L. Smith 1998 *Births and Deaths: Preliminary Data for 1997*. National Vital Statistics Reports 47:4. http://www.cdc.gov/ nchs/data/nvsr47_4.pdf.

Ventura, Stephanie J., Joyce A. Martin, Sally C. Curtin, T. J. Mathews and Melissa M. Park 2000 *Births: Final Data for 1998*. National Vital Statistics Reports 48:3. http://www.cdc.gov/ nchs/data/nvs48_3.pdf.

Verheij, Robert A. 1996 "Explaining urban–rural variations in health: a review of interactions between individual and environment." *Social Science and Medicine* 42(6):923–35.

Vernon, Sally W. 1999 "Risk perception and risk communication for cancer screening behaviors: a review." *Journal of the National Cancer Institute*, Special Issue 25:101–19.

Viby Mogensen, Gunnar 1990 *Time and Consumption: Time Use and Consumption in Denmark in Recent Decades*. Copenhagen: Statistics Denmark.

Victor, David G. and Jesse H. Ausubel 2000 "Restoring the Forests." *Foreign Affairs* 79(6):127–34.

Viel, Jean-François Bruno Challier *et al.* 1998 "Brain cancer mortality among French farmers: the vineyard pesticide hypothesis." *Archives of Environmental Health* 53(1):65–70.

Vitousek, Peter M., John Aber, Robert W. Howarth, Gene E. Likens, Pamela A. Matson, David W. Schindler, William H. Schlesinger and G. David Tilman 1997 "Human alteration of the global nitrogen cycle: causes and consequences." *Issues in Ecology* 1: 3–16. http://www.sdsc.edu/ ~ESA/issues.htm.

Vitousek, Peter M., Paul R. Ehrlich, Anne H. Ehrlich and Pamela A. Matson 1986 "Human appropriation of the products of photosynthesis" *BioScience* 36(6):368–73. http://www.dieoff.org/page83.htm.

Vitousek, Peter M. and Harold A. Mooney 1997 "Human domination of Earth's ecosystems." *Science* 277:494–9.

Vonier, Peter M. D., Andrew Crain, John, A. McLachlan, Louis J. Guillette Jn. and Steven F. Arnold 1996 "Interactions of environmental chemicals with the estrogen and progesterone perceptors from the oviduct of the american alligator." *Environmental Health Perspectives* 104:1,318–22.

Vrijheid, Martine 2000 "Health effects of residence near hazardous waste landfill sites: a review of epidemiologic literature." *Environmental Health Perspectives Supplements* 108(1):101–12.

Walker, Jesse 1998 "Slick characters." *Reason* 29(11):65–8.

Wallensteen, P. and A. Swain 1997 "International freshwater resources: sources of conflicts or cooperation." Background document for CSD 1997. Stockholm: Stockholm Environment Institute.

Walsh, B. Timothy and Michael J. Devlin 1998 "Eating disorders: progress and problems." *Science* 280:1,387–90.

Walsh, James 1996 *True Odds: How Risk Affects Your*

Everyday Life. Santa Monica, CA: Merrit Publishing.

Walter, Dave (ed.) 1992 *Today Then: America's Best Minds Look 100 Years into the Future on the Occasion of the 1893 World's Columbian Exposition*. Helena, MT: American and World Geographic Publishing.

Walter, K. S. and H. J. Gillett (eds.) 1998 *1997 IUCN Red List of Threatened Plants*. Compiled by the World Conservation Monitoring Centre. Gland, Switzerland: IUCN – The World Conservation Union. Searchable database at http://www.wcmc.org.uk/species/plants/plants-by-taxon.htm.

Watson, Rory 1997 "Europe urged to tackle rise in allergies." *British Medical Journal* Vol 314:1,641. http://www.bmj.com/cgi/content/full/314/7095/1641/f.

Wark, Penny 2001 "How to foil the cuddly killer." *The Times*, February 1 2001, http://www.thetimes.co.uk/article/0,,7-76804,00.html.

WCED 1987 *Our Common Future*. ("The Brundtland report.") The World Commission on Environment and Development for the General Assembly of the United Nations. Oxford: Oxford University Press.

WCMC 1998 *Forest Information Service*. World Conservation Monitoring Centre's forest database at http://www.wcmc.org.uk/forest/data/.

WCRF 1997 *Food, Nutrition and the Prevention of Cancer: A Global Perspective*. World Cancer Research Fund and American Institute for Cancer Research. Washington, DC: American Institute for Cancer Research.

Weale, Albert 1992 *The New Politics of Pollution*. Manchester: Manchester University Press.

Weaver, Andrew J. and Francis W. Zwiers 2000 "Uncertainty in climate change." *Nature* 407:6804):571–2.

WEC 1998 "A keynote address to the 30st Conference of the Japan Atomic Industrial Forum, Inc." by Michael Jefferson. *Global Warming and Global Energy after Kyoto*. http://www.wec.co.uk/documents/toyko2.htm (no longer available).

2000 *Survey of Energy Resources 1998*. http://www.worldenergy.org/wec-geis/publications/open.plx?file=default/current_ser.htm.

WEF 2001a *2001 Environmental Sustainability Index*. World Economic Forum, Yale Center for Environmental Law and Policy, Yale University and Center for International Earth Science Information Network, Columbia University. http://www.ciesin.org/indicators/ESI/ESI_01_tot.pdf.

2001b *2001 Environmental Sustainability Index, Data*. World Economic Forum, Yale Center for Environmental Law and Policy, Yale University and Center for International Earth Science Information Network, Columbia University. http://alpha.ciesin/indicators/ESI/esi.xls.

Weinstein, Niel D. 1980 "Unrealistic optimism about future life events." *Journal of Personality and Social Psychology* 39(5):806–20.

Weiss, Dominik, William Shotyk and Oliver Kempf 1999 "Archives of atmospheric lead pollution." *Naturwissenschaften* 86:262–75.

Weiss, K. B., P. J. Gergen and T. A. Hodgson 1992 "An economic evaluation of asthma in the United States." *New England Journal of Medicine* 326(13):862–6.

Wells, Lisa E. and Jay S. Noller 1997 "Determining the early history of El Niño." *Science* 276:966.

Wentz, Frank J. and Matthias Schabel 1998 "Effects of orbital decay on satellite-derived lower-tropospheric temperature trends." *Nature* 394:661–4.

Werner, Alex (ed.) 1998 *London Bodies: The Changing Shape of Londoners from Prehistoric Times to The Present Day*. London: Museum of London.

Wernick, Iddo K., Robert Herman, Shekhar Govind and Jesse H. Ausubel 1996 "Materialization and dematerialization: measures and trends." *Daedalus* 125(3):171–98. http://phe.rockefeller.edu/Daedalus/Demat/.

Western, David and Mary C. Pearl (eds.) 1989 *Conservation for the Twenty-First Century*. New York: Oxford University Press.

Westoff, Charles F. 1974 "Coital frequency and contraception." *Family Planning Perspectives* 6(3):136–41.

Weyant, John P. 1993 "Costs of reducing global carbon emissions." *Journal of Economic Perspectives* 7(4):27–46. http://sedac.ciesin.org/mva/EMF/JW1993.html.

Weyant, John P. and Jennifer N. Hill 1999 "Introduction and overview." *The Energy Journal*, Kyoto Special Issue:vii–xliv.

WFS 1996 *World Food Summit: Technical Background Documents*, vols. I–XV. http://www.fao.org/wfs/final/e/list-e.htm.

White, Andrew, Melvin G. R. Cannell and Andrew D. Friend 1999 "Climate change impacts on ecosystems and the terrestrial carbon sink: a new assessment." *Global Environmental Change* 9:S21–30.

Whitmore, T. C. and J. A. Sayer 1992 *Tropical Deforestation and Species Extinction*. London: Chapman and Hall.

WHO 1986 *The International Drinking Water Supply and Sanitation Decade: Review of Regional And Global Data (as at 31 December 1983)*. Geneva: World Health Organization.

1992 *Global Health Situation and Projections Estimates*. http://www.who.ch/whosis/globest/globest.htm (no longer available).

1997 *Health and Environment in Sustainable Development: Five Years after the Earth Summit. Executive Summary*. Programmes on Health and Environment. World Health Organization. Geneva: World Health Organization. http://www.who.int/environmental_information/Information_resources/htmdocs/execsum.htm.

1998 *The World Health Report 1998: Life in the 21st Century – A Vision for All*. Executive summary. Geneva: World Health Organization. http://www.who.int/whr/1998/exsum98e.htm.

1999a "Malaria, 1982–1997." *Weekly Epidemiological Record* 74:265–71. http://www.who.int/wer.

1999b *The World Health Report 1999: Making a Difference*. Geneva: World Health Organization. http://www.who.int/whr/1999/.

2000a *Air Quality Guidelines*. Geneva: World Health Organization. http://www.who.int/peh/air/Airqualitygd.htm.

2000b *The World Health Report 2000 Health Systems: Improving Performance*. Geneva: World Health Organization. http://www.who.int/whr/2000/index.htm.

2000c *Malnutrition – The Global Picture*. http://www.who.int/nut/malnutrition_worldwide.htm.

2000d *World Health Organization Databank*. http://www-dep.iarc.fr/cgi-bin/cgisql/who.idc.

WI 1984 Worldwatch Institute, Lester Brown *et al.* (eds.), *State of the World 1984*. New York: W. W. Norton.

1991 Worldwatch Institute, Lester Brown *et al.* (eds.), *State of the World 1991*. New York: W. W. Norton.

1993 Worldwatch Institute, Lester Brown *et al.* (eds.), *State of the World 1993*. New York: W. W. Norton.

1994 Worldwatch Institute, Lester Brown *et al.* (eds.), *State of the World 1994*. New York: W. W. Norton.

1995 Worldwatch Institute, Lester Brown *et al.* (eds.), *State of the World 1995*. New York: W. W. Norton.

1997a Worldwatch Institute, Lester Brown *et al.* (eds.), *State of the World 1997*. New York: W. W. Norton.

1997b Worldwatch Institute, Lester Brown *et al.* (eds.), *Vital Signs 1997*. New York: W. W. Norton.

1998a Worldwatch Institute, Lester Brown *et al.* (eds.), *State of the World 1998*. New York: W. W. Norton.

1998b Worldwatch Institute, Lester Brown *et al.* (eds.), *Vital Signs 1998*. New York: W. W. Norton.

1998c Worldwatch Institute. Electronic database.

1998d *Report Calls for Rapid Scaling Up of Efforts to Preserve Health of Forests and Provide Economic Benefits*. Press release, Saturday, 4 April 1998; http://www.worldwatch.org/alerts/pr980402.html.

1999a Worldwatch Institute, Lester Brown *et al.* (eds.): *State of the World 1999*. New York: W. W. Norton.

1999b Worldwatch Institute, Lester Brown *et al.* (eds.): *Vital Signs 1999*. New York: W. W. Norton.

1999c Worldwatch Institute. Electronic database.

2000a Worldwatch Institute, Lester Brown *et al.* (eds.): *State of the World 2000*. New York: W. W. Norton.

2000b Worldwatch Institute, Lester Brown *et al.* (eds.): *Vital Signs 2000*. New York: W. W. Norton.

2000c Worldwatch Institute. Electronic database.

2001a Worldwatch Institute, Lester Brown *et al.* (eds.): *State of the World 2001*. New York: W. W. Norton.

Wiens, John A. 1996 "Oil, seabinds, and science: the effect of the Exxon Valdez oil spill." *BioScience* 46(8):587–97.

Wiese, S. B. O., W. C. L. MacLeod and J. N. Lester 1997 "A recent history of metal accumulation in the sediments of the Thames Estuary,

United Kingdom." *Oceanographic Literature Review* 44(12):1558.

Wigley, T. M. L. 1998 "The Kyoto Protocol: CO_2, CH_4 and climate implications." *Geophysical Research Letters* 25(13):2,285–8.

Wigley, T. M. L., P. D. Jones and S. C. B. Raper 1997 "The observed global warming record: what does it tell us?" *Proceedings of the National Academy of Sciences* 94:8,314–20. http://www.pnap.org.

Willett, Walter C. 1995 "Diet, nutrition, and avoidable cancer." *Environmental Health Perspectives Supplements* 103(8):165–70.

Williams, Michael 1990 "Forests." In Turner *et al.* 1990:179–201.

1994 "Forests and tree cover." In Meyer and Turner II 1994:97–124.

Williams, Michael R., Thomas R. Fisher and John M. Melack 1997 "Solute dynamics in soil water and groundwater in a central Amazon catchment undergoing deforestation." *Biogeochemistry* 38(3):303–35.

Wilson, Edward O. 1992 *The Diversity of Life*. London: Allen Lane.

Wilson, Edward O. and Frances M. Peter (eds.) 1988 *Biodiversity*. Washington, DC: National Academy Press.

Wilson, James D. 1996 *Thresholds for Carcinogens: A Review of the Relevant Science and Its Implications for Regulatory Policy*. Discussion Paper 96–21. Washington, DC: Resources for the Future.

Wilson, Richard 1979 "Analyzing the daily risks of life." *Technology Review* 81(1):41–6.

Wilson, Richard C. 1997 "Total solar irradiance trend during solar cycles 21 and 22." *Science* 277:1,963–5.

Windpower Note 1997 *The Energy Balance of Modern Wind Turbines*. Danish Wind Turbine Manufactures Association, 5th December 1997. http://www.windpower.dk/publ/enbal.pdf.

1998a *Danish Wind Energy 4th Quarter 1997*. Danish Wind Turbine Manufactures Association, 5th February 1998. http://www.windpower.dk/publ/stat9704.pdf.

1998b *Total Installation of Danish Wind Turbines Worldwide 1980–1998*. Danish Wind Turbine Manufactures Association. http://www.windpower.dk/stat/tab11.htm.

Wingo, Phyllis A., Lynn A. G. Ries, Gary A. Giovino, Daniel S. Miller, Harry M. Rosenberg, Donald R. Shopland, Michael J. Thun and Brenda K. Edwards 1999 "Annual report to the nation on the status of cancer, 1973–1996, with a special section on lung cancer and tobacco smoking." *Journal of the National Cancer Institute* 91(8):675–90. http://jnci.oupjournals.org/cgi/reprint/91/8/675.pdf.

Wirl, Franz 2000 "Lessons from Utility Conservation Programs." *Energy Journal* 21(1):87–108.

WMO/UNEP 1994 *Scientific Assessment of Ozone Depletion: 1994 Executive Summary*. World Meteorological Organization Global Ozone Research and Monitoring Project, Report No. 37. United Nations Environment Programme, World Meterological Organization, National Oceanic and Atmospheric Administration, National Aeronautics and Space Administration. http://www.al.noaa.gov/WWWHD/pubdocs/assessment94.html.

1998 *Scientific Assessment of Ozone Depletion: 1998 Executive Summary*. World Meteorological Organization, National Oceanic and Atmospheric Administration, National Aeronautics and Space Administration, United Nations Environment Programme, European Commission. Global Ozone Research and Monitoring Project, Report No. 44. Download at http://www.unep.org/ozone/reports2.htm or http://www.al.noaa.gov/WWWHD/pubdocs/assessment98.html.

WMO/UNESCO 2000 *The World's Water: Is There Enough?* World Meteorological Organization/United Nations Educational, Scientific and Cultural Organization. http://www.unesco.org/science/waterday2000/Brochure.htm.

Wolf, Aaron T. 199. "'Water wars' and water reality." In Steve Lonergan (ed.), *Environmental Change, Adaptation, and Human Security*. Dordrecht: Kluwer Academic, pp. 251–65.

Wolff, Mary S., Paolo G. Toniolo, Eric W. Lee, Marilyn Rivera and Neil Dubin 1993 "Blood levels of organochlorine residues and risk of breast cancer." *Journal of the International Cancer Institute* 85(8):648–52.

Wolfson, Lois and Frank M. D'Itri 1993 *Nitrate – A Drinking Water Concern*. Michigan State University, Institute of Water Research, Extension Bulletin WQ-19. http://www.gem.msu.edu/pubs/msue/wq19p1.html.

Woodard, Colin 1998a "Lessons from 'the Year the Earth Caught Fire'." *Christian Science Monitor*, 4 February 1998. http://www.csmonitor.com/durable/1998/02/04/us/us.4.html.

1998b "Glacial ice is slip-sliding away." *Christian Science Monitor*, 12 October 1998, 91(11):11.

Woodcock, Ashley and Adnan Custovic 1998 "Avoiding exposure to indoor allergens." *British Medical Journal* 316:1,075–8. http://www.bmj.com/cgi/content/full/316/7137/1075.

Woods, Richard G. (ed.) 1981 *Future Dimensions of World Food and Population*. Boulder, CO: Westview Press.

World Bank 1992 *World Development Report 1992 Development and the Environment*. Oxford: Oxford University Press.

1993 *World Development Report 1994: Investing in Health*. Oxford: Oxford University Press.

1994 *World Development Report 1994: Infrastructure for Development*. Oxford: Oxford University Press.

1995a *Trends in Developing Economies 1995*. http://www.ciesin.org/IC/wbank/tde-home.html.

1995b "Press release: earth faces water crisis: worldwide, 40 percent suffer chronic water shortages." Press release of Serageldin 1995.

1996 *Poverty Reduction and the World Bank: Progress and Challenges in the 1990*. Washington, DC: World Bank. Executive Summary.

1997a *World Development Report 1997: The State in a Changing World*. Selected World Development Indicators 1997.

1997b *Monitoring Environmental Progress*; http://www-esd.worldbank.org/html/esd/env/publicat/mep/meptoc.htm (no longer available).

1997c *Annual Report 1997*. http://www.worldbank.org/html/extpb/annrep97/index.htm.

1997d *At China's Table*. Washington, DC: World Bank.

1998a *Poverty Reduction and the World Bank: Progress in Fiscal 1996 and 1997*. http://www.worldbank.org/html/extdr/pov_red/default.htm.

1998b *World Development Indicators 1998*. Selected World Development Indicators 1998. Tables from http://www.worldbank.org/data/archive/wdi/wdi.htm.

1999a *World Development Indicators 1999*. Much of the publication is available at http://www.worldbank.org/data/wdi/home.html.

1999b *World Development Indicators CDROM 1999*.

1999c *Poverty Trends and Voices of the Poor*. http://www.worldbank.org/poverty/data/trends/trends.pdf.

1999d *Annual Report 1999*. http://www.worldbank.org/html/extpb/annrep/content.htm.

1999e *Global Economic Prospects and the Developing Countries: Beyond Financial Crisis*. Washington, DC: World Bank. http://www.worldbank.org/prospects/gep98-99/full.htm.

2000a *World Development Report 1999/2000: Entering the 21st Century*. New York: Oxford University Press. Available at http://www.worldbank.org/wdr/2000/fullreport.html.

2000b *Global Economic Prospects and the Developing Countries*. Washington, DC: World Bank. http://www.worldbank.org/prospects/gep2000/full.htm.

2000c *The 2000 World Development Indicators CDROM*. Some data available at http://sima-ext.worldbank.org/data-query.

2000d *The 2000 World Development Indicators*. Washington, DC: World Bank.

2000e *Global Development Finance 2000. Volume I, Analysis and Summary Tables; Volume II, Country Tables*. Washington, DC: World Bank. http://www.worldbank.org/prospects/gdf2000/.

2000f *Annual Report 2000*. http://www.worldbank.org/html/extpb/annrep/down.htm.

2001a *World Development Report 2000/2001: Attacking Poverty*. Washington, DC: World Bank. http://www.worldbank.org/poverty/wdrpoverty/report/index.htm.

World Water Council 2000 *World Water Vision: Making Water Everybody's Business*. Edited by William J. Cosgrove and Frank R. Rijsberman. London: Earthscan Publications. http://www.watervision.org/clients/wv/water.nsf/dc13a18fccc63f4ac1256767003cc50b/cce1f838f03d073dc125688c0063870f?OpenDocument.

WRI 1996a *World Resources 1996–97*. In collaboration with UNEP, UNDP and the World Bank. New York: Oxford University Press. http://www.wri.org/wri/wr-96-97.

1996b *World Resources 1996–97 Database Diskettes*.

1998a *World Resources 1998–99: A Guide to the Global*

Environment. In collaboration with UNEP, UNDP and the World Bank. New York: Oxford University Press. Data tables can be found at http://www.wri.org/facts/data-tables.html.

1998b *World Resources 1998–99 Database CD-ROM*.

2000a *Deforestation: The Global Assault Continues*. http://www.wri.org/wri/trends/deforest.html.

2000b *The Problem of Forest Loss*. http://www.wri.org/wri/biodiv/intl-ii.html.

2000c *World Resources 2000–2001: People and Ecosystems: The Fraying Web of Life*. In collaboration with UNEP, UNDP and the World Bank. New York: Oxford University Press.

2000d *World Resources 2000–2001 Database CD-ROM*.

Wright, Albert M. 1997 *Toward a Strategic Sanitation Approach: Improving the Sustainability of Urban Sanitation in Developing Countries*. UNDP-World Bank, Water and Sanitation Program. http://www.wsp.org/English/urban-ssa.html

Wrigley, E. A. and R. S. Schofield 1981 *The Population History of England 1541–1871: A reconstruction*. London: Edward Arnold.

WTO 2000 *International trade statistics 2000*. World Trade Organization. http://www.wto.org/english/res_e/statis_e/statis_e.htm.

WWF 1997a *Global Annual Forest Report 1997*. http://www.panda.org/resources/publications/forest/report97/index.htm.

1997b *The Year the World Caught Fire*. By Nigel Dudley, WWF International, Discussion paper, December 1997.

1997c *Eleventh Hour for World's Forests*. Press release, 26 February 1997. http://www.wwf-uk.org/news/news10.htm.

1997d *1997: The Year the World Caught Fire*. Press release, 16 December 1997. http://www.panda.org/forests4life/news/161297_yearfire.cfm.

1997e *Two-Thirds of The World's Forests Lost Forever*. http://www.panda.org/forests4life/news/081097_lostfor.cfm.

1998a *Living Planet Report 1998: Overconsumption is Driving the Rapid Decline of the World's Natural Environments*. Gland: WWF International. http://www.panda.org/livingplanet/lpr/index.htm.

1998b *Protected Forest Area Triples in Brazil's Amazon; Decree Signed by Brazilian President*. Press release, 29 April 1998. http://www.panda.org/forests4life/news/290498_brazprot.cfm.

1998c *The Year the World Caught Fire*. Featured story. http://www.panda.org/news/features/01–98/story3.htm.

1998d *Living Planet Report 1998*. Gland: WWF International. http://panda.org/livingplanet/lpr/index.htm.

1999 *Living Planet Report 1999*. Gland: WWF International. http://www.panda.org/livingplanet/lpr99/.

WWF/IUCN 1996 *Forests for Life*. Gland: WWF International.

Wynder, Enst L. and Gio B. Gori 1977 "Contribution of the environment to cancer incidence: an epidemiologic exercise." *Journal of the National Cancer Institute* 58(4):825–32.

Yang, C.-Y., H.-F. Chiu, J.-F. Chiu, M.-F. Cheng and W.-Y. Kao 1997 "Gastric cancer mortality and drinking water qualities in Taiwan." *Archives of Environmental Contamination and Toxicology* 33:336–40.

Yemaneberhan, Haile and Zegaye Bekele 1997 "Prevalence of wheeze and asthma and relation to Atopy in Urban and Rural Ethiopia." *The Lancet* 350:85–9.

Yohe, Gary and James Neuman 1997 "Planning for sea level rise and shore protection under climate uncertainty." *Climatic Change* 37:243–70.

Yonas, Gerold 1998 "Fusion and the Z pinch." *Scientific American* 279(2):40–5.

Yoon, Carol Kaesuk 1999 "Altered Corn May Imperil Butterfly, Researchers Say." *New York Times*, 05/20/99, 148 (51,528):A1. Text at http://www.connectotel.com/gmfood/ny200599.txt

Zeckhauser, Richard J. and W. Kip Viscusi 1990 "Risk within reason." *Science* 248:559–64.

Zeidler, Ryszard B. 1997 "Climate Change Vulnerability and Response Strategies for the Coastal Zone of Poland." *Climatic Change* 36:151–73.

Zhai, Panmao, Anjian Sun, Fumin Ren, Xiaonin Liu, Bo Gao and Qiang Zhang 1999 "Changes of climate extremes in China." *Climatic Change* 42(1):203–18.

Zhou, Keqian and C. J. Butler 1998 "A statistical study of the relationship between the solar cycle length and tree-ring index values." *Journal of Atmospheric and Terrestrial Physics* 60:1,711–18.

Zilberman, David, Andrew Schmitz, Gary

Casterline, Erik Lichtenberg and Jerome B. Siebert 1991 "The economics of pesticide use and regulation." *Science* 253:518–22.
Zillmann, Dolf and Bryant Jennings 1994 "Entertainment as media effect." In Bryant and Zillmann 1994:437–61.
Zimberoff, T. and B. Mosely 1991 "Bruce Ames." *Omni* 13(5):74–81.

Index